lonely planet

Czech & Slovak Republics

John King
Scott McNeely
Richard Nebeský

Czech & Slovak Republics

2nd edition

Published by

Lonely Planet Publications

Head Office: PO Box 617, Hawthorn, Vic 3122, Australia

Branches: 155 Filbert St, Suite 251, Oakland, CA 94607, USA
10a Spring Place, London NW5 3BH, UK
71 bis rue du Cardinal Lemoine, 75005 Paris, France

Printed by

Colorcraft Ltd, Hong Kong

Photographs by

Mark Daffey
Scott McNeely
Jonathon Smith
John King
Richard Nebeský

Front cover: Detail of the calendar-wheel depicting Bohemian rural life, which is beneath Prague's Astronomical Clock (Richard Nebeský)

First Published

February 1995

This Edition

March 1998

National Library of Australia Cataloguing in Publication Data

McNeely, Scott.
Czech & Slovak Republics.

2nd ed.
Includes index.
ISBN 0 86442 525 2.

1. Czech Republic – Guidebooks. 2. Slovakia – Guidebooks.
I. Nebesky, Richard. II. Title.

914.3704

John King

John grew up in the USA, destined for the academic life (in past incarnations he was a university physics teacher and an environmental consultant), but in a rash moment in 1984 he headed off to China to have a look around. Since then he has eked out a living as a travel writer, encouraged by his wife, Julia Wilkinson, who is also one. Together with their two children they split their time at 'home' between south-west England and remoter parts of Hong Kong. John is also a co-author of LP's *Prague city guide*, and *Karakoram Highway*, *Pakistan*, *Central Asia*, *Russia*, *Ukraine & Belarus*, and *Portugal* travel guides.

Scott McNeely

Scott grew up in Los Angeles and studied at UC Berkeley, and Trinity College in Dublin. Scott has written a half-dozen guidebooks, including the Romania chapter for LP's *Eastern Europe*. Scott also remembers, vaguely, careers as an editor and executive editor in New York and San Francisco. For the past two years he's been travelling around the world (actually, a wide arc plus a few U-turns) from Turkey to Nepal to Thailand. He currently lives in Dublin.

Scott's first trip to the Czech and Slovak republics was in 1990. This time around he spent three glorious months criss-crossing the two countries, fed on a steady diet of dumplings, sauerkraut and roast pork. Most of all, he will miss his blue Škoda Favorit (AEO 78 89).

Richard Nebeský

Richard came into the world one snowy evening in Žižkov, Prague. He got his taste for travelling early in life when his parents dragged him away from the 'pretentious socialist paradise' of Czechoslovakia after it was invaded by the 'brotherly' Soviet troops. A stint on a campus was followed by a working wander trek around the ski resorts of the northern hemisphere and an overland odyssey across south Asia. He joined Lonely Planet in 1987, and since then has been co-author of LP's *Eastern* and *Central Europe* phrasebooks, *Prague city guide*, and has helped to update the guides to *Australia*, *Indonesia*, *Thailand*, *Russia*, *France*, and *Central* and *Eastern Europe*.

From Scott & Richard

Both of us did our best to obtain the most accurate information while researching this guide; however, the moment we turned our backs many things changed, especially due to the floods of July 1997. Remember that the whole world is in motion, and constantly changes. Thus our research dates just as quickly. The key to a good trip is to be flexible, accept that you will not find things exactly as we did and use this book as a guide and not a bible.

Scott wishes to thank the many travellers he met in both countries, many of whom offered useful ideas without knowing it. As helpful were the staff at PIS in Prague and BIS in Bratislava.

Scott would also like to thank the following for their invaluable support and help: Laurence Belgrave, Tom Berger, Judy Boland, David Brown, Peter Carrol, Mark Clare and Mary Clarke, Fionn Davenport, Feargal & Aoife Fitzpatrick, Jacqui Churcher and Dara Fitzpatrick, Kip Gebhardt, Jonathan & Molly Gelber, Kelly Green, Lara Harris & Dave, David &

Michelle Hepler, Kurt & Emily Hobson, Anto Howard, Caroline Liou, Samantha McCaughren, Greg Mooradian, Nichola Murray, Peter Puhvel, Robin & Vari, John Turco, Ada Vassilovski, Annie Ryan & Michael West and Ciara Walsh.

Special thanks to Jennifer Brewer, Ray Klinke, Teal Lewsadder and a wee yellow cottage in Connemara. Double-thanks to Richard Nebeský. And triple-thanks to Jim Stanley, who was accidentally deleted last time around.

Richard would like to thank his father for all his help and invaluable advice, as well as his mother. A very special thanks for priceless information, help and generosity goes to his uncle Luděk, as well as his aunty Zdena and cousin Míša. Blanka, Olin and Průchovy also deserve a very special thank you for their hospitality and putting up with the constant intrusions and questions. And *mnoho dík* to Vikkhi for her jovial and warm company in spirit and in person. Other people he would like to thank are Petr Mařík, Zdena Li, Růžena Bartošová, Vačlav Podhorský, Jeremy Taylor, the staff at tourist information offices and all the travellers who wrote in with their comments. A heartfelt *děkuji* to the co-author Scott McNeely, editor Darren Elder and all other Lonely Planet staff who helped with the production of this book.

From the Publisher

This book was edited by Darren Elder with much-needed assistance from Janet Austin, and proofread by Anne Mulvaney. Louise Klep coordinated the mapping for this edition before going on holidays. The mantle was temporarily taken up by Marcel Gaston before he too departed on holidays. Finally, Andrew Tudor completed layout. Thanks to Andrew and Dan Levin for all their computer wizardry. Ann Jeffree, before also heading off on holidays, did a sterling job drawing several new illustrations. Thanks also to Margie Jung, filling in for people on holidays, for designing the front cover, and Quentin Frayne for his work with the language section.

This Book

The 1st edition of *Czech & Slovak Republics* was written by John King and Richard Nebeský. The current edition was was updated by Richard Nebeský and Scott McNeely. Scott concentrated on Central, South and East Bohemia, South Moravia, Bratislava, West and East Slovakia, and Prague west of the Vltava. Richard concentrated on Prague (east of the Vltava), North and West Bohemia, North Moravia, Central Slovakia and the High Tatras.

Warning & Request

Things change – prices go up, schedules change, good places go bad and bad places go bankrupt – nothing stays the same. So, if you find things better or worse, recently opened or long since closed, please tell us and help make the next edition even more accurate and helpful.

We value all of the feedback we receive from travellers. Julie Young coordinates a small team that reads and acknowledges every letter, postcard and email, and ensures that every morsel of useful information finds its way to the appropriate authors, editors and publishers.

Everyone who writes to us will find their name in the next edition of the appropriate guide and will also receive a free subscription to our quarterly newsletter, *Planet Talk*. The very best contributions will be rewarded with a free Lonely Planet guide.

Excerpts from your correspondence may appear in new editions of this guide; in our newsletter, *Planet Talk*; or in updates on our Web site – so please let us know if you don't want your letter published or your name acknowledged.

Contents

SLOVAK REPUBLIC – 396

BOXED ASIDES

Map Legend

BOUNDARIES

International Boundary
Provincial Boundary
Disputed Boundary

ROUTES

A25 ..... Freeway, with Route Number
Major Road
Minor Road
Minor Road - Unsealed
City Road
City Street
City Lane
Train Route, with Station
M Metro Route, with Station
Cable Car or Chairlift
Ferry Route
Walking Track

AREA FEATURES

Building
Cemetery
Beach
Market
Park, Gardens
Pedestrian Mall
Urban Area
Mountain Range

HYDROGRAPHIC FEATURES

Canal
Coastline
Creek, River
Lake, Intermittent Lake
Rapids, Waterfalls
Salt Lake
Swamp

SYMBOLS

CAPITAL ....National Capital
CAPITAL ....Provincial Capital
CITY ....City
Town ....Town
Village ....Village

Place to Stay
Hostel
Camping Ground
Caravan Park
Hut or Chalet

Place to Eat
Pub or Bar

Airport
Ancient or City Wall
Bank
Border Crossing
Cave
Church
Cliff or Escarpment
Embassy
Golf Course
Hospital
Lookout
Monument
Mosque
Mountain or Hill
Museum
National Park
One Way Street

Parking
Pass
Petrol Station
Police Station
Post Office
Ruins
Shopping Centre
Ski Field
Spring
Swimming Pool
Synagogue
Telephone
Toilet
Tomb
Tourist Information
Transport
Zoo

Note: not all symbols displayed above appear in this book

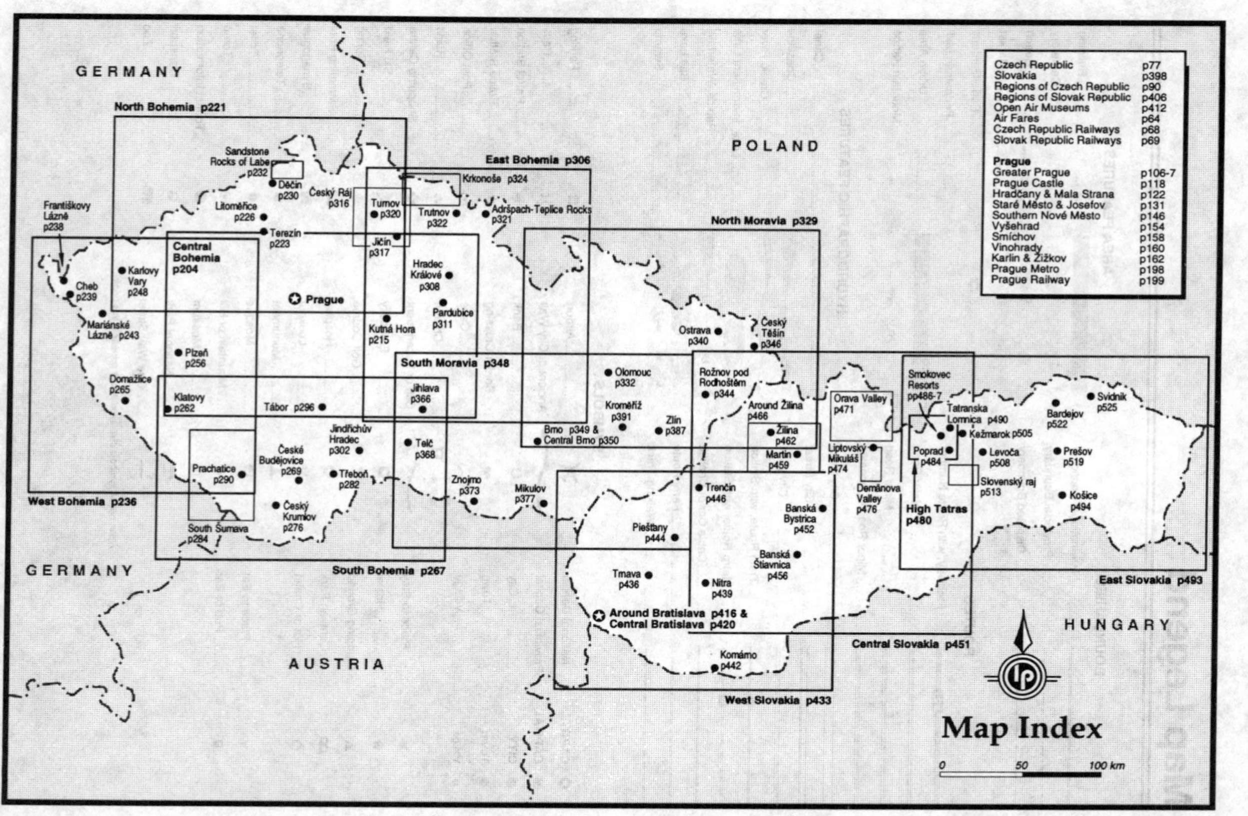

Map Index
Czech Republic p77
Slovakia p398
Regions of Czech Republic p90
Regions of Slovak Republic p406
Open Air Museums p412
Air Fares p64
Czech Republic Railways p68
Slovak Republic Railways p69
Prague
Greater Prague p106-7
Prague Castle p118
Hradčany & Mala Strana p122
Staré Město & Josefov p131
Southern Nové Město p146
Vyšehrad p154
Smíchov p158
Vinohrady p160
Karlín & Žižkov p162
Prague Metro p198
Prague Railway p199
GERMANY
POLAND
AUSTRIA
HUNGARY
North Bohemia p221
East Bohemia p306
North Moravia p329
Central Bohemia p204
West Bohemia p236
South Bohemia p267
South Moravia p348
West Slovakia p433
Central Slovakia p451
East Slovakia p493
High Tatras p480
Sandstone Rocks of Labe p232
Děčín p230
Český Ráj p316
Krkonoše p324
Turnov p320
Trutnov p322
Adršpach-Teplice Rocks p321
Františkovy Lázně p238
Litoměřice p226
Terezín p223
Jičín p317
Karlovy Vary p248
Cheb p239
Prague
Hradec Králové p308
Pardubice p311
Mariánské Lázně p243
Kutná Hora p215
Plzeň p256
Ostrava p340
Český Těšín p346
Domažlice p265
Klatovy p262
Tábor p296
Jihlava p366
Olomouc p332
Rožnov pod Rodhoštěm p344
Around Žilina p466
Orava Valley p471
Smokovec Resorts pp486-7
Tatranska Lomnica p490
Kežmarok p505
Bardejov p522
Svidník p525
Kroměříž p391
Zlín p387
Brno p349 & Central Brno p350
Žilina p462
Martin p459
Liptovský Mikuláš p474
Poprad p484
Levoča p508
Prešov p519
Jindřichův Hradec p302
Telč p368
České Budějovice p269
Prachatice p290
Třeboň p282
Znojmo p373
Mikulov p377
Trenčín p446
Demänova Valley p476
Slovenský raj p513
Košice p494
Banská Bystrica p452
Český Krumlov p276
South Šumava p284
Piešťany p444
Banská Štiavnica p456
Trnava p436
Nitra p439
Around Bratislava p416 & Central Bratislava p420
Komárno p442
0
50
100 km

Introduction

Side-by-side in the heart of Europe sit the Czech and Slovak republics. In many ways they're like orphaned siblings raised separately, reunited just as they came of age, but in the end too different to live together.

Despite common Slavic roots, and more apparent cultural similarities than differences, *České země* (the 'Czech Lands' of Bohemia and Moravia) and *Slovensko* (Slovakia) came of age in different geopolitical neighbourhoods following the collapse of the Great Moravian Empire in the 10th century. For a thousand years both were nearly always under someone else's thumb – the Holy Roman Empire and the Habsburg dynasty for the Czechs, the Hungarian Empire for the Slovaks.

In the 19th century, as the Austrian and Hungarian crowns merged, Czechs and Slovaks began re-exploring their national histories in parallel cultural-revival movements. With the defeat of Austria-Hungary in WWI, they declared joint independence as the doughty new state of Czechoslovakia.

The partnership didn't go down well with Slovaks, who found themselves at the back end of more than just the country's name. Despite agreements to create a single federal state comprising two equal republics, Prague dominated the levers of power, leaving Bratislava a definite second among supposed equals. Three years after the fall of Europe's Communist dominoes in 1989, the two sibling-states suddenly and formally went their independent ways, as Česká Republika and Slovenská Republika – a split due less to mutual hatred than to the incompatible ambitions of their respective politicians.

But they're still bound together in many ways – by marriages, friendships and mutually comprehensible languages, by having shared the horrors of WWII, the daily fear and frustration of the Communist era, the dashed hopes of the Prague Spring and the

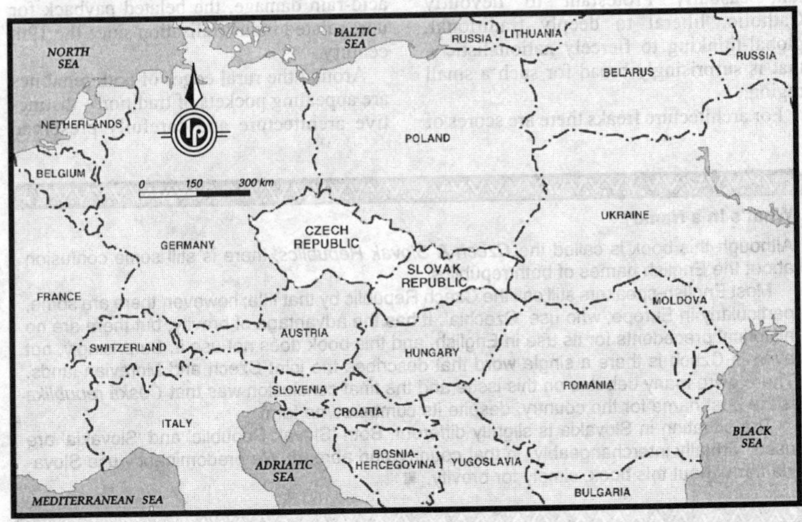

joy of the bloodless 'Velvet Revolution'. Despite the line of new checkpoints between them, foreign visitors will continue to see them as one country for sometime yet.

But with the exception of Prague (now thrust into tourism's big league), most of us know little about this part of what we keep calling 'Eastern Europe' – much to the annoyance of Czechs and Slovaks well aware that, historically and geographically, this is *central* Europe. The feisty Czech Lands in particular have been pivotal in European history – home of the earliest Protestants, flash-point of the Thirty Years' War and one of Hitler's big land-grabs. Western Europeans have been slow to take notice, most infamously Britain's pre-WWII prime minister, Neville Chamberlain, who described Czechoslovakia as 'a far-away country' full of 'people of whom we know nothing', just before signing the Czech Sudetenland over to Hitler.

Czechs and Slovaks are perceived as plain-spoken, even-tempered and cultured people. Beneath the surface they reveal a spectrum of cultural, religious and political influences – German to Polish and Hungarian, casually Protestant to devoutly Catholic, liberal to deeply traditional, global-thinking to fiercely nationalistic – that is surprisingly broad for such a small region.

For architecture freaks there are scores of well-preserved old town centres, plus rural castles and chateaux from Romanesque to fairy-tale Romantic – an amazing trove considering the wars that have raked the region over the centuries. The smallest towns seem to have museums full of home-grown 19th and 20th century art. In larger towns there is enough good-quality classical music, opera and ballet, and in the cities enough modern theatre, cinema, jazz and rock, to keep anyone happy. For backpackers, the generally lower level of tourist development in Slovakia makes it even more attractive.

If you're here for more than about a week, you can easily overdose on chateaux and arcaded town squares. A good antidote is to take a hike or jump on a bike. Both republics are endowed with great natural beauty, from rolling farmland to upland meadows, limestone caves to sandstone canyons and mountains – most notably Slovakia's High Tatras. User-friendly national parks, protected landscape regions and nature reserves are laced with good trails, and the parks are dotted with cheap chalets. Only in the north do you risk stumbling on appalling air pollution and high-altitude acid-rain damage, the belated payback for unregulated industrialisation since the 19th century.

Around the rural edges of both republics are appealing pockets of tradition – distinctive architecture and carefully preserved

What's in a Name?

Although this book is called the *Czech & Slovak Republics*, there is still some confusion about the English names of both republics.

Most English-speakers still call the Czech Republic by that title; however, there are some, particularly in Europe, who use 'Czechia'. It has the advantage of brevity, but there are no historical precedents for its use in English, and this book does not use it. Surprisingly, not even in Czech is there a single word that describes the joint Czech and Moravian lands. There were many debates on this issue and the final conclusion was that *Česká republika* is the best name for the country, despite its cumbersome form.

The situation in Slovakia is slightly different. Both 'Slovak Republic' and 'Slovakia' are used, virtually interchangeably, in that country and abroad. We predominantly use Slovakia throughout this book, simply for brevity. ■

habits, skills, costumes, music and dance that go public at numerous annual folk festivals.

In 1989 the future arrived in the Czech and Slovak republics with a bang, and even in the farthest corners things are changing fast. The heady promises of democracy and capitalism – and of genuine independence for Slovaks – have not proven easy tasks to fulfil. The Czechs struggle with the onslaught of tourists, rising crime rates and the excesses of a nascent market economy, while the Slovaks face high unemployment and a government that verges on authoritarian. Despite all the problems, the chance of seeing these two societies in transformation makes for a fascinating and hugely rewarding journey.

Facts for the Visitor

PLANNING

When to Go

Most Czechs and Slovaks take their holidays in July and August. Hotels, hostels (usually crowded with students on term-break) and tourist sights are more than usually crowded during this time, especially in Prague and the Krkonoše and Tatras mountain-resort areas. Fortunately the supply of bottom-end accommodation increases in large towns during this time, as student accommodation is thrown open to visitors.

European tourists prefer to visit from May to June, and then again over the Easter and Christmas-New Year holiday period, when hordes of German, Austrian and Italian revellers descend on Prague and the mountain resorts.

Centres like Prague, Brno and Bratislava, and the mountain resorts, cater to visitors year-round; Prague is especially beautiful under a mantle of snow. Elsewhere, from October or November through March or April, most castles, museums and other tourist attractions, and some associated accommodation and transport, close down. But hotel prices often drop during this time, and space is plentiful (except in the ski resorts, and except for Christmas-New Year).

In Prague and some North Bohemian and North Moravian industrial centres, the winter burning of low-grade coal for power generation, combined with auto emissions and weather inversions, periodically turns the air thick and foul.

Therefore May to June and September are the prime visiting months, with April and October chillier and sometimes cheaper alternatives. The highland resort regions abound with winter sports from December through to at least March or April, and summer is also a popular time – in these areas the lowest hotel prices are from May to June and October to November.

What Kind of Trip?

Most visitors to the Czech Republic rarely travel beyond Prague, which is a shame considering the number of worthwhile sights within a short distance. A good strategy might be to base yourself in Prague and make short trips to places like Karlštejn Castle, Kutná Hora, Brno, Olomouc and even Bratislava. Package tours are cheap and simple to arrange from Prague.

For a balanced experience in Slovakia you need to visit more than just Bratislava. Unlike Prague, Bratislava doesn't make the best base for touring the country; consider renting a car, joining a tour, or mastering the train and bus timetables.

Both republics are quite safe, and solo travellers report few problems – except perhaps loneliness (in many small towns foreign tourists are a rare sight).

Maps

Country Maps Good maps of the Czech Republic and Slovakia that are available outside the country are those by some German publishers and by Austrian publishers such as Freytag & Berndt. Beware of the Michelin *Czech Republic & Slovak Republic* 1:600,000 map (No 976 in the series) as it doesn't list many of the smaller roads and villages.

Some of the best Czech country maps are by Kartografie Praha: its *Česká republika – automapa* (1:500,000) is good, as are its town plans. There are excellent hiking and cycling maps (1:50,000) produced jointly by Klub Českých turistů and Vojenský karografický ústav (VKÚ). Freytag & Berndt's good multilingual 1:500,000 *Autokarte* (Road Map) has route distances, sights of interest, mountain-shading and other geographical info, and a good index.

VKÚ, a Slovak publisher, produces some of the best maps of the country. There is the *Automapa Slovenská republika* (1:500,000) or the more detailed *Autoatlas Slovenska*

(1:200,000). VKÚ maps are hard to find outside Slovakia, so you may want to try the Austrian Freytag & Berndt *Slovak Republic Road Map* (1:500,000). The German publisher GeoCenter sells similar high-quality maps, all readily available throughout Slovakia.

Regional & Street Maps VKÚ covers both countries' hiking areas with very detailed hiking maps, either at 1:50,000 (green cover) or 1:25,000 (blue cover). Some editions are especially produced with specific information for mountain bikers or skiers, including trail routes.

Freytag & Berndt publishes a good 1:50,000 map of Slovakia's Tatras mountains, in three parts: *Hohe Tatra* (High Tatras) and western and eastern *Niedere Tatra* (Low Tatras). Kartografie Praha and Klub Českých turistů in Prague, and Slovenská Kartografia in Bratislava publish excellent colour-coded regional hiking maps.

Most major tourist towns have several street maps from various publishers but only VKÚ covers most of the major and some minor Slovak towns (the majority of which have a scale of 1:10,000).

You can buy adequate street maps from newsagents, bookshops or travel agencies in most towns big enough to need them, as well as regional maps. Numerous versions are available for Prague and Bratislava.

What to Bring

Of course, bring as little as you can – pack the bare minimum and then cut it in half! You can normally find toilet paper, soap, toothpaste, shampoo, aspirin, insect repellent and razor blades in department stores of most sizable towns, and even cheap clothing in the open-air markets.

Seasoned travellers will already have a secure passport-and-money pouch. Most department stores carry sanitary towels and tampons, but bring a small supply of tampons from home in case you end up stuck in a small town. Hostellers need not bring their own bedding.

Other helpful items are a lightweight day-pack, pocketknife, water bottle, torch, sewing kit, a length of cord (as a washing-line) and a universal sink plug. You may also want sunscreen lotion, lip-salve, sun hat, sunglasses, compass, a few stuff-sacks or plastic bags, and foot powder.

Half a dozen passport-size photos will save you trouble in case of paperwork, though you can also get them en route.

For a suggested medical kit see the Health section of this chapter. For photography prerequisites see the Film & Photography section.

Clothing This depends on where you're going, and when (see Climate in the Facts About the Czech or Slovak republics chapters). Lightweight, drip-dry clothes are easy to carry and easy to wash. You need not take anything dressy, though you might like something modest for top-end restaurants, concerts etc. People dress a bit more conservatively in Slovakia than in the Czech Republic.

The mountains can be cold enough for a sweater and jacket, and at higher altitudes for a coat, cap and gloves, even in summer. In general, many light layers work better than a few heavy ones. Lowland regions can get oven-like in summer. Rain can strike at any time; an anorak, poncho or parka is essential in the mountains, while a cheap umbrella bought when you get there will do in town.

Light walking shoes are adequate unless you are contemplating long or snowy hikes; in any case it is best if they are water proofed. Flip-flops (thongs) help protect against fungal infections in communal showers.

SUGGESTED ITINERARIES

Depending on the length of your stay, you might want to see and do the following things in the Czech and Slovak republics:

Czech Republic

One week

Visit Prague, Kutná Hora, Český Krumlov and České Budějovice.

Two weeks
Visit Prague, Konopiště or Karlštejn, Kutná Hora, Český Krumlov, Telč, Šumava and Litoměřice.
One month
Visit Prague, Konopiště, Karlštejn, Kutná Hora, Tábor, Český Krumlov, České Budějovice, Telč, the Moravské Slovácko region, the Český ráj, Šumava, Litoměřice, Terezín, Mariánské, Lázně, Rožnov pod Radhoštěm and Karlovy Vary.
Two months
Visit Prague, Křivoklát, Konopiště, Karlštejn, Kutná Hora, Tábor, Český Krumlov, České Budějovice, Telč, Brno, Znojmo, Mikulov, the Moravské Slovácko region, the Český ráj, the Adršpach-Teplice rocks, Šumava, Litoměřice, Terezín, Mariánské, Lázně, Rožnov pod Radhoštěm and Karlovy Vary.

Slovakia

One week
Visit Bratislava, Bojnice Chateau, the High Tatra mountains and Levoča.
Two weeks
Visit Bratislava, Bojnice Chateau, Čičmany, the High Tatra mountains, Levoča, Bardejov, Košice and the Slovenský raj.
One month
Visit Bratislava, Bojnice Chateau, Čičmany, Trenčín, the Malá Fatra mountains, Banská Štiavnica, the High Tatra mountains, Levoča, Spiš Castle, Bardejov, Košice, the Slovenský raj and Slovak karst.
Two months
Visit Bratislava, Nitra, Čachtice Chateau, Bojnice Chateau, Čičmany, Trenčín, the Malá Fatra mountains, Martin, Zuberec, Demänova Valley, Banská Štiavnica, Banská Bystrica, the Tatra mountains, Dunajec Gorge, Levoča, Spiš Castle, Bardejov, Bardejovské Kúpele, Svidník, Medzilaborce, Košice, the Slovenský raj and Slovak karst.

THE BEST & WORST

Each republic has its hits, which every traveller should try to experience, but equally each has its must-miss elements.

Czech Republic

The hits in Czech are Prague off-season; Konopiště under a blanket of snow; the human-bone sculptures at the Sedlec Ossuary near Kutná Hora; Český Krumlov, especially its U Matesa pub; Brno and its pubs; tiny Mikulov and Telč with their superb central squares, and the town square of Znojmo; the Moravské Slovácko region during the festival season; multi-day hikes in the pristine Český ráj national park; and the dramatic rock formations at Adršpach-Teplice.

The misses are Prague in July and August: the crowds at Karlštejn Castle; the crowds and high prices at České Budějovice; the southern half of eastern Bohemia; the Moravské Slovácko region outside the festival season; castle tours that last more than 45 minutes; and pork stew at 8 am.

Slovakia

The hits in Slovakia are Bratislava (if you can find cheap accommodation); Bardejov; Čičmany village with its painted houses; the rugged ravines of Slovenský raj; Spiš Castle; the High Tatras mountains for hiking; the *skansen* at Svidník; the wooden churches of East Slovakia; the Slovak National Museum in Martin; the fairy-tale castle of Bojnice; and Jasná in Nízke Tatry for excellent skiing and hiking.

Things to miss in Slovakia include the crowds at Bojnice Castle and along the trails of the High Tatras mountains; the May Day celebrations at námestie SNP in Banská Bystrica, which are just as they were during the Communist years; Martin, because it is 99% prefabricated housing; and the long queues and bribery at the Slovak-Ukrainian border crossing of Vyšné Nemecké-Užhorod.

TOURIST OFFICES

Local Tourist Offices

There's a municipal information office in Prague called the Prague Information Service (PIS); its staff are knowledgeable about sightseeing, food and entertainment. Receptionists in the expensive hotels are often helpful with information, when they're not busy. In all major tourist areas throughout the rest of the Czech Republic there is a network of municipal information centres (*městské informační centrum/ středisko*).

In Slovakia there's a similar network of information centres (*informačné centrum*), many of which are known by the acronym Aices.

Čedok

The former government tourism monopoly, Čedok, has offices around the Czech Republic that you can consult if you wish to change money, or want accommodation, travel or sightseeing arrangements made. It is, however, a travel agency and not a state-run tourist centre. Service varies from office to office – some are quite helpful, others are cold and downright rude. All Čedok offices are oriented towards the top end of the market.

Čedok Offices Abroad Offices outside the Czech Republic include:

Austria
Parkring 10, A-1010 Vienna (☎ 01-512 43 72; fax 512 43 72 85)

France
32 Ave de l'Opéra, 75002 Paris (☎ 01-47 42 74 87)

Germany
Leipzigerstrasse 60, D-10117 Berlin (☎ 030-204 46 44; fax 204 46 23)
Kaiserstrasse 54, 6 Frankfurt am Main (☎ 069-27 40 17; fax 23 58 90)
Allstrasse 1, D-86159 Augsburg (☎ 0821-31 33 81; fax 31 33 82)

Italy
Via Giovanni Lanza 105A, 00184 Roma (☎ 06-48 34 06; fax 482 8397)

Netherlands
Kleinegartmaplatzonen 21, 1017 PR Amsterdam (☎ 020-620 05 86; fax 638 54 41)

Russia
Tversko-Yamskaya ul 33/39, vkhod 7, kv 136, 125 047 Moscow (☎ 0095-978 89 32; fax 978 99 22)

Switzerland
Pelikanstrasse 38, 8001 Zürich (☎ 01-221 3131; fax 221 3141)

UK
53-54 Haymarket, London SW1Y 4RP (☎ 0171-839 4414; fax 01225-480 132)

USA
Victor Corporation (a private company that is a Čedok representative), Suite 3604, 10 East 40th St, New York, NY 10016 (☎ 212-689 9720; fax 481 0597).

Czech Tourist Authority (CCC)

The Czech Tourist Authority (Česká centrála cestovniho ruchu) handles tourist information about sights, museums, festivals etc for the entire Czech Republic. Staff will not book accommodation, but they have plenty of brochures to help you choose.

CCC Offices Abroad The following offices will provide general sightseeing, hotel and transport information:

Canada
Exchange Tower, 2 First Canadian Place, 14th Floor, Toronto M5X 1A6 (☎ 416-367 3432)

UK
96 Great Portland St, London W1N 5RA (☎ 0171-291 9924)

USA
1109-1111 Madison Ave, New York, NY 10028 (☎ 212-288 0830)

CKM

The Czech Republic's youth travel bureau is CKM (Cestovní kancelář mládeže). At the time of writing CKM was planning to rename itself CKM 2000 and, like Čedok, to specialise in upper-end, non-youth travel. Until then CKM's small network of offices will help with transport tickets and sometimes accommodation. CKM has no offices abroad.

Satur

In 1994 Slovakia's national tourist organisation was renamed from Čedok to Satur (Slovenská Agentúra Turisma, or the Slovak Agency for Tourism). It is a national travel agent but also acts as the national tourist information network. At local offices (listed under individual towns) you can get maps and brochures, change money, and sometimes book accommodation and tours.

Satur Offices Abroad At the following Satur offices you can get brochures and arrange package tours and upper-end hotel bookings:

Austria
: Parkring 12, A-1010 Vienna (☎ 01-512 01 99; fax 512 59 16/85)

Germany
: Strausbergerplatz 8/9, D-10243 Berlin Friedrichshain (☎ 030-429 41 13; fax 427 47 56)

Hungary
: Rákoczi út. 15, H-1088 Budapest VIII (☎ 01-118 11 97; fax 138 29 27)

Switzerland
: Gottfried Kellerstrasse 7, CH-8001 Zürich (☎ 01-262 6900; fax 262 6910)

Spa Agencies

Balnea (☎ 02-24 22 76 44; fax 21 10 53 07), Národní 28, Prague 1, is the office to book courses of medical treatment at any spa in the Czech Republic. The Slovak agency is Slovthermae, which has its main office at Radlinského 13 in Bratislava (☎ 07-581 80 or 588 47; fax 580 59), and another at Winterova 29 in Piešťany. See the Health section in this chapter for a list of major spas in the two republics.

VISAS & DOCUMENTS

Passport

Make sure that your passport is not due to expire within eight months of entering the Czech Republic, or within six months of entering Slovakia. Otherwise you may be refused entry or denied the appropriate visa.

Visas

Czech Republic Nationals of all western European countries and New Zealand can visit the Czech Republic for up to 90 days, and citizens of the UK, Irish Republic and Canada for up to 180 days, without a visa. US passport-holders can stay for 30 days without a visa. Australians need a visa but it is free and valid for three months. Citizens of Japan and most other non-European countries still need to pay for a visa, which should be obtained in advance at a consulate.

Visas are only available at three highway border crossings – one from Germany (Waidhaus-Rozvadov) and two from Austria (Wullowitz-Dolní Dvořiště and Klein Haugsdorf-Hatě) – and at Prague's Ruzyně airport (1500 Kč). Elsewhere you'll be refused entry if you need a visa and arrive without one. Visas are never issued on trains. Also note that Slovak visas are not accepted at Czech border crossings and vice versa.

Czech tourist and transit visas are readily available at consulates for about US$33 per visit. You will need two photos per visit (maximum two visits per visa). Don't get a transit visa – it costs the same and cannot be changed to a tourist visa upon arrival. You'll be asked how many days you wish to stay in the Czech Republic, up to a maximum of 30 days, and this number will be written on your visa. You can use your visa at any time within six months of the date of issue. Multiple-entry visas are also available.

All visitors to the Czech Republic can be asked to show a minimum of US$250 or the equivalent in any hard currency, and an air ticket out of the country – though these rules are rarely enforced.

Visa Extensions You can extend a visa (or visa-free stay) for 30 days at police stations inside the Czech Republic for about 200 Kč (1000 Kč if you've already overstayed). The offices handling these matters open for short hours and have long queues, so don't leave it until the last minute. In Prague, apply for visa extensions at the Foreigners' Police & Passport Office (Úřadovna cizinecké policie a pasové služby) at Olšanská 2 in Žižkov, Prague 3.

Slovakia Nationals of all European Union countries, Canada and Switzerland can visit Slovakia for up to 90 days, and UK and Irish Republic citizens for up to 180 days, without a visa. US passport-holders can stay for 30 days without a visa. Nationals of Australia and New Zealand (both about A$30), and South Africa (about US$50) must obtain a visa, which is good for a stay of up to 30 days, commencing within six months of the issue date. Transit visas for 48 hours, double-entry visas for 60 days, and multiple-entry visas for 90 and 180 days are also available.

You'll need one application form, two passport-size photos, and cash or a money order for the fee, which varies with your nationality. Most Slovak embassies in western capitals will accept applications by post if you include a self-addressed envelope with return certified postage, and payment by postal money order; get the forms from them or from a travel agent. Processing is usually immediate for applications in person, and takes about three working days otherwise.

At the time of writing, the only border point where Slovak visas could be issued on the spot (for 30 days at the officials' discretion, and only during business hours) was the automobile checkpoint at Petržalka, near Bratislava in West Slovakia (Berg on the Austrian side).

All visitors are expected to register at the district foreigners' police office within three working days, but this is not necessary if you're staying in hotels.

Technically all visitors to Slovakia must have the equivalent of US$15 for each day they plan to spend in the country, but the law is unevenly enforced.

Visa Extensions If you plan to stay longer than your visa (or visa-free) period, you're expected to register with the authorities within two or three working days of your *arrival*, and apply for a visa extension. In Bratislava go to the Foreigners' Police Office (☎ 549 11 11) at Zahradnická 93. In fact you can go to the foreigners' police office (*Cudzinecká polícia*) in any regional capital, though less English will be spoken.

At the time of writing the fee was 500 Sk for a standard 180 day extension.

Photocopies
Consider keeping copies of vital documents – the first page of your passport and your Czech and Slovak visas (if applicable), credit cards, birth certificate, airline tickets, travellers cheques serial numbers etc – in your money belt, with your travelling companion, and with someone back home.

Driving Licence & Permits
Drivers from the USA, Canada, UK, Australia and New Zealand do not need an International Driving Permit in either republic, only a full domestic licence. You'll also need a certificate of insurance, or 'green card', showing you carry full liability insurance. For more information see the Getting There & Away chapter.

Hostel Card
Hostels in the Czech and Slovak republics do not require a Hostelling International (HI) or affiliate card. That said, HI and IYHF cards entitle you to 20 to 30% discounts at some hostels and junior hotels. Apply for your HI or IYHF card at home.

Student & Youth Cards
ISIC and Euro<26 cards will get you discounts at some hotels and most museums, galleries and theatres. You may even get a discount on air, bus and train tickets. Both can be purchased at most Satur offices, and some CKM and Čedok offices. You'll need a passport-size photo, proof of student status, and the application fee (about US$5.50 and US$7.50, respectively).

Seniors' Cards
Throughout both republics seniors get discounts on museums and galleries. Rail Europe Senior is British Rail International's name for its discount card, and there are equivalents in other western European countries. These and even ordinary domestic ID cards can sometimes be flashed usefully in situations well beyond their intended use.

EMBASSIES
Your embassy can register your arrival, provide referrals to local doctors and dentists, cope with lost or stolen passports and

offer advice on crime and safety. Some consulates even have reading rooms stocked with papers from back home. They will not, however, give you a free ticket home if you run out of money.

Czech Republic

Czech Embassies Abroad The following are the addresses of some Czech embassies and consulates abroad:

Australia
  38 Culgoa Circuit, O'Malley, ACT 2606 (☎ 02-6290 1386; fax 6290 0006)
  Consulate: 169 Military Rd, Dover Heights, NSW 2030 (☎ 02-9371 8877, visa info 9371 8878; fax 9371 9635) – visas are only issued at the consulate
Austria
  Penzingerstrasse 11-13, 1140 Vienna (☎ 1-894 37 41)
Belgium & Luxembourg
  555 rue Engeland, 1180 Brussels-Uccle (☎ 2-374 1203)
  Consulate: 154 Ave Adolphe Buyl, 1050 Brussels (☎ 2-647 5898)
Canada
  541 Sussex Drive, Ottawa, Ontario K1N 6Z6 (☎ 613-562 3875) – only in-person visa applications are accepted
France
  15 Ave Charles Floquet, F-75343 Paris Cedex (☎ 01-40 65 13 00)
Germany
  Ferdinandstrasse 27, 53127 Bonn (☎ 228-91 970)
Hungary
  Rózsa ul. 61, 1064 Budapest VI (☎ 1-132 5589)
Italy
  Via dei Gracchi 322, 00192 Roma (☎ 6-324 4459)
Netherlands
  Paleisstraat 4, 2514 JA The Hague (☎ 070-346 9712)
New Zealand
  Consulate: 48 Hair St, PO Box 43035, Wainuiomata, Wellington (☎ 04-564 6001) – visa applications must be made to the Czech consulate in Sydney, Australia
Poland
  Koszykowa 18, 00-555 Warsaw (☎ 22-678 7221)
Slovakia
  29.augusta 5, Bratislava (☎ 07-536 12 04)
Switzerland
  Muristrasse 53, 3006 Bern 16 (☎ 31-352 3645)
UK & Ireland
  26 Kensington Palace Gardens, London W8 4QY (☎ 0171-243 1115) – the visa office is next door at number 28 (☎ 0171-243 7943)
Ukraine
  Yaroslavov val 34, 252 901 Kiev (☎ 044-212 21 10)
USA
  3900 Spring of Freedom St NW, Washington, DC 20008 (☎ 202-374 9100); 10990 Wilshire Blvd, Suite 1100, Los Angeles, CA 90024 (☎ 310-473 0889)

Foreign Embassies in the Czech Republic Most consulates are open for visa-related business weekdays until noon or 1 pm. Unless stated otherwise, the following are in Prague 1:

Australia
  Na Ořechovce 38, Prague 6 (☎ 24 31 07 43) – this is only an honorary consul, and Australians can get emergency help at the UK embassy; the nearest Australian embassies are in Warsaw and Vienna
Austria
  Viktora Huga 10, Prague 5 (☎ 02-57 32 12 82)
Belgium & Luxembourg
  Valdštejnská 6 (☎ 02-57 32 03 89)
Bulgaria
  Krakovská 6 (☎ 02-24 22 86 46); closed Wednesday
Canada
  Mickiewiczova 6, Prague 6 (☎ 02-24 31 11 08)
Croatia
  V průhledu 9, Prague 6 (☎ 02-312 04 79)
France
  Velkopřerovské náměstí 2 (☎ 02-57 32 03 52)
Germany
  Vlašská 19 (☎ 02-57 32 01 90)
Hungary
  Badeního 1 (☎ 02-36 50 41); closed Friday
India
  Valdštejnská 6 (☎ 02-57 32 02 55)
Ireland
  Tržiště 13 (☎ 02-53 09 11)
Israel
  Badeního 2, Prague 7 (☎ 02-32 24 81)
Italy
  Nerudova 20 (☎ 02-57 32 00 11)
Netherlands
  Maltézské náměstí 1 (☎ 02-57 32 00 94)

New Zealand
Panská 5 (☎ 02-25 41 98) – this is only an honorary consul, and Kiwis can get emergency help at the UK embassy; the nearest NZ embassy is in Bonn
Poland
Václavské náměstí 49 (☎ 02-24 22 87 22)
Romania
Nerudova 5 (☎ 02-57 32 04 94); closed Tuesday and Thursday
Russia
Pod Kaštany 1, Prague 6 (☎ 02-38 19 45)
Slovakia
Pod hradbami 1, Prague 6 (☎ 02-32 05 21)
Slovenia
Pod hradbami 15, Prague 6 (☎ 02-24 31 51 06)
South Africa
Ruská 65, Prague 10 (☎ 02-67 31 11 14)
Switzerland
Pevnostní 7, Prague 6 (☎ 02-24 31 12 28)
UK
Thunovská 14 (☎ 02-57 32 03 55)
Ukraine
Schwaigerova 2, Prague 6 (☎ 02-312 15 77)
USA
Tržiště 15 (☎ 02-57 32 06 63)
Yugoslavia
Mostecká 15 (☎ 02-57 32 00 31)

Slovakia

Slovak Embassies Abroad The following list gives the addresses of some Slovak embassies abroad. There is no Slovak embassy in New Zealand; the nearest is in Canberra, Australia.

Australia
47 Culgoa Circuit, O'Malley, ACT 2606 (☎ 02-6290 1516)
Austria
Armbrustergasse 24, A-1190 Vienna (☎ 1-318 9055/9)
Belgium & Luxembourg
195 Ave Moliére, B-1050 Brussels (☎ 2-343 3505)
Bulgaria
Bulvar Janko Sakazov 9, 1000 Sofia (☎ 2-943 3288)
Canada
50 Rideau Terrace, Ottawa, Ontario K1M 2A1 (☎ 613-749 4442)
Czech Republic, Pod hradbami 1, 160 00 Prague 6 (☎ 2-32 05 07)
Denmark
Vesterled 26, DK-2100 Copenhagen 0 (☎ 31-209 911/2)
France
125 Rue du Ranelagh, 75 016 Paris (☎ 01-44 14 56 00 or 44 14 51 20)
Germany
August-Bier-Strasse 31, D-531 29 Bonn (☎ 228-914 550);
Leipzigerstrasse 36, D-10117 Berlin (☎ 30-204 4007 or 204 4538);
Vollmannstrasse 25d, D-819 25 Munich (☎ 89-910 2067/9)
Hungary
Stefánia út 22 (Népstadion), H-1143 Budapest XIV (☎ 1-251 1660 or 251 5650)
Italy
Via dei Colli della Farnesina, 144 Lotto VI, 00194 Roma (☎ 6-3630 8741)
Netherlands
Parkweg 1, 2585 JG The Hague (☎ 070-416 77 73)
Poland
Litevska 6, 00-581 Warsaw (☎ 22-628 4051)
Russia
ulitsa J Fučíka 17-19, Moscow D-47 (☎ 095-956 4923)
South Africa
930 Arcadia St, Arcadia 0083 Pretoria (☎ 12-342 2051)
Switzerland
Thunstrasse 99, 3006 Bern (☎ 31-352 3646)
UK & Ireland
25 Kensington Palace Gardens, London W8 4QY (☎ 0171-243 0803 or 727 9432)
Ukraine
Yaroslavov val 34, 252 901 Kiev (☎ 044-212 00 08)
USA
2201 Wisconsin Ave NW, Suite 250, Washington, DC 20007 (☎ 202-965 5160 or 445 3804)

Foreign Embassies in Slovakia Australia and New Zealand have no embassies in Slovakia; the nearest are in Vienna. The nationals of unrepresented Commonwealth countries can go to the UK embassy for assistance. The following embassies are all in Bratislava and open for visa-related business only until 1 pm:

Austria
Ventúrska 10 (☎ 07-533 29 86/8)
Bulgaria
Kuzmányho 1 (☎ 07-533 59 71)
Canada
Consulate: Kolárska 4 (☎ 07-536 12 77)

Czech Republic
29.augusta 5 (☎ 07-536 12 04)
France
Hlavné námesti 7 (☎ 07-533 57 45)
Germany
Palisády 47 (☎ 07-531 53 00)
Hungary
Sedlárska 3 (☎ 07-533 05 41)
Poland
Hummelova 4 (☎ 07-531 53 22)
Romania
Fraňa Kráľa 11 (☎ 07-49 16 65)
Russia
Godrova 4 (☎ 07-531 34 68)
South Africa
Jančova 8 (☎ 07-531 15 82 or 531 56 43)
UK & Ireland
Panská 16 (☎ 07-531 00 05)
Ukraine
Radvanská 35 (☎ 07-533 16 72)
USA
Hviezdoslavovo námestie 4 (☎ 07-533 08 61)

CUSTOMS

You can import, tax and duty free, reasonable amounts of personal effects and up to about 3000 Kč/Sk (about US$95) worth of gifts and other 'non-commercial' goods. If you're over 18, you can bring in 2L of wine, 1L of spirits and 250 cigarettes (or equivalent other tobacco products). To avoid problems upon departure, expensive electronic devices – such as video cameras, laptop computers etc – should be declared to customs when you enter either republic.

Before you make any really big purchases in either republic, know how much it will cost to take them out! Theoretically, in the Czech Republic anything above 30,000 Kč (about US$950) worth of consumer goods is dutiable at 22%. In Slovakia, goods valued between 3000 Sk and 8000 Sk are dutiable from 5 to 50% (depending on the type of goods), and anything valued above 8000 Sk is dutiable at up to 100%, plus 6 to 25% VAT depending on the type of goods.

You cannot export genuine antiques. If you have any doubt about what you're taking out, talk to curatorial staff at the National Museum (in Prague or Bratislava) or the Museum of Decorative Arts in Prague, or go to the customs post office (*Pošta celnice/Poštovní colnica*). In Prague it's Pošta 121 Celnice (☎ 02-24 51 17 54), at Plzeňská 139 in Smíchov (metro to Anděl, then three stops west on tram No 4, 7 or 9), which is open Monday and Wednesday from 7 am to 6 pm, and Tuesday, Thursday and Friday until 3 pm. In Bratislava the Poštovní Colnica is at Tomášikova 54 (☎ 07-502 25 01), and it's open weekdays from 8 am to 3 pm (Wednesday from 9.30 am to 6 pm).

In the Czech Republic you can import or export unlimited amounts of Czech and foreign currency. Arriving foreigners may occasionally be asked to prove that they have the equivalent of at least US$250 in convertible currencies.

It is illegal to import or export any Slovak currency. Arriving foreigners in Slovakia are theoretically required to have US$15 per day for each day they plan to spend in the country, but the law is rarely enforced.

If you've saved your encashment receipts you can sell unused Czech and Slovak crowns at your port of exit.

MONEY

The Czech and Slovak republics have separate currencies, the Czech crown (Kč) and the Slovak crown (Sk). The higher inflation rate in Slovakia once meant that the Czech crown was worth a bit more than the Slovak crown. However, following the devaluation of the Czech crown in the summer of 1997, the currencies are essentially equal in value.

US dollars and German marks are the most sensible currencies to pack: they're as welcome as crowns in touristy parts of both republics. Since the introduction of the new US$100 note, many exchange offices and smaller banks are hesitant to accept old-style bills. This will undoubtedly be the case with the soon-to-be released US$50 and US$20 notes.

In both republics, American Express, Thomas Cook and Eurocheques travellers cheques are accepted at most banks, and are relatively easy to replace if lost. American

Express has offices in Prague, and is represented by Tatratour in Slovakia.

In both republics, exchange rates for cash are about 2% lower than for travellers cheques, though commissions are a bit higher. Most banks charge at least 4% to give you *dollars* from travellers cheques.

One warning: Avoid the black market in both republics. The Czech and Slovak currencies are widely convertible, and the black market rates are at best only 1 to 2% higher than bank rates. Basically, people offering to change money on the streets are out to rip you off.

Czech Republic

Costs Food, transportation and admission fees are fairly cheap; it's mostly accommodation that makes the Czech Republic one of the most expensive countries in eastern Europe. If you want to travel on a shoestring, you must spend a little time looking for a cheap place to stay and/or be prepared to rough it. Get out of Prague and your costs will drop dramatically.

By staying at cheap hostels and campsites, sticking to self-catering, pubs and stand-up cafeterias, and going easy on the beer and wine, you might get away with US$15 per person per day in summer. In a private home or better hostel, with meals at cheap restaurants, and using public transport, you can get by on US$25 to US$30. To share a clean double room with bath in a mid-range hotel or pension, and enjoy good local or western meals, plan on at least US$35 to US$50.

In Prague, add a third to half again, and even more if you want to be close to the centre. Having a room to yourself will cost you more. These estimates don't include things like souvenirs, postage and tours. If you spend a lot of time on the move, your costs will be higher.

Outside the summer season, except for Easter and Christmas-New Year, many bottom and mid-range hotels drop their prices by a third or more. Rates may also drop if you take a room for more than a night or two.

A disappointing side of the Czech concept of a 'free market economy' is the official two price system in which foreigners pay around double the local price for most hotel rooms, bus tickets, museum and concert tickets, and sometimes international airline tickets. Some exchange bureaus charge Czechs a lower commission, or none at all, and give better exchange rates to locals than to foreigners. Sometimes simply questioning the price difference results in an 'error correction'; if not, you must either pay the higher price or go elsewhere.

ATMs The easiest way to change money is with your bank card. ATMs (*bankomat*) are everywhere in the Czech Republic, even in smaller towns, and you generally get an excellent rate of exchange. Before leaving find out how much your home bank charges for each ATM transaction (generally US$1 to US$3, plus a foreign currency conversion rate). It's also a good idea to get a four digit PIN (personal identification number). Also note that many ATMs in Europe only have numerical key pads, so memorise your PIN as a number rather than as a word.

Nearly all ATMs in the Czech Republic accept Eurocard. Equally common are MasterCard/Cirrus and Visa/Plus ATMs. One of the largest providers is Komerční banka, which is connected to the MasterCard/Cirrus/Eurocard network. The banks Česká spořitelna and Československá obchodní have ATMs that accept Visa/Plus/Eurocard.

Credit Cards Up-market hotels and restaurants in major tourist centres accept some cards, usually American Express, Visa or MasterCard (Access), and sometimes Eurocard, Diners Club or JCB. Čedok and most other travel agencies accept all of these. Many Prague tourist shops accept credit cards, though some places will charge an extra 1 to 3% as a processing fee.

Lost Credit Cards & Travellers Cheques If your cheques or cards are lost or stolen, the best way to freeze the accounts and get replacements is to call your home office (or the Prague office in the case of American Express or Thomas Cook). Lost Visa cards can also be reported in Prague at ☎ 02-24 12 53 53, MasterCard/Eurocard at ☎ 02-24 42 31 35, American Express at ☎ 02-24 21 99 78 and Diners Club at ☎ 02-673 14 48.

Živnostenská can also help, at its office or via its credit-card hotline (☎ 02-24 23 24 23). It may also let you draw emergency cash on a lost Visa card or MasterCard if you have your account number and passport.

If you're not an American Express or Thomas Cook customer, the fastest way to get emergency money from home is through Western Union at the office of Sport Turist, Národní 33, although you will only be paid in crowns. A funds transfer to a Prague bank can take up to 10 working days.

Currency The unit of Czech money is the *koruna*, or crown, abbreviated Kč (for *Koruna česká*). A crown is divided into 100 *haléřů*, or heller (h). Notes come in 5000, 1000, 500, 200, 100, 50 and 20 Kč denominations. Coins come in 50, 20, 10, 5, 2 and 1 Kč, and 50, 20 and 10 h denominations. Always have a few 2 Kč and 5 Kč coins for use in public toilets, telephones and ticket machines.

All old notes from the days of united Czechoslovakia (identifiable by the words *Korun československých*) ceased to be legal tender in the Czech Republic in October 1993, so beware of being offered Czechoslovak currency.

Exchange Rates Since early 1991 the exchange rate has been fairly steady, with about 9% annual inflation. When this book went to press, the exchange rates for purchase of Czech crowns were:

Australia	A$1	=	25.11 Kč
Austria	AS1	=	2.70 Kč
Canada	C$1	=	24.85 Kč
France	1FF	=	5.63 Kč
Germany	DM1	=	19.04 Kč
Hungary	Ft100	=	17.00 Kč
Japan	¥100	=	29.50 Kč
New Zealand	NZ$1	=	22.54 Kč
Poland	Zł1	=	9.75 Kč
Slovakia	Sk 1	=	0.99 Kč
UK	UK£1	=	57.27 Kč
USA	US$1	=	34.17 Kč

Changing Money Changing money in the Czech Republic can be a hassle as many private exchange offices (especially in Prague) deduct commissions (*výlohy*) of up to 10%. Some of these advertise competitive rates on large boards but don't mention their sky-high commission – if in doubt, ask first. Hotels typically charge 5% commission while Čedok travel agencies charge 2%. Banks take only 2%, but their opening hours are short and they are closed on weekends and holidays.

The Komerční banka is usually efficient about changing travellers cheques for a standard US$2 commission. That said, you should always ask about the commission, as it can vary from branch to branch.

The American Express and Thomas Cook offices in Prague change their own and other companies' travellers cheques without charging commissions, though the American Express rates are slightly worse than those offered by the banks.

Now that the crown is a fully convertible currency it is easy to change a few thousand crowns into foreign currencies. However, if you have more than 5000 Kč to change you will be required to show exchange receipts. It is easy to exchange Czech crowns in Germany, Austria and the Netherlands, and theoretically it should be easy in other EU countries.

Tipping The standard tip in restaurants and taxis is 5 to 10%. The usual protocol at restaurants is for the server to tell you the total food bill and for you, as you hand over the money, to say how much you are paying with the tip included. Tips are appreciated – but not mandatory – at beer halls and bars. A tip of at least 5% is definitely expected at trendy bars in Prague and in other major cities.

Taxes & Refunds The value-added tax (VAT) is only 5% on food but up to 22% on hotel rooms, petrol, restaurant meals and luxury items. This tax is included in the sticker price and not added at the cash register, so you shouldn't notice it directly. If you spend more than US$50 at any shop ask for a VAT refund form – theoretically you can present these at Prague's airport for a refund (though when I tried, customs officials simply laughed and said 'not possible').

Slovakia

Costs Because Slovakia has been much slower to privatise than the Czech Republic, it's likely to remain a bargain for travellers far longer than its neighbour; prices on average are 10% lower than in the Czech Republic.

You'll find food, museum admissions and transport cheap and accommodation quite manageable – except in Bratislava. If you stay in hostels or camp, eat at local beer halls and go easy on souvenirs and imported goods (candy bars, sodas, beer etc) expect to spend about US$15 to US$20 per day. If you're staying in mid-range hotels and pensions and eat at tourist-oriented restaurants, budget at least US$30 to US$40 per day. In Bratislava you'll find it hard to survive on less than US$30 per day in hostels, and between US$35 and US$40 per day in cheap hotels.

ATMs All large towns and most smaller ones have ATMs (*bankomat*) that accept MasterCard/Cirrus and Visa/Plus cards; Eurocards are typically accepted at all ATMs. The bank Slovenská sporiteľňa usually handles Visa/Plus while VÚB (Všeobecná úverová banka) handles MasterCard/Cirrus.

Credit Cards American Express, MasterCard and Visa are widely accepted in Bratislava at up-market hotels, restaurants and tourist shops. Credit cards are less useful outside the capital, though many branches of Slovenská sporiteľňa give crown cash advances from Visa cards at no charge. With MasterCard/Eurocard, go to VÚB, for American Express try Tatratour.

Lost Credit Cards & Travellers Cheques If you need to replace travellers cheques issued by American Express, contact its representative in Bratislava, Tatratour (☎ 07-533 50 12), at Františkánske námestie 3. Other cheques and all credit cards cannot be replaced directly in Slovakia; you'll have to contact your home office or travel agent.

Currency The unit of Slovak money is the *koruna* or crown, abbreviated Sk (for *Slovenská koruna*). A crown is divided into 100 *halierú* or heller (h). Notes come in 5000, 1000, 500, 200, 100, 50 and 20 Sk denominations. Coins come in 10, 5, 2 and 1 Sk, and 50, 20 and 10 h denominations.

Until 1993, Slovakia used recycled Czechoslovak notes, with a special *Slovensko* stamp added. It now has its own notes and coins, and all the old Czechoslovak currency is no longer legal tender.

Exchange Rates The Slovak crown is not freely convertible on world currency markets, though it's easy enough to exchange Slovak crowns for hard currencies in Slovakia, and for Czech crowns in the Czech Republic. At the time of writing the exchange rates for purchase of Slovak crowns were approximately:

Australia	A$1	=	25.22 Sk
Austria	AS1	=	2.71 Sk
Canada	C$1	=	24.96 Sk
Czech Republic	1 Kč	=	1.00 Sk
France	1FF	=	5.65 Sk
Germany	DM1	=	19.12 Sk
Hungary	Ft100	=	18.00 Sk
Japan	¥100	=	29.61 Sk
New Zealand	NZ$1	=	22.60 Sk
Poland	Zł1	=	9.78 Sk
UK	UK£1	=	57.50 Sk
USA	US$1	=	34.30 Sk

Changing Money The easiest place to change travellers cheques is at a branch of

VÚB or the Investičná banka (Investment Bank), where you'll be charged a standard 1% commission to change both travellers cheques and US dollars.

American Express is represented in Bratislava by Tatratour (☎ 07-33 58 52), Františkánské námestie 3, but they charge a 2% commission for exchanging *all* travellers cheques (even those issued by American Express).

Satur offices (see Tourist Offices) deduct 2%. Post offices take 2% on weekdays and 3% on weekends. Banks often give a slightly better rate for travellers cheques than for cash. You'll have no problem exchanging US dollars, German marks, British pounds, Czech crowns and Austrian schillings, but it's harder to change Polish zlotys and Hungarian forints.

Some exchange places might not accept damaged or torn US dollar bills.

Tipping In Bratislava and other major cities, a 5 to 10% tip is expected at upper-end restaurants and in taxis. Elsewhere in Slovakia tips are appreciated but not necessarily expected.

Taxes & Refunds The value-added tax (VAT) in Slovakia is 5% on food and up to 23% on hotel rooms, restaurant meals and luxury items. Satur offices in Bratislava refund 13% of the VAT to all foreign visitors on purchases of more than 1000 Sk (per item).

POST & COMMUNICATIONS

Postal Rates

The two republics' postal services are fairly efficient and not too expensive. In both republics it's safest to mail international parcels from main post offices in large cities.

Mail to Europe (automatically air mail) is 7 Kč/Sk for a letter, 5 Kč/6 Sk for a postcard. To anywhere else by air, a letter is 10 Kč/9 Sk and a postcard 6 Kč/7 Sk. Express service is 10 Kč/Sk extra, and registration is 20 Kč/Sk extra. Aerogrammes are 7 Kč/Sk.

A 2kg parcel to Europe (automatically air mail) is the equivalent of about US$12; to anywhere else it's US$25 to US$27 by air and about half that by sea. Books and printed matter can go for reduced rates in bundles up to 5kg. Larger post offices will let you send parcels of books or printed matter up to 15kg, at even lower rates.

If you are sending anything that looks like an antique, you will probably be sent to the post office's customs clearance office (*Pošta celnice/Poštovní colnica*).

In theory, in the Czech Republic only, anything else can be posted abroad from any major post office. In practice, many postal employees retain Communist-era anxieties about 'regulations', and may send you off to customs clearance if you have anything over 2kg, no matter what it is.

Always ask for a receipt (*paragon*) when mailing anything larger than a letter by air mail or a more expensive mail service. Post-office staff are notorious for charging for such services and then sending the item by surface mail.

Parcels containing glass and crystal will not be accepted by the postal systems of the USA, Australia and New Zealand.

Sending Mail

You can buy stamps in post offices and also from street vendors and newsagents. Letters go in the orange boxes outside post offices and around town.

Receiving Mail

Most larger post offices have a window for poste restante (*uložené zásilky/poste restante*), though the most reliable services are at the main post offices in Prague and Bratislava. You must present your passport to claim mail. Check under your given name too.

Holders of American Express and Thomas Cook credit cards and travellers cheques can have letters sent to the company's Prague offices (see the Prague chapter). The British and Canadian embassies in Prague will hold letters for their citizens for a few months. None will accept registered letters or parcels.

Telephone
In both republics, the current mobile-phone standard is 450MHz, as opposed to the 800MHz standard in the USA and most European countries. At the time of writing a new GSM/800MHz network was being installed in the Czech Republic.

Czech Republic Blue coin telephones accept only 2, 5, 10 and 20 Kč coins and can be used to make local (which cost 2 Kč in Prague), long-distance and international calls. Calls from hotel telephones usually involve substantial extra charges.

A more convenient alternative is a *telekart* (telephone card), good for local, long-distance and international calls. Card telephones are now much more common in Prague than coin-operated ones. Cards are sold in post offices, newsagents and the main telephone bureau; cards come in five different denomination worth from 100 to 300 Kč. It is not advisable to buy cards from people in the streets as you may end up paying more than the card is worth (the number of units should be marked on the back of the card in small print).

When dialling from within the Czech Republic you must add a 0 before the local area code. For directory inquiries call ☎ 120 (Prague) or ☎ 121 (elsewhere in the Czech Republic). Czech Telecom is still replacing the antiquated telephone system with a digital network, so changing telephone numbers will continue to be a problem for a few years to come.

International Calls The Czech Republic's international country code is ☎ 420.

You can make international telephone calls at main post offices; if you are ringing a European town, you will usually be put through right away. Operator-assisted international telephone calls cost US$3 a minute to New Zealand; US$2.50 a minute to Australia, Canada, the USA and Japan; and US$1 a minute to most of Europe. All calls have a three minute minimum. Check the rates with the clerk before placing your call, and ask for a receipt.

To make direct-dial international calls from within the Czech Republic, dial 00, the country code and the phone number. For international directory inquiries call ☎ 0149; for international telephone services call ☎ 0139.

For direct connections to operators in a particular country, either for collect or credit-card calls, dial:

Australia	
Telstra	(☎ 00 420 06101)
Optus	(☎ 00 420 06110)
Canada	(☎ 00 420 00151)
France	(☎ 00 420 03301)
Germany	(☎ 00 420 04949)
Ireland	(☎ 00 420 35301)
Israel	(☎ 00 420 97201)
Japan	(☎ 00 420 08100)
UK	
BT Direct	(☎ 00 420 04401)
Mercury	(☎ 00 420 04450)
USA	
AT&T	(☎ 00 420 00101)
MCI	(☎ 00 420 00112)
Sprint	(☎ 00 420 87187)

Slovakia Coin-operated phones take 1, 2, 5 and 10 Sk coins and can be used for local, long-distance and international calls. They accept extra coins and return the unused ones. Calls from hotel telephones inevitably involve much higher charges.

Telephone cards (*telefónna karta*) in Slovakia are good for local, long-distance and international calls. The cards are sold in post and telephone offices and some newsagents. There are four different types of cards worth from 100 Sk to 400 Sk. Card phones are as common as coin phones, though some remote regions of Slovakia tend to have only coin-operated phones.

When dialling long-distance within Slovakia you must add a 0 before the area code. The Slovak phone system is being modernised, and phone numbers in some regions are scheduled to change over the next few years. For directory inquiries call ☎ 121.

International Calls Slovakia's international country code is ☎ 421.

The easiest way to make international calls is from main post offices or telephone centres, although you can also make them from blue coin and phone-card phones on the street. A three minute call from Slovakia costs about US$3.50 to the UK, and US$5.50 to the USA or Australia. Operator assistance only doubles the cost of the first minute. To make direct-dial international calls dial 00, the country code and the number. Note that reverse-charge calls are not possible to Australia and some other countries.

The following countries have arrangements for direct connections to an operator in that country. However, the numbers seem to work only from Bratislava and other major cities, and then only about 50% of the time:

Australia	(☎ 00 421 061 01)
Canada	(☎ 1800 883 7166)
France	(☎ 0800 990 422)
Germany	(☎ 0130 80 4242)
Japan	(☎ 0039 427)
Netherlands	(☎ 06 022 0442)
UK	
BT	(☎ 0800 89 0420)
Mercury	(☎ 0500 89 0042)
USA	
AT&T	(☎ 1800 428 6608)
MCI	(☎ 1888 422 0042)

Fax, Telegraph & Email

Faxes, telex and telegraph messages can be sent and received in both republics at main post offices in the larger cities. Telegrams are 25 Kč/27 Sk per word to Europe, North America and Australasia.

Fax rates are 50 Kč/Sk to the UK, 85 Kč/Sk to the USA and Australia, and 135 Kč/Sk to South Africa – an A4-size page takes about 1½ minutes. There may be a small per-page charge for receiving faxes. Some hotels and agencies also have fax services, but they tend to charge a lot more.

Email is possible from Internet cafés in Prague and Brno (Czech Republic), and in Bratislava and Banská Bystrica (Slovakia); see the relevant city sections for more details. If you are carrying a laptop computer and a modem, it shouldn't be a problem to make a connection through a telephone line (the telephone tone is 'A'). Most new telephone plugs are US RJ-11 type. If the telephone plug is an old type, it is possible to buy new plugs with adapters in local electronic shops. (For more Internet information see the Online Services section.)

BOOKS

Current Affairs

The Europe-based journalist Timothy Garton Ash's *We the People: the Revolutions of 1989* features gripping first-hand accounts of the revolutions that swept away the region's old guard.

William Shawcross' biography *Dubček & Czechoslovakia* is about the late leader of Prague's original rebuff of Communism, which features a hasty post-1989 update. Another biography is Michael Simmons' *The Reluctant President: A Political Life of Václav Havel.*

A history of the oppressed Slovak nation is described by Stanislav J Kirschbaum in *A History of Slovakia – The Struggle for Survival.*

Essays & Memoirs

Several books by the dissident-turned-president, Václav Havel, offer an 'inside' view. *Disturbing the Peace* is a collection of recent historical musings. *Letters to Olga* is a collection of letters to his wife from prison in the 1980s. *Living In Truth* is a series of absorbing political essays.

Patrick Leigh Fermor's *A Time of Gifts* is the luminous first instalment of the author's trek through Europe, including Czechoslovakia, in the early 1930s.

Fiction

Bruce Chatwin's *Utz* is a quiet, absorbing novella about a porcelain collector in Prague's old Jewish quarter. Jaroslav Hašek's *The Good Soldier Švejk* is good low-brow WWI humour about the trials of Czechoslovakia's literary mascot, written in instalments from Prague's pubs. *Old*

Czech Legends is a compendium of Bohemian legends by Alois Jirásek, a leading light of the Czech National Revival. *The Trial* and *The Castle* are Franz Kafka's complex and claustrophobic masterpieces.

Milan Kundera is one of the Czech Republic's best-known authors-in-exile, who wrote about life under the Communist regime. Probably his best novel is *Joke*; two other notable works are *The Book of Laughter and Forgetting* and *The Unbearable Lightness of Being*. Other good reads are *Cowards* and *The Bride of Texas* by the highly respected Josef Škvorecký, and *The Ship Named Hope* by Ivan Klíma.

Until recently Bohumír Hrabal was one of the Czech Republic's leading contemporary novelists – in 1997 the 83-year-old writer fell to his death from a 5th floor window, trying to feed some birds. His most notable works are *Closely Observed Trains* and *The Little Town That Stood Still*.

The Year of the Frog is one of the latest novels by Martin Šimečka, a Czech-born writer who writes mostly in Slovak. The story follows the life of a young intellectual during the Communist era, who can only work menial jobs because he is barred from college due to his family's anti-government attitudes.

Guidebooks

Lonely Planet For an in-depth look at Prague – not to mention handy colour maps and photos – see Lonely Planet's *Prague* city guide by John King and Richard Nebeský. There are also LP's *Central Europe* and *Eastern Europe* guidebooks, both with sections on the Czech and Slovak republics.

General There are hundreds of coffee-table books on Prague, the Czech and Slovak republics, the High Tatras mountains, you name it – but not all have high-quality colour reproductions. One of the better ones on Slovakia is *Slovensko*, compiled by Eugen Lazišťan, with colour photos from all over the country, including a historical introduction. A good regional book with flora and fauna sections on the Tatras mountains is *Tatry*, by Vladimír Bárta.

ONLINE SERVICES

The Lonely Planet web site has up-to-the-minute travel information and plenty of tips (www.lonelyplanet.com).

EU Net provides regional information, travel tips, and links to related web pages at its Czech site (www.eunet.cz) and Slovak site (www.eunet.sk). EU Net also provides PPP/Slip accounts in both republics. Another service provider with some Czech-related information is CES Net (www.cesnet.cz).

Stay on top of Czech and Slovak news stories courtesy of the Prague Post (www.praguepost.cz) or the news service CTK (www.ctknews.com).

The Czech Ministry of Foreign Affairs has an excellent site packed with country and travel information, and lots of links (www.czech.cz). There's also an Olomouc-specific web site (www.winet.cz/viso.htm).

Central Europe Online is a popular site with lots of links to Czech and Slovak servers (www.ceo.cz).

Bratislava and other major Slovak cities are featured at Slovakia.Com's web site (www.slovak.com) and Slovakia Online (www.savba.sk/logos); the latter provides online reservations at up-market hotels. There's a similar hotel-reservation service in the Czech Republic (www.travel.cz).

CZ Web (www.czweb.com) focuses on Czech business and has a small classified section. It's even possible to post a resumé and search for jobs in the Czech Republic (www.jobs.cz).

A dependable Czech service provider with email/PPP/Slip accounts for 500 Kč per month is @Terminal.CZ in Prague (☎ 02-231 10 93 or 231 20 39; fax 02-231 17 74; www.terminal.cz; email address online@terminal.cz).

NEWSPAPERS & MAGAZINES

Neither republic has an English-language daily, but the weekly *Prague Post* at 40 Kč is good value for visitors. Along with local investigations, regional news and features, it has practical 'facts for the visitor' sections, travel tips, concert and restaurant reviews, and day-by-day arts and entertainment listings.

The Slovak Spectator, a bi-monthly English-language paper published in Bratislava, includes the latest information on what's happening in the city.

The growing business community in Prague is well informed with a glossy monthly magazine *The Prague Tribune* and two weekly newspapers, the *Central European Business Weekly* and the *Prague Business Journal,* which feature business-oriented regional news plus a few entertainment and restaurant listings. The monthly magazine *Business Central Europe,* part of Britain's *The Economist* family, focuses on regional financial and political issues.

Major European and US newspapers and a few magazines are on sale at kiosks and newsagents in larger cities.

RADIO & TV

The BBC World Service broadcasts in Prague (101.1 FM) and Brno (101.3 FM) in English daily at 8 and 10 am, 5 and 10 pm and midnight. BBC English-language programmes are available 24 hours in Bratislava (93.8 FM) and Košice (103.2 FM).

Club VOA – Voice of America pop music and news – is on 106.2 FM, with Czech-language news at half-past each hour. Other Czech radio stations broadcast English-language news; see the *Prague Post* for the latest frequencies.

No Slovak stations have regular English-language programming, though Radio Tatry (102.5 FM) has tourist bulletins in English daily at 7.20 and 9.20 am, and 8.30 pm, with mountain conditions and travel tips. The most independent Slovak radio station is Radio Ragtime (106.6 or 100.3 FM), which has a good mix of jazz and modern rock. Its main competitor is Radio Twist (101.8 or 105.1 FM).

Of the Czech Republic's two state-run TV channels, ČT 2 has Euronews weekdays at around 8 am and noon, and on weekends at around 7 am. There are two other private channels, NOVA and Prima TV, with Czech-language programmes. Anyone with satellite service can receive dozens of European and US cable stations.

Slovakia has two state-run TV channels, STV1 and STV2, as well as two private TV channels, Markíza and VTV. Neither has English-language programming. It's possible to pick up Czech programming in some parts of Slovakia. TVs with satellite connections can receive English-language channels such as the news-oriented Super Channel, Eurosport or HBO.

PHOTOGRAPHY & VIDEO

Basic Kodak and Agfa colour-print films are widely available in Prague, Bratislava and other major tourist centres, as are basic slide films such as Kodak Elite II and Fuji Sensia. Prices are only slightly higher (sometimes even cheaper) than what you would pay back home. Except in Prague, professional films are very difficult to find and serious photographers should bring their own.

Avoid local brands of film, which cannot always be processed in other countries.

You can get prints done in Prague and other tourist centres, for about US$1.50 plus US$0.15 per print. Czech and Slovak photo shops and labs are *not* good places to get slides developed.

Restrictions

It's apparently still forbidden to shoot things like military installations and border checkpoints, but you're unlikely to be stopped from photographing train stations, dams, bridges and other sites once considered 'strategically important'. We've found off-duty soldiers more than happy to be snapped.

Photographing People

Forty-five years with secret police behind every shrub has made some people uneasy about having their pictures taken, so ask them first. A genuine offer to send a print can loosen a potential subject up. Some people dislike you photographing embarrassing things like run-down housing.

'May I take your photograph?' is *Můžu si váš vyfotit?* in Czech, and *Možem si vás odfotit?* in Slovak.

Airport Security

A single dose of airport X-rays used for carry-on bags won't harm slow or medium-speed films, but the effects are cumulative and repeated doses can fog your pictures. Lead 'film-safe' pouches reduce the risk, but if you'll be flying a lot, the best solution is hand inspection. Having all your film in a few clear plastic bags makes it easier.

TIME

The Czech and Slovak republics are both on Central European Time, ie GMT/UTC plus one hour. Clocks are reset to daylight-saving time (DST), one hour ahead, on the last weekend in March and back again on the last weekend in October.

When it's noon in Prague or Bratislava in summer, it's 3 am in San Francisco and Vancouver; 6 am in New York and Toronto; 11 am in London and Dublin; noon in Paris, Berlin, Vienna, Budapest and Warsaw; 1 pm in Kiev; 8 pm (10 pm) in Sydney; and 10 pm (midnight) in Wellington.

For the southern hemisphere, the time is two hours later (in brackets above) during the DST period, April-September inclusive.

Since most central European countries go to DST on identical changeover dates, you'll never have to reset your watch crossing to and from Germany, Austria, Hungary or Poland. Other countries may have slightly different DST dates, which can give rise to one-hour variations in the above shifts during March or October. Australia and New Zealand are on DST when northern-hemisphere countries aren't, which is the reason for the additional time-lag in these countries between April and October.

Czechs and Slovaks quote time on a 24 hour clock so there is no equivalent of 'am' and 'pm'. But they commonly add *ráno* (morning), *dopoledne/dopoludnia* (before noon), *odpoledne/popoludní* (afternoon) or *večer* (evening).

ELECTRICITY

Electricity in the Czech and Slovak republics is 220V AC, 50Hz. Most outlets have the two small round holes common throughout continental Europe; some also have a protruding earth (ground) pin. If you have some other plug or want to use the earth pin, bring a universal adapter. North American appliances will also need a transformer.

WEIGHTS & MEASURES

The metric system is in use. A comma is used at the decimal place and full stops at the thousands, millions etc, plus a dash after prices rounded to the nearest crown. For example, a price of 3000 crowns would be written 3.000,-.

LAUNDRY

As far as we know, only Prague has western-style self-service laundrettes, where a normal load costs 105 Kč to wash and dry. Some top-end hotels have an (expensive) overnight laundry service. Otherwise you must rely on a traditional laundry (*prádelna* in Czech, *čistiareň* or *práčovňa* in Slovak), which can take up to a week! If you'd rather do your own in the hotel sink, bring along a universal sink plug and a bit of line. Detergent is easy to find in the shops.

TOILETS

The hygiene in toilets can vary greatly, and dirty toilets can be one of the most unpleasant experiences of travelling in the Czech and Slovak republics, especially if you have to pay for the use of the toilet. Some attendants in public toilets can be stingy with toilet paper, as they usually only hand over a few miserable pieces.

Public toilets are free in state-run museums, galleries and concert halls, and most cafés and restaurants don't seem to mind non-guests using theirs – ask for *toalet*, *záchod* or WC (pronounced 'vay say'). Elsewhere – in train, bus and metro stations – they're staffed by attendants who ask for a crown or two for use of the toilet and sometimes a further donation to use the washbasin. Men's are marked *muži* or *páni*, women's *ženy* or *dámy*.

HEALTH

Public hygiene in centres like Prague and Bratislava, while not at western European levels, is generally quite good. In rural areas, where standards are lower, you should take the kind of common-sense precautions you would in a developing country – not only with food and personal hygiene but, for example, in contact with animals.

For hikers and campers, ticks sometimes carry infections, the troublesome ones being encephalitis and Lyme disease. In the mountains, you'll need to be prepared for the effects of cold. Prague and some North Bohemian industrial towns are no fun in winter if you have respiratory problems.

Predeparture Preparations

With a little planning before you go, and day-to-day care when you're there, you should have nothing worse than the occasional grumpy stomach in the Czech and Slovak republics.

Health Insurance A policy covering medical treatment is not a bad idea (though UK and German visitors are entitled by treaty to low-cost treatment; see Medical Help in this section). Policies offered by various 'student' travel agencies are good value.

Medical Kit Unless you're only visiting Prague, you might want to carry a small kit for minor problems – eg tweezers, scissors, aspirin, antiseptic, plasters (Band-Aids), a few gauze pads and adhesive tape, alcohol wipes, moleskin (for foot blisters), and a 'plug' for diarrhoea (Imodium, Lomotil or a kaolin preparation like Pepto Bismol).

Iodine water-purification tablets are useful only if you're planning a long hike in the mountains.

Considering the potential for contamination via poorly sterilised needles, some travellers now routinely carry a pack of disposable syringes – available from medical supply shops back home – for any injections while on the road. A doctor's note will help you get them past suspicious customs officials.

Bring whatever medications you might need, as they may not be available here. For any prescription drug, bring the prescription too (with the generic rather than the brand name), as proof of what it is. If you're required to take a narcotic drug, carry a doctor's letter. Always keep medicines in their original, labelled containers and in your hand luggage.

Vaccinations There are no required jabs, but if you expect to spend much time in rural areas, it's wise to protect yourself against hepatitis A and tetanus. Most western travellers will have been immunised against measles and polio in childhood, though your doctor may suggest boosters (required for tetanus every 10 years). Serious campers and hikers may want to consider immunisation for tick encephalitis.

Medical Help

Every sizable town has a *polyklinika*, though few have seen many foreigners. Medical training, equipment and standards of hygiene (and funds for training doctors) are not what most westerners expect, though they are adequate for routine, walk-in problems. Few doctors outside major cities speak English. Prague and Bratislava have special facilities to serve their concentrations of foreign diplomats and business people.

Emergency treatment and non-hospital first aid are free for all foreign visitors (you must show your passport). You must pay for any other hospital treatment unless you're a short-term visitor or long-term

ALL PHOTOS BY RICHARD NEBESKÝ

Folk Costumes of the Czech & Slovak Republics
Rich veins of folk culture still exist in the Czech and Slovak republics. In these regions, which tend to be in the remotest and most rural corners, highly decorative costumes have evolved. The most striking feature is the elaborate embroidery in bright colours and abstract or pictorial designs.

ALL PHOTOS BY RICHARD NEBESKÝ

Folk Festivals
The Czech and Slovak republics have many excellent folk festivals (some, like the Ride of the Kings, are steeped in tradition) where folk arts – such as story-telling, singing, music, dancing, handcrafts – are celebrated by whole communities.

worker from the UK or Germany, in which case you may get cheap or free hospital treatment for urgent problems – as do Czechs and Slovaks in your country – under reciprocal health-care agreements. Others must pay for treatment, normally in crowns, and at least some of it up front; costs are very modest from a western standpoint.

Everybody pays for prescribed medications, though prices are low. Almost every town has a state-run pharmacy, a good place to buy aspirin and vitamin C, though not to fill most western prescriptions.

Basic Rules

Water Locals may say you can drink the tap water, but in remote places – and even in parts of Prague – it's probably not a good idea. If you choose not to, then avoid brushing your teeth in it too, and take your drinks without ice. Bottled water is fairly easy to find.

Food & Drink Most restaurant and take-away food is as hygienic as in the west, but stick with hot, freshly made dishes, and be suspicious of fish and shellfish. When buying dairy or meat products, be sure the shop's refrigerator works – some don't. Bottled milk is nearly always pasteurised, yoghurt is always hygienic, and the dates stamped on them are manufacture dates, not use-by dates.

Czechs and Slovaks are fanatical mushroom and berry hunters. If you want to go, take a local friend with plenty of experience, since many varieties will give you an upset stomach, and some mushrooms are deadly poisonous.

Medical Problems & Treatment

Diarrhoea A change of water or food can bring on the runs, but a few dashes to the loo with no other symptoms is nothing to worry about. Diarrhoea that goes on for days, however, especially with blood or mucus and/or accompanied by a fever, may indicate dysentery or other infection from contaminated food or water. For this you need medical attention. An immediate risk with diarrhoea is dehydration, especially in children.

Tick Encephalitis & Lyme Disease Ticks (*klíště*) are a common nuisance in forests, scrubland and long grass, climbing into the undergrowth to hitch a ride on anything passing by. If you find that one has burrowed into your skin, *don't* pull it off, as that can leave the head in place and increase the risk of infection. Coax it out with Vaseline, oil or alcohol, and try not to touch it even then. If it has been there some time, a red blotch may appear around it.

About 5% of ticks carry tick encephalitis, a virus-borne cerebral inflammation. In this case, the blotches may be several centimetres or more across, sometimes pale in the centre. Headache, stiffness and other flu-like symptoms, as well as extreme tiredness and weakness, appearing a week or two after the bite, can progress to more serious conditions, and even death, without medical care.

This is a risk for hikers and campers from May through September. The best prevention is to wear long trousers tucked into your boots or socks, use insect repellent and check yourself every few hours for the little blighters. You can get a short-lasting vaccine against tick encephalitis in the Czech and Slovak republics, and a vaccine is available in the west that immunises you for years.

Lyme disease is another tick-borne bacterial infection, causing a form of arthritis. It comes from the bite of infected ticks that usually live on deer (sometimes horses), and is usually prevalent from April through September. Appearing as a rash around the bite, it also has flu-like symptoms including aching joints, and it can have serious long-term effects. Early medical attention is important. There's no vaccine.

Animal Bites The only poisonous snake in either republic is the *zmije*, or viper, for which an antivenin is widely available, and is unlikely to be deadly unless you are allergic to the venom. The viper has a wavy black line stretching the length of its grey back. This is only likely to be a risk for hikers and campers, in summer. Vipers are found in and near forests throughout both republics, and are frequently seen sunning themselves on rocks during the day.

Wear boots, socks and long trousers in undergrowth and rocky areas where snakes may be present. Keep your hands out of holes and crevices and be careful when collecting firewood. Keep a snake-bite victim calm and still, wrap the bitten limb tightly – as you would for a sprained ankle – and attach a splint to immobilise it. *Do not* apply a tourniquet or try sucking out the venom! Get medical help. Take the snake if it's unquestionably dead, but don't try catching it if it isn't!

Domestic pets are not an important health risk, except for the rare dog with *slintavka* (rabies). Areas where this is a problem are usually signposted.

HIV & AIDS HIV, the Human Immunodeficiency Virus, develops into AIDS, Acquired Immune Deficiency Syndrome, which is a fatal disease. HIV is a major problem in many countries. Any exposure to blood, blood products or body fluids may put the individual at risk. The disease is often transmitted through sexual contact or dirty needles – vaccinations, acupuncture, tattooing and body piercing can be potentially as dangerous as intravenous drug use. HIV/AIDS can also be spread through infected blood transfusions; some developing countries cannot afford to screen blood used for transfusions.

If you do need an injection, ask to see the syringe unwrapped in front of you, or take a needle and syringe pack with you.

Being an international problem, AIDS has no boundaries. The number of AIDS cases in the Czech and Slovak republics is relatively low compared with many regions worldwide, and STDs are a more common and pressing problem here. However, according to official statistics (as of June 1996) 59 people have died from AIDS in the Czech Republic and just under 300 are HIV positive. Statistics are not available, but there are fewer cases in Slovakia.

Sexually Transmitted Diseases Gonorrhoea, herpes and syphilis are among these diseases; sores, blisters or rashes around the genitals, discharges or pain when urinating are common symptoms. In some STDs, such as wart virus or chlamydia, symptoms may be less marked or not observed at all, especially in women. Syphilis symptoms eventually disappear completely but the disease continues and can cause severe problems in later years. While abstinence from sexual contact is the only 100% effective prevention, using condoms is also effective. The treatment of gonorrhoea and syphilis is with antibiotics. The different sexually transmitted diseases each require specific antibiotics. There is no cure for herpes.

Hypothermia Mountain hikers run a risk of hypothermia, which means the body loses heat faster than it can generate it. It's amazingly easy to go from chilly to dangerously cold through a combination of fatigue, hunger, wind and wet clothing (from rain or sweat), even when the temperature is well above freezing.

Symptoms may include numbness, shivering, muscle cramps, dizzy spells, lethargy, clumsiness, slurred speech, irrational behaviour and violent bursts of energy. You're more likely to recognise symptoms of hypothermia in someone else than in yourself.

To prevent it, dress in easily donned layers. Silk, wool and some synthetics insulate well even when wet – cotton doesn't. A hat makes a big difference, as a lot of heat is lost through the head. A waterproof outer layer is obviously important. Sugary snacks help to generate heat quickly (but aren't good longer term).

To treat it, take shelter and replace wet clothing with dry. Drink hot liquids (not alcohol) and eat easily digestible, high-calorie snacks. In advanced cases it may be necessary to put the victim in a sleeping bag and get in with them. If possible give them a warm (not hot) bath.

The reduced oxygen at high altitudes can cause altitude sickness – headaches, dizziness, breathlessness, and sometimes much more serious problems – but few will fall victim to this even in the High Tatras, since it rarely strikes below 3000m.

Women's Health

Women travellers often find that their periods become irregular or even cease while they're on the road. Remember that a missed period in these circumstances doesn't necessarily indicate pregnancy.

Poor diet, lowered resistance due to the use of antibiotics for stomach upsets, and even contraceptive pills can lead to vaginal infections when travelling. Keeping the genital area clean, and wearing skirts or loose-fitting trousers and cotton underwear, will help to prevent infections.

Yeast infections, characterised by a rash, itch and discharge, can be treated with a vinegar or even lemon-juice douche or with yoghurt. Nystatin suppositories are the

Health Spas

Across the two republics are hundreds of mineral springs whose waters, taken externally or internally, are said to be excellent for all sorts of ailments. The waters often taste quite odd due to their mineral content, ranging from rotten eggs to rust, but you can convince yourself that they are doing you a power of good.

Locals and foreigners – mostly elderly – take the cure at dozens of spas. Although many spa towns make fine trips, the spas themselves are for medical treatment and not really geared for drop-in visits.

A spa course, typically about three weeks, must be booked well in advance. For spas in the Czech Republic contact Balnea (☎ 02-24 22 76 44; fax 21 10 53 07), Národní 28, Prague 1. For Slovak spas book through Slovthermae at Radlinského 13 in Bratislava (☎ 07-581 80 or 588 47; fax 580 59), and at Winterova 29 in Piešťany. Alternatively, ask at any Čedok or Satur office abroad.

Room, board and treatment start at about US$60 per person per day in summer, less in winter, still less for companions not taking treatment.

Some better known spa towns and their specialities are:

Bardejovské Kúpele (East Slovakia): stomach, gall bladder and respiratory diseases
Dudince (West Slovakia): heart disease, circulation disorders, motor and nervous disorders
Františkovy Lázně (West Bohemia): cardiac disease, rheumatism, gynaecological disorders
Jeseník (North Moravia): allergies, respiratory and thyroid diseases
Karlovy Vary (West Bohemia): diseases of the liver, gall bladder, stomach and intestines, metabolic disorders
Luhačovice (South Moravia): respiratory and nervous diseases, stomach disorders
Mariánské Lázně (West Bohemia): diseases of the kidney, urinary tract and skin; metabolic and respiratory disorders
Piešťany (West Slovakia): rheumatism, nervous diseases
Poděbrady (Central Bohemia): heart disease
Sliač (Central Slovakia): vascular, arterial and heart diseases
Teplice (North Bohemia): motor, nervous and vascular disorders
Trenčianske Teplice (West Slovakia): rheumatism, motor conditions, respiratory diseases

Of these, the most venerable, famous and attractive (and heavily touristed) towns are Karlovy Vary and Mariánské Lázně. ■

usual medical prescription. Trichomonas is a more serious infection; symptoms are a discharge and a burning sensation when urinating. If a vinegar-water douche is not effective medical attention should be sought. Metronidazole (Flagyl) is the prescribed drug. With yeast infections or trichomonas, male sexual partners should also be treated.

WOMEN TRAVELLERS

Women (especially solo) may find the atmosphere in most non-touristy pubs a bit raw, as they tend to be male territory. *Kavárny* (coffee shops) often dispense beer and wine too, and are more congenial. *Vinárny* (wine bars) are another good place for drinks and a meal.

To many westerners the Czech and Slovak republics seem to be picking up, sexually speaking, where they left off in 1948. Some newsstands stock dozens of porno titles; even mainstream advertising has no qualms about the occasional naked breast to sell products. The expatriate press in Prague bubbles with arguments about whether this is sexism or freedom of expression, though on the whole locals seem less fussed about the matter than foreigners are.

The darker side is that sexual violence has been on the rise since 1989, at least in Prague. Most Czech women we talked to said they sometimes experience whistling and catcalls. Attacks on local women have happened in all parts of Prague, but statistically speaking women are far safer in the Czech and Slovak republics than in the west. The most dangerous area for women at night is the park in front of Prague's main train station. Women should also avoid deserted and dark streets at night.

There are not many services for women such as refuge or rape crisis centres, but one such crisis centre for women is Prague's White House of Safety (Bílí dům bezpečí; ☎ 02-43 88 33). The White House is only open on Tuesday between 5 and 7 pm.

GAY & LESBIAN TRAVELLERS

Czech Republic

The gay and lesbian monthly magazine *SOHO* provides information for gays, but it is only in Czech. The editor can provide some information for English-speakers in the *SOHO* office (☎ 02-24 25 71 33), Vinohradská 46, Prague 2. There is also an Infocentrum pro ženy (for women; ☎ 02-23 13 23 56), Klimentská 17. A crisis centre for gays is Sokrates Plus (☎ 035-243 31).

Homosexuality is legal in the Czech Republic (the age of consent is 15), but Czechs are not accustomed to seeing gays showing affection to each other in public. That said, their reaction will most likely be nothing more than a surprised look.

Slovakia

Homosexuality has been legal since the 1960s (the age of consent is 16). Gay-bashing is unknown and there is a lot of tolerance towards homosexuals. That said, Slovaks are not accustomed to public displays of gay affection; it's best to be discreet. Officially there are only a few cases of HIV/AIDS in the country, so there is a laissez-faire attitude about the disease.

In Bratislava the local gay organisation is Ganymedes, PO Box 4, Pošta 3, with a few branches around the country – though very few staff speak English. The organisation has a Trust Line (Linka dôvery; ☎ 07-211 54 61), available only on Monday between 6 and 8.30 pm.

For advice about AIDS contact Linka pomoci a prevencie AIDS in Banská Bystrica (☎ 088-75 32 61) or Košice (☎ 095-43 63 17).

DISABLED TRAVELLERS

No attention used to be paid to facilities for disabled people but this is changing slowly. Ramps for wheelchair users in Prague are becoming more common, especially at the more expensive hotels and major street crossings. Transport is a major problem as buses and trams have no wheelchair access.

In Prague only the main train station (hlavní nádraží) and Holešovice train station, as well as a handful of metro stations, have self-operating lifts. Czech Railways (ČD) claims that any larger station in the Czech Republic has ramps and lifts for wheelchairs onto the train but the harsh reality is that the service is poor. McDonald's and KFC entrances and toilets are wheelchair friendly.

Disabled people planning to travel with ČSA need to inform the airline of their needs when booking the ticket. The Stavovské Theatre in Prague has wheelchair access and is equipped for the hearing-impaired.

For more information in the Czech Republic contact the Union of the Disabled (*Sdružení zdravotně postižených v ČR*; ☎ 02-24 81 69 97), Karlínské náměstí 12, Karlín, Prague 8. The wheelchair disabled and the blind also have their organisations: the Prague Wheelchair Users Organisation (*Pražská organizace vozíčkářů*; ☎ 02-232 58 03) at Benediktská 6, Josefov, and the Union of the Blind and Weak Sighted (*Společnost nevidomých a slabozrakých v ČR*; ☎ 02-73 05 52) at Kouřimská 4, Prague 3. The monthly cultural programme booklet *Přehled* (in Czech language only) indicates with a wheelchair symbol if the museum, gallery, cinema or theatre has wheelchair access.

The only organisation in Slovakia is the Slovak Union for the Disabled (*Slovenský zväz tělesně postihnutých*; ☎ 07-36 32 85/6), Jakubovo námestie 12, Bratislava, but again there is little English spoken here.

TRAVEL WITH CHILDREN

There are plenty of activities for children in both republics. Czechs and Slovaks are generally family oriented, with children being part of their daily life. Unfortunately, many theatre performances and films are only in Czech or Slovak.

Restaurants do not specifically cater to children in the western sense, like McDonald's with playgrounds etc. Some restaurants list a children's menu (*dětský jídelníček* in Czech; *detský jedálny lístok* in Slovak), but even if they don't they can usually provide smaller portions for a lower price. Diapers and many other accessories for babies are commonly available in large towns.

A useful source of information is Lonely Planet's *Travel with Children*, by Maureen Wheeler.

Czech Republic

Some of the country's many museums and other activities are ready-made for children. In Prague try the Toy Museum, the National Technical Museum, the Police Museum, the Military Museum or the Transport Museum.

Prague's Petřín Hill is a large park where parents can take a break from sightseeing with their children. In the park itself it is also possible to enjoy the funicular rail, the mirror maze, Petřín Tower, the Štefánik Planetarium and a playground.

There are plenty of theatres that cater to children, but only in Czech. Two of the outstanding ones in Prague are Divadlo Minor, Senovážné náměstí 28, and the other is the marionette theatre Divadlo Špejbla a Hurvínka, Dejvická 38, Prague 6. Programmes for these and many other theatres can be found in *Culture in Prague*, a monthly booklet of cultural programmes.

Slovakia

Great entertainment for children is the week-long Ghost Festival in Bojnice Chateau at the end of April. Many parks have playgrounds and during summer some lakes have boat rental facilities. Other forms of entertainment are circuses that tour around the country and are advertised on street posters. Slovaks also take their children to the folk festivals where there is plenty of music, dancing and food – even children dress up in costumes and perform dances.

DANGERS & ANNOYANCES

Theft

Tourism and heady commercialism have spawned an upsurge in petty (and not-so-petty) crime in Prague and to some extent in

Bratislava. For tourists, the biggest problem is pickpockets, and naturally enough, the prime trouble spots are where tourists gather in crowds. There's no point in being paranoid, but it makes sense to carry valuables well out of reach, eg in a money belt, and to be alert in crowds.

Elsewhere in the two republics, the risk of crime directed at tourists seems fairly remote.

Lost or Stolen Belongings

It's usually helpful to go to your embassy in Prague or Bratislava first. It ought to furnish you with a letter to the police, preferably in Czech or Slovak, requesting a police report (without which you cannot collect on insurance, for example). But since reports in foreign languages don't always go down well with insurance claims officials back home, try to get the embassy to provide their own report in English.

For a police report, go to the main police station in the town where you have had trouble. If your passport has been stolen, Prague, Bratislava and the regional capitals have special police and passport offices for foreigners, where you can apply for a replacement visa.

On the subject of lost or stolen travellers cheques and credit cards, see the Money section earlier in this chapter.

Cross-Border Rip-Offs

British embassies in both republics say they get reports of theft on overnight trains to and from both Berlin and Budapest, with belongings stolen when their owners are asleep.

One couple reported an attempted scam by a Czech border guard on the train to Austria, who tried to collect a US$50 'duty' on a framed poster bought in Prague. When challenged, he mumbled about talking to his superiors and disappeared with the bill of sale, never to return. See the Customs section earlier in this chapter for what is and isn't dutiable.

Racism

You may be surprised at the level of casual prejudice directed at Romanies (Gypsies), whom people are quick to blame for everything (although police statistics actually put much of the blame for petty crime on refugees trying to get to Germany via the two republics). A beauty-pageant contestant in North Bohemia made headlines in 1993 by revealing her aspiration to be a public prosecutor so she could rid her town of Romanies. If you are dark-skinned you may encounter low-level discrimination yourself, though overt hostility towards visitors is unlikely.

There is some hostility between Slovaks and Hungarians, but nothing too serious. Some Slovaks resent the Czechs' higher standard of living, and the fact that Slovakia (unlike the Czech Republic) has been left out of NATO and the EU. But foreigners are largely immune to these types of issues.

LEGAL MATTERS

Penalties for possession of drugs like acid and heroin are harsh and it's unlikely that your embassy can do much to help. It is not illegal to posses a small quantity of marijuana and hashish, but it is illegal to sell it. It's simply not worth the risk to import, export or possess any illegal substances.

If you find yourself under arrest in either republic for any reason whatsoever, you are entitled to call your embassy. Drink-driving is the only time foreigners risk a serious encounter with the law; both republics have a zero blood-alcohol limit for drivers.

Traffic fines are generally paid on the spot (ask for a receipt); for more information on road rules see the Getting Around chapter. The fine for littering is about 100 Kč/Sk.

BUSINESS HOURS

Shops tend to open from 9 am to 5 pm on weekdays and to noon on Saturday (closed Sunday). Smaller shops typically close for an hour or so at lunch time. Department stores may close later, and some have Friday evening hours. Some small food shops open as early as 7 am.

Restaurant hours are notoriously fluid, but most places operate from at least 11 am to 11 pm daily, but some close on Monday. In smaller towns it can be difficult to find something to eat after 9 pm and on Sundays after 6 pm.

Banking hours vary, but the useful banks are open weekdays from 9 am to 5 pm (often closed from noon to 1 pm for lunch). Many exchange offices carry on daily until 11 pm or later, and there are some 24-hour places.

Government office hours are weekdays from 8.30 am to 5 pm, though some tourist offices operate later and on weekends. Prague's main post office is open 24 hours a day, and Bratislava's has weekend hours, though services like poste restante – and all services at other post offices – have shorter hours.

Most museums and galleries in Prague, Brno and Bratislava are open year-round from 9 or 10 am to 5 or 6 pm daily, except Monday and sometimes the first working day after a holiday. You can visit major churches during similar hours, but smaller ones open only for services (usually in the morning).

Most castles, chateaux and other historical monuments outside these cities are open daily in summer, except Monday and the first working day after a holiday, from 9 (sometimes 8) am to 5 or 6 pm, except for an hour lunch break. All except a few close from November through March, with some limited to weekends in April and October.

PUBLIC HOLIDAYS & SPECIAL EVENTS

Czech Republic

The following are public holidays in the Czech Republic, when banks, offices, department stores and many shops close, and public transport is greatly reduced; restaurants, museums and tourist attractions tend to stay open:

1 January
Nový rok (New Year's Day)

March or April
Pondělí velikonoční (Easter Monday) – see the Holidays aside in this chapter

1 May
Svátek práce (Labour Day) – once the obligatory Communist 'holy' day, now it's just a chance for a picnic or a day in the country, often preceded by an all-night party

8 May
Den osvobození (Liberation Day) – a celebration of the liberation of Prague by its citizens in 1945

5 July
Den Cyrila a Metoděje (SS Cyril & Methodius Day) – recalls the Slavs' introduction to literacy and Christianity by the two Greek missionary-monks

6 July
Den Jana Husa (Jan Hus Day) – commemorates the 1415 burning at the stake of the great Bohemian religious reformer

28 October
Den vzniku Československa (Independence Day) – anniversary of the founding of the Czechoslovak Republic in 1918

24-26 December
Vánoce (Christmas)

The following events are either 'significant days' (*významné dny*) or cultural events that happen yearly. Local ones are listed under their relevant places:

6 January
Tři králové (Three Kings Day) – formal end of the Christmas season, sometimes with carols, bell-ringing, gifts to the poor

19 January
Anniversary of Jan Palach's Death – in memory of the Charles University student who in 1969 burned himself to death in protest against the Soviet occupation

7 March
Birthday of Tomáš Garrigue Masaryk – commemorates Czechoslovakia's first president and national father-figure

30 April
Pálení čarodějnic (Burning of the Witches)

5 May
České povstání (Czech Uprising) – anniversary of the 1945 anti-Nazi revolt preceding the arrival of the Soviet army

Holidays

Easter (*Velikonoce*)

Easter, like Christmas, was a work-free holiday under the Communists, though its religious significance and traditions were diluted. Before this time, the end of fasting on Palm Sunday also celebrated the arrival of spring. In an old pagan springtime ritual a figure of sticks and cloth symbolising Death was carried out of the village and drowned or burned. In its place girls returned with green branches decorated with ribbons and eggs, representing spring or summer and the return of Life. Boys used to walk through their villages with rattles, and in a symbolic gesture people used to wash in springs for their rejuvenating effect. There was also a resurrection ceremony on Holy Saturday.

Easter week today is less celebrated though one ritual persists. On Easter Monday a vigorous rite of spring called *pomlázka* takes place, in which Czech men of all ages swat their favourite women on the legs with decorated willow switches. This is supposed to bring rejuvenation, though enthusiastic young boys tend to overdo it. In the Slovak version, men try to throw water on their chosen women. The women respond more peaceably with refreshments and gifts of eggs, hand-painted or otherwise decorated (with different techniques in each region).

This is also the culmination of several days of serious spring-cleaning, cooking and visiting.

The Day of the Witches (*Čarodějnice*)

This is essentially the Czech version of *Walpurgisnacht*, a pre-Christian festival for warding off the evil influence of malign forces, especially witches who, it was believed, rode off on broomsticks to a rendezvous with the Devil. Peasants would clean their properties, gather on the highest hill and burn old brooms to ward off the witches. Later versions involved bonfire competitions between villages.

Now it has become another end-of-winter celebration and an opportunity for all-night bonfire parties. It's also a romantic time, one in which young couples may jump over the

12 May-4 June
The annual *Pražské Jaro* (Prague Spring) – international music festival, with classical music concerts in Prague's theatres, churches and historic buildings; always starts on the anniversary of Smetana's death

September
Prague Mozart Festival

17 November
Start of the Velvet Revolution – anniversary of the beating of nonviolent student demonstrators by security police in Prague, triggering popular outrage and the fall of the Communist government

5 December
Čert a Mikuláš (Devil & St Nicholas)

Slovakia

The following are public holidays in Slovakia, when banks, offices and department stores close. Some restaurants, museums and tourist attractions stay open, but bus timetables are severely cut back. Train transportation is hardly affected.

1 January
Nový rok (New Year's Day), also *Deň vzniku Slovenskej republiky* – anniversary of the founding of the Slovak Republic in 1993

6 January
Tři králové (Three Kings Day) – formal end of the Christmas season, sometimes with carols, bell-ringing, gifts to the poor

March or April
Veľké Nocy (Easter Friday & Monday)

1 May
Sviatok práce (Labour Day) – same as for the Czech Republic, above

dying embers and, next day, boys may cut branches with new green leaves and leave them at the door of a favourite girl.

The Devil & St Nicholas (*Čert a Mikuláš*)

On the evening of 5 December, the Devil and St Nicholas (dressed-up parents or uncles) come to the homes of very young children to find out if they have been good, and leave gifts – usually fruit, nuts and chocolate wrapped in red see-through paper.

The Devil wears a mask or heavy black make-up, horns on his head, an old black fur coat and, preferably, a tail and some chains to rattle. St Nicholas dresses a bit like the Pope, with a tall white hat decorated with a cross, a long white coat and a staff.

Christmas (*Vánoce*)

Christmas Day and Boxing Day were work-free days under the Communists, but like Easter, Christmas has lost much of its religious significance.

Celebrations begin on Christmas Eve, also called *Štědrý večer* ('Generous Evening'), the big day for family meals and gift-giving. Most people wait until the morning of this day to put up their Christmas tree, which is usually a spruce. (The Christmas tradition of nativity scenes and pine-trees doesn't go back all that far, even elsewhere in Europe; they were first introduced into churches in the 18th century, and it was not until the 19th century that people started bringing Christmas trees into their homes and decorating them).

The traditional Christmas Eve dinner starts with carp soup, followed by either carp fried with bread crumbs and potato salad or *kapr na černo* (carp with black sauce). Dessert is usually *vánočka*, a light fruit cake. After dinner everyone attacks the presents under the tree. Some may go to midnight Mass, even non-believers.

There are also religious services on Christmas Day (*Vánoce*), but this is mainly the day for visiting or being with the family – and a big midday meal, typically roast turkey, dumplings, sauerkraut and Christmas biscuits. *Štěpána* (St Stephen's Day or Boxing Day) is everybody's chance to get over it all. ■

5 July
Sv Cyril a Metod (SS Cyril & Methodius Day) – recalls the Slavs' introduction to literacy and Christianity by the two Greek missionary-monks

29 August
Slovenské národné povstanie (Slovak National Uprising) – anniversary of the start of a failed rebellion against the Nazis in Central Slovakia in August-October 1944

1 September
Deň Ústavy Slovenskej republiky (Constitution Day) – celebrating the founding of the Slovak Constitution in 1992

15 September
Sedembolestná Panna Maria (St Mary's Day)

1 November
Sviatok Všetkých svätých (All Saints Day)

24-26 December
Vianoce (Christmas)

The following annual events are 'significant days' or country-wide cultural events:

2 February
Hromnice (Candlemass) 40 days before Easter Monday
Fašiangy (Shrovetide Carnival) – a religious festival preceding Lent, during which masks and costumes are worn in some villages

13 April
Deň nespravodlivo stíhaných – day for victims of persecution

4 May
Výročie úmrtia Milana Rastislava Štefánika – anniversary of the death of MR Štefánik in 1919

8 May
Deň víťazstva nad fašizmom – a celebration of the defeat of Fascism in 1945

Where are the Festivals?

Czech Republic

Blatnice
St Antonínka Pilgrimage – September

Bzenec
Wine Festival – August

Český Krumlov
International Music Festival – late July and early August
Folk Music Festival – mid-September
Pětilisté růže (Five-Petalled Rose) Festival – mid-June

Domažlice
Chod Festival – the closest weekend to 14 August

Hluk
Dolňácké Festival – first weekend of July every four years (next in 2001)

Karlovy Vary
Jazz Festival – March
Dvořák Music Festival – September
International Film Festival – September

Kmochův
Kmochův Festival of brass-band music – June.

Kroměříž
Festival of Summer Music – series of classical concerts from June through September
ARSFILM is a festival of film and art – October
Haná Festival – second week in June.

Kyjov
Kyjovsko Summer Festival – mid-August

Mariánské Lázně
International Music Festival – June or July
Frédéric Chopin Music Festival – Mid-August

Prachatice
Golden Path Celebration – mid-June
Annual Folk Music Festival – last Saturday in February

Prague
Prague Spring International Music Festival – 12 May to 4 June
Mozart Festival – most of September

Plzeň
Liberation Day Celebrations – 8 May
Beer Festivities Festival – October

Rožnov pod Radhoštěm
Easter Traditions
Folkloric Dance & Song Festival – first weekend in July

Strakonice
International Bagpipe Festival – mid-August

Strážnice
International Folk Festival – last weekend in June

Tábor
Hussite Festival – second weekend in September

Velká nad Veličkou
Childrens' folk performances – mid-April
Horňácko Festival – second half of July

Vlčnov
Folk Festival – last weekend of May

Slovakia

Banská Štiavnica
Salamander – Friday nearest to 12 September

Bojnice
International Festival of Spirits and Ghosts – two weeks in late April and early May

Bratislava
Bratislava Music Festival – October
'Cultural Summer' festival – July and August

Červený Kláštor
Zamaguria Folk Festival – mid-June

Gombasek
Hungarian Folk Festival – late June

Komárno
Komárno Days festival – last weekend of April and the first week of May

Košice
East Slovak Folk Festival – mid-June

Svidník
Ruthenian Folk Festival – mid-June

4 August
Deň Matice Slovenskej – anniversary of the founding of the Slovak Matice in 1867
6 October
Deň obetí Dukly – anniversary of the battle of Dukla Pass in 1944
17 November
Deň boja proti totalitě (Day of the fight against totalitarianism) – anniversary of the start of the Velvet Revolution
5 December
Sv Mikulaš (St Nicholas' Day)

ACTIVITIES

Skiing

The Alps it isn't, but downhill skiing is plentiful and popular here. Facilities are fairly good, though queues are long. Rental equipment is OK but skiers who are particular about good-quality gear should bring their own.

The best runs are at Jasná in the Low Tatras. Other favoured spots are the resorts of the High Tatras and the Vrátna dolina (valley) in the Malá Fatra mountains. In the Czech Republic, the Krkonoše mountains have the best skiing, from the resorts of Špindlerův Mlýn, Harrachov and Pec pod Sněžkou. The best time is from late December to early April.

Other ranges with lower peaks, gentler terrain and fine scenery are better suited to cross-country skiing and ski touring. These include the Šumava in western and southern Bohemia, the Jizerský hory in northern Bohemia, the Beskydy and Jeseníky of northern Moravia, and the Veľká Fatra and Slovenský raj in Slovakia.

Accommodation is available in hotels, chalets, cabins or *chata* (mountain huts). For more information contact any Čedok or Satur office, or local *horská služba* (mountain rescue) offices.

Hiking

With a network of some 30,000km of well-marked, well-connected hiking trails, colour-coded to excellent hiking maps, the Czech and Slovak republics are brilliantly equipped for walking or tramping (*trampování/trampovanie* or *turistika*).

The best walking is in the mountains, especially the High Tatras (Vysoké Tatry) and Malá Fatra of Central Slovakia; the Slovak Paradise (Slovenský raj) and Slovak Karst (Slovenský kras) in eastern Slovakia; the Šumava of western and southern Bohemia; the Krkonoše mountains and Bohemian Paradise (Český ráj) in eastern Bohemia; and the Sandstone Rocks of the Labe (Labské Pískovce), also known as České Švýcarsko ('Bohemian Switzerland'), in northern Bohemia.

Camping is now restricted to designated campsites, though many people discreetly camp elsewhere. The alternative is one of the many high-elevation chalets or chaty along major trails (see Accommodation in this chapter for more on these). Open fires are prohibited everywhere. The rules are more stringently enforced in the national parks.

The best maps, generally available in bookshops all over both republics, are Kartografie Praha's *soubor turistických map* series (usually at 1:100,000) and VKÚ's *edice Klub Českých turistů* series (1:50,000) for the Czech Republic; and VKÚ's *turistická mapa* series (1:25,000 or 1:50,000) and Slovenská Kartografia's *edícia turistických map* (1:100,000) series for Slovakia.

Backpacks, hiking boots and other camping gear are easy to find in shops, but campers who are particular about certain high-quality brands should bring gear with them. Mountain weather is incredibly changeable here – even in summer freak snowstorms are possible – and warm, water-resistant clothing is essential.

Mountaineering

Among the most popular climbing areas in the two republics are the Sandstone Rocks of the Labe (Labské Pískovce, also known as České Švýcarsko) in northern Bohemia, and the Adršpach-Teplice rocks in eastern Bohemia. The more modest Bohemian Paradise (Český ráj) is a good area for training. Serious climbers will prefer the High Tatras and Malá Fatra of Central Slovakia.

Considerations for Responsible Hiking

The popularity of hiking is placing great pressure on wilderness areas. Please consider the following tips when hiking and help preserve the ecology and beauty of the Czech and Slovak republics.

Rubbish

- Carry out all your rubbish. If you've carried it in you can carry it out. Don't overlook those easily forgotten items, such as silver paper, orange peel, cigarette butts and plastic wrappers. Empty packaging weighs very little anyway and should be stored in a dedicated rubbish bag. Make an effort to carry out rubbish left by others.
- Never bury your rubbish: digging disturbs soil and ground-cover and encourages erosion. Buried rubbish will more than likely be dug up by animals, who may be injured or poisoned by it. On the other hand, it may take years to decompose, especially at high altitudes.
- Minimise the waste you must carry out by taking minimal packaging and taking no more than you will need. If you can't buy in bulk, unpack small-portion packages and combine their contents in one container before your trek. Take re-usable containers or stuff sacks.
- Don't rely on bought water in plastic bottles. Disposal of these bottles is creating a major problem, particularly in developing countries. Use iodine drops or purification tablets instead.
- Sanitary napkins, tampons and condoms should also be carried out despite the inconvenience. They burn and decompose poorly.

Human Waste Disposal

- Contamination of water sources by human faeces can lead to the transmission of hepatitis, typhoid and intestinal parasites, such as giardiasis, amoebas, and round worms. It can cause severe health risks not only to members of your party, but also to local residents and wildlife.
- Where there is a toilet, please use it.
- Where there is none, bury your waste. Dig a small hole 15cm deep and at least 100m from any watercourse. Consider carrying a lightweight trowel for this purpose. Cover the waste with soil and a rock. Use toilet paper sparingly and bury it with the waste. In snow, dig down to the soil otherwise your waste will be exposed when the snow melts.
- If the area is inhabited, ask locals if they have any concerns about your chosen toilet site.
- Ensure that these guidelines are applied to a portable toilet tent if one is being used by a large hiking party. Encourage all party members, including porters, to use the site.

Washing

- Don't use detergents or toothpaste in or near watercourses, even if they are biodegradable. For personal washing, use biodegradable soap and a water container (or even a lightweight, portable basin) at least 50m away from the watercourse. Widely disperse the waste-water to allow the soil to filter it fully before it finally makes it back to the watercourse.

- Wash cooking utensils 50m from watercourses using a scourer, sand or snow instead of detergent.

Erosion

- Hillsides and mountain slopes, especially at high altitudes, are prone to erosion. It is important to stick to existing tracks and avoid short cuts that bypass a switchback. If you blaze a new trail straight down a slope it will turn into a watercourse with the next heavy rainfall and eventually cause soil loss and deep scarring.
- If a well-used track passes through a mud patch, walk through the mud: walking around the edge will increase the size of the patch.
- Avoid removing the plant life that keeps topsoils in place.

Fires & Low Impact Cooking

- Don't depend on open fires for cooking. The cutting of wood for fires in popular hiking areas can cause rapid deforestation. Cook on a light-weight kerosene, alcohol or Shellite (white gas) stove and avoid those powered by disposable butane gas canisters.
- If you are hiking with a guide and porters, supply stoves for the whole team. In alpine areas, ensure that all members are outfitted with enough clothing so that fires are not a necessity for warmth.
- If you patronise local accommodation, select those that do not use wood fires to heat water or cook food.
- Fires may be acceptable below the tree line in areas that get very few visitors. If you light a fire, use an existing fireplace rather than create a new one. Don't surround fires with rocks as this creates a visual scar. Use only dead, fallen wood. Remember the adage 'the bigger the fool, the bigger the fire'. Use minimal wood, just what you need for cooking. In huts leave wood for the next person.
- Ensure that you fully extinguish a fire after use. Spread the embers and douse them with water. A fire is only truly safe to leave when you can comfortably place your hand in it.

Wildlife Conservation

- Do not engage in or encourage hunting. It is illegal in all parks and reserves.
- Don't buy items made from endangered species.
- Don't assume animals in huts to be nonindigenous vermin and attempt to exterminate them. In wild places they are likely to be protected native animals.
- Discourage the presence of wildlife by not leaving food scraps behind you. Place gear out of reach and tie packs to rafters or trees.
- Do not feed the wildlife as this can lead to animals becoming dependent on trekker hand-outs, to unbalanced populations and to diseases such as 'lumpy jaw'.

Camping & Walking on Private Property

- Seek permission to camp from landowners. They will usually be happy if asked, but confrontational if not.

Park Regulations

- Take note of and observe any rules and regulations particular to the national or state reserve that you are visiting. ■

Caving

Both republics are honeycombed with dramatic caves, the best of which are in the Moravian Karst area, north of Brno. Slovakia has its own Slovak Karst (Slovenský kras), which includes one of the largest caves in central Europe. Another fine cave system is beneath the Demänova Valley in Central Slovakia.

Water Sports

Very popular in both republics are flat-water and white-water canoeing and kayaking on the mountain rivers. It's not easy to find boats for hire, except in peak summer season; Čedok, Satur or local travel agencies may be able to help.

Among prime boating rivers in the Czech Republic is the scenic, but, unfortunately, rather polluted, Sázava, which stretches from western Moravia into Central Bohemia. Equally popular are the upper Vltava and Otava in southern Bohemia. In Slovakia there is the upper Váh, the swift Hornád, which stretches through the narrow gorges of the Slovenský raj (permission is needed from park authorities to use it), and a 16km section of the Dunajec on the Polish border.

White-water canoeing is popular on the Elbe river and below Špindlerův Mlýn in the Krkonoše. On the Vltava river in below the Lipno dam, South Bohemia, there's a famous spot known as the Devil's Currents (Čertovy proudy).

Windsurfing gear is for hire on the Liptovský Mara at Liptovský Mikuláš in Central Slovakia, and on Lipno Lake in southern Bohemia. Water-skiing is also popular on many larger lakes and rivers.

Spas

The spas in both republics are for courses of medical treatment, and most need to be booked. However, you can bring your own glass to the public springs and drink the local water at no cost. Some towns have thermal swimming pools that are open to the public.

For a list of the booking agencies and better known spas, see the Health Spas aside in this chapter.

Fishing

Fishing is governed by considerable restrictions, with limited seasons, and day, week, month and year-long licences. For more information, talk to Čedok in Prague or Satur in Bratislava.

Other Activities

There are plenty of tennis courts, golf courses, horse-riding farms, squash courts, ice-skating rinks (winter only) and fitness centres. Look in the yellow pages or ask at the local tourist offices for more information.

WORK

If you're staying in either republic for longer than six months, you must register as a 'permanent resident', and get a Czech or Slovak green card (which also entitles you to lower fees and hotel rates, as well as duty-free customs clearance). You must submit information on your work and your accommodation, and a medical report. The process takes several months.

Czech Republic

In 1997 the Czech government was on the verge of tightening laws on foreign residency and work permits. At the moment it's possible to apply for a permit from within the Czech Republic (the *Prague Post* estimates that 90% of foreigners working legally in Prague have obtained their work permits on Czech soil). However, the new law (if passed) would require foreigners to apply for work and residency permits in their home countries.

To obtain work legally you need working and resident permits. More information can be found in Prague at the Foreigners' Labour Office (Úřad práce; ☎ 02-24 55 23 34 or 24 55 11 11; metro Anděl), Zborovská 11. The 24 hour foreigners' police hotline in English (☎ 02-61 44 11 19) provides details on how to apply for work and resident permits. A company that employs a foreigner without a work permit faces fines of around US$8000.

You can also talk to the commercial section of your embassy, or the American Chamber of Commerce (☎ 29 98 87 or 26 67 78), Karlovo náměstí 24, Prague 2, about work permits and other matters.

The Business Club (☎ 627 11 19) at Čajkovského 5, Prague 3, is a meeting place for Czech and foreign entrepreneurs. There is also the Economic Chamber of the Czech Republic (☎ 77 21 48), Argentinská 38, Prague 2.

Language Schools Unless you can speak Czech or have a job with a foreign English-speaking company, the most readily available work is English-teaching. It's easier to find a job in provincial towns and your living costs will be much lower. In Prague, look in the Czech advertising paper *Annonce*, the *Prague Post*, several of the expat cafés, and US and UK cultural centres.

There are numerous schools in Prague where you can find short or long-term work teaching English (or other languages). Some trustworthy ones are:

Angličtina Expres
  Pasáž Světozor, Vodičkova 39, Prague 1 (☎ 02-29 06 19)
Berlitz
  Na poříčí 12, Prague 1 (☎ 02-287 20 52)
Canadian Club
  Národní 37, Prague 1 (☎ 02-22 77 95)
London School of Modern Languages
  Belgická 25, Prague 2 (☎ 02-25 68 51)
SPUSA (an agency for English teachers)
  Navrátilova 2, Prague 1 (☎ 02-20 45 63)

Volunteer Work The Klub mladých cestovatelů (KMC; ☎ 02-24 23 06 33; metro Národní Třída), in Prague at Karolíny Světlé 30, organises international work camps from June to August renovating historical buildings, maintaining national parks, teaching children English etc. Contracts are for a minimum of three weeks with no pay, but room and board are provided. The registration fee is US$20. You're supposed to reserve months ahead through volunteer organisations in your home country, but occasionally, when space is available, KMC has accepted foreigners who have turned up without a booking.

Slovakia

The unemployment rate is high in Slovakia, and there are not many opportunities for non-Slovak speakers unless you are working for a foreign company – in which case it is much easier to get the job at home than in Slovakia.

In Bratislava, the American Chamber of Commerce (☎ 07-534 00 00; fax 07-534 05 40), in Hotel Danube at Rybné námestie 1, can help with business queries.

Your best bet is to find a job teaching English, but there are not that many schools in Slovakia. The British Council in Bratislava (☎ 533 10 74), at Panská 17, has an English Teaching Centre; also try the Berlitz Language Centre (☎ 533 37 96; fax 533 38 00), Na Vŕšku 6, Bratislava. There are also occasional ads seeking English teachers (and sometimes other jobs) in *The Slovak Spectator*. Also take a look at Slovakia Online and Slovakia.Com (see the previous Online Services section).

ACCOMMODATION

Accommodation options run the gamut, from campsites to private rooms to hotels at all price levels. You're unlikely to ever get caught out without a place to stay. Most towns have at least one hotel, and even in the smallest village you can usually find someone to rent you a room in their home.

One way to find hostel, campsite or cheap hotel accommodation is to ask at the local tourist office (if there is one). You can also try the local Čedok or Satur office. Some smaller branches are sympathetic to budget travellers' needs, though they will need reminding if a student dorm is what you want. Some can actually book a room for you, but they tack on a hefty fee to do so; they can also book hotels in other towns, though not always cheerfully.

Failing this, stroll around the backstreets and look for signs advertising *Zimmer frei* (German for 'room available'). If this doesn't work, go into a pub and say *Hledám levný hotel* ('I'm looking for a cheap hotel') – and/or *dobrý* (good), *čistý* (clean), *blízký* (nearby).

Unless otherwise noted, this book quotes high-season rates. High season varies from region to region, but is usually April or May through September or October, plus the Easter and Christmas-New Year holidays. Some places drop their rates in the off-season. Major ski areas like the Krkonoše and Tatras mountains have a winter price peak from January to about April that exceeds the summer one, with especially steep hikes at Christmas-New Year. Tourist prices tend to be higher than those for local people.

Be prepared to discover that some of this book's good bargains have succumbed to 'remodelling' only to reappear in grossly expensive forms.

Campsites

Most campsites have pitches for both tents and caravans. Some also have unheated huts or bungalows, which can be good bottom-end options if you have your own transport.

Most campsites don't offer much breathing space, nor much greenery, but they differ widely in attitude and amenities. Typical prices include a per-person rate (about US$2 to US$3, with discounts for kids) plus charges per car or van (US$2 to US$4), caravan (US$2 to US$6), tent (US$1 to US$4) and electrical hook-up. Huts or bungalows, if any, are usually US$4 to US$8 per bed, a few considerably more (some may require payment for all beds). Most campsites have showers, and many have communal kitchens and at least a snack bar. Most are open from about March through October.

These are typical Czech Republic rates; those in Prague are 20 to 40% higher, those in Slovakia about that much lower.

Hostels

A 'hostel' can be anything from a bunk bed in a gymnasium to a double room with shower, the common factor being that filling the other beds is up to them, not you. While some operate year-round, others are sports clubs and student dormitories that only have an appreciable number of beds in the summer. Student hostels with *kolej* in the name are usually of a decent standard, and some have mini-suites.

The number of hostel beds jumps from late June through August when school is out. We have tried to indicate the year-round ones. Typical per-bed prices are US$6 to US$12, but can be as low as US$4 and as high as US$25. Only a few have places to eat on the premises. Except as noted, most do not have curfews.

Czech *ubytovna* and Slovak *ubytovanie* (accommodation) are often used to refer to Spartan overnight facilities belonging to sports clubs or other organisations. Some of these make rooms available to travellers (*turistická ubytovna* or *ubytovanie*), at hostel prices.

Private Rooms

A booming sector of small-scale capitalism in both republics is the renting of rooms in private homes. Touts swarm around Prague's main train stations, most of them honest amateurs with good deals to offer – but check the map and the transport, as some places are way out in the suburbs.

In Prague, the easiest way to find a private room is through an accommodation agency. In smaller towns you can scout any neighbourhood that takes your fancy, for 'Zimmer frei' signs. In very small towns and villages with no hotels or only a deluxe one, this may be the only cheap option.

At the time of writing, typical Prague prices for a double room, with bath and toilet shared with the family, were about US$25 to US$40 per night, and at least US$60 for a room or flat with its own facilities and entrance. Anything near the centre will be 15 to 30% more. Prices elsewhere are lower. Many people offer discounts for longer stays, but put their prices up for Easter, Christmas and some European holidays.

Homestays

In this variant on private rooms, you're the personal guest of a family. American-International Homestays (toll-free in USA ☎ 1-800-876 2048; or ☎ 303-938 8257; fax 303-938 8647; PO Box 7178, Boulder, CO 80306, USA), arranges 17-day trips with homestays in Prague plus Budapest and Kraków, for about US$1800 from New York.

Pensions

Pension or *penzión* used to mean a boarding house – a home or apartment block, family-run and fitted out with locking doors, wash basins, extra toilets, sometimes a café or snack bar. Mostly it still does, though the word has been co-opted by a few high-rise hotels that want to sound homey. Real pensions are a nice compromise between the comforts of a hotel and the personal touches of a private home. But they're not all cheap, and they're often out on the fringes of a town or city.

Mountain Chalets

An additional option in the Krkonoše, Tatras and other mountain areas is the *bouda*, *chata* or *chalupa* (Czech) or *chata* (Slovak) – some call themselves *horský hotel* (mountain hotel).

There are high-altitude lodges, often open year-round, located at intervals along mountain trails or at the top of cable-car or funicular lines. Some are small and Spartan, while others are essentially full-scale hotels. Some can be booked through agencies in lower-elevation towns, while others are first-come-first-served. All have dining facilities of some description. Prices are quite reasonable considering the clean air and splendid views that come with them.

Hotels

In the high season in major tourist centres (eg Prague, the West Bohemian spa towns, and the Krkonoše and Tatras resort areas), you cannot be sure of finding space in a top-end hotel without booking ahead at least a few weeks. Otherwise, if your standards are flexible, you'll not need reservations.

Many hotels rate themselves by a somewhat ambiguous 'ABC' system (though 'four-star' and 'five-star' still signify top-of-the-line places). We have instead divided them according to the price of their most basic double in the high season:

Bottom end – less than about US$40 (1350 Kč/Sk)
Middle – from US$40 to about US$80 (2700 Kč/Sk)
Top end – everything else

Top-end hotel rooms in Prague now cost as much as anywhere in Europe, thanks to a 23% value-added tax, and for Prague we have classified hotels using US$50 and US$100 as the dividing lines.

Some hotels are not what they seem, a four-star hotel charging over US$100 per person a night might not have the facilities or service of western four-star hotels, but might be closer to a two-star hotel. This is a problem in both countries, but especially so in Prague.

It often doesn't occur to some hotel staff that a foreigner might be willing to stay in a room without a bathroom, so if they say it's full, ask if they have anything with shared facilities.

Prices separated by slashes are for single/double or single/double/triple rooms. Single occupancy of a double room is normally more than half the cost of full occupancy, and some places insist you pay the full double rate. Most hotels have only a few single rooms, but these are often available even when larger rooms aren't.

Some refurbished hotels have 'mini-suites', with two or three rooms (each with its own lock) sharing a toilet and shower – a compromise between cheap communal facilities and pricey en suite ones. (In this book, a '1+2+2 mini-suite' means three rooms – one with one single bed and two with two.) Many hotels also have more expensive *apartmá* (meaning suites, not apartments).

Nearly all hotels at mid-range and above have a restaurant and usually a snack bar, night bar and/or café. Prices in the book are without breakfast unless noted.

Major credit cards are accepted by all top-end hotels and many mid-range hotels.

'Hotel Garni' You may see this in some hotel names. It means they're not equipped with a full restaurant and can only offer a simple breakfast – a 'B&B hotel'.

FOOD

For a complete guide to the food of the Czech and Slovak republics, see the Food Guide at the back of the book.

DRINKS

Coffee & Tea

Basic coffee (*káva* or *kafe*) is *Turecká* (Turkish) – hot water poured over ground beans that end up as sludge at the bottom of your cup. *Espreso* is sometimes a fair equivalent of the Italian version. Viennese coffee (*Vídeňská káva*) comes close to its Austrian counterpart. Most tea (*čaj*) is weak, and served with a slice of lemon; if you want it with milk, ask for *čaj s mlékem*.

Nonalcoholic Drinks

Imported, mainly American, soft drinks (*limonády*) are now common. Imported and locally made juice drinks and fruit juices are also easy to find. Mineral water is widely available (few locals drink the tap water). A popular brand is the carbonated Mattoni (called 'Matonka'); another is Dobrá voda ('Good Water', the name of a village near the spring), in carbonated (red top) and non-carbonated (blue top) versions. In Slovakia, more popular brands of mineral water are Salvator or Baldovska.

Most glass bottles can be returned to the point of purchase for a 2 Kč refund.

Beer

Czech beer (*pivo*) is recognised as one of the world's best. Brewing traditions go back to the 13th century (see Plzeň in the West Bohemia chapter). It's said that the Germans learned to love beer from the Czechs.

Beer is served almost everywhere food is served, with the exception of most *vinárna/vináreň* (wine bars). Czechs drink three times as much beer as all soft drinks combined. It is not unusual to see people – sweet old ladies as well as burly young men – having their first half-litre at 6 am in a *bufet*. Most pubs close at 10 or 11 pm, though you can tank up in some big-city bars and clubs all night long.

Most Czech beers are lagers, naturally brewed from hand-picked hops. Czechs like their beer at cellar temperature with a creamy head. Americans and Australians might find this a bit warm. Draught beer normally comes as a *malé pivo* ('small beer', 300mL) or as *pivo* or *velké pivo* ('large beer', 500mL). If you're buying it by the bottle, most beer is either light or dark and *dvanáctka* (12-degree) or *desítka* (10-degree) – this local indicator of its 'gravity', which takes into account its texture and malt content, doesn't correspond to alcohol percentage, but normally the higher the degree, the higher the alcohol content. Most beers are between 3 and 6% alcohol, regardless of the degrees.

The best-known Czech beer is the Plzeňský Prazdroj (Pilsner Urquell), made in Plzeň since 1842. Inside the Czech Republic, of course, you can get this nectar on tap as well as in bottles. Many Czechs prefer the other Plzeň brand, Gambrinus.

The largest Czech beer exporter is not Prazdroj but Budvar in České Budějovice, maker of the original Budweiser (no relation to the insipid American liquid of the same name). This mild, slightly bitter brew is popular in Austria, Germany and Scandinavia. Other good and popular beers are Regent from Třeboň, Radegast from North Moravia, and Krušovice from the town of the same name in Central Bohemia.

Pivo

RICHARD NEBESKY

Beer makes beautiful bodies, or so the Czechs say

Pivo is Czech for beer and the Czech Lands have been famous for centuries as one of the finest producers of the amber liquid. The Czechs drink the largest volume of beer per capita of any country in the world (including Australia). According to figures published by an assocition of small Czech breweries that translated to each Czech drinking 159L per year (the average adult drank 340L).

There are over 80 breweries in the Czech Republic though most pale in comparison to the giant concerns in the USA, Germany and the Netherlands. The four largest breweries are Radegast, Pražské pivovary (Bass), Jihočeské pivovary and Plzeňské pivovary. Bass, the British brewery, owns a major stake in Pražské pivovary (and also Ostravan in Ostrava) and has made the Staropramen label available in the USA, UK and western Europe. One of the oldest brands is Krušovice, which is also the name of the town just outside Prague where the brewery was established in 1581. This label is increasingly seen around the country and the brewery is now the fifth largest in the Czech Republic. Another popular beer is Velkopopovický Kozel from Popovice, not far from Prague.

The largest Czech beer exporter is Budvar, also known by the German name Budweiser. It is not connected in any way to the American brewery Budweiser, whose beer pales in comparison to the far superior, stronger and slightly bitter Czech Budvar. The US brewery has tried to buy the small Czech company, but national pride and government intervention halted the near-disastrous sale. Ever since, the American Budweiser has tried to push the Czech brewery out of the European market by underhanded tactics. In five countries it has succeeded in getting a court order that only allows the US Bud to be sold within their borders.

Czech beers are predominantly lagers fermented by a bottom method. Like in neighbouring Germany, there are no chemicals in the beer. The whole process uses only natural ingredients – water, hops and barley for the fermentation process.

The strong beer culture here is centuries old and is one of the few traditions to survive the Communist era relatively intact. Today the art of beer drinking is celebrated at hundreds of Czech (and to some extent Slovak) festivals. Beer-inspired competitions include speed drinking (the record for 1L of beer is 3.44 seconds) and the largest beer gut to name but a few.

Czechs have many sayings to promote beer drinking, but the claims are often dubious. One of the favourite ones is 'Beer makes beautiful bodies' (Pivo dělá pěkná těla). Brew-your-own fans might adopt, 'Life flourishes in places where beer is brewed' (Kde se pivo vaří tam se dobře daří). ■

Prague's biggest brewery, of the mild Staropramen, is in the suburb of Smíchov. Some pubs brew their own; best known is the strong dark beer made by the U Fleků pub in Prague.

The Slovaks also make some good beers, including well knowns such as Zlatý Bažant (Golden Pheasant), made in Hurbanovo, Topvar from Topoľčany, or Martiner from Martin.

Wine

Wine (*víno*) is not big in the Czech Republic, except in Moravia, though it's available in most restaurants and *hostinců* and of course in vinárny/vinárně. Good wines are available in eateries and shops, though the best tend to be sold only at the wineries. White wines are markedly better than reds. The best domestic label is Vavřinec, a red from south-east Moravia. Frankovka is another good red, and a good dry white is Tramín. Rulandské bílé is a semi-dry white, Rulandské červené a medium red. Czechs who do drink wine tend to prefer sweetish whites.

South-east Moravia is where the best Czech wines come from. People still gather at *vinné sklípky*, semi-underground, family-run wine cellars, for a tipple and a song, though the commercial brands come from large co-operatives. Bohemia's main wine area is around Mělník; the white wines are reasonable, but the reds don't measure up to those in Moravia. A popular summer cooler is *vinný střik*, which is half white wine and half soda, with ice. A popular winter drink is hot wine (*svařené víno/varené víno*).

Slovaks produce and consume far more wine per capita than Czechs. The best wines are mainly from the south and the best region is the Tokaj, along the Hungarian border; better-known labels are Furmint and Tokay. Others come from around Bratislava and the Carpathians, with reds like Kláštorné or whites like Venušíno čáro.

Pub Etiquette

Always ask if a chair is free before sitting down (*Je tu volno?*). Service is normally quick, but if it's slow, chasing the waiter is a sure way to guarantee that you'll be ignored. Your tab is run on a slip of paper left at your table. Tipping is as in a restaurant, ie 5 to 10%, and the bill is usually rounded up to the next 5 or 10 Kč to make it 5%.

Pubs are a strongly male-oriented social scene. Most unaccompanied Czech and Slovak women tend to be more comfortable in vinárny/vinárně. ■

Spirits

Slivovice is a fiery, potent plum brandy said to have originated in Moravia, where the best brands, like Jelínek, still come from. If you have a sweet tooth, try the cherry liqueur *griotka*. There are other hard spirits and sweet liqueurs made from fruit, such as *meruňkovice/marhulovica* (apricot brandy). Borovička is made from juniper berries.

Probably the most unusual Czech liqueur is a herbal spirit called Becherovka, which is from the spa town of Karlovy Vary. Another popular bitter spirit is Fernet. A good brandy is Myslivecká. Imported whisky, cognac and vodka are widely available if you cannot get used to local brands. Spirits are drunk neat and often as chasers. Most are served cold. A popular year-round hot drink is *grog* – half rum, half hot water and lemon.

The deadliest spirit is not slivovice but *absinth*, which is made from wormwood, and due to its high alcohol content of 75% is banned in most countries. It is legal here but there is still some controversy about its safety – any drink with an alcoholic content this high can cause serious health problems. The local distillery Hills Liqueurs began producing absinth again in 1991, as it was banned from the 1950s until 1990. The correct way to drink absinth is to soak a cube of sugar in a glass of absinth, and then light the cube. When the sugar has melted, stir it into the glass. Now, it is ready. It is not easy to describe the taste of the green spirit, but it does have a slight soapy flavour.

ENTERTAINMENT

Long before the Czech and Slovak republics appeared on the map, Czechs and Slovaks were expressing their national aspirations through the arts. Today both republics provide fertile ground for everything from classical music to avant-garde cinema to heavy-metal music.

Prague's is the richest and most eclectic scene, with a bewildering array of entertainment, some of it first class. The city has become a European centre for jazz and rock as much as for classical music. Prague, Bratislava and Brno have their own annual music festivals, with international artists and composers among the Czech and Slovak favourites. Most towns of any size have a drama theatre and a concert hall, as well as cinemas and a shifting array of discos and clubs.

Refer to the Public Holidays & Special Events section in this chapter for information about festivals and other regular events. Local events are described under specific localities.

Tickets

For classical music, opera, ballet and theatre, you can often find a ticket or two on sale at the box office immediately before concert time.

If you can't be bothered or you want a sure seat in advance there are several options: try Čedok or Satur, your hotel or a travel agency. Prague is awash with ticket agencies, but all of them add their own charges to the box-office price. Touts may offer you tickets at the door, but their mark-ups tend to be the biggest.

Many places have discounts for students and seniors, and sometimes, for the disabled. At the box office, foreigners normally pay the same price as locals for the same seat.

For rock and jazz clubs, just front up at the door.

Classical Music, Opera & Ballet

Prague has the most classical offerings, with half a dozen concerts of varying quality almost every day in summer. There's also the well known Pražské jaro (Prague Spring) annual music festival from 12 May to 2 June (see Entertainment under Prague for more information about it), and various similar festivals. Bratislava and Brno also have classical music festivals.

České Budějovice, Karlovy Vary, Plzeň and other cities have quite a bit to offer as well. Even many smaller towns or regions have respectable orchestras and ballet troupes, along with a steady stream of guest performers. Prices on the whole are quite modest.

Many venues close during July and August (when Czechs and Slovaks traditionally go on holiday), but there are frequent small concerts in churches, chateaux and other historical buildings at that time.

Theatre

Most big towns have a classical drama theatre, and Prague and Bratislava also have a clutch of avant-garde venues, though there's little in English. The Estates Theatre in Prague does offer simultaneous English translation for selected plays, however. Prague's famous multimedia Laterna Magika, as well as its mime and 'black-light' theatres, depending little on the spoken word, are accessible to all. In Prague you can also find musicals and revues.

Jazz

Prague has half a dozen well-established regular jazz venues. Both Bratislava and Prague have annual jazz festivals – Bratislava in September and Prague in October.

Rock

Prague has a high-energy club scene (see the Entertainment section in the Prague chapter). Punk and heavy metal have also taken root in Ustí nad Labem and other industrial centres of northern Bohemia.

For current Prague, northern Bohemia and some Bratislava listings and reviews, see the entertainment pages of Prognosis and the Prague Post – and look out for posters.

Pubs, Clubs & Other Nightlife

Even small towns may have a disco, and you may find a live band playing at the local top-end hotel. In the smallest towns, however, things go pretty quiet after the pubs close at 10 or 11 pm.

Cinemas

Most sizable towns have at least one *kino* (movie theatre). There are about 30 of them in Prague and 20 in Bratislava, where you're as likely to catch a first-run western film – dubbed or subtitled – as a local product. In newspaper cinema listings, a dubbed film is indicated by *dabing*, and subtitles by *titulky* or *anglické titulky* (English subtitles).

Museums

Every town seems to have a museum, though some are little more than dusty collections of old furniture and stuffed animals. Prague and Bratislava each have fairly grand National Museums and these, and the regional capital and city historical museums, have specialised collections such as decorative arts, restored historical buildings and the like.

Admission charges are typically 5 Kč/Sk to 30 Kč/Sk. Very often youth, student and senior discounts are available for the asking.

Also of interest are several *skansens*, open-air collections of traditional-style houses and other buildings, set in rural areas of both republics. Probably the best of these are at Rožnov pod Radhoštěm in northern Moravia, and at Zuberec in Central Slovakia's Orava Valley.

SPECTATOR SPORT

Ice Hockey

Ice hockey (*lední hokej*) is a very popular sport, and the Czech ice-hockey team has a successful history dating back to the early days of the European and world championships. The national team always finishes near the top, and has won the European title 17 times and the world title seven times. The Czech team finished third at the 1997 European championships. One of the best Czech league teams in recent years has been HC Petra Vsetín, from North Moravia.

The first separate Slovak national team was only formed in 1993. In the 1994 Winter Olympics Slovakia finished a disappointing seventh after losing only two games in the whole series. At the 1997 European championships the Slovak team finished ninth. One of the best Slovak league teams is HC Slovan Bratislava.

There are rinks all over both republics where local games can be seen. The season runs from September through April.

Tennis

When it comes to Czech sports stars, most westerners think of tennis (*tenis*). But you won't run into Ivan Lendl or Martina Navrátilová here: they're now US citizens. The new hero is Jana Novotná, who won the bronze medal at the 1996 Olympics, and was also the runner-up in 1996 and 1997 at Wimbledon. Tennis tournaments are common in Prague (on Ostrov Štvanice), and the Škoda Czech Open is held there in early August.

Soccer

Soccer (*fotbal*) is the most popular sport in either republic. Although never as successful as the ice-hockey team the Czechoslovak national soccer team twice made the final (both times losing) of the World Cup – in 1934 (Italy) and 1962 (Chile). In Olympic competition the Czechoslovak team has won the gold medal (1980) and the silver (1964) once each.

The Czech national team has been more successful in the European championships, winning twice this century; in 1996 the Czech team lost 2-1 to Germany. In the Czech national league, SK Slavia Praha has been one of the leading teams.

A Slovak national team was only formed in 1993, but there is a long tradition of local league teams, two of the best being SK Slovan Bratislava and FC Košice. The season is September through December and March through June.

Horse Racing
Horse racing (*dostihy*) is popular in Prague (eg at Velká Chuchle) from May through October. There is also a strenuous (for the horses) steeplechase course at Pardubice. Tickets are cheap and usually available at the tracks.

THINGS TO BUY
The privatisation of retailing since 1989 has radically changed the shopping scene in the two republics, at least in the cities, and consumer goods are now easily obtainable and mostly of good quality. While imports carry western European prices, locally made products are mostly affordable for local people, and cheap for westerners.

Antiques & Artwork
If you have bought what you think is a genuine antique or a piece of museum-quality art, which could cause trouble at customs on the way out, talk to a specialist – eg curatorial staff at the National Museum in Prague or Bratislava, or inspectors at the customs post office (*Pošta celnice/Poštovní colnica*) in Prague or Bratislava. Usually, anything made before 1920 is likely to be illegal to export. See Customs earlier in this chapter.

Books
Books are a great gift or souvenir, and many shops stock reference books and good-quality coffee-table books about the major tourist centres. Recommended bookshops are listed under each town.

Gems
Locally mined semiprecious stones, such as amber, rubies and Czech garnets, are good value and popular as souvenirs or gifts. Amber (*jantar*), seen everywhere in the tourist zones, is better value here than over the border in Germany. This fossilised tree resin is usually honey yellow in colour, although it can be white, orange, red or brown. The ruby (*rubín*) is a dark red stone, and the Czech garnet (*český granát*) is usually red but can be many other colours, or colourless.

There are many jewellers around central Prague, such as Václavské náměstí (Wenceslas Square), Na příkopě, Národni and Karlova ulice, and popular tourist towns such as Karlovy Vary.

Glass & Crystal
One of the Czech Republic's best buys is Bohemian crystal – anything from simple glassware to stupendous, multicoloured works of art. Prices aren't radically different from shop to shop, though they're lower outside the tourist centres. Very few shops will ship abroad. If you want to do it yourself, you'll have to take your purchases, unsealed, to a customs post office.

Music
Good buys are classical CDs of the works of national composers such as Smetana, Dvořák, Janáček, Suk, Martinů or Slovakia's Johann Hummel, as well as folk music – even the cheerful Bohemian brass-band music called *dechovka*. There are almost as many CD and tape shops as bookshops in the major centres.

Souvenirs
Prague in particular overflows with souvenirs for sale. Much of it is junk, but there is some quality work. Look for painted eggs, marionettes, wooden and straw dolls and other toys, wooden utensils and gingerbread moulds, ceramic ware with traditional designs, linen and blouses with traditional stitching, lacework, Mucha posters, and prints of old maps.

A handful of hawkers still sell Soviet military paraphernalia and *matryoshka* dolls (look inside, as some don't have all the dolls they should).

Getting There & Away

This chapter is about getting in and out of the Czech and Slovak republics. Because their transport systems remain quite intertwined, travel *between* the republics is treated in the Getting Around chapter.

Scheduled international flights (except inter-republic ones) arrive only at the two capitals, Prague and Bratislava. There are some 18 rail crossings into the two republics. By road, visitors can enter the Czech Republic at over 30 points and Slovakia at about 15, and the list is growing all the time (this doesn't count crossings between the republics). You can arrive in Bratislava by passenger boat from Vienna and even Budapest.

Students, and people aged under 26 or over 59, can get some big travel discounts. See the Train section of this chapter about rail passes, and the Documents section of the Facts for the Visitor chapter about getting student, youth and senior ID cards.

AIR

Airports & Airlines

The high season for air travel to the Czech and Slovak republics is roughly June or July through September, plus the Easter and Christmas-New Year holidays.

The only international airports are Ruzyně in Prague and Ivánka in Bratislava (if you count inter-republic flights, the other long-distance airports – Ostrava in the Czech Republic and Poprad and Košice in Slovakia – are also 'international').

Prague is connected worldwide by some two dozen international carriers, including ČSA (České aerolinie), the state-run airline. Air Ostrava is a new Czech airline with flights to Nuremberg (Germany).

Although ČSA has a few direct flights to Bratislava from North America, there are many more worldwide connections there via Prague; another common option is to fly to Vienna or Frankfurt and take a train or bus from there.

Bratislava is also linked to Zürich, Munich, Stuttgart, Frankfurt and dozens of cities worldwide by the Slovak carrier Tatra Air.

Buying Tickets

Buying tickets in the Czech and Slovak republics won't save you much money, so if you're going only there, take advantage of the lower cost of a return (round-trip) ticket bought at home.

Except during fare wars, airlines themselves don't usually offer the cheapest tickets. For these you must shop around the travel agencies. Look for adverts in major newspapers' travel sections, and watch for special offers. Besides the fare, check the airline, route, schedule, long layovers and any restrictions. The lowest prices often have strings attached.

In the UK and the USA, the cheapest flights are often offered by obscure bucket shops that don't even appear in the telephone book. Many are honest and solvent, but some may take your money and disappear, to reopen elsewhere under a new name. You're safest if an agency belongs to a national body like the American Society of Travel Agents (ASTA), the Association of British Travel Agents (ABTA) or the Australian Federation of Travel Agents (AFTA).

If you're uneasy about an agency, offer only a deposit – say, 20% – until you have the ticket. If its staff insists on 100% cash up front, consider going elsewhere. Once you have the ticket, ring the airline to confirm that you're actually booked on the flight.

You may decide to pay a little more for the safety of a better-known agent. Very convenient are agencies who specialise in finding low fares, like Trailfinders (UK), Council Travel (USA), Travel Cuts (Canada) and STA Travel (worldwide).

If you have a favourite airline, call and

ask the name of its 'consolidator', the agency selling its discounted tickets either directly or to other agencies. The consolidator is likely to have the cheapest fares for that airline.

Fares quoted here are approximate, and based on advertised rates at the time of writing. None of them constitutes a recommendation for any airline.

Reconfirmation To minimise your chances of being 'bumped' from an onward or return flight because of overbooking, reconfirm directly with the airline at least 72 hours before departure.

Travellers with Special Needs
If you're in a wheelchair, or vegetarian, or taking the baby, or terrified of flying, let the airline know when you book, so it can make arrangements. Most are happy to do so. Remind the airline when you reconfirm and again when you check in.

Young children who don't occupy a separate seat usually travel for a fraction of the adult fare. Children up to about 12 years of age can usually occupy a seat for half to two-thirds of the full fare.

North America

ČSA flies directly to Prague from New York four times a week (US$850), and jointly with Air Canada from Montreal two or three times weekly. But the cheapest way is probably to fly to London and buy an onward ticket there.

Council Travel and STA Travel sell discounted tickets in the USA from offices all around the country. Council's national toll-free number is ☎ 1-800-223 7402, STA Travel's is ☎ 1-800-777 0112. Another agency recommended by individual travellers is Travel Avenue (☎ 312-876 1116), 10 S Riverside Plaza, Chicago, IL 60661. For an ISIC card-holder, a return fare to Prague in high-season would be about US$950 from New York, and about US$100 more from the west coast.

Canada's best bargain-ticket agency is Travel Cuts, with some 50 offices in major cities. The parent office (☎ 416-979 2406) is at 187 College St, Toronto M5T 1P7. Their July fares are around C$950.

Europe

Discount air travel is big business in London. In addition to the travel sections of the major dailies, check the Travel classifieds in London's weekly *Time Out* and *TNT* entertainment magazines. A good bargain-ticket agency, especially for those aged under 26, is Campus Travel (☎ 0171-730 3402), 52 Grosvenor Gardens, London SW1W 0AG. Also try Trailfinders (☎ 0171-937 5400), 42-50 Earl's Court Rd, Kensington, London W8 6EJ; and STA Travel (☎ 0171-937 9921), 86 Old Brompton Rd, London SW7, and 117 Euston Rd, London NW1. All three have branches across the UK.

Another agency aimed at independent travellers to central Europe is Regent Holidays (☎ 0272-211 711), 15 John St, Bristol BS1 2HR.

Flying London-Prague (about two hours) can be cheaper than the train. Campus Travel has charter flights from UK£175 return (less for under-26s, ISIC cardholders and their dependants). British Airways, ČSA and British Midland (☎ 0345-554 554) have daily direct flights; these and KLM also fly from other UK cities. The best ordinary discounted summer fare is about UK£175, around the same in the low season.

If Bratislava is your destination, flying via Vienna is about UK£150 return plus the bus or train link. You can also fly into Prague and back from Vienna for about the same price, plus the Prague-Bratislava fare. Campus Travel has a UK£320 summer return fare from London or Manchester to Bratislava.

A reliable source of bargain tickets on the continent is NBBS Travels (☎ 020-638 17 36), Leidsestraat 53, 1017 NV Amsterdam. A discounted return ticket to Prague from Amsterdam is about UK£180, and about UK£100 from Berlin, Vienna, Warsaw or Budapest.

Air Travel Glossary

Apex Apex, or 'advance purchase excursion' is a discounted ticket which must be paid for in advance. There are penalties if you wish to change it.
Baggage Allowance This will be written on your ticket: usually one 20kg item to go in the hold, plus one item of hand luggage.
Bucket Shop An unbonded travel agency specialising in discounted airline tickets.
Bumped Just because you have a confirmed seat doesn't mean you're going to get on the plane – see Overbooking.
Cancellation Penalties If you have to cancel or change an Apex ticket there are often heavy penalties involved; insurance can sometimes be taken out against these penalties. Some airlines impose penalties on regular tickets as well, particularly against 'no show' passengers.
Check-In Airlines ask you to check in a certain time ahead of the flight departure (usually 1½ hours on international flights). If you fail to check in on time and the flight is overbooked the airline can cancel your booking and give your seat to somebody else.
Confirmation Having a ticket written out with the flight and date you want doesn't mean you have a seat until the agent has checked with the airline that your status is 'OK' or confirmed. Meanwhile you could just be 'on request'.
Discounted Tickets There are two types of discounted fares – officially discounted (see Promotional Fares) and unofficially discounted. The lowest prices often impose drawbacks like flying with unpopular airlines, inconvenient schedules, or unpleasant routes and connections. A discounted ticket can save you other things than money – you may be able to pay Apex prices without the associated Apex advance booking and other requirements. Discounted tickets only exist where there is fierce competition.
Full Fares Airlines traditionally offer first class (coded F), business class (coded J) and economy class (coded Y) tickets. These days there are so many promotional and discounted fares available from the regular economy class that few passengers pay full economy fare.
Lost Tickets If you lose your airline ticket an airline will usually treat it like a travellers cheque and, after inquiries, issue you with another one. Legally, however, an airline is entitled to treat it like cash and if you lose it then it's gone forever. Take good care of your tickets.
No-Shows No-shows are passengers who fail to show up for their flight, sometimes due to unexpected delays or disasters, sometimes due to simply forgetting, sometimes because they made more than one booking and didn't bother to cancel the one they didn't want. Full-fare passengers who fail to turn up are sometimes entitled to travel on a later flight. The rest of us are penalised (see Cancellation Penalties).
On Request An unconfirmed booking for a flight (see Confirmation).
Open Jaws A return ticket where you fly out to one place but return from another. If available this can save you backtracking to your arrival point.

Australasia

Flight Centres International and STA Travel are major dealers in cheap airfares, each with offices throughout Australia and New Zealand. In Australia, Flight Centres' (☎ 13 16 00) main offices are at 19 Bourke St (☎ 03-9650 2899) and 317 Swanston St (☎ 03-9663 1304) in Melbourne, Vic 3000; and 82 Elizabeth St, Sydney, NSW 2000 (☎ 02-9235 3522). The main STA Travel offices are at 224 Faraday St, Carlton, Vic 3053 (☎ 03-9347 6911); 855 George St,

Overbooking Airlines hate to fly empty seats and since every flight has some passengers who fail to show up (see No-Shows), airlines often book more passengers than they have seats. Usually the excess passengers balance those who fail to show up but occasionally somebody gets bumped. If this happens guess who it is most likely to be? The passengers who check in late.
Promotional Fares Officially discounted fares like Apex fares which are available from travel agents or direct from the airline.
Reconfirmation At least 72 hours prior to departure time of an onward or return flight you must contact the airline and 'reconfirm' that you intend to be on the flight. If you don't do this the airline can delete your name from the passenger list and you could lose your seat. You don't have to reconfirm the first flight on your itinerary or if your stopover is less than 72 hours. It doesn't hurt to reconfirm more than once.
Restrictions Discounted tickets often have various restrictions on them – advance purchase is the most usual one (see Apex). Others are restrictions on the minimum and maximum period you must be away, such as a minimum of 14 days or a maximum of one year (see Cancellation Penalties).
Standby A discounted ticket where you only fly if there is a seat free at the last moment. Standby fares are usually only available on domestic routes.
Tickets Out An entry requirement for many countries is that you have an onward or return ticket, in other words, a ticket out of the country. If you're not sure what you intend to do next, the easiest solution is to buy the cheapest onward ticket to a neighbouring country or a ticket from a reliable airline which can later be refunded if you do not use it.
Transferred Tickets Airline tickets cannot be transferred from one person to another. Travellers sometimes try to sell the return half of their ticket, but officials can ask you to prove that you are the person named on the ticket. This is unlikely to happen on domestic flights, but on an international flight tickets may be compared with passports.
Travel Agencies Travel agencies vary widely and you should ensure you use one that suits your needs. Some simply handle tours while full-service agencies handle everything from tours and tickets to car rental and hotel bookings. A good one will do all these things and can save you a lot of money but if all you want is a ticket at the lowest possible price, then you really need an agency specialising in discounted tickets. A discounted ticket agency, however, may not be useful for other things, like hotel bookings.
Travel Periods Some officially discounted fares, Apex fares in particular, vary with the time of year. There is often a low (off-peak) season and a high (peak) season. Sometimes there's an intermediate or shoulder season as well. At peak times, when everyone wants to fly, not only will the officially discounted fares be higher but so will unofficially discounted fares or there may simply be no discounted tickets available. Usually the fare depends on your outward flight – if you depart in the high season and return in the low season, you pay the high-season fare.

Sydney, NSW 2000 (☎ 02-9212 1255); and, in New Zealand, at 10 High St, Auckland (☎ 09-309 0458).

The *Sydney Morning Herald* and the Melbourne *Age* both have good weekend travel sections that have dozens of advertisements for bucket shops and late bargains.

The Australian and New Zealand, and Czech and Slovak national carriers, have cooperative deals but don't fly to each other's countries. In high-season the best available return fare from Melbourne or Sydney is about A$2200 with Qantas and ČSA (twice a week, via Singapore). In low-season it's about A$500 less, and ČSA throws in a free internal flight. You can also change at Frankfurt or Vienna. Air New Zealand and ČSA have similar deals; sometimes it can actually be cheaper to fly via the USA. Check with the ČSA booking office in Sydney (☎ 02-9247 6196).

The fastest (but not cheapest) way to Prague is with Lauda Air, which has several flights a week from Melbourne (via Sydney) to Vienna, with a two hour wait for the Austrian Airlines hop to Prague.

BUS

This is the cheapest way to travel across Europe. It's easiest to book with Eurolines, a consortium of coach companies with offices all over Europe. Coaches are comfortable, air-conditioned and as fast as the train, and they stop frequently for food and bodily functions. Services to Prague and Bratislava are comprehensive – there are direct buses from Amsterdam, Paris, Munich, Berlin and dozens of other major European cities.

Eurolines goes to Prague from London's Victoria coach station daily in summer for UK£90 return (UK£80 for people aged under 26 and over 59); book through any National Express office. Smaller lines that go from London for a few pounds less are Kingscourt Express (☎ 0181-673 7500) and Capital Express (☎ 0171-243 0488). Eurolines charge UK£99 return from London to Bratislava. All fares are 10 to 15% cheaper if you book from within the Czech and Slovak republics. London-Prague takes 22 hours, London-Bratislava about 24 hours.

Eurolines also has regular buses to Prague, Brno and Bratislava from Vienna.

For quick trips around Europe, both Eurolines and the new Eurobus have bus passes. The Eurolines Pass (in the UK ☎ 01582-404 511) covers 18 major European tourist cities for 30 or 60 days for UK£234/282. Youth and senior discount passes are also available.

Eurobus has two interlocking circuits taking in about 23 cities, including London, Prague, Vienna, Budapest and Munich. The two month pass bought in the UK is about UK£185/230 for people under/over 26. There is also a two week pass, and one and three month passes. The bus departs every two days and theoretically you can get on and off wherever you want. However, at peak season you'll have to book sectors well ahead. Eurobus has an information line in the USA (☎ 800-727 2437, ext 6143) and in the UK (☎ 0181-991 1021). In the UK, STA Travel or Campus Travel can book seats and also sell the passes.

TRAIN

Trains go daily to Prague from most major European cities. Fares quoted here are based on advertised rates at the time of writing. In summer you should book at least a few weeks ahead.

In the UK, it's cheapest to buy tickets through British Rail International (☎ 0171-834 2345), Victoria station, London SW1V 1JY; or Eurotrain at Campus Travel (0171-730 3402), 52 Grosvenor Gardens, London SW1W 0AG. A 2nd class return ticket from London via Cologne – the cheapest and most direct of half a dozen routes – is UK£280 (UK£208 for under-26s), plus about UK£10 for a couchette or UK£25 for a sleeper. Tickets are good for two months and you can break your journey anywhere en route. London-Prague takes 25 to 30 hours.

Prices for international trains are cheaper if you book in Prague or Bratislava. Some sample 2nd class international train fares from Prague are: US$35 to Budapest (nine hours), US$35 to Kraków (10 hours), US$25 to Vienna (six hours), US$29 to Warsaw (12 hours) and US$45 to Berlin (5½ hours).

There's no need to book domestic rail travel before you get there.

Rail Passes

If you plan to travel widely in Europe, the following special tickets and rail passes may be better value for getting to and out of the Czech and Slovak republics but not within them. It is still cheaper to buy local tickets for travelling around either republic than to travel with the passes below. Some of these may have different names in different countries.

Inter-Rail Pass This UK£275 pass gives people aged under 26 unlimited 2nd class travel for one month on most of the state railways of western and central Europe (except their own country). The cheaper 'Zone D' pass for people under 26 and for travel in the Czech Republic, Slovakia, Hungary, Poland, former Yugoslav countries, Romania and Bulgaria costs UK£185 for 15 days. If you want to go out of this zone into another then a two zone pass, valid for a month, is UK£220. There's also an Inter-Rail pass for people aged 26 and over that costs UK£215 for 15 days or UK£269 for one month.

Circuit Tour Ticket This fixed-route return ticket (Eurotrain's version for those aged under 26 is called an Explorer ticket) links six or eight major European cities, going out one way and returning another. Two Eurotrain routes that include Prague are UK£262 and UK£286; British Rail International has a non-youth version for UK£312, plus 1st class options.

Czech Explorer Pass This Eurotrain pass is UK£23 for a week's unlimited 2nd class travel within the Czech and Slovak republics (UK£33 for 1st class). It's available to people aged under 26, ISIC card-holders, teachers and their spouses and children. It can be difficult to buy and many conductors are not familiar with the ticket, so most do not know what to do with it when you present it.

Euro-Domino Freedom Pass If you don't plan to be on the move all that much, this pass allows a few days per month of unrestricted train travel within a particular country. In the Czech and Slovak republics, for example, any three/five/10 days in a designated month is UK£39/59/89 respectively, travelling in 2nd class (for people under 26 it's UK£29/39/69).

Eurail Pass This pass, for 1st and 2nd class travel in a limited number of European countries, is meant for non-Europeans and is normally only sold outside Europe. At present the Eurail Pass is not valid in the Czech and Slovak republics, however, this may change.

Warning

The overnight Prague-Berlin and Prague-Budapest trains have become notorious for bold thefts from sleeping passengers, so keep a grip on your bags.

International Train Departures

You can front up to the window for international tickets (*mezinárodní jízdenky* or *medzinárodný lístok)* in a big-city train station, but it's easier to make international bookings (and get any discounts you're entitled to) through a reliable travel agency. Some are identified under individual towns. There's often a ČD (České dráhy, or Czech Railways) agency in bigger stations, and the local Čedok or Satur office may not be the cheapest but is usually competent.

See the Getting Around chapter for more about buying train tickets in the Czech and Slovak republics.

CAR & MOTORCYCLE

For more about driving between and within the two republics, including traffic rules, fuel and Czech-Slovak border crossings, see the Getting Around chapter.

International Border Crossings

The box below lists international border crossings for cars, buses and motorbikes (including the crossings where tourist visas can be issued on the spot). See the Getting Around chapter for information on crossing between the two republics. Note that there is only one crossing from Austria to Slovakia, at Petržalka.

Documents

Drivers from the USA, Canada, UK, Australia and New Zealand don't need an International Driving Permit; only a full domestic licence, along with the vehicle registration. If you're arriving in someone else's car, avoid potential headaches by carrying a notarised letter from the owner, saying you're allowed to drive it.

You'll also need a certificate of insurance or 'green card', normally valid for three months, showing you carry full liability insurance. This card is available from your insurer (sometimes for a small fee). Without this or other proof of acceptable insurance, you'll be required to take out a short-term policy at the border, for about US$120 per month for a car, US$30 per month for a motorcycle. Insurance is not available at all border crossings, and it's highly recommended carry your own proof of insurance.

In your car you need to carry a first-aid kit, a red-and-white warning triangle, as well as display a nationality sticker on the rear.

BICYCLE & WALKING

A border crossing that is limited to pedestrians and cyclists links Horní Malá Úpa in the Krkonoše mountains to Ogorzelec in Poland. There are also other border points limited to people on foot, bicycle or moped; see the aside in this chapter. Otherwise, 'self-propelled' travellers may officially cross only at designated border points.

Some customs posts will stamp your passport, some don't bother. It's best to ask for this to be done, if only so you know when your visa expires.

SEA

From May to September, hydrofoils ply the Danube twice daily between Bratislava and Vienna (600 Sk one way, 950 Sk return); in April and October the service is reduced to four times per week. From April to October hydrofoils also go daily from Bratislava to Budapest (1750/2800 Sk).

DEPARTURE TAXES

Flying internationally to and from either republic, the departure tax (which applies to flights between the two republics as well) is 350 Kč from Prague and 300 Sk from Bratislava. This is normally included in the price of any ticket bought from a travel agency.

ORGANISED TOURS

After decades of being the only game in town, Čedok and Satur have garnered the widest range of short breaks and package tours to the republics – though not necessarily at the lowest prices.

Depending on choice of accommodation and entertainment, their land-only cost (ie not including the cost of getting there and back) for a two night Prague visit is US$190 to US$250 per person in a double with breakfast – with cheaper winter versions. Longer visits with out-of-city excursions are also available. A two night break in Bratislava is US$150 to US$200. They also offer driving tours (your car, their local tours and accommodation), fly-drive packages (book only your flight and car) and various escorted coach tours around the republics.

Čedok and Satur offices abroad (listed under Tourist Offices in the Facts for the Visitor chapter) can make the arrangements or furnish the names of local agents that sell their packages.

From the USA

American-International Homestays (☎ 303-642 3088; toll-free in the USA, 1-800-876 2048; PO Box 17541, Nederland, CO 80466) organises multi-city homestays in which host families act as de facto guides to their city. The 17-day programmes (Prague plus Budapest, Kraków or Berlin) are US$2449 including return airfare from New York, or US$1699 with a one-way airfare from New York. It also arranges ordinary bed & breakfast accommodation at US$49/79 per single/double (a minimum three day tour). Homestay tours with guides, local transport, accommodation and dinner are US$99/179.

From the UK

New Millennium (☎ 0121-711 2232; 20 High St, Solihull, W Midlands B91 3TB) runs coach tour holidays from five to 10 days to Prague for UK£169 per person, to Bratislava for UK£190 per person. Travelsphere Holidays (☎ 01858-410 818; Compass House, Rockingham Rd, Market Harborough LE16 7QD) offers an eight day trip with three nights in Vienna and four in Prague with flight, transfer and accommodation included from UK£399. A Prague 'city break' (with a UK£30 to UK£60 flight supplement) with Travelscene (☎ 0181-427 4445; 11-15 St Ann's Rd, Harrow, Middlesex HA1 1AS) starts at UK£329 for three nights, UK£430 for seven nights; more depending on the season and quality of accommodation. Tours to Bratislava start at UK£370 for three nights.

The Czech Tourist Centre (☎ 0171-794 3263; 16 Frognal Parade, London NW3 5GH) offers half and full-day bike tours and city tours in Prague from UK£18. Martin Randall Travel (☎ 0181-742 3355; 10 Barley Mow Passage, Chiswick, London W4 4PH) offers a five to six day art tour guided by an art historian for around UK£800.

From Australasia

One agency organising tours to the Czech and Slovak republics from Australia is Eastern Europe Travel Bureau at 75 King St, Sydney, NSW 2000 (☎ 02-9262 1144) and at 343 Little Collins St, Melbourne, Vic 3000 (☎ 03-9600 0299). It's an agent for Čedok and Satur, and its packages include a two night tour in Prague from A$174 or a six night tour of the Czech Republic from A$1420. There is also a two night Bratislava tour from A$194.

WARNING

The information in this chapter is particularly vulnerable to change: prices for international travel are volatile, routes are introduced and cancelled, schedules change, special deals come and go, and rules and visa requirements are amended.

Airlines and governments seem to take a perverse pleasure in making price structures and regulations as complicated as possible. You should check directly with the airline or travel agent to make sure you understand how a fare (and the ticket you might buy) works. In addition, the travel industry is highly competitive and there are many lurks and perks.

The upshot of this is that you should get opinions, quotes and advice from as many airlines and travel agents as possible before you part with your hard-earned cash. The details given in this chapter should be regarded as pointers and are not a substitute for your own careful, up-to-date research.

Getting Around

This chapter is about getting around within the Czech and Slovak republics, as well as between them.

AIR

ČSA is the national carrier of the Czech Republic. Slovakia, as yet, has no national carrier but there has been talk of the government creating one. Two smaller carriers are Slovak airline Tatra Air, with connections from and within Slovakia, and Czech airline Air Ostrava, which operates between Prague and Ostrava. For details on airline booking offices, see the Getting There & Away sections under Prague and Bratislava.

There are five main airports: Prague Ruzyně (PRG) and Ostrava (OSR) in the Czech Republic; Bratislava Ivánka (BTS) and Košice (KSC) in Slovakia. In the Czech Republic, Brno has a smaller airport.

The chart below shows inter-republic and major internal connections. The figures indicate the respective airline's one-way fares at the time of writing, for tickets purchased within either republic. For passengers aged under 25 and over 69, the airlines offer discounts of about 5% on most flights. Local and foreign passengers pay the same fares.

Domestic Air Services

There is only one regular connection within the Czech Republic, Prague-Ostrava on Air Ostrava. Within Slovakia there is only the Bratislava-Košice flight with Tatra Air.

Inter-Republic Flights

From Prague, ČSA has three flights a day to Bratislava and two a day to Košice. Tatra Air flies Prague-Bratislava twice a day, but only on weekdays.

BUS

ČSAD, the old Czechoslovak state bus company, has now split into ČSAD (Česká automobilová doprava, or Czech Bus

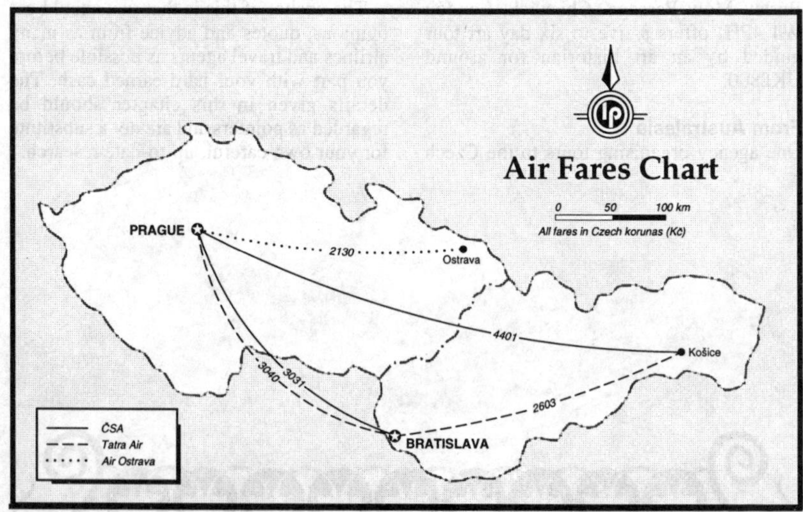

JOHN KING

RICHARD NEBESKÝ

RICHARD NEBESKÝ

JOHN KING

RICHARD NEBESKÝ

RICHARD NEBESKÝ

RICHARD NEBESKÝ

RICHARD NEBESKÝ

Handcrafts
The Czech and Slovak republics also boast a rich tradition of finely detailed handcrafts. In addition to clothing, everyday tools, utensils, music instruments, linen, furniture and entire buildings are decorated in special ways.

JONATHAN SMITH

RICHARD NEBESKÝ

RICHARD NEBESKÝ

RICHARD NEBESKÝ

RICHARD NEBESKÝ

RICHARD NEBESKÝ

RICHARD NEBESKÝ

RICHARD NEBESKÝ

JONATHAN SMITH

Prague
The capital of the Czech Republic boasts many fine examples of architectural styles. The Renaissance domes of St Michael Church (top middle) lend the city a Tuscan look, but the Baroque and Art Nouveau (typified by the ornate features of the top left building) styles dominate.

Bus Timetable Symbols

⚒	workdays (normally Monday to Friday)
S	Saturdays if not a state holiday
†	holidays
N	holiday just before a workday
b	⚒ and S
g	daily except Saturdays
a	Saturdays and holidays only
P	workday following a holiday only
V	workday before holidays
c	Fridays and schooldays only
r	not on 24 Dec.
x	stops on request
MHD	stop situated in an urban mass transit area
⟩	bus takes another route
I	bus doesn't stop there

Transport) in the Czech Republic, and SAD (Slovenská autobusová doprava) in Slovakia.

Long-distance coach connections tend to be faster, more frequent and marginally pricier than train connections, and remoter locations require fewer transfers. Most sizable towns are linked by several buses a day. Foreign and local travellers pay the same fares.

The Czech Republic has at least two private lines too, with prices a shade less than ČSAD's. From Prague, Čebus and Český národní expres go to Brno.

Buying a Bus Ticket

Few travel agencies book internal coaches, though some may have timetable information. Short-haul tickets are sold on the bus, long-distance tickets usually at the station. You can hand the clerk a scrap of paper with your destination, departure time (24 hour clock) and date (month in Roman numerals) and get the nearest thing on offer, or wrestle with the timetables.

Big stations like Florenc in Prague have charts with all the route numbers for each major destination and all the departure times for each route number, plus timetables for every route. To figure out when the next bus leaves, you'll probably have to look at more than one timetable. They'll drive you cross-eyed, peppered with symbols showing the days buses do and don't run. The box below explains the most common ones, but be ready for local variations.

Taking a Bus Between the Republics

Your coach may not stop at the border check between the two republics, but you'll avoid hassles later (mainly over how long you've been in the country) if you insist on stopping for an entry stamp in your passport.

TRAIN

ČSD, the old Czechoslovak state rail company, was split into ČD (České dráhy, or Czech Railways) and ŽSR (Železnica Slovenskej republiky, or Railways of the Slovak Republic), which have a combined network that is among Europe's densest. Most major cities are linked by several trains a day. Travel is cheap by western standards. Foreign and local passengers pay the same fare, and kids aged under 12 ride for half-price. The Prague-Bratislava fare is 280 Kč one way. For more information see the Rail & Bus Fare aside.

Buying a Train Ticket

The fastest trains are SC (SuperCity), EC/IC (EuroCity/InterCity), and express

Train Timetable Symbols

∄	after the name of the station = tickets issued on train only
✕	in the train column = dining car included
🚌	in the train column = train includes sleeping cars or couchettes
R	in the train column = for indicated cars, reservation is possible
[R]	in the train column = train with obligatory seat reservation
🛏	in the train column = the train carries only sleeping cars or couchettes
♿	in the train column = there is a coach for wheelchairs
x	in front of time descriptions = request train stop only
🚲	the notes have information on transport of bicycles
〉	train travels on another line
|	train doesn't stop at this station
①	Monday ② Tuesday ③ Wednesday ④ Thursday ⑤ Friday ⑥ Saturday ⑦ Sunday
⚒	workdays only (normally Mon-Fri)
†	holidays (except 24 Dec., 1 & 8 May, 5 Jul.) and 2 Jan. only
Ⓝ	the last rest day before a workday (except 28 Oct. or 27 Dec.)
Ⓟ	the first workday following a holiday (except 29 Oct. or 28 Dec.)
Ⓢ	Saturdays (except 26 Dec. & 2 Jan.) and 24 Dec. only
Ⓐ	the last workday before Ⓢ or † (except 27 Oct. and 31 Dec.)
Ⓑ	except Saturday
Ⓒ	Saturdays and holidays and 2 Jan only
Ⓓ	workdays and Saturdays only
Ⓔ	⚒ and Ⓝ
Ⓚ	not on Ⓝ
Ⓗ	not on Ⓟ

(*rychlík/rýchlik*), which are shown in shaded columns and bold print in timetables (and on the two railways maps in this book all are grouped together as Express Trains). They're often reservation-only, marked with an R in a box; an un-boxed R means reservations are recommended. 'Fast trains' (*spěšný vlak/spešný vlak*) make more stops but cost a bit less; times are printed in bold on timetables. Slowest of all are the local trains (*osobní vlak/osobný vlak*).

You can buy an unreserved ticket (*jízdenka/lístok*) right up to departure time, or make a reservation (*místenka/miestenka*) up to an hour beforehand. You must buy the ticket before, or at the same time as you make, the reservation. You can get a seat (*místo/miesto*), and on longer routes a couchette (*lehátkový vůz/ležadlo*) or sleeper (*spací vůz/spací vozeň*). On fast trains, if ordinary (*jednoduchý*) places are sold out, 1st class (*prvotřídní/prvotriedny*) ones will probably be available for about 50% more.

Most travel agencies won't make domestic train reservations. If you're buying your own ticket, it's easiest to write down your destination, departure time (24 hour clock) and date (month in Roman numerals) for the clerk. If you don't specify anything else, you'll probably get a one-way, 2nd class ticket on a local train. 'Return' (round-trip) is *zpáteční/spiatočný*. The Train & Bus Symbols aside in this chapter lists some useful symbols found in train timetables.

It is also possible for passengers to transport a car. This is a new service, which started in June 1997, and is only possible on the route between Prague and Poprad. The cost to transport the car and a couchette for the driver is 988 Kč. Canoes can also be transported in special carriages, and bicycles are transported in the normal cargo carriages.

See the Getting There & Away chapter for information on special tickets and passes that can reduce the cost of train travel in the two republics.

CAR & MOTORCYCLE

The Czech and Slovak republics are covered by a network of generally good roads, though they often follow old routes through villages and small towns, with sudden sharp bends and reduced speed limits. There is about 900km of European-style motorways (freeways), the main ones being the D1 or E50/E65 between Prague, Brno and Olomouc, the D2 or E65 between Brno and Bratislava, and the D5 or E50 between Prague and Plzeň.

Most of the major motorways now have an annual 800 Kč/200 Sk toll charge (see the country map) and this is payable at most border crossings or at automobile organisations in both countries. You can be fined up to 5000 Kč/Sk if you are caught on a freeway without the toll sticker displayed on the right-hand side of the vehicle's windscreen.

Motorways and country roads tend to have light traffic, since only about 60% of Czechs and 51% of Slovaks own cars. On the whole, Czech and Slovak drivers are reasonably considerate and appreciate you being in return.

See the Getting There & Away chapter for information about documents, insurance and external border crossings.

Border Crossings Between the Republics

The new Czech-Slovak border functions just like any other border in Europe and, at the time of writing, there were 15 official border crossings. Czechs and Slovaks flash their documents to the guards and barely stop when crossing the border checks, but foreign drivers are more thoroughly checked. The most well-used border crossing and probably most foreigner-friendly one is on the E65 Highway at Kúty, between Brno and Bratislava.

Road Rules

As in the rest of continental Europe, you drive on the right-hand side of the road. The legal driving age is 18. *Don't drink if you'll be driving*: regulations permit *no* blood alcohol, and penalties are severe.

Speed limits vary in built-up areas from 40 to 50km/h between 5 am and 11 pm, and 90km/h at night. On major roads the limit is 90km/h, and on motorways 120km/h (in Slovakia it's only 110km/h). The official speed limit at the country's many rail crossings is 30km/h but you're better off stopping and looking, since many well-used crossings have no barriers and some don't even have flashing lights.

If the car has seatbelts, they must be worn by all passengers. Children under 12 years of age may not sit in the front seat. Horns may only be used to signal danger or that you're about to overtake someone. You may not use your horn at all in Bratislava, nor during the night in central Prague.

Riders of motorbikes greater than 50cc must wear helmets and goggles, and their passengers must also wear helmets. The motorcycle's headlight (on low beam) must be on at all times. The maximum speed for motorbikes, even on major highways, is 90km/h.

Road Signs Standard European signs are in common use throughout both republics. Some that may be unfamiliar to Britons and non-European visitors are:

Blue disk with red border and red slash – no parking
Blue disk with red border and crossed red slashes – no stopping
White disk with red border – no vehicles allowed
Red disk with horizontal white line – no entry
White triangle (point down) with red border – give way to crossing or merging traffic
Yellow diamond on white background – you have the right of way; a black slash through it means you *don't* have the right of way anymore

In cities and towns, keep a sharp eye out for *pěší zóna* signs, indicating pedestrian-only

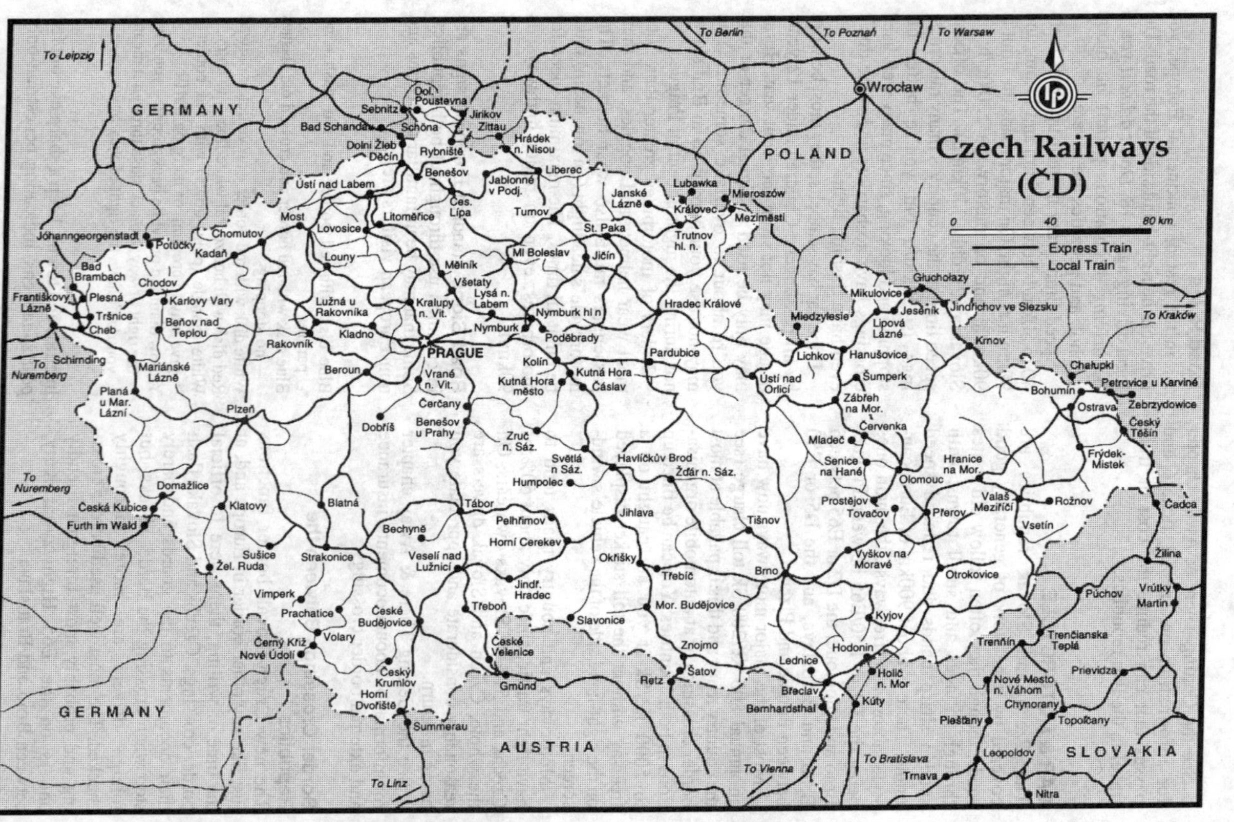

Czech Railways
(ČD)
0
40
80 km
Express Train
Local Train
To Warsaw
To Poznań
To Berlin
To Leipzig
To Kraków
To Bratislava
To Vienna
To Linz
To Nuremberg
To Schirnding
POLAND
GERMANY
SLOVAKIA
AUSTRIA
Wrocław
Gluchołazy
Mikulovice
Jeseník
Jindřichov ve Slezsku
Krnov
Chałupki
Bohumín
Petrovice u Karviné
Zebrzydowice
Český Těšín
Ostrava
Frýdek-Místek
Čadca
Žilina
Vrútky
Martin
Púchov
Prievidza
Trenčianska Teplá
Trenčín
Topoľčany
Chynorany
Nové Mesto n. Váhom
Piešťany
Leopoldov
Nitra
Trnava
Rožnov
Vsetín
Valaš. Meziříčí
Otrokovice
Hranice na Mor.
Přerov
Olomouc
Červenka
Lipová Lázně
Šumperk
Hanušovice
Zábřeh na Mor.
Lichkov
Międzylesie
Mladeč
Senice na Hané
Prostějov
Tovačov
Vyškov na Moravě
Kyjov
Hodonín
Holič n. Mor
Kúty
Břeclav
Lednice
Bernhardsthal
Brno
Tišnov
Ústí nad Orlicí
Mieroszów
Meziměstí
Lubawka
Královec
Trutnov hl. n.
Hradec Králové
Pardubice
Janské Lázně
St. Paka
Jičín
Liberec
Hrádek n. Nisou
Zittau
Jiříkov
Jablonné v Podj.
Turnov
Ml Boleslav
Nymburk hl n
Poděbrady
Nymburk
Lysá n. Labem
Všetaty
Mělník
Kralupy n. Vlt.
PRAGUE
Kolín
Kutná Hora
Čáslav
Kutná Hora město
Havlíčkův Brod
Žďár n. Sáz.
Třebíč
Mor. Budějovice
Znojmo
Šatov
Retz
Jihlava
Okříšky
Slavonice
Světlá n. Sáz.
Humpolec
Zruč n. Sáz.
Pelhřimov
Horní Cerekev
Jindř. Hradec
České Velenice
Gmünd
Třeboň
Tábor
Veselí nad Lužnicí
Bechyně
Čerčany
Benešov u Prahy
Vraně n. Vlt.
Dobříš
České Budějovice
Summerau
Český Krumlov
Horní Dvořiště
Strakonice
Volary
Prachatice
Černý Kříž
Nové Údolí
Vimperk
Blatná
Beroun
Kladno
Lužná u Rakovníka
Rakovník
Louny
Lovosice
Litoměřice
Ces. Lípa
Benešov
Rybniště
Dol. Poustevna
Sebnitz
Schöna
Dolní Žleb
Děčín
Bad Schandau
Ústí nad Labem
Most
Chomutov
Kadaň
Plzeň
Klatovy
Sušice
Žel. Ruda
Domažlice
Česká Kubice
Furth im Wald
Potůčky
Johanngeorgenstadt
Karlovy Vary
Bečov nad Teplou
Chodov
Mariánské Lázně
Planá u Mar. Lázní
Cheb
Tršnice
Plesná
Bad Brambach
Františkovy Lázně

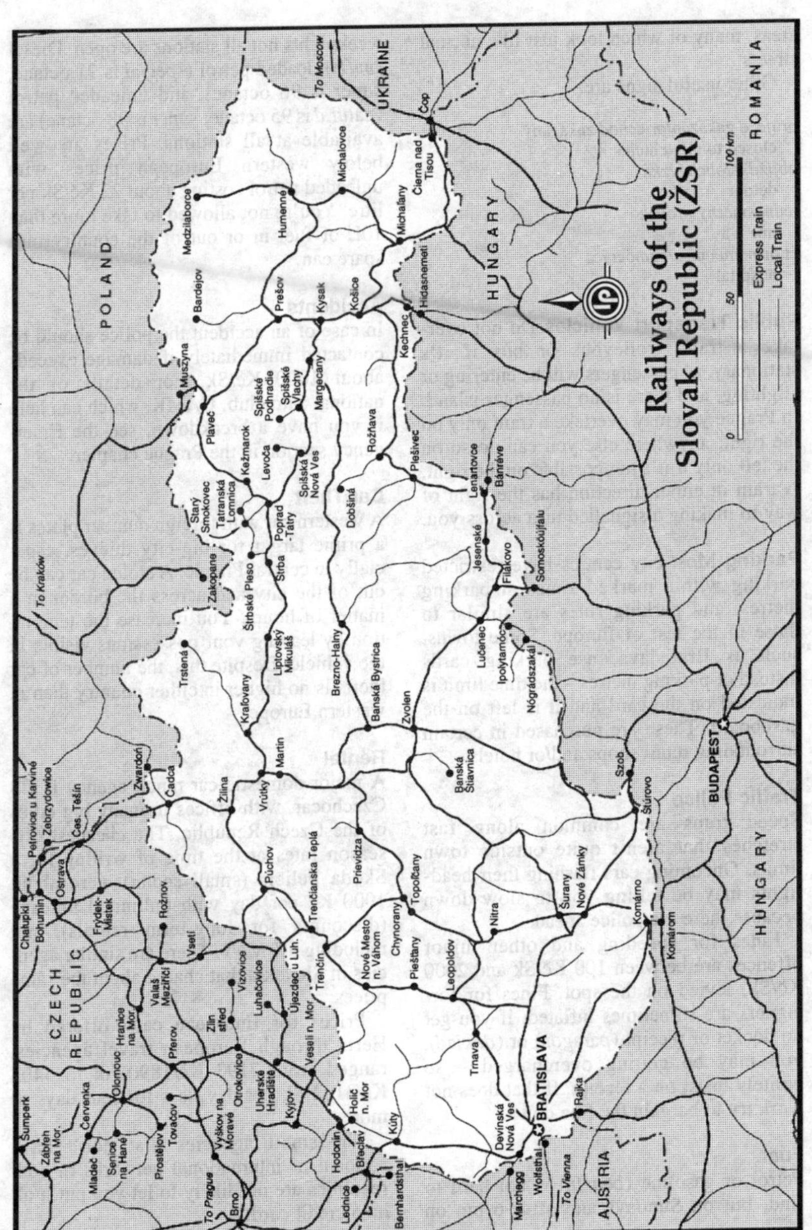
Railways of the Slovak Republic (ŽSR)
Express Train
Local Train
0
50
100 km
POLAND
UKRAINE
HUNGARY
ROMANIA
CZECH REPUBLIC
AUSTRIA
To Kraków
To Moscow
To Prague
To Vienna
BRATISLAVA
BUDAPEST
Košice
Prešov
Žilina
Martin
Vrútky
Zvolen
Banská Bystrica
Brezno-Halny
Poprad -Tatry
Spišská Nová Ves
Levoča
Kežmarok
Plaveč
Muszyna
Bardejov
Medzilaborce
Humenné
Michalovce
Michaľany
Čierna nad Tisou
Čop
Kysak
Margecany
Spišské Vlachy
Spišské Podhradie
Rožňava
Plešivec
Dobšiná
Kechnec
Hidasnemeti
Lenartovce
Bánréve
Jesenské
Fiľakovo
Somoskőújfalu
Lučenec
Ipolytamóc
Nógrádszakál
Banská Štiavnica
Štúrovo
Szob
Komárno
Komárom
Nové Zámky
Šurany
Nitra
Leopoldov
Trnava
Piešťany
Topoľčany
Chynorany
Prievidza
Nové Mesto n. Váhom
Trenčín
Trenčianska Teplá
Púchov
Čadca
Zwardoń
Kraľovany
Trstená
Liptovský Mikuláš
Štrba
Štrbské Pleso
Zakopane
Tatranská Lomnica
Starý Smokovec
Devínska Nová Ves
Marchegg
Wolfsthal
Rajka
Kúty
Holíč n. Mor
Hodonín
Břeclav
Bernhardsthal
Lednice
Brno
Kyjov
Veselí n. Mor
Újezdec u Luh.
Uherské Hradiště
Otrokovice
Luhačovice
Vizovice
Zlín střed
Vsetín
Valaš. Meziříčí
Rožnov
Frýdek-Místek
Ostrava
Bohumín
Chałupki
Petrovice u Karviné
Zebrzydowice
Čes. Těšín
Přerov
Hranice na Mor.
Olomouc
Červenka
Šumperk
Zábřeh na Mor.
Mladeč
Senice na Hané
Prostějov
Tovačov
Vyškov na Moravě

areas, many of which look just like normal streets.

Other useful signs are:

průjezd zakázán/priechod zakázaný
closed to all vehicles
objížďka/obchádzka
detour
jednosměrný provoz
one way
H or *nemocnice/nemocnica*
hospital

Public Transport Vehicles Do not overtake a tram, trolleybus or bus if it's stationary, as passengers will be entering or alighting, and there is no passenger island. In Prague you may overtake a tram only on the right; anywhere else you can do so on the left only if it's not possible on the right. A tram in either direction has the right of way in making a signalled turn across you.

Parking Most city centres have restricted parking within marked zones at parking metres, and parking rules are similar to those in the rest of Europe. Some towns, such as Bratislava, use parking cards instead of parking metres – the time limit is indicated on the card and it is left on the dashboard. These are purchased in certain surrounding retail shops and/or hotels.

Traffic Police

Speed traps are common along fast stretches that aren't quite outside town limits. Oncoming cars flashing their headlights may be telling you to slow down because there are police ahead.

Fines for speeding and other minor offences are between 100 Kč/Sk and 2000 Kč/Sk, levied on the spot. Fines for foreigners are sometimes inflated; if you get no docket or receipt (*paragon*) or (*doklad*), you may be getting overcharged – so politely insist on a receipt. If that does not work try to bargain the fine down.

Fuel

Petrol or gasoline (*benzín*) is not hard to find, but on Sundays and after 6 pm on weeknights not all stations are open. Diesel (*nafta*), leaded petrol (*special* is 91 octane, *super* is 96 octane), and unleaded petrol (*natural* is 95 octane, *super* is 98 octane) are available at all stations. Prices are well below western European prices with unleaded petrol costing about 22 Kč/Sk per litre. You're not allowed to take more than 10L of fuel in or out of the country in a spare can.

Accidents

In case of an accident the police should be contacted immediately if damage exceeds about 1000 Kč/Sk. For details of the national auto club, UAMK, which can help if you have a breakdown, see the Emergency section in the Prague chapter.

Car Theft

A western car with foreign number plates is a prime target for big-city thieves, especially in central Prague. A stolen car can be out of the city and across the border in a matter of hours. You increase the temptation by leaving your possessions visible in the vehicle. Despite this, the number of car thefts is no higher in either country than in western Europe.

Rental

A major domestic car-rental agency is CS Czechocar, with offices in many big cities of the Czech Republic. The cheapest off-season rates at the time of writing for a Škoda Felicia (small sedan) were about 1000 Kč per day with unlimited mileage (discounts for long-term rentals), not including 5% VAT. There are similar agencies in Slovakia that charge about the same prices.

Prices for European cars, offered by Hertz through European travel agencies, ranged from 2193 Kč/1890 Sk to 4403 Kč/3102 Sk per day, less for four days or more.

The small agencies that don't have national or international networks in both republics are not likely to let you put it all on a credit card.

BICYCLE

One of the best ways to enjoy the Czech and Slovak republics is from the saddle of a bike, as confirmed by numerous cyclists' letters to Lonely Planet. Many Czechs and Slovaks are keen cyclists too.

One of the authors of this book has cycled across central and South Bohemia, southern Moravia, plus the beautiful Malá Fatra mountains of Central Slovakia. Some other fine regions for riding are the spa towns of western Bohemia; the foothills of the Šumava mountains in southern and western Bohemia; the Třeboň lake region of southern Bohemia; the south-east corner of Moravia around Znojmo, Břeclav, Hodonín and Uherské Hradiště; the flat southern border regions of Slovakia; and the demanding but splendid High Tatras.

It is advisable to get hold of regional hiking maps, and stick to minor roads where possible, both for your safety and for your own enjoyment of rural areas. If you have a mountain bike, any level, low-lying walking trails are another scenic option. Motorists tend to give cyclists a wide birth, though narrow country roads are still a threat, especially at night. Big cities are no fun to ride in, due to heavy traffic, pollution, tram tracks (especially when wet) and cobblestones.

A mountain bike or sturdy touring bike with at least 18 gears is probably the best choice, since so much of both republics is hilly. There are plenty of cycling shops and repair centres in Prague and other large towns, but for rural riding you should carry all essential spare parts. Security – a good lock and chain for the frame and both wheels – is essential, as bikes are popular targets for theft.

You can take your bike on the trains quite safely. Present your ticket at the railway luggage office and fill out a tag, to be attached to the bike, with name, address, departure station and destination. The charge is usually 10% of your own fare; don't lose that receipt! Strip the bike of anything easily removed. Collect it from the freight carriage as soon as you arrive. If you're short on time, take the bike straight to the freight carriage (normally at the rear or the front of the train) and the conductor will load it for a small fee.

You can also take a bike on international trains, but it must be presented to customs (at the train station of your departure) at least four days before departure. They will see that it goes on the right train to get there at the same time you do.

Bicycles can be transported on buses but at the discretion of the driver.

For details of cycling in Prague, and also if you want to take bicycles on the metro, see the Getting Around section at the end of the Prague chapter.

Rental

There are one or two bicycle-rental places in sports shops in Prague and popular tourist areas like Vysoké Tatry, as well as in a few up-market hotels in Prague, Bratislava and a handful of tourist towns like Český Krumlov, but it's not easy to rent them in most other parts of the Czech and Slovak republics. Throughout this book we note places where you can.

HITCHING

Hitching is never entirely safe anywhere in the world. Travellers who decide to hitch should understand that they are taking a small but potentially serious risk. Those who choose to hitch will be safer if they travel in pairs, and let someone know where they are planning to go.

That said, many Czechs and Slovaks, women included, do hitch and do pick up hitchhikers, and it can be an easy and friendly way to get around.

BOAT

On the whole, most Czech and Slovak rivers are too shallow for passenger transport. In the Czech Republic in summer boats go along the Vltava between Prague and Slapy, and on the Labe between Děčín and Hřensko. In summer in Slovakia there are regular boats along the Danube between Bratislava, Gabčíkovo and Komárno.

LOCAL TRANSPORT

Most towns of any size have at least a bus (*autobus*) system, and often trolley-buses (*trolejbus*) as well. Bigger towns may have a network of trams (*tramvaj/električka*) serving the central area. Prague has an extensive and efficient metro (underground) system.

On the whole, service is frequent and reliable. Typical hours of operation are 5 am to 11 pm or midnight. Prague, Brno and Bratislava also have limited night-time services.

Depending on the town, a ride is just 5 Kč/Sk to 10 Kč/Sk, with big discounts for kids aged from 10 to 16 and for parents accompanying very young children. Kids aged under 10 and the elderly ride free.

Tickets are sold individually or in discounted books at public transport offices, newsstands, tobacco kiosks, and from machines at major big-city stops; in one or two towns you buy them on board. In most places a single ticket is valid for all forms of transport. In Prague, Brno and Bratislava you can also buy multi-day and monthly passes, good for unlimited travel.

You validate your ticket by punching it in a little machine on board (or in Prague's metro station lobbies). It's an honour system, but inspectors pop up fairly often and are keen to levy instant fines on anyone without a valid ticket.

Taxi

Most towns have at least a few taxis for hire. Prague, however, is plagued with crooked taxi-drivers (for some of the problems involved in taxi-hire there, and ways to cope with them, see the Getting Around section in the Prague chapter), but taxi-drivers in Brno, Bratislava and smaller towns are more courteous and will generally treat you fairly.

valleys of the Morava, Becva and Odra rivers, the only lowland corridor across the Czech Republic. Though this is the most densely populated part of the republic, the hills to both sides offer some of its most peaceful travelling.

The country is nearly encircled by low hills and thickly wooded mountain ranges, beloved by Czechs and their neighbours for winter skiing and summer walking. High-elevation chaty (mountain chalets) and small-town pensions make long-distance treks feasible.

The northern Bohemian ranges – the Krušné hory and Krkonoše – offer extraordinary landscapes like the sandstone 'sculptures' of Labské Pískovce, Český ráj (the Bohemian Paradise) and Adršpach-Teplice, though these and the Jeseníky of Moravia are afflicted at higher elevations with appalling acid rain damage. With mountains full of coal and other minerals, northern Bohemia and Moravia underwent intense industrialisation in the 19th century, and the Communists topped the tide with steel, machinery and other heavy industry.

Around the edges of the republic are several picturesque enclaves of traditional culture – architecture, speech, customs, dress and in some cases music – which over the centuries have withstood Habsburg incursions and creeping urbanisation. These

Czech Republic

Most foreigners who hear 'Czech Republic' think 'Prague', and indeed since 1989 Prague has, for better or worse, become one of the top tourist destinations in Europe. Other familiar attractions are the Bohemian spa towns, particularly the starchy old trio of Karlovy Vary (Karlsbad), Mariánské Lázně (Marienbad) and Františkovy Lázně (Franzenbad). And everybody knows about the beer – the world-famous amber brew of Plzeň (Pilsen).

All these high-profile attractions could be 'done', tour-group style, in five or six days. But there's much more to the Czech Lands – the historical regions of Bohemia and Moravia – than this, and they could keep you fascinated for months if you let them. Moravia (including a slice of Silesia in the north) is perhaps more of a surprise for being less well known.

Those who enjoy world-class architecture needn't spend all their time in Prague. The republic overflows with well-restored historical centres lined with Gothic, Renaissance and Baroque façades. Among the richest are Kutná Hora in Central Bohemia; Cheb, Loket and Domažlice in western Bohemia; Olomouc in northern Moravia; and Telč and Kroměříž in southern Moravia.

Of the scores of castles and chateaux, both ruined and restored, the most splendid are probably Křivoklát and Karlštejn in central Bohemia; Hluboká, Rožmberk and Orlík in southern Bohemia; Pernštejn and Vranov in southern Moravia; and several in the Olomouc region. An historical spot of another kind is the site of one of the pivotal battles of the Napoleonic Wars, at Austerlitz, now Slavkov, just east of Brno.

Cyclists will appreciate the undulating Bohemian plateau, drained by the Vltava, the republic's longest river, and its parent river, the Labe, and dotted with castles and modest villages. A natural path through Moravia is the 'Moravian Gate', the linked valleys of the Morava, Bečva and Odra rivers, the only lowland corridor across the Czech Republic. Though this is the most densely populated part of the republic, the hills to both sides offer some of its most peaceful travelling.

The country is nearly encircled by low hills and thickly wooded mountain ranges, beloved by Czechs and their neighbours for winter skiing and summer walking. High-elevation *chaty* (mountain chalets) and small-town *penzions* make long-distance treks feasible.

The northern Bohemian ranges – the Krušné hory and Krkonoše – offer extraordinary landscapes like the sandstone 'sculptures' of Labské Pískovce, Český ráj (the Bohemian Paradise) and Adršpach-Teplice, though these and the Jeseníky of Moravia are afflicted at higher elevations with appalling acid-rain damage. With mountains full of coal and other minerals, northern Bohemia and Moravia underwent intense industrialisation in the 19th century, and the Communists upped the ante with steel, machinery and other heavy industry.

Around the edges of the republic are several picturesque enclaves of traditional culture – architecture, speech, customs, dress and in some cases music – which over the centuries have withstood Habsburg incursions and creeping urbanisation. These independent-spirited regions offer relief from the omnipresent old-town squares lined with pastel-painted houses. Among them are Chodsko in western Bohemia, peaceful Walachia in northern Moravia and, best of all, Moravské Slovácko in southern Moravia, with its succession of jolly summer and autumn festivals. The best of the country's several *skansens* (open-air museums of traditional architecture and furnishings) is at Rožnov pod Radhoštěm.

A less fortunate local culture was that of the Jews. A chilling reminder of the horror that overtook them is the ghetto-fortress of Terezín in northern Bohemia. Most larger towns also bear sad traces of their pre-WWII Jewish communities in the form of neglected synagogues and graveyards.

Facts about the Czech Republic

HISTORY

The written history of the Czechs goes back just over 1000 years, to a record from November 822 that mentions the Bohemians and Moravians at a gathering of the representatives of the lands of the Frankish Empire at Frankfurt. In typical fashion the Czechs were even then playing second fiddle; they would later spend 300 years under total domination by the Habsburg Empire, followed by German and Russian quasi-rule. But even under the thumb of powerful neighbours, the Czechs have had a disproportionate impact on European history – for example the Czech rejection of Roman Catholicism in 1418, resulting in the Hussite Wars; the revolt against Habsburg rule in 1618, which set off the disastrous Thirty Years' War; the French and British handover of Czechoslovakia to Hitler in 1938 in an effort to forestall WWII; the 1948 Communist putsch; and the 1968 Soviet-led invasion.

Prehistory

The first evidence of human habitation in the Czech Lands is more than 600,000 years old. More numerous clues were left by mammoth-hunters in the last Ice Age, about 25,000 years ago. Permanent farming communities were established around 4000 BC in the low-lying regions of the Czech Republic, and the area was inhabited by various Celtic and Germanic tribes before the arrival of the Slavs in the 6th century AD. It was from a Celtic tribe, named the Boii by the Romans, that Bohemia (Boiohemum in Latin, Böhmen in German) got its name. Strangely enough, this word has never been used by Czechs for themselves or their country, only by others.

The Slavs & the Great Moravian Empire

Slav tribes arrived from eastern Europe in several waves in the late 5th and early 6th centuries. Soon after their arrival they were conquered by the nomadic Avars. It was not until 623-24 that the Frankish trader Samo reunified the Slav tribes and defeated the Avars. Samo ruled for about 35 years, but after his death his empire fell apart.

The short-lived Great Moravian Empire (830-906) had its beginnings in the rule of Mojmír I (830-46) who, with other Moravian tribes, seized the Nitra region and banished its ruler, Prince Pribina. In addition to Moravia, this empire came to include western Slovakia, Bohemia, Silesia, parts of eastern Germany, south-eastern Poland and northern Hungary. Its capital is not known, but most of its archaeological remains have been found in present-day Moravia.

It was the Great Moravian Empire's second ruler, Rastislav (846-70), who asked the Byzantine emperor at Constantinople to send Christian emissaries to his empire and introduce Christianity to the region. The missionaries Cyril and Methodius arrived in 836, with a Bible written in the Cyrillic alphabet; when it was translated into Slavic, the Slavs acquired a written language for the first time.

In frequent conflict with the Carolingian Empire and later with the East Frankish Empire, the Moravians withstood all attacks, but were undone by internal conflicts, especially with the Czechs, who finally broke away. Constant raids by the Magyars in the early 10th century led ultimately to the collapse of the empire.

Přemysl Dynasty

Prague Castle was founded in the 870s by Prince Bořivoj as the main seat of the Přemysl dynasty, though the Přemysls failed to unite the squabbling Czech tribes until 993. In 950, German King Otto I conquered Bohemia and incorporated it into his Holy Roman Empire. The Přemysl princes then ruled on the Germans' behalf until

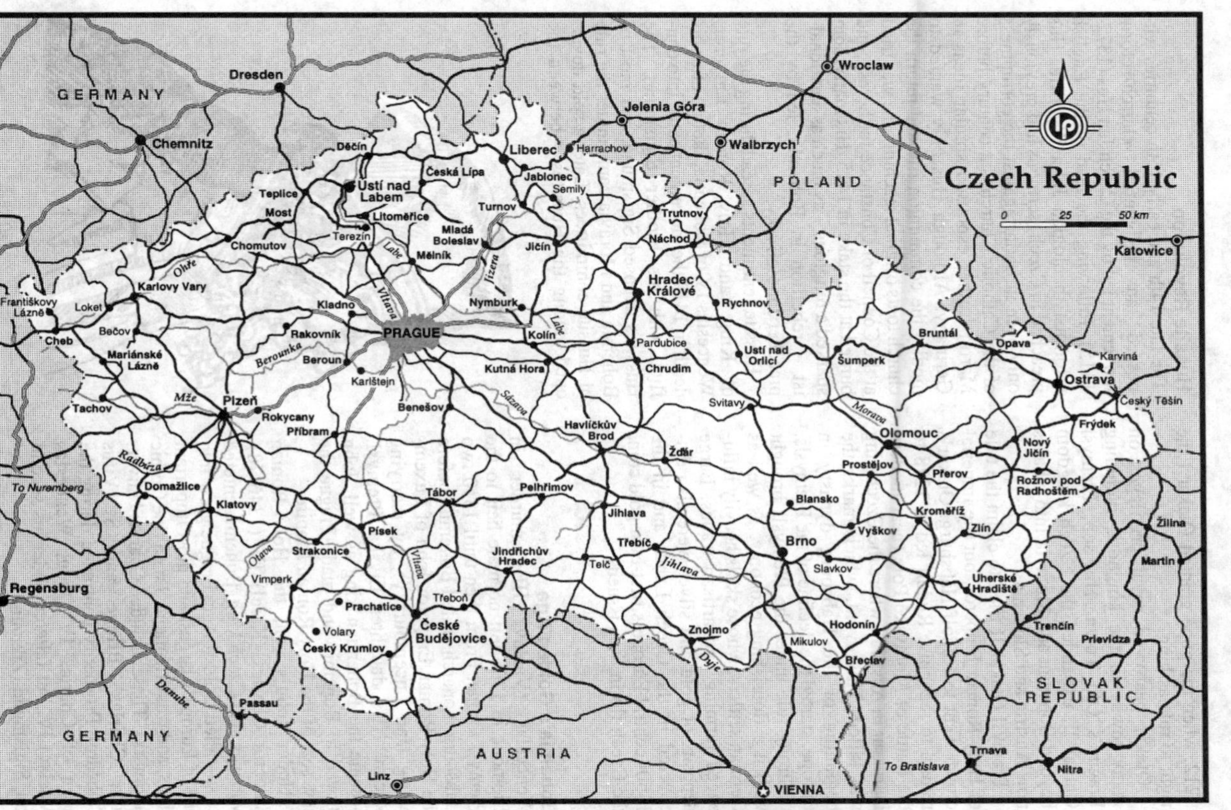

CZECH REPUBLIC

1212, when the pope granted Otakar I the right to rule as king.

Otakar bestowed royal privileges on many towns in the kingdom, including Prague's Old Town. His son, Přemysl Otakar II, expanded the Czech kingdom beyond Bohemia and Moravia into what is now Austria and Slovenia.

Přemysl Otakar II tried to claim the title of Holy Roman Emperor, but the imperial crown went to Rudolf Habsburg. Otakar's refusal to recognise Rudolf led in 1278 to the Battle of Moravské Pole (near modern Dürnkrut in Austria), where the Czech king was killed. This event, which marks the beginning of the Habsburg dynasty in Europe, started the decline of the Přemysls.

Strong rule under the Přemysls brought with it a flourishing economy, as well as German settlers, whose skills heavily influenced farming and artisan trades. Large deposits of gold and silver were also discovered in the Czech Lands and in the 1350s central Europe's first-ever gold coin, the Czech florin, was issued.

Bohemia's Golden Age

Wenceslas (Václav) III's murder in Olomouc in 1306 left no male heir to the Přemysl throne. From then until 1310 two Habsburg monarchs ruled Bohemia, before the Holy Roman Emperor John of Luxembourg (Jan Lucemburský), by marrying Václav III's daughter Elyška Přemysl, became the Bohemian king as well. John moved to Bohemia and made Prague the new seat of the Holy Roman Empire.

Under John's son, the Holy Roman Emperor Charles (Karel) IV (1346-78), who was also Czech king, Bohemia entered its so-called Golden Age. Prague grew into one of Europe's largest and most important cities, and was ornamented with fine Gothic landmarks. These included Charles University, Charles' Bridge and St Vitus Cathedral. Prosperity continued during the reign of Charles IV's son, Wenceslas (Václav) IV, but faltered under his second son, Sigismund (Zikmund).

Hussite Revolution

The late 14th and early 15th centuries witnessed an influential church-reform movement led by the Czech Jan Hus (1372-1415), following the lead of the English reformist theologian John Wycliffe. Hus preached in Czech (sermons had previously only been in Latin) against the corruptness of the Catholic Church – a century before Martin Luther espoused similar ideas in Germany. Although Hus only wanted to modify the communion rite and return the church to its original teachings, he was tried at the Council of Constance for heresy, and burned at the stake in 1415. His martyrdom sparked a religious – as much as a nationalist – rebellion in Bohemia, led by the preacher Jan Želivský.

Hussite sentiments spread during the rule of King (and Holy Roman Emperor) Wenceslas IV of Bohemia, though after his death in 1419 the movement came into conflict with his brother Sigismund. The Hussites deposed Sigismund, and most of Bohemia and Moravia came under the rule of Hussite committees. Later a split developed among the Hussites – between the

Jan Hus

radical Taborites, who advocated total war on Catholics, and the moderate and mainly aristocratic Utraquists, who were only interested in reforming the church.

The spread of Hussitism and Hussite power had threatened the Catholic status quo all over Europe. In 1420 combined Hussite forces under the military leader Jan Žižka successfully defended Prague against the first in a series of anti-Hussite crusades, which had been launched by Sigismund on the authority of the pope. Though they were up against larger and better equipped forces, the Hussites repeatedly went on the offensive and raided deep into Germany, Poland and Austria.

In 1434 the Utraquists accepted Sigismund's return in exchange for religious tolerance; the Taborites kept fighting, only to be defeated by the combined forces of the Utraquists and Sigismund's army the same year at the Battle of Lipany, near Kolín.

The throne later came into the hands of George of Poděbrady (Jiří z Poděbrad), who ruled from 1458 to 1471 (with the backing of Utraquist forces) as Bohemia and Moravia's only Hussite king. Though centuries ahead of his time in suggesting, among other things, a European council to solve international problems by diplomacy rather than war, George failed to sway European rulers or the pope. After his death, Bohemia was ruled by the Polish Jagiellon dynasty. Two weak kings ruled until 1526, but real power in Bohemia continued to lie with the Protestant Utraquist nobles, the so-called Bohemian Estates.

Habsburg Rule

In 1526 the Czech kingdom again came under the control of the Catholic Habsburgs. After an unsuccessful Utraquist uprising, Prague was deprived of its royal privileges, though it remained the Bohemian capital. In the second half of the 16th century, however, the Czech kingdom experienced great prosperity under Emperor Rudolf II, with Prague becoming the seat of the Habsburg Empire. Rudolf established great art collections, and renowned artists and scholars were invited to his court.

Then, on 23 May 1618, the Bohemian Estates, protesting against both the Habsburgs' failure to deliver on promised religious tolerance and the loss of their own privileges, ejected two Habsburg councillors from an upper window of Prague Castle (they survived with minor injuries). This famous defenestration sparked the Thirty Years' War, which was to devastate much of central Europe and shatter Bohemia's economy.

The Bohemian Estates elected Frederick of the Palatinate, the so-called 'Winter King', as their ruler. But his weak leadership, and low troop morale, caused the crucial Battle of the White Mountain (8 November 1620) to be lost almost before the first shots were fired. The Winter King fled, the 27 nobles who had started the revolt were executed, and the fate of the Czechs was sealed for the next three centuries.

The Czechs lost their rights and property, and almost their national identity, through forced Catholicisation and Germanisation. Saxons occupied Prague and much of Bohemia in 1631 and 1632; Swedes also seized large parts of the kingdom. By 1648, the population of the Czech Lands had been reduced by up to 40% in many areas.

With power in the hands of mainly non-Czech Catholic nobles, the country suffered economically as well. The Habsburgs moved their throne back to Vienna, and Prague was reduced to a provincial town for over a century.

The country again suffered extensive damage in the War of the Austrian Succession (1740-48) and the Seven Years' War (1756-63), which pitted the armies of Habsburg Empress Maria Theresa against those of Frederick the Great of Prussia. Bohemia and Moravia were the scene of much of the fighting; Prague was attacked three times between 1741 and 1757.

With the loss of most of Silesia to Prussia, the Habsburgs began to encourage economic development more widely in the empire. Centralist administrative reforms under the Habsburgs curtailed some of the powers of the nobility, spreading the tax burden more evenly. Serfdom was abolished between 1781 and 1785, and religious freedom was allowed.

Czech National Revival

In the 19th century, Bohemia and Moravia, like many other European countries, were swept by nationalistic sentiments. In Prague, where the so-called Czech National Revival (České národní obrození) flourished, the movement's initial expression was in literature, journalism and theatre. The movement was the result of several factors. Educational reforms by Empress Maria Theresa had given even the poorest of Czechs access to schooling and greater knowledge. A vocal middle class was emerging with the Industrial Revolution. And Austrian economic reforms, as well as changes in industrial production procedures, were forcing Czech labourers into the bigger towns, thereby cancelling out the influence of large, pre-existing German minorities.

The nationalist revival found its voice, however, not in political figures, since political activity was banned under the Habsburgs, but among the regenerators of the Czech language, notably the linguists Josef Jungmann and Josef Dobrovský, and the author of the *History of the Czech Nation*, František Palacký.

The Czech Lands joined in the 1848 revolutions that swept across Europe – Prague was the first city in the Austrian Empire to rise in favour of reform. Though the revolution was soon crushed, Czechs continued to demand free use of their own language in all walks of life. They also continued to agitate for complete independence.

CZECH REPUBLIC

The Sokol Movement

Among the disparate elements that contributed to the Czech National Revival was a movement based on physical exercise. Sokol was started in 1862 by two friends, Miroslav Tyrš (1832-84), a professor of art history at Charles University in Prague, and the German-Czech Jindřich Fügner (1822-65).

The idea of Sokol was based on a tradition of physical education in Bohemia stretching back to Renaissance times, incorporating the ideas of the writer and philosopher Comenius. Even so, the movement's foundation was primarily nationalistic; it was to be a Czech counterbalance to the 'Turner' movement in Germany, which was a national physical education organisation based loosely on Darwin's principle of the survival of the fittest.

Tyrš developed this idea by suggesting that nations die when they lose moral, physical and intellectual qualities. To Tyrš, the pursuit of physical exercise not only led to a healthy body but also a healthy mind. By bringing people together they could forge a sense of nationhood, thus strengthening the physical and moral fibre of the nation.

To help achieve his aim Tyrš wrote a booklet called *Tělocvičová soustava* (Physical Education Constitution), laying out a set of exercises. Today, they could be compared to aerobics, as the principle was based on several repetitive sequences. There were different formats for men, women and children, graded according to age.

Tyrš and Fügner also envisaged Sokol as a central element of the Czech army, to be used in any future conflict with the Austrian monarchy. After the failure of the 1848 Revolution and 1849 uprising, which had been followed by a wave of police oppression against the Czech nationalists, the need for unity had become even more apparent. The role of Sokol grew during the Czech National Revival as its activities became connected with the cultural and political events of the times.

WWI & the Founding of Czechoslovakia

The dream of an independent state began to be realised during WWI. Czechs and Slovaks had no interest in fighting for their Austrian and Hungarian masters, and many defected to Czech and Slovak legions to fight against the Germans and Austrians. Meanwhile, Tomáš Garrigue Masaryk, Edvard Beneš and the Slovak Milan Štefánik began to argue the case for independence.

Eventually Czechs and Slovaks agreed to form a single federal state of two equal republics, confirmed in agreements signed in Cleveland in 1915 and Pittsburgh in 1918. President Wilson was motivated by his long-term goal of forging closer ties between Europe and the USA under the aegis of the League of Nations, the unsuccessful precursor to the United Nations.

On 28 October 1918, as WWI drew to a close, the new Czechoslovak Republic was declared, with Allied support. Prague became the capital, and the popular Tomáš Garrigue Masaryk became the first president.

The First Republic experienced an industrial boom – mainly in Bohemia and Moravia, which contained most of the new country's industry – until the Great Depression of the 1930s.

WWII

Czechoslovakia was not left to solve its problems in peace. In the mid-1930s, most of Bohemia's three million German-speakers fell for the dream of a greater Germany, particularly those living in the Sudetenland (ie in north-western Bohemia near the German border). The German-speaking Sudeteners had plenty of sympathy for Nazi Germany, mostly due to a long history of discrimination at the hands of the Czechs

The Austrian government continuously hounded the movement and it continued to exist under uneasy conditions. In November 1915 Sokol was banned in the Austrian Empire, even as legions were formed in France, Italy and Russia to fight against the Axis powers for Czech independence. After the independence of Czechoslovakia on 28 October 1918, Sokol was quickly renewed, helping the army and police with their duties, though once these were organised, it reverted to a physical education organisation – which it remained until 1939.

The Communist putsch of February 1948 seemed to be the beginning of the end of Sokol, even though it numbered about 85,000 members. The movement, which had struggled for a free nation developed on democratic principles, could not coexist with the Communist dictatorship.

The new government tried to de-politicise Sokol by making it a national sports organisation. Most of its leaders were either arrested or expelled. In the 1950s the movement ceased to have any formal existence, the Communists only keeping the idea of Sokol rallies, which they renamed Spartakiáda, and then limiting their number by only holding them every five years.

The Sokol rallies in fact have a long tradition going back to 1882, when the first rally was held on Střelecký Island. Sokol even built a stadium for this purpose in 1934 at Strahov which, according to the *Guinness Book of Records*, is the largest in the world, with room for 240,000 spectators and 40,000 Sokol gymnasts.

Sokol has been revived since 1989, though most members are from pre-Communist days. A Sokol rally in the summer of 1994 attracted big crowds of young and old people, suggesting that the movement draws on pervasive and enduring sentiments within Czech society. ■

and the region's high unemployment. When Hitler demanded the Sudetenland in 1938, the Czechs prepared for war.

The British and French governments pressed the Czechoslovak president, Beneš, to give up these lands for the sake of European peace – the fateful 'appeasement' policy proposed by Britain's prime minister, Neville Chamberlain. Against the advice of his generals and other politicians, Beneš agreed, then resigned.

In October 1938, under the infamous Munich Agreement between the Germans, French, British and Italians (the Czechs were notably absent), the Nazis occupied the Sudetenland. The Poles took part of Silesia in northern Moravia, and the Hungarians seized Ruthenia and southern areas of Slovakia. On 15 March 1939, Germany occupied all of Bohemia and Moravia, declaring the whole region a 'protectorate'.

Although Bohemia and Moravia suffered little material damage in the war, many of the Czech intelligentsia were killed in retaliation for the assassination, in Prague, of Reichsprotektor Heydrich (carried out by Czechoslovak parachutists trained in Britain). In response, the Germans wiped out most of the Czech underground. In the meantime, tens of thousands of Czech Jews perished in concentration camps.

On 5 May 1945, the population of Prague, together with many Russian renegades under General Vlasov, rose against the German forces as the Red Army approached from the east. US troops had reached Plzeň, but held back in deference to their Soviet allies. The Germans, granted free passage out of the city by the victorious Czech resistance, began pulling out on 8 May. Most of Prague was thus liberated before Soviet forces arrived the following day. (Liberation Day is now celebrated on 8 May, and not, as under the Communists, on 9 May.)

Communism

After the war, Czechoslovakia was reestablished as an independent state. One of the government's first acts was to order the expulsion of Sudeten Germans from the Czech borderlands. By 1947 nearly 2.5 million Sudeteners had their Czech citizenship revoked and their lands confiscated, and were then forcibly expelled to Germany (mostly Bavaria). Sudeten Germans received neither restitution nor apologies from subsequent Czech governments. (These atrocities, in fact, soured Czech-German relations until 1997, when Prime Minister Klaus and German chancellor Kohl signed a declaration of mutual apology.)

In the 1946 elections the Communists became the largest party, with 36% of the popular vote, and formed a coalition government with other socialist parties. But tensions grew between Communists and democrats, and in February 1948 the Communists staged a coup d'état with the backing of the Soviet Union. A new constitution established the Communist Party's dominance, and government was organised along Soviet lines. Thousands of non-Communists fled the country.

The 1950s was an era of harsh repression and decline as Communist economic policies nearly bankrupted the country. Many people were imprisoned, and hundreds were executed or died in labour camps, often for little more than a belief in democracy. A series of Stalinist purges was organised by the Communist Party, during which many people, including top members of the party itself, were executed.

The Prague Spring

In the 1960s, Czechoslovakia enjoyed a gradual liberalisation, peaking under the reformist general secretary of the Czechoslovak Communist Party, the former Slovak party leader Alexander Dubček. He had replaced Antonín Novotný as president on 5 January 1968, and his subsequent reform plans bespoke a popular desire for full democracy and an end to censorship – 'socialism with a human face', as the Communist Party called it in its April 1968 'Action Programme'.

Soviet leaders, unable to face the thought

of a democratic society within the Soviet bloc, crushed the short-lived 'Prague Spring' with an invasion by 200,000 Soviet and Warsaw Pact troops on the night of 20 August 1968. By the end of the first day, 58 people had died. Passive resistance followed; street signs and numbers were removed from buildings throughout the country to disorient the invaders.

In 1969, Dubček was replaced by the orthodox Dr Gustav Husák and exiled to the Slovak forestry department. Around 14,000 Communist Party functionaries and 500,000 members who refused to renounce their belief in 'socialism with a human face' were expelled from the Communist Party and lost their jobs. Many educated professionals were made street-cleaners and manual labourers. Totalitarian rule was re-established, and dissidents were routinely imprisoned.

In 1977 the trial of a rock group, the Plastic People of the Universe, inspired a group of 243 writers, artists and intellectuals to sign a public demand for basic human rights, *Charta 77* (Charter 77). This became a focus for opponents of the regime. Prominent among these was the playwright Václav Havel who, with other leading members of the group, suffered severe persecution and imprisonment.

Václav Havel

The 'Velvet Revolution'

The Communist regime under Miloš Jakeš, who had taken over from Husák in 1987, remained in control until after the fall of the Berlin Wall in late 1989; the regime continued even without the support of the newly outward-looking Kremlin.

But on 17 November 1989 things changed. Prague's Communist youth movement organised an officially sanctioned demonstration in memory of nine students executed by the Nazis in 1939. A peaceful crowd of 50,000 was cornered in Národní street, some 500 were beaten by the police and about 100 were arrested. There is a theory that it was the reformist government faction, including reformists in the StB (state security), who wanted to set up the confrontation to trigger further public outrage and precipitate the fall of the hard-line government.

The following days saw constant demonstrations by students, artists and writers, and finally by most of the populace, culminating in a rally of 750,000 people on Letná Hill. Leading dissidents, with Havel at the forefront, formed an anti-Communist coalition that negotiated the government's resignation on 3 December. A 'Government of National Understanding' was formed, with the Communists as minority members. Havel was elected president of the republic by the federal assembly on 29 December, and Alexander Dubček was elected speaker of the national assembly.

The days after the 17 November demonstration have become known as the 'Velvet Revolution' *(Sametová revoluce)*, because there were no casualties. The downside of this nonviolent transformation is that no-one has ever been tried for crimes under the former regime; ex-Communists who killed, tortured and oppressed their fellows still walk free, while many who fought the Communists and were sentenced by them have still not been pardoned.

(In September 1992 Dubček was seriously injured in a car accident near Prague, and died on 7 November. Conspiracy theorists have been busy ever since.)

CZECH REPUBLIC

Václav Havel

The Czech Republic's president, Václav Havel, is a rarity in the world of politics, being a writer and former dissident.

Born on 5 October 1936 in Prague, Havel completed his matriculation then unwillingly headed towards a career as a laboratory technician. His yearning for the artistic world took him into the theatre, where he worked as a stage technician in the ABC Theatre and from 1960 as an assistant director and a literary adviser in the divadlo na Zábradlí. In 1963 his first play, *The Garden Celebration* (Zahradní slavnost), saw the light of day at the same theatre. Its theme was the oppressive political system in Czechoslovakia.

This and other plays of his were banned from public performance after 1968. Further persecution pushed him towards helping to found an opposition group, 'Charta 77', which became one of the main targets of the police system. Despite four spells in jail, he kept writing, his works being published by *samizdat* (underground) presses and in the west. Two of his better-known works are *Letters to Olga* (*Dopisy Olze, 1983*), a compilation of 144 letters he sent to his former wife from prison, and the play *Largo desolato* (1984).

In the Velvet Revolution Havel led the artists who joined students to bring down the fall of the Communist regime through constant street demonstrations. He also took part in the formation of Civic Forum, the main reform party. His prominence in the revolution led to him being elected (on 29 December 1989) as the president of Czechoslovakia. However, the obligations of the presidential office took him away from both writing and Civic Forum, and only in 1991 did he manage to publish *Summer Meditations* (Letní přemítání), his outline of the problems Czechoslovakia faced and how he would like to solve them. The split with Slovakia saw him elected president of the Czech Republic. Recent years have not been kind to Havel. His wife died of cancer in 1996, and in the same year he had one of his lungs removed. Havel remarried in 1997.

Comparisons have been made between Havel and former President Tomáš Garrigue Masaryk. Although Havel's political career is still too short to be assessed, and although he did not, strictly speaking, found a new nation, both men, within the same century, freed Czechoslovakia from foreign ideological domination. Interestingly Havel and Masaryk, though believing in Czechoslovakia as a nation, found themselves caught up in the problem of reconciling the aims of Czechs and Slovaks. Havel also remains, just as Masaryk was, profoundly democratic and committed to individual rights. ■

The 'Velvet Divorce'

The major concerns of the new government were to ensure the first free elections since 1946, and to begin an economic transformation by privatising most industry and returning property to its pre-1948 owners. Free elections to the federal assembly in June 1990 were won by Občanské hnutí (OH, Civic Forum) and its Slovak counterpart, Verejnost' proti násilu (VPN, People Against Violence).

Yet with the strong central authority provided by the Communists gone, old antagonisms between Slovakia and Prague re-emerged. The federal parliament tried to stabilise matters by approving a constitutional amendment in December 1990, which gave each of the Czech and Slovak republics full federal status within the Czech and Slovak Federative Republic (ČSFR), as Czechoslovakia was now known. These moves failed to satisfy Slovak nationalists.

Meanwhile the Civic Forum had split into factions over differences on economic policy creating the right-of-centre Občanská demokratická strana (ODS, Civic Democratic Party) led by Václav Klaus, and the left-of-centre Civic Forum led by Jiří Dienstbier. As finance minister, Klaus forced through some tough economic policies, the success of which gave the ODS a slim victory in the Czech Republic in the June 1992 elections.

In Slovakia's 1992 elections, the Hnutí za demokratické Slovensko (HZDS, Movement for a Democratic Slovakia), founded by Vladimír Mečiar on a platform of Slovak independence and a slower approach to a market economy, won a slim majority.

On the federal level, Václav Klaus' ODS took 48 seats in the 150 seat federal parliament, while 24 seats went to Mečiar's HZDS. The former Communists came second in both republics, with the Left Bloc (KSCM-LB) winning 19 seats in the Czech Republic and the Party of the Democratic Left (SDL) winning another 10 seats in Slovakia.

The incompatibility of Klaus and Mečiar soon became apparent, with the former pushing for shock-therapy economic reform while the latter wanted state intervention to save key industries in Slovakia. Finally they decided (or Klaus persuaded Mečiar) that splitting the country was the best solution. Many people, including President Havel, called for a referendum, but even a petition signed by a million Czechoslovaks was not enough for the federal parliament to agree on how to arrange it. In the end Havel resigned because the parliament was incapable of agreeing to a new president.

Thus on 1 January 1993 Czechoslovakia ceased to exist for the second time this century. Prague became the capital of the new Czech Republic, and Havel was promptly elected its first president. Some, though not all, Slovaks danced in the streets. Both new republics became members of the United Nations on the same day, 19 January.

Since the Divorce

Thanks to Klaus' economic policies, booming tourism and a solid industrial base, the Czech Republic started strongly. Unemployment was negligible, shops were full, and many cities were getting face-lifts.

Although, things weren't so rosy in 1997. The crown was floated, suffering a devaluation of around 10%, and unemployment rose to 4.5%. There is also an acute shortage of affordable housing, steeply rising crime, severe pollution and the health system is deteriorating. As this book was being printed, the government was reeling and the polls were showing they were losing support.

The 1996 elections, in which 76.4% of the population voted, gave the governing ODS only 29.6%, while the major opposition, the Social Democrats (ČSSD), tripled their vote to 26.4%. Neither party could form a majority government. The governing coalition formed a minority government with 99 out of 200 seats. In order that the ODS-led coalition could govern, a deal was struck in which ČSSD parliamentary support was given in exchange for some lower ministerial positions, the exclusion of certain policies the ČSSD found unpalatable and the appointment of opposition leader Miloš Zeman as speaker of the parliament. The ultra-orthodox Communist Party, which still believes in the dictatorship of the proletariat, gained 10.3% of the total vote.

In July 1997, the Czech Republic was invited to become a full member of the North Atlantic Treaty Organisation (NATO), a joint US-European security structure that promises mutual defence in case of an armed invasion. This has supplanted the old Soviet-sponsored Warsaw Pact. For most Czechs, NATO membership signals that country's final break with Communism.

In 1997 the European Union (EU) also began membership talks with the Czech Republic – the country is expected to join as a full member by 2003. EU membership promises to revolutionise the Czech economy, allowing all EU citizens to live and work legally in the Czech Republic and vice versa.

Czech Rulers

Rulers of the Great Moravian Empire
Mojmír I 830-46
Rastislav 846-70
Svatopluk 870?-894
Mojmír II 894-906

Czech Přemysl Princes
Bořivoj ?- 894?
Spytihněv I ?-915?
Vratislav I 915?-921?
Wenceslas (Václav) ?-935? ('Good King Wenceslas')
Boleslav I 935?-972
Boleslav II 972-99
Boleslav III 999-1002
Vladivoj 1002-03
Boleslav III 1003
Jaromír 1003
Boleslav Chrabrý 1003-04
Jaromír 1004-12
Oldřich 1012-33
Jaromír 1033-34
Oldřich 1034
Břetislav 1035-55
Spytihněv 1055-61
Vratislav II 1061-92 (from 1085 King of Bohemia, under the Holy Roman Empire)
Konrád I 1092
Břetislav II 1092-1100
Bořivoj II 1101-07
Svatopluk 1107-09
Vladislav I 1109-17
Bořivoj II 1117-20
Vladislav I 1120-25
Soběslav I 1125-40
Vladislav II 1140-72 (from 1158 Elector of the Holy Roman Empire)
Bedřich 1172-73
Soběslav II 1173-78
Bedřich 1178-89
Konrád Ota II 1189-91
Wenceslas (Václav) II 1191-92
Přemysl Otakar I 1192-93
Jindřich Břetislav 1193-97
Vladislav Jindřich 1197

Czech Přemysl Kings
Přemysl Otakar I 1197-1230 (king from 1212)
Wenceslas (Václav) I 1230-53
Přemysl Otakar II 1253-78
Wenceslas (Václav) II 1278-1305
Wenceslas (Václav) III 1305-06

Habsburg Kings
Henry of Carinthia (Jindřich Korutanský) 1306
Rudolf I 1306-07
Henry of Carinthia (Jindřich Korutanský) 1307-10

Luxembourg Kings
John of Luxembourg (Jan Lucemburský) 1310-46

GEOGRAPHY

The Czech Republic is a landlocked country of 78,864 sq km (about one-third the size of the UK) squeezed between Germany, Austria, Slovakia and Poland. The main regions are Bohemia in the west and Moravia in the east. Within Moravia is a small southern part of the historical region called Silesia, the rest of which is in present-day Poland.

Roughly speaking, Bohemia is a 500m-high plateau surrounded by low mountains, forming a basin drained by the Labe (upper Elbe) river and its tributary, the Vltava (Moldau); the latter is the republic's longest river at 430km. The Labe-Elbe eventually empties into the North Sea. Prague, the capital of the Czech Republic and of Bohemia, sits astride the Vltava about 30km above its junction with the Labe.

The encircling mountains are Bohemia's natural frontiers. Along the German border are the Šumava in the south-west, the Český les (Bohemian Forest) in the west and the

Charles (Karel) IV 1346-78
Wenceslas (Václav) IV 1378-1419
(The Hussite Wars 1419-34)
Sigismund (Zikmund) 1436-37

Habsburg Kings
Albert (Albrecht) II 1437-39
Ladislav the Posthumous (Ladislav Pohrobek) 1453-57

Czech King
George of Poděbrady (Jirí z Poděbrad) 1458-71

Jagillonian Kings
Vladislav II 1471-1516
Louis (Ludvík) 1516-26

Habsburg Kings
Ferdinand I 1526-64
Maxmilian II 1564-76
Rudolf II 1576-1611
Matthias (Matyáš) 1611-19
Ferdinand II 1620

Protestant King
Frederick of the Palatinate (Fridrich Falcký) 1619-20

Habsburg Rulers
Ferdinand II 1620-37
Ferdinand III 1637-57
Leopold I 1657-1705
Joseph (Josef) I 1705-11
Charles (Karel) VI 1711-40
Maria Theresa (Marie Terezie) 1740-80
Charles Albert I (Karel Albert) of Bavaria (1741-43)
Joseph (Josef) II 1780-90
Leopold II 1790-92
Franz (František) II 1792-1835
Ferdinand V 1835-48

Austro-Hungarian Emperors
Franz Joseph (František Josef) I 1848-1916
Charles (Karel) I 1916-18

Presidents of Czechoslovakia
Tomáš Garrigue Masaryk 1918-35
Edvard Beneš 1935-38
Semil Hácha 1938-39
(German Occupation 1939-45)
Edvard Beneš 1945-48
Klement Gottwald 1948-53
Antonín Zápotocký 1953-57
Antonín Novotný 1957-68
Ludvík Svoboda 1968-75
Gustav Husák 1975-89
Václav Havel 1989-92

Presidents of the Czech Republic
Václav Havel 1993-

Krušné hory (Ore Mountains) in the northwest (across which the Labe cuts into Germany). At the Polish border rise the Krkonoše (Giant Mountains), highest of the Sudeten Range that continues east into Moravia. The republic's highest peak is Sněžka (1602m), in the Krkonoše.

South Bohemia's most unusual landscape is the Třeboňsko, a region of broad fields and bogs around České Budějovice, which since the 16th century has been gradually braided into a network of hundreds of linked fish-ponds and artificial lakes. The Czech Republic's largest artificial lake, the 489 hectare Rožmberk, which was engineered way back in 1590, is near Třeboň. The biggest dam in the republic, the 4870 hectare Lipno, which is in the Šumava mountains near the Austrian border, is also in South Bohemia.

Moravia is mostly lowlands, drained by the river Morava flowing south to the Danube and thence to the Black Sea, and by the Odra (Oder), which rounds the eastern end of the Sudeten Range into Poland, and flows on to the Baltic Sea.

Moravia does have a few mountains: in the east are the Bílé Karpaty (White Carpathians) and Javorníky, beyond which is Slovakia, and in the north are the Sudetens. To the south-west are gentler highlands. The 120 sq km Moravian Karst north of Brno features limestone caves, subterranean lakes and the Macocha Abyss, which is 138m deep.

CLIMATE

The damp continental climate of most of the Czech Republic is characterised by warm, showery summers and cold, snowy winters. Spring and autumn feature generally changeable conditions. Although the Czech Republic enjoys marginally milder weather than Slovakia, variations across and between them are small compared with those between low and high elevations.

July is the hottest month everywhere; January the coldest. A typical 24 hours in Prague or Brno from June to August sees the mercury range from about 13°C to 23°C. From December through to February, temperatures push below freezing even in the lowlands, and are bitter in the mountains. Wide variations from 'normal' are also normal; the cities often surpass 30°C in summer and -15°C in winter.

There is no real 'dry season'; February and March, the driest months, see precipitation about one day in three, compared with about one in two during the wettest months of June, July and August. The long, sunny hot spells of summer tend to be broken by sudden, heavy thunderstorms.

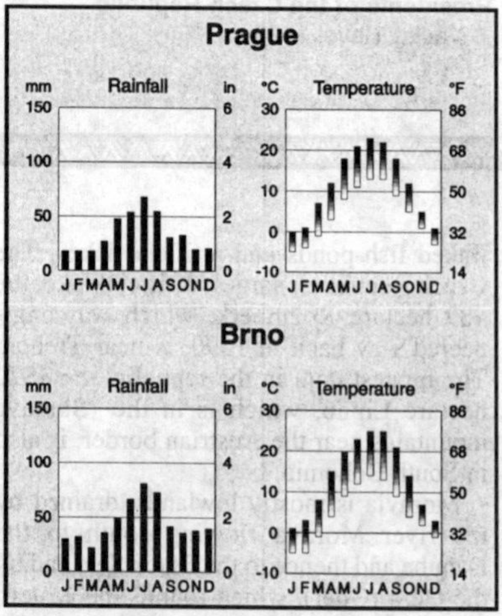

Prague

Rainfall (mm / in) — Temperature (°C / °F)

J F M A M J J A S O N D

Brno

Rainfall (mm / in) — Temperature (°C / °F)

J F M A M J J A S O N D

ECOLOGY & ENVIRONMENT

Most tourists would describe a typical Czech Republic scene as pretty towns and rolling countryside under clear skies. In fact, parts of the republic are among the most highly polluted corners of the world. The origins of the problem go back to the Industrial Revolution, but its seriousness is the result of the single-minded industrial-development policies of successive Communist governments.

One 1980s story that indicates the level of environmental awareness at that time is of a worker awarded a labour medal for saving electricity. His secret? He figured that since no-one sees factory smoke at night, the trick was to operate the plant's smokestack filters only during the day.

Industry emits some 1,400,000 tonnes of sulphur annually, mainly from the burning of low-grade brown coal. The air in parts of northern Bohemia and Moravia, as well as Saxony (south-east Germany) and Polish Silesia – an area known as the 'Black Triangle' – can be almost unbreathable, exceeding even the liberal levels permitted by Czech regulations. Weather inversions can also turn Prague's air dangerously foul.

In many cities the burning of coal for household heating has been replaced by natural gas, although pollution levels have not decreased significantly, especially in Prague where car emissions have increased. This pollution creates choking smogs in winter, and at certain times the sulphur dioxide levels in Prague have been many times higher than official safety levels.

Even so, the forests of northern Bohemia

have been devastated by acid rain; in parts of the eastern Krušné hory not a single tree has been left standing. Conifers in the Krkonoše mountains are stricken by air-borne pollutants blown in from Polish Silesia. In the last couple of years the situation has marginally improved.

In the republic's major industrial areas, rates of cancer, respiratory diseases and deformities are many times higher than the world average. The country's normal life expectancy is not only lower than the European average by eight years, but has actually declined since the 1960s. According to World Bank statistics, around 3% of deaths are due to air pollution, and child deaths due to respiratory diseases are 2.4 times higher in highly polluted areas than in 'unpolluted' areas.

From a policy standpoint there seem to be few alternatives for a country that cannot yet afford major remedial measures, though many people feel the government is not doing all it can. Public attention focuses more on a better standard of living than on the environment.

A nuclear generating station is at Dukovany (between Znojmo and Brno), while another is being built at Temelín (south-west of Tábor). The Austrian government has expressed fears that the Temelín plant will be unsafe.

FLORA & FAUNA

Despite centuries of clear-felling for cultivation, forests – mainly oak, beech and spruce – still cover about one-third of the country. Dwarf pine is common near the tree line (1400m). Above it there is little but grasses, shrubs and lichens.

Most remaining virgin forest is in inaccessible mountain areas. Over half of the high-altitude forest in northern Bohemia – especially in the Krušné hory, Jizerské hory and Krkonoše mountains – have been killed or blighted by acid rain from unregulated industrial development. Moravian forests have fared somewhat better.

The most common types of wildlife in the mountains are lynx, marmots, otters, marten and mink. In the woods and fields there are pheasants, partridges, deer, ducks and wild geese. Rarer are eagles, vultures, osprey, storks, bustards and grouse.

National Parks & Reserves

Though national and local authorities have set aside numerous natural areas, the emphasis seems to be on visitor use rather than species protection.

The Czech Republic's largest park, founded in 1991, is the 685 sq km Šumava National Park, in western and southern Bohemia. The other large park is the 380 sq km Krkonoše National Park in eastern Bohemia. Both are well known as winter ski resorts.

Far more scenic is the small (92 sq km) Bohemian Paradise Protected Landscape Region, founded in 1955. This is part of the much larger Český ráj (Czech Paradise) nature area.

Another highlight is the Adršpach-Teplice Rocks State Nature Reserve in eastern Bohemia, with sandstone pinnacles and caves spread over 20 sq km.

GOVERNMENT & POLITICS

The Czech Republic is an independent state and a parliamentary democracy headed by the president, who is elected by the parliament for a five year term. The president is the head of state, but it is the prime minister, with the *vláda* (cabinet), who wields the most power. Parliament can also override the president's veto on most issues by a simple majority,

The cabinet is composed of the prime minister, vice president and ministers. The prime minister is chosen by the president, who then advises on the selection of other members of the cabinet.

The parliament is composed of two chambers: the *poslanecká sněmovna* (House of Representatives) has 200 delegates who are voted in for a four year term; the *senát* (Senate) has 81 senators who are voted in for a six year term. Both chambers are elected by citizens of the Czech Republic who are 18 years and over.

Czechoslovakia remained hobbled by the old Communist constitution even after its first post-Communist democratic government was elected in 1990. The present Czech constitution was passed by the parliament in December 1992.

At the time of writing, the president was Václav Havel and the prime minister was Václav Klaus of the Občanská demokratická strana (ODS, Civic Democratic Party), which formed a minority coalition after the inconclusive 1996 elections. The next presidential elections are scheduled for 1998.

The traditional lands of the Czech Republic, Bohemia and Moravia, are divided into nine administrative *kraje* (regions), consisting of Prague, Brno and five regions in Bohemia, and two regions in Moravia (North Moravia includes part of the historical region of Silesia). These are further subdivided into 75 *okresy* (districts). There has been much talk of reorganising these inefficient, Communist-era divisions.

The traditional flag of Czechs and Moravians was equal horizontal bands, white above red. But because two other nations, including the republic's northern neighbour Poland, have the same flag, the old federal flag has been retained, with a blue triangle driving a wedge into the white and red bands. This created a flap with Slovakia, which wanted a payment of millions of crowns for the Czechs' contravention of an earlier agreement not to use the old federal symbols.

The national coat of arms has four parts – two with the Czech white twin-tailed crowned lion on a red background, one with the Moravian red and white chequered eagle on a blue background, and one with the Silesian black eagle on a gold background.

ECONOMY

Bohemia and Moravia have specialised in light industry since the Industrial Revolution, and during the 1930s their combined industrial output was second only to that of Germany in central Europe. Under Communist rule, industry and agriculture were nationalised and heavy industry was introduced along Stalinist lines.

Steel and machinery production are the main forms of heavy industry. Other important products include armaments, vehicles, cement, ceramics, plastics, cotton and beer. In the later years of Communist rule the country's industrial equipment was approaching obsolescence and there was much economic inefficiency. Increased production was sought with scant regard for the environment, and in recent years the price has been paid in terms of public health.

The largest industrial area is around Ostrava in North Moravia, with coal-mining, chemicals, a steel mill and car production. The rugged Tatra trucks are built at Kopřivnice near Ostrava. The main Škoda works are at Plzeň but the Škoda car factory is at Mladá Boleslav. Thanks to a partnership with Volkswagen, the quality of the Škoda automobile has been greatly enhanced in recent years.

In 1894 Tomáš Baťa founded the Baťa shoe factory at Zlín, east of Brno, which today produces over a quarter of a million pairs of shoes a week.

Privatisation

Since 1991, privatisation has taken place in three stages. From the beginning, privatisation has been dogged by rumours of corruption, such as former Communist Party officials skimming off the assets of firms, and free-market advocates grabbing control of choice companies by dubious means.

The first stage of privatisation was the restitution to the original owners of some 100,000 small businesses and commercial properties confiscated by the Communists. Then about 30,000 small retail outlets or service facilities throughout the former Czechoslovakia were auctioned off to owner-operators.

This stage is now complete and the third and most difficult stage of privatising 1500 medium and large-sized companies is almost finished. There are about 100 large-sized companies (including the major banks) left that will be progressively privatised over the next couple of years.

The third stage of privatisation has been carried out mainly by a voucher scheme the government devised in which hundreds of millions of shares in 1200 state corporations arbitrarily valued at US$9 billion were distributed to Czechs at near giveaway prices. Every adult citizen was entitled to purchase 1000 voucher points for 1000 Kč. The points could be used to bid for shares in companies being privatised; many people assigned their points to investment funds that would act on their behalf. The system was completed in several rounds from 1992 to 1994. In April 1993 the Prague stock market opened, and trading began in June of that year.

Performance

Despite some major banking scandals in 1997, the performance of the Czech economy remains one of the best in the former Eastern bloc, second only to Slovenia's. The country's manageable inflation rate (7.3% in 1996), an increasing gross domestic product (GDP) growth rate (4.4% in 1996), and a healthy industrial growth rate (7.4% in 1996) are all outshone by a low unemployment rate (just 4.5% in 1997) and the recording of budget surpluses until 1996 when it recorded a deficit. The average monthly wage in 1996 was US$360.

The apparent success of the economy seemed to be due to the government's pragmatic strategies and its privatisation system, but this suffered a significant hiccup in 1997. Foreign investment has been decreasing due to insufficient business laws and the inability of the law to prosecute swindlers. The growing weakness of the economy, especially the lowering growth rate, is due to the government's policy of not privatising the largest firms (to keep unemployment low) especially the major banks, who own major stakes in many of the newly privatised companies. Despite this the economy is not in crisis, but the public is losing confidence in the government.

Of great help to the economy is the ever-increasing number of foreign tourists. In 1996, over 17 million tourists visited the Czech Republic and spent US$2.8 billion.

In 1988, 53% of Czechoslovakia's exports went to the Warsaw Pact countries, but in 1995 that area absorbed only 17% of Czech exports, while 55% went to the EU. The same trend appears in import statistics. The Czech Republic's largest trading partners by far (in both the import and export categories) are Germany, Slovakia, Austria, Poland, Italy and the former USSR countries, with most of the trade in both directions being in manufactured goods, machinery and transportation equipment. This is in spite of the fact that exports to western Europe are partly blocked by quotas and tariffs. Trade with Slovakia has dropped more than 50% since separation (Slovakia bought 17% of Czech exports in 1996).

POPULATION & PEOPLE

According to the most recent census, in 1991, the Czech Republic has a population of 10.3 million, with a population density of 130.7 people per sq km. Of these, about 95% identified themselves as ethnic Czechs, 3% Slovaks, 0.6% Polish, 0.5% German, 0.3% Gypsy and 0.2% Hungarian.

In 1996 the population growth rate was -0.3%. Abortion is widely practised. The nation also has an amazingly high divorce rate (40%). The average life span is 75 years for men, 81 years for women.

Czechs, like the Slovaks and Russians, belong to the Slav group of peoples, which is divided into East, West and South Slavs. Poles, Czechs, Slovaks and Lusatians (Sorbs) belong to the West Slav group.

The issue of Moravian and Silesian nationality has been raised by the former HSD-SMS (the Movement for Autonomous Democracy – League for Moravia & Silesia). The census figures show that in Moravia itself, 33% consider themselves Moravian and 1% Silesian, compared to 61% Czech.

Romanies, or Gypsies (*romové* or *cikáni*), one of the most conspicuous minorities, are thought to be descended from migrants from India in the 15th century. They have always experienced particular hostility in central Europe, which now seems to be on the increase. Their numbers here have increased sharply since the 1950s, both from births and from migration into the republic for work. The Communist government tried to integrate them into Czech society, with mixed success.

There is a small Vietnamese minority, originally brought here as guest workers. They have also faced racism, and claim to be underpaid. Their future is uncertain; the government would like to see most of them return to their homeland.

The major cities and their populations are: Prague (1,214,000), Brno (388,000), Ostrava (327,000), Plzeň (173,000) and Olomouc (106,000).

EDUCATION

Education is compulsory from age six to 16 and is fully funded by the state at all levels; even newly established private schools receive subsidies. The Czech Republic has three universities: Universita Karlova (Charles University) in Prague, Universita Masarykova (Masaryk University) in Brno, and Universita Palackého (Palacký University) in Olomouc.

The literacy rate is about 98%. About 41% of Czech citizens have had full secondary education, and 5% have had higher education. A problem at present is finding money to publish new textbooks at western standards, especially in computer and biological sciences. The Czech Republic's impending membership in the EU has forced economic and political-science faculties to reinvent their curricula.

Even so, the resources available in Czech schools are at least on a par with their western counterparts, particularly in the sciences and mathematics (in the old Czechoslovakia, an amazing 55% of all advanced degrees were in science and engineering). But this is offset, say Czechs, by students' general inability to think independently, a hangover from Communist educational attitudes.

ARTS

Architecture

The earliest (Slavic) buildings in Bohemia and Moravia were made of wood and have not survived. The earliest nonperishable structures were stone Romanesque rotundas, though most of these have since been incorporated into larger churches. Remains of one of the earliest basilicas, from the 9th century, can be seen at Mikulčice in southern Moravia. From the 12th century, fortifications, bridges, castles, churches, monasteries and merchants' houses were also built of stone.

The 13th century saw the appearance of the Gothic style in buildings and entire town centres, leading to the typical square, surrounded by arcaded houses, that survives

Architectural Styles

Romanesque This style dates from the 10th to 13th centuries. A typical Romanesque church has thick walls, closely spaced columns and heavy, rounded arches.

Gothic The Gothic style predominated in the Czech and Slovak lands from the 13th to 16th centuries. It represented not just a new aesthetic but new engineering that permitted thinner walls and, in churches, taller, more delicate columns and great expanses of stained glass. Distinctive features (such as seen in the Cathedral of St Barbara, Kutná Hora, below) included pointed arches and external 'flying buttresses' to support the thinner walls.

Renaissance The 16th century saw a new enthusiasm for classical forms and an obsession with grace and symmetry. Czech versions, especially in houses and chateaux, featured elaborate gables and rooftops, and exterior walls covered with sgraffito, in which fanciful designs are cut through the plaster into deeper, darker coloured layers.

Baroque This resplendent, triumphal style is closely associated with the rebuilding (and the re-imposition of Catholicism) in the region after the Thirty Years' War. Emotional sculpture and frescoes, and rich, gilded ornamentation all seem designed to awe.

Rococo This is essentially late, over-the-top Baroque. Florid in the extreme, elaborate and 'lightweight', it was popular with architects in the late 18th century.

Revivalist Styles Neo-classical, neo-Gothic and neo-Renaissance styles appeared in the late 1700s and 1800s. Neo-classicism favoured grand colonnades and pediments, and often huge, simple, symmetrical buildings. Renaissance and Gothic revival styles played a part in the so-called Czech National Revival movement.

Modern At the turn of the century, the decorative and sensual style called Art Nouveau produced some of the republic's most striking buildings. Unique to Czechoslovakia was the fruitful development of cubist architecture, and Prague has some surprisingly elegant examples. ■

RICHARD NEBESKÝ

in many towns today. Ecclesiastical architecture flourished in the 14th century, under Charles IV, especially in the works of Peter Parler. The leading late-Gothic architects Benedikt Rejt and Matěj Rejsek are noted for their complex vaulting, including the style known as diamond vaulting.

Italian architects seconded to Bohemia in the early 16th century brought Renaissance styles in chateaux, summer palaces and merchants' houses. A unique 'Czech Renaissance' style evolved, with ornamental stucco decorations that often featured legendary or historical scenes.

The 1620 victory of the Habsburgs at the Battle of the White Mountain was followed by the imposition of an Italian Catholic and Baroque style. The Jesuit order was foremost in building and renovating many churches along Baroque lines, and in the early 18th century Germanic landowning families created a rich 'Czech Baroque' style in palaces throughout the Czech Lands. The best-known practitioners of Baroque architecture were the Bavarian father-and-son team of Kristof and Kilian Ignatz Dientzenhofer, the Italian designer and sculptor Giovanni Santini, and the Czech František Kaňka.

In the 19th century came numerous 'revivalist' movements – neo-classical, neo-Gothic, neo-Renaissance – which in their later stages coincided with the Czech National Revival movement.

As in the rest of Europe, Czech architecture in the early 20th century came under the spell of Art Nouveau, known as *secese* in Bohemia, *Sezessionstil* in Austria and *Jugendstil* in Germany. Some of the finest Art Nouveau works are the Obecní dům (Municipal House) and structures built for the 1891 Terrestrial Jubilee Exhibition at Holešovice, in Prague. Under the influence of Jan Kotěra, some of Art Nouveau's more fanciful tendencies gave way to a functionalist approach, as embodied in Gahura's work at Zlín (South Moravia) for the Baťa shoe company.

Cubism, which had a strong influence on pre-WWI architecture, can be seen throughout Prague in houses built by Josef Chochol and Josef Gočár. The latter's finest work is the House of the Black Virgin (dům U černé Matky Boží) on Celetná.

The Communist era was, architecturally, a wasteland. The 1960s saw vast, badly needed housing estates springing up all over the country, but the era produced little of quality.

Most architectural efforts in recent years have focused on restoration; the preservation of tourist sights has been a priority, and since the Velvet Revolution both state-funded and private restoration work has moved into high gear.

Painting

Romanesque illuminated manuscripts and church frescoes (such as at Znojmo's rotunda) are the earliest examples of graphic art in the region. Byzantine influences start to appear in the late 13th century, and Gothic in the early 14th (such as in Strakonice Monastery). The finest manuscripts in central Europe – the vibrantly coloured *Brno Law Book* and Bibles and books made for Arnošt z Pardubic in the Brno Municipal Museum – show the standard Italianate style acquiring a distinct Czech slant. The gem of Czech Gothic art is a trio of late 14th century altar panels by the anonymous Master of the Třeboň Altar, in the St George Convent in Prague Castle.

The Renaissance period produced no outstanding native-born Czech artists, the field of book illumination continuing as the main genre. Subsequently, 17th and early 18th century artists like Petr Brandl, Karel Škréta and Václav Reiner concentrated on religious subjects for their church patrons.

In the late 18th and early 19th centuries Czech realism, coinciding in its later stages with the Czech National Revival, brought an appreciation of everyday subjects in painting. Prominent names are the portraitist Antonín Machek, Antonín Mánes and his better-known son Josef, Václav Brožík and Vojtěch Hyanis. Josef Mánes was the first to develop what might be called a 'Czech national style', concentrating on Czech and Slav people; some of his best paintings can be seen in the gallery of 19th century art within the Convent of St Agnes in Prague. Mikuláš Aleš is regarded as one of the best artists of folk and national themes.

Possibly the best-known, late 19th century Czech artist is Alfons Mucha, whose early work decorated Art Nouveau posters in Paris. The most outstanding of his works is a series of 20 large canvasses called the Slav Epic, which are presently in Moravský Krumlov (see the South Moravia chapter). Czech landscape art developed in the works of Anton Kosárek and Julius Mařák, and was followed by a wave of impressionism and symbolism under artists like Antonín Slavíček (some of whose works can be seen in Průhonice Castle) and Max Švabinský.

In the early 20th century Prague became a major European centre for avant-garde art, centred on a group of artists who called themselves Osma (the Eight). Leading cubist painters included Josef Čapek and Emil Filla. Between the two world wars functionalism evolved and flourished in a group called Devětsil, led by the adaptable Karel Teige. Surrealists included Zdeněk Rykr, Josef Šíma and Jindřich Štýrský.

After WWII, Communist art brought little of interest, but several underground artists are worth mentioning. Mikuláš Medek's abstract and surrealist art was occasionally exhibited in obscure galleries; Jiří Kolář was an outstanding graphic artist as well as a poet. Some never-exhibited work of the postwar years has begun surfacing since 1989. Modern artists such as Milena Dopitová and František Skála use junk and everyday items to express their social statements.

Sculpture

Medieval sculpture, like medieval painting, served religious ends, though kings and wealthy patrons were first carved in the later 13th century. Sculpture shed its dependence on architecture around the 12th century, moving from ornamentation to realism in a flourish of Madonnas and crucifixions. Wood was the common medium. At the end of the 14th century a more decorative style emerged, as in the work of the Master of the Krumlov Madonna. Gothic realism in the latter 15th century culminated in the work of the Master of Sorrows from Žebrák, which is in the St George Convent in Prague Castle.

Top-quality Baroque religious sculpture sprouted in public places as part of the anti-Reformation drive by the Habsburgs against the Protestant Czechs. This included hundreds of Marian columns erected in gratitude to the Virgin for protection against the plague. Two outstanding sculptors of the time were Matthias Braun and the realist Ferdinand Maxmilian Brokoff. An important figure at the end of the 18th century, Ignác František Platzer, was commissioned to produce statues all over Prague.

Czech sculpture declined until a revival in the mid-19th century through Václav Levý. In the later 19th century Josef Václav Myslbek dominated the field with his Romantic Slav style, which was to influence Rodin; his monument to St Wenceslas is in Prague's central square. One of Myslbek's students, Stanislav Sucharda, produced brilliant Symbolist metal pieces, as well as the stone and bronze Palacký Monument in Nové Město.

Sculpture even had its impressionist exemplars, such as Ladislav Šaloun and Josef Mařatka. The prominent cubist Otto Gutfreund switched to realism in the 1920s, influencing the next generation of Jan Lauda, Karel Pokorný and Karel Dvořák.

The Communist era produced little sculpture of value officially, but there were many interesting works produced 'underground'.

Literature

The earliest literary works were hymns and religious texts in Old Church Slavonic, replaced by Latin during the late 11th century. Among the first true Czech texts were the *Legends of St Wenceslas* from the 10th century, and the hymn *Hospodine,*

CZECH REPUBLIC

pomiluj ny (Lord Have Mercy On Us). An important 12th century Latin work was a history of Bohemia, *Kosmova kronika* (the Kosma Chronicle).

The 13th century saw not only religious works but those of legends such as *Alexandreis* (Alexander the Great), and a more detailed Bohemian history, the *Dalimilova kronika.* Only in the 14th century did real Czech literature get under way, one of the earliest pieces being the anonymous *Legendy sv Kateřiny* (Legends of St Catherine).

Hussitism introduced a new kind of literature, starting with religious tracts such as Jan Hus' *De orthographia Bohemica* and continuing along revolutionary lines with anti-Catholic hymns, poems and chronicles.

Prose in the 16th and 17th centuries took up humanism, morality, chronicles, daily life, travel and poetry. Two good pieces of the times are the *Kosmografie* of Zikmund z Půchova, and the Hussite *Kralická bible* (Kralice Bible), which became a standard of the literary Czech language.

After the Battle of the White Mountain, Czech literature entered a dark age. The Czech language practically ceased being used in literature, though it stayed alive in villages and among exiles. The best-known author-in-exile was Jan Ámos Komenský (known in the west as Comenius), who wrote in Czech and Latin on education and theology. His most famous work is *Labyrinth světa a ráj srdce* (The Labyrinth of the World and Paradise of the Heart), written in 1632.

Literature of the 18th century was written mainly in Latin or German. The frustration of Czech scholars unearthing their own history in an alien tongue was one factor in a growing movement for the revival of the Czech language – and the Czech nation. The Czech National Revival was set in motion at the start of the 19th century by Josef Dobrovský and Josef Jungmann, who separately developed a Czech literary language closer to the vernacular, and by František Palacký, who wrote a seminal history of Bohemia and Moravia.

Major movements often call forth major figures, and in the Czech case it was Karel Hynek Mácha. Possibly the greatest of all Czech poets, he was a leading Romanticist of the early 19th century; his most famous work, *Máj* (May), came to symbolise the spring of the new movement.

Romanticism took hold in the mid-19th century with some outstanding pieces on country life: Božena Němcová's *Babička* and Karel Erben's *Kytice.* The radical political journalist Karel Havlíček Borovský lampooned the Habsburgs. Famous (though not distinctly anti-Habsburg) is his excellent and fairly scurrilous poem, *Křest svatého Vladimíra* (The Baptism of St Vladimír).

Czech history formed the source of inspiration for poets such as Jan Neruda and Svatopluk Čech, as well as for Alois Jirásek at the end of the 19th century. Jirásek, with his *Staré pověsti české* (Old Czech Legends), reinterpreted Czech legends from the arrival of Czechs in Bohemia to the Middle Ages, and wrote nationalist historical novels, his best being *Temno* (Darkness).

One of Bohemia's greatest writers – and certainly the best-known today – was Franz Kafka, who, with a circle of other German-speaking Jewish writers in Prague, played a major role in the literary scene at the beginning of this century.

In the years between the two world wars, Karel Čapek was probably the best-known author, with his novel *Rossum's Universal Robots* (from which the word 'robot' entered the English language). His contemporaries included the author Jaroslav Hašek, whose *The Good Soldier Švejk* is still widely read today. Poets of the time included Jaroslav Seifert (awarded the Nobel Prize for Literature in 1984) and Vítěslav Nezval.

The early Communist period produced its quota of socialist realists and little else, but the 1960s saw a resurgence. Writers like Josef Škvorecký, Milan Kundera, Bohumír Hrabal, Ivan Klíma, Věra Linhartová, Zdena Salivarová and many others drafted their first masterpieces during the years of liberalisation (but before 1968). After the Warsaw Pact invasion some left, while others stayed and wrote for the underground *samizdat* press, or had their manuscripts smuggled to the west.

Škvorecký and Kundera, writing mainly about Communist oppression in Czechoslovakia, became widely known in translation. Other figures were the philosopher Jan Patočka, the poet Jiří Kolář, and of course the playwright Václav Havel. However, probably the best contemporary writer is still Hrabal.

Theatre

Certain forms of theatre existed in pre-Christian festivals, and some have remained part of village life for centuries. In feudal times the church organised religious plays in Latin. In the 13th century some plays appeared in Czech, performed by non-clergy, and drama began to take on themes of everyday life.

Czech-language theatre did not develop fully until the 16th century. Themes, mostly biblical, were used to make comparisons between contemporary and biblical times. Historical drama developed from this. At Prague's Charles University, drama was performed in Latin and also used as a form of teaching. Some of the best plays, known as *schola ludus*, or school games, were also written by the educator Comenius in the 17th century.

After the Battle of the White Mountain, Czech-language theatre survived only in villages until the Czech National Revival, while non-Czech theatre took the stage in the form of Counter Reformation plays written by Jesuits. The first purpose-built theatres were built in the 19th century.

In 1785, Czech reappeared at the Nostické (now Stavoské or Estates) Theatre, and Prague became a centre for Czech-language theatre. Major 19th century playwrights included Josef Kajetán Tyl and Ján Kolár. Drama, historical plays and fairy tales contributed to the Czech National Revival, with the first professional companies appearing in Prague and Brno.

Nonetheless, no venues specifically for independent Czech-language theatre existed until 1862, when the Prozatimní divadlo (Temporary Theatre) opened in Prague. Others soon appeared. The first permanent Czech theatre was opened in 1883 in Prague.

In the early years of the First Republic the leading lights among playwrights were the novelist Karel Čapek and the brilliant František Langer. The comedy duo of Voskovec & Werich (or V&W, as they were known), at the Osvobozené divadlo (Liberated Theatre) in Prague, produced some of the best theatre of the years between the two world wars. Actor and playwright EF Burian was known for experimental drama.

During the Communist years, classical theatre was of a high quality, but the modern scene was stifled. Exceptions included the excellent pantomime of the Black Theatre (Černé divadlo), and the pioneering *Laterna Magika* by Alfréd Radok.

Some excellent plays, including those by Václav Havel, went unperformed locally because of their anti-government viewpoint, but appeared in the west. In the mid-1960s, free expression was explored in Prague's divadlo na Zábradlí (Theatre on the Balustrade), with works by Ladislav Fialka, Havel, and Milan Uhde, and by the comedy duo of Jiří Suchý and Jiří Šlitr. Suchý is still performing today and has a successful show.

Marionette & Puppet Theatre Marionette plays have been popular since the 16th century, and puppet plays since before that. This form peaked in the 17th and early 18th centuries. A legendary figure was Matěj Kopecký (1775-1847), who performed original pieces. The composer Bedřich Smetana also wrote two plays for marionettes.

Marionette theatre became a children's entertainment until a revival in this century. Marionette theatres opened in Prague and

Plzeň. Plzeň's Feriálních osad Theatre was the home of Josef Skupa's legendary puppets Špejbl & Hurvínek, who still perform in Prague. Even under Communism, puppet and marionette theatre was officially approved of and popular, and Czech performances ranked among the best in the world. They also feature in the well known films of Jiří Trnka.

Music

Classical Although there were pre-Christian folk songs, dances and music, the earliest written description of them is by the Arab explorer Ibrahim ibn Jakub who, passing through Bohemia in 965 AD, described string and woodwind instruments used by the Slavs. The earliest musical instrument found by archaeologists is an 11th or 12th century lute.

The church tried to replace folk songs with Christian hymns, and introduced Gregorian plainsong. At this time nearly all songs were in Latin; just four hymns in Czech are known from the 14th century. However, the Hussites, drawing on folk themes, created distinctively Czech hymns and laid the foundations for future Czech music. A handful of old Hussite melodies persist in German Protestant hymns. In turn, the post-Hussite era saw new growth in folk music.

Following the Habsburg victory at the Battle of the White Mountain, Czech music above the village level survived only among a few musicians composing and playing at the courts of other European rulers. The most notable of these expatriates was Jan Dismas Zelenka, who worked in Dresden in the 18th century.

The flowering of a Czech spirit in music took place in the mid-19th century. Bedřich Smetana, the first great Czech composer, created a national style by incorporating folk songs and dances into his classical compositions. His best-known pieces are the operas *Prodaná Nevěsta* (The Bartered Bride) and *Dalibor a Libuše*, and the symphonic-poem cycle *Má vlast* (My Country). Despite increasing deafness over the last 10 years of his life, Smetana carried on composing.

Antonín Dvořák, who started out as an apprentice butcher, is perhaps everyone's favourite Czech composer. Among his best-known works are his symphony *From the New World* (composed in the USA while lecturing there for four years), his *Slavonic Dances* of 1878 and 1881, the operas *The Devil & Kate* and *Rusalka*, and his religious masterpiece, *Stabat Mater*.

Leoš Janáček's interest in Moravian folklore is reflected in his music. Though never as popular as Smetana and Dvořák at home, he has come to be recognised as a gifted and original composer. Better-known compositions include the opera *Jenůfa*, the towering *Glagolitic Mass* and the orchestral work *Taras Bulba*. One of his finest, though less well-known, pieces is the opera *Stories of Liška Bystrouška*.

Other more recent composers are Zdeněk Fibich, Josef Suk and Bohuslav Martinů.

Jazz Jazz has been popular with amateurs and professionals since the mid-1930s, though mostly as an accompaniment to dancing. A pioneer of dance jazz was pianist, composer, singer, publisher and eventually bandleader RA Dvorský. Other star bands have included EF Burian's Červené sedmy, the Ježkův Orchestr, Gramoklub and the Karla Vlacha Orchestr.

After WWII Czech musicians were at the forefront of European jazz, but this came to an end with the 1948 Communist putsch. In the late 1950s the Prague radio station had a good band led by Karel Krautgartner.

Restrictions were gradually lifted in the 1960s. One of the top bands was the SH Quintet, though it only played for three years at Prague's Reduta Club, the first Czech professional jazz club. Another was the Junior Trio, with Jan Hamr and the brothers Miroslav and Allan Vitouš, who all escaped to the USA after 1968. Jan Hamr (keyboards) became prominent in 1970s American jazz-rock as Jan Hammer, and even received a Grammy for the *Hawaii Five-O* theme. Miroslav Vitouš (bass) also rose to fame in several American jazz-rock groups.

Since the Velvet Revolution the jazz scene in Prague has exploded.

Rock & Pop Rock, since its birth in the 1950s, was always banned by the authorities because of its western-American 'corrupting influence'. Pop music was allowed, but mainly harmless local clones of western groups like ABBA. Of the two most popular Czech pop stars of the 1960s, Karel Gott and Helena Vondráčková, it was Gott who had the longer hair – and he was even banned from TV for a short time because of it. Some 1960s stars like Marta Kubišová disappeared from screens after the 1968 invasion, never to perform in public again.

The pioneers of Czech Big Beat, Sputnici, formed as a band in 1959. They were the most well known of the 1960s big beat bands that mainly played their own versions of American hits.

Rock found fans among political dissidents like Václav Havel, but remained like them an underground movement, with a handful of bands playing to small audiences in obscure pubs and country houses. Raids and arrests were common. The Plastic People of the Universe gained international fame by being imprisoned after a 1970s show trial intended to discourage underground music. The tactic was successful only temporarily and by the mid-1980s there was a lively underground scene.

Since 1989, rock has become legitimate and bands have proliferated, playing all styles in today's music world, even rap. The rock-club scene in Prague is booming. Well-established bands on the home front include pop-oriented Jerusalem, hard-rock Alice, the grunge band Support Lesbiens and Lucie Bílá, who sounds like a toned-down Nina Hagen. Newer talent on the alternative scene includes Načeva, who is compared to Patti Smith by some and Iva Bittová. At the top of the pops is the ever-popular Buty, who draw large crowds at concerts.

One of the bands that has made it on the European scene is heavy-metal band Krabathor who have released an album in Germany and hold more concerts outside the country than at home. A band that fuses rock with the traditional folk music from their home town of Vizovice, south-eastern Moravia, is Fleret. More successful is the punk-oriented Narajama, who use folk music sounds of the dulcimer in their compositions.

Probably the largest Communist-era punk and underground music scene was in Teplice, in northern Bohemia, which had about four times as many bands as in Prague. Today, Teplice and nearby Ústí nad Labem are still the hub of the punk band movement; the grim, heavily polluted, industrial north seems a perfect nihilist setting for such music. On the other hand, the popular skinhead band Orlík was disbanded after three years by its leader when he decided that skinheads were becoming too involved with racist violence.

CZECH REPUBLIC

Cinema

The grandfather of Czech cinematography, JE Purkyněv, made rudimentary animated films in the 1850s, and Jan Kříženecký was making slapstick films as early as 1898, but it wasn't until 1908 that the Czech film industry took off.

In the 1930s many films were produced at the newly built Barrandov studios in Prague. One that was popular abroad, especially in France, was *Stavitel chrámů* (The Cathedral Builder, 1919), directed by Karel Degl and Antonín Novotný. Cinematographically better but less popular was *Macocha*, by Antonín Fencl. In 1921, an American-Czechoslovak co-production of *Jánošík*, about the legendary 17th century Slovak 'Robin Hood', produced two versions – a domestic version showing his execution, and one for the Americans with the hero escaping and living happily ever after.

The first film ever to show full frontal nudity, *Extase* (Ecstasy), was directed by

Gustaf Machatý in 1932. A hit (and a scandal) at the 1934 Venice Festival, even the pope objected to its screening in Venice. Revealing all was one Hedvige Kiesler, who went on to Hollywood fame as Hedy Lamarr. Another Czech, Hugo Haas, directed an excellent adaptation of Karel Čapek's anti-Nazi science fiction novel *Bílá smrt* (White Death, 1937) before finding fame in Hollywood. Two stars of Czech comedy between the two world wars, Voskovec & Werich, also produced some well-known films, including *Pudr a benzín* (Powder and Petrol, 1931) and *Hej rup!* (Heave-Ho, 1934).

The Nazi invasion limited the movie industry to nationalistic comedies, but three outstanding films were made between 1945 and the Communist takeover in 1948 – *Předtucha* (Premonition, 1947) and *Krakatit* (1948), both by Otakar Vávra, and Alfréd Radok's *Daleká cesta* (The Long Journey, 1949), which used radically new lighting and camera work. The latter dealt with the deportation of Jews to concentration camps, and was banned by the Communists for two decades.

The only good work among many low-quality propaganda films in the 1950s had historical themes, such as *Císařův pekař* (The Emperor's Baker) and *Pekařův císař* (The Baker's Emperor), both directed by Martin Frič in 1951 – though these still managed to incorporate plenty of socialist propaganda.

The 'New Wave' of Czech cinema began in 1963, but ended five short years later with the Soviet-led invasion. It was from the early 1960s onwards that Czech films began to win international awards. The young directors of the time escaped censorship because they were among the first graduates of the Academy of Film under Communist rule, and therefore assumed to be ideologically 'clean'.

Among the earliest and best were *Černý Petr* (Black Peter, 1963; the American version was called *Peter & Paula)* and *Lásky jedné plavovlásky* (Loves of a Blonde; 1965) by Miloš Forman, who fled following the Soviet invasion, later to become a successful Hollywood director with films like *One Flew Over the Cuckoo's Nest*, *Amadeus* and *The People vs Larry Flint*.

Other well-known works by this generation of film-makers are *A pátý jezdec je strach* (And the Fifth Horseman is Fear, 1964) by Zbyněk Brynych, *Démanty noci* (Diamonds of the Night, 1964) by Jan Němec, *Intimní osvětlení* (Intimate Lighting, 1965) by Ivan Passer, and *Sedmikrásky* (Daisies, 1966) by Vera Chytilová. The lyrical and mildly satirical *Rozmarné léto* (Capricious Summer, 1968) was an early work by Jiří Menzel, who also gained wide recognition abroad.

Films critical of the post-invasion regime were made during 1969 and 1970, but were promptly banned from public screening. The most outstanding of these were *Spalovač mrtvol* (The Cremator of Corpses) by Juraj Herz, *Žert* (The Joke) by Jaromil Jireš, *Ucho* (The Ear) by Karel Kachyňa, and *Nahota* (Nakedness) by Václav Matějka. Probably the best among the films of the next two Communist decades was the comedy *Vesničko má středisková* (My Sweet Little Village, 1985) by Jiří Menzel, a subtle look at the workings and failings of socialism in a village co-operative. In the post-Communist era, Zdeněk Svěrák is the only director who has managed to make good and entertaining films. His 1994 hit *Akumulátor* was the most expensive Czech film produced to date. In 1996, it was surpassed at the box office by the internationally acclaimed *Kolja*, which managed to score the two big film prizes of 1997 – the best foreign film awards at the Cannes Film Festival and the US Academy Awards. The film is about a Russian boy being brought up by a Czech bachelor.

Prague itself has become a major star in big-budget Hollywood films; *Amadeus* was shot here (Miloš Forman thought the backstreets of Malá Strana look more like old Vienna than any part of modern-day Vienna), as were *Kafka* and *Mission Impossible*.

Folk Arts

For a complete guide to folk art in the Czech and Slovak republics see the Folk Arts section in the Facts about Slovak Republic chapter later in the book.

SOCIETY & CONDUCT

Most Czechs are polite and mild-mannered, with a good sense of humour; they are hospitable and fairly conservative socially. You may also see them being rude to one another in public places like shops and hotels. This is perhaps a forgivable hangover from the routine drudgery and anxiety of life under totalitarianism; however, it is showing signs of diminishing.

It is customary to say 'good day' (*dobrý den*) when you enter a shop, café or quiet bar, and 'goodbye' (*na shledanou*) when you leave. Most elderly people seem pleased to be greeted at any time. On public transport, young people readily give up their seats to the elderly and sick and to women who are pregnant or carrying small children.

If you are invited to a local's home, take some flowers for your hosts (but not dried flowers or an even number of flowers, both are symbols of the dead), and perhaps sweets if you know they have young children. Remember to remove your shoes as you enter the house, unless you're told not to bother.

When attending a concert or other performance in one of the older theatres, men usually wear a suit and tie, and women a conservative dress or suit. Foreigners tend to be the only ones who don't. Casual dress is fine for more contemporary entertainment and in smaller venues.

RELIGION

Czechs were introduced to Christianity in the 10th century by the 'Apostles of the Slavs', the Greek monks Cyril and Methodius. Christianity became the state religion under St Wenceslas (sv Václav), Duke of Bohemia from 925 to 929 and patron saint of the Czechs.

Czechs remained loyal to the pope until the end of the 14th century, when reformers like Jan Hus began to demand the simpler and more accessible practices of early Christianity. The protracted Hussite Wars following Hus' martyrdom turned Bohemia into a hotbed of anti-Catholicism. Hussitism eventually lost its military edge, but Bohemia remained a Protestant and independent-minded part of the Holy Roman Empire for two more centuries, and a focus of the struggle between the two churches.

After Protestant Czechs were defeated in the Battle of the White Mountain in 1620, they lost not only their religious but their political and national independence. The Habsburgs forced Roman Catholicism on a nation that never took to that doctrine as feverishly as it did to Protestantism.

Communist suppression dealt a blow to all religions. The state was officially declared atheistic, most religious institutions were closed and many clergy were imprisoned. An underground religious network persisted, with priests performing rites secretly. Sadly, the Vatican refused to ordain those priests after the 1989 Velvet Revolution, when full religious freedom was restored and many churches were reopened. Churches today are poorly attended, and then mainly by the elderly, though there has been a slight rise in church membership and a big jump in the numbers of children attending religious education.

The largest church is the Roman Catholic Church, with 40% of Czechs calling themselves Catholics. The next largest church is the Hussite Church, with some 400,000 members, and there are numerous other Protestant denominations, the largest being the Evangelical Church of Czech Brethren, with about 180,000 members.

The history of the Jews in the republic goes back to the 10th century – Josefov in Prague is one of the oldest Jewish quarters in Europe. Beginning with the rule of the Austrian Emperor Joseph II, Jews were treated like other citizens of the empire.

At the formation of Czechoslovakia, Jews comprised just 1% of the population, but around 70% of those Jews in the

František Tomášek

František Tomášek was a cardinal and head of the Roman Catholic Church in Czechoslovakia from 1965 to March 1991, mostly under Communist rule, during which he was regarded, with Alexander Dubček and Václav Havel, as a symbol of popular opposition to the regime.

Tomášek was born in Studenka, Moravia, in 1899. After completing his studies and military service, he studied for the priesthood at Olomouc, and was ordained in 1922. In 1938 he was awarded a first doctorate from the Cyril & Methodius theological faculty there.

With the Communist putsch in Czechoslovakia, the church lost ground. In 1949 Pope Pius XII named Tomášek the auxiliary bishop of Olomouc, but the government then outlawed any appointment that didn't have its approval. A year later all monasteries and most other church institutions were closed, and many clergy, including Tomášek, were packed off to labour camps.

Tomášek was released in 1953 and allowed to serve in a small rural parish. His elevation to apostolic administrator of the archdiocese occurred when Archbishop Josef Beran, who was away in Rome to accept a cardinal's hat, was not allowed back into the country.

'Prague Spring' reforms returned the church's rights in 1968, but these were again revoked after the Soviet-led invasion. Tomášek was appointed to the college of cardinals by Pope Paul VI in 1976, but the title was given to him in secret for fear of reprisals. A year later he was made archbishop of Prague.

In the 1980s Tomášek began openly to criticise the government, and his struggle for human and religious rights gained him the respect of the dissident 'Charter 77' movement. He led an unsuccessful campaign against abortion reforms in 1986, and supported a layman named Navratil in submitting a 600,000 signature petition demanding religious freedom.

As Czechoslovakia shook off Communism in 1989, Tomášek lived to see the church's freedoms restored. Though he resigned as cardinal in March 1991 due to ill health, he had the pleasure of welcoming his friend Pope John Paul II to Prague's St Vitus Cathedral in April 1990. ■

country before WWII were killed by the Nazis. Communist rule was another tragic time for Jews, with anti-Semitic show trials centring on the Jewish prime minister Rudolf Slánský. Jewish participation in public life revived under Dubček, only to be followed by a new wave of anti-Semitism in the 1970s, largely due to Soviet policies in the Middle East.

Prague still has the largest Jewish community in the republic, with about 6000 members; smaller ones are in Ostrava and Brno.

LANGUAGE

Except in tourist parts of Prague, Brno and Bratislava, most Czechs and Slovaks speak no English, though many older people speak German. Russian was compulsory in school under Communism, so most can speak it, but prefer not to.

The Czech and Slovak languages, along with Polish and Lusatian, belong to the West Slavonic group of Indo-European languages. Czech is the mother tongue of about 10 million people; Slovak of about five million. The two languages are very closely related, and mutually understandable.

English-speakers must abandon some linguistic habits to speak Czech or Slovak. The Czech tongue-twister *strč prst zkrz krk* ('stick your finger through your neck') will give you an idea of what you're up against;

another one is the word *řeřicha* (nasturtium). These are about as bad as it can get! It's not easy to learn the pronunciation from print; however, the language is spelt as it is spoken and once you become familiar with the sounds, it can be easily read.

Throughout this book, words separated by a slash are the Czech/Slovak words; where a single word is given, it's the same in both languages. For a complete pronunciation guide to the Czech language, see the Language Guide at the back of the book.

Prague

Prague (Praha in Czech) is like a history lesson come to life. As you walk among the long stone palaces or across Charles' Bridge, with the Vltava flowing below and pointed towers all around, you'll feel as if history had stopped in the 18th century.

This storybook city in the centre of Bohemia experienced two architectural golden ages: a Gothic period under Holy Roman Emperor Charles IV and a Baroque period during the Counter-Reformation. There's also an incredible smorgasbord of Romanesque, rococo and Art Nouveau architecture, all packed into Prague's compact, complex medieval city centre.

Unlike Warsaw, Budapest and Berlin, which were major battlefields during WWII, Prague escaped almost unscathed; after the war, lack of modernisation prevented haphazard development. Since 1989, however, central Prague has been swamped by capitalism as street vendors, cafés and restaurants take over streets and parks as they did prior to 1948.

Today, almost a decade after the fall of the Czech Republic's Communist government, Prague is a city of over a million inhabitants, the seat of government and the leading centre of the country's intellectual and cultural life. Known already for its musical and literary life, and in this century for ground-breaking visual arts and cinema, today's Prague is also a magnet for top-flight jazz, rock and post-rock music.

Prague has also become one of Europe's favourite tourist destinations; in summer the hotels are full to bursting and the city's narrow lanes are choked with tour groups, weekenders and school children. Thousands of young westerners have settled here as artists, consultants and entrepreneurs, leading journalists in the early 1990s to effuse about a 'new Left Bank'.

How you feel about Prague's current tourist glut may depend on where you're coming from. If you're arriving from London, Paris or Rome it may all seem quite normal. But if you've spent time elsewhere in eastern Exurope, you may begin to feel that Prague is little more than a tacky tourist trap. But you'll feel infinitely better about Prague after dinner in a small pub, a late-night walk along Charles' Bridge, or a concert in a grand Baroque palace.

You'll go crazy trying to see the best of Prague in less than about four days, and you could easily spend weeks.

HIGHLIGHTS

- Visit Prague Castle and the awesome St Vitus Cathedral
- Explore the quiet and rarely crowded back lanes of Hradčany
- Visit the Municipal House and admire its superb Art Nouveau details
- Stroll through the eerie old Jewish cemetery in Josefov
- Watch the colourful Astronomical Clock strike the hour and see the 12 Apostles march past nodding to the crowd

HISTORY

Permanent farming communities were established around 4000 BC in the north-western parts of Prague, and the area was inhabited continuously by Germanic and Celtic tribes before the arrival of the Slavs in the 6th century.

Prague Castle was established in the 870s by Prince Bořivoj as the seat of the Přemysl dynasty, with Vyšehrad an occasional alternative in the 10th and 11th centuries (see Vyšehrad in this chapter for more on the mythical founding of Prague). King Přemysl Otakar I bestowed royal privileges on Staré Město, and Malá Strana was established in 1257 by Otakar II.

During the reign of Charles (Karel) IV, Prague experienced its so-called Golden Age, and grew into one of the largest cities on the continent, acquiring its fine Gothic face, and landmarks including Charles University, Charles' Bridge and St Vitus Cathedral.

Jan Hus and other church reformers preached here against the corruptness of the Catholic Church. Hus' death at the stake in 1415 sparked a nationalist rebellion in Bohemia, led by the Prague Hussite preacher Jan Želivský. After the death of Wenceslas IV in 1419, the city was ruled by various Hussite committees. In 1420, Hussite forces led by General Jan Žižka successfully defended the city against an anti-Hussite crusade launched by Emperor Sigismund.

In 1526 the Catholic Habsburgs were again elected to rule Bohemia. After an unsuccessful Bohemian Estates uprising, Prague lost its royal privileges, though it remained the Bohemian capital. But in the later 16th century the city experienced a rebirth under Emperor Rudolf II, and was made the seat of the Habsburg Empire.

In 1618 two Habsburg councillors were flung from an upper window in Prague Castle, sparking the Thirty Years' War. The crucial Battle of the White Mountain, just west of Prague, in 1620 confirmed Habsburg power, and the nobles who had instigated the revolt were executed in Staroměstské náměstí (Old Town Square). Saxons occupied the city between 1631-32, Swedish troops seized Hradčany and Malá Strana in 1648, and (unconquered) Staré Město suffered months of bombardment. Prague's population shrank from 60,000 in 1620 to 24,600 in 1648.

Eventually the Habsburgs moved back to Vienna and Prague was reduced to a provincial town, although it got a major Baroque face-lift over the next century, particularly after a great fire in 1689. Prague's four towns – Staré Město (Old Town), Nové Město (New Town), Malá Strana and Hradčany – were made a single unit by imperial decree in 1784.

Prague was the centre of the 19th century Czech National Revival, and the first city in the Austrian Empire to rise in favour of reform during the ill-fated revolutions that swept Europe in 1848. Landmarks of this period include the National Theatre, the National Museum and the New Town Hall. In 1861, Czechs defeated Germans in Prague council elections and edged them out of power forever, though the shrinking German minority still wielded substantial influence well into the 1880s.

As WWI drew to a close, Czechoslovakia declared its independence, with Prague as the capital. On 1 January 1922, Greater Prague was established by the absorption of several surrounding towns and villages, becoming a city of 677,000. By 1938 the population had grown to one million.

Prague was occupied during WWII but suffered little of the physical damage wreaked elsewhere. Reichsprotektor Reinhard Heydrich was assassinated in the city in June 1942; the Czech paratroopers who did the deed were betrayed in their hiding place in the Church of SS Cyril & Methodius, committing suicide with their last bullets.

After the February 1948 Communist coup, Prague settled into a slow decline. The 'Prague Spring' of 1968 was crushed by Warsaw Pact troops on the night of 20-21 August; Prague was one of their first objectives, as Soviet special forces needed Ruzyně airport for Soviet transport planes.

On 17 November 1989, marchers in Prague commemorating the execution of nine students by the Nazis 50 years earlier were beaten by the police, setting in motion the extraordinary, nonviolent 'Velvet Revolution' that within a fortnight brought

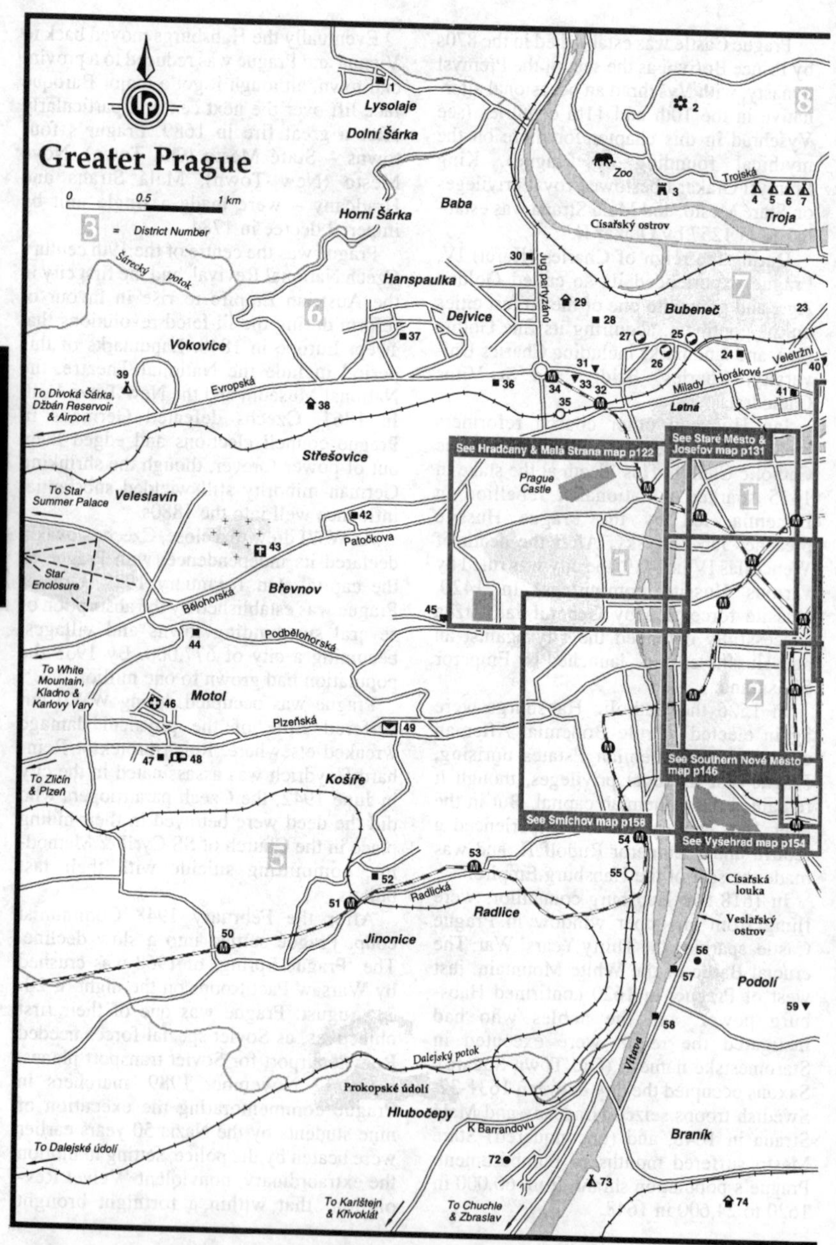
Greater Prague
0
0.5
1 km
3 = District Number
Lysolaje
Dolní Šárka
Horní Šárka
Baba
Zoo
Trojská
Troja
Císařský ostrov
Šárecký potok
Hanspaulka
Jug partyzánů
Dejvice
Bubeneč
Vokovice
Evropská
Milady Horákové
Veletržní
Letná
To Divoká Šárka, Džbán Reservoir & Airport
Střešovice
See Hradčany & Malá Strana map p122
Prague Castle
See Staré Město & Josefov map p131
To Star Summer Palace
Veleslavín
Patočkova
Star Enclosure
Břevnov
Bělohorská
Podbělohorská
To White Mountain, Kladno & Karlovy Vary
Motol
Plzeňská
To Zličín & Plzeň
Košíře
See Southern Nové Město map p146
See Smíchov map p158
See Vyšehrad map p154
Radlická
Radlice
Císařská louka
Veslařský ostrov
Jinonice
Podolí
Vltava
Dalejský potok
Prokopské údolí
Hlubočepy
K Barrandovu
Braník
To Dalejské údolí
To Karlštejn & Křivoklát
To Chuchle & Zbraslav

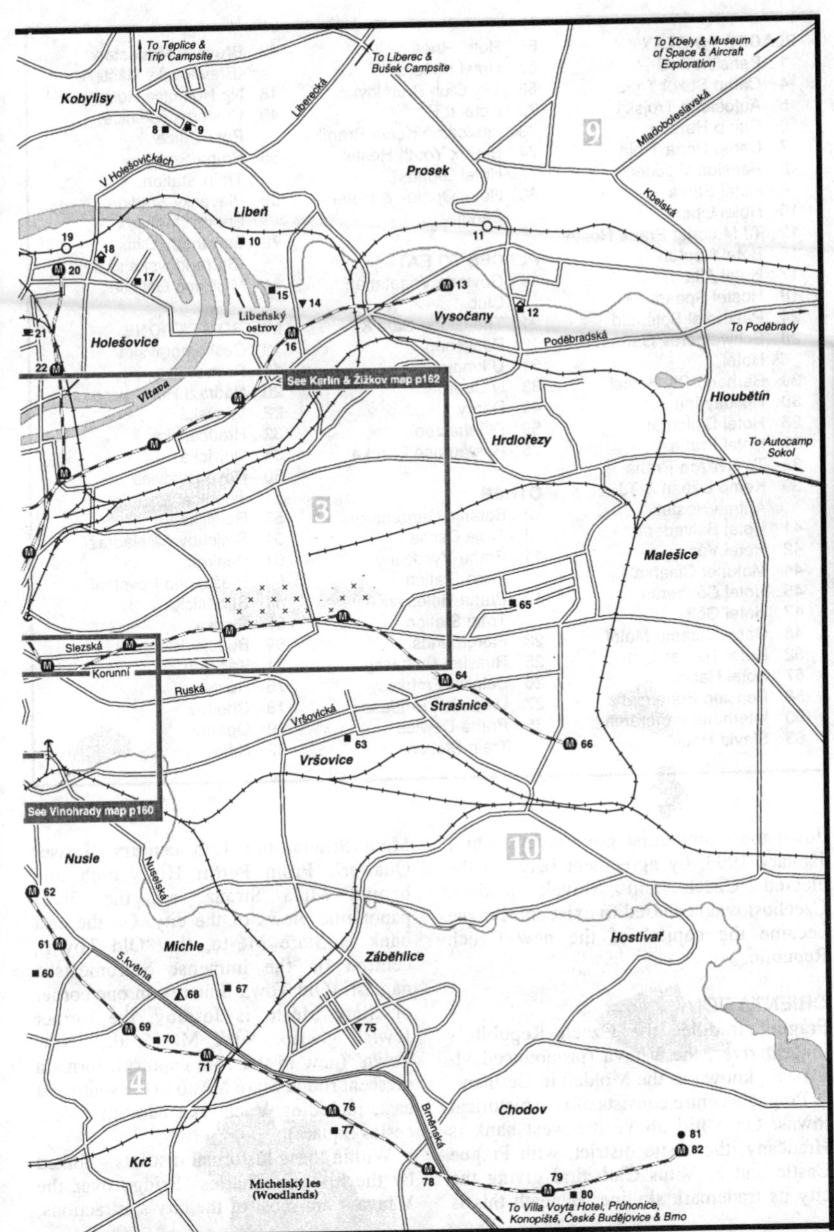

CZECH REPUBLIC

PLACES TO STAY
1 Pension BoB
4 Camp Sokol Troja
5 Autocamp Trojská
6 Camp Herzog
7 Camp Dana Troja
8 Pension V sudech
9 Hotel Stírka
10 Hotel Libeň
12 TJ Motorlet Praga Hostel
15 Botel Neptun
17 Hotel Alta
18 Hostel Spoas
24 Parkhotel Spléndid
28 Schweigerov Gardens Hotel
29 Berhanu CK Hostel
30 Holiday Inn
36 Hotel Diplomat
37 Hotel Praha
38 TJ Hvězda Praha
39 Kemp Džbán & TJ Aritma Hostel
41 Hotel Belveder
42 Hotel Váza
44 Motorlet Císařka
45 Hotel Coubertin
47 Hotel Golf
48 Caravancamp Motol
52 Hotel Tourist
57 Botel Racek
58 Pension Bohemians
60 Interhotel Panorama
63 Slavia Hotel
65 Hotel Rhea
67 Hotel Kačerov
68 Sky Club Brumlovka
70 Hotel ILF
73 Intercamp Kotva Braník
74 Braník Youth Hostel
77 Hotel Globus
80 Hotel Opatov & Hotel Sandra

PLACES TO EAT
14 Góvinda Vegetarian Club
21 The Globe Café & Bookshop
31 U kmotra
33 U Cedru
40 Derby
59 Dlouhá zeď
75 Restaurace Eureka

OTHER
2 Botanic Gardens
3 Troja Castle
11 Praha-Vysočany Train Station
19 Praha-Holešovice Train Station
23 Fairgrounds
25 Russian Embassy
26 Belgian Embassy
27 Ukrainian Embassy
35 Praha-Dejvice Train Station
43 Břevnov Monastery (Břevnovský klášter)
46 Na Homolca Hospital
49 Customs (Celnice) Post Office
55 Praha-Smíchov Train Station
56 Plavecký Stadión Sports Complex
72 Barrandov Cliffs (Barrandovské skály)
81 Multikino Galaxie

METRO STATIONS
13 Českomoravská
16 Palmovka
20 Nádraží Holešovice
22 Vltavská
32 Hradčanská
34 Dejvická
50 Nové Butovice
51 Jinonice
53 Radlická
54 Smíchovské Nádraží
61 Pankrác
62 Pražského Povstání
64 Strašnická
66 Skalka
69 Budějovická
71 Kačerov
76 Roztyly
78 Chodov
79 Opatov
82 Háje

down the Communist government. On 1 January 1993, by agreement between the elected Czech and Slovak leaders, Czechoslovakia ceased to exist and Prague became the capital of the new Czech Republic.

ORIENTATION

Prague straddles the Czech Republic's longest river, the Vltava (pronounced vl-TA-va), known as the Moldau in German.

Prague's centre consists of five historical towns. On a hill above the west bank is Hradčany, the castle district, with Prague Castle and St Vitus Cathedral giving the city its trademark skyline. Beneath this is Malá Strana, the 13th century 'Lesser Quarter'. From Petřín Hill, south and behind Malá Strana, are the finest panoramic views of the city. On the east bank is Staré Město, the 'Old Town', centred on the immense Staroměstské náměstí (Old Town Square). In one corner of Staré Město is Josefov, the former Jewish ghetto. Nové Město, the 'New Town' (new in the 14th century), forms a crescent round Staré Město to the south and east, including Václavské náměstí (Wenceslas Square).

Within these historical districts – linked by the historic Charles' Bridge over the Vltava – are most of the city's attractions, best appreciated on foot. Beyond the centre are the suburbs of 19th and 20th century Prague.

The city is divided into 10 postal districts – Prague 1, and parts of Prague 2 to the south, cover the historical centre. Ruzyně airport is 17km to the west of the city.

Maps

Numerous maps are available at Prague newsagents, bookshops and travel agencies for around 75 Kč.

The most precise and readable map of the city's historical heart and surrounding suburbs is Kartografie's *Praha – plán středu města* (1:10,000). It also includes transport information, index, metro map, and (on the back) a brief description of the major historical sights.

Other useful maps are Kartografie Praha's *Praha – plán města* (1:20,000) and Žaket's *Praha – plán města* (1:23,000). The Prague Information Service gives out a free map (*Praha – plán města*) of Prague's historical centre.

If you are staying in Prague for a significant amount of time, Kartografie's pocket atlas *Praha – plán města* (1:20,000) is invaluable – it covers all of Prague and also provides a lot of information on the sights, hotels, restaurants and transport.

Public transportation maps showing metro routes as well as day and night routes for trams and buses are available from DP offices (for locations of these see Public Transport in the Getting Around section later in this chapter).

Some shops still sell older maps with out of date information. A map's copyright blurb or cover will show its publication date – stay away from maps printed before 1994. The maps in this guide are for orientation only and you should purchase a city map as soon as you arrive.

INFORMATION

Tourist Offices

There are several tourist organisations that provide varying levels of information and services.

Prague Information Service (PIS) The very helpful Prague Information Service (Pražská informační služba) is a municipal agency with city information, entertainment listings and accommodation services. It also offers guided tours, a telephone information service (☎ 54 44 44 or 187) and dozens of useful English-language booklets – including the monthly *Cultural Events* and *Prague Guide* – that list museums, galleries, theatres, bars, clubs, you name it.

Summer hours for all offices are weekdays from 9 am to 7 pm, and weekends from 9 am to 5 pm. Offices generally close two hours earlier in the off-season.

Main Office, Na příkopě 20 (metro náměstí Republiky): concert and theatre tickets, and maps. Accommodation provided by AVE (in same office).

Old Town Hall (☎ 24 81 61 21; fax 24 81 61 72; metro Staroměstská or náměstí Republiky): maps, concert and theatre tickets, and accommodation service. City tours handled by Pragotour (in same office).

Main Train Station (Hlavní nádraží; metro Hlavní nádraží): concert and theatre tickets, and maps

Malostranská Bridge Tower (open summer only; metro Malostranská): concerts and theatre tickets, and maps

Czech Tourist Authority (CCC) The Czech Tourist Authority (Česká centrála cestovniho ruchu; ☎ 24 21 14 58), at Národní 37, has information about sights, museums, festivals etc for the whole of the Czech Republic. It does *not* handle accommodation in Prague. The office is open daily from 10 am to 6 pm.

Čedok The Czech Transport Office (Česká dopravní kancelář), better known by its acronym Čedok, is the state-run tour operator and travel agency. It's not a tourism-promotion office, but makes money by organising things for tourists (both Czech and foreign), so don't expect a lot of advice on doing things independently.

That said, the main office at Na příkopě 18 is a pretty good one-stop shop for maps, accommodation bookings, excursions, concert and theatre tickets, and all types of onward travel bookings. The smaller Pařížská and Rytířská offices are also good for the above-mentioned services. The tiny Ruzyně airport and Hilton Hotel offices provide only basic services. Following is a list of the Prague offices; all are open weekdays from 8.30 am to 6 pm, Saturday from 9 am to 1 pm:

Main Office, Na příkopě 18 (☎ 24 19 76 42; fax 24 22 23 00; metro Můstek)
Rytířská 16 (☎ 26 36 97; metro Můstek)
Pařížská 6 (☎ 231 69 78; metro Staroměstská)
Hilton Atrium Hotel, Pobřežní 1, Prague 8 (☎ 24 84 20 42)
Ruzyně airport, Prague 6 (☎ 367 08 02)

CKM The Youth Travel Office (Cestovní kancelář mládeže) is the youth-travel equivalent of Čedok. At the time of writing there was a rumour that CKM was rechristening itself CKM 2000 and attempting to shed its student/youth focus. In the meantime it's a good place to buy a student, Euro26 or Hostelling International (HI) card, purchase student-discount travel tickets (for those under 26) and arrange cheap accommodation. Its two branch offices in Prague are located at:

Main Office, Jindřišská 28 (☎ 26 85 32; metro Hlavní nádraží): weekdays from 9 am to 1 pm and 2 to 5 pm, and Saturday to noon
Žitná 12 (☎ 24 91 57 67 or 24 21 79 54; metro Karlovo náměstí): weekdays from 9 am to noon and 1 to 6 pm

Publications

Several advertiser-supported tourist handbooks are sold at travel agencies and newsstands. Best of the lot is the quarterly *Welcome to Prague*. There is also the monthly *Prague Guide*, with useful information on transport, banks, embassies, travel agents, clubs, and up-market shops and restaurants. For free detailed information on entertainment, museums and galleries see PIS's monthly booklet *Prague Cultural Events* and the bi-monthly pamphlet *Do města Downtown*. Or you can buy the monthly *Culture in Prague* or *Přehled* (in Czech only) programme booklets. A variety of free magazines are strewn around the bars and cafés; a good one for club listings and articles on Prague's underground scene is the monthly *Think*.

The gay and lesbian magazine *SOHO* has plenty of information on the city's gay clubs and special events. The SOHO editorial offices (☎ 24 25 71 33 or 21 38 40) are at Vinohradská 46, Prague 2, if you're looking for specific advice.

Prague Card

If you're only in Prague for a short time a good way to save money would be to get a Prague Card. Available at the American Express office on Václavské náměstí, it costs 430 Kč and is valid for three days and includes unlimited travel on public transport, entry to 44 museums and galleries, and a free tourist guide to the city.

Foreign Consulates

For a list of foreign embassies in Prague, see the Embassies section in the Facts for the Visitor chapter.

Visa Extensions Apply for a visa extension at the Foreigners' Police & Passport Office (Úřadovna cizinecké policie a pasové služby) at Olšanská 2 in Žižkov, Prague 3. It's a 10 minute walk from the Florenc metro station, or take tram No 9 from Václavské náměstí.

Use Entrance B and queue up at any door inside. You must have a good reason to extend your visa, and bring any documentation that may be helpful. After processing you'll be sent to Entrance A, where there's a photo booth (200 Kč for the required two photos) and a cashier (200 Kč for a two month extension). Take your paperwork back to Entrance B for final processing.

The office is open Monday, Tuesday and Thursday from 7.30 to 11.45 am and 12.30 to 2 pm, Wednesday from 7.30 to 11.30 am and 12.30 to 5 pm, and Friday from 7.30 am to noon.

Money

The easiest way to change money is with your bank card – ATMs (*bankomat*) are everywhere in Prague, and you generally get an excellent rate of exchange (note that your home bank often takes a US$1 to US$3 commission per transaction). Nearly all ATMs accept Eurocard. Equally common are MasterCard/Cirrus and Visa/Plus ATMs.

Avoid small exchange offices like the ubiquitous Chequepoint or Exact Change, which charge from 4 to 10% commission (95 to 150 Kč minimum) or 1% commission but offer much lower rates. You're far better off with one of the main foreign-exchange banks:

American Express, Václavské náměstí 56, Prague 1 (☎ 24 21 99 92; fax 24 22 77 08): weekdays from 9 am to 6 pm (to 7 pm in summer), and Saturday to noon (Saturday and Sunday to 3 pm in summer)

Československá obchodní banka, Na příkopě 14, Prague 1: weekdays from 8 am to 5 pm

Komerční banka, Na příkopě 33, Prague 1: weekdays from 8 am to 5 pm

Thomas Cook, Staroměstské náměstí 5, Prague 1 (☎ 24 81 71 73 or 24 81 81 73) or Národní 28, Prague 1 (☎ 21 10 52 72): both open weekdays from 9 am to 6 pm, and Saturday to 5 pm

Živnostenská banka, Na příkopě 20: weekdays from 8 am to 9.30 pm, and Saturday from 1.30 to 5.30 pm

American Express or Thomas Cook travellers cheques can be converted to crowns free of charge (4 to 8% commission to receive dollars or pounds) at the American Express and Thomas Cook offices. Most banks charge 1 or 2% commissions for travellers cheques; hotels charge about 5%.

For cash, Živnostenská charges 2%. Česká obchodní's exchange machine charges 1%.

If it's late and you need to change money, a handful of private exchange desks on Václavské náměstí stay open 24 hours in summer, but they give awful rates.

A couple of warnings: beware of places that post the *selling* rates, which are much higher than the *buying* rates they'll pay you, and places that advertise slightly higher rates without mentioning the high commission charges. There is also no black market here, so people offering to change money on the street are usually thieves.

Cash Advances Most Prague banks (and their ATMs) will give you Visa and MasterCard cash advances with no commission. American Express cardholders can get commission-free advances from its office. If you plan to use your credit card at an ATM, make sure you know the PIN (personal identification number).

Credit Cards In Prague, most hotels and many restaurants and shops accept American Express, Visa or MasterCard, and sometimes Eurocard, Diner's Club, Access or JCB. Čedok and most travel agents accept all of these.

Post & Communications

The main post office is at Jindřišská 14, Nové Město, just off Václavské náměstí. It is open 24 hours a day for postage, parcels, telegrams, faxes and unassisted telephone calls.

The main telephone bureau (from 7 am to 11 pm) is to the left inside the main post office's front entrance, and the fax/telegram/telex bureau (24 hours a day) is to the right. Information is at window 30. Most other services, and all services at the city's 115 other post offices, are available weekdays from 8 am to 6 pm, and Saturday until noon.

Letters Buy stamps at windows 22 to 26 and 36 to 39 in the main post office, or from street vendors or PNS newsagents. Letters go in the orange boxes.

Parcels From the main post office you can send parcels weighing up to 2kg at window 24. Send international and Express Mail Service (EMS) parcels from window 7.

Parcels weighing between two and 15kg do not have to be taken to Pošta 121 Celnice

CZECH REPUBLIC

(☎ 24 51 17 54), Plzeňská 139, Smíchov (metro to Anděl, then three stops west on tram No 4, 7 or 9), but you will end up there anyway, as most postal employees retain Communist-era anxieties about regulations. You have to fill in three forms. It's open Monday and Wednesday from 7 am to 6 pm, and Tuesday, Thursday and Friday until 3 pm.

Poste Restante Pick up poste restante mail (*uložené zásilky*) in the main post office at window 28, weekdays from 7 am to 8 pm, and Saturday to 1 pm. Mail should be addressed to Poste Restante, Hlavní pošta, Jindřišská 14, 110 00 Praha 1, Czech Republic. You must present your passport to claim mail (check under your first name, too). Mail is held for one month.

Holders of American Express and Thomas Cook cards and travellers cheques can have letters sent to the Prague offices (see the earlier Money section); the British and Canadian consulates will hold letters for their citizens for a few months. None of them will accept registered letters or parcels.

Telephone In addition to coin-phones, Prague has lots of card-phones. Telephone cards (*telekarty*) are sold in post offices, newsagents and in the main post office at windows 22 to 26; there are five different denominations, worth between 100 and 300 Kč.

Prague's area code is ☎ 02.

Travel Agencies

All of the organisations listed earlier under Tourist Offices in the Information section offer tours of the city, as well as being able to help with all your travel needs.

In addition, several offices around Prague sell tickets on buses to western European cities, which usually work out cheaper than the trains (though they're less comfortable). Some good deals can be had at Čedok, such as bus tickets (with Eurolines) to Amsterdam, London and Paris. Even cheaper tickets to the same destinations with Czech bus companies are also possible at Čedok and through other agencies.

Another travel agent, Bohemiatour, Zlatnická 7, has international bus tickets to many European cities, as does the Eurolines representative in Prague, ČSAD Klíčov (☎ 24 21 34 20), Opletalova 37.

The Czech Railways (ČD) Travel Agency (☎ 24 21 48 86), at Hlavní nádraží train station and its other office (☎ 66 71 09 31) at Holešovice train station, sells train and bus tickets to points all over western Europe. It also has cheap youth airfares.

Bookshops

One of the best English-language bookshops is Big Ben (☎ 231 80 21; metro náměstí Republiky), Malá Stupartská 5, Nové Město.

Knihkupectví Orbis, Václavské náměstí 42, has a good selection of maps, and local as well as foreign guidebooks.

Nadas (metro náměstí Republiky), Hybernská 5, sells train timetables (*jízdní řád*).

Bohemian Ventures, náměstí Jana Palacha 2, Josefov, in the Faculty of Philosophy building, has an excellent selection of paperbacks in English, including English translations of works by Czech authors.

Topičovo Knihkupectví (metro Národní Třída), Národní 11, also has English-language books and at slightly lower prices.

There are two cafés with English-language bookshops: U knihomola (☎ 627 77 67; metro náměstí Míru) at Mánesova 79, and The Globe (☎ 66 71 26 10; metro Vltavská) at Jankovského 14 in Holešovice.

Cultural Centres

If you're looking for newspapers or information about other cultures, try these centres:

France
: Institut Français de Prague, Štěpánská 35 (☎ 24 21 66 61)

Germany
: Goethe Institut, Masarykovo nábřeží 32 (☎ 24 91 57 25)

Hungary
Hungarian Cultural Centre, Rytířská 25 (☎ 24 22 24 24): Monday to Friday from 8 am to 6 pm
Poland
Polsky institut, Václavské náměstí 19 (☎ 24 21 47 08/9)
Slovakia
Slovak institut, Purkyňova 4 (☎ 24 91 56 29 or 29 09 93)
UK
The British Council, Národní 10 (☎ 24 91 21 79/83): weekdays from 9 am to 4 pm; British newspapers and magazines, and Sky TV
UK Embassy, Thunovská 14, Malá Strana: reading room
USA
American Center for Culture and Commerce (USIS), Hybernská 7A (☎ 24 23 10 85): US newspapers, magazines and reference books, plus a business reference service and occasional events

Newspapers & Magazines

The weekly English-language *Prague Post* (40 Kč) has local news and features, travel tips, concert and restaurant reviews, and day-by-day arts and entertainment listings. (For more information see the Newspapers & Magazines section in the Facts for the Visitor chapter.)

Major European and American newspapers and a few magazines are on sale at kiosks in the tourist areas, at the main train station and the airport.

Radio

BBC World Service news and cultural programming is broadcast locally on 101.1 FM, weekdays from 5.30 to 6 pm. Club VOA (Voice of America) has pop music and news on 106.2 FM. BBC and VOA are also easy to receive on short-wave. Radio 1 (91.9 FM) has a 15 minute 'Central Europe Today' news programme in English, weekdays from 7 am, and a music and magazine programme also on weekdays from 11.10 am or on Saturday from 7 pm. Radio Prague (92.6 or 102.7 FM) has its news and current affairs 'Radio Prague Calling' programme weekdays from 5.30 pm. These programmes change regularly so it is best to refer to the 'On Radio' section in the *Prague Post*. The FM dial is full of Czech DJs playing western and local pop and rock.

Left Luggage

There is a 24 hour left-luggage office (*úschovna*) on Level 1 at the main train station, Praha hlavní nádraží. The station also has day-use lockers, as do most other train stations and the Praha-Florenc long-distance bus station.

Lost or Stolen Belongings

Tourism has spawned an epidemic of petty crime in Prague. Where tourists are concerned, this mainly means pickpockets. The prime trouble spots are of course where tourists gather in crowds, such as Prague Castle, Charles' Bridge, Old Town Square (especially by the Astronomical Clock), the entrance/exit to the Old Jewish Cemetery, Václavské náměstí (Wenceslas Square), Ruzyně airport, the metro and on other public transport (especially tram Nos 9 and 22).

If you lose something or it's stolen, your embassy ought to give you a letter to take to the police, preferably in Czech, asking for a police report (without which you cannot collect from your insurance). Try to get the embassy to provide its own report in English too. The UK embassy has this down to a science, and will also help you get in touch with relatives or your bank to get more money.

For a police report, go to the Prague 1 police station at Bartolomějská 1 or Konviktská 6, but if the theft occurred in another district you have to go to that district's main police station. If your passport has been stolen, apply for a replacement visa at the Foreigners' Police & Passport Office at Olšanská 2 in Žižkov (see the Visa Extensions section earlier in this chapter).

For anything except travel documents, you might get lucky at the city's Lost & Found Office (*ztráty a nálezy*; ☎ 24 23 50 85), Karoliny Světlé 5, north of the National Theatre; there's also one at the airport (☎ 20 11 42 83). If you left something behind on

CZECH REPUBLIC

public transport contact MHD (☎ 24 98 24 20) at Na bojišti 5, Prague 2.

Laundry

Prague's first self-service laundry (*samoobslužná prádelna*) is the expatriate-run Laundry Kings (☎ 312 37 43) in Prague 6. A normal load costs about 105 Kč to wash and dry, and there's also a drop-off service. It's open weekdays from 6 am to 10 pm, and weekends from 8 am. From metro station Hradčanská, take the 'Praha Dejvice' exit, turn left into Dejvická and it's at No 16.

Other self-service laundromats are Laundryland (☎ 25 11 24) at Londýnská 71, off náměstí Míru, Prague 2, and Prague Laundromat (☎ 25 55 41; metro náměstí Míru) at Korunní 14, Prague 2.

Locally run laundries are hard to find, and a load can take up to a week. There are a couple of 24 hour quick service dry cleaners/laundromats, such as Astera (☎ 24 23 73 35) at Jindřišská 5, which charges 50 to 80 Kč per item for dry cleaning. Another is Aura Rapid Service (☎ 25 10 04) at Francouzská 15, Prague 2; they also repair clothing.

Also look in the Yellow Pages (Zlaté stránky) under *prádelny* (laundries). Hotels sometimes offer pricey services.

Medical Services

Prague's best hospital – equipped and staffed to western standards – is Na Homolce Hospital, Na Homolce 724, Motol, Prague 5; take bus No 167 from Anděl metro station. This used to be just for diplomats and Communist Party bigwigs, and to most Praguers (*pražáci*) it's still the 'rich people's hospital'. The foreigners' polyclinic and emergency entrance (☎ 52 92 21 44, from 6.30 am to 3.30 pm; ☎ 52 92 20 43 or 52 92 11 11, after hours) are on the north side, 2nd level. There's a separate children's clinic (☎ 52 92 20 43).

Among several of the new private clinics is the Canadian Medical Centre (☎ 316 55 19, weekdays from 8 am to 6 pm; ☎ 0601-21 23 20, other hours), at Veleslavínská 30/1, with English-speaking doctors, 24 hour medical aid and a pharmacy. It's the seventh stop on tram No 20 or 26 from Dejvice metro station.

District clinics have after-hours emergency services (from 7 pm to 7 am and all weekend). The city's biggest polyclinic is at Antala Staška 80 in Prague 4 (☎ 692 89 70), south-west of metro station Budějovická. The Prague 1 clinic (☎ 24 22 25 20) is at Palackého 5, off Jungmannova in southern Nové Město. For Prague 2 the Všeobecná fakultní nemocnice (☎ 24 96 11 11) is at U nemocnice 2, south of Karlovo náměstí.

Dental Services There are dental clinics at Na Homolce Hospital (☎ 52 92 21 55, from 6.30 am to 3.30 pm; ☎ 52 92 20 43 or 52 92 11 11, after hours), and the big Prague 4 polyclinic (see the previous Medical Services section). District clinics for after-hours emergencies include those at Vladislavova 22, opposite Národní Třída metro station (☎ 24 22 76 63).

Pharmacies There are plenty of pharmacies (*lekárna*), and most city districts have one that stays open 24 hours a day. For Prague 2 it's Lékárna U sv Ludmily (☎ 25 81 89; metro Náměstí Míru) at Belgická 37, and for Prague 6 it's U stříbrného orla (☎ 32 75 12) at Vítězné náměstí 12.

Emergency

Emergency telephone numbers in Prague include:

Municipal Police	☎ 156
Police	☎ 158
Fire	☎ 150
Ambulance	☎ 155
Road accidents	☎ 77 34 55
	☎ 77 75 21
	☎ 154

WALKING TOURS

We have detailed three good walking tours around Prague's centre, but for more specific information about the city's sights see the following sections.

CZECH REPUBLIC

Walk 1 – Royal Way

The Royal Way (Královská Cesta) is the ancient coronation route to Prague Castle. The part of it through Staré Město and Malá Strana takes you past some of the city's finest sights. From Václavské náměstí (Wenceslas Square), walk up Na příkopě to náměstí Republiky, from where this tour starts.

Facing náměstí Republiky is the Art Nouveau façade of Prague's most delicate building, the **Municipal House** (Obecní dům). It also has several good restaurants, a rip-roaring club, and a pub. Next door, swathed in scaffolding as it has been for years, is the 15th century **Powder Tower** (Prašná brána).

Go under the tower and west into Celetná. On the corner is the Old Fruit Market (Ovocný trh), which is one of the earliest cubist façades in a city famous for them. Nearby is the **House at the Black Madonna**. Westwards towards Staroměstské náměstí, Celetná is a virtual open-air museum of pastel Baroque façades.

Backtrack a bit and turn off the Royal Way, north into Králodvorská. This area, the Králův dvůr (Royal Court), was once a royal stables. On U Obecního domu is the Art Nouveau Hotel Paříž, built in 1907 and recently restored.

Turn left into Jakubská; at the west end, facing Malá Štupartská, is **St James Church**, famous for its pipe organ and acoustics. The entire block across from the church was once a medieval inn, the **Týn Court.** Turn right and go around it by way of the quiet Týnská passage.

Admire the beautiful north door of the Týn Church and turn left behind it to emerge back into Celetná and the Royal Way. Pass No 3, Franz Kafka's boyhood home from 1896 to 1907, and No 2, where his family lived in 1888-89, and you're in **Staroměstské náměstí** (Old Town Square). See Walk 2 for a tour round the square.

Left and beyond the Old Town Hall tower, the corner building covered in Renaissance sgraffito is the dům U minuty, another Kafka house. Beyond this is Malé náměstí, with a Renaissance fountain and some fine Baroque and neo-Renaissance façades.

You're now looking at the Old Town tower of **Charles' Bridge**. Cross the bridge, through the crowds of tourists, hawkers and pickpockets and the rows of Baroque statues, and soak up the views of Prague Castle.

The western end of Charles' Bridge crosses the island Kampa, separated from Malá Strana by the Čertovka channel. Walk beneath the Malá Strana bridge towers and you're on Mostecká.

At the top of Mostecká is Malostranské náměstí, bisected by trams and centred around one of Prague's finest Baroque structures, the **Church of St Nicholas**. Cross the square to Nerudova, one of Prague's most picturesque streets, which is named after the poet Jan Neruda who lived at No 47. On many of Nerudova's mostly Baroque façades there are colourful emblems that have given these buildings their popular names.

Continue along Úvoz to the Church of St Roch and the Strahov Monastery behind it, then backtrack via Loretánská to Hradčanské náměstí (or short-cut up Nerudova on Ke Hradu) and the entrance to **Prague Castle**. Don't miss the view of the city from the corner of the square, with Petřín Hill off to the right. It's easy to see why Czechs call Prague the 'city of 100 spires'.

Walk 2 – Václavské Náměstí to Staroměstské Náměstí

This tour starts on Václavské náměstí (Wenceslas Square) at Prague's most famous landmark, the equestrian **statue of St Wenceslas**, the 10th century 'good King Wenceslas' of the Christmas carol. Just below it is a modest memorial to those who died for their resistance to Communism, including Jan Palach. Looming above the statue is the neo-Renaissance National Museum.

Below the statue stretches Václavské náměstí, a focal point of Czech history since the 19th century. On 24 November 1989 the obituary of Czech Communism was pronounced by Alexander Dubček and Václav Havel from the balcony of the Melantrich building at No 36, on the west side. Among the square's turn-of-the-century buildings, the finest is probably the 1906 Art Nouveau Grand Hotel Evropa at No 25.

At the bottom of the square is the **'Golden Cross'**, the intersection with Na příkopě, one of the city's premier shopping streets; it marks part of the ancient ditch around Staré Město (Old Town).

Take a little detour, west from the intersection, around the metro entrance to Jungmannovo náměstí and the beautiful 14th century **Church of Our Lady of the Snows**. By its Gothic north door is a bizarre cubist street lamp.

Back at the 'Golden Cross', the onward extension of Václavské náměstí is Na můstku, where a footbridge once crossed the moat into Staré Město.

Na můstku ends at Rytířská, and a one block detour east takes you to Prague's oldest theatre and finest neo-classical building, the Tyl or **Estates Theatre**, where Mozart's opera *Don Giovanni* premiered in 1787. Next door is the **Karolinum**, birthplace of central Europe's oldest university. Na můstku then crosses an open-air market on Havelská.

Squeezing through Melantrichova, you emerge into pastel-painted Staroměstské náměstí. Join the crowd awaiting the hourly performance of the **Astronomical Clock** on the 14th century Old Town Hall; climb the tower for postcard views of the city. Just to your right is the city's best source of tourist information, the Prague Information Service (PIS).

The square's centrepiece is the Art Nouveau bronze **statue of Jan Hus**. Across to the right (east) is the spiky-topped Gothic Týn Church, and next to it, behind Jan Hus, is the Kinský Palace, probably the city's finest rococo façade. In the north-west corner of the square is the wedding-cake Baroque Church of St Nicholas.

Walk 3 – Josefov

Prague's Jewish community was confined to a walled ghetto in Staré Město in about the 13th century, and it was not until 1848 that the walls came down. A drastic clearance at the turn of the century brought the ghetto to an end as a community.

At the bottom of Maiselova, on Staroměstské náměstí's north-west corner, is the birthplace of Franz Kafka, though the building itself is new since then; beside it is a private Kafka Exhibition. Maiselova runs north into the heart of Josefov. In the second block is the neo-Gothic **Maisel Synagogue**. Beyond the pink Jewish Town Hall, in the third block, is the **Old-New Synagogue**, Europe's oldest active synagogue, completed about 1270. Beside it is the 16th century High Synagogue.

Left down U starého hřbitova are the walls of the melancholy **Old Jewish Cemetery**, Europe's oldest surviving Jewish burial ground – spared, ironically, by a Nazi plan for a memorial to an 'extinguished race'. Continuing along the cemetery wall, a left turn into Břehová brings you to **17.listopadu**, across which is the Charles University Law Faculty. The street's name ('17 November') refers to students killed in a 1939 anti-Nazi demonstration, and to the clubbing of students 50 years later that triggered the fall of Czechoslovakia's Communist government.

Turn left to reach No 2, the **Museum of Decorative Arts**, with a trove of eye-popping 16th to 19th century furnishings (and a good coffee shop). Across the road is the **Rudolfinum**, interwar seat of the Czechoslovak parliament and now home of the Czech Philharmonic.

From náměstí Jana Palacha (Jan Palach Square; beside the Rudolfinum) you will catch your first views of Prague Castle. Turn left (east) into Široká, where the 16th century **Pinkas Synagogue** is now a memorial to the Bohemian and Moravian victims of the Nazis. The eponymous 'hero' of Bruce Chatwin's *Utz* had his fictional home in this street, overlooking the cemetery.

Two blocks on, in a sudden change of atmosphere, you come to Pařížská, testament to Prague's turn-of-the-century infatuation with Art Nouveau architecture. Turning left, you can see right up Pařížská, across the river to the **Letná Gardens**, where a gigantic metronome slowly bobs, on the spot once occupied by a 14,000 tonne statue of Stalin. The first right on Pařížská brings you into Bílkova. A block along, at Elišky Krásnohorské 10 and 12, are Prague's last purely cubist façades.

If your feet are sore, take the next right along Bílkova into Dušní and head back to Staroměstské náměstí. If you're game for a bit more, continue to the end of Bílkova, left into Kozí and right into U milosrdných, to Prague's oldest Gothic structure, the **former Convent of St Agnes**, now housing the National Gallery's collection of 19th century Czech art.

Return to Staroměstské náměstí via Haštalské náměstí, Kozí and Dlouhá.

PRAGUE CASTLE

Prague Castle (Pražský hrad; simply called *hrad* by the Czechs) is the most popular sight in Prague; if you don't like crowds, come early or late in the day. According to the *Guinness Book of Records*, it's the largest ancient castle in the world – 570m long, an average of 128m wide and occupying 7.28 hectares. Remarkably, the surrounding complex of churches and former ecclesiastical buildings covers an additional 38 hectares.

The castle's history goes back to the 9th century, when Prince Bořivoj established a fortified settlement here. It grew as rulers made their own additions, which explains its mixture of styles. The castle was for centuries the home of Bohemia's kings; since 1918 it's been used by Czech presidents, though the current president, Václav Havel, has chosen to live in his own house on the outskirts of the city.

The castle has had four major reconstructions, from that of Prince Soběslav in the 12th century to a classical face-lift under Empress Maria Theresa. In the 1920s, President Masaryk contracted a Slovenian, Josef Plečnik, to renovate the castle.

First Courtyard

On either side of the main gate at the west end are the *Battling Titans* by Ignác Platzer (1767-70). The **castle guards** below them are known to crack smiles now and then. Havel hired the costume designer for the film *Amadeus* to replace their Communist-era khaki uniforms with the present ones, reminiscent of the First Republic. The guard is changed every hour from 5 am to 11 pm, but the most spectacular display is at noon, with everything from an exchange of banners to a 15 minute fanfare by a six piece brass band.

The pointy flagpoles in the first courtyard are among Plečnik's controversial 1920s additions.

Second Courtyard

The second courtyard is entered through the Baroque **Matthias Gate** (1614). The Spanish Hall (Španělský sál) and Rudolf Gallery (Rudolfova galerie) here are the most beautiful in the castle, but like all the other western parts of the castle they're only for state use.

The **Chapel of the Holy Cross** (kaple sv Kříže, 1763), on the right, was once the treasury of St Vitus Cathedral; now it's the ticket office and castle information centre. In the middle of the courtyard is a Baroque fountain and a 17th century well with Renaissance lattice work.

At the northern end, the **Prague Castle Gallery**, which is open daily, except Monday, from 10 am to 6 pm (until 5 pm in winter), features 16th and 17th century European and Czech paintings and sculptures, in what was once a stable.

A detour past the gallery crosses the Powder Bridge (Prašný most), built in 1540. The Stag Moat (Jelení příkop) below it was later used for raising game animals, hence the name. To the left is a gate into a bomb shelter started by the Communists in the 1950s but never completed, with tunnels that run under most parts of the castle.

Castle Services & Approach Routes

In some ways Prague Castle is a mini-town, with all sorts of services within its walls. The castle itself is open daily from 5 am to midnight from April to October, and to 11 pm the rest of the year. Most sights are open daily from 9 am to 5 pm (to 4 pm in winter), although the hours vary.

Information An information centre (☎ 24 37 33 68) in the second courtyard's Chapel of the Holy Cross is open from 9 am to 5 pm (until 4 pm in winter). There are maps posted around the castle. Call to pre-arrange guided tours in English (you can also arrange these on the spot).

Tickets Buy castle tickets at the Chapel of the Holy Cross in the second courtyard. The 100 Kč ticket (50 Kč for students) is valid for three days and includes most sights within the castle complex – except the Convent of St George, Lobkovic Palace and Burgrave's Palace. Guides are available for 50 Kč per hour.

Post Office The post office is in the third courtyard, opposite the main entrance to St Vitus Cathedral.

Money The Chequepoint exchange office, by the post office, charges a 10% commission and is open during regular castle hours.

Emergency The castle police station is on Vikářska, but its main function is to look after the president and the castle. For serious problems visit the main city police at Konviktská 14 in Staré Město.

Approach Routes Most approaches to the castle require some walking. The usual ones are from the trams in Malostranské náměstí, up Nerudova and Ke Hradu to the main gate; and from Malostranská metro station, up the Old Castle Steps (Staré zámecké schody). The approach with the least walking is along U Prašného mostu from the Pražský hrad stop on tram No 22. ■

Royal Garden The Royal Garden (Královská zahrada), on the far side of the Stag Moat, is open daily from March through October from 10 am to 6 pm. Ferdinand I built a Renaissance garden here in 1534. To the left of the entrance from U Prašného Mostu (Powder Bridge street) is the Lion's Court (Lví dvorek), recalling the animals that were once kept here in Prague's first private zoo.

The most beautiful of the garden's buildings is the **Ball-Game House** (Míčovna) built by Bonifác Wohlmut in 1569, but it's only open for exhibitions. The Habsburgs played an early version of badminton here.

Walking east through a well-kept park popular for its tulips and azaleas – Europe's first tulip garden, from where they later went to the Netherlands – you come to the bronze **Singing Fountain** (Zpívající fontána) and the **Summer Palace** (Letohrádek), also (and incorrectly) called the Belvedere Palace. The palace, built between 1538-64, is the most authentic Italian Renaissance building outside Italy, with arcades and a copper roof that looks like an inverted ship's hull. It houses temporary modern art exhibitions.

West of the Royal Garden is the former **Riding School**, which was built in 1695 and is now a venue for temporary modern art exhibitions.

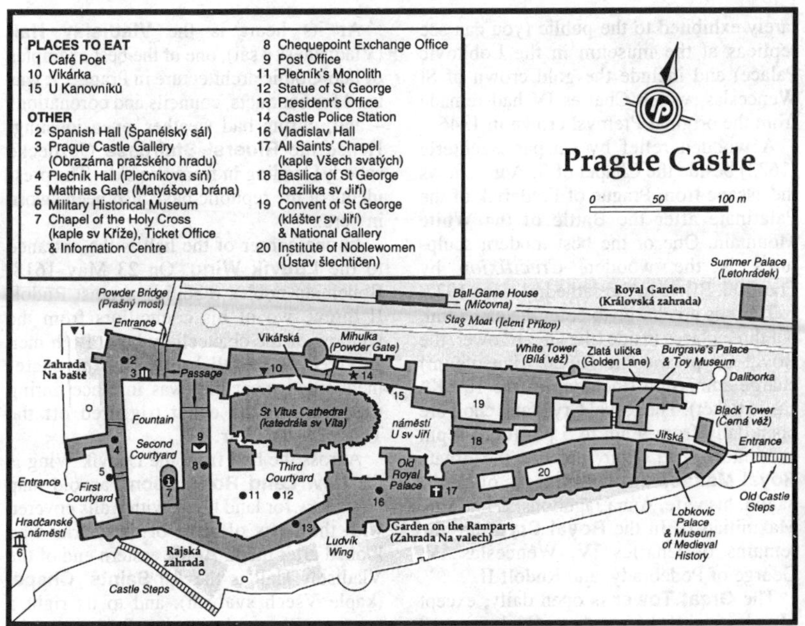

Third Courtyard

Entering from the second courtyard brings you straight to the main entrance of St Vitus Cathedral, the largest in the country, with a main steeple 97m high.

St Vitus Cathedral Blackened by age and pollution, St Vitus Cathedral (katedrála sv Víta) occupies the site of a Romanesque rotunda first built by Duke Wenceslas in 929 and enlarged in the 11th century.

The cathedral's foundation stone was laid in 1344 by Charles IV. His architect, Matthias of Arras, began work in the French Gothic style but he died eight years later. The German Peter Parler completed much of the structure in a freer, late-Gothic style before he also died, in 1399. Details were added in Renaissance and Baroque styles over the following centuries. Yet it was only in 1861, during the Czech National Revival, that a concerted effort was made to finish Parler's work. Many architects were involved, most notably Josef Mocker, and the job was finally completed in 1929.

The doorways are richly decorated with carvings of historical and biblical scenes, the most beautiful being the *Mosaic of Last Judgment* (1370-71) on the southern doorway, the **Golden Gate** (Zlatá brána). Its wrought-iron gate has scenes of people at work – a blacksmith, shoemaker, butcher.

The interior is enhanced by traditional and modern stained-glass windows. Of its numerous side chapels, the most beautiful is the **Chapel of St Wenceslas** (kaple sv Václava), built in the 14th century by Peter Parler and full of frescoes and more than 1300 semiprecious stones.

On the south side of this chapel, a small door – locked with seven locks – hides a staircase leading to the Coronation Chamber above the Golden Gate, where the Czech **crown jewels** are held. They're rarely exhibited to the public (you can see replicas at the museum in the Lobkovic Palace) and include the gold crown of St Wenceslas, which Charles IV had remade from the original Přemysl crown in 1346.

A wooden relief by Caspar Bechterle (1623) beside the Chapel of St Anne shows the escape from Prague of Frederick of the Palatinate after the Battle of the White Mountain. One of the best modern sculptures is the wooden *Crucifixion* by František Bílek, in the cathedral since 1927.

There is no charge to enter the cathedral, but three places inside (the Great Tower, the Royal Crypt and the Royal Mausoleum) charge admission (included in the 100 Kč castle ticket). The Royal Crypt and choir are open daily from 9 am to 5 pm (until 4 pm in winter). The choir includes the ornate **Royal Mausoleum** with images of Ferdinand I, his wife, Anna Jagellonská, and son, Maxmilián II. In the **Royal Crypt** are the remains of Charles IV, Wenceslas IV, George of Poděbrady, and Rudolf II.

The **Great Tower** is open daily, except Monday and if the weather is bad, from 10 am to 4 pm, and on a clear day the views are great. You can also study part of the 1597 clockworks. One of the bells, the Sigismund Bell, is the largest in Bohemia, made by Tomáš Jaroš in 1549.

In the courtyard facing the cathedral's southern entrance is Plečnik's 16m granite **monolith** (1928) dedicated to the victims of WWI. At the south-east end of the courtyard, a gate leads to the **Garden on the Ramparts** (Zahrada Na valech), an elegant manicured space with fine views over the city. The grass areas are considered sacred here and if you bend even one blade, you risk a verbal ear-bashing in Czech on the virtues of STAYING OFF THE GRASS.

Old Royal Palace The Old Royal Palace (Starý Královský Palác) is one of the oldest parts of the castle. Dating from 1135, it was originally a castle for Czech princesses; from the 13th to the 16th century it was the king's palace. It is open daily from 9 am to 5 pm (to 4 pm in winter).

At its heart is the **Vladislav Hall** (Vladislavský sál), one of the best examples of late-Gothic architecture in Prague. It was used for banquets, councils and coronations – and, during bad weather, even jousting. Hence the **Riders' Staircase** (Jezdecké schody) leading in from one side. The presidents of the republic have also been sworn in here.

In one corner of the hall is the entrance to the **Ludvík Wing**. On 23 May 1618, Bohemian nobles rebelling against Rudolf II threw two of his councillors from the window of the chancellery here. Both men survived, their fall broken by the excrement-filled moat that was in place during that era, but the event triggered off the Thirty Years' War.

Across the hall from the Ludvík Wing is the **New Land Rolls Room**, an old map repository for land titles, with walls covered with the coats of arms of the clerks who looked after them. At the eastern end of the Vladislav Hall is the **All Saints' Chapel** (kaple Všech svatých), and to its right a terrace with good views of Prague and its surrounds.

Náměstí U sv Jiří

Náměstí U sv Jiří (St George Square) is the plaza behind the cathedral, and the heart of Prague Castle. The Castle Police have an office here, in the north-west corner.

Convent of St George The very plain-looking Convent of St George (klášter sv Jiří) was Bohemia's first convent, established in 973 by Boleslav II, and closed and converted to an army barracks in 1782. It's now a branch of the National Gallery, which is open daily, except Monday, from 10 am to 6 pm. This is not covered by the 100 Kč castle ticket – you must pay an extra 50 Kč (15 Kč for students; free on the first Friday of each month). Here you'll find an excellent collection of Czech Gothic, Renaissance and Baroque art, including the jewel of 14th century Czech Gothic art, a trio of panels by the Master of the Třeboň Altar.

Basilica of St George The Basilica of St George (bazilika sv Jiří) is the striking church adjoining the convent, which was established in the 10th century by Vratislav I (the father of St Wenceslas), and is the best preserved Romanesque structure in the Czech Republic. What you see is mostly the result of attempts between 1887-1908 to give it back a pure Romanesque look. The Přemysl princes are buried here. It's open daily from 9 am to 5 pm (to 4 pm in winter). Unlike the adjoining convent, the Basilica of St George is included in the 100 Kč castle ticket.

Inside are some fine, partially preserved frescoes. Beside the altar is an unusual statue of St Ludmilla lying down with hands at prayer. On the left wall is a hole that enabled the nuns from the convent next door to communicate with the rest of the world. The basilica's acoustics make it a good venue for classical concerts.

Mihulka Powder Tower

The 20m Mihulka Powder Tower (Prašná věž), on the north side of St Vitus, was built at the end of the 15th century as part of the castle's defences. Later it was the workshop of the cannon and bell maker Tomáš Jaroš, who cast the bells of St Vitus. Alchemists employed by Rudolf II worked here. It got its name in the 19th century from the *mihule* (lamprey eels) bred in the area. Today it's a museum of alchemy, bell and cannon forging, and Renaissance life in Prague Castle, which is open daily from 9 am to 5 pm (to 4 pm in winter). Admission is included in the 100 Kč castle ticket.

On the wall opposite the entrance is a peculiar clock: a globe with the days of the week written in Czech, around which a little plane is meant to fly every hour, though it hasn't worked for years.

Jiřská Ulice

Off Jiřská, along the northern wall of the castle, is Zlatá ulička (**Golden Lane)**, also known as Goldsmiths' Lane (Zlatnická ulička). Its tiny colourful cottages were built in the 16th century for the sharpshooters of the castle guard, and later used by goldsmiths. In the 18th and 19th centuries they were occupied by squatters, and later by artists like Kafka (who stayed at No 22 in 1916-17) and the Nobel-laureate poet Jaroslav Seifert. Today, many are souvenir shops.

At the west end of the lane is the **White Tower** (Bílá věž), where the Irish alchemist Edward Kelley was imprisoned by Rudolf II for failing to discover the secret of changing iron to gold. At the east end is the **Daliborka** tower, which got its name from the knight Dalibor of Kozojed, imprisoned here in 1498 for supporting a peasant rebellion, and later executed. According to an old tale, during his imprisonment he played a violin, which could be heard throughout the castle. Smetana based his opera *Dalibor* (1868) on the tale.

Just inside the eastern gate, with its Black Tower (Černá věž), is the **Lobkovic Palace** (Lobkovický palác), built in the 1570s. On the 1st and 2nd floors is a good museum of Czech history from the arrival of the Slavs until 1848. Exhibits include copies of the Czech crown jewels (the originals are locked up in St Vitus Cathedral), the sword of Prague's executioner Jan Mydlář (who lopped off the heads of 27 rebellious Protestant nobles in Old Town Square in 1621) and some of the oldest marionettes in the Czech Republic. It's open daily, except Monday, from 9 am to 5 pm. Admission – which is not included in the castle ticket – is 30 Kč (15 Kč students).

Opposite Lobkovic Palace is the Burgrave's Palace (Purkrabství) and its **Toy Museum** (Muzeum hraček), open daily from 9.30 am to 5.30 pm; entry costs 40 Kč. It claims to be the world's second largest toy museum, with exhibits going back to Greek antiquity.

HRADČANY

Hradčany is the residential area around the west gate of Prague Castle. In 1320 it was made a town in its own right. Before it became a borough of Prague in 1598, it twice suffered heavy damage: in the Hussite

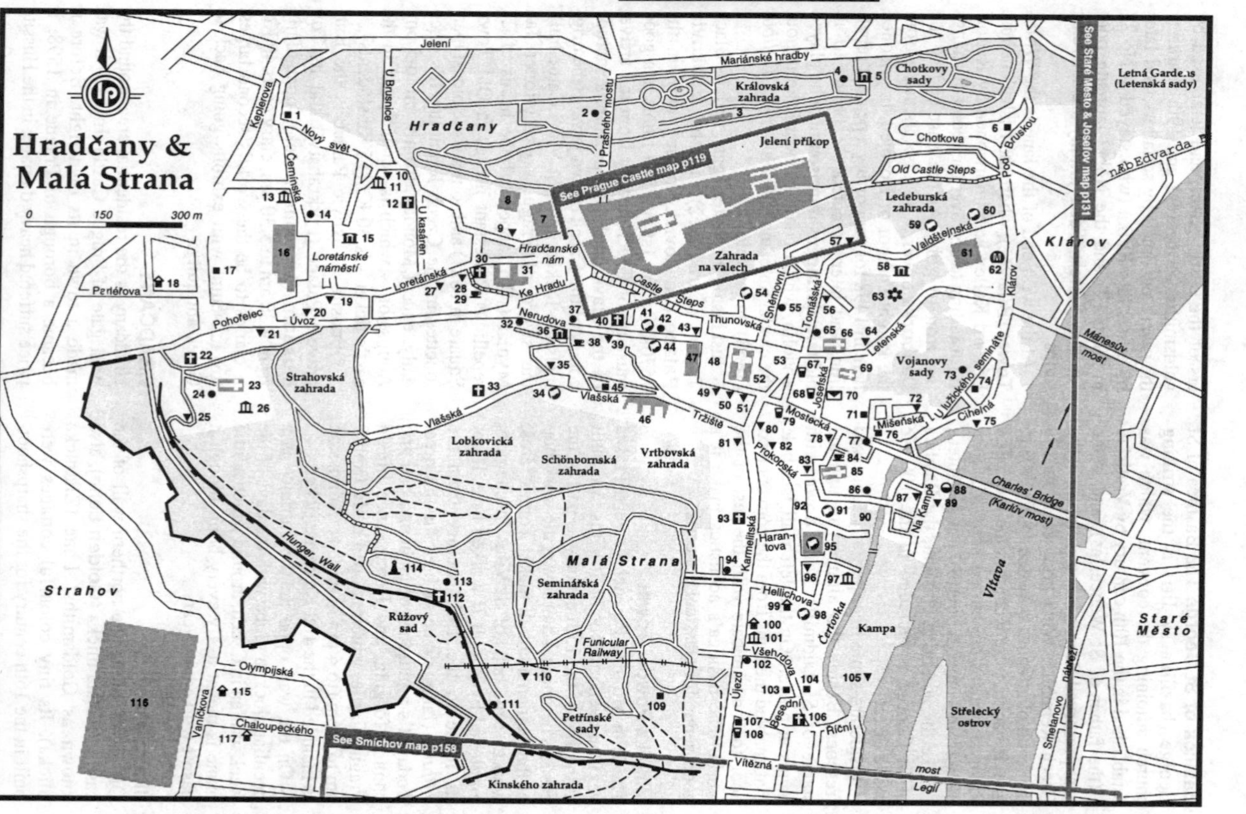
Hradčany &
Malá Strana
0
150
300 m
See Staré Město & Josefov map p131
See Prague Castle map p119
See Smíchov map p158
Letná Gardens
(Letenská sady)
Chotkovy sady
Královská zahrada
Jelení příkop
Zahrada na valech
Old Castle Steps
Castle Steps
Ledeburská zahrada
Vojanovy sady
Vrtbovská zahrada
Schönbornská zahrada
Lobkovická zahrada
Strahovská zahrada
Seminářská zahrada
Petřínské sady
Kinského zahrada
Růžový sad
Hunger Wall
Funicular Railway
Charles' Bridge
(Karlův most)
Mánesův most
most Legií
Vltava
Střelecký ostrov
Kampa
Čertovka
Hradčany
Malá Strana
Klárov
Staré Město
Strahov
Hradčanské nám
Loretánské náměstí

PLACES TO STAY

1 Pension U raka
6 Hotel Hoffmeister
17 Hotel Savoy
18 Kolej Komenského Hostel
45 Hotel Sax
71 Hotel Pod věží
74 Hotel U Páva
76 Hotel U tří pštrosů
99 Hostel Sokol
100 Entrance to Hostel Sokol
103 U Kiliána
104 Hotel Kampa
107 Hotel U Kříže
109 Travellers' Hostel
115 ESTEC Hostel
117 Hostel SPUS

PLACES TO EAT

9 U Labutí
10 U zlaté hrušky
19 Pivnice U Černého vola
20 Malý Buddha
21 Sate indonéské kuchyně
25 Peklo Restaurant
27 Renthauz
28 U stará radnice
29 Literární kavárna U zavěšeného kafe
35 Restaurant Faros
38 Zapomenutá Čajovna
39 U zeleného čaje
43 Hostinec U kocoura
49 Circle Line & Avalon Grill
50 U tří zlatých hvězd
51 Jo's Bar
56 Waldštejnská hospoda
57 Pálffy Palác club restaurace
64 Pivnice U sv Tomáše
72 U Bílé kuželky
75 Restaurace Čertovka
78 U sněděného krámu
80 J+J Mašek & Zemanova
81 U malého Glena
82 Vinárna U maltézských rytířů
83 Mazlova vinárna U malířů
84 Chiméra
87 U zlatých nůžek
89 U staleté báby
96 U modré kachničky
105 Rybářský klub
110 Nebozízek Restaurant

OTHER

2 Former Riding School
3 Ball-Game House (Míčovna)
4 Singing Fountain (Zpívající fontána)
5 Summer Palace (Letohrádek)
7 Archbishop's Palace (Arcibiskupský palác)
8 Šternberk Palace (Šternberský palác)
11 Galerie Nový Svět
12 Church of St John of Nepomuk (kostel sv Jana Nepomuckého)
13 Gambra Surrealist Gallery
14 Capuchin Monastery
15 Loreta
16 Černín Palace (Černínský palác)
22 Church of St Roch (kostel sv Rocha) & Miro Gallery
23 Strahov Monastery & Church of the Assumption of Our Lady (kostel Nanebevzetí Panny Marie)
24 Strahov Library
26 Strahov Gallery (Strahovská obrazárna)
30 Church of St Benedict (kostel sv Benedikta)
31 Schwarzenberg Palace & Military Museum
32 House of Two Suns (dům U dvou slunců)
33 Church of St Charles Borrome (kostel sv Karla Boromejského)
36 Bretfeld Palace
37 House at the Golden Horseshoe (dům U zlaté podkovy)
40 Church of Our Lady of Unceasing Succour (kostel Paní Marie ustavičné pomoci)
42 House at the Three Fiddles (dům U tří housliček)
47 Liechtenstein Palace
48 Malostranské náměstí
52 Church of St Nicholas (kostel sv Mikuláše)
53 Malostranské náměstí
55 Former Parliament House (Sněmovna)
58 Wallenstein Palace (Valdštejnský palác)
61 Wallenstein Riding School (Valdštejnská jízdárna)
62 Malostranská Metro Station (Line A)
63 Entrance to Wallenstein Garden (Valdštejnská zahrada)
65 House at the Golden Stag (dům U zlatého jelena)
66 Church of St Thomas (kostel sv Tomáše)
67 Malostranská beseda
68 Blue Light
69 Church of St Jospeh (kostel sv Josefa)
70 Post Office
73 Entrance to Vojan Park (Vojanovy sady)
77 Malá Strana Bridge Tower (Malostranská mostecká věž)
79 Scarlett O'Hara's
85 Church of Our Lady Below the Chain (kostel Panny Marie pod řetězem)
86 John Lennon Wall
88 Kampa Boat Landing
90 Velkopřerovské náměstí
92 Maltézské náměstí
93 Church of Our Lady Victorious (Kostel Panny Marie Vítězné)

continued over page

CZECH REPUBLIC

continued from previous page

94 Prague Spring (Pražské jaro) Box Office
97 MXM Gallery
101 Tyrš Museum (Tyršovo muzeum)
102 Bugaboo
106 hurch of St John at the Laundry (Kostel sv Jan na prádle)
108 Klub Újezd
111 Štefánik Observatory & Planetarium (Štefánikova hvězdárna)
112 Church of St Lawrence (Kostel sv Vavřince)
113 The Maze (bludiště)
114 Petřín Tower (Petřínská rozhlendna)
116 Strahovský Stadium (stadion)

EMBASSIES & CONSULATES
34 German Embassy
41 Italian Embassy
44 Romanian Embassy
46 US Embassy
54 UK Embassy
59 Polish Embassy
60 Belgian Consulate
91 French Embassy
95 Netherlands Embassy
98 Swedish Embassy

CZECH REPUBLIC

Wars and in the Great Fire of 1541. After this, palaces were built in place of the older townhouses, some by Habsburg nobility in hopes of cementing their power at Prague Castle.

Today Hradčany reaches as far as Pohořelec and the Strahov Monastery. There are a few government offices around Hradčanské náměstí and along Loretánská, but the rest is basically residential.

Hradčanské Náměstí

Hradčanské náměstí has kept its shape since the Middle Ages. At its centre is a plague column by Ferdinand Brokoff (1726). Several former canons' residences (Nos 6 to 12) have richly decorated façades.

The imposing **Schwarzenberg Palace** (Šwarcenberský palác) sports a sgraffito façade that stands out from the others. The Schwarzenbergs acquired the palace in 1719; it's now a pre-WWI Museum of Military History, which is open daily, except Monday, May through October from 10 am to 6 pm. Don't miss the special exhibit of tin soldiers.

Opposite is the rococo **Archbishop's Palace** (Arcibiskupský palác), bought and remodelled by Archbishop Antonín Bruse of Mohelnic in 1562, and the seat of archbishops ever since. Its wonderful interior, including a chapel with frescoes by Daniel Alexius (1600), is only open to the public on the day before Good Friday.

Diagonally behind it is the Baroque **Sternberk Palace** (Šternberský palác; 1707), home to the **National Gallery** (enter through the unassuming archway and walk down the lane) and its splendid collection of 19th and 20th century European art. The ground floor has a very good French art collection, and on the 1st floor are 14th to 16th century European paintings. It's open daily, except Monday, from 10 am to 6 pm; entry costs 50 Kč (free admission on the first Friday of each month). In summer the gallery hosts the odd classical concert. The café here is pleasant and not over-priced.

Loretánské Náměstí

From Hradčanské náměstí it's a short walk to Loretánské náměstí, created early in the 18th century when the **Černín Palace** (Černínský palác) was built. This palace today houses the foreign ministry. In 1948, the foreign minister Jan Masaryk, son of the founding president of Czechoslovakia, allegedly fell to his death from his bathroom window while desperately trying to escape from his Czech secret service tormentors. The new Communist government (which at the time claimed he committed suicide) would have had good reasons to get rid of this democrat and staunch anti-Communist, but the truth about the incident may never be known.

At the north end of the square is a **Capuchin Monastery** (1600-1602), the oldest operating monastery in Bohemia; it's closed to the public.

The Loreta Without a doubt, the square's main attraction is the Loreta, an extraordinary Baroque place of pilgrimage founded by Benigna Kateřina Lobkovic in 1626 to resemble the house of the Virgin Mary (the Santa Casa), which legend says was carried by angels to the Italian town of Loreto as the Turks were advancing on Nazareth. The duplicate **Santa Casa** (Svatá chýše) – with a stunning silver altar – is in the centre of the courtyard.

Across from it is the **Church of the Nativity of Our Lord** (kostel Narození Páně), built in 1737 by Kristof Dientzenhofer, with a bizarre interior. There are two skeletons, of Spanish saints Felicissima and Marcia, dressed in nobles' clothing with wax masks over their skulls inside.

Also in the Loreta complex is the **Chapel of Our Lady of Sorrows** (kaple Panny Marie Bolestné), featuring a crucified bearded lady, St Starosta (St Liberatou to the Spanish), daughter of a Portuguese king who promised her to the king of Sicily against her wishes. After a night of tearful prayers she awoke with a beard, the wedding was called off, and her father had her crucified. She was later made patron saint of the needy and godforsaken.

The Loreta's most eye-popping sight is the **treasury** on the 1st floor. Though its treasures have been looted at least four times over the centuries, there are still plenty of gem-encrusted chalices and sumptious jewels. Most valuable is an 89.5cm-tall monstrance called the Prague Sun (Pražské slunce), made of solid silver with plenty of gold and 6222 diamonds.

Above the Loreta's entrance are 27 bells, made in Amsterdam in the 17th century, that play *We Greet Thee a Thousand Times* every hour to an open-mouthed audience of tourists and locals.

The Loreta is open daily, except Monday, from 9 am to 12.15 pm and 1 to 4.30 pm; entry costs 40 Kč.

Strahov Monastery The Strahov Monastery (Strahovský klášter) was founded in 1140 by Vladislav II for the Premonstratensians. Today's structure, completed in the 17th and 18th centuries, functioned until the Communist government closed it and imprisoned most of the monks (they have recently returned).

Just to the north is the 1612 **Church of St Roch** (kostel sv Rocha), home to the **Miro Gallery**, which has everything from medieval icons to Andy Warhol prints. It's open daily, except Monday, from 10 am to 5 pm; entry costs 20 Kč.

The heavy white structure in the middle of the courtyard is the **Church of the Assumption of Our Lady** (kostel Nanebevzetí Panny Marie), built in 1143. Mozart allegedly played the organ here.

The monastery's biggest attraction is the **Strahov Library** (Strahovská knihovna), just to the south of the churches. This is the largest monastic library in the Czech Republic. You can look but you can't go into the two storey Philosophy Hall (Filozofický sál), with its carved floor-to-ceiling shelves lined with beautiful old tomes. Covering the ceiling is the *Struggle of Mankind to Gain Real Wisdom*, a fresco by Franz Maulbertsch. Down the hallway is the Theology Hall, with a ceiling fresco by Siard Nosecký. The library is open daily, except Monday, from 9 am to noon and 1 to 5 pm; entry costs 50 Kč.

Walk farther south to the second courtyard and the **Strahov Gallery** (Strahovská obrazárna), with Gothic icons and a smattering of Baroque and rococo paintings. It's open daily, except Monday, from 9 am to noon and 12.30 to 5 pm; entry costs 25 Kč.

MALÁ STRANA

Malá Strana (Lesser Quarter) clusters at the foot of Prague Castle. Though most tourists climb to the castle on the Royal Way, along Mostecká and Nerudova, the narrow side streets of this Baroque quarter have plenty to offer. Almost too picturesque for its own good, it's now a favourite movie and commercial set.

Malá Strana started in the 8th or 9th century as a market settlement. In 1257 Přemysl Otakar II granted it town status.

Fortifications were built by Charles IV – the so-called 'Hunger Wall' (Hladová zeď).

Malá Strana was twice nearly destroyed – during battles between the Hussites and the Prague Castle garrison in 1419, and in the Great Fire of 1541. Renaissance buildings and palaces replaced destroyed houses. In the 17th and 18th centuries the Baroque churches and palaces that give Malá Strana its present charm were built. The largely residential quarter is an historical reserve.

Nerudova Ulice

Nerudova, part of the Royal Way, is architecturally the quarter's most important street. Most of its old Renaissance façades were later 'Baroquefied'. Many still have their original shutter-like doors.

At No 47 is the **House of Two Suns** (dům U dvou slunců), an early Baroque building where the Czech poet Jan Neruda lived from 1845 to 1891. At No 34 is the **House at the Golden Horseshoe** (dům U zlaté podkovy), so-called for the statue of St Wenceslas, whose horse was said to have a gold horseshoe. The first pharmacy in Hradčany opened next door in 1749, and is still operating.

On the corner with Janský vršek is **Bretfeld Palace**, which Josef of Bretfeld made a centre for social gatherings starting in 1765; among his guests were Mozart and Casanova. At No 24 is the Baroque **Church of Our Lady of Unceasing Succour** (kostel Paní Marie ustavičné pomoci). From 1834 to 1837 it was the Divadlo U Kajetánů, a theatre that featured Czech plays during the Czech National Revival.

Most houses have emblems of some kind on them. At No 18 is one built in 1566 and named after St John of Nepomuk, patron saint of the Czechs. The **House at the Three Fiddles** (dům U tří housliček) was originally a Gothic building, rebuilt in Renaissance style in the 17th century. It once belonged to a family of violin-makers.

Úvoz, Nerudova's uphill extension, takes you to the Strahov Monastery, with fine views over the city.

Malostranské Náměstí

This is really two squares, with the Church of St Nicholas – Malá Strana's primary landmark – between them. It has been the hub of Malá Strana from the 10th century, though it lost some of its character at the turn of this century when Karmelitská was widened. Today it's a mixture of official buildings and touristy restaurants, with a tram line through the middle.

What is today a nightclub and restaurant called Malostranská beseda, at No 21, was the **Old Town Hall**, where in 1575 the non-Catholic nobles wrote the so-called *Czech Confession* (České konfese), a pioneering demand for religious tolerance addressed to the Habsburg emperor and eventually passed into Czech law by Rudolf II in 1609. In practice the demands were not fully met, and Czech nobles gathered again on Malostranské náměstí on 22 May 1618, this time at No 18, the Smiřický Palace. The next day they flung two Habsburg councillors out of a window in Prague Castle, setting off the Thirty Years' War.

Church of St Nicholas The beautiful and heavily decorated church with the huge green cupola is the Church of St Nicholas (kostel Sv Mikuláše) – one of central Europe's finest Baroque buildings. (Don't confuse it with the other Church of St Nicholas on Staroměstské náměstí.) Work was commenced by Kristof Dientzenhofer between 1732-35; his son Kilian Ignatz continued the work in the following decade, and Anselmo Lurago finished the job in 1755.

Ongoing renovations are responsible for all the scaffolding. The church is scheduled to be 'unveiled' in the summer of 1998; in the meantime, the interior remains open to the public.

The **ceiling fresco** (1770) by Johann Kracker portraying the life of St Nicholas is the largest fresco in Europe. In the first chapel on the left is a mural by Karel Škréta, into which he has painted the church official who kept track of him as he worked; he is looking out through a window in the

CZECH REPUBLIC

upper corner. The most original of the church's paintings is the *Death of St Francis Xavier* by František Palko, which can be seen in the third chapel.

The church is open daily from 9 am to 5 pm (to 4 pm on concert days and in winter); entry costs 20 Kč.

Below the Castle to Klárov

The **Castle Steps** (Zámecké schody) were originally the main route to the castle; the houses around them were built later. The steps merge at the top into Thunovská. Around the corner at Sněmovní is the **Parliament House** (Sněmovna) in the Thun Palace; today it houses parliament, but historically it was also the seat of the national assembly, which on 14 November 1918 deposed the Habsburgs from the Czech throne.

At Tomášská 4 is the **House at the Golden Stag** (dům U zlatého jelena), with a statue (1726) by Ferdinand Brokoff of St Hubert and a stag with a cross between its antlers.

Wallenstein Palace On Valdštejnské náměstí is the first of the monumental Baroque structures built by Albrecht of Wallenstein, general of the Habsburg armies. The Wallenstein Palace (Valdštejnský Palác), built between 1623-29, displaced 23 houses, a brickworks and three gardens. It was financed by Wallenstein's confiscation of properties from Protestant nobles who lost the Battle of the White Mountain. It's now occupied by the Ministry of Culture.

Beside the palace is the huge, geometrically designed **Wallenstein Garden** (Valdštejnská zahrada), open daily from May to September from 8 am to 7 pm; entry is free. In summer concerts are often held here. At the east end of the garden, the **Wallenstein Riding School** (Valdštejnská jízdárna) is home to changing exhibitions of modern art. It's open daily, except Monday, from 10 am to 6 pm.

Other Parks & Gardens The quiet **Vojan Park** (Vojanovy sady), entered from U lužického semináře, is all that remains of Prague's oldest park, established in 1248. Up the hill towards Dejvice is **Chotek Park** (Chotkovy sady), Prague's first public park, established in 1833.

South of Nerudova to Kampa

The buildings in Vlašská and Tržiště were neglected during the Communist era, and lower Tržiště is getting a total face-lift. Vlašská has another Lobkovic Palace, this one home to the **German embassy**. In summer 1989 it was besieged by thousands of East Germans trying to get into West Germany.

The fine Baroque **Vrtbov Garden** (Vrtbovská zahrada), entered through the house at No 25 on the corner of Karmelitská and Tržiště, has statues and vases by Matthias Braun and a terrace with good views of Prague Castle and Malá Strana.

In Karmelitská is the unimposing 1613 **Church of Our Lady Victorious** (kostel Panny Marie Vítězné). On its central altar is a waxwork figure of the baby Jesus brought from Spain in 1628, the so-called **Infant of Prague** (Pražské jezulátko), also known by its Italian name of Bambino di Praga. It's alleged to have worked numerous miracles – including saving Prague from the plague and from the destruction of the Thirty Years' War. It's still visited by a steady stream of Roman Catholic pilgrims from around the world. The Infant's wardrobe consists of 60 costumes donated from all over the world, changed in accordance with a religious calendar.

Maltézské Náměstí This quiet square got its name from the Maltese Knights, Czech crusaders who established a monastery beside the Church of Our Lady Below the Chain (kostel Panny Marie pod řetězem) in 1169. All that remains today are sections of the church. Beyond the statue of St John the Baptist is a music school; listen for classical melodies drifting out from the windows.

A short way east is Velkopřevorské náměstí and, opposite the French embassy, the **John Lennon Wall** (Lennonova zeď). After his death, Lennon became a pacifist hero among young Czechs, and the wall served as a monument to him and his ideas. Most western pop music was banned by the Communists, and some Czech musicians who played it went to jail. Beatles lyrics began appearing on the wall in the 1980s, and the secret police never managed to keep the wall clean. Nowadays, lightweight graffiti has buried the potent political messages.

Kampa Island Lying off the Malá Strana bank, with Charles' Bridge passing over one end, this is the most picturesque of Prague's islands. In the 13th century the town's first mill, the Sovovský mlýn, was built on Čertovka (Devil's Stream) separating Kampa from the mainland, and other mills followed. The island was settled in the 16th century; it was once used as farmland and was home to a popular pottery market.

The area along the stream and under Charles' Bridge is sometimes called 'Prague's Venice' because the buildings rise straight out of the water. **Na Kampě** square below the bridge, with its sunny cafés, makes a pleasant diversion.

The southern part of Kampa is a park, ideal for summertime naps and picnics. Near the tip of the island is another wall venue for graffiti artists. The views of Staré Město from here are excellent.

CZECH REPUBLIC

Around Újezd

On Říční is one of the oldest Gothic buildings in Malá Strana, the **Church of St John at the Laundry** (kostel sv Jana Na prádle), built in 1142 as a local parish church. Inside are the remains of 14th century frescoes. In 1784 it was converted to a laundry (hence the name). In 1935 it was reconsecrated by the Czechoslovak Hussite Church.

At Újezd 40 is the **Tyrš Museum** (Tyršovo muzeum), with exhibits on the history of Czech sport, including the Sokol movement that mobilised the masses in the name of sport early this century. It's all in Czech but some staff speak English. For 5 Kč you can listen to a multilingual tape. It's open daily, except Monday, from 9 am to 4.30 pm (Sunday from 10 am).

Petřín Hill

The 318m Petřín Hill (Petřínské sady), simply called Petřín by Czechs, is actually a network of eight parks – Strahovská, Lobkovická, Schönbornská, Vrtbovská, Seminářská, Kinského, Růžový and Petřínské. Together they comprise the largest green space in Prague. It's great for cool, quiet walks and outstanding views of the city. Once upon a time there were also vineyards, and a quarry from which most of Prague's Romanesque and Gothic buildings were assembled.

Petřín is easily accessible from Hradčany and Strahov, or you can ride the **funicular railway** (*lanová dráha*) from Újezd (at U lanové dráhy) up to Růžový Park. It runs from 9.15 am to 8.45 pm, for the same price as a bus ride (and you can use city transit tickets), though it seems to be out of order many months of the year.

Just south of the funicular railway terminus is the **Štefánik Observatory & Planetarium** (Štefánikova hvězdárna). It's open daily, except Monday, April to August from 2 to 7 pm and 9 to 11 pm, and Saturday and Sunday from 10 am to noon, 2 to 7 pm and 9 to 11 pm; during the rest of the year, hours are shorter. For 10 Kč you can view the stars if it's clear, and look at the exhibition.

North of the terminus on the summit is the **Petřín Tower** (Petřínská rozhledna), a 60m Eiffel Tower lookalike built in 1891 for the Prague Exposition. You can climb its 299 steps (20 Kč) daily from June through September from 9.30 am to 8 pm, until 6 pm in April, May and October, and on weekends only to 5 pm from November through March. Probably the best views over Prague are from here, and on clear days you can see the forests of Central Bohemia.

On the way to the tower you cross the so-called **Hunger Wall** (Hladová zeď), running from Újezd to Strahov, fortifications completed in 1362 under Charles IV. The name comes from the fact that it was to be built by the poor of the city in return for food.

Below the tower is the **Maze** (bludiště), also built for the 1891 Exposition and later moved here. Inside is a mirror maze that is good for a laugh, and a diorama of the 1648 battle between Praguers and Swedes on Charles' Bridge. It's open daily from March to October from 10 am to 4 pm, and on weekends only in November.

Opposite is the **Church of St Lawrence** (kostel sv Vavřince), with a ceiling fresco depicting the founding of the church in 991 at a pagan site. In the Middle Ages executions took place in the area. Close by is the **Chapel of the Tomb of Christ** (kaple Božího hrobu), from where the Stations of the Cross (Křížová cesta) commence along the Hunger Wall, part of the way down to Malá Strana. Each station is a small chapel with a painting of Jesus struggling through Jerusalem to his crucifixion.

STARÉ MĚSTO & JOSEFOV

A settlement and marketplace existed on the east bank of the Vltava by the 10th century. In the 12th century this was linked to the castle district by the Juditín Bridge, forerunner of the Charles' Bridge, and in 1231 Wenceslas I honoured it with a town charter and the beginnings of a fortification. This Old Town – Staré Město – has been Prague's working heart ever since. The town walls are long gone, though still traced by Národní třída, Na příkopě and Revoluční streets.

Staré Město shared in the boom when Charles IV gave Prague a Gothic face befitting its new status as capital of the Holy Roman Empire. Charles founded the Karolinum (Charles University) in Staré Město in 1348, and began the Charles' Bridge in 1357. When Emperor Josef II amalgamated Prague's towns into a single city in 1784, the Old Town Hall became its seat of government.

Many of Staré Město's buildings have Gothic insides and Romanesque basements. To ease the devastation of frequent flooding by the Vltava, the level of the town was gradually raised, beginning in the 13th century, with new construction simply rising on top of older foundations. A huge fire in 1689 contributed to an orgy of rebuilding in the re-Catholicised 17th and 18th centuries, giving the formerly Gothic district a heavily Baroque face.

The only intrusions into Staré Město's medieval layout have been appropriation for the Jesuits' massive college, the Klementinum, in the 16th and 17th centuries, and the 'clearance' of Josefov, the Jewish quarter, at the end of the 19th century.

At the centre of everything is Staroměstské náměstí (Old Town Square). If the maze of alleys around it can be said to have an 'artery', it is the so-called Royal Way, the ancient coronation route to Prague Castle.

Josefov

The slice of Staré Město within Kaprova, Dlouhá and Kozí streets contains the remains of the once-thriving mini-town of Josefov, Prague's once thriving Jewish ghetto.

The 'State Jewish Museum' (Státní židovské muzeum) is an umbrella-word for what's left of the Jewish Quarter – half a dozen synagogues, the town hall, a ceremonial hall and the powerfully melancholy Old Cemetery. In a grotesquely ironic act, the Nazis spared these to be a 'museum of an extinguished race' – thanks to which they have instead survived as a memorial to seven centuries of oppression. The Old-New Synagogue is still used for religious services; the others have been converted to exhibition halls for Europe's biggest collection of sacred Jewish artefacts, many of them saved from demolished Bohemian synagogues.

All are open from 9 am to 6 pm but closed to the public on Saturday. Sadly, the 360 Kč ticket (students 270 Kč) to the Jewish Museum (Old Cemetery, Ceremonial Hall and Maisel, Pinkas and Klaus synagogues) and the Old-New Synagogue is a rip-off – Czechs pay only 70 Kč. It is

CZECH REPUBLIC

Kafka's World

Literary Prague at the turn of the century was a unique melting pot of Czechs, Germans and Jews. Though he wrote in German, Franz Kafka is a son of Prague; he lived here all his life, haunting the city and haunted by it, needing it and hating it. One could look at *The Trial* as a metaphysical geography of Staré Město, its Byzantine alleys and passages breaking down the usual boundaries between outer and inner, private and personal; and *The Castle* is the best example of the brooding presence in the anonymous and depersonalised world of all of Kafka's novels.

Most of Kafka's life was lived around Josefov and Staroměstské náměstí (Old Town Square). He was born on 3 July 1883 in an apartment beside St Nicholas Church; only the stone portal remains from the original building. As a boy, he lived at: Celetná 2 (1888-89); 'U minuty', the Renaissance corner building that's now part of the Old Town Hall (1889-96); and Celetná 3 (1896-1907), where his bedroom window looked into Týn Church. He took classes between 1893-1901 at the Old Town State Gymnasium in the Kinský Palace on the square, and for a time his father, Hermann, ran his clothing shop on the ground floor there.

On the south side of the square, at No 17, Berta Fanta ran an intellectual salon in the early 1900s to which she invited fashionable European thinkers of the time, including Kafka and fellow writers Max Brod (Kafka's friend and biographer), Franz Werfel and Egon Erwin Kisch.

After earning a law degree from the Karolinum in 1906, Kafka took his first job. From 1907 to 1908 he worked (unhappily) as an insurance clerk with the Italian firm Assicurazioni Generali at Václavské náměstí 19. At Na poříčí 7 in northern Nové Město is the former headquarters of the Workers' Accident Insurance Co, where he toiled on the 5th floor from 1908 until his retirement in 1922.

The last place where he lived with his parents (1913-14) – and the setting for his horrific parable, *Metamorphosis* – was a top-floor flat across Pařížská from St Nicholas Church, facing Staroměstské náměstí. At the age of 33 he finally moved into a place of his own at Dlouhá 16 (on the narrow corner with Masná) where he lived from 1915 to 1917, during which time he also spent a productive winter (1916-17) at a cottage rented by his sister at Zlatá ulička (Golden Lane) 22, inside the Prague Castle grounds. By now ill with tuberculosis, he took a flat for a few months in 1917 at the Schönborn Palace at Tržiště 15 in Malá Strana (now the US embassy).

Kafka died in Vienna on 3 June 1924 and is buried in the New Jewish Cemetery in Žižkov. ■

also possible to buy a 200 Kč ticket (students pay 150 Kč and Czechs 50 Kč) just for the Jewish Museum and a 160 Kč ticket (Czechs pay 20 Kč) just for the Old-New Synagogue. The tickets for the Jewish Museum and the Old-New Synagogue can be bought at the Pinkas or Klaus synagogues. Mantas Travel Agency, Maiselova 15, sells tickets for the Old-New Synagogue only.

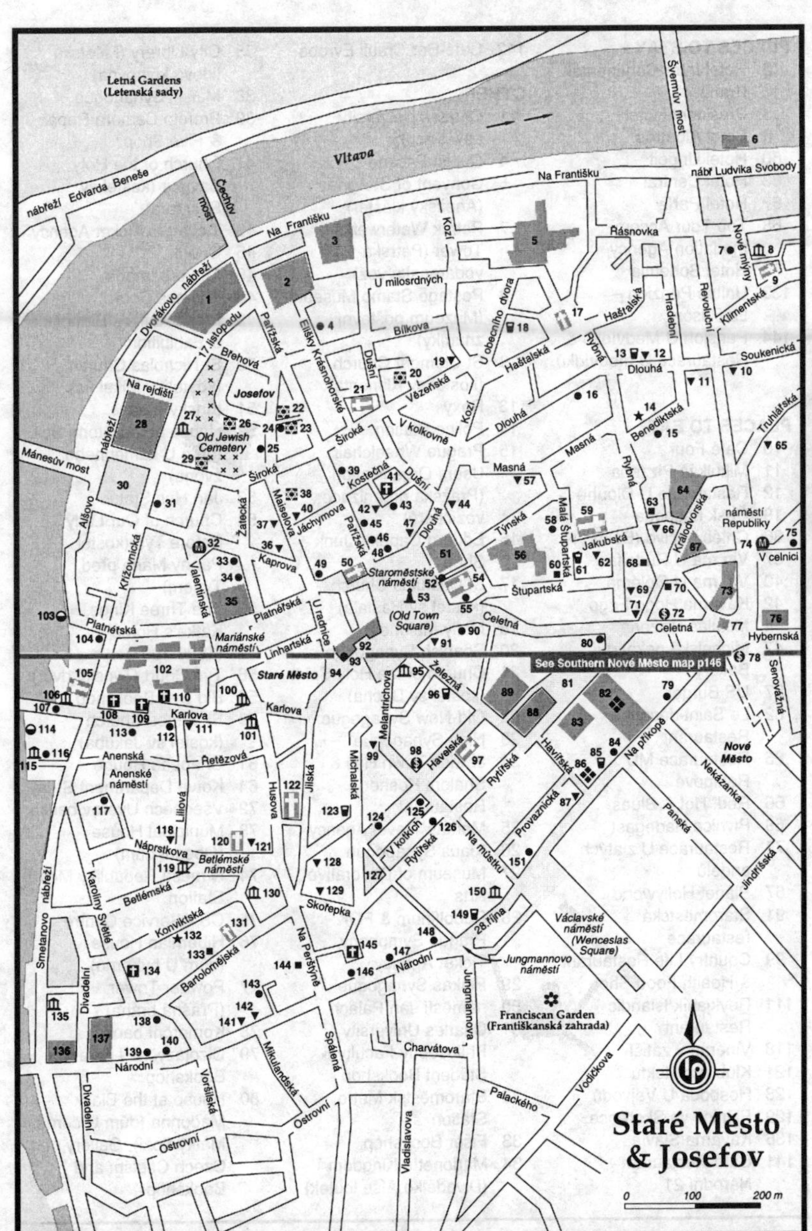

Letná Gardens
(Letenská sady)
Vltava
Švermův most
nábř Ludvíka Svobody
Na Františku
nábřeží Edvarda Beneše
Čechův most
Dvořákovo nábřeží
17.listopadu
Pařížská
Elišky Krásnohorské
U milosrdných
Kozí
Řásnovka
Revoluční
Nové mlýny
Klimentská
Hradební
Haštalská
Rybná
U obecního dvora
Bílkova
Břehová
Na rejdišti
Josefov
Old Jewish Cemetery
Dušní
Vězeňská
Dlouhá
Soukenická
Benediktská
Truhlářská
V kolkovně
Široká
Mánesův most
Masná
Kostečná
Maiselova
Jáchymova
Žatecká
Alšovo nábřeží
Křižovnická
Valentinská
Kaprova
Staroměstské náměstí
(Old Town Square)
Týnská
Malá Štupartská
Jakubská
Štupartská
Králodvorská
náměstí Republiky
V celnici
Celetná
Hybernská
Platnéřská
Mariánské náměstí
Linhartská
U radnice
Staré Město
See Southern Nové Město map p146
Senovážná
Karlova
Melantrichova
Železná
Michalská
Jilská
Husova
Havelská
Rytířská
Havířská
Na příkopě
Nové Město
Nekázanka
Panská
Jindřišská
Anenská
Anenské náměstí
Řetězová
Liliová
Náprstkova
Betlémské náměstí
Betlémská
Karoliny Světlé
Smetanovo nábřeží
Konviktská
Bartolomějská
Skořepka
Na Perštýně
V kotcích
Provaznická
Na můstku
28.října
Václavské náměstí
(Wenceslas Square)
Jungmannovo náměstí
Národní
Jungmannova
Franciscan Garden
(Františkanská zahrada)
Divadelní
Mikulandská
Spálená
Charvátova
Vorsilská
Ostrovní
Vladislavova
Palackého
Vodičkova
Staré Město
& Josefov
0
100
200 m
CZECH REPUBLIC

PLACES TO STAY

2 Hotel Inter-Continental Praha
3 President Hotel
6 Botel Albatros
60 Hotel Ungelt
63 Hotel Central
67 Hotel Paříž
68 Top Tour Accommodation Agency
70 Hotel Bohemia
133 Unitas Penzion – La Prison
144 Pension U Medvídků & Restaurace U medvídků

PLACES TO EAT

10 Café Four
11 Mikulkáš Pizzeria
12 Restaurace U Dlouhé
19 Česk hospoda
36 Chléb pečivo (Bakery)
37 Vin rna U Rudolfa
40 Vin rna U Golema
42 Kavárna Hogo Fogo
44 Mikuláš Pizzeria
47 Michelské pekařství Bakery
57 US Burger
62 Le Saint-Jacques Restaurant
65 Restaurace MD Rettigové
66 Red, Hot & Blues
69 Pivnice Radegast
71 Restaurace U zlatých andělů
87 Planet Hollywood
91 Staroměstská restaurace
99 Country Life Restaurant & Health Food Shop
111 Reykjavík Islandic Restaurant
118 Vinárna v zátiší
121 Klub Architektů
128 Hospoda U Vejvodů
129 Pivnice ve Skořepce
136 Kavárna Slavia
141 Café-Restaurant Národní 21
142 Café-Bar Craull Evropa

OTHER

1 Charles University Law Faculty
4 Cubist Façade
5 Convent of St Agnes (Anežský klášter)
7 Petrsk Waterworks Tower (Petrská vodárenská vež)
8 Postage Stamp Museum (Muzeum poštovní známky)
9 St Clement Church (kostel sv Klimenta)
13 Roxy
14 Police Station
15 Prague Wheelchair Users Organisation (Pražská organizace vozíčkářů)
16 Eduard Čapek's Junk Shop
17 St Castulus Church (kostel sv Haštala)
18 Molly Malones
20 Spanish Synagogue
21 Church of the Holy Spirit (kostel sv Ducha)
22 Old-New Synagogue
23 High Synagogue
24 Jewish Town Hall & Shalom Kosher Restaurant
25 Mantas Travel Agency
26 Klaus Synagogue
27 Museum of Decorative Arts
28 Rudolfinum & FOK Prague Symphony Ticket Agency
29 Pinkas Synagogue
30 náměstí Jan Palach
31 Charles University Philosophy Faculty & Student Bookshop
32 Staroměstsk Metro Station
33 Fišer Bookshop
34 Marionette Kingdom (Divadélko Aíše loutek)
35 City Library (Městská lidová knihovna)
38 Maisel Synagogue
39 Profoto Camera Repair & Film Shop
41 Church of the Holy Saviour (kostel sv Salv tora)
43 Ticketpro Ticket Agency
45 Čedok
46 Theatre Image
48 Thomas Cook
49 Franz Kafka's Birthplace & Exhibition
50 St Nicholas Church (kostel sv Mikul še)
51 Kinský Palace
52 House at the Stone Bell (dům U kamenného zvonu)
53 Jan Hus Statue
54 Church of Our Lady Before Týn (kostel Panny Marie před Týnem)
55 The Three Kings, Kafka's Home (1896-1907)
56 Týn Court (Týnský dvůr)
58 Big Ben Bookshop
59 St James Church (kostel sv Jakuba)
61 Chapeau Rouge
64 Kotva Department Store
72 Všeobecn Úverov banka
73 Municipal House (Obecní dům)
74 N mestí Republiky Metro Station
75 ČSA Service Centre
76 Hibernian House (dům U hybernů)
77 Powder Tower (Prašná brána)
78 Komerční banka
79 Cizojazyčná Literatura Bookshop
80 House at the Black Madonna (dům U černé Matky boží), Gallery of Czech Cubism and Bookshop

81 Old Fruit Market (Ovocný trh)
82 Myslbek Shopping Complex
83 Kolowrat Theatre
84 Fotoplus
85 Klub X
86 Dětský dům Department Store
88 Tyl (or Estates) Theatre (Tylovo divadlo)
89 Karolinum
90 Kafka's Home (1888-89)
92 Old Town Hall (Staroměstská radnice), Astronomical Clock & Prague Information Service
93 Dům U minuty, Kafka's Home (1889-96)
94 Malé námestí
95 Museum of Czech Glass (Muzeum českého skla)
96 Železná Jazz Club
97 Church of St Gall (kostel sv Havla)
98 Bank of Austria
100 Prague House of Photography
101 Czech Museum of Graphic Arts (České muzeum výtvarních umění)
102 Klementinum
103 Boat Rental
104 V Andrle Antique Shop
105 Church of St Francis Seraphinus (kostel sv Františka Serafinského)
106 Křižovník Gallery (galerie Křižovníků)
107 Old Town Bridge Tower (Staroměstská mostecká věž)
108 Church of the Holy Saviour (kostel sv Salvátora)
109 Assumption Chapel (Vlašská kaple Nanebevzetí Panny Marie)
110 St Clement Church (kostel sv Klimenta)
112 The Golden Snake (U zlatého hada)
113 Ta Fantastika Theatre
114 Boat Rental
115 Bedřich Smetana Museum
116 Opera Mozart Theatre & Lávka Disco
117 Theatre on the Balustrade (Divadlo Na zábradlí)
119 Náprstek Museum (Náprstkovo muzeum)
120 Bethlehem Chapel (Betlémská kaple)
122 St Giles Church (kostel sv Jiljí)
123 U staré paní Jazz Club
124 Havelská Market
125 Albatros Bookshop
126 Hungarian Cultural Centre
127 Old Coal Market
130 Jednorožec s Harfou Gallery
131 St Bartholomew Church (kostel sv Bartoloměje)
132 Police Station (Prague 1)
134 Chapel of the Holy Cross (kaple sv Kříže)
135 Hollar Gallery
137 Academy of Science
138 City lost & found (Ztráty a nálezy)
139 Viola Building & Viola Jazz Club
140 Topičovo Bookshop
143 Highland Group International (Internet) Café
145 Church of St Martin in the Wall (kostel sv Martina ve zdi)
146 Western Union (at Sport Turist)
147 Czech Tourist Authority (Česká centrála cestovního ruchu)
148 Kodak Processing Lab
149 Batalion
150 Wax Museum (muzeum voskových figurin)
151 Knihkupectví Na můstku (Bookshop)

Old-New Synagogue Completed about 1270, the Old-New Synagogue (Staronová synagóga) is Europe's oldest active synagogue and one of Prague's earliest Gothic buildings. You step down into it because it predates the raising of Staré Město's streets against floods.

Men must cover their heads (a hat or bandanna serves better than the complimentary paper *yarmulkas*). Around the central chamber are an entry hall, a winter prayer hall, and the room from which women watch the men-only services. The interior, with a pulpit surrounded by a 15th century wrought-iron grille, looks much as it would have 500 years ago. The 17th century scriptures on the walls were recovered from beneath a later 'restoration'. On the east wall is the Holy Ark that holds the Torah scrolls. In a glass case at the rear there are little lights beside the names of prominent deceased that light up on the anniversary of their death.

With its steep roof and 'crowstep' gables, this looks like a place with secrets, and at least one version of the golem legend ends

The Jews of Prague

Prague's Jewish community was first moved into a walled ghetto in about the 13th century, in response to directives from Rome that Jews and Christians should live separately. Subsequent centuries of persecution and official repression culminated in Ferdinand I's threat, only grudgingly withdrawn, to throw all Jews out of Bohemia.

The reign of Rudolf II saw honour bestowed on Prague's Jews, a flowering of Jewish intellectual life, and prosperity in the ghetto. Mordechai Maisel (or Maisl), mayor of the ghetto, Rudolf's finance minister and Prague's wealthiest citizen, bankrolled some lavish redevelopment. Another major figure was Judah Lõw ben Bezalel, or Rabbi Lõw, prominent theologian, chief rabbi, student of the mystical teachings of the cabbala, and nowadays best known as the creator of the mythical golem – an artificially created human being made of mud from the Vltava and brought to life by supernatural means.

When they helped repel the Swedes on the Charles' Bridge in 1648, Prague's Jews won the favour of Ferdinand III – to the extent that he had the ghetto enlarged. But a century later they were driven out of the city for over three years, to be welcomed back only because Praguers had begun to miss their business. In the 1780s Emperor Joseph II outlawed many forms of discrimination, and in 1848 the ghetto walls were torn down and the Jewish quarter was made a borough of Prague, named Josefov in honour of the emperor.

The demise of the Jewish quarter (which had slid into squalor as its Jewish population fell) came between 1893-1910 when it was cleared, ostensibly for public health reasons, slashed through the middle by Pařížská and lined with new Art Nouveau housing.

The community itself was all but wiped out by the Nazis, with almost three-quarters of the city's Jews dying of starvation or exterminated in camps. The Communist regime slowly strangled what was left of Jewish cultural life, and thousands emigrated. Today a few thousand Jews live in Prague, compared with some 50,000 in the 1930s. ■

RICHARD NEBESKÝ

here: the creature, left alone on the sabbath, runs amok; Rabbi Löw rushes out in the midst of a service, removes its magic talisman and carries the lifeless body into the synagogue's attic, where some insist it still lies.

The synagogue closes at 2 pm on Friday.

High Synagogue Opposite the Old-New Synagogue is the elegant 16th century High Synagogue (Vysoká synagóga), so-called because its prayer hall is upstairs. The building also houses a bookshop on its ground floor.

Jewish Town Hall Built by Maisel in 1586 and given its rococo façade in the 18th century, the Jewish Town Hall (Židovská radnice) is closed to the public except for the Shalom Kosher Restaurant on the ground floor. It has a clock tower with one Hebrew face whose hands, like the Hebrew script, run 'backwards'.

Klaus Synagogue In the Baroque Klaus Synagogue (Klauzová synagóga; 1694), by the cemetery, is a good exhibit on Jewish artefacts and ceremonies of birth, death, worship and special holy days.

Ceremonial Hall The Ceremonial Hall (Obřadní síň), by the cemetery entrance, was built around 1906. It has a collection of paintings and drawings by children held in the Terezín (Theresienstadt) concentration camp during WWII.

Pinkas Synagogue The handsome Pinkas Synagogue (Pinkasova synagóga), on Široká, was built in 1535 and used for worship until 1941. After WWII it was converted into a powerful memorial, with the names, birth dates, and the date of disappearance of the 77,297 Bohemian and Moravian victims of the Nazis, inscribed across wall after wall. 'Renovated' away during the Communist era it has been painstakingly reconstructed. There is now a ticket office to the Jewish Museum and the entrance to the Old Jewish Cemetery here.

Maisel Synagogue The neo-Gothic Maisel Synagogue (Maiselova synagóga), Maiselova 10, replaced a Renaissance original built by Maisel and destroyed by fire. It houses another exhibit of synagogue silver, textiles, prints and books.

Spanish Synagogue Named after its striking Moorish interior, the Spanish Synagogue (Španělská synagóga; 1868) is being reconstructed and should be open to the public by 1998.

Old Jewish Cemetery Founded in the early 15th century, the Old Jewish Cemetery (Starý židovský hřbitov) is Europe's oldest surviving Jewish cemetery, truly a monument to dignity in the face of humiliation. It has a palpable atmosphere of mourning even after two centuries of disuse (it was closed in 1787).

Some 12,000 crumbling stones (some brought from other, long-gone cemeteries) are heaped together, but beneath them are perhaps 100,000 graves, piled in layers because of space limitations. Most stones contain the name of the deceased and his/her father, the date of death (and sometimes of burial), and poetic texts. Elaborate markers from the 17th and 18th centuries have bas-relief and sculpture, some of it indicating the deceased's occupation and lineage.

The oldest standing stone (now replaced by a replica), from 1439, is that of Avigdor Karo, a chief rabbi and court poet to Wenceslas IV. The most prominent graves, marked by pairs of marble tablets with a 'roof' between them, are near the main gate. They include those of Mordechai Maisel and Rabbi Löw.

You enter the cemetery beside the Ceremonial Hall on U starého hřbitova. This is one of Prague's most popular sights, and the queue of chattering tour groups tends to break its spell.

Since this cemetery was closed, burials have been at the New Jewish Cemetery in Žižkov. Remnants of another old Jewish burial ground are at the foot of the TV tower in Žižkov.

Pařížská Třída Despite their association with the demise of the Jewish quarter, Pařížská třída ('Parisian Avenue') and adjacent streets are themselves a kind of museum. The ghetto was cleared at a time of general infatuation with the French Art Nouveau style, and its old lanes were lined with courtly four and five-storey residential buildings with stained glass and sculptural flourishes.

Museum of Decorative Arts The wonderful Museum of Decorative Arts (Umělecko-Průmyslové muzeum) of European and Czech 'applied art' arose as part of a European movement to return to aesthetic values sacrificed to the Industrial Revolution. Its four halls of 16th to 19th century furniture, tapestries, porcelain and a fabulous trove of glasswork are a feast for the eyes. Don't miss the rococo grandfather of all grandfather clocks in room No 3.

Labels are in Czech but English texts are

available in each room. What you see is only a fraction of the collection; other pieces appear now and then for single-theme exhibitions. The museum's French neo- Renaissance quarters, built in 1890, are at 17.listopadu 2, opposite the Rudolfinum. It's open from 10 am to 6 pm, except Monday and holidays.

Rudolfinum & Náměstí Jana Palacha
Náměstí Jana Palacha (or Palachovo náměstí; Jan Palach Square) is a memorial to the Charles University student who in January 1969 set himself alight in Václavské náměstí in protest of the Soviet invasion. Across the road on the philosophy faculty building, where Palach was a student, is a plaque with a spooky death mask.

Presiding over the square is the Rudolfinum, home of the Czech Philharmonic. This and the National Theatre, both designed by the architects Josef Schulz and Josef Zítek, are considered Prague's finest neo-Renaissance buildings. Completed in 1884, the Rudolfinum served between the wars as the seat of the Czechoslovak parliament. The basement has a good classical CD shop. Upstairs is the galerie Rudolfinum with temporary art exhibitions; open daily, except Monday, from 10 am to 6 pm.

The street into the square from the north is called 17.listopadu (17 November), which now has a dual meaning. It originally honoured students killed in an anti-Nazi demonstration in 1939. Exactly 50 years later, students marching in memory of that day were clubbed by police, triggering the national outrage that brought the Communist government down.

Charles' Bridge
Charles' Bridge (Karlův most) was first started by Charles IV near the foundations of the earlier Judith Bridge (Juditín most; named after Vladislav I's queen), washed away by floods. Designed by Peter Parler, it was completed about 1400, though it got Charles' name only in the 19th century. Despite occasional flood damage, it withstood wheeled traffic for 600 years without a shudder – thanks, legend says, to eggs mixed into the mortar – until it was made pedestrian-only in the 1970s. Many of the statues are a later addition (mostly Baroque) and are now copies. Some of the originals are in an exhibit in the casemates under the walls at Vyšehrad, others are in the lapidarium at the Fairgrounds in Holešovice.

Crossing the bridge is everybody's favourite Prague activity. By 9 am it's a 500m-long fairground, with an army of tourists running the gamut of hawkers and buskers, beneath an outer rank of imposing Baroque statues.

In the crush, don't forget to look at the bridge itself and the grand views up and down the river. In summer you can climb up into the old defensive towers at either end for a few crowns; they're normally open from 10 am to 6 pm. To have the bridge more or less to yourself in the high season you'd have to get here by about 8 am.

Gangs of pickpockets work the bridge during the day, so watch your valuables.

On the Staré Město side of Charles' Bridge at Křižovnické náměstí 3 is the **Křižovník Gallery** (galerie Křižovníků), which has an arch of the Judith Bridge. There are also an underground chapel with stalactite decorations and a gold treasure of the Křižovník Order – all for 30 Kč. It's open daily except Monday from 10 am to 6 pm.

Staroměstské Náměstí
The 1.7 hectare Staroměstské náměstí (Old Town Square; also called Staromák) has been Prague's heart since the 10th century, and was its main marketplace until the beginning of this century.

Despite over-the-top commercialism and swarming tourists, it's impossible not to enjoy the place – the cafés spilling onto the pavement, the buskers, performing dogs and horse-drawn beer wagons. Its pastel gingerbread Baroque and neo-Renaissance buildings have been recently restored, their façades revealing barely a hint of the square's harrowed history.

Czech History in Staroměstské náměstí (Old Town Square)

Staroměstské náměstí (Old Town Square) has been the scene of some momentous events in Czech history:

1338: John of Luxembourg grants Staré Město the right to a town hall, and a private house is purchased for the purpose
1422: Execution of Jan Želivský, the Hussite preacher who led Prague's first defenestration (literally the act of throwing somebody out of a window), touching off the Hussite Wars
1437: Execution of 57 more Hussites
1458: Election of the Hussite George of Poděbrady as King of Bohemia, in the Town Hall
21 June 1621: Beheading of 27 Protestants after the Battle of the White Mountain
1784: The town hall becomes the governmental seat of a newly unified Prague city
6 July 1915: Unveiling of the statue of Jan Hus on the 500th anniversary of his martyrdom
2 November 1918: The 270-year-old column commemorating the end of the Thirty Years' War is toppled
8 May 1945: Nazi SS units try to demolish the Old Town Hall as German troops begin pulling out after three days of fighting against Prague residents; the following day, the Red Army marches in
21 February 1948: Klement Gottwald proclaims a Communist government from the balcony of the Kinský Palace
21 August 1968: Warsaw Pact tanks roll across the square as the 'Prague Spring' comes to an end; the Jan Hus statue is draped in black. ■

RICHARD NEBESKÝ

Jan Hus Statue Ladislav Šaloun's brooding Art Nouveau sculpture of Jan Hus dominates the square just as Hus' mythic memory dominates Czech history. It was unveiled on 6 July 1915, the 500th anniversary of Hus's death at the stake. The steps at its base – being almost the only place in the square where you can sit down without having to pay for something – are a magnet for footsore visitors.

A brass strip on the pavement nearby is the so-called **Prague Meridian**. Until 1915 the square's main ornament was a 17th century column; commemorating the Habsburg victory in the Thirty Years' War, whose shadow used to cross the meridian at high noon. Three years after the Hus statue went up, and five days after Czechoslovakia's declaration of independence, the column was toppled by jubilant Praguers.

Old Town Hall The Old Town Hall (Staroměstská radnice), founded in 1338, looks like a row of private buildings with a tower at the end – the result of having been gradually assembled from existing buildings by a medieval town council short on funds.

The arcaded building at the corner, covered with Renaissance sgraffito, is called **dům U minuty**. Kafka lived in it as a child just before it was bought for the town hall.

A Gothic chapel and a neo-Gothic northern wing were destroyed by Nazi shells in 1945, on the day before the Soviet army marched into Prague. The chapel has been laboriously reconstructed.

A plaque on the tower's east face contains a roll call of the 27 Czech Protestant nobles beheaded in 1621 after the Battle of the White Mountain; crosses on the ground mark the spot where the deed was done. Another plaque commemorates a critical WWII victory by Red Army and Czechoslovak units at Dukla Pass in Slovakia.

It is *de rigueur* to wait for the hourly show by the hall's splendid **Astronomical Clock** (*orloj*). You can also view selected rooms of the town hall, the Gothic chapel and the apostles from behind the scenes for 30 Kč. The hall's best feature is the **view** from the 60m tower, open from 9 am to 6 pm daily (Monday from 11 am to 5 pm) and certainly worth the 30 Kč price.

Opposite the Old Town Hall at No 27 is the **Museum of Czech Glass** (Muzeum českého skla), open daily from 10 am to 9 pm. For the high entrance fee of 50 Kč you get a small exhibit of glass, and are shown how glass is made – and that is supposed to entice you to buy the overpriced kitsch glass made in front of your eyes.

St Nicholas Church The Baroque wedding cake in the north-west corner of the square is St Nicholas Church (kostel sv Mikuláše), built in the 1730s by Kilian Dientzenhofer. (It's not to be confused with St Nicholas Church, the masterwork of Kilian and his father, in Malá Strana.) He managed to work considerable grandeur into a very tight space, wedged at the time behind the north wing of the Old Town Hall, which was destroyed in 1945. Frequent chamber concerts are held beneath its stucco decorations, a visually splendid (but acoustically mediocre) setting.

On the corner of Maiselova is the tiny privately operated **Franz Kafka Exhibition** (Expozice Franze Kafky), which is the author's birthplace. The mediocre exhibit full of photographs is open Tuesday to Friday from 10 am to 6 pm, and Saturday to 5 pm. At the same address is a new gallery of Jan Sudek, the famous Czech photographer (he experimented with light and form). It was due to open in mid-1997.

Kinský Palace Fronting the late-Baroque Kinský (or Goltz-Kinský) Palace (Palác Kinských), at No 12, is probably the city's finest rococo façade, completed in 1765 by the redoubtable Kilian Dientzenhofer. From its balcony in February 1948 Klement Gottwald proclaimed Communist rule in Czechoslovakia.

Here the National Gallery stages changing exhibitions drawn from its collection of prints and 19th and 20th century graphics; there's also a good music shop.

House at the Stone Bell Next door at No 13, its 14th century Gothic dignity rescued in the 1960s from a second-rate Baroque renovation, is the House at the Stone Bell (dům U Kamenného Zvonu), named after the house sign at the corner of the building. Inside, two restored Gothic chapels now serve as a private gallery of modern art and a chamber-concert venue.

Church of Our Lady before Týn The early-Gothic, spiky-topped 'Týn Church' (kostel Panny Marie Před Týnem) is oddly appealing outside, but smothered in heavy Baroque inside. It's strangely hidden behind the four storey, almost contemporaneous Týn School. The entrance is up a passage beside the Caffé Italia.

Two of its most striking features are a huge rococo altar on the north wall, and the beautiful north-east entrance. On the south wall are two tiny windows that once afforded a view inside from the house at Celetná 3 – one from the bedroom of the teenage Kafka during the period 1896-1907. The Danish astronomer Tycho Brahe, one of Rudolf II's most illustrious 'consultants' (who died in 1601 of a burst bladder

CZECH REPUBLIC

Astronomical Clock

The Old Town Hall tower was given a clock in 1410 by the master clockmaker Mikuláš of Kadaně; this was improved in 1490 by one Master Hanuš, producing the mechanical marvel you see today. Legend has it that Master Hanuš was afterwards blinded so he could not duplicate the work elsewhere, and in revenge crawled up into the clock and disabled it. (Documents from the time suggest that he carried on as clock master for years, unblinded, although the clock apparently didn't work properly until it was repaired in about 1570.)

Four figures beside the clock represent 15th century Praguers' deepest civic anxieties: Vanity, Greed (originally a Jewish money-lender, cosmetically altered after WWII), Death and Pagan Invasion (represented by a Turk). The four figures below these are the Chronicler, Angel, Astronomer and Philosopher.

On the hour, Death rings a bell and inverts his hourglass, and a parade of Apostles passes two windows, nodding to the crowd: on the left side, Paul (with a sword and a book), Thomas (lance), Jude (book), Simon (saw), Bartholomew (book) and Barnabas (parchment); on the right side, Peter (with a key), Matthew (axe), John (snake), Andrew (cross), Philip (cross) and James (mallet). At the end a cock crows and the hour is rung.

On the upper face, the disk (A) in the middle of the fixed part depicts the world known at the time – with Prague (B) at the centre, of course. The gold sun (C) traces a circle through the blue zone of day, the brown zone of dusk (*CREPUSCULUM* in Latin) in the west (*OCCASUS*, D on the diagram), the black disk (E) of night, and dawn (*AURORA*) in the east (*ORTUS*, F on the diagram). From this the hours of sunrise and sunset can be read. The curved lines (G) with black Arabic numerals are part of an astrological 'star clock'.

The sun-arm (H) points to the hour (adjusted for daylight-saving time) on the Roman-numeral ring (I); the top XII is noon and the bottom XII is midnight. The outer ring (J), with Gothic numerals, reads traditional 24-hour Bohemian time, counted from sunset; the number 24 (K) is always opposite the sunset hour on the fixed (inner) face.

The moon (L), with its phases shown, also traces a path through the zones of day and night, riding on the offset moving ring (M). On the ring you can also read which houses of the zodiac the sun and moon are in. The hand with a little star at the end of it (N) indicates stellar time.

The calendar-wheel beneath all this astronomical wizardry, with 12 seasonal scenes in praise of rural Bohemian life, is a duplicate of one painted in 1866 by the Czech Revivalist Josef Mánes. You can have a close look at the beautiful original in the Museum of the City of Prague (see the Nové Město section). Most dates are marked with the name of the relevant saint; 6 July is in honour of Jan Hus. ■

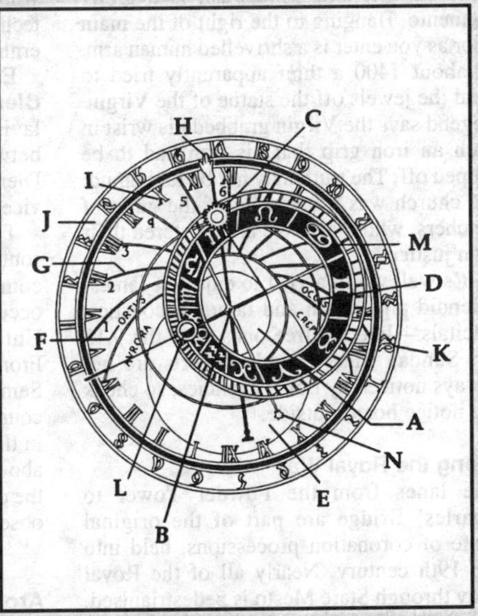

CZECH REPUBLIC

during a royal drinking-bout), is buried near the chancel.

The church's name comes from a medieval courtyard for foreign merchants, the **Týn Court** (Týnský dvůr or just Týn), behind it on Štupartská. One side of the courtyard complex has been renovated as the Hotel Ungelt.

The Týn Church is an occasional concert venue, and has a very grand-sounding pipe organ.

St James Church

The long and tall Gothic St James Church (kostel sv Jakuba), behind the Týn Court on Štupartská, began in the 14th century as a Minorite monastery church. It got a beautiful Baroque face-lift in the early 18th century. Pride of place goes to the over-the-top tomb of Count Jan Vratislav of Mitrovice, 18th century lord chancellor of Bohemia, on the north aisle.

In the midst of the impressive ceiling frescoes, gilt and whitewash is a grisly memento. Hanging to the right of the main door as you enter is a shrivelled human arm. In about 1400 a thief apparently tried to steal the jewels off the statue of the Virgin. Legend says the Virgin grabbed his wrist in such an iron grip that his arm had to be lopped off. The truth may not be far behind: the church was a favourite of the guild of butchers, who may have administered their own justice.

It's well worth a visit to enjoy St James' splendid pipe organ and famous acoustics. Recitals – like the free ones after the 9.15 am Sunday Mass – and concerts are not always noticed by ticket agencies, so check the notice board outside.

Along the Royal Way

The lanes from the Powder Tower to Charles' Bridge are part of the original route of coronation processions, held into the 19th century. Nearly all of the Royal Way through Staré Město is pedestrianised. We follow the coronation route in reverse direction from Charles' Bridge.

Klementinum To boost the power of Rome in Bohemia, Ferdinand I invited the Jesuits to Prague. Selecting one of the city's choicest bits of real estate, the Jesuits set to work in 1578 on Prague's flagship of the Counter-Reformation, the Church of the Holy Saviour (kostel sv Salvátora).

After gradually buying up most of the adjacent neighbourhood, the Jesuits broke ground in 1653 for their college, the Klementinum, which by the time of its completion a century later was second in size only to Prague Castle. When the Jesuits fell out with the pope in 1773, all of it became part of Charles University.

The western façade of the **Church of the Holy Saviour** faces Charles' Bridge, its sooty stone saints glaring down at merrymakers and the traffic ripping through Křižovnické náměstí. Alongside the church, Karlova bends in front of the little round **Assumption Chapel** (vlašská kaple Nanebevzetí Panny Marie), which was completed in 1600 for the Italian artisans who worked on the Klementinum (it is still technically the property of the Italian government).

East on Karlova you can look inside **St Clement Church** (kostel sv Klimenta), lavishly rehabilitated in Baroque style between 1711-15, to plans by Kilian Dientzenhofer. It's now Anglican, with services in English on Sunday at 11 am.

The three churches form most of the southern wall of the Klementinum, a vast complex of beautiful rococo halls now occupied by the Czech National Library. Unfortunately, it's closed to the public. From gates on Křižovnická, Karlova and Seminářská you can detour through several courtyards, and inside the library entrance in the south-east courtyard is a tiny exhibit about the Klementinum. In a courtyard at the centre of the complex is an 18th century observatory tower.

Around the Klementinum Beside the Staré Město tower of Charles' Bridge is the 17th century **Church of St Francis**

Seraphinus (kostel sv Františka Serafinského), its dome decorated inside with a fresco of the Last Judgment. The church belongs to the Order of Knights of the Cross, the only Bohemian order of crusaders.

Just south of the bridge, at the site of the former mill, is Novotného lávka, a pedestrian lane full of sunny, overpriced *vinárny*, and a grand view of the bridge and castle. At No 1, the private **Opera Mozart Theatre** is a venue for chamber concerts, opera and Sunday jazz (see Entertainment). A **museum** devoted to Bedřich Smetana, Bohemia's sentimental favourite composer, is upstairs but was closed at the time of writing.

At Karlova 18, on the corner of Liliová, the building called **The Golden Snake** (U zlatého hada) was Prague's first coffee house, opened in 1708 by an Armenian named Deomatus Damajan. It's now a T-shirt shop with an espresso machine in the corner, serving coffee in paper cups – tasteless in every sense. The whole surrounding neighbourhood in fact seems to have acquired a few too many T-shirt and cute wooden-toy shops.

At Husova 19-21, on the corner of Karlova, is a good modern-art gallery, the **Czech Museum of Graphic Arts** (České muzeum výtvarních umění; ☎ 24 22 20 68).

At Žatecká 1 is an old theatre called **Marionette Kingdom** (Říše loutek), which got a new lease on life when the respected Kladno puppet troupe moved in with a puppet show for adults – Mozart's opera *Don Giovanni* at 490 Kč a throw has been a sellout for several years now. The name 'National Marionette Theatre' was a joke that has stuck.

Malé Náměstí In the 'Little Square', the south-western extension of Staroměstské náměstí (Old Town Square), is a Renaissance fountain as well as a 16th century wrought-iron grille. Several fine Baroque and neo-Renaissance exteriors decorate some of Staré Město's oldest structures.

Celetná Ulice This pedestrianised lane from Staroměstské náměstí to the Powder Tower is an open-air museum of well-groomed, pastel-painted Baroque façades over Gothic frames.

But the most interesting façade only dates from 1912: Josef Gočár's delightful cubist front on the so-called **House at the Black Madonna** (dům U černé Matky Boží). It's at No 34, on the corner of the Old Fruit Market (Ovocný trh), with its Baroque predecessor's Madonna house-marker. It houses a small exhibit of **Czech Cubism** (Český kubismus), which flourished between 1911-19, on the 4th and 5th floors, while the lower floors have temporary exhibits. It is open daily, except Monday, from 10 am to noon and 1 to 6 pm.

Powder Tower The 65m-tall Powder Tower (Prašná Brána) was started in 1475 for King Vladislav II Jagiello, at the site of one of Staré Město's original 13 gates. After the defenestration of the mayor in 1483, the king wisely moved up to Prague Castle and the tower was left unfinished. The name comes from its use as a gunpowder magazine in the 18th century. Josef Mocker rebuilt, decorated and steepled it between 1875-86 with its neo-Gothic icing. It's open daily between 10 am and 6 pm.

Municipal House Don't miss the Municipal House (Obecní dům or just 'dům'), Prague's most beautiful building, with an unrivalled Art Nouveau interior and a façade that looks like a Victorian Easter egg.

The site was that of the royal court, seat of Bohemia's kings from 1383 to 1483, and only demolished at the turn of this century. Between 1906-12 the 'dům' was built in its place – a lavish joint effort by around 30 of the leading artists of the day, a cultural centre that was to be the architectural climax of the Czech National Revival.

The exterior mosaic, *Homage to Prague*, is set between sculptures representing the oppression and rebirth of the Czech people. You enter beneath a wrought-iron and glass canopy into an interior that is Art Nouveau down to the door knobs.

The restaurant and the *kavárna* flanking the entrance are like museums of design, and the basement club is like a gallery. Upstairs are half a dozen amazing salons – including the Lord Mayor's Hall, done up entirely by Alfons Mucha, whose paintings and posters have made him an international symbol of Art Nouveau, and Smetana Hall, Prague's largest concert hall.

Among symbolic moments here have been the proclamation of an independent Czechoslovak Republic on 28 October 1918, and meetings between Civic Forum and the Jakeš regime in November 1989.

Around the Municipal House Across náměstí Republiky looms **Hibernian House** (dům U hybernů). In 1810 this monstrous empire-style façade was affixed to a 17th century monastery church by the Viennese architect Georg Fischer, and it became the Prague Customs House. It's now an exhibition hall.

At U Obecního domu 1 is another Art Nouveau gem, the **Hotel Paříž**, built in 1907.

Na příkopě The name means 'on the moat', and with Národní and Revoluční this street marks the moat (filled in at the end of the 18th century) outside the old Staré Město walls.

This street was the haunt of Prague's German café society in the 1800s. Today it is, along with Národní, the main shopping precinct, lined with banks, bookshops, tourist cafés and a few interesting buildings:

No 20, Živnostenská banka headquarters: has a very grand Art Nouveau interior completed in 1896 by Osvald Polívka, co-architect of the Municipal House

No 19-21, Myslbek: a new (1996) and trendy shopping complex with a rather basic glass front, built by the Paris-based Caisse des dépots et consignations

No 18, Čedok headquarters: also by Polívka (1912) and linked with No 20 by a bridge over Nekázanka

RICHARD NEBESKÝ

The Municipal House is one of Prague's most beautiful buildings

No 16, Church of the Holy Cross (kostel sv Kříže): leaden empire-style block by Georg Fischer

No 12, House at the Black Rose (U černé růže): upstairs is a charming neo-Renaissance interior by Josef Fanta (1880)

No 10, Sylva-Taroucca Palace: a rococo masterpiece by Kilian Dientzenhofer (1751), and the oldest building on the street

Na příkopě runs north-west from Václavské náměstí as 28.října ('28 October'; Czechoslovak Independence Day). Just past the entrance to the metro, on the left, you can see part of a Gothic structure. Developers must have dreams about this junction – nicknamed the 'Golden Cross' (Zlatý kříž) – because it's a charmless spot now with postcard vendors and loitering heavies.

The brand-new **Wax Museum** (Muzeum voskových figurin), 28.října 13, has the usual selection of world figures and who's who in Czech history, most of which bear little resemblance to the people they are supposed to represent. It is overpriced at 120 Kč and the only worthwhile thing to see is the 'scenographic technology' display called *The Magic Prague in Storm of History*. It's an impressive display centred around a TV screen and combining images of Prague in mirrors arranged around the room. It is open daily from 10 am to 8 pm.

St Gall's Market Area

About 1230 a new market quarter, Havelské Město or St Gall's Town (named after the 7th century Irish monk who helped introduce Christianity to Europe), was laid out for the pleasure of the German merchants invited into Prague by Wenceslas I.

Modern-day Rytířská and Havelská streets were at that time a single plaza, surrounded by arcaded merchants' houses. Specialist markets included those for coal (Uhelný trh) at the west end and for fruit (Ovocný trh) at the east end. In the 15th century stalls a centre aisle of stall was built down the middle.

Havelská Market All that remains of St Gall's market today is the flower and vegetable market on Havelská, and the clothes hawkers in adjacent V kotcích. No match for the original, it's still Prague's most central open-air market.

Looking down on it, and as old as St Gall's Town itself, is the **Church of St Gall** (kostel sv Havla). Jan Hus and his predecessors preached church reform here. Its present shapely Baroque face was added in 1723. The Czech Baroque painter Karel Škréta (1610-74) is buried in the church.

At the west end of Havelská is Old Coal Market (Uhelný trh), and nearby the plain 12th century **Church of St Martin in the Wall** (kostel sv Martina ve zdi), a parish church enlarged and Gothicised in the 14th century. The name comes from its having had the Staré Město wall built around it. In 1414 the first-ever Hussite communion service *sub utraque specie* ('with both bread and wine', from which the name 'Utraquist' derives) was held here.

Karolinum Charles University – central Europe's oldest university, founded by Charles IV in 1348 – took as its original home the so-called Röthlow House at Železná 9. With Protestantism and Czech nationalism on the rise, Hus became rector in 1402 and soon persuaded Wenceslas IV to slash the voting rights of the university's German students, prompting thousands of them to leave Bohemia.

After the Battle of the White Mountain, the building, called the Karolinum, was handed over to the Jesuits, who gave it a Baroque renovation. When they were booted out in 1773 the university took it back. Damage in WWII led to remodelling and expansion.

Charles University now has faculties all over Prague, and the Karolinum serves mainly for academic ceremonies. Its finest room is the high-ceiling assembly hall upstairs. Gothic traces in the Chapel of SS Cosmas & Damian were built around 1370 (before it was made part of the university) and renovated by Josef Mocker in 1881, whose extraordinary oriel sticks out of the building's south wall. A good private gallery of modern Czech artists now occupies the ground floor.

Estates Theatre Beside the Karolinum at Železná 11 is Prague's oldest theatre and its finest neo-classical building. Opened in 1783 as the Nostitz Theatre (after its founder, Anton von Nostitz-Rieneck), it was patronised by upper-class German Praguers. It came to be called the Estates Theatre (Stavovské divadlo) – the Estates being the traditional nobility – by which name it's again known.

True Mozart fans know it as the venue for the premieres of his operas *Don Giovanni* in 1787 and *La Clemenza di Tito* in 1791. It's the only European opera house that remains, unaltered, from Mozart's day.

After WWII it was renamed the Tyl Theatre (Tylovo divadlo) in honour of the 19th century Czech playwright Josef Kajetán Tyl, whose play *Kde domov můj?* (Where is my home?) inspired the Czech national anthem, which also had its premiere in the theatre. Its Czech-language plays occasionally include simultaneous English translation. The theatre is equipped for disabled and hearing-impaired visitors.

Around the corner at Ovocný trh 6 is the 17th century Kolowrat Theatre, now also a National Theatre venue.

North-East Staré Město

The surviving buildings of the former **Convent of St Agnes** (klášter sv Anežky) are Prague's oldest standing Gothic structures, now finely restored and used by the National Gallery.

In 1234 the Franciscan Order of the Poor Clares was founded by the Přemysl King Wenceslas I, who made his sister Agnes (Anežka) its first abbess. Agnes was beatified in the 19th century, and with timing that could hardly be accidental, Pope John Paul II canonised her as St Agnes of Bohemia just weeks before the revolutionary events of November 1989.

In the 16th century the buildings were handed over to the Dominicans, and after Joseph II dissolved the monasteries they went to ruin. They've only been restored in the last few decades, and work is ongoing.

The complex consists mainly of the cloister and two churches in French Gothic style. In the **Sanctuary of the Saviour** (svatyně Salvátora) are the graves of St Agnes and Wenceslas I's queen Cunegund, and the Chapel of Virgin Mary. To the south is the smaller **Church of St Francis** (kostel sv Františka), which has a chancel where Wenceslas I is buried. Part of its ruined nave and other rooms have been rebuilt as a chilly concert and lecture hall.

The 1st floor of the **cloister** now holds the National Gallery's permanent collection of 19th century Czech paintings and sculptures, and in the last room a shifting show of works by other European artists who influenced them. Included is an eclectic selection from Josef Mánes, the foremost painter of the Czech National Revival. Don't miss the luminous little landscapes of Josef Navrátil.

Everything is open daily, except Monday, from 10 am to 6 pm. Normal admission is 50 Kč, students 15 Kč, and free for the disabled – and free for all on the first Sunday of each month. It's at U milosrdných 17, on the corner of Anežská (take any tram along Revoluční, or bus No 207 from Jan Palach Square).

The winding lanes around St Agnes and Háštalské náměstí retain a feeling of earlier times. Only furious lobbying by residents and Prague intellectuals saved from the same clearance that ravaged Josefov at the turn of the century.

South-West Staré Město

The meandering lanes and passageways in the quarter from Karlova south to Národní are Prague's best territory for aimless wandering. When the crowds thin out early or late in the day, this area can cast such a spell that it's a surprise to return to the 20th century outside its borders.

Bethlehem Chapel On Betlémské náměstí is one of Prague's most important churches, the Bethlehem Chapel (Betlémská kaple), which is the birthplace of Hussitism.

Reformist Praguers won permission for a chapel where services could be held in Czech instead of Latin, and in 1391 proceeded to build the biggest chapel Bohemia had ever seen, for 3000 worshippers. Architecturally, it was a radical departure, with a simple square hall focussed on the pulpit rather than on the altar. Jan Hus preached here from 1402 to 1412, marking the emergence of the church-reform movement from the free-talking safety of the campuses of Charles University (where he was rector).

In the 18th century the chapel was torn down. Remnants were rediscovered around 1920 and – because Hussitism had official blessing as an antecedent of Communism – the whole thing was painstakingly reconstructed from 1948 to 1954 in its original form, based on old drawings, descriptions, and traces of the original work in the outer walls that were still standing. It's now a national cultural monument.

Only the wall facing the street is brand new. You can still see some original bits in the east wall: the pulpit door, several windows and the door to the preacher's quarters. These quarters, including rooms used by Hus and others, are apparently original too; they're now used for exhibits. The wall paintings are modern, based on old Hussite tracts. The indoor well predates the chapel. Additional buildings are now being reconstructed.

It's open daily from 9 am to 6 pm, with an English text available at the door. Every year on the night of 5 July, the eve of Hus' burning at the stake in 1415, a commemorative celebration is held here, with speeches and bell-ringing.

Náprstek Museum At the west end of Betlémské náměstí is a small museum founded by Vojta Náprstek, a 19th century industrialist with a passion for both anthropology and modern technology. His ethnographical collection has exhibits from American, Australian and Pacific Ocean cultures. It is open daily, except Monday, from 9 am to noon and 12.45 to 5.30 pm. (His technology exhibits are now in the National Technology Museum in Holešovice).

St Giles Church With stocky Romanesque columns, tall Gothic windows, and oozing Baroque inside, St Giles Church (kostel sv Jiljí) is a good place to appreciate the range of Prague's architectural history.

The church, on the corner of Zlatá and Husova, was founded in 1371. The proto-Hussite reformer Jan Milíč of Kroměříž preached here before the Bethlehem Chapel was built. The Dominicans got it during the Counter-Reformation, built a cloister next door and 'Baroquefied' it in the 1730s. Václav Reiner, the Czech painter who did the ceiling frescoes a few years before his death, is buried here.

Chapel of the Holy Cross A tiny Romanesque rotunda at the west end of Konviktská, the Chapel of the Holy Cross (kaple sv Kříže) is one of the oldest buildings in Prague. It started out as a parish church in about 1100. Saved from demolition and restored in the 1860s by a collective of Czech artists, it still has the remnants of some 600-year-old wall frescoes. It is open to the public from 1 to 5 pm on weekends, and Mass is on Tuesday and Sunday at 5 pm.

Police & Secret Police Staré Město's charm goes a bit cold along Konviktská and Bartolomějská, and not just because the block between them is full of police offices. Before November 1989, the block was occupied by the StB (Státní bezpečnost, or State Security), the hated secret police. Czechs are still understandably twitchy about police of any shade, and it's a common supposition that a few former StB officers are still around, in new uniforms.

Backing onto Bartolomějská is an old convent and the once-charming 18th century **St Bartholomew Church** (kostel sv Bartoloměje), for a time part of the StB complex and recently returned to the Franciscans. The church is closed to the public, but the enterprising Unitas Penzion has rented space from the nuns, and guests can now spend the night in refurbished StB prison cells, including one where Václav Havel spent a night (see the Places to Stay section).

NOVÉ MĚSTO

Nové Město means 'New Town', although this crescent of land east and south of Staré Město was only 'new' when it was founded by Charles IV in 1348. Its outer fortifications were knocked down in 1875. The layout has been essentially preserved, although most surviving buildings are from the 19th and early 20th centuries. Many blocks are honeycombed with dark, pedestrian-only passages, some lined with shops, cafés and theatres.

Nové Město extends from Revoluční and Na příkopě east out to Wilsonova and the main railway line, and south of Národní almost to Vyšehrad. Its focus is Václavské

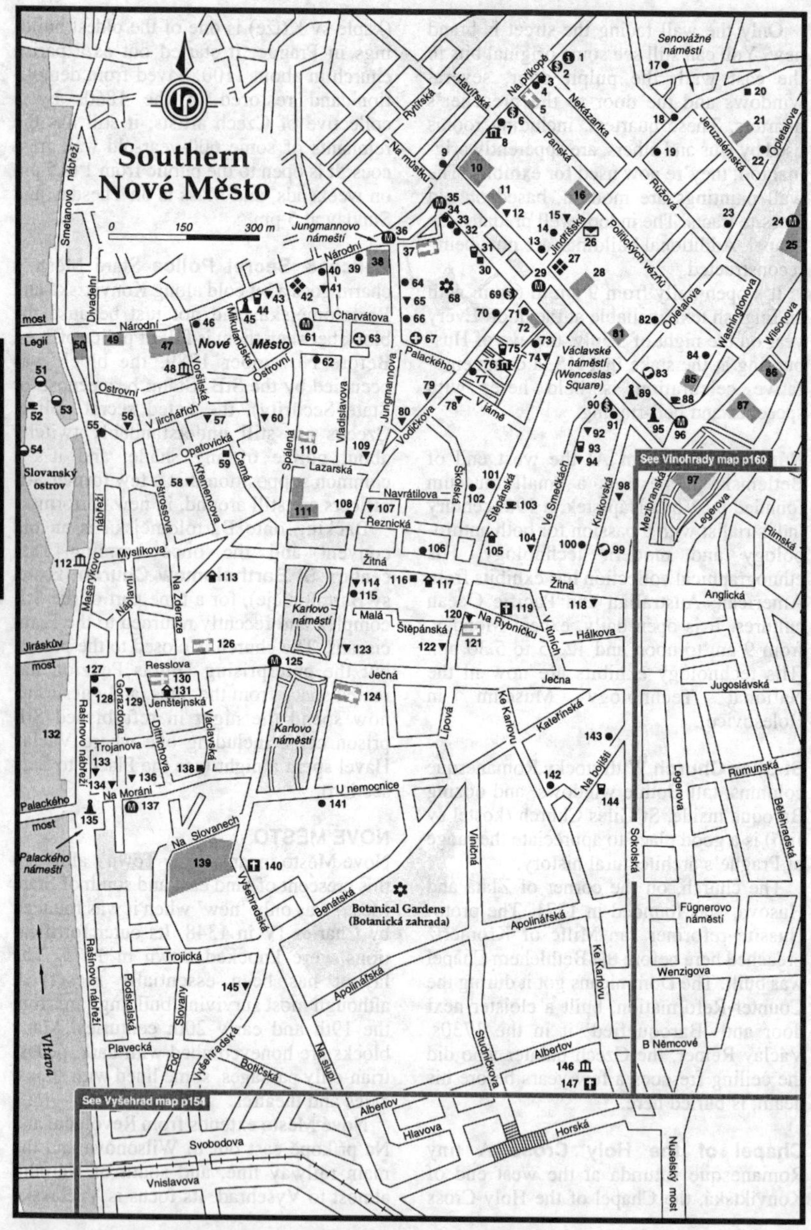
Southern Nové Město
0
150
300 m
Jungmannovo náměstí
Senovážné náměstí
Národní
Charvátova
Nové Město
Ostrovní
Václavské náměstí (Wenceslas Square)
Palackého
Vodičkova
V jámě
Lazarská
Navrátilova
Řeznická
Žitná
Karlovo náměstí
Malá Štěpánská
Ječná
Resslova
Jenštejnská
Trojanova
Na Moráni
U nemocnice
Na Slovanech
Botanical Gardens (Botanická zahrada)
Benátská
Apolinářská
Trojická
Plavecká
Botičská
Vyšehradská
Albertov
Hlavova
Horská
Svobodova
Vnislavova
Vltava
Slovanský ostrov
Smetanovo nábřeží
Masarykovo nábřeží
Rašínovo nábřeží
Most Legií
Jiráskův most
Palackého most
Palackého náměstí
See Vinohrady map p160
See Vyšehrad map p154
Anglická
Jugoslávská
Rumunská
Bělehradská
Fügnerovo náměstí
Wenzigova
B Němcové
Sokolská
Legerova
Mezibranská
Římská
Wilsonova
Washingtonova
Opletalova
Politických vězňů
Jindřišská
Panská
Na příkopě
Havířská
Rytířská
Na můstku
Nekázanka
Jeruzalémská
Růžová
Štěpánská
Ve Smečkách
Krakovská
Školská
V tůních
Na Rybníčku
Hálkova
Ke Karlovu
Kateřinská
Na bojišti
Viničná
Studničkova
Lípová
Spálená
Vladislavova
Jungmannova
Mikulandská
Voršilská
V jirchářích
Opatovická
Křemencova
Pštrossova
Myslíkova
Na Zderaze
Náplavní
Gorazdova
Dittrichova
Václavská
Divadelní
Podskalská
Na slupi
Nuselský most
CZECH REPUBLIC

PLACES TO STAY

11 Ambassador Hotel & Hotel Zlatá Husa
16 Hotel Palace
20 Libra Q Hotel
28 Grand Hotel Evropa & IfB
30 Hotel Adria
59 Hotel Koruna
81 Hotel Jalta & kino Jalta (Cinema)
85 Hotel Esplanade
105 Hostel in Club Habitat
113 Hostel in Club Habitat
116 CKM Juniorhotel
117 CKM Hostel & Travel Agency
131 Hlávkova kolej Hostel
138 City Hotel Morán

PLACES TO EAT

12 McDonald's
15 Paris-Praha kavárna
16 Delicatesse Buffet
41 Monica cukrárna
43 Gany's
52 Café
56 Pivnice U zpěváčků
57 Pizzeria Kmotra
58 U Fleků Beer Hall
60 Kavárna Velryba
65 Restaurace U Mázlů
74 Mayur Indický Snack Bar& Restaurant
78 U Purkmistra
79 McDonald's
80 Buffalo Bill's Tex-Mex Bar & Grille
88 Bonal Café
92 Sport Bar
94 Smečky dietní restaurace
98 Česká hospoda v Krakovské
103 Kavárna Cybeteria
104 Pohádka
107 Italská cukrárna
109 Country Life Restaurant & Health Food Shop
114 Pizza Taxi
118 Dátá Santóš Restaurace & Sokol Summer Hostel
120 Ice Cream Parlour
122 Jihočeská restaurace U Šumavy
123 Vinárna U Čížků
129 Diogenes
133 Vinárna Nad přístavem
134 Restaurace U Pomníku
136 Šnek Bar
145 U Čínského labužníka

OTHER

1 Prague Information Service
2 Živnostensk banka
3 Čedok
4 BTI Ticket Agency
5 Church of the Holy Cross (kostel sv Kříže)
6 Česk obchodníbanka
7 House at the Black Rose & Moser Glass Shop
8 Sylva-Taroucca Palace
9 Knihkupectví Na můstku (Bookshop)
10 Koruna Palace
13 Former Office of Assicurazioni Generali (Kafka's workplace 1907-08) & Polish Cultural Centre
14 Astera Laundry
17 Soho
18 Jindřišsk Tower (Jindřišsk věž)
19 CKM Accommodation & Travel Agency
21 Jubilee (Jubilejní) or Great Synagogue (Velk synagóga)
22 Eurolines representative Judr Jan Hofman, ČSAD Praha-Klíčov Travel Agency
23 Autoklub Bohemia Assistance
25 Main Train Station (Praha hlavní nádraží)
26 Main Post Office
27 Krone Department Store
31 Disco Astra
32 Peterkův dům
33 Baťa Shoe Store
34 Lindt Building
37 Church of Our Lady of the Snows (kostel Panny Marie Sněžné)
38 Adria Palace & Theatre
39 Balnea Spa & Travel Agency
40 Thomas Cook & Václav Špála Gallery
42 Tesco (Mj) Department Store
44 Reduta Jazz Club & Rock Café
45 Memorial to students clubbed by police on 17 November 1989
46 British Council
47 Church & Convent of St Ursula (sv Voršila)
48 Novásín Gallery
49 Nov Scéna (Laterna Magika) Theatre
50 National Theatre (Národní divadlo)
51 Boat Rental
53 Boat Rental
54 Boat Rental
55 Goethe Institute
62 Slovak institut & Bookshop
63 All-night Dental Clinic
64 Popron Music Shop
66 Supraphon CD Shop
67 All-night Emergency Medical Clinic
68 (Franciscan Garden) Františkansk zahrada
69 Československá obchodní banka
70 Kino Světozor (Cinema)
71 Wiehl House
72 Melantrich Building & Jídelna uzeniny
73 Ticketpro's Melantrich Ticket Agency
75 Lucerna Bar
76 Lucerna Palace
77 U Nováků Building & Variete Praha
82 ČTK Photo Developing Lab
83 Polish Embassy & Cultural Centre
84 A-rent a car
86 State Opera House (Statní opera)
87 National Assembly & Radio Free Europe
89 Memorial to Victims of Communism
90 American Express
91 Kino Blaník (Cinema)

continued over page

continued from previous page

93 Dramatic Club (Činoherní klub)
95 St Wenceslas Statue
97 National Museum (Národní muzeum)
99 Bulgarian Embassy
100 AghaRTA Jazz Centrum
101 Institut Français de Prague & Café
102 Rent a Bike
106 CKM Travel Agency
108 New Town Hall (Novoměstská radnice)
110 Holy Trinity Church (kostel Nejsvětější Trojice)
111 Municipal Courthouse
112 Mánes Gallery
115 Cyklocentrum Bicycle Shop
119 Rotunda of St Longinus (rotunda sv Longinus)
121 St Stephen Church (kostel sv Štěpána)
124 St Ignatius Church (kostel sv Ignáce)
126 Church of SS Cyril & Methodius(kostel sv Cyrila a Metod ěje)
127 Dancing Building (Tančící budova)
128 President Havel's Flat
130 Church of St Wenceslas in Zderaz (kostel sv Václava na Zderaze)
132 Central Quay (Vltava Cruise Boats)
135 František Palacký Monument
139 Emmaus (also Na Slovanech) Monastery
140 Church of St John of Nepomuk on the Rock (kostel sv Jana Nepomuckého naSkalce)
141 Všeobecná fakultní nemocnice
142 Villa Amerika & Antonín Dvořák Museum
143 Prague Transport Department (Dopravní podnik)
144 U kalicha
146 Police Museum
147 Church of the Assumption of the Virgin Mary & Charlemagne (kostel Nanebevzetí Panny Marie a Karla Velikého)

METRO STATIONS

24 Hlavní nádraží
29 Můstek
35 Můstek
36 Můstek
61 Národní Třída
96 Muzeum
125 Karlovo Náměstí
137 Karlovo Náměstí

náměstí (Wenceslas Square), a broad, 750m-long boulevard lined with turn-of-the-century buildings, sloping down from the National Museum towards Staré Město.

Postage Stamp Museum

Philatelists will love the tiny Postage Stamp Museum (muzeum Poštovní Známky), at Nové mlýny 2, near the north end of Revoluční, with its drawers of old postage stamps. It's open daily, except Monday, from 9 am to 5 pm.

Across the street is the **Petrská Waterworks Tower** (Petrská vodárenská věž), built about 1660 on the site of earlier wooden ones. From here, wooden pipes once carried river water to buildings in Nové Město.

Museum of the City of Prague

At Na poříčí 52, near the Florenc metro station, is the Museum of the City of Prague (muzeum Hlavního Města Prahy), built between 1896-98. The ground floor is devoted to the period up to the Battle of the White Mountain in 1620. Upstairs are knick-knacks including the Old Town Hall clock's 1866 calendar-wheel with Josef Mánes' beautiful panels.

But what everybody comes to see is Antonín Langweil's astonishing 1:480 scale model of Prague as it looked between 1826-34. It's most rewarding after you get to know Prague a bit, so you can spot the changes. Other drawings, paintings and woodcuts offer earlier 'snapshots' of the city.

The museum is open daily, except Monday, from 9 am to 6 pm. It's excellent and a bargain at 10 Kč (students 5 Kč), and there's a good English text for the asking.

Jindřišská Tower

This former watchtower or bell tower, squarely at the end of Jindřišská, was built in the 15th century.

Around the corner at Jeruzalémská 7 is the Moorish-looking Jubilee Synagogue

(Jubilejní synagóga), also called the Velká (Great) Synagogue, which dates from 1906.

Main Train Station

Have a look at the fading Art Nouveau elegance of the original section of the main train station (hlavní nádraží), designed by Josef Fanta and built between 1901-09. The exterior and vaulted interior are full of bas-relief women's faces from around the world. Under the central dome a plaque says *Praga: mater urbium* (Prague, Mother of Cities), where you can also have a drink in the new kavárna.

National Museum

Looming above Václavské náměstí is the neo-Renaissance bulk of the National Museum (Narodní muzeum), designed in the 1880s by Josef Schulz as an architectural symbol of the Czech National Revival.

The museum was founded in 1818 primarily as a museum of science, but its rocks, fossils, stuffed animals, archaeological displays and coins are pretty routine, and devoid of English labels.

Perhaps most appealing is the building itself, especially the grand stairwell, and the upper gallery of the 'pantheon' with (strangely without women) murals of Czech legend and history by František Ženíšek and Václav Brožík, and pink-bottomed cherubs by Vojtěch Hynais.

The light-coloured patches on the façade of the museum are patched-up bullet holes. In 1968, Warsaw Pact troops apparently mistook the museum for the radio station or the seat of government, and raked it with gunfire.

The museum is open from 10 am to 6 pm, except the first Tuesday of each month. The 40 Kč admission (students 15 Kč) is waived on the first Monday of each month.

Across the road to the east is the former **National Assembly** building (1973), which retains within its walls the former Stock Exchange (1936-38) and today houses Radio Free Europe. The next building beyond it is the Smetana Theatre or **State Opera Theatre** (Statní opera).

Václavské Náměstí

A horse market in medieval times, Václavské náměstí (Wenceslas Square; also called Václavák) got its present name during the nationalist upheavals of the mid-19th century, and since then it has been the scene of a great deal of Czech history. A giant Mass was celebrated in the square during the revolutionary upheavals of 1848. Here in 1918 the new Czechoslovak Republic was celebrated.

In January 1969, in protest against the Warsaw Pact invasion, university student Jan Palach set himself on fire on the steps of the National Museum, before staggering into the square and collapsing. The next day around 200,000 people showed up to honour him. It was four agonising days before he died.

Following the 17 November 1989 beating of students on Národní třída, thousands gathered here in anger, night after night. A week later, in a stunning mirror-image of Klement Gottwald's 1948 proclamation of Communist rule in Staroměstské náměstí, Alexander Dubček and Václav Havel stepped onto the balcony of the Melantrich building to a thunderous and tearful ovation, and proclaimed the end of Communism in the Czechoslovak Republic.

At the top of the square is Josef Myslbek's muscular equestrian **statue of St Wenceslas** (sv Václav), the 10th century pacifist Duke of Bohemia, 'Good King Wenceslas' of the Christmas carol – never a king but decidedly good. Flanked by other patron saints of Bohemia – Prokop, Adalbert, Agnes and Wenceslas' grandmother Ludmilla – he has been plastered with posters and bunting at every one of the square's historical moments. Near the statue, where Jan Palach fell, is a small **memorial** to him and other anti-Communist rebels.

In contrast to the solemnity of this shrine, the square beyond it has become a monument to the capitalist urge, a gaudy gallery of cafés, shops, greedy cabbies and pricey hotels. Noteworthy buildings include:

RICHARD NEBESKÝ

Statue of St Wenceslas, the same 'Good King Wenceslas' from the Christmas carol

No 1, Koruna palác (1914): Antonín Pfeiffer's Art Nouveau design with a tower; also note its tiny façade around the corner on Na příkopě
No 4, Kysela's Lindt Building: finished one year before the Baťa Shoe Store, it is one of the republic's first constructivist buildings
No 6, Baťa Shoe Store: designed by Ludvík Kysela in 1929 for Tomáš Baťa, the art patron, progressive industrialist and founder of the worldwide shoe empire
No 12, Peterka House (Peterkův dům; 1901): Jan Kotěra's Art Nouveau design
No 25, Grand Hotel Evropa (1906): the square's most beautiful fading building, Art Nouveau inside and out; have a peep at the French restaurant at the rear of the ground floor, and at the 2nd floor atrium
No 34, Wiehl House (1896): named after its designer, Antonín Wiehl; its façade is decorated with neo-Renaissance murals by Mikuláš Aleš and others
No 36, Melantrich Building: from its balcony Havel and Dubček spoke in November 1989

At the bottom, Václavské náměstí intersects the up-market shopping street of Na příkopě (described under Staré Město) at the so-called 'Golden Cross'.

West of Václavské náměstí

Lucerna Passage The most elegant of Nové Město's many passages runs beneath the Lucerna Palace at Štěpánská 61, bounded by Štěpánská, Vodičkova and V jámě. It was designed by Václav Havel, the president's grandfather (and is still partially owned by the president's sister-in-law). The Art Nouveau Lucerna complex includes theatres, a cinema, shops, a rock club-cum-restaurant, and cafés.

Of numerous entrances to the complex, the most handsome is beneath the 1902 **U Nováků** building at Vodičkova 30, itself with one of Prague's finest Art Nouveau façades, complete with mosaics of country life.

Church of Our Lady of the Snows The most sublime attraction in the neighbourhood is the Gothic Church of Our Lady of the Snows (kostel Panny Marie Sněžné) at the bottom end of Václavské náměstí. It was started in the 14th century by Charles IV but only the chancel was ever completed, which accounts for its proportions, seemingly taller than it is long. Charles had intended it to be the grandest church in Prague; the nave is higher than that of St Vitus, and the altar is the city's tallest. It was a Hussite stronghold, ringing to the sermons of Jan Želivský, who led the 1419 defenestration that touched off the Hussite Wars.

While you're here, go round and look at the church's fine Gothic entryway (and the bizarre cubist street-lamp nearby). Rest your feet in **Františkanská zahrada**, a former monastery garden built by the Franciscans, now a peaceful park in the middle of the block.

Along Národní Třída Národní třída is central Prague's 'high street', a stately row of mid-range shops and grand government buildings – above all is the National Theatre, at the Vltava end. The following are some attractions you'll encounter on a stroll west from Jungmannovo náměstí.

Fronting Jungmannovo náměstí at Národní 40 is an age-blackened, imitation Venetian palace known as the dům Látek (Cloth House) or **Adria palác**. Beneath it is the Adria Theatre, original home of Laterna Magika and meeting place of Civic Forum in the heady days of the 'Velvet Revolution'. From here, Dubček and Havel walked through the Lucerna Passage to their 24 November 1989 appearance on the balcony of the Melantrich building.

The **plaque** reading '17.11.89' with a hand making a peace sign, on the wall near No 16, is in memory of the students clubbed here on that date, an event that pushed the Communist government towards its final collapse a few days later.

West of Voršilská, the lemon-yellow walls of the **Convent of St Ursula** (klášter sv Voršila) frame a pink church, which has a lush Baroque interior that includes a battalion of apostle statues. Out the front is St John of Nepomuk, and on the building's lower right niche is a statue of St Agatha holding her severed breasts.

Across the road at No 7 is the fine Art Nouveau façade (by Osvald Polívka) of the **Viola Building**, former home of the Prague Insurance Co, with the huge letters *PRAHA* around five circular windows, and mosaics spelling out *život*, *kapitál*, *důchod*, *věno* and *pojišťuje* (life, capital, income, dowry, is insurance). Down the passage is the Viola Jazz Club. The building next door, a former publishing house, is also a Polívka design.

On the south side at No 4, looking like it has been bubble-wrapped by Christo, is Nová Scéna, the 1983 'New National Theatre' building, home of **Laterna Magika**. This pioneering multimedia production combining professional music and live actors with projected images was humbly born at the other end of the street in the Adria Theatre, but has become a permanent tourist attraction here.

Finally, facing the Vltava across Smetanovo nábřeží, is the **National Theatre** (Národní divadlo), neo-Renaissance flagship of the Czech National Revival, funded entirely by private donations and decorated inside and out by a roll call of prominent Czech artists. Architect Josef Zítek's masterpiece burned down within weeks of its 1881 opening but, incredibly, was funded again and restored under Josef Schulz in less than two years. It's now mainly used for ballet and opera performances.

Across from the theatre is the **Kavárna Slavia**, known for its river views and comically awful service, once *the* place to be seen or to grab an after-theatre meal, and only just open again after renovations.

Masarykovo Nábřeží About 200m south of the National Theatre along Masarykovo nábřeží is a grand Art Nouveau building at No 32, once the East German embassy, now occupied by the **Goethe Institut**.

Opposite this is **Slovanský ostrov** (Slav Island), a sleepy, dog-eared sandbank with river views and gardens, named after Slav conventions held here since 1848. On a wharf facing the river is a café, from where you can ride between the two Vltava weirs for 45 minutes in a 12 seat cruise boat, if there are enough people to fill it. If it's solitude you want, around the north tip of the island there are three little boat-hire places (see the Getting Around section). In the middle of the island is a 19th century meeting hall. At the south end is Šitovská věž, a 15th century water tower (once part of a mill) with an 18th century onion-dome roof.

Opposite the south end of the island is the **Mánes Gallery**, established in the 1920s by a group of artists headed by painter Josef Mánes as an alternative to the Czech Academy of Arts, and still one of Prague's better showcases for contemporary art.

Karlovo náměstí
At over seven hectares, Karlovo náměstí (Charles Square) is Prague's biggest square, although it's more of a park than a square. Presiding over it is **St Ignatius Church**

(kostel sv Ignáce), a 1660s Baroque *tour de force* designed by Carlo Lurago for the Jesuits, which is worth a look for its huge stone portal and lavish interior.

The square's historical focus is the **New Town Hall** (Novoměstská radnice) at the north end, built when the 'New Town' was new. From its windows several of Sigismund's Catholic councillors were flung to their deaths in 1419 by followers of the Hussite preacher Jan Želivský, giving 'defenestration' (literally, the act of throwing someone out of a window) its meaning and Czechs a new political tactic, and touching off the Hussite Wars. (The present tower, however, was added 35 years later.)

The white edifice along the square's north end and up Spálená is the Municipal Courthouse. The Baroque palace at the south end is known as Faust House (Faustův dům; Faust was a German mythical magician and alchemist) because of popular associations with Rudolf II's Irish court alchemist, Edward Kelley, who toiled here trying to convert lead into gold.

Resslova to the west, and Žitná and Ječná to the east; bisect central Prague. The intersection of Resslova with the square is the city's nocturnal transport hub; all eight night-time tram routes pass through here (see the Getting Around section).

Resslova Ulice

The Baroque **Church of SS Cyril & Methodius** (kostel sv Cyril a Metoděj), a 1730s work by Kilian Dientzenhofer and Paul Bayer at the corner of Resslova and Na Zderaze, was the hiding place of seven Czechoslovak paratroopers who took part in the assassination of Reinhard Heydrich, the Nazi governor of Bohemia and Moravia, in June 1942. During the German siege of the church, all were killed or committed suicide. In savage revenge for the assassination, the Germans obliterated the village of Lidice, west of Prague (see the Central Bohemia chapter).

Across Resslova is the 14th century Gothic **Church of St Wenceslas in Zderaz** (kostel sv Václava na Zderaze), the former parish church of Zderaz, a village that predates Nové Město. On its west side are bits of a wall and windows from its 12th century Romanesque predecessor.

Rašínovo Nábřeží

Though you can't go inside, this is where President **Václav Havel** first chose to live in preference to Prague Castle; his flat faces the river from the top floor of the nondescript building at Rašínovo nábřeží 78, near the corner with Resslova. Today he lives in a villa on the outskirts of Prague.

On the corner of Rašínovo nábřeží and Resslova is the most unusual and beautiful modern structure known as the **Dancing Building** (Tančící dům). Its shape suggests motion so strongly as it curves and bulges out above the footpath, that the architects originally called it the (Fred) Astair & (Ginger) Rogers Building. Surprisingly, the juxtaposition between the old and new in this heavy Art Nouveau area blends the building splendidly into its surroundings. It was completed in 1996 from a design by Vlado Milunć and the American architect Frank O Gehry.

From here the Vltava is lined in both directions with *fin-de-siècle* apartment houses. Two blocks south, in Palackého náměstí, is Stanislav Sucharda's extraordinary **monument to František Palacký** – an Art Nouveau swarm of haunted bronze figures around an intense statue of the 19th century historian and giant of the Czech National Revival.

Emmaus Monastery

A block inland from Palackého náměstí, at Vyšehradská 49, is the Emmaus Monastery (klášter Emauzy), originally named the Monastery at the Slavs (klášter Na Slovanech). It was completed in 1372 for a Slavic order of Benedictines by order of Charles IV, who persuaded the pope to allow the Old Church Slavonic liturgy here, possibly in hopes of undermining the Orthodox Church in neighbouring Slavic states. These un-Roman Catholic beginnings probably saved it from Hussite plundering. Spanish Benedictines later renamed it Emmaus.

The monastery's Gothic **St Mary Church** (kostel Panny Marie) was damaged by Allied bombs in February 1945. It wears its scars proudly. A few ceiling frescoes are still visible. The asymmetrical spires, added in the 1960s, look vaguely out of place.

Across Vyšehradská is the 1739 **Church of St John of Nepomuk on the Rock** (kostel sv Jana Nepomuckého na Skalce), one of the city's most beautiful Dientzenhofer churches. Just south on Na slupi is a large, peaceful **botanic gardens**, open every day.

East of Karlovo náměstí

Though full of hospitals, the area east of Karlovo náměstí and the botanic gardens has a few delights. Wedged between Žitná and Ječná is the 14th century **St Stephen Church** (kostel sv Štěpána), with a 15th century tower, 17th and 18th century chapels, and a neo-Gothic face-lift by Josef Mocker in the 1870s.

Behind it on Na Rybníčku is one of Prague's only three surviving round Romanesque chapels, the **Rotunda of St Longinus** (rotunda sv Longina), built in the early 12th century. It's unfortunately closed to the public.

The most arresting building in the quiet neighbourhood south of Ječná is the **Villa Amerika** at Ke Karlovu 20. This 1720, French-style summerhouse designed by (you guessed it) Kilian Dientzenhofer is now a museum dedicated to the composer Antonín Dvořák, open daily except Monday from 10 am to 5 pm.

Around the corner at Na bojišti 12 is the **U kalicha** (At the Chalice) pub. Here the hapless Švejk is arrested at the beginning of Jaroslav Hašek's comic novel of WWI, *The Good Soldier Švejk* (which Hašek cranked out in instalments from his own local pub). U kalicha is milking the connection, as you'll see from the German tour buses outside.

At the southern end of Ke Karlovu is a little church with a big name, **Church of the Assumption of the Virgin Mary & Charlemagne** (kostel Nanebevzetí Panny Marie a Karla Velikého), founded by Charles IV in 1350 and modelled on Charlemagne's burial chapel in Aachen, Germany. In the 16th century it acquired its fabulous ribbed vault, which used a revolutionary unsupported span that was attributed by some to witchcraft. The monastery buildings next door house a humdrum **Police Museum**.

Below the church you can find some of Nové Město's original fortifications, and look out at the Nuselský most (Nusle Bridge), which leaps the valley of the Botič creek to Vyšehrad, with six lanes of traffic on top and the metro inside.

VYŠEHRAD

Archaeologists know that the early Slavic tribes set up camp near Hradčany, but mythical Prague was born at Vyšehrad ('High Castle'), a crag above the Vltava south of the Botič creek valley (or Nusle valley, after the suburb through which it runs).

According to legend, the wise chieftain Krok built a castle here in the 7th century. Libuše, the cleverest of his three daughters, prophesied that a great city would rise here. Taking as her king a ploughman named Přemysl, she founded Praha and the Přemysl line of Czech rulers.

Vyšehrad may in fact have been settled as early as the 9th century. Boleslav II (972-99) may have lived here for a time. There was a fortified town by the mid-11th century. Vratislav II (1061-92) moved here from Hradčany, beefing up the walls, adding a castle and several churches. His successors stayed until 1140, when Vladislav II returned to Hradčany.

Vyšehrad then faded away; until Charles IV, aware of its symbolic importance, repaired the walls and joined them to his new town, Nové Město. He built a small palace, and decreed that coronations of the Bohemian kings should begin with a procession from here to Hradčany.

Nearly everything was wiped out during the Hussite Wars. The hill remained a ruin

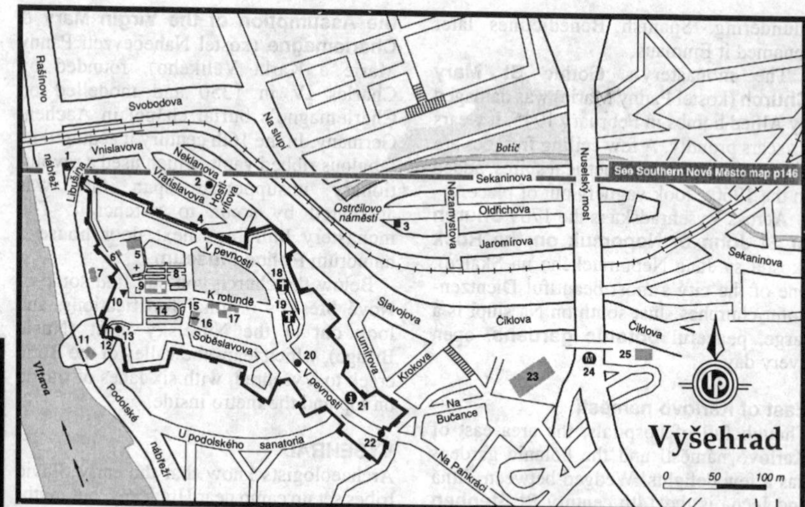

– except for a township of artisans and traders – until after the Thirty Years' War, when Leopold I refortified it.

The Czech National Revival generated new interest, both scholarly and romantic, in Vyšehrad as a symbol of Czech history. Painters painted it, poets sang about the old days, Smetana set his opera *Libuše* here. Many fortifications were dismantled in 1866, and the parish graveyard was converted into a national memorial cemetery.

Since the 1920s the old fortress has been a quiet park, with splendid views of the Vltava valley and a spot in Czech hearts. It's a great place to stroll, shake off the urban blues, and catch a bit of Prague's mythical flavour.

Vyšehrad Complex

Orientation From Vyšehrad metro station, head west past the Palace of Culture (Palác kultury) to the Tábor Gate (Táborská brána). Inside are the remains of another gate, the Špička, which includes an information centre and a café. Farther is Leopold Gate (Leopoldova brána), the most elegant of the fort's gates. The Táborská and Leopoldova were erected, and the Gothic Špička pulled down, in the course of refortification after the Thirty Years' War.

A steeper entrance through the 1842 Brick Gate (Cihelná brána, also called Pražská or Vyšehradská brána) is up from the No 18 or 24 trams on Na slupi or the No 7 tram on Svobodova. Check the fine views into the Nusle valley from the north-east bastion.

A more demanding route is up the long stairs from tram No 3 or 17 on the riverside drive, directly to Vyšehrad Cemetery.

Rotunda of St Martin The little chapel Rotunda of St Martin (rotunda sv Martina) is Vyšehrad's oldest standing building. In the 18th century it was used as a powder magazine. The door and frescoes date from a renovation about 1880.

Nearby are a 1714 plague column and the Baroque St Mary Chapel in the Ramparts (kaple Panny Marie v hradbách), dating from about 1750, and behind them the remains of the 14th century Church of the Beheading of St John the Baptist (kostelík Stětí sv Jana Křtitele).

PLACES TO STAY
3 Hotel Union
25 Hotel Forum

PLACES TO EAT
10 Restaurace na Vyšehradě

OTHER
1 Cubist House
2 Cubist House
4 Brick Gate (Cihelná brána) & Visitors' Map
5 Cultural Hall (Kulturní sín), in New Provost's House (Novéproboštsví)
6 Old Provost's House
7 Cubist Houses
8 Vyšehrad Cemetery (Vyšehradský ha) & Slavín Monument
9 Church of SS Peter & Paul (kostel sv Petra a Pavla)
11 Libuše's Bath
12 Galerie Vyšehrad
13 Foundations of Charles IV's Palace
14 Vyšehrad Gardens (Vyšehradské sady) & Myslbek statues
15 Old Archdeaconry (Staré děkanství) & Snack shop
16 Foundations of St Lawrence Basilica (bazilika sv Vavřince)
17 Former New Archdeaconry (Nové děkanství)
18 St Mary Chapel in the Ramparts (kaple Panny Marie v hradbách), Plague Pillar & remains of the Church of the Beheading of John the Baptist (kostelík Stětí sv Jana Křtitele)
19 Rotunda of St Martin (rotunda sv Martina)
20 Leopold Gate (Leopoldova brána)
21 Information Centre, Remains of Špička Gate & Café
22 Tábor Gate (Táborská brána), Visitors' Map & Café
23 Palace of Culture (Palác kultury)
24 Vyšehrad Metro Station

Vyšehrad Cemetery For Czechs the Vyšehrad Cemetery (Vyšehradský hřbitov) may be the hill's main attraction. In the 1880s and 90s the parish graveyard was made into a memorial cemetery for the cultural good and great of the land. For the real heroes, an elaborate pantheon called the Slavín (loosely, 'Hall of Fame'), designed by Antonín Wiehl, was added along the north side in 1894.

The Slavín's 50 or so graves and the 600 or so in the rest of the cemetery include those of Smetana and Dvořák, writers Karel Čapek, Jan Neruda and Božena Němcová, painter Alfons Mucha, and sculptor Josef Myslbek; a directory is at the entrance. Some of the most beautiful headstones bear names few foreigners will recognise. It's open daily in summer from 8 am to 6 pm, off-season from 9 am to 5 pm.

The Prague Spring music festival kicks off each 12 May, the anniversary of Smetana's death, with a procession from his grave to the Municipal House.

Church of SS Peter & Paul Vratislav II's Church of SS Peter & Paul (kostel sv Petra a Pavla) has been built and rebuilt over the centuries, culminating in a neo-Gothic transformation by Josef Mocker in the 1880s. The towers were added in 1903, and most of its interior frescoes were only added in the 1920s.

South of the church are the Vyšehrad Gardens (Vyšehradské sady), with four sculptures by Josef Myslbek, based on Czech legends. Libuše and Přemysl are in the north-west corner; in the south-east are Šárka and Ctirad. Šárka, one of a renegade army of women who fled across the Vltava after Libuše's death, was chosen as a decoy to trap Ctirad, captain of the men's army. Unfortunately, she fell in love with him, and after her cohorts had done him in, she threw herself into the Šárka valley (see North-West Outskirts later in this section) in remorse. The women were later slaughtered by the men of Hradčany in a final battle.

Casemates Within Vyšehrad's ramparts are many vaulted casemates (*kasematy*). At the Brick Gate, is the beginning of a guided tour through several of these chambers, now used for exhibitions and for storage of some original Baroque statues from the Charles' Bridge (others are at the Lapidárium in Holešovice). At the entrance to the casemates is also a small exhibit of Vyšehrad and Prague fortifications.

Other Attractions For a few crowns you can look at the foundations of the 11th century Romanesque **St Lawrence Basilica** (bazilika sv Vavřince). Ask for the key next door in the snack bar by the old archdeaconry.

In front of the south-west bastion are the foundations of a small **palace** built by Charles IV, which was dismantled in 1655. Perched on the bastion is the **Galerie Vyšehrad**, with temporary exhibitions, which is open daily, except Monday, from 9.30 am to 5.30 pm. Below the bastion are some ruined **guard towers** poetically named 'Libuše's Bath'.

In the north-west corner, in the former **New Provost's House** (Nové proboštství; 1874), you can catch a concert every Sunday afternoon in the high season (except July and August), ranging from jazz to chamber music.

Cubist Architecture

If you've taken the trouble to come out to Vyšehrad, don't miss a clutch of Prague's famous cubist buildings in the streets north of the Brick Gate. Cubist architecture, with its eye-catching use of elementary geometric forms, is more or less unique to the Czech Republic, particularly Prague.

The best of the lot is a simple, striking façade by the dean of Czech cubist architects, Josef Chochol, at Neklanova 30. Others by Chochol are at Libušina 3, and a villa on Rašínovo nábřeží, just before it tunnels beneath Vyšehrad rock. All date from around 1913. Other works by lesser lights can be spotted around the neighbourhood.

HOLEŠOVICE

This patch of Prague in the Vltava's 'big bend' sprang from two old settlements – Holešovice and the fishing village of Bubny. Both remained small until the arrival of industry in the mid-19th century, along with the construction of Hlávkův Bridge (1868) linking the area to Nové Město, a horse-drawn tram line, a river port and the Fairgrounds. The area became a part of Prague in 1884.

Holešovice today is an 'up-and-coming' neighbourhood, with a few good restaurants, bars and cafés, plus lots of young American, Aussie and European expatriates wandering the streets.

Fairgrounds

This vast exhibition area is the venue for a big and popular annual fair in March, when it's full of rides, candyfloss, and half of Prague having fun. Some older buildings were built for the 1891 Terrestrial Jubilee Exposition, including the Prague Pavilion (Pavilón hlavního města Prahy), which houses the Lapidárium, and the Palace of Industry (Průmuslový palác).

It's a popular weekend destination, if only for a sausage, a beer and some *dechovka* (Bohemian brass-band music). There is a 20 Kč admission charge if the **Křižík Fountain** (Křižíkova fontána) is doing its thing – namely an hourly display of water jets to recorded music; Tuesday to Friday from 6 to 9 pm, weekends from 3 to 9 pm. It's best after sunset, when it's aglow with coloured lights.

Dětský svět is a children's theatre with regular weekend performances. The **Maroldovo Panorama** is an impressive 360° diorama of the Battle of Lipany in 1434, which was a Hussite civil war battle where the Hussite Taborites lost to Hussite Utraquists; it's open Tuesday to Friday from 2 to 5 pm, weekends from 10 am.

The **Lapidárium** is a repository of some 400 sculptures from the 11th to the 19th centuries, removed from Prague's streets and buildings to save them from demolition or pollution. They include bits of Staroměstské náměstí's Marian column (torn down by a mob in 1918), and several original statues from Charles' Bridge. It's open Tuesday to Friday from noon to 6 pm, weekends from 10 am to 12.30 pm and 1 to 6 pm.

Get to the Fairgrounds on tram No 12 from nádraží Holešovice metro station; get off at the Výstaviště stop.

Stromovka Park

Stromovka Park, to the west of the Fairgrounds, is Prague's largest park. In the Middle Ages it was a royal hunting preserve, and is sometimes referred to as Royal Deer Park (Královská obora). Rudolf II had rare trees planted and several lakes dug (fed from the Vltava by a canal that still functions). You can get here across the Vltava via Císařský ostrov.

Stromovka has a **Planetárium**, open Monday to Thursday from 8 am to noon and 1 to 6 pm, Friday from 8 to noon, and weekends from 9.30 am to 5 pm. Overall, it's not as good as the Štefánik Observatory planetarium on Petřín Hill.

National Technology Museum

The National Technology Museum (Národní technické muzeum), Kostelní 42, has a transport exhibit including aeroplanes, locomotives, Škoda and Tatra cars from the 1920s and 30s, and an impressive motorbike collection. You can take a tour down a mineshaft, or learn about photography, astronomy or timepieces. The museum is open daily, except Monday, from 9 am to 5 pm; entry costs 20 Kč (free on the second Sunday of each month). From the Vltavská metro station, take tram No 1 or 25 four stops to Letenské náměstí and walk down Nad štolou and Muzejní streets.

Letná

Letná is a vast open area between Hradčany and Holešovice, with a bland assembly area to the north and a park, the **Letná Gardens** (Letenské sady), to the south. It also has postcard-perfect views of the city and the Vltava bridges. In 1261 Přemysl Otakar II held his coronation celebrations here.

The present layout dates from the early 1950s, when a 30m, 14,000 tonne statue of Stalin, the biggest monument to the man in the Eastern bloc, was erected by the Czechoslovak Communist Party, only to be blown up in 1962. Today in its place stands a peculiar **giant metronome**. Skateboarders enjoy the area.

Letná used to be the site of May Day military parades, similar to those in Moscow. In late 1989, some 750,000 people demonstrated here in support of what became known as the Velvet Revolution. In 1990 Pope John Paul II said an open-air Mass here to over a million people.

The Hanavský pavilón in the south-western corner is a charming but pricey Art Nouveau restaurant, built by Otto Prieser for the 1891 Terrestrial Jubilee Exposition.

SMÍCHOV

Smíchov is a dirtier, rougher neighbourhood that few tourists make an effort to see. In some ways Smíchov is reminiscent of pre-1989 Prague, with its handsome Baroque and Art Nouveau façades covered in thick layers of dirt and pollution. The streets of Smíchov have few souvenir shops, and working-class Czechs far outnumber the tourists.

Smíchov became part of Prague in 1838 as the suburb grew into an industrial quarter, full of chimney stacks, railway yards and the Staropramen brewery. The tone of the neighbourhood is still industrial, except where northern Smíchov meets the southern end of Malá Strana.

Kinský Gardens (zahrada Kinských)

In the peaceful Kinský Gardens (zahrada Kinských) on the south side of Petřín Hill is the wooden **Church of St Michael** (kostel sv Michala), built in the 1760s and transferred here, log by log, from the village of Medveďov in what was formerly the Czech Ukraine. Such structures are rare in Bohemia, though still common in Ukraine and north-eastern Slovakia.

The Pink Tank

Smíchov meets Malá Strana at náměstí Kinských, formerly náměstí Sovětských

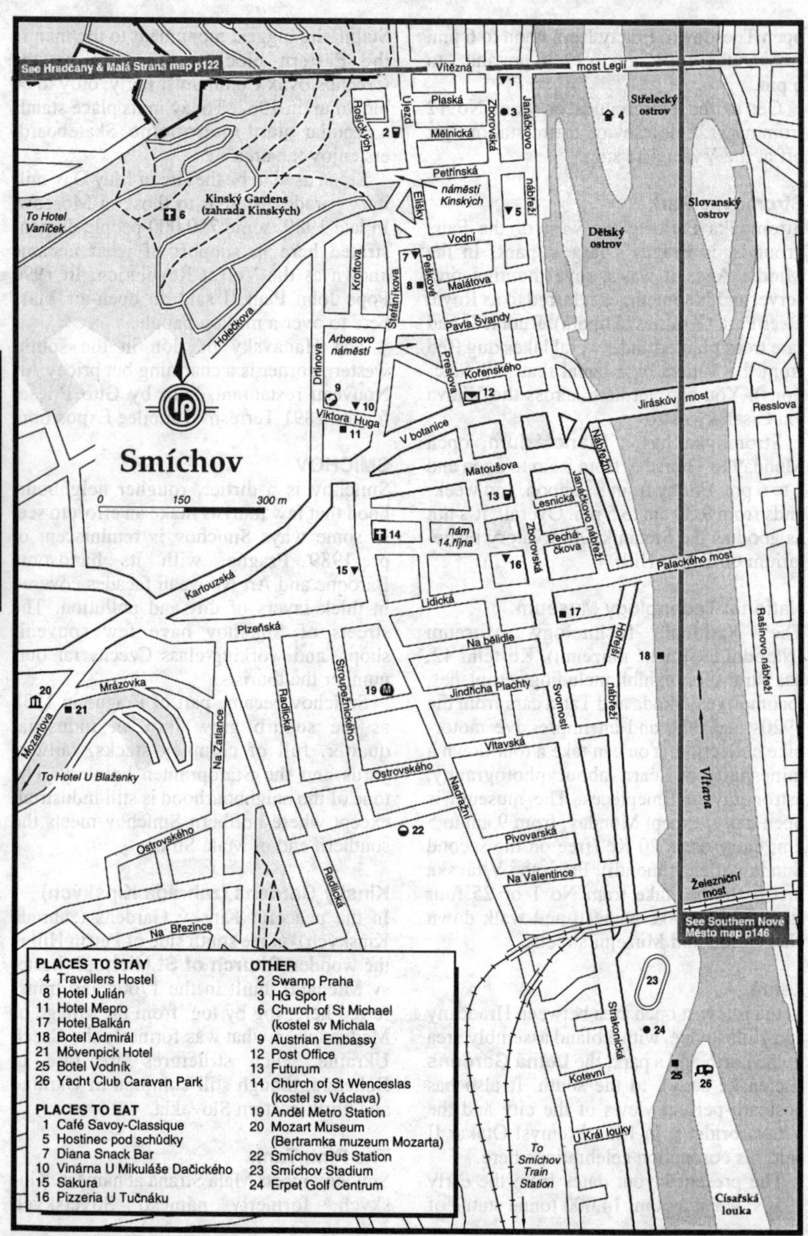

CZECH REPUBLIC

tankistů (Square of Soviet Tank Drivers), which was named in memory of Soviet soldiers who marched into Prague on 9 May 1945. At the intersection stood tank No 23, allegedly the first to enter the city under General Lelyushenko – in fact, the general had no such JS1 heavy tanks, and this one was a later donation to the city.

In 1991, artist David Černý decided that the tank, being a weapon of destruction, was an inappropriate monument to the Soviet soldiers, and painted it pink. The authorities had it painted green again, and charged Černý with a crime against the state. This infuriated many parliamentarians, and 12 of them painted the tank pink again. Their parliamentary immunity saved them from arrest and secured the release of Černý.

After complaints from the former Soviet Union, the tank was removed. Only a grassy patch remains, where each 9 May a few die-hard Communists celebrate their Liberation Day.

Bertramka

Mozart stayed at this elegant 17th century villa during his visits to Prague in 1787 and 1791, as guest of composer František Dušek. Here he finished his opera *Don Giovanni*. Today the house, at Mozartova 169, houses a modest **Mozart Museum** (Bertramka muzeum Mozarta). Summer concerts and other events are held here, and the adjacent café is a pleasant respite from hectic Smíchov. The museum is open daily from 9.30 am to 6 pm (to 5 pm in winter); entry costs 50 Kč. Take tram No 4, 7 or 9 from the Anděl metro station.

TROJA

Facing the Vltava north of the 'big bend' is the recently renovated **Troja Castle** (Trojský zámek), a 17th century Baroque chateau with a mob of stone giants on the balustrade above its French gardens. On the walls and ceiling of the main hall is a vast, sycophantic mural depicting the Habsburgs in full transcendental glory. The chateau houses part of the National Gallery's collection of 19th century Czech paintings and sculptures. It's open daily, except Monday, from 10 am to 6 pm (gardens to 7 pm); entry costs 80 Kč.

Across the road is the city **zoo**, with 1960 animals caged or fenced on 45 hectares of wooded, hillside grounds. Pride of the place, at the top of the hill, goes to a herd of Przewalski's horses, little Mongolian steppe-dwellers that have been successfully bred here. A rackety funicular railway climbs the hill for a few crowns in the summer. The zoo is open daily from 9 am to 6 pm. Outside the entrance is a good place to eat, *Restaurant Altán u Rudolfa II*, and another cheaper and plainer *restaurace* (open to 10 pm) and an outdoor beer hall.

It's a short walk north to a branch of the **botanic gardens**, open daily from April through October from 9 am to 6 pm.

To reach Troja, take bus No 112 from nádraží Holešovice metro station. Or, in summer (except Monday), take the boat: excursions leave the pier by Palackého most at 9.30 am and 1.30 pm (Troja is the final stop), and return at noon and 5 pm. A round-trip ticket is 40 Kč.

VINOHRADY

Vinohrady is the district south-east of the National Museum and main train station. The name refers to vineyards that grew here centuries ago.

Náměstí Míru

Vinohrady's physical and commercial heart is náměstí Míru (Peace Square), dominated by the brick neo-Gothic **St Ludmilla Church** (kostel sv Ludmily). Right behind it at No 9 is the neo-Renaissance **National House** (Národní dům, also called Kulturní dům), with exhibit and concert halls. On the north side of the square is the 1909 **Vinohrady Theatre** (divadlo na Vinohradech), a popular drama venue.

Though relatively close to the centre of Prague, the tree-shaded neighbourhood south from the square to Havlíčkovy sady, with genteel, turn-of-the-century mansions in every 'neo' style, makes a peaceful stroll.

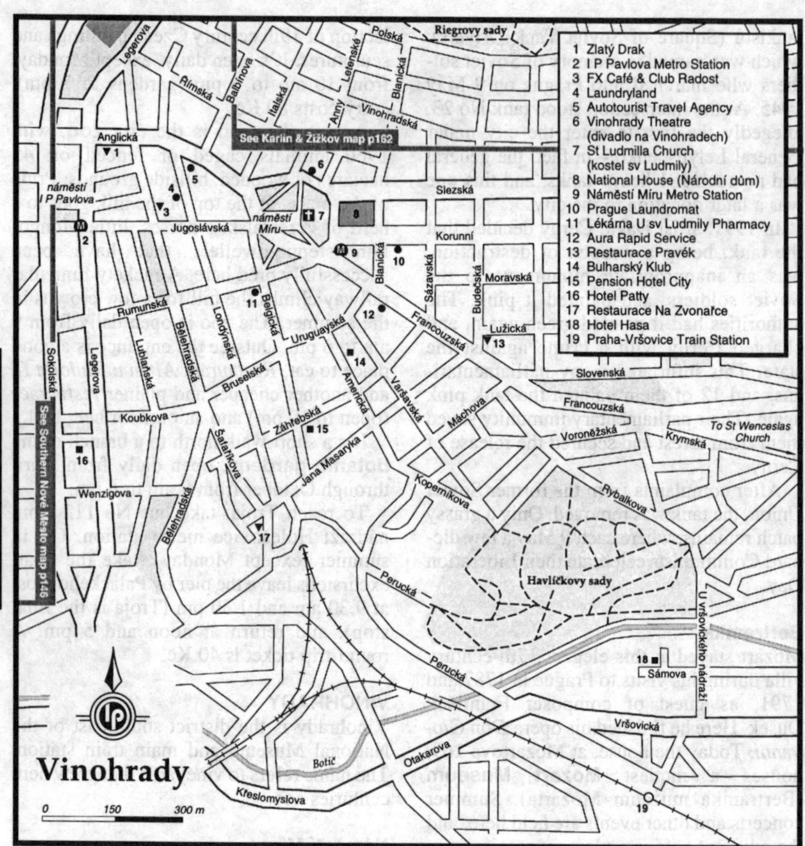

Church of the Most Sacred Heart of Our Lord

With its perforated brickwork, outsize clock tower and ultra-simple interior, the Church of the Most Sacred Heart of Our Lord (kostel Nejsvětějšího Srdce Páně) is brash and lovely at the same time and is probably Prague's most original church. Completed in 1932, it is the work of Josef Plečnik, the Slovenian architect who also raised a few eyebrows with his additions to Prague Castle. It's in náměstí Jiřího z Poděbrad, by the metro station of the same name.

St Wenceslas Church

Another surprise from the same period is Josef Gočár's 1930 constructivist St Wenceslas Church (kostel sv Václava), with its fragile-looking tower, climbing a hillside at náměstí Svatopluka Čecha. To get to it take tram No 4 or 22 from Karlovo náměstí, or walk the 800m east from Havlíčkovy sady.

ŽIŽKOV

Named after the one-eyed Hussite hero, General Jan Žižka, who whipped Emperor

Sigismund of Luxembourg and his army on a hill here in 1420, Žižkov has always been a rough-and-ready neighbourhood, working class and full of revolutionary fervour well before 1948, but now it's fairly middle class. The turn-of-the-century streets near the centre are slowly getting a face-lift now, but many are run-down and depressing. There is little for visitors except the highest concentration of pubs in Prague, some nightclubs, views from Žižkov Hill and Prague's futuristic TV Tower, and several melancholy cemeteries.

Žižkov (or Vítkov) Hill

The famous battle of 1420 took place on this long mound separating the Žižkov and Karlín districts. From beside the colossal 1950 equestrian statue of the general you can enjoy superior views across Staré Město to Prague Castle.

Behind you is the grandiose **National Memorial** (Národní památník), completed around 1930 as a memorial to the Czechoslovak 'unknown soldier' but hijacked as a mausoleum for the Communist leader Klement Gottwald (whose body, mummified Lenin-style, is said to have been mostly latex by the time it was finally put in the ground). The memorial is now closed, weedy and neglected.

From Florenc or the main train station, walk along Husitská; after the first railway bridge, climb to the left up U památníku. Battle enthusiasts may enjoy the **Military Museum** (muzeum odboje a dějin armády) on the way up.

TV Tower

Prague's tallest, ugliest landmark is the 216m TV Tower (Televizní věž), erected in the 1970s. For 25 Kč you can ride a high-speed elevator up for views right out past the edges of the city. But you're actually *too* high to see the city skyline or much detail, so it's a bit of a disappointment.

The tower was built on the site of a **Jewish cemetery** that operated until 1890, after Josefov's was shut. What's left of the cemetery is just north of the tower. The area is called Mahlerovy sady (Mahler Park), but even though there is plenty of grass only a few trees are growing in the cemetery.

The tower's viewing area is open from 11 am to 10 pm, and the Restaurace Bohemia (at 63m) from 11 am to midnight. It's a few blocks north-east of the Jiřího z Poděbrad metro station.

Olšany Cemetery & the Grave of Jan Palach

Jan Palach, the university student who set himself on fire in January 1969 after the Soviet invasion, was buried in Olšany Cemetery (Olšanské hřbitovy), Prague's main cemetery. When his grave became a focus for demonstrations, the remains were moved in 1974 to his home village, but were re-interred here in 1990.

The cemetery was founded in 1680 during a plague epidemic. Its oldest stones are in the north-west corner, near the 17th century **St Roch Chapel** (kaple sv Rocha).

From Flora metro station, walk east on Vinohradská to the central entrance or take any tram one stop. Turn right and walk about 50m to Palach's grave. The cemetery is open from 8 am to 7 pm from May through September, to 6 pm in March and April, and from 9 am to 4 pm in winter.

New Jewish Cemetery

Franz Kafka is buried in this sad, overgrown graveyard, opened around 1890 when the previous Jewish cemetery – now at the foot of the TV Tower – was closed. The entrance is beside Želivského metro station, and the grave of Kafka and his parents is to the right, about two-thirds of the way along the front wall. Men should cover their heads (a handkerchief will do). The cemetery is closed on Friday and Saturday.

NORTH-WEST OUTSKIRTS

The area north-west of Prague's centre stretches from eastern Dejvice out to the vast housing estates in the north. It also takes in the green Šárka valley and the great battleground at White Mountain.

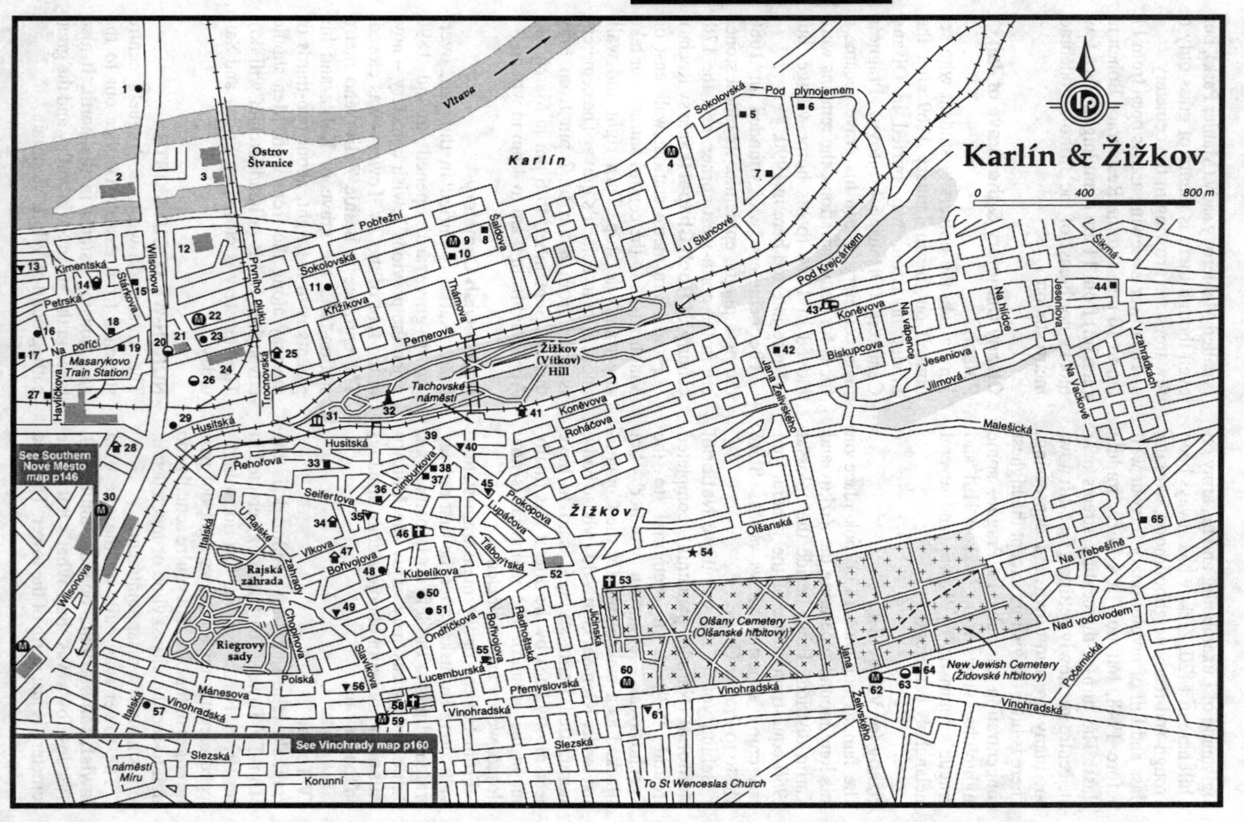
Karlín & Žižkov
0
400
800 m
Vltava
Ostrov Štvanice
Karlín
Žižkov
Žižkov (Vítkov) Hill
Tachovské náměstí
Masarykovo Train Station
Olšany Cemetery (Olšanské hřbitovy)
New Jewish Cemetery (Židovské hřbitovy)
Riegrovy sady
Rajská zahrada
náměstí Míru
See Vinohrady map p160
See Southern Nové Město map p146
To St Wenceslas Church
Wilsonova
Prvního pluku
Thámova
Šaldova
Sokolovská
Křižíkova
Pobřežní
Pernerova
Husitská
Řehořova
Seifertova
Cimburkova
Vinohradská
Jičínská
Slavíkova
Polská
Chopinova
Mánesova
Slezská
Korunní
Lucemburská
Bořivojova
Ondříčkova
Kubelíkova
Táboritská
Lupáčova
Prokopova
Koněvova
Roháčova
Jana Želivského
Malešická
Na Třebešíně
Nad vodovodem
Počernická
Jeseniova
Na Vackově
V zahrádkách
Šikmá
Na hlídce
Na vápence
Jilmová
Biskupcova
Pod Krejcárkem
U Sluncové
Pod plynojemem
Havlíčkova
Na poříčí
Petrská
Kimentská
Stárkova
Trocnovská
Olšanská
Radhošťská
Přemyslovská
Vlkova
U Rajské zahrady
Italská

PLACES TO STAY
5 Hotel Olympik
6 Hotel Olympik-Garni
7 Hotel Čechie
8 Hotel Karl-Inn
10 Hotel Brno
12 Atrium Hotel
14 Kolej Petrská
15 Hotel Opera
17 Hotel Atlantic
18 Hotel Harmony
19 Hotel Axa
25 TJ Sokol Karlín Hostel
27 Renaissance Hotel
28 Kolej Jednota Hostel & Universitas Tour Accommodation Agency
33 Hotel Ostaš
34 Purple House Hostel
36 Hotel Ariston
37 Hotel Bilý Lev
38 Hotel Kafka
41 TJ Sokol Žižkov Hostel
42 Hotel Vítkov
43 Autocamping Žižkov
44 Hotel Jarov
47 Clown & Bard Hostel
52 Olšanka Hotel
64 Hotel Don Giovanni
65 Hotel Velodrom

PLACES TO EAT
13 U Góvindy
35 Restaurace Confucius
40 Restaurace Viktoria
45 U radnice
49 Restaurace U koleje
55 Tabák Kaaba Café
56 U knihomola
61 Crazy Daisy Restaurant

OTHER
1 Belmondo Revival Music Club Vltavská
2 Winter Sports Stadium
3 Tennis Centre
11 Union of the Disabled (Sdružení zdravotně postižených v ČR)
16 Bohemiatour
20 Ceres Bus Tickets and Station
21 Prague City Museum
23 Čebus Bus Tickets
24 Karlín Music Theatre (Hudební divadlo)
26 Florenc Bus Station
29 Aqua club 2000 (formally Borsalino)
30 Main Train Station (Praha hlavní nádraží)
31 Military Museum
32 Jan Žižka Monument & National Memorial
39 Prokopovo námestí
46 St Procopius Church (Kostel sv Prokopa)
48 Palác Akropolis
50 Former Jewish Cemetery
51 TV Tower (Televizní věž)
53 St Roch Chapel (kaple sv Rocha)
54 Foreigners' Police & Passport Office
57 Stop City Apartment Agency
58 Sacred Heart Church (kostel Nejsvětějšího Srdce Páne)
63 Želivského Long-Distance Bus Stand

METRO STATIONS
4 Invalidovna
9 Křižíkova
22 Florenc
30 Hlavní nadraží
59 Jiřího z Poděbrad
60 Flora
62 Želivského

Dejvice
This neighbourhood is north-west of Hradčany, and is easy to reach by metro (on the A line) and by tram or bus. In summer numerous student hostels and private rooms become available here, and many tourists will no doubt find themselves sleeping in this unassuming but perfectly pleasant part of Prague.

Near the northern edge of Hradčany, at Mickiewiczova 1, is the **Bílkova Villa**, designed by the sculptor František Bílek in 1911 for his own residence. Now it's a museum to his unconventional stone and wood reliefs, religious works, drawings and ceramics; open daily, except Monday, from 15 May to 15 October from 10 am to 6 pm.

Nearby at Tychonova 4-6 are two **cubist houses** designed by architect Josef Gočár for his own use. Take tram No 18 one stop from Hradčanská metro station to Chotkovy sady.

In the north of Dejvice, the unusual villa suburb of **Baba** was a 1930s project by a team of cubist artists and designers to build cheap, attractive single-family houses. A similar project was the **Hanspaulka** suburb to the south, built between 1925-30.

Šárka Valley
This valley of the Šárka Stream (Šárecký potok) is one of Prague's best known nature parks. It's named after the female warrior Šárka, who threw herself off a cliff here (see Vyšehrad for more about this sad legend). The most attractive area is among the rugged cliffs at **Divoká Šárka**, near the Džban reservoir where the stream rises. You can swim in the reservoir.

From the terminus of the No 2 or 26 tram

(from Dejvická metro station), it's about 7km on a red-marked trail to the suburb of Baba, where the stream empties into the Vltava. There's a bus stop right beside the river here, or walk south to the terminus of tram Nos 20 and 25 opposite the Holiday Inn on Jugoslávských partyzánů. No matter where you stop along the valley, you can find a bus to bring you back to central Prague.

White Mountain

The 381m White Mountain (Bílá hora), on Prague's western outskirts, was the site of the 1620 Protestant defeat that ended Czech independence for almost 300 years. The only reminder today is a small monument in the middle of the field. Take tram No 8 from Hradčanská metro station, or tram No 22 from Malostranská metro station, to the end of the line.

Star Summer Palace

In 1530 Ferdinand I established a hunting reserve on a verdant hill east of White Mountain. In 1556 one Archduke Ferdinand of Tyrol built a Renaissance summer palace here in the shape of a six-pointed star. Inside the Star Summer Palace (Letohrádek hvězda) is a museum dedicated to two leading lights of the Czech National Revival: Alois Jirásek (1851-1930), who wrote powerful stories based on Czech legends, and the artist Mikuláš Aleš (1852-1913).

It's open daily, except Monday, from 10 am to 5 pm. Take the same trams towards White Mountain, only get off at the second-last stop, Malý Břevnov.

Břevnov Monastery

The Břevnov Monastery (Břevnovský klášter) is the oldest Benedictine monastery in the Czech Republic, established in 993 by Boleslav II and Bishop St Vojtěch Slavníkovec. The two men, from opposing and powerful families intent on dominating Bohemia, met at Vojtěška spring, each having had a dream that this was the place to establish a monastery. The name of the monastery comes from *břevno* (beam), for the beam laid across the spring where they met.

In 1993, on the 1000th anniversary of the monastery's founding, the restored 1st floor with its fine ceiling frescoes, and the crypt with the original foundations and a few skeletons, were opened to the public for the first time. Restoration work is continuing. The monastery was a secret-police archive until 1990.

The present monastery building and the nearby Baroque **Church of St Margaret** (kostel sv Markéty) were completed in 1720 by Kristof Dientzenhofer. Jan Patočka (1907-77), a leading figure of the Charter 77 movement, is buried in the **cemetery** behind the monastery. He died after interrogation by the secret police.

The church and parts of the monastery can be seen with a tour on Saturday at 9 and 10.30 am, and 1, 2.30 and 4 pm, on Sunday at the same times but starting at 10.30 am. Take the same trams towards White Mountain, but get off two stops earlier at the Břevnovský klášter stop.

SOUTH-WEST OUTSKIRTS

This part of Prague has few accessible tourist sights, though the **Barrandov Cliffs** (Barrandovské skály), a unique geological formation named after the French geologist Joachim Barranda who explored the area, is one of them. Nearby are the well known Barrandov film studios.

Good for a pleasant hike are the scenic **Prokopské** and **Dalejské valleys** (*údolí*), along the Dalejský potok between the suburbs of Hlubočepy and Jinonice. The 8km trail starts from near the corner of Novoveská and Pod Vavřincem in southern Jinonice; from Jinonice metro station, take bus No 130 or 149 one stop to Sídliště Jinonice. The trail ends at Haladova Garden in Hlubočepy, from where you can catch bus No 104 or 120 from Hlubočepská to the Smíchovské nádraží metro station.

Zbraslav

This town 10km south of Prague was only

incorporated into greater Prague recently, although as early as 1268 Přemysl Otakar II had established a hunting lodge and chapel here, later to be rebuilt as a Cistercian monastery. In 1784 the monastery was turned into a **castle** that today houses what may be the republic's best museum of 19th and 20th century Czech sculpture.

Enter its garden from Zbraslavské náměstí. The ground floor has exhibits of 19th century sculpture, including a large collection by Josef Myslbek, the country's leading sculptor at the turn of the century.

At the time of writing the museum was closed for renovations, although the gardens remain open. Take bus No 129, 165, 241, 243 or 255 from Smíchovské nádraží metro station.

SOUTH-EAST OUTSKIRTS

Several huge, unkempt woodlands lie at the edges of the city. One of the biggest is **Michelský les** and the adjoining **Kunratický les**, which is straight out of Roztyly metro station. Michelský les has a mini-zoo and a snack bar with beer and sausages.

NORTH-EAST OUTSKIRTS

Out on the north-east edge of the city you can take a close look at a Russian MiG fighter plane. The **Museum of Aircraft & Space Exploration** (muzeum letectví a kosmonautiky; ☎ 20 20 75 04), on Mladoboleslavská in the Kbely district (Prague 9), has exhibits on aeronautics and space flight, including the exploits of Russian cosmonauts. It's open daily, except Monday and Friday, from 10 am to 6 pm. Take bus No 185 or 259 from the Českomoravská metro station.

MUSEUMS & GALLERIES

Museums

Museum admission charges are typically 15 to 40 Kč, except where noted. Often youth, student and senior discounts are available for the asking.

Dvořák Museum, Villa Amerika, Ke Karlovu 20, Nové Město, Prague 2 (☎ 29 82 14): daily, except Monday, 10 am to 5 pm

Kafka Exhibition, corner of Maiselova and Staroměstské náměstí (Old Town Square): Tuesday to Friday from 10 am to 6 pm, Saturday to 5 pm

Křižovník Gallery, Křižovnické náměstí 3: daily, except Monday, 10 am to 6 pm

Lapidárium, Výstaviště (Fairgrounds), Holešovice: Tuesday to Friday from noon to 6 pm, weekends from 10 am to 12.30 pm and 1 to 6 pm

Military Museum, U památníku 2, Žižkov, Prague 3: daily, except Monday, 9 am to 5 pm; history from WWI

Mozart Museum, Bertramka, Mozartova 169, Smíchov: daily from 9.30 am to 6 pm (to 5 pm in winter); 50 Kč

Museum of Czech Glass, Staroměstské náměstí (Old Town Square) 27: daily 10 am to 9 pm

Museum of Czech History, Lobkovic Palace, Jiřská 3, Prague Castle: daily, except Monday, 9 am to 5 pm; until 1848

Museum of Decorative Arts, 17.listopadu 2, Josefov: daily, except Monday, 10 am to 6 pm

Museum of Military History, Schwarzenberg Palace, Hradčanské náměstí 2, Hradčany: daily, except Monday, May to October from 10 am to 6 pm; pre-WWI

Museum of the City of Prague, Na poříčí 52, Karlín: daily, except Monday, 9 am to 6 pm

Náprstek Museum of Asian, African and American Cultures, Betlémské náměstí, Staré Město: daily, except Monday, 9 am to noon and 12.45 to 5.30 pm

National Museum, Václavské náměstí 68, Nové Město: daily, except the first Tuesday of each month, 10 am to 6 pm; free on the first Monday of each month

National Technology Museum, Kostelní 42, Holešovice: daily, except Monday, 9 am to 5 pm

Postage Stamp Museum, Nové mlýny 2, Nové Město: daily, except Monday, 9 am to 5 pm

Smetana Museum, Novotného lávka 1, Staré Město: closed for renovations

State Jewish Museum (Old Jewish Cemetery, synagogues and other buildings in Josefov): daily, except Saturday, 9 am to 6 pm; 360 Kč ticket to Jewish Museum (Old Cemetery, Ceremonial Hall and Maisel, Pinkas and Klaus synagogues) and Old-New Synagogue; 200 Kč ticket for Jewish Museum; 160 Kč ticket for Old-New Synagogue. Tickets can be bought at Pinkas or Klaus synagogues; Mantas Travel Agency, Maiselova 15, only sells tickets for the Old-New Synagogue

Wax Museum, 28.října 13: daily from 8 am to 8 pm; 120 Kč

State-Run Galleries

National Gallery venues cost 20 to 50 Kč, though all give a sizable discount to students. Many are free on the first Friday of each month. It is also possible to buy a daily (100 Kč) or three day (200 Kč) ticket for all the galleries.

The National Gallery has four permanent collections, which are all open daily, except Monday, from 10 am to 6 pm, located at:

Sternberk Palace, Hradčanské náměstí 15, Hradčany (☎ 20 51 46 34): 14th to 20th century (and especially 19th and 20th century) European art.
Convent of St Agnes, U milosrdných 17, Staré Město (☎ 24 81 06 28): 19th century Czech painting and sculpture
Convent of St George, Prague Castle (☎ 53 52 46 ext 11): Czech Gothic and Renaissance art
Zbraslav Castle, Zbraslav: 19th and 20th century Czech sculpture

In addition the National Gallery has changing exhibitions at the following venues:

Kinský Palace, Staroměstské náměstí (Old Town Square) 12, Staré Město (☎ 24 81 07 58)
Rudolfinum, náměstí Jana Palacha (Jan Palach Square), Josefov
Riding School, U Prašného mostu 55, Prague Castle

Prague Municipal Gallery venues are free to all on the first Tuesday of each month. All venues are open daily, except Monday, from 10 am to 6 pm

House at the Stone Bell, Staroměstské náměstí 13 (☎ 24 81 0 36)
Old Town Hall on Staroměstské náměstí (Old Town Square; ☎ 24 48 27 51)
City Library, Mariánské náměstí, Staré Město: occasional exhibitions of contemporary Czech art
Troja Castle, Troja, Prague 7: 19th century Czech painting and sculpture
Bílkova villa, Mickiewiczova 1, Prague 6

Private Galleries

These include both exhibition and sales galleries. Most charge from 5 to 25 Kč. Some may close for weeks at a time, so call ahead to the more remote ones. Lots of other small galleries come and go.

Behémot Gallery, Elišky Krásnohorské 6, Josefov (☎ 231 78 29): open daily, except Monday, from noon to 7 pm; Czech avant-garde art
Czech Museum of Graphic Arts; Prague Municipal Gallery, Husova 19-21, Staré Město (☎ 24 22 20 68): open daily, except Monday, from 10 am to noon and 1 to 6 pm
Hollar Gallery, Smetanovo nábřeží 6, Staré Město: daily, except Monday, 10 am to 1 pm and 2 to 6 pm; contemporary Czech graphics
Galerie Nový Svět, Nový Svět 5, Hradčany: daily 10 am to 6 pm
Gambra Surrealist Gallery, Černínská 5, Hradčany: daily, except Monday and Tuesday, noon to 6 pm, weekends only from November to February
Jednorožec s Harfou, Průchodní 4, Staré Město: Monday to Friday from 11 am to 11 pm, weekends from noon to 10 pm; art by the physically and mentally disabled
Karolinum, Ovocný trh 3, Staré Město: daily, except Monday, 10 am to 6 pm
Mánes Gallery, Masarykovo nábřeží 250, Nové Město (☎ 29 18 08): daily, except Monday, 10 am to 6 pm; contemporary Czech art
MXM Gallery, Nosticova 6, Malá Strana (☎ 53 15 64): daily, except Monday, noon to 6 pm
Nová síň, Voršilská 3, Nové Město: daily, except Monday, 10 am to 1 pm and 2 to 6 pm; contemporary Czech art
Prague House of Photography, Husova 23, Staré Město (☎ 24 23 20 22): daily from 11 am to 6 pm
U prstenu Gallery, Jilská 14, Staré Město (☎ 26 28 58): daily from 11 am to 7 pm; 'Grotesque Humour and Fantastic Art'
Václav Špála Gallery, Národní 30 (☎ 24 21 30 00): daily, except Monday, 10 am to 1 pm and 2 to 6 pm; contemporary Czech art
Via Art Gallery, Resslova 6, Nové Město (☎ 29 25 70): Tuesday to Friday from noon to 6 pm, weekends from 1 to 5 pm

ACTIVITIES

Contact Prague Information Service for a full list of Prague's sports halls and complexes.

Prague International Marathon

The Prague International Marathon started

in 1989 and is now an annual event attracting more foreigners than Czechs. Entries have to be in 10 days before the race. In 1997 it was run in early June and the entry fee was US$50 for foreigners and 200 Kč for Czechs. For more information contact the main office (☎ 29 91 63) at Záhořanského 3.

Swimming

You can take a swim at the Plavecký stadión (swimming stadium) sports complex in Podolí, Prague 4. An Olympic outdoor pool is open weekdays from 6 am to 9.45 pm, and weekends from 6 am to 7.45 pm; an indoor pool is open at least on weekends, year-round. It costs about 35 Kč for the day from May through September, and about 15 Kč an hour in winter. A two hour sauna session is 75 Kč.

The complex, with restaurant and snack bar, is on Podolské nábřeží. Take tram No 3 from Václavské náměstí to the Dvorce stop, from where it's a five minute walk. Take flip-flops (thongs) for the grotty shower. Theft is a problem, even from lockers, so leave your valuables at the desk.

Tennis

Among many places to play tennis is the prestigious Štvanice club (TJ Slavoj Praha; ☎ 232 46 01) on Ostrov Štvanice (Štvanice Island); take tram No 3 from Václavské náměstí. The cheaper Tenis areál Strahov is in Strahov, Prague 6; take bus No 149 or 217 from Dejvická metro station to the Koleje Strahov stop.

Cycling & Rowing

See the Getting Around section of this chapter for details on hiring bicycles and row boats.

Ice Skating

There are many places to skate in winter. When it's below zero, parts of certain parks are sprayed with water and turned into ice rinks. Or try the rinks (*zimní stadióny*) at HC Konstruktiva (☎ 49 63 81), Mikuleckého 1441, Braník, open on weekends from 1 to 3 pm; or Štvanice in the winter-sports complex on Ostrov Štvanice, Holešovice, open Friday from 7.30 to 10 pm, Saturday from 1 to 3.30 pm, and Sunday from 7.30 to 10 am.

It is also possible to skate on the ice rink at the Sparta Sport Hall next to the Fairgrounds in Bubeneč. If you're a guest at the Hotel Hasa in Vinohrady, you can use the adjacent rink free of charge.

Golf

The Czech Republic has 13 golf courses, but only four have 18 holes. Prague has only one nine-hole golf course, the Golf Club Praha (☎ 651 24 64), Na Moráni 4, Motol, Prague 5, behind the Hotel Golf at Plzeňská 215A.

Or you can practice at the indoor Erpet Golf Centrum (☎ 57 32 12 29), at Strakonická 510 in southern Smíchov. It costs 200 Kč per hour to use the facilities (sauna, weight room etc), plus 200 Kč per hour for the driving range or 110 Kč per hour for the putting green. Non-members are welcome daily from 8 am to 2 pm.

The closest 18 hole course overlooks Karlštejn Castle. It costs 1000 Kč to play on weekdays and 1400 Kč on weekends and holidays. The course (☎ 0311-947 16) is on the south bank of Berounka river; from Karlštejn village head south-west uphill towards the village of Liteň and the course is on your left.

Other Activities

Pool and billiards are popular and there are many clubs in the city. One popular place is Billiard Club at Národní 22. American-style lanes for tenpin bowling are at Hotel Forum (☎ 61 19 11 51), Kongresová 1, Prague 4 (metro Vyšehrad). It costs 250 Kč per person for one hour including a ball, and shoes are about 30 Kč extra. Squash can also be played in several places around town, including Esquo-Squash-Centrum (☎ 20 51 36 09) at Strahov Stadium, Prague 6. It costs around 100 Kč per hour.

There's a year-round facility for horseriding at Jezdecké středisko (Riding Centre)

Zmrzlík, Zmrzlík 3, Řeporyje, Prague 5; take bus No 256 from Nové Butovice metro station to the Zmrzlík stop.

There are several fitness centres around Prague with pools, saunas, massage, weight-lifting rooms and tennis courts; see PIS for a list of centres and opening times. One of the largest is Sportovní areál Masopol (☎ 471 08 31) at Libušská 320, Prague 4; take bus No 113 or 171 from Kačerov metro station.

LANGUAGE COURSES

The Institute of Linguistics & Professional Training of Charles University (fax 24 22 94 97), Jindřišská 29, 11000 Praha 1, runs a three week summer course for foreigners from mid-July to early August. Participants have the choice of studying in Prague (US$873, including accommodation) or at Poděbrady, 50km east (US$997, including accommodation and all meals). Single rooms are US$81 extra per month and group excursions are additional. Students at Poděbrady are able to use the facilities of the local spa. The application deadline is 15 June. No prior knowledge of the Czech language is required and everyone is welcome.

Charles University also offers regular 10-month winter courses (from September to June) for those interested in further study at Czech universities or specialisation in Slavic studies at a foreign university. (Students wishing to have credits transferred to their home university should obtain written approval from the head of their department before enrolling.)

The cost of tuition and materials is US$2458 with 25 hours a week of instruction, US$3212 with 35 hours weekly. You can also opt for one or two four-month semesters at US$1250 each (25 hours a week). Special six-week language courses (US$423 tuition) are available from time to time and individual tutors can be hired at US$18 an hour. Participants are eligible for inexpensive accommodation in student dormitories, and in addition to Prague, you can study at Dobruška, Mariánské Lázně, Poděbrady or Teplice.

CZECH REPUBLIC

ORGANISED TOURS

Čedok has the widest selection of English-language city tours and out-of-city excursions, which can be arranged at its offices at Na příkopě 18 (☎ 24 19 76 43), Pařížská 6 (☎ 231 69 78), or Rytířská 16 (☎ 26 36 97). Following are some worthwhile possibilities; only the 'Historic Prague' tour is offered year-round:

Old Prague on Foot: three hour walking tour of Staré Město and Josefov; Friday at 9.30 am; 300 Kč

Historic Prague: three hour dash around the city by coach, with a walk through Hradčany and Prague Castle; Monday to Saturday at 10 am; 550 Kč

Panoramic Tour of Prague: two hours by coach around the edges of the historical centre, recommended only for those unable/unwilling to walk; Wednesday, Friday and Saturday at 11 am; 350 Kč

PIS offers excellent tours of historical places in Prague, some of which are not normally accessible to the public. More information is available from PIS offices (see Tourist Offices section) or directly from Prague History (Pražská vlastivěda; ☎ 231 11 27 or 24 81 61 84), a branch of PIS that runs the tours. Pragotour (☎ 24 48 25 62), in the PIS office at Old Town Hall, Staroměstské náměstí, arranges group tours and private guides.

Some smaller, independent agencies are Martin-Tour (☎ & fax 24 21 24 73) at Štěpánská 61, and Premiant City Tour (☎ 24 23 00 72) at Palackého 1; both also have tours outside of Prague. A problem with smaller outfits is that they may lump customers speaking various languages into one group and split the talking time between them, leaving no room for questions.

SPECIAL EVENTS

The following are the dates of major events in Prague:

30 April

Pálení Čarodějnic (Burning of the Witches): in Prague the Czech version of Walpurgisnacht, a pre-Christian festival for warding off evil, is an opportunity for all-night, end-of-winter bonfire parties on Kampa island and in suburban backyards

12 May to 4 June
: *Prague Spring (Pražské jaro) International Music Festival*: classical music concerts in theatres, churches and historic buildings; kicked off on the anniversary of Bedrich Smetana's death (12 May) with a procession from his grave at Vyšehrad to the Municipal House (Obecní dům); see the Entertainment section for information on getting tickets

Mid-May
: *Prague International Book Fair*

Late May or Early June
: *Prague International Marathon* – see the Activities section for more information

September
: *Mozart Festival*

24 December to 1 January
: *Christmas-New Year* – while most Czechs celebrate an extended holiday, Prague is engulfed by revellers from all over Europe and the tourist season is on again, briefly and furiously

PLACES TO STAY

Prague hotel space is tighter, and rates more inflated, than anywhere else in the Czech Republic. A bed shortage and a 23% hotel tax have made Prague one of Europe's most expensive places to stay – though not for Czechs, who generally pay 20 to 80% less than foreigners for hotel accommodation.

You can find something habitable in Prague without booking ahead, in any season. But during the high season – roughly April through September, plus the Christmas-New Year and Easter holidays – you cannot count on space in top-end hotels (nor in some mid-range places) without booking ahead at least a few weeks.

Independent travellers will no doubt be disappointed by Prague's hostels – most are quite basic, a bit expensive and a tram or metro ride from the centre. Private rooms fill the gaps, but most of these are equally far off in the suburbs.

There are exceptions to every rule, and with persistence and plenty of patience it's possible to find something decent nearish to the centre. Yet save yourself a pounding headache by booking in advance, at least for the first night or two.

Unless noted, prices given here are for a basic double with attached shower and WC, in the high season. Prices separated by slashes are for single/double or single/double/triple rooms.

Camping

Don't expect wide-open spaces. They're cheek-by-jowl, and differ mainly in attitude and amenities. Prices are about 100 Kč per person, plus 150 Kč per van or caravan or 100 to 200 Kč per tent. Some campsites have unheated bungalows at 150 to 200 Kč per bed. All have showers and most have communal kitchens and a snack bar. Most are on the outskirts of the city, and are open from mid-March through October.

Hostels

A 'hostel' can be anything from a bed in a gymnasium to a double room with shower – the common factor being that filling the other beds is up to them, not you. Some operate throughout the year; others are sports clubs and student dormitories that only have beds in the summer. We have indicated the year-round ones.

Typical per-bed prices are 300 to 350 Kč, but they can be lower or much higher. Few have places to eat on the premises.

Private Rooms

A booming business in Prague is the renting of rooms in private homes. Touts swarm the arrival platforms of the main train station, hoping to lure new arrivals. If you go this route, check the location on a map and don't pay until you have seen the room. It's also a good idea to pay by the night, rather than all up front.

The easiest way to find a private room is through an accommodation agency (see below). Away from the city centre, a double room with shared bath and WC is 700 to 1000 Kč; one with its own facilities and entrance is at least 1200 Kč per night, a bit less off-season.

Hotels

We organise hotels by the price of their

most basic double in the high season. 'Bottom end' means less than about 1500 Kč per double; 'middle' is 1500 Kč to about 3500 Kč; and 'top end' is everything above that. Some places have lower rates off-season.

Unless noted, prices are for a room with attached shower and WC. If they say they're full, ask if there's anything with shared facilities. In addition to being cheaper, these can be quite grand: the 'common bath' down the hall is often a private WC with a bathtub.

Accommodation Agencies

Following are some reputable agencies – our favourites being AVE, CKM and Universitas Tour. Most can arrange private rooms, and many can get cheaper rooms in pensions and hotels.

American Express (☎ 24 21 99 92), Václavské náměstí 56: hotel rooms from 1500 Kč
AVE, with offices upstairs at the main train station (☎ 24 22 32 26; fax 24 23 07 83), Holešovice train station and the airport: open daily from 6 or 7 am to 10 or 11 pm; offering private, hostel and hotel rooms
Bohemiatour (☎ 231 39 17; fax 231 38 06), Zlatnická 7, Nové Město: pensions and private rooms
Čedok, Na příkopě 18 (☎ 24 19 76 43; fax 24 22 23 00), Staré Město; Pařížská 6 (☎ 231 69 78), Josefov; and the airport (☎ 36 78 02): all offer private rooms from 1000 Kč and pricier hotels
CK Intercity (☎ 24 61 76 66), Masarykovo train station: open weekdays from 9 am to 8 pm; mostly private rooms
CKM (☎ 26 85 32), Jindřišská 28, Staré Město: open weekdays from 9 am to 1 pm and 2 to 5 pm, Saturday to noon; with youth-oriented accommodation in hostels (20% IYHF/HI discount), cheaper hotels and some private homes from 1000 Kč
CKM (☎ 24 91 57 67), Žitná 12, Nové Město: open weekdays from 8 am to 6 pm
ESTEC (☎ 52 12 50), Vaníčkova 5/1, Prague 6: student travel agency with dormitory accommodation in hostels and student colleges
Flat-Finders (☎ 96 14 36 97 or 0603-45 33 85): pricey flats for long-term visitors
Pragotur (☎ 231 12 35), inside PIS office at Old Town Hall, Staroměstské náměstí: open weekdays in summer from 8 am to 6 pm, weekends from 8.30 am to 4 pm; mainly private homes from 1000 Kč per person
Prague Suites (☎ 24 22 99 61), Melantrichova 8, Staré Město: rooms and apartments in private homes from US$19 (in the suburbs)
Stop City (☎ 24 22 24 97), Vinohradská 24, Vinohrady: open daily from 11 am to 8 pm; private apartments only
Top Tour (☎ 232 10 77; fax 24 81 14 00), Rybná 3, Staré Město: mostly expensive luxury private homes
Universitas Tour (☎ 26 04 26; fax 24 21 22 90), Opletalova 38, near main train station: open daily from 8.30 am to 5.30 pm; a recommended stop if you're after a hostel (there's one upstairs), also some private, pension and hotel rooms
Vesta (☎ 24 61 71 20), main train station: hostels and its own Hotel Kafka in Žižkov
Wasteels (☎ 24 61 74 54), main train station: cheaper hotels, hostels, private homes

Hradčany & Malá Strana (Prague 1)

Hostels In July and August every student dormitory block in the cluster opposite Strahov Stadium accepts tourists. In the off-season only the *ESTEC Hostel* (☎ 52 12 50 or 52 73 44; fax 52 73 43), block 5, Vaníčkova 5, and the nearby *Hostel SPUS* (☎ 57 21 07 64), block 4, accept travellers. At either beds in doubles are about 240 Kč each, with shared showers and WC. Breakfast is an extra 50 Kč. Reception, in the Hostel SPUS, is only open weekdays from 8 am to 1 pm, and to noon on weekends. From Dejvická metro station, take bus No 217 south to the Kolej Strahov stop.

The quiet *Kolej Komenského* (☎ 35 20 41), Parléřova 6, a 15 minute walk west of Prague Castle, has modern single/double rooms for around 550/750 Kč with breakfast. It's crowded year-round, so call in advance. From the Malostranská metro station take tram No 22 (direction Bílá Hora) to the Pohořelec stop; the hostel is 100m north.

A small and dirty but very central place is the *Hostel Sokol* (☎ 57 00 73 97), Hellichova 1, with dorm beds for 200 Kč. There is also a kitchen. The entrance to the hostel is at Újezd 42; walk through the passage and dial 397 at the door that leads to the apartments.

There is a network of six summer-only Travellers' Hostels conveniently spread around the city centre. In this area the *Travellers' Hostel* (☎ 53 31 60) is at U lanové dráhy 3; take tram No 12 or 22 from Malostranská metro station to the Újezd stop, walk up U lanové dráhy from Újezd, turn left in the park, and walk under the funicular bridge. The hostel is the large lone building surrounded by trees. Dorm beds cost 250 Kč per person.

Hotels – middle Near the southern end of Kampa, Všehrdova 13, is *U Kiliána* (☎ 561 81 40; fax 73 41 10), a friendly pension-restaurant with lots of character. Single /double rooms are 2000/2400 Kč.

Opposite, at No 16, is the deluxe *Hotel Kampa* (☎ 57 32 05 08; fax 57 32 02 62), set in a fully renovated 17th century armoury. Rooms with all the trimmings, including breakfast, are 2200/3500 Kč (less 10% off-season).

Nearby, at Újezd 20, is the new, 16 room *Hotel U Kříže* (☎ 53 33 26; fax 53 34 43). It's central but on a noisy main street. The restaurant here is good. Rooms are 2900/3200 Kč.

Another new spot in a quiet corner of Hradčany is *Hotel Sax* (☎ 53 84 22; fax 53 84 98), Jánský vršek 328/3, on the corner of Vlašská. The building is ultra-modern, and the prices – 2700/3400 Kč – are not too bad considering the location.

Hotels – top end The cheapest up-market option is *Hotel U Pava* at U Lužického semináře 32, a small 11 room place charging 3800/4000 Kč for a single/double. Top-floor rooms have stunning views of Prague Castle. Street noise is the only drawback.

Hotel U tří pštrosů (☎ 57 32 05 65; fax 57 32 06 11), Dražického náměstí 12/76, is opposite the Malá Strana tower on Charles' Bridge. Overpriced rooms with bath, WC and breakfast start at 4400/6000 Kč.

Across the road in a handsome (and pink) townhouse, at Mostecká 2, is the new *Hotel Pod věží* (☎ 53 37 10; fax 53 18 59). Comfortable rooms are 3900/5300 Kč.

The six room *Pension U raka* (☎ 20 51 11 00; fax 20 51 05 11), Černínská 10/93, is set in a beautiful warren of narrow and peaceful streets. Rooms are 6300/6900 Kč – and are regularly booked out.

Hotel Hoffmeister (☎ 561 81 55; fax 53 09 59), Pod Bruskou 9, is at the northern end of Malá Strana, with a pleasant courtyard for drinks and meals. Rooms are 5600/6400 Kč, and there's an underground carpark.

Hotel Savoy (☎ 24 30 24 30; fax 24 30 21 28), in a restored 19th century palace at Keplerova 6, is priced at 6900/7300 Kč and usually frequented by politicians and movie stars. Enjoy the sauna and fitness centre.

Staré Město & Josefov (Prague 1)

Hotels – bottom end One of the better deals in Staré Město is *Pension u Medvídků* (☎ & fax 24 21 19 16) at Na Perštýně 7, where beds in smallish rooms cost 615 Kč per person. Bookings are recommended.

Highly recommended is the *Unitas Penzion – La Prison* (☎ 232 77 00; fax 232 77 09) at Bartolomějská 9, in space rented from a convent that was once a Czech secret-police jail. President Václav Havel was held here for a day, and if it's available you can stay in the very room (No P6). Quiet rooms with common WC and showers are 920/1100/1500/1750 Kč for a single/double/triple/quad with breakfast. Book ahead if you can; the place is getting famous.

Hotels – middle A three-star hotel with a one-star exterior is the *Central* (☎ 24 81 27 34; fax 232 84 04) at Rybná 8. Clean rooms are 2330/2820/3300 Kč with breakfast. Visa cards are accepted.

Hotels – top end The splendid Art Nouveau *Hotel Paříž* (☎ 24 22 21 51; fax 24 22 54 75), U Obecního domu 1, is now a historic monument. Even if you can't afford it (5900/6200 Kč and up, with breakfast), make sure you have a look.

In Týn Court (Týnský dvůr), at Štupartská 1, is the *Hotel Ungelt* (☎ 24 81 13 30;

fax 231 95 05), with eight elegant suites. Singles are 5150 Kč, doubles 6030 Kč, and quads 7530 Kč.

At the north end of Pařížská, at náměstí Curieových 5/43, the *Hotel Inter-Continental Praha* (☎ 24 88 11 11; fax 24 81 12 16) has luxury rooms from 8700/9280 Kč, but not very good restaurants. Behind it, facing the river at No 100, is the *President Hotel* (☎ 231 48 12; fax 231 87 56), which has rooms for 5850/6200 Kč.

Northern Nové Město (Prague 1 & 8) These listings include a few places east of Wilsonova in Karlín (Prague 8), which are near Florenc but most easily reached from northern Nové Město.

Hostels The ageing *Kolej Jednota* (☎ 26 04 26), Opletalova 38, has beds for 355 Kč with breakfast, in summer – ISIC cards get a bed for 245 Kč. In the lobby is the Universitas Tour agency, which can also book you into several other hostels. One is *Kolej Petrská* (☎ 231 64 30) at Petrská 3, in a dreary neighbourhood but near trams and food on Na poříčí; a single/double in a mini-suite is 530/1100 Kč with breakfast.

CK Vesta travel agency (☎ 24 22 57 90) at the main train station has a hostel in the station's roof. A bed is 300 Kč in three, four or six-bed dorms. There are also a handful of doubles with bath and WC for 900 Kč per person.

If you're on a rock-bottom budget, try the year-round *Raketa Hostel* (☎ 21 61 70 14), Na Florenci 2, inside the railyard at Masarykovo station. Basic but fairly clean rooms with shared facilities are 330 Kč per bed. You can also book this with Vesta in the main train station. If this isn't cheap enough, try *TJ Sokol Karlín* (☎ 26 09 55), Malého 1, Karlín, Prague 8, a truly down-and-out place just east of Florenc bus station. Beds are 220 Kč. You must clear out from 8 am to 6 pm.

Hotels – bottom end A well priced place for its location, at Senovážné náměstí 21, is the *Libra Q Hotel* (☎ 22 10 55 36), which has dorm beds from 280 Kč, and rooms for 750/810/1200/1400 Kč with shared facilities or 890/1250/1480 Kč including bath and WC.

Hotels – middle A recommended mid-range place is the faded *Hotel Opera* (☎ 231 56 09, 231 25 23), Těšnov 13/1743, near Florenc. Threadbare but clean rooms are 1600/1700 Kč without shower or WC, 1850/2000 Kč with shower, 3340/3690 Kč for both, with breakfast. Walk-in prospects look good, and credit cards are accepted.

A good off-season bargain is the floating hotel, *Botel Albatros* (☎ 24 81 05 41; fax 231 97 84), on nábřeží Ludvíka Svobody. Spartan cabins with tiny shower and WC are 2000/2800 Kč in summer, and discounted by almost half in the off-season. It has a restaurant and café, and connections by tram No 3 to Václavské náměstí.

Na poříčí, though noisy, has tram connections and plenty of food. Two group-oriented hotels there have the occasional spare room. The pleasant *Atlantic* (☎ 24 81 23 78/5; fax 232 21 72), at No 9, has rooms with TV and breakfast for 3200/4100/5100 Kč, including rooms for disabled visitors, and it accepts credit cards. The plain *Axa* (☎ 24 81 25 80; fax 232 21 72), at No 40, is 1800/3100 Kč, and has a pool and sauna.

Hotels – top end Central Europe's biggest hotel is the Hilton's 788 room *Hotel Atrium* (☎ 24 84 11 11; fax 24 84 23 78), Pobřežní 3, Karlín, Prague 8, which also boasts a glass roof, swimming pool, four restaurants – the lot. It's luxurious and modern inside but you would never guess that from its ugly outside. Single/double rooms in this business-oriented spot start at 7600/8250 Kč. Opposite Masarykovo train station is the *Renaissance* (☎ 21 82 23 00; fax 21 82 23 33), V celnici 7, with rooms starting at 6200/6800 Kč. It's chiefly for groups and business people.

A nice place for the money is the modest *Hotel Harmony* (☎ 232 00 16; fax 231 00 09), Na poříčí 31, with huge, clean doubles for 3500 Kč (the quieter ones face Biskupská), and a pleasant restaurant.

Rooms with TV and bath at Best Western's friendly *Hotel Meteor Plaza* (☎ 24 22 06 64; fax 24 21 30 05), Hybernská 6, just east of the Powder Tower, are somewhat overpriced at 4500/5000/5900 Kč with breakfast.

Southern Nové Město & Vyšehrad (Prague 1 & 2)

These hotels are all south of Národní and Na příkopě.

Hostels & Cheap Hotels A recommended hostel is the quiet *Hlávkova kolej* (☎ 29 00 98) at Jenštejnská 1, Prague 2, two blocks from Karlovo náměstí metro station. Mini-suites are 1600 Kč, including breakfast.

A cheaper hostel is east of Karlovo náměstí along dreary Žitná, Prague 2: the *CKM Hostel*, upstairs from CKM's accommodation agency at No 12. It's 500 Kč per bed, with a 20% HI discount. Don't confuse this with the *CKM Juniorhotel* (☎ 24 22 28 11; fax 29 13 20) at No 10, which has rooms with WC, shower and TV for 1500/2200/2820 Kč with breakfast, but it's usually booked out.

The *Hostel in Club Habitat* (☎ 29 03 15) is in two locations near Karlovo náměstí. One is at Na Zbořenci 10 and the other at Štěpánská 14. Accommodation is in rooms with two or more beds for 350 Kč per person.

Hotels – middle One of Prague's architectural gems, the fading Art Nouveau *Grand Hotel Evropa* (☎ 24 22 81 17; fax 24 22 45 44), Václavské náměstí 25, actually has some run-down mid-range rooms without bath for 1280/2160/2790 Kč, and with bath for 2450/3400/4350/5200 Kč. These prices all include breakfast, which was the worst buffet we had in three months in the country. You'll have to book well ahead.

In a lane south of Národní, at Opatovická 16, is the *Hotel Koruna* (☎ 24 91 51 74; fax 29 24 92), where rooms with bath and WC are 1650/2850/3600 Kč, including breakfast.

Hotels – top end A block off Václavské náměstí, at Panská 12, is the Art Nouveau *Hotel Palace* (☎ 24 09 31 11; fax 24 22 12 40), which is aimed at business people. In addition to the good-value Delicatesse Buffet (see Places to Eat) it has two pricier restaurants. Rooms start at 7540/8900 Kč with breakfast – or how about the Presidential Apartment at 28,670 Kč?

On Václavské náměstí are more top-end places. At No 5-7, the *Ambassador* and *Zlatá Husa* (☎ 24 19 31 11; fax 24 23 06 20) form a single four-star establishment with lots of restaurants, and 5600/6700 Kč rooms, mainly for groups. Rooms at the snooty, five-star *Hotel Jalta* (☎ 24 22 91 33; fax 24 21 38 66), at No 45, are 5600/6600 Kč in summer, with breakfast.

Across the square, the newish *Adria* (☎ 21 08 12 00; fax 242 110 25), at No 26, has rooms with bath and satellite TV for 4280/5180 Kč with breakfast, and a flash vinárna and a café. At Washingtonova 19, opposite the Opera House, is the *Hotel Esplanade* (☎ 24 21 17 15; fax 24 22 93 06) with rooms from 5250/6890 Kč.

Near the river, at Na Moráni 15, is another Best Western, the *City Hotel Moráň* (☎ 24 91 52 08; fax 29 75 33), which has good access to trams and the metro. Rooms with bath, WC, fridge and satellite TV are 4940/5880 Kč, including breakfast.

Just below Vyšehrad, at Ostrčilovo náměstí 4, is the *Hotel Union* (☎ 692 75 06; fax 692 72 89). The plain and clean rooms are 2815/3380 Kč, including breakfast. It's on the No 24 tram line to Václavské náměstí. The cloistered, high-rise *Hotel Forum* (☎ 61 19 12 38; fax 61 19 16 73), beside Vyšehrad metro station, Nusle, Prague 4, has western European-class service and rooms for 6235/7090 Kč.

Bubeneč & Holešovice (Prague 7)

Hostels In north-east Holešovice is the year-round, very basic *Hostel Spoas* (☎ 80 48 91), Jankovcova 63A. Turn left out of nádraží Holešovice metro station, cross over the highway, and follow the signs for five minutes. Space in a six bed dorm is 220

Kč. Don't wander alone late at night, as the neighbourhood isn't so great.

Hotels – middle The pleasant *Parkhotel Splendid* (☎ 37 33 51; fax 38 23 12), Ovenecká 33, charges 1320/1600 Kč for a single/double with breakfast. It's in a quiet, semi-secluded spot. From Vltavská metro station, take tram No 25 two stops to Letenské náměstí.

The ageing, seven storey *Hotel Belveder* (☎ 37 47 41; fax 37 03 55), Milady Horákové 19, is in the heart of Holešovice, with rooms including breakfast for 2350/3150 Kč. Take tram No 1 two stops from Vltavská metro station.

Best Western's *Hotel Alta* (☎ 80 02 52; fax 66 71 20 11), Ortenovo náměstí 22, is in the far north-east corner of Holešovice. It's mainly used by business travellers. Rooms are 2470/3090 Kč. From nádraží Holešovice metro station, take tram No 12 or 25 one stop east.

Hotels – top end Overpriced rooms – 3120/3760 Kč with breakfast – at the 11 storey *Parkhotel* (☎ 24 31 23 76; fax 24 31 61 80), at Veletržní 20, reflect its proximity to the Fairgrounds. From metro station nádraží Holešovice, take tram No 12 west to the third stop.

Smíchov (Prague 1 & 5)

Camping The *Yacht Club Caravan Park* (☎ 54 09 25; fax 54 33 05), at the tip of the Císařská louka island, has fine views across to Vyšehrad. From Anděl metro station, take tram No 12 four stops to Lihovar; it's a 20 minute walk from there.

Hotels – bottom end Near Anděl metro station, at třída Svornosti 28, is *Hotel Balkán* (☎ & fax 54 07 77). It's definitely shabby but a good deal at 1000/1300 Kč.

Hotels – middle In the quiet streets above Bertramka is the elegant *Hotel U Blaženky* (☎ 24 51 10 54; fax 24 51 10 29), U Blaženky 1, with rooms for 2315/2730 Kč and a semi-fancy restaurant. From Anděl metro station, take bus No 137 or 508 four stops to the Malvazinky stop.

Closer to the action in north Smíchov is *Hotel Mepro* (☎ 54 91 67; fax 561 85 87), Viktora Huga 3, a swank modern spot with rooms for 2000/2400 Kč.

Smíchov's newest hotel is also the nicest – *Hotel Julián* (☎ 53 51 37; fax 54 75 25), Elišky Peškové 11, priced at 2280/2680 Kč with shower and WC. You can even email reservations (casjul@vol.cz).

Smíchov has two older floating hotels, a weird idea but actually quite nice when you're sitting on deck at sunset. Cheaper is the 70 room *Botel Vodník* (☎ & fax 54 77 04), near Strakonická, at 1100/1600 Kč with breakfast. It's a five minute walk from Smíchovské nádraží metro station.

The nearly identical *Botel Admirál* (☎ 57 32 13 02; fax 54 96 16), Hořejší nábřeží, near Palackého bridge, is priced at 2190/2300 Kč.

Hotels – top end A massive hotel and entertainment complex in eastern Smíchov called the *Mövenpick Hotel* (☎ 57 15 11 11; fax 57 15 31 31), Mozartova 261/1, which is mainly popular with tour groups. Rooms with the works are 3500/4600 Kč.

Troja & Kobylisy (Prague 7 & 8)

Camping Along Trojská in Troja (Prague 7) are four campsites, all about 10 minutes from nádraží Holešovice metro station on bus No 112: *Camp Dana Troja* at No 129 (Trojská bus stop), *Autocamp Trojská* (☎ 688 60 35; fax 854 29 45) at No 375/157 (Kazanka bus stop), *Camp Herzog* (☎ 689 06 82) at No 161, and dreary *Camp Sokol Troja* (☎ & fax 688 11 77) at No 171a (Čechova Škola bus stop). Autocamp Trojská has a grassy site (just like the other campsites), ISIC discounts, satellite TV, bungalows (210 Kč per bed), and rooms in the house.

Hotels – bottom end *Pension V sudech* at Zenklova 217 in Kobylisy, Prague 8, is about 100m up the hill from the No 12 tram line (Okrouhlická stop), which leaves from

Palmovka metro station. This is part of the Na Vlachovce restaurant (☎ 688 02 14) and there are cabins with two beds each, bath and WC for 900 Kč per person.

Hotels – middle A recommended mid-range place is the quiet *Hotel Stírka* pension (☎ 688 18 27; fax 84 74 88) at Ke Stírce 11/78, Kobylisy, Prague 8. Rooms with WC, shower and TV are 1400/2100/2600 Kč, and less than half that in the off-season; credit cards are accepted. You can also book it through the AVE agency. Take tram No 25 from nádraží Holešovice metro station to the Ke Stírce stop.

Karlín & Libeň (Prague 8)

Hotels – bottom end Doubles with common facilities are reasonable for only 700 Kč at *Hotel Libeň* (☎ 683 40 09; fax 683 40 14), Zenklova 37, Libeň. The *Botel Neptun* (☎ 66 31 01 43 or 66 31 05 41) is a floating hotel at U Českých loděnic in Libeň. Cabins with WC, shower and fridge are 1010/1400 Kč. There are eateries in the neighbourhood. From Palmovka metro station, walk five minutes north on Zenklova, turn left at Elznicovo náměstí and follow the channel.

Hotels – middle The *Hotel Brno* (☎ 24 81 18 88; fax 24 81 04 32), Thámova 26, beside the Křižíkova metro station, is a pretty good deal at 1460/2140/2580 Kč (if paying with credit card an extra fee is charged). It has a small restaurant. Around the block, at Šaldova 54, is the well-run *Hotel Karl-Inn* (☎ 24 81 17 18; fax 24 81 26 81). Very comfortable rooms are 3100/3600 Kč and cards are accepted.

A five minute walk from Invalidovna metro station is the small *Hotel Čechie* (☎ 66 19 41 01), U Sluncové 618, Karlín, with good walk-in prospects. Rooms are 2000/3200 Kč with breakfast (less in winter), but the restaurant is very overpriced. There are also some sporting facilities in the hotel complex.

Hotels – top end Also near the Invalidovna metro station are the *Olympik* (☎ 66 18 11 11; fax 66 31 05 59), Sokolovská 138, priced at 2360/3460 Kč, and the *Olympik-Garni* (☎ 684 55 01), U Sluncové 14, for 2000/3000 Kč with breakfast. Both are popular with groups. In 1995, there was a fire in the Hotel Olympik in which seven foreign tourists died.

Vinohrady & Žižkov (Prague 2 & 3)

Camping The very central *Autocamping Žižkov* (☎ & fax 644 20 61), Koněvova 141A, is just 3km from the heart of Prague but only open in July and August.

Hostels A recommended place in Žižkov is the year-round *TJ Sokol Žižkov* (☎ 27 49 38; fax 27 48 42) at Koněvova 19, with beds for 230 Kč. There's also a sauna. It offers breakfast (extra) but the neighbourhood has a few adequate restaurants. Take bus No 133 or 207 from Florenc metro station, or bus No 168 from the main train station, two stops to Tachovské náměstí.

A new and popular place in the heart of Žižkov is the *Clown & Bard Hostel* (☎ 27 24 36) at Bořivojova 102. Beds in dorms cost 200 Kč, and in rooms from 250 Kč per person. Beverages are sold daily from 8 am to 1 am in the hostel's café. Nearby, at Krasova 25, is the *Purple House* (☎ 27 14 90), where space in four-bed rooms is 300 Kč. There is also a kitchen. They are both near tram Nos 5, 9 and 26.

Hotels – bottom end Good value in Vinohrady is the *Bulharský Klub* (☎ 25 25 15) at Americká 28. It's an older but cheerful hotel popular with eastern Europeans. Rooms are 850/1300 Kč with shower and WC. It has a small restaurant and is close to a tram route.

At the *Hotel Velodrom* (☎ 77 07 37 or 781 57 48; fax 781 67 40), Nad Třebešínem III, Vackov, Prague 10, bunk beds in mini-suites are 270 Kč with breakfast. It also has hotel-style double rooms at 1350 Kč, and a restaurant with hotel prices (there's nowhere else to eat). The Velodrom is a 15 minute walk from Želivského metro station in a web of residential streets that all have Třebešín in their names – go east along the Jewish Cemetery, take the first left and then the second right into Na Třebešíně, follow it for a block, then go diagonally across a park and one block east.

Another good place is *Hotel Kafka* (☎ 27 31 01), Cimburkova 24, Žižkov, with clean rooms for 1050/1600/1950 Kč. The neighbourhood is dreary, but near the trams, such as the No 9 to Václavské náměstí.

South of Havlíčkovy Park, at Sámova 1, is the *Hotel Hasa* (☎ 72 37 51/2; fax 72 37 53). Comfortable rooms are 780/1360/1800 Kč. It's 15 minutes by tram No 24 from Václavské náměstí.

Hotels – middle A good deal in dreary inner Žižkov is *Hotel Bílý Lev* (☎ 27 11 26; fax 27 32 71) at Cimburkova 20, where rooms with breakfast are 1300/2400/3400 Kč. A few blocks west is another bright spot, the small *Hotel Ostaš* (☎ 627 93 86; fax 627 94 18) at Orebitská 8, with a good restaurant and pleasant rooms for 1560/2800 Kč with breakfast. Take tram No 5, 9 or 26 from the main train station or bus No 133 or 207 from Florenc.

The *Olšanka Hotel* (☎ 67 09 22 02; fax 27 33 86), Táboritská 23 (enter at the rear), has overpriced rooms with shower, WC and TV for 1900/2500 Kč with breakfast. Walk-in prospects are poor.

The *Hotel Vítkov* (☎ 27 93 40/7; fax 27 93 57), Koněvova 114, Žižkov, has overpriced, threadbare rooms for 1980/2600 Kč with breakfast; credit cards are accepted. It's 15 minutes from Václavské náměstí on tram No 9.

In Vinohrady, a recommended place is the well-run *Pension Hotel City* (☎ & fax 691 13 34), Belgická 10, in a quiet neighbourhood two blocks from náměstí Míru metro station. There are 20 very plain rooms, some with bathtubs (1050/2080 Kč) and some without (1034/1396 Kč). There are restaurants nearby.

Hotels – top end The new Austrian-built, 241 room *Hotel Don Giovanni* (☎ 67 03 16 03; fax 67 03 67 04), Vinohradská 157A, Prague 3, next to the Želivského metro and bus stations, is ugly but has good service. This four-star luxury hotel is also suitable for business people and has rooms costing from 4100/5180 to 13,440 Kč (for the presidential suite), including a huge buffet breakfast.

Dejvice & North-West Outskirts (Prague 6)

Camping The year-round *Kemp Džbán* (☎ 36 85 51; fax 36 13 56), Nad lávkou 3, Vokovice, is part of the Aritma sports complex (and some 200m on from the sports ground). Facilities also include huts and bungalows.

Hostels The year-round *TJ Aritma* (☎ 36 85 51; fax 36 13 65), at the same address as Kemp Džbán (see Camping above), has beds in doubles and five-bed rooms for 220 Kč, and a restaurant.

The small *TJ Hvězda Praha* (☎ 316 51 04), at Za lány in Střešovice, has beds for 200 Kč. From Dejvická metro station take tram No 2, 20 or 26 four stops to Horoměřická.

A 20 minute walk from Dejvická metro station, at Terronská 28, the good-value *Berhanu CK Hostel* (☎ & fax 24 31 11 07) costs 200 Kč per person in a double. There are also triples and quads available, all with shower and WC. Anyone with an LP guide apparently gets a 10% discount.

Hotels – bottom end Rooms with bath and WC at *Hotel Váza* (☎ & fax 20 51 32 83), at Na Petynce 45 in Střešovice, are 670 Kč per person with breakfast. From Hradčanská metro station take bus No 108 or 174 three stops to Kajetánka.

The helpful, family-run *Pension BoB* (☎ & fax 311 78 35), at Kovárenská 2 in Lysolaje, has rooms with two or more beds, shower and WC for 700 Kč per person, including breakfast. There's a bar and secure parking. Take bus No 160 from Dejvická metro station to the Žákovská stop.

Hotels – middle The *Hotel Coubertin* (☎ 35 28 51; fax 35 40 69) is at Atletická 4 in Strahov, near the Strahovský stadión. Rooms with breakfast are 1630/2180 Kč. Take bus No 143 from Dejvická metro station.

Hotels out towards Ruzyně airport, in the suburb of Veleslavín, are the *Krystal* (☎ 316 52 26; fax 316 42 15) at José Martiho, with rooms for 1400/1800 Kč, including breakfast (bus No 119 from Dejvická metro station), and the *Obora* (☎ 36 77 79; fax 316 71 25) at Libocká 271/1, with rooms for 1950/2400 Kč, including breakfast.

Hotels – top end Dejvice's newly renovated *Schweigerov Gardens Hotel* (☎ 32 00 05; fax 32 02 25) at Schweigerova 3 has rooms with all the extras starting at 3400/4000 Kč, including breakfast.

In Dejvice at Koulova 15, the Soviet-style International Hotel, which is a tower of a building, has been recast as a *Holiday Inn* (☎ 24 39 38 77; fax 311 83 00). It was originally built for the army. Rooms start at about 4500/5200 Kč with breakfast.

Dejvice's two top-quality hotels are the *Diplomat* (☎ 24 39 41 11; fax 24 39 42 15; email diphoprg@mbox.vol.cz) at Evropská 15, with rooms from 6000/7200 Kč, and the *Praha* (☎ 24 34 11 11; fax 24 31 12 18) at Sušická 20, starting at 6000/6800 Kč.

South-West Outskirts (Prague 5)

Camping *Caravancamp Motol* (☎ 52 47 14) is on Plzeňská in Motol, below the Hotel Golf. From Anděl metro station, take tram No 4, 7 or 9 seven stops to the Hotel Golf. *Pension Eva*, in Zličín, also has a campsite (see Hotels following).

Hostels At the year-round *Motorlet Císařka* (☎ 52 61 42), at Podbělohorská 97 in Císařka, quads are 320/400 Kč per person without/with shower. From Anděl metro station, take bus No 191 to the fourth stop.

Hotels – bottom end The big *Hotel Tourist* (☎ 52 96 20 62; fax 52 64 69), at Peroutkova 531/81 in Košíře, has rooms for 750/1200 Kč. From Anděl metro station, take bus No 137 to the end of the line and walk back several hundred metres.

Pension Eva (☎ 301 92 13), at Strojírenská 78 in Zličín, has rooms for about 380 Kč per person, and an adjacent campsite. From Václavské náměstí, take tram No 9 to the end of the line, then bus No 164 to the third stop.

Hotels – middle The drab but clean *Hotel Golf* (☎ 52 32 51; fax 52 21 53), at Plzeňská 215A in Motol, has rooms with shower, WC and TV for 900/1375 Kč.

South-East Outskirts (Prague 4 & 10)

Camping A peaceful campsite with a view across the Vltava is *Intercamp Kotva Braník* (☎ 46 13 97; fax 46 61 10), at the end of the tram lines in Braník, Prague 4, 25 minutes south of the city centre.

Sky Club Brumlovka (☎ & fax 42 35 19), Vyskočilova 2, Michle, Prague 4, is right off 5.května (Highway E50/65), and 500m east of Budějovická metro station (take bus No 118 or 178 one stop). It takes telephone bookings and offers student discounts.

Hostels The *Braník Youth Hostel* (☎ 46 26 41), Vrbova 1233, Prague 4, is a large 10 storey hostel on the southern side of Prague. Bus No 197 from Anděl metro station and bus Nos 196, 198 and 199 from Smíchovské nádraží metro station pass the hostel. It's 300 Kč per person, breakfast included, and an HI card is not required.

Another popular place is the unfriendly *Hostel Boathaus (Wesico)* (☎ 402 10 76), V náklích 1A (Prague 4), where dorm beds are 230 Kč. To get here from the main train station, take tram No 3 at Jindřišská (direction: Modřany) to the tram stop at Černý kůň and follow the hostel signs to the river.

Hotels – bottom end A recommended place along the river is *Pension Bohemians* (☎ & fax 643 04 48) at Modřanská 51 in Podolí, Prague 4. Doubles with hot breakfast are 1350 Kč, and walk-in prospects are good. From Václavské náměstí take tram No 3 for 10 minutes, walk around the back and go to the top floor.

Hotels – middle The *Botel Racek* (☎ 61 21 43 83; fax 61 21 43 90) is a quiet floating hotel at Na Dvorecké louce in Podolí, Prague 4. Spartan cabins with shower and WC are 2000/2500 Kč with breakfast (40% less off-season). Walk-in prospects are good on weekdays, credit cards are accepted, and there's a restaurant. It's a five minute walk from the No 3 or 17 tram stop, 10 minutes from the city centre.

The business-oriented *Hotel ILF* (☎ 42 25 55; fax 42 36 92), Budějovická 15, Michle, Prague 4, has plain, carpeted rooms from 2000/2800 Kč with breakfast; cheaper ones might be booked through Top Tour. There's a dining room, and a smoky pivnice down the road. It's a block from Budějovická metro station.

The small *Hotel Kačerov* (☎ & fax 61 21 08 92), Na úlehli 1200, Kačerov, Prague 4, has rooms for 800/1200 Kč with breakfast, good walk-in odds, a decent restaurant but a shifty bar. It's a 10 minute walk (or bus No 106, 139 or 182) under the highway from Kačerov metro station.

The *Slavia Hotel* (☎ 67 31 24 71; fax 74 49 50), at Vladivostocká 10 in Vršovice, Prague 10, has spiffy rooms for 1500/1950 Kč with breakfast, and a restaurant. Credit cards are accepted. From Strašnická metro station, take tram No 7 west for two stops, or tram No 19 to the terminus; the hotel is to the right of the sports complex at the No 19 terminus.

On the edge of the Michelský woodlands in Prague 4 is CKM's smartly run *Hotel Globus* (☎ 792 77 00; fax 792 00 95), Gregorova 2115, Roztyly. Rooms with bath and TV are 1900/2600 Kč with breakfast, which is good value in this range; some rooms are outfitted for disabled guests. The hotel has a restaurant and pivnice. Walk-in prospects are good. It's five minutes from Roztyly metro; walk up left of the trees and turn right on Gregorova.

A pair of hotels sit on the edge of a housing estate near Opatov metro station, about 20 minutes from the centre. Walk east from the station towards two brown tower blocks. On the left is *Hotel Opatov* (☎ 793 13 08; fax 791 48 48) at Jonášova 2141. A one-plus-two mini-suite is 1400 Kč for one, 2000 Kč for two with breakfast, or a great bargain for three. The other is the glum *Hotel Sandra* (☎ 791 11 58; fax 795 16 21), Bardounova 2/2140, with rooms for 785/1240 Kč, including breakfast.

Hotels – top end Rooms in the high-rise *Interhotel Panorama* (☎ 61 16 11 11; fax 42 62 63), at Milevská 7 in Pankrác, Prague 4, are 4700/5400 Kč with breakfast. It's just around the corner from the Pankrác metro station.

The small *Villa Voyta* (☎ 472 55 11; fax 472 94 26) is in a fine Art Nouveau house at K Novému dvoru 54/124, Lhotka, Prague 4 – past the southern edge of our Greater Prague map. Its elegant rooms are targeted at business people and cost 4100/4900 Kč with breakfast. There's a very good restaurant here. Take bus No 113, 171, 189 or 215 south from Kačerov metro station to the Sídliště Krk stop, and walk three blocks west on Na Větrově.

North-East Outskirts (Prague 8 & 9)

Camping There are more campsites out in Prague 8 and 9 than anywhere else, some out past the edge of our Greater Prague map.

On the fringes of Prague 9 is *Autocamp Sokol* (☎ 72 75 01), on Nad Rybníkem in Dolní Počernice; from Palmovka metro station, take bus No 250 or 261 to the Dolní Počernice stop, then walk for 10 minutes.

To the north, at U parku 6 in Březiněves, Prague 8, is the *Bušek* (☎ 859 18 52; fax 22 36 17). From the No 12 terminus, take bus No 258 to the end of the line.

Also in Prague 8 is *Triocamp* (☎ & fax 688 11 80), at Obslužná 43 in Dolní Chabry, about 40 minutes from the city centre. From nádraží Holešovice metro station, take bus No 175 to Kobyliské náměstí, change to bus No 162 and go four stops.

Hotels The *Pension Praga* (☎ 66 31 07 32) is at U Lidového domu 11 in Vysočany, Prague 9. From the Českomoravská metro station, walk 700m east on Ocelářská and cross Freyova. A double is 1200 Kč, including shower, WC and breakfast. In Staré Strašnice, Prague 10, the uninspiring highrise *Hotel Rhea* (☎ 77 90 48/1; fax 77 06 23), V úžlabině, has mini-suites for 1620/2000 Kč, but there's little food in the neighbourhood. From Želivského metro station, take tram No 11 to the Zborov stop.

PLACES TO EAT

Tourism has had a heavy impact on the Prague restaurant scene. Cheaper restaurants have almost disappeared from the historical centre, while many places in the old town, the castle district and along Václavské náměstí are now patronised almost exclusively by tourists. If you're on a low budget it's worth walking a few streets away from the tourist centres or taking the metro to an outlying station and eating there.

Opening hours are volatile, so you may want to check them for yourself. Main courses can stop well before closing time, with only snacks and drinks after that.

We list price ranges for the main *hotová jídla* (ready-to-serve courses) and *jídla na objednávku* (courses to order). Plan on paying half to two-thirds more than this if you order side dishes and drinks.

Beer, Dumplings and McPork

Czech cuisine is typically central European, with German, Austrian, Polish and Hungarian influences. It's very filling, usually with meat, dumplings, potato or rice topped with a heavy sauce, and typically served with a vegetable or sauerkraut.

The standard meal, offered in just about every restaurant, is *'knedlo, zelo, vepřo'* (bread dumpling, sauerkraut and roast pork). Caraway seed, salt and bacon are the most common flavourings – most Czech chefs are rather generous with salt. Everything is washed down with alcohol, mainly beer (and lots of it). It's not diet food.

Prague's restaurant scene is changing remarkably fast, yearly sprouting dozens of new ethnic and international restaurants. Yet the Czech palate has proven rather stubborn – even McDonald's was forced to cater to the Czechs' fondness for swine with its McBůček burger, which replaces the beef with a slab of fried pork. ■

Reservations

In the high season, an advance booking is essential for dinner at an upper-end restaurant; for places near the city centre you may have to plan a few days ahead. Elsewhere and at other times you'll have few problems being served.

Most places that serve tourists have someone who can speak some English, but if you'd rather dispense with bookings, try eating at odd hours, such as having lunch at 11.30 am and dinner at 6 pm. Many pubs will serve you meat and dumplings at any time of day.

Self-Catering

There are food shops (*potraviny*) and supermarkets (*samoobsluha*) everywhere, the best but most expensive being in department stores near the city centre, such as in the basement of the glitzy Krone on Václavské náměstí, or in the Kotva department store off náměstí Republiky. The cheapest are Bílá labuť on Na poříčí or Tesco on Národní. One of the new large supermarkets in Staré Město is Pronto in the old Tržnice, which can be entered from either Rytířská or 28.října.

There aren't many open-air produce markets in the city. The biggest one near the centre is the pricier daily market along Havelská, south of Staroměstské náměstí (Old Town Square). Other inexpensive ones are in Dejvice (from Dejvická metro station, walk south-east on Dejvická

The Traps of Eating Out in Prague

Prague restaurants are notorious for overcharging. A survey by the Czech Commercial Inspectorate found that some 37% of their restaurant inspectors were overcharged, so you can imagine what happens to foreigners. Some places in tourist areas have two menus – one in Czech and one in foreign languages with higher prices. You might be charged considerably more for wiener schnitzel than for *telecí řízek*, which is the same thing.

If there's no menu, go elsewhere. If the menu has no prices, ask for them. Don't be intimidated by the language barrier; know exactly what you're ordering. When the waiter says 'rice or potatoes?' it may well cost you extra; learn how to say 'does it cost extra?' (*platí se zato zvlášť?*). Return anything you didn't order and don't want, such as bread, butter or side dishes. Don't just leave it to one side.

Finally, check your bill; better yet, estimate it before you let go of the menu. If you pay with a credit card, be sure the date and the price have been clearly and correctly entered, and keep in mind that unscrupulous proprietors may make several imprints of your card and copy your signature – try not to lose sight of it.

Many Prague restaurants have a cover charge (*couvert*), typically 10 to 20 Kč. In some places condiments like ketchup and mustard are not free, but if they charge you when you haven't used them, politely decline. ■

towards the railway line); at Bubenské nábřeží in southern Holešovice (closed Sunday); and a small one at Arbesovo náměstí in southern Malá Strana.

Early Breakfast

Plenty of buffets are open by 8 am, but you may not fancy soup and sausage at that time of day. Most restaurants that can do a western-style breakfast don't open until 10 or 11 am. But there's hope. On the 1st floor at Národní 22, *Gany's* kavárna, open from 8 am to 11 pm, has a reasonable Swedish-table breakfast that includes fried eggs and ham for 100 Kč, and it's all in grand Art Nouveau surroundings. The *Red, Hot & Blues*, Jakubská 12, does the only real western-style fry-up from 9 am daily, and their more expensive brunches on weekends finish at 4 pm. The *kavárna* (coffee bar), at the rear of the *Paris-Praha* shop at Jindřišská 7, does croissant sandwiches daily from 8.30 am. The 350 Kč Swedish-table breakfast at *Hotel Don Gioavanni*, Vinohradská 157A, Prague 3, has an expensive, though large, selection of brunch food – but the coffee is terrible.

Hradčany & Malá Strana (Prague 1)

Prague Castle There might be room among the tourist groups at *Vikárka* (☎ 55 51 58), Vikářská 39, where inventive Czech main courses are 150 to 350 Kč. A cheaper place is the passable upstairs bistro *U Kanovníků*, also on Vikářská (but check your bill closely). For cake and good coffee, or an ordinary meal from 120 to 275 Kč, try *Café Poet*. It's on Na baště, left of the castle's main gate, and is open daily from 10 am to 6 pm. At Hradčanské náměstí 11 is *U Labutí*, which has a cheap beer hall (60 to 120 Kč) and a more expensive garden dining area (200 to 350 Kč).

Hradčany Loretánská is lined with places serving Czech and international meals. The moderately priced *U stará radnice* (☎ 20 51 11 40), at Loretánská 1 in the former Hradčany town hall, is the least pretentious eatery in the neighbourhood, and is open daily from 10 am to 10 pm. Down the street at No 13 is *Renthauz*, with above-average Czech dishes from 80 to 150 Kč and a sunny terrace overlooking the city. It's open daily to 8 pm.

For inexpensive beer, coffee and snacks try the friendly *Literární kavárna U zavěšeného kafe* (Literary Café of the Hanging Coffee), on the Castle Steps at No 7.

In Hradčany's quiet backstreets, at Nový svět 3, is *U zlaté hrušky* (☎ 53 11 33), a quiet, elegant place popular with politicians. The set menu is 350 Kč, with entrées starting at 200 Kč.

At the upper end of Hradčany, on Loretánské náměstí, *Pivnice U Černého vola* is a pub with hot snacks and cheap beer. A bit farther up, at Pohořelec 3, is the excellent *Sate indonéské kuchyně* (☎ 20 51 45 52), with authentic Indonesian noodle dishes from 85 to 110 Kč. It's open daily to 10 pm. The oriental tearoom *Malý Buddha*, Úvoz 46, has a variety of Asian teas and vegetarian dishes, and is open daily from 2 to 10.30 pm.

The up-market *Peklo* restaurant (☎ 57 32 01 09) is uphill from Strahov Monastery in a small smoky cellar; the name means 'hell', not for the atmosphere but because monks used to do penance here. The food is Italian and Czech, and ranges from 300 to 450 Kč. It's open daily from 6 pm (the bar stays open to 4 am).

Nerudova & Around *Hostinec U kocoura*, Nerudova 2, is one of President Havel's favourites. Basic but delicious Czech meals here are 60 to 110 Kč – try the smoked chicken. The crowds are heavy at lunch time. At No 19, *U zeleného čaje* serves and sells teas from around the world, as well as light salads and sandwiches, daily to 7.30 pm. *N Pizzeria*, at No 37, is nothing fancy, just a good place for cheap pizzas (100 Kč) and pastas. It's open daily to 10 pm. One of the better spots for tea or a snack is the tranquil, incense-filled teahouse *Zapomenutá Čajovna*, in a courtyard at Jánský vršek 312/8.

For Greek food priced under 220 Kč try *Restaurant Faros* (☎ 53 34 82) at Šporkova 5, open daily from noon to 3 pm and 6 to 11 pm. It's a sedate place, mainly popular with workers from the nearby German and Italian embassies.

The swank *Lobkovická Vinárna* (☎ 53 01 85), Vlašská 17, has an excellent wine list plus a continental menu lightly spiced with Czech dishes (200 to 350 Kč). It's open daily from noon to 3 pm and 6.30 pm to midnight.

Malostranské Náměstí & Around On the square, at No 7, is the trendy *Jo's Bar*, where the young expat crowd comes for sandwiches and surprisingly decent Mexican food (80 to 110 Kč). It's open from 11 am to 2 am and has a two-beers-for-one happy hour weekdays from 5 to 6 pm, plus a weekend brunch.

The best thing about *U malého Glena*, Karmelitská 24, is its weekend brunch (to 3 pm), with bagels and other western-style dishes. There's a bar downstairs with live music most nights. Across the road is the small, friendly *U svatého Václava*, with decent Czech dishes for 95 to 180 Kč. Nearby, at No 30, is the mouthwatering deli and food shop *J+J Mašek & Zemanova*.

Back on the square, *U tří zlatých hvězd* (☎ 53 96 60), Malostranské náměstí 8, has four-course Czech lunches for 200 Kč, though the a la carte menu (up to 500 Kč) is superior. It's open daily from 11.30 am to 4 pm.

On the square, at No 12, are the adjoining *Circle Line* (☎ 53 03 08) and *Avalon Grill* (☎ 53 02 76). The Circle Line (on the ground floor) is very posh, with a superb wine list and unique items like brill with ham or Basque-style pepper fondue, plus 850 Kč French set menu (open 6 pm to midnight). The Avalon Grill (upstairs) is a more informal bar and grill, with pastas, salads and meat dishes from 150 to 350 Kč (open 11 am to 1 am). Both are closed Sunday.

North-east from the square, at Letenská 12, is *Pivnice U sv Tomáše* (☎ 53 67 76), a beer hall with Czech standards plus a few vegetarian dishes, all are less than 180 Kč.

The rather more exotic menu at *Waldštejnská hospoda* (☎ 53 61 95), an ornate beer hall on the corner of Valdštejnské náměstí and Tomášská, includes deer and wild pig for up to 350 Kč. It's open daily to 11.30 pm.

Another spot with great atmosphere is the *Pálffy Palác club restaurace* (☎ 51 32 54 18), tucked away on the 1st floor of the Pálffy Palace at Valdštejnská 14. It serves mainly fish or meat dishes with mouthwatering sauces from 120 to 250 Kč.

Charles' Bridge & Around Opposite Kampa island, at Cihelná 22, is *Restaurace Čertovka* (☎ 53 88 53), which is OK for a meal or a drink, though its main attraction is the view of Charles' Bridge. Small main courses are 120 to 200 Kč. In summer there's live piano music on Thursday evenings.

The area's cheapest (and least touristy) beer hall is *U Bílé kuželky* at Mišeňská 12, with Czech dishes for 80 to 120 Kč.

Just north of the Malá Strana bridge tower, at Dražického náměstí 4, is the excellent but very expensive *Restaurace U Patrona* (☎ 53 15 12), with Czech and continental main dishes for 400 to 700 Kč and a four-course set menu for 1250 Kč.

U sněděného krámu (☎ 53 17 95), Lazeňská 19, has a Czech and international menu with plenty of entrées for less than 200 Kč, and old-Prague decor. It's open daily to 11 pm.

Down the street is the *Chiméra*, a self-styled gallery and café, ideal for an afternoon of newspaper reading. The menu has coffees, beer, ice creams and light snacks.

At Maltézské náměstí 11 is one of Prague's best and most expensive French restaurants, the *Mazlova vinárna U malířů* (☎ 57 32 03 17). Main courses are 700 to 900 Kč, and the four-course set menu is 1500 Kč. It's open daily from 7 to 10 pm.

Around the corner at Prokopská 10 is the *Vinárna U maltézských rytířů* (☎ 53 63 57), a place for that romantic dinner or quiet business lunch. The service is fast and pleasant, and the food is very good (main dishes 200 to 300 Kč). It's open daily from 11 am to 11 pm.

Kampa & Southern Malá Strana Na Kampě square has several eateries. *U zlatých nůžek* (☎ 24 51 01 10) at No 6 has salads and Czech dishes for 100 to 120 Kč.

A good mini-splurge is *U staleté báby* (☎ 53 15 68) at No 15, a modern space with fish tanks and Art Deco fixtures, plus a sunny outdoor garden. Pastas and meat dishes are 300 Kč and up. Around the corner is the cheaper *U staleté báby pivnice*, a bar-restaurant with excellent pizzas (80 to 110 Kč). Both are open daily from 10 am to 10 pm.

At the southern end of Kampa is a good fish restaurant, the *Rybářský klub* (☎ 53 02 23). Main courses are 100 to 190 Kč.

The elegant *U modré kachničky* (☎ 57 32 03 08), Nebovidská 6, is on a quiet side street, perfect for a romantic evening. Meat or fish dishes at 200 to 450 Kč are good value. Try the duck with one of the unusual sauces. It's open daily from noon to 4 pm and 6.30 to 11 pm.

The first stop on the funicular railway up Petřín Hill is at the *Nebozízek Restaurant* (☎ 53 79 05), Petřínské sady 411, with a varied menu of Czech and seafood dishes from 150 to 350 Kč. The salads are good, and the steaks and wines are excellent, as are the views.

Josefov (Prague 1)

Kavárna Hogo Fogo (☎ 231 70 23), Salvátorská 4, is great for a coffee hit or lunch, and the music's good. A big list of vegetarian dishes are righteously priced under 100 Kč. It's open Sunday to Thursday from 11.30 am to midnight, Friday and Saturday to 2 am.

Vinárna U Golema (☎ 232 81 65) and *Vinárna U Rudolfa* (☎ 232 26 71) are right across Maiselova from one another, at Nos 8 and 5. U Golema is a quiet wine bar with fish, poultry and meat dishes from 100 to 180 Kč, and is open daily from 11 am to 10 pm. U Rudolfa is probably better, a grill with fine meat dishes cost – from 90 to 130 Kč. It's open from 10 am to 10 pm.

Shalom (☎ 231 89 96), in the Jewish Town Hall at Maiselova 18, is a kosher restaurant, with set lunches (11.30 am to 2 pm) from 120 to 350 Kč.

Inside the Museum of Decorative Arts, 17.listopadu 2, is a smoky *coffee house* with light meals and good music, which is open from 10.30 am to 10.30 pm on weekdays, to 6 pm on weekends. The *Česká hospoda* pub (☎ 231 73 30), Vězeňská 9, has uneven food and service and the Czech food costs 65 to 210 Kč; it's closed on Sunday.

Staré Město (Prague 1)

Around Staroměstské Náměstí Restaurants around Staroměstské náměstí (Old Town Square) tend to be predatory, but the food can be splendid. Worth a try is *Staroměstská restaurace* (☎ 24 21 30 15), Staroměstské náměstí 19, not far from the Old Town Hall. Food and beer prices on the square outside are up to 60% higher than those charged inside. The meaty Czech and international menu is extensive (65 to 250 Kč) and the food good with pleasant service. Try the fruit dumplings.

A good upmarket French restaurant with pleasant service, whose proprietor speaks a few languages, is *Le Saint-Jacques* (☎ 232 26 85) at Jakubská 4. Mains cost from 160 to 450 Kč. Try the steaks or frogs' legs.

Among the various expat bars that are frequented by tourists and Czechs alike is *Chapeau Rouge*, on the corner of Malá Štupartská and Jakubská. It gets crowded and its staff suffer from surliness – that famous Czech waiter disease. It's open daily from 4 pm to 4 am.

Around Dlouhá A very good bakery at Dlouhá 1, *Michelské pekařství*, is open weekdays from 6.30 am to 6.30 pm, Saturday from 7 am to noon, and Sunday from 3.30 to 7 pm. A cheap alternative is *US Burger* (☎ 231 59 83), Masná 2, open weekdays from 10.30 am to 9 pm, which has hamburgers, fishburgers, good chicken dishes and Mexican food; nothing costs more than about 80 Kč.

Restaurace U Dlouhé (☎ 231 61 25), Dlouhá 35, serves tasty, reasonably priced Czech food (main courses from 60 to 180 Kč) daily from 11 am to 11 pm. At Dlouhá 8 is a pizza joint with good but unusual pizzas with too many toppings, including a dessert one with chocolate. *Mikulkás Pizzeria* (☎ 231 00 18), open daily from 11.30 am to at least 10 pm, has pizzas for 53 to 103 Kč per person. Look out for their display pizzas in a glass stand in front of the restaurant. Another pizza place is at Benediktská 16 (☎ 231 67 27); bookings at both are recommended.

Among the string of Irish pubs around Prague that serve Guinness and Irish whiskies is *Molly Malones*, tucked away in the northern part of Staré Město at U obecního dvora 4. There is an ambient candle-lit atmosphere here, suiting the old part of Prague outside.

Around Náměstí Republiky *Red, Hot & Blues* (☎ 231 46 39), Jakubská 12, offers burgers or Texas chilli for 99 Kč and New Orleans specials like shrimp creole for up to 289 Kč, plus wicked desserts and 'bottomless' coffee. It's open from 9 am to about midnight, with traditional jazz playing and the occasional live gig.

At Celetná 29 is *Restaurace U zlatých andělů* (☎ 232 82 37), which has a varied menu and main courses from 68 to 285 Kč. At Templová 2, off Celetná, is *Pivnice Radegast* with fast but not the most pleasant service, although the traditional Czech food is very good and inexpensive for the location. Perhaps the best menu item is the guláš with dumplings (54 Kč). It's open daily from 11 am to midnight and is popular with young Czechs.

Municipal House The Municipal House (Obecní dům), at náměstí Republiky 5, provides an unmatched Art Nouveau setting for good food and drink. To the left as you enter is the *Kavárna Obecní dům*, with pricey (although nothing is over 120 Kč) pastries and coffee, salads and sandwiches until late.

To the right of the entrance is *Francouzská restaurace*, with good French cuisine for 195 to 480 Kč; try the beef burgundy with celery purée. In the basement is the inexpensive but touristy *Plzeňská restaurace* with Czech pub food from 60 to 95 Kč per main dish.

Around Havelská *Country Life*, Melantrichova 15, is Prague's finest stand-up joint. It's a health-food shop and wholesome vegetarian salad-and-sandwich bar where you can fill up for under 80 Kč. It's jammed at lunch time, so go early or ask for a takeaway. It's open Sunday from noon to 6 pm, Monday to Thursday from 8.30 am to 7 pm, and Friday from 8.30 am to 2.30 pm.

Around Betlémské Náměstí *Hospoda U Vejvodů* (☎ 24 21 05 91), in an ancient building at Jilská 4, is a traditional pub serving Czech standard fare for 27 to 200 Kč. Service is unhurried, though you'll have time for a beer before you sit down. It's open daily from 11 am to 11 pm.

The architect's club restaurant *Klub Architektů* (☎ 61 50 17 60), in an underground cellar at Betlémské náměstí 5, is popular for food or coffee. Their Czech and international dishes have unusual combinations; there are also vegetarian dishes (all under 90 Kč).

The Icelandic restaurant *Reykjavík* (☎ 24 22 92 51), Karlova 20, has some excellent seafood dishes (210 to 390 Kč), along with chicken and meat dishes. Try the 'salmon pocket', with vegetables that are steamed to a crunchy perfection.

Perhaps one of the finest restaurants in the city is the *Vinárna v zátiší* (☎ 24 22 89 77) at Liliová 1, as it has some excellent international and Czech dishes with a difference. The mains cost from 300 to 500 Kč; for something totally different try the duck leg with herb dumplings. There are some vegetarian dishes for around 200 Kč.

North of Národní Třída *Restaurace U medvídků* (☎ 24 22 09 30), at Na Perštýně 7 just off Národní, is a popular beer hall/wine bar/no-smoking restaurant with an outdoor garden, with the usual meat-heavy dishes (80 to 190 Kč). It's open daily from 11.30 am to 11 pm.

In the passage at Národní 4 is an Internet café, the *Highland Group International Café* (☎ 21 08 52 84), where one hour on the Internet costs 120 Kč. It's open weekdays from 9 am to 9 pm, and weekends from 3 to 10 pm.

Northern Nové Město (Prague 1)
Café Four, Soukenická 2, offers pizza, trout, salads and apple pie. At the vegetarian *U Góvindy* (☎ 24 81 60 16), Soukenická 27, a 'donation' of at least 50 Kč gets you a generous, imaginatively seasoned set meal of hot vegetables, soup, salad, rice, cake and herbal tea. It's run by Hare Krishnas but nobody's preaching. It's open Monday to Saturday from 11 am to 5 pm.

At Truhlářská 4 is the vaguely rustic *Restaurace MD Rettigové* (☎ 231 44 83), named after Magdalena Dobromila Rettigová, a 19th century exponent of a culinary Czech National Revival. The menu is serious (poultry and meat for 120 to 200 Kč, specials like roast goose and frogs' legs for up to 300 Kč) and the food is good.

Pizzeria Mamma Mia (☎ 231 47 26), Na poříčí 13, rustles up very good pizzas in a wood-fired oven (49 to 200 Kč for two people). It's open daily from 11 am to 11 pm, Sunday from 5 to 10 pm.

Southern Nové Město (Prague 1 & 2)
Main Train Station The old station (level 4) has *Fantova kavárna*, a cafeteria, under the cupola and surrounded by the Art Nouveau splendour.

Around Václavské Náměstí The square is lined with atmospheric places where you generally pay over-the-top prices. One good exception is the *Delicatesse Buffet* in the Hotel Palace, on the corner of Panská and Jindřišská, which is open daily from 11 am to 7 pm with a 60 Kč salad bar and a few meat dishes – very good value.

Another good place is the *Mayur Indický Snack Bar* (☎ 24 22 67 37), on the other side of the square at Štěpánská 63. Deprived spice-heads will weep over the reasonable curries, soups, salads and fresh tandoori bread; there are also vegetarian dishes (all 99 to 185 Kč). It's open daily from noon to 11 pm. Next door is the *Mayur Indický Restaurant*, with larger but more expensive main courses.

On the square at No 57, the *Bonal Café* has good sandwiches, pastries and coffee; two doors down it has a patisserie. In the Melantrich building, at No 36, is a sausage shop called *Jídelna – uzeniny* with a popular stand-up buffet that serves soups, goulash, chicken and the best bread dumplings in central Prague. It's open daily from 7 am to 7 pm.

Just off the square, on the corner of Na příkopě and Havířská, some of those famous Hollywood stars opened a *Planet Hollywood* restaurant. It has the usual Hollywood paraphernalia and American favourites like hamburgers, pastas, fajitas and salads at premium prices. Nothing is over 375 Kč and 500mL of beer is 50 Kč.

West of Václavské Náměstí At Vodičkova 9 you can sample the salsa-hot cuisine of the Texas-Mexico border at *Buffalo Bill's Tex-Mex Bar & Grille* (☎ 24 21 54 79), open from noon to midnight. At Vodičkova 26, the unpretentious beer hall *U Purkmistra* (☎ 24 22 71 03) has a meaty, good-value Czech menu (100 to 200 Kč) and cheap beer. It's open daily from 9 am to 11 pm.

The cafeteria-style *Country Life*, Jungmannova 1, has fresh vegetarian salads, sandwiches, pizza and goulash at great prices (fill up for under 60 Kč). It's crowded at lunch time, so come early or late; it's open Monday to Thursday from 8.30 am to 6.30 pm, Friday to 3 pm.

For great ice cream try *Italská cukrárna* at Vodičkova 4.

At Ve Smečkách 26, *Smečky dietní restaurace* serves boring, low-calorie courses for less than 64 Kč, weekdays only from 10 am to 2.30 pm. It has some vegetarian dishes and even a macrobiotic menu. At No 3, the plain *Pohádka* pub (☎ 236 27 69) has cheap Gambrinus beer and all-night hours (daily from 9 am to 7 am).

For sports fans there is the *Sport Bar*, Ve Smečkách 30, with TV screens all around showing Eurosport programmes; open daily from 9 am to 2 pm. If you're craving American-style fast food (burgers up to 120 Kč and salads from 35 Kč) and the company of expats, this is the place for you.

Around the block at Krakovská 20, the pub *Česká hospoda v Krakovské* (☎ 26 15 37) serves plain Czech food (with light or dark Braník beer) for under 100 Kč, daily from 10 am to 11 pm. The small cosy place gets crowded, so it might be wise to book ahead. For tastier food in duller and less-crowded surroundings try the *Jihočeská restaurace U Šumavy*, Štěpánská 3, which is closed Saturday.

Closer to Václavské náměstí, at Štěpánská 18, is the Internet café *Kavárna Cybeteria* (☎ 24 23 30 24; email info @cybeteria.cz). Connections are 50 Kč for 30 minutes.

Národní Třída The modest *Café-Restaurant Národní 21* (☎ 26 75 19), Národní 21, has Czech standard fare and Italian dishes from 95 to 220 Kč. The pseudo Art Nouveau *Café-Bar Craull Evropa* (☎ 26 20 80), at No 23, has snacks downstairs from 8 am, and a pricey (90 to 700 Kč) Czech and international restaurant upstairs, daily from noon to midnight.

Across the road, on the 1st floor at No 22, is a kavárna called *Gany's* (☎ 29 76 65), open from 8 am to 11 pm. Czech courses (plus some vegetarian dishes) are 70 to 240 Kč. The buffet breakfast is 100 Kč.

South of Národní Třída *Restaurace U Mázlů* (☎ 26 12 72), Jungmannova 26, offers Czech dishes (plus more interesting fare like trout and venison) for 70 to 190 Kč. Service is quick, there's an English-language menu, and it's open daily from 11 am to 11 pm.

For a sugar-and-caffeine hit try *Monica cukrárna*, down an alley at Národní 32 and open daily from 9 am to 7 pm (Saturday from 10 am, Sunday from 11 am).

A place with absent-minded service, but

interesting music is the *Kavárna Velryba* (☎ 241 23 91), Opatovická 24. It's an arty café-bar with good coffee and heaps of tasty, mainly vegetarian food at ridiculously low prices (less than 89 Kč per dish), and it's open daily from 11 am to 2 am.

Pizzeria Kmotra (☎ 24 91 58 09) makes non-greasy pizzas (53 to 145 Kč) from scratch in the basement at V jirchářích 12, with lots of cheap beer to wash it down. Hours are 11 am to 1 am – though the crowds are thick by 8 pm.

The jolly drinking and eating rooms at the *U Fleků* (☎ 29 89 59) beer hall, Křemencova 11, are a Prague institution, increasingly clogged with tour groups high on oompah music and the tavern's own 13 degree black beer (39 Kč for a 400mL glass). Food prices are shamelessly touristic (150 to 300 Kč). You might still find an empty seat by 7 pm on a weekday; it's open daily from 9 am to 11 pm.

For Indian vegetarian food and teas try *Dátá Santóš* (☎ 24 21 78 62) at Žitná 42, open weekdays from 1 to 10 pm and Saturday from 3 to 8 pm.

Pivnice U zpěváčků, on the corner of Vojtěšská and Pštrossova, is a good cheap pub if you like mixing with young dropouts.

On the west side of Slovanský ostrov is an unexceptional *café* with exceptional views to accompany an afternoon beer or snack.

Karlovo náměstí The *Pizza Taxi* Italian restaurant (☎ 29 57 62), Karlovo náměstí 28, has a huge menu of mediocre pizzas and pasta (pizza for one from 82 to 170 Kč). It's open daily from 11 am to 11 pm. *Vinárna U Čížků* (☎ 29 88 91), at No 34, serves Czech dishes for 150 to 280 Kč daily from noon to 3.30 pm and 5 to 10 pm. Both are a few minutes from the Karlovo náměstí metro station.

Near the Vltava The following places are all within a few blocks of Karlovo náměstí metro station, and close to tram No 3 from Václavské náměstí.

The small but popular fish restaurant *Vinárna Nad přístavem* (☎ 29 86 36), at Rašínovo nábřeží 64, has tasty main dishes from 90 to 230 Kč. The carp is excellent. Down the road at No 10, the friendly *Šnek Bar* café (☎ 29 73 21) offers 'Chinese' food and meaty variants on Czech dishes for a modest 66 Kč, daily from 11 am to about 11 pm (Sunday from 2 pm to midnight). At No 1, *Restaurace U Pomníku* serves meat and fish dinners for less than 90 Kč.

At the central quay, from where the river cruise boats leave, *Restaurant Vltava* (☎ 29 49 64) serves decent fish and Chinese dishes from 70 Kč, daily from 11 am to 10 pm. It's great on a warm evening, though summer-afternoon sunlight turns it into a solar oven.

South of Karlovo náměstí *U Čínského labužníka* (☎ 24 91 14 77), Vyšehradská 39, offers authentic Chinese food for 105 to 405 Kč, and several vegetarian dishes. It's open Monday to Saturday from 11 am to 3 pm and 5.30 to 11 pm. Take tram No 24 from Václavské náměstí.

Vyšehrad (Prague 2)

Within the Vyšehrad complex there's a café in the remains of Špička Gate, and a snack bar by the remains of the St Lawrence Basilica. The new and pricey *Restaurace na Vyšehradě*, Štulcova 2, has a very meat and fish-oriented Czech menu for 120 to 320 Kč. It's open daily between 10 am to 10 pm.

Holešovice (Prague 7)

The best pizza in Holešovice comes from *Pizzeria San Pietro*, Milady Horákové 63, which is often packed on Saturday and Sunday nights.

The Globe (☎ 66 71 26 10), Janovského 14, is a perennially popular café and bookshop, with a refreshing mix of sandwiches, soups, pastas and leafy salads, plus a delicious weekend brunch. It's open daily from 10 am to midnight (in winter to 11 pm).

Just up the street is *Na krušárně*, Šternberkova 3, a smart-looking bar and restaurant serving standard Czech dishes for less than 100 Kč, daily to midnight.

The trendy and raucous *Derby*, Dukelských hrdinů 20, is all about pizza, lots of beer and loud alternative rock.

Restaurant U divadla (☎ 87 94 87), Sochora 9, is a modern, newly renovated eatery with standard Czech dishes for 60 to 100 Kč.

There are two Chinese restaurants near the Fairgrounds: *Hong Kong* (☎ 37 13 70) at Letenské náměstí 5, and *China Restaurant* (☎ 87 00 16) at Janovského 36. Both serve authentic noodle dishes and tasty soups from 90 to 150 Kč. In terms of tone, the latter is more formal.

Smíchov (Prague 1 & 5)

One of Smíchov's few up-market restaurants is *Café Savoy-Classique*, an airy high-ceilinged space, popular with Prague's nouveau riche. Head to the bar while you wait for a table. Pastas and meat dishes are 180 to 250 Kč.

The decor at *Diana Snack Bar* (☎ 53 17 35), Elišky Peškové 17, is 1960s in the best sense. Come for coffee or a light meal (80 to 120 Kč).

Vinárna U Mikuláše Dačického, Viktora Huga 2, and *Hostinec pod schůdky*, Zborovská 46, serve no-nonsense Czech meals for less than 90 Kč. Both are off the beaten path. The former is open daily from 4 pm to 1 am, the latter from 10 am to 10 pm.

Pizzeria U Tučňáků, náměstí 14.října, has above-average pizzas for 60 to 90 Kč.

The up-market *Sakura* (☎ 54 23 48), Štefánikova 7, serves sushi, tempura and udon noodles in a twee Japanese setting. The sushi set menu is a staggering 2200 Kč; a la carte sushi is 150 to 400 Kč. The cheapest noodle dishes are 320 Kč.

Libeň (Prague 8)

A refuge for vegetarians and paupers is the *Góvinda Vegetarian Club* (or *U Góvindy*; ☎ 683 72 26) at Na hrázi 5, just north of Palmovka metro station. A 'donation' of at least 45 Kč gets you a generous set-meal of hot vegetable, soup, salad, rice, cake and herbal tea. It's run by the Hare Krishnas and is open weekdays from noon to 6 pm.

Žižkov (Prague 3)

A good local meeting place that includes a sauna (40 Kč per hour) is the *U radnice* (☎ 27 57 60) at Havlíčkovo náměstí 7. It has good Czech food and dishes cost from 38 to 90 Kč. Take tram No 26 from náměstí Republiky to tram stop Lipanská. *Restaurace U koleje* (☎ 627 41 63), Slavíkova 24, is an unpretentious vinárna with carefully prepared Czech dishes for less than 120 Kč. It's four blocks north of Jiřího z Poděbrad metro station, open only on weekdays from 11 am to 10 pm.

Restaurace Confucius (☎ 27 57 36), Seifertova 18, which is on the corner of Přibyslavská, is a quiet Chinese place with attentive service and generous helpings for less than 120 Kč. It's open daily from 11 am to 3 pm and 5.30 to 11 pm.

The inexpensive *Restaurace Viktoria* (☎ 27 63 60), just two blocks north at Prokopovo náměstí, has dishes for under 60 Kč. It's open daily from 11 am to 11 pm. From Václavské náměstí take tram No 9.

The small but pleasant *Tabák – Kaaba café*, Lucemburská 15, sells newspapers and magazines (even the *Prague Post* and some other foreign-language publications). It closes daily at 10 pm. Not far away at Kubelíkova 27 is the alternative Palác Akropolis, which, on the corner with Víta Nejedlého, also has the *Akropolis Theatre* café (☎ 27 21 84) inside. There is a bar and some inexpensive vegetarian dishes are served that include salads with names such as 'vitamin shock'.

South of Olšanský Cemetery is the popular *Crazy Daisy restaurant* (☎ 67 31 03 78), Vinohradská 142, opposite the Flora metro station. The seafood dishes (crevettes and salmon) are tasty and fairly priced (70 to 130 Kč). It also offers good Czech-style meatless dishes plus large salads; daily from 11 am to 11 pm.

Vinohrady (Prague 2)

In addition to underground decor, the *FX Café,* Bělehradská 120, has great salads, imaginative soups and vegetarian dishes plus pita sandwiches and cakes. It stays open daily from 11.30 am to at least 5 am. Weekend brunch is from 11 am to 3 pm. It's part of the Club Radost complex (see Entertainment), two blocks east of IP Pavlova metro station or a 10 minute walk from the top of Václavské náměstí.

U knihomola (☎ 627 77 67), Mánesova 79, is a bookshop-café that serves light French dishes weekdays from 10 am to 11 pm, Saturday until midnight, and Sunday from 11 am to 8 pm.

A Chinese restaurant in the same area, at Anglická 6, is *Zlatý drak* (☎ 24 21 81 54). It's open daily from 11.30 am to 3 pm and 6.30 to 10.30 pm. Main dishes are 100 to 170 Kč. At Budečská 6, south-east from náměstí Míru, *Restaurace Pravěk* (☎ 24 25 22 87) offers duck, venison, wild boar and their version of a Stone Age pizza for 90 to 300 Kč per course, plus beer and wine. There are also some meatless dishes.

Down where Vinohrady spills into the Nusle valley is *Restaurace Na Zvonařce* (☎ 24 25 27 75), in a residential area at Šafaříkova 1. The patio commands a wide view across the valley. 'Plzeň-style' Czech dishes are good value for less than 60 Kč. It's open daily from 11 am to 11 pm. Take tram No 6 from IP Pavlova metro station, or walk 10 minutes from náměstí Míru.

CZECH REPUBLIC

Dejvice & North-West Outskirts (Prague 6)

Dejvice has a few interesting spots near Vítězné náměstí. *U Cedru* (☎ 312 29 74), Národní obrany 27, is an up-market Lebanese restaurant with dishes like chopped lamb, tabouleh salad and stuffed vine leaves priced under 200 Kč.

U kmotra (☎ 312 24 57), Eliášova 27, is a quiet, pleasant spot for Italian and Czech dishes under 130 Kč; open daily to 11 pm.

The popular *Budvarka* (☎ 32 89 89), on the corner of Wachterlova and Svatovítská, is good for a drink or something from the simple Czech menu (60 to 120 Kč).

Dejvická sokolovna, Dejvická 2, is nothing fancy, just a simple beer hall with simple food and very cheap beer.

U zlatého ražně (☎ 24 31 11 61), Československé armády 22, has a few vegetarian choices plus typical Czech treats like smoked tongue, all priced 100 to 150 Kč. It's open daily to 11 pm.

South-East Outskirts (Prague 4)

The *Dlouhá zeď* (Great Wall) Chinese restaurant (☎ 692 23 74), Pujmanové 10/1218 in Pankrác, a five minute walk from Pankrác metro station, has had mixed reports about its service and main dishes (100 to 600 Kč). It's open daily, except Monday, from 11 am to 3 pm and 5.30 to 11 pm.

The *Restaurace Eureka* (☎ 76 11 15), Roztylské náměstí 2, has big helpings of Czech and international dishes for less than 150 Kč, and several kinds of salad. From Roztyly metro station, take bus No 118 to the Roztylské stop (a few minutes walk from the restaurant).

ENTERTAINMENT

Prague features a bewildering array of entertainment, from jazz to rock, ballet to bluegrass, highbrow drama to ice hockey. Prague is now as much a European centre for jazz and alternative rock as for classical music.

It's a changing scene, too. For reviews, up-to-the-minute venues and day-by-day listings, see the 'Night & Day' section of the *Prague Post*. The bi-monthly pamphlet *Do města Downtown*, free at bars and restaurants, lists clubs, galleries, cinemas, theatre events etc. The monthly *Prague Cultural Events* booklet, available at PIS, focusses more on opera, ballet and classical music.

Tickets

For classical music, opera, ballet, theatre and some rock concerts – even the most thoroughly 'sold-out' events – you can often find a ticket or two on sale at the box office during the half-hour or so before show time. Many venues have discounts for students and seniors, and sometimes for the disabled. Non-Czechs normally pay the same price as Czechs – though at special events like the Prague Spring, tickets for foreigners can be up to 600% more expensive than for Czechs.

If you can't be bothered, or you want a sure seat, Prague is awash with ticket agencies. Their advantage is convenience: most are computerised and quick, and accept credit cards. Their drawback is the service charge, usually 10 to 15% of the ticket's face value. Touts will sell you a ticket at the door, but avoid them unless all other avenues have been exhausted.

For rock and jazz clubs, just show up at the door, though for well known acts tickets are also sold through the following agencies and it is usually recommended to buy them in advance. Melantrich is usually the best place to buy tickets for rock concerts.

Following are some reliable agencies. The main 'wholesalers' are BTI, FOK, IfB and Ticketpro. The others are apt to get their tickets from these agencies and then resell them to you (at a higher price):

American Express (☎ 24 21 99 92), Václavské náměstí 56

BTI: Na příkopě 16, Staré Město (☎ 24 21 50 31); Salvátorská 6, Josefov (☎ 24 22 78 32)

Čedok: Na příkopě 18, Staré Město (☎ 24 19 76 42); Pařížská 6, Josefov (☎ 231 69 78); Rytířská 16, Staré Město (☎ 26 36 97)

FOK (☎ 24 89 32 27), Rudolfinum at náměstí Jana Palacha, Staré Město: mainly for the Prague Symphony

IfB (☎ 24 22 72 53), Václavské náměstí 27

Melantrich (☎ 24 21 50 18), in the passage of Václavské náměstí 36

Ticketpro's Melantrich: in the passage Rokoko, Václavské náměstí 38, Nové Město (☎ 24 21 50 18) – good for rock and pop concerts; Ticketpro at PIS, Old Town Hall, Staroměstské náměstí 1, Staré Město (☎ 24 48 20 18); and Na příkopě 20, Staré Město (☎ 26 40 20); or check out their web page (www.ticketpro.cz)

Classical Music, Opera & Ballet

There are half a dozen concerts of one kind or another almost every day in summer, a fine soundtrack to the city's visual delights. Many are chamber concerts by aspiring musicians in the city's churches – gorgeous but chilly (take an extra layer, even on a summer day).

The *Křižík Fountain* (Křižíkova fontána; ☎ 20 10 32 80) at the Fairgrounds (Výstaviště), Holešovice, Prague 7, has classical and occasionally even electronic or rock music performances while jets of water shoot to various heights. This is even more spectacular at night when coloured lights illuminate the jets of water. The one-hour shows commence at 7, 8 and 9 pm in summer and at 4, 5 and 6 pm in spring and autumn.

The following are some major venues:

Hradčany
: *St George Basilica*, Prague Castle; *Lobkovic Palace*, Prague Castle; *St Vitus Cathedral*, Prague Castle; *Wallenstein Palace*, Valdštejnské náměstí

Malá Strana
: *St Nicholas Church*, Malostranské náměstí; *Nostitz Palace*, Maltézské náměstí 1

Nové Město
: *State Opera Theatre* (☎ 26 53 53), Wilsonova 4 – mainly opera and ballet, box office open from 10 am to 5.30 pm (closed weekends between noon and 1 pm); *Villa Amerika* (Dvořák museum), Ke Karlovu 20 – special Dvořák concerts

Vyšehrad
: *New Provost's House* – 3.30 pm Sunday afternoon concerts in summer; *Congress Center*, Palace of Culture, 5.května 65 (next to Vyšehrad metro station) – recitals, chamber concerts, pop concerts

Staré Město & Josefov
: *House at the Stone Bell*, Staroměstské náměstí 13; *Rudolfinum* (☎ 24 89 31 11), 17.listopadu – box office open from 10 am to 12.30 pm and 1.30 to 6 pm (and for one hour before performances), access for wheelchairs; *Convent of St Agnes*, U milosrdných 17; *Church of Our Lady Before Týn*, Staroměstské náměstí; *Church of St Francis Seraphinus*, Křižovnické náměstí; *National Theatre* (☎ 24 91 26 37), Národní třída 2 – mainly opera and ballet, box office at the Nová Scéna at Národní 4, open 10 am to 6 pm (closed weekends between 12.30 and 3 pm); *Chamber Opera Prague* (Opera Mozart; ☎ 24 21 47 97), Novotného lávka 1 – chamber concerts, opera and Sunday jazz; box office open from 1 to about 6 pm; *Smetana Hall*, Obecní dům, náměstí Republiky 5; *Estates (Stavovské) Theatre* (☎ 24 21 50 01), Železná 11 – opera as well as drama, equipped for the hearing-impaired and has wheelchair access

(wheelchair-bound people can book up to five days in advance), for bookings go to Kolowrat Theatre or to National Theatre box office at Národní 4 (open only 30 minutes before performances); *Chapel of Mirrors,* Klementinum

Holešovice
Fairgrounds (Výstaviště)

Smíchov
Villa Bertramka (Mozart Museum, ☎ 54 38 93), Mozartova 2/169 – special Mozart concerts

Prague Spring

This is the Czech Republic's best known annual cultural event, and now also a major tourist event. It begins on 12 May, the anniversary of Bedřich Smetana's death, with a procession from his grave at Vyšehrad to the Municipal House (Obecní dům), and then a performance is held of his work *My Homeland* (Má vlast). It runs until 2 June. The beautiful venues are as big a draw as the music.

If you want a guaranteed seat at a Prague Spring concert, book it by mid-March. Write to Prague Spring (MHF Pražské jaro), Hellichova 18, Malá Strana, 118 00 Praha 1 (☎ 53 02 93; fax 53 60 40); there's also a web site (www.festival.cz). Bookings can also be made through Ticketpro (☎ 24 81 40 20; fax 24 81 40 21), Salvátorská 10, Josefov, 110 00 Praha 1.

Occasional seats may be available as late as the end of May – watch the papers. The cheapest tickets are sold from the official box office at Hellichova 18, off Karmelitská in Malá Strana. It's open weekdays from 10 am to 6 pm during the run-up to the festival, and until 5 pm during the festival.

Jazz

The following clubs all have a cover charge of about 30 to 60 Kč, except as noted; some double as bars and restaurants:

Malá Strana
Blue Light (☎ 55 87 23), Josefská 1 – bar with live music most nights; *Malostranská beseda* (☎ 53 90 24), Malostranské náměstí 21 – jazz on some nights at 8.30 pm; *U malého Glena* (☎ 90 00 39 67), Karmelitská 23 – restaurant with jazz downstairs most nights from 9 pm

Staré Město
U staré paní Jazz Club (☎ 26 49 20), Michalská 9 – jazz nightly between 9 pm and midnight; *Viola Jazz Club* (☎ 24 22 08 44), Národní 7 – occasional live gigs, mainly on a Saturday at 8.30 pm; *Železná Jazz Club* (☎ 24 21 25 41), Železná 16 – nightly jazz from 9 pm to midnight, club opens at 3 pm

Southern Nové Město
Reduta Jazz Club (☎ 24 91 22 46), Národní 22 – one of the city's oldest clubs, with live jazz daily from 9 pm to whenever, a stiff 90 to 120 Kč cover charge, advance bookings can be made here from 3 pm; *AghaRTA Jazz Centrum* (☎ 24 21 29 14), Krakovská 5 – nightly jazz, open weekdays from 10 am to midnight, bands from 9 pm

Rock & Whatever

Prague has a high-energy music scene, with plenty of rock, metal, punk, rap etc at over three dozen legitimate DJ and live-music venues. There are also a few unlicensed places with changing addresses that tend to be grotty and massively overcrowded. The clubs listed here are at least semireputable. Except as noted, they have a bar and usually a dance floor, and a cover charge of 30 to 100 Kč:

Hradčany & Malá Strana
Klub Újezd, Újezd 18 – bar open daily 2 pm to late, loud live bands most nights; *Malostranská beseda* (☎ 53 90 24), Malostranské náměstí 21 – one of Prague's larger venues; *Scarlett O'Hara's,* Mostecká 12 (in the courtyard behind McDonald's) – Irish bar for serious drinking, with occasional live Irish and rock bands; *Strahov 007,* block 7, student dormitory complex, across the road from Strahovský stadium (take bus No 217 from either Dejvická or Anděl metro stations to Strahov) – cheap beer and raw DJ disco and some live rock, daily except Sunday from 7.15 pm to midnight; *U malého Glena* (☎ 90 00 39 67), Karmelitská 23 – restaurant upstairs, bar and music venue downstairs (music from 9 pm)

Staré Město & Josefov
Batalion (☎ 26 01 17), 28.října 3 – mainly upcoming Czech heavy metal bands or DJs, open 24 hours and music starts nightly from 9 pm; *Rock Café,* Národní 22 – open weekdays from 10 am to 3 am (weekends from 8 pm), DJ and live rock, and a café downstairs

Southern Nové Město
Lucerna Music Bar (☎ 24 21 71 08), Vodičkova 36 – predominantly Czech performers playing anything from jazz and blues to pop and underground, the 'klub' is open from 6 pm to 6 am (concerts usually start at 9 pm) and the café from 11 am to 5 pm

Vinohrady & Žižkov
Club Radost FX (☎ 25 12 10), Bělehradská 120, Vinohrady, near IP Pavlova metro station – DJ and occasional live music daily from 9 pm to 4 am (plus early-evening fixtures from 6 to 9 pm, eg Sunday poetry night, open-mike acoustic music every other Wednesday) the adjacent *FX Café* is open to 4 am; *Propast* (☎ 90 00 33 71), Lipanská 3 – a true punk venue, open daily from 5 pm to 3 am

Holešovice
Belmondo Revival Music Club Vltavská (☎ 755 10 81), Bubenská 1, in blocky building at top of pedestrian overpass near Vltavská metro station – a dance club with local bands, open daily from 8 pm to 1 am; *O'Brien's Pub*, Janovského 36 – first-rate Irish bar with music only occasionally, come for the Guinness; *Pokrok Klub*, Keramická 3 – very odd bar in the back of an art gallery, with occasional music and performance art

Smíchov
Futurum (☎ 54 44 75), Zborovská 7 – DJ, tribal disco and occasional live heavy metal, open nightly from 9 pm; *Swamp Praha* (☎ 531 99 42), Újezd 5 – DJ disco, rock and heavy metal nightly (music from 9 pm)

Clubs & Discos

With few exceptions, Prague's dance clubs cater to teenagers weaned on MTV Europe and techno/tribal beats. Most venues open late (after 9 pm) and keep the music going until 4 or 5 am. Clubs have notoriously short life spans; check the *Prague Post* for current listings.

Hradčany & Malá Strana
Club 001, Strahov student dormitory complex, across the road from the Strahovský stadium (take bus No 217 from either Dejvická or Anděl metro stations to Strahov) – techno from 9 pm to 4 am; *Disco Club 011*, not far from Club 001 –open from 10 pm to 2.30 am

Staré Město & Josefov
Arkadia Club, 3rd floor, Na příkopě 22 – DJs play reggae, soul, American latino, African music and rap nightly from 10 pm to 4.30 am; *Lávka* (☎ 24 21 47 97), Novotného lávka 1 – a typical disco that plays top-40 hits daily from 9 pm to 5 am

Southern Nové Město
Disco Astra, Václavské náměstí 22 – one of several discos around the square playing mainly techno, 9 pm to 4 am; *Variete Praha* (☎ 24 21 59 45), Vodičkova 30 – old-style international variety show and artistic programme nightly from 8 pm to 2 am (closed Monday)

Vinohrady & Žižkov
Aqua Club 2000 (☎ 627 80 63), Husitská 7 (bus No 133 or 207 from Florenc metro station) – a lesbian and gay as well as straight place with nightly disco (closed Sunday), from Thursday to Saturday there's a transvestite show; *Club Radost FX*, Bělehradská 120, Vinohrady, near IP Pavlova metro station – DJ and occasional live music, nightly from 9 pm to 4 am

Smíchov
Futurum, Zborovská 7 – DJs play techno and tribal nightly from 9 pm to 5 am (to 8 am Friday and Saturday)

Alternative Venues

These are joint theatre-clubs with an underground look and feel. These mainly experimental venues have bands (anything from blues to grunge), art exhibitions, plays or films.

Klub X (☎ 24 21 60 73), Na příkopě 15, Staré Město – nightly from 9 pm
Palác Akropolis (☎ 697 64 11), Kubelíkova 27, Žižkov, Prague 3 (metro station Jiřího z Poděbrad) – shows normally start at 7.30 pm
Roxy (☎ 24 81 09 51), Dlouhá 33, Staré Město – open nightly from 5 pm to 1 am, performances from 9 pm

Theatre

Probably Prague's most famous theatre is *Laterna Magika* (Magic Lantern), a multimedia show interweaving dance, opera, music and film, which caused a stir when it premiered in 1958 at the Brussels World Fair. Since moving from its birthplace in the basement of the Adria Palace into Nová Scéna – the 'New National Theatre' building at Národní 4 – the various shows have evolved from the old-style 'Kouzelný cirkus' to the more contemporary 'Odysseus'. It is clever, expensive, mainstream entertainment, mainly for tourists.

Čedok may tell you it's booked out, but you may bag a leftover seat at the box office on the day before a performance, or if people fail to claim their tickets half an hour beforehand. Tickets are about 500 Kč (575 Kč from Čedok). The box office (☎ 24 91 41 29) is open on weekdays from 10 am to 8 pm, and on weekends from 3 pm.

Big-name musicals like *Dracula* and *Cats* have been performed at the *Theatre Pyramida* (☎ 37 11 42) in the Fairgrounds in Holešovice, and at the *Palace of Culture* (Palác kultury; ☎ 643 28 68), Congress Hall, 5.května 65, Nusle, Prague 4.

Other venues for drama, experimental theatre, musicals and revues are:

Staré Město & Josefov

Theatre on the Balustrade (Divadlo Na Zábradlí; ☎ 24 22 19 33), Anenské náměstí 5 – box office open from 2 to 7 pm and on performance days two hours before the show starts; *Kolowrat Theatre* (☎ 24 21 50 01), Ovocný trh 6 – box office open from 10 am to 6 pm on weekdays, plus weekend performance days from 10 am to 12.30 pm and 3 to 6 pm; *National Marionette Theatre* (Říše loutek; ☎ 232 34 29), Žatecká 1 – the Kladno puppet troupe does sell-out performances of Mozart's *Don Giovanni*; *Estates (Stavovské) Theatre* (☎ 24 21 50 01), Ovocný trh 1 – drama and opera, some plays include simultaneous translation on headphones, for advance bookings go to the Kolowrat Theatre or to the National Theatre box office at Národní 4; equipped for the hearing-impaired and has wheelchair access (wheelchair-bound people can book up to five days ahead); *Theatre Image*, Pařížská 4, Josefov – black-light and mime theatre

Southern Nové Město

Dramatic Club (Činoherní Klub; ☎ 24 21 68 12), Ve Smečkách 26; *Reduta Theatre* (☎ 24 91 2 46), Národní 22 – part of the jazz club of the same name, drama performances at 7 pm on selected evenings

Vinohrady

Vinohrady Theatre (☎ 24 25 76 01), náměstí Míru 7 – box office open Monday to Saturday from 10 am to 7 pm

Karlín

Karlín Music Theatre (Hudební divadlo v Karlíně; ☎ 24 81 62 13), Křížíkova 10, near Florenc – musicals and operettas

Cinema

Prague has about 30 movie theatres (*kino*). Some show Czech films, while a majority show first-run western films in their original language with Czech subtitles. Admission is from 35 to 100 Kč. For listings try the 'Night & Day' section of the *Prague Post* or the free bi-monthly pamphlet *Do města Downtown*.

The highest concentration of cinemas is around Václavské náměstí: *Blaník* at No 56, *Hvězda* at No 38, *Jalta* at No 43 and the *Praha* at No 17. Nearby is the *Lucerna* at Vodičkova 36.

Prague's first multicomplex eight-screen cinema, complete with a bar, is the *Multikino Galaxie*, Arkalycká 874, Prague 4, a two minute walk from the Háje metro station (line C).

SPECTATOR SPORT

Ice Hockey

One of the best national teams is HC Sparta Praha. You can see them play in winter at the ice rink of the Sparta Sport Hall next to the Fairgrounds in Bubeneč (take tram 12 one stop from nádraží Holešovice metro station). Other games are played at HC Slavia Praha's zimní stadión on Na hroudě in Vršovice, Prague 10.

The season runs from September until early April, and cheap tickets are available at the rinks for the mainly weekend games.

Tennis

Tennis tournaments can be seen on Ostrov Štvanice (tram No 3 from Václavské náměstí). The Škoda Czech Open is usually played here in early August.

Soccer

SK Slavia Praha has been one of the leading teams in the national league, along with AC Sparta Praha. Each has a stadium where you can see matches, mostly on Sunday after-

CZECH REPUBLIC

JONATHAN SMITH

MARK DAFFEY

MARK DAFFEY

Prague
Top Left: Looking down on the street cafés of Old Town Square.
Top Right: A busker on the streets of Staré Město, Prague's old town.
Bottom: The mix of architectural styles lining the Vltava are caught in the morning light.

MARK DAFFEY

SCOTT McNEELY

South Bohemia

Top: The dramatic scene looking up to the 16th century Krumlov Castle, Český Krumlov.

Bottom: The village of Holašovice is known for its 19th century 'folk Baroque' country houses, barns and churches that feature fine carvings or are richly painted.

noons. The season runs from September to December and March to June.

SK Slavia Praha Stadium is on Vladivostocká in Vršovice, Prague 10; take tram No 4, 19 or 22 from Karlovo náměstí. AC Sparta Praha Stadium is at Milady Horákové in Bubeneč, Prague 7; take tram No 5 from the main train station.

Horse Racing

Check this out at the Chuchle Racecourse (závodiště; ☎ 581 08 53) on Radotínská in Velká Chuchle, Prague 5; take bus No 172 from Smíchovské nádraží metro station. Races usually start at noon and 2 pm on Sunday, from May to October. Contact PIS about other venues and events, as these constantly change. Tickets are cheap and usually available at the track.

THINGS TO BUY

The privatisation of retailing since 1989 has radically changed Prague's shopping scene. Consumer goods are easily obtainable and mostly of good quality. Imports carry western European prices, but Czech products are affordable for Czechs and cheap for westerners.

The main shopping streets are Václavské náměstí and the streets along the edge of Staré Město: Na příkopě, 28.října and Národní třída.

Department Stores

Prague's major department stores include the following:

Bílá Labut, Na poříčí 23, Nové Město, and a smaller store on the corner of Václavské náměstí and WilsonovaDětský dům, Na příkopě 15, Staré Město
Kotva, náměstí Republiky 8, Staré Město
Krone, corner of Václavské náměstí and Jindřišská
Tesco, Národní 26, Nové Město

Kotva has a patisserie, photo supplies and processing, a photocopy shop and groceries, along with the traditional stuff. Krone is a German joint venture, with German prices.

Open-Air Markets

Along Havelská and V kotcích, south of Staroměstské náměstí (Old Town Square), is a daily market with fruit, vegetables, clothing and souvenirs. A fruit and vegetable market is behind Tesco. Another is at Bubenské nábřeží, on the south side of Holešovice, which is open daily, except Sunday.

One in Dejvice (from Dejvická metro station, walk south-east on Dejvická towards the railway line) has fruit and vegetables, other foodstuffs and cheap clothing. There's also a small one at Arbesovo náměstí in southern Malá Strana.

Bookshops

Prague is full of interesting bookshops (*knihupectví*), and those that stock English-language titles tend to have an increasing amount of books on Czech history, culture or translations of well-known Czech writers. There are also plenty of coffee-table books and paperback English classics. Following are the best of the lot for English-speaking book junkies:

Albatros, on the corner of Havelská and Melantrichova: children's books and classical CDs
Big Ben (☎ 231 80 21), Malá Štupartská 5: smallish but well stocked with only English-language books
Bohemian Ventures, Charles University Philosophy Faculty bookshop (☎ 231 95 16), náměstí Jana Palacha 2, Staré Město: some Czech history and Czech writers among the Penguin Classics
Cizojazyčná literatura, Na příkopě 27: many books about Prague and the Czech Republic
The Globe, Janovského 14, near Strossmayerovo náměstí in Holešovice: pleasant bookshop-cum-coffee shop
Knihkupectví Na můstku, Na příkopě 3: good selection of city and country maps
Knihkupectví Orbis (☎ 24 21 73 35), Václavské náměstí 42: good selection of maps and guidebooks
Nadas (☎ 24 61 75 39), Hybernská 5: publishes train and bus timetables, and is good for Prague maps and guidebooks
Topičovo knihkupectví (☎ 24 81 14 15), Národní 11: plenty of English-language books and guidebooks, including Lonely Planet

U knihomola (☎ 627 77 67), Mánesova 79, metro náměstí Míru: largest selection of English-language books including Lonely Planet guidebooks; there's also a café

Glass & Crystal

One of Prague's best buys is Bohemian crystal, which ranges from simple glassware to stupendous works of art, and is sold at about three dozen places in the shopping streets. Prices aren't radically different from shop to shop, though they are highest in the city centre.

The city's most exclusive (and expensive) crystal shop is Moser, which is worth a browse for the decor as well as the goods. It's in an originally Gothic building called House at the Black Rose (dům U černé růže) at Na příkopě 12.

Some shops around Jungmannovo náměstí and Národní advertise that they will ship abroad. If you want to do it yourself, you will have to take your parcel, unsealed, to the customs post office (see Customs in the Facts for the Visitor chapter).

Junk

You may not need a door knob, rusty bed springs or a cracked teapot, but drop in anyway at Dlouhá 32 and look around the wonderful old hardware/household-equipment shop of Eduard Čapek, founded before WWI and doing a roaring trade ever since.

Music

Good buys are classical CDs of the works of Czech composers such as Smetana, Dvořák, Janáček and Martinů, as well as folk music – even *dechovka* (brass-band 'polka' music) if you are into that sort of thing.

There are almost as many CD and tape shops as bookshops. A good one for classical music is in the basement of the Rudolfinum at Jungmannova 20, Nové Město. The AghaRTA Club has its own jazz music shop at Krakovská 5, Nové Město, which is open weekdays from 3 pm to midnight, and weekends from 7 pm. The Albatros bookshop at Národní 29 has a big selection of rock CDs and tapes, and its branch on the corner of Havelská and Melantrichova has classical CDs.

If you have problems finding anything specific, try Popron, the largest music store in the Czech Republic, at Jungmannova 30 in Nové Město.

Souvenirs

There is a vast array of souvenirs for sale, with some quality work among the junk. Look for painted Easter eggs, marionettes, wood and straw toys, wooden utensils, ceramic ware with traditional designs, linen with traditional stitching, and Bohemian lacework. You'll find many stores selling along the heavily touristed Royal Way and on Václavské náměstí. A large shop full of wooden toys and ceramics is L&L, at Husova 8. Moderately priced traditional ceramics can be found at Keramika, in the passage at Václavské náměstí 41. Česká lidová řemesla, Národní 37, sells wooden folk objects and toys as well as blue dyed table cloths.

Sporting Goods

Good tents and camping equipment are hard to find. HG Sport, at Zborovská 60 in Smíchov, has rafting, kayaking and hiking gear at premium prices. Dům Sportu, Jungmannova 28, Nové Město, has general sports equipment, as do the big department stores. A good place for bags, backpacks and ice-hockey equipment is Opus, Vodičkova 7, off Václavské náměstí. Locally manufactured equipment is moderately priced. Another good camping store is Hudy Sport at Slezská, Vinohrady, Prague 2. For snowboards, skis and trendy outdoor clothing try Bugaboo at Všehrdova 27 in southern Malá Strana.

GETTING THERE & AWAY

Air

Prague Ruzyně, the Czech Republic's only international airport, is on the western outskirts of the city.

The arrivals hall has several currency exchange offices, including IPB banka with normal bank exchange rates (2% commission, no minimum), as well as Visa and MasterCard ATMs. The accommodation agency AVE is reliable, although it does charge high commissions. There is also a 24 hour left-luggage office (20 Kč daily per bag), and five pricey car-rental agencies. A Čedok desk (☎ 36 78 02; open daily from 8 am to 6 pm, to 8 pm April to October) has maps and information, and can book cars and mid-range hotels.

Prague Ruzyně is the hub of ČSA's domestic and international network, with several flights a day to many Czech cities and numerous international connections; see the Getting There & Away chapter for information about airlines and fares. ČSA's Service Centre (☎ 20 10 41 11; metro náměstí Republiky), V celnici 5, is open daily from 7 am to 6 pm.

Airline Booking Offices Airlines with Prague offices include:

Aeroflot (☎ 24 81 26 83), Pařížská 5
Air Algeria (☎ 24 22 91 10), Žitná 23
Air Canada (☎ 231 26 75), Revoluční 13
Air France (☎ 24 22 71 64), Václavské náměstí 10
Air India (☎ 24 21 24 74), Václavské náměstí 15
Air Ostrava (☎ 24 03 27 32), Ruzyně airport
Air Ukraine (☎ 069-662 77 30), 28.října 19
Alitalia (☎ 24 81 00 79), Revoluční 5
Austrian Airlines (☎ 231 18 72), Revoluční 15
Balkan Bulgarian Airlines (☎ 20 11 45 83), Ovocný trh 11
British Airways (☎ 24 81 37 28), Ovocný trh 8
British Midland (☎ 24 23 92 80), Washingtonova 17
Delta (☎ 24 23 22 58), Národní 32
El Al (☎ 24 21 73 49), Václavské náměstí 48
Finnair (☎ 24 21 19 86), Španělská 2
Georgian Airways (☎ 232 57 42), Petrská 8
KLM (☎ 24 22 86 78), Václavské náměstí 37
LOT (☎ 231 75 24), Pařížská 18
Lufthansa (☎ 24 81 10 07), Pařížská 28
Malév Hungarian (☎ 24 81 26 71), Pařížská 5
Sabena (☎ 20 11 43 23), Ruzyně airport
SAS (☎ 24 21 47 49), Rytířská 13
Swissair (☎ 24 81 21 11), Pařížská 11
Syrian Arab Airlines (☎ 32 21 53), Ruzyně airport
Tatra Air (☎ 20 11 35 34), Ruzyně airport
Varig (☎ 52 75 75), Jenišovská 27

Bus

International Nearly all international buses leave from Florenc station, outside the Florenc metro station – although Eurolines buses leave from Želivského metro station. At least one of the five ticket windows (*Vnitrostátní a mezinárodní místenky*) sells both domestic and international tickets; window 5 seems most consistent.

Overall it is much simpler to book through a good agency. The price is the same, and you're more likely to get discounts. All Čedok and CKM offices (see the Tourist Offices section earlier) book international bus tickets. Following are some other reliable agencies (they don't all book the same destinations):

Bohemiatour (☎ 24 21 62 55), Zlatnická 7, northern Nové Město: low-price trips to surrounding countries
Capital Express (☎ 87 03 68), U Výstaviště 3, Prague 7: good deals to London Victoria
ČD, level 2 of main train station (☎ 24 22 58 49); Holešovice train station (☎ 24 21 79 48)
JUDr Jan (☎ 24 21 34 20), Opletalova 37, Nové Město (opposite main train station): the main Prague agent for Eurolines
Kingscourt Express (☎ 49 92 56; info 61 21 16 68), Antala Staška 60, near metro station Budějovická

Domestic Long-distance coaches and most regional buses depart from Florenc station. Some regional buses start from stands near metro stations Anděl, Hradčanská, nádraží Holešovice, Palmovka, Radlická, Roztyly, Smíchovské nádraží, and Želivského.

Agencies do not book seats on domestic buses, but Čedok and others can tell you which stand is best for a particular trip – or indeed whether you're better off taking the train. You might get some help from ČSAD's information line (☎ 24 21 10 60; daily 6 am to 8 pm).

Florenc offers a maze of charts, although they're next to impossible to sort out. One gives the route numbers and departure platforms for each major destination. Others give all departure times for each route number. Then there are timetables for every route. To figure out when the next bus leaves, you'll probably have to look at timetables for more than one route number. You can buy your own regional timetables from the Nadas bookshop, Hybernská 5, northern Nové Město.

Short-haul tickets are sold on the bus. Long-distance domestic tickets are sold in Florenc, weekdays from 6 am to 6.30 pm, Saturday from 6.30 am to 1 pm, and Sunday from 8 am to 3 pm.

There are at least two private coach lines that cost a shade less than ČSAD. Čebus (☎ 24 81 19 36), Sokolovská 28, Prague 8, goes to Brno; tickets can be booked through the travel agency Trakie (☎ 232 50 93), on Ke Štvanici near Florenc and open weekdays from 9 am to 8 pm, and weekends from 10 am to 8 pm. Český národní expres (☎ 232 27 31), at Čermákovă 10, Prague 10, goes to Brno; its office near the City Museum on Křížíkova is open weekdays from 5.30 am to 6.45 pm, Saturday from 6.30 am to 6.30 pm, and Sunday from 9.45 am to 6.45 pm.

CZECH REPUBLIC

Train

International Most international trains arrive at the main station, Praha hlavní nádraží, three blocks from Václavské náměstí. International trains between Berlin and Budapest often stop at Praha-Holešovice (metro nádraží Holešovice) on the northern side of the city.

International tickets are sold at the main train station. At Praha-Holešovice station, most windows sell international tickets, but only window No 1 books international couchettes.

If you'd like to let someone else do the ticket-buying work, go to any train station and look for the state railway office, ČD (České dráhy); there are several at the main train station. You can also try Čedok (see the Tourist Offices section earlier in this chapter).

In Prague, information about connections is available on ☎ 24 21 76 54 or 24 61 40 30. Station lobbies have timetables on rotating drums.

Domestic Most domestic trains arrive at the main station or Masarykovo nádraží, two blocks north of it. Others where you might end up are Praha-Dejvice (two blocks from metro station Hradčanská), Praha-Smíchov (adjacent to metro Smíchovské nádraží), Praha-Vysočany north-east of the centre (bus No 185, 209, 259 or 278 to/from metro station Českomoravská), and Praha-Vršovice (tram No 24 to/from Václavské náměstí).

Hlavní nádraží handles trains to Benešov (one hour; 49km), České Budějovice (2½ hours; 169km), Cheb via Plzeň (four hours; 220km), Karlovy Vary via Chomutov (four hours; 199km), Košice (10 hours; 708km), Mariánské Lázně (three hours; 190km), Plzeň (two hours; 114km) and Tábor (1½ hours; 103km).

Trains to Brno (3½ hours; 257km) and Bratislava (5½ hours; 398km) may leave from either Hlavní nádraží, Holešovice or Masarykovo nádraží.

Trains to Kutná Hora (1½ hours; 73km) depart from Holešovice or, more frequently, Masarykovo nádraží. Karlštejn trains always depart from Smíchov.

At the main station, domestic tickets (*vnitrostátní jízdenky*) are sold on level 2 at the odd-numbered windows on the left-hand side, and also at windows 2, 4 and 6 on the right-hand side.

Main Train Station At Prague's main train station (Hlavní nádraží) you disembark at level 3 into a swarm of currency exchanges, accommodation offices and people offering places to stay. Get your bearings and a map at the helpful PIS booth on level 2 (open weekdays from 10 am to 5 pm, weekends to 4 pm), or at the information office on level 3. There's a metro station entrance on level 2, and city trams and buses stop outside the north (right) end of level 3 and out the front on Opletalova. Public transport information is available at the DP booth beside the metro entrance.

Level 1 has a 24 hour left-luggage office (*úschovna*) and day-use lockers (set your own combination inside the door, insert two

5 Kč coins, close it and turn the handle). There are showers beneath level 2.

If you arrive in the wee hours without a hotel booking, store your bags and take a long walk until sunrise. At night Hlavní nádraží is a magnet for pickpockets, crazies and drunks, and a bad place to hang out. Exchange and accommodation offices generally close from 11 pm to at least 6 am. The closest hostel with a night desk is Kolej Jednota at Opletalova 38, just north of the station. The closest 24 hour currency exchange is at the Hotel Jalta on Václavské náměstí.

International tickets are sold at the even-numbered windows (from 12 to 24) on the right-hand side of level 2. International couchettes and seat reservations are handled at the yellow-signed office downstairs near the metro entrance. Couchettes to Slovakia (Bratislava and Košice) are sold downstairs at windows 16 to 24.

GETTING AROUND

Prague's compact historical centre is best appreciated on foot, with the help of good, cheap public transport. Pollution, traffic congestion and vibration damage to old buildings have led to the construction of pedestrian-only zones and restrictions on vehicle traffic.

The Airport

City bus Nos 119 and 254 (which runs at irregular times) ply between Ruzyně airport and the Dejvická metro station every half-hour or so from 4.30 am to 11.30 pm (buy a 10 Kč bus ticket at the airport from the lobby newsstand or the yellow machine near Čedok). The trip takes about 40 minutes, including the metro trip to/from the city centre.

A private company, Welcome Touristic Prague, runs comfortable shuttle buses between the airport and the ČSA Service Centre at V celnici 5 (metro náměstí Republiky) for 100 Kč (buy tickets on board). These shuttles run daily from 7 am to 7 pm at least every half-hour.

Cedaz is another private company that runs a microbus between the airport and náměstí Republiky, once an hour from 5 am to 10 pm; the microbus also picks up passengers at Evropská, near the Dejvická metro station. Buy the 110 Kč ticket from the driver.

There are also two taxi companies, Airport Fix-Cars and ALM Car, which are required by the airport authority to offer a fixed-price service into Prague for 550 Kč. Book a taxi at the airport information desk. This is the only safe way to take a taxi from the airport; trust no-one else.

Public Transport

It costs 10 Kč for a ticket (*jízdenka*) to ride Prague's trams, buses, metro and intra-city 2nd class trains (but not express trains). Tickets are 5 Kč for children aged six to 15, and for excess luggage and bicycles. Kids under six ride free.

Validate your ticket by punching it in the little orange (sometimes yellow) machines in metro station lobbies and on buses or trams. Once validated, each ticket allows an unlimited number of transfers – from bus to tram to metro etc – for either 60 minutes (weekdays from 5 am to 8 pm) or 90 minutes (weekdays from 8 pm to 5 am and 24 hours on weekends). There is also a short-hop 6 Kč ticket that can only be used for 15 minutes on buses and trams, or for riding the metro no more than four stations; it's invalid on night trams and buses.

Tickets are sold from the yellow machines in metro stations (read the operating instructions carefully as the procedure is not straightforward), and individually or in discounted books at newsstands, Trafiky shops, PNS and other tobacco kiosks, and at offices of the city transport department (Dopravní podnik, or DP). There are DP ticket offices in all metro stations, plus DP information centres at the following four metro stations: Muzeum and Můstek (daily from 7 am to 9 pm) and Karlovo náměstí and nádraží Holešovice (daily to 6 pm). The DP information centres sell tickets, maps and timetables for all day and night services.

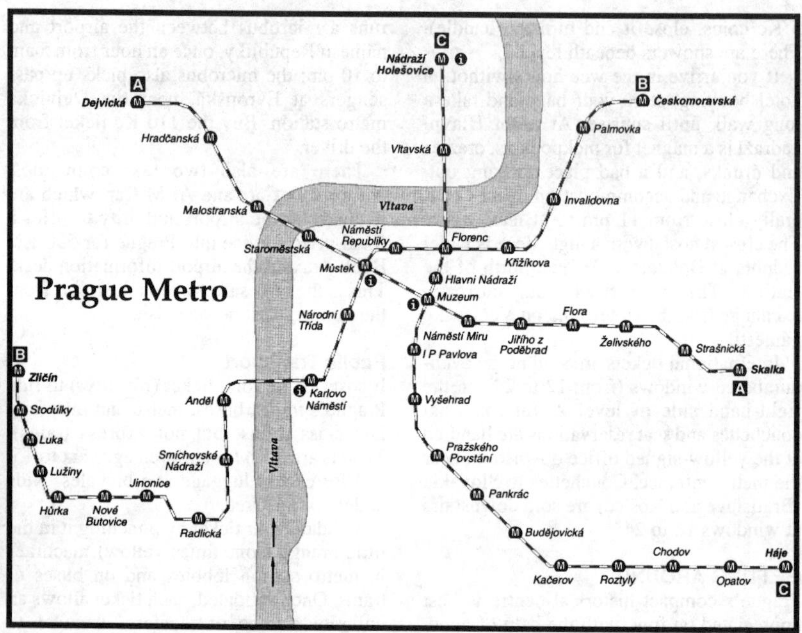

Automated ticket machines in most metro stations also sell short-term passes: 24 hours (50 Kč), three days (130 Kč), seven days (190 Kč) and 15 days (220 Kč). The pass is not valid until you fill in your full name and birthdate, and validate it in the machine. Longer-term visitors may want to get a one (320 Kč), three (860 Kč) or 12 month (2700 Kč) pass (*měsíční jízdenka*). These are sold between the 25th and 8th of the month in the DP office at Na bojišti 5 (near metro station IP Pavlova), at DP information offices and at about half the city's metro stations. The pass itself is a stamp (placed in a plastic wallet with a photo ID card) that needs to be filled in with your passport number and the zone it is used in – if the pass is not completely filled in you could be fined 200 Kč. To apply for one of these passes bring your passport and one passport-size photo to any DP information office. The pass remains valid one day before and three days after the valid date, allowing time to 'switch' to a new pass.

Tickets are inspected very regularly, and if you're caught without a valid ticket or pass they can fine you 200 Kč on the spot.

Tram & Bus The metro is quickest as far as it goes, but trams are much more relaxed. Buses cover all the areas that trams miss. Most trams and buses operate daily from 4.30 am to 11.30 pm, though a few run only at peak hours. Routes and schedules are posted at each stop. Tram numbers have one or two digits, buses three.

There is limited night service on certain lines from midnight to 5 am, usually running at roughly 40-minute intervals: tram Nos 51 through to 58 all pass the corner of Lazarská and Spálená (north of Karlovo náměstí) so you can transfer, and bus Nos 501-506, 508-510 and 512 connect with the trams. These are indicated by reverse-colour signs at stops. An invaluable purchase is DP's map, *Noční provoz* (Night Service).

On weekends and national holidays between April and October vintage tram cars are used on a special sightseeing route. Tram No 91 goes round-trip from in front of the Fairgrounds (Výstaviště) via Malostranské náměstí, the National Theatre, Václavské náměstí and the Masarykovo train station. It costs 10 Kč (kids 5 Kč) to ride, and ordinary tickets and passes cannot be used on this line.

Metro Prague's 43 station network is safe, reliable and clean. Trains run daily from 5 am to midnight.

A polite recorded voice announces each station. Before departing it warns, *'Ukončete výstup a nástup, dveře se zavírají'* (Finish getting on and off, the doors are closing). As the train pulls away it says, *'Příští stanice...'* (The next station is...), perhaps noting that it's a *přestupní stanice* (transfer station). When you disembark, signs point you towards the *výstup* (exit) or to a *přestup* (connecting line).

Train Prague's integrated public transport system also includes travel on 2nd-class trains. The rules are fairly complex and if you plan to take advantage of this system, see one of the DP information offices for more information.

Car & Motorcycle

Driving in Prague is no fun. Trying to find your way around – or to park legally – while coping with trams, lunatic Czech drivers and pedestrians, and police on the lookout for a little *baksheesh*, will make you wish you'd left the car at home.

Ease the trauma by avoiding weekday

CZECH REPUBLIC

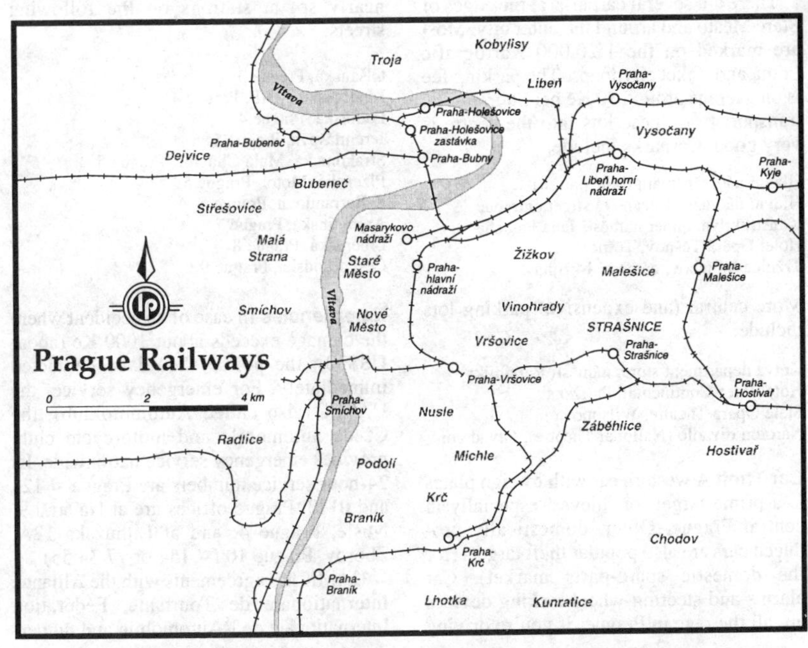

peak-traffic hours – in central Prague from 4 pm onwards (on Friday as early as 2 pm). Try not to arrive or leave on a Friday or Sunday afternoon or evening, when half the population seems to head to and from their weekend houses.

Central Prague has many pedestrian-only streets, including Václavské náměstí, parts of 28.října and Na příkopě, most of Staroměstské náměstí (Old Town Square) and some streets leading into it. They are marked with *Pěší zóna* (Pedestrian Zone) signs, and only service vehicles and taxis are allowed in these areas.

Parking Street parking in most of Prague 1 is regulated by permit-only and parking meter zones. Meter time limits range from two to 24 hours. Parking in one-way streets is normally only allowed on the right-hand side. Traffic inspectors need little encouragement to fine you, clamp your wheels or tow your car away.

There are several carparks at the edges of Staré Město and around the outer city. Most are marked on the 1:20,000 Kartografie Praha and Žaket city maps. The parking fee is on average around 30 Kč per hour. Public transport from these lots into the centre is very good. Carparks include:

Hlavní nádraží (main train station)
Hlavní nádraží, Bolzanova street entrance
Konstruktiva, under náměstí Jana Palacha
Hotel Opera Těšnov, Těšnov
Tržnice Smíchov, náměstí 14.října

More central (and expensive) parking lots include:

Kotva department store, náměstí Republiky
Hotel Inter-Continental, Pařížská
State Opera Theatre, Wilsonova
Národní divadlo (National Theatre), Divadelní

Car Theft A western car with foreign plates is a prime target for thieves, especially in central Prague. Older, domestically produced cars are also popular theft targets (for the domestic spare-parts market). Car alarms and steering-wheel locking devices are all the rage in Prague; if you're driving your own car in Prague, consider bringing a locking device. Despite this, the chances of your car being stolen are not higher than at home. Also popular are smaller items like windscreen wipers, antennas and car emblems. Of course, don't leave your possessions visible in the vehicle.

Tram Rules In Prague you may overtake a tram only on the right, and only if it is in motion. Where there is no passenger island, you must stop for any tram taking on or letting off passengers. A tram has the right of way when making any signalled turn across your path. For more road rules, see the Getting There & Away chapter.

Fuel Leaded and unleaded petrol are sold at over 25 stations in Prague. Petrol stations are marked on newer street maps, including Kartografie Praha's *Plán města Praha* (1:20,000). Opening hours are typically 8 am to 7 or 8 pm. Expect 24 hour service, or nearly so, at stations on the following streets:

Olšanská, Prague 3
Modřanská AGIP, Prague 4
Podolská, Prague 4
Jeremiášova, Prague 5
Strakonická, Malá Chuchle, Prague 5
Plzeňská, Motol, Prague 5
K Barrandovu, Prague 5
Argentinská, Prague 7
Liberecká, Prague 8
Českobrodská, Prague 9

Emergencies In case of an accident where the damage exceeds about 1000 Kč (about US$30), the police should be contacted immediately. For emergency service, the ÚAMK (also called Automotoklub), the Czech automobile and motorcycle club, provides emergency service nationwide. Its 24-hour service numbers are Prague ☎ 123 and 0123. Prague offices are at Na strži 9, Nusle, Prague 4; and at Limuzská 12A, Zborov, Prague 10 (☎ 154 or 77 34 55).

ÚAMK has agreements with the Alliance Internationale de Tourisme, Fédération Internationale de l'Automobile and numerous national auto and tourist clubs. If you're a member of one of these, ÚAMK will help you on roughly the same terms as your own club would. If not, you must pay for all services.

Other places offering round-the-clock repair services throughout the republic are ABA (Autoklub Bohemia Assistance, also known as Autoklub české republiky; ☎ 0124), and they have an information centre (☎ 26 26 51) at Opletalova 29, or Autoturist (☎ 154 or 24 22 59 18) at náměstí Republiky 6.

Spare parts (other than for Škodas) can be harder to find, but most well-known models can be repaired at a basic level by at least one garage in Prague. Repair shops for major foreign brands include:

Fiat
  K Ryšánce 16, Prague 4 (☎ 42 01 64)
Ford
  Na křivně 1, Prague 4 (☎ 643 11 42); Černokostelecká 116, Prague 10 (☎ 70 65 40)
Chrysler, Peugeot & Simca
  Novostrašnická 46, Prague 10 (☎ 782 15 01)
Nissan & Ford
  Severní XI, Prague 4 (☎ 76 67 53)
Honda
  Za opravnou 1, Prague 5 (☎ 52 26 51)
Mercedes
  Jeremiášova 11, Prague 5 (☎ 52 32 29)
Renault, Hyundai, Daewoo & Dacia
  Ďáblická 2, Prague 8 (☎ 88 73 83)
Toyota
  Weberova 5, Prague 5 (☎ 52 53 24)
Volkswagen
  K Vltavě 1114, Prague 4 (☎ 402 58 02); Mezi lány 22, Prague 5 (☎ 57 21 16 48)
Most models
  Uni Car Service, Dudkova 187, Prague 9 (☎ 855 25 68)

Car Rental Prague's inexpensive (and small) car-hire companies charge 500 to 800 Kč per day or 13,000 to 15,000 Kč per month for the cheapest models. Of the following agencies, CS Czechocar is the most reliable:

CS Czechocar (☎ 61 22 20 79; fax 61 17 24 32), Palác kultury (entrance 9), Prague 4, opposite Vyšehrad metro station
Josef Stašek (☎ 39 85 78), 194 Horoměřice, north-west Lysolaje, Prague 6
Discar Marcel Vlasák (☎ 687 05 23), Hovorčovice 192, Prague 9, north of Třeboradice
Koospol Servis (☎ 24 36 23 02; fax 316 41 49), Evropská 178, Prague 6

Mainstream agencies tend to charge 1000 to 2000 Kč or more per day for a basic model. They have desks at the airport, as well as the following offices in Prague 1:

A-Rent Car (☎ 24 21 15 87; fax 24 21 20 32), Washingtonova 9
Avis (☎ 21 85 12 56; fax 21 85 12 29), Klimentská 46
Budget (☎ 24 88 11 11), Hotel Inter-Continental, náměstí Curierových
Eurodollar (☎ 90 00 47 08; fax 29 72 63), Masarykovo nábřeží 4, Prague 2
Europcar (☎ 24 81 12 90), Pařížská 26
Hertz (☎ 29 78 36; fax 292 11 47), Karlovo náměstí 28, Prague 2

Taxi

Prague is plagued with unscrupulous cabbies who are regulated by weak laws. All official taxis are white in colour, have a 'taxi' light on top, and must use a meter, with rates displayed on the door. At the time of writing, the 'recommended free-market price' a registered taxi could charge was 10 Kč flagfall plus 15 Kč per km (8 Kč per km if you're travelling round-trip). This is the rate Czechs are expected to pay, though foreigners are generally asked to pay two to four times as much (some tourists have been asked for as much as 1000 Kč per km!). It might be easier to agree on a price before you get in the taxi.

Hailing a taxi on the street is inviting trouble, and even a Czech-speaking middleman may not help much, as Czechs are not immune to taxi rip-offs. If you do take one, find out the approximate fare in advance and ask the driver to use the meter (*zapněte taximetr, prosím*). If it's 'broken', find someone else. Before paying, ask for a receipt (*paragon*), with the driver's name and signature, taxi ID number, car registration number, distance and fare shown. If you get the rare driver who willingly turns on the meter, he probably deserves a tip. The taxi stands at Václavské náměstí and Staroměstské náměstí (Old Town Square) are notorious for rip-offs. Especially at night, some taxi drivers will not use a meter but will charge a set price from the city centre to the suburbs between 250 Kč and 350 Kč, depending on the distance.

It's much safer to telephone for a taxi. From our experience the following taxi companies, both with 24 hour service, generally have honest drivers: AAA (☎ 3399 or 312 21 12 or 61 04 33 99) and RTAX (☎ 472 14 53 or 472 12 27).

Bicycle

Prague is not a brilliant place to ride a bike. Traffic is heavy, the pollution can be choking, and there are no bicycle lanes. The cobblestones in older streets will loosen your teeth, and tram tracks are treacherous, especially when wet. Have a good lock and chain for both wheels and frame – western bikes are a popular target. Spare parts are available in the city's numerous bike shops, but scarcer outside Prague.

If you're at least 12 years old you can take your bicycle on the metro for an extra 5 Kč. You must keep it near the last door of the rear carriage and only two bikes per carriage are allowed. You may not take a bike on board weekdays from 5.30 to 8.30 am and 2.30 to 5.30 pm, nor at any time when the carriage is full, nor if there's already a pram in the carriage.

Bicycle Rental The only place that rents bicycles to the public seems to be A Landa (☎ 24 25 61 21) at Šumavská 33, Prague 2. Their mountain bikes cost 150 Kč per day or 100 Kč for more than three days. Some major hotels occasionally rent bicycles to their guests.

Boat

In summer, cruise boats of Prague Passenger Shipping (Pražská paroplavební společnost; ☎ 29 83 09 or 90 00 08 22) chug up and down from the central quay (*centrální přístaviště*) on the east bank north of Palackého most. The closest metro station is Karlovo náměstí (exit to Palackého náměstí).

Most photogenic is a two hour jaunt north to Hradčany and south to Vyšehrad; it runs daily from May through to 27 October at 11 am, 3.30 and 6 pm (also 9 pm June to August), and costs 200 Kč. At 10.30 am, 2.30 and 4.30 pm a 1½ hour trip goes north around Střelecký ostrov and south to the outskirts of Prague at Barrandov cliffs, for 200 Kč, including cake and coffee. If there are enough passengers, a one hour trip goes to Barrandov and back daily, except Monday, every hour from 10 am to 4 pm. Other boats go up and down while you lunch, snack or dine expensively on board.

Every day, except Monday, boats go north to the zoo and chateau at Troja, departing at 9.30 am and 1.30 pm and stopping at Kampa, Čechův most and nádraží Holešovice for 50 Kč return. On weekends at 9 am (plus Friday from early June to mid-September), a boat goes the 40km south (upstream) through a wild, green landscape to Štěchovice, which is almost to the big dam across the Vltava at Slapy, arriving back at 6.30 pm. This fine escape is 150 Kč return.

Other cruises that run throughout the day include a two hour sightseeing cruise with lunch (550 Kč) or a three hour cruise with dinner (775 Kč). From the Kampa landing next to Charles' Bridge there are 45-minute cruises (220 Kč) from 11.45 am to 6.45 pm (daily, except Monday).

All river transport shuts down in winter.

Boat Rental If you just want a quiet float on the river to watch the sunset, consider renting a row boat or pedal-boat on Slovanský ostrov, though you can't take these beyond the upstream and downstream weirs. Another place that rents rowing boats by the hour is just north of Charles' Bridge on the Staré Město side, at the end of Platnéřská, off Křižovnická. A third place is part of Klub lávka, which is just south of Charles' Bridge (enter from Novotného lávka).

Central Bohemia

The Central Bohemian countryside – mostly flat, sometimes gently hilly – is essentially the low-lying centre of the Bohemian plateau. These fertile agricultural and lightly wooded lands are drained by the Labe (Elbe to Germans), its tributary the Vltava (the Czech Republic's longest river) and two main Vltava branches, the Berounka and Sázava.

Central Bohemia is rich in rural landscapes, good walks and fine architecture, often in the middle of nowhere – a hamlet full of Gothic homes, a neo-classical farmhouse, an old castle. Virtually all of Central Bohemia is within a 90 minute train or bus ride of Prague, accessible on day trips with or without overnight stays.

Highlights, for our money, are Křivoklát Castle, photogenic Karlštejn Castle, the silver-mining town of Kutná Hora and, barely beyond Prague's city limits, the park at Průhonice. Be ready for summer crowds at Karlštejn and Konopiště castles in particular. Staying the night lets you see these places in a kinder light, when the tour buses have gone back to Prague.

HIGHLIGHTS

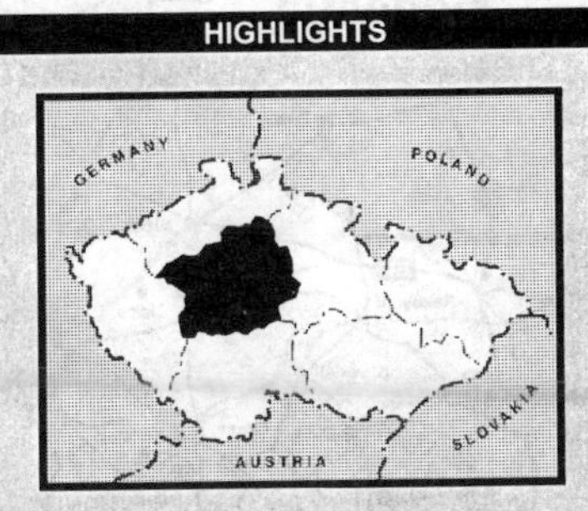

- Visit the ghoulish Sedlec Ossuary in Kutná Hora, decorated with the bones of monks and plague victims
- Go wine-tasting in a 13th century cellar at Mělník Chateau
- Tour the impregnable, meticously restored castles at Karlštejn, Český Šternberk and Konopiště
- Soak up the serenity of Průhonice park, one of the finest in Europe

Castles & Chateaux

Take note of opening times before you go. Most of the region's castles, chateaux and other historical monuments are open daily during the summer, but are closed on Monday, the first working day after a holiday, and also from November through March. A few open on weekends in April and October. Karlštejn and Křivoklát castles stay open year-round except Christmas Eve and New Year's Day. The Lidice memorial and the Mělník chateau are open seven days a week. A useful booklet with background information and month-by-month opening hours is *Castles & Chateaux in the Czech Republic*, sold at Čedok and some Prague bookshops.

The risk of theft has prompted most castles and chateaux to admit visitors only in guided groups, though most will let you pay the Czech price (typically less than 30 Kč) and lend you a written English narrative. If you want to catch every detail, be prepared to fork out 60 to 150 Kč for an English-language tour (available only at the major tourist sights).

Walks

Only a few walks are noted in this chapter, but there are over 50 itineraries mapped and described (in Czech) on Kartografie Praha's excellent map, *Výlety do okolí Prahy* (Excursions to the Outskirts of Prague). Trails are well marked and colour-coded.

Organised Tours

If you're short on time or want to let someone else make the plans, Čedok and other

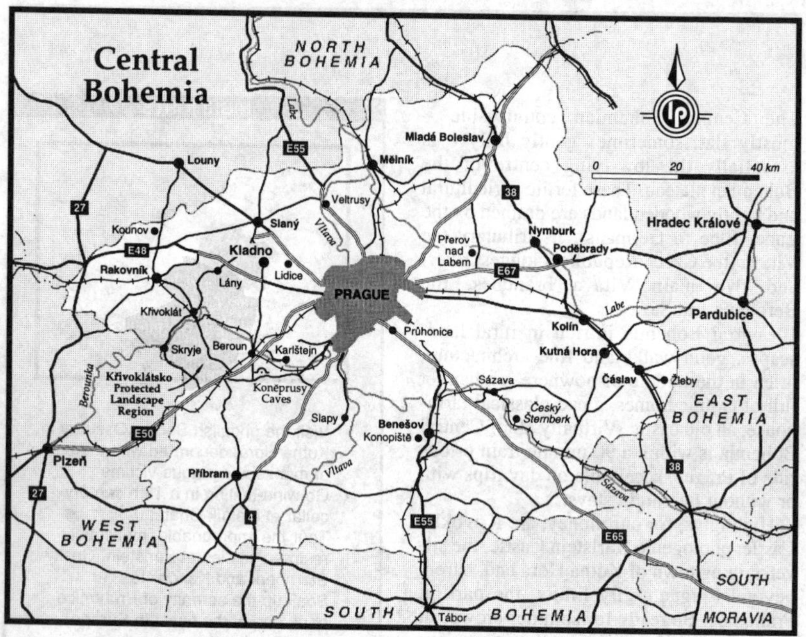

operators (see Organised Tours in the Prague section) have a range of expensive all-day excursions from Prague during the summer months. Among Čedok's offerings are (price per person, lunch included):

Karlštejn and Konopiště castles – Tuesday, Thursday and Sunday; 1700 Kč
Karlštejn Castle – Saturday and Friday (in summer); 1100 Kč
Kutná Hora & Český Šternberk – Thursday and Sunday; 1600 Kč

PRŮHONICE

In a village just beyond the Prague city limit is a photogenic 13th century **chateau**, restored at the end of the 19th century in a romantic mix of neo-Gothic and neo-Renaissance styles. It fronts onto a 250 hectare landscaped park, one of the finest of its kind in Europe.

The chateau, once the property of Count Arnošt Emmanuel Sylva-Taroucca, is now occupied by the Botanical Institute of the Czech Academy of Sciences. The rooms are off-limits, though you can snoop around the veranda. The only survivor in anything like its original form is the little **Church of the Birth of Our Lady** (kostel Narození Panny Marie) beside the chateau, consecrated in 1187 and with some of its frescoes, dating from 1330, still visible. This too is closed, unless you attend the 5 pm Sunday Mass.

However, the park, now a state botanical and horticultural preserve, is the main attraction. On weekends it's packed with day-tripping Czech families, but on a drizzly weekday morning you could literally have the exotic gardens, sweet-smelling woods and three artificial lakes to yourself. In May, thousands of species of rhododendrons come out in all colours of the rainbow. Through it runs the Botič brook (which empties into the Vltava at Vyšehrad).

Admission is 15 Kč, and a map of the park, with some English, is available at the entrance.

Getting There & Away

On weekdays, buses leave every 30 to 60 minutes all morning from the ČSAD stand (not the city bus stop) at Prague's Opatov metro station, on the C line. The 15 minute trip is 10 Kč. On weekends there are more buses (and more visitors).

KONOPIŠTĚ

Midway between Prague and Tábor, 2km west of Benešov train station, is the French-style castle of Konopiště, which dates from 1300. It received a handsome neo-Gothic face-lift in the 1890s from its last and best-known owner, Archduke Franz Ferdinand d'Este, successor to the Austro-Hungarian throne, whose June 1914 assassination set off WWI.

The man was an obsessive hunter, as you will see from a tour through the dark, wood-panelled castle, packed with a grossly over-the-top collection of dead animals and an armoury of hunting weapons. In 25 years he dispatched several hundred-thousand creatures on the 225 hectare estate (and kept a tally of them all).

Nowadays the animals are back, and the English-style wooded grounds – dotted with lakes, gardens and a statuary – are a much-appreciated antidote to the heavy tourist scene around the castle.

Orientation & Information

The nearest town is Benešov. Its train and bus stations are opposite one another and less than five minutes on foot from the town square, Masarykovo náměstí (turn left out of the train station, walk one longish block and turn right on Tyršova). Česká spořitelna, on the main square, does foreign exchange and has a MasterCard/Visa ATM. Benešov's area code is ☎ 0301.

The castle is 2km away in the opposite direction from town, a fine half-hour walk through the estate. Cross the bridge over the railway lines, take the first left into Ke stadiónu and the third right down Spartakiádní. Drivers can go straight down Konopišťská from the bridge.

Castle

The castle is divided into three long tours that tend to become tiresome inventories of every item on display. For Tours I and II you can join a Czech group for 40 Kč, or take a 100 Kč English-language tour. Tour III costs 120 Kč and 190 Kč, respectively, making it the most expensive attraction in the Prague region.

Tours I and II take in the archduke's trophies, a forest of mounted heads, antlers, claws and teeth. Tour I looks at the stately rooms with their Italian cabinets, Dürer graphics and Meissen porcelain. Tour II takes in the hunting weapons, the chapel and a plush mens' party room.

Tour III is limited to groups of just 10 people, as the exhibits are highly prized and include the archduke's living quarters, study, bedrooms, and the music saloon of Princess Žofie.

If that's not enough, go around the back to see the archduke's St George fetish: scores of paintings, statues and other renderings of the mythical dragon-slayer (and this is only some 10% of the hoard) in a purpose-built private gallery.

Konopiště castle is open daily, except Monday, April to October from 9 am to noon and 1 to 4 pm (to 5 pm May through August).

Places to Stay & Eat

The only accommodation near the castle is *Hotel Myslivna* (☎ 224 69), a luxury chalet 500m beyond Konopiště. Rooms are 400 Kč per person. The hotel's restaurant is aimed at tour groups on large budgets. Instead try the snack bar in the adjacent carpark.

In Benešov, *Hotel Pošta* (☎ & fax 223 55), at Tyršova 162 just off the main square, is clean and a good bargain at 380/760 Kč for a single/double room. The adjoining restaurant is simple but OK. Much closer to the train station is the new *Hotel Mymír*

(☎ & fax 247 61), a reasonable deal at 600/850 Kč.

Two monstrous motels sit south-west of town at the edge of the Konopiště estate. *Motel Švarc* (☎ 256 11), on Ke stadiónu, has featureless doubles with toilet and shower for 850 Kč, plus a restaurant. The similar *Motel Konopiště* (☎ 227 32) also has a campsite, which is open from May to September.

Getting There & Away

Benešov is a pleasant train ride, through broadly rolling farmland and forest, from Prague's Hlavní nádraží station. Trains go every 1½ hours, and the trip takes just over an hour. Most trains to and from Tábor (one hour; 54km) and České Budějovice (two hours; 120km) also stop here.

A convenient bus for day-trippers leaves Prague's Roztyly metro station at 9.20 am, stops at Benešov at 10.25 am, and continues to Český Šternberk, arriving at 1.20 pm. The last bus leaves Český Šternberk at 6.15 pm, Benešov at 8 pm, and arrives back in Prague at 10 pm.

SÁZAVA MONASTERY

Sázava Monastery (Sázavský klášter) was founded in the 11th century as a centre of Orthodox Christianity; it was the first place in Bohemia to conduct services in Old Church Slavonic, though the brethren were booted out of Bohemia a few decades later. Rebuilt in the 13th century and defaced by a heavy-handed Baroque renovation, it served as a private chateau in the 19th century.

The monastery's Gothic chapter hall was rediscovered under whitewash and masonry during excavations in the 1940s, and restored in the 1970s. These ancient bits are really the only reason to drop by, and only if you're already on your way to or from Český Šternberk (see the following section).

Though you must join a tedious Czech-language tour through the monastery, an English-language text is available. The cloister has displays on archaeology, with side rooms given over to the history of Slavonic Bohemia. The over-the-top rococo monastery church includes a reconstructed crypt.

Star of the show is the chapter hall, with all the Baroque renovations scraped away to reveal the original Gothic chamber, complete with fragmentary frescoes like those at Prague's Emmaus Monastery (another former centre of the Slavonic liturgy).

Getting There & Away

Get off the train to/from Český Šternberk at Sázava Černé Budy. Go behind the station, cross the tracks, descend the hill, cross the Sázava river and make for the monastery church steeple. It's a 15 minute walk – a sign by the station that puts it at 4.5km presumably predates the bridge.

ČESKÝ ŠTERNBERK

This hulking fortress, on a sheer ridge above the Sázava river, dates back to the 13th century. It probably owes its survival not only to its impregnable position, but to its having been in the same family, the Šternberks, for almost its entire life.

It succumbed to heavy Baroque remodelling in the 17th and 18th centuries, and the only remaining traces of its Gothic personality are in the fortifications. Nowadays its most impressive features are the views up from the river, and out from the castle windows.

The scenery on the train journey up the Sázava river valley – deep woods, steep contours and limestone crags – is itself probably worth the ride.

Orientation

Don't get off at Český Šternberk station, but one stop on at Český Šternberk zastávka, across the river from the castle. A road and a shorter footpath climb around behind the castle.

Castle

The tedious 45 minute tour reveals an Italian Baroque renovation, very heavy on stucco. Such highlights as there are include the rococo **St Sebastian Chapel** (kaple sv Šebastiána) and the **'Yellow Room'**, with fine views over the countryside. From here you can see trees marking out a 17th century French-style park across the river, the only part of a planned Šternberk chateau that was completed before the money ran out.

The castle is open daily, except Monday, June to August from 9 am to 6 pm, in May and September to 5 pm, and in April and October on weekends only to 4 pm. Tours in Czech are 25 Kč and in other languages 100 Kč. The last tours commence an hour before closing.

Places to Stay & Eat

Hotel Tesla (☎ & fax 0303-551 02) is at a quiet spot on the river, a 25 minute trek downstream on the castle side, but was closed at the time of writing. Just above the train stop (zastávka) in a manor-type building is *Parkhotel Český Šternberk* (☎ 0303-551 08), with smallish but clean rooms with shower for 650 Kč per person, including breakfast. The hotel.also has a restaurant. The castle has a pricey *vinárna*. The *Restaurace pod hradem* in the hamlet below has cheap eats.

Getting There & Away

Change at Čerčany on the Prague-Benešov railway line (see the Konopiště section earlier). From Čerčany, trains lumber up the Sázava valley about every 2½ hours, taking about 1¼ hours to Český Šternberk.

Buses also run from Prague to Český Šternberk (see the Konopiště section).

KARLŠTEJN

Karlštejn was founded by Charles IV in 1348 as a hideaway and royal treasury for the imperial crown jewels. Perched on a crag above the Berounka river, looking taller than it is wide, Karlštejn is one of the most splendid and photogenic castles in Bohemia – and therefore the most popular, with coachloads of tourists trooping through all day. Arrive early to beat the crowds.

Heavily remodelled in the 19th century, it's now in amazingly good shape. The best views are from the outside, so if the tours are sold out, relax and enjoy a good tramp in the woods (see the following Walks section).

Orientation & Information

It's a 10 minute walk from the station to the village (turn right and follow the weathered metal signs), and another 10 minutes up to the castle through a gamut of overpriced restaurants and souvenir shops. Karlštejn's area code is ☎ 0311.

Castle

The south-facing palace is where most of the open rooms are, including a handsome **audience hall** and the **imperial bedroom**. You must use your imagination since they have been stripped of their furnishings. Several scale models indicate how drastic the 19th century renovation was.

North of the palace is the **Marian Tower** (Marianská věž), with Charles' private quarters and the **Church of Our Lady** (kostel Panny Marie), with fragments of its beautiful original frescoes. Charles' private St Catherine Chapel (kaple sv Kateřiny) is in a corner of the church.

The centre of the complex is the **Great Tower** (Velká věž), where the royal regalia, jewels and relics were kept. At its heart is the lavish **Chapel of the Holy Cross** (kaple sv Kříže), furnished in gilt and inlaid with thousands of semiprecious stones and scores of panels by Master Theodoric, Bohemia's best-known painter of the time. Sadly it's closed to the public, and you must settle for photographs and a scale model in the sacristy behind the Church of Our Lady.

Below the castle, on the road towards the carpark, is the **Museum of Nativity Scenes** (Muzeum betlémů) in the 14th century parsonage (*fara*). There are 25 pieces made from all types of materials, including wood, tin, bread and sugar.

Foreigners are expected to buy a 150 Kč guided tour, commencing when there are enough people who speak your language.

But you can try in your best Czech for a 90 Kč ticket and tag along with a Czech group. Cameras are an extra 50 Kč.

The castle is open year-round except at lunch time (noon to 1 pm), on Mondays, and on Christmas Eve and New Year's Day as follows: in July and August from 9 am to 7 pm; May, June and September to 6 pm; April and October to 5 pm; and the rest of the year to 4 pm.

Walks

On a red-marked path east from Karlštejn village it is 7km via Mořinka (not Mořina) village into the **Karlík valley** (Karlícké údolí), a nature reserve where you may find the remains of Charles IV's Karlík Castle, which was abandoned in the 15th century. Karlík village, 1km down the valley, has a 12th century rotunda. A road and a green-marked trail run 1.5km south-east from there to Dobřichovice, on the Prague-Beroun railway line.

From Srbsko, one train stop west of Karlštejn, another red trail climbs up the wooded Buboviský valley, 8km to the ridge-top **Monastery of St John Under the Rock** (klášter sv Jan pod Skálou), allegedly once an StB (secret police) training camp. About 1.5km farther on a blue-marked trail, just beyond the highway, is Vráž, where you can catch buses back to Beroun or to Prague.

Either walk can be done in under three hours, not counting return transport.

Places to Stay

There's a *campsite* on the north side of the river, 500m west of the bridge, and the *Hotel Mlýn* (☎ 68 42 08) down the south side of the river, east of the bridge, with single/double rooms from 600/900 Kč.

The cheapest option in town is the bright-yellow *Penzión U královny Dagmar* (☎ 68 46 14; fax 68 46 15), a well-kept mini-hotel that is located where the road turns up towards the castle. Rooms are 680/900 Kč. The restaurant here is good.

To escape the crowds try the tranquil, family-run *Pension Slon* (☎ 68 45 50), where rooms with shared facilities are 500/900 Kč. From the train station, turn right and right again over the tracks, then follow the elephant-shaped signs for 300m.

Considering its central location on the village square, *U Janů* serves typical Czech dishes at fair prices, from 80 to 120 Kč.

Getting There & Away

Karlštejn is on the Beroun railway line, which starts at Prague's Smíchov station. Local trains depart at least hourly for the 40 minute, 12 Kč trip; express trains don't stop here. There are return departures from Karlštejn until at least 7 pm.

BEROUN

Beroun has impressive old town gates and fragments of 14th century walls, but it's mainly a good jumping-off point for Křivoklát and Karlštejn castles, the Koněprusy Caves, and hikes in the beautiful Berounka river basin.

Orientation & Information

The main square, Husovo náměstí, is a 10 minute walk straight out (north) of the train station. The bus station is east of the square, across the river.

The tourist office (☎ 54 31 33), on the main square inside the Pasáž na Nové shopping arcade, has maps and a list of local accommodation, and is open weekdays from 8 am to 4 pm. Agrobanka and its MasterCard/Visa ATM are off the main square near the Plzeňská brána clock tower.

Beroun's area code is ☎ 0311.

Places to Stay & Eat

Hotel Český dvůr (☎ & fax 214 11), Husovo náměstí 86, has basic single/double rooms with toilet and shower for 400/800 Kč. A bit nicer is *Hotel Parkán* (☎ 214 23) at Hornohredební 162, 20m from the clock tower, with doubles from 900 Kč. The small *Hotel Venedik* (☎ 244 04), na příkopě 11, is just past the tourist office behind Prague Tower (Pražská brána). Doubles with bath are 1000 Kč; the restaurant here is worth a look.

At *Hotel U Blažků* (☎ 213 76), north off the square at Česká 176, a double room with breakfast costs 1050 Kč. The place on Havlíčkova with the illuminated 'hotel' sign is *Hotel Litava* (☎ 252 65), with doubles at 1360 Kč.

Restaurace Alena, on the main square at No 175, is a step up from the local beer halls.

Getting There & Away

Beroun is a beautiful 40 minute ride from Prague along the Berounka river. Express trains leave every three hours from Prague's main train station, while local trains depart hourly from Prague's Smíchov station. An unreserved seat is 14 Kč.

KONĚPRUSY CAVES

The tour through these impressive limestone caves (Koněpruské jeskyně), 6km south of Beroun and 600m deep, reveals colourful formations, the bones of humans and a woolly rhinoceros, and a 15th century underground forge used to make counterfeit coins.

Buses run at odd intervals from Beroun's train station to Koněprusy village, below the caves. Go by midday to be sure of a bus back; the caves-office will know the return times (on weekends buses are few and far between).

The caves are open daily from April to October. From April to September opening times are 8 am to 4 pm (to 5 pm from June to August and on weekends in May). In October, the hours are weekdays 8 am to 3 pm, weekends 8.30 am to 3.30 pm. Take a pullover: it's a chilly 10°C down there.

KŘIVOKLÁT

Křivoklát is a drowsy village beside the Rakovnický potok, a tributary of the Berounka river. Half the pleasure of visiting **Křivoklát Castle** is the getting there – by train up the wooded Berounka valley.

The castle was built in the late 13th century as a royal hunting lodge; in the 15th century Vladislav II gave it its present Gothic face. There's no hunting anymore, as much of the upper Berounka basin, one of Bohemia's most pristine forests, is now included in the Křivoklát Protected Landscape Region and is a UNESCO 'biosphere preservation' area.

The valley is dotted with holiday bungalows and hemmed in by limestone bluffs. On weekdays you'll find none of the crowds associated with places like Karlštejn.

Orientation & Information

From Hotel Sýkora, climb up the road about 10 minutes to the castle turn-off. If you're driving, there's a petrol station farther up the hill. Křivoklát's area code is ☎ 0313.

Castle

Scarred on the outside by clumsy renovations, the castle's best features are inside. Its **chapel** is one of the Czech Republic's finest, with unaltered late-Gothic interiors full of intricate polychrome carvings. The altar is decorated with angels carrying instruments of torture – perhaps not surprising in view of the castle's use in the 16th century as a political prison.

Right under the chapel are the **prison** and torture chambers. The **Knights' Hall** features a permanent collection of late-Gothic religious sculpture and painted panels. Across one end of the 1st floor is the 25m-long **King's Hall**, the second-biggest non-church Gothic hall in the republic, after Vladislav Hall in Prague Castle.

The castle is covered on two tours. Tour I lasts 75 minutes and costs 40 Kč for a Czech guide, 60 Kč for an English-speaking guide. Tour II lasts 35 minutes and is 30/50 Kč, respectively.

Křivoklát is open daily, except Monday and at lunch (noon to 1 pm), June through August from 9 am to 5 pm, in May and September to 4 pm, and in March, April and October through December to 3 pm.

Walking from Křivoklát to Skryje

If you've got the gear and an extra day or two, consider walking the fine 18km trail (marked red) south-west up the Berounka

Křivoklát Castle was originally built as a royal hunting lodge

valley to Skryje. It starts on the west side of Rakovnický potok near the train stop. Beyond the bridge to Roztoky are the **Nezabudice Cliffs** (Nezabudické skály), part of a state nature reserve, and the village of Nezabudice. Across the river from Týřovice village is **Týřov**, a 13th century French-style castle used for a time as a prison and abandoned in the 16th century. Around this is another nature reserve.

The summer resort of **Skryje** has some old thatched houses. You can also walk down the other side of the valley for a closer look at Týrov Castle. There are local buses down the valley to the train at Roztoky, or on to Beroun.

Places to Stay & Eat

There are three *campsites* in the area, the first about 3km up the Berounka at Višňová; another is across the river at Branov (cross at Roztoky); and there's also one at Skryje.

The friendly *Hotel Sýkora* (☎ 981 14) in Křivoklát village has doubles with shower for 550 Kč and a beer hall with inexpensive meals. It's closed Monday so rooms have to be booked in advance for Sunday and Monday.

Otherwise, from the castle turn-off, climb on up the road for about 500m to the plain *Hotel U Černých* (☎ 983 11), which has doubles for about 500 Kč.

Getting There & Away

You can get from Prague to Křivoklát and back on a long day trip, but staying a night at Beroun makes it easier. Rakovník-bound trains leave Beroun every two hours or so; Křivoklát is 50 minutes up the line. There are occasional direct trains to Křivoklát from Prague's Smíchov station.

LIDICE

When British-trained, Czechoslovak paratroops assassinated Reichsprotektor Reinhard Heydrich in June 1942, the Nazis took a savage revenge. Picking – apparently at random – the mining and foundry village of Lidice, 18km north-west of Prague, they proceeded on 10 June to obliterate it from the face of the earth. All its men were shot, all the women and the older children shipped to the Ravensbrück concentration camp, and the younger children farmed out to German foster homes. The village was systematically burned and bulldozed so that no trace remained. Of its 500 inhabitants, 192 men, 60 women and 88 children eventually died.

The atrocity electrified the world and triggered a campaign to preserve the village's memory and create a kind of symbolic Lidice. The site is now a green field, eloquent in its silence, dotted with a few memorials and the reconstructed foundations of a farm where most of the men were shot and buried.

Nearby is a **museum** that recreates the village in photographs and text, and also has chilling SS film of its destruction. It's opposite the Prague-Kladno bus stop, and is open daily from 8 am to 5 pm; entry costs 30 Kč.

An astonishing and beautiful sculptural group of 82 children, a 20 year project by Prague artist Marie Uchytilová, is due to be erected here, pending the raising of enough private funds to have the plaster casts bronzed.

Places to Stay & Eat

If you're caught out, or want to explore the region more, not far to the west is the dreary smokestack town of Kladno, which has some cheap accommodation.

Year-round hostel accommodation is 150 Kč a bed at *Domov mládeže*, 5.května 1879. From the Hotel Kladno, cross the street and walk about one and a half blocks.

Hotel Kladno (☎ 0312-66 16 67), where single/double rooms with bath and WC are about 1200/1500 Kč, is at náměstí Sítná on the Prague-Kladno bus line, two stops before Kladno station. *Pension Tonička* (☎ 0312-2759) has suites with shared toilet for 750/950 Kč, including breakfast. It's at Bendlova 2037; from the Hotel Kladno, cross the bridge, turn left and it's a block in.

Two adequate *restaurants* are just off náměstí Starosty Pavla near the Kladno bus station, and the Hotel Kladno's eatery is not too pricey.

Getting There & Away

Lidice is on the bus line to Kladno, half an hour from Prague. Buses go from Dejvická metro station every 30 to 60 minutes, and a few go from Florenc. Direct (*přímý spoj*) buses to Kladno don't stop at Lidice, but anything serving Buštěhrad does.

KOUNOV STONES

The so-called Kounov Stones (Kamenné řady u Kounova) are a grid of over 2000 small menhirs (standing stones), dating from Neolithic (late Stone Age) times. Their exact use is still a mystery, but they were most likely part of an astronomical calendar-observatory. They're similar to sites found around western Europe, but are the only array of its kind in central and eastern Europe.

This is only for those with a real interest in such sites. Stonehenge it's not – most of the stones are less than a metre across, and buried in tall grass. Over the years many bigger ones have been taken as convenient and cheap building materials.

The surviving stones form a grid about 300m west to east and 450m north to south. Over the largest rock (called Gibbon on the map at the site), it was possible to observe sunrise on the summer solstice; the winter solstice sunrise was observed over another one to the south-east, long since dug up. Sunset was observed above a rock in the south-west (called Pegas on the map).

Getting There & Away

Getting there is a pain unless you have a car. Kounov village is 6km west of Hředle, which is 10km north of Rakovník on the Rakovník-Louny road. Or it's an hour by late-morning bus (weekdays only) from Louny, with few return options; Louny is 1¼ hours from Prague's Florenc bus station (last bus at 10 am).

At Kounov, turn north by a pond; 1.5km up the hill, past the railway line there is a signposted trailhead. After walking for two up the track, fork right onto a nature trail with diagonal green markings for 20 minutes, then go through the woods and around an open field. The stones are at nature-trail signboard No 7.

MĚLNÍK

Mělník, on a prominent hill above the confluence of the Vltava and Labe rivers, began as a 9th century Slavic settlement. Mělník's chateau was the second home of Bohemia's queens from the 13th century until the time of George of Poděbrady. A solidly Hussite town, it was demolished by Swedish troops in the Thirty Years' War, after which the castle was rebuilt as the present chateau you see today.

Mělník is the centre of Bohemia's small wine-growing region. Tourist brochures feature photos of the hill's steep south face, topped by the chateau and covered in scrawny vines. There are healthier vineyards in the area, the best of them descended from Burgundy vines imported by Charles IV.

This is the type of place you come to for an easy and relaxed day exploring and enjoying some pleasant wine-tasting. It's a perfect day trip from Prague.

CZECH REPUBLIC

Orientation

Turn right out of the bus station and take the first left on Jaroše, which climbs up to the old town. Beyond the old gate tower, bear right into náměstí Míru, an arcaded square lined with pastel-tinted Renaissance and Baroque façades. Take the first left along Svatováclavská to Mělník Chateau and the Church of SS Peter & Paul.

Information

The tourist information centre (☎ 62 75 03), náměstí Míru 31, sells maps and historical guides, and can help with accommodation. It's open weekdays (and on summer weekends) from 9 am to 5 pm. Komerční banka on náměstí Míru has a MasterCard/Visa ATM.

Mělník's area code is ☎ 0206.

Chateau

The Renaissance chateau was acquired by the Lobkovic family in 1739. Since getting it back from the state in 1990, they've opened it to the public (daily from 10 am to noon and 1 to 5 pm).

On the hour, for 60 Kč, you can take a tour through the **former living quarters** on the top floor, crowded with the family's rich collection of Baroque furniture and 17th and 18th century paintings, including a series of beautiful lunettes on the life of St Wenceslas by Karel Škréta and his students. Additional rooms are given over to changing exhibits of modern works.

At half-past each hour you can look at the 13th century **wine cellars** for 20 Kč; a cellar tour plus wine-tasting costs 60 Kč. A shop in the courtyard sells the chateau's own label.

Independent of the family's operations is a dreary **Regional Museum** (Okresní muzeum) on the 1st floor, with exhibits on wine-growing and baby prams. It's open daily, except Monday, April through October from 10 am to 5 pm.

Church of SS Peter & Paul

The 15th century Gothic church, the kostel sv Petra a Pavla, with Baroque furnishings and tower, is worth a look. Remnants of its Romanesque predecessor have been incorporated into the rear of the building, south of the bell tower.

The old **crypt** is now an ossuary, packed with the bones of some 10,000 people dug up to make room for 16th century plague victims, and arranged in macabre patterns. It's open to the public daily, except Monday, from 9.30 am to noon and 12.30 to 4 pm; entry costs 30 Kč. Tickets and information are available at the snack bar across the street.

Viewpoint & Walks

The view from behind the chateau takes in the confluence of the Vltava and the Labe, and a once-busy 10km canal. The big bump on the horizon to the north-west is a hill called Říp where, legends say, the brothers

Čech and Lech stopped on a journey from the Far East; the former stayed and founded the Czech nation, the latter went on to sire the Poles.

Lobkovic vineyards carpet the wedge of land between the Vltava and the canal. A pleasant walk could include the thickly wooded Hořínský Park, to the right of the canal, as well as a look at the canal lock, still in use, and the ruins of Hořín, the old Lobkovic family home.

Places to Stay

There's a good campsite, *Autokemp Mělník* (☎ 62 38 56), in the north-eastern part of the town at Klášterní 717.

Look for 'Zimmer frei' (private room) signs around town; there's one behind the church at Česká 4, with beds for 300 Kč per person. Another is *Vila Evropa,* Jaroše 736, on the road up from the bus station. Beds here are 350 Kč per person.

The run-down *Hotel Zlatý Beránek* (☎ 62 23 70), náměstí Míru, has very basic single/double rooms with shared facilities for 300/500 Kč. If you have a car stay instead at *Hotel Ludmila* (☎ 62 24 23), on the road to Prague in the southern part of town in Pražská. Rooms with bath and shower are 500/700 Kč.

Places to Eat

The best local red and white wines are both called Ludmila, after the favourite local saint and grandmother of St Wenceslas. You can taste them in the chateau: on the ground floor are the *U Soutoku* restaurant, with a smashing view of the countryside and very good food (main dishes are around 120 Kč), and a pricier *vinárna.* Both are only open in summer, from 10 am to midnight.

The snug *Stará škola* vinárna behind the church has views to rival the chateau's, and modest prices. It's open in summer only, daily from 11 am to 11 pm.

Off-season try *U Tomášé,* at Svatováclavská 15 right by the chateau, with cheap but good food and a decent selection of wine.

Getting There & Away

Buses run to Mělník from Prague's Florenc bus station and Holešovice metro station at least hourly, taking about 45 minutes.

VELTRUSY

This primly symmetrical chateau was built in the early 18th century as a summer retreat for the aristocratic Chotek family. As the Choteks had collaborated with the Nazis in WWII, the Czechoslovak government seized the chateau and chucked them out. They sold off the furnishings to pay their debts, so the presently assembled period furniture and porcelain has all come from elsewhere, giving the interior a contrived look.

The Baroque and rococo interiors are worth a look, especially the woodwork, the Asian-motif wallpaper and the frescoes (representing the four quarters of the day) on the ceiling of the pompous central dome. The 'men's salon' was redecorated from top to bottom as a set for the film *Amadeus* – and then never used.

Of more interest are the 120 hectares of landscaped grounds, whose beautiful woods are salted with little follies, including an old mill, artificial ruins and an Egyptian pavilion, complete with Sphinx.

The chateau is open daily, except Monday, May through August from 8 am to 5 pm, in September from 9 am to 5 pm, and in April and October from 9 am to 4 pm. They'd like to sell you a 40 Kč English tour but may let you go round with an English text for 10 Kč. It's not worth a trip from Prague, but makes a good add-on to a day in Mělník (if you have a car).

Places to Eat

The *Restaurace Terasa* by the chateau may not be open unless there are groups around. There's a dreary *pivnice* near the bus stand.

Getting There & Away

Buses run every hour or two from Prague's Florenc bus station and Holešovice metro station, and there are hourly connections between Veltrusy and Mělník. From the bus stand it's a few hundred metres to an old gate at the south end of the estate, plus a five minute walk through the woods. If you're driving there's a carpark just west of the chateau.

PŘEROV NAD LABEM

In this village east of Prague is the **Labe River Region Ethnographic Museum** (Polabské národopisné muzeum), the oldest of Bohemia's open-air museum of traditional architecture. It was established in 1895, soon after the first museum of its type opened in Stockholm (the Swedish word for such a museum, *skansen*, has stuck). Contrived as skansens are, they are a unique help in visualising life of an earlier day.

This one was started around a Přerov house that was already here: the 'Old Bohemian Cottage', which is dressed in herringbone timber-cladding and carved ornaments. Other buildings have been brought in piecemeal from around the region – over a dozen houses, as well as belfries, pigsties, decorated beehives and a pigeon house. Staff tend gardens and raise bees using traditional methods.

The museum is open daily, except Monday, May through October from 9 am to 5 pm, and on weekends in April and November from 9 am to 4.30 pm. Entry is 50 Kč, plus 10 Kč for a detailed English brochure.

Getting There & Away

Buses to Poděbrady from Prague's Palmovka metro station (about half a dozen during the day) stop at an isolated petrol station about 35 minutes from Prague. From there it's a 20 minute walk north to the village. Give yourself about 1½ hours, including the walk. Nymburk-bound buses stop in front of the skansen four times a day but there is only one on the weekend; the trip takes about 40 minutes.

KUTNÁ HORA

It's hard to imagine today, but in its time Kutná Hora was, after Prague, Bohemia's most important town. In 1996 it was added to UNESCO's World Heritage List.

In the late 13th century, silver ore was found in these hills, and a town sprouted. In 1308, Wenceslas II imported a team of Italian minters and established a royal mint here. The town's power grew, splendid churches and palaces rose, and in 1400 Wenceslas IV moved the royal residence to Kutná Hora. In less than 150 years Kutná Hora had grown from literally nothing to become one of Europe's biggest, richest towns and Bohemia's economic mainstay.

In the 16th century the silver began to run out and decline set in, hastened by the Thirty Years' War. A Baroque building boom came to an end with a devastating fire in 1770.

Today Kutná Hora may be a fraction of its old self, but with a pastel-hued square dotted with cafés, and façades ranging from Gothic to cubist, comparisons with Prague are hard to resist. Kutná Hora is certainly as densely picturesque as the Czech capital, and blessed with warmer people, better budget accommodation and fewer visitors. It's further blessed with the ossuary chapel in Sedlec, a nearby suburb (see the Around Kutná Hura section). Decorated with the bones of some 40,000 monks and plague victims, Sedlec's chapel is incredibly macabre – and far more interesting than Brno's Capuchin Monastery.

One caveat: don't come on a Monday, as most sights are closed.

Orientation

The historical centre is compact enough to see on foot. Most attractions lie between the central square, Palackého náměstí, and the Cathedral of St Barbara in the south-west corner of town.

The bus station is a five minute walk north of the town centre. Although there's a train station here, trains from Prague stop only at Sedlec, 3km to the north-east.

The easiest way to visit Kutná Hora on a day trip is to arrive on the morning express train from Prague's Masarykovo nádraží train station, then walk 10 minutes from Kutná Hora's Hlavní nádraží train station to the ossuary chapel in Sedlec. From there

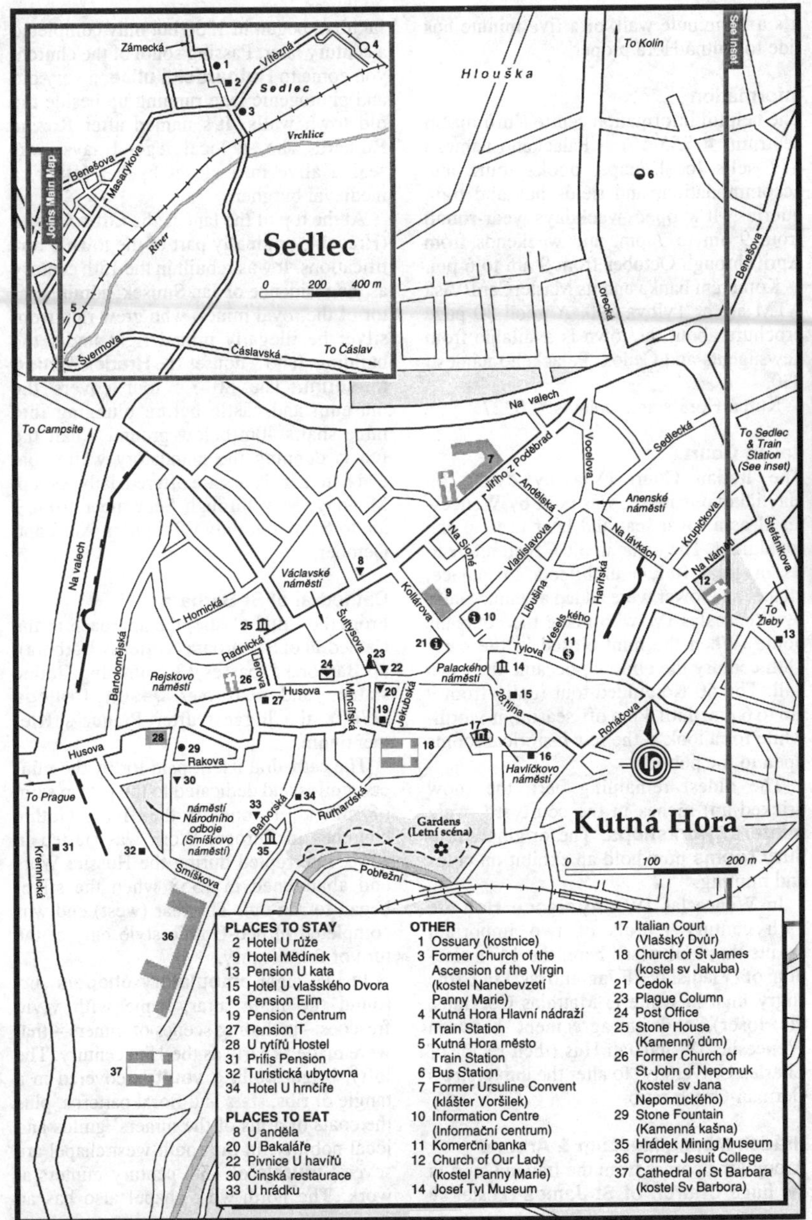
Sedlec
Zámecká
Vítězná
Sedlec
Vrchlice
Benešova
Masarykova
River
Joins Main Map
0 200 400 m
Švermova
Čáslavská
To Čáslav
See Inset
To Kolín
Hlouška
Lorecká
Benešova
Na valech
To Campsite
Jiřího z Poděbrad
Vocelova
Sedlecká
To Sedlec & Train Station (See inset)
Andělská
Anenské náměstí
Na Sioné
Vladislavova
Na lávkách
Krupičkova
Na Náměti
Štefánikova
Václavské náměstí
Kollárova
Libušina
Havířská
Veselského
To Žleby
Hornická
Šultysova
Radnická
Tylova
Palackého náměstí
Rejskovo náměstí
Lierova
Husova
Minciřská
Jekubská
28. října
Rohačova
Bartolomějská
Husova
Rakova
Havlíčkovo náměstí
To Prague
náměstí Národního odboje (Smíškovo náměstí)
Barborská
Ruthardská
Gardens (Letní scéna)
Kutná Hora
0 100 200 m
Kremnická
Smíškova
Pobřežní
PLACES TO STAY
2 Hotel U růže
9 Hotel Mědínek
13 Pension U kata
15 Hotel U vlašského Dvora
16 Pension Elim
19 Pension Centrum
27 Pension T
28 U rytířů Hostel
31 Prifis Pension
32 Turistická ubytovna
34 Hotel U hrnčíře
PLACES TO EAT
8 U anděla
20 U Bakaláře
22 Pivnice U havířů
30 Čínská restaurace
33 U hrádku
OTHER
1 Ossuary (kostnice)
3 Former Church of the Ascension of the Virgin (kostel Nanebevzetí Panny Marie)
4 Kutná Hora Hlavní nádraží Train Station
5 Kutná Hora město Train Station
6 Bus Station
7 Former Ursuline Convent (klášter Voršilek)
10 Information Centre (Informační centrum)
11 Komerční banka
12 Church of Our Lady (kostel Panny Marie)
14 Josef Tyl Museum
17 Italian Court (Vlašský Dvůr)
18 Church of St James (kostel sv Jakuba)
21 Čedok
23 Plague Column
24 Post Office
25 Stone House (Kamenný dům)
26 Former Church of St John of Nepomuk (kostel sv Jana Nepomuckého)
29 Stone Fountain (Kamenná kašna)
35 Hrádek Mining Museum
36 Former Jesuit College
37 Cathedral of St Barbara (kostel Sv Barbora)

it's a 15 minute walk or a five minute bus ride to Kutná Hora proper.

Information

The helpful information centre (Informační centrum; ☎ 755 56) at Palackého náměstí 377 sells local maps, books tours and accommodation, and fields bus and train queries. It's open weekdays year-round from 9 am to 7 pm, and weekends from April through October from 9 am to 6 pm.

Komerční banka and its MasterCard/Visa ATM are at Tylova 390. A good 30 page brochure about the town is available from newsagents and Čedok, Palackého náměstí 330.

Kutná Hora's area code is ☎ 0327.

Italian Court

The Italian Court (Vlašský dvůr), on Havličkovo náměstí, was built by Wenceslas II as a royal seat and later used as the royal mint. The name in old Czech refers to its original Italian architects. A palace, chapel and tower were added a century later by Wenceslas IV, who made the court his home. When the mint closed in the early 18th century the building became the town hall. The 50 Kč guided tour (daily from 9 am to 6 pm, until 4 pm off-season) is worthwhile for a look at the few historical rooms open to the public.

The oldest remaining part, the (now bricked-up) niches in the courtyard, were **minters' workshops**. The original **treasury rooms** now hold an exhibit on coins and minting.

In Wenceslas IV's **Audience Hall** are 19th century murals of two important events that took place here: the 1471 election of Vladislav II Jagiello as king (the angry man in white is Matthias Corvinus, the loser), and an agreement between Wenceslas IV and Jan Hus (then rector of Charles University) to alter the university's German-Czech ratio.

Hrádek Mining Museum & Around

Around the corner from the Italian Court is the huge **Church of St James** (kostel sv Jakuba), begun in 1330 but only completed a century later. Passing south of the church, you come to **Ruthardská ulice**, a very old and photogenic lane running up beside the old town walls. It's named after Rozina Ruthard who, a local legend says, was sealed alive in a closet by her father, a medieval burgher.

At the top of the lane is the **Little Castle** (Hrádek), originally part of the town's fortifications. It was rebuilt in the 15th century as the residence of Jan Smíšek, administrator of the royal mines, who grew rich from silver he illegally mined right under the building. It now houses the **Hrádek Mining Museum**. The 80 Kč tour covers the museum and castle before plunging into mine shafts 40m below ground – half the fun is donning the mandatory white coat and hard hat. Tours are offered daily, except Monday, May through September from 9 am to 6 pm, but only till 5 pm in April and October.

Cathedral of St Barbara

From the Little Castle, the approach to the Cathedral of St Barbara (kostel sv Barbora), up Barborská, passes 13 crumbling Gothic statues and a former **Jesuit College** (1700), the biggest after Prague's Klementinum.

The cathedral itself, paid for by the miners' guilds and dedicated to the patron saint of miners, is one of the finest Gothic churches in Europe. Work was started in 1380, interrupted during the Hussite Wars and abandoned in 1558 when the silver began to run out. The rear (west) end was completed in neo-Gothic style only at the turn of this century.

Inside, eight **ambulatory chapels** surround the main altar, some with vivid frescoes – including scenes of miners – that were made as early as the 15th century. The lofty, bright **ceiling vault** is covered in a tangle of ribs, stars and floral patterns, plus the coats of arms of the miners' guilds and local nobility. In the south-west chapel are several **murals** of 15th century minters at work. The north-west chapel also has an eye-popping mural of the Vision of St Ignatius.

The cathedral is open daily, except Monday, from 9 to 11.30 am and 1 to 5.30 pm, but only till 3.30 pm in the off-season; entry costs 20 Kč.

On the hillside below the cathedral is the former **Corpus Christi Chapel** (kaple Božího těla), built in the 14th century.

Around the Old Town

From the Jesuit College, walk through náměstí Národního odboje (also called Smíškovo náměstí) and turn left on Husova to see bits of the **old city walls**. Return along Husova to Rejskovo náměstí, with its 1495 Gothic **stone fountain** (Kamenná kašna).

Cross via Lierova to Radnická. The Gothic confection at No 183 is the **Stone House** (Kamenný dům), a burgher's house dating from 1490, adorned with a high triangular gable bearing figures of knights jousting.

East and then south is Šultysova, once part of the town's medieval marketplace. It's now lined with handsome townhouses – in particular the **Marble House** (dům U Marmorů) at No 173. At the bottom of the street is a 1715 **plague column**.

Cross Palackého náměstí and walk down Tylova to No 9, the **Josef Tyl Museum**, birthplace of the 19th century playwright who wrote *Where is My Home?*, later to become part of the Czech national anthem. It's open only for special exhibitions, usually held a week or so each month.

Cross the square again to Kollárova and turn right onto Jiřího z Poděbrad. Two blocks down is the unfinished former **Ursuline Convent** (klášter Voršilek), with a 1743 chapel by Kilian Dientzenhofer. In the convent is an exhibit of furnishings from various chateaux in Central Bohemia.

Places to Stay

Camping Basic *Camping Santa Barbara* (☎ 2051) is north-west of town off Česká, near the cemetery (u hřbitova). It's open from May through September.

Hostels A friendly, welcoming place to stay is the hostel *U rytířů* (☎ 2256) at Rejskovo náměstí 123, across the street from the large Gothic well in the middle of the road. The 20 rooms vary in price and start at 200 Kč per person. Most rooms are doubles with private bath.

Turistická ubytovna (☎ 3463), náměstí Národního odboje 56, is a basic dormitory with a reception that only opens from 8 to 9 am and 5 to 6 pm. Space in a four bed dorm is 125 Kč per person.

Private Rooms The information centre books private rooms for 250 to 450 Kč per person.

Pensions You get good value at *Pension U kata* (☎ 750 96), Uhelná 569, which has rooms with private shower and WC for 185 Kč per person. Downstairs is a lively beer hall. In the same price range is *Prifis Pension*, at Kremnická 5.

Pension Elim (☎ 3129), Havličkovo náměstí 548, is basic but comfortable at 390 Kč per person.

The up-market *Pension T* (☎ 2413), Husova 117, is impeccably central and charges 390 Kč per person for rooms with bath and WC.

A good splurge is *Pension Centrum* (☎ 4218), Jakubská 57, with fully equipped doubles for 980 Kč.

Hotels The *Hotel Mědínek* (☎ 2741), a modern four storey place on Palackého náměstí, is a bit expensive at 900/1200 Kč for a single/double with bath and breakfast.

A better choice is *Hotel U hrnčíře* (☎ 2113), Barborská 24, just down the street from the Hrádek. The five doubles in this down-to-earth inn are 800 Kč each, including breakfast.

The top-end choice is *Hotel U vlašského Dvora* (☎ 4618; fax 4627) at 28.října 511. Doubles with the works are 1290 Kč; the on-site sauna is much appreciated.

Places to Eat

U hrádku, at Babaroská 12, is a quiet café

with a small but good food menu; it's closed Monday.

Kutná Hora is well stocked with beer halls: *U anděla*, Václavské náměstí 8, has a decent if typical pub menu and is less smoky than the nearby *Pivnice U havířů* on Šultysova (closed Monday). The latter has a more sedate 'Irish Pub' at the back.

Across the road, *U Bakaláře* has better, more expensive dishes and is open daily until at least 10 pm.

The *Čínská restaurace*, náměstí Národního odboje 48, has delicious Chinese dishes from 80 to 150 Kč. It's closed from 2 to 5 pm and on Monday.

Getting There & Away

Bus Long-distance buses leave from Prague's Florenc metro station about six times a day. The 1¼ hour trip is 40 Kč. Buses also leave seven times daily from the ČSAD stand on Počernická, near Prague's Želivského metro station. The weekend service is greatly reduced, and the few buses that do run go mostly to and from the ČSAD stand.

Train No trains go directly from Prague to Kutná Hora. Three or four each day go from Prague's Masarykovo station to Kutná Hora Hlavní nádraží in Sedlec, 3km north of town, taking about an hour.

It's easiest to walk from the station into Kutná Hora (first stopping at the ossuary in Sedlec). However, about 10 trains a day link Kutná Hora Hlavní nádraží to the Kutná Hora město station, which is adjacent to the old town. Alternatively, from the Sedlec station there are local buses direct to Kutná Hora's old town.

Car The fastest route is Highway 12 via Kolín and Sedlec; the prettiest is Route 333 via Kostelec.

Getting Around

Local (*městská doprava*) buses on Masarykovo go to and from the train station and Sedlec every 20 to 30 minutes. Buy tickets from the driver.

AROUND KUTNÁ HORA

Sedlec & the Ossuary Chapel

Today Sedlec is a suburb of Kutná Hora, but it's been around longer, since the founding of Bohemia's first Cistercian monastery there in 1142.

After a 13th century abbot brought back some earth from Jerusalem and sprinkled it on the monastery's graveyard, its popularity mushroomed. Demand was augmented by plague epidemics, and within a century there were tens of thousands of graves, and bones began to pile up. The small 14th century All Saints' Chapel (kaple Všech Svatých) was pressed into service as an **ossuary** (kostnice).

When Joseph II abolished the monasteries, the Schwarzenberg family bought this one, and in 1870 a Czech woodcarver named František Rint arranged the bones into the ghoulish attraction's now on display in the chapel cellar. There are bone chalices and bone crosses; the Schwarzenberg coat of arms in bones; and an extraordinary chandelier made from at least one of every bone in the human body. Rint even signed his name in bones, at the foot of the stairs.

The ossuary is open daily all year-round from April through October from 8 am to noon and 1 to 6 pm, and from November through March from 9 am to noon and 1 to 4 pm. Admission is 20 Kč, plus 25 to snap photos.

Down on the main road is the monastery's **Church of the Ascension of the Virgin** (kostel Nanebevzetí Panny Marie), renovated at the start of the 18th century by Giovanni Santini in his 'Baroque-Gothic' style, unique to Bohemia. Sadly it is now part of a tobacco factory and closed to the public.

Places to Stay Morbid types who want to sleep near all those bones should try the *Hotel U růže* (☎ 741 15), at Zámecká 52 just down the road from the ossuary. It's a posh little spot priced at 650/1400 Kč for a single/double with bath, WC and satellite TV.

Getting There & Away Sedlec is 3km from Kutná Hora by local bus. Some buses stop by the church, some opposite the ossuary, two blocks up Zámecká. It's an easy 15 minute walk from Kutná Hora's Church of Our Lady straight up Masarykovo.

Žleby Chateau

This beautiful chateau, 18km south-east of Kutná Hora, dates from at least the 13th century. Its fairy-tale appearance is the result of renovation by Duke Vincent Karl Auersperg in the latter 19th century – a sugary Gothic-Renaissance style meant to conjure up visions of medieval castles.

The Auerspergs lived here until 1945, when they fled to Austria, leaving everything behind. The chateau is therefore in immaculate – and authentic – shape, and offers a glimpse of how the other half was living in Czechoslovakia earlier in this century.

Inside it's all armour and mounted firearms, wood panelling and leather wallpaper, rococo flourishes and a treasure trove of old furniture. Highlights include the **Knights' Hall** with a huge Baroque cupboard and rows of Czech and German glass; and the **Duchess Study**, with a replica Rubens on the ceiling and a fantastic door of inlaid wood.

The chateau is open daily, except Monday, May to August from 8 am to 4 pm (from 9 am in September). In April and October it's open only on weekends from 9 am to 4 pm. Admission is 50 Kč. There are no crowds here, save the occasional coach tour.

Getting There & Away The chateau is 50 minutes from Kutná Hora by bus (15 Kč). There's only one suitable direct connection, which leaves about 2.15 pm and returns about 5.30 pm. There are a dozen options if you change at Čáslav. Ask for Žleby náměstí, the square at the foot of the chateau. Check return times, as buses peter out soon after 5 pm

Kolín

Kolín, on the Labe river, is a friendly old town seldom visited by tourists. It has a picturesque central square (Karlovo náměstí) with a Baroque Marian column (1682) and fountain (1780) in the middle. A block away is the towering Gothic **Church of St Bartholomew** begun by Petr Parléř. The **City Museum** (closed Monday) is next to this church (also closed Monday). The Kmochův Festival of brass-band music is held in Kolín every June.

Orientation & Information The town centre is next to the river, a 15 minute walk from the adjacent bus and train stations. There is an exchange counter and a MasterCard ATM at Agrobanka, Kutnohorská 56/821. Kolín's area code is ☎ 0321.

Places to Stay & Eat The *Turistická ubytovna zimní stadion* (☎ 270 93), Brankovická 27, has beds in triple rooms at 175 Kč; take bus No 3 from the train station. There's a good restaurant at the zimní stadion, open daily until 10 pm.

The *Hotel Savoy*, Rubešová 61, was closed at the time of writing. Nearby is the new *Vinárna/Pension Pod věží* (☎ 238 77) at Parléřova 40, just off Kutnohorská, where single/double rooms are 900/1200 Kč including bath and breakfast.

Getting There & Away Buses run regularly from Kolín bus station to Kutná Hora, 12km south by road. Kolín is also a major junction on the Prague-Košice railway line, with frequent service to and from Prague (62km, one hour).

North Bohemia

HIGHLIGHTS

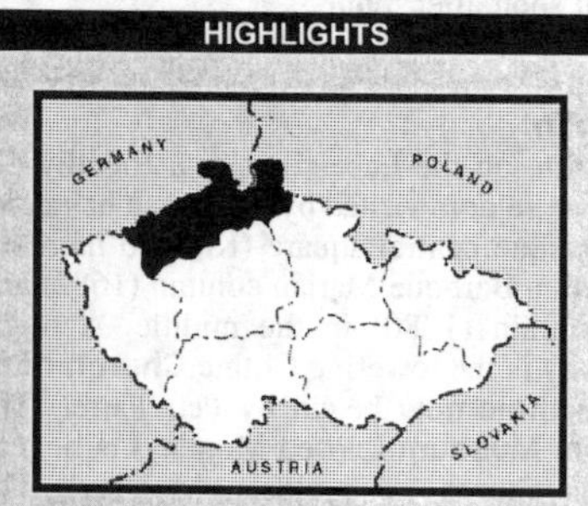

- Visit the picturesque town of Litoměřice
- A former Nazi concentration camp, the fortress of Terezín is now a poignant memorial to the Holocaust
- Marvel at the excessive rococo interior of Ploskovice chateau
- Go on one of the many superb hiking trails or simply check out the rock formations of the Sandstone Rocks of Labe

Tourists tend to be shy of North Bohemia, perceived as little more than an arc of polluted factory towns at the feet of the republic's border-mountains – the Krušné hory (Ore Mountains), Lužické hory and Jizerské hory.

In the 19th century, north Bohemia was the focus of the most intense industrialisation anywhere in the present-day Czech and Slovak republics, fed by the ore and coal mines of the Ore Mountains. This extraordinary inheritance made the newborn Czechoslovak nation an instant economic giant – and was the cause of alarm when the region's large German population focussed on their ethnic ties with Nazi Germany. In WWII, Allied bombs wrought havoc on several towns, including the regional administrative capital, Ústí nad Labem.

After the war, the region's Germans were brutally expelled and the Communists resumed industrialisation with a vengeance. Development since the war, probably more than in the two previous centuries, has led to appallingly high incidences of cancer and birth defects – and the death by acid rain of vast areas of mountain forest. Privatisation now compounds the misery with unemployment and dislocation.

The irony is that the Czech Republic's gathering economic strength, in comparison to Slovakia, owes much to this region. The country's reputation for artisanship also rests heavily on Northern Bohemian traditions – for example, the glass and crystal of Nový Bor and other towns, the porcelain mined and fired at Klášterec nad Ohří, the textiles of Liberec and the costume jewellery of Jablonec nad Nisov.

There is in fact more to see here than factories. North of Děčín, where the mighty Labe exits to Germany (as the Elbe) through a deep notch called the Bohemian Gate, the mountains offer abundant hiking (though acid rain has spoiled some of the views). Eastward there are several protected landscape regions, including the beautiful Sandstone Rocks of Labe (Labské pískovce), and a string of handsome Germanic towns. A not so well regarded attraction are the prostitutes and brothels along the 12km section of Highway E55 between Cínovec and Dubí.

TEREZÍN

Even were it not for their savage use by the Nazis, the massive strongholds at Terezín (Theresienstadt in German) would be awesome. They were founded in 1780 by Emperor Joseph II (and named after his mother, Empress Maria Theresa) as a state-of-the-art bulwark against the Prussians, but they never saw any action. In the 19th century the town within the Main Fortress was made a garrison, while the so-called

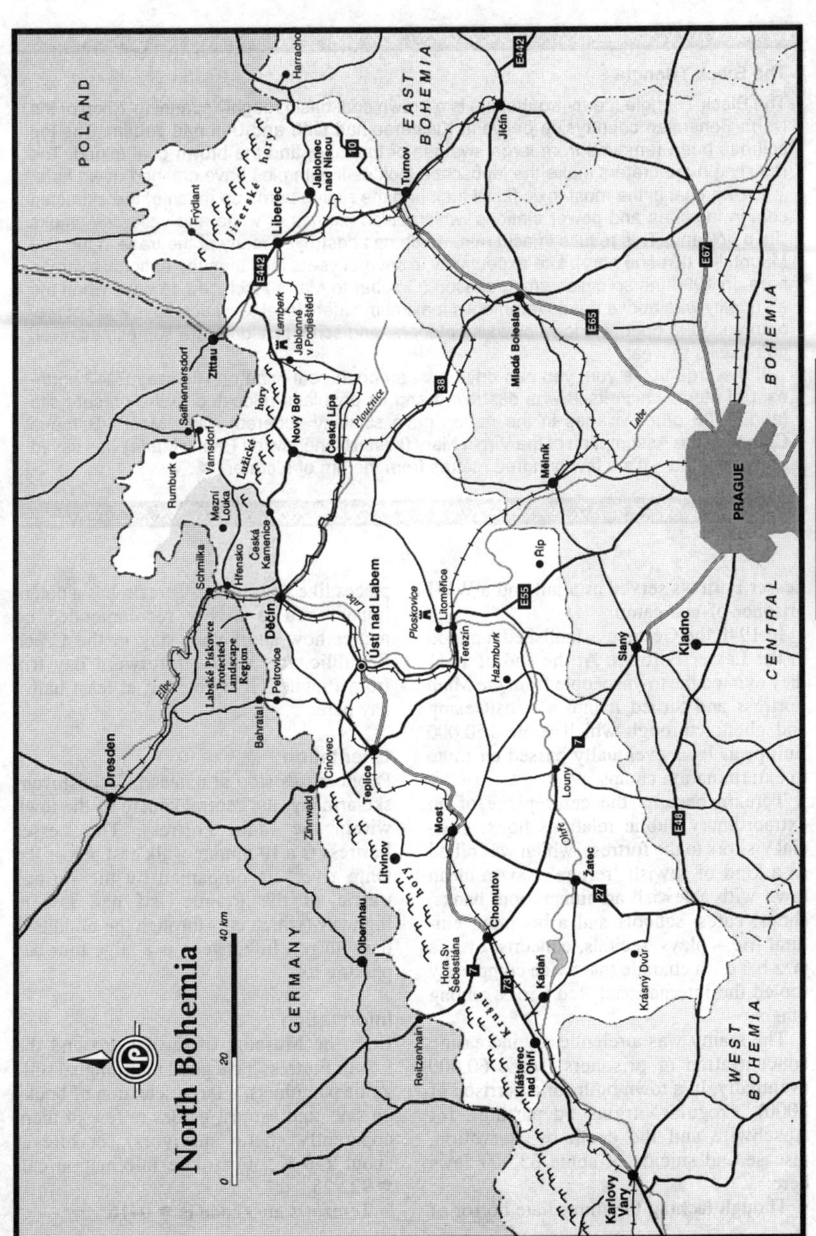
North Bohemia
0
20
40 km
POLAND
GERMANY
EAST BOHEMIA
CENTRAL BOHEMIA
WEST BOHEMIA
Harracho
Jičín
E442
10
Turnov
Jablonec nad Nisou
Liberec
Frýdlant
Jizerské hory
E442
Lemberk
Jablonné v Podještědí
Zittau
Seifhennersdorf
Rumburk
Varnsdorf
Lužické hory
Nový Bor
Česká Lípa
Ploučnice
38
Mladá Boleslav
E65
E67
Mělník
Labe
PRAGUE
Kladno
Slaný
Říp
E55
Mezní Louka
Schmilka
Hřensko
Česká Kamenice
Děčín
Labe
Ústí nad Labem
Ploskovice
Litoměřice
Terezín
Hazmburk
Labské Pískovce Protected Landscape Region
Petrovice
Bahratal
Elbe
Dresden
Cínovec
Zinnwald
Teplice
Most
Litvínov
Louny
7
Ohře
E48
Žatec
27
Chomutov
Kadaň
Krásný Dvůr
Hora Sv Šebestiána
7
73
Krušné hory
Olbernhau
Reitzenhain
Klášterec nad Ohří
Karlovy Vary

The Black Triangle

The Black Triangle (černý troûhelník) is a brown coal basin roughly spanning 70km of the North Bohemian countryside between Klášterec nad Ohří and Ůstí nad Labem. The top soil has been removed from large swathes of the land, and the brown coal mined. The resulting huge craters make the landscape look as if asteroids have crashed down here.

Brown coal is the most toxic fossil fuel, and the region burns up much of the extracted coal in factories and power stations, which belch plumes of white and yellowish smoke like a volcano. This results in acid rain, which has destroyed many of the trees in the Ore Mountains (Krušné hory). Life expectancy is several years less than the national average here. In 1996 the so-called smog season (October to March) included 45 days when the air quality was above the government's maximum safety level. On such days it is not recommended to open windows or walk outdoors, and school children are sometimes given gas masks to wear.

If the urge takes you, you can drive past an open coal mine on Highway E442 northeast of Most, which itself was destroyed and its populace relocated to the present site (about 100 other villages in the region have similarly suffered). Only Most's Baroque Church of the Assumption of the Virgin Mary (kostel Nanebevzetí Panny Marie) was saved and relocated – it's a few hundred metres from the rim of a crater. ■

Lesser Fortress served as a jail and a WWI prisoner-of-war camp.

In 1940 the Gestapo established a prison in the Lesser Fortress. At the end of 1941 they evicted the townspeople from the Main Fortress and turned it into a transit camp and ghetto, through which some 150,000 European Jews eventually passed en route to extermination camps.

Terezín became the centrepiece of an extraordinary public relations hoax. Official visitors to the fortress, which was billed as a kind of Jewish 'refuge', saw a clean town with a Jewish administration, banks, shops, cafés, schools and a booming cultural life – plays, recitals, concerts, even a jazz band – a charade that twice completely fooled the International Red Cross, among others.

The reality was a relentlessly increasing concentration of prisoners (some 60,000 eventually, in a town built for a garrison of 5000), regular trains departing for Auschwitz and the death by starvation, disease and suicide of some 35,000 Jews here.

Though lacking the immediate horror of places like Auschwitz, Terezín has a potent impact and is highly recommended no matter how short your stay in the Czech Republic. It's a straightforward day trip from Prague. Give yourself at least half a day here.

Orientation

Public buses stop at náměstí Československé armády, the central square of the town within the Main Fortress. The Lesser Fortress is a 10 minute walk east across the Ohře river, accompanied by the furious traffic of the Prague-Ústí nad Labem highway (which cuts through the middle of the village). In between is a huge tour-bus parking lot.

Information

Both the Museum of the Ghetto and the Lower Fortress have good multilingual self-guide pamphlets, a large selection of books on sale, and earnest guides (a few of them apparently ghetto survivors) for hire at about 220 Kč. For more information call ☎ 922 25.

Terezín's area code is ☎ 0416.

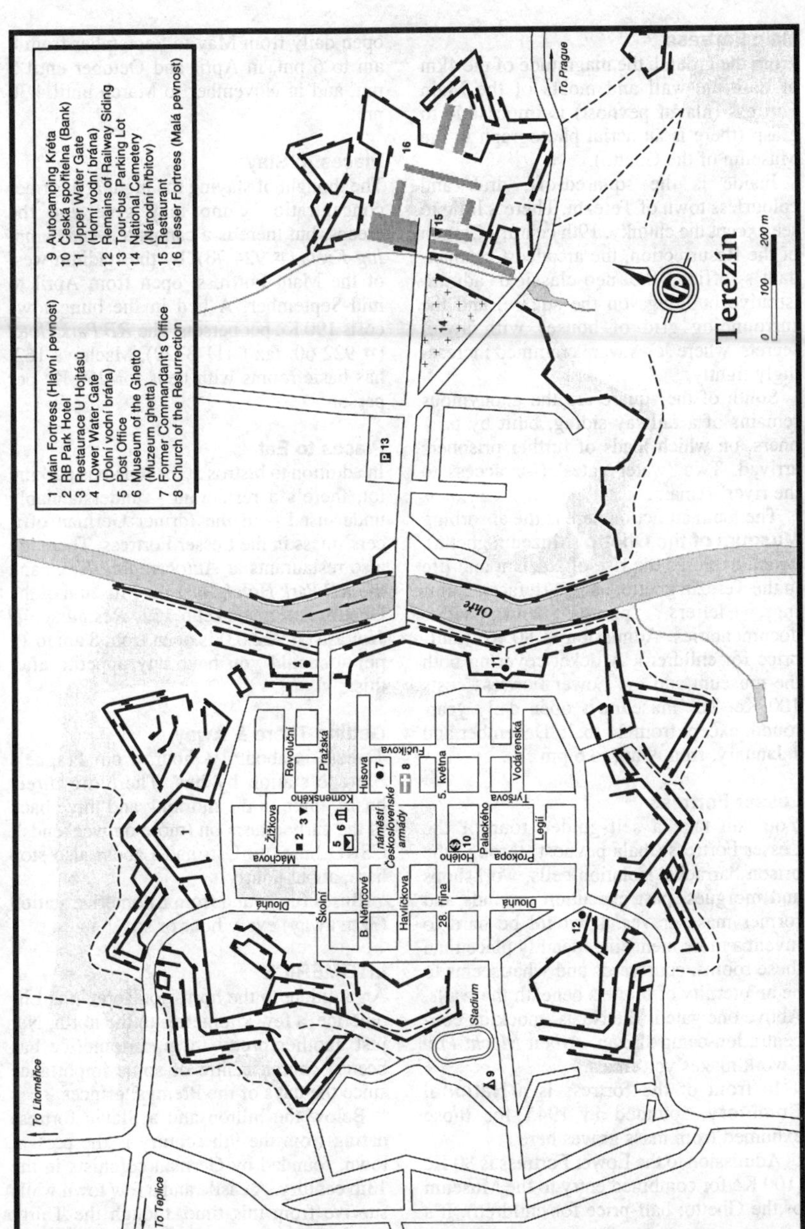
Terezín
1 Main Fortress (Hlavní pevnost)
2 RB Park Hotel
3 Restaurace U Hojtášů
4 Lower Water Gate
(Dolní vodní brána)
5 Post Office
6 Museum of the Ghetto
(Muzeum ghetta)
7 Former Commandant's Office
8 Church of the Resurrection
9 Autocamping Kréta
10 Česká spořitelna (Bank)
11 Upper Water Gate
(Horní vodní brána)
12 Remains of Railway Siding
13 Tour-bus Parking Lot
14 National Cemetery
(Národní hřbitov)
15 Restaurant
16 Lesser Fortress (Malá pevnost)
To Prague
To Litoměřice
To Teplice
Ohře
Stadium
Máchova
Žižkova
Revoluční
Pražská
Komenského
Husova
Fučíkova
náměstí Československé armády
5. května
Vodárenská
Tyršova
Palackého
Hollého
Prokopa
Legií
Dlouhá
Školní
B. Němcové
Havlíčkova
28. října
P 13
0
100
200 m

Main Fortress

From the ground, the magnitude of the 4km of multiple wall and moats of the Main Fortress (hlavní pevnost) is impossible to grasp (there is an aerial photograph in the Museum of the Ghetto).

Inside is the squared-off, drab and colourless town of Terezín. There's little to see except the chunky, 19th century Church of the Resurrection, the arcaded Commandant's office, the neo-classical administrative buildings on the square, and the surrounding grid of houses with awful secrets, where Jews were crammed increasingly tightly.

South of the square are the anonymous remains of a railway siding, built by prisoners, on which loads of further prisoners arrived. Two 'water gates' (for access to the river) remain.

The main attraction here is the absorbing **Museum of the Ghetto** (Muzeum ghetta), which explores the rise of Nazism and life in the Terezín ghetto, using artefacts, paintings, letters, photos and video documentaries. Admission is 80 Kč (half-price for children). A ticket covering both the museum and the Lower Fortress costs 100 Kč. The museum is open daily year-round, except from 24 to 26 December and 1 January, from 9 am to 6 pm.

Lesser Fortress

You can take a self-guided tour of the Lesser Fortress (malá pevnost) through the prison barracks, isolation cells, workshops and morgues, past execution grounds and former mass graves. It would be hard to invent a more menacing, deathly place than these rooms, courtyards and what seems to be an eternity of tunnels beneath the walls. Above one gate is the Nazis' mocking concentration-camp slogan, *Arbeit Macht Frei* ('work makes you free').

In front of the fortress is a **National Cemetery**, founded in 1945 for those exhumed from mass graves here.

Admission to the Lower Fortress is 80 Kč (100 Kč for combined entry to the Museum of the Ghetto; half-price for children). It's open daily from May to September from 8 am to 6 pm, in April and October until 5 pm, and in November to March until 4.30 pm.

Places to Stay

The thought of staying the night at a former concentration camp may give you the creeps, but there is a campsite, *Autocamping Kréta* (☎ 924 73), by the stadium west of the Main Fortress, open from April to mid-September. A bed in the bungalows costs 190 Kč per person. The *RB Park Hotel* (☎ 922 60; fax 0411-3729), Máchova 162, has basic rooms with beds for 260 Kč per person.

Places to Eat

In addition to bistros at the tour-bus parking lot, there's a restaurant – understandably under-used – in the former German officers' mess in the Lesser Fortress. There are also restaurants at *Autocamping Kréta* and the *RB Park Hotel*. Near the Museum of the Ghetto at Komenského 152, *Restaurace U Hojtášů* (☎ 922 03) is open from 8 am to 11 pm – should you have any appetite after this.

Getting There & Away

Terezín is about 1¼ hours from Prague's Florenc station by bus. There are direct buses, three in the morning and three back in the early afternoon (more on weekends). ČSAD buses to Ústí nad Labem also stop here, about hourly.

Buses run to and from Litoměřice station (3km away) every hour or so.

LITOMĚŘICE

An antidote to the horror of Terezín is Litoměřice, a few kilometres to the north. Not just another pretty town, Litoměřice has been a church centre of some importance since the days of the Přemysl princes.

Below the hilltop and a Slavic fortress dating from the 9th century is the present town, founded by German colonists in the 13th century. A castle and a few town walls survive from this time, though the Thirty

ALL PHOTOS BY JOHN KING

North & West Bohemia

Top: Ploskovice Chateau's exterior is spectacular, but its interior is where the beauty lies.
Middle: The view of the village of Loket nad Ohří from the castle.
Bottom: The Colonnade and singing fountain of Marianské Lázně.

RICHARD NEBESKÝ

RICHARD NEBESKÝ

RICHARD NEBESKÝ

RICHARD NEBESKÝ

SCOTT McNEELY

JOHN KING

A	B
C	D
E	F

East & South Bohemia

A A farmhouse near Volyně
B Horní Vltavice
C Rožmberk nad Vltavou
D Renaissance houses in Holašovice
E The castle at Orlík nad Vltavou
F Opočno Castle is one of the region's finest

Years' War eradicated much of the Gothic personality of this fervently Hussite town.

In the early 18th century, architect Ottavio Broggio, who was born in the town, designed new churches and renovated old ones, in honour of Litoměřice's new status as a royal seat and bishopric by order of Ferdinand III.

Orientation

Litoměřice sits on the north bank of the Labe at the confluence with its tributary, the Ohře. From the train station or adjacent bus station, the old centre begins just across the road to the west, past the best preserved of the 14th century town walls. Walk down Dlouhá to the central square, Mírové náměstí.

Information

The Municipal Information Centre (Městské informační centrum; ☎ 2136) is in the House at the Chalice, the present town hall, and has information on accommodation and transport, and also sells maps. It's open on weekdays from 8 am to 6 pm and weekends from 9.30 am to 4 pm. An earnest Čedok office (☎ 2588) is at Dlouhá 47.

Komerční banka, Mírové náměstí 37, has a Visa/MasterCard ATM. The post and telephone office is on Osvobození, two blocks north of Mírové náměstí. Litoměřice's area code is ☎ 0416.

Mírové Náměstí

Dominating this attractive square is the Gothic tower of **All Saints Church** (kostel Všech svatých), built in the 13th century and 'Broggio-ised' in 1718. Beside it, with multiple gables, pointy arches and a copper-topped tower, is the handsome Gothic **Old Town Hall** (Stará radnice), with a small town museum inside. During the summer months it is possible to join a tour to visit 366m of the **catacombs** (historické sklepy). The entrance is through the Radniční sklípek restaurant, but it might be easier to phone ☎ 73 43 06 or the Municipal Information Centre first.

Most striking is the Renaissance **House at the Black Eagle** (dům U Černého orla; 1560) at No 12, covered in sgraffito biblical scenes. A few doors down is the present town hall, in the **House at the Chalice** (dům U Kalicha; 1539), with a massive Hussite chalice on the roof.

The piece of Baroque fruitcake that almost hits you in the eye from the other end of the square is the **House of Ottavio Broggio**.

An excellent local art exhibit is found at the **Museum and Gallery of Litoměřice Diocese** (muzeum a galerie litoměřické diocéze) at No 16, the oldest standing house on the square. The staff are keen to show you the collection that includes paintings and statues from St Stephen Cathedral, modern paintings and naive art that is spread around several burgher houses. One house has a wooden panel ceiling painted with floral designs, while another has an original wooden Gothic roof frame built entirely without a single nail. The museum is open Tuesday to Sunday from 9 am to noon and 1 to 6 pm (October to March until 5 pm); entry costs 14 Kč.

Around the Square

Another Broggio original, built for the Jesuits, is just south of the square. The pink and white **Church of Annunciation of Our Lady** (kostel Zvěstování Panny Marie) has a neglected exterior and a stripped interior. Over a little footbridge from it is the former Jesuit college.

West of the square at Michalská 7 is another house with a Broggio face-lift, now home to the good **North Bohemia Fine Arts Gallery** (Severočeská galerie výtvarného umění; ☎ 4127). Its pride and joy is a set of panels on the life of the Virgin from the **Litoměřice Altarpiece**, one of Bohemia's most famous works of Renaissance art, by the anonymous 'Master of Litoměřice' (whose work also graces Prague's St Vitus Cathedral). The museum is open daily, except Monday, from 9 am to 6 pm.

Other Litoměřice monastery churches of the Counter-Reformation include the

CZECH REPUBLIC

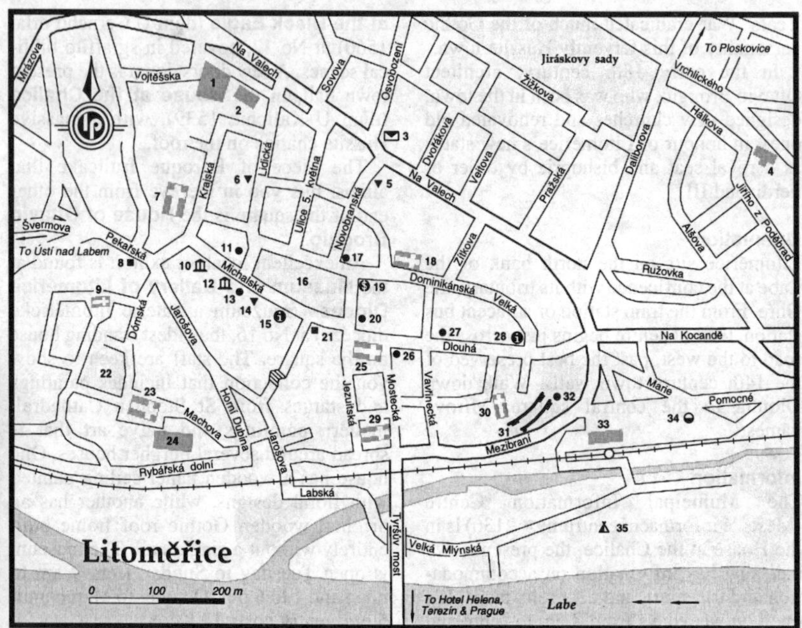

PLACES TO STAY

4 Lovochemie Hotel
8 Penzion U pavouka
21 Hotel Salva Guarda & House at the Black Eagle (dům U Černého orla)
35 Autocamp Slavoj

PLACES TO EAT

1 Parnas & Cultural Centre (dům kultury)
5 Pekárna Kodys & Hamele Bakery
6 Pivnice Kalich
14 Radniční sklípek & Catacombs (historické sklepy)

OTHER

2 Castle
3 Post & Telephone Office
7 St Michael Church (kostel sv Michala)
9 St Wenceslas Church (kostel sv Václava)
10 North Bohemia Fine Arts Gallery (Severočeská galerie výtvarného umění)
11 House of Ottavio Broggio
12 Museum and Gallery of Litoměřice iocese (muzeum a galerie litoměřické diocéze)
13 Bookshop
15 House at the Chalice (dům U Kalicha) & Municipal Information Centre (Městské informační centrum)
16 Mírové náměstí
17 Bookshop
18 St James Church (kostel sv Jakuba)
19 Komerční banka
20 Old Town Hall (Stará radnice)
22 Dómské náměstí
23 St Stephen Cathedral (katedrála sv Štěpána)
24 Bishop's Palace
25 All Saints Church (kostel všech svatých)
26 Fruit & Vegetable Shop
27 Supermarket (samoobsluha)
28 Čedok Travel Agency & Tourist Information
29 Church of Annunciation of Our Lady (kostel Zvěstování Panny Marie)
30 St Ludmilla Church (kostel sv Ludmily)
31 Old Town Walls
32 Old Town Bastion
33 Train Station
34 Bus Station

remains of the St Michael Church (kostel sv Michala), west of the fine arts gallery, the St James Church (kostel sv Jakuba), which is north-east of the square on náměstí Dominikanské, and St Ludmilla Church (kostel sv Ludmily), east of the centre.

Cathedral Hill

South-west of Mírové náměstí is the weedy **Dómské náměstí**, site of an ancient Slavic fortress and, despite its abandoned appearance, the town's historical heart. On the way (along Dómská from the fine arts gallery), don't miss Broggio's finest work, the little **St Wenceslas Church** (kostel sv Václava; 1716), a true Baroque gem.

At the top of Cathedral Hill (dómský pahorek) is the town's oldest church, the huge **St Stephen Cathedral** (katedrála sv Štěpána), built in the 11th century and rebuilt in the 17th. Spacious and Romanesque in shape, a tall arch reaches out like an arm to an 1880s belfry. Behind it is the renovated former **Bishop's Palace**.

Castle

The town's heavily reconstructed 14th century castle is north of Mírové náměstí, up Lidická. Not a very interesting building to begin with, it now has a massive, ugly cultural centre (dům kultury) attached to it like a barnacle.

Places to Stay

Čedok can help with private accommodation for about 600 Kč 800 Kč. *Autocamp Slavoj* (☎ 6694), with tent spaces and bungalows, is on an island called Střelecký ostrov (Shooting Island), directly south of the train station. It's open May through September.

The best bargain in town is *Penzion U pavouka* (☎ 6703), Pekařská 7, where small doubles are 550 Kč, including breakfast. Another well-priced place is the basic, high-rise *Lovochemie Hotel* (☎ 5451; fax 5452), a factory hostel with a big 'SCHZ' sign on the roof at Vrchlického 10, a 15 minute walk north-east of the main square. Singles/doubles with WC, shower and satellite TV start at 460/770 Kč, and there's a breakfast restaurant.

Overpriced but comfortable rooms with shower and toilet at the *Hotel Helena* (☎ 5179), Želetická 10-12, are 700/1400 Kč, including breakfast. It's a 15 minute walk south across the river. The best place in town is the well-positioned three-star *Hotel Salva Guarda* (☎ 3296) in the House at the Black Eagle, Mírové náměstí 12, with cosy rooms from 800/1200 Kč. This formally Gothic house was rebuilt in Renaissance style in 1576.

Places to Eat

Radniční sklípek (☎ 6626), Mírové náměstí 21, is a basement wine bar (vinárna) with main courses from 20 Kč 100 Kč. On the corner of the old town hall is a decent coffee and ice-cream shop.

At Novobranská 18, *Pekárna Kodys & Hamele* is a good bakery for coffee and something gooey, and on Lidická there's the noisy old *Pivnice Kalich*. *Parnas* is a boring café-restaurant in the cultural centre, with courses under 90 Kč. *Vinárna Bašta*, in a former old-town bastion at Pokratická 91, is open from noon to at least midnight (11 pm on Sunday, closed on Monday).

Do-it-yourselfers will find a better-than-average fruit and vegetable shop and a supermarket (samoobsluha), both on Dlouhá.

Getting There & Away

There are bus connections between Litoměřice and Terezín (only a few kilometres away) every 30 to 60 minutes.

Litoměřice is about 1¼ hours from Prague. ČSAD buses from Prague to Ústí nad Labem stop here hourly. The train trip is very tedious.

PLOSKOVICE

This chateau is probably one of the few secular works by the ubiquitous Ottavio Broggio. It has more personality than any of his churches in Litoměřice, the more so for the deliciously excessive rococo interior

CZECH REPUBLIC

renovations by painter Josef Navrátil, part of an overhaul for Emperor Ferdinand V carried out in the 1850s.

Chateau

The guided tour of the chateau takes in about 10 rooms used by the emperor and empress (the tour's in Czech, but you can borrow an English text). Highlights include the emperor's ostentatious bedroom, with unusual bidet, and the stunning main hall at the rear, with murals by Václav Vavřinec Reiner representing the four corners of the world. Most of the chateau's other murals are by Josef Navrátil (who was certainly free of excess humility: on the ceiling of the empress' study he painted himself beside her favourite sculptor, Benvenuto Cellini).

Arcaded galleries to either side of the main house, and a basement grotto, are closed to the public. At the rear is a stately, manicured garden, complete with peacocks.

The chateau (☎ 0416-8692) is open daily, except Monday, May through August from 8 am to 5 pm, from 9 am to 4 pm in September, and on weekends and holidays in April and October. Entry costs 20 Kč (free for students, the disabled and children up to six years old).

Getting There & Away

Ploskovice is a 20 minute bus trip from Litoměřice. Take bus No 47350, bound for Třebušín, departing four or five times a day; check return times with the driver, since the bus stop at Ploskovice may have no times posted. The bus stops in the village square, around the corner from the chateau.

DĚČÍN

This Labe river port (whose name comes from Děčané, the Slavic tribe who were the first settlers here) is mainly a base for visiting the Labské pískovce (the Sandstone Rocks of the Labe, the so-called 'Czech Switzerland') or making connections in or out of the country. According to the Department of Environment, Děčín has made the best progress towards becoming an environmentally clean city. It has cut the burning of coal by 50% per annum since 1990, which has lowered the emission of sulphur dioxide from an annual average of 160 micrograms to 41 micrograms.

Děčín's one real historical attraction is its huge, brooding castle (zámek Děčín), founded in the final years of the Přemysl kings and last used as a Soviet army garrison after the 1968 Warsaw Pact invasion. It has been closed to the public since 1968, and is currently undergoing renovations, but the tiny surviving old town and a ride to the top of Shepherd's Wall might still warrant a few hours here.

Orientation

The town has two quite distinct centres – Děčín proper, on the east bank of the Labe, and Podmokly on the west, at the foot of an escarpment called Shepherd's Wall (Pastýřská stěna). The Děčín side has what few historical attractions there are, most hotels and better food, while Podmokly has the train and bus stations.

Information

The marginally helpful Čedok (☎ 226 78), at Prokopa Holého 8 in Podmokly, is open on weekdays from 8 am to 4 pm. Around the corner on Tržní is the Foreigners' Police office. There are post offices south of the train station in Podmokly, and at náměstí Svobody on the Děčín side; the town's area code is ☎ 0412.

There's a Komerční banka with a MasterCard ATM at Radniční 19, Děčín, and a ČSOB on the corner of Zbrojnická and Československých legií, Podmokly, with a Visa ATM. A small Kodak-franchise photo shop is on Plzeňská, behind the ČSOB bank in Podmokly.

Old Town & Castle

A minuscule section of old-town Děčín has been preserved at the foot of the castle, along pedestrianised U brány ulice. What ought to be the centrepiece is the **Church of the Holy Cross** (kostel sv Kříže), but its high-domed Romanesque exterior is undergoing only half-hearted restoration and its frescoed Baroque interior is going to seed. From here a walled avenue, the so-called Long Ride (Dlouhá jízda), climbs to the castle, with a separate covered walkway along one side.

Děčín Castle was founded in 1305 by the Přemysl King Václav III. The 'Baroque-fied' Renaissance chateau inside is said to have 'as many rooms as the year has days'. Among its distinguished visitors was Frédéric Chopin, who composed a waltz (in A flat major) here in 1835. The castle passed into the hands of the Czechoslovak state in 1932. After 1968 it served as a Soviet army garrison, and has been closed to the public ever since. Sufficient funds for restoration are constantly lacking, so the castle could well remain closed for a while.

Console yourself with the very beautiful **Rose Gardens** (Růžová zahrada) beside the castle, accessible from the Dlouhá jízda, or via a footpath from the church to a rear entrance. The gardens are open daily, except Monday, May through September from 10 am to 5 pm; entry costs 20 Kč.

Stone Bridge

Art historians might be interested in the melancholy stone footbridge over the Ploučnice river, with a slowly crumbling Baroque sculptural group by Jan Brokoff (whose work also decorates Charles' Bridge in Prague). It's south of the castle, surrounded by weeds and traffic flyovers on U starého mostu.

Shepherd's Wall

On the Podmokly side, 130 steps and a 7 Kč ride in a lift (*výtah*) take you up this cliff, several hundred metres over the river, with a startling bird's-eye view over the castle and Děčín side. There's a small **zoo** just behind the little chateau at the top. If you're caught out – the lift stops at 7 pm – walk down Žižkova into Podmokly.

Regional Museum

In an 18th century palace at Československé mládeže 1, the good Regional Museum (okresní muzeum) has few foreign visitors and an eager staff. The best displays focus on the castle (including its earlier versions and various royal and aristocratic owners) and shipping on the Labe (the latter is good for kids too, very hands-on). Who'd have guessed that for 200 years until 1886, some Labe boats pulled themselves along a 720km chain between Mělník (Central Bohemia) and Hamburg! The museum is open daily, except Monday, from 9 am to noon and 1 to 5 pm, and entry costs 20 Kč.

Places to Stay

The *Campsite Pod zámkem* (☎ 227 55) is right below the castle, next door to a thermal swimming pool (koupaliště).

The bottom-end *Hotel Pošta* (☎ 228 31), on Masarykovo náměstí, has grotty doubles with shared facilities for 190 Kč per person, and a smoky beer hall. Two doors down at No 60, the up-market *Hotel Česká koruna* (☎ 220 93; fax 222 71) has singles/doubles for 1017/1716 Kč with buffet breakfast (which is open to non-guests too).

South of the centre at U starého mostu 4 is the newish *Pension Nela* (☎ 235 66), with comfortable, surprisingly quiet singles/doubles with shower and WC for 540/950 Kč, including breakfast – good value but a long walk. Book ahead in summer. The Nela also has a restaurant.

In Podmokly, there's the inexpensive *Hotel Bílý lev* (☎ 221 86) on the corner of Prokopa Holého and Teplická.

Places to Eat

Zámecká vinárna (☎ 247 50), U brány 21, has tasty meaty main courses for under 100 Kč. *Bar Kapitán*, on Radniční opposite Masarykovo náměstí, looks appealing and has been recommended.

Over in Podmokly, there's a *café-restaurant* at the chateau at the top of Shepherd's Wall. The *Restaurace Arizona*, Husovo náměstí 9, is a friendly bar-café serving tasty Czech standard fare dressed up with American-sounding names. It's open from 10 am to 10 pm daily, and can also do an impressive big vegetable salad.

Around the block at Teplická 23 is

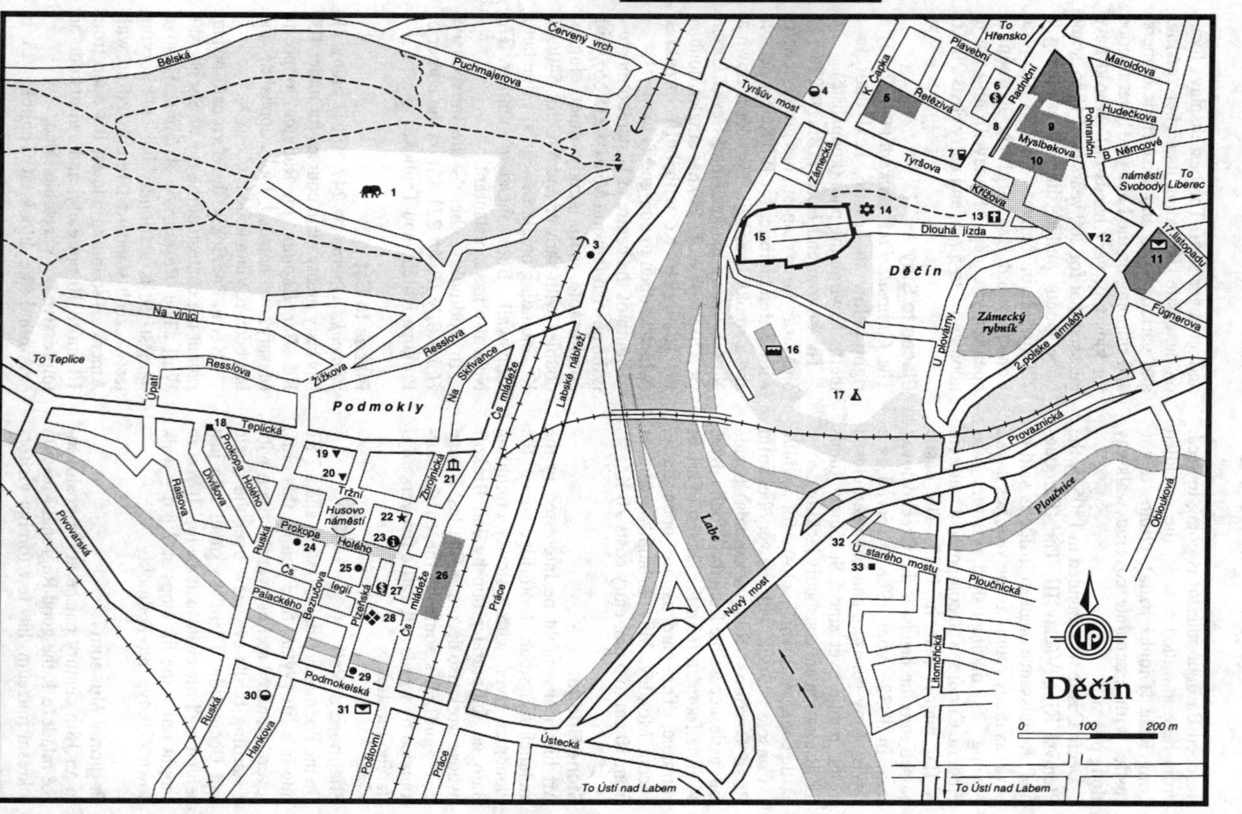
Děčín
Děčín
Podmokly
Labe
Zámecký rybník
Tyršův most
Nový most
To Ústí nad Labem
To Ústí nad Labem
To Teplice
To Hřensko
To Liberec
Pohraniční
Maroldova
Hudečkova
B. Němcové
náměstí Svobody
17 listopadu
Fügnerova
Oblouková
Ploučnice
Ploučnická
U starého mostu
Litoměřická
Provaznická
2 polské armády
U plovárny
Dlouhá jízda
Křížova
Tyršova
Řetězová
Plavební
Radniční
Myslbekova
K. Čapka
Zámecká
Červený vrch
Puchmajerova
Labské nábřeží
Čs mládeže
Práce
Na Skřivance
Resslova
Žižkova
Teplická
Zbrojnická
Tržní
Husovo náměstí
Prokopa Holého
Legií
Plzeňská
Poštovní
Podmokelská
Bezručova
Palackého
Ruská
Hankova
Divišova
Raisova
Úpatí
Na Vinici
Bělská
Pivovarská
Ústecká
0
100
200 m

PLACES TO STAY
9 Hotel Pošta
10 Hotel Česká koruna
17 Campsite Pod zámkem
18 Hotel Bílý lev
33 Pension Nela

PLACES TO EAT
2 Chateau & Café-Restaurant
7 Bar Kapitán
12 Zámecká vinárna
19 Restaurace Asia
20 Restaurace Arizona

OTHER
1 Zoo
3 Lift (výtah) to Shepherd's Wall
4 River Ferry Terminal
5 Kotva Department Store
6 Komerční banka
8 Masarykovo náměstí
11 Post Office
13 Church of the Holy Cross (kostel sv Kříže)
14 Rose Gardens (Růžová zahrada)
15 Děčín Castle (zámek Děčín)
16 Swimming Pool
21 Regional Museum (Okresní muzeum)
22 Foreigners' Police
23 Čedok Travel Agency
24 Bookshop
25 Photo Shop
26 Train Station
27 ČSOB banka
28 Korál Department Store
29 ČSAD Bus Information & Booking Office
30 Bus Station
31 Post Office
32 Stone Bridge

Restaurace Asia, with OK meaty Chinese dishes for 80 Kč to 180 Kč; open Tuesday to Saturday from 11 am to 10 pm.

Getting There & Away

Three buses a day come from Florenc station in Prague, a two to 2½ hour trip. There's a ČSAD office adjacent to the bus station for information and pre-booking. Fast trains go to and from Prague about eight times a day, via Ústí nad Labem.

Děčín is on the main road and railway line to Dresden, and has many European train connections, including 10 a day to Dresden and onwards.

The only passenger service along the river runs twice daily to and from Hřensko between April and September on weekends and public holidays. The one-way fare is 50 Kč.

Getting Around

Most municipal bus lines run between the train station and Masarykovo náměstí, so you can take any bus if you want to travel between Podmokly and Děčín. Bus tickets (7 Kč) are available from automated machines on the bus.

SANDSTONE ROCKS OF LABE

The road north from Děčín runs up the scenic and steep Labe valley. **Hřensko**, 12km away on the German border, is Bohemia's lowest point (115m); here, through a slot in its northern mountain border, the entire north Bohemian watershed empties into Germany, and the Labe becomes the Elbe. The western bank is already Germany (Saxony) 3km before you reach Hřensko. The road is lined with stalls offering homeward-bound German weekenders their last chance for a bit of cheap glassware or bottle of Becherovka.

A roughly 5km by 35km strip along the border is a protected landscape region called the Sandstone Rocks of Labe, or Labské pískovce, one of Bohemia's characteristic 'rock towns' (others are Český ráj and Adršpach-Teplice Rocks in East Bohemia). Called the 'Bohemian Switzerland' (Český Švýcarsko) by Czech and Germans on both sides of the border, and indeed the meadows and chalets look a bit Swiss – though the steep gorges and dramatic sandstone formations don't.

The part east of the road to Hřensko, called the **Jetřichovice Walls** (Jetřichovické stěny), offers leisurely walking, plus boat jaunts through the deep gorge of the Kamenice river. The most popular (and crowded) attraction is a huge natural stone bridge called the Pravčická brána.

Orientation & Information

Wedged picturesquely at the Labe's rocky confluence with the Kamenice, Hřensko is

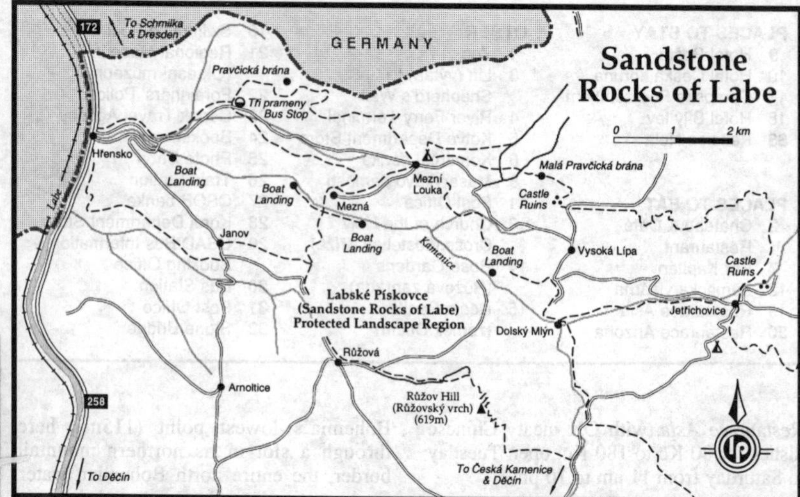

a handy reference point but an expensive place to linger. A good information centre and foreign exchange office is here, at the turn-off east up the Kamenice valley. At the northern end of Hřensko is the German border crossing towards Dresden.

A road and several walking trails roughly follow the Kamenice from Hřensko to Česká Kamenice. Along or near it, the villages of Mezní Louka, Mezná, Vysoká Lípa and Jetřichovice offer food, accommodation and access down into the gorge or up into the rocks.

The map to have, especially if you're walking, is Kartografie Praha's 1:50,000 *Českosaské Švýcarsko* (Bohemia-Saxon Switzerland).

Walks

You can wander for days through here if you like, thanks to cheap village accommodation.

If you're short on time, a well-worn nature trail (*naučná stezka*), marked with a green diagonal slash, lets you take in the region's highlights in one long day. From Hřensko it runs beside the road for 3km to a bus stop at Tři prameny, 2km up to the Pravčická brána natural bridge and 6km back to the road at Mezní Louka. From there it plunges 2.5km into the Kamenice gorge below Mezná and returns to Hřensko – part of the way by boat (see the following section). A variation that skips the gorge is the yellow-marked trail from Mezná back to Tři prameny.

A 'grand tour' of the Jetřichovické stěny is a red-marked high trail that follows the nature trail from Hřensko to Mezní Louka (11km) and then continues to Jetřichovice (15km), with options to spend the night at Mezní Louka or Vysoká Lípa. Additional attractions en route include a smaller stone bridge, the Malá Pravčická brána, and castle ruins north of Vysoká Lípa and just east of Jetřichovice.

A quite different and somewhat shorter alternative follows a blue-marked trail from Mezní Louka down into the Kamenice gorge at Dolský Mlýn, and a yellow trail back out to Jetřichovice.

Pravčická Brána Some 16m high and 30m long, with postcard views south to the 619m cone of Růžovský vrch (Růžov Hill), this is probably Europe's finest natural bridge, and on a par with those in the Canyonlands of the USA. If you just want to see the bridge, get off a Hřensko-Vysoká Lípa bus at Tři prameny and walk up for 2km. It is a real tourist trap because if you want to get close to Pravčická brána, you have to walk past the hotel-restaurace Sokolí hnízdo, which will cost you 45 Kč.

Kamenice Gorge On the dammed-up stretches of the Kamenice above and below Mezná, you can break your hike with a placid float on the river at the bottom of a dramatic slot of the canyon. Whatever the weather up above, it's mossy, damp and cool down here.

If you're just interested in the boat trip, you still have to walk – 2km from Hřensko to the lower end; a steep, sharp 1.5km below Mezná to the middle; or 3km down a blue trail from Mezní Louka to the upper end. From the upper end you could also continue south-east to Vysoká Lípa or Jetřichovice.

Each stretch is 35 Kč; just wait at the landing and a boat will be along, normally within half an hour. The boats run daily from May to August and weekends in April and October.

Places to Stay

You'll hardly go 2km along the road without seeing *Zimmer frei* (room available) signs. Some villages also have campsites, fairly cheap pensions, and pricier hotels. The closer to Hřensko, the higher the price. Čedok in Děčín can book ahead for you but will add a fat fee.

In Hřensko, a noted tourist junction, accommodation can be difficult to find in summer. There are several places to stay, including the *Hotel Labe* at 456 Kč per person and the *Hotel u Lípi* (☎ 912 17), with reasonable singles/doubles at 255/510 Kč. Farther up the valley is the brand-new and expensive *Hotel Praha*.

In Mezní Louka, 11km on, are the *Hotel Mezní Louka* and a *campsite*, including bungalows. Mezná has a small hotel, several pensions, and private rooms in handsome log and half-timbered houses. Vysoká Lípa has private rooms. About 1.5km south of pretty Jetřichovice is a *campsite*.

Getting There & Away

Buses run from Děčín to Hřensko (20 minutes) and from Děčín via Česká Kamenice to Jetřichovice (one hour) every two or three hours.

Border Crossing The Hřensko information agency says there are *no* buses on the German side. The nearest are 11km inside Germany at Schmilka, which go to Dresden. The train from Děčín to Dresden, on the other side of the river Labe/Elbe, no longer stops opposite Hřensko.

The last bus from Hřensko to Děčín leaves at about 6.30 pm.

Getting Around

Buses run between Hřensko and Mezná four times a day, and between Česká Kamenice and Mezná three or four times a day. If you're driving, there is no parking *at all* from Hřensko to Mezní Louka. The fine is 5000 Kč.

JABLONNÉ & LEMBERK CHATEAU

The castle of Lemberk (or Löwenberg; 'Lion Mountain'), on the outskirts of Jablonné v Podještědí, was founded in 1240 by Havel Markvartic, head of a north Bohemian feudal aristocratic family. Its best-known resident was Havel's frail Moravian wife, Zdislava, beatified in 1907 (and now slated for sainthood) for her exemplary Christian life.

Later owners turned the castle into a comfortable Gothic and then Renaissance chateau. It owes its present Baroque face to Albrecht of Wallenstein, the Habsburg general who grew rich on confiscated Hussite property (see the Jičín section in the East Bohemia chapter), and the family of one of his officers who contrived to keep the castle after Wallenstein's murder.

The last private owners, the Auerspergs (who also owned Žleby Chateau in Central Bohemia), lent the castle to the German army during WWII. The state has been renovating it since 1971, recently re-opening parts of the building in anticipation of Zdislava's canonisation.

Though out of the way as a trip from Prague, it's worth visiting en route to/from Děčín or Český ráj in East Bohemia. You and the occasional Zdislava pilgrims should have it more or less to yourself.

Orientation & Information

The chateau is in the hamlet of Lvová on the outskirts of Jablonné v Podještědí, midway between Česká Lípa and Liberec. It's a 10 minute climb up through scented woods from the Lvová stop on the Česká Lípa-Liberec train.

Alternatively, get off the bus or train at Jablonné, make for the domes of St Lawrence Church a few hundred metres up the hill, have a look in at the mummies in the crypt and then walk 3.5km (about 40 minutes) north-east on a green-marked trail to the chateau.

St Lawrence Church & Mummies

This big church on náměstí Míru is St Lawrence Church (kostel sv Vavřince), completed in 1722, and is apparently where Zdislava is buried. Beneath the building is a crypt, open to the public, with mummified corpses dating from the 17th and 18th centuries, amazingly well preserved thanks to a clever ventilation system. (Other, better-known, mummies are at the Jesuit church in Klatovy, south of Plzeň; see the West Bohemia chapter.)

Lemberk Chateau

The chateau foundations and shape are still Gothic, the tower renovations are Renaissance and the chateau is Italian Baroque, with heavy stucco ornamentation. Ongoing renovations mean it's a pretty chaotic scene.

A tedious 45 minute, Czech-language tour of the west wing takes in a big open-hearth kitchen, rooms full of furniture and church furnishings, and a great upstairs hall that has a ceiling with 70 panels (dating from 1608) depicting German proverbs and Aesop's fables. There are also several rooms with breathless exhibits on Zdislava.

A few rooms are used for changing exhibitions. Check this out, as it may give you a look at the most interesting part of the chateau, a little upstairs Baroque chapel beside the castle tower – and possibly the tower too. Outside the gate are several preserved North Bohemian half-timbered houses.

The chateau is open daily, except Monday, May through September from 9 am to 5 pm, and in April and October on weekends only from 9 am to 4 pm. Entry costs 20 Kč with a Czech guide or 40 Kč with an English-speaking guide (if available).

Places to Stay

Jablonné has no hotels, but there is a *campsite* with bungalows just north of the train station and highway, a sports-club *hostel* by the stadium up Švermová from the train station, and there are *private rooms*.

Places to Eat

The good vinárna *Gabel* is in the corner of Jablonné's main square, the *Restaurace Lev* is nearby, and there's a cheap eatery at the train station. Just east of the chateau in Lvová village is the tourist *Restaurace pod Zámkem*.

Getting There & Away

The slow train between Liberec and Česká Lípa runs every hour or two; Jablonné is about an hour from Liberec. Česká Lípa is easily reached by train from Děčín.

Jablonné is on long-distance bus routes linking Karlovy Vary (West Bohemia), Děčín, Liberec and the Krkonoše resorts (East Bohemia). One bus a day makes the three hour trip from Prague. All buses stop at the train station.

CZECH REPUBLIC

West Bohemia

For Czechs, the appeal of West Bohemia surely lies in its landscapes and recreational possibilities. Over 40% is covered in dense woodlands. The German border is lined with venerable mountain ranges – the Ore Mountains (Krušné hory), the Bohemian Forest (Český les), and Šumava – loved by hikers, cyclists, boaters and skiers alike.

A swathe of the Šumava in western and southern Bohemia is one of the republic's newest national parks; this and the adjacent protected landscape region are part of a 'green island' straddling the border with Bavaria, and one of Europe's few remaining zones of pristine wilderness. Other protected landscape regions are the 640 sq km Slavkov Forest (Slavkovský les) around Karlovy Vary and Mariánské Lázně, and a bit of the Křivoklátsko extending from Central Bohemia.

For visitors, a major drawcard is the region's elegant old spa towns, especially the 'big three' of Karlovy Vary (Karlsbad), Mariánské Lázně (Marienbad) and Františkovy Lázně (Franzenbad) – not merely because of their curative cold and hot springs but because of a sedate and cultured atmosphere that rubs off on even the most dedicated philistine.

And for everybody there's Plzeň, the home of arguably the best amber beer in the world.

The prettiest town centres in which to read western Bohemia's architectural record are Cheb, Loket and Domažlice. The Chodsko region near Domažlice offers glimpses of a traditional way of life that has resisted change for at least seven centuries.

HIGHLIGHTS

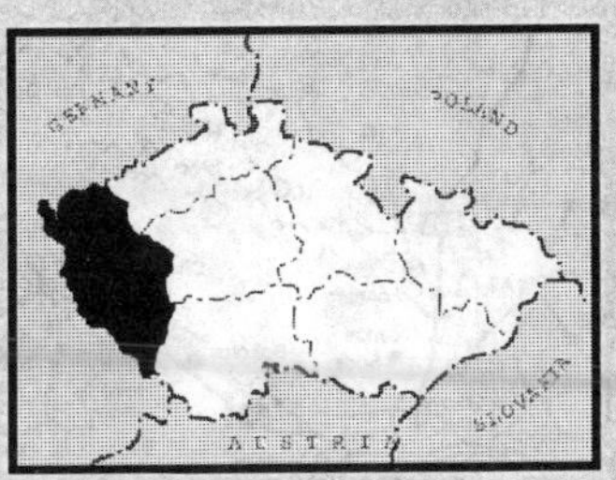

- Take a health spa or soak up the atmosphere in one of the region's three big spa towns: Karlovy Vary, Mariánské Lázně or Františkovy Lázně
- Visit the quaint town of Loket nad Ohří with its impressive Gothic castle
- Marvel at the extraordinary Baroque Gothic style architecture of the Abbey Church of the Holy Virgin, Kladruby
- Visit the picturesque town of Domažlice and see the Chodsko region's unique local folk traditions

Spa Towns

See one of these, just to see it. There's more to them than ordinary sanatoria – extraordinary wedding-cake architecture, an earnest cultural life, and peaceful vibes. The health risk, once you've admired the façades and had a brisk hike, is death by boredom.

Of the 'big three', Karlovy Vary is the biggest, most urbanised and most accessible, with by far the finest collection of buildings. Mariánské Lázně offers the best terrain and the cleanest, most bracing air. Both are on the edge of the hilly, forested Slavkov Forest Protected Landscape Region. Františkovy Lázně is the quietest (and dullest). The others – Jáchymov (for radioactive treatment), Konstantinovy Lázně and the children's spas of Lázně Kynžvart and Kyselka – are not worth a visit, unless of course you're there for the cure.

'High season', when the Bavarian tour buses pour in and the hotels fill up, is from May through September or October, plus the Easter and Christmas-New Year period.

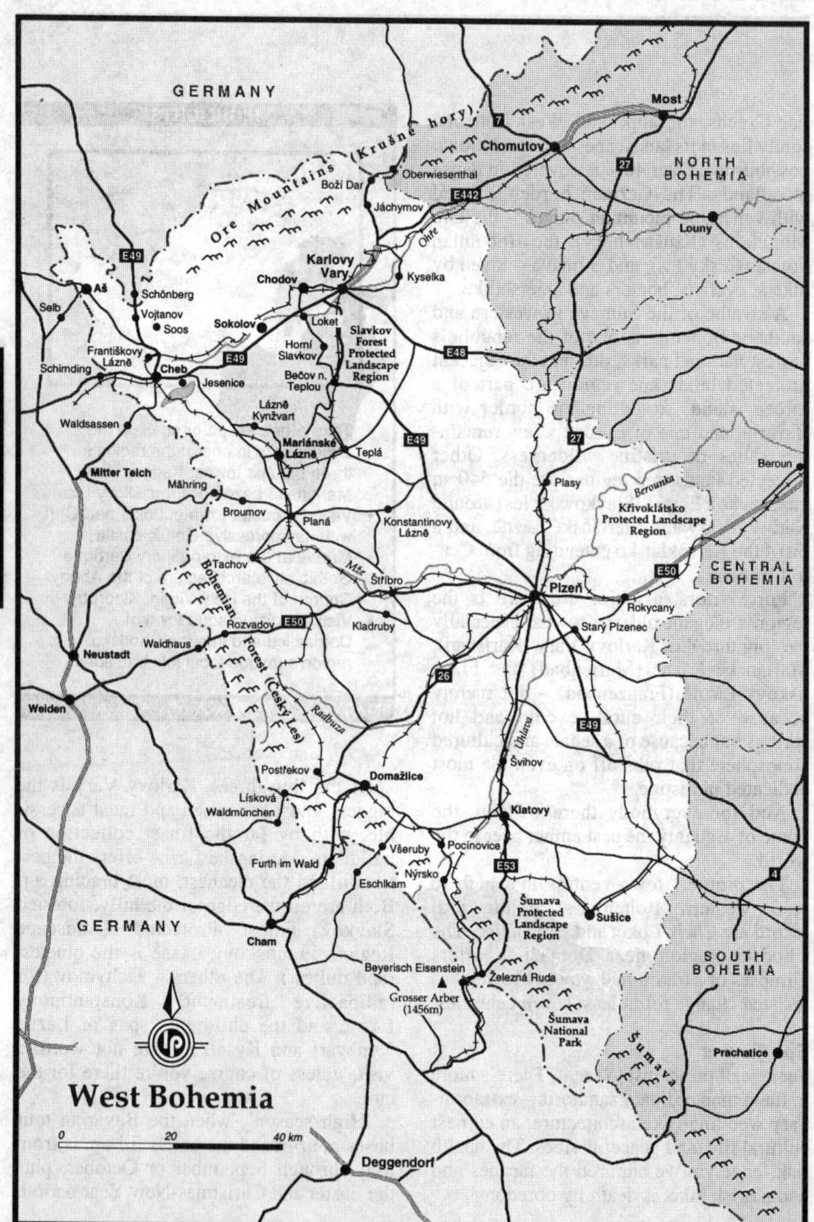

West Bohemia
GERMANY
Ore Mountains (Krušné hory)
Most
Chomutov
NORTH BOHEMIA
Oberwiesenthal
Boží Dar
Jáchymov
Louny
Ohře
Karlovy Vary
Chodov
Kyselka
E49
Aš
Schönberg
Vojtanov
Soos
Selb
Sokolov
Loket
Slavkov Forest Protected Landscape Region
Horní Slavkov
Františkovy Lázně
Schimding
Cheb
Jesenice
E48
Bečov n. Teplou
Waldsassen
Lázně Kynžvart
Mariánské Lázně
Teplá
27
Mitter Teich
Plasy
Beroun
Berounka
Mähring
Broumov
Planá
Konstantinovy Lázně
Křivoklátsko Protected Landscape Region
Tachov
Mže
Stříbro
Bohemian Forest (Český Les)
CENTRAL BOHEMIA
E50
Plzeň
Rokycany
Kladruby
Rozvadov
Waidhaus
Starý Plzenec
Neustadt
26
Weiden
Radbuza
Úhlava
Švihov
Postřekov
Domažlice
Lísková
Waldmünchen
Klatovy
Všeruby
Pocínovice
Nýrsko
E53
Furth im Wald
Eschlkam
4
Šumava Protected Landscape Region
Sušice
Cham
Beyerisch Eisenstein
Železná Ruda
SOUTH BOHEMIA
Grosser Arber (1456m)
Šumava National Park
Šumava
Prachatice
7
E442
0
20
40 km
Deggendorf

Hotel prices tend to drop outside the high season, but even then accommodation and food prices are comparable with those in Prague.

FRANTIŠKOVY LÁZNĚ

Prim, symmetrical Františkovy Lázně (population 5400) is the quietest and least interesting of the 'big three' spas but somehow quaint; even the surrounding terrain is flat and undemanding.

The spa was founded in 1793 as Franzenbad, named after the Habsburg Emperor Franz II; famous guests have included Beethoven, Goethe and the Czech writer Božena Němcová. Its 25 salty springs are best known for the treatment of female infertility. Unless you're here for the cure, you can't bathe in the water, though you can try drinking the stuff.

Orientation

This is the republic's westernmost spa, 5km north of Cheb and 6km south of the German border crossing at Vojtanov.

There's no bus station; you should get off the long-distance bus at the 'Sady' (gardens) stop, opposite the Hotel Centrum. From the train station it's a 600m walk south-west down Nádražní and across the Municipal Gardens (*Městské sady*). Once in the centre – arranged neatly to either side of the pedestrianised main street, Národní – you'll find it exhaustively signposted.

Information

There's a small Čedok (☎ 94 22 09) office at Národní 5 that can advise on accommodation and sells maps. It's open weekdays from 9 am to 4.30 pm and Saturday from 9 to 11.30 am. Česká spořitelna, on Anglická, has a foreign exchange desk and a Visa ATM. The post office is on Boženy Němcové.

Františkovy Lázně's area code is ☎ 0166.

Things to See & Do

Aside from the relentlessly neo-classical façades, all painted the same colour, there is the parish **Church of the Raising of the Cross** (kostel Povýšení sv Kříže) on Ruská, one of Bohemia's few empire-style churches, and the town's central spring, the **Františkův pramen**, at the south end of Národní.

If these haven't stirred you, neither will the exhibits on the spa's history at the **Municipal Museum** (Městské muzeum), Dr Pohoreckého 8, which is open weekdays from 10 am to noon and 1 to 5 pm and weekends from 10 am to 4 pm. Entry costs 15 Kč.

About 2km south-west of the city centre you can rent a boat on Rybník (fishpond) Amerika, or swim at Rybník Jadran. In summer a mini-train (*mikrovláčka*) runs to the lakes and back every half-hour or so from a terminal on Máchova.

Six kilometres north-east of town, in the hamlet of Hájek, is the **Soos nature reserve**, featuring peat-bogs with gas springs, mud volcanoes and bizarre salt-water plants.

Places to Stay

Autocamping Amerika (☎ 94 25 18), open from May through September on Rybník Amerika, is 70 Kč plus 90 Kč for each person and vehicle. It also has double and quad bungalows from 220 to 760 Kč, and a restaurant and beer hall. Another cheap option is a *private room.*

About 1km out of the town centre, on the road towards Cheb at Americká 27, is *Pension Josef* (☎ 54 29 69) with smallish doubles at 850 Kč, including breakfast. Doubles with shower at the *Hotel Slovan* (☎ 94 28 41/2), Národní 5, start at 1190 Kč. The *Hotel Centrum* (☎ 94 31 56/7), Anglická 41, has rooms with shower, WC, TV and fridge from 1105 Kč. Perhaps the classiest place to stay is the four-star *Spa Hotel Three Lilies* (☎ 54 24 15), Národní 3, with luxurious singles/doubles priced from 1700/2720 Kč.

These prices are with breakfast, but don't include the 'spa tax': 15 Kč per bed per night from April through September; 10 Kč the rest of the year.

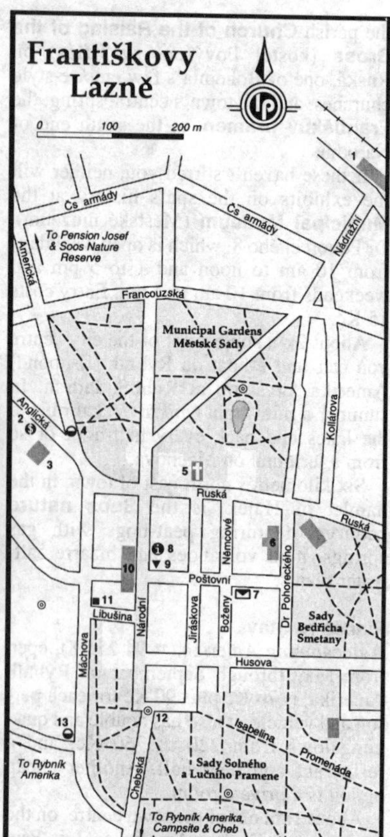

1 Train Station
2 Česká spořitelna
3 Hotel Centrum
4 Long-Distance Bus Stop
5 Church of the Raising of the Cross (kostel Povýšení sv Kříže)
6 Municipal Museum (Městské muzeum)
7 Post Office
8 Čedok Travel Agency & Tourist Information
9 Restaurant in Lázeňský Hotel Pošta
10 Hotel Slovan & Café
11 Spa Hotel Three Lilies
12 Františkův pramen (spring)
13 Terminal of Mini-train (mikrovláčka) to Rybník Amerika

Places to Eat

The café inside *Hotel Slovan* is OK and inexpensive; in fact the hotel seems to have more eateries than rooms – a restaurant, two cafés, a grill, a vinárna and a snack bar. The restaurant in the *Lázeňský Hotel Pošta*, across from the Slovan, has good food (mains from 72 to 125 Kč). There's also a *restaurant* (☎ 94 24 21) at the campsite.

Getting There & Away

The bus is faster, more direct and more frequent than the train. One daily bus comes direct from Prague via Karlovy Vary (four hours); about three a day come from Plzeň (1¼ hours). For additional long-distance options, and international connections, go via Cheb, which has buses to Františkovy Lázně every 15 to 30 minutes.

CHEB

The grimy industrial centre of Cheb (pronounced 'kheb', and long known as Eger; population 32,000) is the first, or last, town that many overland visitors to the Czech Republic see. It is in fact one of Bohemia's more architecturally fascinating towns, with a history that's more German than Czech.

In 1167, at the site of an older Slavic settlement by the Ohře, the crusader Frederick I Barbarossa built one of a line of royal dwellings-cum-strongholds on the eastern front of the Holy Roman Empire. Around it grew the town of Eger, fed by German immigration and enriched by trade between Bohemia and Bavaria.

The Přemysl kings slowly got a grip on the region, and it became part of Bohemia in 1322. The staunchly Catholic town, though held to ransom by the Hussites in 1430, prospered under the Hussite King George of Poděbrady.

Cheb's strategic location made it a military football in the Thirty Years' War, and it suffered badly. It was in Eger in February

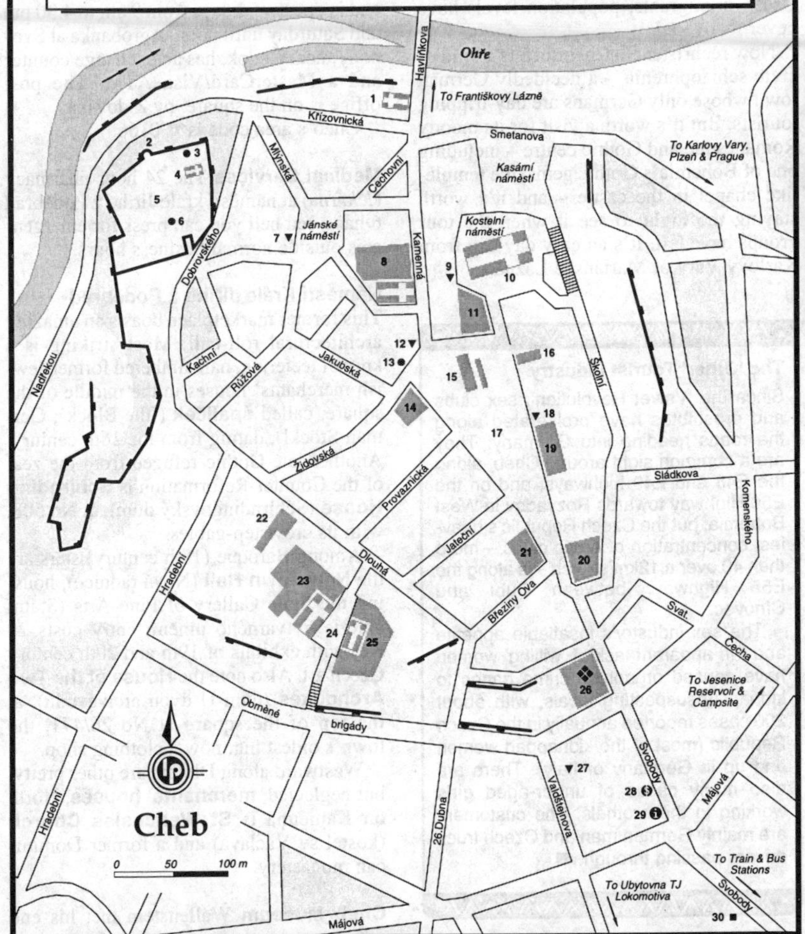

CZECH REPUBLIC

1634 that the Habsburg general, Albrecht of Wallenstein, was assassinated, probably under orders from Ferdinand II.

The growth of nearby spas brought the town back to life in the 19th century. Always a hotbed of pan-Germanism, and of the Sudeten German Party in the 1930s, the region welcomed the German army with open arms in September 1938. After WWII, tens of thousands of Germans were brutally expelled. Despite financial inducements for Czech immigrants, population levels have never recovered.

Now rechristened, Cheb suffers a kind of civic schizophrenia – a decidedly German town whose only Germans are day-tripping tourists. But it's worth a visit for its moody Romanesque and Gothic centre – including one of Bohemia's Gothic gems, the temple-like chapel in the castle – and it's worth staying the night to see it when the tour groups have left. It's an easy day trip from Karlovy Vary or Mariánské Lázně.

The 'Other' Tourist Industry

Since the 'Velvet Revolution', sex clubs and prostitutes have proliferated along the roads heading into Germany. They are a common sight around Cheb, along the E48 and E49 highways, and on the E50 Highway towards Rozvadov in West Bohemia, but the Czech Republic's heaviest concentration of erotic clubs – more than 40 over a 12km stretch – is along the E55 Highway, between Dubí and Cínovec.

The sex industry's insatiable appetite and the apparent lack of 'willing' women have caused organised crime gangs to kidnap unsuspecting locals, with about 200 cases reported annually in the Czech Republic (most of the kidnapped women end up in Germany or Italy). There are also many cases of under-aged girls working in the brothels. The customers are mainly German men and Czech truck drivers passing through. ■

Orientation

From the adjacent bus and train stations it's a 1km trek west and north-west along dismal Svobody to the old town's main square, the sloping, triangular náměstí krále Jiřího z Poděbrad (King George of Poděbrady Square).

Information

A helpful Čedok office (☎ 43 39 51) is at Májová 31, on the corner with Svobody, and is open weekdays from 9 am to 4.30 pm and Saturday until noon. Agrobanka at Svobody, near Čedok, has an exchange counter and a MasterCard/Visa ATM. The post office is on the square, by Židovská.

Cheb's area code is ☎ 0166.

Medical Services The 24 hour pharmacy (*lékárna*) at náměstí krále Jiřího z Poděbrad 6 has a red bell you can press for emergencies outside normal business hours.

Náměstí Krále Jiřího z Poděbrad

This former marketplace boasts an amazing architectural roll-call. Most striking is a knot of teetering, half-timbered former Jewish merchants' houses in the middle of the square, called **špalíček** ('the Block'; German Stöckl), dating from the 16th century. Another late-Gothic refugee from the zeal of the Counter-Reformation is **Schirnding House** (Schirndingovský dům), at No 508, with its crowstep-gables.

Among Baroque (18th century) stars are the **New Town Hall** (Nová radnice), housing the State Gallery of Fine Arts (Státní galerie výtvarného umění; entry costs 20 Kč) with exhibits of 19th and 20th century Czech art. Also note the **House of the Two Archdukes** (dům U dvou arcivévodů), at the top of the square at No 26/471, the town's oldest inn, now a clothing shop.

Westward along Dlouhá are other pretty, but neglected, **merchants' houses**. North on Kamenná is **St Wenceslas Church** (kostel sv Václava) and a former Dominican monastery.

Cheb Museum Wallenstein met his end

while staying at the pink Renaissance Pachelbel House (Pachelblův dům), at No 492 at the north end of the square. This and the adjacent house are now the Cheb Museum (Chebské muzeum), open daily, except Monday, from 9 am to 5 pm; entry costs 15 Kč.

On the ground floor is a gallery of 20th century paintings of the town – which show the town's decline quite graphically. Archaeology and town history exhibits upstairs have nothing in English. At the end of it all is a mock-up of the bedroom where Wallenstein was run through, a moment re-enacted in multiple illustrations, plus a map of the events of that day.

St Nicholas Church

The giant, Baroque St Nicholas Church (kostel sv Mikuláš) is chiefly of interest for its age (13th century) and Romanesque basilica plan, its ambitious scale, and some surviving frescoes on the columns inside.

Františkánské Náměstí

On the left as you enter this quiet square, beyond Dlouhá, is the former **St Clare Church** (kostel sv Klára) and monastery, a fine piece of high Baroque by Kristof Dientzenhofer, now a concert and exhibition hall. On the right is the Gothic Church of The Herald of the Virgin Mary (kostel Zvěstování Panny Marie), its Franciscan cloister now used for museum administration.

Cheb Castle

The red-brick fortress, mostly in ruins except for its towers, is a must-see because it's a rare thing, a Romanesque castle (and the biggest in Bohemia), and because of its extraordinary chapel.

Only the north-east corner walls of the **palace** are still standing, its multiple arched windows hinting at former elegance. Westward are the foundations of a later building where four officers loyal to Wallenstein were killed just before him.

The star attraction is the little, square **Chapel of SS Erhard & Ursula** (kaple sv Erharda a Uršuly). In the very early-Gothic lower storey (perhaps once a crypt), four thick granite pillars, each carved differently, support a vaulted ceiling. Upstairs is a sublime version of the same thing, with delicate, late-Gothic marble columns, again each different. The upstairs room once had its own entrance from the castle.

Above the moat-bridge, the dusty, thick-walled **Black Tower** (Černá věž) offers views of the river, old-town rooftops and distant apartment blocks from its 18.5m top. In an adjacent building is a tantalising **archaeological exhibit** on Chebsko (the Cheb region), unfortunately without English captions.

To appreciate the scale of the fortifications, take the steep path leading down to Křížovnická, past the round, late-Gothic **Mlýnská věž** (Mill Tower) and the longest surviving stretch of town walls.

The castle is open daily, except Monday, from June through August from 9 am to noon and 1 to 6 pm, in May and September to 5 pm, in April and October to 4 pm. There are no tours, but a pidgin-English text is available.

St Batholomew Church

The 14th century St Batholomew Church (kostel sv Bartoloměj) has been deconcecrated and is now used as a gallery of Bohemian Gothic statues, which is open Wednesday to Sunday from 9 am to 4 pm.

Places to Stay

Čedok can help with local and regional accommodation, for a fee. There is a *campsite* (☎ 315 91) 6km east of the city centre at Dřenice, by the Jesenice reservoir (vodní nádrž Jesenice), open from mid-May through September. The lake area is a popular place for relaxation while the surrounding woods are also good for walks.

Snug, clean rooms of all sizes at the *Hotel Hradní dvůr* (☎ 42 20 06; fax 42 24 44), Dlouhá 12, are 430 Kč for singles without a shower, and doubles/triples with a shower and WC are 1070/1310 Kč; all rates include breakfast. On náměstí krále Jiřího z

CZECH REPUBLIC

Poděbrad, the *Hotel Hvězda* (☎ 42 25 49; fax 42 25 46) has doubles with shower from 1000 Kč, with breakfast.

Outside the 'tourist zone' at Svobody 32 is the *Hotel Slavie* (☎ 43 32 16), where a single/double with shower and WC is 510/870 Kč.

Places to Eat

Cheb has plenty of bistros and cafés aimed at tour groups, with high prices and small helpings. Among better-value places is the *Staročeská restaurace* (☎ 42 21 70), Kamenná 1, with well-prepared Czech, western and Chinese dishes under 130 Kč. The *Metropolitan restaurace*, on the square, has good vegetable soup and courses up to 120 Kč.

Also recommended are the beer hall on Kostelní náměstí, opposite the St Nicholas Church, and the *Rybárská bašta* fish restaurant (☎ 319 51) at the Jesenice reservoir.

Decent cheap food is available at the restaurants of the *Hvězda* and *Hradní dvůr* hotels. There is a small open-air market beside the Prior department store on Obrněné brigády. Away from the tourist zone, on quiet Jánské náměstí, is the *Kavárna pod Kaštanem*, where you can enjoy a quiet coffee or an inexpensive glass of Gambrinus.

Getting There & Away

The bus is the way to go. There are three coaches a day from Prague, at least six each from Karlovy Vary and Mariánské Lázně, and four from Plzeň. Regional buses run between Cheb and Františkovy Lázně every half-hour or so.

Express trains from Prague are more frequent but take much longer than the bus. For shorter trips – eg from Plzeň, Františkovy Lázně or Karlovy Vary – there are several fast trains a day, though they're pricier than ordinary trains.

Cheb is also a convenient point for international train connections.

MARIÁNSKÉ LÁZNĚ

Mariánské Lázně was founded, as Marienbad (population 15,500), in 1817 by the abbot of the nearby Teplá Monastery, and a local physician, who knew a good thing when they saw it. Most of its extravagant empire and Art Nouveau mansions and hotels date from the late 19th century, when this was *the* civilised place to get fit and have a little fun.

On a visit at the age of 72, the German poet (and spa-freak) JW Goethe wrote of his love for Ulrike von Lewetzow, the 16-year-old daughter of a local hotelier, in his *Marienbad Elegy*. Franz Kafka spent perhaps the only happy time of his life here with Felice Bauer, shortly before he died of tuberculosis in 1924. Here also Nikolai Gogol wrote *Dead Souls* and Richard Wagner composed *Lohengrin*. Frédéric Chopin was a frequent visitor. The place became a favourite of royalty too, especially the British monarch, Edward VII. Nowadays, it's open to all.

Among Mariánské Lázně's attractions are its bracing clean air and its setting among thickly forested hills (elevation 630m). Good hikes provide relief from the slow-motion pursuits of sanatorium guests, and the crowds of ageing German tourists looking for places to eat.

Unlike Karlovy Vary, Mariánské Lázně isn't feasible as a day trip from Prague.

Orientation

Mariánské Lázně stretches like a 4km ribbon along its main axis, Hlavní třída. From the adjacent bus and train stations at the southern, 'business' end of town, it's 2km on trolleybus No 5 to the spa area's main bus stop, opposite the Hotel Excelsior.

The spa area is a network of paths, parks and 39 therapeutic springs – centred on the photogenic Colonnade (Kolonáda) and surrounded by streets of ageing hotels and mansions. Mírové náměstí has a summer kavárna and an open-air stage. The spa is at the southern toe of a hilly protected landscape region called the Slavkov Forest (Slavkovský les), which spills down around both sides of it.

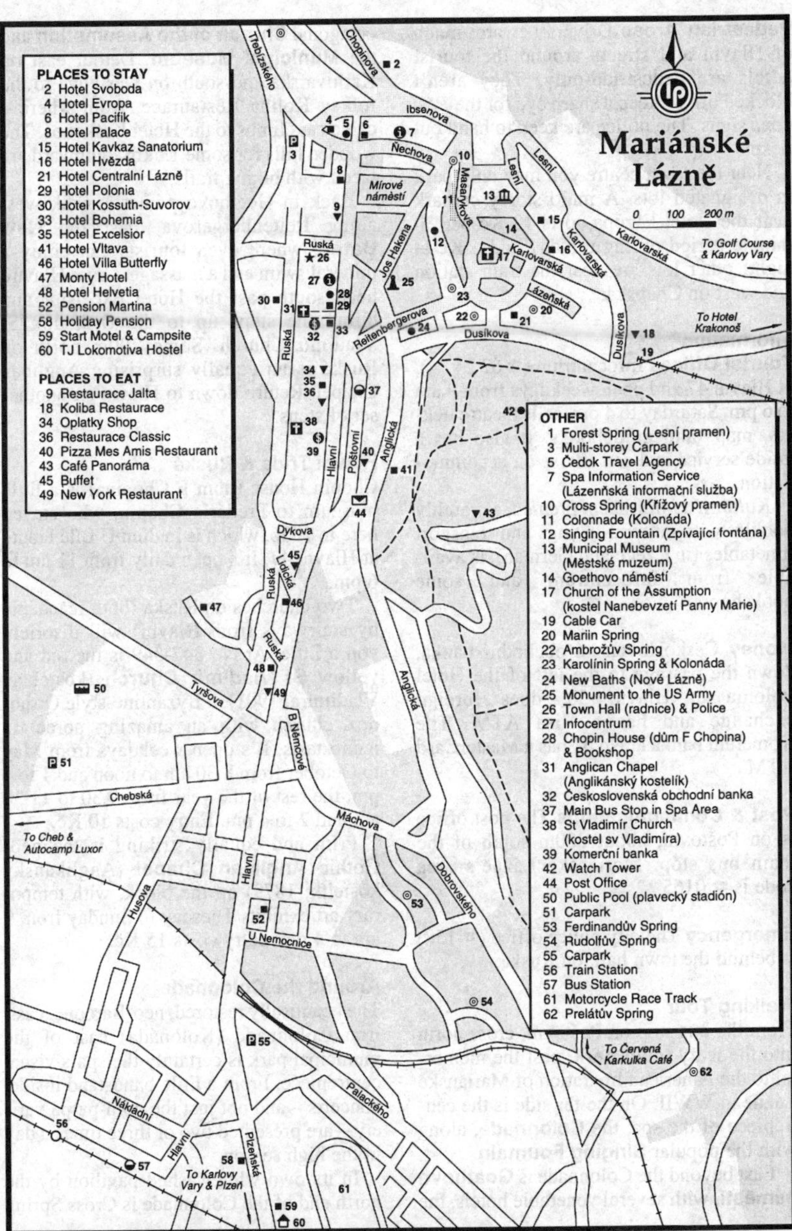
Mariánské Lázně
0 100 200 m
PLACES TO STAY
2 Hotel Svoboda
4 Hotel Evropa
6 Hotel Pacifik
8 Hotel Palace
15 Hotel Kavkaz Sanatorium
16 Hotel Hvězda
21 Hotel Centralní Lázně
29 Hotel Polonia
30 Hotel Kossuth-Suvorov
33 Hotel Bohemia
35 Hotel Excelsior
41 Hotel Vltava
46 Hotel Villa Butterfly
47 Monty Hotel
48 Hotel Helvetia
52 Pension Martina
58 Holiday Pension
59 Start Motel & Campsite
60 TJ Lokomotiva Hostel
PLACES TO EAT
9 Restaurace Jalta
18 Koliba Restaurace
34 Oplatky Shop
36 Restaurace Classic
40 Pizza Mes Amis Restaurant
43 Café Panoráma
45 Buffet
49 New York Restaurant
OTHER
1 Forest Spring (Lesní pramen)
3 Multi-storey Carpark
5 Čedok Travel Agency
7 Spa Information Service (Lázenňská informační služba)
10 Cross Spring (Křížový pramen)
11 Colonnade (Kolonáda)
12 Singing Fountain (Zpívající fontána)
13 Municipal Museum (Městské muzeum)
14 Goethovo náměstí
17 Church of the Assumption (kostel Nanebevzetí Panny Marie)
19 Cable Car
20 Mariin Spring
22 Ambrožův Spring
23 Karolínin Spring & Kolonáda
24 New Baths (Nové Lázně)
25 Monument to the US Army
26 Town Hall (radnice) & Police
27 Infocentrum
28 Chopin House (dům F Chopina) & Bookshop
31 Anglican Chapel (Anglikánský kostelík)
32 Československá obchodní banka
37 Main Bus Stop in Spa Area
38 St Vladimír Church (kostel sv Vladimíra)
39 Komerční banka
42 Watch Tower
44 Post Office
50 Public Pool (plavecký stadión)
51 Carpark
53 Ferdinandův Spring
54 Rudolfův Spring
55 Carpark
56 Train Station
57 Bus Station
61 Motorcycle Race Track
62 Prelátův Spring
To Golf Course & Karlovy Vary
To Hotel Krakonoš
To Cheb & Autocamp Luxor
To Karlovy Vary & Plzeň
To Červená Karkulka Café
Třebízského
Chopinova
Ibsenova
Ňechova
Mírové náměstí
Masarykova
Lesní
Karlovarská
Lázeňská
Dusíkova
Ruská
Jos Hakena
Reitenbergerova
Hlavní
Poštovní
Anglická
Dykova
Lidická
Tyršova
B Němcové
Chebská
Máchova
Dobrovského
Husova
U Nemocnice
Palackého
Nákladní
Plzeňská

Pedestrian Areas Drivers beware: much of Hlavní and streets around the tourist hotels are pedestrian-only. They aren't blocked off, so keep a sharp eye for the *Pěší zóna* signs. The police are keen to hand out tickets.

Near the town centre you may only park in designated lots. A multi-storey carpark near the Hotel Evropa costs 12 Kč per 30 minute period during the day and 4 Kč at night; other lots are near the train station and west on Chebská.

Information

Tourist Offices Infocentrum (☎ 62 24 74), at Hlavní 47 and open weekdays from 9 am to 6 pm, Saturday to 4 pm, sells theatre tickets, maps and guidebooks. It also has a guide service and can advise on accommodation.

Kulturní a informační přehled, a monthly booklet with cultural listings and transport timetables (in Czech and German), is available from Infocentrum and some bookshops.

Money Československá obchodní banka, down the passage to the left of the Hotel Polonia at Hlavní 50, does foreign exchange and has a Visa ATM. The Komerční banka at No 51 has a MasterCard ATM.

Post & Communications The post office is on Poštovní, about 200m south of the main bus stop. Mariánské Lázně's area code is ☎ 0165.

Emergency The city police office (☎ 158) is behind the town hall, on Ruská.

Walking Tour

From the bus stop on Poštovní, cross north into the leafy **town park**, past the memorial to the American liberation of Mariánské Lázně in WWII. On the far side is the centrepiece of the spa, the **Colonnade**, along with the popular **Singing Fountain**.

East beyond the Colonnade is **Goethovo náměstí**, with several venerable hotels, the octagonal **Church of the Assumption** and the **Municipal Museum**. Detour east on Karlovarská and south on Dusíkova to the folksy Koliba Restaurace, from where a cable car climbs to the Hotel Krakonoš. The wooded hills for some 1.5km southward are laced with hiking trails.

Back in Goethovo náměstí, walk west along Reitenbergerova, past the **New Baths**, where even tourists can enjoy a mineral swim and a massage. Cross Hlavní, head south past the Hotel Excelsior and climb the steps up to the Orthodox St Vladimír Church. Some 200m north on Ruská is an equally surprising Anglican Chapel. Return down to Hlavní on another set of steps.

Hlavní Třída & Ruská

Chopin House (dům F Chopina) is a little museum to Frédéric Chopin, who stayed here in 1836, which is in dům U Bílé labutě at Hlavní 47. It's open daily from 11 am to 6 pm.

Two churches on Ruská (both reachable by stairways from Hlavní) will disorient you a little. At No 347-349 is the red and yellow **St Vladimír Church** (kostel sv Vladimíra; 1901), a Byzantine-style Orthodox church with an amazing porcelain iconostasis. It's open weekdays from May to October from 8.30 am to noon and 1 to 4 pm, the rest of the year from 9.30 to 11.30 am and 2 to 4 pm. Entry costs 10 Kč.

Prim and equally striking is the neo-Gothic **Anglican Chapel** (Anglikánský kostelík; 1879) up the block, with temporary art exhibits Tuesday to Sunday from 9 am to 4 pm; entry costs 15 Kč.

Around the Colonnade

The beautifully restored, neo-Baroque, cast-iron Colonnade (Kolonáda) east of the municipal park is certainly the spa's visual centrepiece. From a little bandstand inside, concerts – and not just the oom-pa-pa variety – are presented two or three times a day in the high season.

In its own whitewashed pavilion by the north end of the Colonnade is Cross Spring

(Křížový pramen), the spa's first spring. At the other end is the crowd-pleasing Singing Fountain (Zpívající fontána), leaping and spraying to recorded classical music every two hours all day (the programme is in the *Kulturní a informační přehled* booklet).

Statues in the squeaky-clean municipal park (no dogs, no bicycles, no smoking even) include a monument to the liberation of the town by the US army on 6 May 1945.

Goethovo Náměstí

This manicured square, edged with extravagant turn-of-the-century buildings, probably looks much as it did when King Edward VII stayed here in his favourite hotel, now called the Hotel Kavkaz sanatorium.

At No 11, the site of a house where Goethe stayed (after whom the Goethe Square derives its name) on his last visit to Mariánské Lázně, is a ho-hum **Municipal Museum** (Městské muzeum; ☎ 2740), which is open daily, except Monday, from 9 am to 4 pm with an hourly video-tape history of the town and a mock-up of Goethe's room. Entry costs 30 Kč.

Opposite is the bulky, eight-sided **Church of the Assumption of Virgin Mary** (kostel Nanebevzetí Panny Marie), built in 1848 in 'neo-Byzantine' style.

Hikes

In the wooded hills on both sides of the spa, a dozen trails, colour-coded according to difficulty, wind past pavilions, springs and cafés. Wilderness it isn't (some paths are even signposted with cardiac energy use data!), but pleasant it is. The routes are shown on some city maps, and on mapboards at the south end of the Colonnade.

A popular trail climbs to the Café Panoráma, round past an old stone watch tower (100 steps up to a sweeping view over the trees) and on to the Červená karkulka Café. Mortals can descend from here to buses on Hlavní (total less than 4km). Those here for the cure can carry on for a 7km round trip.

An easier loop trail heads north past Forest Spring (Lesní pramen) to the Lunapark Café, which is said to have afternoon tea dances!

Baths & Swimming

The only place where tourists can soak in spring water is the New Baths (Nové lázně; ☎ 3001) on Reitenbergerova. A 'carbonic bath' is about 320 Kč, and a massage is 230 Kč. It's open weekdays from 7 am to 3 pm.

A public pool (*plavecký stadión*), southwest of the city centre off Tyršova, is open Tuesday to Friday from 2 to 8 pm and Saturday from 9.30 am to 7 pm. The pool in the nearby Monty Hotel (☎ 4682), Příkrá 218, is open to non-guests daily from 1 to 8 pm and costs 100 Kč.

Special Events

The town has a lively summertime cultural life, including an International Music Festival in June or July, a week-long Frédéric Chopin Music Festival in mid-August, and frequent outdoor concerts. It bears no relation whatever to Alan Resnais' proto-psychedelic 1960s film, *Last Year at Marienbad.*

Places to Stay

Mariánské Lázně has over three dozen hotels. The best rooms are booked up in the high season, but Čedok will help you find something, even at the bottom end. Unless noted, hotel prices don't include the 'spa tax' of 20 Kč per bed per night (at least in the high season).

The Hotel Krakonoš is the only hotel that isn't in or near the pedestrian zone. Drivers staying at most of the other hotels should plan on the extra cost of overnight parking.

Places to Stay – bottom end

Campsites, Motels & Hostels The plain, noisy *Start Motel* (☎ 62 20 62), and a campsite with bungalows and shabby prefabricated motel rooms for 290 Kč, is on Plzeňská, 300m south of the train station turn-off. A bit farther on is the *TJ Lokomotiva* (☎ 62 39 17) sports club hostel (book in by 5 pm), with beds for 140 Kč.

Autocamp Luxor (☎ 3504), also with bungalows, is 2km west out along Chebská road (to the suburb of Velká Hleďsebe) and 1km south – easy with a car, though you could take trolleybus No 6 from the town centre to Velká Hleďsebe and walk from there. It's open May through September.

Hotels The *Krakonoš* (☎ 62 26 24; fax 62 23 83) is in a crumbling 1900s palace in the hills east of the town centre. Old rooms with shower but common WC are 335 Kč per person; new doubles with shower and WC are 610 Kč per person, including breakfast (and tax). With a hostel card it's 300 Kč per person. Walk-in odds are good, and you can choose from four restaurants. The location is awkward – by bus No 12 (8 Kč) every 60 to 90 minutes, or by cable car from the Koliba Restaurace (if it is operating), or about 25 minutes by foot.

The least expensive choice near the town centre is *Hotel Evropa* (☎ 62 20 63; fax 62 54 08) at Třebízského 101. Singles/doubles are 400/600 Kč without shower or WC, and 600/950 Kč with facilities. You may have to persist to get one of the cheaper rooms.

Other tourist spots are the *Hotel Kossuth-Suvorov* (☎ 62 28 61), Ruská 77/76, where rooms with shared facilities are 450/600 Kč, with shower and WC 510/790 Kč.

The pension *Martina* (☎ 62 36 47), Jiráskova 6, rents small flats with shared bath at 650 Kč per double. *Holiday Pension* (☎ 62 31 94), Plzeňská 98, has doubles for 1000 Kč, including breakfast.

Some spa hotels (sanatoria) are open to tourists if you book through the Spa Information Service (Lázeňská informační služba; ☎ 62 21 70) at Mírové náměstí 104/6, open weekdays from 7 to 11 am and noon to 4 pm. The mid-range places it deals with have street-side rooms with shared facilities and breakfast for around 1000 Kč (850 Kč off-season). These include the *Svoboda* (☎ 62 46 64) at Chopinova 393, *Pacifik* (☎ 62 30 06) at Mírové náměstí 84, *Hvězda* (☎ 62 57 71) at Goethovo náměstí 7, *Centrální Lázně* (☎ 62 59 51) at Goethovo náměstí 1, and *Vltava* (☎ 62 25 72) at Anglická 475.

CZECH REPUBLIC

Places to Stay – middle

Hotel Helvetia (☎ 62 26 29), Hlavní 230, has modern rooms with TV, shower and WC for 1500/1900 Kč, including breakfast. Another classy place is *Hotel Bohemia* (☎ 62 32 51; fax 62 29 43), Hlavní 100, with nice rooms for 1800/2300 Kč.

Places to Stay – top end

Most hotels at the north end of Hlavní are being renovated and transformed into expensive places. They have high standards with all the trimmings. *Hotel Palace* (☎ 62 22 22; fax 62 42 62) at No 67 charges 2550/3400 Kč, and the *Hotel Villa Butterfly* (☎ 62 62 01; fax 62 62 10) at No 655 charges 2500/3300 Kč.

Places to Eat

Eating grandly must be part of 'the cure', as Mariánské Lázně is full of elegant, high-priced restaurants. If you long for a beer hall with spotty tablecloths and loud talk, a place that comes close is the *Restaurace Jalta*, upstairs at Hlavní 43, with a menu of Czech dishes for 40 to 120 Kč. Cheaper is the new *pivnice* under the Hotel Helvetia with good Czech main courses for under 65 Kč. At Hlavní 145 is a *buffet* with good salads.

Restaurace Classic (☎ 62 28 07), a few doors south of the Hotel Excelsior and open from 10 am to midnight, has a varied international menu with main courses from 70 to 160 Kč, plus vegetarian choices for around 60 Kč. The *Pizza Mes Amis Restaurant*, Poštovní 330, has a large menu and pizzas for less than 100 Kč.

The touristy *Koliba Restaurace* (☎ 62 51 69), Dusíkova 592, east of the town centre, serves grilled game and other specialities from 11 am to 11 pm, which are best washed down with Moravian wines. The rustic *Café Panoráma* (☎ 5321), on Pod Panoramou in the woods above town, is good for lunch or coffee as it's only open from 2 to 5 pm.

Oplatky Spa patients kill the taste of the water with big, round, sweet wafers called *oplatky*, sold for about 3.50 Kč each at a few spa hotels or speciality shops; one is just to the right of the Hotel Excelsior, another is by the Cross Spring.

Entertainment

Several nights a week, jazz bands play at the *New York Restaurant*, Hlavní 233, from 8 pm to 11 pm. Its food and cocktails are recommended by locals.

Getting There & Away

Ten fast trains a day run from Prague (three to 3½ hours away) all via Plzeň (1¼ hours away), and more from Cheb. Buses from Prague, Plzeň and Cheb are less frequent (up to seven a day) and take as long as the train. The train journey from Karlovy Vary is slow but scenic.

The *Kulturní a informační přehled* booklet (see the Information section) has current bus and train timetables.

Getting Around

On buses and trolleybuses, drop 5 Kč into the box on boarding; there are no tickets and no day passes. The No 12 bus to the Hotel Krakonoš is 8 Kč.

AROUND MARIÁNSKÉ LÁZNĚ

Teplá Monastery

Founded in 1193, the Premonstratensian Monastery (Premonstrátský klášter) at Teplá had become by the 16th century one of the richest landowners in Bohemia. Among its holdings was Mariánské Lázně itself.

Ravaged over the centuries by fire, peasant rebellions and the Thirty Years' War, it took its present Baroque shape at the hands of the father-and-son architects, Kristof and Kilian Ignatz Dientzenhofer, in the early 18th century. Though a bit run down now (it served as an army barracks during the Communist years), it boasts a sturdy Romanesque church that has survived almost intact from 1232, and a lavish turn-of-the-century library, which includes rare manuscripts and first printings among its 80,000 books.

The monastery (☎ 922 64) is open daily, except Monday, May through October from 9 am to 4.30 pm, to 3 pm the rest of the year (closed January). Organ and chamber concerts are held here in summer.

Places to Stay If you can afford the mid-range prices, stay at the *Klášterní hospic* (The Cloister Hospice; ☎ 0169-922 64; fax 923 12), in a section of the monastery that has been converted into a hotel. The modern singles/doubles with shower, WC and TV cost 870/1520 Kč, including breakfast.

Getting There & Away Teplá village is on the Mariánské Lázně-Karlovy Vary railway line. By car, take the Karlovy Vary road for 7km and turn east. The monastery is 2km south-east of the village.

KARLOVY VARY

Karlovy Vary (population 60,000) is the oldest of the Bohemian spas, and probably the second most popular tourist city in the Czech Republic, after Prague. It's also the most beautiful of the 'big three' spas and, despite the crowds, the most accessible. However, you can't just pop in for a sulphurous bath or gas-inhalation therapy, but you can sample the waters till your teeth float.

Legend says the first of the 12 warm springs here was discovered by Emperor Charles IV while on a hunting trip, when one of his dogs fell into it while chasing a stag. In fact the springs were already well known by then, but Charles did have a hunting lodge built near the biggest one in 1358, and granted town status to 'Charles Spa' a few years later.

The waters were found to be good for digestive and metabolic complaints. The first spa establishments appeared in 1522, and Karlsbad, as it was known, became a fashionable watering-place for European aristocrats. Early royal visitors included Russian Tsar Peter the Great (in 1711 and 1712), Frederick I of Prussia and Empress

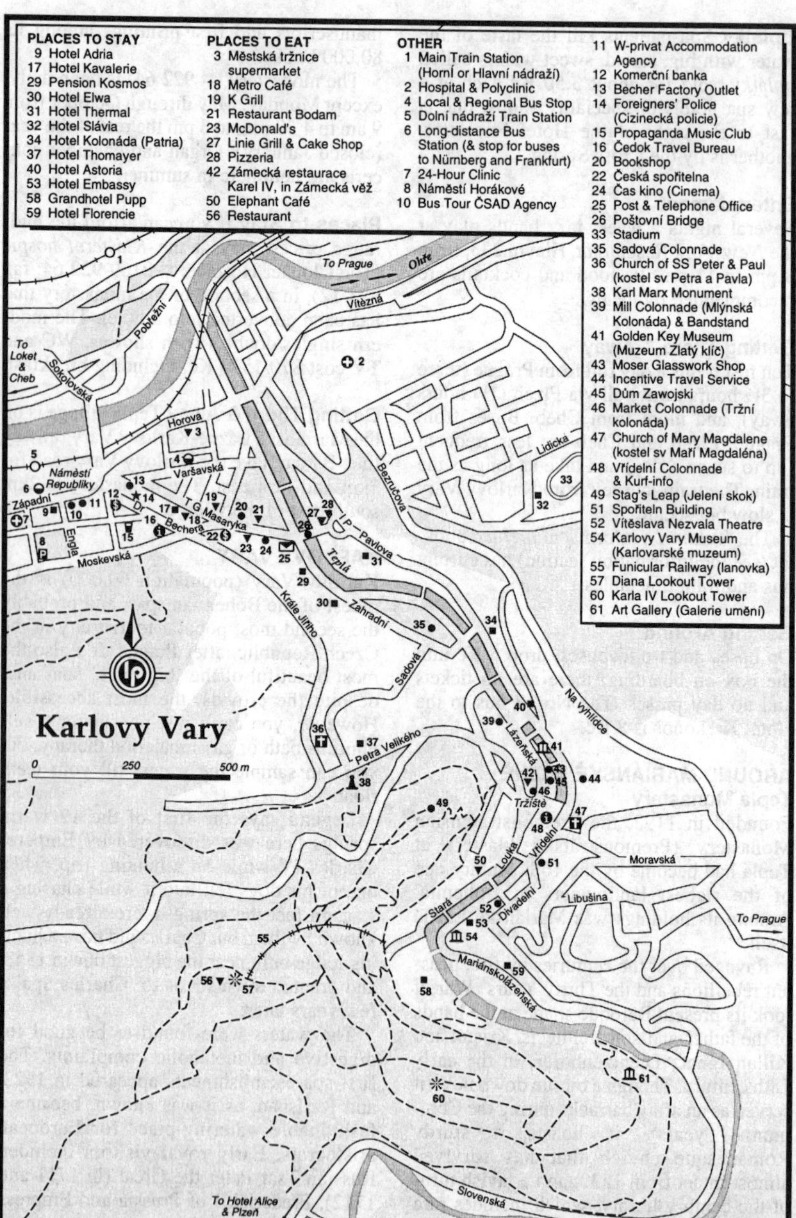
PLACES TO STAY
9 Hotel Adria
17 Hotel Kavalerie
29 Pension Kosmos
30 Hotel Elwa
31 Hotel Thermal
32 Hotel Slávia
34 Hotel Kolonáda (Patria)
37 Hotel Thomayer
40 Hotel Astoria
53 Hotel Embassy
58 Grandhotel Pupp
59 Hotel Florencie
PLACES TO EAT
3 Městská tržnice supermarket
18 Metro Café
19 K Grill
21 Restaurant Bodam
23 McDonald's
27 Linie Grill & Cake Shop
28 Pizzeria
42 Zámecká restaurace Karel IV, in Zámecká věž
50 Elephant Café
56 Restaurant
OTHER
1 Main Train Station (Horní or Hlavní nádraží)
2 Hospital & Polyclinic
4 Local & Regional Bus Stop
5 Dolní nádraží Train Station
6 Long-distance Bus Station (& stop for buses to Nürnberg and Frankfurt)
7 24-Hour Clinic
8 Náměstí Horákové
10 Bus Tour ČSAD Agency
11 W-privat Accommodation Agency
12 Komerční banka
13 Becher Factory Outlet
14 Foreigners' Police (Cizinecká policie)
15 Propaganda Music Club
16 Čedok Travel Bureau
20 Bookshop
22 Česká spořitelna
24 Čas kino (Cinema)
25 Post & Telephone Office
26 Poštovní Bridge
33 Stadium
35 Sadová Colonnade
36 Church of SS Peter & Paul (kostel sv Petra a Pavla)
38 Karl Marx Monument
39 Mill Colonnade (Mlýnská Kolonáda) & Bandstand
41 Golden Key Museum (Muzeum Zlatý klíč)
43 Moser Glasswork Shop
44 Incentive Travel Service
45 Dům Zawojski
46 Market Colonnade (Tržní kolonáda)
47 Church of Mary Magdalene (kostel sv Maří Magdaléna)
48 Vřídelní Colonnade & Kurf-info
49 Stag's Leap (Jelení skok)
51 Spořiteln Building
52 Vítěslava Nezvala Theatre
54 Karlovy Vary Museum (Karlovarské muzeum)
55 Funicular Railway (lanovka)
57 Diana Lookout Tower
60 Karla IV Lookout Tower
61 Art Gallery (Galerie umění)
To Prague
Ohře
Vítězná
Pobřežní
To Loket & Cheb
Sokolovská
Horova
Náměstí Republiky
Varšavská
Západní
T G Masaryka
Dr Bechera
Engla
Moskevská
Bezručova
Lidická
I P Pavlova
Teplá
Zahradní
Krále Jiřího
Sadová
Na vyhlídce
Lázeňská
Petra Velikého
Tržiště
Vřídelní
Louka
Stará
Divadelní
Moravská
Libušina
To Prague
Mariánskolázeňská
Slovenská
To Hotel Alice & Plzeň
Karlovy Vary
0 250 500 m

Maria Theresa. By the late 18th century this was a world-class health resort.

Karlovy Vary became a centre for the arts too. The playwright Johann Schiller honeymooned here, and Goethe returned 13 times. Visiting composers have included Bach, Beethoven, Brahms, Wagner, Tchaikovsky, Schumann, Liszt and Grieg. Here Dvořák's symphony *From the New World* premiered in 1884. The spa hosts an annual Dvořák Autumn Festival in September.

Most of the present buildings date from the late 19th and early 20th centuries – a visual feast of 'neo' styles and Art Nouveau.

Many visitors attribute their sense of well being to the so-called '13th spring', the famous Becherovka herb liqueur, made here to a secret recipe of one Dr David Becher, who around 1790 first analysed the Karlovy Vary springs.

Thanks to efficient bus transport, Karlovy Vary is feasible even as a day trip from Prague. But thanks to its popularity, especially with German holiday-makers, it's as expensive as Prague for accommodation and food.

Orientation

Karlovy Vary sits at 450m, at the confluence of the Ohře and tributary Teplá rivers. The business end of town is by the Ohře, centred on Dr Bechera, while the spa sprawls for 3km up the Teplá valley, in the northern corner of the steep, wooded Slavkov Forest (Slavkovský les) Protected Landscape Region.

Trains from Cheb, Plzeň and Prague, and most international connections, arrive at the upper station (horní nádraží), also called main station (hlavní nádraží), a 10 minute walk from the other side of the Ohře. Those from Mariánské Lázně and the south use the lower station (dolní nádraží), on the spa side of the Ohře.

Long-distance coaches and international buses to Nuremberg and Frankfurt use stands by lower train station. The main junction for city and regional buses is on Varšavská.

There are pedestrian zones along the Teplá valley, but thanks to exempted delivery and construction vehicles traffic along here is only marginally less threatening than elsewhere in town.

Information

Tourist Offices Kurf-info (☎ 322 40 97), at Vřídelní Colonnade, is the municipal information centre, providing ticket bookings, guide services, accommodation, and spa treatment.

A helpful Čedok office (☎ 322 29 94) is at Dr Bechera 21. The bookshop at TG Masaryka 12 has regional maps.

You can buy the monthly multilingual booklet *Promenáda*, full of information on spa history, cultural events, transport and other practicalities, from news kiosks, bigger hotels or Kurf-info.

Money Near the Tržnice city bus station, the Komerční banka, Bělehradská 13, has a MasterCard ATM (open weekdays from 8 to 5 pm). Not far away at TG Masaryka 14, Česká spořitelna has a Visa ATM. The American Express agent is Incentive Travel Service (☎ 322 53 17), which is at Vřídelní 51.

Post & Communications The main post and telephone office at TG Masaryka 1 is open daily from 7.30 am to 7 pm (Saturday to 1 pm, Sunday to noon). Karlovy Vary's area code is ☎ 017.

Medical & Emergency Services The Foreigners' Police Office (Cizinecká policie) is just inside a passage off Dr Bechera 24. A 24 hour clinic (☎ 246 79) is at Krymská 2a. A dental clinic is at the same address (☎ 323 08 94), but is only open weekdays from noon to 8 pm, weekends from 8 am.

Around the Colonnades

The spa proper starts at Poštovní Bridge, where rows of turn-of-the-century mansions face off against the monstrous Communist-era (1976) **Hotel Thermal** sanatorium.

The 12 distinct springs are housed in or

near five colonnades (*kolonády*) along the Teplá. The first is the whitewashed and wrought-iron **Park Spring Colonnade** (Sadová kolonáda).

Farther on is the biggest and most popular, the neo-Renaissance **Mill Colonnade** (Mlýnská kolonáda; 1881), with five different springs, rooftop statues depicting the months of the year, and a little bandstand (see the Entertainment section). The Petra Restaurant, opposite, is the spot (but not the original building) where Peter the Great allegedly stayed in 1711.

Straight up Lázeňská is a gorgeous Art Nouveau (1901) building called **dům Zawojski**. Next door you can do some very up-market **window shopping** along Stará Louka at the Moser glasswork shop at No 28 (see the Things to Buy section). Across the road is the **Market Colonnade** (Tržní kolonáda) with its delicate white 1883 woodwork; one of its two springs is the spa's oldest, pramen Karla IV. Behind this is the Castle Colonnade (Zámecká kolonáda) and a castle tower, the **Zámecká věž**, erected in place of Charles IV's hunting lodge after it was destroyed by fire in 1604.

The steam billowing from the direction of the river comes from the ugly 1975 **Hot Spring Colonnade** (Vřídelní kolonáda). Inside is the spa's biggest, hottest spring, pramen Vřídlo (Sprudel to Germans), belching 15m into the air. People lounge in the geyser room for the vapours, or sample the waters from a line of progressively cooler taps in the next room.

After we had visited this area we received word that the building housing the geyser had been closed for urgent repairs, however, we do not know how extensive the repairs are or how long they will take to complete.

East of the Teplá

Here your eye may be caught by the curvaceous, creamy white façade of the **Church of Mary Magdalene** (kostel sv Maří Magdaléná; 1737) across the river. Whatever your thoughts on the excesses of Baroque architecture, it's hard not to fall for this confection by Kilian Ignatz Dientzenhofer, whose work so shaped Prague.

Southward on Moravská is a striking phalanx of **mansions** from neo-Gothic (such as No 4, where Dvořák stayed in 1879) to Art Nouveau (the Spořitelna building on Divadelní náměstí) to cubist. Across the square is the 1886 **Municipal Theatre** (Městské divadlo).

Upper Valley

Back on the west side you can have coffee at the classic and classy Elephant Café. Or peek into the concert hall and two-storey-high dining rooms of the gigantic, neo-Baroque **Grandhotel Pupp**, the spa's first hotel and still top of the line after two centuries.

About 500m past the Pupp is the municipal **Art Gallery** (for more information see Museums & Galleries below).

Orthodox Church

On Krále Jiřího, a backstreet lined with sanatorium hotels, is the incongruous but deluxe little Church of SS Peter & Paul (kostel sv Petra a Pavla), with five polished onion domes and vaguely Art Nouveau exterior murals.

Museums & Galleries

There's an art gallery and two relatively interesting museums in town if the weather is bad or if you have some time to kill:

Art Gallery (Galerie umění; ☎ 243 87), Goethova stezka 6: open daily, except Monday, from 9 am to noon and 1 to 5 pm; modest collection of 20th century Czech art

Karlovy Vary Museum (Karlovarské muzeum; ☎ 262 52), Nová Louka 23: open Wednesday through Sunday from 9 am to noon and 1 to 5 pm; Karlovy Vary history and natural history, Czech glasswork, church furnishings

Golden Key Museum (Muzeum Zlatý klíč; ☎ 238 88), Lázeňská 3: open Wednesday through Sunday from 9 am to noon and 1 to 5 pm; paintings of the spa from the Karlovarské Theatre

Hikes

For relief from all this grandeur (and from the service traffic), climb steeply up from the Teplá into sun-dappled woods full of paths, statues and decaying pavilions.

It's about 1.5km from the Grandhotel Pupp to a hilltop lookout (*vyhlídka*) called Diana, with a melancholy garden restaurant and an old lookout tower with a view of the spa. The woods on the way back down are sprinkled with monuments, including one to that old bourgeois Karl Marx, who visited Karlsbad three times between 1874-76.

Alternatively you can ride a **funicular railway** (*lanovka*) from behind the Pupp, a five minute one-way trip to Diana for 20 Kč or a return trip for 30 Kč. It runs every 15 minutes from 9 am to 6 pm, every day. Jelení skok (Stag's Leap), the promontory where Charles IV's dog scared up that mythical deer, is 500m north-east from an intermediate stop on the funicular. Another lookout tower is on vyhlídka Karla IV, south of the Pupp.

If you're feeling ambitious, it's 17km on a very fine blue-marked trail, via the Diana lookout, along the Ohře to the romantic castle and village of Loket nad Ohří (see the Around Karlovy Vary section).

Special Events

The Karlovy Vary Film Festival, held in May, always features the year's top films as well as attracting plenty of stars. Recently, it has also been ranked in the same category as the film festivals in Cannes, Venice and Berlin.

Places to Stay

Accommodation is as dicey and pricey as in Prague. The demise of three inexpensive places has put a squeeze on budget travellers. Several agencies can help, though they won't always have places near the town centre.

Unless noted, prices don't include the 'spa tax' (15 Kč per bed per night).

Accommodation Agencies Čedok can suggest *private rooms*, typically from about 372 Kč per person with private facilities. A travel agency called W-privat (☎ 322 22 85; fax 277 68), náměstí Republiky 5, can arrange private, pension and hotel rooms. Another place to try is Kurf-info.

Places to Stay – bottom end

Camping A campsite with bungalows is open in the high season at the *Motel Březová* (☎ 322 51 01). It's up the Teplá valley, about 6km on bus No 7 from Varšavská; drivers follow Plzeň signs southward on Bezručova. The *Rolava* campsite (☎ 452 24) is on a little lake of the same name, about 3km north-west of town. The *Sasanka* campsite (☎ 331 11 30) is in Sadov, about 6km north on the road to Ostrov.

Hotels Near the town centre at Západní 1 is the *Hotel Adria* (☎ 237 65), with plain doubles/triples with shower and WC for 640/1080 Kč. The newish *Hotel Kavalerie* (☎ & fax 322 96 13), TG Masaryka 43, has cosy single/double rooms with shower and WC for 750/1000 Kč, including breakfast.

The streets around the spa have a few small pensions for 500 to 600 Kč per person. A good one is *Pension Kosmos* (☎ 322 31 68), Zahradní 39, where rooms with shower and WC are 316/480 Kč.

The sports-club hostel *Hotel Slavia* (☎ 322 72 71/4) is by a stadium at Lidická 12 in Drahovice (take bus No 1 east three stops from Varšavská or walk for 20 minutes). Rooms with shower, WC and TV start at 573/700/1146/1370 Kč, and there's a restaurant.

Places to Stay – middle

The pleasant *Hotel Kolonáda (Patria)* (☎ 322 20 10; fax 322 26 70), IP Pavlova 8, in the heart of the spa, has a restaurant, sauna and rooms with shower and WC for 1710/2400 Kč, with breakfast.

The *Hotel Embassy* (☎ 322 11 61; fax 322 31 46), Nová Louka 21, has lovely 19th century decor. Its smallish rooms are definitely worth 1820/2970 Kč, including breakfast and parking.

Some spa hotels (sanatoria) will take in

tourists. Doubles with shower and WC at the *Astoria* (☎ 322 82 24/8), Vřídelní 23, and *Florencie* (☎ 322 55 01/3), Mariánskolázeňská 25, are about 1900 Kč. The *Elwa* (☎ 322 84 72/4), Zahradní 29, and *Thomayer* (☎ 322 53 01/3), Petra Velikého 16, are about 3800 Kč.

Places to Stay – top end

Feeling wicked? Doubles at the *Grandhotel Pupp* (☎ 310 91 11; fax 322 40 32), Mírové náměstí 2, start at 5000 Kč (about 20% less off-season).

Places to Eat

Food prices, especially in and around the colonnades, will come as a shock unless you've just arrived from Prague or Plzeň. In the pricier restaurants, be sure you get a menu with prices. And check your bill; 'mistakes' happen.

A good cheap place is the popular grill and cake shop called *Linie*, just across the Poštovní Bridge. There's a little *pizzeria* a few doors down. Across the road is a complex with several unexciting restaurants, and down at TG Masaryka 20 is a grill with fried chicken. In the market hall (Městská tržnice) supermarket is a good and inexpensive *buffet*.

A good, clean, mid-range place is the *Metro Café* at TG Masaryka 27, with Czech dishes for under 115 Kč. A decent upscale place is the *Zámecká restaurace Karel IV* (☎ 322 72 55), in the Zámecká věž and open from noon to 1 am.

Self-Catering By the bus stop on Varšavská is a big supermarket in the market hall.

Breakfast The *Hotel Adria's* restaurant does a passable western breakfast from 7 am, though you'll probably pay more for less.

Oplatky The correct way to take your spring water (which the locals drink from the 'spa cup' or *lázeňský pohárek*) is with these tasty, sweet wafers. You can buy them at the Městká tržnice supermarket, or from an oplatky shop past the pizzeria at Poštovní Bridge.

Entertainment

Karlovy Vary's main theatre is the *Vítězslava Nezvala Theatre* (divadlo Vítězslava Nezvala), which is on Divadelní náměstí, not far from the Vřídelní Colonnade, but it was undergoing renovations at the time of writing. From mid-May to mid-September concerts are held in the colonnade daily, except Monday. There are also all kinds of concerts held daily around town – for more information see *Promenáda* or Kurf-info.

The *Propaganda Music Club*, Jaltská 7, has occasional live bands or just taped modern pop music nightly. It's open daily from 5 pm to 3 am, and until 6 am on weekends.

Among the many cultural events are the Jazz Festival in March, the Dvořák Singing Contest in June, the International Magicians Meeting in July, the Dvořák Autumn Festival in September, and the International Festival of Touristic Films also in September.

Seeing a movie at *Čas kino*, TG Masaryka 3, is another option.

Things to Buy

There's Becherovka herb liquor, of course – in every shop and in bottles of every imaginable size. The Becher factory outlet is at TG Masaryka 57. Group tours of the Becher factory are by advance arrangement only, such as through Čedok.

Should you fancy something pricier and more lasting, take a look at the Moser glasswork shop at Lázeňská 28. The Moser factory, on the Cheb road in the western outskirts, has a huge showroom and a museum of historical glasswork (which is free of charge). It's open weekdays from 9 am to 5 pm and Saturday until 3 pm, and part of the factory can be visited weekdays between 9 am and 1 pm.

Karlovy Vary porcelain is also well known, and not just those funny spa cups. The top local name is Pirkenhammer.

Getting There & Away

To or from Prague or Plzeň, buses are faster and more frequent than trains – typically 2½ hours from Prague, compared with four to five hours by train. A seat reservation (*místenka*) is recommended for Prague (a day or two ahead) and for international connections (a week or more).

For domestic ČSAD and international bus bookings, go to the Bus Tour ČSAD agency (☎ 322 50 35) at náměstí Republiky 7, weekdays only from 6 am to 6 pm. Coaches depart from the stops on Jaltská and travel to Plzeň seven times a day, to Prague at least 10 times a day, and to Brno once a day. Buses to Mariánské Lázně (about seven a day) go from lower train station. There are departures to Nuremberg and Frankfurt three times a week, and Amsterdam once a week, from lower train station.

Karlovy Vary's small airport is only for charters and private flights, though ČSA has a booking office (☎ 322 57 60) at the Grandhotel Pupp.

Getting Around

Local buses run at 20 or 30 minute intervals; routes are posted at the stop on Varšavská. Bus tickets (6 Kč) are sold in kiosks, and machines at major stops.

A 24 hour taxi service is Willy Taxi (☎ 322 30 30). Parking is a problem and there is a two hour limit at parking meters. A large underground carpark is under náměstí Horákové – an hour costs 10 Kč or 24 hours is 180 Kč.

LOKET NAD OHŘÍ

In the 12th century the Bohemian Prince (later King) Vladislav II built a castle on a rock in a loop of the river Ohře that is so extreme it almost makes an island. In the 14th century, King John of Luxembourg jailed his son (the future Charles IV) in this castle for several months in fear of being deposed by him.

The river's embrace has kept the surrounding walled village of Loket from growing beyond its medieval size, and the resulting storybook setting is almost too romantic. Goethe certainly thought so, and came here often between 1807 and 1823. This is in fact where the 72-year-old poet first met and fell for 16-year-old Ulrike von Lewetzow.

Loket's German name is Elbogen, and it's been famous by that name since 1815 for the manufacture of porcelain, as have the neighbouring towns of Horní Slavkov (Schlackenwald) and Chodov (Chodan). You can look at some fine examples in the town, and do a bit of shopping too.

The castle and village make a charming afternoon outing from Karlovy Vary.

Orientation & Information

The bus from Karlovy Vary provides a cinematic, near-360° look at the town, almost completely circling it on approach. From the public bus stop across the river it's easy to appreciate the size and strength of the castle-fortress.

Česká spořitelna, TG Masaryka 32, has an exchange counter.

Town

The narrow, curving square, náměstí Masaryka, has a fair share of handsome **Gothic façades**. But one of the most attention-getting buildings is the neo-Gothic **Hostinec Bílý kůň** (White Horse Inn), where Goethe stayed.

In the early-Baroque **town hall** (radnice) are a few bits of glass and porcelain, and lots of old spa cups, masquerading as a 'museum of ceramics' (open daily from 9 am to noon and 1 to 5 pm; entry costs 7 Kč). There's more to see in the castle and in the town's **ceramics showrooms**, including a shop selling Loket's own Epiag brand.

Two old **gate towers** are still standing, one at the north-east end of the square, another down a steep cobbled lane by the town hall. Outside the gate towers is the tiny Baroque **St Anne Chapel** (kaple sv Anny), now empty inside.

Castle

The red and white parish Church of St

Wenceslas (kostel sv Václava), dating in its present form from the early 18th century, is on your way to the castle.

The castle was built on the site of an earlier Romanesque fort, of which the only surviving bits are the tall square tower, and fragments of a rotunda and palace. Its present late-Gothic look dates from the late 14th century. From 1788 until 1947 it was used (and abused) as the town prison. The town, not the state, did the good restoration work in the 1970s.

A tour isn't necessary, and the complementary English text on the castle's history has little on the exhibits inside – several cutaway sections from archaeological work on the castle, and two rooms full of luscious ceramics, are barely enough to whet the appetite. Check out the postcard views of the village and forest from the tower.

The castle is open daily, except Monday, from 9 am to noon and 1 to 5 pm (until 4 pm from November to March). Entry costs 20 Kč with a Czech text or 50 Kč with an English text.

Places to Stay & Eat

Goethe's favourite suite at *Hostinec Bílý kůň* was No 103, but sadly the hotel has been closed for several years. The reasonably priced *penzion* at Kostelní 4, on the way to the castle from TG Masaryka, has rooms with TV, shower and WC for 250 Kč per person. The newish *Hotel Goethe* (☎ 0168-68 41 84), TG Masaryka 21, has a restaurant and charges 720/1040 Kč for a single/double. The not-so-friendly *Hotel Actus* (☎ 68 41 03), a few doors away, has similar prices.

Getting There & Away

Loket is 25 minutes by bus from stop No 11 in Karlovy Vary's lower train station. There are seven departures per day on weekdays, fewer on weekends. The tedious train trip requires a change at Sedlo.

You could even walk from Karlovy Vary, on a very fine 17km trail (marked blue) beside the Ohře; see Hikes in the Karlovy Vary section.

PLZEŇ

Plzeň was founded in 1295 by Přemysl King Václav II as Nový Plzeň, to succeed the much older Starý Plzeň (now Starý Plzenec, 9km to the south-east) as western Bohemia's administrative capital – which it still is, seven centuries on. By the 14th century the fortified, solidly Catholic Plzeň was Bohemia's third largest town after Prague and Kutná Hora.

Among other things, Václav II granted to some 260 Plzeň burghers the exclusive right to brew beer. By the time of the Thirty Years' War there were 26 separate basement breweries, each with its own beer hall – though many of the products were not particularly drinkable. In 1842 the crafty brewers pooled their experience, installed 'modern' technology and founded a single municipal brewery, with spectacular results. Their golden beer, labelled Plzeňský Prazdroj (*prazdroj* is old Czech for 'the original source' – Pilsner Urquell in German), is now one of the world's best, and most imitated, beers.

At the same time, Plzeň began to industrialise. Its other famous name, the Škoda Engineering Works, was founded in 1869 and prospered as a manufacturer of armaments. Since WWII it has been known mainly for the ubiquitous Škoda car (made at another branch in Mladá Boleslav), as well as locomotives and industrial machinery. In the midst of post-1989 euphoria, Volkswagen offered Škoda a staggering US$1 billion development loan, and the German car manufacturer now has an important stake in the company.

In 1995, Plzeň's population was 173,000, making it the fourth largest city in the Czech Republic after Prague, Brno and Ostrava. Thanks to its factories, it's not a very pretty town. But it is an interesting one, definitely worth a day's exploration – with cheap lubrication by Prazdroj.

Orientation

Plzeň sits near the confluence of four sizable rivers, two of which, the Mže and the Radbuza, flow past the old town centre.

The central bus station (centrální autobusové nádraží) is west of the town centre, a 15 minute walk down Husova to the main square, náměstí Republiky. The main train station (hlavní nádraží) is as far again on the other side; turn right under the tracks and left (west) on Americká, and cross the Radbuza, and the second, third and fourth right turns will take you into náměstí Republiky.

Information

Tourist Offices The Municipal Information Centre (Městské informační středisko; ☎ 723 65 35), náměstí Republiky 41, can provide information and reserves accommodation, organises guides, sells city transport tickets, maps and guidebooks, and changes currencies. It's open daily in summer from 9 am to 5 pm, and the rest of the year weekdays from 10 am to 4.30 pm. Its annual *Plzeň* booklet has plenty of cultural and practical information.

Čedok (☎ 722 26 09) is at Prešovská 10. CKM (☎ 723 63 93), Dominikánská 1, books international travel and can help with cheap accommodation; weekdays from 8 am to 6 pm (Friday to 5 pm).

Motorists in need of assistance can turn to the Autoklub Plzeň (☎ 722 07 36) at Havlíčkova 6 or Autoturist (☎ 722 00 06) at Sady Pětatřicátníků 3.

Money Komerční banka, Zbrojnická 4, has an exchange counter and a MasterCard ATM. There is a Visa ATM at Československá obchodní banka, Americká 60, opposite Tesco.

Post & Communications The post and telephone office is on Solní. Plzeň's area code is ☎ 019.

Online Services The *Net Café – internetová kavárna* is on the 1st floor at Americká 34.

Bookshops A good bookshop with maps, postcards, posters and CDs is at Dřevěná 2.

Cultural Centres The American Centre in Plzeň (☎ 723 77 22/3; fax 723 77 25), Dominikánská 9, is mainly a business resource centre, with a restaurant-bar (open daily to midnight) and CNN news. Send an email (amcenter@mbox.vol.cz) or browse its Internet site (www.vol.cz/AMCENTER).

Emergency The Foreigners' Police (Cizinecká policie) office is beside Čedok at Prešovská 10.

Náměstí Republiky

The square, bright and pleasant but constantly rumbling with traffic and trams, is dominated by the gargantuan Gothic **St Bartholomew Church** (kostel sv Bartoloměje), its size accentuated by its isolation. Have a look inside at the delicate marble 'Pilsen Madonna' (dating from about 1390) on the main altar.

A mere 301 steps bring you 62m up the church's 102m **tower**, the highest steeple in Bohemia, for views across the city. It's open daily, except Monday, from 10 am to 6 pm; entry costs 18 Kč.

Plzeň is less plastered with Baroque façades than many Bohemian towns. The best Renaissance structures in the old centre are in and around the square. Check out **Chotešov House** at No 106/13 and a lovely old thing, the **Gerlach House**, around the corner at Dřevěná 344/4. These jointly house a good ethnographic museum that's currently under renovation (see the Museums & Galleries section).

One of the most charming buildings in Bohemia is Plzeň's sooty old **town hall** (radnice). The bottom four floors, built in 1558, are pure Italian Renaissance. A few years later the top floor, tower, multiple gables and little brass flags were added; all it needs is a liveried ensemble doing trumpet fanfares from the roof. The sgraffito on the front dates from this century. In front is a 1681 **plague column** (one Czech tourist brochure calls it a 'pest column').

On the west side at No 234/35 is the 1710 **Archdeacon's House** (Arciděkanství) by Jakub Auguston, a local boy who made good.

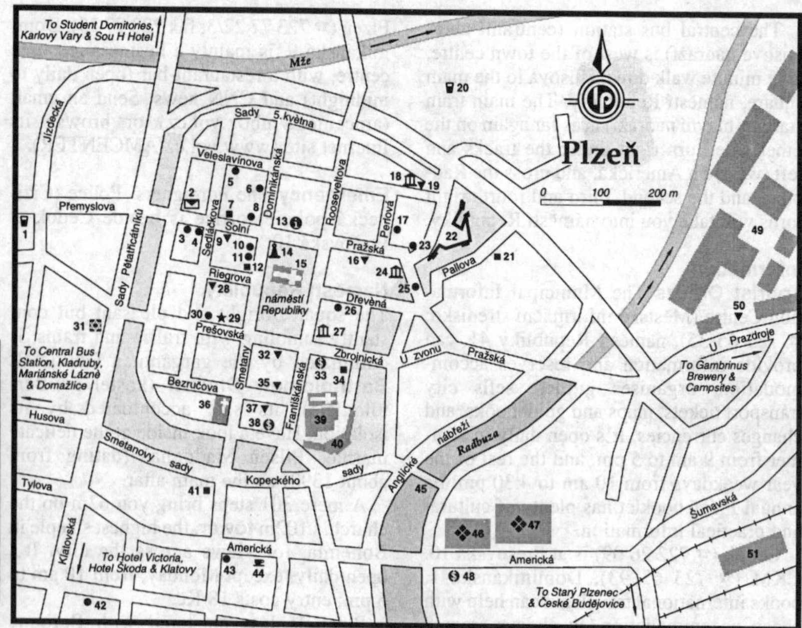

The south half of the square becomes a boisterous open market every Friday.

Underground Plzeň

A deceptively plain house at Perlová 65 turns out to be one of the city's best preserved Renaissance homes. It's also from here that you can descend into an extraordinary museum of early Plzeň, a honeycomb of passages, cellars and wells under the old centre.

The earliest were probably dug by out-of-work silver miners for Plzeň burghers in the 14th century – perhaps for beer production, or defence, or both. The latest date from the 19th century. Some 500m of them are open to the public, of an estimated 11km excavated in the 1970s and 80s.

Wealthier people had long had wells in their cellars. Over-use led to severe water shortages until a municipal water system was established in the 15th century. When wells dried up they were buried, often filled with rubbish, and these have yielded an amazing trove of artefacts. The tunnels are dotted with exhibits of wooden water pumps, mining tools, pewter, pottery and – to the surprise of some historians – Czech glass dating back to the 14th century.

The damp tunnels are open daily, except Monday and Tuesday, from 9 am to 4.30 pm, and are definitely worth the 30 Kč price. A good English text is available. You end up in a complex beneath the water tower on Pražská.

Bring a pullover (it's chilly); a torch will let you peer into the darkest corners.

Assumption Church & Franciscan Monastery

South of the square on Fratiškanská is the Assumption Church (kostel Nanebevzetí Panny Marie), its early-Gothic origins betrayed by the low ceiling and thick pil-

PLACES TO STAY
- 7 Pension Bárová
- 12 Hotel Central
- 21 Hotel Rosso
- 34 Hotel Continental
- 41 Hotel Slovan

PLACES TO EAT
- 9 Pizzerie
- 16 Pivnice U Salzmanů
- 19 Pivnice Na Parkánu
- 28 Pivnice U Šenku
- 32 Fénix bistro
- 35 Moravská vinárna
- 37 Vinárna Zlatý hrozen
- 44 Net Café internetová kavárna
- 50 Restaurace Na Spilce

OTHER
- 1 Zach's Pub
- 2 Post & Telephone Office
- 3 House with Mikuláš Aleš Mural
- 4 House with Mikuláš Aleš Mural
- 5 Second-Hand Bookshop
- 6 American Center in Plzeň
- 8 CKM Travel Agency & Restaurant-Club U Dominiku
- 10 House with Mikuláš Aleš Mural
- 11 Archdeacon's House (Arciděkanství)
- 13 Tourist Centre & Town hall (radnice)
- 14 Plague Column
- 15 St Bartholomew Church (kostel sv Bartoloměje) & Tower
- 17 Entrance to Underground Passages
- 18 Brewery Museum (Pivovarské muzeum)
- 20 Subway Club
- 22 Fragments of Old Town Walls
- 23 Water Tower (vodárenská věž)
- 24 Art Gallery, in Former Butchers' Stalls
- 25 Prague Bridge (Pražský most)
- 26 Bookshop
- 27 Ethnographic Museum, in Chotešov House & Gerlach House
- 29 Foreigners' Police (Cizinecká policie)
- 30 Čedok Travel Agency
- 31 Great Synagogue
- 33 Komerční banka
- 36 St Anne Church (kostel sv Anny) & Former Monastery
- 38 Československá obchodní banka
- 39 Assumption Church (kostel Nanebevzetí Panny Marie) & Franciscan Monastery (klášter Františkánů)
- 40 West Bohemian Museum (Zapadočeské muzeum) & West Bohemian Gallery (Zapadočeská galeria)
- 42 Autoklub Plzeň
- 43 Cinema Elektra (Kino Elektra)
- 45 Pedestrian Bridge
- 46 Shopping Centre & House of Culture
- 47 Tesco Department Store
- 48 Československá obchodní banka & ATM
- 49 Prazdroj (Urquell) Brewery
- 51 Main Train Station (Hlavní nádraží)

lars. You enter past an unusual crucifix with a clean-shaven Christ nailed to the cross by only one hand and one foot.

In the former Franciscan monastery (klášter Františkánů) next door, the West Bohemia Museum has assembled fine church statues from Gothic to Baroque. But the real reason to visit is to see the little **St Barbara Chapel** (kaple sv Barbory) on the east side of the cloister, unaltered since it was built in the 13th century, bearing the remains of frescoes from as early as the 15th century, beneath an elegant ribbed vault. The whole complex was under renovation at the time of writing.

Elsewhere Around Náměstí Republiky

The streets of Nový Plzeň's original checkerboard layout are good for browsing.

At least three buildings – two on Solní and one on náměstí Republiky – bear bright murals by **Mikuláš Aleš**, a central figure of the so-called 'National Theatre generation' of the Czech National Revival.

At the end of Pražská is a stone **water tower** (vodárenská věž) from 1530, part of the first town water system (this one supplied fountains in the square until the beginning of this century). It now houses a private gallery. Opposite is a former arcade of medieval **butchers' stalls** (*masné krámy*), which is now a good gallery of new Czech art. It's open daily, except Monday, from 10 am to 6 pm, Saturday to 1 pm, and Sunday from 9 am to 5 pm.

Heading out through a town gate that's no longer there, you cross the **Prague Bridge** (Pražský most) over a moat that's no longer there. Turning left brings you to some weedy, reconstructed bits of the **old town walls**.

South of the square on Smetany is the very Baroque **St Anne Church** (kostel sv Anny), another work by Jakub Auguston. The former Premonstratensian **monastery** next door is now part of a State Science Library.

Prazdroj (Urquell) Brewery

Across the Radbuza is the brewery (*pivovar*) that put Plzeň on the map, entered through the gate that has graced the label of its beer since 6 October 1842. For 30 Kč individual visitors can join a one hour tour on weekdays at 12.30 pm – with a film, visits to the brewing rooms and chilly fermentation cellars, and, of course, beer-tasting.

Head east on Pražská, cross the river and bear left on U Prazdroje; the gate is by a pedestrian bridge, 750m from náměstí Republiky. Through a similar gate 500m on is the Gambrinus brewery. Sorry, mate, no tours at that one.

Great Synagogue

The neo-Renaissance Great Synagogue (Velká synagóga) across Sady Pětatřicátníků is one of Europe's biggest synagogues, built in 1892 by the 2000 or so Jews who lived here then. The city and state have apparently shown no interest in saving the synagogue, now locked up and in shameful disrepair. Out of an office at Smetanovy sady 5, Plzeň's present Jewish community, perhaps 100 in all, is going for broke with a private appeal for funds.

Museums & Galleries

Brewery Museum This museum is in a restored malt house, so you can learn all about how beer was made (and drunk) in the days before Prazdroj was founded. Highlights include a mock-up 19th century pub similar to the one that was actually here, a tiny working model of a steam brewery, old wooden beer steins and beer mats through the ages. All have English captions, bless 'em, and there's a good English text. It's on Veleslavínova and open daily from 10 am to 6 pm. Entry costs 40 Kč.

Ethnographic Museum With clothing, utensils, mock-up interiors and excellent displays on traditional holidays and celebrations, the dusty Ethnographic Collection (národopisné sbírky) of the West Bohemian Museum is a good place for visualising earlier days. Check out the Chod bagpipes, too (see the Chodsko section). It's housed in two historic buildings that are of as much interest as the contents; enter at náměstí Republiky 106/13. It was closed for restoration at the time of writing.

West Bohemian Museum The magnificent agglomeration of building that makes up the West Bohemian Museum (Západočeské muzeum) is mixed with revivalist styles built between 1897-1901. The museum is closed for restoration, though the West Bohemian Gallery (Západočeská galerie) is open with temporary, mostly modern, art exhibits Tuesday to Friday from 10 am to 6 pm, Saturday to 1 pm, Sunday from 9 am to 5 pm.

Special Events

Plzeň celebrates the official Czech holiday for Liberation Day earlier than the rest of the country, because it was liberated by the US army two days earlier on 6 May 1945.

In Plzeň this is always celebrated with a huge parade of Czechs dressed in US army surplus from WWII, and driving Jeeps and armoured vehicles. There is also a country and western music festival.

Since 1992 Plzeň has held a *Pivní slavností* (Beer Festival) in early October – only fitting for the beer-making capital of a nation that claims to drink more per capita than any other. Afterwards, everybody staggers off to München, Germany.

Places to Stay

Čedok can arrange private accommodation, of which it says there is plenty, for about 350 Kč per double with shower and WC. The Municipal Information Centre has private rooms in the centre for around 620 Kč per person, including breakfast. CKM has private rooms from around 300 Kč.

Places to Stay – bottom end

Camping The camping grounds *Bílá Hora* (☎ 53 49 05) and *Ostende* (☎ 52 01 94) have bungalows and are both open from May through September. They're on opposite sides of Velký Bolevecký rybník, a lake about 6km north of the city centre and accessible (tediously) by public transport (take bus No 20 from near the train station).

Hostels The *Sou H* (☎ 28 20 12) is a year-round hostel (ubytovna) at Vejprnická 56, about 3km west of town but easily accessible on tram No 2 (direction: Skvrňany) from the train or bus station. Beds are 165 Kč per person.

Similarly priced beds are available at *TJ Lokomotiva* (☎ 480 41), Úslavská 75, not far behind the train station. Ask CKM Student Travel about other hostels and accommodation possibilities in student dormitories. Western Bohemian University has pricier student dormitories (☎ 22 30 49 or 22 30 66) at Bolevecká 30, open to visitors all year round. Take tram No 4 two stops north from Čedok.

Hotels Two staid places near the city centre have a few rooms with shared facilities. Singles/doubles at the *Hotel Continental* (☎ 723 64 79; fax 722 17 46), Zbrojnická 8, are good value at 548/802 Kč with breakfast; credit cards are accepted. It also has rooms with TV and shower but shared WC for about 960/1460 Kč, or with bath and WC for 1492/2150 Kč. The rooms at the *Hotel Slovan* (☎ 722 72 56; fax 22 70 12), Smetanovy sady 1, with shared facilities are 580/900 Kč, though you may have to persist to get one. Rooms with shower and WC are 1380/1800 Kč.

Only a handful of spacious rooms with shower and WC are available for 510/850 Kč at *Pension Bárová* (☎ 723 66 52), Solní 8. Book ahead.

Places to Stay – middle

Sticking its dull, ugly face into náměstí Republiky at No 33 is the Communist-era *Hotel Central* (☎ 722 67 57; fax 722 60 64), where posh rooms with shower, WC and satellite TV are about 1420/2548 Kč.

The modern *Hotel Victoria* (☎ 722 10 10; fax 27 66 12) has rooms starting at 1280/1690 Kč. It's about 1km from the centre; take tram No 4 south on Sady Pětatřicátníků to Borská and walk a block west to No 19.

Places to Stay – top end

The new and central *Hotel Rosso* (☎ 22 64 73; fax 22 72 54) at Pallova 12 has smallish but comfortable rooms for 980/1780 Kč, plus a pricey French-Czech restaurant. Rooms at *Hotel Škoda* (☎ 27 52 52; fax 27 63 22), náměstí Českých bratří 10, two blocks west of the Victoria, start at 1295/1950 Kč.

Places to Eat

Pivnice Na Parkánu, Veleslavínova 4, beside the Brewery Museum, has standard Czech courses for under 120 Kč, service at a snail's pace, and music on Friday nights. A decent pizza-for-one is about 70 Kč at *Pizzerie*, Solní 9, open daily from 10 am to 10 pm.

Pivnice U Šenku, on the corner of Riegrova and Sedlačková, has Czech standard fare for less than 120 Kč, while *Vinárna Zlatý hrozen*, on Bezručova, charges 70 to 150 Kč.

Fénix bistro, náměstí Republiky 18, is a good, inexpensive self-service buffet. Not far from the square is the well known *Pivnice U Salzmannů*, Pražská 8. This is a Plzeň institution, known for high-quality food (main courses 40 to 180 Kč) and fine beer, though a bit touristy.

Restaurace Na Spilce is a jolly, 600-seat tourist trap run by the Prazdroj Brewery, up the road from the gate. Locals insist it's good; in any case it's handy if you're there for a brewery tour. Czech main courses are 32 to 140 Kč, and it's open daily from 11 am to about 10 pm.

A popular bar with younger locals and students is *Restaurant-Club U Dominiku* next to the CKM office, with taped rock music and pool tables. It's open daily from 11 am to midnight. Another popular hangout is *Zach's Pub*, at Palackého náměstí 2 and open daily until 1 am, with Guinness and some English beers.

Breakfast The *Hotel Continental* has a small but reasonable all-you-can-eat buffet breakfast, though the exotic coffees from Burundi and India aren't offered during breakfast. Non-guests pay a steep 100 Kč.

Entertainment

For entertainment, try the *JK Tyla Theatre* (Divadlo JK Tyla) or the ultramodern *House of Culture* (dům kultury) beside the river. The JK Tyla Theatre also has interesting tours of the backstage area and dressing rooms, in Czech only, from late June to August. If loud rock in a packed club with graffitied walls is your scene then head for *Subway* (☎ 22 28 96) at Truhlářská 21, just off the overpass beyond the corner of Rooseveltova and Sady 5.května.

Getting There & Away

Czechs claim the best way from Prague to Plzeň is by train, a 1½ to two hour trip, with at least 13 fast or express departures every day. But buses leave Prague for Plzeň about every hour all day, taking 1½ hours and seat reservations aren't necessary.

To and from Karlovy Vary, buses are quicker (about 1½ hours) and more frequent (about seven a day) than the train (no direct services anyway). Other frequent long-distance bus connections are from Cheb and Mariánské Lázně, and from České Budějovice.

The Bus Tour ČSAD agency at the bus station is mainly for international connections.

Getting Around

Buy 6 Kč tickets for the buses, trolleybuses and trams from kiosks and tabák shops, or from machines at major stops; there are no day passes.

AROUND PLZEŇ

Kladruby

A Benedictine abbey was founded here in 1115 by Prince Vladislav I. Following repeated plundering in the Thirty Years' War, the Counter-Reformation abbots undertook a major face-lift of the buildings by two of the most prominent Bohemian artists of the time, Giovanni Santini and Kilian Ignatz Dientzenhofer.

The main attraction is the **Abbey Church of the Holy Virgin**, rebuilt between 1712-26 by Santini in an extraordinary 'Baroque Gothic' style seen nowhere outside Bohemia (an earlier Santini work in this style is the abbey church at Sedlec, near Kutná Hora). Bohemia abounds in fine but often repetitive architecture; here is something very different, and a pleasure to look at.

The church has the original floorplan of a Romanesque basilica, the longest in Bohemia (85m). The church itself, Santini's design from the fantastically complex vaulting right down to the pews, is an improbable marriage of Baroque flamboyance and Gothic severity that would verge on tongue-in-cheek if it weren't so beautiful. At the left front is the tomb of Vladislav I, among the few Přemysl rulers not buried either at Prague Castle or Zbraslav.

The standard tour also includes the cloisters, with several dozen allegorical sculptures from the workshop of the celebrated Baroque sculptor Matthias Bernard Braun. Of the monastery buildings themselves (not on the tour), the west wing is the Old Prelature (Abbot's residence), now a church library. The Baroque east wing is the so-called New Convent, built to a design of Dientzenhofer between 1729-39, and now beautifully renovated.

The monastery (☎ 0183-773) is open daily, except Monday, for hourly group tours from June through August from 9 am to noon and 1 to 6 pm, to 5 pm in May and September, and to 4 pm in April and October. It's closed to drop-in visitors the rest of the year.

Getting There & Away Kladruby village is about 35km west of Plzeň, just south of Stříbro. Getting there without a car is tricky. There is one daily bus to and from Prague (via Plzeň) taking about 3¾ hours. Changing buses at Stříbro gives you additional options from Plzeň.

From Kladruby's main square, walk (in the direction of the parish church) 1.5km to the monastery.

KLATOVY

Klatovy, 42km south of Plzeň, is considered the west Bohemian 'gateway' to the Šumava mountains, and merits a few hours if you're on your way there. Founded in 1262 by Přemysl Otakar II, the town was to pay for its Hussite leanings with forced re-Catholicisation and military harassment in the Thirty Years' War. But it actually did quite well under the Habsburgs and the Counter-Reformation, foreshadowed here by the founding of a Jesuit hostel in 1636. It sports a small, fairly attractive Renaissance and Baroque centre, though no match for the romantic views it offers of afar.

Orientation

The main train station and the bus station are about 1.5km from the central square, náměstí Míru. Take bus No 1 or 2 from either one.

Information

A first-rate private agency for information about Klatovy and the Šumava region – plus currency exchange – is Pergolia Informservis (☎ 235 15; fax 251 56), beside the old town hall at náměstí Míru 63. It's open weekdays from 9 am to 1 pm and 1.30 to 6 pm.

Komerční banka, on the corner of náměstí Míru and Křížová, changes money weekdays between 8 am and 5 pm, and also has a 24 hour MasterCard/Visa ATM.

The main post office is west of the town centre on Domažlická. Klatovy's area code is ☎ 0186.

Black Tower & Around

Clustered around this prominent Gothic watch tower is the most interesting part of the old town. The Black Tower (Černá věž) was completed in 1557, and given the present roof, with its multiple pointy pyramids, in 1872 after the old one blew off in a storm. The astronomical clock was added later. The name reflects either that the tower was never plastered over, or that it has burned down three times.

You can climb it for the views, the best being south to the Šumava. While catching your breath on the way up, you can admire the clockworks. It's open May through September from 9 am to noon and 1 to 5 pm, April and October to 4 pm, and closed the rest of the year.

Next door is the late 16th century **town hall**. The handsome neo-Renaissance façade was added only in 1925, by architect Josef Fanta.

Jesuit Church & Jesuit Hostel

Opposite the Black Tower is the sober-faced Baroque Jesuit Church of the Immaculate Conception & St Ignatius, worth a visit for its extraordinary *trompe l'oeil* frescoes. Towering over the tiny main altar is a painting of the immense altar and domes the Jesuits probably wished they had. Completed in 1656, the church burned down twice, to be finally restored by Kilian Ignatz Dientzenhofer in 1722.

CZECH REPUBLIC

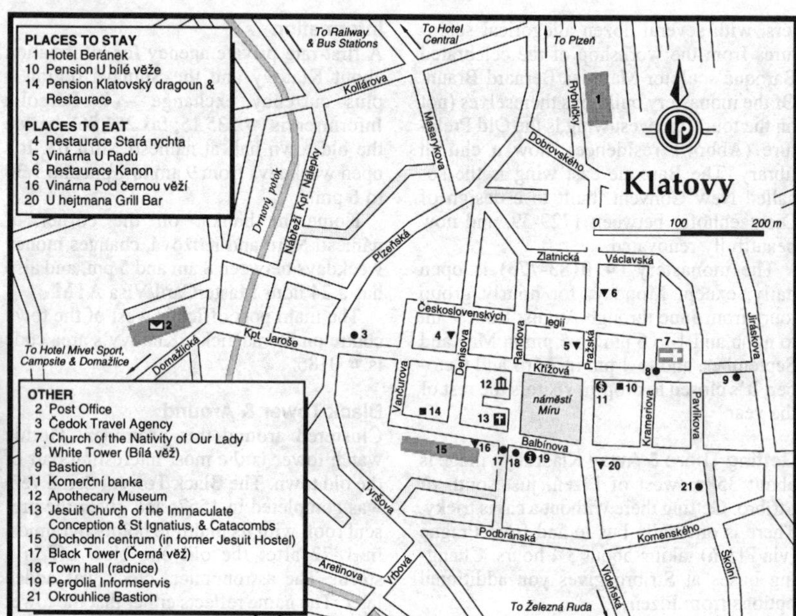

Across Balbínova is the former Jesuit hostel. After the Jesuits were forced out of Bohemia, the two-block-long building was subdivided for a school, a brewery and an army barracks. It's now a department store and shopping mall called Obchodní centrum.

Catacombs

Klatovy's most popular, and ghoulish, attraction lies *beneath* the Jesuit church: a crypt with over 200 corpses in surprisingly good condition (for corpses), including Jesuit monks and many of the region's 17th and 18th century most notable people. The secret to their preservation was cunningly designed natural air-conditioning, although the arrival of tourists in recent years raised the humidity and temperature just enough so that many of the cadavers resumed their decay and had to be buried. Only a few of the remainders are now on view.

With its own well, and secret access to the church tower, the catacombs were also intended as a siege shelter. Once accessible only from the church, they now have their own entrance at the right-hand side of the church. They're open in April and October on weekends and Monday from 9 am to noon and 1 to 4 pm, between May and September from Tuesday to Sunday until 5 pm.

As you return to the street in search of the living, a cheerful notice says, 'if you enjoyed this visit, perhaps you would be interested in other places where you can see crypts with mummies'. (We've checked the list out, for those who *are* interested, and have noted them elsewhere in this book.)

Apothecary Museum

A few doors down the west side of náměstí Míru is the White Unicorn (U bílého jednorožce) Apothecary, with its original lavish rococo furnishings from the 17th and

CZECH REPUBLIC

18th centuries. It was a working pharmacy until the 1960s, and is now a museum (and a UNESCO-protected cultural monument). It's open daily, except Monday, May through October from 9 am to noon and 1 to 5 pm. The tour requires a minimum of five people.

Next door at No 149 is the **Galerie U bílého jednorožce** with mostly modern art exhibits.

White Tower & Archdeacon's Church

East of náměstí Míru is another of Klatovy's towers, a Renaissance belfry called the White Tower (Bílá věž; 1581). Nearby is the town's oldest church, the early-Gothic (16th century) Archdeacon's Church of the Nativity of Our Lady, restored by Josef Fanta early in this century.

A block east is one of the surviving **bastions** of the old town walls. Another, a round bastion called Okrouhlice, is beside a path between Balbínova and Komenského.

Šumava Mountains

South-east of Klatovy the ancient, rounded Šumava range along the German (and Austrian) border begins. This range, which contains some of Bohemia's most pristine mountains, forms one the Czech Republic's newest national parks, and lies mainly in South Bohemia. Its West Bohemian parts – including the tourist centres of Železná Ruda, Špičák and Hojsova Stráž – are included with the rest of the Šumava region in the South Bohemia chapter.

Places to Stay

There are plenty of *private rooms* in town, and a *campsite* with bungalows about 5km west on the Domažlice road.

The Pergolia agency (see the Information section) can help with accommodation in town and in the Šumava region. It recommends the *Pension U bílé věže* (☎ 233 85), Křížová 165, at about 250 Kč per bed. Another pension, the *Královský dragoun* (☎ 240 88), is past the other side of the square at Balbínova 6, and has singles/doubles from 700/800 Kč.

The most central hotel, the *Beránek* (☎ 223 48), Rybničky 506/2, is also the sleaziest, with a lobby serving as an extension of the adjacent bar. Overpriced doubles with shower and common bath are 655 Kč.

The three-star *Hotel Central* (☎ 245 71; fax 247 45), Masarykova 300, has rooms with shower, WC and TV for 1130/1530 Kč, including breakfast. The *Hotel Mivet Sport* (☎ & fax 209 10), Domažlická 609, has noisy triples and quads with shared facilities for 185 Kč per bed or with private facilities for 240 Kč, as well as a sauna and a popular, smoky beer hall. It's a 1.2km walk from the town centre (west on Domažlická, north on Nerudova), or take bus No 2 to the Zimní Stadión stop.

Places to Eat

Our choice is the small *Vinárna U Radů* (☎ 245 94), on Pražská, with Czech standard fare from 38 to 140 Kč. Other good places in this range are the *U hejtmana* grill bar (☎ 206 50) in the south-east corner of the square, and the *Klatovský dragoun* restaurant (☎ 240 88) on Balbínova, despite the too-cute menu.

Other restaurants suggested by local friends are the *Kanon* on Pražská and the *Stará rychta* on Denisova.

The vinárna *Pod černou věží* (☎ 231 79), in Obchodní centrum at Balbínova 59, erupts with disco music later in the evening.

Getting There & Away

In general, bus is the most convenient way to get here – from Prague (three hours) about three times a day, Plzeň (one hour) five times, and Domažlice (45 minutes) five times. If you're carrying on south to Železná Ruda at the German border, trains are better, with four fast ones each day.

Chodsko Region

Chodsko (pronounced 'khodsko') is the Bohemian border region where the Bohemian Forest (Český les) and Šumava ranges splice together. The Chods, a sturdy, independent people traditionally from 11 villages in an arc from Postřekov to Pocínovice, were first entrusted with patrolling the Bavarian border by King John of Luxembourg in 1325, in return for formal exemption from feudal servitude.

After the Thirty Years' War the Habsburgs reneged, handing over the region to favoured courtiers and generals. When these refused to honour the old agreements, the Chods took up arms, briefly and disastrously. But their way of life, neither Bohemian nor Germanic, survives in unique customs and speech, in tidy fields and trim, prosperous-looking villages in the smooth hills around Chodsko's administrative centre, Domažlice.

Only on special occasions are you likely to hear Chod *dudy* (bagpipes), clarinet and violin music or catch sight of Chod women's long printed dresses and aprons. One such occasion is the annual summer Chod Festival (Chodské slavnosti), held in Domažlice on the Friday and weekend after 14 August, St Lawrence (sv Vavřinec) Day.

CZECH REPUBLIC

DOMAŽLICE

Domažlice was already a customs settlement by the 10th century. In 1266 King Přemysl Otakar II made it a fortified town, with a layout that has survived to the present. Its very beautiful, very Baroque old centre, spiked with tall towers, is once again under assault by Bavarian armies – of tourists this time.

It's a fairly sombre place, with few hotels, and probably best as a short day trip from Plzeň or Klatovy.

Orientation

From the joint train and local bus station it's about 1km north-west on Masarykova and Husova to the main square, náměstí Míru. A few trains, such as those from Planá, also stop at Domažlice město station, which is 500m from the town centre via Jiráskova and Chodská. The ČSAD bus station is on the corner of Poděbradova and Prokopa Velikého.

Information

The local Čedok office (☎ 2266) at náměstí Míru 129 is little more than an up-market travel agency. IPB banka, on the corner of the square at Branská, changes money and has a MasterCard ATM. The post office is at the west end of the square.

Domažlice's area code is ☎ 0189.

Náměstí Míru

The narrow, 500m-long square is a pleasure to explore, a kind of museum of Baroque arcades and Gothic and Renaissance burghers' houses. It's closed at the east end by the 13th century **Lower Gate** (Dolní brána) and a Gothic gatehouse.

Dominating the square is the slightly leaning tower of the **Dean's Church of the Nativity of the Virgin** (Děkanský kostel Narození Panny Marie), a little gem in cream and gold by Kilian Ignatz Dientzenhofer – bright and open, not the usual Baroque whipped cream. Note the *trompe l'oeil* altarpiece. It's a long climb up the 56m **tower**, but the views of the town and the Šumava are fine (open daily, except Monday, April to September from 9 am to noon and 1 to 5 pm; entry costs 10 Kč).

Across the square is the neo-Renaissance **town hall**. A block west is a house where the Czech writer **Božena Němcová** lived and worked between 1845-47, and beyond it the Gothic monastery **Church of the Assumption** (kostel Nanebevzetí Panny Marie).

Chod Castle & Chodsko Museum

South-west of the square, and as old as Domažlice itself, is the town castle. The castle was gutted by fire in 1995 and at the time of writing restoration work was still in progress.

Jindřich Jindřich Museum

You can get a good look at some aspects of the Chod lifestyle – such as handcrafts, clothing, a typical home – at a little museum based on the collections of a composer named Jindřich Jindřich, who lived here in the 1960s. It's just outside the Lower Gate.

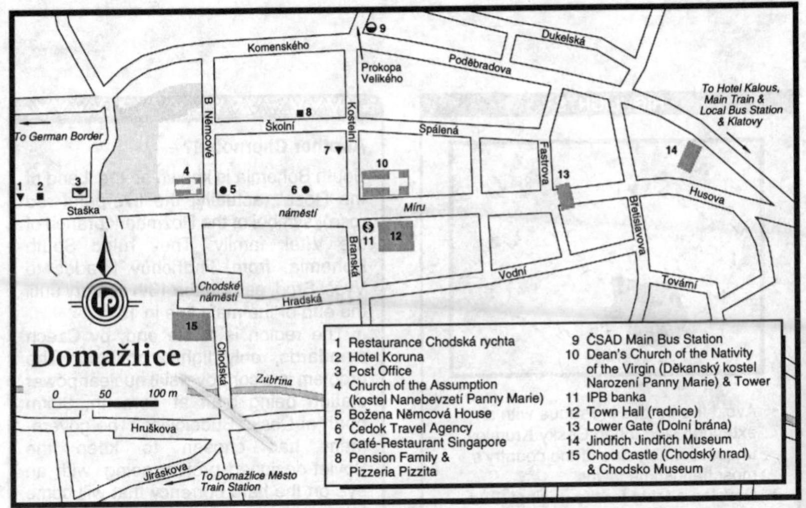

It's open daily, except Monday, from mid-April to mid-October from 8 am to noon and 1 to 4 pm, and the rest of the year in the mornings only.

Places to Stay

The *Hotel Kalous* (☎ & fax 2305), at Masarykova 377 on the road from the train station, has plain rooms with shower or bath, but shared WC, for 470 Kč per bed. At Staška 69 is the uncheerful *Hotel Koruna* (☎ 2279), which is small and full much of the time, with beds at 300 Kč per person. Better value are the numerous pensions around town. Try the small *Pension Family* (☎ 5962), Školní 107, where rooms cost from 330 Kč per person.

Places to Eat

A place that serves good Czech and international dishes is the *Café-restaurant Singapore*, on Kostelní. It has main courses from 90 to 185 Kč and is open daily, except Monday, from 9 am to 5 pm. Around the corner at Školní 107 is the reasonable *Pizzeria Pizzita.*

There's also a basic pivnice at the *Hotel Koruna.* A few doors up at Staška 63 is the new up-market *Restaurace Chodská* rychta with a large selection of Czech meat and fish courses from 60 to 290 Kč. It's open from 10 am to 10 pm.

Getting There & Away

Trains run to Domažlice from Plzeň every hour or two (in 1¾ hours, or half that time on two expresses from Prague to Germany), and from Klatovy four times a day. There are also six buses a day from Klatovy and two express buses to Prague and Plzeň.

South Bohemia

HIGHLIGHTS

- Avoid the hordes in Prague with an extended side trip to Český Krumlov, unquestionably one of the country's most handsome towns
- Develop a taste for the original 'Budweiser' beer at the Budvar Brewery in České Budějovice
- Take a ferry (in summer) between Orlík and Zvíkov castles, then hike back along tranquil forest trails

Another Chernobyl?

South Bohemia is known as the 'Land of the Rose' (actually, the five-petal red rose), symbol of the Rožmberk branch of the Vítek family. They ruled South Bohemia, from Jindřichův Hradec to Vyšší Brod, early in the 13th century until the end of the male line in 1611.

The region is fertile and, by Czech standards, only lightly polluted. The problem is a controversial nuclear power station being built at Temelín, 30km north of České Budějovice. The government has chosen to keep the Soviet-designed project going, with an eye on the hard currency that will come from selling energy to foreign markets. Yet environmentalists warn that even a small accident could destroy 30% of the country's most productive cropland. Not to mention the five-petal rose. ■

South Bohemia is a land of lakes, forests and fields, sprinkled with quaint villages that mix a Bavarian or Austrian flavour with Czech Baroque folk motifs. The countryside is enhanced by some 5000 carp ponds, many dating from the Middle Ages, not to mention the photogenic Hussite stronghold of Tábor and the striking castles at Hluboká, Rožmberk, Orlík and Červená Lhota. Apart from České Budějovice and a few pockets in the northern part of the region, there's relatively little industry.

South Bohemia's rolling hills are bisected by the Vltava river, flowing north to Prague from the Šumava mountains. The tame mountains here – the highest point is Mt Plechý at 1378m – are popular with Czech hikers and cyclists. The Třeboň lake district is another good spot to embrace nature.

Foreign travellers flock to České Budějovice and smaller, more striking Český Krumlov. The rest of South Bohemia is seemingly off the beaten track, though frequent bus and rail services mean nothing is more than a few hours away.

České Budějovice Region

ČESKÉ BUDĚJOVICE

České Budějovice is South Bohemia's regional capital and largest city, with a population of 97,000. This colourful medieval conurbation is halfway between Plzeň and Vienna, set in a flat plain at the confluence

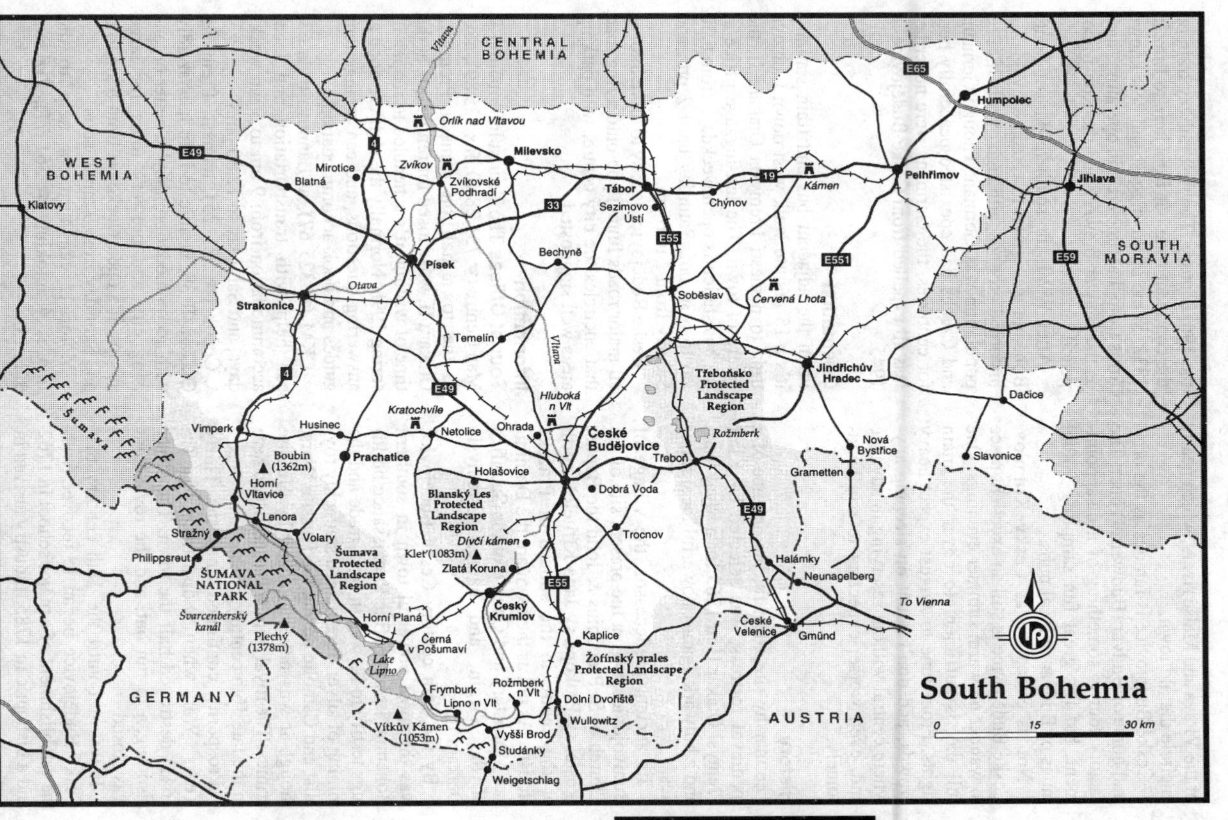
CENTRAL BOHEMIA
Vltava
WEST BOHEMIA
SOUTH MORAVIA
GERMANY
AUSTRIA
Humpolec
E65
Orlík nad Vltavou
4
E49
Milevsko
Mirotice
Zvíkov
Zvíkovské Podhradí
Blatná
Klatovy
Tábor
Sezimovo Ústí
33
19
Kámen
Chýnov
Pelhřimov
Jihlava
E55
E551
E59
Bechyně
Písek
Otava
Strakonice
Soběslav
Červená Lhota
Temelín
Vltava
Jindřichův Hradec
Třeboňsko Protected Landscape Region
Hluboká n Vlt
Kratochvíle
Dačice
Vimperk
Husinec
Netolice
Ohrada
České Budějovice
Rožmberk
Nová Bystřice
Slavonice
Boubín (1362m)
Prachatice
Třeboň
Gramatten
Holašovice
Dobrá Voda
Horní Vltavice
Šumava
Blanský Les Protected Landscape Region
Lenora
Stražný
Volary
Dívčí kámen
Trocnov
Philippsreut
Šumava Protected Landscape Region
Kleť (1083m)
Zlatá Koruna
Halámky
Neunagelberg
ŠUMAVA NATIONAL PARK
Český Krumlov
To Vienna
Švarcenberský kanál
Plechý (1378m)
Horní Planá
Černá v Pošumaví
Kaplice
České Velenice
Gmünd
Lake Lipno
Žofínský prales Protected Landscape Region
Frymburk
Lipno n Vlt
Rožmberk n Vlt
Dolní Dvořiště
South Bohemia
Vítkův Kámen (1053m)
Wullowitz
Vyšší Brod
Studánky
Weigetschlag
0
15
30 km

of the Vltava and Malše rivers, which neatly encircle the old town.

České Budějovice is famous as the original home of Budvar (Budweiser) beer. The factory tour is something of a disappointment, but it's great fun sampling 500ml mugs of Budvar in local pubs.

Not as evocative as Český Krumlov, České Budějovice is still an excellent place to wander on warm summer evenings. One full day is sufficient to cover the main sights. From June to August expect heavy crowds, and don't count on sleeping anywhere central without reserving in advance and, even worse, expecting to pay handsomely.

History

The marshy site, ideal for the defence of a medieval fortress, was selected by King Přemysl Otakar II in 1265 for a royal town and a bulwark against powerful local families.

Its ancient predecessor, the village of Budivojovice, was at the present site of the Church of St Procopius & John the Baptist (kostel sv Prokopa sv Jana Křtitele), north of the centre in the suburb of Pražské sídliště. As old as the town are the Dominican Monastery and Church of the Sacrifice of the Virgin, and náměstí Přemysla Otakara II.

By the 14th century České Budějovice was the most powerful town in southern Bohemia. Its many fine Renaissance buildings testify to its wealth from trade and the mining of silver. It remained staunchly royalist and Catholic during the Hussite Wars, though it was never attacked by Hussite armies. The royal mint was established here in the late 16th century.

Prosperity continued until the Thirty Years' War, when a disastrous fire (in 1641) destroyed half the town. The silver also began to run out, and the royal mint was closed.

It was not until the 18th century that České Budějovice began to recover, with the establishment of a major school in 1762 and a bishopric in 1785. Industry arrived in the 19th century. The first railway train on the continent rode out from here to Linz in 1832. Some of the biggest and best known firms from that time are still operating, such as the Budvar brewery and the Koh-i-noor pencil factory.

After WWI, the southern part of South Bohemia was given to Czechoslovakia on historical grounds, although over half of its population was German. Though Germans and Czechs had coexisted peacefully here for centuries, the Germans were nevertheless all expelled from České Budějovice in 1945.

Orientation

From the adjacent bus and train stations, it's a 15 minute walk west down Lannova třída to náměstí Přemysla Otakara II, the centre of town. The left-luggage office at the bus station is open weekdays from 6.30 am to 6.30 pm, Saturday until 2 pm, and Sunday from 2 to 6 pm.

České Budějovice is easy to drive into, as all major roads funnel you onto a ring road that encircles the city centre, with parking areas well signposted.

Information

Tourist Offices The Tourist Information & Map Centre (☎ 731 28 40; fax 525 89), next to the town hall on náměstí Přemysla Otakara II, was closed for renovation at the time of writing; it's scheduled to reopen in spring 1998. Normally the staff are good at answering questions, and can arrange tour guides and book accommodation.

CKM (☎ 325 67), at Lannova třída 63, can help with transportation and local accommodation from 9 am to 5 pm weekdays, and Saturday to 12.30 pm.

Čedok (☎ 521 25), náměstí Přemysla Otakara II 39, is able to help haphazardly with accommodation; they're better organising city and brewery tours for large groups. It's open weekdays from 8 am to 6 pm, Saturday from 9 am to noon.

Motorists can turn for help to the Jihočeský autoklub (☎ 361 77), Žižkova třída 13.

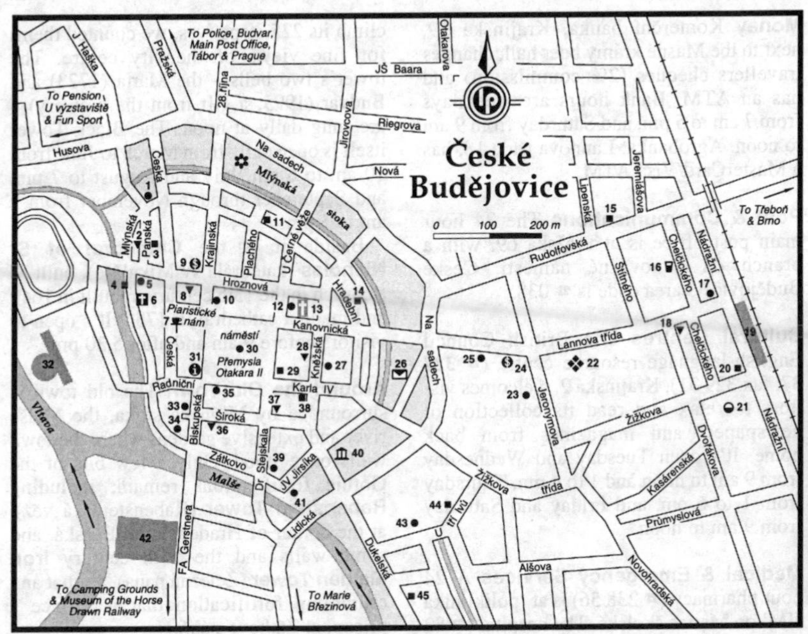

PLACES TO STAY

3 Petra Privat
4 Pension Klika
11 Hotel Bohemia
14 Pension Centrum
15 Hotel Hobit
20 Hotel Grand
29 Hotel Zvon & Bufet Zvon
38 Hotel Malý pivovar
44 Hotel U tří lvů
45 AT Pension

PLACES TO EAT

2 Víno z Panské
7 Cukrárna U kláštera
8 Masné krámy Beer Hall
18 Bufet Central
28 Pivnice Na dvorku
36 Restaurace U Paní Emy
37 Uzenářství Labužník

OTHER

1 Rabenštejn Tower (Rabenštejnská véž)
5 Armoury (zbrojnice)
6 Dominican Monastery (Dominikánský klášter)
9 Komerční banka
10 British Council
12 Black Tower (Černá věž)
13 Cathedral of St Nicholas (katedrála sv Mikuláše)
16 London Bar
17 CKM
19 Vlakové nádraží Train Station
21 Bus Station
22 Prior Department Store
23 Children's Theatre (Malé divadlo)
24 Agrobanka
25 CTS Travel Agency
26 Main Post Office
27 Concert Hall & Church of St Ann
30 Samson's Fountain (Samsonova kašna)
31 Tourist Information & Town Hall
32 Swimming Pool
33 Bishopric (Biskupství)
34 Iron Maiden Tower (Železná pana)
35 Čedok
39 South Bohemia Theatre (Jihočeské divadlo)
40 Museum of South Bohemia (Jihočeské muzeum)
41 Městský dům kultury
42 Ice Skating Rink
43 Dům kultury & Divadelní sál DK

Money Komerční banka, Krajinská 19, next to the Masné krámy beer hall, changes travellers cheques (2% commission) and has an ATM. Bank hours are weekdays from 7 am to 5 pm, and Saturday from 9 am to noon. Agrobanka, Lannova třída 18, has a MasterCard/Visa ATM.

Post & Communications The 24 hour main post office is at Pražská 69, with a branch on Senovážné náměstí. České Budějovice's area code is ☎ 038.

Cultural Centres The British Council English-language resource centre (☎ 327 37; fax 329 31), Krajinská 2, welcomes visitors to relax and read its collection of newspapers and magazines from back home. It's open Tuesday and Wednesday from 9 am to noon and 1 to 4 pm, Thursday from 1 to 6 pm, and Friday and Saturday from 9 am to noon.

Medical & Emergency Services A 24 hour pharmacy (☎ 238 56) is at 'poliklinika JIM' on Matice školské. The hospital (☎ 82 19 11) is at B Němcové 54, and the police station (☎ 287 57) is at Pražská 5.

Things to See

Náměstí Přemysla Otakara II At 133 square metres, this is the biggest plaza in the Czech Republic, surrounded by exquisite arcaded Gothic, Renaissance and Baroque buildings and centred around **Samson's Fountain** (Samsonova kašna; 1727). The formerly Renaissance **town hall** (1555) received a Baroque face-lift in 1731 at the hands of AE Martinelli. The allegorical figures on the town hall balustrade – Justice, Wisdom, Courage and Prudence – are matched by four bronze dragon gargoyles.

A horse-drawn carriage can be hired on the square for a tour of the town; the going rate is 500 Kč for 30 minutes. Kids can ride ponies along the square for about 100 Kč.

Just off the square on U Černé věže is the dominating 72m Gothic-Renaissance **Black Tower** (Černá věž), built in 1553. For 6 Kč climb its 225 steps (yes, we counted them) for fine views of the city centre. The tower's two bells – the Marta (1723) and Budvar (1995; a gift from the brewery) – are rung daily at noon. The Black Tower itself is open daily from March to June from 10 am to 6 pm, July and August to 7 pm, and September through November from 9 am to 5 pm.

Beside it is the **Cathedral of St Nicholas** (katedrála sv Mikuláše), built as a church in the 13th century, rebuilt in 1649 and made a cathedral in 1784. It's open to visitors before 9 am and after 5.30 pm.

Around the Old Town The old town is surrounded by Mlýnská stoka, the Malše river and extensive gardens where the town walls once stood. Only a few bits of the Gothic fortifications remain, including **Rabenštejn Tower** (Rabenštejnská věž), at the corner of Hradební and Panská, and some walls and the 15th century **Iron Maiden Tower** (Železná pana), a squat and crumbling fortification that was once a prison, at Zátkovo nábřeží.

On Hroznová, past Krajinská, are the **Butchers' Shops** (Masné krámy), a former meat market dating from 1554, now a popular tourist restaurant. Farther along Hroznová, on Piaristické náměstí, is the Church of the Sacrifice of the Virgin (kostel Obětování Panny Marie) and a former **Dominican Monastery**, which is slightly rundown but has a splendid pulpit. You enter the church from the Gothic cloister. Beside the church is a medieval **armoury** (*zbrojnice*) that was later used to store salt until it could be sent down the Vltava to Prague.

Return up to Česká, turn right and follow it to Radniční. Another right onto Biskupská takes you past the 18th century **bishopric** (*biskupství*). This and a garden behind it are accessible through a small gate in the wall. It's open daily from May through September from 8 am to 6 pm.

Follow Zátkovo to Dr Stejskala. Pass the South Bohemian Theatre (Jihočeské divadlo) and continue to JV Jirsíka and turn right into Dukelská, where you'll find the **Museum of South Bohemia** (Jihočeské muzeum), with its extensive collection on history, books, coins, weapons and wildlife. It's open daily, except Monday, March through November from 9 am to noon and 12.30 to 5.30 pm; entry costs 20 Kč.

A small **Museum of the Horse-Drawn Railway** (Památky koněspřežní železnice) is south of the centre at Mánesova 10, near the Koh-i-noor factory, and open daily, except Monday, May through September from 9.30 am to noon and 12.30 to 5 pm.

Budvar Brewery Advance bookings (☎ 770 52 01) are required to visit this modern brewery (*pivovar*), and only groups of five or more will be accepted. A one hour tour costs 100 Kč, while a 90 minute tour with beer-tasting is 180 Kč. It is easier to make a booking with a tourist office.

Budvar's brewery is on Pražská at the corner of K Světlé, in an industrial area several kilometres north of the city centre (take bus No 2 or 4). It lacks the picturesque appearance of the Urquell Brewery in Plzeň; ease the pain with a beer and pub lunch at the on-site Restaurace Budvarka.

Places to Stay

Accommodation is especially tight in July and August, so book in advance or call the tourist office before arriving.

Camping The *Dlouhá Louka Autocamp* (☎ 731 17 57; fax 531 41), Stromovka 8, is a 20 minute walk south-west of town (take bus No 6 from in front of the dům kultury). Tent space is available here from May to September, and motel single/double rooms (580/980 Kč with breakfast) are available year-round. The showers are clean and the water hot, but beware of bar prices.

Stromovka Autocamp (☎ 534 02 or 288 77), just past Dlouhá Louka Autocamp, has three and four-person bungalows for 480/575 Kč. It's open April through October.

Hostels In summer, the information centre arranges accommodation in dormitories from around 350 Kč per person. From July to September, the *Kolej jihočeské university* (☎ 770 35 57), Studentská 800/15, has beds from 300 Kč in twin rooms. It's best to book in advance with CKM.

The closest thing to a travellers' hostel is *Pension U výstaviště* (☎ 724 01 48), 30 minutes from the city centre at U výzstaviště 17. You pay 250 Kč for one of 12 beds and use of the kitchen and common room. In summer call for a free lift from the stations (not guaranteed), or take bus No 1, 14 or 17 from outside the bus station to the fifth stop (U parku); the pension is about 100m up the right-hand street.

Private Rooms The information centre books private rooms from 350 Kč per person. Another agency with similarly priced rooms is CTS (☎ 539 68), at Lannova třída 6.

A dependable choice is *Marie Březinová* (☎ 599 96) at U Malše 14, a side street that runs east from Lidická. Double rooms cost 800 Kč, and Mrs Březinová appreciates advance reservations.

It's much the same at *Petra Privat* (☎ 372 30), Panská 23, except the cost is 400 Kč per person.

Pensions Small private pensions around town are a better deal than the hotels, but you ought to ask to see the room before accepting it.

Pension Centrum (☎ 520 30) is at Mlýnská stoka 6, just off Kanovnická as you enter the old town. Double rooms with bath are 1000 Kč, including breakfast.

Doubles at the stupendously pleasant *Pension Klika* (☎ & fax 371 56), Zátkovo 17, are well worth it for 1000 Kč.

South of the city centre is the friendly *AT Pension* (☎ & fax 731 25 29), Dukelská 15, priced at 800/950 Kč for a single/double.

Hotels The basic *Hotel Grand* (☎ 565 03), Nádražní 27, opposite the train station, needs major renovations but is quite OK considering the price of 640/880 Kč for a single/double. Also near the station is the threadbare *Hotel Hobit* (☎ 354 38), Rudolfonská 25, with noisy rooms overlooking the street for 550/950 Kč.

Of Budějovice's four luxury hotels, least appealing is the blocky *Hotel U tří lvů* (☎ 599 00), on the street of the same name, priced from 1100/1490 Kč. *Hotel Bohemia* (☎ & fax 731 13 81), Hradební 20, has far more character, and is on a quiet side street, and charges 1290/1690 Kč.

The deluxe *Hotel Zvon* (☎ 731 13 83; fax 731 13 85) is on the main square and charges accordingly – 1395/2430 Kč. Around the corner is the newly renovated *Hotel Malý pivovar* (☎ 731 32 85; fax 731 32 87), a better deal at 1490/1890 Kč.

Places to Eat

Bufet Central, Lannova třída 32, is handy for a self-service breakfast on the way to the train station. It's open weekdays from 6 am and Saturday from 7 am. *Bufet Zvon*, another stand-up buffet with early hours, is on the main square next to Hotel Zvon.

A butcher's shop called *Uzenářství Labužník* at Dr Stejskala 3 has great chlebíčky (open sandwiches) and a variety of salads and sausage meats.

The *Masné krámy* (Butcher's Shop) beer hall, in the old meat market on the corner of Hroznová and 5.května, has been a town institution for centuries. Now it's touristy and expensive, but still worth a look for the ambience.

A more local, no-frills beer hall is *Pivnice Na dvorku*, Kněžská 11, which is open daily to 11 pm. The food here is good.

The wine bar *Víno z Panské*, Panská 14, with wholesome vegetarian and chicken dishes is open weekdays to 9.30 pm. Local wine is served straight from the barrel.

At the popular *Restaurace U Paní Emy*, Široká 25, international courses with fish and chicken are under 200 Kč.

Cafés The *Cukrárna U kláštera*, Piaristické náměstí 18, just off the main square, is great for coffee and cakes (closed Sunday).

Café filharmonie, in the concert hall at the corner of Karla IV, is perhaps the town's most elegant café.

Entertainment

There are two cultural centres, both near the Museum of South Bohemia. The old *Městský dům kultury* is by the river at JV Jirsíka, and the new *dům kultury* is south-east of the museum. You've a better chance of hearing music at *Divadelní sál DK*, behind the newer dům kultury.

The *South Bohemian Theatre*, by the river on Dr Stejskala, usually presents plays in Czech, plus the occasional opera and concert. The *Church of St Anne*, Kněžská 6, functions as a concert hall. The *Children's Theatre* (Malé divadlo) has puppet shows and the like.

Jazz bands play on summer evenings at *Kulturní dům Hroznová* on the corner of Hroznová and Palackého.

The *London Bar*, Chelčického 13, serves reasonable Guinness (39 Kč) in a cavernous pub-like space; it's closed Sunday.

Getting There & Away

Bus For shorter distances you're better off travelling by bus. Service to Brno (182km; four hours) is via Telč (100km; two hours).

A bus to Vienna's Mitte Bahnhof departs from the bus station on Friday, and to Linz (via Český Krumlov) on Wednesday and Saturday. In July and August this bus operates daily, except Sunday, with two onward buses to Salzburg. Pay the driver.

Train There are fast trains to Plzeň (136km; two hours), Tábor (66km; one hour), Prague (169km; 2½ hours) and Jihlava (132km; two hours).

Twice a day there are trains to and from Linz, Austria (125km; three hours). Three times a day you can go to Linz with a change of trains at the border stations (Horní Dvořiště and Summerau). Connections with trains between Prague and Vienna are made at České Velenice, 50km south-east of České Budějovice. One daily train runs directly to and from Vienna (Franz-Josefsbahnhof).

Getting Around

The city is well connected by bus. Services start winding down after 8 pm and stop by midnight. The main taxi stand (☎ 233 17) is at Lannova 1.

To rent a car, talk to Čedok or visit Europcar/Rekrea (☎ 731 22 90) at Široká 12 (closed weekends).

Bikes can be hired for 200 Kč a day at Fun Sport, just west of the stadium at Husova 43. The city centre's pedestrian zones are open to cyclists – just look out for pedestrians not looking where they're going. The cycle routes are in Geodézie's *České Budějovice* (1:20,000) map.

AROUND ČESKÉ BUDĚJOVICE

Dobrá Voda

On a hill east of České Budějovice is Dobrá Voda, with the Baroque-style Church of the Virgin of Sorrows (kostel Panny Marie Bolestné) designed by Kilian Ignatz Dientzenhofer. Local buses stop here irregularly; inquire at the tourist office.

Trocnov

Another easy trip is the village of Trocnov, 12km south-east of České Budějovice. This is the birthplace of Jan Žižka, the Hussite military leader, and it has a statue and a small museum dedicated to him. From Budějovice there are at least six daily buses.

Holašovice

South Bohemia is well known for its picturesque, 19th century 'folk Baroque' country houses and barns, which are ornately carved and sometimes richly painted. Some of the best examples are in the tiny village of Holašovice, 15km west of České Budějovice.

Traditionally, holidays and festivals have been celebrated in just such a setting, around a large square, complete with a pond and a chapel. Each spring maypoles are still erected in many village squares, to cele-

Jan Žižka

The Hussite Count Jan Žižka was born in Trocnov, just outside České Budějovice, in 1376. He spent his youth at King Wenceslas IV's court and fought as a mercenary in Poland, returned to the Czech kingdom at the beginning of the Reformation and became the leader of the Taborites (see the Tábor section). His brilliant military tactics were responsible for all the Hussite victories, from the 1420 battle of Žižkov onwards. Although losing both eyes in two separate battles, Žižka died not in battle but by catching the plague in 1424.

Žižka's army was highly organised and was the first to use a system of wagons with mounted artillery – the earliest tanks in history. These vehicles allowed him to choose where to draw up position, taking the initiative away from the crusaders and making them fight where he wanted. The technique proved almost invincible.

The Hussites successfully used their mobile artillery to subdue their enemies for a further 10 years, until the Taborites were defeated by the rival Hussite faction of the Utraquists in 1434. Surprisingly Žižka's invention was not incorporated into other armies until the Swedish king Gustavus II Adolphus adopted it two centuries later. ■

brate the end of winter – but the ponds are mostly neglected, polluted and weedy. There is nowhere to stay in Holašovice, and getting here without a car is virtually impossible.

Kratochvíle

This attractive Renaissance chateau was completed in 1589 for the Rožmberk family, and is decorated inside with stucco reliefs and murals based on classical mythology. Kratochvíle is also home to an interesting **Museum of Animated Film**, with examples from notable Czech producers like Jiří Trnka, Karel Zeman and Hermína Týrlová.

The chateau is open daily, except Monday, May through September from 9 am to noon and 1 to 5 pm, on weekends only in April and October; entry costs 20 Kč. Take a bus to Netolice from České Budějovice (one hour; seven daily) or Prachatice (30 minutes; four daily), and walk the remaining 1.5km.

HLUBOKÁ NAD VLTAVOU

The attraction of this small village (population 4800) 10km north of České Budějovice is its white castle, which is on a hill above the Vltava river and visible from afar. Hluboká Castle was built by the Přemysl rulers in the second half of the 13th century. In 1662 it was taken from the Protestant Malovec family for their support of an anti-Habsburg rebellion, and sold to the Bavarian Schwarzenbergs. It got its present appearance in 1871 and, with its many towers and neo-Gothic Tudor touches, is considered by most to be an imitation of Windsor castle. Architects sniff at the over-the-top Romanticism, but it is justly the second-most visited castle in Bohemia, after Karlštejn.

If summertime accommodation is tight in České Budějovice, consider spending a night or two in this peaceful village and visiting Budějovice on day trips.

Information

The information centre (☎ 96 53 29), opposite the church at Masarykovo 35, is open daily (except Monday, and November to March) to book hotels and pensions from 9 am to 4 pm. Česká spořitelna, Masarykovo 38, changes money and has a MasterCard/Visa ATM. Hluboká nad Vltavou's area code is ☎ 038.

Castle

The 45 minute tour of the heavily decorated interior includes Venetian glass chandeliers, Flemish tapestries, porcelain, weapons, hunting trophies, a library of 12,000 rare books, and incredible inlaid wood ceilings, walls and floors that took 40 years to complete. A tour in English or German costs 120 Kč, plus an extra 80 Kč for cameras. The castle is open daily, except Monday, as follows: 9 am to 4 pm in April and October, to 5 pm in May and September, and from 8 am to 5 pm from June through August. Unless the castle is extremely crowded, tours do not run from 12.30 to 1 pm (lunch time). For you intrepid off-season travellers, the castle grounds are open year-round, free of charge.

South Bohemian Aleš Gallery

This superb gallery – known to Czechs as the Alšova jihočeská galérie – is to the right of the castle gate, in a former riding school (*jízdárna*). On display is a permanent collection of Czech religious art from the 14th to 16th centuries, plus 17th century Dutch masters and changing exhibits of modern artists. It's open daily year-round, except Monday, from 9 to 11.30 am and noon to 4 pm (until 6 pm in summer); entry costs 15 Kč.

Places to Stay

The information centre can recommend private rooms. Also watch for '*Zimmer frei*' or '*privát*' signs along Masarykovo.

Autokemping Křivonovska (☎ 96 52 85), 3km north of Hluboká at Křivonovska, has bungalows for 200 Kč per person and is open from 15 May through September.

Just outside of town is the pleasant, clean *Penzion Club* (☎ 96 53 18), part of the

Sportovní areál tennis centre 1.5km east of the information centre (turn left out of the office, walk downhill to the main road and go left onto Podskalí). If it's not full a bed costs 300 Kč.

More central is the *Family Pension* (☎ 96 55 36) on 28.října, near the police station and past Hotel Bakalář. Doubles are 700 Kč.

Apartments Hluboká (☎ & fax 96 67 77), Masarykovo 972, has fully equipped rooms for 600 Kč per person. The adjacent *Hotel Bakalář* (☎ & fax 96 55 16) is overpriced at 1000/1260 Kč for a single/double room.

If money is no object, *Hotel Štekl* (☎ & fax 96 64 12), directly opposite the castle, has doubles that run the gamut from small (2650 Kč) to big (3050 Kč) to massive (4050 Kč).

Places to Eat

U Rozlů Bufet, at Masarykovo 38, is a basic stand-up spot with meals under 40 Kč. A good place for dumplings and beer is *Restaurace na Růžku*, at the east end of Masarykovo. More up-market (and touristy) is *Restaurant Eleonora*, on the road up to the castle; a full meal here costs about 150 Kč.

Getting There & Away

Buses run from České Budějovice to Hluboká's main square every 30 to 60 minutes. The town has two train stations with connections to České Budějovice; the Plzeň line stops at Hluboká nad Vltavou, 3km south-west of the castle, and the Prague line at Hluboká nad Vltavou-Zámostí, 2km east of the castle.

AROUND HLUBOKÁ

The Baroque **Ohrada Castle** is about 2km south-west of Hluboká, between Bezdrev and Vlunický lakes. Ohrada was originally a hunting lodge built for the Schwarzenbergs in 1715; now it's a museum of hunting and forestry, featuring wildlife, hunting trophies and some hideous furniture made from deer antlers. It's open daily, except Monday, April through October from 8.30 am to 6 pm; entry costs 30 Kč. Beside it, local species of animals are caged in a small zoo.

Public transport is not very regular, but the castle is a pleasant walk from Hluboká. Or see if Penzion Club has extra bicycles for hire.

ČESKÝ KRUMLOV

Český Krumlov is one of Europe's most beautiful towns, with a well-preserved historical centre that was added in 1992 to UNESCO's World Heritage List. Its castle is the second largest in the Czech Republic after Prague Castle – and just as dominant, high on a hill above the Vltava.

Český Krumlov looks stunning at night, when the hilltop castle is flooded with light and the old town's cobbled streets are shrouded in shadow. The only caveat is Krumlov's popularity: summertime crowds can be daunting, making accommodation a bit tight.

History

The town was first mentioned in writing in 1253, when the barons of Krumlov built the castle and ruled the area. In 1302 it came into the hands of the Rožmberks (see the Třeboň section later), and in the late 16th century Vilém Rožmberk rebuilt the castle in Renaissance style. The lords of Rožmberk, who were seated here, possessed the largest estate in Bohemia; it was later given to the Eggenbergs in 1622 and to the Schwarzenbergs in 1719, who owned the castle until 1945.

Despite expanding suburbs and industry, the town declined after WWII, and only in the last few years has an effort been made to restore the historical centre. Money, of course, is the main problem. In 1994-95 the municipal government put 250 houses up for sale – which represented an amazing 75% of all the structures built from the Middle Ages to the 17th century – with an eye to restoring the dog-eared old town with private funds.

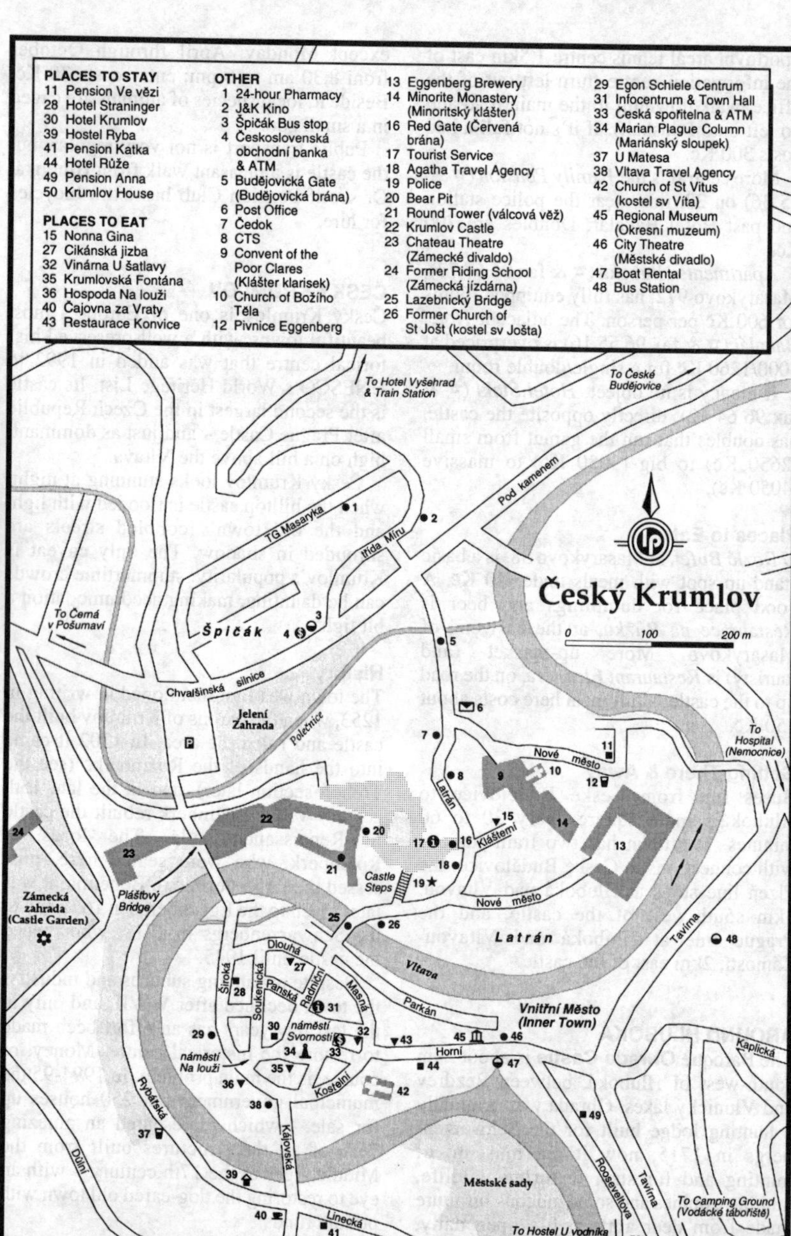
PLACES TO STAY
11 Pension Ve věži
28 Hotel Straninger
30 Hotel Krumlov
39 Hostel Ryba
41 Pension Katka
44 Hotel Růže
49 Pension Anna
50 Krumlov House
PLACES TO EAT
15 Nonna Gina
27 Cikánská jizba
32 Vinárna U šatlavy
35 Krumlovská Fontána
36 Hospoda Na louži
40 Čajovna za Vraty
43 Restaurace Konvice
OTHER
1 24-hour Pharmacy
2 J&K Kino
3 Špičák Bus stop
4 Československá obchodní banka & ATM
5 Budějovická Gate (Budějovická brána)
6 Post Office
7 Čedok
8 CTS
9 Convent of the Poor Clares (Klášter klarisek)
10 Church of Božího Těla
12 Pivnice Eggenberg
13 Eggenberg Brewery
14 Minorite Monastery (Minoritský klášter)
16 Red Gate (Červená brána)
17 Tourist Service
18 Agatha Travel Agency
19 Police
20 Bear Pit
21 Round Tower (válcová věž)
22 Krumlov Castle
23 Chateau Theatre (Zámecké divaldo)
24 Former Riding School (Zámecká jízdárna)
25 Lazebnický Bridge
26 Former Church of St Jošt (kostel sv Jošta)
29 Egon Schiele Centrum
31 Infocentrum & Town Hall
33 Česká spořitelna & ATM
34 Marian Plague Column (Mariánský sloupek)
37 U Matesa
38 Vltava Travel Agency
42 Church of St Vitus (kostel sv Víta)
45 Regional Museum (Okresní muzeum)
46 City Theatre (Městské divadlo)
47 Boat Rental
48 Bus Station
To Hotel Vyšehrad & Train Station
To České Budějovice
Pod kamenem
TG Masaryka
třída Míru
Český Krumlov
0 100 200 m
To Černá v Pošumaví
Špičák
Chvalšinská silnice
Jelení Zahrada
Polečnice
Nové město
Latrán
Klášterní
To Hospital (Nemocnice)
Castle Steps
Zámecká zahrada (Castle Garden)
Plášťový Bridge
Dlouhá
Široká
Soukenická
Panská
Radniční
Masná
Vltava
Parkán
náměstí Svornosti
náměstí Na louži
Horní
Kostelní
Vnitřní Město (Inner Town)
Tavírna
Kaplická
Rybářská
Kájovská
Dlouhá
Linecká
Rooseveltova
Městské sady
To Camping Ground (Vodácké tábořiště)
To Hostel U vodníka

Orientation

Conforming to the hills and the Vltava's bends, Český Krumlov has an irregular shape and steep, winding streets that make it a confusing place to navigate. The castle tower and Church of St Vitus are helpful landmarks.

From the main bus station it's a short walk west to the Inner Town (Vnitřní Město), centred on náměstí Svornosti. The Lazebnický Bridge (Lazebnický most) takes you to Latrán, a warren of shops and run-down townhouses beneath the castle.

The main train station is in the northern part of Český Krumlov, a steep 20 minute downhill walk to the castle (turn right from the station, take the first left and continue downhill on třída Míru).

Stay out of the city centre if you're driving, as parking is permit-only. There are public parking lots around the edges of the old town.

Information

Tourist Offices Infocentrum (☎ & fax 71 11 83), náměstí Svornosti 1, books accommodation (10% fee) and concert tickets, sells maps, and organises guided tours. You can even email the office with questions (ck-info@ck.bohem-net.cz). The office is open Monday to Saturday from 9 am to 5 pm.

Vltava Travel Agency (☎ & fax 71 19 78), Kájovská 62, books accommodation and arranges various sporting activities, such as fishing, canoeing etc. It's open daily from 9 am to 5 pm.

Tourist Service, Zámek 57, sells maps and provides town information, but it doesn't book accommodation. The same applies for Čedok (☎ 71 14 06), which is at Latrán 79.

Money The Česká spořitelna branch at náměstí Svornosti has a MasterCard ATM, changes travellers cheques and gives Visa cash advances. At Chvalšinská silnice, near the Špičák bus stop there is a branch of Československá obchodní banka, and it has a Visa ATM.

Post & Communications The telephone centre is in the post office at Latrán 81. It's open weekdays from 7 am to 6 pm and Saturday until 11 pm. Český Krumlov's area code is ☎ 0337.

Emergency The police (☎ 71 14 06) are located in the castle on Zámek. A hospital (*nemocnice*; ☎ 719 11) is at Hřbitovní 424, one block east of the bus station. The 24 hour pharmacy (*lékárna*; ☎ 3403) is on TG Masaryka, past the castle and towards the train station.

Latrán & Krumlov Castle

Krumlov Castle, the city's most photogenic sight, looms high above the old town. Approaching from below, cross the wooden **Lazebnický Bridge** (Lazebnický most) to Latrán and climb to the courtyard via the **Castle Steps** (Zámecké schody). A more traditional approach is from the north via **Budějovická Gate** (Budějovická brána; 1598); pass the post office and Čedok, and go through the **Red Gate** (Červená brána) into the castle's first courtyard.

Below the entrance bridge are three brown – and, frankly, unhappy – bears, traditional residents since the 16th century. Through a passageway are the second and third courtyards, covered in sgraffito. Between these is the ticket office.

There are two tours of the castle. The so-called 'Rožmberk Tour' is of the older parts, built by the Rožmberks; at the time of writing this tour was cancelled due to renovations, though you can still climb the multi-coloured **Round Tower** (válcová věž), painted in 1590 by Bartholomew Beránek, for 25 Kč.

The other tour takes in the Baroque and rococo sights, including the extraordinary **Masquerade Ballroom** (Maškarní sál), painted in 1748 with life-size figures enjoying themselves at a ball. The artist, one J Lederer, has painted himself by a window on the courtyard side, drinking a cup of coffee.

Just across the bridge behind the castle is the rococo **Chateau Theatre** (Zámecké divaldo; 1767), open only during performances. Behind this, a ramp to the right leads up to the former **Riding School** (Zámecká jízdárna), now a restaurant; note the Cherubs above the door offering the head and boots of a vanquished Turk. Above the school are the Italian-style **castle gardens**, which sprawl impressively and include the 'Bellarie' summer pavilion.

The castle is open daily, except Monday, as follows: in April and October from 9 am to noon and 1 to 3 pm, May through August to 5 pm, and in September to 4 pm. Admission is 100 Kč including the tour (English-language tours are offered erratically, so arrive early and inquire about the day's schedule).

Back outside in Latrán are a decaying **Minorite Monastery** (Minoritský klášter) and a former armoury, which is now the **Eggenberg Brewery**, built in 1630 and modernised with steam machinery in 1881. It's closed to the public, so grab a beer at its pub (see Entertainment).

Inner Town

Travelling south from the castle along Latrán you pass the former Church of St Jošt (kostel sv Jošta) on the way to Lazebnický Bridge, from where the Inner Town opens up. Turning right into Parkán takes you to Na ostrově, a small island with good views across the river to the castle.

Below the square is the **Egon Schiele Centrum**, in a former brewery at Široká 70. Open daily from 10 am to 6 pm, this private gallery, established in 1993, houses 50 watercolours and sketches by the Viennese painter Egon Schiele (1890-1918), who lived briefly in Krumlov in 1911, raising local hackles by hiring young girls as nude models. For this and other municipal sins he was eventually driven out. Entry costs a steep 100 Kč.

Continue on Široká and Na louži, and turn left to náměstí Svornosti, with its 16th century **town hall** (*radnice*) and **Marian Plague Column** (Mariánský sloupek), erected in 1716. Several houses have valuable stucco and painted decorations, such as the hotel at No 13 and the house at No 14.

Back at the square, follow Horní uphill and past Kostelní to the 14th century **Church of St Vitus** (kostel sv Víta). Its mixed Gothic and Baroque interior is worth

RICHARD NEBESKÝ

The Vltava almost completely encircles Český Krumlov's inner town a look. Continue on Horní past the 1588 **Jesuit College** (Jesuitská kolej), now housing the Hotel Růže.

Up on the left is the **Regional Museum** (Okresní muzeum), featuring folk art from the Šumava region, archaeology, history, fine arts, furnishings and weapons. The highlight is a room-size ceramic model of Český Krumlov as it was in 1800. The museum is open Tuesday to Friday from 9 am to noon and 12.30 to 4 pm, weekends from 1 to 4 pm; entry costs 20 Kč.

Activities

In summer you can rent boats from an outlet at Myší díra, below Hotel Růže. Canoes and small rubber rafts are available from 300 to 700 Kč per day. It is possible to do trips to Lake Lipno, Vyšší Brod and České Budějovice; inquire at the Vltava Travel Agency (see Tourist Offices earlier).

Hotel Růže rents bicycles, and it's a pleasant two hour ride south-west to Lake Lipno, involving a climb then a drop to the lake and a great downhill run on the way back.

Special Events

Infocentrum sells tickets to major festivals, including the International Music Festival in late July and early August, and the Folk Music Festival in mid-September. The Pětilisté růže (Five-Petalled Rose) Festival in mid-June features three days of street performances, parades and medieval games.

Places to Stay

Camping A *camping ground* is on the right (east) bank of the Vltava, about 2km south of town. The facilities are basic (no showers) but the management is friendly, the location idyllic and the price (25 Kč per person) reasonable. It's open from June to August. The staff organise one-hour canoe trips down the river.

Hostels The *U vodníka* (☎ 71 19 35), Po vodě 55, is situated right next to the Vltava in a street below Rooseveltova. Space in one of two four-bed dorms is 180 Kč per person, or in one of three double rooms for 250 Kč per person. Cooking facilities are available, there's a small English library and a nice garden out the back.

The affiliated and similarly priced *Krumlov House* (☎ 5675), nearby at Rooseveltova 68, has a study area and a washing machine.

The intimate *Hostel Ryba* (☎ 71 18 01), at Rybářská 5, has 16 dorm beds priced at 180 Kč each. It's on a footpath overlooking the Vltava.

All three hostels are open year-round.

Private Rooms & Pensions Expect to pay between 400 Kč and 500 Kč per person for a private room, often with breakfast included. Inquire at Infocentrum, the Vltava Travel Agency, CTS (☎ 5781) at Latrán 67, or Agatha Agency (☎ 71 15 30) at Latrán 44. If all else fails, Rooseveltova near the bus station is chock-a-block with pensions.

Pension Anna (☎ & fax 71 16 92), at Rooseveltova 41, has large doubles for 950 Kč and a sunny terrace.

Pension Na věži (☎ & fax 71 17 42), Nové město 28, is in a Gothic tower with handsome – if oddly shaped – doubles for 1000 Kč.

The best bargain is *Pension Katka* (☎ 71 19 02) at Linecká 51, priced at 500/900 Kč for a single/double.

Hotels *Hotel Vyšehrad* (☎ 5311), a three storey inn on a hill north of town between the train station and the city centre, has single/double rooms with shower at 650/1100 Kč.

Good value in the old town is *Hotel Straninger* (☎ & fax 2276), Široká 49, with doubles only for 1500 Kč.

The atmospheric *Hotel Krumlov* (☎ 71 15 65), on náměstí Svornosti, has fully equipped rooms for 1000/1550 Kč.

The expensive *Hotel Růže* (☎ 71 11 41; fax 71 11 28), Horní 153, is in a Jesuit college dating from 1588. Rooms are 1490/2380 Kč.

Places to Eat

For cheap eats try *Krumlovská Fontána*, náměstí Svornosti 8, a Czech-style buffet with early hours (from 7 am; closed Sunday).

Hearty, cheap pub grub is no problem at the boisterous *Cikánská jizba*, Dlouhá 31. The szeged goulash is tops.

Vinárna U šatlavy, on Šatlavská just off náměstí Svornosti, was once the town jail, and the medieval setting seems to enhance the flavour of its home-made sausages, cheese and wine.

Hospoda Na louži, on náměstí Na louži, is less smoky than most pubs and serves good South Bohemian meals for around 150 Kč.

Krumlov's best pizzas and pastas come from *Nonna Gina*, Klášterní 52.

A good splurge is *Restaurace Konvice*, attached to the hotel of the same name at Horní 144.

Cafés One spot deserves special mention, the peaceful *Čajovna za Vraty*, Rybářská 40, with its range of teas and light snacks. It's closed Monday.

Entertainment

There are occasional plays at the castle theatre and in the castle gardens, plus frequent classical music at the *City Theatre* (Městské divadlo); check with Infocentrum.

U matesa, on Rybářská, is ideal for a quiet late-night drink. At the other extreme is *Pivnice Eggenberg*, a bacchanal beer hall attached to the brewery, with a pool table upstairs.

J&K Kino, on třída Míru, screens films daily in summer.

Getting There & Away

About eight local trains a day run from České Budějovice, a one hour trip. Buses run all day from České Budějovice (40 minutes) and about 10 times a day from Rožmberk nad Vltavou (45 minutes). From Prague the train takes about four hours, with a change at České Budějovice. Buses are slightly pricier and half an hour faster.

AROUND ČESKÝ KRUMLOV

The nature reserve of **Blanskÿ les** is good hiking territory, particularly near the summit of the **Kleť** (1083m), which boasts fine views of the Šumava region. In winter it is a ski resort. A year-round chair lift climbs to the summit from the carpark above Krasetín, which is a 2km walk from Holubov, where the Český Krumlov-České Budějovice train stops.

Kleť can also be reached on foot via a green-marked trail from near Český Krumlov's main train station. Other trails are marked on Kartografie Praha's *Českobudějovicko* (1:100,000) map.

ZLATÁ KORUNA

Above the Vltava in the wee village of Zlatá Koruna is one of the country's best-preserved Gothic structures, a Cistercian monastery (Cisterciácký klášter) founded in 1263 by Přemysl Otakar II to demonstrate his power in the region.

Originally called the Saintly Crown of Thorns, the monastery in later, wealthier days was renamed the Gold Crown (Zlatá Koruna). The monastery cathedral (*konventní chrám*), completed at the end of the 13th century, is clearly Gothic in spite of its Baroque face-lift. The walled complex also houses a **Museum of South Bohemian Literature** (Památník písemnictví jižních Čech).

The entire complex – entered at the rear through a functioning convent – is open daily, except Monday, April through October from 8.30 am to 4.30 pm. A mandatory guided tour costs 30 Kč.

Places to Stay & Eat

There are private rooms here and in the adjacent village of Rájov (which also has the *Restaurace Na kovárně*), a 1.5km downhill walk.

About 50m before the monastery is *Ubytovna Zlatá Koruna* (☎ 0337-841 31), housed in the House of Culture & Sport (dům Kultury a tělevýchovy). Its dorms are open from June through August, and cost 200 Kč a bed.

CZECH REPUBLIC

Across the bridge at the bottom of town is the basic *Zlatá Koruna Autocamp*, open from May through September. The adjacent *Česka CK* (☎ 038-798 89 36) organises canoe and kayaking trips.

The only restaurant as such is the *Koruna*, opposite the monastery and open from 3 to 10 pm (closed Tuesday).

Getting There & Away

Bus is easiest from Český Krumlov. Six a day make the 20 minute trip. Less frequent ones come from České Budějovice.

Many local trains on the České Budějovice-Český Krumlov line stop at Srní, which is a 20 minute walk from Zlatá Koruna.

AROUND ZLATÁ KORUNA

The brawny, ruined **Dívčí kámen**, a castle on an outcrop above the Vltava, was founded by the Rožmberks in 1349 but abandoned in 1541. It's an easy 4km walk on a red-marked trail by the river, north from Zlatá Koruna. There's nowhere to stay here. Trains stop at nearby Třišov.

TŘEBOŇ

This spa town of about 9000 people has a picturesque old section with most of its defensive walls still standing. The narrow main square has some fine Baroque and Renaissance façades, and Třeboň's castle is worth a look, but a one day visit is plenty. Even residents admit their town is known mainly for the flavoursome local fish and another delicacy, Regent beer.

The area was settled during the 12th century and a castle was established by the Rožmberks in 1374. The town's greatest growth came around the turn of the 16th century under Petr Vok, the last of the Rožmberk line, and his brother Vilém. In 1660 it became the property of the Schwarzenbergs. In the 17th and 18th centuries the town suffered from wars and fires.

Orientation

Old Třeboň can only be entered through its three venerable gates. From the main square, Masarykovo náměstí, it's easy to find your bearings.

The main train station is north-west of the old town, a 20 minute walk or a local bus ride away. There's also a smaller station on the same line, 10 minutes by foot north-east. The main bus station is 20 minutes due west, off Svobody.

Information

The Municipal Information Centre (Informační středisko; ☎ 72 11 69) at Masarykovo náměstí 146 can help with private accommodation. The map to get for this region is Klub českých turistů Praha's *Třeboňsko* (1:50,000).

Change money or use the MasterCard/Visa ATM at Česká spořitelna at Masarykovo náměstí 100. The main post office is at Seifertova 588. Třeboň's area code is ☎ 0333.

Around Masarykovo Náměstí

The main attractions are the Renaissance and Baroque houses on the square and within the town walls, which date from 1527. Don't miss the **town hall** and the **House at the White Horse** (dům U bílého koníčka) on the square, and **St Giles Church** (kostel sv Jiljí) and the **Augustine Monastery** (Augustinský klášter) on Husova. On Trcnovské náměstí the run-down **brewery** (*pivovar*) has been home to Regent beer, one of Bohemia's oldest and best beers, since 1379. Unfortunately it's closed to the public.

Třeboň Castle

The castle (*zámek*), recently renovated, includes a museum with a small collection of furniture and porcelain. The mandatory guided tour (20 Kč) also includes a grand chamber filled with Rožmberk arms. Enter through a gate (opposite Březanova) from Masarykovo náměstí or via the courtyard off Rožmberská. The ticket office is in the tower. The castle itself is open daily, except Monday, May through August from 9 am to 5 pm, and on weekends only to 4 pm in April and September through October.

CZECH REPUBLIC

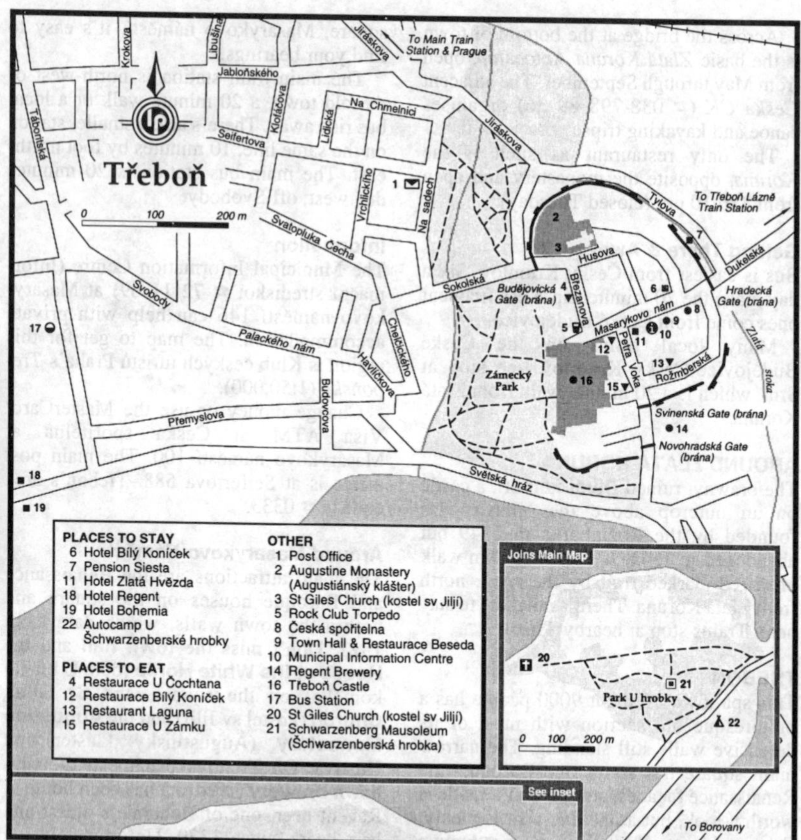

Schwarzenberg Mausoleum

Many Schwarzenbergs have taken their last rest in this 1877 neo-Gothic tomb in the Park U hrobky, on the other side of the pond from Třeboň. It's a pleasant area for a picnic, especially if you strike a sunny day. Take note that cycling is prohibitedin the park.

Entry to the Schwarzenberg Mausoleum (Švarcenberská hrobka) costs 15 Kč and it's open daily, except Monday, May through September from 9 to 11.30 am and 1 to 4 pm.

Places to Stay

Pickings are slim here. The cheapest is *Autocamp U Schwarzenberské hrobky* (☎ 2586), south of town near the Schwarzenberg Mausoleum, on the road to Borovany. Bungalows are 200 Kč per person. Otherwise inquire at the information office about private rooms, which start at 300 Kč per person.

A good choice in town is *Pension Siesta* (☎ 2324), on Tylova overlooking a canal. Rooms in this big green house are 380 Kč per bed.

Třeboň's cheapest hotel is the *Bílý Koníček* (☎ & fax 72 11 23), which is on Masarykovo náměstí, built in 1544. Smallish but reasonable rooms cost 490/700 Kč for a single/double. Also on the square is *Hotel Zlatá Hvězda*, temporarily closed at the time of writing.

A 20 minute walk from town and on opposite sides of the road are the mediocre *Hotel Regent* and *Hotel Bohemia*, which, oddly enough, share the same phone line (☎ 72 13 94). Both charge about 1000/1500 Kč.

Places to Eat

The hotel *Bílý Koníček* is a pleasant restaurant with Czech and international meals; the fish dishes are worth trying.

Restaurace Beseda, with an entrance through the town hall, and *Restaurace U Zámku* at Žižkovo náměstí 51, are simple and popular. Also, the Beseda has a wine bar, the *Bluegrassland vinárna*, attached to it, which is open until 2 am.

The more up-market *Restaurace U Čochtana* at Březanova 7 is open daily to 11 pm. A similar spot is the *Restaurant Laguna* on Rožmberská.

Entertainment

In summer the *Rock Club Torpedo*, on Masarykovo náměstí, doubles as a rowdy bar and late-night disco.

Getting There & Away

Bus is best from České Budějovice (25 minutes; about every hour) and Jindřichův Hradec (30 minutes; nine a day). Třeboň is a stop on the daily Prague-Tábor-Vienna railway line. On a local train from Tábor, you must normally change at Veselí nad Lužnicí; the whole trip from Tábor takes about an hour.

AROUND TŘEBOŇ

A good **forest walk** begins at Masarykovo náměstí, following a green-marked trail east out of Třeboň. This joins a blue-marked trail that runs north-east to Na kopečku, past Rožmberk Pond, through Stará Hlína to Hodějov Pond. From here a yellow trail runs west to Smítka, where it joins a red trail heading north to Klec and a primitive campsite.

From there, for nearly 20km, the red trail runs north, past more ponds, forests and small villages to Veselí nad Lužnicí, a major railway junction. Camping is allowed only in official campsites throughout the protected landscape region.

Šumava

The Šumava (Böhmerwald in German) is a heavily wooded mountain region stretching for about 125km along the border with Austria and Germany. Its importance lies in its large, tranquil, thinly populated forests, which are relatively undamaged by acid rain. Although only one small patch, the Boubín Virgin Forest (Boubínský prales), is regarded as completely untouched, the Šumava's overall pristine state makes it a unique asset.

The Boubín Virgin Forest region has been a nature reserve since 1858. The 1630 sq km Šumava Protected Landscape Region (Chráněná krajinná oblast, or CHKO) was established in 1963. In 1990 UNESCO declared this a biospheric reservation. The adjacent Bavarian Forest gained this status in 1981, and together they comprise central Europe's largest forest complex. In April 1991, 685 sq km of the CHKO became the Šumava National Park (Národní park Šumava). This and the CHKO now make up the biggest single state-protected area in the Czech and Slovak republics.

The Šumava – actually two rounded ranges with high plains and moors between them – are among the oldest mountains in the Czech Republic. The highest point is the 1456m Grosser Arber (Velký Javor to Czechs) on the Bavarian side; the highest peak on the Czech side is Plechý (1378m), west of Horní Planá.

The mighty Vltava rises in the Šumava,

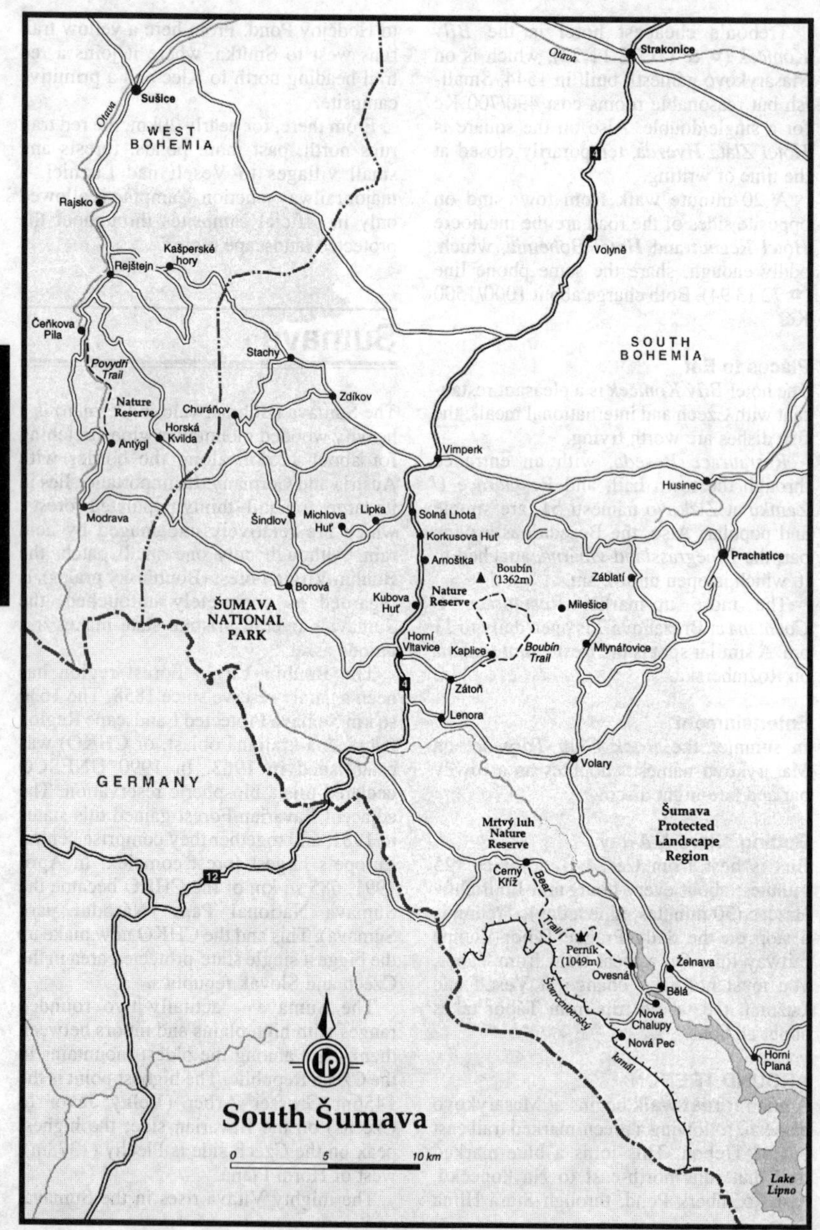
Strakonice
Otava
Sušice
Otava
WEST BOHEMIA
4
Rajsko
Volyně
Kašperské hory
Rejštejn
Čeňkova Pila
SOUTH BOHEMIA
Stachy
Povydří Trail
Zdíkov
Nature Reserve
Churáňov
Horská Kvilda
Antýgl
Vimperk
Husinec
Modrava
Šindlov
Michlova Huť
Lipka
Solná Lhota
Korkusova Huť
Prachatice
Arnoštka
Boubín (1362m)
Záblatí
Borová
Nature Reserve
Milešice
ŠUMAVA NATIONAL PARK
Kubova Huť
Horní Vltavice
Kaplice
Boubín Trail
Mlynářovice
4
Zátoň
Lenora
Volary
GERMANY
Šumava Protected Landscape Region
Mrtvý luh Nature Reserve
12
Černý Kříž
Bear Trail
Perník (1049m)
Ovesná
Želnava
Bělá
Nová Chalupy
Švarcenberský kanál
Nová Pec
Horní Planá
South Šumava
0
5
10 km
Lake Lipno

as do five other major rivers. The five major lakes are Plešné, Prášilské, Mláka, Čertovo and Černé, which is the largest at 18.4 hectares, and 39m deep. Two canals, the Vchynický and Schwarzenberg, built in the early 1800s to transport logs, sadly scar the region.

The only wildlife left behind by past hunting are birds, though deer have been re-introduced. Otters, owls and lynx are also staging a comeback.

Most of the Šumava is now open for trekking (*turistika*). The mountainous terrain rules out cycling on most hiking trails, though the many dirt roads are good for an adventurous and challenging ride. There are also many possibilities for boating.

Czechs and Bavarians appreciate the Šumava for skiing and ski-touring, the most popular areas being Železná Ruda, Špičák and Hojsova Stráž in the west, and Zadov, Churáňov and the Lipno Lake area in the east. The weather is cooler and wetter than in the rest of South Bohemia.

Part of the attraction for Czechs is undoubtedly their interest in the unknown – this was a closed border area during the Communist years. As in other parts of the former Eastern bloc, the Šumava border was a virtual prison-camp fence – two rows of electrified barbed wire, with a strip of earth between them that was regularly turned to show any fresh footprints. Most habitations near this border were either demolished or abandoned. The electrified fences are gone now, but some concrete bunkers, built in the 1920s against a possible German invasion, remain.

Maps

The best hiking map is Klub českých turistů's *Šumava* (1:50,000), which includes elevations, marked trails, all roads, types of accommodation, plus a legend that includes English. A must for cyclists is ShoCart's *Šumava Trojmezí velká cyclo-turistická* (1:75,000) map. Both are available at regional tourist offices and bookshops.

Getting There & Away

There are several train routes into the Šumava, such as from Plzeň and Klatovy, Strakonice or České Budějovice. Another rail option might be from the German side.

NATIONAL PARK WALKS

Of the many trails to choose from, we list only three here; it's easy to devise your own walk with the help of the maps. A very long but interesting walk is along most of the length of the national park, from Nová Pec, at the northern tip of Lake Lipno, up to Nýrsko, south-west of Klatovy.

The national park must be entered on designated trails, with camping only at designated sites. Fires can only be lit at those campsites. The colour-coded trails are well marked with distance and walking-time information. If you pass a trail intersection and don't see a marker within about 300m, return to the intersection and try again. Also note that some parts of the reserve are totally off-limits: watch for signs proclaiming '*Vystup zakázán*' (do not enter).

Bear Trail

A recommended walk is along the Bear Trail (Medvědí stezka) past Bear Rock (Medvědí kámen), where the last bear in Bohemia was killed in 1856. This is the oldest walking trail in the Šumava. It starts at the Ovesná train stop and ends at a train stop in Černý Kříž (Black Cross), 14km and six hours later. There's a pension here in case you're dead-tired. Part of the going is hard, along rocky formations of the Jelení vrchy and up to the 1049m summit of Perníku. Avoid this section in bad weather.

The trail continues past Deer Lake (Jelení jezírko), Jelení village, the Schwarzenberg Canal and tunnel, Medvědí kámen memorial (engraved *Bären Stein*, and about 50m off the trail), and along Hučivý stream into Černý Kříž.

Povydří

One of the Šumava's best trails is along the Vydra river, especially in the area called Povydří, between Čeňkova Pila and Antýgl.

Vydra means 'otter', and the river got its name from the many otters that used to live in it. Today only a few otters live high up in the mountains because their main food supply, the trout, can no longer live in the river (fertilisers used in nearby fields have made the water too acidic).

Starting at Čeňkova Pila, the trail goes along the Vydra to Modrava, taking you past Turnerova hut (*chata*), Antýgl, the right side of the Vchnicko-tetovský Canal, Rokyta and finally to Modrava. This is an easy and very scenic 14km trail, taking about five hours. It is also possible to start farther down the river at Rejštejn.

Boubínský Prales

The 46 hectare Boubín Virgin Forest, around the peak of Boubín (1362m), was one of the world's first nature reserves, founded in 1858. Beech, spruce and pine predominate, with some trees estimated at over 400 years old. Much of the original 138 hectares of forest was destroyed by a windstorm in 1870. Ironically, these centuries-old trees have been left alone due to damage by coring beetles; the forest itself is out of bounds to visitors.

If you have a car, the easiest approach is via the carpark at Kaplice, where there is a basic campsite. From here it's an easy 2.5km to U pralesa lake, on a green and then blue trail. In July and August there is a snack kiosk at the lake. To reach Boubín, stay on the blue trail along the boundary of Boubín prales. After 6km you reach Křížova Smrč, and from there it's 1.5km to the top of Boubín.

A longer and more enjoyable walk is between Kubova Huť and the zastávka Zátoň train stop (not Zátoň town, which is 2km away). The trail is 17.5km long and, from Kubova Huť, passes Johnův kámen, Boubín, Křížová Smrč, Boubín Forest, U pralesa lake and the Kaplice campsite before terminating at the Zátoň train stop. Give yourself at least five hours.

Places to Stay & Eat

In dreary Volary, doubles at *Hotel Bobík* (☎ 0338-92 53 51), a monstrous high-rise in the town centre, are 680 Kč. Far better is *Pension Kukačka* (☎ 038-922 32) at Česká 76, two blocks behind the Bobík.

Lenora's pensions are hard to find from the train station (head 10 minutes downhill to the main road). The best bet in this peaceful village is *Zámeček Hotel Lenora* (☎ 0339-988 61), with doubles in a former hunting lodge for 720 Kč; the restaurant here is also good. Across the road is *Pension Lenora* (☎ 0339-988 13), priced at 290 Kč per person.

In Zátoň try *Penzion Boubín* (☎ 0339-981 81) at 250 Kč per bed, or the similarly priced *Pension Zátoň* (☎ 0339-981 09).

In Horní Vltavice, *Hostinec u Vltavy* (☎ 0339-981 02) charges 300 Kč per bed. Nearby, *Autokemp Horní Vltavice* is open from May through September and also has cottages.

Little Kubova Huť is a ski resort in winter, and the large *Hotel Armika* (☎ 0339-987 26) has single/double rooms with TV, shower and WC for 1100/1550 Kč, with free use of their tennis courts, swimming pool, sauna and mountain bikes. The same hotel's *Pension Hubert* is 880/1100 Kč with breakfast.

At Rejštejn you can try *Pension Kizek* (☎ 0187-92 25 27) or the basic and cheaper *Turistická ubytovna Klášterský mlýn*. Farther on at Čeňkova Pila is *Pension Bystřina* (☎ 0187-992 21) and a basic *campsite*. In Antýgl there is only the *Autocamp Antýgl*, open from May to October. In Modrava there is *Penzion Arnika* (☎ 0187-993 49) and a basic *campsite*.

Getting There & Away

Up to 10 trains a day run between Volary and Strakonice, stopping at Lenora and two other stations – zastávka Zátoň and Horní Vltavice, both of which are several kilometres from their respective towns (Kubova Hut' and Vimperk). From Volary you can get a train to Prachatice (40 minutes) or Horní Planá (35 minutes).

Buses also cover these routes, less frequently. On weekdays there are five runs on the very scenic 21km Vimperk to Lenora route, via Kubova Hut' and Horní Vltavice. Between Sušice and Modrava a bus runs four times a day, less on weekends.

Border Crossings There are border crossings to Germany south of Vimperk. A 24 hour vehicle and pedestrian crossing at Strážný, to Phillippsreuth, can be reached by local bus from Horní Vltavice. Another at Stožec, to Haidmühle, is for pedestrians and cyclists only, and is open from 9 am to 9 pm. A third option is the pedestrian-only crossing from Nové Údolí to Dreisessel, but is closed from November through March.

ROŽMBERK NAD VLTAVOU

This beautifully positioned hilltop castle dominates the quiet village and valley below – the castle makes for a spectacular sight when reflected in the Vltava. Rožmberk has yet to be overtaken by tourism, and though accommodation here is sparse, consider spending a night far from the madding crowd.

The so-called Upper Castle, built in the mid-13th century, was destroyed by fire in 1522; the only reminder today is the crumbling **Jakobín Tower** in the trees above. The 1330s **Lower Castle** was rebuilt in Renaissance style in the 1550s. It's said to be haunted by a ghost called the White Lady (Bílá paní), the long-suffering wife of one of the Rožmberks.

After the Battle of the White Mountain the castle came into the hands of the Buquoy family. All the paintings, sculpture, porcelain, furniture, weapons and some particularly nasty torture instruments are all from their era. The treat of the tour is the **Banquet Hall**, covered in 16th century Italian frescoes. One fresco, behind a grille, is encrusted with jewels confiscated during the Thirty Years' War.

The castle is open daily, except Monday, June through August from 9 am to 4.15 pm, to 3.15 pm in May and September, and on weekends only to 3.15 pm in April and October. Entry costs 50 Kč, including a mandatory tour (usually in Czech).

Places to Stay & Eat

The village below has some private rooms starting from 350 Kč per person. Also try asking at local restaurants, some of which offer B&B lodging in summer.

Pension U mostu (☎ 0337-9834) was temporarily closed for renovations when we visited, but was due to reopen in summer 1998. In the same building is the popular *Zámecká restaurace.* Also try *Restaurace-Pension U Vltavy* (☎ & fax 0337-74 98 35), with singles/doubles for 700/900 Kč.

If you have your own transport, stay at the excellent *Hotel Studenec* (☎ & fax 0337-74 98 18), 1.5km out on the road to Český Krumlov. Rooms are 470 Kč per person, 570 Kč with breakfast. It also hires out canoes and bikes. Beyond the Hotel Studenec is the primitive *Tábořiště U bílého mostu* campsite, which is only open in summer.

Serious horse-lovers should contact *Dvůr Metlice* (☎ 0337-74 98 14; fax 74 98 73), 2.5km from Rožmberk. All-inclusive, week-long riding and camping trips start at 13,500 Kč per person.

Getting There & Away

About 10 buses a day come from Český Krumlov, a 45 minute trip, continuing on to Vyšší Brod.

VYŠŠÍ BROD

The town is known for the Cistercian monastery around which it grew, though it has some worthy late-Gothic and Baroque buildings of its own. Rather than make a special trip, stop (along with hordes of Austrian day-shoppers) on the way someplace else. It's only 8km to the Austrian border and 24km to Český Krumlov.

Cistercian Monastery

This fortified monastery was founded by Vok Rožmberk in 1259, though it was not completed until the late 14th century. It successfully withstood two Hussite assaults in the 15th century. Later owners were the Eggenbergs and, in the 18th century, the Schwarzenbergs. It was closed by the Com-

CZECH REPUBLIC

munists in 1950 and its monks imprisoned. After half a century of neglect major repairs began in 1990.

Today it has one of Bohemia's finest Gothic buildings, the **Chapter House** (Kapitulní síň), completed in 1285, its roof supported by a single pillar. A highlight is its 70,000 volume library, founded with the monastery. The Large Library Hall is entered by a secret door through a bookcase in the Small Library Hall. Note the gold-leaf rococo ceiling.

The monastery is open daily except Monday, May through September from 8.30 to 11.30 am and 12.30 to 5 pm, and to 4 pm in April and October. The mandatory tour costs 50 Kč.

CZECH REPUBLIC

Places to Stay & Eat

There are two *campsites*, one between the monastery and the river and one above the monastery, both with bungalows and both open from May through September.

At the top end of the main square, Hotel Šumava (% 0337-74 65 74) charges 250 Kč per person; the adjoining beer hall is smoky but otherwise OK. At the square's lower end, Hotel Panský dům (% 0337-926 69) is a step up in comfort, with doubles for 600 Kč.

A good spot for lunch is the *Restaurace U candrů*, which is on the main square at No 36.

Getting There & Away

The town is on a rail spur, 20 minutes from Rybník, which is on the well-serviced České Budějovice-Austria line. There are about 10 trains a day from Rybník, and it's about 1¼ hours from there to České Budějovice.

Frymburk-bound buses run about 10 times a day from Český Krumlov via Rožmberk nad Vltavou to Vyšší Brod (one hour).

Border Crossings Two 24-hour vehicle and pedestrian crossings to Austria are near Vyšší Brod: Studánky to Weigetschlag, and Dolní Dvořiště to Wullowitz.

LAKE LIPNO

Lipno Lake, the largest artificial body of water in the Czech Republic, backs up behind a dam 8km west of Vyšší Brod. The whole area is a popular – but frankly mediocre – summer resort for Czechs and Germans. Its main attractions are water sports and walking.

Orientation

The largest town along the lake is Horní Planá, a major centre with accommodation, shops and transport. The smaller towns of Frymburk and Černá v Pošumaví can also be used as bases to explore the area.

Information

In Horní Planá, KIC Infocentrum (☎ 976 98), náměstí 8, sells hiking and cycling maps, arranges accommodation, and fields most transport questions. It's open week-days from 9 am to 4 pm.

The local area code is ☎ 0337.

Places to Stay & Eat

Along the lakefront, especially the eastern shore, there are literally dozens of camp-sites and pensions, but few hotels. Without a booking in July or August, your only hope is a campsite, most of which open from May through September. Everybody drops their prices outside the summer season.

Horní Planá Two campsites are on the road to the ferry dock, about 1km from the main square: *Autocamping U pláže* (☎ 972 35), with two-person bungalows for 800 Kč, and *Caravancamp na Pláži*, 100m farther along.

Three good pensions line Horní Planá's main square: *Pension-Restaurace Inka* (☎ 974 05), *Pension Paula* (☎ 972 29) and the basic *Hotel Smrčina* (☎ 972 28). All three charge about 550/1000 Kč for a single/double.

Černá v Pošumaví *Pension Rex* (☎ 961 42), on the edge of this small village by the lake, charges 500/950 Kč. The adjacent *Autokemping Olšinách* (☎ 961 87) has bun-galows for 400 Kč per person.

Frymburk Expensive *Camping Frymburk* (☎ 952 84), on the north edge of town, charges about 50% more than other campsites in the Lipno area. On Frymburk's main square try *Restaurace-Pension Markus* (☎ 954 18) at 550 Kč per person, or the deluxe *Hotel Maxant* (☎ & fax 952 29) at 650/1150 Kč.

Getting There & Away

Up to six trains a day travel from České Budějovice (two hours away) to the Volary stop at Horní Planá. From Volary, trains go to Prachatice (40 minutes) and beyond seven times a day.

About 10 buses per day go along the lake from Horní Planá through Černá v Pošumaví, Frymburk and Lipno nad Vltavou. Many continue to Český Krumlov (1¼ hours).

Getting Around

Apart from local buses, ferries make regular crossings from Horní Planá, Dolní Vltavice and Frymburk, for about 10 Kč per person and 50 Kč per car. From June to September there is a boat service from Lipno nad Vltavou to Horní Planá via Přední Výtoň, Frymburk and Černá v Pošumaví.

PRACHATICE

Embedded among the modern streets of Prachatice is one of the best-preserved Renaissance old towns in Bohemia, surrounded by an almost unbroken 14th century fortification. You can easily take in all the sights, including the worthwhile city museum, in a few hours.

The town of Prachatice was founded in 1325 as a trading post along the important Golden Trail (Zlatá stezka), bringing salt from Bavaria in return for Czech grain. Hussites under General Jan Žižka conquered it in 1420; as a reward for its later return to the royalist fold in 1436, King Sigismund made it a royal town.

After a fire in 1507, Prachatice, by then in the hands of the Rožmberks, was rebuilt. Most of the Renaissance structures to be seen today come from that time. Petr Vok, the last of the Rožmberks, sold it to Rudolf II in 1601, but the town sided with the Protestants during the rebellion of the Czech nobles, and in 1620 it was heavily damaged by one of Rudolf II's generals, Buquoy. During the rule of later aristocratic families Prachatice stagnated, though one result of the neglect was the survival of the town walls.

Orientation

The main train station is at the end of Nádražní, the continuation of Zvolenská, a 10 minute walk east of the old town. The main bus station is a bit closer, at the corner of Nádražní and Nebahovská.

The old town is a pedestrian zone. The only carpark is at the north end of Velké náměstí.

Information

Tourist Offices Infocentrum (☎ 225 63), inside the City Theatre, can book accommodation weekdays from 7.30 am to 4 pm. For transport tickets try Čedok (☎ 225 31) at Zvolenská 30.

Money Investiční banka at Velké náměstí 7 has a foreign-exchange desk.

Post & Communications The post and telephone office is at the corner of Pivovarská and Malé náměstí; Prachatice's area code is ☎ 0338.

Things to See

As you come from either the bus or train station, along Zvolenská and Malé náměstí, in front of you are the 14th century **town walls**, beefed up in 1620. On the left is the **Chapel of St John of Nepomuk** (kaple sv Jana Nepomuckého).

Enter the old town and historic Velké náměstí through the **Lower Gate** (Písecká brána). Through the gate, on the left, behind the heavily decorated Heydl House (Heydlův dům) at No 30, is the 16th century **Literary School** (Literátská škola), where Jan Hus is said to have studied.

In front of you is the 14th century **St**

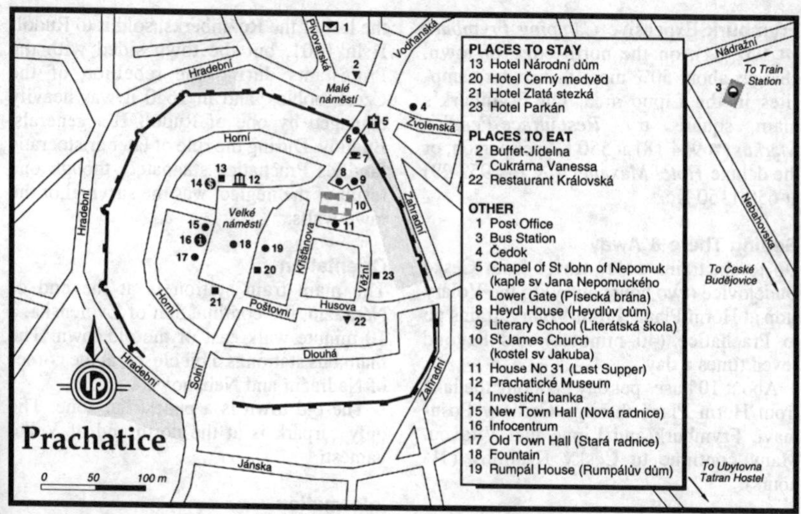

James Church (kostel sv Jakuba), with a little park behind it. The house on the south side at No 31 bears a sgraffito depicting the Last Supper.

At Velké náměstí 41 is **Rumpál House** (Rumpálův dům), a former brewery covered with Renaissance battle scenes. Opposite are the **Old Town Hall** (Stará radnice; 1571) and the neo-Renaissance **New Town Hall** (Nová radnice; 1903), both covered in sgraffito.

At No 13 is the **Prachatické Museum**, built as a palace in 1572 by the Rožmberks; it still has the town's finest façade, plus a collection of arms and old postcards (closed Monday). Entry costs 15 Kč.

Special Events

Prachatice goes fairly wild during the mid-June Golden Path Celebration (Slavnosti zlaté stezky), with medieval costumes, fencing tournaments and fireworks. An annual folk music festival is held on the last Saturday in February.

Places to Stay & Eat

Infocentrum can help with private rooms (from 300 Kč per person). Cheapest in town is the summer-only *Ubytovna Tatran* hostel (☎ 234 74) in the stadium on U stadionu, for about 170 Kč per bed.

At Velké náměstí 169, the *Hotel Národní dům* (☎ 215 61) has doubles for 480 Kč without shower and 640 Kč with, and an adequate restaurant. Reception is open from noon to 6 pm.

Hotel Zlatá stezka (☎ 218 41), across the square, has doubles with shower and WC for 515 Kč, and with shower only for 420 Kč.

A step up in quality is the *Hotel Černý medvěd* (☎ 235 09) at Velké náměstí 42, with single/double rooms priced at 600/1100 Kč.

The deluxe *Hotel Parkán* (☎ & fax 218 68), Věžní 51, charges 800/1250 Kč. The terrace here is a good spot for a beer.

Buffet-Jídelna, on Malé náměstí, is fine for a quick, cheap breakfast. The popular *Restaurant Královská*, Husova 106, has good southern Bohemian dishes for 60 to 260 Kč. For coffee and some cake by the town walls try *Cukrárna Vanessa,* at Kostelní náměstí 28.

Getting There & Away
Prachatice is on a minor line from Volary to Čicenice (45 minutes away), where it joins the České Budějovice-Plzeň main line.

There are four buses a day to Prague, 10 to České Budějovice, and departures all day to Husinec and Vimperk.

HUSINEC
The small village of Husinec is 5km north of Prachatice, from where there are regular bus connections. It has only one attraction: the house where the reformist preacher Jan Hus is thought to have been born around 1371, together with a museum.

The main square, Prokopovo náměstí, has a statue of Hus that was erected in 1958. The **Jan Hus House** (dům Jana Husa) and the small museum at No 37 are open daily, except Monday, May through September from 8 to 11.30 am and 1 to 4 pm; entry costs 10 Kč. In early July this is the scene of a Jan Hus commemoration, with a remembrance ceremony, cultural events and exhibitions.

There are no hotels here and only one restaurant, *U Toma*, up from the museum.

VIMPERK
This is a pleasant town (population 8100) with a castle on a hill – but not much else. The castle, founded at the end of the 13th century, was rebuilt in Renaissance style in 1560, with Baroque alterations in 1734; only Vlčkova Tower (Vlčkova věž) remains from the Gothic original. Bohemia's first calendar was printed here in 1484.

The town grew around the castle, prospering from trade along the so-called Golden Trail (Zlatá stezka) between Bavaria and Bohemia. Some Gothic and Renaissance houses still remain in the square, along with the Gothic **Black Tower** (Černá věž).

The castle has a small museum – its glass exhibits are a reminder that Vimperk has manufactured glass since the 16th century – that is open daily, except Monday, May through October from 9 am to noon and 1 to 4 pm; entry costs 30 Kč.

Orientation & Information
The train and bus stations are 3km from the castle and old town; turn left onto the highway and continue downhill. Buses to town are frequent in the morning, less so in the afternoon. A small information kiosk opposite Hotel Anna seems permanently closed. Vimperk's area code is ☎ 0339.

Places to Stay & Eat
In a busy location opposite the train station is the threadbare *Hotel Boubín* (☎ 210 10), Špidrova 45, which costs 285 Kč per person. More appealing is the adjacent *Hotel Růže* (☎ 216 16), at 200/480 Kč for a single/double. Both have very basic restaurants.

In the old town, both *Hotel Zlatá hvězda* and *Hotel Vltava* were closed for renovations at the time of writing. The only alternative is the deluxe *Hotel Anna* (☎ 220 50), right off the main highway at Kaplířova 168, with doubles for 1510 Kč.

Autocamp Hajná Hora (☎ 221 13), open from June through August, is 1.25km from the bus stop on 1.máje.

Getting There & Away
Vimperk is about an hour from either end of the Strakonice-Volary railway line, with about eight trains a day, through beautiful mountain and forest scenery.

Buses are less frequent to Strakonice, but faster to Prachatice (30km), Písek (55km), České Budějovice (79km) and Prague (140km), which has over 10 departures per day.

ŽELEZNÁ RUDA & AROUND
The name of this popular western Šumava ski resort means 'Iron Ore', which gives a hint to the town's mining origins in the 16th century. There is a little museum on mining and glass-making, and the wooden Church of St Mary of Hvězda with a big onion-dome, but the main thing to do in summer is to walk.

Orientation
The train station for the village of Železná

Ruda is 2km from the German border, at an elevation of about 750m.

Along the road to Nýrsko, a green-marked trail climbs (4km in all) north to Špíčák, a ski area in a saddle (Špíčácké sedlo) at about 1000m. About 7km beyond the saddle, at 900m, is another village and ski area, Hojsova Stráž.

Walks

About 2.5km from the village towards the saddle is a year-round chair lift to a lookout tower at the summit of **Pancíř** (1214m). Alternatively, there's a red-marked trail up to it from the saddle.

From **Špíčák** you can also climb to the Šumava's two largest glacial lakes. The 18 hectare **Black Lake** (Černé jezero) is 4.5km north-west on a yellow-marked road. Smaller **Devil's Lake** (Čertovo jezero) is 2.5km south-west of the saddle, by trail only. Both lakes are on a red-marked trail that continues north-westward along the border for about 25km.

Places to Stay

There are plain *campsites* 1km north-east of Železná Ruda on the road to Čachrov, and at Brčálník, about midway between Špíčácké sedlo and Hojsova Stráž.

There are plenty of hotels, though better value are private rooms (watch for signs).

Getting There & Away

Železná Ruda is easiest to reach by train from Plzeň (three hours; about six direct trains a day) or Klatovy (1½ hours; 12 a day). About half of these continue across the border to Bayerisch Eisenstein; the border is open 24 hours.

Písecko Region

PÍSEK

Písek (population 30,000) is an industrial town with an extremely handsome historical centre set on the banks of the Otava river, spanned by the oldest bridge in Bohemia. North of town the Otava widens near its junction with the Vltava and the Orlík dam. The surrounding region, called Písecko, is a traditional gold-panning area, and the town's name comes from the sand (*písek*) from which the gold was separated.

The town and castle, plus a church and monastery, were founded in 1243 by Přemysl Otakar II. The town prospered from its position on the Golden Trail trading route, and Charles IV established salt and grain storage houses here. Písek backed the Hussites, but was taken and virtually emptied by Habsburg forces early in the Thirty Years' War. It enjoyed a kind of rebirth with the logging trade in the late 18th century.

The poet Frána Šrámek (1877-1952), whose poems have inspired a number of directors to make films in the town, lived here. Písek also has one of the finest museums in Bohemia.

Orientation

The train and bus stations are near each other, 1km south of the city centre. To get to the centre walk up Nádražní, turn right at Budovcova, left at Chelčíkeho, cross Alšovo náměstí, and take Jungmannova to the main square, Velké náměstí.

Information

Infocentrum (☎ 21 35 92), Fügnerovo náměstí 42, overlooks the river one block north of Velké náměstí and is open weekdays from 10 am to 5 pm. Čedok (☎ 2886) is on the east side of Velké náměstí. No less than four banks (with ATMs) line the main square. Písek's area code is ☎ 0362.

Things to See

The 13th century **castle** was never rebuilt after a 1510 fire. Only the original right wing remains today, hidden inside a courtyard just off the main square. Nowadays it houses the superb **Prácheňské muzeum**, with first-rate displays on the Nazi and Communist eras. It's open daily, except Monday, from 10 am to 6 pm; entry costs 10 Kč.

Next door is the Baroque **town hall**, which replaced the castle's left wing. **Putim Gate** (Putimská brána) is the only section left from the castle's original fortifications.

There are some finely decorated Renaissance and Baroque houses on Velké náměstí and Jungmannova. Mikuláš Aleš (see the Around Blatná section) designed the sgraffito decoration of the Hotel Otava. Most enjoyable is a walk along the Otava near the stone **Kamenný Bridge**, dating from the second half of the 13th century and the oldest in Bohemia, even predating Prague's Charles' Bridge.

Special Events

The Písecko region's preoccupation with gold-panning is celebrated each August by a panning championship, which is held anywhere between Slaník, a few kilometres east of Strakonice, and Kestřany, near Písek.

Places to Stay

The cheapest lodgings are in the summer-only *Hotelová ubytovna* hostel (☎ 2200) in the Písek Winter Stadium (zimní stadion Písek), where a bed in a triple with shower and WC is 225 Kč. Take bus No 1 from the train or bus station north to the corner of Čelakovského and U Výstaviště; the hostel is on U Výstaviště.

The cheapest – and nicest – hotel is *Hotel Pod skálou* (☎ & fax 21 47 53) at Podskalí 156 (most easily approached from Putim Gate), with rooms and a restaurant overlooking the river. Rooms, most with shower and WC, are 400/800 Kč for a single/double. The *Hotel Otava*, Komenského 56, is closed for renovations.

A good mid-range option is the *City Hotel* (☎ 21 56 34) at Alšovo náměstí 35, with modern rooms for 670/925 Kč. More expensive is *Hotel Bílá růže* (☎ 21 49 31) at Šrámkova 169, just off Velké náměstí. Doubles with the works are 1550 Kč.

Places to Eat

Ristorante Venezia, in an arcade just off the main square, has above-average pizzas (75 Kč) and pastas (50 to 65 Kč). *Restaurace Candis*, Jungmannova 32, has hearty pub food and is open daily to midnight. Elegant *U Přemysla Otakara II*, adjacent to the museum, is Písek's best splurge.

Getting There & Away

Trains pass through Písek on their way to Plzeň (2½ hours; eight daily), České Budějovice (30 minutes), Tábor (1¾ hours) and Prague (four hours; eight daily). Plzeň requires a change at Ražice, and České Budějovice a change at Protivín. There are also buses to these and regional destinations, such as Blatná (10 a day) and Orlík (six a day).

STRAKONICE

This industrial town of 25,000 at the confluence of the Otava and Volyňka rivers has little to offer, except being famous for its *dudy* (Czech bagpipes) and ČZ motorbikes. It began as a village beside the 13th century castle of the Bavor family of Strakonice. When parts of Bohemia were liberated by the US army in 1945, General Patton based himself here.

Orientation & Information

The train and bus stations are next to each other about 1km south-east of the city centre. Strakonice's area code is ☎ 0342.

Things to See

In the remains of the castle is a regional **museum** on gold panning and local industry, including a collection of dudy. It's open daily, except Monday, from 8 am to 4 pm.

Of Velké náměstí's sgraffitoed buildings, the finest is the former **town hall** by Mikuláš Aleš; others are the municipal headquarters (*městký úřad*), Investiční banka, and a building opposite the Městká spořitelna bank.

Special Events

In mid-August the castle hosts an International Bagpipe Festival (Mezinárodní dudový festival).

Places to Stay & Eat

Autokemping Podskalí (☎ 246 93), open from May through September, is a long walk west out of town and past the castle, along the Otava. A hostel called *Restaurace – ubytování Palermo* (☎ 32 12 72), in the winter stadium at Luční 454, has beds in quads for 185 Kč each; take bus No 4 or 6 from the train station or walk the 1km.

Hotel Dudák (☎ 32 13 05), Alfonse Šťastného 171, near the train station, is 250/500 Kč for a single/double. Closer to the town centre is the *Hotel Bílý Vlk* (☎ 224 35), directly opposite the castle at Komenského 29, with doubles from 420 Kč.

A good choice off Velké náměstí is *Hotel Fontána* (☎ 32 14 40) at Lidická 203, priced at 720/1000 Kč and has an excellent restaurant. Top of the line is the high-rise *Hotel Bavor* (☎ 32 13 00), 300m from the castle at Na ohradě 31, priced at 1100/1550 Kč.

Getting There & Away

There are regular direct trains to Plzeň, Blatná, Vimperk and Tábor, but Prague, České Budějovice and Písek involve changes. Buses cover these same destinations and are a bit faster.

BLATNÁ

Blatná's name comes from the *blata* (fens) in the district that were drained and made into ponds. The town's sole attraction is its castle, which is worth a look if you're driving through the area.

Things to See

The 13th century **Vodní hrad** (Castle on the Water) was rebuilt several times before a major restoration in the mid-19th century, and it's currently being prettified for tourists. A 50 minute tour takes in the Hunting Room (Lovecký sál), with furniture made from stag horns. The castle is open daily, except Monday, May through September, and on weekends only in April and October, from 10 am to noon and 1 to 4 pm. The castle is connected by a bridge to the large **English Garden** (anglický park), ideal for picnics.

General Patton stayed in the castle in May 1945. The Communists in their time did not allow the town's liberation by US forces on 5 May to be celebrated, but since 1990 it has been, with gusto.

The **Cathedral of the Virgin** (chrám Panny Marie), across from the castle on náměstí Míru, is one of Bohemia's most valuable late-Gothic structures, with an older Romanesque sacristy inside the Gothic walls.

Places to Stay & Eat

Blatná's only hotel, the *Beránek*, was closed at the time of writing. Inquire about private rooms at Turistické informační středisko (☎ 0342-3902) on náměstí Míru (closed Sunday). *Hospůdka Blatná*, opposite the church, is a quiet pub with OK food.

Getting There & Away

Blatná is a one hour train ride north from Strakonice, with 10 connections daily. To or from Plzeň, change at Nepomuk. For Prague, change at Březnice. There are also up to 10 buses a day to Písek.

AROUND BLATNÁ

About 11km east of Blatná is **Mirotice**, the birthplace of Mikuláš Aleš (1852-1913). He was the foremost artist of Bohemia's so-called 'National Theatre generation', which focused on folk and nationalistic themes from Czech history. His designs decorate houses in Písek and Strakonice. The house where he was born burned down in 1901 but was rebuilt in 1952.

The village is just west of the Písek-Březnice road, with several buses a day travelling the 20km to Písek.

ORLÍK NAD VLTAVOU

Though still one of the finest castles in the republic, Orlík has been vigorously renovated to the point of sterility; in summer it's also oppressively crowded. (A more authentic experience is the nearby Zvíkov Castle.) Orlík's main asset is its setting – on a cliff-lined bay encircled by trees. The castle was once high above the Vltava, but the Orlík dam has filled the valley almost to the castle's lower walls.

Orientation

The town of Orlík is a 10 minute walk from the lake and castle.

Orlík Castle

The original early-Gothic castle dates from the 13th century. After fires in 1514 and 1802, it was rebuilt and extended. The last Czech owner, Krištof ze Švamberka, lost the castle after the Battle of the White Mountain, when it fell into Austrian hands; the Schwarzenbergs held it from 1719 until 1945, when it was seized by the state.

In 1992 it was returned to the Schwarzenbergs, and the one hour castle tour is mainly about them and their life here. The highlight is a magnificently carved wooden ceiling that took four years to complete. In the thickly wooded gardens is the **Schwarzenberg Mausoleum** (Švarcenberská hrobka). From here you can access a network of scenic, peaceful hiking trails. From late May to early October, small boats ply the lake on 50-minute tours; the pier is just below the castle.

The castle itself is open daily, except Monday, May through August from 9 am to 5 pm, and to 4 pm in April, September and October.

Places to Stay & Eat

In the centre of the village is the *Restaurace U Cvrků* (☎ 0362-84 11 24), with cheap basic food and bungalows (summer only) for 250 Kč per person. *Penzion ubytovna*, 2km south of the village before the Žďákov Bridge (Žďákovský most), has cottages and dorm rooms from June through August.

Next to the castle is *Zámecký hostinec U Toryka*, with Czech courses for 60 to 130 Kč.

Getting There & Away

Up to six daily Prague-Písek buses stop near Orlík Castle; Orlík is 1½ hours from Prague.

If you're considering continuing on to Zvíkov Castle (see next section), consider going by boat. A regular service along the Orlík dam to Zvíkov stops at Orlík Castle twice each day, except Monday, in July and August, and on weekends only in June and until mid-September. The timetable is subject to frequent changes; for information it's best to call ☎ 0362-961 97. The fare from Orlík to Zvíkov Castle is 26 Kč.

ZVÍKOV CASTLE

This small Gothic castle, built by the Přemysl princes in the 13th century, commands a better position than Orlík. The castle sits high above the lake, at the point where the Otava and Vltava rivers enter it. During the rebellion of the Czech Estates in 1618, a garrison of 140 men successfully defended the castle against 4000 Habsburg troops. Unlike most other Bohemian castles, this one was never renovated and so has kept a medieval look.

A self-guided tour takes in furniture, weapons and a frescoed ballroom (*taneční sál*), plus a chapel with an altar featuring the Deposition of Christ and Veneration of the Three Kings (Oplakávání Krista a Klanění Tří králů), all in one painting. The castle is open daily, except Monday, May through September from 9 am to noon and 1 to 4.30 pm, and on weekends to 3.30 pm in April and October. Entry costs 20 Kč.

Places to Stay & Eat

Unless you have a car, it is difficult to see both Zvíkov and Orlík castles without staying the night. At the village of Zvíkovské Podhradí, a walk of just over 1km from Zvíkov Castle, there are private rooms available. Also here is the *Hotel Zvíkov* (☎ 0362-89 96 59; fax 89 96 55), which has comfortable single/double rooms for 1200/1850 Kč plus a summer-only hostel with beds for 380 Kč. Eateries include the hotel and the cheaper *Zvíkovská restaurace u Váňů*.

Getting There & Away

Several buses a day cover the 20km from Písek to Zvíkovské Podhradí. Alternatively, it is a fine 14km (six hour) walk on a marked trail beside the lake between the castles of Zvíkov and Orlík. Cyclists will need to use the minor road a bit farther inland.

North-Eastern Region

This traditionally rural corner of Bohemia, including the Českomoravská vysočina (Czech-Moravian Uplands) extending into southern Moravia, is historically important as the heartland of the Hussite movement led by Jan Žižka and Prokop Holý. The district administrative town of Jindřichův Hradec was the seat of the powerful Vítek family, masters of the land until the 16th century.

Highlights of the area include the Hussite town of Tábor, the chateau of Červená Lhota, and the Renaissance and Baroque façades of Pelhřimov and Slavonice.

TÁBOR

God's warriors, the Hussites, founded Tábor in 1420 as a military bastion in defiance of Catholic Europe. The town was organised according to the biblical precept that 'nothing is mine and nothing is yours, because the community is owned equally by everyone'. New arrivals threw all their worldly possessions into large casks at the marketplace and joined in communal work. This extreme nonconformism helped to give the word Bohemian the connotations we associate with it today. Planned as a bulwark against Catholics in České Budějovice and farther south, Tábor (population 37,000) is a warren of narrow broken streets with protruding houses that were intended to weaken and shatter an enemy attack. Below ground, catacombs totalling

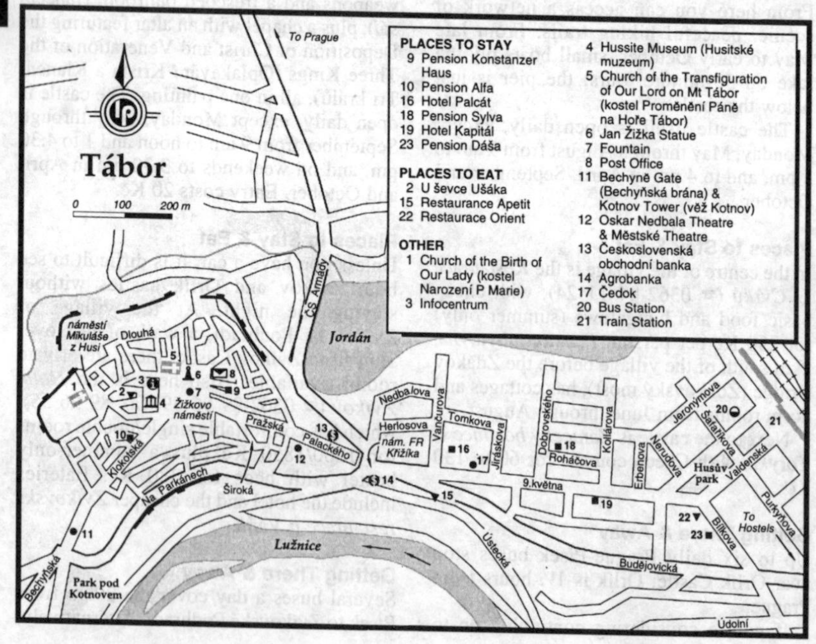

14km provided a refuge for the defenders. Give yourself at least one full day here.

History

Archaeological evidence suggests that Tábor was a Celt settlement about 100 BC. A castle and town called Hradiště were established by Přemysl Otakar II in the 13th century, only to be burned down in 1277 by the Víteks. In the 14th century the lords of Sezimové z Ústí built a castle here, of which all that remains is the single Kotnov Tower.

In 1420 the town achieved fame as the home of the Hussites, militant peasants who took up the cause of the martyred Jan Hus, and for over a decade this was the heart of their movement. After the Taborites' defeat at the Battle of Lipany in 1434, the town's significance declined.

Jordán Lake, west of the town, dates from this era and is the oldest artificial lake

The Hussites

When Jan Hus was burned for heresy at Constance in 1415, the consequences were far greater than the Catholic authorities could have foreseen. His death caused a religious revolt among the Czechs, who had seen Hus' adoption of the Czech mass as a step towards national self-determination. Hus himself had not intended such drastic revolution, focussing on a translation of the Latin rite, and the giving of both bread and wine to all the congregation instead of to the clergy alone. But for many the time was ripe for church reform.

Hus himself was born around 1372 in Husinec, South Bohemia. Of a poor background, he nevertheless managed to become a lecturer at Charles University in Prague, though it was not until 1402 that he was ordained a preacher. His aim was a return to the original doctrines of the church – tolerance, humility, simplicity – but such a message had political overtones for a church that treated forgiveness as an opportunity to make money.

Tried on a trumped-up charge of heresy at Constance, in present-day Germany, Hus was burned at the stake on 6 July 1415. The trial was doubly unjust, in that Hus had been given a safe conduct by the Holy Roman Emperor Sigismund.

In Bohemia many nobles offered to guarantee protection to those who practised religion according to Hus' teachings, and Hussite committees became widespread. The movement split over its relationship with the secular authorities, with the moderate Utraquists siding in 1434 with the Catholic Sigismund.

The more radical Taborites, seeing themselves as God's warriors, fought the Catholics in every way. As the military base for the Hussites, Tábor – named after the biblical Mt Tabor – was successfully defended by a mainly peasant army under Jan Žižka (see Trocnov, South Bohemia) and Prokop Holý.

In addition to the spread of Hussite ideas to many towns in the Czech Lands, the movement attracted supporters from other Protestant sects in Europe. Many converged on Tábor; some were too radical even for the Taborites, and groups like the Adamites and Pikarts, whose behaviour verged on lawlessness and total abandon, were suppressed. However, all groups joined against the invading crusading armies of the Holy Roman Empire.

Hussite ideals were never extinguished in Bohemia. Although the Utraquists became the dominant force after defeating the Taborites in the Battle of Lipany in 1434, the peace treaty that the Hussites signed with Rome guaranteed religious freedom for the movement. It took almost 200 years before Protestantism was suppressed in the Czech Lands by the Catholic Habsburg rulers following the Battle of the White Mountain. ■

in Bohemia, the dam having been built in 1492. Another first for the town was the completion of Austro-Hungary's first electric train service between Bechyně and Tábor in 1903.

Orientation

The old town is a 10 minute walk west from the train and bus stations through Husův park and along 9.května. The latter runs to náměstí FR Křižíka, from where Palackého and Pražská lead through the old town to Žižkovo náměstí. The left-luggage office at the bus station closes at 7 pm, so use the 24 hour facility at the train station.

Information

Tourist Offices The helpful Infocentrum (☎ 25 23 85), Žižkovo náměstí 2, books accommodation and guided tours weekdays from 9 am to 5 pm, Saturday from 9 am to noon, and Sunday from 1 to 6 pm (October through March, Tuesday to Friday from 9 am to 4 pm).

Čedok (☎ 25 22 35) is at 9.května 1282.

Money Agrobanka at náměstí FR Křižíka has a MasterCard ATM, as does the Československá obchodní banka at Palackého 5. Čedok's exchange counter doesn't charge a commission.

Post & Communications The post office, incorporating the telephone centre, is in the pink building just off Žižkovo náměstí. Tábor's area code is ☎ 0361.

Things to See

Start on Palackého and go west past the **Oskar Nedbal Theatre** (Divadlo Oskara Nedbala) to the handsome main square, Žižkovo náměstí. On every side it's lined with late-Gothic, Renaissance and Baroque houses, a **fountain** (1567) with a statue of the Hussite commander Jan Žižka, and two stone tables that the Hussites probably used for religious services.

On the square's northern side is the **Church of the Transfiguration of Our Lord on Mt Tábor** (kostel Proměnění Páně na hoře Tábor), built in 1440-1512 and known for its vaulting and the neo-Gothic altar. In July and August its **tower** is open for a sweeping view of Tábor (30 Kč).

The other imposing building on Žižkovo náměstí is the early-Renaissance town hall (1521), now the **Hussite Museum** (Husitské muzeum), with a copy of a peasant wagon mounted with cannons, the ingenious prototype tank invented by Jan Žižka. Also here is the entrance to a 650m stretch of **underground passages** (*podzemní chodby*), which is only open for visits when a group of five people forms. The passages, constructed in the 15th century as refuges during fires or times of war, were also used to store food and to mature beer. The museum is open daily, except Monday and weekends during the off-season, from 8.30 to 11 am and 11.30 am to 4 pm; entry costs 40 Kč. Tunnel tours are an extra 32 Kč.

The arch at Žižkovo náměstí 22, beside the Old Town Hall, leads into Mariánská and then Klokotská, which runs south-west to **Bechyně Gate** (Bechyňská brána), now a small historical museum focussing on the lives of peasants.

Kotnov Castle, founded here in the 12th century, was destroyed by fire in 1532; in the 17th century the ruins were transformed into the current brewery. The remaining 15th century **Kotnov Tower** can be climbed from the Bechyně Gate museum for a sweeping view of Tábor and the Lužnice river. Both the museum and tower are open daily, except Monday, mid-May through September from 8.30 am to 4 pm.

Special Events

The annual Hussite Festival of Tábor, held on the second weekend in September, features food, drink and locals dressed in Hussite costumes.

Places to Stay

Camping *Autokemping Malý Jordán* (☎ 321 03), open from mid-June through September, is 1.5km north of town near Lake Jordán. Only a few buses a day come here. Two-person bungalows are 300 Kč.

Hostels At Bydlinského 2474, 1.5km south of the stations, are two high-rise, year-round hostels, *SOU spojů* (☎ 25 97 20) and *Domov mládeže* (☎ 25 47 56). Dorm beds at both are 180 Kč per person. From the stations walk south-east on Purkyňova, veer right onto Hromadkova, then keep straight for 10 minutes.

Private Rooms & Pensions Infocentrum books private rooms from 300 Kč per person.

Closest to the stations is *Pension Dáša* (☎ 25 62 53), Bílkova 735, a deluxe spot with a carpark and garden, priced at 450 Kč per person. The house next door offers private rooms for 350 Kč per person.

Pension Sylva, Roháčova 668, has doubles for 800 Kč, and a good attached restaurant.

The friendly *Pension Alfa* (☎ 25 61 65), Klokotská 107, is right in the centre of town, with doubles for 650 Kč. Reception is open from 10 am to 4 pm.

Equally convenient is *Pension Konstanzer Haus* (☎ 25 30 30), Střelnická 220, priced at 490/780 Kč for a single/double.

Hotels There are only two expensive hotels in town. The new *Hotel Kapitál* (☎ 25 60 96/7), 9.května 617, is a better overall deal at 980/1550 Kč for a single/double. The bland six storey *Hotel Palcát* (☎ 25 29 01), 9.května 2467, is where German tour groups always stay. Rooms are 790/1200 Kč.

Places to Eat

It looks run-down and there is no sign, but *Restaurance Apetit*, náměstí FR Křižíka 1878, is actually an airy beer hall with a pleasant terrace.

Standard Bohemian cuisine is available at the *Beseda Restaurant*, next to the church on Žižkovo náměstí.

U ševce Ušáka, just off the main square, serves decent Bohemian food for less than 100 Kč.

Restaurace Orient, upstairs at Bílkova 1, offers tasty Chinese dishes daily to 11 pm.

Entertainment

Tábor's two theatres, the *Městské divadlo* and *Divadlo Oskara Nedbala*, are next to one another on Palackého třída.

Getting There & Away

Tábor is on the main railway line between Prague and Vienna. The line from České Budějovice to Prague also passes through here. Travelling from Tábor to Telč by train you must change at Horní Cerekev and Kostelec u Jihlavy. Otherwise take a bus to Jihlava (74km) and another bus on to Telč (29km).

To Plzeň (113km) or Brno (158km) it's easier to take a bus. Buses to Jihlava, Brno and Třeboň leave every few hours. The posted timetable bears numerous footnotes, so reconfirm your departure time at the information window.

AROUND TÁBOR

Chýnov Cave

The Chýnov Cave (Chýnovská jeskyně) was discovered in 1863 and has been open to the public since 1888. A narrow passage descends 37m to the colourful stalagmites formed by slowly dripping, mineral-laden water. A small cave, it's no match for those in the Moravian Karst (see the South Moravia chapter). There are 30-minute tours daily, except Monday, May through September from 9 am to 5 pm.

The cave is a 4km walk on a blue-marked trail north-east from the train station at Chýnov, itself four stops east of Tábor on the Pelhřimov line.

Soběslav

During the Hussite Wars Soběslav, 18km south of Tábor, was Oldřich Rožmberk's main defensive stronghold against the Hussite armies.

The main attractions of this small town are its two double-naved Gothic churches: the **St Vitus Church** (kostel sv Víta) and the **Church of our Lady** (kostel Panny Marie). The latter is notable for its tower, built in 1487, and an elaborate vaulted ceiling in the crypt.

BECHYNĚ

This quiet spa town (population 5700) 20km south-west of Tábor has a photogenic central square and a castle perched on a cliff above the Smutná creek, at the point where it joins the Lužnice river. The castle is one of many founded by Přemysl Otakar II and later owned by a succession of noble families, including the Rožmberks. The run-down castle is unfortunately closed to the public, as is the nearby Franciscan Monastery.

Things to See

In the 15th century the town grew famous for its ceramics. The **South Bohemian Aleš Gallery** (Alšova Jihočeská galerie), in a former brewery on náměstí TG Masaryka, documents the evolution of Bechyně ceramic ware. It's open daily, except Monday, May through October from 9 am to noon and 12.30 to 5 pm; entry costs 20 Kč.

The nearby **Franciscan Church**, with fine vaulting and a dazzling clock tower, is only open for services.

There's a small **Firefighting Museum** (Hasičské muzeum) in a former synagogue on Široká, which has some displays of several great old fire engines. It's open daily, except Monday, May through October from 9 to 11.30 am and 1 to 5 pm; entry costs 10 Kč.

Places to Stay & Eat

It's a five minute walk from the train station to Libušina and its two hotels: *Hotel U draka* (☎ 0361-81 10 53) and the new *Hotel Jupiter* (☎ 0361-96 21 31; fax 96 19 22). The Hotel U draka is cheaper (doubles 750 Kč), while the Hotel Jupiter is more quiet and refined (doubles 1200 Kč). Both have good adjoining restaurants.

Continue down Libušina to náměstí TG Masaryka and the very plain *Hotel Panská* (☎ 0361-96 11 19), priced at 600/850 Kč for a single/double.

Hospoda u Města Bechyně, on náměstí TG Masaryka, has cheap and reasonable Czech meals.

Getting There & Away

The adjacent bus and train stations are a 10 minute walk south-west from náměstí TG Masaryka.

Bechyně is at the end of the narrow-gauge rail link from Tábor, built in 1903. Eight trains a day come from Tábor (50 minutes). Buses are faster to Písek (three daily) and České Budějovice (seven daily).

KÁMEN

The Czech word for rock, *kámen*, lends itself to the great boulder that **Kámen Castle** sits on, and which gives it a commanding view of the surrounding countryside. Founded in the 13th century, the castle was renovated in the 17th century in early-Baroque style.

Apart from a few historical displays, the castle's main attraction is a **Motorcycle Museum** (Muzeum Motocyklo), featuring Czech motorbikes from 1899 to the 1960s, including late-model Jawas and ČZs, in their time among the best in the world. It's open daily, except Monday, May through September from 8 am to noon and 1 to 5 pm, and on weekends only in April and October from 9 am to noon and 1 to 4 pm.

There are no restaurants or hotels in wee Kámen.

Getting There & Away

Up to seven daily Tábor-Pelhřimov buses stop at Kámen.

PELHŘIMOV

The old centre of this industrial town (population 17,000) straddling the Bělá river, still has many Renaissance and Baroque houses, most of which face onto the main square, Masarykovo náměstí. The original settlement, around the St Vitus Church on Svatovítské náměstí, burned down in 1289.

Orientation

The train station is 1.5km south of the old town; to reach it turn left onto Nádražní, follow it past the bus station (keep sharp left) and take Poděbradova left up to the main square.

Information

The information centre (☎ 269 24) at Masarykovo náměstí 1 is open weekdays from 8 to 11 am and noon to 4 pm. The nearby Agrobanka has a MasterCard/Visa ATM. Pelhřimov's area code is ☎ 0366.

Things to See

Most of the Renaissance houses on and around the square were rebuilt in Baroque style after a devastating fire in 1766. One at Masarykovo náměstí 13 was given a striking cubist face by Pavel Janák in 1913 – another Janák creation is the yellow and red Drechsel House (Drechselův dům) at Strachovská 331. Also on the square is the uninspiring **Pelhřimov Muzeum**; it's closed Monday, and entry costs 12 Kč.

In the courtyard behind the museum is a **statue of St Václava**, guarding the entrance to the tiny **castle** (*zámek*), completed in 1554 for the Lords of Říčany. It has a small exhibit of furnishings; the most interesting room is the frescoed Music Hall (*hudební sál*). The castle is open weekdays from 9 am to 4 pm and weekends from 10 am to noon; entry costs 20 Kč.

Just north of the castle is the **Church of St Bartholomew** (kostel sv Bartoloměj), with its 61m clock tower.

Places to Stay

The information centre has lists of cheap pensions and hotels.

The convenient *Hotel Grand* (☎ 212 37), just off the main square at Palackého 69, is priced at 350/700 Kč for a single/double. Reception is on the 2nd floor, above a beer hall.

A cheaper option is the *Sporthotel* (☎ 251 60), in a sports complex at Nádražní 1536, near the bus station, where dorm beds are 115 Kč. There's also a cheap, but smoky restaurant.

Places to Eat

For breakfast or a snack try the *Mléčné lahůdky* at Masarykove náměstí 28. The only advantage of the *Restaurace u Vlasáků*, Solní 855, is that it's open on Sunday until 10 pm, when everything else is closed.

Getting There & Away

Pelhřimov is on the Jihlava-Tábor railway line, 1¼ hours from Tábor. For Jihlava, change at Horní Cerekev. Buses run reasonably frequently to Tábor, Jihlava and Kámen. Long-distance buses run to Prague (2¼ hours; up to five a day) and Brno (two hours; up to three).

RICHARD NEBESKÝ

Superb Renaissance houses line Masarykovo náměstí in Pelhřimov

JINDŘICHŮV HRADEC

Who would have guessed that quiet Jindřichův Hradec (population 21,800) was in the Middle Ages one of Bohemia's most important towns? Its central square and lakeside castle, situated between the Nežárka river and Vajgar Lake, are striking. The town, prospering from its position on a trade route from Austria, suffered three great fires in 1435, 1773 and 1801; the result is a broad spectrum of architecture from the 15th to the 19th centuries. Of course, some people come simply to gawk at the world's largest mechanised Nativity scene.

Orientation

The adjacent bus and train stations are 20 minutes by foot from the city centre; to reach the main square walk south down Nádražní, turn left past the church onto Klášterská and continue south down Panská to the main square, náměstí Míru.

Information

Infocentrum (☎ 228 44), Panská 136, can help with accommodation weekdays from 8 am to 5 pm, Saturday until 11 am. The adjacent Čedok office (☎ 36 10 99) changes money for a 2% commission. If you need money, there's a MasterCard/Visa ATM on the main square. Jindřichův Hradec's area code is ☎ 0331.

Castle

Jindřich Vítek, a member of the most powerful feudal family in southern Bohemia in the early 13th century, founded the original Gothic castle here, sections of which are preserved in the third courtyard. The remainder was renovated in the 16th century with lavish murals and furniture. The highlight is the frescoed, Italianate Rondel garden pavilion, done for the Lords of Hradec in 1591 by Baldassare Maggi. The castle is open daily, except Monday, April through October from 9 am to 5 pm.

There are three mandatory tours to choose from: tour 'A' includes the Baroque and neo-classical sections; tour 'B', the most interesting, covers the medieval fortifications and a dazzling 13th century chapel; while tour 'C' covers the Renaissance bits. Each costs 30 Kč.

CZECH REPUBLIC

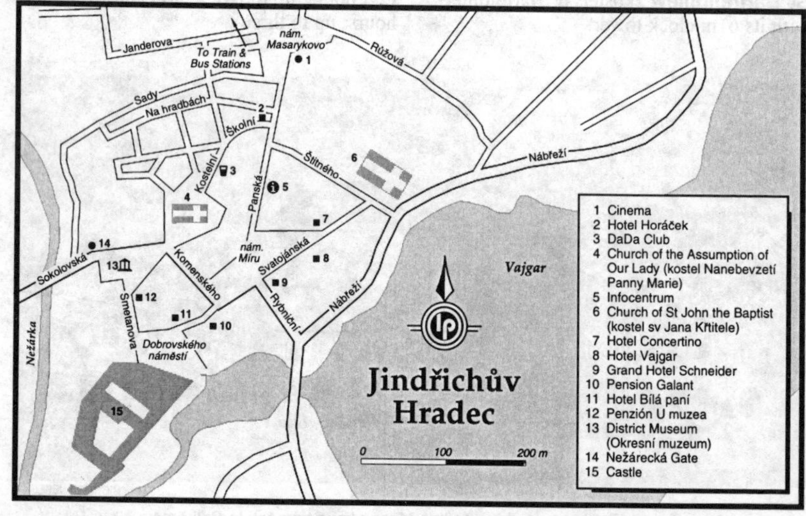

Around the Old Town
Bits of the old town walls still remain. To the east is a poorly preserved gate, the **Nežárecká brána** (1466). The main square (náměstí Míru) has several late-Gothic, Renaissance and Baroque houses, the most notable being the sgraffitoed **Langrův dům** (No 139, at the north end) and its vaulted archway.

The **Church of the Assumption of Our Lady** (kostel Nanebevzetí Panny Marie), behind the town hall (*radnice*), has a good cycle of 17th century frescoes. The **Church of St John the Baptist** (kostel sv Jana Křtitele) is noteworthy for some 600-year-old frescoes, including one of St Louis of Toulouse.

District Museum
The Jesuit seminary opposite the former Jesuit College on Komenského now houses the District Museum (Okresní muzeum). The foremost attraction is an extraordinary mechanical **Nativity scene** completed by one Tomáš Krýza in 1756, after 60 years of labour. The scene comprises over 1000 handcrafted figurines and fills an entire room.

The museum is open daily, except Monday, April through December from 8.30 am to noon and 12.30 to 5 pm, and including Monday in July and August; entry costs 30 Kč.

Places to Stay
Hostel Dormitory beds at the *Zimní stadion TJ Slovan* (☎ 36 17 99), off Jarošovská north of náměstí Masarykovo are available only in July and August, and cost 200 Kč per person.

Private Rooms & Pensions Infocentrum books private rooms for about 350 Kč per person. The cheapest pension in town is the *Perla* (☎ 36 16 39) at Nádražní 299, with doubles from 750 Kč.

In the centre try *Pension Galant* (☎ 36 24 46) at náměstí Míru 178, or *Penzión U muzea* (☎ 36 16 98) at Smetanova 17. A double at either is 900 Kč.

Hotels *Hotel Bílá paní* (☎ & fax 220 59), Dobrovského 5, is a quiet 10 room inn with single/double rooms at 700/1100 Kč. Cheaper but far less comfortable is *Hotel Horáček* (☎ 36 14 56), Panská 102 (enter off Školní), where rooms are 390/750 Kč.

Three hotels line the main square, the nicest being *Hotel Concertino* (☎ 36 23 20) at No 41, for 990/1870 Kč. The others are *Hotel Vajgar* (☎ & fax 36 12 71) at No 162 and *Grand Hotel Schneider* (☎ 36 12 52) at No 165, both with doubles for 1200 Kč.

Places to Eat
The hotels have a near monopoly on restaurants. Try Hotel Horáček for cheap Czech meals in a smoky beer hall, or Hotel Bílá paní for less smoke and a greater menu selection. A good splurge is *U zlatá husa* (The Golden Goose) inside Hotel Concertino.

Entertainment
A *cinema* (kino) on náměstí Masarykovo shows films nightly year-round. The *DaDa Club*, Kostelní 73, is the local hipster bar.

Getting There & Away
Jindřichův Hradec is on the railway line between České Budějovice (one hour) and Jihlava (1¼ hours). Some trains to Jihlava continue to Brno (3½ hours). The best train to Prague is via Veselí nad Lužnicí.

It's probably easier to take a bus for nearish places like Telč (one hour; nine daily), Tábor (two hours; five daily), Pelhřimov (1¾ hours; four daily), Třeboň (1¼ hours; nine daily) and Slavonice (1½ hours; eight daily).

ČERVENÁ LHOTA
This romantic, faded pink chateau sits on an outcrop in the middle of a lake. It got its name ('Red Lhota') in 1641 from its innovative bright-red roof tiles. The 14th century Gothic fortress was rebuilt into a Renaissance castle that was later adapted into a Baroque style. In the second half of the 18th century the jovially named German composer Karl Ditters von Dittersdorf lived

here. Červená Lhota makes an excellent day trip from Jindřichův Hradec.

It is possible to visit the empire-style interior daily in June, July and August from 9 am to noon and 1 to 5 pm; daily, except Monday, in May and September to 4 pm; and only on weekends in April and October to 4 pm. Entry costs 50 Kč. Even when closed, the chateau's grounds are great for strolling.

Getting There & Away

On weekdays there are four daily buses from either Soběslav or Jindřichův Hradec, each about half an hour away. Weekend transport is sporadic.

SLAVONICE

This border town of 2600 in the Czech-Moravian Uplands, founded in 1277, has a unique collection of 16th century Renaissance houses, some with rich sgraffito decorations and vaulted ceilings. UNESCO has listed the old centre as an historical town preserve.

In Communist times, Slavonice was as close to the border as ordinary people were allowed to live. Farther villages were evacuated, sometimes destroyed, and roads and railway lines were ripped up. The castle near Slavonice was destroyed for a different purpose – the making of a film for a western company.

Orientation & Information

From the train station it's a five minute walk north-east along Nádražní to Slavonice's old town. The bus station is a two minute walk north of the main square, náměstí Míru. Slavonice's area code is ☎ 0332.

Old Town

The town's architectural treasures are around náměstí Míru, Horní náměstí and Boženy Němcové. The sgraffito at Horní náměstí 88 depicts the Habsburgs and figures from Greek mythology. The 1599 **town hall** stands out, as does the high tower of the Gothic **Church of the Assumption of Our Lady** (kostel Nanebevzetí Panny Marie), surrounded by 14th to early 16th century houses on náměstí Míru.

Also on the square is a small **museum** with some artefacts from the abandoned village of Pfaffenschlag. It's only open from May through August – Tuesday to Thursday from 3 to 6 pm and Friday to Sunday from 9 am to 6 pm. Entry costs 8 Kč.

Places to Stay & Eat

In addition to private rooms there is the friendly *Besídka penzion* (☎ 932 93) at Horní náměstí 522, which has dormitory beds for 300 Kč (though it gets booked out in July) and a good, cheap restaurant. It's closed on Sunday.

Hotel Alfa (☎ 932 61) at náměstí Míru 482 has doubles with shared facilities for 350 Kč.

Getting There & Away

Slavonice is at the end of a minor railway line that goes through Telč (one hour; nine daily) to Kostelec u Jihlavy. The bus from Prague takes 3½ hours to Dačice, where you must change for Slavonice.

Border Crossing Just over 1km south of Slavonice is a vehicle and pedestrian border crossing, to Fratres in Austria, open daily from 8 am to 8 pm.

East Bohemia

East Bohemia's main attractions are its forested uplands, including the amazing natural sandstone rock formations of the Český ráj and Adršpach-Teplice. Less compelling (except for skiers) are the Krkonoše (Giant Mountains), the highest massif in the Czech Republic. Several major rivers rise in the Krkonoše, including the Labe (Elbe), which crosses Bohemia and Germany to the North Sea. The Krkonoše today form a natural border with the Silesian region of Poland – a decidedly friendly border.

This swathe of Bohemia also has some of the broadest lowlands in the country – mainly the fertile basin of the Labe, where it drops out of the mountains. Close by is the region's administrative centre, Hradec Králové, with a fine Renaissance old town and easy access to smaller, equally handsome towns such as Pardubice and Jičín.

HIGHLIGHTS

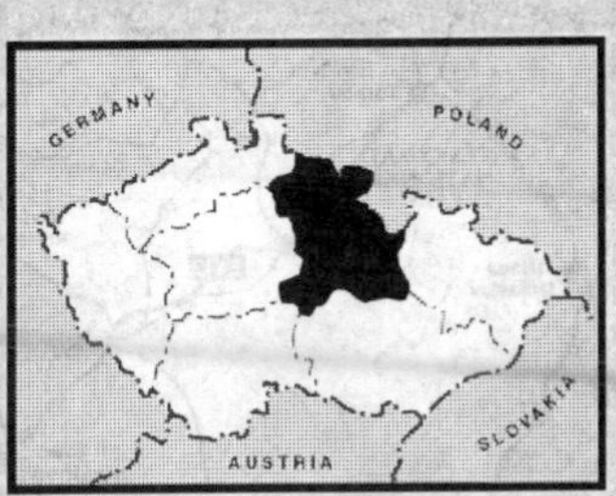

- See one of the country's finest Renaissance town squares, plus impressive Art Nouveau and functionalist architecture, in Hradec Králové
- Spend a few days in the Český ráj National Park, threaded with hiking trails and dotted with ruined castles and dramatic sandstone rock formations
- Scramble up sheer cliff faces, conquer the mighty Wolf Canyon hiking trail and explore sandstone 'rock towns' in the Adršpach-Teplice Protected Landscape

HRADEC KRÁLOVÉ

Sprawling Hradec Králové (population 100,000) lacks the energy and handsome façades of nearby Pardubice, yet there are some worthwhile sights, notably the main square (Velké náměstí) and the Gallery of Modern Art. The heavily industrialised suburbs are home to ČKD (a diesel engine manufacturer) and the Petrof piano plant.

The hill at the confluence of the Labe and the Orlice is a natural place for a stronghold – and there has been one here since at least the 9th century. The Přemysl rulers fixed it up as a castle, and since the 12th century Hradec Králové has been eastern Bohemia's administrative centre.

Growing rich on trade, Hradec Králové was Bohemia's second most important town, after Prague, by the 14th century. At that time it was made a seat of Bohemia's widowed queens (the town name means 'Queens' Castle') – a mixed blessing, as the immense double brick walls subsequently built around the town began slowly to strangle its growth.

Ardently Hussite, Hradec Králové was occupied by Swedish troops during the Thirty Years' War, after which serious decline set in, though the church kept busy with new construction. With the merging of the Austrian and Hungarian thrones in the 19th century, defences were beefed up even more. The Prussians never even tried to get in, managing instead to thrash the Austrians just east of town in 1866.

In the following decades the walls were pulled down. Thus released, Hradec Králové expanded explosively, guided by some far-sighted planning. Nové Město, the 'new town', bears both the Art Nouveau and severe functionalist imprint of Bohemia's leading turn-of-the century architects, particularly Jan Kotěra and his

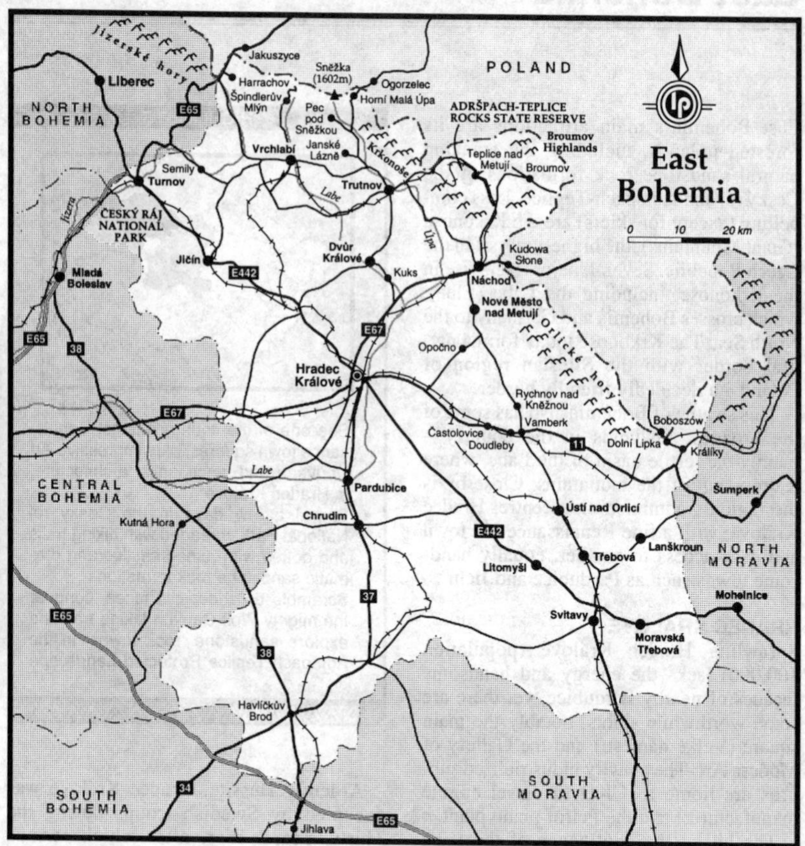

student Josef Gočár. In the 1920s, Gočár designed at least half a dozen local buildings and is credited (for better or worse) for the overall appearance of large parts of Nové Město.

Orientation

Staré Město, the old town, is squashed between the Labe and Orlice rivers. Nové Město begins west of Československé armády, but reveals its own personality only from the Labe west to the railway line.

From the train station (or the bus station in front of it) it's a five minute walk east into the heart of Nové Město, or 20 minutes to Staré Město. Trolleybus Nos 2, 3 and 7 go from the train station to the edge of Staré Město.

Information

Tourist Offices The information centre (Informační centrum; ☎ 551 16 50), Havlíčkova 836 (not the travel agency next door), sells maps and helps with accommodation; it's open on weekdays from 9 am to noon and 1 to 5 pm. In summer a small information kiosk opens inside the former town hall on Velké náměstí.

CK Svobodná cesta (☎ 324 11), in the train station, has a good selection of cheap private rooms, and opens on weekdays from 7.30 to 11.30 am and 12.15 to 3.30 pm. Čedok (☎ 323 21), Gočárova 63, sells maps and bus/rail/air tickets.

On a good day the above offices stock *Města Downtown*, a free bi-monthly guide to cinemas, clubs and theatres.

Money Komerční banka and its MasterCard/Visa ATM are on Masarykovo náměstí in Nové Město. Inside the train station is a Česká spořitelna Visa ATM.

Post & Communications The main post office, which also has a 24-hour telephone office, is opposite the train station. Another post office is on Tomkova, near Velké náměstí. Hradec Králové's area code is ☎ 049.

Emergencies The city police and Foreigners' Police are in the complex on the north side of Riegrovo náměstí, the square by the train station.

Staré Město

The old town's architectural heart is at the west end of **Velké náměstí** (Big Square, also known as Žižkovo náměstí). The oldest structure here is the brick Gothic **Church of the Holy Spirit** (kostel sv Ducha), founded in 1307. Dour outside, the church is plain and lofty inside, illuminated by decorative stained glass. The Silesian-style towers were added in the 14th century.

Next door is the 68m Renaissance belfry known as the **White Tower** (Bílá věž), built in 1589 and no longer very white. The tower's original 16th century clock was ruined by a storm in 1828; the current clock dates from a 1993 renovation. Next door is the plain Baroque **St Clement Chapel** (kostel sv Klimenta).

Facing the square, the twin-towered, 15th century former **town hall** (*radnice*) looks abandoned – the plan is to convert it into commercial office space. To the south of the square, at the end of a row of pastel-painted former canons' residences, is the municipal brewery, behind a guarded gate.

Sturdy arcades line the north side of the square; opposite is the Jesuits' **Church of the Assumption of the Virgin** (kostel Nanebevzetí Panny Marie), light and pretty inside in spite of its Baroque baggage. This and the adjacent Jesuit College and Bishop's Palace date from the 17th century, when a bishopric was established in Hradec Králové. Tucked beside the church is a Josef Gočár addition, a staircase down to Komenského ulice.

A definite highlight of Hradec Králové is the regional **Gallery of Modern Art** (Galérie moderního umění), on the main square at Nos 139-140. In the handsome and sunny Art Nouveau building (designed by Osvald Polívka) is a superb collection of late 19th and 20th century Czech painting and sculpture, with changing modern exhibitions on the ground floor and in a roof-top gallery. It's open daily, except Monday, from 9 am to noon and 1 to 6 pm; entry costs 12 Kč.

The eastern extension of Velké náměstí is the less photogenic **Malé náměstí** (Little Square), also known as Husovo náměstí.

Nové Město – East of the River

Nové Město begins from Československé armády, although the strip east of the Labe – including Kotěra's derelict Hotel Bystrica and its once-splendid restaurant – has fallen into serious neglect, in contrast to the clean-cut neighbourhoods west of the river.

Where Palackého meets the river is the **East Bohemia Regional Museum** (Krajský muzeum vychodních Čech), a graceful Art Nouveau building of red brick, designed by Kotěra, with seated giants on either side of the door. Inside are old photos, clockworks, mammoth bones and a fascinating scale model of Hradec Králové dating from 1865, showing the fortress that bound the town for four centuries. The museum is open daily, except Monday, from 9 am to noon and 1 to 5 pm.

CZECH REPUBLIC

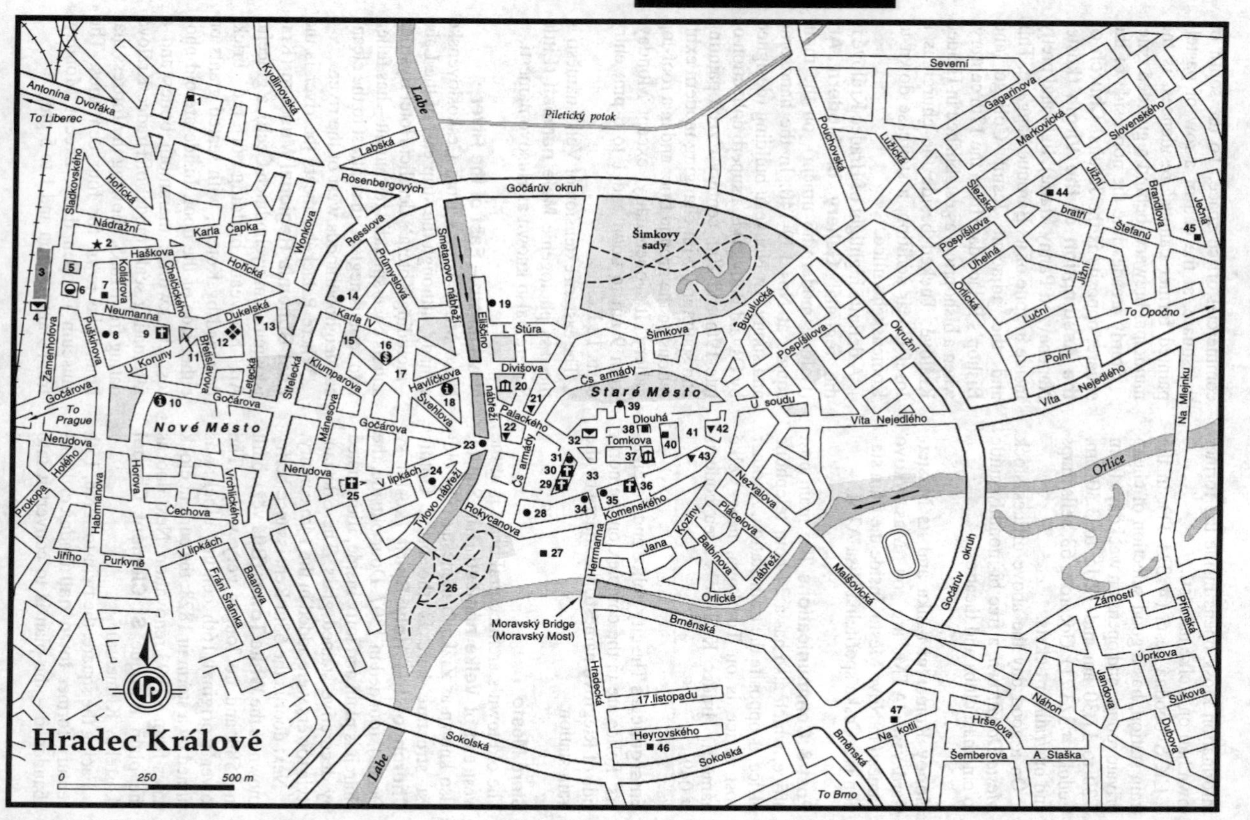

PLACES TO STAY

1 Ubytovna Astra
7 Hotel Černigov
27 Hotel Stadión
38 Pension U sv Lukáše
40 Pension U Jana
44 Hotel Alessandria
45 Pension Petr
46 Ubytovna ZVU
47 Hotel Garni

PLACES TO EAT

13 Open-air Market
21 Salamandr
22 Restaurace Asie
42 Bufet v Tunelu
43 Černý kůň

OTHER

2 Police
3 Train Station
4 Main Post Office
5 Riegrovo náměstí
6 Long-distance Bus Stand
8 ČAD Information Office
9 Church of the Blessed Heart of Our Lord (kostel Božího Srdce Páně)
10 Čedok
11 Náměstí 28.října
12 Tesco Department Store
14 Kino Centrál
15 Batkovo náměstí
16 Komerční banka
17 Masarykovo náměstí
18 Information Centre (Informační centrum)
19 Filharmonie Hradec Králové
20 East Bohemia Regional Museum (Krajský muzeum vychodních Čech)
23 Pražský Bridge
24 State Grammar School (Státní gymnázium)
25 Ambrosian Chapel (Ambrožů sbor)
26 Jiráskovy sady
28 Municipal Brewery
29 Church of the Holy Spirit (kostel sv Ducha)
30 White Tower (Bílá věž) & St Clement Chapel (kostel sv Klimenta)
31 Former Town Hall (radnice)
32 Post Office
33 Velké náměstí
34 Bishop's Palace
35 Jesuit College
36 Church of the Assumption of the Virgin (kostel Nanebevzetí Panny Marie)
37 Gallery of Modern Art (Galérie moderního umění)
39 Klicperovo divadlo (theatre)
41 Malé náměstí

Down at the confluence of the two rivers is **Jiráskovy sady**, a woody park with gardens, a carousel and an appealing 16th century wooden church brought from Ukraine in 1935. The park is linked to the west side of Nové Město by a footbridge across the municipal hydroelectric weir.

Nové Město – West of the River

Handsome, pastel-painted and almost too tidy is Gočár's showpiece square, boxy **Masarykovo náměstí**, which best shows his wider vision for the city. Nowadays it's linked by a pedestrian-only mall to the more lively square, **Batkovo náměstí**.

To the south are several brick school buildings designed by Gočár and built between 1925 and 1928. The most interesting is the **State Grammar School** (Státní gymnázium), with a severe façade that suggests an open book. Nearby is another arresting Gočár work, the wedge-shaped Protestant **Ambrosian Chapel** (Ambrožů sbor).

On náměstí 28.října, hunt down the functionalist **Church of the Blessed Heart of Our Lord** (kostel Božího Srdce Páně), with a dramatic – though cold and harsh – arched space inside.

Places to Stay

Hotels are not cheap, so ask the tourist offices (but not Čedok) about private rooms (starting at 250 Kč per person). The nearest *campsite* is at Stříbrný rybník, about 5km east of the centre (take bus No 17).

Hostels Two multi-storey hostels offer accommodation year-round, though they're often fully booked by workers from local construction sites. Most convenient is *Ubytovna Astra* (☎ 61 11 33), the white building with yellow trim at Vocelova 802. *Ubytovna ZVU* (☎ 230 81), Heyrovského 1171, is part of the pharmaceutical college. Both have singles/doubles with private showers and communal toilets for 150/300 Kč.

Pensions & Hotels A double with bath at the newly renovated (but still ageing) *Hotel*

Stadión (☎ 551 46 64), Komenského 1214, is 980 Kč (no singles). You won't save any money sleeping on the outskirts of town at *Pension Petr* (☎ 415 71), Ječná 125, *Hotel Alessandria* (☎ 415 21), třída SNP 733, or *Hotel Garni* (☎ 526 33 75), Na kotli 1147. Each has fully equipped doubles with bath for 1200 Kč, 1470 Kč and 1200 Kč, respectively.

It's better to stay somewhere more central. *Pension U Jana* (☎ 241 55) at Velké náměstí 137 and *Pension U sv Lukáše* (☎ 521 06 16) at Úzká 208 are both new and very deluxe, with private bath and breakfast for 1000/1300 Kč. The up-market, multistorey *Hotel Černigov* (☎ 581 41 11), opposite the train station at Riegrovo náměstí 1494, charges 1990 Kč for doubles with bath.

Places to Eat

Down at Malé náměstí 10-12, the restaurant and pivnice *Černý kůň* has Czech standard fare for 60 Kč to 110 Kč per course. Across the square at No 125 is the cheap *Bufet v Tunelu*, a point-and-serve counter open weekdays to 7 pm, weekends to 4 pm.

Next to the town hall on Velké náměstí is *Hospoda pod věží*, a quiet beer hall with above-average Czech food. Nearby on the corner of Tomkova and Špitálska is the loud, smoky, quite fun *Pivnice Na hradě*; which has basic pub food if the kitchen staff are in the mood.

The trendy snack bar *Salamandr*, Palackého 83, is good for a break from dumplings. The same goes for the Chinese-Thai *Restaurace Asie* at Eliščino 304, with main dishes priced from 110 Kč to 180 Kč.

Buy groceries at the Tesco department store on Dukelská, or fresh produce at the adjacent open-air market.

Entertainment

Classical concerts are regularly held at the *Filharmonie Hradec Králové*, Eliščino 777. Most theatre productions at the *Klicperovo divadlo* on Dlouhá are in Czech. A convenient cinema is the aptly named *Kino Centrál* at Karla IV 774.

Getting There & Away

By ČSAD bus, Hradec Králové is 1½ hours from Prague and about three hours from Brno, with departures all day long. ČSAD has an information office on Puškinova, near the bus stop.

There are about 10 fast trains a day to Prague, three to Brno. The ČD travel agency in the train station will book international but not domestic trains; Čedok books both.

PARDUBICE

Pardubice, East Bohemia's 'second city' after Hradec Králové, was founded in about 1340 at the junction of the Labe and Chrudimka rivers. In 1491 the whole region became the property of a Moravian noble family, the Pernštejns, who fixed up the town castle and moved in. Over the next century, with the help of Italian artisans and the unexpected assistance of two devastating fires, the Pernštejns gave Pardubice a wholly new Renaissance face.

Though only a fraction of the Pernštejns' legacy remains today (thanks to the work of a Swedish siege army in the Thirty Years' War), Pardubice's architecturally unified and recently restored historical centre makes it a worthy day trip from Hradec Králové, or even from Prague. Pardubice may have fewer overall sights than Hradec Králové, but it's more intimate and far less hectic. Among Czechs the town is known for the annual Great Pardubice Steeplechase, held here since 1874, with older roots in aristocratic stag hunts.

Orientation

Ulice Míru, the artery of 'new' Pardubice, is a 15 minute walk east along Palackého from the bus and train stations (or take any bus or trolleybus). On the east side of náměstí Republiky is a Gothic gate-tower into the old centre, Pernštýnské náměstí.

Note that some Pardubice maps spell Pernštejn as 'Pernštýn'.

Information

Pardubice has one lonely tourist office, and

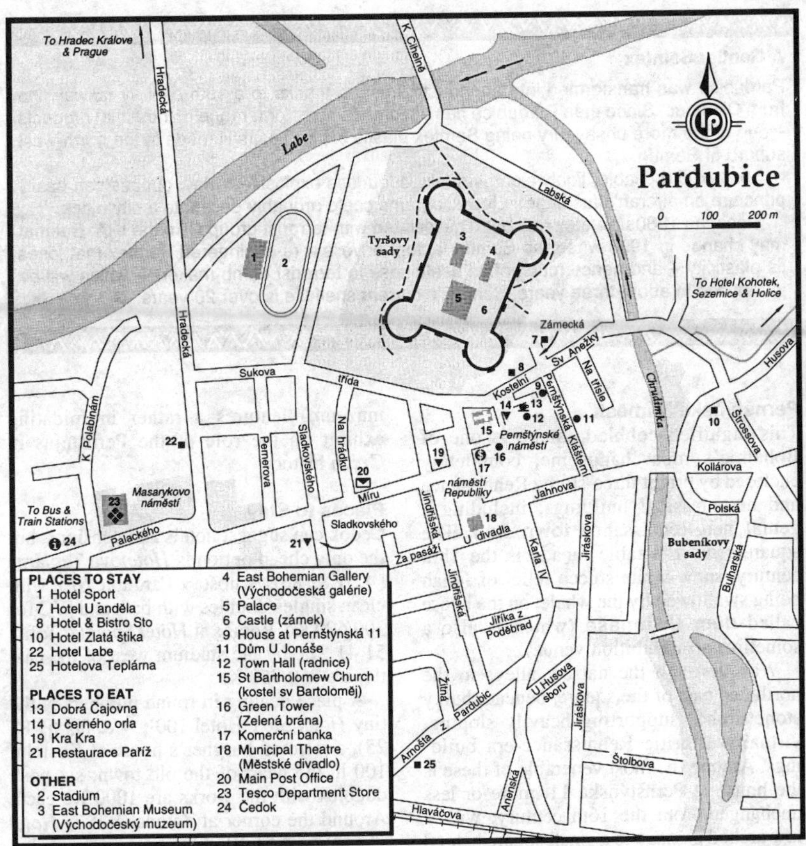

a surprisingly helpful Čedok office (☎ 51 15 21) at Palackého 1947; inquire here about private rooms. Komerční banka, on náměstí Republiky beside the gate-tower, has a MasterCard/Visa ATM in its lobby. The main post office is on Míru, two blocks past McDonald's.

Pardubice's area code is ☎ 040.

Náměstí Republiky

Though sundered by fume-belching traffic, this modern square is home to three of Pardubice's oldest and most interesting buildings. The most arresting, with its 'crowstep' gables and needle-thin tower, is **St Bartholomew Church** (kostel sv Bartoloměj), dating originally from the 13th century. Its present form dates from about 1515, when it was rebuilt after being razed by the Hussites.

At the other end of the square is the Art Nouveau **Municipal Theatre** (Městské divadlo). On the east side, brandishing flags and pointy gables, is the neglected 16th century **Green Tower** (Zelená brána).

A Gentler Semtex

Pardubice was transformed into an industrial centre thanks to a 19th century railway line from Olomouc. Since then Pardubice has become famous for a range of industrial products – one of the more unsavoury being Semtex plastic explosives, still made in the north-west suburb of Semtín.

Semtex is a pliable, lightweight, virtually odourless explosive. A few ounces can easily puncture an aircraft's fuselage; a few kilograms could probably decimate a city block.

Since the 1980s Semtex has been associated with terrorist groups like the IRA. But that may change in 1998 when the Semtín factory unveils a re-engineered Semtex that loses its plasticity – and hence much of its usefulness to terrorist bomb makers – which will be introduced in about three years. Semtex's current shelf life is over 20 years. ■

Pernštýnské Náměstí

This dignified cobbled square is one of Bohemia's most handsome, completely enclosed by bright three-storey Renaissance and neo-classical buildings, including a genial neo-Renaissance **town hall**. The square's most notable façade is the 18th century, snow-white stucco relief of Jonah being swallowed by the whale, on the house called **dům U Jonáše** (which is also a sometime art-exhibition venue).

Walk through the narrow alleys to the north and east of the square, beneath bulky stone arches supporting heavily sloping, virtually arthritic Renaissance-era buildings. Among the most venerable of these is the house at Pernštýnská 11, more or less unchanged from the 16th century, with a low arched passage to a small square behind it.

Pardubice Castle

You enter the castle (*zámek*) from Zámecká. Brooding in the inner court is the very neglected palace, in the early stages of restoration; opposite, in two already completed wings, are a superb gallery and a museum. The **East Bohemian Gallery** (Východočeská galérie), open daily except Monday from 10 am to 5 pm, has a permanent collection of 19th and 20th century Czech art, including unexpected modern sculptures around the grounds. The **East Bohemian Museum** (Východočeská muzeum) features a rather intimidating exhibit on the role of the Pernštejns in Czech history.

Places to Stay

Čedok can suggest hotels and pensions, but the only cheap option is *Hotelová Teplárna* (☎ 51 82 80), Arnošta z Pardubic 675, with clean singles/doubles with bath and WC for 300/600 Kč. Rooms at *Hotel Sport* (☎ & fax 51 41 22), by the stadium west of the castle, are 750/950 Kč.

A place dealing in round numbers is the tiny *Hotel Sto* ('Hotel 100'; ☎ & fax 51 88 25), a restored burgher's house at Kostelní 100 in the heart of the old town; six posh doubles with the works are 1000 Kč each. Around the corner at Zámecká 25 is *Hotel U anděla* (☎ 51 40 28), a cozy inn priced at 800/1200 Kč.

The deluxe *Hotel Labe* (☎ 51 72 86; fax 51 72 81), Masarykovo náměstí 2633, costs 1790/1890 Kč. The *Hotel Zlatá štika* (☎ 51 81 11), just across the river Chrudimka, has rooms at similar rates.

Places to Eat

On Sladkovského, *Restaurace Paříž* is open daily from 7 am to 11 pm and serves quality fish and meat dishes; main courses range from 60 Kč to 150 Kč.

U černého orla is an animated beer hall on Pernštýnské náměstí, with pub food that's above average.

Kra Kra, in the pedestrian tunnel beneath náměstí Republiky, has excellent food and relatively cheap Guinness on tap.

The quiet *Bistro Sto*, beside the Hotel Sto, serves a fine goulash with dumplings, but beware the pricey beer.

For tea and pastries in a smoke-free environment head across the square to *Dobrá čajovna* at Pod Sklípky 112.

Getting There & Away

Pardubice is 30 minutes from Hradec Králové by bus or train. Buses go about every half-hour, trains hourly (tickets from machines in the station).

A visit is feasible as a day trip from Prague, best by fast train (1¼ hours; about hourly). ČSAD buses take two hours.

OPOČNO

One of the finest castles in the region, with a history full of plots and intrigue, looms over the village of Opočno, approximately 25km north-east of Hradec Králové.

There was a Přemysl fortress at Opočno by the 11th century. After a later owner, Jan Městecký, abandoned the Hussite cause, the followers of the Hussite military hero Jan Žižka trashed the place.

In the 16th century the fortress was converted into the neo-Romanesque chateau you see today by the Trčkas, one of Bohemia's richest families. The last of the line, Adam Erdmann Trčka, was killed in 1634 in the course of a plot to assassinate Ferdinand II. The emperor then sold the chateau to the Italian Colloredo family, who lived in it right up until 1945.

In 1813, King Friedrich Wilhelm II of Prussia, Austrian Chancellor Metternich and Russian Tsar Alexander II met here in the course of forming their 'Holy Alliance' against Napoleon.

The staid, pastel chateau is impressive partly because it still looks lived-in. The owner at the turn of this century, Josef II Colloredo-Mannsfeld, filled one end of the castle with his hunting trophies and artefacts from Africa and the Americas. Other highlights are the tiny, tall St Anne chapel, and a striking collection of 16th to 18th century Italian paintings housed in two galleries.

All that remains of the older fortress is one cylindrical tower. The restored Baroque houses outside the chateau are worth a look, as is Zámecký park, the very fine English-style parklands that wrap around the chateau, entered about halfway up the hill.

The chateau is open daily, except Monday, May to August from 9 to 11.30 am and 12.30 to 4.45 pm, and on weekends only from 10 to 11.30 am and 12.30 to 3.45 pm in April and October. The short tour lasts 50 minutes and costs 30 Kč. A longer 75 minute tour covers a tedious collection of arms and costs 40 Kč. The park is open daily from 7 am to 8 pm.

Orientation & Information

The joint train and bus stations are 1.5km from the castle: follow Nádražní to Kupkovo náměstí then veer right on Zámecká. The chateau is a five minute climb from Opočno's renovated central square. Lucia Tour (☎ 425 10), in the town hall on Kupkovo náměstí, sells maps and can suggest

Opočno Holy Trinity Church

CZECH REPUBLIC

accommodation options on weekdays from 8 am to 5 pm, and on Saturday from 9 am to noon. There's a Visa ATM in the lobby. Opočno's area code is ☎ 0443.

Places to Stay & Eat

The *Zámecký hotel & restaurace* (☎ 421 25), next to the chateau, charges 300 Kč per person for standard, clean rooms. *Private rooms* (summer only) cost about the same at Třckovo náměstí 13. For a cheap Czech lunch try the beer hall *U slunce*, off Kupkovo náměstí on the road to the chateau.

Getting There & Away

Buses run from Hradec Králové every hour or so, taking an hour. From Prague there are three buses a day, taking 2½ hours.

ČASTOLOVICE & AROUND

The 13th century stronghold of Častolovice, 30km south-east of Hradec Králové, was renovated as a Renaissance chateau at the end of the 16th century; it passed into the hands of the Šternberk (Sternberg) family in 1694, and then into the hands of the state at the end of WWII. The Šternberks recently reclaimed it, repairing the Communist-era pillage and opening some of its 150 rooms to visitors.

Highlights of the tour include a vast Knights' Hall with biblical scenes on the ceiling, the family's fine collection of 17th to 19th century furniture, portraits of every one of the Czech kings, and a laid-back, un-museum-like atmosphere. The chateau is surrounded by a staid, English-style park. Both are open daily, except Monday, April through October from 9 am to 6 pm.

The chateau makes an easy excursion from Hradec Králové, or you could make a long day trip full of chateaux and castles (but not on Monday, when they're closed), including those at **Kostelec** and **Doudleby nad Orlicí** (respectively about two and 7km beyond Častolovice on Highway 11), and at **Rychnov nad Kně nou** (a few kilometres on to Vamberk and 5km north on Highway 14). In fact there are said to be some 30 castles and chateaux, from Romanesque to Renaissance, in a 50 sq km area around Hradec Králové.

Vamberk itself, a traditional centre for handmade bobbin-lace, has a Museum of Lacework (Muzeum krajky). Its St Procopius Church (kostel sv Prokopa), which is undergoing some repair work, is said to have a crypt with some 40 mummies in good condition.

Getting There & Away

Buses run about hourly from Hradec Králové; Častolovice takes 40 minutes. All the castles (except Rychnov) are on the railway line from Hradec Králové, and costs under 10 Kč.

At least two buses a day go to Častolovice and Vamberk from Prague's Florenc station, taking under three hours via Hradec Králové.

KUKS

A minor German nobleman and art patron named Franz Anton von Sporck (Špork in Czech), having discovered a mineral spring on his land beside the Labe, 30km north of Hradec Králové, set out to make an impression on his neighbours. From 1694 to 1724 he built a deluxe spa complex, complete with baths, infirmary, chapel, racecourse, theatre, gardens, guest houses and a chateau for himself. The concerts, salons, hunts and lavish parties at this upper-class Baroque 'resort' made it briefly a rival to the West Bohemian spa-towns.

In 1740, two years after Sporck's death, a massive flood washed away many of the buildings and destroyed the spring, and the complex went to ruin. All that remains today are the chapel and infirmary, a big staircase leading nowhere, and a fine collection of statues by Matthias Bernard Braun (1684-1738), one of Bohemia's master Baroque sculptors.

Non-Czech visitors are rare at Kuks, save for the odd busload of Austrian package-tourists. Consider stopping if you're in the area, otherwise give it a miss. Kuks is open daily, except Monday, May through September from 9 am to 6 pm, and on weekends only in April and October to 4 pm. The hour-long tour costs 50 Kč.

Infirmary & Crypt

From afar, the grimy Baroque survivors look haunted. Up close, the first thing you come to is a rusty gate to the Sporck family crypt, bearing a gilt skull-and-crossbones with snakes coming out of the eyes.

The front terrace is lined with Braun's strong allegorical **statues**, vices to one side and virtues to the other, all women. These are replicas; the originals, moved indoors to protect them from acid rain, are one highlight of the 45 minute guided tour. Our favourites were all vices – craftiness, calumny and despair!

The other attraction is a beautiful **apothecary**, filled with little drawers and bottles and surmounted by a carved unicorn's head. Our guide claimed it had been in continuous operation until 1945, and needed almost no restoration work; other sources say it's an almost total reconstruction.

A small **picture gallery** has several paintings of Kuks before disaster struck, and a huge, self-important portrait of Sporck. At the rear is a garden lined with strange little statues of dwarves by Braun.

Braunův Betlém

About 3km west of Kuks is 'Braun's Bethlehem', an al fresco 'gallery' with several extraordinary religious sculptures – hermits, saints and biblical scenes, some with little grottoes behind them – all but one by Braun, hewn directly from the rock outcrops scattered through the woods. This is all that remains of another Sporck project, which once had fountains, chapels and free-standing sculpture as well. It was vandalised in the 18th century for building materials.

Getting There & Away

Buses come from Hradec Králové about hourly, stopping at Kuks village, across the Labe from the infirmary. South of the infirmary is a whistle stop on the railway line.

To get to Braunův Betlém, walk west on a red-marked path from Kuks village or on a yellow path from the infirmary. By car, drive 3km west from Kuks village to Žíreč, turn left, cross the railway and climb for 2km to a carpark on the far side of the woods; it's a 10 minute walk from there.

Český Ráj

The Český ráj (Bohemian or Czech Paradise) is a maze of low hills, sandstone 'rock towns' and volcanic basalt fingers, all set against a backdrop of gently rolling woods and farmland. Threaded with walking trails, the Český ráj rises gradually northward into the foothills of the Krkonoše mountains, dotted at the highest points with ruined castles. Spend a few days hiking here and it's easy to see why the landscape inspired poets, sculptors and painters of the Czech National Revival, and why it's so popular with Czech holidaymakers.

A small part (92 sq km) was designated the Bohemian Paradise Protected Landscape Region in 1955 (with talk of future expansion), though 'Český ráj' is used loosely for a much wider area.

There are two so-called 'gateways' to the Český ráj – Turnov and Jičín. Of the two, Jičín is by far the more interesting and appealing. A major road and a poky little railway line link the two towns, and there's plenty to see and do within walking distance of the train stations.

Information

Tourist offices in Jičín and Turnov stock hiking and cycling maps, and can book accommodation.

The best map for roads and trails is Kartografie Praha's 1:100,000 *Český ráj a Poděbradsko (No 13)* or, for greater detail, klub českých turistů's *Český ráj* (1:50,000). The best map for the Prachovské skalý formations is Geodézie ČS' *Plán města Jičín – Prachovské skalý*, which looks like a cheap leaflet (but isn't).

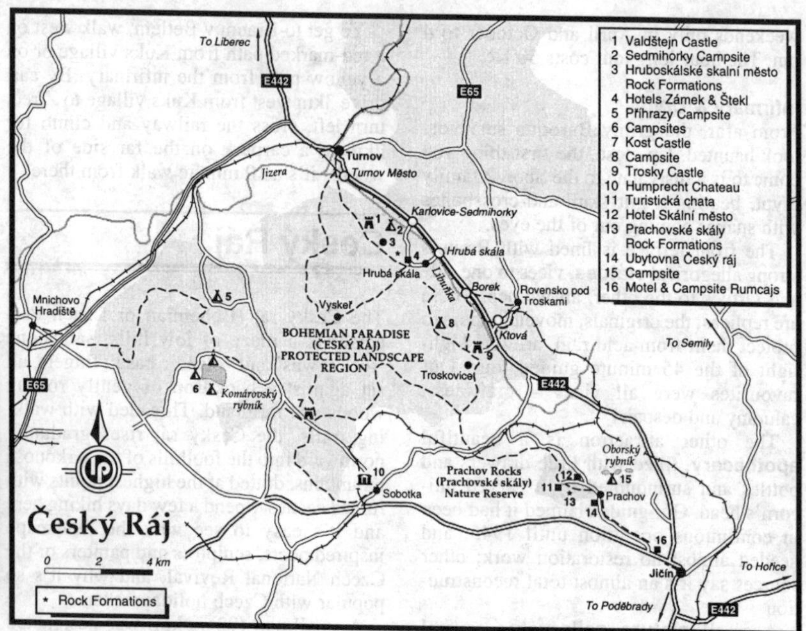

Walks

A good short option is to catch a train to Jičín and, early next morning, a bus to the Prachovské skalý formations, with plenty of walking trails to pass a full day (plus accommodation).

Option two is to catch a train from Jičín (or Turnov) to Hrubá skála and cover in one long day Trosky Castle, the rock formations at Hruboskálské skalní město and finally Valdštejn Castle (13km total) before catching a return train via Turnov Město.

Longer walks are also feasible: it's about 32km on the most direct (red) trail from Jičín to Turnov. If you've got the gear, it's worth taking a leisurely two or three days, camping en route.

Getting There & Away

During the day, trains run from Hradec Králové to Jičín and Turnov every hour or two.

A local train chugs between Turnov and Jičín about every two hours, and local buses service all the villages that aren't near the railway line.

JIČÍN

Wallenstein (Valdštejn), the Habsburg general who grew rich on property confiscated after the Battle of the White Mountain, decided he liked Jičín and had an old castle transformed into an ostentatious residence here between 1625-33. His plans to rebuild much of the town were cut short by his assassination in Cheb in 1634. He's buried at the nearby town of Mnichovo Hradiště.

Orientation

Husova runs a block north from the bus station, or 700m north from the train station. Head west along it towards Žižkovo náměstí and continue beneath the red-topped gate-tower into the main square,

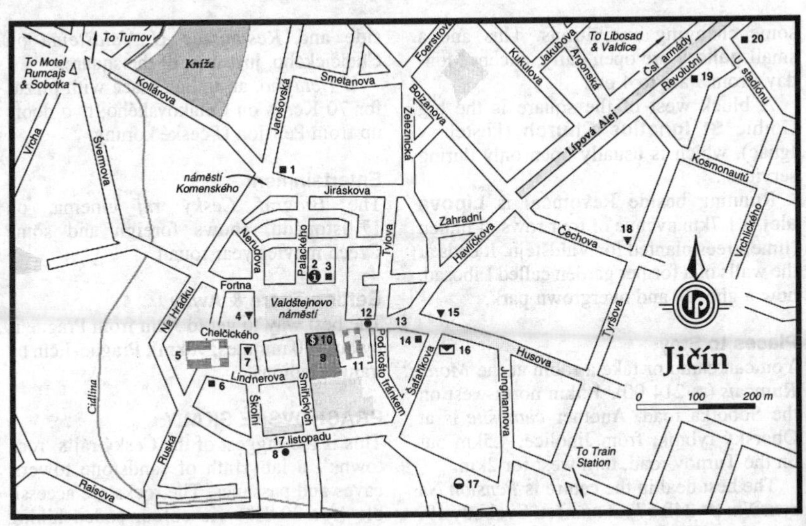

PLACES TO STAY
1 Pension Rieger
3 Pension U české koruny
6 Pension Na rynečku
14 Hotel Paříž
19 Pension J&K Albrechtovi
20 Hotel Start

PLACES TO EAT
4 Vinárna U Anděla
7 Restaurace U Valdštejna
15 Restaurace Volf
18 Restaurace Šuang-Si

OTHER
2 Information Centre
5 St Ignatius Church (kostel sv Ignác)
8 Biograf Český ráj (cinema)
9 Valdštejn Chateau
10 Komerční banka
11 St James Church (kostel sv Jakuba)
12 Valdická Gate (Valdická brána)
13 Žižkovo náměstí
16 Main Post Office
17 Bus Station

Valdštejnovo náměstí. Both of the squares and much of Husova have been pedestrianised.

Information

The extremely helpful information centre (☎ & fax 243 90) on Valdštejnovo náměstí sells hiking maps, books accommodation and has transport schedules; it's open on weekdays from 9 am to 5 pm, and on Saturday from 8.30 am to 12.30 pm. Komerční banka is on the main square, but its MasterCard/Visa ATM is adjacent to the information centre. Jičín's area code is ☎ 0433.

Things to See

For 8 Kč you can enjoy a bird's-eye view of town from the Gothic **Valdická Gate** on Valdštejnovo náměstí, open daily from 9 am to 5 pm, May to August. You enter the square past the un-steepled Jesuit **St James Church** (kostel sv Jakuba), Renaissance outside and Baroque inside.

The square and its well-preserved Renaissance façades are dominated by the **chateau** built by Valdštejn's Italian architects. A rather uninspiring **Regional Museum** (Okresní muzeum) spreads through eight halls of the chateau, with archaeology, local history, applied arts and some changing exhibitions. This and a small **gallery** are open daily, except Monday, from 9 am to 4 pm.

A block west of the square is the big Gothic **St Ignatius Church** (kostel sv Ignác), which is usually open only during services.

Running beside Revoluční is **Lípová alej**, a 1.7km avenue of four rows of linden (lime) trees planted for Valdštejn. It ends at the walls of a former garden called Libosad, now a ghostly and overgrown park.

Places to Stay

You can camp or take a room at the *Motel Rumcajs* (☎ 214 00), 1.5km north-west on the Sobotka road. Another *campsite* is at Oborský rybník; from Jinolice, 4.5km out on the Turnov road, turn west for 2km.

The best deal in the centre is *Pension Na rynečku* (☎ 248 57) at náměstí Svobody 19, a steal at 350 Kč per person – though it's often booked solid on weekends.

Hotel Paříž (☎ 227 50; fax 245 10), Žižkovo náměstí 3, is threadbare but not unbearably so. Basic singles/doubles are 450/630 Kč, with private bath and WC 650/970 Kč.

More up-market is *Pension U české koruny* (☎ 212 41), on the main square at No 77. Doubles with breakfast are 990 Kč.

Beyond the centre are the deluxe *Pension Rieger* (☎ 254 80) on náměstí Komenského, with fully kitted doubles for 1100 Kč, and the very basic *Pension J&K Albrechtovi* (☎ 225 44) at Revoluční 712, with quiet rooms for 180 Kč a bed and meals by arrangement.

Hotel Start was closed for renovations at the time of writing.

Places to Eat

Tasteful, quiet *Restaurace Volf* at Husova 39 has top-rate Czech courses for 50 Kč to 100 Kč. The Chinese *Restaurace Šuang-Si*, Čechova 266, is open daily until 10 pm with courses for 60 Kč to 80 Kč.

Valdštejnovo náměstí sprouts buffets and snack bars in summer; more substantial fare is served at *Vinárna U Anděla* on the west side and *Restaurace U Valdštejna* on Chelčického, just west of the square.

U Henryho, an Italian place with pizzas for 70 Kč, is on Čelakovského, two doors up from Pension U české koruny.

Entertainment

The *Biograf Český ráj* cinema, on 17.listopadu, shows foreign and some Czech movies year-round.

Getting There & Away

The best way to get to Jičín from Prague is by bus (90 minutes; 90km); Prague-Jičín by train is tedious.

PRACHOVSKÉ SKÁLY

This is the biggest of the Český ráj's 'rock towns', a labyrinth of sandstone towers, caves and passages. The rocks are accessible (for 20 Kč) via colour-coded hiking trails from three points: Ubytovna Český ráj (red trail), Hotel Skální město (blue trail) and the Turistická chata (green or red trail). All three trails eventually meet up. A full loop on the green trail takes two hours and covers the main sights.

Places to Stay & Eat

Chata and hotels here are overrun in summer, when you're better off booking ahead from Jičín. The best choices are *Ubytovna Český ráj* and the *Turistická chata* (☎ 0433-3541), both with basic hostel-style dorm rooms for 120 Kč per person, plus good, cheap hot meals. Both are open from mid-April through September. Considerably pricier, *Hotel Skální město* (☎ 0433-351 13; fax 351 38) has fully equipped singles/doubles with private bath and WC for 680/1150 Kč. There's a good restaurant here.

Getting There & Away

From Jičín, buses run right past these places about every two hours; stops are labelled 'Holín (Prachov Skalní město)' to the hotel or 'Holín (Turistická chata)'. Or you could walk it, a relatively easy 8km hike from the Rumcajs Motel at Jičín; the yellow trail gets farthest from the road.

HRUBÁ SKÁLA & VALDŠTEJN CASTLE

Another 'rock town', Hruboskálské skalní město is a dull uphill hike from the Hrubá skála train station; turn right across the tracks and follow the blue trail 3km to the Hotel Štekl carpark. From here, follow the red trail south-east to Trosky Castle (6.5km) or north-west to Hruboskálské skalní město (1.5km) and Valdštejn Castle (another 1.5km).

The 13th century castle was used variously by Hussite rebels, bandits and Albrecht of Wallenstein (Valdštejn), and is being slowly renovated. Valdštejn Castle is open daily, except Monday, April to October from 9 am to 4 pm; entry for self-guided tours costs 10 Kč.

Places to Stay

Sedmihorky Campsite (☎ 0436-91 61 34), 1.5km from the Karlovice-Sedmihorky train stop, charges 40 Kč per person and 40 Kč per tent, and is open from April to October.

Guarding the trail heads are two year-round hotels: the *Hotel Zámek* (☎ 0436-39 11 70), an atmospheric castle with sweeping views, and the adjacent, less thrilling *Hotel Štekl* (☎ 0436-91 62 84). Doubles with bath and breakfast are 800 Kč at the Zámek and 980 Kč at the Štekl.

Getting There & Away

Buses are rare; the most convenient access to Hruboskálské skalní město is from the train stations at Hrubá skála or Turnov Město (red trail; 5.5km). Express trains do not stop at either station, though at least 10 daily local trains serve Turnov-Jičín and Turnov-Hradec Králové (via Jičín).

TROSKY CASTLE

These dramatic castle ruins, perched on twin basalt towers, are visible for miles around. Built in around 1380 by Honoratus of Vartenburg, the strategically placed castle has changed hands madly over the centuries; in addition to its many lawful owners was a gang of 15th century robbers who terrorised the countryside for several years.

The higher tower is called Panna (the Virgin), and the other is Bába (the Granny). Panna and some lower walls were restored in the early 1990s, and work on Bába is under way. Visitors can only climb to the saddle between them, though even from there the view is good.

The castle is open daily, except Monday, May through September from 8 am to 5 pm, and on weekends only from 9 am to 4 pm in April and October.

Places to Stay & Eat

At the foot of the towers, ruining any photo taken from the south, is the sprawling *Hotel & Restaurace Trosky* (☎ & fax 0436-912 90), starting at 320 Kč per person. Or follow the green trail 1km south to the basic *Svitačka campsite*, priced at 40 Kč each.

Getting There & Away

The odd bus from Turnov stops below the hotel, from where it's 500m up to the castle. Better alternatives for walkers are local trains (not express) to Ktová plus a 2km hike up the green trail, or to Borek plus a 4km walk up a blue trail. It's also possible to walk from Hruboskálské skalní město.

TURNOV

Turnov has plenty of cheap lodgings and is a convenient Český ráj gateway, however, it's incredibly dull.

Orientation

The centre of town is náměstí Českého ráje. The train station is about 1km away, across the river on Nádražní. Regional buses (eg to/from Jičín) stop at the big bus station by the river; Prague and other long-distance buses deposit you by the train station.

Information

The information centre (☎ 255 00) on náměstí Českého ráje stocks hiking maps and books local and regional accommodation; it's open on weekdays from 9 to 11 am and noon to 4 pm.

CZECH REPUBLIC

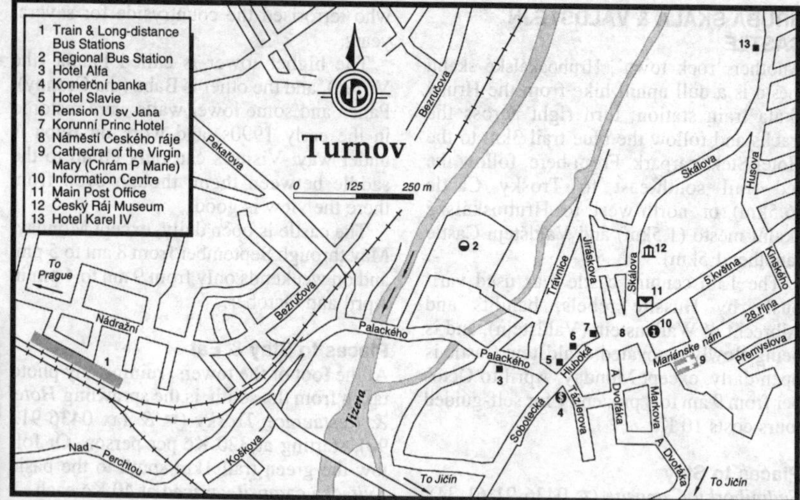

Komerční banka, on Sobotecká, has an exchange office and MasterCard/Visa ATM. The main post office is on náměstí Českého ráje at Skálova. Turnov's area code is ☎ 0436.

Český Ráj Museum

This plain museum at Skálova 71 features local archaeology, history, mineralogy and ethnography; entry costs 20 Kč. It's open daily, except Monday, year-round from 9 am to 4 pm.

Places to Stay & Eat

The information centre can help with private rooms and other cheap places. Spacious, modern doubles with breakfast are only 600 Kč at *Hotel Alfa* (☎ 213 38), Palackého 211. Equally comfortable are *Hotel Slavie* (☎ 222 46) at Hluboká 146 and *Pension U sv Jana* (☎ 233 25) at Hluboká 142. Both charge 350/700 Kč.

Behind the dreary face of the *Hotel Karel IV* (☎ 238 55), Žižkova 501, is a fairly decent hotel and restaurant, with doubles with shower and WC for 640 Kč, plus breakfast.

Turnov's top spot is the *Korunní Princ Hotel* (☎ & fax 242 12) at náměstí Českého ráje 137, with the works for 900/1260 Kč.

There's a shortage of restaurants in Turnov; the best of the bunch is upstairs at Pension U sv Jana.

Getting There & Away

To and from Prague there are direct trains, and around 10 buses a day, with more on weekends.

Adršpašsko-Teplické Rocks

The Český ráj may have the best known of the Czech Republic's 'rock towns', but the most rugged and dramatic rock formations are the Adršpašsko-Teplické skály. They lie in the Broumovská vrchovina (highlands) east of the Krkonoše, in a knob of eastern Bohemia that juts into Poland.

Slabs of sandstone have been worn by

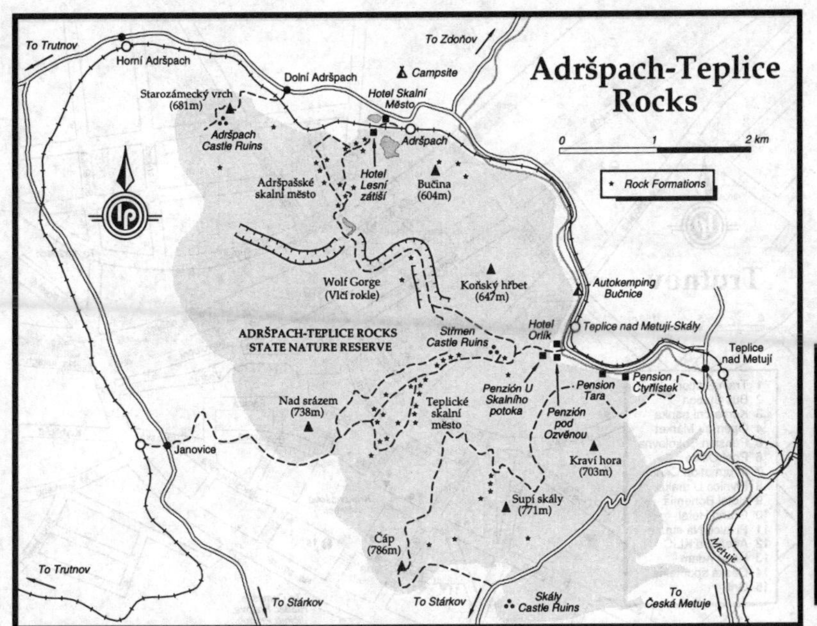

exposure and fissured by water and frost to form giant towers and terraces – a scene fit for *The Lord of the Rings*.

You can stroll along well-marked paths, scramble up for the view over 20 sq km of deep pine forest, or get together with local guides for some serious climbing. In summer the trails are heavily trodden, and you may have to book accommodation a week or more ahead, unless you're camping; in winter (snow lingers as late as mid-April) you'll have this stunning landscape mostly to yourself.

There are actually two clusters of formations, hence the mouthful of a name – Adršpach Rock Town (Adršpašské skalní město) and Teplice Rock Town (Teplické skalní město). They now comprise a single state nature reserve, lying about 15km east of the district capital of Trutnov.

At each 'rock town' you must pay a small admission charge of 25 Kč, and you can pick up a *Adršpašsko-Teplické skály a Ostaš* (1:25,000) trail map.

TRUTNOV

If you've come this far, you're more interested in woods and rocks than in yet another cobbled square lined with Renaissance façades. Even so, Trutnov is a pleasant place to pick up information, book hotels and change to the Teplice train. The lack of cheap accommodation is Trutnov's major drawback.

Orientation

The main square, Krakonošovo náměstí, is 500m south-east of the bus station along Horská, and a bit farther along from the train station across the Úpa river.

Information

Trutnov's information centre (☎ 6426), at Krakonošovo náměstí 72, has hiking maps

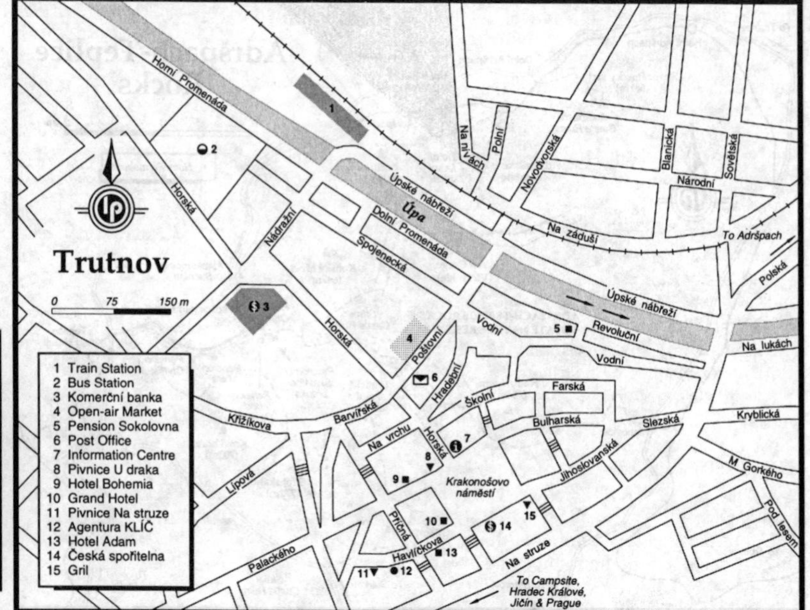

and a list of private rooms; it's open on weekdays from 8.30 am to 12.30 pm and 1 to 5 pm, and on Saturday from 8.30 am to noon.

Komerční banka is just down from the bus station, and Česká spořitelna is on the main square; both have ATMs. The post office is on Poštovní. Trutnov's area code is ☎ 0439.

Places to Stay

The only cheap option is a private room – inquire at the information centre or Agentura KLÍČ (☎ 2200), at Halíčkova 15.

Dolce camping (☎ 2763), on a reservoir about 5km south-west of the centre, is open from mid-June to mid-September. *Pension Sokolovna* (☎ 3348), above the seedy Restaurace Sokolovna near the river, supposedly has beds for 150 Kč. When we visited there was a 'problem' and all the rooms were 'broken'.

The *Grand Hotel* (☎ 81 19 01), Krakonošovo náměstí 120, is the town's cheapest and most comfortable place to stay, with doubles with bath for 1000 Kč.

Up-market options include *Hotel Bohemia* (☎ 81 19 51) at Palackého 81, with singles/doubles with bath for 1000/1450 Kč, and *Hotel Adam* (☎ 81 19 55) at Havlíčkova 10, priced at 1150/1650 Kč. The Adam has a much appreciated sauna.

Places to Eat

Good places on the square include a small stand-up *grill* and the smoky, raucous *Pivnice U draka*. A more classy, less smoky beer hall is *Pivnice Na struze*, at Havlíčkova 19. There is an open-air produce market by the post office.

Getting There & Away

Buses run to Trutnov throughout the day

from Prague, Hradec Králové and the main Krkonoše centres. Though there are no buses from Trutnov to the rocks, there are trains every two hours or so to Teplice nad Metují and Adršpach. Note that express trains do not stop at Teplice nad Metují-Skály; walk or change to a local train at Teplice nad Metují.

TEPLICKÉ SKALNÍ MĚSTO

About 200m west of the Teplice nad Metují-Skály train station is the Hotel Orlík and a carpark, from where a blue-marked trail climbs the valley of the **Skalní potok** (Rocky Stream), making a 7km loop lined in its upper reaches with stone giants.

About 1km along, those not subject to vertigo or shortness of breath can detour by stairs and ladders up to a look-out called **Střmen**. This and neighbouring formations were the site of a 13th century, eyrie-like wooden castle, destroyed in 1447 on the defeat of the Hussites hiding out in it.

Two scenic trails continue onwards to Adršpašské skalní město. From the blue loop-trail's west end, follow the green then a second blue trail 4km to a yellow trail, which meanders 3km north up **Vlčí rokle** (Wolf Gorge). Much shorter is a yellow trail that starts just before Střmen and continues 4km north up Wolf Gorge.

Places to Stay & Eat

Autokemping Bučnice, 300m north-west of the Teplice nad Metují-Skály train station, has tent sites for 35 Kč per person and 30 Kč per tent, and bungalows with bedding for 100 Kč per person. It's open May through September.

If you can get one, a single/double with shared facilities at the *Hotel Orlík* (☎ & fax 0447-933 66) is good value at 340/700 Kč, and the restaurant is excellent. Similar rooms at the adjacent *Penzión pod Ozvěnou* (☎ 0447-932 54) are 300 Kč per bed.

Just up the trail is the stream-side *Penzión U Skalního potoka* (☎ 0447-932 49), where quads with/without shower and WC are about 360/270 Kč, with kitchen privileges. In the same price range as Hotel Orlík are *Pension Tara* (☎ 0447-933 48) and *Pension Čtyřlístek* (☎ 0447-933 41).

All of the above close in winter and usually reopen by early March.

ADRŠPAŠSKÉ SKALNÍ MĚSTO

These rock formations are easiest to reach from Adršpach's train station; turn left onto the main road and left again at Hotel Skalní město. The green trail makes a 2.5km loop past the Czech Republic's tallest sandstone towers. You can detour south on the yellow trail (via Wolf Gorge) to the Teplice nad Metují-Skály train station.

Places to Stay & Eat

A *campsite* 500m north of the train station (via the yellow trail) is open May through September. At the time of writing, *Hotel Skalní město* (☎ 0447-938 23) was closed for renovations, though its excellent beer hall was open. The adjacent *Hotel Lesní zátiší* (☎ & fax 0447-938 19) has doubles for 1180 Kč.

Krkonoše

The Krkonoše (Giant Mountains, or Riesengebirge in German) are part of the Sudeten Range, stretching across the 'top' of Bohemia and Moravia. They're really two parallel ranges separated by a broad, marshy depression, the higher northern ridge forming the border with Poland's Silesia region. The 363 sq km **Krkonoše National Park** (Krkonošský národní park) was established in 1963 (its Polish counterpart is the Karkonoski Park Narodowy).

Rounded with age and cut by wide, shallow lateral valleys covered in spruce forests, these are indeed the Czech Republic's giants, topped by Sněžka (1602m), the highest mountain in the country. Four sizeable rivers rise here – the Mumlava, Jizera, Úpa and mighty Labe (Elbe).

The Krkonoše are the republic's most popular mountains, particularly for skiing.

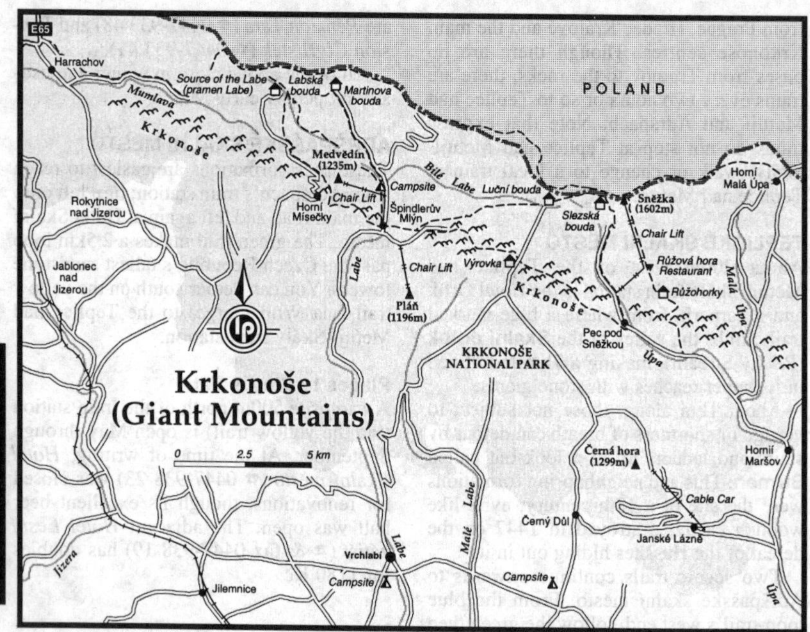

The walking is good too, though high-altitude summer weather is inconsistent, often cold and wet, and at lower elevations the chalet villages and access roads look dreary once the snow melts. Count on crowds in winter and high summer, especially on weekends.

Being a national park has not protected the Krkonoše's forests. Estimates suggest that as much as 25% have been badly damaged by acid rain (and then, in their weakened state, by insects), due to massive industrialisation in northern Bohemia. It's startling and depressing to come across vast areas of dead trees in what's meant to be a protected landscape.

Orientation

Most 'villages' in the park are simply unattractive resorts – essentially with a few services and innumerable places to sleep and eat. The main centres are Harrachov for skiing and Špindlerův Mlýn and Pec pod Sněžkou for walking.

The national park headquarters are at Vrchlabí, which is sometimes referred to as the park's 'gateway', but in fact the bigger resort centres inside the park have better information, and it's easy to reach many of them directly from Prague and Hradec Králové.

Information

National park information centres at Vrchlabí, Harrachov, Rokytnice nad Jizerou, Špindlerův Mlýn and Pec pod Snežkou have brochures, maps and at least some good advice on accommodation. For up-to-date trail and weather information, go to the nearest Mountain Rescue Service (Horská služba) office.

Kartografie Praha has a *Krkonoše* (1:50,000) map, complete with blow-ups of the main resort centres and colour-coded hiking trails. There is also a two-part, 1:25,000 map of the park.

Warning
Despite the modest elevations, it's usually windy and *very cold* year-round at higher elevations. Even in summer, mountain fog creates a hypothermia risk (see Health in the Facts for the Visitor chapter). Don't go up without sturdy shoes, extra layers, rain protection and water. If the mist rolls in, consider turning back.

Activities
There are **walking** trails galore, including the red-marked Cesta česko-polského přátelství (Czech-Polish Friendship Trail) along much of the border ridge. Couch potatoes, and travellers with children, can get up into the high country via year-round chair lifts at Pec pod Snežkou (to the summit of Sněžka) and Špindlerův Mlýn, and via a cable car at Janské Lázně.

Link roads, some with limited or no public access, are a treat for **cycling** enthusiasts. And of course there's **skiing** in winter. It's possible to rent ski equipment, at least at Pec pod Snežkou.

Places to Stay
There are literally hundreds of hotels and chalets in the park. The hotels tend to be full year-round, but in the summer many chalets at lower elevations are used for pension or private accommodation – with good walk-in prospects, so there's no need to book ahead. For two people, figure on about 700 Kč and up, with breakfast.

The local word for a mountain hut, chalet or hotel is *bouda (b.* on maps), a term originally used for the shepherds' huts at these spots. Other more or less equivalent Czech terms are *chata* and *chalupa.* There are some comfortable, and popular, *boudy* along the high-elevation trails. You should try to book these at least a few days ahead; inquire at a park information centre.

Getting There & Away
Buses are the most convenient way into the Krkonoše, with numerous daily direct connections from Prague to Pec pod Snežkou and Špindlerův Mlýn (three to 3½ hours), and others via Hradec Králové, Vrchlabí and Trutnov. Pec pod Snežkou also has direct bus links from Brno.

The nearest fast-train junctions are Vrchlabí and Trutnov, with connections to Harrachov, Rokytnice nad Jizerou and Svoboda nad Úpou.

Getting Around
Limited bus connections exist among the resort centres, such as three a day between Pec pod Snežkou and Janské Lázně and about six a day between Pec pod Snežkou and Špindlerův Mlýn.

VRCHLABÍ

This dreary town has few hotels or places to book accommodation, but you may have to change buses or trains here.

Orientation & Information
The town stretches inconveniently like a ribbon along the Labe. From the (adjacent) bus and train stations it's 1.5km north to the town centre at náměstí Masaryka; cross the river and take the second right on Slovanská, which becomes Krkonošská. Náměstí Míru is a further 250m north.

A park information centre (☎ 210 11), at náměstí Míru, offers maps, brochures and souvenirs, and opens daily from 9.30 am to 4 pm. Vrchlabí's area code is ☎ 0438.

Museums
The park service has a permanent exhibition on Krkonoše ecology in a former monastery on Husova, west off náměstí Míru, and another on local history and handicrafts, by the park information centre. Both are open daily, except Monday, from 9 am to 4 pm.

Places to Stay
There are quite a few *'Zimmer frei'* (room for rent) signs south of the centre. For a cheap sleep, try *Sportovní hala*, a sports centre just over the river from the bus station; the office is upstairs. The glum *Hotel*

CZECH REPUBLIC

Labuť (☎ 229 64), Krkonošská 188, has doubles/triples with bath for 1000/1400 Kč. Another central option is *Pension Gól* (☎ 231 66), Frügnerova 1288, priced at 400 Kč per person.

Vejsplachy campsite (☎ 221 96), open June through September, is several kilometres south-west of the centre on Pražská třída, the road to Prague.

Getting There & Away

Vrchlabí is 2½ hours from Prague, and ČSAD has eight to 10 buses a day. Buses run frequently all day to Špindlerův Mlýn, Pec pod Snežkou and Janské Lázně.

ŠPINDLERŮV MLÝN

At 780m, Špindlerův Mlýn is the Krkonoše's largest winter recreation centre, which is about the only polite thing there is to say about this strip of high-rise hotels. After Pec pod Snežkou, this is probably the second best ski resort in the Czech Republic.

Orientation & Information

From the bus stop, the Mountain Rescue Service (Horská služba; ☎ 934 30) is 500m east, after a right turn at the post office. The national park information centre (☎ 932 28) is 1.5km up the Labe valley road, beside the campsite. Špindlerův Mlýn's area code is ☎ 0438.

Things to See & Do

A **chair lift** runs north-west to the top of Medvědín (1235m) and back for 60 Kč, and another runs south up Pláň (1196m) and back for 45 Kč.

You can hike up to the **Labe headwaters** on a blue-marked trail heading north and north-west. At the top of a nasty 200m ascent at the end of the valley is the Labská bouda chalet; the source of the Labe (*pramen Labe* on maps) is about 800m farther on, along the red trail. Return to Špindlerův Mlýn on the red trail south via Horní Mísečky, or on a green trail east via Martinova bouda, making a round-trip of five to six hours.

Places to Stay

A basic *campsite* (☎ 935 34), open May through September, is 1.5km up the valley road from the bus stop. The park information service can offer advice on finding private rooms.

At last count there were 24 hotels and 12 pensions in town – shop around for the best price. The Svatý Petr road has the most options, notably the cheap *Hotel Panorama* (☎ 933 52) at No 136.

PEC POD SNEŽKOU

'Pec under Sněžka' (or just Pec), sitting about 770m beneath the highest peak of the Krkonoše (1602m Sněžka), is probably the most popular centre in summer. The highest ski resort in the Czech Republic, this is most likely to have the best skiing, but it's not the Alps.

Orientation & Information

Near the bus stop is a cheerful gallery and information service called Veselý Výlet (Jolly Jaunt), open daily from 8 am to 6 pm, with maps, postcards, excursion ideas and accommodation advice. It also publishes an excellent free newsletter full of regional lore and relevant excursions.

The national park information centre (☎ 96 22 13), 200m up the hill at No 172, is open weekdays from 8 am to noon and 1 to 3 pm, and weekends from 8 to 10 am. A further 400m along is the Mountain Rescue Service (Horská služba). Pec pod Snežkou's area code is ☎ 0439.

Climbing Sněžka

This is a three hour climb or five hour round trip. From near the Hotel Horizont, climb the green-marked Čertový schody (Devil's Staircase) trail north-west to a chalet at Výrovka, then north up the red ridge trail to Luční bouda chalet.

A blue trail crosses a marshy area to Slezská bouda on the Polish border, from where you make your assault on the treeless summit of Sněžka. The peak is bang on the border (Poles call it Śnieżka). You must share your triumph, and the grand views, with Czech and Polish guards and an army of tourists who have come up the easy way, by chair lift from both sides.

From Sněžka, take the yellow ridge trail south to chalets at Růžohorky, and then descend along a steep green trail back to Pec.

If you can't handle the climb, walk 300m back from the bus stop and about 1.5km up the valley of the Úpa to the **chair lift**, or *lanovka*, and ride right to the top. The two stage trip (65 Kč return) takes half an hour each way. There's a restaurant halfway up, at Růžová hora.

Places to Stay

The hillsides above Pec are thick with chalets, many open to tourists in summer. The Velká Úpa road has the best selection of pensions – try the *Čertice* (☎ 96 22 69) at No 191, priced at 350/700 Kč.

Getting Around

At the park boundary near Horní Maršov is a highway checkpoint where drivers must buy a parking permit, which costs a whopping 100 Kč a day in the carpark below the Sněžka chair lift or 25 Kč in the centre of Pec.

North Moravia

HIGHLIGHTS

GERMANY
POLAND
SLOVAKIA
AUSTRIA

- Spend a few hours admiring the region's architecture and cultural past at the Walachian Open-Air Museum, Rožnov pod Radhoštěm
- Stop off in Olomouc to catch the proletariat astronomical clock, and while you're there take in the fine architecture of this underrated university town
- Go for a walk to the top of Radhošť, and while you're there stay the night in one of the chalets

When they consider Moravia, most travellers think of Brno and the Moravian Karst in the south. And it's true, the northern half of Moravia is more industrialised and more polluted than the rustic south, due partly (as in Bohemia) to the mining of rich deposits of iron ore and other minerals. This was once the centre of Czechoslovakia's overheated arms industry, which is now in decline.

But North Moravia – which includes part of the historical region called Silesia – also has some of the Czech Republic's most fertile lowlands (the Morava and Bečva valleys), some of its least tamed mountains (the Jeseníky), the culturally unique Walachia region in the gentle Beskydy hills, and a first-rate museum of traditional architecture at Rožnov pod Radhoštěm.

Though dreary Ostrava is the region's administrative centre and largest city, the beautiful, sooty old university town of Olomouc is its historical capital, and its cultural and commercial heart.

Jeseníky Mountains

The Jeseníky range takes up roughly half of northern Moravia, in the form of two quite different ranges. The rugged Hrubý Jeseník rises 1500m in the north-west corner of the region. It's here that you'll find Moravia's highest peak, Praděd (1491m) – apparently on a clear day you can see both the Krkonoše of eastern Bohemia and the Tatras of central Slovakia from its peak. The surrounding Hrubý Jeseník Protected Landscape Region (Chráněná krajinná oblast Hrubý Jeseník) is still home to deer

Silesia

Historically, this once German-speaking region, occupying the basin of the Odra (German: Oder) river in Poland and Moravia, has variously belonged to Poland, Bohemia, the Habsburgs, and Prussia. Geographical factors even resulted in its division into Black, White and Green Silesia.

This century has seen the boundaries of 'Austrian' (Czechoslovak) Silesia and Prussian Silesia being juggled, then Prussian Upper Silesia being ceded to Poland, and at the end of WWII most of Prussian Lower Silesia going to Poland too.

German-speakers throughout both the Moravian and Polish parts of the region have all been driven out since WWII. ■

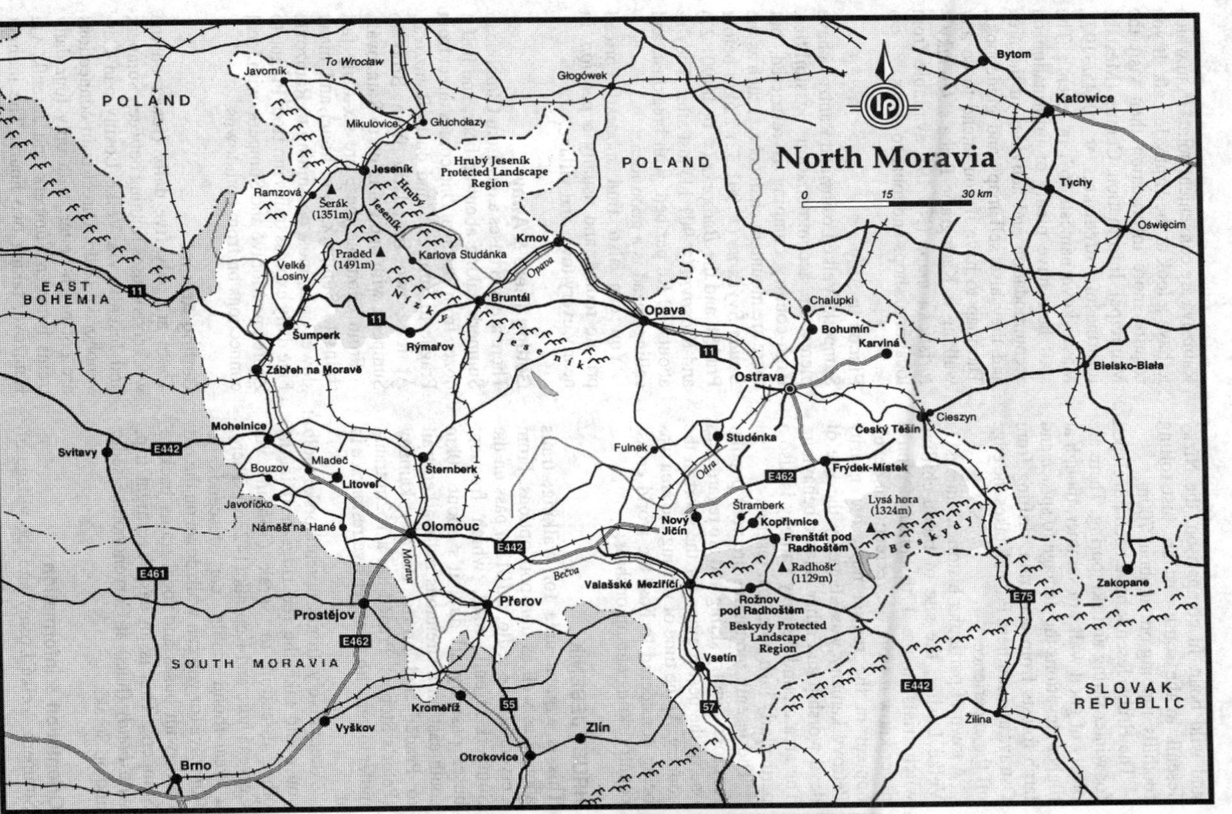
North Moravia
0
15
30 km
To Wrocław
Javorník
POLAND
Mikulovice
Głuchołazy
Głogówek
POLAND
Bytom
Katowice
Tychy
Oświęcim
Jeseník
Hrubý Jeseník Protected Landscape Region
Hrubý Jeseník
Ramzová
Šerák (1351m)
Praděd (1491m)
Karlova Studánka
Krnov
Opava
Velké Losiny
EAST BOHEMIA
11
Bruntál
Nízký Jeseník
Opava
Chałupki
Bohumín
Karviná
Šumperk
Rýmařov
Zábřeh na Moravě
Ostrava
Bielsko-Biała
Cieszyn
Český Těšín
Mohelnice
Svitavy
E442
Studénka
Fulnek
Mladeč
Bouzov
Litovel
Šternberk
Frýdek-Místek
E462
Odra
Javoříčko
Štramberk
Lysá hora (1324m)
Nový Jičín
Kopřivnice
Náměšť na Hané
Olomouc
Frenštát pod Radhoštěm
Beskydy
E442
Radhošť (1129m)
E461
Bečva
Morava
Valašské Meziříčí
Zakopane
Přerov
Rožnov pod Radhoštěm
E75
Prostějov
Beskydy Protected Landscape Region
E462
SOUTH MORAVIA
Vsetín
E442
SLOVAK REPUBLIC
Kroměříž
55
57
Žilina
Vyškov
Zlín
Otrokovice
Brno

and wild boar. In comparison, the Nízký Jeseník to the south-east are just rolling foothills, topping out at about 700m.

The Hrubý Jeseník have been developed for winter skiing and ski touring. There are plenty of good walks in summer, though at higher elevations the damage to spruce and larch forests from acid rain, drifting from Ostrava and southern Poland, takes the edge off the experience.

A town of particular historical interest is Velké Losiny, the site of blood-chilling witch trials in the 17th century. You'd never know it from the recreational development in the region now, but nearby Petrovy kameny was allegedly the site of devil worship and other satanic behaviour. The area around Petrovy kameny is also a particularly lush botanical reserve.

The Jeseník mountains are very popular for cross-country skiing and are regarded as one of the best regions for the sport in the country. At the time of writing the area was being considered to host the world cross-country skiing championships.

HRUBÝ JESENÍK

This is a great area for walking; trails abound as well as transport options. From Červenohorské sedlo, a 1013m pass on the Šumperk-Jeseník road, which frequent buses pass by all day, it's about 10km south-east on a strenuous red-marked trail to Praděd and on to Petrovy kameny (Peter's Stones). Praděd has a 162m transmitter tower with an expensive *restaurace* in it.

Alternatively, from Červenohorské sedlo you could take the red ridge-trail in the other direction to Serák (1351m) via Červená hora and Keprník (1423m). There, a year-round cable car descends to Ramzová (or you can walk down on the red trail), with buses and local trains back to Šumperk. This is an easy overnight trip, with *boudy* (huts) at Červenohorské sedlo and on Serák.

Orientation & Information

Šumperk, Velké Losiny and the village of Ramzová are convenient points from which to have a look at the Hrubý Jeseník. If you require more information then visit the Municipal Information Centre (Městské informační středisko; ☎ 0645/3197), Masarykovo náměstí 167, in Jeseník. The staff here have plenty of information on accommodation and activities in the area and they also sell maps and guidebooks. The map to have if you intend to do any walking is Kartografie Praha's *Jeseníky – turistická mapa* (No 19), available from local bookshops and tobacco shops.

Places to Stay

Šumperk, Velké Losiny and Ramzová have plenty of accommodation possibilities. High-country camping is restricted, but there are mountain chalets here, such as the *Bouda Švýcárna* (☎ 901 32) 2.5km before Praděd, and the *Barborka* (☎ 0646-901 27) and *Kursovní* (☎ 901 11) just after. They're about 400 Kč per bed, with breakfast, and calling ahead is a good idea.

You can also find modestly priced private rooms, and usually a *penzión*, in nearly every town and village.

Getting There & Away

There are two buses a day from Olomouc to Šumperk, taking about an hour, and half a dozen from Ostrava. One comes direct from Prague to Šumperk (and on to Ramzová). At least two run daily from Brno to Šumperk, with one going on to Ramzová.

From Olomouc there are six daily fast trains to Šumperk (one hour) and many slower ones, most continuing to Ramzová. Five daily express trains run from Prague to Zábřeh na Moravě and Šumperk, with local connections on from both towns.

Getting Around

There are only five daily (fewer on the weekends) buses running between Šumperk and Jeseník, via Velké Losiny nad Červenohorské sedlo. Direct train connections are not much better, with only four daily trains between Šumperk and Jeseník, via Ramzová, taking two hours. The indirect trains on this line are more frequent but require at least one change, usually at Hanušovice.

VELKÉ LOSINY

Velké Losiny, today a minor spa town, was from 1496 to 1802 the seat of the powerful Žerotín family. A factory (with a small museum) established here by the family still produces handmade paper.

Žerotín Chateau

The striking, U-shaped *zámek*, with three storeys of arcades rising above its courtyard, and lavish parklands, is one of Moravia's best preserved Renaissance properties, inside and out. The 25 Kč group tour in Czech (there's an English text) takes in lots of empire furniture and a 16th century tiled stove said to be one of the oldest in either republic, as well as portraits of the Žerotíns and paintings collected by them. It steers clear of the actual room – the grotesquely named Hall of Justice – where the infamous trials took place, and goes into little detail about them.

The chateau (☎ 0649-23 53 80) is open daily, except Monday and the day after a national holiday, May through September from 8 am to noon and 1 to 5 pm (to 4 pm in September), and on weekends only (to 4 pm) in April and October.

Getting There & Away For getting to Šumperk, see the preceding section on the Hrubý Jeseník. From there, Velké Losiny is a 20 minute train ride, with about eight departures a day. The chateau is about 1km south-west on a green-marked path from the train station, through the old spa.

Olomouc

Olomouc, a town of 100,000 in a broad, fertile stretch of the Morava river basin, is one of the Czech Republic's most underrated places. It's a youthful, laid-back university town, friendly and cheap, with cobbled streets and the largest trove of historical architecture outside Prague – and hardly a tourist in sight. Despite a somewhat bedraggled, sooty outskirts, its historical centre is certainly northern Moravia's most beautiful town.

Legend says it was founded by Julius

CZECH REPUBLIC

The Boblíg Inquisition

In the 17th and 18th centuries this part of North Moravia was swept by a wave of witch and vampire hysteria that makes the Salem witch hunts, happening in the USA at the same time, look like a Sunday outing.

In 1678 the Žerotíns hired František Boblíg to undertake the role of inquisitor in eradicating what they saw as ungodly and superstitious practices.

The inquisitor fulfilled his commission with zeal. Over the course of 15 years, with the help of weak-minded church and civilian officials, he accused scores of people, mostly women, of satanic practices and witchcraft. He tortured them to extract confessions of impiety, and had them put to death, often at the stake. When nobles in Šumperk grew critical of the amount of property that Boblíg and his 'judges' were confiscating from their victims, he accused them of being implicated with the devil, too.

Almost 15 years after they had started, the increasingly terrified Žerotíns were persuaded by King Leopold I to take steps to end the persecutions, and the murderous Boblíg was forced to retire. It is recorded that he died of natural causes at an advanced age; despite causing the deaths of over 100 innocent people, he was never punished. ■

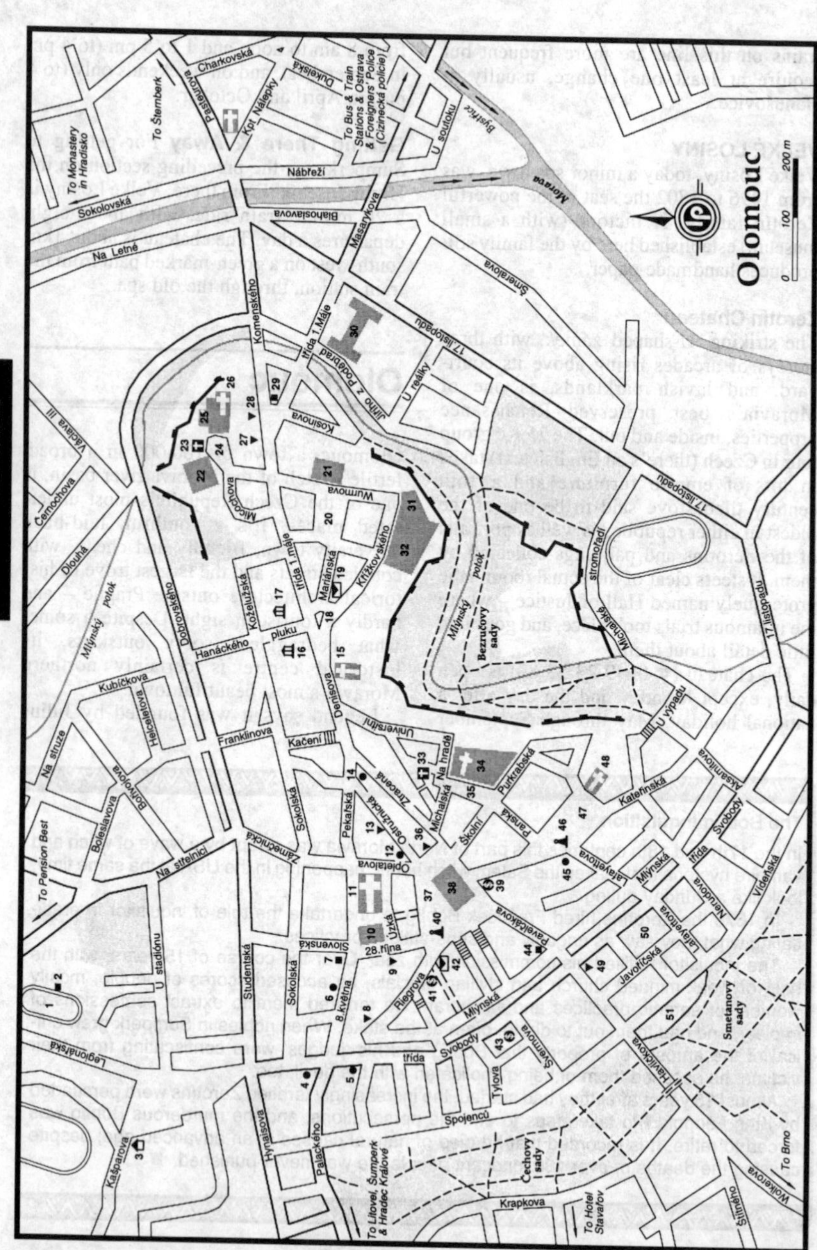
Olomouc
0 100 200 m
To Monastery in Hradisko
To Šternberk
Charkovská
Pasteurova
Dukelská
Kpt. Nálepky
To Bus & Train Stations & Ostrava
Foreigners' Police (Cizinecká policie)
Nábřeží
U soutoku
Bystřice
Morava
Sokolovská
Na Letné
Blahoslavova
Masarykova
Komenského
Šmeralova
17.listopadu
třída 1.Máje
Jiřího z Poděbrad
U reálky
Kosinova
Václava III
Černochova
Dlouhá
Mlýnský potok
Dobrovského
Wurmova
Mičochova
Křížkovského
Mariánská
Koželužská
Hanáckého pluku
Denisova
Bezručovy sady
stromořadí
Michalské
U výpadu
Kubíčkova
Helceletova
Na struze
Franklinova
Kačení
Univerzitní
Na hradě
Purkrabská
Kateřinská
Aksamitova
Svobody
Vídeňská
Bolívarova
Boleslavova
To Pension Best
Na střelnici
Zámečnická
Sokolská
Pekařská
Ztracená
Ostružnická
Michalská
Školní
Panská
Lafayettova
Mlýnská
Nerudova
třída
Opletalova
Pavelčákova
Javoříčská
Smetanovy sady
U stadiónu
Studentská
Slovenská
Úzká
28.října
8.května
Riegrova
Mlýnská
Havlíčkova
Legionářská
Svobody
třída
Tylova
Sternova
Hynaisova
Palackého
Kašparova
Spojenců
Čechovy sady
To Litovel, Šumperk & Hradec Králové
Krapkova
To Hotel Stavařov
Stiboreho
Wolkerova
To Brno

PLACES TO STAY

2 Hotel Gól
3 Hostel Plavecký stadion
7 Hotel Národní dům
29 Hotel Palác
30 Student Hostel
44 Hotel Gemo

PLACES TO EAT

8 Vinárna Matěj
9 Mikulovská vinárna
13 Pekárna Tiefenbach
27 Centrum bufet
28 Neptun Fish Restaurant
36 Kavárna a cukrárna Mahler
49 Drápal Restaurant

OTHER

1 Football Stadium (Fotbalový stadion)
4 DPMO (Municipal Transport Office)
5 Čedok
6 Kodak Mini-lab
10 Prior Department Store
11 St Moritz Cathedral (chrám sv Mořice)
12 Tycho bookshop (knihkupectví)
14 CKM
15 Church of St Mary of the Snows (kostel Panny Marie Sněžné)
16 Olomouc Museum of Art (Olomoucký muzeum umění) in the Musical Theatre (Hudební divadlo)
17 Natural History Museum (Vlastivědné muzeum)
18 Náměstí Republiky
19 Main Post & Telephone Office
20 Biskupské náměstí
21 Archbishop's Palace (Arcibiskupský palác)
22 Former Deanery
23 St Anne Chapel (kaple sv Anny)
24 Václavské náměstí
25 Přemysl Palace (Přemyslovský palác)
26 St Wenceslas Cathedral (dóm sv Václava
31 Student Union (Stavovská unie studentů) & Kavárna Terasa
32 Palacky University (Universita Palackého)
33 Chapel of St Jan Sarkander (kaple sv Jana Sarkandera)
34 St Michael Church (kostel sv Michala) & Dominican Seminary
35 Žerotínovo náměstí
37 Horní náměstí
38 Town Hall (radnice), OIS (Olomoucká informační služba) & Kavárna Caesar
39 Česká spořitelna
40 Trinity Column (Sousoší Nejsvětější trojice)
41 Komerční banka & ATM
42 Branch Post & Telephone Office
43 Komerční banka
45 Hauenschild Palace & Hanack restaurace
46 Marian Plague Column (Mariánský morový sloup)
47 Dolní náměstí
48 Annunciation of St Mary Church (kostel Zvestování Panny Marie)
50 Palachovo náměstí
51 Turn-of-the-century Houses

Caesar. After Moravia and Bohemia were united in the 11th century, it became a major seat of administrative power, and in 1063 a bishopric. Olomouc looks fit to be a capital city, and indeed was the Moravian capital from the 12th century until it was occupied and looted by Swedish troops between 1642-50. It has been the seat of the metropolitan archbishop of Moravia since 1777. Industrialisation passed Olomouc by until well into this century.

Orientation

The main train station (*hlavní nádraží*) is on the main square, Horní náměstí, 2km east over the Morava river and its tributary the Bystřice (take tram No 1, 2, 5 or 6). The bus station is 1km farther east (take tram No 5 or 6).

The old town itself, around the two linked squares of Horní (Upper) and Dolní (Lower) náměstí, is easily seen on foot. Horní náměstí, with the beautiful old town hall at the centre, is pedestrianised. Around the old town's eastern lobe, centred on náměstí Republiky, are buildings of the university and the archbishopric.

Information

Tourist Offices On the north side of the town hall is the Olomouc Information Service (Olomoucká informační služba, or OIS; ☎ 551 33 85; fax 522 08 43). Open daily from 9 am to 7 pm it's good for town information, maps and accommodation advice. Find out more detailed information on its world wide web site (www.winet.cz/viso.htm).

CZECH REPUBLIC

Čedok (☎ 522 88 31), náměstí Národních Hrdinů 4, open weekdays from 9 am to noon and 1 to 5 pm, is helpful but mainly for accommodation. CKM (☎ 522 21 48), Denisova 4, sells ISIC, HI and other cards, and can advise you on bottom-end accommodation; weekdays from 9 am to noon and 1 to 5 pm.

A good source of road and hiking maps is the Tycho bookshop (*knihkupectví*) at Ostružnická 3.

Money Komerční banka is west of Horní náměstí on třída Svobody, but its MasterCard ATM is at the Riegrova 1 branch. There's a Visa ATM and exchange counter at Česká spořitelna, Horní náměstí 17.

Post & Communications The main post and telephone office is on náměstí Republiky, and there's a branch on Horní náměstí. International calls are possible from both locations.

Olomouc's area code is ☎ 068.

Cultural Centres The British Council and the French Regional Centre operate small language-resource centres upstairs at the university's student union (Stavovská unie studentů) at Křížovského 14. On the ground floor is a small bookshop.

Emergency The Foreigners' Police (Cizinecká policie; ☎ 551 51 11 or 522 33 33) are in the police building at Smetanova 14, near the train station.

Horní Náměstí & Around

The splendid, polymorphous **town hall** (*radnice*) in the middle of the square was built in 1378, though its present appearance and needle-like tower date from 1607. Note the oriel window of the 15th century chapel on the south side. The 10 Kč entry fee allows you to climb the tower. It's open daily between March and October from 11 am to 11.30 am and 3 to 5 pm. Don't miss the astronomical clock on the north side, grotesquely remodelled by the Communists so that each hour brings a procession of wooden proletarians instead of saints.

Beside the town hall sits the phenomenal **Trinity Column** (Sousoší Nejsvětější trojice; 1754), a column to end all columns. Built between 1716-54 to a design by V Render, a local sculptor, it is supposedly the biggest single Baroque sculpture in central Europe. In its blackened complexity it is surprisingly reminiscent of the Buddhist shrine at Borobudur in Indonesia.

In the square are two of the city's six **Baroque fountains**. Around the perimeter stand a medley of Renaissance, Baroque and empire façades.

Down Opletalova is Olomouc's original parish church, the vast **St Moritz Cathedral** (chrám sv Mořice), Gothic through and through, which took almost 130 years to

Fountains of Olomouc

Olomouc boasts six impressive Baroque fountains:

Hercules Fountain (Herkulova kašna): Horní náměstí, by Michal Mandík, 1688, the oldest
Caesar Fountain (Caesarova kašna): Horní náměstí, by Jiří Schuberger, 1724, the biggest and best known
Mercury Fountain (Merkurova kašna): near Prior department store, by Filip Sattler, 1730, one tourist brochure actually calls Mercury the 'god of business'
Tritons Fountain (Kašna Tritonů): náměstí Republiky, by Václav Render, 1709
Neptune Fountain (Neptunova kašna): Dolní náměstí, by Michal Mandík, 1695
Jupiter Fountain (Jupiterova kašna): Dolní náměstí, by Václav Render, 1707 ■

complete (1412-1540). The west tower is from its 13th century predecessor. Inside it's an amazing island of peace – or of thundering glory if its organ, the biggest in Moravia, is in action.

The modern fits pretty neatly around the old in Olomouc, with the hideous exception of the Prior department store that now shares St Moritz's little square, which is like having a Sherman tank in your parlour. Nowhere in the republic (except Jihlava) is there a building so out of place and worth tearing down.

Dolní Náměstí

The 1661 **Church of Annunciation of St Mary** (kostel Zvěstování Panny Marie), with plain mosaic and round windows, stands out with its sobriety and beautifully simple interior. Quite another matter is the rapidly ageing Renaissance confection with a bay window across from it, the 16th century **Hauenschild Palace**. The square also sports its own Marian plague column (Mariánský morový sloup).

The old town's most picturesque bits are the narrow lanes east of the two squares, leading to the town's commanding, green-domed landmark, the **St Michael Church** (kostel sv Michala), with its incredibly muscular Baroque interior. Among the furnishings is a rare painting of a pregnant Virgin Mary. Wrapped around the entire block is an active **Dominican seminary** (Dominikánský klášter). Surprisingly, the square, Žerotínovo náměstí, is named after the landowning family (the Žerotins) who set in motion Velké Losiny's gruesome 17th century witch trials (for more information see the Bohlí Inquisition aside in this chapter).

Nearby is the tiny round **Chapel of Saint Jan Sarkander** (kaple sv Jana Sarkandra), named after a local priest who died under torture in 1620 for refusing to divulge confessions made to him. It's built on the site of the jail where he died, and part of the jail is said to be preserved in the cellar.

The 1997 Floods

The July 1997 floods were the worst on record. At one time one-third of the Czech Republic was under water. The worst affected areas were East Bohemia and North Moravia, while parts of North Bohemia, South Moravia and north-western Slovakia were also swept up by the deluge.

At the time of writing there were still some railway lines and bridges out of operation but by the time you read this they are expected to be fully operational. The damage was exceptionally high, running into millions of dollars and over 40 people were reported dead. The floods disrupted the transportation network, made thousands homeless and ruined much of the agricultural produce. ■

Náměstí Republiky & Around

The original Jesuit college complex, founded in 1573, stretched along Univerzitní and into náměstí Republiky. It included the Baroque **Church of St Mary of the Snows** (kostel Panny Marie Sněžné) full of frescoes and reputed to have fine acoustics.

Across the road at Denisova 47, upstairs from the Musical Theatre (Hudebné divadlo), is the **Olomouc Museum of Art** (Olomoucký muzeum umění; ☎ 522 84 70), an excellent gallery with changing displays from a collection of 20th century Czech painting and sculpture, plus shows of contemporary artists; entry is a bargain at 20 Kč (free every Wednesday). It's open daily, except Monday, from 9 am to 5 pm. Beside this in a former convent, is the **Regional History Museum** (Vlastivědné muzeum).

Detour away from the mad traffic on třída 1.máje and up Křížovského, past the 17th century canons' residences that now house part of **Palacký University** (Universita Palackého). The sunny *kavárna* at the student union is a good place for a coffee break.

Around the corner in Biskupské náměstí is the **Archbishop's Palace** (Arcibiskupský palác; 1685), not so much interesting as merely huge. The monolith on the south side of the square is a former armoury (1711).

Přemysl Palace & St Wenceslas Cathedral

In the peaceful, pocket-sized Václavské náměstí, in the north-east corner of the old centre, site of the town's original castle, are the most venerable of Olomouc's historical buildings.

Originally a Romanesque basilica, consecrated in 1131, the **St Wenceslas Cathedral** (dóm sv Václava) was rebuilt several times before being thoroughly 'neo-Gothicised' inside and out in the 1880s. An exposition in the crypt includes over-the-top reliquaries, postage stamps on church themes, and an ostrich egg used as a ballot box in the selection of the Olomouc bishops.

Pride of place goes to the remnants of the early 12th century **Přemysl Palace** (Přemyslovský palác; 9 am to noon and 1 to 5 pm Tuesday to Sunday; 20 Kč). Once thought to be a royal palace, it's now known to have been built for Bishop Jindřich Zdík. A detailed English text walks you through a cloister with 15th and 16th century frescoes on the original walls, up to the archaeological centrepiece, the bishops' rooms with their Romanesque walls and windows (it was only rediscovered in 1867) and artistry unequalled elsewhere in the Czech Republic, even in Prague Castle. Downstairs, surviving 16th century frescoes in the Chapel of St John the Baptist (kaple sv Jana Křtitele; 1262) include angels with instruments of torture (a sign of ecclesiastical approval?).

To the left of the palace is the **St Anne Chapel** (kaple sv Anny), and beyond it the long, yellow walls of the former **deanery** where Wenceslas III, last of the Přemysl line, was mysteriously assassinated in 1306. This building is now part of Palacký university.

Monastery in Hradisko

From the palace, you can stroll east on Komenského (towards a little pink and green Orthodox church) for a view up the Morava to the onion-domed bulk of a former Benedictine monastery, founded by the Přemysls in 1078 (and once the biggest monastery in central Europe) in the district of Hradisko. It's now a military hospital, closed to the public.

Other Attractions

In the south-west of the town on Vídeňská, past blocks of run-down Art Nouveau flats around Palachovo náměstí, are four wonderfully fanciful turn-of-the century houses, all in a row, each with walled gardens, multiple gates and towers, but, sadly, all now gone to seed.

Similar houses are dotted nearby on the edge of Smetanovy sady, one of the large parks that enclose the historical centre to the west and east (and which are also worth a stroll through).

Places to Stay

OIS and CKM can advise you on private and hotel rooms. At the time of writing CKM was sending people only to *Penzion Best* (☎ 285 06), Na Střelnici 48, just north of the centre (take bus No 18), where single/double rooms cost 490/880 Kč. Čedok too will help, but slaps on big fees if you let it book for you. Though there aren't many hotels, walk-in prospects seem good in general.

Bottom End The *Hostel Plavecký stadion* (☎ 41 31 81), Legionářská 11, has basic doubles for 380 Kč. Another cheap place is *Hotel Stavařov* (☎ 541 39 40), U místní dráhy 1, just west of the city centre along Tylova, where basic rooms start from 190/380 Kč.

The overpriced *Hotel Gól* (☎ 522 98 13), on the eastern side of the football stadium off U stadiónu, a five minute walk north-west of the centre, has doubles for 880 Kč.

Middle The *Hotel Národní dům* (☎ 522 48

06/7; fax 522 48 08), 8.května 21, has clean rooms with WC and shower or bath for 720/1420 Kč, with breakfast, and a good and not-too-pricey restaurant. At třída 1.máje 27 is the *Hotel Palác* (☎ 522 40 96; fax 522 32 84), where rooms including shower and WC are 625/1650 Kč.

The new four-star *Hotel Gemo* (☎ 522 20 65; fax 286 25), Pavelčákova 22, has elegant rooms from 1856/2568 Kč.

Places to Eat

There are numerous vinárna and pubs (hospody) that serve respectable meals, such as *Mikulovská vinárna* (☎ 522 03 54) on 28.října opposite the Prior department store, with main courses for under 120 Kč, and the *Hanacká restaurace* at Dolní náměstí 29, which has local specialities for under 109 Kč.

Bistros, bars, cake shops (cukrárna) and open-air cafés (kavárna) are plentiful around Horní náměstí. The classy *Kavárna a cukrárna Mahler* at Hlavní náměstí 11 is a nice place to enjoy coffee and cake. Good bread, rolls and Czech pastries (koláče) can be found aplenty at *Pekárna Tiefenbach*, Ostružnická 13.

Probably the best daytime value in town is the clean, cheerful, cafeteria-style *Centrum bufet* at třída 1.máje 23, serving soups, fish, hot courses and a dozen delicious salads from 8 am to 5 pm on weekdays only. You can eat well here for about 50 Kč.

The student union's bright *Kavárna Terasa*, at Křížovského 14, is open from 11 am to midnight on weekdays and 3 pm to midnight on weekends.

Three other possibilities are the *Neptun* fish restaurant at Komenského 5, with mid-range fish courses (55 to 168 Kč) daily from 11 am to 11 pm (until 8 pm on Sunday); the *Vinárna Matěj* at Riegrova 22; and the trendy *Restaurant Drápal*, on the corner of Svobody and Havlíčkova, has a cosy wooden decor and its meatless main courses start from 45 Kč and other mains are under 250 Kč.

Ice-cream vendors and vegetable and fruit stalls draw large queues in the 'funnel' between Horní and Dolní náměstí.

Getting There & Away

There are five or six buses and many direct trains a day from Ostrava; the bus takes about two hours. From Brno (a 1½ hour trip) there are about 15 buses a day, but five direct fast trains. The best connection from Prague (3½ hours) is by fast train, with 13 a day from Praha hlavní nádraží and others from Masarykovo, Holešovice and Smíchov.

Bratislava has poor bus links but one direct fast train. From the transport hub of Žilina there are three daily direct buses and three fast trains.

Getting Around

The bus fare is 7 Kč if you buy it from the usual *tabák* and other stores, or 9 Kč from the driver for a duration of 35 minutes. A 24 hour transport pass (*denní jízdenka*) for 36 Kč is available from the municipal transport office, DPMO, on the corner of Legionářská and Palackého, and at the main bus station (Monday to Saturday from 8 am to 8 pm).

AROUND OLOMOUC

For excursions in a wide arc around Olomouc, get hold of the multilingual booklet *Hrady, zámky, muzea a vybrané památky* (Castles, Palaces, Museums & Selected Sights), from OIS.

Šternberk Castle

Šternberk Castle (Hrad Šternberk), 15km north of Olomouc, was founded in the late 13th century by the aristocratic family of the same name. It got a Renaissance face-lift about 1480, and its present fairy-tale Romantic look from one Duke Jan II of Liechtenstein around 1886. It's now open to the public, with historical interiors from Gothic to Baroque (thanks to Duke Jan's redecorations) plus an interesting museum of clocks. The chapel features Gothic artwork, including traces of murals.

The castle is open daily, except Monday,

May through September from 8 am to 5 pm, and weekends in April and October from 9 am to 4 pm; entry costs 30 Kč.

It's about 300m up the hill from the town's pleasant main square, Hlavní náměstí. In fact the real landmark here is the **Parish Church of the Annunciation of Our Lord** (farní kostel Zvěstování Páně) on the way up. In contrast to its bombastic Baroque façade, the interior is spacious, sparsely furnished and topped with fine ceiling murals. Off to the right is a former Augustinian monastery.

Getting There & Away This is an easy day trip from Olomouc. Hourly trains take about 25 minutes and the less frequent buses from the main bus station take 35 minutes.

Bouzov Castle & Javoříčko Caves

The very handsome **Bouzov Castle** (hrad Bouzov) dates back at least to the 14th century, and in the 17th century came into the hands of the Order of Teutonic Knights. The Order's own Grand Master liked it so much he had it renovated in neo-Gothic style and moved his summer country seat here in 1901. The Order was abolished in 1939 and the castle occupied and looted by the Nazis during WWII.

It's under renovation now, so you can only see a few rooms. It's open daily, except Monday, May through September from 9 am to 4 pm, and on weekends and holidays only in April and October from 9 am to 3 pm. For more information call ☎ 068-544 62 01.

From the castle it's a 5km walk south on a blue-marked trail (or you can take the occasional local bus) to Javoříčko and the impressive local underground attraction, the **Javoříčko Caves** (Javoříčské jeskyně). Bring an extra layer or two as it gets quite chilly down there. There are cave tours Tuesday to Sunday from May through September from 8 am to noon and 12.30 to 4 pm, and in April and October to 3 pm. Entry costs 25 Kč.

RICHARD NEBESKÝ

Bouzov Castle is a former residence of the Grand Master of the Teutonic Knights

You can either stay the night or continue north-east on a scenic red-marked trail for 8km to Bílá Lhota. Another 4km on are the smaller **Mladeč Caves** (Mladečské jeskyně) at Mladeč, and a farther 5km on is Litovel.

Places to Stay & Eat Šternberk has the modern three-star *Hotel M* (☎ 0643-41 17 42; fax 41 17 42), Čechova 11, near the post office, with spacious single/double rooms for 775/1140 Kč, including breakfast, TV, bath and WC. *Chata Jeskyňka* (☎ 0644-9241), by the caves, has inexpensive rooms at hostel rates, and serves cheap Czech dishes. It's very popular in summer, so book ahead if you want to stay the night. There's a small hotel at Mladeč.

Getting There & Away This can be done in a long day trip if you're out of Olomouc by about 7 am. Buses depart every hour or two (fewer on weekends) for Litovel, where you must change for Bouzov (seven buses a day); from Olomouc to Bouzov will take at least 2½ hours. There appear to be few convenient buses between Litovel and Javoříčko and only two between Bouzov and Javoříčko. Mladeč has good connections to Litovel and Olomouc. Check onward bus times at every stop.

Ostrava

Ostrava, administrative capital of North Moravia, is the Czech Republic's biggest producer of coal and steel, its biggest industrial centre, and third most populous city (328,600). It's a blast from the Communist past, a gritty workers' stronghold where the new mood of entrepreneurship has yet to take hold.

The Velvet Revolution seems to have passed Ostrava by. With its public buildings and public health already eaten away by decades of unchecked pollution, its self-esteem now seems to be in danger as the old state subsidies disappear. While the centre's renaissance is in full swing and there is a respectable cultural life, some outer areas – such as en route to the main train station – are as derelict as if there had just been a war.

For tourists there's little reason to stop, except that this is a transport junction on a major route to and from Poland.

Orientation

Ostrava is an incredibly sprawling city, with only a tiny part of use to visitors – mainly the southern end of Nádražní, where banks and hotels cluster, and Masarykovo náměstí, a few blocks east, with its shops and restaurants.

Most trains use the main station, Ostrava hlavní nádraží; it's 2.5km south on Nádražní to the city centre via tram No 2, 8 or 14. From the small Ostrava-střed train station, and the main bus station, it's about 1km north-east to the centre; catch tram No 2, 12 or 14 going north (right) on Vítkovická in front of the bus station.

A constant irritant for visitors is that few buildings have numbers on them.

Information

Tourist Offices The Municipal Information Centre (Městské informační centrum, or MIC; ☎ 23 39 13), Nádražní 7/686, has plenty of information about the town, accommodation and maps. It's open daily from 9 am to 6 pm and weekends until 1 pm.

CKM (☎ 611 44 83) is at 28.října 102, open weekdays from 9 am to 6 pm and Saturday from 10 am to 1 pm. Čedok (☎ 23 15 63) is at 30.dubna 2B, open weekdays from 9 am to 5 pm.

Foreign Consulates If you need a visa for Poland (eg Australians, New Zealanders, Canadians) you can get one in 10 minutes at the friendly Polish consulate (☎ 622 28 22), weekdays from 8.30 am to noon. Bring two passport-size photos. It's at Blahoslavova 4, left of the new town hall; from Nádražní walk four blocks east on Československobratrská and two blocks north on Sokoloská, or take trolleybus No 102 or 103 on Československobratrská to the Nová radnice stop.

Money For foreign exchange, Česká národní banka is at Nádražní 4, IPB banka at No 6, and Komerční banka at No 12.

Post & Communications The post office is three blocks east of Nádražní on Dvořákova. Ostrava's area code is ☎ 069.

Emergency The Foreigners' Police (Úřadovna cizinecké policie) office is two blocks east of Nádražní on the corner of Milíčova and Československobratrská.

Things to See

The city's oldest public building is the **former town hall** (Stará radnice) on Masarykovo náměstí. Inside is the small **Ostrava Museum** (Ostravské muzeum), open weekdays from 9 am to 5 pm and

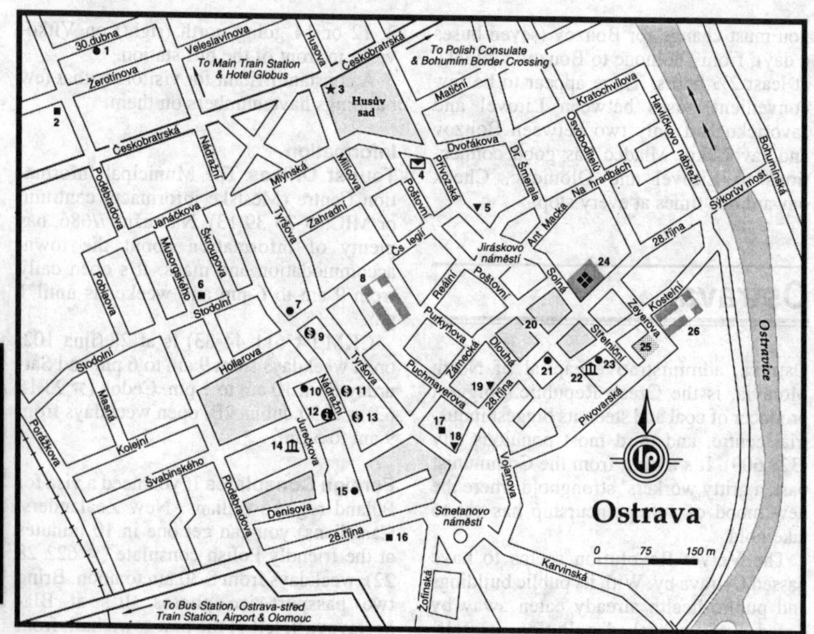

weekends from 9 am to 1 pm (but closed on public holidays), with regional natural history, archaeology and history, including the 20,000-year-old tiny statue of Petřkovická Venus.

To the east on Kostelní náměstí is the appealing **St Wenceslas Church** (kostel sv Václav). The late-Gothic building has a Baroque face on Romanesque foundations and is complete with little side rotundas (unfortunately, it was locked when we visited). Two blocks eastwards from Nádražní, on Československých legií, is a heavy neo-Renaissance basilica, the parish **Church of the Divine Saviour** (chrám Božského Spasitele), which dates from 1889.

An **Art Museum** (dům umění) with a modest collection of 20th century Czech art is at Jurečkova 9. It's open Tuesday to Friday from 10 am to noon and 12.30 to 6 pm, and weekends to 3 pm.

Places to Stay

Čedok can help with *private rooms*, which are the cheapest option. MIC can advise on all kinds of accommodation options.

Otherwise, at the upper end of Nádražní is *Hotel Globus* (☎ 22 20 40; fax 21 36 60), No 186, which has single/double rooms without facilities for 430/630 Kč and with facilities for 630/830 Kč. The friendly, central *Hotel Palace* (☎ 611 21 22), 28.října 59, has threadbare rooms with shared facilities for 600/800 Kč and including facilities for 1200/1800 Kč with breakfast. Get a rear room otherwise you'll listen to screeching trams all night. The *Hotel Brioni*, Stodolní 8, is being renovated.

Further up the scale, the business-oriented *Polský dům* (☎ 23 20 01; fax 23 50 62), in a faded 1899 Art Nouveau building at Poděbradova 53, has doubles with WC, bath and TV from 1770 Kč, and accepts some credit cards. The *Hotel Imperial*

PLACES TO STAY
- 2 Polský dům
- 6 Hotel Brioni
- 16 Hotel Palace
- 17 Hotel Imperial

PLACES TO EAT
- 5 Bistro
- 18 Pivnice Radegast
- 19 McDonald's
- 25 Fruit & Vegetable Market

OTHER
- 1 Čedok
- 3 Foreigners' Police (Úřadovna cizinecké policie)
- 4 Post Office
- 7 Bookshop
- 8 Church of the Divine Saviour (chrám Božského Spasitele)
- 9 Komerční banka
- 10 ČSA
- 11 IPB banka
- 12 Municipal Information Centre
- 13 Česká národní banka
- 14 Art Museum (dům umění)
- 15 Bookshop
- 20 Masarykovo náměstí
- 21 Bookshop
- 22 Ostrava Museum (Ostravské muzeum)
- 23 Former Town Hall (Stará radnice) & Vinárna Klub umělců
- 24 Laso Department Store
- 26 St Wenceslas Church (kostel sv Václav)

(☎ 611 66 21; fax 611 20 65), Tyršova 6, has two restaurants, a night club and rooms with the works from 2200/5400 Kč, including breakfast.

Places to Eat

Vinárna Klub umělců, in the cellar of the former town hall on Masarykovo náměstí, is open weekdays from 11 am to 8 pm with a small menu of Czech courses for under 90 Kč. At the rear of the Hotel Imperial is *Pivnice Radegast* with a good selection of local specialities. Its four-course daily menu (nabídka dne) for 94 Kč is good value.

For some obscure reason, *McDonald's* has an outlet here, on 28.října behind the Hotel Imperial. Much better and healthier are the salads and other buffet-style dishes at the *Bistro*, Přívozská 6. There's a fruit and vegetable market opposite St Wenceslas Church in Kostelní náměstí.

Getting There & Away

The private carrier Air Ostrava flies daily to and from Prague. You can book tickets at ☎ 248 43 22 or from the ČSA office (☎ 23 37 65) on the 2nd floor at Jurečkova 20. There are five or six buses and several direct trains every day to Olomouc.

It's 15km from central Ostrava to the Polish border crossing at Bohumín, linking Katowice. At the main train station you can catch one of dozens of fast trains passing each day from Prague and Brno to the border. There are also fast trains and buses from Ostrava to the border crossing at Český Těšín (see that listing later), linking Kraków.

Getting Around

The Došnov airport is at least 10km southwest of the centre. There is no public bus to the airport. A private bus leaves from the bus station on náměstí Jiřího z Poděbrad, in the suburb of Vítkovice, an hour before departure, and also meets each incoming flight (for details ask MIC).

The same tickets are used for all Ostrava's buses, trolleybuses and trams. Buy them in the main train station, at MIC, newsagents and other small shops. There are 5 Kč tickets for 15 minutes, 9 Kč for 45 minutes, and 24 Kč for 24 hours. Big backpacks need an extra ticket.

Western Beskydy

The Western Beskydy (Západní Beskydy) hills are the modest western end of an outrider range to the Carpathians that arcs into Poland and Ukraine (and into eastern Slovakia as the Lower Beskydy). The rounded, wooded countryside around the Rožnovská Bečva and Vsetínská Bečva valleys, dotted

Walachia

Walachia (also spelled Wallachia; in Czech it's Valašsko) is the region of the western Beskydy into which a semi-nomadic sheep-farming people, the Vlachs, moved in the 15th century. Nobody is sure where they came from – eastern Poland or Slovakia, western Ukraine or Romania. Walachia was also the name of a principality on the lower Danube that was the forerunner of the Romanian state, and it's at least plausible that there is an old connection.

The major towns of Moravian Walachia are Vsetín and Valašské Meziříčí, which were hotbeds of resistance to Catholicism in the 17th century.

By the 18th century the Vlachs had been absorbed into the Habsburg Empire, and had intermarried with Moravians and Slovaks. But they have managed to preserve some of their rural way of life, including the unique carved timber architecture you can see in the *skansen* at Rožnov pod Radhoštěm or, better yet, in the course of exploring the Beskydy. ■

with the rough-and-ready log homes and peaceful farmsteads of Walachia, feels straight out of a storybook. Most of the Western Beskydy is a protected landscape region.

The hills themselves, topping out on Lysá hora (1324m), are delightful for walking and are also popular for winter sports. The map to have is Kartografie Praha's *Beskydy* (1:100,000) No 42 trail map.

The region's best known attraction is the skansen at Rožnov pod Radhoštěm, the biggest and best of many such expositions across the Czech and Slovak republics.

ŠTRAMBERK

This peaceful village, east of the industrial centre of Nový Jičín, presents the face of authentic Walachia. Its rough-cut, low-gabled timber houses look inviting, and the air smells of wood-smoke (or it can also stink of brown coal smoke). Towering over it on the highest hill is the single remaining bastion of a ruined castle.

The Municipal Information Centre (Městské informační centrum; ☎ 0656/401 01) is at Náměstí 9.

The path up from the north end of the too-cute little village square passes through a stone gate inscribed '*Cuius Regio – Eius Religio – 1111*' (whose place – his place). On the slopes are the remains of Gothic castle walls, and at the top you can climb 166 steps to the top of the bastion – a 42m tower called Trúba – for vertiginous views across the Walachian landscape. The tower is open daily from April through October from 9 am to 5 pm; entry costs 10 Kč. There's also a restaurant next door.

Just north off the village square is a museum on local archaeology, folk furniture, art and daily implements. It's open daily, except Monday, April through November from 9 am to noon and 1 to 5 pm (mornings only on weekends); entry costs 5 Kč. South of the square is the interesting **Muzeum Zdeňka Buriana**, which is named after the painter of Stone Age people, but the museum seemed temporarily closed at the time of writing.

Places to Stay & Eat

The older doubles with shared facilities at the quiet *Hotel Šipka* (☎ 0656-85 21 81), on the square, are good value at 320 Kč per bed. Modern ones with facilities and TV are 900 Kč. There's a restaurant and beer hall. The new *Hotel Gong* (☎ 0656/72 10 36), Zauliční 410, has rooms for 950/1550 Kč, including breakfast, and there's also a stylish restaurant with tasty pricier dishes. Try the local speciality with the peculiar name of *Štramberské uši* (Štramberk ears) –

a conically shaped gingerbread with honey and spices that can be served with cream. According to legend, the ears originally belonged to the unfortunate captured Tatar invaders.

Getting There & Away

Nový Jičín is a stop for most Olomouc-Ostrava coaches, and from there local buses run two times a day to Štramberk's square. However, the most enjoyable way to get here is on foot through the hills; 8km on a red-marked trail that you can get onto in front of Nový Jičín město train station or across the river from Nový Jičín horní nádraží station.

Alternatively you can catch a local train from Studénka on the Olomouc-Ostrava railway line. From the Štramberk station it's a 15 minute walk to the square.

KOPŘIVNICE

A short bus ride from Štramberk is the industrial town of Kopřivnice with a very good museum of Tatra cars. This is also the birthplace of the famous Czech runner and Olympic medallist Emil Zátopek, as well as the painter of Stone Age people, Zdeňek Burian. Today it's mostly known as the home of the vehicle manufacturer Tatra, which mainly produces large trucks. Its **Technical Museum Tatra** (Technické muzeum Tatry) is in a lane south of Štefánikova, opposite the poliklinika. For fans of old cars, trucks and other vehicles, the Tatra company has put on display 60 of its prized products, including its first car, the 'Präsident' (1897). The Tatra products have always had a very good name and reputation for high quality and reliability. The company originally specialised in passenger cars and trucks but since the later days of Communist rule most of the production has shifted to trucks and limousines, for use mainly by diplomats. The museum is open daily from October to December and February to April from 8 am to 4 pm; entry costs 20 Kč.

There are seven buses and five trains a day to and from Štramberk.

ROŽNOV POD RADHOŠTĚM

Rožnov pod Radhoštěm ('Rožnov-under-Radhošť) is a resort town best known for its museum of traditional wooden architecture, first opened in 1925 and a showcase for Walachian houses, farms and workplaces of the 18th to 20th centuries, brought piecemeal from around the Beskydy region.

The tourist crush (and hotel crunch), and a heavy schedule of contrived 'folk events', occurs on summer weekends. Beat the tour-bus crowd by staying the night and fronting up at the museum at 8 am; on a summer weekday morning you could have it to yourself for several hours.

A completely different culture is on display for about a week around 4 July every year, when Texans of Czech descent pour into Rožnov for a week-long Independence Day jamboree, complete with BBQs, a rodeo and truckloads of Radegast beer. Hotel space is nonexistent then. More interesting are whole weekend folk festivals such as Easter Traditions or the Folkloric dance and song festival on the first weekend of July.

Orientation

From the adjacent train and bus stations it's a five minute walk east across the river to the main square, Masarykovo náměstí. The museum is another 10 minutes east on Palackého.

Information

The helpful information centre (Informační centrum; ☎ 521 59), on the corner of Videčská and Nádraží, has maps, pamphlets and information about accommodation, restaurants and transportation. It is open daily between June and September from 8 am to 8 pm, and the rest of the year only to 6 pm. Čedok (☎ 550 97), good for maps and last-ditch accommodation help, is at Sokolská 56, south of Masarykovo náměstí.

Česká spořitelna, on the corner of Masarykovo náměstí and Lázeňská, has a Visa ATM and an exchange counter. The post office is on náměstí Míru.

Rožnov's area code is ☎ 0651.

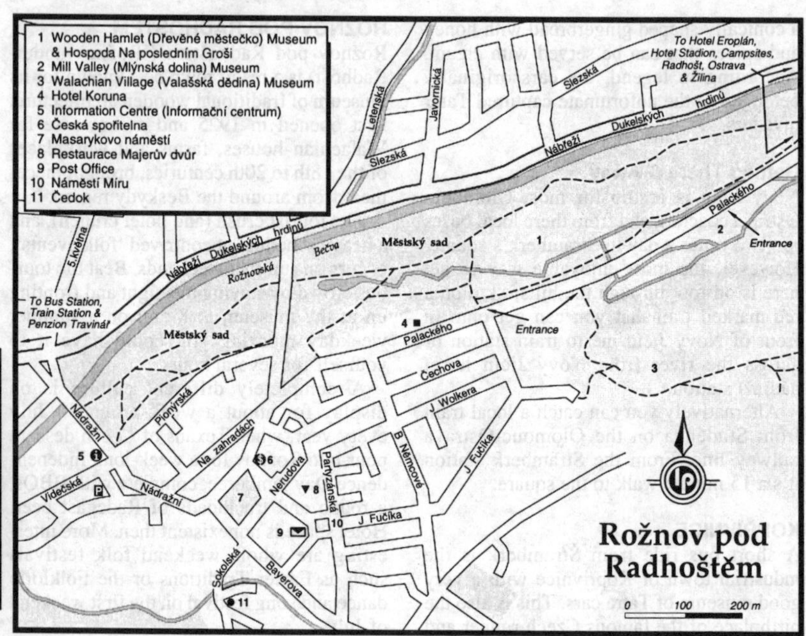

Walachian Open-Air Museum
Actually three separate museums, the Walachian Open-Air Museum (Valašské muzeum v přírodě) is an impressive effort to keep a grip on the region's architectural and cultural past. Multilingual maps and inventories of the buildings are free at the entrances. Each museum costs 30 Kč during weekdays and 40 Kč on the weekends, while a combined ticket is 75/100 Kč respectively.

Walachian Village The biggest and best of the three museums is the Walachian Village (Valašská dědina), which climbs right up to a ridge with fine views. It's an attempt to reconstruct an entire shepherds' village, right down to the orchards and livestock, which are raised by traditional methods. It's open daily from mid-May through August from 9 am to 5.30 pm, and until 5 pm in September.

Wooden Hamlet The Wooden Hamlet (Dřevěné městečko) is the most fun, with its Walachian-style *hospoda* (pub) where you can actually get a beer and a good Moravian meal. Other highlights are a pretty church from the village of Větřkovice and a collection of wooden beehives decorated with smirking faces. This one is open daily from May through September from 8 am to 6 pm; October through to mid-November from 8.30 am to 3.30 pm; and Tuesday to Sunday from 9 am to 4 pm between mid-December and March.

Mill Valley The Mill Valley (Mlýnská dolina) is a very interesting collection of various water-driven mills and an operating smithy and miller. It's open daily from mid-April through May and September through to mid-October from 8.30 am to 5 pm, and from June through August from 8 am to 6 pm.

Walking up Radhošť

It's 5.5km on a red-marked trail from the Wooden Hamlet museum, past Rožnov campsite and up to Černá hora (885m), and then a farther 2.5km on up the ridge to fine views from Radhošť (1129m).

From there it's 3.5km on a blue trail to a saddle below Tanečnice peak; on the way, you pass a wooden idol of a pre-Christian mountain spirit called Radegast (after whom the pleasant local beer is named), and a little wooden church. From Tanečnice a year-round chair lift descends to Ráztoka, where you can catch a bus back to Rožnov pod Radhoštěm.

Places to Stay

Camping & Motel About 1km east of the museum are two deluxe campsites, *Sport* (☎ 558 58) and *Rožnov* (☎ 554 42). Other campsites are at Dolní Bečva, 5km east on the Žilina road, and at Prostřední Bečva.

Hotels The hostel-like *Penzion Travinář* (☎ 552 13), Zemědělská 572, has very plain rooms with shared facilities for 180 Kč per bed. Next to the Sport campsite, in the stadium, is the *Hotel Stadion* (☎ 544 96), a rather basic hostel with inexpensive rooms. Damp doubles with shower and WC at the *Hotel Koruna* (☎ 558 77), on Palackého near the museum, are about 500 Kč.

The comfortable three-star *Hotel Eroplán* (☎ 558 35) at Horní Paseky 451 has modern doubles with shower, WC and TV for 1580 Kč, including breakfast.

Chalets on Radhošť If you fancy staying the night there are some comfortable chalet-hotels up on the mountain, including the *Radegast* near Radhošť, the *Lyžařská chata* near the idol, and the *Tanečnice* at the top of the chair lift. Talk to Čedok in Rožnov.

Places to Eat

Some locals recommend the *Restaurace Majerův dvůr* (☎ 531 58) at Nerudova 141; it's through the courtyard on the left. The fish, chicken and meat dishes are under 140 Kč. The restaurant at the *Hotel Koruna* serves cheap, good meals, including vegetarian dishes. There are several other small eateries around Masarykovo náměstí, and an open-air market on the square.

You could also try the touristy *Hospoda Na posledním Groši* ('At the Last Penny'; ☎ 545 17) in the Wooden Hamlet museum.

Getting There & Away

Buses are the simplest way to get here. There is one direct bus to and from Prague (a 5½ hour trip) and another via Brno. There are also four from Brno (three hours), and three from Olomouc. To get here by train requires at least one change at Valašské Meziříčí (13km away) which is on the Prague-Košice main railway line where many express trains stop.

ČESKÝ TĚŠÍN

An international border was laid through the middle of this town at the end of WWI using the natural division of the Olše river: to the west is Český Těšín in the Czech Republic, and to the east is Cieszyn in Poland. Most of the original town, and all the interesting historical sights, ended up on the Polish side (refer to LP's *Poland* guidebook). The only reason to be here is if you have arrived from, or are off to, Poland.

Orientation

The river is the border, with separate crossings for each direction: the Hlavní Bridge (Hlavní most) is for entering the Czech Republic, the Střelniční most for leaving. From the railway tracks on the Czech side, each bridge is about 500m along a street of the same name. Český Těšín's bus station is west of the tracks, via a pedestrian underpass on Hlavní or an automobile underpass on Viaduktova.

The town has a one-way street system that will send drivers up the wall.

Information

The helpful Regional Information Centre (Regioální informační centrum; ☎ 567 73), Hlavní 12, is open weekdays from 8 am to 6 pm and Saturday from 9 am to 4 pm.

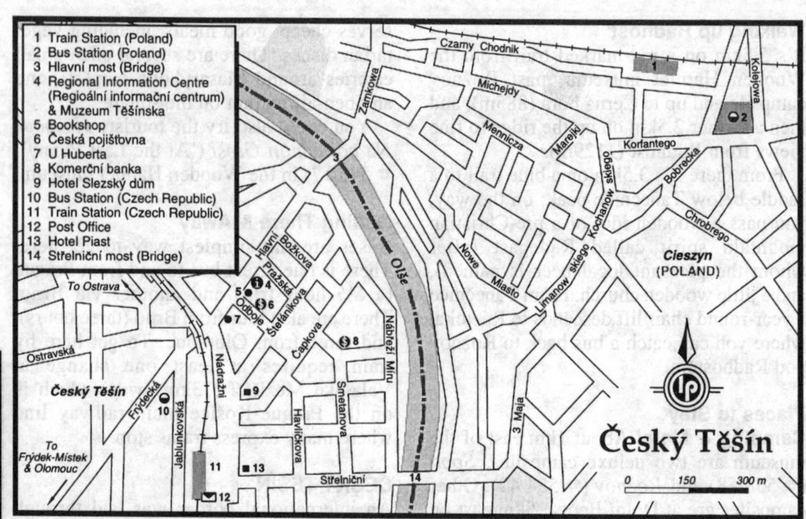

The Česká pojišťovna, Odboje 1, and the Komerční banka, Smetanova 5, have exchange counters, as does the post office beside the train station. Český Těšín's area code is ☎ 0659; Cieszyn's is ☎ 0386.

Těšín Regional Museum

If you need to kill some time check out the Muzeum Těšínska, which is next to the Regional Information Centre and has a local regional historical exhibit.

Places to Stay & Eat

There are two hotels opposite the train station. The friendly *Piast* (☎ 71 15 60; fax 71 15 64), Nádražní 18, has single/double rooms without facilities for 600/800 Kč and with WC and shower for 990/1090 Kč, including breakfast. Nearby, the uptight *Slezský dům* (☎ 571 41) has basic rooms for 550/780 Kč. There are also several motels out on the road to Olomouc.

If you've just arrived from Poland, *U Huberta*, Hlavní 3, is a great introduction to the country's beer halls, and also serves meals.

Getting There & Away

Five fast or express trains depart in the afternoon and evening via Olomouc (three hours away) to Prague (six hours), and seven via Žilina (one hour) and Poprad (three hours) to Košice (4½ hours).

Six fast trains stop at Ostrava main station, though only one arrives before 10 pm. Local trains run to Ostrava all day, but only to outlying stations, from where you must take a tram about 5km to the centre.

Coaches leave four or five times a day for Ostrava, where you can change for Olomouc and other destinations. On the Polish side, there is an express coach every hour or two to Katowice, plus several per day for Kraków.

South Moravia

South Moravia boasts beautiful historical towns like Telč and Kroměříž, some of the republic's most handsome medieval buildings – in particular Pernštejn and Vranov castles and Lednice chateau – and the rich and colourful folk traditions of the Moravské Slovácko region. The Czech Republic's energetic 'second city', Brno, has much of Prague's charm but without the oppressive crowds.

This is also the birthplace of several Czech luminaries, including founding president, TG Masaryk, composer Leoš Janáček and artist Alfons Mucha.

Travellers who enjoy the outdoors will also find plenty in this relatively unpolluted region, including good walking and cycling for those who don't mind a few hills, and the incredible karst caves of the Moravský kras.

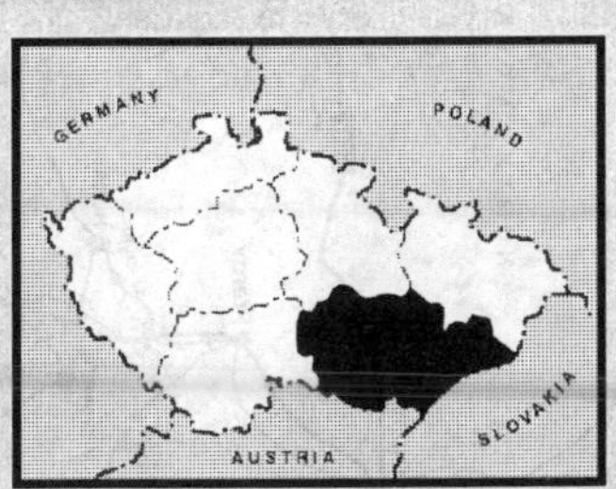

- Visit the under-appreciated city of Brno, with all the charm and architectural drama of Prague, minus the crowds
- In summer, go festival hopping in the Maravské Slovácko, one of central Europe's richest traditional folk regions
- Visit Telč and its perfectly preserved, highly photogenic Renaissance square, one of the finest in Moravia
- Stop in Moravský Krumlov and see Alphons Mucha's series of 20 large canvases called the *Slav Epic*

Brno

Brno, halfway between Budapest and Prague, has been the capital of Moravia since 1641; the modern city, with a population of about 388,000, is the second largest in the Czech Republic. Brno has a rich cultural life and its compact centre (most of which is a pedestrian zone) holds a variety of worthwhile sights, without the summertime crowds that overwhelm Prague. If you enjoy museums, bars and the diversions of city life, you'll like Brno for a few days.

History

The present suburb of Líšeň was a Slav fort, Staré Zámky, at the time of the Great Moravian Empire. Around 1000 AD a settlement was founded on the Svratka river, where the suburb of Staré Brno now stands.

In the 11th century a castle was built on Petrov Hill by the Přemysl princesses, and the town that formed around it had acquired a defensive wall by the middle of the 13th century. At this time another castle was built on Špilberk Hill. During the reign of John of Luxembourg, Brno became an important centre of arts and trade. In the late 1300s it became Moravia's capital, and most of Brno's monasteries date from then.

This predominantly Catholic town sided with King Sigismund in the Hussite Wars; the Hussites tried to take it twice but failed. In the mid-15th century Brno sided again with an enemy of the Czechs, Matthias Corvinus (Matyáš Korvín). Later in the 16th century Brno turned Protestant and joined the unsuccessful anti-Habsburg rebellion by the Czech Estates. In the ensuing Thirty Years' War, the town was able to

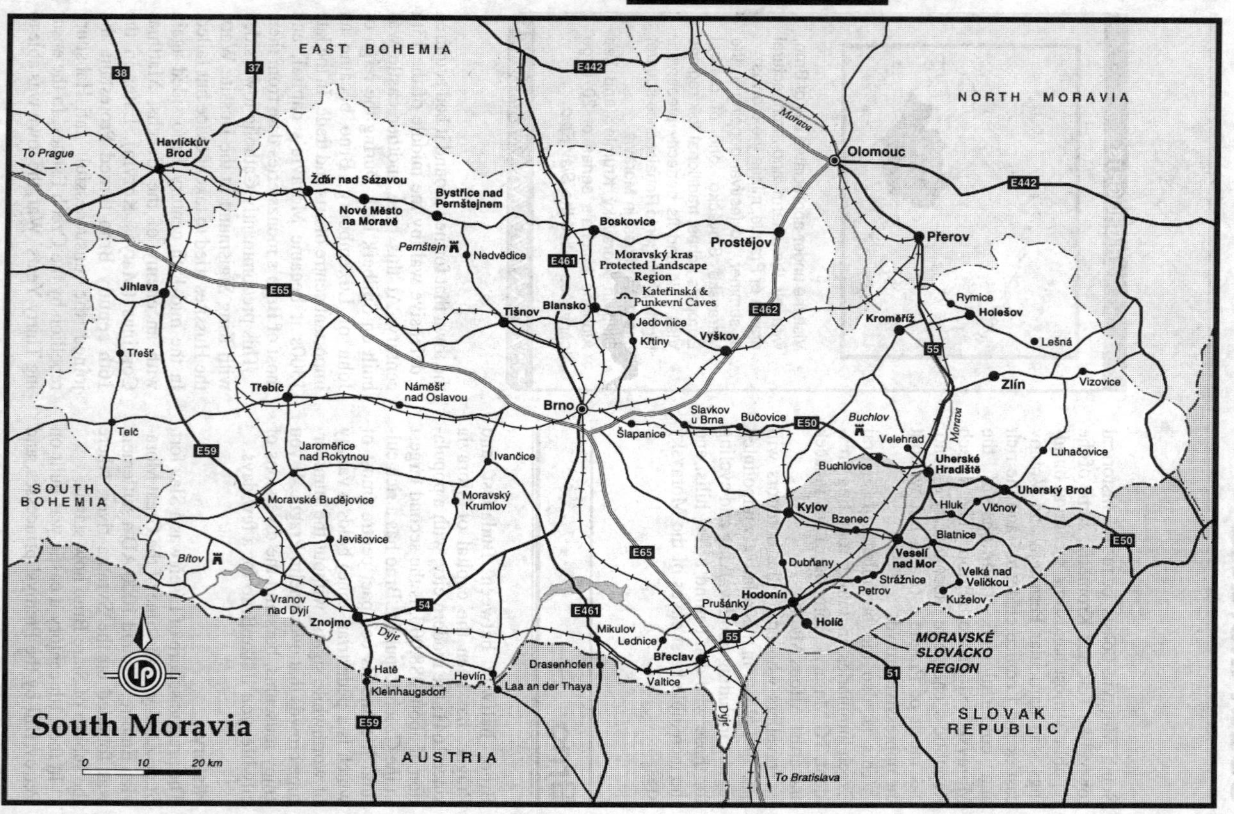
EAST BOHEMIA
NORTH MORAVIA
SOUTH BOHEMIA
AUSTRIA
SLOVAK REPUBLIC
MORAVSKÉ SLOVÁCKO REGION
To Prague
To Bratislava
Havlíčkův Brod
Žďár nad Sázavou
Nové Město na Moravě
Bystřice nad Pernštejnem
Pernštejn
Nedvědice
Boskovice
Moravský kras Protected Landscape Region
Kateřinská & Punkevní Caves
Prostějov
Olomouc
Morava
Přerov
Jihlava
Třešť
Tišnov
Blansko
Jedovnice
Křtiny
Vyškov
Kroměříž
Rymice
Holešov
Lešná
Zlín
Vizovice
Třebíč
Náměšť nad Oslavou
Brno
Slavkov u Brna
Bučovice
Šlapanice
Buchlov
Velehrad
Telč
Jaroměřice nad Rokytnou
Ivančice
Buchlovice
Uherské Hradiště
Luhačovice
Uherský Brod
Moravské Budějovice
Moravský Krumlov
Kyjov
Bzenec
Hluk
Vlčnov
Blatnice
Jevišovice
Veselí nad Mor
Bítov
Dubňany
Velká nad Veličkou
Strážnice
Petrov
Kuželov
Vranov nad Dyjí
Znojmo
Dyje
Prušánky
Hodonín
Holíč
Mikulov
Lednice
Břeclav
Drasenhofen
Hatě
Hevlín
Laa an der Thaya
Valtice
Kleinhaugsdorf
South Moravia
0
10
20 km
38
37
E442
E442
E461
E65
E462
55
E59
E50
E50
E65
54
E461
55
51
E59

successfully defend itself against the Swedes from 1643 to 1645. After the war Brno underwent extensive Baroque reconstruction.

The botanist Gregor Mendel (1822-84) established the modern science of heredity through his studies of peas and bees at the Augustinian monastery in Brno. After the Brno-Vienna railway was completed in 1839, Brno developed into a major industrial centre. As the most important town in the Czechoslovak state after Prague, it also acquired a university and, in the 1920s, some major exhibition buildings (still used to host Brno's many trade fairs).

Orientation

The town is dominated by Špilberk Castle, on the hill of the same name; vying for attention are the spires of the Church of SS Peter & Paul on Petrov Hill.

Brno's main train station (*hlavní nádraží*) is at the southern edge of the old town centre. Opposite the station is the beginning of Masarykova, a main thoroughfare that leads north to triangular náměstí Svobody, the

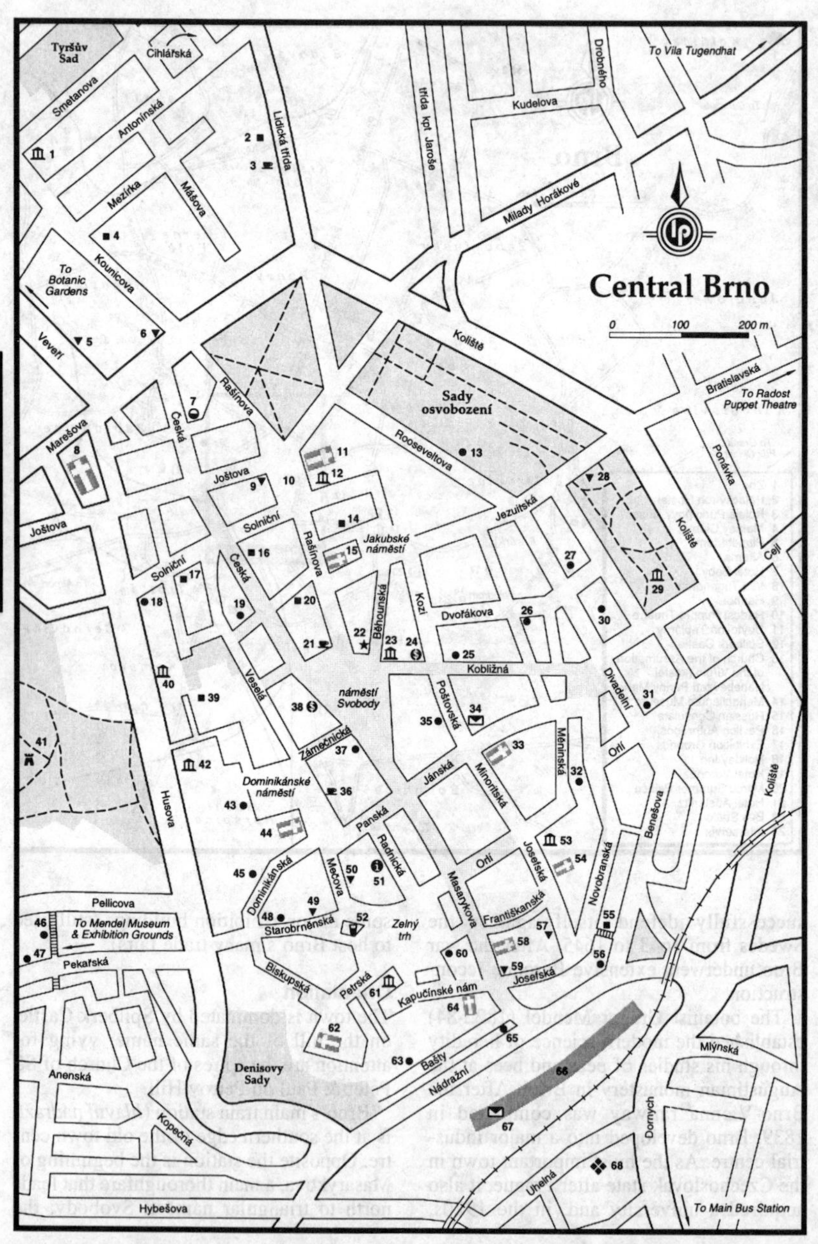
Central Brno
0
100
200 m
Tyršův Sad
Cihlářská
Smetanova
Antonínská
Lidická třída
Mezírka
Mášova
Kounicova
To Botanic Gardens
Veveří
Rašínova
Česká
Marešova
Joštova
Solniční
Veselá
Husova
Pellicova
To Mendel Museum & Exhibition Grounds
Pekařská
Anenská
Kopečná
Hybešova
Denisovy Sady
Petrská
Biskupská
Starobrněnská
Dominikánská
Dominikánské náměstí
Mečova
Radnická
Panská
Zámečnická
náměstí Svobody
Běhounská
Jakubské náměstí
Kozí
Zelný trh
Kapucínské nám
Bašty
Nádražní
Masarykova
Františkánská
Josefská
Orlí
Minoritská
Jánská
Poštovská
Koblížná
Dvořákova
Jezuitská
Rooseveltova
Sady osvobození
Koliště
třída kpt Jaroše
Drobného
Kudelova
Milady Horákové
To Vila Tugendhat
Bratislavská
To Radost Puppet Theatre
Ponávka
Cejl
Divadelní
Měnínská
Novobranská
Benešova
Mlýnská
Dornych
Uhelná
To Main Bus Station

PLACES TO STAY

2 Hotel Slovan
4 Hotel Continental
14 Hotel U sv Jakuba
16 Hotel Avion & Molly Malone's Pub
17 Hotel Slavia
20 Hotel Pegas & Pivnice Pegas
39 Hotel International-Best Western
55 Grand Hotel

PLACES TO EAT

3 @Internet Café
5 Zlatý drak
6 Pivnice Zemský dům
9 U dvou kozlů
21 Café Wein
28 Zemanova kiavárna
36 Cajovna
49 Sklípek U rytíře
50 Vinárna Pod radničím kolem
57 Restaurace Gourmand
59 Adria

OTHER

1 Leoš Janáček Memorial Museum (Památník Leoše Janáčka)
7 'Česká' Tram & Trolley-bus Stop
8 Red Church (Červený kostel)
10 Moravské náměstí
11 Church of St Thomas (kostel sv Tomáše)
12 Místodržitelský Palace & Moravian Gallery
13 Janáček Theatre (Janáčkovo divadlo)
15 Church of St James (kostel sv Jakuba)
18 Meeting House (Besední dům)
19 CKM 2000
22 Police Station
23 Ethnographic Museum (Etnografické muzeum)
24 Komerční banka
25 Late-night Pharmacy (Lékárna)
26 Geokart
27 Theatre Booking Office (Předprodej)
29 City Art Gallery & House of Culture (dům umění)
30 Mahenovo Theatre (Mahenovo divadlo)
31 Kino Kapital
32 Měnín Gate (Měninská brána)
33 Church of St John (kostel sv Janů)
34 Main Post Office (Pošta 1)
35 Kino Alfa
37 Knihkupectví Bookshop
38 Komerční banka
40 Pražákův Palace & Moravian Gallery
41 Špilberk Castle
42 Applied Arts Museum (Uměleckoprůmyslové muzeum)
43 New Town Hall (Nová radnice)
44 Church of St Michael (kostel sv Michala)
45 Former Dominican Monastery (Dominikánský klášter)
46 Cubist House (No 11)
47 Autoturist
48 BVV Fair Travel (American Express)
51 Information Office & Old Town Hall (Stará radnice)
52 Livingstone
53 Technical Museum
54 Church of St Joseph (kostel sv Josefa)
56 ČSA Airlines
58 Church of St Mary Madgalene (kostel sv Máří Magdalény)
60 Reduta Theatre (Reduta divadlo)
61 Moravian Museum (Moravské zemské muzeum)
62 Cathedral of SS Peter & Paul (katedrála sv Petra a Pavla)
63 Autoklub České republiky
64 Church of the Holy Cross (kostel sv Kříže)
65 Čedok
66 Main Train Station (Hlavní nádraží)
67 24-hour Post Office (Pošta 2)
68 Tesco Department Store

centre of town. The bus station (*autobusové nádraží*) is 800m south of the train station, beyond the Tesco department store – to get to Tesco go through the pedestrian tunnel under the train tracks, then follow the crowd along the elevated walkway.

There are two left-luggage offices in the train station, one upstairs opposite the lockers, another downstairs by thc tunnel to the platforms. Both are open from 4 am to 10 pm (10 Kč per bag). The left-luggage office at the bus station is open daily from 6.15 am to 10 pm.

Half the city centre is a pedestrian zone, and most parking here is permit-only. There are metered carparks around the rim of the city centre, plus a guarded 24 hour carpark at Hotel International (240 Kč per day).

Maps One of the latest and best new maps is GeoCart's *Brno Plán města* (1:15,000).

Information

Tourist Offices The information office (Kulturní a informační centrum; ☎ 42 21 10 90), in the old town hall at Radnická 8, has computers that can answer almost any question. Rooms are booked for a 10% commission. It also sells the monthly event guide *Kam v Brně*. More useful is the free bi-monthly *Do města Downtown*, with full listings of cinemas, bars etc. The office is open weekdays from 8 am to 6 pm, weekends from 9 am to 5 pm.

Motorists can turn to the Autoklub České republiky (☎ 42 21 50 30), Bašty 8, or to Autoturist (☎ 43 23 20 33), Pekařská 24.

Foreign Consulates The Consulate General of the Russian Federation, Hlinky 146, opposite the fairgrounds, is open Monday, Wednesday and Friday from 9 am to 1 pm.

Visa Extensions The Foreigners' Police, at Kounicova 24 on a northbound extension of Rašínova, has information about Czech visa extensions. This is also the place to report a lost passport. Look for the separate entrance between the main police station and the post office; it's open Monday and Wednesday from 8 am to noon and 1 to 4 pm, Tuesday from 8 am to 1 pm, and Friday from 7 to 11 am and noon to 3 pm.

Money Two branches of Komerční banka, at náměstí Svobody 21 and on the corner of Kozí and Kobližná, change travellers cheques (2% commission), give Visa cash advances, and have MasterCard/Visa ATMs.

American Express is represented by BVV Fair Travel (☎ & fax 42 21 65 07), Starobrněnská 20.

Čedok at Nádražní 10/12 charges a 2% commission for their exchange services.

There's another MasterCard/Visa ATM in the shopping arcade below the train station. In the station proper, Taxatour charges a 5% commission to change money and is open daily from 7 am to 10 pm.

Post & Communications The main post office (Pošta 1) is at Poštovská 3-5. The 24 hour post office (Pošta 2), by the train station on Nádražní, is good for international telephone service and poste restante. Brno's area code is ☎ 05.

Travel Agencies České dráhy travel agency, next to the international ticket office in the train station, sells bus tickets to western Europe.

Čedok (☎ 42 32 12 67), Nádražní 10/12, sells international bus and train tickets, as does CKM 2000 (☎ 42 21 60 99) at Skrytá 2.

Bookshops Knihkupectví, náměstí Svobody 18, has a good selection of English-language books. For maps and travel guides try Geokart at Vachova 8.

The British Council Resource Centre (☎ 42 21 60 14), at Opletalova 6, has a reading room with a good supply of current newspapers and magazines from the UK.

Medical & Emergency Services The police station is at the corner of náměstí Svobody and Běhounská. The hospital is at Bratislavská 2. First aid (☎ 511 31 13), náměstí 28.října 23, is available Monday to Friday from 7 pm to 6 am, and 24 hours a day on weekends. A late-night pharmacy (☎ 42 21 09 30) is at Kobližná 7.

City Centre

Church of the Holy Cross From the main train station head up Masarykova to Kapucínské náměstí. At No 5 is the Church of the Holy Cross (kostel sv Kříže) and the adjoining **Capuchin Monastery** (Kapucínský klášter), completed in 1651.

The monastery's ghoulish attraction lies in its **crypt** (*krypta*) – some 150 mummies were deposited here prior to 1784, including 24 monks, and rooms full of the clothed skeletons of monks and aristocrats. It's open Tuesday to Saturday from 9 am to noon and 2 to 4.30 pm, and Sunday from 11 to 11.45 am and 2 to 4.30 pm. Entry costs 20 Kč, plus 10 Kč for a handy English text.

Moravian Museum & Around Turn left out of the monastery to reach the former Ditrichstein Palace (Ditrichštejnský palác), which houses the Moravian Museum (Moravské zemské muzeum) and its so-so collection of folk dresses and crafts; entry costs 12 Kč.

In a courtyard around to the right, at Muzejní 1, is the **Biskupský Yard Museum**, with one of the country's better natural history displays; entry costs 20 Kč. Both are open daily, except Monday, from 9 am to 5 pm.

The cobbled **Cabbage Market** (Zelný trh) has been Brno's marketplace since the 13th century. There's still a daily market with everything from fresh fruit and vegetables to flowers. The unusual **Parnas Fountain** (kašna Parnas) was designed in 1695 by the Viennese architect JB Fischer von Erlach. Carp were once sold from its waters at Christmas.

The nearby **Reduta Theatre** (Reduta divadlo), at No 4, is where Mozart performed in 1767; the operettas usually presented are on hold until it's restored.

Cathedral of SS Peter & Paul From the top of the Cabbage Market take Petrská to Petrov Hill, site of the domineering Cathedral of SS Peter & Paul (katedrála sv Petra a Pavla). Climb its tower (15 Kč) for great views of Brno.

The 14th century cathedral, said to have been built on the site of a pagan temple to Venus, has been reconstructed many times since then. The highly decorated, 11m-high main altar with figures of SS Peter and Paul was carved by the Viennese sculptor Josef Leimer in 1891. Also note the unfinished Stations of the Cross by Jiří Marek (1960). The Renaissance **Bihop's Palace** (closed to the public) adjoins the cathedral.

Old Town Hall & Around From Biskupská you can digress left into the pleasant **Denisovy sady** park, which has statues, an obelisk and a music pavilion. Back on Biskupská, turn right onto Starobrněnská and go past the **former brewery** at No 20.

On the left, at Mečová 5, is the back of the **Old Town Hall** (Stará radnice). About 3m up is what looks like the face of a man.

According to a tale, a Brno councillor who plotted with the Hussites to surrender the town in 1424. The plan was overheard by Borro, Emperor Sigismund's court clown, while a prisoner of the Hussites. Borro escaped and told the story, and the councillor was sealed alive in the wall.

Ahead of Their Time

Oddly enough, the brawny bells of the Cathedral of SS Peter & Paul ring noon each day at 11 am, in commemoration of the Swedish siege of Brno in 1645. Legend says Swedish General Torstenson, having failed to conquer Brno after a week-long battle, decided to launch a final attack, with one caveat: if his troops could not prevail by noon he would call off the siege.

At 11 am the Swedes were about to scale the town walls when a cannon ball hit the cathedral tower. Seeing the Swedes on the verge of victory, the tower keeper had the inspired idea of ringing noon. True to his word, General Torstenson broke off the attack and the city was saved. ■

The original early 13th century building – which became the town hall in 1343 – has been incorporated into today's structure. A peculiar sight by the entrance on Radnická is a Gothic portal with a crooked middle turret, made by Anton Pilgram in 1510. According to legend, he was not paid the agreed amount by the council for the portal and, in revenge, left the turret (above the statue of Righteousness) crooked.

The town hall **tower**, raised by 5m during repairs in 1905 so as not to disappear among the newly built houses around it, offers a magnificent view of Zelný trh and the city; entry costs 8 Kč.

What legend calls a dragon, hanging from the ceiling at the entrance, is in fact an Amazon River crocodile, donated by Archprince Matyáš in 1608. Also here is a wheel made as part of a bet in 1636 by the Lednice cabinet maker Jiří Birek; it's cut from a single tree, and he supposedly rolled it 40km to Brno in a single day.

The Old Town Hall is open daily from April through September from 9 am to 5 pm.

Technical Museum & Around Cross Zelný trh to Květinářská and go over Masarykova into Františkánská, where you'll find the **Church of St Mary Magdalene** (kostel sv Máří Magdalény) and the adjacent Franciscan Monastery, founded in 1451. Turn left into Josefská. On the right is the **Church of St Joseph** (kostel sv Josefa).

In the former Franciscan Convent at No 1 is a **Technical Museum** (Technické muzeum), which was closed for renovations at the time of writing. Hopefully it will retain the Panorama, a machine built in 1890 that offers continuous 3-D showings of the wonders of the world.

Next turn right into Orlí, at the end of which is the **Měnín Gate** (Měninská brána), built around 1600, with a dull museum inside (closed Monday).

From here turn back along Jánská to the **Church of St John** (kostel sv Janů) and the Minorite Monastery founded in 1230. The Minorites have been here for 750 years and are the only order in Moravia still in their original medieval quarters. The well-preserved ceilings in the pivnice U tří kníž, at Jánská 88, are also worth a look.

Náměstí Svobody & Around Turn right into Masarykova and follow it to the busy náměstí Svobody. At No 17, is the **Schwarz Palace** (Schwarzův palác), with an outstanding 16th century façade by Giorgio Gialdi.

Opposite at No 10 is the **House of the Four Mamlases** (dům U čtyř mamlasů), which has on its lower façade statues of grimacing figures trying to hold up both the building and their trousers simultaneously. Created by Germano Wanderley in 1928, they aroused much controversy over whether they were in good taste.

The square dates from the early 13th century, when it was called Dolní trh (the Lower Market). Its plague column dates from 1680. On the corner of the square and Kobližná is the **Palác Říkovský z Dobrčic**, also known as the House at the Red Ox (dům U rudého vola). At Kobližná 4, the Schrattenbachův palác has a niche with a 1637 statue of the Madonna.

At Kobližná 1 is a good **Ethnographic Museum** (Etnografické muzeum); 25 Kč buys admission to all three exhibitions – folk culture, Moravian puppets, and 18th and 19th century decorative shooting targets. It's open daily, except Monday, from 9 am to 5 pm.

Běhounská northwards brings you to Jakubské náměstí and the plain but towering 15th century **Church of St James** (kostel sv Jakuba). It has a Baroque pulpit with reliefs of Christ dating from 1525. Also here is the Baroque tomb of the French Protestant Raduit de Souches, who died leading the defence of Brno in 1697.

Near a south-facing Gothic window in the church tower is a statue that has caused much controversy over the years. To some it resembles a man flashing his bare bottom at the town, to others a couple making love – in fact, it's probably Siamese twins.

Dominikánské Náměstí & Around From náměstí Svobody, Zámečnická leads west to Dominikánské náměstí, a humble square dominated by the **Church of St Michael** (kostel sv Michala), which has an interesting ornate main altar (1759) by Josef Winterhalter.

Also facing the square is the 16th century **New Town Hall** (Nová radnice) with its impressive courtyard, stairways and frescoes.

Church of St Thomas & Around The Church of St Thomas (kostel sv Tomáše), with a soaring nave in the purest Gothic style, abuts a 14th century Augustinian Monastery that today houses a branch of the Moravian Gallery (see the following section).

Along Joštova, past the neo-Renaissance Assembly (zemská sněmovna), stands the Evangelical Comenius Church (kostel JA Komenského), better known as the **Red Church** (Červený kostel) for its red-brick exterior; it was built between 1862-67 to a design by H Ferstel. Left down Husova at the corner of Komenského náměstí is the **Meeting House** (Besední dům), one of the best works of 19th century Danish architect Theofil Hansen; nowadays it's home to Brno's philharmonic orchestra.

Moravian Gallery There are three branches in Brno of the Moravian Gallery (Moravská galerie), all open daily, except Monday, from 10 am to 6 pm. Entry is free on Friday.

Adjoining the Church of St Thomas is the **Místodržitelský Palace**, with a fine collection of Gothic, Baroque and 19th century Moravian art; entry costs 15 Kč.

The second branch, the **Applied Arts Museum** (Uměleckoprůmyslové muzeum), at Husova 14, has a permanent collection of furniture and glassware from the 1700s to the 1960s. Entry costs 30 Kč.

Up the road at Husova 18 is the third branch, inside the **Pražákův Palace**, with 19th and 20th century Czech art and sculpture impressively displayed inside. Entry costs 20 Kč.

Špilberk Castle

Špilberk Castle, founded in the early 13th century, was often used as a residence by the Czech kings. It always played an important role in the defence of the city, and was once connected by a covered tunnel to the old Brno Gate (now Šilingrovo náměstí). In the 18th century the castle was made into a military fortress, with a prison later called the Prison of the Nations because of its international guest list of rebels against the Austro-Hungarian Empire. The prison was closed in 1853, but was again put to use by the occupying Nazis in WWII.

Some of Špilberk's casemates (*kasematy*) – the dark, chilly corridors beneath the bastions – are now a museum of prison life. Explore it without a guide daily, except Monday, June through September from 9 am to 5 pm; entry costs 20 Kč. The castle is approachable only on foot, up the hill through the cool gardens.

Back on Husova, at the corner with Pellicova, there is a 1914 **cubist house** by František Uherka. From Husova, walk through Šilingrovo náměstí and left into Dominikánské, with a former **Dominican Monastery** (Dominikánský klášter).

Outside the Old Town

Near Špilberk Castle Over Špilberk Hill from the old town, on the corner of Úvoz and Pekařská, is the **Church of the Assumption of the Virgin** (kostel Nanebevzetí Panny Marie), regarded as Brno's finest late-Gothic building. Inside is the oldest painting on wood in the Czech Republic, the so-called Black Madonna (Černá Madona) from the late 13th century.

Around the corner at Mendlovo náměstí 1, in part of the Augustinian Monastery, is a museum called the **Mendelianum**, devoted to one of the monks who lived here, the botanist Gregor Johann Mendel (1822-84). It was Mendel who fathered modern genetics with his pioneering work on the common garden pea. The museum is open on weekdays from 8 am to 5 pm, except in July and August when it's open until 6 pm. Take tram No 18 or 20 from the train station to Mendlovo náměstí.

North of the Centre At the corner of Smetanova 14 and Kounicova, a short walk from the old town, is the **Leoš Janáček Memorial Museum** (Památník Leoše Janáčka), a house-museum dedicated to the composer. Janáček was born in Hukvaldy (North Moravia) but lived in Brno from childhood until his death in 1928. It's open Monday from 1 to 4 pm, and Tuesday to Thursday from 9 am to noon. His grave is in the Krematorium in Jihlavská (take bus No 62 or tram No 6, 7 or 8 from Nádražní).

Janáček is the least known of the 'big three' Czech composers, the others being Smetana and Dvořák. All were exponents of 'musical nationalism', incorporating folk music into their pieces, but some of Janáček's music explored other harmonies that were ahead of their time. It was not until around 1900 that he established an international reputation with his opera *Jenůfa*.

Farther north, on adjacent Veveří (to the west), is the city's **Botanic Garden** (Botanická zahrada); from the centre take tram No 10 or 13.

Vila Tugendhat, a modern functionalist building at Černopolní 45, in the suburb of Černá Pole, is the work of the well-known German architect Ludwig Mies van der Rohe (1886-1969), and a shrine for students of modern architecture. Hired by some rich newlyweds to build them a home, Mies turned it into one of the first true open-plan houses. Though many of the original fittings are gone, it is still worth a look and is open Wednesday to Sunday from 10 am to 3 pm. Take tram No 5, 9 or 17 from Moravské náměstí up Milady Horákové to Černopolní, then walk north.

Exhibition Grounds & Around A competition to design the Exhibition Grounds (Výstaviště), in the suburb of Pisárky (take bus No 137 from the Red Church's south side) near the bank of the Svratka, was won by Josef Kalous of Prague. The buildings were built by the Brno architect Emil Králík, and the exhibition opened in 1928. It is now a year-round trade-fair venue. In addition to the Palace of Industry (Průmyslový palác), other interesting buildings include the post office, Congress Hall (Kongresová hala), and New House (Nový dům), built in fine Bauhaus style.

There is also an older, empire-style summer palace, the **Zámeček Bauerova rampa**. In the space between Rybářská and Křížkovského is the quaint **Mitrov Summer Palace** (Letohrádek Mitrovských) with a garret roof, built around 1780.

Other Museums & Galleries Changing art exhibitions are held at the **City Art Gallery** in the House of Culture (dům umění), Malinovského náměstí 2. It's open daily, except Monday, from 10 am to 6 pm, and entry is free on Wednesday.

Across the Svratka river from the Exhibition Grounds is **Pavilon Anthropos**, with an interesting exhibit on evolution, and a reconstructed mammoth. It's open daily, except Monday, April through November from 8.30 am to 5 pm; entry costs 10 Kč.

Tram enthusiasts might enjoy the **Tram Museum** (Muzeum tramvají) at Holzova 4 in Líšeň. The **planetarium** is at Kraví hora (tram No 4 to náměstí Míru), and a **zoo** (Zoologická zahrada) is at Bystrc-Mniší hora.

Special Events

The annual Czech Republic 500cc Grand Prix is held at Brno's Masarykův circuit (*okruh*) at the end of August. At this time Brno and the area around are packed solid with visitors. Special buses run to the circuit.

Places to Stay

In February, April, September and October Brno hosts numerous international trade fairs, and advance reservations are recommended as hotels fill and walk-in rates increase by about 25%.

Camping Just beyond Modřice, 12km south of the city, is *Motel Boubrava* (☎ 43 32 12 27), where camping costs 50 Kč per person and 100 Kč per tent. Two-bed cab-

CZECH REPUBLIC

ins are 200 Kč. The restaurant is good and is open year-round. From the centre take tram No 2 or 6 to the end of the line, then walk the remaining 3km. Otherwise take a local train to Popovice, 500m from the camping ground – but get times of returning trains before leaving Brno, because there is no information readily available at Popovice.

Hostels There are two year-round dorms and three that open in summer only (July to August).

Year-Round Most convenient is *Interservis* (☎ 45 23 42 32), south of the centre at Sladkého 13. Beds in double rooms are 200 Kč per person. From the train station take tram No 9 or 12 south to the end of the line, go through the underpass and follow Luzňá east three blocks, then turn right on Lomená. The hostel is the tall modern building about two blocks down on your left.

Palacký roh – vysokoškolské koleje (☎ 41 32 12 63) is at Kolejní 2, block K-1, on the northern side of the city, and has expensive singles/doubles at 390/800 Kč. This large student complex is easy to reach by taking tram No 13 north to the end of the line, and then trolleybus No 53 the rest of the way to the hostel.

Summer Only Just east of the centre at Špitálka 11, *Ubytovna Teplárny* (☎ 45 16 11 11, extension 3500) offers comfortable triple rooms at 250 Kč per bed. From the City Art Gallery, walk east along Cejl to No 52, then right onto Radlas and right again onto Špitálka.

Nearby at Tkalcovská 5 is *Ubytovna Tkalcovská* (☎ 45 16 22 50), with dorm beds from 190 Kč.

North of the city centre, the student dormitory at *Koleje Purkyňovy* (☎ 41 12 01 11), Purkyňova 93, block C-2, rents beds in double and triple rooms for 200 Kč per person. From the 'Česká' stop, take tram No 12 north to the end of the line; the dorm is on the left.

Private Rooms Čedok arranges rooms in private homes from 350 Kč per person a night. Most are far from the city centre but can easily be reached on public transport. The information office and Taxatour (☎ 42 21 33 48), in the train station, both arrange private rooms from 400 Kč per person (plus 10% commission).

Hotels – City Centre The plain *Hotel Avion* (☎ 42 21 50 16; fax 42 21 40 55), Česká 20, is reasonable at 650/850 Kč for a single/double without bath, and 850/1100 Kč with bath.

The musty, ageing *Hotel U sv Jakuba* (☎ 42 21 07 95), Jakubské náměstí 6, costs 800/1200 Kč with shower.

Hotel Pegas (☎ & fax 42 21 12 32), Jakubská 4, is on a quiet street right in the centre of town. Bright and clean rooms with bath and breakfast are 975/1490 Kč.

Just north of town is the bland *Hotel Slovan* (☎ 41 32 12 07) at Lidická 23, with fully equipped rooms for 1090/1490 Kč.

It may be an ugly high-rise, yet there's an odd appeal to the hyper-modern *Hotel Continental* (☎ 41 51 91 11), Kounicova 6. Rooms with all the trimmings are 1190/1790 Kč.

Of central Brno's three top-end spots, the nicest is the *Grand Hotel* (☎ 42 32 12 87; fax 42 21 03 45), at Benešova 18/20, and priced at 2400/3600 Kč. The others are the *Hotel Slavia* (☎ 42 32 12 49) at Solniční 15/17 and the *Hotel International-Best Western* (☎ 42 12 21 11) at Husova 16. Rooms at both start at 1700/2300 Kč.

Hotels – Outside the Centre The following cater mostly to business people and trade-fair goers: *Hotel Voroněž* (☎ 43 14 13 77), Křižkovského 47, priced at 2550/4000 Kč; *Hotel Austerlitz-Best Western* (☎ 43 21 13 95), Táborského 3, at 1680/3000 Kč; and the *Holiday Inn* (☎ 43 12 21 11), Křižkovského 20, at 2800/5000 Kč.

A less stuffy splurge is *Hotel Boby* (☎ 727 21 33) at Sportovní 2a, part of a massive entertainment complex (bars, nightclubs, shops etc), priced at 2800/5600 Kč.

Places to Eat

Brno has some excellent beer halls. Top of the list is *Pivnice Pegas*, a true micro-brewery inside Hotel Pegas. It's definitely touristy, but plenty of fun.

Equally classy is *U dvou kozlů* at Joštova 1, with good pub food and two pool tables upstairs.

Vegetarians will appreciate the small salad bar at nearby *Pivnice Zemský dům*, Kounicova 1 (closed Sunday).

Another must for vegetarians is *Haribol*, a Hare Krishna buffet off Lidická at Lužanecká 4, which is open weekdays from 11 am to 5 pm.

Two spots for pub grub and a good beer are *Vinárna Pod radničím kolem*, in a smoky cellar at Mečová 5, and humble *Sklípek U rytíře* at Starobrněnská 14.

Zemanova kavárna, in the park on Jezuitská, is a semi-fancy bistro popular with theatre-goers.

Elegant, soothing *Adria*, on the corner of Josefská and Masarykovo, is good for coffee, desserts and full-blown meals (try the pastas), though cheap it is not.

Restaurace Gourmand, downstairs at Josefská 14, specialises in French cuisine and local wines at prices that are fair for what you get (closed Sunday).

Zlatý drak, Veveří 4, has authentic but expensive Chinese dishes (150 Kč and up).

There's a well-stocked supermarket in the basement of the *Tesco* department store, behind the train station.

Cafés Have a caffeine fix and surf the world wide web (1 Kč per minute) at the *@Internet Café*, Lidická 17 (closed Sunday). *Café Wein*, upstairs at náměstí Svobody 2, is a good spot for people-watching, but the food is miserable. The small and smoke-free *Čajovna*, Dominikánské náměstí 6/7, serves at least 40 types of exotic teas.

Entertainment

Despite a reputation as dullsville, Brno has plenty of things to do at night, but you must hunt around a bit. The free bi-monthly guide, *Do města Downtown*, has invaluable listings.

Classical Music & Theatre Except in midsummer when the artists are on holiday, Brno's theatres offer excellent performances. In Brno, you are expected to dress up a bit.

Opera, operettas and ballet are performed at the modern *Janáček Theatre* (Janáčkovo divadlo), Sady osvobození, which opened in 1966.

The nearby neo-Baroque *Mahenovo Theatre* (Mahenovo divadlo; 1882), a beautifully decorated theatre designed by the famous Viennese architects Fellner and Hellmer, presents operettas, and classical drama in Czech.

When it reopens try to see an operetta at the historic *Reduta Theatre* (1734), Zelný trh 3.

The *State Philharmony Brno*, in Besední dům, Komenského náměstí 8, has regular concerts. Tickets can be bought on the ground floor weekdays from 1 to 5 pm.

For tickets to the Janáček, Mahenovo and Reduta theatres, go to *Předprodej*, Dvořákova 11, a small booking office behind the Mahenovo Theatre, open weekdays from 9 am to 5.30 pm, Saturday to noon.

Puppet Theatre Don't miss the *Radost Puppet Theatre*, Bratislavská 32, which has shows on Sunday at 10 am and 2.30 pm. It's kids' stuff but great fun.

Cinemas Brno's outstanding 'art house' cinema is *Kino Art*, at Cihlářská 19, a short walk past Hotel Slovan. *Kino Alfa* at Poštovská 8 and *Kino Kapital* at Divadelní 3 are both in the city centre.

Bars & Clubs Two popular bars in the city centre are the stylish *Livingstone*, Starobrněnská 1, and the cosy Irish pub *Molly Malone's*, adjacent to Hotel Avion.

For live music you must go farther afield. *Mersey Club*, at Minská 15, is a dive bar in the best sense, with alternative bands and

DJ mixes. From the 'Česká' stop take tram No 3 or 11 four stops north to Tábor.

Alterna, Kounicova 48, Block B, is a hip student club with live jazz every Sunday at 8 pm. From 'Česká' take trolleybus No 134 or 136 three stops north.

A night at the massive *Boby Centrum*, Sportovní 2, can seriously overload the senses, with two bars, a disco, nightclub, café and restaurants. From the intersection of Koliště and Cejl take bus No 67 north.

Things to Buy

Forte Plus music store, náměstí Svobody 22, has a good selection of Czech CDs, and the staff don't mind playing things for you. Hudy Sport, at Veveří 13, stocks high-quality camping and hiking gear with prices to match.

Getting There & Away

Air Brno's Tuřany airport is 7.5km south-east of the train station, along Křenová (which becomes Olomoucká). ČSA (☎ 42 21 07 39), Nádražní 4, has scheduled flights from Brno to Prague, Frankfurt, London, Moscow, Paris and more.

Bus Two companies, Český Národní Expres and Čebus, run buses between Prague and Brno. Tickets are available from their offices opposite the Grand Hotel – this is often easier than going all the way to the bus station.

For short trips buses are faster and more efficient than the trains, especially to Telč, Trenčín, Znojmo, Vranov, Mikulov, Strážnice, Kroměříž and Zlín. The Euroline bus to Vienna (Mitte Bahnhof) departs from platform No 20 at the bus station twice a day (300 Kč; 127km).

Train Brno is a major rail hub, with frequent main line connections to Prague (three hours; 257km), Bratislava (two hours; 141km), Vienna (via Břeclav), Budapest and Berlin. Within Moravia there are direct trains to Břeclav, Jihlava, Třebíč, Žďár nad Sázavou, Blansko, Přerov, Ostrava, and Veselí nad Moravou. Reserve couchettes or sleepers in the station at window Nos 24 to 29.

Getting Around

The MHD at Benešova 22 sells tickets and monthly passes for public transport, weekdays from 6 am to 6 pm and weekends from 7 am to 4 pm. Single tickets cost 8 Kč and are valid for 60 minutes (with two changes). Tickets are also available from *tabák* shops.

Around Brno

CZECH REPUBLIC

MORAVIAN KARST

The Moravian Karst (Moravský kras) is a beautiful, heavily wooded hilly area north of Brno, carved with canyons and honeycombed with some 400 caves. One karst cave (Punkevní) and the Macocha Abyss are open year-round, an easy and very worthwhile day trip from Brno. A handful of other caves open in summer only.

Karst formations are the result of the seepage of faintly acidic rainwater through limestone, slowly dissolving it and, over millions of years, creating hollows and fissures. In caves, the slow drip of this water produces extraordinary stalagmites and stalactites.

Getting There & Away

Unless you have a car, the simplest way in is by train from Brno to Blansko, and by bus (or hitching) from there. At the time of writing there were no organised tours to the caves, though Čedok in Brno should have the latest details.

Blansko

Blansko (population 22,000) is little else other than a good jumping-off point. The only thing of interest in town is a small **museum** about the caves, which is opposite Hotel Dukla and open daily, except Monday, from 9 am to 5 pm (off-season from 8 am to 4 pm).

Orientation & Information The dull main

square, náměstí Svobody, is a 15 minute walk north-east of the train station. From the latter, the bus station is directly across the Svitava river.

A tourist office right outside the train station sells maps and advance tickets to the Punkevní and Kateřinská caves, fields transport questions, and can help with accommodation. It's open weekdays from 7 am to 4 pm, Saturday from 7.30 to 9.45 am. Blansko's area code is ☎ 0506.

Places to Stay & Eat Directly opposite the bus station is *Hotel Macocha* (☎ 41 97 06), with doubles for 900 Kč. Walk up Nádražní past the Macocha, cross Masarykova and continue on Sušilova to the cheaper *Hotel ČKD Blansko* (☎ 549 87), at Husova 1, priced at 400/750 Kč. If you turn left on Masarykovo instead, 400m ahead is *Hotel Dukla* (☎ 550 03), on náměstí Republiky, and priced at 500/800 Kč. All the hotels have restaurants.

Getting There & Away The 22km from Brno takes half an hour, and there are 14 trains a day. Off-season, the only train that meets the bus to Skalní Mlýn departs Brno at 6.55 am, arriving in Blansko at 7.31 am – leaving you about four minutes to catch the bus (see Getting There & Away in the following section). Buses direct from Brno are less frequent – up to nine daily on weekdays but only two on weekends. Be warned that some Blansko-bound buses depart from Brno's bus station, while others depart from a stand opposite the Grand Hotel; confirm in advance at Čedok or the tourist office.

Skalní Mlýn & the Caves

Skalní Mlýn is the administrative centre for the two most popular caves, Punkevní and Kateřinská. At the far end of the Skalní Mlýn carpark are two offices: the first sells 'Eko-Train' and gondola tickets to reach Punkevní Cave and the Macocha Abyss (it's possible simply to walk) the second, called Ústřední informační služba (☎ & fax 553 79), sells the actual entrance tickets to Punkevní and Kateřinská.

Arrive as early as possible in the crowded summer season and on weekends, as Punkevní can sell out by 11.30 am. Also consider buying Punkevní or Kateřinská ticket vouchers (for a small extra fee) at Blansko's tourist office; the vouchers give you priority and are redeemable at the Skalní Mlýn ticket office.

Punkevní is open daily year round, May through September from 8.20 am to 3.50 pm, October through April to 2 pm. Entry costs 70 Kč. Kateřinská is open daily from May through September from 8.20 am to 3.30 pm, in October and January through April until 2 pm; entry costs 25 Kč.

Punkevní & the Macocha Abyss From the Skalní Mlýn carpark, either walk 15 minutes to Punkevní Cave (Punkevní jeskyně) or pay 30 Kč for the 'Eko-Train' to shuttle you (every 30 minutes). Once you reach the cave, the 75 minute tour winds through caverns studded with the requisite stalagmites and stalactites, then continues by boat on the underground Punkva river. The tour ends at the bottom of the Macocha Abyss (propast Macocha), which is quite wide and almost 140m deep. Visitors either walk to the abyss or – with a pre-purchased ticket obtained at the Skalní Mlýn carpark – ride the gondola (40 Kč).

Kateřinská Cave This cave is only 300m from the Skalní Mlýn carpark, yet it is much less crowded. The 30 minute tour covers two massive chambers, one of which hosts music concerts on summer weekends.

Other Caves The least-visited cave is the smallest one, **Balcarka jeskyně**, a pleasant 2km walk from Skalní Mlýn (or there are eight daily buses from Blansko on weekdays, two on weekends). Balcarka is open daily from April through September from 8 am to 3.15 pm (in October until 2 pm), on weekends in February and March from 10 am to 1 pm; entry costs 25 Kč. On the way to Balcarka jeskyně is a turn-off to the upper rim of the Macocha Abyss. There is a restaurant and snack bar here, but no public transport. From the road to Balcarka is about 3km.

The fourth cave, **Sloupsko-Šošuvské jeskyně**, is near the village of Sloup, and is only worth it if you have a car or bike. It was closed for renovations in 1997; inquire in Skalní Mlýn for current opening times.

Places to Stay & Eat The *Hotel Skalní Mlýn* (☎ 41 81 13), opposite the ticket offices, is priced at 1190/1490 Kč (less 40% off-season). The restaurant here is good. In summer the hotel hires bikes (150 Kč per day).

Near the Macocha Abyss is the summer-only *Útulna U Macochy*, with dorm beds for 200 Kč per person.

Getting There & Away Most convenient is the *autobusový okruh*, a tour bus from the Blansko bus station that hits all the caves for just 50 Kč. It operates from May through September at one or two-hour intervals from 7.40 am to noon. It only goes if there are at least 15 passengers.

Otherwise you can take a train from Brno to Blansko, and a bus from Blansko (stand No 6) to Skalní Mlýn; at the time of writing departures from Blansko were at 7.35 am (year-round), 8.15 am (May to September) and 11 am (June to August), returning to Blansko at 11.30 am (June to August), 3.25 pm (year-round) and 5.10 pm (April to September). On foot it's 5.3km from Blansko's train station to Skalní Mlýn's carpark. To get there turn right across the bridge onto the highway, left at Hotel ČKD Blansko, and follow the signs to Hotel Skalní Mlýn.

Local Churches

There are several other stops worth making as long as you're here. The charming church in the village of **Křtiny**, 14km northeast of Brno, was built according to a design by the great Baroque architect Giovanni Santini, in 1712-50. There is an annual pilgrimage to this church every St Anne's Day (sv Anny), on the last weekend in July or the first weekend in August.

If you are into more modern work, check out the interiors of the village churches at **Jedovnice** and **Senetářov**. They contain work that has only been seen in public since the end of Communist rule, including Medek's Stations of the Cross in Senetářov, which is particularly striking. Find the caretaker (*kaplan*) or priest (*kněz*) if you want to visit these churches.

PROSTĚJOV

Prostějov (population 50,900) dates back to a castle built here in 1213. A few hours is plenty to see the few sights.

Orientation & Information

From the adjoining train and bus stations, head straight up Svatoplukova for 10 minutes to the main square, náměstí TG Masaryka.

In the town hall on the main square, Informační a Turistická Kancelář (☎ 52 92 22) can help with accommodation (closed Sunday). Prostějov's area code is ☎ 0508.

Things to See

The remains of the castle are 200m north of the main square at Pernštýnské náměstí 8; it's now a **museum** with changing art exhibits and sgraffito by J Köhler. The museum is open daily, except Monday, from 9.30 am to noon and 1 to 5 pm; entry costs 5 Kč. Another museum, in the **Old Town Hall** (Stará radnice) on náměstí TG Masaryka, features history and traditional handcrafts, including two rooms of ceramics from the Haná region. It's open at the same times as the castle museum; entry costs 10 Kč.

František Bílek (1872-1941) painted the Stations of the Cross in the **Cathedral of the Ascension of the Holy Cross** (Chrám Povýšení sv Kříže) on Filipcovo náměstí.

Places to Stay & Eat

The cheapest hotel is *Hlavní nádraží* (☎ 245 59), next to the train station, where doubles with shower and TV are 350 Kč. At central *Hotel Avion* (☎ 245 61), náměstí E Husserla, doubles without/with shower are

300/750 Kč. Top of the line is the *Grandhotel* (☎ 33 23 11) at Palackého 3-5, priced at 2490 Kč per double, with satellite TV and breakfast. All the hotels have restaurants to match their price range.

Getting There & Away

Prostějov is on the Brno-Olomouc main line, two hours from Brno and half an hour from Olomouc, with 12 direct trains a day.

The Karel Psota Autoexpress is a local private bus company whose Znojmo-Brno-Olomouc bus stops here daily. Buy tickets as normal at bus stations.

VYŠKOV

Vyškov (population 23,100), on the Haná river, is worth a visit only if you have a *serious* interest in folk museums – and a car.

Things to See

The oldest building in town is the Gothic **Archbishop's Castle** (Arcibiskupský zámek), rebuilt between 1667-95 in Renaissance style according to a design by Tencalla. It's behind the town hall and through the carpark. The local museum it now houses, along with the usual archaeology and history, has an interesting section on the folk traditions of the Haná region, of which Vyškov is part. Note the beehive made from a tree trunk, a mock-up room from a peasant house, and the furniture and souvenirs brought back by local professor Alois Musil from his travels in Arabia. The museum is open weekdays from 8 am to 4 pm, and on Sunday from April through October.

On the main square, Masarykovo náměstí, is a Baroque fountain, a plague column and the Renaissance **Town Hall Tower** (Radniční věž), restyled in the Baroque era. You can climb the tower, but only on Monday and Wednesday from 8 am to 5 pm.

Places to Stay & Eat

All accommodation is farther from the city centre than the train station. *Hotel Dukla* (☎ 0507-226 22), on Dědická, has single/double rooms for 400/700 Kč. The restaurant here is simply OK. Or try the cheap and basic *Hostinec U městské brány* on Masarykovo náměstí.

Getting There & Away

Vyškov is 40 minutes or so from Brno on the train to Přerov. Bus links include eight a day to Prostějov, 10 to Kroměříž, and three to Blansko.

SLAVKOV U BRNA & AROUND

Slavkov u Brna is better known to foreigners by its German name, Austerlitz. This was the scene of the pivotal Battle of the Three Emperors in 1805, when Napoleon defeated the combined (and superior) forces of Austrian Emperor Ferdinand I and Russian Tsar Alexander I. For more information see the Battle of Austerlitz aside.

Orientation & Information

From Slavkov's dreary train station, turn left onto the highway, go past the bus station, and continue straight up Palackého náměstí to the chateau. Slavkov's area code is ☎ 05.

Things to See

Napoleon stayed for several days at **Slavkov Chateau**, where the treaty with Austria was signed. Built around 1700 to a design by Martinelli, the chateau was enlarged in the mid-18th century and its rooms adorned with stucco decorations and ceiling murals. The tour includes exhibits on Napoleon and the Kounice paintings in the gallery of the **Chapel of the Holy Cross** (kaple sv Kříže).

The chateau is open daily, except Monday, June through August from 8 am to 5 pm; and April, May, September and October from 9 am to noon and 1 to 4 pm. Entry costs 20 Kč.

Complete the Austerlitz circuit with a trip to Pracký kopec, a hill 12km east of Slavkov where the battle was actually decided. At the site is a 1912 **Peace Monument** (Mohyla míru) to those who fell and a small **museum** about the battle. It's open daily, except Monday, year-round from 9 am to 6.30 pm (to 3.30 pm in the off-season); entry costs 18 Kč.

Unfortunately, Pracký kopec is difficult to reach by public transport and hard to find. You can try getting a bus from Brno to Prace, from where it's a 3km walk south to the top of the hill. On the Brno-Slavkov train, get off at Ponětovice and walk 4km south through Prace.

Places to Stay & Eat

In addition to some private rooms around town (from 200 Kč per person; watch for the signs), there is the absurdly expensive *Hotel Soult* (☎ & fax 44 22 71 48), opposite the train station, with doubles only for 1200 Kč. Far superior is the central *Hotel Sokolský dům* (☎ & fax 422 11 03), at Palackého náměstí 75, priced at 350/700 Kč for a single/double. The restaurant here is quite good.

Across the street, *Hostinec U černého Lua* has cheap, hearty pub grub.

Getting There & Away

Slavkov is 21km east of Brno and easily reached by bus (seven daily) and train (nine daily). The trip takes about 45 minutes by bus or train.

PERNŠTEJN

This majestic late 13th century castle, on a hill above the small town of Nedvědice, is one of the Czech Republic's best preserved late-Gothic castles. From the 1450s to the 1550s it was enlarged and rebuilt in several stages, as the residence of the leading Moravian noble family of Pernštejn.

Among its attractions are the small towers that were part of the original and very solid-looking fortifications. Tours of the interior, refurbished in the 18th and 19th centuries, include the castle chapel (1570), a Baroque Knights' Room and library.

The castle is open daily, except Monday, May through September from 9 am to noon and 1 to 4 pm (to 5 pm in July and August), and on weekends in April and October to 3 pm. The 90 minute tour costs 45 Kč.

CZECH REPUBLIC

Battle of Austerlitz

The battle took place 10km west of Slavkov, around the village of Šlapanice, on 2 December 1805 – the anniversary of Napoleon's coronation as emperor. A day before the battle, Napoleon evacuated the Pracký plateau, hoping that the allies would occupy the site. Allied troops advanced on the French through the fog-filled lowlands the next morning, their plan being to attack the French right flank and cut off supply lines from Vienna. But under cover of the fog Napoleon regrouped and, when the fog lifted, counterattacked, recapturing the plateau. By the afternoon the allies were defeated, suffering losses five times higher than the French. Austria signed a peace treaty and the Russian troops returned home.

The Battle of Austerlitz led to the disintegration of the anti-Napoleon coalition and to a new European political map. It is re-enacted annually in December. ■

Places to Stay

In Nedvědice there are private rooms – try *Pod hradem* at the castle's base for 300 Kč per person – or the *Hotel Atelier* (☎ 0505-963 17) in the town centre, with modern doubles for 685 Kč.

Getting There & Away

There are many daily trains from Brno to Nedvědice, with a change to a local train at Tišnov; each leg takes about half an hour. The local train continues to Žďár nad Sázavou and rejoins the Brno-Prague main line.

Without a car the surest way to Pernštejn from Nedvědice is on foot. There are only three daily buses on weekdays and one on weekends.

TIŠNOV

En route from Brno to Pernštejn is the cross-shaped **Cistercian Convent** (founded in 1233) in the Tišnov suburb of Předklášteří. It's worth a look if you have the time. The beautifully carved *Porta coeli*, a Romanesque-Gothic portal, dates from the early 13th century. It also has a six-part vault (the first of its kind in Moravia) above the presbytery, and the windows are in Romanesque rosette style.

The convent is on the west side of town, across the Svratka river.

NÁMĚŠŤ NAD OSLAVOU

Náměšť' (population 5100) is known for its 13th century **castle**, which is on a hill above the Oslava river. Its present Renaissance face, largely the work of architect Leonardo Garvi, dates from the 16th century.

The most interesting parts of the castle tour are 24 Renaissance and Baroque tapestries, and a library adorned with stucco work and murals. The 30 Kč tour is offered daily, except Monday, May through September from 9 am to noon and 1 to 5 pm (until 6 pm in July and August), on weekends only to 4 pm in April and October.

Places to Stay & Eat

Try not to get stuck here – the only hotel is the shabby *Schliksbier* (☎ 0509-3332), at Masarykovo 55, with doubles from 550 Kč. Far better is the tiny *Pension Fontána* (☎ 0509-3108), Brněnská 594, priced at 350/650 Kč for a single/double.

Restaurace U Karlíčka at the castle serves good Moravian food. There are several basic restaurants and cafés around the main square.

Getting There & Away

Náměšť' is 26km west of Brno and is easy to reach by bus. The bus station is a five minute walk east from the main square, and the train station is north-east a few minutes farther on.

The train station is also on a minor rail link between Brno and Třebíč, with regular connections. It is more practical to take buses if you are going on to Mikulov, Znojmo, Jaroměřice nad Rokytnou or Moravský Krumlov.

MORAVSKÝ KRUMLOV

Moravský Krumlov, 27km south-west of Brno, stands in an idyllic setting in the valley of the Rokytná river, with the Church of St Florián sitting alone on a hill above the town. Nearby is the village of Ivančice, where the artist Alphons Mucha was born in 1860. In fact, the main reason to visit Moravský Krumlov is to view an awesome, breathtaking series of 20 canvasses by Mucha depicting scenes from Czech and Slav history.

Mucha Gallery

The gallery is housed inside a neglected Renaissance chateau 100m off the main square. Inspired by Slav history, Mucha's Slav Epic (Slovanská Epoje) cycle is unlike the Art Nouveau style of the artist's Paris posters, and is worth a dozen textbooks on history. They border on science fantasy, full of wild-eyed priests, medieval pageantry and battlefield carnage, all under brooding northern skies. Mucha worked abroad for several years but returned to his newly independent homeland in 1918 to help design its banknotes and stamps. No building other than this one could be found to accommodate these huge paintings, which he worked on between 1912 and 1930.

The chateau is open daily, except Monday, April through October from 9 am to noon and 1 to 4 pm; entry costs 25 Kč.

Places to Stay & Eat

Hotel Jednota (☎ 0621-32 23 73), náměstí TG Masaryka 27, has basic doubles for 540 Kč, and a decent restaurant.

Getting There & Away

The train station is about 2km from náměstí TG Masaryka, though local buses aren't good about meeting the 12 daily trains that come through from Brno (under an hour away). From Brno five buses a day (three on weekends) stop on Moravský Krumlov's main square.

Jihlavsko Region

This is the region on the Moravian side of the Czech-Moravian Uplands (Českomoravská vysočina), continuing down to the Austrian border. It includes the pleasant city of Jihlava and the postcard-perfect town of Telč, as well as the chateau at Jaroměřice nad Rokytnou. It's an ideal cycling region, gently hilly and dotted with pretty villages.

JIHLAVA

Jihlava's first real growth and prosperity came with the mining of silver and the founding of a royal mint during the 14th century.

Despite being marred by a huge department store and a carpark, the central square – one of the country's largest at 36,650 sq metres – still has many Renaissance houses, and in the southern part of the old town parts of its medieval bastions survive. Take a break from architecture and churches at the superb local zoo.

Orientation

There are two train stations. The main station (Jihlava hlavní nádraží), for trains to and from Brno, Třebíč and Prague, is 2km north of the centre; take trolleybus B or B1 to the main square, Masarykovo náměstí.

The Jihlava město station, for trains to Tábor and České Budějovice, and the bus station at the corner of Tolstého and Jiráskova, are a five minute walk north of the old town.

Information

Tourist Office Turistické informační středisko (☎ 280 34), on Masraykovo náměstí, arranges local accommodation weekdays from 9 am to 5 pm, and on Saturday (in summer only) from 9 am to noon.

Money No less than five banks line the main square. Spořitelna, at the corner of Masarykovo náměstí and Křížová, charges 1% for travellers cheques and 2% for cash, and has a MasterCard/Visa ATM.

Post & Communications The main post and telephone office is at the corner of Masarykovo náměstí and Komenského. Jihlava's area code is ☎ 066.

Things to See

The Gothic **Church of St James** (kostel sv Jakuba), on Jakubské náměstí, has a gilt Renaissance baptismal font and a Baroque chapel. In the 13th century **Church of the Virgin Mary** (kostel Panny Marie), to the west on Minoritská, are some Gothic frescoes and the oldest picture of the town, a 16th century work showing the defeat of Zikmund Křižanovský z Rokštejna by the local residents in 1402.

In the Baroque **Church of St Ignatius** (kostel sv Ignáce; 1689), on Masarykovo náměstí, are an emaciated Christ, some Tepper frescoes on the vaulted ceiling, and a fine main altar.

A late-Gothic house with a Renaissance face at Masarykovo náměstí 58 is the **Highlands Museum** (Muzeum Vysočiny), which includes fine Gothic, Renaissance

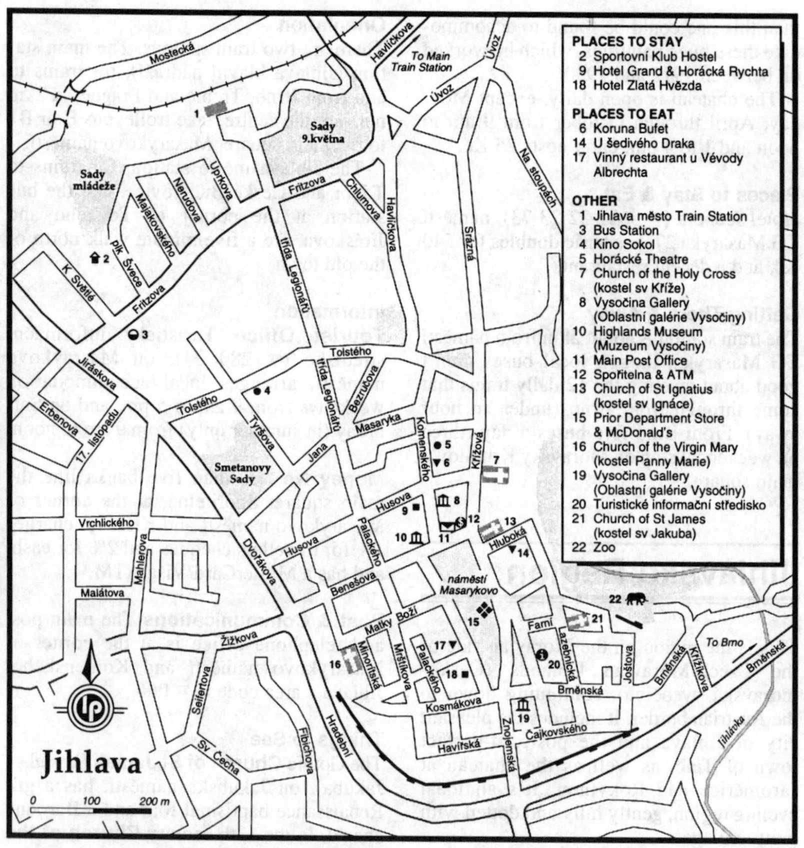

and Baroque interiors, and a display of folk arts and handcrafts. It's open daily, except Monday, from 9 am to 5 pm; entry costs 10 Kč.

The **Vysočina Gallery** (Oblastní galérie Vysočiny) displays Czech art and sculpture from the 1930s to 60s in two locations: one at Komenského 10, and the other at Masarykovo náměstí 24. Both charge 20 Kč for entry and are open daily, except Monday, from 9 am to 5 pm.

A real highlight is Jihlava's **zoo** a 10 minute walk from the main square. Over 400 animals – notably three Sumatra tigers, snow leopards and a dozen species of monkeys – are kept in open-air, mostly bar-free compounds. It's open daily year-round; entry costs 30 Kč.

Places to Stay

A year-round *campsite* (☎ 278 38) is at Pávov, 4km north from Jihlava beside the Prague-Brno motorway and linked by buses from town.

The summer-only *Sportovní Klub* hostel (☎ 265 93), opposite the bus station on K

Světlé, has beds for around 200 Kč. The tourist office books private rooms from about 350 Kč per person.

Hotel Zlatá Hvězda (☎ 294 21), Masarykovo náměstí 32, has single/double rooms with shower and WC for 960/1160 Kč. The up-market *Hotel Grand* (☎ 235 41; fax 731 01 99), Husova 3, is 890/1490 Kč. Next door is the smaller, more modern *Horácká Rychta* (☎ 227 21), with doubles for 1050 Kč.

Places to Eat

Hotel Grand has a popular café and restaurant. For breakfast there's the cheap *Koruna Bufet* at Komenského 18 (closed Sunday).

Vinný restaurant u Vévody Albrechta, Masarykovo náměstí 41, has a good international menu with main courses for 85 to 285 Kč. In the same price range is *U šedivého Draka*, a semi-formal Chinese restaurant on Hluboka.

Entertainment

The tourist office has a schedule for the *Horácké Theatre* (Horácké divadlo). Otherwise catch a film at *Kino Sokol*, on Tolstého.

Getting There & Away

Jihlava hlavní nádraží is for trains to and from Brno, Třebíč and Prague; and Jihlava město for trains west to Tábor and České Budějovice. Buses are quicker to Žďár nad Sázavou (six a day) and Telč (12 a day).

ŽĎÁR NAD SÁZAVOU

Žďár is an uninspiring industrial town of 27,000 people, about 35km north-east of Jihlava. Its main sights – the Cistercian Monastery and the Church of St John of Nepomuk, both by the architect Giovanni Santini – are just barely worth the bother of getting here.

Orientation & Information

The monastery is 3km north of the train and bus stations, which are next to each other. The central square, náměstí Republiky, is 1km north-west of the adjoining stations; follow Nádražní straight for 10 minutes. Local buses pass the monastery from the stations, hourly on weekdays and less frequently on weekends. Tini Tour (☎ 258 08), in the Old Town Hall on náměstí Republiky, can help with accommodation weekdays from 9 am to 5 pm.

Žďár's area code is ☎ 0616.

Cistercian Monastery

The Cistercian Monastery (klášter Cisterciáků), founded in 1252, was burned down by the Hussites in 1422. A reconstruction began in 1638, and Giovanni Santini started work here in 1702, though he never completed the project. In it, he attempted to combine the medieval with the Baroque in a distinctive dark-and-light style. His **Church of the Virgin** (kostel Panny Marie) contains an altar by Řehoř Thény. The former monastery stables are now a museum devoted to Santini. Another section has a **Book Museum** (Muzeum knihy) on the evolution of writing, calligraphy and printing. Both are open daily, except Monday, May through September from 9 am to 5 pm, and on weekends from 8 am to 4 pm in April and October.

Church of St John of Nepomuk

Closer to town on a hill called Zelená Hora (Green Mountain) is a peculiar Santini church in the shape of a five-pointed star.

According to legend, John of Nepomuk's tongue was cut out for not revealing royal confessions, and he was thrown off Prague's Charles' Bridge to his death. Five stars are said to have appeared above the spot where he drowned. Thus the Church of St John of Nepomuk (kostel sv Jana Nepomuckého) is chock-full of 'tongue' motifs, and circles of five stars.

Places to Stay & Eat

There are two comfortable hotels around náměstí Republiky – *Hotel U labutě* (☎ 229 49) at No 70, where single/double rooms with shower and WC are 500/700 Kč, and the nearby *Hotel Fit* (☎ 235 08) at Horní 30, priced at 450/650 Kč. Both have decent restaurants.

Getting There & Away

Žďár is on the Brno-Prague main line, with about 14 connections a day; Brno is 1½ hours away. There are up to five daily buses to Třebíč and six to Jihlava.

TELČ

Telč (population 6000) was founded in the 14th century by the feudal lords of Hradec as a fortified settlement, with a castle separated from the town by a strong wall. The artificial ponds on each side of Telč provided security and a sure supply of fish. After a fire in 1530, Lord Zachariáš, then governor of Moravia, ordered the town and castle rebuilt in the Renaissance style by Italian masons. Profits from gold and silver mines allowed Lord and Lady Zachariáš to enjoy a regal lifestyle.

After the death of Zachariáš in 1589, building activity ceased and the complex you see today is largely as it was then. The main square of this most charming of Czech

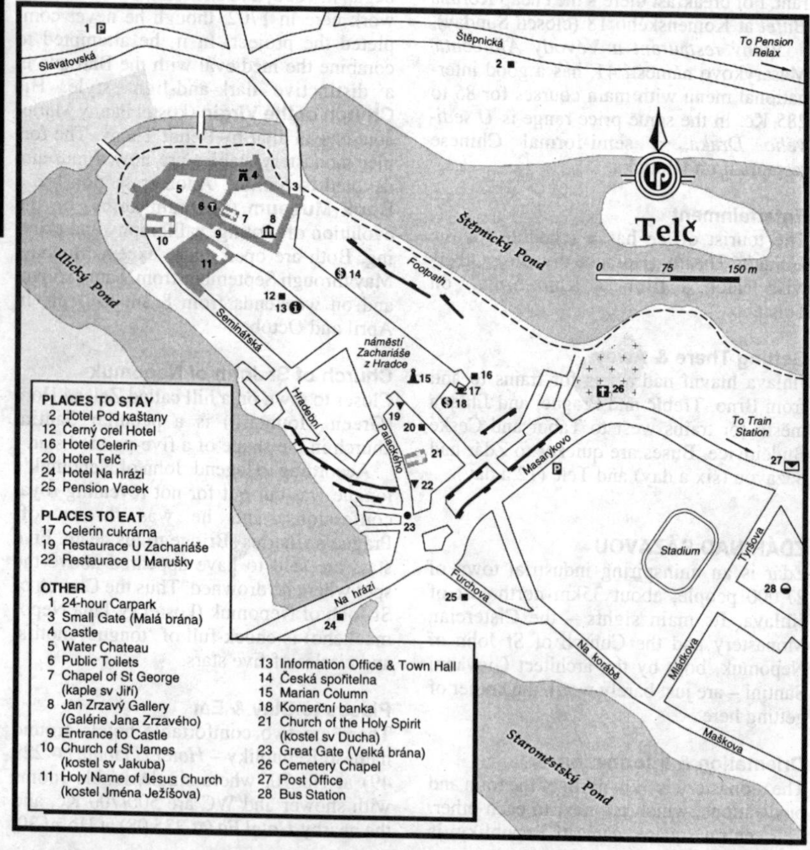

towns is unmarred by modern constructions, and the fire hall at náměstí Zachariáše z Hradce 28 is evidence of local concern to keep it that way. In 1992, Telč was added to UNESCO's World Heritage List.

Orientation

The old centre, including náměstí Zachariáše z Hradce and the castle, is nearly surrounded by two ponds – a fine setting, though the town's sewage has only recently stopped being dumped into them. The train and bus stations (one street apart) are a 10 minute walk south-east of the town centre. A left-luggage service is available at the train station 24 hours a day – ask the stationmaster.

Information

Tourist Office An information office (☎ 96 22 33) just inside the town hall provides the usual services and can book accommodation. It's open in summer only, weekdays from 9 am to 4 pm.

Money Česká spořitelna, náměstí Zachariáše z Hradce 21, changes travellers cheques for 1% commission and gives Visa cash advances. Komerční banka, on the square at No 40, has a MasterCard ATM.

Post & Communications The post office is on Staňkova, a block from the train station. The telephone section is open weekdays from 7.30 am to noon and 1 to 5.30 pm, Saturday from 8 to 11 am.

Telč's area code is ☎ 066.

Things to See

Castle Telč's Renaissance castle, part of which is known as the Water Chateau, was rebuilt from the original Gothic structure between 1553-56 by Antonio Vlach and between 1566-68 by Baldassare Maggi. In the ornate **Chapel of St George** (kaple sv Jiří), opposite the ticket office, are the remains of the castle's founder, Zachariáš z Hradce.

There are two tours – *Trasa A* takes you

CZECH REPUBLIC

RICHARD NEBESKÝ

Telč's main square is bordered on three sides by these stunning Renaissance houses

through the Renaissance chateau and *Trasa B* through the castle apartment rooms. While you're waiting for your guide, visit the local **historical museum** (enter from the chateau courtyard), with a scale model of Telč in 1895, or the small **Jan Zrzavý Gallery** (galérie Jana Zrzavého).

The castle and chateau are open daily, except Monday, May through August from 9 am to noon and 1 to 5 pm; and to 4 pm in April, September and October. Entry costs 25 Kč. The gallery and museum are open from March through November, Tuesday to Friday from 9 am to noon and 1 to 4 pm, Saturday from 9 am to 1 pm.

Other Attractions Telč's stunning town square is bordered on three sides by 16th century Renaissance houses, built on the ruins of their Gothic predecessors after the 1530 fire. Though from another era, the Baroque **Marian column** (1717) in the square does not detract from the town's overall character.

Dominating the town centre are the Gothic towers of the **Church of St James** (kostel sv Jakuba) and the Baroque **Holy Name of Jesus Church** (kostel Jména Ježíšova), completed in 1667 as part of a Jesuit College.

North out of the square is a narrow lane to the old town's **Small Gate** (Malá brána), through which is a large English-style park surrounding the duck ponds (once the town's defensive moat). The park is good for restful walks and picnics.

Southwards down Palackého towards the **Great Gate** (Velká brána) is the imposing Romanesque **Church of the Holy Spirit** (kostel sv Ducha), from the early 13th century. Outside the Great Gate you can walk along bits of Telč's remaining bastions.

Places to Stay

Private Rooms The information office can book private rooms from 300 Kč per person. There are several 'Zimmer frei' signs advertising private rooms east along Štěpnická, and on náměstí Zachariáše z Hradce at Nos 12, 32 and 58.

Pensions & Hotels The ageing but friendly *Hotel Pod kaštany* (☎ 721 30 42), Štěpnická 409, just outside the old town, charges 400/800 Kč for a single/double with bath.

If it's full try *Pension Relax* (☎ 721 31 26), 300m farther east along Štěpnická at Na posvátné 29. Equally appealing is *Pension Vacek* (☎ 721 30 39) on Furchova. Both charge about 350/750 Kč.

The *Černý orel Hotel*, at náměstí Zachariáše z Hradce 7, was closed for renovations at the time of writing. A good alternative is the modern *Hotel Celerin* (☎ & fax 96 24 77), on the main square at No 43, and priced at 1020/1120 Kč.

The drab and dreary *Hotel Telč* (☎ 96 21 09), Na můstku 37, charges 900/1150 Kč.

The 15 room *Hotel Na hrázi* (☎ & fax 721 31 51), Na hrázi 78, is a fine splurge, with fully equipped doubles at 1660 Kč.

Places to Eat

The restaurant at *Hotel Celerin* is quite good. The more basic restaurant at *Hotel Pod kaštany* has cheaper beers.

Restaurace U Zachariáše, on the main square, is the spot for a simple Moravian pub lunch.

The newish *Restaurace U Marušky*, Palackého 29, serves hearty, delicious Moravian cuisine. The adjacent (but signless) *Pod věží* is a bit more fancy and has a sunny garden terrace.

For coffee and cakes try *Celerin cukrárna*, on the square at No 1/43.

Getting There & Away

The railway line through Telč is fairly useless, as it ends at Slavonice on the Austrian border. For a train to Telč on the Tábor-Jindřichův Hradec line, change at kostelec u Jihlavy; there are connections to Telč about nine times a day.

Frequent buses go from Telč to Jihlava, Znojmo (via Vranov nad Dyjí) and Bítov. Buses travelling between České Budějovice and Brno stop at Telč about five times a day – it's about a 100km, two hour trip from either city. Seven buses a day run to Prague

(2½ hours; 210km). Telč's bus station is unstaffed; tickets are sold by the drivers and timetables are posted.

TŘEBÍČ

This polluted industrial city of 400,000, west of Brno, is not worth a trip for its own sake, but does have a few things to see if you're driving through the area.

Orientation & Information

The train station is on a hill south of the city centre, a 15 minute walk from the main square, Karlovo náměstí. The bus station is at Komenského náměstí, five minutes west of the main square.

A tourist office at Karlovo náměstí 56 can help with maps, accommodation, and foreign exchange, weekdays from 8 am to 7 pm, and Saturday to 1 pm.

Třebíč's area code is ☎ 0618.

Things to See

The **Benedictine Monastery** (Klášter benediktínů), around which the town originally grew, was founded in 1101 and rebuilt, shoddily, as a chateau at the end of the 17th century. A museum here has a small collection of Nativity scenes, but little else of interest; it's open daily, except Monday, from 8 to 11.30 am and 1 to 5 pm (to 4 pm in winter). Also in the complex is the **St Procopius Church** (kostel sv Prokopa), with an attractive chancel and carved north portal (Portal Paradisi). Admission to each is 20 Kč.

A short walk east from the monastery is the former Jewish ghetto. Only two synagogues and a cemetery remain – in fact, of the town's 290 Jews who survived WWII, only about 10 are still alive. The 1639 **Old Synagogue** (Stará synagóga) on Tiché náměstí now belongs to the Hussite Church; the **New Synagogue** (Nová synagóga), at Bohuslavova 42, is in serious disrepair. The wall around the 17th century **Jewish cemetery** (Židovský hřbitov), on Hradeck, 600m north of the Old Synagogue, was recently completed by its venerable caretaker and a group of local students.

Places to Stay & Eat

Autokemping Poušov (☎ 716 41) is 2km west of town, and open from May through September.

The very basic *Hotel U Podlipný* (☎ 211 10), at Nádražní 25, opposite the train station, charges 225 Kč per person. The top-end *Hotel Alfa* (☎ 5916), Znojemská 1235, at the southern edge of town, has doubles for 680 Kč.

On Karlovo náměstí there are several inexpensive places to eat; try *U hroznu* at No 52.

Getting There & Away

Třebíč is on a main line between Brno (1¾ hours away) and Jihlava (one hour away), with 12 trains a day. There are two buses a day to Telč, four to Jihlava, and five to Žďár nad Sázavou.

JAROMĚŘICE NAD ROKYTNOU

This small village's claim to fame is that it has one of Europe's largest Baroque chateaux, a typical example of Counter-Reformation architecture of the new nobility, in this case Johann von Questenberg.

A tour of the red-and-white striped castle includes the Hall of the Forefathers (Sál předků), with inlaid wood ceiling, and the stucco-decorated Dance Hall (Taneční sál). It's open daily, except Monday, May through September from 9 am to noon and 1 to 5 pm, and on weekends only in April and October; entry costs 10 Kč. Tours are in Czech, with an English text.

The 18th century Baroque **St Margaret Church** (kostel sv Markéty), which is also in the grounds, boasts a large cupola with a busy fresco by Karel Tepper. The interior can only be seen by asking the caretaker (*správce*); you'll find him opposite the entrance to the church at No 130 náměstí Míru.

In the large French and English-style gardens is a theatre where the first Czech opera, *O původu Jaroměřic* (The Origin of Jaroměřice) by František Míča, had its première in 1730.

Places to Stay

The only place to stay is at the *Opera Hotel* (☎ & fax 0617-44 02 32) on Komenského náměstí, which has spacious single/double rooms with shower and WC for 445/700 Kč.

Getting There & Away

Jaroměřice, 14km south of Třebíč, is best reached by bus. The station is a five minute walk north-west of the castle and main square. The train station is 2km away in the village of Popovice.

There are up to six buses a day from Brno, and 12 from Třebíč and Moravské Budějovice.

MORAVSKÉ BUDĚJOVICE

This town 6km south-west of Jaroměřice has a museum of pre-industrial crafts and trades. There are mock-ups of the workshops of saddlemakers, wheelwrights, carpenters, potters, cobblers, blacksmiths and more. Part of the museum is in the town castle and part in the former butchers' stalls (*masné krámy*). The exhibits are open daily, except Monday, May through September from 8 am to noon and 2 to 5 pm.

From here, Znojmo is 30km south-east by rail on the Znojmo-Okříšky line, with 10 trains a day.

South Moravian Borderlands

This is a lowland agricultural and light-industrial region, running along the Austrian border roughly from Znojmo to Břeclav. Much of the borderlands were owned, from the Middle Ages until the end of WWII, by the Lichtenstein family, who built most of the castles and churches here. Its highlights include the castles at Lednice and Vranov, and the small, handsome town of Mikulov.

The region was once home to a large German-speaking minority. They were expelled after WWII, leaving a legacy of tidy, prosperous-looking villages. Among Czechs the borderlands are famous for a local delicacy, Znojmo pickled gherkins (*Znojemské sladkokyselé okurky*). The borderlands also produce excellent wines, with the region around Mikulov offering some of the very best.

Large parts of south-east Moravia are fairly flat and ideal for cycling. One of the most appealing areas is between Lednice and Valtice.

ZNOJMO

For such a big and busy town, modern-day Znojmo (population 39,000) maintains a pleasant old centre with an unusually large number of religious buildings, marred only by a huge department store on the main square. Unjustly, few travellers do more than speed through on their way to and from nearby Austria.

Znojmo has a long history: a fortified settlement was built here by the 7th century. In the 9th century, in the era of the Great Moravian Empire, the Slavs established a settlement around the Church of St Hipolita. This important bulwark against Austria was always highly regarded by the Czech kings. It was also an important trading centre.

Orientation

Most sights, hotels and eateries are centred on náměstí TG Masaryka, Horní náměstí north of it, and the castle to the west.

The bus and train stations are 10 minutes by foot from náměstí TG Masaryka. From the bus station head up Tovární, turn left at náměstí Republiky, and right onto Vídeňská. From the train station, walk straight up 17.listopadu and, at the roundabout (Mariánské náměstí), veer left onto Pontassievská.

Information

Tourist Office Informační středisko (☎ 22 43 69), in the Znojemská beseda building at náměstí TG Masaryka 22, books rooms and arranges tours, but is only open in summer,

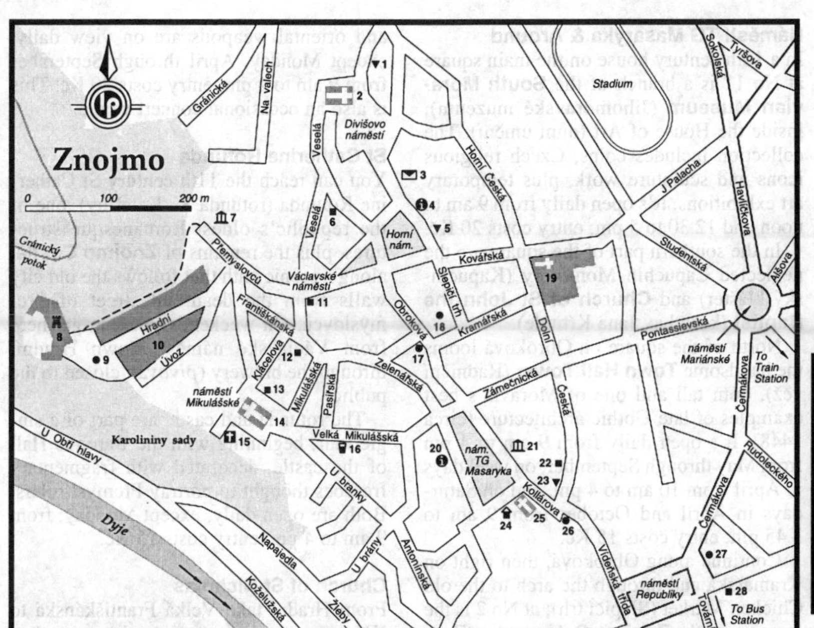

PLACES TO STAY

- 6 Pension Archa
- 11 Pension Austis
- 12 Hotel Kárník
- 13 Café-Pension Havelka
- 22 Pension U Huberta
- 24 Turistická ubytovna
- 28 Hotel U divadla

PLACES TO EAT

- 1 Marco Polo
- 5 Restaurace Morava
- 23 Bistro Art

OTHER

- 2 Church of St Michael (kostel sv Michala)
- 3 Post Office
- 4 Čedok
- 7 South Moravian Museum
- 8 Znojmo Castle
- 9 St Catherine Rotunda (rotunda sv Kateřiny)
- 10 Brewery
- 14 Church of St Nicholas (kostel sv Mikuláše)
- 15 St Wenceslas Chapel (kaple sv Václava)
- 16 Na věčnosti
- 17 Town Hall Tower
- 18 Znojmo Catacombs (Znojemské podzemí)
- 19 Church of the Holy Cross (kostel sv Kříže)
- 20 Informační středisko
- 21 South Moravian Museum
- 25 Church of St John the Baptist (kostel sv Jana Křtitele)
- 26 Vlk Tower (Vlková věž)
- 27 South Moravian Theatre (Jihomoravské divadlo)

on weekdays from 8 am to 8 pm, and Saturday to noon.

Money Znojmo has few banks in the centre; foreign exchange is best handled at Čedok (☎ 22 66 35), Horní náměstí 15, which is open weekdays from 9 am to 4 pm, and Saturday to noon.

Post & Communications The main post and telephone office is at Horní náměstí 13. Znojmo's area code is ☎ 0624.

Náměstí TG Masaryka & Around
In a 16th century house on the main square at No 11 is a branch of the **South Moravian Museum** (Jihomoravské muzeum), inside the House of Art (dům umění). The collection includes coins, Czech religious icons and sculpture work, plus temporary art exhibitions. It's open daily from 9 am to noon and 12.30 to 5 pm; entry costs 20 Kč.

In the southern part of the square are the neglected Capuchin Monastery (Kapucínský klášter) and **Church of St John the Baptist** (kostel sv Jana Křtitele).

North of the square on Obroková looms the handsome **Town Hall Tower** (Radniční věž), 66m tall and one of Moravia's best examples of late-Gothic architecture (circa 1448). It's open daily from 9 am to 4 pm from May through September, on weekdays in April from 10 am to 4 pm, and on Saturdays in April and October from 9 am to 3.45 pm; entry costs 15 Kč.

Continue along Obroková, then right on Kramářská and through the arch to the old Chicken Market (Slepičí trh); at No 2 is the entrance to the **Znojmo Catacombs** (Znojemské podzemí). In the 14th century the town's cellars were linked by some 27km of tunnels, which were used for storage and defence. They're open the same hours as the Town Hall Tower, but the 30 Kč tours only set off with seven or more people.

East on Kramářská is the 13th century **Church of the Holy Cross** (kostel sv Kříže) part of an active Dominican monastery. The early-Gothic church got a Baroque face-lift in the 1780s.

Other Squares
North of Horní náměstí, via Divišovo náměstí, is Jezuitské náměstí and the Jesuit **Church of St Michael** (kostel sv Michala), a 'Baroquified' Romanesque church at the highest point of the old town.

From here Veselá leads to Václavské náměstí, where a right turn into Přemyslovců takes you to a former Minorite Monastery at No 6, now a branch of the **South Moravian Museum**. Exhibits on crafts and trades, geology and archaeology, and oriental weapons are on view daily, except Monday, April through September from 9 am to 4 pm; entry costs 20 Kč. This is also an occasional concert venue.

St Catherine Rotunda
You can reach the 11th century St Catherine Rotunda (rotunda Sv Kateřiny), one of the republic's oldest Romanesque structures, plus the remains of **Znojmo Castle**, along a scenic path that follows the old city walls from the dead-end street of Přemyslovců. On weekends you can get here from Václavské náměstí down Hradní, through the brewery (*pivovar*; closed to the public).

The rotunda and castle are part of a single tour, beginning with the Baroque Hall of the castle, decorated with fragmentary frescoes thought to portray Přemysl rulers. Both are open daily, except Monday, from 9 am to 4 pm; entry costs 15 Kč.

Church of St Nicholas
From Hradní take Velká Františkánská to Klácelova and turn right into náměstí Mikulášské. Ahead is the Church of St Nicholas (kostel sv Mikuláše), once Romanesque, but rebuilt as the present monumental Gothic structure. It's prized for its interior, mainly the nave and presbytery.

In a side chapel near the entrance is the so-called 'Bread Madonna'. According to legend, during the Thirty Years' War a box beneath this image was always found to be full of food, no matter how much was removed. The church is only open for services and concerts. Beside the church is the Orthodox **St Wenceslas Chapel** (kaple sv Václava).

Places to Stay
Informační středisko books private rooms from 300 Kč per person.

Hostel Basic dorm beds are available for under 150 Kč at the central *Turistická ubytovna* (☎ 22 47 09), in the Capuchin Monastery on náměstí TG Masaryka. You must check in between 6 and 10 pm.

Pensions The excellent *Pension U Huberta* (☎ 701 02), at Dolní Česká 38, charges 400/800 Kč for single/double rooms with a shared bath. Equally central but more expensive are *Pension Austis* (☎ 24 19 49) at Václavské náměstí 5, *Café-Pension Havelka* (☎ 22 01 38) at náměstí Mikulášské 3, and *Pension Archa* (☎ 22 50 62) at Vlkova 4.

Hotels Cheapest is the newly renovated *Hotel U divadla* (☎ 22 45 16) at náměstí Republiky 16, priced at 500/1100 Kč with private bath. A good choice in the town centre is *Hotel Kárník* (☎ 22 68 26) at Zelenářská 25, with smallish doubles starting at 1000 Kč.

Places to Eat

Restaurace U Huberta, attached to the pension of the same name, serves pub food that's a step up in quality and flavour. *Hotel Kárník* also has a good – though pricey – restaurant.

Worth trying at Horní náměstí 17 is the mid-range *Restaurace Morava*, with South Moravian and international courses under 225 Kč (closed Sunday). For cheaper and faster fare try *Bistro Art*, on Dolní Česká. The all-vegetarian *Marco Polo*, on Divišovo náměstí, is sadly only open for lunch, weekdays from 10.30 am to 2 pm.

Entertainment

You can try the *South Moravian Theatre* (Jihomoravské divadlo), at náměstí Republiky, for a taste of opera. Classical concerts are sometimes held in *St Nicholas Church*. Ask Informační středisko for details.

Znojmo's alternative scene, such as it is, centres on the funky cellar bar *Na věčnosti*, at Velká Mikulášská 11. It's open daily, except Tuesday, from 5 pm to rather late.

Getting There & Away

Bus Fast direct buses run to Brno as often as the trains, and to Jihlava four times a day. Prague is three hours away by bus, with up to three daily services. Locally, about 10 daily buses go to Moravský Krumlov. Private buses also run to and from Olomouc (via Brno).

Train There are 10 direct trains a day to Břeclav (taking 1½ hours), which stop at Mikulov, 50 minutes away. Eight direct trains run daily to Brno (two hours), some with a change at Hrušovany nad Jevišovkou; eight daily trains also service Jihlava (two hours).

VRANOV NAD DYJÍ

Appearing to rise right out of the plain, west of Znojmo, is beautiful Vranov Castle. Closer up you see that it sits atop a cliff over the Dyje river. The castle can be reached across a bridge, about 1km uphill from the quiet town. Vranov's area code is ☎ 0624.

Castle

The castle's Gothic core dates from the 14th century. The rest was rebuilt in Baroque style in the 17th and 18th centuries. Most of the castle, including its chapel, is the work of the renowned Baroque architect, JB Fischer von Erlach.

Most prized is the oval **Hall of the Ancestors** (Sál předků), with some famous frescoes by Johann Michael Rottmayr. The castle has many ornate Baroque rooms, from the time when the 18th century Spanish princess Maria Anna Pignatelli lived here. There is a royal bath that looks like a modern hot tub, and two elegant ceramic stoves in the Pignatelli bedroom.

The castle is open for 40 Kč tours daily, except Monday, July and August from 9 am to noon and 1 to 6 pm, to 5 pm in May, June and September, and only to 4 pm on weekends in April and October. A separate tour covers the 1698 chapel and frescoes.

Places to Stay & Eat

The cheapest place to stay is *Penzión Autokemp U Jelena* (☎ 972 60) at Zámecká 202, which also calls itself Drops. Beds are about 150 Kč.

There are two hotels on the village square, the older *Pod zámkem* (☎ & fax 972 16) at No 45, with doubles for 700 Kč, and the newer *Pension Country Saloon* (☎ 972 38) at No 35, which has a good restaurant, and is priced at 500/600 Kč for a single/double.

Getting There & Away

There are up to nine daily bus connections from Znojmo, 20km away. In July and August only, two daily buses run the 26km to and from Bítov, departing Vranov at 8.15 am and 1.20 pm, and Bítov at 10.25 am and 5.10 pm.

BÍTOV

The 11th century **Bítov Castle** was rebuilt in early-Gothic style, and extended during the 15th to 17th centuries. Because of major renovations, there's little to see now except a small exhibit on the castle's history and reconstruction, and the frescoed castle chapel. It's open daily, except Monday, May through September from 9 am to noon and 1 to 5 pm (to 6 pm in July and August), and on weekends to 4 pm in April and October.

The castle is 3km north-west of Bítov village, and unless you have your own wheels, you must walk (follow the road north from the main square, past Hotel Bítov). If you're driving from Znojmo, don't be fooled by the derelict ruins of Cornštejn Castle, a few kilometres south-west of Bítov village, continue past them to Bítov.

Places to Stay

Autokemping Bítov Horka (☎ 0624-973 53), beneath the castle near the lake, is open from June through September. Otherwise try your luck at the large, chalet-style *Hotel Bítov*, 500m north of the village square; it was closed for renovations at the time of writing.

Getting There & Away

Buses are infrequent from Znojmo and Jihlava. The best connection is from the train station at Šumná, which is serviced by several trains from Znojmo, Jihlava and beyond.

CZECH REPUBLIC

JEVIŠOVICE

Jevišovice (population 1200), 17km north of Znojmo, is unusual because it has three castles – but don't make a special trip.

There are only ruins of the **Old Castle** (Starý hrad), on a cliff on the left bank of the Jevišovka river. Human artefacts from this site date back to around 3000 BC. The Renaissance **Old Chateau** (Starý zámek) is on an outcrop on the right bank, and the neo-Gothic **New Chateau** (Nový zámek), built in 1879, is in an English Garden (Anglický park) on the south edge of town. The Old Chateau has a small museum, with unusual musical instruments and apparently the largest collection of 'folk furniture' in the republic. It's open daily, except Monday, in June and July, and weekends only in April, May and August through October.

MIKULOV

Picturesque Mikulov (population 7700) and its sprawling castle sit on a hill in the flat wine-growing region of Pálava, a UNESCO-designated biospheric reservation. It's pleasant to linger over the village's Renaissance and Baroque houses and churches, though in a pinch all the sights could be covered in a long afternoon. Mikulov used to have a large Jewish population, and there is still a synagogue and Jewish cemetery here.

There is some good hiking in the nearby Pavlovské Hills (Pavlovské vrchy), with ruined castles and great views of the surrounding Mikulovsko region.

Orientation

From the train station, turn right onto 28.října, left onto Nádražní, and right onto Hraničářu to Piaristů. The bus station is a bit closer to town at the corner of Piaristů and 28.října.

Information

Tourist Office The Regional Tourist Centre (☎ & fax 2855), Náměstí 32, is a good source for information on the town and region, including maps for hiking. It can also organise tours and accommodation, and is open daily in summer from 8 am to 7 pm, weekdays in the off-season from 8.30 am to 5 pm.

Money Česká spořitelna, at Náměstí 19, has a Visa ATM. Komerční banka, at Piaristů 2, has a MasterCard ATM. Both have exchange desks.

Post & Communications The post and telephone office is at Česká 7. Mikulov's area code is ☎ 0625.

Castle

A Slav fortified settlement once stood here, replaced later by a Romanesque fort of which nothing remains today. The present walls and towers are part of the castle built in the 13th century. The heavy Baroque renovations were the work of the Dietrichstein family, who owned it from 1575 until 1945. The castle was burned down by the Germans in February 1945, and has been painstakingly restored.

A castle **museum** includes local archaeology and natural history, paintings and weapons, but the best bits are on regional folk traditions and wine-making. In the cellar is the largest wine barrel in central Europe, made by Kryštof Secht of Brno in 1643. The 390kg barrel has a capacity of 101,000L, though it's now unusable.

The castle is open daily, except Monday, May through September from 8 am to 5 pm, and from 9 am to 4 pm in April and October; entry costs 15 Kč.

Other Attractions

The now-restored 15th century **synagogue** (*synagóga*) at Husova 13 was damaged during WWII and neglected during Communist rule. The **Jewish Cemetery** (Židovský hřbitov), founded in the 15th century, is off Brněnská, under Kozí hrádek hill. You can get the key from the house at Brněnská 28.

The town's main square, called simply Náměstí, has many houses of interest, including the **town hall** at No 1 and the sgraffitoed **Canons' Houses** (kanovnické domy) at No 4. At No 5 is the **Dietrichstein Burial Vault** (Dietrichštejnská hrobka), closed to the public.

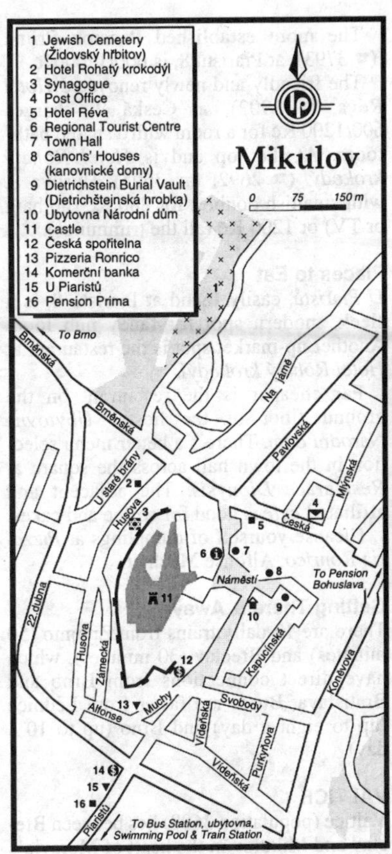

Places to Stay

The *Ubytovna Národní dům* (☎ 2576), Náměstí 9, has dormitory-style beds for about 200 Kč. Another reasonable hostel is at the swimming pool near the bus station, on the corner of Piaristů and 28.října.

Pension Bohuslava (% 2253), Venušina 2, at the end of Koněvova, is basic but cheap at 350/700 Kč for a single/double.

CZECH REPUBLIC

The more established Pension Prima ((☎ 3793), at Piaristů 8, is 600/1200 Kč.

The friendly and newly renovated *Hotel Réva* (☎ 3902), at Česká 2, charges 600/1200 Kč for a room with a shared bathroom. At the top end is *Hotel Rohatý krokodýl* (☎ 2692; fax 3695), Husova 8, with smallish doubles for 880 Kč (no bath or TV) or 1200 Kč (all the trimmings).

Places to Eat

U Piaristů, easily found at Piaristů 8, is a sleek, modern spot for fancy pub food. Another up-market spot is the restaurant at *Hotel Rohatý krokodýl.*

Far cheaper is the restaurant on the ground floor of the hostel *Ubytovna Národní dům.* There's a better menu selection in the town hall across the square at *Restaurace Dionysis.* The adjacent and affiliated *café* is good for coffee and cakes.

Cleanse yourself of dumplings at *Pizzeria Ronrico,* Alfonse Muchy 6.

Getting There & Away

There are 12 daily trains from Znojmo (50 minutes) and Břeclav (30 minutes), which have direct connections from Brno and Bratislava. Buses are faster from Lednice (up to eight a day) and Brno (up to 10 a day).

VALTICE

Valtice (population 3600) lies between Břeclav and Mikulov in the heart of Moravia's prime wine region. The town and its castle were one of the main residences of the Lichtenstein family, who owned it for five and a half centuries. This powerful aristocratic family had almost 100 estates in Moravia, many of which were confiscated from the Protestant Czech Estates when they lost the Battle of the White Mountain in 1620.

All the Lichtensteins' property was itself confiscated in 1945 for their collaboration with the Nazis. They are now trying to reclaim some of it, though the republic's 1990 restitution laws apply only to 1948 or later confiscations.

Valtice and Lednice are known in the Czech Republic as Valtilednicko, and the area that encompasses both towns was declared a UNESCO protected region in 1997 because it is the most architecturally valuable region in the country.

Orientation

The train station is on the northern edge of town, on the road to Lednice. Buses stop on the main road, where it meets náměstí Svobody.

Castle

The 12th century Gothic castle on náměstí Svobody has had face-lifts over the years, and is now recognised as one of the country's finest Baroque structures, with work by JB Fischer von Erlach and the Italian architect Domenico Martinelli.

The castle tour lingers over all the belongings and furnishings left behind as the Lichtensteins fled from the advancing Soviet army in 1945. Of interest are the walls themselves, plastered with 7.5kg of gold.

The castle is open daily, except Monday, May through August from 8 am to noon and 1 to 5 pm, and on weekends in April and October from 9 am to 4 pm; entry costs 30 Kč (an English text is available). In mid-August each year, Valtice holds a Baroque Music Festival (Zámecké Barokní Léto) in many parts of the castle, complete with a party and fireworks.

In front of the castle is the **Church of the Assumption of the Virgin** (kostel Nanebevzetí Panny Marie), with a Rubens painting behind the main altar. Next door is a dull agricultural museum.

Places to Stay & Eat

Restaurace Besední dům (☎ 0627-941 20), on the main road to Mikulov at No 173, 300m from náměstí Svobody, has dorm-style beds for under 140 Kč, and a cheap restaurant. For a treat you could stay in the castle; the *Hotel Hubertus* (☎ 0627-945 37) there has spacious doubles for 900 Kč, and a mid-range restaurant.

CZECH REPUBLIC

For a simple, hearty lunch try *Restaurace Albero* at náměstí Svobody 12.

Getting There & Away

There are 12 daily trains to Břeclav (with connections to Brno, Zlín and Bratislava) and Mikulov. From Mikulov the train continues to Znojmo. The train to Břeclav also stops at Valtice, a 13 minute ride away. There are up to seven buses a day to Lednice.

LEDNICE

Lednice (population 2364) literally means 'fridge', though it doesn't seem any colder than the rest of the region. It's best known for its neo-Gothic **chateau** (1856) by J Wingelmüller, preceded by Gothic, Renaissance and Baroque versions. The Lichtensteins held it from 1582 until 1945.

This is one of the more popular chateaux in the country, and gets very crowded in July and August, and on weekends. The luxurious interior is open for group tours daily, except Monday, in May and August from 9 am to noon and 1 to 6 pm, to 5 pm in September, and on weekends in April and October from 9 am to 4 pm; entry costs 40 Kč.

To the left of the chateau museum is a ho-hum **National Agricultural Museum** (Národní zemědělské muzeum), which also has weapons on display for some reason. To the right is a **greenhouse** (*skleník*) with a collection of exotic flora from around the world. The castle's extensive grounds, complete with lakes and the odd pavilion, are excellent for long summer walks. A highlight is the Turkish-style **minaret**, which is about a 2km round trip.

Places to Stay & Eat

The *Apollo* campsite (☎ 0627-984 14) is 2km south of Lednice on the road to Břeclav, opposite Mlýnský rybník. There are also four and five-bed bungalows for 355 and 530 Kč respectively.

Opposite the chateau is the new *Hotel Mario* (☎ 0627-983 96), with doubles for 1250 Kč and a popular restaurant. About 50m farther, at Podivínská 90, is the more basic *Pension Jordán* (☎ 0627-981 19) with its spacious doubles for 800 Kč. Just beyond is the massive *Hotel Harlekin* (☎ 0627-34 03 01), a mini-resort that boasts a fitness room, disco, restaurant and more. Doubles are 1320 Kč.

Getting There & Away

The train station is in the southern part of town, on the road to Valtice. Lednice is on a branch line from Břeclav, from where there are frequent connections to Hodonín and Zlín, Brno, Prague or Bratislava. Buses are less frequent to Břeclav, and there is just one daily bus to Brno on working days.

AROUND LEDNICE

The flat region around Lednice is fairly easy to explore on foot or by bicycle (though there's no bike hire so you'd have to bring your own wheels). If you can get hold of Kartografie Praha's *Jižní Morava* or a similar map, you can spend an interesting day exploring some of the smaller scattered chateaux, temples and pavilions that the Lichtensteins built around Lednice.

Just over 2km east of Lednice, on a green or yellow-marked trail through forests and meadows, is the rarely visited but picturesque, partly ruined **Janův Castle** (Janův hrad). In one room is a collection of stuffed wildlife of the region. It's open daily, except Monday, June through August from 9 am to 4 pm, with shorter hours in April, May, September and October.

Most of the buildings can be visited on a red-marked trail south from Lednice. Past the Apollo campsite, south of Mlýnský rybník, are the **Apollo Temple** (Apollónův chrám; 1817) and the **Nový dvůr Stables** (1890). Nearby is the **Three Graces Temple** (Chrámek Tří Grácií; 1825).

After you pass two ponds, a yellow trail digresses to Hlohovec, where north of town is **Hraniční Chateau** (Hraniční zámek; 1816). Or you can continue on the red trail to **Rendezvous Temple** (1810-12) and then to Valtice, from where a blue trail leads north to **Belvedér** (1818), Hlohovec and Hraniční Chateau. On a rise in the southern part of Hlohovec village there are wine cellars, where you might be able to taste and buy some of the local product.

From Hlohovec take the yellow trail joining the dead-straight Valtice-Lednice road to return to Lednice.

Moravské Slovácko Region

Moravské Slovácko (Moravian Slovácko), essentially the basin of the lower Morava river, is one of central Europe's richest surviving repositories of traditional folk culture. During the summer festival season, it's one of the more interesting places to spend time in either republic. The only hitch is transportation – outside the festival season, bus services are infrequent and hardly cover the small towns.

Geographically, Moravské Slovácko lies between the Chřiby hills (south-east of Brno) and the White Carpathians (over the border in western Slovakia). Its towns and villages are strung roughly from Břeclav to Uherské Hradiště, and to Holíč in western Slovakia.

Ethnically and culturally Moravské Slovácko also spans the border, being neither particularly Moravian nor Slovak, but something in between. Tomáš Garrigue Masaryk, the founding president of the Czechoslovak Republic, was born in the large Slovácko town of Hodonín, of Slovak and Moravian parentage.

The region's special flavour arises not only from a mild climate (incidentally favouring production of the republic's best wine) but from the character and temperament of the people – friendly, easy-going and full of life, with a feel for the arts.

The result is an extraordinary reservoir of colourful traditions in speech, dress, and building and decorating styles. Annual festivals are held frequently, at which singing, dancing and music are the norm, and traditional food is washed down with ample amounts of local wine.

In terms of traditional dress Slovácko has three main regions: eastern, including the centres of Veselí nad Moravou, Strážnice and Velká nad Veličkou; western, including the Hodonín area, and Holíč in Slovakia; and northern, around the towns of Kyjov, Bzenec and Ždánice.

Folk dress, heavily decorated with embroidery and lace, includes a head covering and dress for women, hat, shirt (and sometimes a waistcoat) and trousers for men, and boots or leather thongs for all. These often differ according to the age of the wearer.

The houses in many villages are still painted in traditional white with a blue band around the bottom, many embellished with painted flowers or birds. Good souvenirs include the famous local pottery, often decorated with floral and other designs, as well as embroidery and woodcarvings.

Special Events

The best time to see folk dress, and to hear the local music – some of it very impromptu – is during a regional festival. The following are some major ones (more details are given under Strážnice, Blatnice and Vlčnov in this section):

Blatnice – St Antonínka pilgrimage; September
Bzenec – Wine festival; August
Hluk – Dolňácké festival; first weekend of July every four years (next in 2001)
Kyjov – Kyjovsko summer festival; on a weekend in mid-August
Strážnice– International Folk Festival; last weekend in June
Velká nad Veličkou – Children's folk performances, mid-April; Horňácko festival with folk music and dance, on a weekend in the second half of July
Vlčnov – Folk Festival; last weekend of May

Wine Cellars

The region's distinctive wine cellars, or *vinné sklepy*, are generally open for tastings from mid-May through to late September. In places such as Petrov (3km south-west of Strážnice), where they are called *plže*

Tomáš Garrigue Masaryk

In the 1920s and 30s the name of Masaryk became synonymous with the 'First Republic', which Tomáš Garrigue Masaryk helped to create, and of which he became the first president.

The town of Hodonín saw the birth of Tomáš Masaryk (he added the name of his American wife after their marriage) on 7 March 1850. The first child of a Slovak father and a German-speaking Moravian mother, Masaryk had a background that is a typical blend of the region's nationalities.

Masaryk's Czech national awareness began during his school days in Brno, when he studied at a German school, and where he was at the forefront of the Czech student movement. At the beginning of WWI he went abroad and took up the struggle to free Czechoslovakia from the Austro-Hungarian Empire. Later he played a leading role in organising legions of Czech and Slovak prisoners of war in Russia, France and Italy to fight the Axis powers. During the whole of WWI he and two colleagues, Edvard Beneš and Milan Rastislav Štefánik, constantly held talks with French, English, Russian and American leaders to make the new Czech and Slovak nation a reality.

The dream came true on 28 October 1918. Only 14 days later Masaryk was voted the country's first president. He was subsequently re-elected three times – in 1920, 1927 and 1934. Throughout his presidential life he strove to make Czechoslovakia an independent, democratic state among its European equals. Basing his philosophy and vision on both nationalist and religious tenets, Masaryk's uncompromising honesty made him enemies. But his deep moral, humanistic and democratic beliefs eventually brought universal esteem. Following his resignation in 1935, the National Assembly bestowed on him the title of 'President and Liberator' (president Osvoboditel). ■

instead of vinné sklepy, they are partially underground; in Vlčnov they are more like huts (vinařské búdy). You can spot the ones in Petrov by their whitewashed walls, with a blue stripe around the base.

In some villages wine cellars constitute virtually a separate village, such as at Raštíkovice, where they are north of the village, or at Prušánky. Normally they are within the village boundaries. At Petrov, they are congregated near the train station.

These wine cellars usually have tables and benches outside where guests are entertained. After giving you a few samples your host might even invite you to a friend's place to try other varieties. Take your own containers if you want to buy wines.

Buses around these villages (except to Petrov) are erratic and it's easier to reach them by car – though remember that drink-driving attracts heavy penalties.

STRÁŽNICE

Strážnice (population 6100), 13km north-east of Hodonín, is the best known of Slovácko's towns, largely because of its annual International Folk Festival, held at the end of June. It also has an excellent skansen and a small chateau.

Orientation

The train and bus stations are a few minutes walk from the small, bland main square, Předměstí; walk straight out of the train station, turn right onto the main road and follow it for 200m before turning left.

Information

An agency called Irra (☎ 33 21 84), Předměstí 388, has information about the town and region and can organise tours, horse riding and winery trips (but not accommodation). It's open weekdays from 8 am to 5.30 pm.

The Česká spořitelna bank adjoining Hotel Černý orel has a foreign exchange desk and a MasterCard/Visa ATM.

Strážnice's area code is ☎ 0631.

Things to See

Only two of the Renaissance **town gates**, the Veselská brána and Hodonínská brána, are left from the town's defensive wall. The originally Gothic castle (1261-64) was rebuilt as a neo-Renaissance **chateau** in the mid-19th century, and today it is a museum, which includes good displays on the folk culture of the Slovácko region. From Předměstí walk north on kostelní, turn right and cross náměstí Svobody to Rybářská, and go left up Bzenecka. The chateau is open daily, except Monday, May through October from 8 am to 5 pm; entry costs 20 Kč.

Across the road and slightly closer to town is a **skansen** with a large collection of Slovácko buildings from the last century, including smithies, wineries, barns and colourfully decorated beehives. Most houses are furnished. The skansen is open at the same times as the chateau.

Special Events

The three day International Folk Festival, also called the Strážnice Festival, was the first such festival held in the Czech Republic, back in 1945. It gave a major boost to the preservation of traditional dress, music and dance.

Most of the festivities go on in the chateau's park, including open-air stage performances and impromptu jams, and food stalls with plenty of beer, wine and spirits. There are entry fees into the park, as well as to various performances. One of the highlights is a procession from the town's main square to the chateau's garden. There are also children's shows in the skansen.

Places to Stay & Eat

North of town, 1km beyond the chateau, is *Autokemping Strážnice* (☎ 33 20 37), with plenty of spaces, though you should book ahead around festival time. It also has rooms and bungalows for 140 to 155 Kč a bed, plus a restaurant and buffet.

There are two hotels facing the main square. The *Černý orel* (☎ 94 21 28) at

Traditional music is just one of the features of the region's many folk festivals

Předměstí 33 has comfortable single/double rooms for 785/1105 Kč, including breakfast. Opposite, the *Strážnice-Flag* (☎ 33 20 59; fax 33 20 99) has doubles with all the trimmings for 1265/1540 Kč, plus a pricier international restaurant and wine bar.

For an early, cheap breakfast or hot dishes, soups, salads and cakes, try the *bufet* in the Danaj shopping centre on Předměstí. In the skansen is the touristy (and tourist-priced) *Restaurace Skanzen*, with international and South Moravian dishes. *Zámecká vinárna*, in the castle, serves good South Moravian food, and is also popular for a late drink.

Getting There & Away

Strážnice is connected with Veselí nad Moravou and Hodonín by old electric trains, with regular daily service. For Uherské Hradiště or Břeclav you must change in Rohatec (a 15 minute ride from Strážnice). Břeclav and Veselí nad Moravou have regular links to Brno, Prague and elsewhere.

Buses to Veselí nad Moravou (10 minutes), Hodonín (15 minutes) and Petrov are more frequent, with about 10 daily connections. For Zlín, there is only one daily bus, or you can change at Uherské Hradiště.

KUŽELOV

On a hill above this little village in the foothills of the White Carpathians is one of the last five surviving **windmills** in Moravia and Silesia. In the 19th century there were almost 700 registered windmills, used for making flour, but most have given way to modern technology.

Kuželov's Dutch-style windmill, which can be rotated to face the wind, was built in 1842 and worked until 1945. In 1973 the Technical Museum of Brno began restoring it to working order.

The old caretaker will show you how it works, and take you through a little museum full of old furnishings, clothing and utensils. It's only open on weekends and holidays (unless you're in a group) from April through October from 9 am to noon and 1 to 5 pm; entry costs 5 Kč.

There is nowhere to stay here, and buses are scarce, with four on weekdays from Strážnice (19km) and six from Veselí nad Moravou (28km); on weekends there is only one bus from each. By car, the turn-off for Kuželov is 2km south of Velká nad Veličkou.

BLATNICE

Blatnice is 5km west of Veselí nad Moravou, and is known for the St Anthony Pilgrimage, which is held on the weekend nearest the period 13 to 16 September. The colourful pilgrimage takes place around the **Chapel of St Anthony** (kaple sv Antonína), built in the 17th century. Many of the pilgrims are dressed in traditional dress, and the songs and music are traditional as well.

VLČNOV

There is little to see in Vlčnov, apart from some decorated houses and the village's 40 or so wine cellars (here called búdy) – unless you're here for the annual Jízda králů (Ride of the Kings) folk festival.

The closest accommodation is in Uherské Hradiště (15km away), to which there are several daily buses (many more are added during the festival). There is a 25 Kč admission fee into the village during the festival.

Jízda Králů Festival

This festival features not only singing and dancing but the traditional Ride of the Kings, which is both a celebration of spring's new crops and a young men's rite of passage, thought to date back to the old European festival of Whitsuntide. The only other village to do this is nearby Hluk (where it happens only every four years); elsewhere, it had died out by the 1940s. The two day festival happens on the last weekend of May, with the Ride of the Kings on the Sunday.

The king, who must be chaste, is always chosen from among 10 to 12-year-old boys, while helpers can be up to 18 years old. The king may not speak or smile, so he holds a rose in his teeth throughout the ceremony.

He and two helpers dress in women's clothing. According to legend King Wenceslas escaped undetected; the women's clothing symbolises him wearing a disguise and the rose is a symbol of his silent escape. The horses are decorated with ribbons and paper flowers. Starting from the home of the king the ride winds through the village, while the helpers, calling out old verses in the king's honour, ask for gifts for him, upon which people stuff money in the helpers' boots.

UHERSKÉ HRADIŠTĚ

This energetic town (population 27,000) has a pleasant main square and several gardens, plus two worthwhile museums. It is a hub for regional buses, making it a good base if you can find cheap accommodation (not easy in summer).

Orientation

The Uherské Hradiště train station is southwest of the city centre, at the corner of Nádražní and Spojovací, but it's only on a rail link between two main lines. Břeclav-Přerov trains, including those from Hodonín and Rohatec, stop in the northern suburb of Staré Město. Brno-Slovakia trains, including those from Kyjov, stop in the southern suburb of Kunovice. City bus No 1 plies the route between Staré Město and Kunovice stations, via the city centre, while bus No 4 connects Uherské Hradiště and Staré Město stations.

The bus station is at Velehradská třída, near the Centrum department store. To get to the main square, Masarykovo náměstí, walk west along Obránců míru as far as Velehradská and turn left along Krátká and Šromova to the square.

Information

The bookshop Portal (☎ 55 61 13), Masarykovo náměstí 35, sells town maps; out front is a computerised kiosk with town information.

Komerční banka and its MasterCard/Visa ATM are at Masarykovo náměstí 1232.

Uherské Hradiště's area code is ☎ 0632.

Památník Velké Moravy

The archaeological site called Památník Velké Moravy (Great Moravia Monument) is thought by many Czech archaeologists to be a major centre of the 9th century Great Moravian Empire. Many of the artefacts found here – such as jewellery, weapons, a canoe and ice-skates made from bone – have been collected in the museum. You can also see the foundations of buildings dating back to the 8th century.

The museum is open from April through October, on weekdays from 8.30 am to 4.30 pm, and on weekends from 8.30 am to noon and 12.30 to 5 pm; entry costs 10 Kč. It's on Jezuitská in Staré Město, a 30 minute walk north of the city centre. To get here from the main square walk east on Havlíčkova to the highway (Velehradská třída), turn left and cross the Morava river, continue along Hradišťská, turn right into Velkomoravská and take the second left at Jezuitská. Alternatively take bus No 4 from the bus station on Obránců míru; it stops near this corner, two stops past the bridge.

Slovácké Museum

In addition to an excellent collection of traditional folk dress, tools and ceramics, this museum has an unusual example of 'folk art', an exhibit of 17th to 19th century shooting targets (from the days of local civil-defence militias) featuring politicians, musicians, mythological characters, animals and birds.

The museum is open Monday to Saturday from 9 am to noon and 12.30 to 5 pm; entry costs 10 Kč. It's in Smetanovy Park (Smetanovy sady), behind the cinema at the intersection of Havličkova and the main highway.

Places to Stay & Eat

The year-round, so-called *Autokemp Kunovice* (☎ 5371) is not a campsite at all, though it has beds for 200 Kč, and a communal kitchen. It's on the edge of the suburb of Kunovice; take city bus No 2 to the Trin store on Lidická, go eastwards in the direction of Uherský Brod and ask.

Easier to find is *Pension Schneider* (☎ 400 42) at Dvořákova 1210, near its intersection with Velehradská třída, opposite the Slovácké Museum. Doubles here are 500 Kč.

There are two hotels in the city centre, both with decent restaurants. The ageing and musty *Hotel Fojta* (☎ 55 12 37), at Masarykovo náměstí 155, has plain single/double rooms with shared facilities from 460/920 Kč. The far superior *Hotel Grand* (☎ 55 15 11), Palackého náměstí 349, is priced at 740/1090 Kč, including breakfast.

Getting There & Away

Trains to and from Hodonín and Rohatec stop at the Staré Město station, while those to and from Kyjov use the Kunovice station (see the Orientation section).

There are up to eight daily buses to Buchlovice (11km), five to Zlín (30km), four to Brno (109km), and four to Mikulov.

BUCHLOVICE

The Baroque **Buchlovice Chateau** was built back in the 1700s, probably to a design by Martinelli, with ornate stucco decorations. On display are the furnishings left behind by the Berchtold family, who fled advancing Soviet forces in 1945. Outside is a garden full of flowers and preening peacocks.

You pay 5 Kč to enter the garden and 30 Kč for a chateau tour, which are held daily in July and August from 9 am to noon and 1 to 6 pm. In May, June and September it's open daily, except Monday, from 8 am, and in April and October on weekends only from 9 am to noon and 1 to 5 pm.

Places to Stay & Eat

Autokemp Smrďavka (☎ 0632-953 67) is 2km west of the main square. In July and August a local bus plies the route. A bed in a bungalow is 160 Kč, and one in a caravan is 75 Kč. The only hotel in town has been closed awaiting renovation for several years.

In Buchlovice's main square, *Restaurace Záložná* has cheap and tasty South Moravian fare.

Getting There & Away

Up to 10 daily buses stop here en route between Uherské Hradiště and Kunovice.

BUCHLOV CASTLE

Buchlov Castle, sitting majestically in the Chřiby hills, was built in the 13th century, and although enlarged since, has not been restyled since its founding. The Berchtold family, its last owners, turned it into a museum during the 19th century.

This simple and appealing place has none of the over-wrought decoration of the Baroque style. Rooms are sparsely furnished but interesting. As in most medieval castles there are plenty of weapons and a few instruments of torture on display.

It's open daily, except Monday, May through August from 8 am to 5 pm, in September from 9 am to 4 pm, and in April and October on weekends from 9 am to 3.45 pm. The one hour tour costs 20 Kč. The closest place to stay is Buchlovice.

Getting There & Away

The castle turn-off is off the Brno highway, 4km west of Buchlovice, though for those on foot or a bike it's uphill all the way. Up to 10 daily buses between Uherské Hradiště and Kunovice stop at the castle turn-off, from where it's a pleasant 2km walk through the forest.

VELEHRAD

Another worthwhile sight near Uherské Hradiště is the **Cistercian Monastery** (klášter Cisterciáků) at Velehrad. The monastery and a church were founded here in 1205, and this was originally thought to be the ancient capital of the Great Moravian Empire. More importantly, though mistakenly, it was long considered to have been the archepiscopal seat of St Methodius, who may have died in the area in 885. Pilgrims have flocked to the shrine for centuries, not least Pope John Paul II in 1990.

The monastery was damaged during the

Hussite Wars and abandoned until the 17th century. Its late-Romanesque church was rebuilt in Moravian Baroque style between 1681 and 1710 by GP Tencalla. Under the church is a lapidarium with the remains of the original basilica, and a 17th century crypt. It's open daily, except Mondays in October and November, April through November from 9 am to noon and from 1 to 4 pm; entry costs 10 Kč.

There are up to eight buses during weekdays (fewer on weekends) from Uherské Hradiště (10km).

Zlín Region

ZLÍN

This place is essentially the country's best known shoe factory, and it's difficult to escape the fact. However, it's worth a brief – very brief – visit just to see what happens when a philanthropic millionaire gets to plan a whole town.

Zlín has a tradition of film-making, its studios having first promoted Baťa shoes, and later branching out. More than 2000 films have been made in Zlín's studios over the last 50 years, including about 600 animations, with the best known being those of Hermína Týrlová and Karel Zeman. Zlín is also the birthplace of playwright Tom Stoppard, born as Thomas Straussler in 1937 (his father worked at the Baťa factory).

Orientation

The train station (Železniční stanice) stands just off Gahurova, south of the river. The much larger bus station is a few hundred metres closer to the centre. All the town's sights are within walking distance of the unexceptional main square, náměstí Míru.

Information

Tourist Office The Informační Centrum (☎ 721 02 40), in the town hall on náměstí Míru, arranges accommodation weekdays from 7 am to 5 pm, and Saturday from 8 am to noon.

The People's Shoe

Before its present incarnation, humble Zlín was one village among many, pleasantly situated in a broad valley. Its present form, a herringbone pattern of streets radiating from the main thoroughfare, dates from 1894 when Tomáš Baťa, the omnipresent shoe manufacturer, began to expand his enterprise (Baťa had made a fortune from the sale of boots to the Austrian army in WWI).

Baťa began by commissioning a total environment for his workers, with housing, entertainment and sports facilities all close together so that workers could 'relate' to their work. The system was evidently successful: between 1910 and 1930 the town's population trebled to 36,000 souls.

Geographically, the shoe production line is central to everything – an enormous production facility right in the centre of town (sadly, you can't visit the shop floor). Much of the architecture was designed during the 1920s by František Gahura and Vladimír Karfík, in a functionalist brick and plate-glass combination that isn't as bad as it sounds.

Baťa, and later his son, grew the company into a sizable multinational, which the leftist government happily nationalised as soon as it could in 1945. The Communists in 1949 renamed the town Gottwaldov, after the then leader, to try and expunge its capitalist history (it has only recently regained its original title). Much of Baťa's enterprise remains the property of the state, though the family recently was given a shop in Prague's Václavské náměstí (small consolation for Mr Baťa and his former family empire). ■

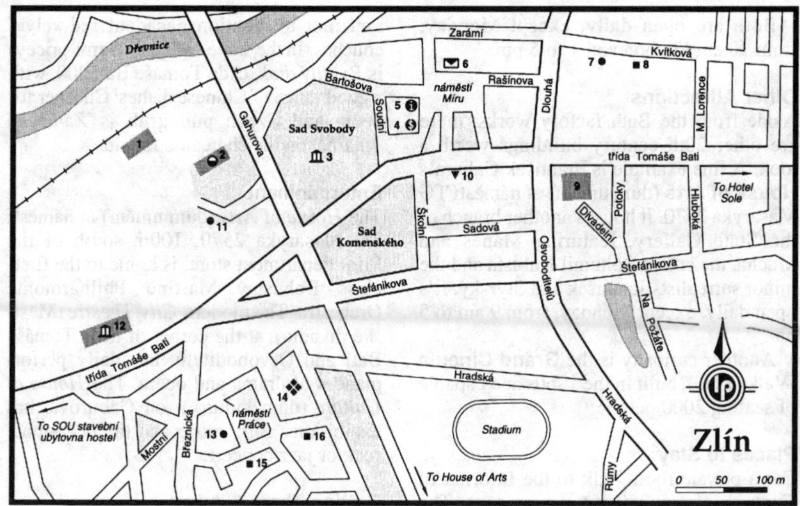

Money Komerční banka, on náměstí Míru, changes foreign currency (1.5% commission). Čedok (☎ 268 68), at Kvítková 80, charges a 2% fee.

Post & Communications The main post and telephone office is on náměstí Míru. Zlín's area code is ☎ 067.

Shoe Museum
The Shoe Museum (Obuvnické Muzeum) is in the basement of Baťa's 15 storey headquarters, the Správní budova Svit, at třída Tomáše Bati 1970. Inside are interesting exhibits on footwear from around the world and through the ages, naturally with emphasis on Baťa's. Open from Thursday through Sunday from 10 am to noon and 1 to 5 pm.

Zlín Chateau
This castle with Renaissance (1578-81) and Baroque reincarnations now houses the **Regional Museum of South-East Moravia** (Oblastní muzeum jihovýchodní Moravy), and has displays of folk-music instruments and utensils from the Slovácko and Haná regions; entry costs 20 Kč.

PLACES TO STAY
8 Hotel Ondráš
15 Interhotel Moskva
16 Hotel Garni Zlín

PLACES TO EAT
10 Ruchlý drak

OTHER
1 Train Station (Železniční stanice)
2 Bus Station
3 Zlín Chateau & Museum
4 Komerční banka
5 Informační Centrum
6 Post Office
7 Čedok
9 City Theatre (Městské divadlo)
11 House of Culture (Dům kultury)
12 Shoe Museum & Svit Administrative Building
13 Grand Cinema (Velké kino)
14 Prior Department Store

Upstairs is a branch of the **State Gallery** (Státní galerie), with permanent displays of 20th century Czech art and sculpture; entry costs 10 Kč.

Both are open daily, except Monday, from 10 am to noon and 1 to 5 pm.

Other Attractions

Aside from the Baťa factory works, there are other 20th century buildings worth a look. A fine example is František Gahura's **House of Arts** (dům umění) at náměstí TG Masaryka 2570. It houses another branch of the State Gallery, featuring Mánes and Mucha, the cubist Bohumil Kubista and the minor surrealists Janoušek and Štýrský. It's open daily, except Monday, from 9 am to 5 pm.

Another curiosity is the **Grand Cinema** (Velké kino), built in the 1960s and capable of seating 2000 people.

Places to Stay

For a private room, talk to the Informační Centrum (from 250 Kč per person). The hostel *SOU stavební ubytovna* (☎ 791 42 00), at třída Tomáše Bati 1268, has beds from May through August for around 115 Kč, but you need to check in before lunch.

Zlín's hotels are all fairly expensive. The cheapest is *Hotel Garni Zlín* (☎ 721 19 41; fax 366 60) at náměstí TG Masaryka 1335, next to the Interhotel Moskva, with decent doubles for 1200 Kč, including breakfast, TV, shower and WC.

Hotel Sole (☎ 721 04 58), at třída Tomáše Bati 3692, charges about the same but is 1km from the city centre towards Slušovice, by bus No 31 or 54.

Hotel Ondráš (☎ 721 01 78), at Kvítková, near Čedok, has doubles with all the trimmings (no singles) for 1100 Kč.

The fanciest and most expensive is *Interhotel Moskva* (☎ 836 11 11; fax 365 93) at náměstí Práce 2512, considered an exceptional example (by Karfík) of 1930s functionalism. Single/double rooms are 1190/1360 Kč; it also has several restaurants, a café and 24 hour exchange office.

Places to Eat

Zlín is a culinary black hole – most people eat at street stalls and stand-up buffets. *Hotel Garni Zlín* has an excellent restaurant, not to mention decadent red-velvet couches. In the same category (semi-pricey) is *Rychlý drak*, třída Tomáše Bati 200, with a good range of Chinese dishes. Cheaper for beers and Czech pub grub is *Zámecká vinárna*, on the chateau's far side.

Entertainment

The *House of Arts* (dům umění) at náměstí TG Masaryka 2570, 100m south of the Prior department store, is home to the first-class Bohuslav Martinů Philharmonic Orchestra. The modern *City Theatre* (Městské divadlo), at the corner of třída Tomáše Bati and Osvoboditelů, has daily performances of drama and opera. The *House of Culture* (dům kultury), on Gahurova, has exhibitions, folk music and the occasional rock or jazz concert.

Getting There & Away

Zlín's train station is on a dead-end spur. To go anywhere requires at least one change of trains, usually at Otrokovice, 11km and 20 minutes away on the Břeclav-Přerov main line. For Brno, change at Veselí nad Moravou. For Bratislava, change at Břeclav. Frequent northbound connections go to Přerov (half an hour away), Olomouc and Ostrava.

Buses are faster but less frequent in general; up to five a day go to Uherské Hradiště, 14 to Luhačovice, and 10 to Kroměříž.

VIZOVICE

This town of 4500, 15km east of Zlín, is the home of the Jelínek distillery, makers of some of the country's finest *slivovice* (plum brandy), and home of the annual Trnkobraní festival in early September.

The rather ordinary **Vizovice Chateau**, 100m off the main square, does have some good exhibits on traditional trades and crafts. It's open daily, except Monday, April through September from 10 am to 5 pm; entry costs 20 Kč.

There are regular daily train and bus connections here from Zlín.

LEŠNÁ

The attractions of tiny Lešná, 8km north of Zlín, are a Romantic-style chateau and a better-than-average zoo. Their joint entrance is 20m from the Zlín bus stop opposite the sprawling Restaurant Lešná (with a decommissioned aeroplane out back for the kids to play in).

Lešná Chateau (1887-93) is an over-decorated concoction of towers and shutters. Inside it is heavily decorated with paintings, porcelain and carved wood panelling. It's open daily, except Monday, May through August from 9 am to 5 pm, in September to 4 pm, and on weekends only in April and October from 10 am to 4 pm. The guided tour costs 25 Kč.

The surrounding **zoo** is in an English-style park, with many animals free to roam within fairly large enclosures, though the lions, bears and tigers remain caged. It's open daily year-round from 8 am to 5.30 pm; entry costs 35 Kč.

There are at least 14 daily buses from Zlín (30 minutes), reduced to six on weekends.

LUHAČOVICE

About 18km south-east of Zlín is Moravia's biggest spa, a peaceful town complete with leafy parks, promenades and colonnades endlessly dispensing mineral water. In 1668 a Brno physician, Jan F Hertod von Totenfeldt, publicised the health benefits of the mineral springs of this unknown town below Lukov Castle.

The town was not fully developed into a spa until 1902, by a Dr František Veselý. Together with the Slovak architect Dušan Jurkovič, he gave the town its distinctive rustic architecture, which incorporates Walachian farmhouse motifs and is set off by the surrounding forests. This is one of Moravia's more enjoyable spa towns, a sylvan spot suited to complete relaxation.

Orientation

The train and bus stations are at the south-west end of town; walk out of the stations, turn left onto Masarykova and continue past the police station. Farther up is the post office, on the left. From here the street Dr Veselého leads up to the spa area.

Information

The agency Luha (☎ 93 39 80), near the post office at Masarykovo 950, arranges accommodation and has a good selection of maps. The best for hikers is GeoCart's *Městský plan Luhačovice* (1:8000). The office is open weekdays from 9 am to noon and 1 to 4 pm, and Saturday from 9 am to 1.30 pm.

Luhačovice's area code is ☎ 067.

Things to See

Among the more interesting of Luhačovice's Tudoresque houses are **Jestřábí dům** and **Vodoléčebný ústav** on L Janáčka, and **Jurkovičův dům** on Dr Blaha.

The spa snakes along beside a creek, spanned by bridges and lined with trees, spa-hotels and fountains. Two spas that flow year-round and are meant for drinking are **Ottovka** in the gazebo by the tennis courts, and **Aloiska** behind the Palace Sanatorium.

Many spa hotels offer specialised treatment – paraffin packs, four-chamber baths, you name it. The average 'cure' lasts about a week; contact the spa's main office, Lázně Luhačovice (☎ 9311; fax 93 25 26), at Lázeňské náměstí 436.

The **Luhačovice Museum** (Muzeum v Luhačovicích), near the tennis courts, has a small collection of painted Easter eggs (*kraslice*), ceramics, embroidery and other folk art. It's open from April through October on Tuesday, Thursday and Saturday from 9 am to noon and 1 to 5 pm, and on Sunday between noon and 5 pm; entry costs 10 Kč.

Places to Stay

There is plenty of accommodation in all ranges, including private rooms (Luha can help with these). *Autokemping Luhačovice* (☎ 93 33 18) is at the Údolní Dam (Údolní přehrada), 3km north of town along the creek, or via bus No 7. A bed in a chalet is

120 Kč. The site is only open from May through September.

Hotel prices rise as you go from the train station area towards the spa. *Hotel Havlíček* is a former bargain at Masarykova 163, though it was closed for renovations at the time of writing.

Hotel Litoval (☎ 93 30 40), at Dr Veselého 158, is ageing but admirably cheap at 220/440 Kč with shared bath. A few doors down at No 169 is *Hotel Vltava* (☎ 93 21 23), with up-market doubles for 1500 Kč, including breakfast.

Other mid-range options include the old but elegant *Hotel Alexandria* (☎ 93 27 50; fax 93 37 35) at Masarykova 567, with bath, WC and cable TV for 1060/1550 Kč. Down the road at No 174 is the small *Pension Karina* (☎ 93 28 48), priced at 400/800 Kč.

Places to Eat

As in all Czech spa towns, sweet wafers are a popular snack, which are eaten warm one at a time. For cheap eats try *Restaurace U Šimů* at Masarykova 108. For a bit more style try the restaurant in *Hotel Alexandria* or the *Divadelní kavárna*, in the pink theatre building above the inhalatorium.

Getting There & Away

Buses are easier and quicker than trains from most destinations, with up to 12 a day from Zlín and seven from Uherský Brod.

KROMĚŘÍŽ

Kroměříž (population 29,000), the highlight of the Zlín region, is also known as Hanácké Athény (the Athens of Haná). This was the seat of the powerful and affluent bishops of Olomouc from the 12th to 19th centuries (Olomouc was the Moravian capital from the 12th to 17th centuries). The bishops' Baroque chateau and immense gardens are the town's main attraction.

German colonists began arriving in the 13th century, when the town was fortified. The town was practically destroyed by the Swedes in the Thirty Years' War, but in 1664 the bishops undertook their major Baroque construction effort. The castle was rebuilt by the Italian architects Tencalla and Lucchese to a commission by a bishop, Charles II of Liechtenstein-Kastlekorn. In the mid-18th century, Kroměříž and the castle were damaged during an occupation by the Prussian army, and later from a fire.

Orientation

If you're arriving at the train or bus stations, get onto Hulínská and cross the river. The interesting bits of town are centred around the chateau and Velké náměstí.

Information

Tourist Office The municipal Kroměříž Information Office (Informační kancelář města Kroměříže; ☎ & fax 212 19), at Kovářská 3, can help with accommodation, money exchange, guides and maps. It's open weekdays from 8 am to 6 pm, and Saturday from 9 am to 1 pm (also summer Sundays from 9 am to noon). Čedok (☎ 222 24) is at Tovačovského 3161.

Money Česká spořitelna, on Velké náměstí, has an exchange office and Visa ATM. Banka Haná, Riegrovo náměstí 182, has a MasterCard/Visa ATM.

Post & Communications The main post and telephone office is on the corner of Oskol and Denkova. A second branch is in the train station. Kroměříž's area code is ☎ 0634.

Archbishops' Chateau

Just north of Velké náměstí is the Archbishops' Chateau (Arcibiskupský zámek) with its 84m tiered Baroque **tower**. It takes a full 1½ hours to tour the lavish interior, with rococo ceilings and murals painted by Franz Anton Maulpertsch and Josef Stern. The **Manský Hall** (Manský sál) has Maulpertsch's skilful ceiling paintings. The biggest and best known room is the **Assembly Hall** (Sněmovní sál), where scenes for the film *Amadeus* were shot, and where concerts are occasionally held. The **library** includes impressive collections of coins and globes along with the old books.

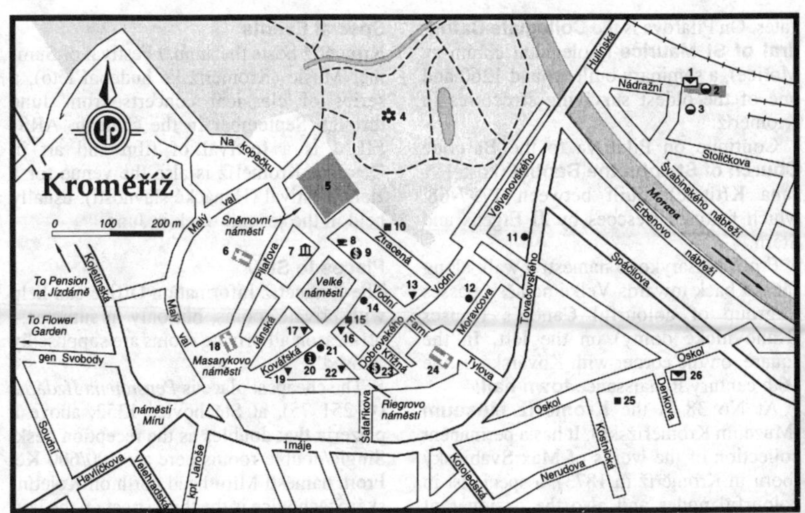

PLACES TO STAY
10 Pension Lilie
15 Hotel Bouček
25 Hotel Oskol

PLACES TO EAT
8 Kavárna U zámku
13 AB Bistro
16 Avion samoobslužná restaurace
17 Radniční sklípek
19 U Mana
22 Starý pivovar

OTHER
1 Post Office
2 Train Station
3 Bus Station
4 Podzámecká Garden (Podzámecká zahrada)
5 Archbishops' Chateau
6 Collegiate Cathedral of St Maurice (Kolegiátní chrám sv Mořice)
7 Kroměříž Museum (Muzeum Kroměřížska)
9 Česká spořitelna
11 Čedok
12 Jewish Town Hall
14 U zlatého lva
18 Church of St John the Baptist (kostel sv Jana Křtitele)
20 Kroměříž Information Office
21 Town Hall
23 Banka Haná
24 Church of the Assumption of Our Lady (kostel Nanebevzetí Panny Marie)
26 Main Post Office

The chateau is open daily, except Monday, May through September from 9 am to 5 pm, and only on weekends and holidays in April and October; entry costs 40 Kč.

It costs another 20 Kč to see the **Chateau Gallery** (Zámecká obrazárna), which has a valuable collection of Italian, German and Dutch masters from the 16th and 17th centuries. Pride of place goes to Titian's *Flaying of Marsyas.*

At the rear of the chateau is **Podzámecká Garden** (Podzámecká zahrada), one of the largest historical gardens in the country, with 64 hectares of ponds, trees, flowerbeds and pavilions, designed in the 17th century by Lucchese. You enter from Vejvanovského.

Around the Old Town

Leaving the castle through Sněmovní náměstí, on the right is the **Mill Gate** (Mlýnská brána), one of three remaining gates. On Pilařova is the **Collegiate Cathedral of St Maurice** (Kolegiátní chrám sv Mořice), a seminary built around 1260 and one of the oldest surviving structures in Kroměříž.

Continue on Pilařova to the Baroque **Church of St John the Baptist** (kostel sv Jana Křtitele), built between 1737-68, which features frescoes by JJ Etgens and Stern.

From Masarykovo náměstí a walk along Jánská back towards Velké náměstí passes a group of colourful Canon's Houses (Kanovnické domy) on the left. In the square, on the corner with Kovářská, is the 16th century Renaissance **town hall**.

At No 38 is the **Kroměříž Museum** (Muzeum Kroměřížska). It has a permanent collection of the works of Max Švabinský (born in Kroměříž in 1873), a specialist in colourful nudes and also the designer of many of Czechoslovakia's early postage stamps. The museum is open daily, except Monday, from 9 am to noon and 1 to 5 pm; entry costs 10 Kč.

The museum is in one of the original Gothic buildings that belong to the Capitol Houses (Kapitulní domy), rebuilt in Renaissance and later Baroque styles. House No 40 retains some of the Renaissance sgraffito. At No 30 is the town's oldest pharmacy (*lékárna*), **U zlatého lva**, which was established in 1675. The cobblestone square also has a decorative fountain and plague column.

From Velké náměstí, take Vodní and continue along Farní, past the **Church of the Assumption of Our Lady** (kostel Nanebevzetí Panny Marie). On the left is Moravcova, and halfway down is one of the few reminders of the town's Jewish history, the old **Jewish Town Hall** (Židovská radnice) at the centre of what was once the Jewish town.

A final attraction is the 17th century Baroque **Flower Garden** (Květná zahrada), with a frequently photographed rotunda by Lucchese and a colonnade by Tencalla. Enter from Gen Svobody, west of the city centre.

CZECH REPUBLIC

Special Events

Kroměříž hosts the annual Festival of Summer Music (Kroměřížské hudební léto), a series of classical concerts from June through September in the chateau. ARS-FILM is a festival of film and art in October. Kroměříž is also the venue for a Haná Festival (Hanácké slavnosti), usually held in the second week in June.

Places to Stay

The Kroměříž Information Office can help with private rooms, but only in summer – off-season all private rooms are supposedly 'closed'.

The cheapest place is *Pension na Jízdárně* (☎ 251 75), at Štěchovice 1352, above a pizzeria that doubles as the reception desk. Single/double rooms here are 400/600 Kč. From náměstí Míru head north on Kojetínská; Štěchovice is the third street on the left.

Pension Lilie (☎ 238 71), Ztracená 67, is an excellent choice in the city centre. Comfortable doubles (no singles) are 700 Kč with shower and WC.

At the time of writing there were only three hotels to choose from. Cheapest but farthest out is *Hotel Hvězda* (☎ 229 14), Osvoboditelů 182, in the panelák (prefab) housing area called sídliště Vážany; take bus No 2 or 4 south along Velehradaská. Decent doubles with shower and WC are 650 Kč.

A 10 minute walk from Velké náměstí is the Communist-era *Hotel Oskol* (☎ 242 40), at Oskol 3203, with doubles for 1075 Kč, including WC and shower. The recently restored *Hotel Bouček* (☎ & fax 257 77), on Velké náměstí itself, has doubles without/with bath for 1280/1660 Kč.

Places to Eat

For a quick and cheap breakfast, lunch or early dinner, try the self-service *Avion samoobslužná restaurace* on Velké náměstí, beside the Hotel Bouček.

AB Bistro, at the corner of Vodní and Farní, has good Czech and international food, including meatless meals and fresh salads, from 30 to 150 Kč.

Popular beer halls with simple food include *U Mana* at Kovářská 13, and *Starý pivovar* next to the town hall.

A little expensive, but worth it, is the *Radniční sklípek*, in a cellar on Kovářská. Czech and international dishes cost 90 to 180 Kč.

Good cakes and cheap coffee are the theme at *Kavárna U zámku*, Velké náměstí 41.

Getting There & Away

Kroměříž is about 60km east of Brno and 50km south of Olomouc. Getting here by train requires at least one change – at Kojetín (9km away) when coming from Brno and Olomouc, or at Hulín (8km away) when coming from Břeclav, Uherské Hradiště or Slovakia. There are frequent connections all day from these transfer points. There are up to 10 buses a day to Zlín, seven to Olomouc, 20 to Brno, 10 to Vyškov, and four to Uherské Hradiště and Prague.

RYMICE

This sleepy village of less than 600 people, about 13km north-east of Kroměříž, has a few 19th century farmhouses. Two with thatched roofs – No 14 on the main square and No 6 in a side street – are actually mini-museums showing the house and shop of a blacksmith and a saddlemaker. They're open on weekends from May through September from 9 am to 5 pm.

public

organisation, the Matica Slovenska; Prešov, where the Slovak Soviet Republic was declared in 1919; and Banská Bystrica, the cradle of the ill-fated Slovak National Uprising.

Compared to the Czech Republic, visitors to Slovakia will find a more religious and conservative people, very conscious of their own heritage. The Slovak Republic – which has a generally pastoral environment though blighted in places by post-WWII industrialisation – is blessed with surviving pockets of traditional speech, habits and hospitality. It also has a richer and more volatile ethnic mix, including some 600,000 Hungarian speakers in the south and about 150,000 Romanies (Gypsies) in the east.

Overall, in Slovakia, prices are lower, the infrastructure less developed, and services fewer. This is an economy that seems to have done less well out of the 'Velvet Divorce' than the Czech Republic, and Slovaks sometimes feel conscious of the disparity between themselves and their neighbours, and when they do they tend to take solace in wine rather than beer.

Slovak Republic

The Slovak Republic (also known as Slovakia) is not as well beaten a tourist route as the Czech Republic. And those tourists who do venture over its borders usually don't get beyond the capital, Bratislava, and the High Tatras resorts – although the south and east are among the most traditional, ethnically diverse and interesting parts of the country.

The country's biggest drawcard is a vast, user-friendly patchwork of forested mountain ranges, which are all part of the great Carpathian range that arcs across central Europe. Naturally it's a favourite with walkers, mountaineers, cyclists, skiers, potholers and other outdoor enthusiasts. There are five national parks, a dozen other protected landscape areas and numerous state nature preserves.

The republic's longest river, the Váh, rises in the High Tatras. After worming its way through the mountains, it crosses the Danubian plain – just about the only lowlands in Slovakia – and finally joins the Danube (Dunaj to Slovaks) itself along the southern border. The *považie* ('along the Váh'), once the main trade route between the Mediterranean and the Baltic, is dotted with castles and their ruins.

Across the republic there are over 150 chateaux and castles, the finest and grandest being Spišský hrad, near Levoča, and Orava and Trenčín in Central Slovakia – all testimony to a millennium of Hungarian domination. Among scores of renovated old town centres are some of the former Hungarian Empire's most important towns, as well as several that played a role in the rebirth of the Slovak state – Martin, home of the first Slovak cultural-promotion organisation, the Matica slovenská; Prešov, where the Slovak Soviet Republic was declared in 1919; and Banská Bystrica, the cradle of the ill-fated Slovak National Uprising.

Compared to the Czech Republic, visitors to Slovakia will find a more religious and conservative people, very conscious of their own heritage. The Slovak Republic, which has a generally pastoral environment, though blighted in places by post-WWII industrialisation, is blessed with surprising pockets of traditional speech, habits and artisanship. It also has a richer and more volatile ethnic mix, including some 600,000 Hungarian-speakers in the south and about 350,000 Romanies (Gypsies) in the east.

Overall, in Slovakia, prices are lower, the infrastructure less developed, and services fewer. This is an economy that seems to have done less well out of the 'Velvet Divorce' than the Czech Republic, and Slovaks sometimes feel conscious of the disparity between themselves and their neighbours. And when they do, they tend to take solace in wine rather than beer!

Facts about the Slovak Republic

HISTORY

Europe's youngest country, the Slovak Republic emerged in 1993 from 74 years of junior partnership in Czechoslovakia. Though the two republics share many traits, they are definitely not the same country. Nor do their histories form a seamless narrative, despite many common threads.

Early Days

The historical record of Slovakia doesn't become distinguishable from that of Bohemia and Moravia until around the 7th century AD, though the archaeological record indicates a human presence here for nearly as long as in the Czech Lands.

The earliest known groups to have settled in Slovakia were the Illyrians around the 5th century BC, followed shortly by the Celts. These were pushed out by Germanic Markoman and Quadi tribes in 100 BC.

Forces of the Roman Empire occupied parts of the Danube region of southern Slovakia and made frequent raids north, but were unable to dislodge the Germanic tribes settled there. In the 5th century Slavs began to filter into Slovakia. The whole area was overrun by Avars in the 6th century. Although a brief union of Slav tribes emerged in 623 under Samo, no cohesive power emerged until the Great Moravian Empire.

Great Moravian Empire

In 833 AD, the prince of Moravia captured Nitra and formed the Great Moravian Empire, which included all of modern-day Central and West Slovakia, the Czech Republic and parts of neighbouring Poland, Hungary and Germany. The empire converted to Christianity with the arrival of the Thessaloniki brothers and missionaries, Cyril and Methodius, in 863. To facilitate the translation of the Bible, Cyril created the first Slavic alphabet, the forerunner of contemporary Cyrillic.

In 907, the Great Moravian Empire collapsed as a result of the political intrigues of its rulers and, more specifically, invasion by Hungary. (The Great Moravian Empire is the only period when Slovakia and the Czech Lands were united in a meaningful way, until the founding of Czechoslovakia in 1918.) By 1018 the whole of Slovakia was annexed to Hungary and remained so for the next 900 years, although the Spiš region of East Slovakia belonged to Poland from 1412 to 1772.

Magyar (Hungarian) Rule

After the fall of the Great Moravian Empire, Slovakia was under constant attack by the Magyars and Poles. Most of the Slovak lands were to remain, with short breaks, part of the Magyar (Hungarian) Empire for the next nine centuries.

During early Hungarian rule, in the time of Béla IV (1235-70), industry blossomed, especially mining (silver, copper, gold) and trade (gold, amber, fur). In 1237 Slovakia was invaded by Tatars from the east, who shattered the region's developing economy. In response the Hungarian king invited settlers, mainly Saxon German artisans, into the area to help rebuild the mercantile base. After a more serious Tatar wave between 1241-42, directed against Hungary as well, further German immigration took place, the history of which can still be read in the mining towns along Slovakia's eastern border.

Slovaks did not take easily to Hungarian domination, and their history is full of rebellions. For a decade or two in the early 14th century a powerful renegade warlord named Matúš Čák effectively ruled much of what is now Slovakia from Trenčín (in western Slovakia), until his death in 1321. Another short break from Hungarian rule came with Hussite raids starting in 1428, aimed at Catholics and their property; in the early 1430s Hussites actually ruled much of Slovakia, until their defeat at the Battle of

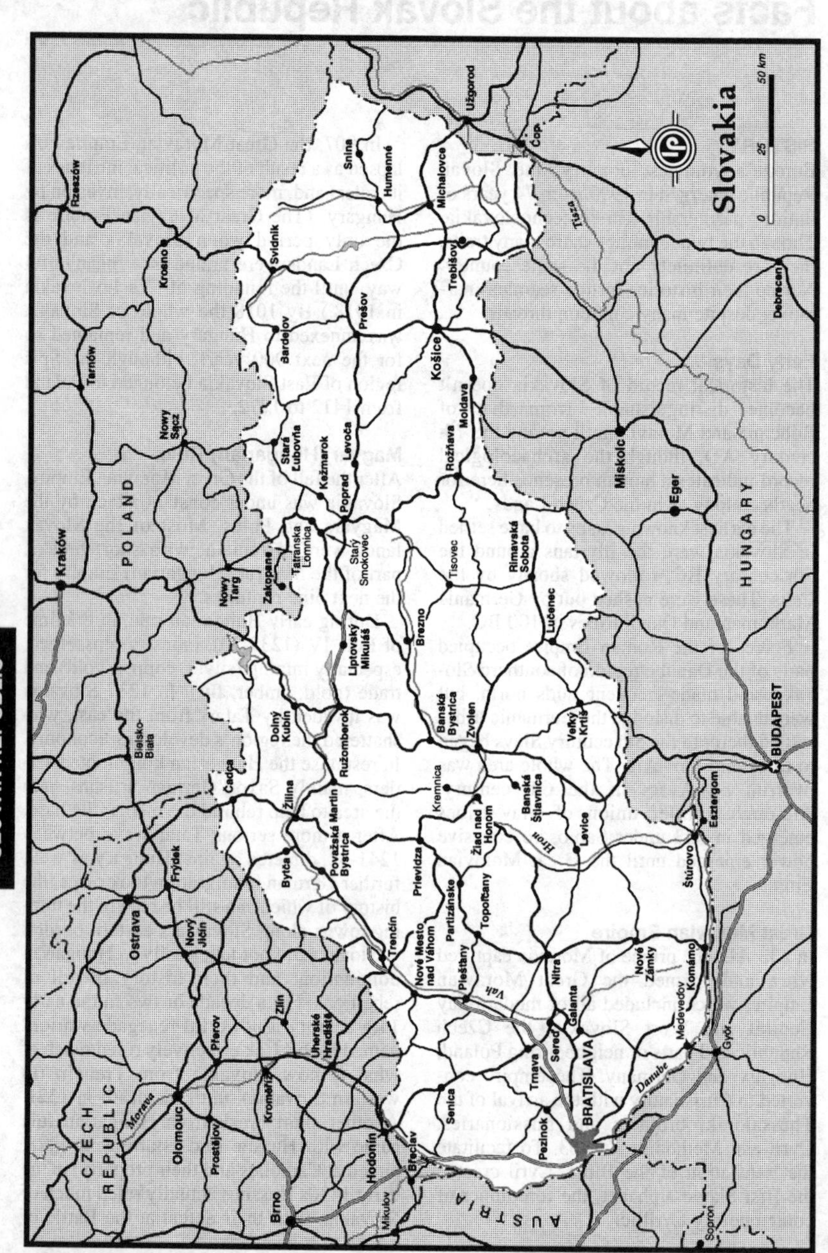
Slovakia
0
25
50 km
POLAND
CZECH REPUBLIC
HUNGARY
AUSTRIA
Kraków
Rzeszów
Tarnów
Krosno
Nowy Sącz
Nowy Targ
Zakopane
Bielsko-Biała
Ostrava
Frýdek
Nový Jičín
Olomouc
Přerov
Zlín
Kroměříž
Prostějov
Brno
Uherské Hradiště
Hodonín
Břeclav
Mikulov
Morava
Čadca
Žilina
Bytča
Považská Bystrica
Martin
Trenčín
Nové Mesto nad Váhom
Piešťany
Váh
Senica
Trnava
Pezinok
BRATISLAVA
Sereď
Galanta
Danube
Dolný Kubín
Ružomberok
Liptovský Mikuláš
Tatranská Lomnica
Starý Smokovec
Poprad
Kežmarok
Stará Ľubovňa
Levoča
Bardejov
Svidník
Prešov
Snina
Humenné
Michalovce
Trebišov
Košice
Moldava
Rožňava
Užgorod
Čop
Tisza
Debrecen
Miskolc
Eger
BUDAPEST
Esztergom
Štúrovo
Komárno
Nové Zámky
Nitra
Levice
Hron
Banská Štiavnica
Žiad nad Honom
Kremnica
Banská Bystrica
Zvolen
Brezno
Tisovec
Rimavská Sobota
Lučenec
Veľký Krtíš
Prievidza
Partizánske
Topoľčany
Medveďov
Győr
Sopron

Lipany in 1434. High taxes and harsh working conditions led to an uprising in 1514 by Juraj Dáža, with an army of 50,000 peasants rebelling against their Hungarian masters, which was ruthlessly suppressed.

When Hungary suffered a major defeat by Ottoman Turks at Mohács in 1526, it was the Austrian Habsburgs, already Holy Roman emperors and rulers of the Czech Lands, who assumed the Hungarian crown. The fall of Buda (part of modern Budapest) to the Turks in 1536 saw the Hungarian capital moved to Bratislava. Many of the subsequent conflicts, of Hungarian nobles siding with Turks in continuous efforts to dislodge the Habsburgs, were played out in Slovakia.

In 1683, with the help of the Polish King Ján Sobieski, the Habsburgs defeated the Turks, practically at the gates of Vienna, and the Turks were driven out of central Europe for good. However, Bratislava's spell as the Hungarian capital then came to an end.

For over a century Slovakia remained little more than a backwater, part of Habsburg Hungary, though in the second half of the 18th century Empress Maria Theresa and Emperor Joseph II made life easier for Slovaks with educational and labour reforms, including basic schooling for all children. Later, in the 19th century, serfdom was abolished in Slovakia, and economic development, including the appearance of a garment industry, began to gather pace. Mines and foundries were established, accounting in 1860 for some 75% of Hungary's production in these industries.

Slovak National Revival

The late 18th century had seen a national cultural awakening in Slovakia, much of it a reaction against Hungarian domination, in step with a similar struggle by Czechs against their Germanic overlords. One of its early leaders was Anton Bernolák, who founded the Slovak Learned Society (Slovenské učené tovarišstvo) in Modra, western Slovakia, in 1792.

Early on the movement gained momentum with Slovak intellectuals who saw a chance to subvert the Austro-Hungarian aristocracy. Yet the movement failed to inspire the Slovak lower classes until the 1840s, when Ľudovít Štúr, a major figure in the Slovak cultural renaissance, called for a Slovak literary language that would make nationalist ideas more accessible to the mass of Slovak people (Slovaks had hitherto used the Czech language in their literature).

By 1848 revolutions were widespread in Europe, and Slovakia was ripe for change. Slovak volunteer units formed in many parts of the country to fight the no-longer united Hungarians and Austrian Habsburgs, themselves under pressure from Austrian rebels.

Due to Russian intervention, however, the Habsburgs were able to reassert authoritarian control. They annulled the Hungarian constitution and made German the main language, even in Hungary. In 1867 the Austrian Empire, after losing a war with Prussia, was forced to join with the Hungarians in a 'dual monarchy', and under the new Austro-Hungarian Empire the Slovaks were subjected to an even more brutal programme – 'Hungarisation'. This policy forbid all languages but Hungarian to be taught in Slovak schools, and large swathes of land were confiscated for the use of Hungarian settlers, causing poverty and famine throughout Slovakia.

Nonetheless, throughout this time, the gradual awakening of a Slovak national consciousness continued, and 1863 saw the founding of the cultural and educational foundation known as Matica slovenská. This was a major milestone in the Slovak National Revival, confronting Hungarisation head-on (for more information see the Martin section in the Central Slovakia chapter).

WWI & WWII

At the turn of the century, Slovak intellectuals began cultivating closer relations with the Czechs, who were themselves dominated by the Austrians. Some Slovak intellectuals thought that the Czechs and Slovaks could, together, roll back the Hungarians and then separately nurture their distinct national identities. And the notion of a joint Czech-Slovakian entity fighting against the Austro-Hungarians quickly became reality following the outbreak of WWI.

Throughout the war both Czech and Slovak nationalists lobbied the USA, UK and France for a generous postwar settlement. Eventually the Czechs and Slovaks agreed to form a single federal state of two equal republics. The deal was brokered in the USA by President Wilson and formalised in the 1918 Pittsburgh Agreement. Thus on 28 October 1918, the new Czechoslovak Republic was declared, with Tomáš Garrigue Masaryk as its first president.

In the late 1920s an industrial base was finally established in previously agrarian Slovakia. Yet slow development, an influx of Czech bureaucrats, and the breaking of the promise of a Slovak federal state (as stipulated in the Pittsburgh Agreement) generated calls for Slovak autonomy.

In the 1930s, as the world plunged into depression, Czechoslovakia began to unravel. Unemployment in Slovakia approached 50%, and the federal government in Prague was demonised for its inability to offer relief. In the 1935 elections, more than 60% of the Slovak vote went to the Communists and right-wing nationalist groups that were agitating for an independent Slovak state.

Somewhat ironically, the first truly separate Slovak state was founded as a result of the Munich Agreement and the German occupation of the Sudetenland. In November 1938, after the Czech President Beneš had given in to French and British demands to let the Germans take the region, Slovaks declared their urgent wish for autonomy. The Czech government was in no position to refuse; Hungary had seized parts of Ruthenia and southern Slovakia, including Košice, and the Carpathian Rusins were making similar demands for territory. On 14 March 1939, the day before Hitler declared that Bohemia and Moravia were to be a German 'protectorate', the separate state of Slovakia was announced.

The government of the new state was to be headed by Jozef Tiso, leader of the nationalist Hlinkova slovenská ľudová strana (HSĽS, Hlinka Slovak National People's Party), which had been seeking autonomy from the Czechs. Tiso immediately banned all opposition political parties and instituted censorship along Nazi lines. In 1941 the HSĽS promulgated its own 'Jewish Code', and drew up its own list of Jewish targets (during the war 73,500 Jews were deported from Slovakia to the Nazi extermination camps).

Not all Slovaks supported this Nazi puppet state, and in August 1944 the Slovak National Uprising (Slovenské národné povstanie, or SNP) took place, led by units of the Slovak army and partisans. It was quashed after two months by German troops, apparently invited by Tiso. This short, ill-fated uprising is today remembered in monuments and street names all over Slovakia.

Communism

The Slovak state collapsed in April 1945. The second Czechoslovakia, established after the war, was to have been a federal state. But following the Communist takeover in February 1948 the administration once again became centralised in Prague. Many of the Slovaks who resisted the new Communist dictatorship – both anti-Communists and Slovak nationalists – were ruthlessly eliminated by execution, torture and starvation in labour camps.

Although the 1960 constitution granted Czechs and Slovaks equal rights, only the 'Prague Spring' reforms introduced in 1968 by Alexander Dubček (a rehabilitated Slovak Communist) actually implemented this concept. In August 1968 Soviet troops invaded Czechoslovakia and quashed all of Dubček's reforms except for the declaration – at least on paper – of separate but federated Czech and Slovak republics. The real power, however, remained in Prague.

SLOVAK REPUBLIC

Slovak Rulers

Rulers of the Great Moravian Empire
Mojmír I 830-46
Rastislav 846-70
Svatopluk 870?-94
Mojmír II 894-906

A Polish King
Boleslav Chrobry ?-1018

Hungarian Kings of the Árpád Dynasty
Geza 972-97
St Stephen I 997-1038
Peter 1038-41
Samuel Aba 1041-44
Peter 1044-46
Andreas I 1046-61
Béla I 1061-63
Solomon 1063-74
Geza I 1074-77
Ladislas I 1077-95
Koloman 1095-1114
Stephen II 1114-31
Béla II 1131-41
Geza II 1141-61
Stephen III 1161-62
Ladislas II 1162
Stephen IV 1162
Stephen III 1162-73
Béla III 1173-96
Emerich 1196-1204
Ladislas III 1204-05
Andreas II 1205-35
Béla IV 1235-70
Stephen V 1270-72
Ladislas IV 1272-90
Andreas III 1290-1301

Mixed Dynasties
Charles Robert (Karol Robert) 1301-42
Louis the Great 1342-82
Mary 1383-87
Sigismund (Zikmund) 1387-1437
Albert (Albrecht) II Habsburg 1437-39
Elizabeth 1439-40
Vladislav I Jagiello 1440-44
Ladislas 1444-45
János Hunyadi 1445-58
Matthias Corvinus 1458-90
Vladislav II Jagiello 1490-1516
Louis (Ludvík) II 1516-26
John Szapolyai 1526-40

Habsburg Rulers
Ferdinand I 1540-64
Maxmilian II 1564-76
Rudolf II 1576-1611
Matthias 1611-19
Ferdinand II 1619-37
Ferdinand III 1637-57
Leopold I 1657-1705
Joseph (Josef) I 1705-11
Charles (Karel) VI 1711-40
Maria Theresa (Marie Terezie) 1740-80
Joseph (Josef) II 1780-90
Leopold II 1790-92
Franz (František) II 1792-1835
Ferdinand V 1835-48

Austro-Hungarian Emperor
Franz Joseph (František Josef) I 1848-1916
Charles (Karel) I 1916-18

Presidents of Czechoslovakia
Tomáš Garrigue Masaryk 1918-35
Edvard Beneš 1935-38
Emil Hácha 1938-39

President of the Slovak Republic
Jozef Tiso 1939-45

Presidents of Czechoslovakia
Edvard Beneš 1945-48
Klement Gottwald 1948-53
Antonín Zápotocký 1953-57
Antonín Novotný 1957-68
Ludvík Svoboda 1968-75
Gustav Husák 1975-89
Václav Havel 1989-92

President of the Slovak Republic
Michal Kováč 1993-

Alexander Dubček survived the Soviet putsch of 1968 and even outlived Communism

The 'Velvet Divorce' & Independence

The fall of Communism in Czechoslovakia during 1989 led to a resurgence of Slovak nationalism and agitation for Slovak autonomy. In February 1992 the Slovak parliament rejected a treaty that would have perpetuated a federal Czechoslovakia.

The rift deepened with the June 1992 elections, which, in Slovakia, brought to power the left-leaning nationalist Movement for a Democratic Slovakia (HZDS), headed by Vladimír Mečiar, a firm believer in Slovak independence. (In 1991 Mečiar had been dismissed by the Slovak National Council from his post as prime minister because of both his autocratic temperament and revelations of involvement with the former secret police.)

In July, goaded by Mečiar's fiery rhetoric, the Slovak parliament voted to declare sovereignty. Mečiar held negotiations with his Czech counterpart, Václav Klaus, as neither was able to form a stable government. Despite numerous efforts the two leaders could not reach a compromise. In August 1992 it was agreed that the federation would peacefully dissolve on 1 January 1993.

The early days of independence were taken up by the still unresolved matters of dividing the remaining federal assets between the two republics. Within 15 months Mečiar's dictatorial rule – and his reluctance to embark on privatisation when Slovakia needed it most – reduced a government with a comfortable majority to one in minority, due to defections of his ministers. The minority government had little chance to stay in power for long. Mečiar even managed to alienate his ally, President Michal Kováč, by accusing him of 'corrupt, immoral and destabilising acts'.

As a result, on 11 March 1994 the Slovak parliament passed a vote of no-confidence in the prime minister. A broad coalition of parties was formed, with Mečiar's former foreign minister Jozef Moravčík as the new prime minister. An interim government was put in place until the 1994 elections, which promptly passed the second stage of the privatisation scheme (initiated in 1992), in case Mečiar was re-elected.

In September 1994, however, the HZDS won the general elections with 34.9% of the vote, and Mečiar formed a new coalition government with an extreme left-wing and a right-wing party. Most Slovaks voting for Mečiar were pensioners, farmers, and people living in rural villages; students and city dwellers tended to vote for leftish parties like the Democratic Union of Slovakia (DU).

Immediately after the elections, Mečiar cancelled the sale of state-owned enterprises, halted Slovakia's privatisation scheme and threatened independent radio stations and newspapers with legal action if they dared criticise the government.

It's estimated that since 1994, some 4000 civil servants have been fired for their liberal (ie anti-Mečiar) political beliefs. A law passed in 1995 recognises Slovak as the

President vs Prime Minister

Michal Kováč and Vladimír Mečiar do not like each other. At one time, Kováč, the Slovak president, and Mečiar, the prime minister, were both close political allies, both members of the HZDS (Movement for a Democratic Slovakia) party, and Kováč became president essentially because of Mečiar's support.

The falling out happened because Kováč disagreed with Mečiar's authoratarian rule. Since then Kováč believes Mečiar has mismanaged the economy and ruined Slovakia's chances for early entry into the EU and NATO – in fact, in 1997 both organisations denied Slovakia membership.

Thus, in 1994, the president asked parliament for a vote of no-confidence in the government. Mečiar was duly ousted and many Slovaks breathed a collective sigh of relief.

But Mečiar is an ex-amateur boxer, a tough-talking man with an insatiable desire for power. When Mečiar promised to get even with Kováč, few people took him seriously – until the 1994 elections, when Mečiar's party won 34.9% of the popular vote and 61 of the parliament's 150 seats. Despite the mediocre results, Mečiar formed a coalition with the ultra-nationalist Slovak National Party (SNS) and the socialist Association of Slovak Workers (ZRS), giving him 83 seats and control of the government.

And then things got weird. In August 1995 the son of President Kováč, Michal Jr, was kidnapped. According to *Time* magazine, 'armed men halted his car just outside Bratislava, forced him into another vehicle, blindfolded and beat him, and applied electric shocks to his genitals. They poured a bottle and a half of whisky down his throat, drove him across the border to Austria and dumped him, unconscious, outside a police station.'

The subsequent investigation uncovered some curious facts – mainly that members of the SIS, Slovakia's secret police, carried out the kidnapping on orders from 'the highest levels of government'. Shortly afterwards, two detectives on the case were suddenly sacked, and a crucial witness was killed in a mysterious car explosion.

The investigation has since faded into obscurity, though many Slovaks believe Mečiar ordered the kidnapping to embarrass President Kováč. Not surprisingly, Mečiar continues to insist that there is no evidence of SIS or government involvement – even though an Austrian court ruled that the SIS was indeed responsible for the bizarre abduction of Michal Jr. ■

Vladimir Mečiar

only official language, meaning that, officially, the large Hungarian minority cannot use their mother tongue in public places. A separate law passed in 1995 to protect the Slovak Republic allows for the arrest of *anyone* criticising the government.

Not surprisingly, many Slovaks are starting to lose their patience with Mečiar's heavy-handed rule. The passing of anti-democratic laws has also brought criticism from human rights organisations, European leaders and US President Clinton. According to one European parliamentarian, Mečiar's policies show 'insufficient respect for democracy, human and minority rights, and the rule of law'.

Partly for these reasons, in 1997 both the European Union (EU) and the North Atlantic Treaty Organisation (NATO) decided not to extend membership to Slovakia. Many Slovaks blamed the Mečiar government for not doing more to join the EU, by far Slovakia's largest trading partner after the Czech Republic. (Slovaks were less upset by the rebuff from NATO – only 46% voted to join the organisation in a controversial 1997 referendum.)

Immediately following the EU announcement, President Kováč called for Mečiar's resignation and demanded early elections. Mečiar, however, seems likely to survive until at least the next parliamentary elections in October 1998.

GEOGRAPHY

With an area of some 49,035 sq km, Slovakia is about half the size of Portugal. Bordered by Austria, Hungary, Ukraine, Poland and the Czech Republic, it sits on the western end of the great Carpathian mountain chain that arcs up through Romania and western Ukraine. Almost 80% of Slovakia is over 750m above sea level.

Much of Slovakia is steep, forested mountains, and these are probably its most endearing feature, among not only European tourists but legions of Slovak hikers and skiers. Best known are two parallel branches of the western Carpathians – the massive High Tatras (Vysoké Tatry), rising to about 2500m and spilling over into Poland, and the Low Tatras (Nízké Tatry), reaching about 2000m in Central (and bits of eastern) Slovakia. The republic's highest peak, the 2655m Gerlachovský štít, is in the High Tatras.

At the eastern end of the Low Tatras is the Slovenský raj (Slovak Paradise), one of five national parks in the republic, featuring a karst landscape similar to that in southern Moravia in the Czech Republic. There are several thousand limestone caves, mainly in central Slovakia, of which a dozen are state-protected and open to the public.

South of the Low Tatras is a third Carpathian branch, the lesser known Slovenské rudohorie (Slovak Ore Mountains). Also much loved by outdoor enthusiasts are two subsidiary ranges of the Tatras, the Malá Fatra and Veľká Fatra. Slovakia faces the Czech Republic across mountains as well – the modest White Carpathians (Bílé Karpaty) and Javorníky.

The main exceptions to all this high relief are southern lowland regions, which are also Slovakia's main agricultural areas. The Danube (Dunaj) and two tributaries form much of Slovakia's south-western boundary with Hungary. Descending from the heart of the High Tatras, the Váh – Slovakia's longest river at 433km – joins the Danube in a broad, fertile basin in the south-west. At the edge of this depression, on the banks of the Danube, is the republic's capital, Bratislava. A smaller south-eastern basin extends on into the Ukrainian steppe.

Slovakia's largest natural lake is the 217.9 hectare Velké Hincovo in the High Tatras. Its biggest dam is the 3501 hectare Orava, west of the High Tatras near the Polish border.

CLIMATE

Slovakia is characterised by cold, harsh winters and temperate – if wet – summers. June and July are the wettest months, with rainfall on average once every two days. Summer temperatures are mild, with an average day registering a low of about 13°C and a high of 24°C. Resorts in the High Tatras will be at least 5°C cooler and high elevations can approach freezing, even in August.

There are no 'dry seasons', though Slovakia's southern lowlands are noticeably

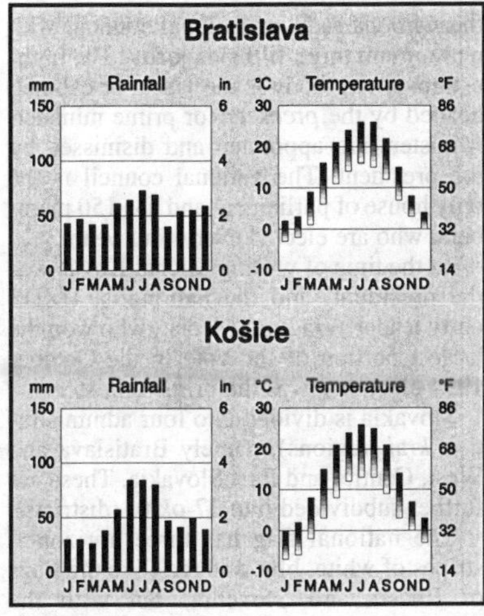

drier and almost balmy in spring. At higher altitudes in spring and summer the weather is changeable and ranges from thunderstorms to simply overcast.

Early fall – at the cusp of harvest time when trees start shedding their leaves – is perhaps the most pleasant time of year, with an average daytime high temperature of 20°C. Winter brings 40 to 100 days of snow cover (about 130 in the mountains), plus fog in the lowlands. Between December and February Slovakia sees few tourists, except skiers who don't mind the -5°C temperatures (up to -30°C at the highest altitudes).

ECOLOGY & ENVIRONMENT

Compared to the Czech Republic, Slovakia is less industrialised and consequently has not been as badly damaged by pollution; overall, its rivers and forests are in far better shape than the Czech Republic's. That said, Slovakia's larger towns suffer from air pollution, Bratislava and Košice especially, but also Banská Bystrica, Žilina and Trenčín.

Slovakia's extraordinary physical beauty, especially in the north, somehow throws the damage into sharper relief. The tranquil, sometimes wild upper-mountain valleys all seem to have a permanent haze hanging over them; look at car windows after a shower, to see what comes down with the rain.

Slovakia has significant deposits of iron ore, manganese, copper, zinc and lead. It is short of energy resources, and most petroleum and gas has to be imported (at present from Russia).

Slovakia's first nuclear power station was built in the 1970s at Jaslovské Bohunice, near Trnava; a second plant is to be completed by 1998 at Mochovce, east of Nitra. These Soviet-designed VVER-440 facilities supply nearly half of Slovakia's electricity, but the safety of the Jaslovské Bohunice facility has been questioned.

The Gabčíkovo hydroelectric project, on the Danube west of Komárno, became very controversial after Hungary backed out of the joint project in 1989 because of environmental considerations. Gabčíkovo produces enough electricity to cover the needs of every home in Slovakia and its canal allows the largest river vessels to reach Bratislava year-round.

FLORA & FAUNA

Slovakia's most diverse wildlife area – home to bears, wolves, lynx and other wild cats, marmots, otters and mink – is the High Tatras, and most of these animals are protected from hunting within the High Tatra National Park. One animal protected even outside national parks is the chamois, a mountain antelope, which was for a time near extinction but is now making a tentative comeback. Deer, pheasants, partridges, ducks, wild geese, storks, grouse, eagles and vultures can be seen throughout the countryside.

Forests, mainly beech and spruce, still cover 40% of the Slovak Republic despite centuries of deforestation and the effects of acid rain.

National Parks

There are five national parks in Slovakia: Malá Fatra (east of Žilina), Nízké Tatry (between Banská Bystrica and Poprad), Vysoké Tatry (north of Poprad), Pieniny (along the Dunajec River), and Slovenský raj (near Spišská Nová Ves).

The most accessible and popular national parks are the Vysoké Tatry and the Slovenský raj. The former is well suited for short and multi-day mountain hikes, generally at elevations above 1200m. The summer high season runs from late June to August. In winter the region has numerous downhill and cross-country skiing trails. The Slovenský raj is flatter and has fewer steep, strenuous trails, making it popular with Slovak families on weekend outings.

GOVERNMENT & POLITICS

Slovakia is a parliamentary republic. The government is elected every four years by proportional representation for parties getting more than 5% of the popular vote.

The head of the government is the president, who is elected for a five year term by the *národná rada*, or national council, with a minimum three-fifths majority. The highest governing body is the *vláda*, or cabinet, headed by the *predseda*, or prime minister. Ministers are appointed and dismissed by the president. The national council is the only house of parliament and has 150 members, who are elected every four years.

At the time of writing Michal Kováč was the president, and the nationalist HZDS party leader, Vladimír Mečiar, who won the largest portion of the vote in the October 1994 elections, was the prime minister.

Slovakia is divided into four administrative *kraj* (regions), namely Bratislava and West, Central and East Slovakia. These are further subdivided into 37 *okres* (districts).

The national flag has three horizontal stripes of white, blue and red (like the flags of Russia and Slovenia) but with the national coat of arms (a double-barred cross rising from the central of three mountains) superimposed.

ECONOMY

For centuries Slovakia was a backward agricultural area from which people sought

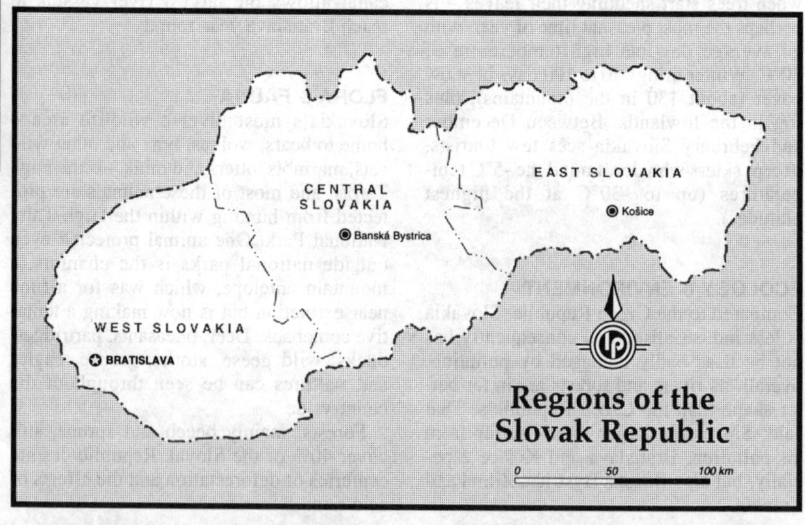

SLOVAK REPUBLIC

to escape through emigration (today, nearly two million people of Slovak origin live in the USA). In 1918 Slovakia united with the far more advanced Czech Lands, stimulating limited industrial development. During WWII, however, most existing Slovak factories were adapted to the needs of the German war effort, and later the Communists developed heavy industry and arms production – 65% of the former Czechoslovakia's military production came from Slovakia.

Attempts since 1989 to convert these plants to other uses have led to widespread unemployment in central Slovakia and created severe problems for Slovakia's heavy manufacturing industry. In 1996 unemployment in Slovakia was 13.7%, and the average wage was US$315 a month.

Under Communism, agriculture was neglected and the connection of farmers to their land was disturbed by Soviet-style collectivisation. Agriculture remains an important part of the economy, despite the small amount (only 1.78 million hectares) of arable land. The main crops are wheat, maize (corn), sugar beet, barley, potatoes, rye and oats. The principal livestock are pigs, cows and sheep. The major fruit and tobacco-growing area is along the Váh River, and vineyards are widespread in southern Slovakia. Slovakia's cooperative farms are now owned by those who work on them – with a maximum of 150 hectares per person. Before the privatisation of state farms was put on hold, only a fraction of land was in private hands.

Until 1994 heavy industry was experiencing difficulties as a result of the loss of markets in former Eastern bloc countries, an inability to export to protectionist western Europe, inferior products, inefficiency, and high company debt.

By 1995 the economy was visibly improving, growing by 7.4%, even though some of the above ills still plagued Slovakia (apparently, 50% of companies in 1995 did not make a profit and would have gone bankrupt if not for government subsidies).

In 1996 the economy continued to improve slowly, reflected in a modest inflation rate (6.2%) and a healthy GDP growth rate (6.9%). The country's trade deficit was US$2.8 billion (a bit worrying after a negligible trade deficit in 1995). Slovakia's main trading partners are the Czech Republic, Germany, Austria, Italy, Hungary and the countries of the former Soviet Union. Most of Slovakia's exports are in convenience foods and raw materials, provided by several major state-owned giants including Bratislava Slovnaft and East Slovak Ironworks Košice. Slovakia's external debt (US$4.6 billion in 1995) is one of the lowest in central Europe.

One of the main problems affecting the economy is the lack of direct foreign investment: a mere US$850 million in the first half of 1996. This is a reflection of the Slovak government's 'socially oriented' market economy and the temporary suspension of the privatisation process commenced in 1990 by the former Czechoslovak government. Until late 1992 in Slovakia, privatisation was carried out exactly as in the Czech Republic. Since 1993 this has slowed to a crawl, mainly for political reasons – Prime Minister Mečiar does not want to repeat the mistakes of Russia, where privatisation is seen by voters as corrupt and benefiting only the rich. As a result, Mečiar has allowed only a few large-scale privatisations (and even these are embroiled in scandal).

Despite pervasive problems with the Slovak privatisation scheme, most hotels, restaurants and shops have been privatised. Yet private-sector growth is likely to remain flat over the next few years, partly because of the EU's decision in 1997 not to extend membership to Slovakia.

POPULATION & PEOPLE

Slovakia has a population of 5,378,000, of which 85.7% are Slovaks, 10.6% Hungarians, 1.4% Romanies (Gypsies) and 1% Czechs. The 600,000 ethnic Hungarians live mostly in southern and eastern Slovakia. It is estimated that there might actually be 350,000 to 500,000 Romanies in Slovakia, though most claim Slovak or Hungarian nationality. The population density is 107.5 people per sq km.

The population growth rate is about 0.3%. The average life span for men is 69, and for women 77. The largest cities are Bratislava (population 452,000), Košice (241,000), Nitra (87,000), Prešov (92,000), Banská Bystrica (84,000), Žilina (86,000) and Trnava (70,000).

The September 1992 Slovak constitution guarantees the rights of minorities, with three-quarters of Hungarian children receiving schooling in their mother tongue. For historical reasons, some antagonism exists between Slovaks and Hungarians. The Slovak government aggravated the situation in 1996 by passing a law making Slovak the country's only official language.

Eighty thousand Slovakian Gypsies escaped Nazi extermination because the Germans didn't actually occupy Slovakia until after the Slovak National Uprising in late 1944. The Communists gave the Gypsies homes and jobs, but their nomadic culture has been destroyed in the process. Lately, as heavy industrial jobs have disappeared, many Slovakian Gypsies have migrated to the Czech Republic. As elsewhere in eastern Europe, there is much prejudice against Gypsies.

Slovakia's Jews weren't as lucky as the Gypsies. Beginning in March 1942, 60,000 Jews were deported to Nazi death camps in Poland by Slovak fascists, and another 30,000 were rounded up in the Hungarian-occupied part of southern Slovakia. Many of those who survived emigrated to Palestine after the war, and the number of Jews in Slovakia today is very small.

EDUCATION

Slovakia has a high proportion of educated citizens, and a 99% literacy rate. Nearly all schools are government-run, and students must complete year nine (around 15 years of age). Slovakia has two universities: in Bratislava there's the Univerzita Komenského (Comenius University) and in Košice is Univerzita Šafárika (Šafárik University). About 3.6% of Slovaks have had higher education.

Most schools teach in the Slovak language, though some elementary and high schools use minority languages as well – mainly Hungarian, with some Ukrainian. In the Communist years, the substantial Rusin minority was taught in Ukrainian, but there is presently little interest in Rusin for teaching purposes.

Though younger Slovaks, like Czechs, have grown up under a Communist educational system that stifled free thought, they are still among the best educated people in the world, with 63% having completed secondary school.

ARTS

Architecture

One of the oldest architectural relics in Slovakia is the Romanesque remains of a Benedictine monastery (1002) at Diakovce, south-east of Trnava. Nitra's St Emeram Cathedral also has a tiny 11th century Romanesque chapel, said to incorporate the remains of the first Christian church in the Czech and Slovak republics, which was founded here in 833.

Among Slovakia's finest late-Gothic works are the St Martin Cathedral in Bratislava, the mausoleum chapels of Spišské Podhradie and Spišský Štvrtok, and the town houses of Kremnica, south of Martin. Other Gothic masterpieces are the Cathedral of St Elizabeth in Košice and the Church of St James in Levoča. Some of the country's best Renaissance buildings are the town hall in Bardejov, the church and nearby houses in Fričovce (eastern Slovakia), and the restored castles at Zvolen and Bratislava. Slovakia's grandest and most photogenic fortress, Spišský Castle, dates from 1209.

The Baroque style, with a Viennese flavour, was appreciated by wealthy Slovak aristocrats and merchants of the 17th century. A fine example is the 1637-built University Church of St John the Baptist in

SLOVAK REPUBLIC

Trnava, with beautiful stucco decorations and a grand high altar.

Art Nouveau arrived in Slovakia from Vienna and Budapest. One of the style's more prominent structures is the Church of St Elizabeth in Bratislava, designed by Hungarian architect János Ödön Lechner. The lesser-known of the two Slovak architects with the name Dušan Jurkovič designed a quaint peasant house in Skalica. His more famous namesake worked mainly in the Czech Republic, where all his most notable works are, including the bath house at Luhačovice.

The Communist era also left some monumental structures such as the Nový (SNP) Bridge in Bratislava.

Painting & Sculpture

Among the earliest examples of painting in Slovakia are the remains of 12th century Romanesque frescoes in the church at Dechtice and in the Chapel of the Twelve Apostles at Bíňa. Notable Gothic frescoes can be found in the Spiš region, such as the anonymous work in the church at Veľká Lomnica, and the magnificent 15th century panel paintings that adorn the Church of St James in Levoča and the Cathedral of St Elizabeth in Košice. Some of Slovakia's best Gothic paintings are the icons in the old wooden churches of eastern Slovakia, such as in the Church of St Francis of Assisi in Hervartov, near Bardejov.

Slovakia's most outstanding Gothic craftsman-sculptor was Pavol of Levoča, whose moving painted-wood figures are the highlights of the Church of St James in Levoča and the Church of Our Lady in Banská Bystrica. Fine stone sculptures by Master Štefan of Košice are in the Cathedral of St Elizabeth in Košice.

Among notable Baroque painters were Ján Kupecký and Jakub Bogdan, though the most decorative Baroque works in Slovakia are the frescoes by Jan Kracker in the Jasov Chateau, near Košice, and the rococo frescoes of Antonín Maulpertsch in the chapel of Trenčianske Bohuslavice.

Two products of the Baroque era, with a religious slant, are the treasured 1736 lower iconostasis, by Andrej Gajecký in the Orthodox Church of SS Cosmas & Damian in Lukov, near Bardejov, and a 1780 rococo iconostasis in the Greek-Catholic church in Jedlinka.

Sculpture of the Baroque era is best exemplified by the Austrian Georg Raphael Donner, who worked in Bratislava in the early 18th century. Some of his finest pieces are in the St Johann Capistran Chapel in Bratislava; his masterpiece, an equestrian statue, of St Martin and the Beggar, is in Bratislava's St Martin Cathedral.

The Slovak National Revival in the 19th century brought a crop of painters eager to do justice to the new movement, including the portraitist Petr Bohúň, Ladislav Medňanský, who was known for his vivid landscapes, and Dominik Skutecký, who drew scenes of daily life in the area around Banská Bystrica.

While Slovak art took its major influences from Hungary before WWI, it looked to Bohemia after the birth of Czechoslovakia. Prominent 20th century Slovak artists who favoured landscapes and scenes of daily life were Martin Benka and Ľudovit Fulla. Under Communism, Július Bártfay sculpted numerous WWII monuments and contributed, though less successfully, to the Red Army memorial outside Bratislava.

In recent years political art has been competing for attention against older influences. This trend has seen the emergence of Stano Filko from banishment under Communism; his art is known for its use of military objects. The younger artists Klára Bočkayová and Martin Knut draw on naive folk art to depict a more autobiographical vision.

Literature

Slovaks had no literary language until 1790, when Anton Bernolák published his *Slovak Grammar*, followed in 1827 by a Slovak dictionary – early landmarks in the gathering Slovak National Revival. Among writers who took up the new language with enthusiasm were Ján Holý, who wrote several epics about national heroes, as well as lyrics and poems, and Jozef Bajza with his novel *René*.

Bernolák's pioneering work was based on the dialect of his home town, Trnava. The 19th century nationalist and linguist Ľudovít Štúr improved upon this in 1884, creating a grammar based on central Slovak dialects, and it is not surprising that writers of this era produced romantic fiction with a heavy 'folk' flavour. One of the first works from the 'Štúr generation' was the original and stylish *Marína*, by Andrej Sládkovič. The towering figure of the time was the Pan-Slavic poet and hero of the 1848 revolution, Janko Kráľ, who barely escaped execution by the Hungarians.

Drama and comedy flourished in the 1850s and 60s. Seminal figures were the dramatist Ján Chalupka, and Ján Palárik who wrote popular comedies. The Austro-Hungarian monarchy continued to oppress the Slovaks through the elimination of Slovak-language secondary education, and it was through literature that Slovaks fought back for political and national rights.

Poetry was their strongest suit. Slovakia's best-known poet at the turn of this century was Pavol O Hviezdoslav, whose works have been translated into several foreign languages. Other outstanding poets of the era were Svetozár H Vajanský, who was preoccupied with the links between the Slovak and Russian nations, and Ivan Krasko, whose *Verše* (Verses) is regarded as one of the masterpieces of Slovak literature.

Among post-WWI Slovak literary landmarks are Petr Jilemnický's immense, leftist, and visionary *Kronika* (Chronicle), describing the SNP and full of workers and anti-wealthy capitalist themes. The brilliant village tales of Božena Slančíkova.

SLOVAK REPUBLIC

Music

Classical The mid-14th century *Bratislava Missal* is one of the earliest pieces from an epoch that has left few musical traces, and is a fine example of the first 'domestic' liturgical work in Slovakia.

In the 17th century, German and Italian polyphonic music became popular and influential. There was a wide interest in these foreign models, both in public and for domestic performance. Two important composers of the time were Kašpar Plotze and Jan Schimbraczký. During the 18th century the works of Haydn, Mozart and Beethoven echoed in the courts of the nobility. Of Slovak composers, the most prominent at this time were Juraj Jozef Zlatník, and Anton Zimmermann, a cathedral organist who composed cantatas, symphonies, concertos and chamber music. Another contemporary was Georg Druschetzky, known for his solo, orchestral and chamber pieces.

Slovaks began to redefine their folk song heritage in the 19th century, and Slovak composers of the time often used folk motifs in their classical compositions. Only Ján Levoslav Bella and Mikulás Schneider-Trnavský, however, achieved any substantial fame. Among Bella's best works are the opera *Kovář Wieland* and the symphonic poem *Fate & Dreams*.

More recently the symphonies of Alexander Moyzes have become established as probably the best Slovak compositions of the mid-20th century. One of Moyzes' students, Dezider Kardoš, has written the country's most innovative post-WWII music, especially his Second Symphony, *Hero's Ballad* and *Concerto for Orchestra*. The most prominent modern Slovak composer is Ladislav Burlas.

Jazz & Rock The development of jazz began in Slovakia in the 1950s, though the only outstanding band was the Traditional Jazz Studio, led by P Smetáček. The jazz boom was short-lived, as rock'n'roll took over as popular entertainment, but some good jazz bands did appear in the 1960s, among them the Traditional Club Bratislava, Combo 4, the Bratislava Jazz Quartet and Medik Quintet.

The Slovak modern music scene is small and not all the world music trends are represented. One of the main reasons for this is probably the lack of performance venues. The singer Paľo Habera is one of the longest-established pop artists. His former and still popular band, Team, produced their first single in 1986 and recently released their sixth album. OBD is a Bratislava-based rock group with some very talented musicians who are classical-trained. Fans of 'death metal' will enjoy the innovative band Apoplexy, who formed in 1991 and are from Myjava.

Cinema

Few Slovak films were made before WWII. An early epic feature, which flopped at the box office, was *St Wenceslas* (1929), directed by Jan Kolár. Cinematography saw a real evolution after the war, typified by the light-hearted *Cathy* (1949), by Ján Kádar.

In the 1960s the film industry came into its own. Among the best Slovak 'New Wave' directors are Ján Kádar, with *Smrt si říká Engelchen* (Death Calls Itself Engelchen, 1963); and Elmar Klos, who directed *Obžalovaný* (The Accused, 1964) and *Obchod na korze* (The Shop on Main Street, 1965), which won an Oscar and depicted the failure of individuals to rise above selfishness in the face of Nazism.

During the Czechoslovak era many films were made with combined Czech and Slovak crews, so it is a simple task to say a film was either Czech or Slovak – these films were Czechoslovak.

Folk Arts

Slovakia's most interesting pockets of traditional culture are in the north-eastern regions of Slovakia: Spiš, Bardejov, Svidník and Humenné. Throughout these areas you'll find older women (but only a few men) wearing traditional clothing, mainly embroidered skirts, shawls, jackets, fur coats, colourful belts and shoes.

In addition to clothing, even everyday tools, utensils, musical instruments, linen, furniture and entire buildings may be decorated with elaborate folk designs. Buildings may not only have a unique architectural style, but also be adorned with carved or moulded plaster, or intricately painted. In some areas, like Kostice in southern Moravia, villagers draw designs on windows with soap or on the ground with fine sand at times of religious festivals.

Other traditional art forms are carved toys and religious statues. Local artists may show off their skills by painting Easter eggs, glass bottles and pots. Even food may be decorated or shaped.

Traditional Slovak folk instruments include the *fujara* (a 2m-long flute), the *gajdy* (bagpipes) and the *konkovka* (a strident shepherd's flute). Folk songs helped preserve the Slovak language during Hungarian rule, and in eastern Slovakia ancient folk traditions are still a living part of village life. The songs tell of love, lament, anticipation and celebration.

In some of the poorest, remotest and most rural corners of the Czech Republic are rich veins of folk culture. The excessive use of the 'happy peasant' as a Communist propaganda tool probably put many city people right off the idea of folk culture, but the Communists unwittingly helped many traditions to survive by overlooking these areas when it came to economic development. The country's many folk festivals – particularly in southern Moravia – are refocussing attention on this heritage.

Folk arts are preserved in many forms – stories and songs, music and dance, skills and handicrafts, food and drink, speech, clothing, architectural styles – which first received serious scrutiny in the course of the mid-19th century national revival. In fact, little of the physical evidence for folk traditions reaches much farther back than this, because of the perishability of traditional materials (one major exception being pottery) and the ravages of the Thirty Years' War.

The richest and best preserved traditions are in the Moravské Slovácko (Moravian Slovácko) region of south-eastern Moravia, the Chodsko region around Domažlice and, more modestly, Walachia in northern Moravia. The most interesting of these traditional pockets in Slovakia is the Spiš region, followed by Eastern Slovakia.

The two very different routes for the preservation of traditional ways are private transmission in the family and public transmission through museums and festivals. Most of the latter, held in summer or autumn, bring neighbours together for an old-fashioned good time, livened by music and dancing troupes from around the country (and even abroad), and brightened with traditional dress.

Skansens Both countries are dotted with open-air museums of traditional architecture and furnishings called *skansens* – derived from the Swedish word for the first one that opened in Stockholm in 1891. Most are collections of houses, barns, churches and other buildings transported piecemeal from around the region, and stocked with typical furniture, linen, clothing, utensils, tools and decorations. The better ones make an attempt to show not just individual buildings but whole communities.

Over the Czech and Slovak republics there are 15 skansens. It's hard to say which is the best, although the first one to open, in 1925 in Rožnov pod Radhoštěm (North Moravia), is certainly one of the finest.

Some skansens are venues for festivals. Those at Strážnice in South Moravia and Svidník in East Slovakia host well-known international folk festivals.

Music The basic traditional musical instruments were flutes and drums. Bagpipes were also popular, and though you don't hear them often, a core of musicians is trying to keep this instrument and its music alive. Most music played today is polka-like, with fiddle, bass, clarinet, and sometimes dulcimer, trumpet, fujara – a long wooden tube, like the Australian didgeridoo – or accordion. There are almost always dances to go with the music, and in some regions unaccompanied songs as well.

Folk Dress Folk dress has evolved from the simple garments of everyday life, with highly decorated versions for Sunday, holidays and special events like weddings. The most striking feature is usually elaborate embroidery in bright colours and abstract or pictorial designs. They may vary in specific

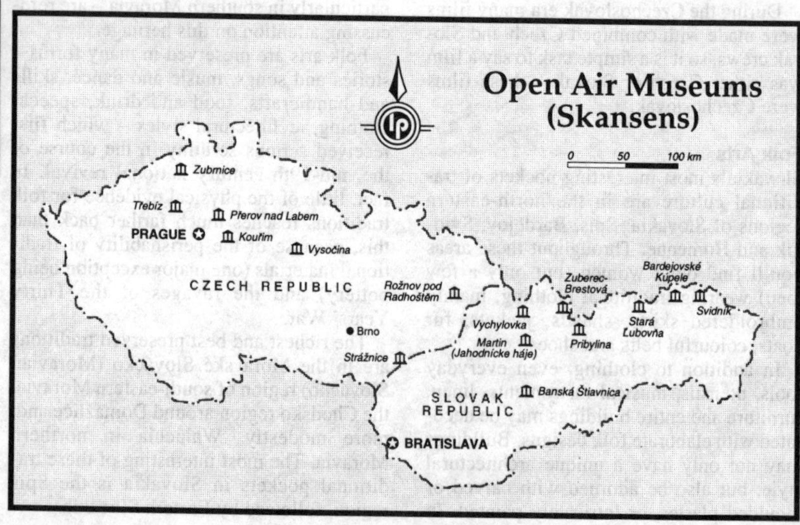

ways according to the season and the age and marital status of the wearer.

In a very few places you may still see such clothing (mainly on women) virtually any day. But it's less and less common because young people, who are not so interested, want to avoid the cost and effort of making traditional gear.

The big regional variations in traditional dress can be categorised in any number of ways: west (Bohemia and central Moravia) versus east (the Carpathians, the rest of Moravia and Slovakia); or north (Polish and western Ukrainian) versus south (Austrian, Hungarian, South Slav and Romanian). The western Czech Republic has few actual folk dresses to be seen, but specific styles of headgear, shawls, belts and shoes abound. The eastern Czech Republic and Slovakia contain the most attractive, with hand-sewn shirts, skirts, aprons, jackets, fur coats, pants, shawls and scarves for both men and women. The Moravské Slovácko region of south-eastern Moravia shows the most pronounced variations in dress between villages.

SOCIETY & CONDUCT

It is customary to say 'good day' (*dobrý den*) when you enter a shop, café or quiet bar, and 'goodbye' (*do videnia*) when you leave. Slovaks are generally friendly and very approachable. On public transport, it's customary to give up your seat to the elderly and sick and to women who are pregnant or carrying small children.

The differences between a Czech and a Slovak might not be obvious to most foreigners. However, keep in mind that Slovaks have always had to play second fiddle to Czechs in Czechoslovakia – most of the world knew the people only as 'Czechs'. Consequently Slovaks are very touchy on nationality issues.

(Also see the Society & Conduct section in the Facts About the Czech Republic chapter for more on ways to avoid offending your Slovak hosts.)

RELIGION

The first Christian church in Slovakia was founded at Nitra by the non-Christian but crafty Prince Pribina in 833. Slovakia's religious history parallels that of the Czech Lands, though Slovaks today, including the young, are far more devout church-goers than the Czechs. People often stop at church on the way home from work, and fill the churches to overflowing on Sunday.

There are 15 registered churches in Slovakia. The Roman Catholic is the largest, with about 1,200,000 declared members. It's led by the Archbishop of Trnava, Ján Sokol. The two main Protestant churches are the Evangelical Church of the Augsburg Confession, with 369,000 members, and the Reformed Christian Church of Slovakia, with 150,000.

Jews have been in Slovakia since the 13th century. They numbered 137,000, or 4% of the population of Slovakia, at the founding of Czechoslovakia in 1918. Bratislava was the centre of Jewish Orthodox education, with a well known *yeshiva*, or university, founded in 1806.

Slovakia's wartime government left a black mark in the country's history, allying itself with Hitler's Germany, which saw around 73,500 Slovak Jews removed to concentration camps by the Nazi SS and the Slovak Hlinka guards. After the war most survivors left for Palestine and, later, Israel. Today, only about 3000 Jews remain in the country.

LANGUAGE

For a complete pronunciation guide to the Slovak language, see the Language Guide at the back of the book.

Bratislava

HIGHLIGHTS

CZECH REPUBLIC
POLAND
HUNGARY

- Take a stroll down Michalská, one the city's most picturesque streets, and then enjoy a meal in one of the restaurants
- See some of the country's finest museums, from the Slovak National Gallery to the Museum of Jewish Culture
- Take a leisurely river cruise on the ferry from the Slovak National Museum to the clifftop ruins of Devín Castle
- Spend an afternoon admiring the old town's architecture

SLOVAK REPUBLIC

Bratislava (Pozsony in Hungarian, Pressburg in German) is the capital of the Slovak Republic and, with a population of 441,000, the country's largest city by far. Bratislava straddles the Danube river about 55km downstream from Vienna, at the edge of the Danubian plain and within sight of the southern end of the Lesser Carpathian mountains.

There's no denying that Bratislava is marred by grotesque Stalinist architecture, not to mention high-rise apartment blocks that rise starkly around the city's perimeter.

The surprise is that Bratislava is actually a cheerful, energetic place with a respectable collection of Baroque architecture, some excellent museums and galleries, an active cultural (especially musical) life, a thriving café and bar scene – and relatively few tourists other than Austrian and Czech day-trippers.

You could easily spend two or three days enjoying Bratislava and the surrounding area. The lone drawback is a *serious* lack of cheap accommodation.

History

There was a Celtic settlement on the site of Bratislava Castle by the 1st century BC, and later a Roman camp. A 5th century Slav fort – called Brezalauspurch – grew into an important citadel of the Great Moravian Empire. With the empire's defeat in 906 by the Magyars, this became an administrative centre of the growing Hungarian kingdom.

In the 12th century a royal market was established in the surrounding settlement, and in 1291 the Hungarian King Andrew III made it a royal borough. By the 14th century it had become a busy commercial centre, at the intersection of several major trade routes. In 1465 King Matthias Corvinus founded the first Hungarian (and Slovak) university here, the Academia Istropolitana.

When King Ludovic Jagiello died at the Battle of Mohács in 1526, the Habsburgs took over the combined Bohemian and Hungarian states. With the Turks' occupation of Buda, the Hungarian capital was moved to Bratislava in 1536, and the town's heyday began, peaking under Empress Maria Theresa. Wealthy burghers and Viennese aristocrats built grand palaces, many of them still standing. Musical life flourished; frequent visitors included Haydn, Mozart, Beethoven and, later, Liszt.

Then, as the Turks fell back, Josef II in 1783 ordered most government functions back to Buda, and Pressburg fell on hard times. During the Napoleonic Wars, French troops reached the city. After Napoleon defeated Austria at the Battle of Austerlitz, the December 1805 Treaty of Pressburg, which deprived Austria of much of its territory, was signed in the Primatial Palace.

Slovak national awareness began to grow in the 19th century; one of its leading figures, Ľudovít Štúr, lived and published in the city. In the Primatial Palace, Ferdinand V in 1848 signed his name to one of Štúr's demands, the abolition of serfdom.

Following the 1867 amalgamation of the Austrian (Habsburg) and Hungarian crowns, a policy of 'Hungarisation' made life miserable for Slovaks, who after WWI finally threw in their lot with the Czechs. On 1 January 1919 the city, with its Slovak name Bratislava, became part of the new Czechoslovakia, and set to work re-establishing its 1000-year-old Slovak identity.

After Germany invaded Czechoslovakia in WWII, a Slovak puppet state was declared, with Bratislava as its capital. The August 1944 Slovak National Uprising (Slovenské národné povstanie or SNP) overthrew this state, but was itself crushed by the Nazis. The Russians liberated the city on 4 April 1945.

Over the next 30 years Bratislava was ruthlessly modernised. In 1972, Slovak Communist officials cut the ribbon on their pride and joy, the Nový Bridge and flyover, which had been constructed upon the city's bulldozed old Jewish quarter. The following year, the vast Petržalka housing estates were begun.

On 1 January 1993, Bratislava became the capital of the sovereign Slovak Republic. Over the last few years the city centre has been extensively renovated, with a few major projects – recobbling old town streets, painting historical façades – scheduled for completion in 1999.

Orientation

Most of Bratislava is on the north bank of the Danube. The city's historical heart, the old town (Staré mesto), is a confusing but compact half sq km (much of it now pedestrian-only) marked out by the castle, námestie SNP and Hviezdoslavovo námestie. From here Bratislava has grown north-eastward in the form of the new town (Nové mesto) and the bland high-rise suburbs beyond it.

The city's most obvious landmark is the hyper-modern Nový Bridge (Nový most, formerly known as most SNP), straddled by the Staromestská roadway. South across the bridge is the 'model socialist' suburb of Petržalka, home to some 170,000 Bratislavans.

Bratislava's main train station (Hlavná stanica) is several kilometres north of town. Tram No 1 runs from the lower level of this station to námestie Ľ Štúra near the city centre. Or walk downhill to Šancová, veer right and cross over the pedestrian bridge, and continue south down Štefánikova. A few trains also use the Bratislava-Nové Mesto station, less conveniently located on the north-eastern side of the city.

The main bus station (*autobusová stanica*) is in a convenient modern building on Mlynské nivy, a little over 1km east of Štúrova behind a lonely skyscraper; to reach the city centre turn left out of the main doors and make a quick right onto Mlynské nivy (which becomes Dunajská).

Headaches for drivers include pedestrian areas around the old town and the Hotel Forum, numerous (and poorly marked) one-way streets, limited parking and sharp-eyed traffic police on Hviezdoslavovo námestie. Parking in the city centre is fairly restricted, so consider paying 30 Sk an hour (the going rate) at a private carpark.

Maps The most current map is *Bratislava – Mapa mesta* by AAA. Map freaks can go to the source and buy maps of almost anywhere in Slovakia at Slovenská Kartografia, Pekná cesta 17, which is off Račianska (eastbound trams No 3, 5 or 11). Geodézia Bratislava, Pekná cesta 15, has topographical maps of western Slovakia.

Information

Tourist Offices General information about the city is supplied by the Bratislava Information Service (BIS; ☎ 533 37 15), at Klobučnícká 2, with a second branch at the main train station. Both offices sell city

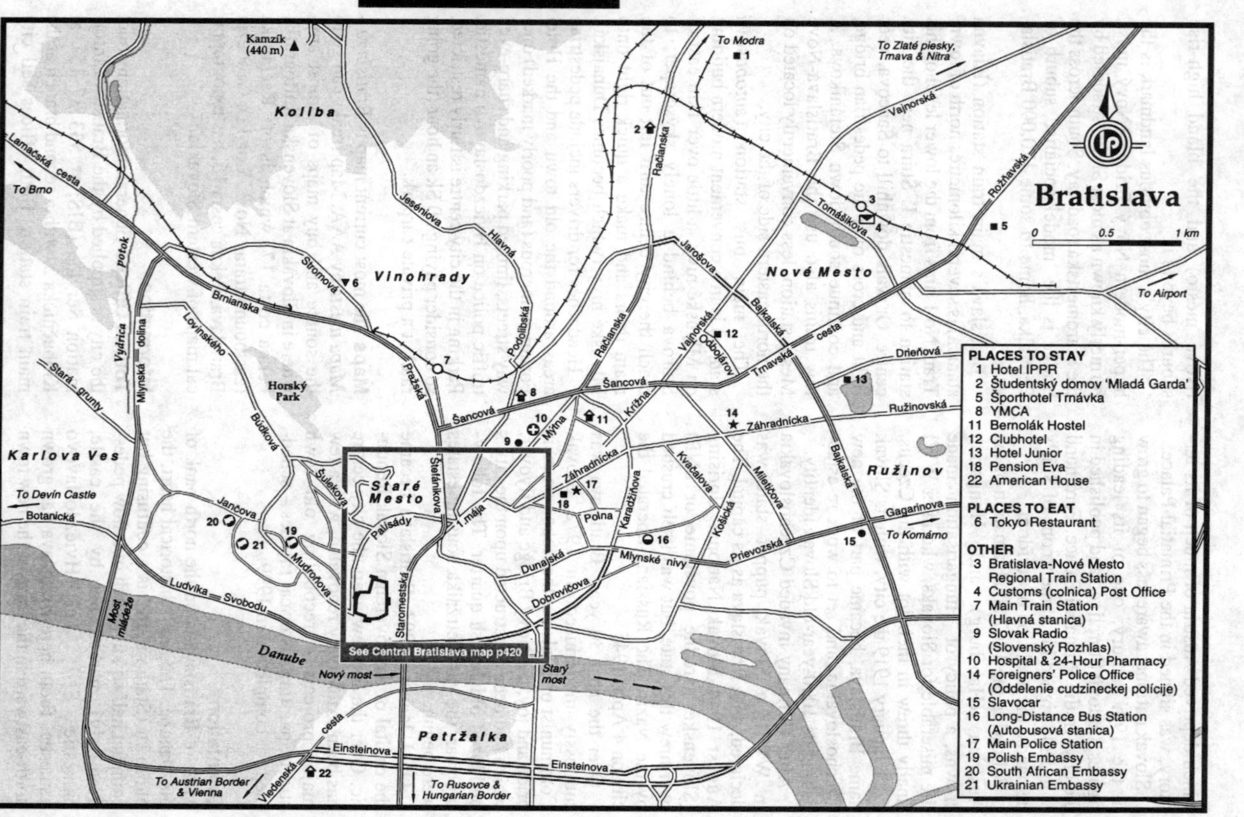
Bratislava
0 0.5 1 km
PLACES TO STAY
1 Hotel IPPR
2 Študentský domov 'Mladá Garda'
5 Športhotel Trnávka
8 YMCA
11 Bernolák Hostel
12 Clubhotel
13 Hotel Junior
18 Pension Eva
22 American House
PLACES TO EAT
6 Tokyo Restaurant
OTHER
3 Bratislava-Nové Mesto Regional Train Station
4 Customs (colnica) Post Office
7 Main Train Station (Hlavná stanica)
9 Slovak Radio (Slovenský Rozhlas)
10 Hospital & 24-Hour Pharmacy
14 Foreigners' Police Office (Oddelenie cudzineckej polícije)
15 Slavocar
16 Long-Distance Bus Station (Autobusová stanica)
17 Main Police Station
19 Polish Embassy
20 South African Embassy
21 Ukrainian Embassy
Kamzík (440 m)
Kolba
Vinohrady
Nové Mesto
Ružinov
Karlova Ves
Staré Mesto
Petržalka
Horský Park
Danube
To Modra
To Zlaté piesky, Trnava & Nitra
To Airport
To Brno
To Devín Castle
To Komárno
To Austrian Border & Vienna
To Rusovce & Hungarian Border
See Central Bratislava map p420
Nový most
Starý most
Most mládeže
Lamačská cesta
Jeséniova
Hlavná
Stromová
Brnianska
Lovinského
Stará grunty
Vydrica potok
Mlynská dolina
Búdková
Pražská
Podolibská
Račianska
Jarošova
Vajnorská
Rožňavská
Tomášikova
Bajkalská
Trnavská cesta
Obojárov
Šancová
Križna
Drieňová
Ružinovská
Záhradnícka
Mýtna
Šulekova
Štefánikova
Jančova
Palisády
1. mája
Mudroňova
Ludvika Svobodu
Botanická
Polna
Karadžičova
Kvačalova
Miletičova
Košická
Gagarinova
Prievozská
Mlynské nivy
Dunajská
Dobrovičova
Staromestská
Einsteinova
Viedenská cesta

maps and can arrange accommodation (50 Sk reservation fee). The former is open weekdays from 8 am to 4.30 pm (to 7 pm in summer), Saturday from 8.30 am to 1 pm. The latter is open weekdays from 9 am to 6 pm, Saturday to noon.

The biweekly English-language paper *The Slovak Spectator* is a good source of information on what's happening in Bratislava. Less helpful is the Slovak-language pamphlet *Kam v Bratislave* (Where in Bratislava), with listings for museums, galleries and theatres.

Foreign Consulates For a list of foreign embassies in Bratislava, see the Embassies section in the Facts for the Visitor chapter.

Visa Extensions For visa or passport inquiries go to the Foreigners' Police Office (Oddelenie cudzineckej polície) at Záhradnícka 93. It's open Monday, Tuesday and Friday from 8 am to 12.30 pm, Wednesday from 8.30 am to 12.30 pm and 1 to 5 pm. To get there take tram No 12 from námestie SNP and get off at the corner of Záhradnícka and Miletičova.

Money Bratislava has a bank and ATM on almost every corner. The ubiquitous Všeobecná úverová banka (VÚB) has several offices around town, including an exchange office at the main train station (open daily from 7.30 am to 6 pm). It's hidden to one side of the corridor, behind the 'Internationale Kasse', opposite the main hall from the left-luggage office. There's also a Visa ATM in the station. Another VÚB branch is upstairs in the bus station, open Monday to Thursday from 8 am to noon and 1.30 to 5 pm, Friday from 8 am to noon. In the centre of town is yet another VÚB branch on the corner of Poštová and Obchodná. They all charge 1% commission to change travellers cheques. The Poštová branch gives cash advances on Visa and MasterCard.

The local American Express agent is Tatratour (☎ 533 50 12), Františkánské námestie 3, which charges a 2% commission to change travellers cheques. American Express cardholders can get cash advances.

Post & Communications Mail addressed c/o poste restante, 81000 Bratislava 1, can be collected at window No 6 at the main post office, námestie SNP 34, which is open weekdays from 7 am to 8 pm, Saturday from 7 am to 1.30 pm. Letters from abroad are held for one month.

To mail a parcel go to the office marked 'podaj a výdaj balíkov', through the next entrance at námestie SNP 35. You can also mail parcels at the customs (*colnica*) post office opposite the train station.

Bratislava has two 24 hour international phone centres: at Kolárska 12 and in the main train station.

Bratislava's area code is ☎ 07.

Travel Agencies Satur (☎ 566 15 75), Jesenského 5-9, can arrange air tickets, accommodation and tours in Slovakia, as well as international air, train and bus tickets. It also books stays at health spas.

Bookshops The Big Ben Bookshop (closed Sunday), Michalská 1, stocks a wide range of titles in English, as well as Lonely Planet guides. Knihy Slovenský spisovateľ, on the corner of Rybárska brána and Laurinská, sells useful hiking maps. Interpress, on Sedlárska next to the Dubliner, stocks international newspapers and magazines.

Cultural Centres The Bulgarian Cultural Centre, Panská 1, has more to do with souvenirs than information. The following are authentic centres that host cultural exhibitions and mini-festivals:

British Council
  Panská 17 (☎ 533 10 74)
Goethe Institut
  Konventná 1 (☎ 531 52 81)
Institut Française
  Sedlárska 7 (☎ 533 46 62)
Hungarian Cultural Centre
  Somolitského 1 (☎ 49 42 00)
Polish Cultural Centre
  námestie SNP 27 (☎ 536 82 40)

Laundry Improkom, at Laurinská 16, offers one-day and cheaper three-day services. It's open weekdays from 8 am to 6 pm, and Saturday from 8 am till noon.

Medical & Emergency Services For medical emergencies call ☎ 444 44. The main outpatient clinic (☎ 49 65 80) is at Mýtna 5 and has a 24 hour pharmacy. Another 24 hour pharmacy (*lekáreň*) is at námestie SNP 20.

The main police station (*polícia*) is at Sasinkova 23. For the foreigners' police, see the earlier Visa Extensions section.

Walking Tour

Hodžovo Námestie to Mirbach Palace

This long walk starts at Bratislava's deluxe Hotel Forum on Hodžovo námestie. Elegance of an earlier day is typified by the 18th century Grassalkovich Palace across the square. Stroll down shady Poštová – crossing Obchodná, a good street for cheap food and wine (see the Places to Eat section later) – to námestie SNP, with its rather bleak monument to the Slovak National Uprising.

Another block east and you're in the major shopping district and tram junction of Kamenné námestie. Detour south for a block or two along Špitálska to see the elegant 'neo-style' buildings where it becomes Štúrova. Head west on Laurinská, then right on Uršulínska into Primaciálne námestie, dominated by the fine classical Primatial Palace. Beside it is the green-roofed Old Town Hall.

The lane beside the town hall leads to Hlavné námestie, once Bratislava's central market. Turn right immediately into Františkánské námestie, past the Jesuit Church to the yellow Franciscan monastery church, after which the square is named. Opposite, the handsome rococo Mirbach Palace is now a branch of the Municipal Gallery.

Mirbach Palace to St Martin Cathedral

Beyond the palace, bear left on Zámočnícka to the old town's one surviving tower, the St Michael Tower (Michalská veža), which you can climb for views over the city centre. Southward runs picturesque Michalská and its extension Ventúrska, lined with late-Baroque palaces, plus some good mid-range eateries. In lower Michalská the University Library occupies the former home of the royal Hungarian parliament.

Detour down a passage beneath the library to the St Clare Church and convent, and round the block into Kapitulská, one of Bratislava's oldest streets. This leads south to the city's most prominent Gothic building, the St Martin Cathedral, the old Hungarian Empire's coronation church, now under siege by the Nový Bridge.

St Martin Cathedral to the Danube Turn east into Panská and detour briefly up Ventúrska to the buildings of Slovakia's first university, the 15th century Academia Istropolitana. Back on Panská is the Baroque Pálffy Palace, now another branch of the Municipal Gallery.

A right on Rybárska brána (Fishermen's Gate) takes you across Hviezdoslavovo námestie, dominated by the neo-Renaissance Slovak National Theatre. Continue down Mostova, past the beautiful neo-Baroque building called Reduta, home of the Slovak Philharmonic, to the Danube's embankment. Eastward you can see the original bridge across the Danube, across which a tram used to run all the way to Vienna. Turning west past the Slovak National Gallery on Rázusovo nábrežie, you have a direct view of the juggernaut Nový Bridge.

If you have the energy, top off your tour by crossing back to St Martin Cathedral and going under the highway, then climbing the royal stairway to Bratislava Castle, where you can enjoy the breeze and the views across the city.

Bratislava Castle & Around

From St Martin Cathedral, cross under the roadway to the **Castle Steps** (Zámocké schody), but don't go up them yet, carry on a bit north along Židovská (Jewish St) – one of the few surviving reminders of the

SLOVAK REPUBLIC

former Jewish quarter that was pulled down for the Nový Bridge.

At Židovská 1, just metres from the seething flyover traffic, is a handsome, wedge-shaped rococo burgher's house called the House of the Good Shepherd (dom U dobrého pastiera) after its façade statue. Inside is a small **Clock Museum** (múzeum hodín), open daily, except Tuesday, from 10 am to 5 pm. Opposite is the **Decorative Arts Museum** (múzeum umeleckých remesiel), open daily, except Tuesday, from 11 am to 5 pm.

Ahead 50m is the excellent **Museum of Jewish Culture** (múzeum židovskej kultúry) at Židovská 17, with displays in English on Slovakia's much-persecuted Jews. It's open daily, except Saturday, from 11 am to 5 pm; entry costs 30 Sk.

Head back towards the Clock Museum and turn right up Beblavého, an old lane now tarted up with pricey wine bars, to rejoin the Castle Steps. A bit farther up is Corvinus Gate (Korvínova brána) and the imposing Bratislava Castle.

The fortress, 100m above the river, took its present shape in the 15th century, when it was beefed up against the Hussites. The castle was heavily remodelled by Maria Theresa in the 18th century. When the Hungarian capital reverted to Buda, the castle became a seminary and later a military barracks, gutted by fire in 1811 and bombed in WWII. In the 1950s the Communists rebuilt it as the prime ministerial headquarters.

The castle itself is a cold, plain box on the outside, with towers stuck on in the 17th century. Inside are government offices and two branches of the **Slovak National Museum** (Slovenské národné múzeum) – furniture and folk crafts (20 Sk) on the 3rd floor, plus a small archaeological exhibit (10 Sk) immediately inside the castle entranceway. Both are open daily, except Monday, from 10 am to 5.30 pm.

North of the castle but still within the walls is the fun **Museum of Folk Music** (Hudobné múzeum), filled with a staggering variety of folk pipes, whistles, drums and more. In summer check the posted schedule of live performances. It's open daily, except Monday, from 10 am to 5 pm; entry costs 10 Sk.

From the castle's ramparts you can see Austria (3km south-west) and, on a clear day, Hungary (16km south), although with the Nový Bridge and the mind-numbingly vast housing estates of Petržalka, the view is not so much beautiful as awesome. The Slovak national parliament meets in the modern complex that overlooks the river, just beyond the castle.

Historical Centre

Around Kapitulská Across from the castle is the 14th century **St Martin Cathedral** (dóm sv Martina), Bratislava's foremost Gothic structure – a rather modest building considering this was where at least nine Hungarian Habsburg kings and eight queens were crowned from 1563 to 1830 (the steeple is topped by a golden crown in place of a cross). Inside is a 1734 statue by Georg Raphael Donner, Austria's best-known Baroque sculptor, of St Martin cutting off the corner of his cloak for a beggar. The cathedral and nearby buildings are slowly going to pieces due to vibrations from bridge traffic; restorations belatedly began in 1997.

Kapitulská runs north from the cathedral, and is one of the city's oldest streets, once lined with the homes of the clergy. At the end is the **Church of the Clarissine Order** (kostol Klarisiek), founded by the Cistercians in the 13th century. The church and an exhibit of medieval art are closed for renovations.

Michalská, Ventúrska & Panská From the church veer right up Baštová and turn left on Michalská. Facing nearby Hurbanovo námestie is the old town's only surviving watchtower, **St Michael Tower** (Michalská veža), with a 14th century base, 16th century top and 18th century steeple. Go inside for displays of antique weapons and good views over the old town. It's open daily, except Tuesday, from 10 am to 4.30 pm; entry costs 10 Sk.

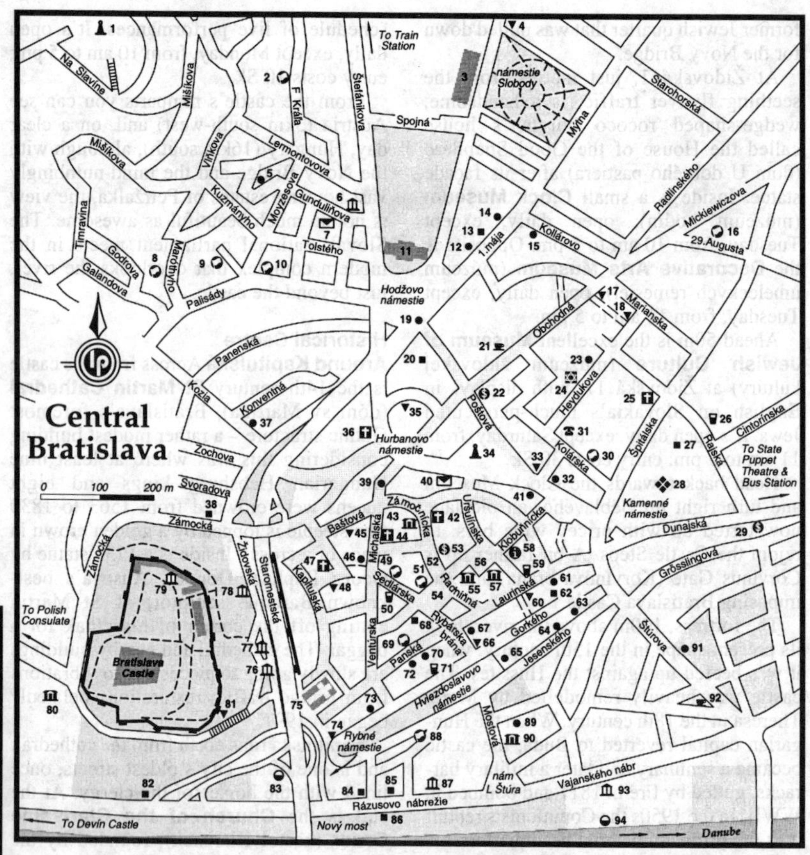

In front of the tower, a footbridge crosses an old moat, now converted into a garden serving as the 'summer reading room' (*letná čitáreň*) of the city library. Between the two tower gates, at Michalská 26, is a passage to the garden, open daily, except Sunday, from 10 am to 7 pm from May through September.

A stone's throw south of the tower at Michalská 28, in a building called U červeného raka (At the Red Crayfish), is one of Bratislava's oldest pharmacies, now an extraordinary **Pharmaceutical Museum** (Expozícia farmácie), open daily, except Monday, from 10 am to 4.30 pm; entry costs 10 Sk.

Continue south down photogenic Michalská and its extension, Ventúrska, both lined with the old palaces, built after the Hungarians moved their capital here in 1536, that give the historical centre its late-Baroque face.

Don't overlook the tiny **St Catherine Chapel** (kaplinka sv Kataríny) at Michalská 8, consecrated in 1325 as a monastery church and given a face-lift in the 19th

PLACES TO STAY
13 Hotel Tatra
20 Hotel Forum
27 Hotel Kyjev
38 Chez David Penzión & Restaurant
62 Gremium Penzión & Café
68 Hotel Perugia
82 Pension Rybársky cech
84 Hotel Danube
85 Hotel Devín
86 Botel Gracia

PLACES TO EAT
4 Umag Pizzeria
17 Vegetariánská jedáleň
18 Smíchovský dvor
21 Caffé Soirée
33 Cukráreň Jezbera
35 Pizza Hut
45 Vináreň pod Baštou
48 U dežmára
60 Divesta vegetariánská
66 Food Market; Spaghetti & Co
74 Korzo Restaurant
81 Modrá hviezda
92 Café Krym

OTHER
1 Slavín War Memorial
2 Romanian Embassy
3 Archbishop's Palace
5 Hungarian Cultural Centre
6 Police Museum (Múzeum polície)
7 Post Office
8 Russian Embassy
9 Bulgarian Embassy
10 German Embassy
11 Grassalkovich Palace
12 Kino Tatra
14 Kino Hviezda
15 Nová scéna Theatre
16 Czech Embassy
19 DPB Office
22 Všeobecná úverová banka
23 Tatra Air
24 Synagogue
25 Church of St Elizabeth (Kostol sv Alžbety)
26 Charlie's Pub
28 Tesco Department Store
29 Všeobecná úverová banka
30 Canadian Consulate
31 International Telephone Office
32 House of Culture (Dom kultúry)
34 Námestie SNP & Monument
36 Church of the Holy Trinity (Kostol Trinitárov)
37 Goethe Institut
39 St Michael Tower (Michalská veža)
40 Main Post Office
41 Polish Cultural Centre
42 Church of the Annunciation (Kostol Zvestovania-Františkáni)
43 Mirbach Palace (Mirbachov palác)
44 St Catherine Chapel (Kaplinka sv Kataríny)
46 Big Ben Bookshop
47 Church of the Clarissine Order (Kostol Klarisiek)
49 Hungarian Embassy
50 The Dubliner
51 French Embassy
52 Františkánske námestie
53 Tatratour (American Express agent)
54 Hlavné námestie
55 Old Town Hall (stará radnica)
56 Primaciálne námestie
57 Primate's Palace (Primaciálný palác)
58 Bratislava Information Service (BIS)
59 Piano Bar
61 Improkom Laundry
63 Satur
64 Pokladňa - Kassa Ticket Office
65 Slovak National Theatre (Slovenské národné divadlo)
67 Knihy Slovenský spisovateľ (bookshop)
69 UK Embassy
70 British Council
71 Danglár Klub
72 Bratislava Municipal Gallery (Galéria mesta Bratislavy)
73 Kino Mladosť
75 St Martin Cathedral (Dóm sv Martina)
76 Decorative Arts Museum (Múzeum umeleckých remesiel)
77 Clock Museum (Múzeum hodín)
78 Museum of Jewish Culture (Múzeum Židovskej kultúry)
79 Museum of Folk Music (Hudobné múzeum)
80 Slovak National Parliament
83 Bus to Devín Castle
87 Slovak National Gallery (Slovenská národná galéria)
88 US Embassy
89 Slovak Philharmonic (Slovenská filharmonia)
90 Reduta Palace
91 ČSA Airline Office
93 Slovak National Museum (Slovenské národné múzeum)
94 Hydrofoil Terminal

century. At Michalská 1 is one of the buildings making up the huge University Library (Univerzitná knižnica) that served as the Hungarian diet, or parliament, in the 18th and 19th centuries; now parts of it house the Big Ben Bookshop (see earlier Bookshops section). A passage here leads to the St Clare Church.

Another library building at Ventúrska 13 has a concert pavilion where nine-year-old

Franz Liszt gave his first recital in 1820. Down the street at Ventúrska 10, which was one of several palaces owned by the Pálffy family, another child, six-year-old Wolfgang Amadeus Mozart, performed here in 1762; the building is also called **Mozart House** (Mozartov dom).

At the bottom of Ventúrska turn left onto Panská. At No 19 is the **Bratislava Municipal Gallery** (galéria mesta Bratislavy) inside the stunning Pálffy Palace (Pálffyho palác). On display is a mix of Slovakian impressionists and post-impressionists, plus modern graphic art on the top floor. It's open daily, except Monday, from 10 am to 5 pm; entry costs 20 Sk.

Hlavné Námestie & Františkánske Námestie Once the centre and main market of the old town, Hlavné námestie is now a sleek, touristy plaza with a splendid fountain. Among the burghers' houses around it, note the very handsome 1912 Art Nouveau building on the south-west side. On the north-west corner is the French embassy and Institut Française.

The square's northern extension is Františkánske námestie. Along its eastern side, to the right of Tatratour, is the **Church of the Holy Saviour** (kostol Najsvätejšieho Spasiteľa), a 17th century Protestant church later 'Baroquified' by the Jesuits. Immediately north are the Franciscan **Church of the Annunciation** (kostol Zvestovania-Františkáni) and monastery that give the square its name. The latter is one of Bratislava's oldest churches, completed in 1297 but thoroughly altered by subsequent renovations.

Opposite is the 1770 **Mirbach Palace** (Mirbachov palác), with a small collection of Renaissance religious art, plus modern graphic design on the ground floor. It's open daily, except Monday, from 10 am to 5 pm; entry costs 20 Sk.

Old Town Hall This 13th century Gothic building, with a Renaissance courtyard and green-roofed neo-Gothic annexe, is one of the most appealing in the old town. It's now mostly taken up by the interesting **Municipal Museum** (Mestské múzeum), which has torture chambers in the casemates and an extensive collection housed in finely decorated rooms. You enter the museum from the picturesque inner courtyard, where concerts are held in summer. It's open daily, except Monday, from 10 am to 4.15 pm; entry costs 10 Sk.

Turn left out of the courtyard to Radničná 1, home to the not so interesting **Museum of Wine Production** (múzeum vinohradnícko-vinárska), which is open Wednesday to Sunday from 10 am to 4.30 pm; entry costs 10 Sk. During summer wine-tastings are sometimes held in its cellar.

Primaciálne Námestie The austere, quiet square behind the Old Town Hall is dominated by one of Slovakia's finest neo-

RICHARD NEBESKY

The Renaissance courtyard and neo-Gothic annexe of the Old Town Hall

SLOVAK REPUBLIC

classical buildings, the **Primatial Palace** (Primaciálný palác), completed in 1781 for the bishops of Esztergom, the Hungarian primates. The façade is topped with a 150kg cast-iron bishop's hat. Enter to see the Hall of Mirrors where Napoleon and the Austrian Emperor Franz I signed the Treaty of Pressburg on 26 December 1805, following the Battle of Austerlitz. In the municipal gallery on the 2nd floor are rare English tapestries from the 1630s. The palace is open daily, except Monday, from 10 am to 5 pm; entry costs 20 Sk. Classical concerts are held here in summer.

Just off the square, behind BIS in a courtyard at Klobučnícka 2, is the **Hummel Music Museum.** It's in the former home of German composer and pianist Johann Hummel (1778-1837), although it's likely to be only of interest to die-hard Hummel fans.

Hviezdoslavovo Námestie to the Danube

Narrow Hviezdoslavovo námestie traces a filled-in moat outside the old town walls. It's named after Pavol Orságh Hviezdoslav, Slovakia's favourite poet, whose statue sits in the centre. Presiding over the square is the neo-Baroque **Slovak National Theatre** (Slovenské národné divadlo), the city's premier opera and ballet venue, completed in 1886. At the western end is Rybné námestie (Fish Square), which is all that remains of the city's old fish market – yet another victim of the Nový Bridge.

South of the square on Mostová is the beautiful Art Nouveau **Reduta Palace**, completed in 1914 as a dance hall. It's now Bratislava's main concert hall, though the Slovak Philharmonic (Slovenská filharmonia) has its own hall around the corner.

East of Mostová is the **Slovak National**

Helicopter Blades or Haloes

Many people wonder why so many statues have golden-looking helicopter blades on top of their heads. Are they pigeon poop protectors? Is it a case of flying statues? No, actually it's a halo that indicates the statue is of a saint.

A very important part of Baroque Catholic religion was a reverence of saints. This cult of sainthood was foreign to the Czechs until early into the 17th century; during the Protestant era idolising martyrs of the church was against the Protestant doctrine. The Catholicisation period began after the Czech Protestants lost the Battle of the White Mountain in 1620 and the Austrian Habsburgs, who were feverishly Catholic, reinstated the Catholic religion throughout the Czech Lands. The statues of saints were part of the propaganda and brainwashing campaign used to convert the population. These statues adorned squares, buildings and crossroads everywhere. Big, flashy churches were also built, and crosses, many with Christ on them, were popping up like mushrooms all over the place.

As usual there is one exception to the halo rule. The saint Jan Nepomucký does not appear with the standard helicopter blades above his head, but a circle of stars. No, he didn't get hit on the head like in a cartoon – each statue of a saint has some significant symbol that distinguishes them for easy recognition from all others. Jan Nepomucký was thrown off Charles' Bridge in Prague and drowned; according to legend the stars appeared above the water indicating the spot where his body lay. ■

RICHARD NEBESKÝ

Museum (Slovenské národné múzeum), Vajanského nábrežie 2, featuring exhibits on archaeology, natural history and geology. It's open daily, except Monday, from 9 am to 5 pm; entry costs 20 Sk.

More interesting is the ultra-modern **Slovak National Gallery** (Slovenská národná galéria) farther up the riverfront at Rázusovo nábrežie 2. This is Slovakia's biggest combined gallery and museum collection, with a good Gothic section and rotating exhibits of modern art. It's open daily, except Monday, from 10 am to 6 pm; entry costs 25 Sk.

Námestie SNP & Around

The central feature of námestie SNP is a bronze monument – dubbed by locals the 'Angry Family' – to the failed anti-fascist uprising for which the square is named. In November 1989 huge crowds assembled here in the days leading up to the fall of Communism, and it was also here that Slovak nationalists gathered before the Velvet Divorce from the Czech Republic. The square is too vast to be friendly, though there are some cafés and useful shops, as well as the main post office.

Westward on Hurbanovo námestie, across from the St Michael Tower, is the city's finest Baroque church, the **Church of the Holy Trinity** (kostol Trinitárov), worth a look for the *trompe l'oeil* dome painted on the ceiling.

Two blocks north-east of námestie SNP, at Heydukova 11-13, is the city's only remaining **synagogue** (closed to the public). Around the block on Špitálska is the 18th century **Church of St Elizabeth** (kostol sv Alžbety), which is named after Bratislava's only home-grown saint, the daughter of the Hungarian King Andrew.

East of námestie SNP is **Kamenné námestie**, a major shopping district (as evidenced by the gigantic department store) and tram junction. The blocks of Štúrova just south of the square contain many fine revivalist ('neo') style buildings dating from the end of the 19th century.

SLOVAK REPUBLIC

Námestie Slobody & Around

The Communist leader Klement Gottwald tried to erect a shrine to himself here, though only the vast square and giant bronze 'Fountain of Friendship' remain (actually, it's supposed to be a lime-flower, a symbol of the Slav people). In the north-west corner is a pedestal which once supported a huge statue of Gottwald, but it was knocked down in 1989.

West across the road is the former **Archbishop's Palace**, which was completed in 1765 as the summer residence of the Hungarian bishops of Esztergom, who obviously knew how to live well. Now it is used as government offices.

On the north side of the square is the Ministry of Telecommunications. Beyond it, the modern building that seems to be standing on one foot is the headquarters of Slovak Radio (Slovenský rozhlas), and a concert hall.

Southward, beyond the Faculty of Engineering of Comenius University, are gardens and the immense rococo **Grassalkovič Palace**, commissioned in 1760 by Count Grassalkovich, head of the Hungarian Court Chamber. It's closed to the public. A few blocks east, at Gundulićova 2, is the small but interesting **Police Museum** (múzeum polície), which is open Tuesday to Saturday from 10 am to 5 pm.

Slavín Hill

On Slavín Hill, north-west of námestie Slobody, is a cemetery and garden with fine views over the city. Towering over it is the **Slavín War Memorial**, an enormous pillar erected in 1960 in memory of the 6000 Soviet soldiers who died pushing the Nazis out of western Slovakia.

To get here, take trolleybus No 214 west from Hodžovo námestie to the end of the line, and climb for 1km up Timravina and Mišíkova. Alexander Dubček lived in enforced isolation at Mišíkova 46 from 1968 until his 'resurrection' in 1989, and afterwards until his death in November 1992.

Kamzík Hill

Looming above and beyond Slavín Hill is Kamzík Hill (440m), the final southern bump of the Lesser Carpathians. It rises 300m above the Danube and is covered with woods and trails.

If you feel like a good hike, take trolleybus No 213 from Hodžovo námestie through the vineyards of Vinohrady to the end of the line in the Koliba district. A red-marked trail climbs past a memorial to a 1683 victory over the Turks at Vienna, to the summit, where there's a café and a 200m TV tower.

Carry on up the red trail to a yellow trail, bearing left down this to the valley of the Vydrica stream (Vydrica potok). Walk down-valley past several ponds to Partisan Meadow (Partizánska lúka), cross under Red Bridge (Červený most) and catch the No 212 trolleybus back down to Hodžovo námestie.

The 6km walking part of the journey takes about two hours. A longer trip would entail taking the yellow trail all the way from the main train station.

Special Events

The city's biggest musical event is the annual Bratislava Music Festival (Bratislavské hudobné slávnosti, or BHS), held in October. From early September, bookings can be made through BIS. Opera and ballet tickets during the same period are available from the National Theatre box office (see the Entertainment section).

In July and August the city puts on a 'Cultural Summer' festival, with chamber concerts in St Clare Church, Mirbach Palace and the University Library; opera and drama in the picturesque courtyard of the Old Town Hall, and trumpet concerts from its tower; plus jazz, folk music, brass bands and films.

The city also hosts a well known international children's book illustration fair, the Bienále ilustrácií Bratislava (BIB), in late September and early October of odd-numbered years.

Places to Stay

In July and August it's fairly easy to sleep cheaply in Bratislava, though don't expect to be in the city centre. The rest of the year, cheap accommodation is extremely hard to find, so try to arrive early (not on a Sunday) and head straight to BIS or Satur (see the Travel Agencies section earlier), both of which book student dorms, private rooms and pensions. Reservations are recommended year-round, even at up-market hotels.

The nearest *campsites* are at Zlaté piesky (see below).

Hostels *Hotel Junior* (☎ 23 43 40), at Drieňová 14, in the eastern suburbs beside a large pond, is open year-round and has comfortable double rooms for 450 Sk per person (YHA or student cardholders) or 1100 Sk (everyone else). This place is often full with groups; try calling ahead. Take tram No 8 from the train station or bus No 34 or 54 from the east side of námestie Slobody.

The shabby but friendly *YMCA* (☎ 39 80 05), on the corner of Šancová and Karpatská, is open year-round and has 13 doubles, six triples and one five-bed room, all for 200 Sk to 250 Sk per bed, but it's often full. Reception is upstairs; downstairs are a cinema, bar and restaurant. From the train station walk downhill and turn left on Šancová.

In July and August you can try the 12 storey *Bernolák* (☎ 49 77 21) at Bernolákova 1, about five blocks east of the YMCA – continue east on Šancová, then, at the three way intersection, turn right onto Radlinského and left onto Bernolákova. Beds in doubles are 350 Sk per person. There's a swimming pool and disco (audible throughout the building).

Študentský domov 'Mladá Garda' (☎ 25 31 36), Račianska 103, north-east of town (tram No 3 from the train station), has accommodation from July to mid-September only. The communal showers are hidden way down in the basement.

South of the city centre in Petržalka is the

summer-only *American House* (☎ 83 88 90), at Kremnická 7, with beds in a dorm for 350 Sk each, including breakfast. From the train station take bus No 47 and get off at the second stop after the Nový Bridge.

Private Rooms Satur arranges private rooms for 300 Sk to 450 Sk per person. It has a wider range of rooms than BIS, which rents private rooms starting from 350 Sk per person. Both charge a 50 Sk commission. Annoyingly, private rooms are more expensive off-season.

Pensions Cheap and convenient, *Pension Rybársky cech* (☎ 531 83 34; fax 531 83 33), at Žižkova 1, charges 800 Sk for clean doubles (no singles) and has a good upper-end restaurant.

Advance reservations are a must at the popular *Gremium Penzión* (☎ 32 18 18; fax 533 06 53), in the heart of the city centre at Gorkého 11. There's one single for 680 Sk and four doubles without/with bath for 930/1130 Sk, all including breakfast.

Chez David Penzión (☎ 531 38 24; fax 531 26 42), Zámocká 13, is clean and modern, on the site of the old Jewish ghetto directly below the castle. The eight double rooms are overpriced at 1770/2770 Sk without/with bath. Breakfast is included.

Just outside the city centre *Pension Eva* (☎ & fax 36 33 81), off Mickiewiczova at Moskovská 5, has singles/doubles without bath for 1200/1600 Sk. From the train station take tram No 2 or 8.

Hotels – Bottom End The two storey *Športhotel Trnávka* (☎ 522 34 97), Nerudova 8, next to a small stadium north-east of town, is seedy and rooms are small. But it's cheap at 335/470/705 Sk with shared bath for singles/doubles/triples. Take trolleybus No 215 from Cintorínska, near Hotel Kyjev; or No 219 eastbound from Palárikova, just down the hill from the main train station.

Ask BIS about *Hotel IPPR* (☎ 525 70 35), Nobelova 16, north-east of the city centre, which sometimes rents rooms at 200 Sk per person. Going directly there is risky as it's often booked by groups.

Clubhotel (☎ 25 63 69), just off Vajnorská at Odbojárov 3, has rooms with shower (but shared WC) that are good value at 620/910 Sk.

Hotels – Middle The permanently anchored and ageing *Botel Gracia* (☎ 533 21 32; fax 533 21 31) sits in the Danube near Nový Bridge. It's small, respectably clean, and the top-deck terrace is pleasant on summer afternoons. Single/double rooms with bath are 1600/2200 Sk.

There's a certain charm to the hyper-modern, 1960s-era *Hotel Kyjev* (☎ 32 20 41; fax 32 68 20) in the city centre at Rajská 2. Rooms with bath are 1850/2000 Sk.

Less appealing is *Hotel Tatra* (☎ 32 12 78) at námestie 1.mája 5, which was badly renovated in the 1980s. Rooms are 1870/2470 Sk.

Hotels – Top End The most affordable splurge is the elegant *Hotel Devín* (☎ 533 36 40; fax 533 06 82) by the river at Riečna 4. Single/ double rooms come fully equipped and cost 2650/3450 Sk.

With only 11 rooms, *Hotel Perugia* (☎ 533 18 18; fax 533 18 21), at Zelená 5, is popular with business travellers looking for peace and quiet. Luxurious doubles are 4880 Sk.

The ultimate in comfort and cost are the *Hotel Danube* (☎ 534 08 33; fax 531 43 11), at Rybné námestie 1, and the *Hotel Forum* (☎ 34 81 11; fax 31 46 45), at Hodžovo námestie 2, respectively priced at 4960/5630 Sk and 4900/5900 Sk.

Zlaté Piesky There are bungalows, a motel, a hotel and two camping grounds at Zlaté piesky (Golden Sands), which is near a clear blue lake 7km north-east of Bratislava. Tram Nos 2 (from the main train station) and 4 (from the city centre) terminate at Zlaté piesky. You can hire rowing boats and sailboards here in summer and there are also tennis courts.

As you cross the bridge from the tram

stop you'll see *Hotel Flora* (☎ 25 79 88) on your left. Doubles here are 480/540 Sk without/with shower (no singles).

Next to the Flora is a lakeside *campsite* (☎ 25 73 73) with 50 four-bed cottages without bath and 20 three-bed bungalows with private bath. Tent camping is possible and the facility is open from mid-April to mid-October.

A poorer *campsite* with run-down three-bed bungalows at 600 Sk a triple is nearby (but not on the lake). Camping is handled at the reception but the bungalows are controlled by *Motel Evona Zlaté piesky* (☎ 25 73 65), a couple of minutes away. The motel's 35 double rooms with bath are 600 Sk (no singles). Motel Evona is open year-round, but the bungalows are only available from mid-May to September.

Places to Eat

Central Bratislava has some reasonably priced restaurants, and plenty of cheap cafeteria-style buffets. Up-market places tend to cater to business people on hefty budgets. Vegetarians will find a surprising number of meatless places.

Budget One of the few places to get an early breakfast is *Cukráreň Jezbera*, námestie SNP 11, which opens at 6.30 am from Monday to Saturday. The stand-up buffet in the basement, which you enter from around the corner, opens an hour later but not at all on Saturday.

Enough good things can't be said about two sit-down vegetarian buffets: *Vegetariánská jedáleň*, downstairs and entered through a passageway at Obchodná 68, open weekdays from 11.30 am to 3 pm; and *Divesta vegetariánská* at Laurinská 8, open weekdays from 11 am to 3 pm.

A *food market* on the corner of Hviezdoslavovo námestie and Rybárska brána (open daily from 10.30 am to 10 pm), has a dozen cuisines at individual counters in the stand-up section. Or sit down in the adjacent *Spaghetti & Co*, which has excellent pastas (60 Sk to 95 Sk) and pizzas (70 Sk to 110 Sk), and is open daily to 1 am.

The pizzas served at *Umag Pizzeria*, on the corner of námestie Slobody and Žilinská, are among the best in town. A more central pizza place is the *Pizza Hut* on Drevená. The salad bar here is decent.

In the beer hall category – smoky, simple, cheap – are *Smíchovský dvor* at Marianska 6 and *U dežmára* at Klariská 1.

One supermarket worth a mention is the massive *Tesco* at Kamenné námestie; the food section is beneath Little Caesar's Pizzeria.

Cafés The *Gremium Café*, Gorkého 11, has a good atmosphere and is the place to sip coffee and read the newspaper.

The *Múzeum Café*, on the east side of the Slovak National Museum, has coffee, a small food menu, and computers to surf the Web (70 Sk per hour); it's open daily, except Monday, to 9 pm.

Caffé Soirée, Obchodná 29, doubles as an art gallery.

Café Krym, on Štúrova, has a (drunk's) bar and a mellow, well-lighted room for coffee drinkers.

Top End A slightly up-market but still affordable place is the *Korzo Restaurant*, Hviezdoslavovo námestie 11. Entrées start at 65 Sk.

Café London, part of the British Council at Panská 17, serves excellent meals but is usually very crowded; lunch with a beer typically runs to about 100 Sk. It's open weekdays from 9 am to 9 pm.

Vináreň pod Baštou, in a cellar at Baštová 3, serves authentic Slovak meals and has a good wine selection.

Modrá hviezda, Beblavého 14 on the way up to the castle, features local dishes such as cheese pie. The menu is in English.

Chez David Penzión, Zámocká 13, has a full-service kosher restaurant that's up-market but not intolerably so. A full meal costs about 150 Sk. It's open Sunday to Thursday to 10 pm, Friday to 3 pm.

Jasmín, near the Clock Museum at Židovská 5, is a classy Chinese spot with a 158 Sk set menu; it's closed Sunday.

The *Tokyo Restaurant* (closed Sunday), Stromová 16, 20 minutes from the train station via Pražská, serves sushi, sashimi, udon and a variety of pricey Japanese dishes. Good value is the 70 Sk lunch box.

Entertainment

Opera & Ballet Opera and ballet are presented at the *Slovak National Theatre* (Slovenské národné divadlo) on Hviezdoslavovo námestie (often closed Sunday). The local opera and ballet companies are outstanding.

Tickets are sold at the 'Pokladňa-Kassa' office (open weekdays from noon to 6 pm) on the corner of Jesenského and Komenského námestie, behind the national theatre building. An hour before the performance, ticket sales are at the theatre itself, but they're usually sold out (*vypredané*).

Classical Music The Slovak Philharmonic (*Slovenská filharmonia*) is based in the neo-rococo Reduta Palace (built in 1914) at Palackého on the corner of Mostová, across the park from the national theatre. The ticket office (open weekdays from 1 to 5 pm) is inside the building.

Drama The *Nová scéna* theatre, Kollárovo námestie 20, presents operettas, musicals and drama (the latter in Slovak, so check first). The ticket office is open weekdays from 12.30 to 7 pm and an hour before the performance, but the tickets are usually sold out.

There's often something happening at the *House of Culture* (dom kultúry), námestie SNP 12.

Puppet Theatre The *State Puppet Theatre* (Štátne Bábkové divadlo), Dunajská 36, puts on puppet shows for kids, usually at 9 or 10 am and sometimes again at 1 or 2 pm. It's good fun.

Bars & Clubs *Charlie's Pub*, Špitálska 4 (entry is from Rajská), has loud pop music, TVs all around and people dancing among the tables. There is a 30 Sk cover charge on weekends. It's one of the most popular meeting and drinking places in town, and is open nightly from 6 pm to 4 am, and until 6 am on Friday and Saturday.

If there are tourists in town, you're sure to meet them at *The Dubliner*, Sedlárska 6, a massive Irish pub with an open fire and good Guinness (65 Sk). Some nights there's live music.

Danglár klub, Hviezdoslavovo námestie 18 (downstairs through the smaller entrance to one side), is open Monday to Saturday from 8 pm or so. The bar staff are friendly and the club is popular with the young alternative crowd.

The *Piano Bar*, Laurinská 7, is a busy spot with live piano music on Friday and Saturday nights.

GUnaGU divadlo, in the basement of the Čierny havran restaurant at Františkánske námestie 10, mixes live jazz with DJ discos and performance art.

Cinemas In the same complex as Charlie's Pub, Špitálska 4, are Bratislava's best art cinemas: *Marilyn, Charlie, Lumiere* and *Voskovec & Werich*. Other cinemas in the city centre include *Kino Mladosť* at Hviezdoslavovo námestie 17, *Kino Tatra* at námestie 1.mája 5, and *Kino Hviezda* at námestie 1.mája 9. Films are generally shown in the original language with Slovak subtitles, and admission prices are low.

Getting There & Away

Air Ivánka airport is 8km north-east of the centre. Tatra Air (☎ 36 67 58), at Heydukova 29, has daily flights to and from Košice (2073 Sk one way, 4145 Sk return), Prague (3500/7000 Sk), Kiev and Zürich. ČSA (☎ 36 10 73), at Štúrova 13, has daily flights to Pragu and Košice. Satur and many other travel agents can book these flights.

Bus At Bratislava's main bus station (SAD/Eurolines information, ☎ 526 13 12), on Mlynské nivy, you can usually buy your ticket from the driver, but check first at the information counter. Advance tickets for the buses marked 'R' on the timetable may be purchased from the AMS counter. The footnotes on this timetable are in English.

Ten express buses a day run to Prague (one hour faster than the train for about the same price; 250 Sk one way). Other buses leaving Bratislava daily include six to Košice (402km), four to Bardejov (457km), three to Prešov (429km), and two each to Banská Štiavnica and Tatranská Lomnica.

Eight buses a day connect Vienna (Mitte Busbahnhof) to Bratislava (330 Sk; 64km). In Bratislava buy your ticket for this bus at the ticket window inside the station.

Other international Euroline buses leaving from the bus station go to Brussels (weekly), Budapest (330 Sk; daily), Cologne (weekly), Frankfurt (2470 Sk; twice weekly), Kraków (weekly), London (3700 Sk; three times a week), Munich (four times a week), Paris (2050 Sk; three times a week), Sofia (twice weekly) and Thessaloniki (weekly). Tickets may be purchased (using crowns) either at the international ticket window in the bus station or at the adjacent Eurolines office.

Beware of buses that transit the Czech Republic, as you could be 'kicked off' at the border if you need, and don't have, a visa.

Train Train services to and from Košice (via Poprad, Žilina and Trenčín) are fairly frequent and couchettes are available on the night train. There's also a daily service to Prague.

All express trains between Budapest and Prague call at Bratislava. There are four local trains a day between Vienna (Südbahnhof) and Bratislava's main train station (260 Sk; 64km; 1¼ hours). One nightly train departs for Moscow but there's no direct service to Poland. International train tickets are available at the station.

Hungary Two local trains a day run from Bratislava's Nové Mesto (regional) station to Gyor, Hungary (280 Sk; 90km; two hours), via Rajka. The ticket office at Nové Mesto will sell you a ticket only as far as the border (50 Sk) and you must pay the Hungarian conductor the balance. Otherwise buy a through ticket at the main train station or from Satur the day before. If you don't want to bother getting an international train ticket, take a local train or bus to Komárno and walk across the bridge to Komárom in Hungary.

Boat From May to September, hydrofoils ply the Danube between Bratislava and Vienna (600 Sk one way, 950 Sk return; two daily); in April and October service is reduced to four times weekly. From April to October hydrofoils also head daily from Bratislava to Budapest (1750/2800 Sk). Children aged 15 years and under and students pay half-price.

Tickets and information are available at the hydrofoil terminal, Fajnorovo nábrežie 2. In late summer the service can be interrupted because of low water levels.

Getting Around

The Airport The only way to reach Ivánka airport (8km) is on city bus No 24 from the train station.

Bus & Tram Public transport in and around Bratislava is based on an extensive tram network complemented by bus and trolleybus. Orange automats at tram and trolleybus stops sell tickets (7 Sk per ride, no transfers), but make sure that the green light is on before inserting coins. (At the time of research, Bratislava was considering switching to a zone-fare system similar to Prague's, with single tickets valid for unlimited travel within a 60 minute period. BIS should have the latest details.)

Tourist tickets (*turistické cestovné lístky*) valid for 24 hours (35 Sk), 48 hours (65 Sk) or seven days (105 Sk) are sold at the Dopravný podnik Bratislava (DPB) office in the underground passageway below Hodžovo námestie. It's open weekdays from 6 am to 7 pm. These tickets are also sold at the window marked 'MHD' next to the taxi stand in front of the main train station. The validity of the ticket begins immediately upon purchase, so buy one only when you need it.

Vehicles run from 4.30 am to 11.30 pm; from midnight to 4 am, special night buses run on routes out of námestie SNP. Schedules are posted at all stops. Trams are numbered 1 to 12, buses 21 to 65, express buses 101 to 127, and trolleybuses 208 to 220.

Taxi Bratislava's taxis all have meters and drivers are far less likely to try to overcharge you than those in Prague. Downtown Bratislava is small enough for you to be able to walk almost anywhere.

Rental Car Europcar (☎ 534 08 41) is in the lobby of the Hotel Danube. Hertz (☎ 534 81 55) has a desk in the lobby of Hotel Forum. Hertz and Europcar also have desks at Ivánka airport. You'll get better rates at Slavocar (☎ 521 31 19), past the bus station at Prievozská 30.

Around Bratislava

DEVÍN CASTLE

The Hungarians' main military bulwark in this region was not Bratislava Castle but another one at the confluence of the Morava and Danube rivers at Devín, 9km west of Bratislava – the westernmost point of the Hungarian Empire.

Devín has been settled for at least as long as Bratislava. The first walled buildings date from Roman times. The Great Moravian Prince Rastislav fortified this and the adjacent hills in the 9th century. A small fort was built in the 13th century, and a palace added in the 15th century by the aristocratic Garay family. Subsequent owners, especially the Bathorys in the 16th century, made their own modifications. In 1809 Napoleon's army reduced it all to ruins.

The 19th century Slovak nationalist Ľudovít Štúr encouraged the designation of Devín as a 'national cultural monument' and symbol of Slovak national history – similar to Prague's Vyšehrad.

The promontory, which looks across to Austria on the far bank, was of course a prickly place in Communist days. Indeed the entire river bank from Bratislava was lined with huge razor-wire fences. The road along the river, now unfenced, makes a shady, pleasant day trip to the castle, especially on a weekday. There's a mediocre café outside the castle grounds.

Things to See

Left of the path just past the cashier are some Roman foundations. Farther on the left are foundations of a 15th century **guardhouse**, and beyond it a 16th century gate. Before you reach the castle, a dirt track detours south to the reconstructed foundations of a 9th century church, with a grand view across and down the Danube.

Just across the castle moat on the left is what remains of the Bathorys' 16th century **palace**, with an exhibit of artefacts on the lower level. Straight ahead is the Garays' 15th century well, and around in the left-hand (south-eastern) corner their fortified palace. At the west end is the 13th century citadel, under restoration.

Below, the dark 'stain' in the Danube is the clearer waters of the entering Morava. On the plain beyond the Morava, near Dürnkrut (Austria), the Czech King Přemysl Otakar II died in battle fighting Rudolf I's imperial troops in 1278.

The castle is open daily, except Monday, May through October from 10 am to 5 pm.

Getting There & Away

On weekdays and summer weekends, bus No 29 departs Bratislava about every half-hour from the stand beneath the Nový Bridge; the very last stop is at the castle's carpark (20 minutes).

Alternatively, if you're feeling robust, ride tram No 4 from Kamenné námestie or tram No 9 from Hurbanovo námestie, west to the end of the line in the suburb of Karlova Ves, from where Devín is a two hour walk on the red-marked path, which goes via Devínska kobyla.

Highly recommended is the Bratislava-Devín ferry, which operates daily (except Sunday) from May through October. It leaves from the landing opposite the Slovak National Museum at 9 and 11.10 am and 2 pm, returning at 10.30 am and 12.40 and 4 pm. Boats will not leave without at least 30 passengers. The cost is 180 Sk return.

West Slovakia

HIGHLIGHTS

- Step back into the Middle Ages in the handsome walled old town of Trnava
- Indulge yourself with a mud bath and massage at the low-key spa town of Piešťany
- Enjoy some of the region's most evocative religious architecture in Nitra, a former princely seat and bishopric

West Slovakia contains much of the republic's lowlands, in the form of the vast Danubian plain and the valley of the Váh. Aside from Nitra, most of the region's attractions – gentle hills studded with derelict castles, and one macho fortress at Trenčín – are near both the railway and the E75 Highway from Bratislava to Žilina (in Central Slovakia).

Walkers can find solitude and modest views in the White Carpathians (Bílé Karpaty) and the Lesser Carpathians (Malé Karpaty) west of the Váh. Another Carpathian finger, the Považský Inovec range, runs south of Trenčín. A fourth, the Tribeč range, peters out at Nitra. Views across the lower Váh are only spoiled by the eight monster cooling towers of Slovakia's first nuclear power station, about 12km north-east of Trnava.

The Danube forms the region's entire southern border. In 1992 Slovakia began diverting the river through a 40km concrete canal, as part of the vast Gabčíkovo hydro-electric project started in 1977 by Czechoslovakia and Hungary. Hungary later withdrew, and has joined the Czech Republic and the European Union (EU) in demanding a closer look at the project's ominous environmental impact.

LESSER CARPATHIANS

Stretching for 100km north-east from Bratislava are the Lesser Carpathian (Malé Karpaty) mountains. They are gently undulating, not dramatically scenic but pleasant for walks and hikes.

On the slopes of the Carpathians grow most of Slovakia's wine grapes, the vineyards extending right down into Bratislava's Vinohrady district, and with a car or on a bicycle it's easy to go wine-tasting through the region. The map *Malokarpatská viná cesta* (1:75,000), available at Aices in Modra, lists local wineries, castles and colour-coded walking trails .

Modra

Modra village, where the Slovak nationalist Ľudovít Štúr (1815-56) spent his later years, provides some of Slovakia's best red and white wines (as well as celebrated ceramics). The town is a popular stop on summer wine-tasting tours, and the village centre has several *vináreň* to choose from.

The only notable sight is the **Ľudovíta Štúra Museum**, in the former town hall on Štúrova. Often it's open when it looks closed; ring the buzzer to see Štúra's writing desk plus a wee display of medieval Modra relics. It's open Tuesday to Friday year-round from 8 am to 4 pm, Saturday in summer from 9 am to 3 pm; entry is 10 Sk.

Orientation & Information Tiny Modra is centred around Štúrova, a street that runs past the hotel and bus stop before changing its name to Dukelská.

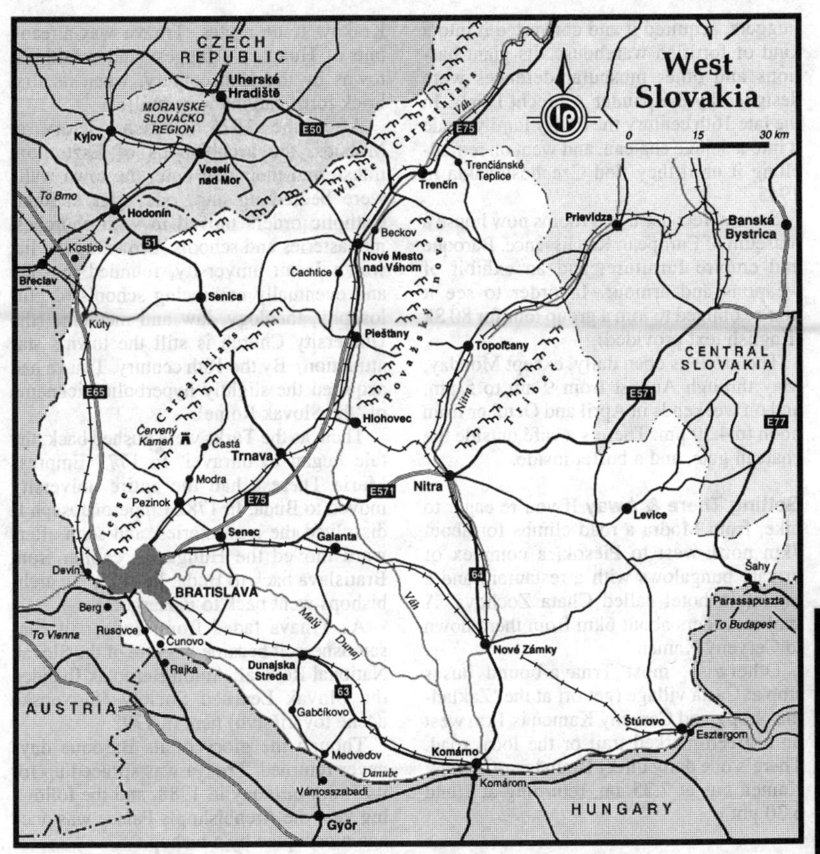

Aices (☎ 92 43 02), Štúrova 84, sells maps and can help with accommodation, weekdays from 9 am to 4 pm. Nearby, Tatra banka has a MasterCard/Visa ATM. Modra's area code is ☎ 0704.

Places to Stay & Eat Your only choice is the *Hotel Modra* (☎ 92 47 22) at Štúrova 111, which charges a reasonable 280 Sk per person for its basic rooms. A good spot for food and local wines is *Hostinec U tarkan* at Štúrova 46.

Getting There & Away Buses leave for Modra several times every hour from Bratislava's regional station on Bajkalská, and less often from the main bus station. The trip takes about an hour. From Trnava there are six daily buses (two on weekends).

Červený Kameň

About 5km north-east of Modra looms the castle of Červený Kameň, originally built in the 1230s by Queen Constance, wife of Czech King Přemysl Otakar I. In the 15th century a German merchant family, the

Fuggers, acquired it and converted it into a kind of fortified warehouse. Its giant bastions and other muscular defences were designed by the painter Albrecht Dürer. In the late 16th century the Pálffy family made it into a deluxe chateau, and went on remodelling it until they fled Czechoslovakia in 1945.

Several reconstructed rooms now house a museum of European Renaissance, Baroque and empire furniture, and an exhibit of weapons and armour. In order to see it you're obliged to join a group tour for 80 Sk (English text provided).

The castle is open daily, except Monday, May through August from 9 am to 5 pm, and on weekends in April and October from noon to 4.30 pm. There's a café outside the chateau gate, and a buffet inside.

Getting There & Away If you're eager to hike, from Modra a road climbs for about 7km north-west to Piesok, a complex of private bungalows with a restaurant and a mountain hotel called Chata Zochova. A trail meanders about 6km from there down to Červený Kameň.

Otherwise, most Trnava-bound buses stop at Častá village (get off at the 'Zakladina' stop), and Červený Kameň is 1km west on a green-marked trail or the local road. There's one daily direct Bratislava-Červený Kameň bus at 7.25 am, returning at 1 and 5.30 pm.

SLOVAK REPUBLIC

TRNAVA

Trnava (population 70,000) is Slovakia's oldest town, the first to get a royal charter as a free borough (from Hungarian King Béla IV in 1238). Though badly marred by modern development, its handsome fortified old town, a legacy of almost three centuries as Hungary's religious centre, merits a day trip from Bratislava, perhaps even an overnight stop. The town is friendly, low-key and cheap.

History

Lying on the Prague-Budapest and Vienna-Kraków trade routes, Trnava was already one of Hungary's biggest and wealthiest towns by the 13th century, when its first brick fortifications were built.

After the 1526 Turkish victory at Mohács, the archbishops of Esztergom transferred their seat here, the town walls were beefed up and, one after another, Catholic orders moved in with churches, monasteries and schools. Crowning the list was a Jesuit university, founded in 1635 and eventually embracing schools of philosophy, theology, law and medicine (the University Church is still the town's star attraction). By the 18th century, Trnava had acquired the slightly hyperbolic nickname of 'the Slovak Rome'.

Then, as the Turks were pushed back, the tale began to unravel. In 1777 Empress Maria Theresa had the entire university moved to Buda. In 1782 Emperor Joseph II dissolved the monasteries, and soon afterward moved the Hungarian capital from Bratislava back to Buda. In 1820, the archbishops went back to Esztergom.

As Trnava faded from Hungarian consciousness, it became a centre of the Slovak National Revival; Anton Bernolák founded the Slovak Learned Society (Slovenské učené tovarišstvo) here in 1792.

Though the glory of its Baroque days never returned, Trnava was spruced up for its 750th birthday in 1988, and the following year the Archbishop's Palace was once again occupied by a bishop.

Orientation

The bus and train stations are south-west of the old town, across the Trnavka stream. The heart of town is Trojičné námestie, and the main shopping street is pedestrianised Hlavná.

Information

Tourist Office The best source for accommodation listings and maps is Trnava Information Service (TINS) (☎ 51 10 22), in the Municipal Tower at Trojičné námestie 1. It's open weekdays from 8 am to 6 pm, weekends from 10 am.

Money Banks on Hlavná námestie include Slovenská sporiteľňa (Visa ATM) and Prvá komunána (MasterCard/Visa ATM). Both have currency exchange offices. A third ATM is in the train station.

Post & Communications The main post and telephone office is at Trojičné námestie 4. Trnava's area code is ☎ 0805.

Travel Agencies Satur (☎ 51 11 51), Vajanského 1, books domestic and international tickets by bus and rail.

Medical & Emergency Services The police (☎ 253 00) are in the Old Town Hall on Hlavná. The hospital (☎ 200 51) is 500m south of the old town on Andreja Žarnova.

Around Trojičné Námestie

Restored 13th century brick **town walls** stretch almost completely around the historical centre. In the west wall is the **Bernolák Gate** (Bernolákova brána), the only surviving tower gate.

Through the gate and past the Franciscans' 1640 **Church of St James** (kostol sv Jakuba) is the main square, **Trojičné námestie**. It's dominated by a Renaissance watch tower, the **Mestská veža**, built in 1574 but with a Baroque top, plus an original sgraffito buried under Baroque whitewash. The 17th century **Trinity Column** in the square, removed by the Communists in 1948, was replaced in 1989 by popular demand.

Around the square is a muddle of the town's best and worst architecture. Among the best are Slovakia's first stone theatre, the 1831 **Trnava Theatre** (Trnavské divadlo), and the 1793 **Old Town Hall** just south on Hlavná. Among the worst are the domineering modern blocks of the House of Culture (dom kultúry) and the massive Obchodný dom shopping centre.

North of the square on Štefánikova is the Jesuits' twin-towered **Trinity Church** (Jezuitský kostol), built in 1729; its exuberant Baroque interior is outdone by a striking side chapel with stuccoed columns and tiled ceiling. East on Hviezdoslavova is the Baroque Ursuline **Church of St Anne** (kostol sv Anny).

University District

In the Baroque neighbourhood around the old university is one of Slovakia's finest churches, the huge **University Church of St John the Baptist** (Univerzitný kostol sv Jána Krstiteľa), designed by Pietro Spezzo and built by Italian and Viennese artisans for the Jesuits between 1629-37. Though severe outside, it's all lush Baroque and rococo inside, with a beautiful altar reaching to the ceiling.

Staid former colleges line Hollého and Univerzitné námestie. The town's first seminary (Oláhov seminár), founded by Archbishop Mikuláš Oláh in 1566, now houses a **Museum of Book Culture** (múzeum knižnej kultúry), in recognition of Trnava's history of printing (the first press opened in 1577) and Slovak-language scholarship. It's directly opposite the Cathedral of St Nicholas and open weekdays from 8 am to 4 pm.

Cathedral of St Nicholas & Around

Named after the patron saint of merchants, the Cathedral of St Nicholas (dóm sv Mikuláša) was founded as a Gothic parish church in about 1380, and promoted to a cathedral when the archbishops arrived from Esztergom. It was given a Baroque face-lift in the 17th century, and a new interior in the 18th century. Beside it, decorated with the ecclesiastical coats-of-arms, is the old clerical homestead, the Renaissance **Archbishop's Palace** (Arcibiskupský palác).

West of here on Halenárska is a dilapidated former synagogue that now houses the quirky **Galéria Jána Koniarka**, with rotating exhibits of ultra-modern art. More compelling than the art is the synagogue's interior, left in a half-ruined state. It's open daily, except Monday, from 10 am to 4 pm, and entry costs 10 Sk. Around the corner on Havlíka is an active **synagogue**, which is only open to worshippers. Both were built

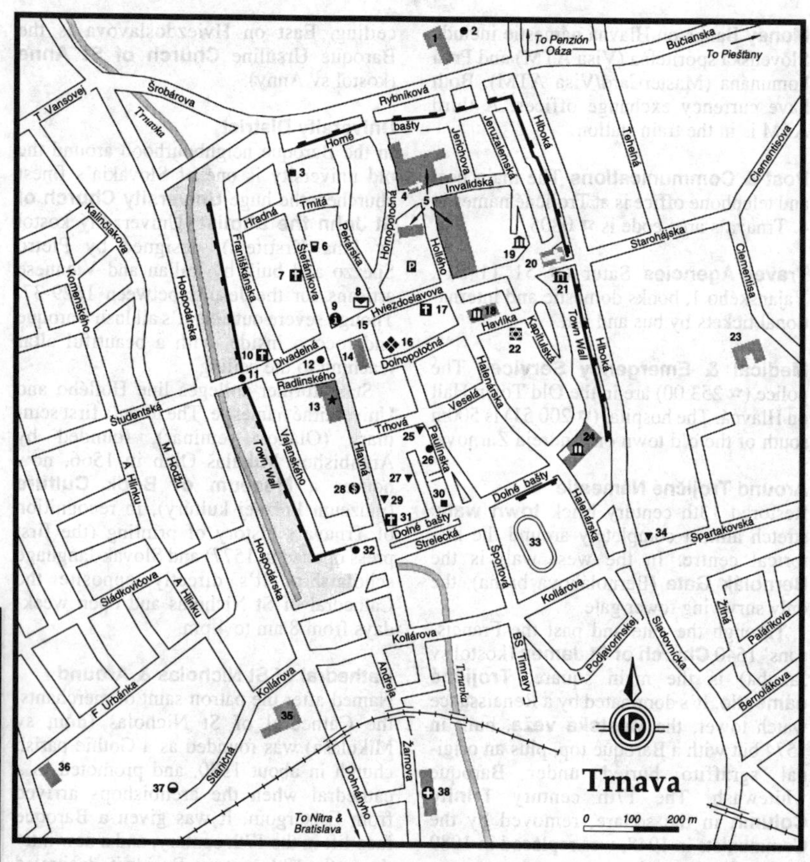

SLOVAK REPUBLIC

by the small Jewish community that settled in Trnava at the end of the 19th century.

South from St Nicholas is picturesque **Kapitulská ulica**. Lined with burghers' houses fronting Gothic basements and Renaissance façades, and full of shady trees, the street has a feeling of gentle decay.

West Slovakia Museum

South from Kapitulská is the handsome former Clarist convent, dating from 1239. After the dissolution of the monasteries by Emperor Joseph II it was used as a veterans' home and a mental hospital until the 1950s. American pilots were apparently hidden here during WWII.

Now it houses the excellent West Slovakia Museum (Západoslovenské múzeum). Some of it is fairly incomprehensible for non-Slovak speakers, but not the folk dress and crafts, exhibits of Slovakian Olympic medallists, and the antique menorahs and Torahs from the local Jewish community.

June through September the museum is

PLACES TO STAY		OTHER (cont.)			
1	Hotel Slávia	6	Piváreň Barbakan	18	Galéria Jána Koniarka
3	Hotel Apollo	7	Trinity Church (Jezuitský kostol)	19	Museum of Book Culture (Múzeum knižnej kultúry)
23	Budovateľ Hostel	8	Post Office	20	Cathedral of St Nicholas (dóm sv Mikuláša)
30	Hotel Tyrna	9	Trnava Information Service (TINS)	21	Archbishop's Palace (Arcibiskupský palác)
36	Hotel Skloplast	10	Church of St James (kostol sv Jakuba)	22	Synagogue
PLACES TO EAT		11	Bernolák Gate (Bernolákova brána)	24	West Slovakia Museum (Západoslovenské múzeum)
25	Pizzeria Corleone	12	Trnava Theatre	26	Kino Hviezda
27	U Michala	13	Old Town Hall & Police	28	Slovenská sporiteľňa
29	Pivnica pod baštami	14	House of Culture (dom kultúry) & Sundu Restaurant	31	Church of St Helen (kostol sv Helena)
34	McDonald's	15	Trojičné námestie	32	Satur
OTHER		16	Department Store (Obchodný dom)	33	Stadium
2	Kino Oko	17	Church of St Anne (kostol sv Anny)	35	Train Station
4	University Church of St John the Baptist (Univerzitný kostol sv Jána Krstiteľa)			37	Bus Station
5	University			38	Hospital

open daily, except Monday, from 9 am to 5 pm; the rest of the year it's open Tuesday to Friday from 8 am to 4 pm, weekends from 11 am. Entry costs 5 Sk.

Church of St Helen

Finally, don't miss Trnava's oldest building, the small, sad Church of St Helen (kostol sv Helena), built in the early 14th century and, except for a 19th century steeple, pure early-Gothic.

Places to Stay

With the temporary closure of *Hotel Tyrna* (due to reopen in 1998 as the deluxe Hotel Karpaty), Trnava has scant tourist accommodation. Cheapest is *Penzión Oáza* (☎ 50 12 18), a 15 minute walk north of the centre at J Hajdóczýho 19, with singles/doubles priced at 450/850 Sk. The up-market choice is *Hotel Apollo* (☎ 51 19 37) at Štefánikova 23, with all the extras for 1300/1450 Sk.

Otherwise try one of the factory and sports-club hostels – basic but comfortable, and quite cheap. Closest to the centre is *Hotel Slávia* (☎ 50 12 54), in the Domov stavárov at Námestie Jozefa Herdu 2, with 2+3 mini-suites with shower and WC for 250 Sk per person.

The plain but clean hostel *Budovateľ* (☎ 411 62), Clementisa 12, has rooms with attached shower and WC for 290/560 Sk. From the Cathedral of St Nicholas, follow the pedestrian bridge to the end, go right on Clementisa and continue 200m past Centrum Royal.

Another workers' hostel, *Hotel Skloplast*, is closed for renovations.

Places to Eat

Pivnica pod baštami, Hlavná 43, is an up-market beer hall with Slovak dishes starting at 80 Sk (closed Sunday). Its alter ego is the humble *U Michala* on Orolská, serving cheap, basic but wholesome Slovak meals from 11 am to 9 pm (closed Sunday).

Pizzeria Corleone, on Trhová, serves outstanding pizzas (60 to 95 Sk) and fair pastas from 10 am to 11 pm (closed Sunday).

A good splurge is *Sundu*, a swank Chinese eatery on the 2nd floor of the House of Culture, with views over the main square. Authentic entrées are 80 to 130 Sk.

You could cobble together a decent breakfast and lunch at two places next to TINS: *Maxim Baguette*, with fresh, healthy sandwiches for 30 Sk, and *Cukráreň Pukky club*, with cakes and coffee.

Locals are mighty proud of the recently finished *McDonald's*, on Spartakovská.

Entertainment
There are cultural – especially musical – programmes and exhibitions during the summer, particularly at the *Trnava Theatre*; see TINS.

The local 'cool' bar is *Piváreň Barbakan*, on Štefánikova; it's smoky and quiet upstairs, cavernous and noisy downstairs. Avoid the food here. A nameless bar across the street has a pool table.

The most central cinemas are *Kino Hviezda* on Paulínska and *Kino Oko* adjacent to Hotel Slávia.

Getting There & Away
There are a dozen fast or express trains a day from Bratislava's main train station, and several more from Bratislava-Nové Mesto, taking half an hour. Buses run all day from Bratislava's main terminal, though only a few are direct or express service.

By car, Trnava is about 50km from Bratislava.

NITRA

Nitra (population 88,000), sprawling beneath a castle in a bend of the Nitra river, is the oldest documented settlement in Slovakia. It's also the site of the first Christian church in the Czech and Slovak republics, founded by an atheistic but crafty prince named Pribina in 833.

The surviving old centre – particularly the castle and its cathedral – can be appreciated in one day, or even on a long day trip from Bratislava.

History

After Pribina's patch was absorbed into the Great Moravian Empire in 833, Nitra was made a princely seat and bishopric. The first church is gone, but the clerical grip has persisted. In 1302 the Nitra bishops assumed feudal control of the region, strangling its development for almost five centuries.

The Turks pounded the town in the 16th century and nearly wrecked it in the 17th. Industrialisation set in during the 19th century, and Nitra has since grown into the republic's third largest city after Bratislava and Košice. As it comes to grips with post-1989 realities, historical sites seem to be getting only marginal attention. In fact, most money has been pumped into Nitra's sprawling Agricultural University and the surrounding Agrokomplex, a series of convention centres that hosts Slovak and foreign business travellers throughout the year.

Orientation

At the foot of the castle is the former clerical enclave called the Upper Town (Horné Mesto). Southward are the remnants of the Lower Town (Dolné Mesto), sometimes referred to as the Old Town (Staré Mesto), centred on the grandiose Svätoplukovo námestie. The Lower Town's axes – Štefánikova and Štúrova – cross beside the big district market. Svätoplukovo námestie, Kupecká and upper Štefánikova have been pedestrianised.

Information

Tourist Office The helpful staff at NISYS (☎ 41 09 06), Štefánikova 46, offer the usual accommodation services, weekdays from 8 am to 6 pm, Saturday to 1 pm.

Money Všeobecná úverová banka has an exchange office and MasterCard ATM at Štefánikova 44. Across the street is Slovenská sporiteľňa and its Visa ATM.

Post & Communications The main post and telephone office is on Svätoplukovo námestie. Nitra's area code is ☎ 087.

Travel Agencies Satur (☎ 52 36 11), Štefánikova 52, is open weekdays from 8.30 am to 4 pm.

Lower Town

Because of Turkish attacks, aristocratic rebellions against Hungary, a 1793 fire and post-Communist redevelopment, little is

SLOVAK REPUBLIC

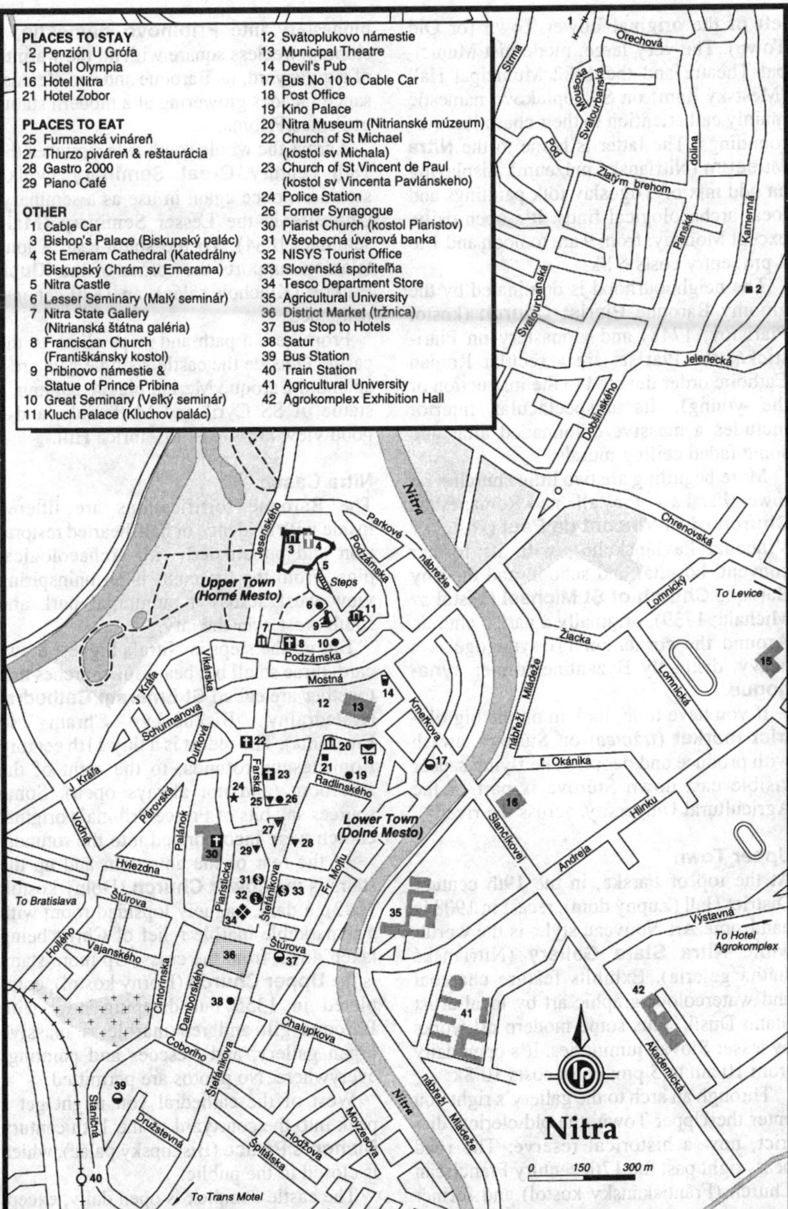
PLACES TO STAY
2 Penzión U Grófa
15 Hotel Olympia
16 Hotel Nitra
21 Hotel Zobor
PLACES TO EAT
25 Furmanská vináreň
27 Thurzo piváreň & reštaurácia
28 Gastro 2000
29 Piano Café
OTHER
1 Cable Car
3 Bishop's Palace (Biskupský palác)
4 St Emeram Cathedral (Katedrálny Biskupský Chrám sv Emerama)
5 Nitra Castle
6 Lesser Seminary (Malý seminár)
7 Nitra State Gallery (Nitrianská štátna galéria)
8 Franciscan Church (Františkánsky kostol)
9 Pribinovo námestie & Statue of Prince Pribina
10 Great Seminary (Veľký seminár)
11 Kluch Palace (Kluchov palác)
12 Svätoplukovo námestie
13 Municipal Theatre
14 Devil's Pub
17 Bus No 10 to Cable Car
18 Post Office
19 Kino Palace
20 Nitra Museum (Nitrianské múzeum)
22 Church of St Michael (kostol sv Michala)
23 Church of St Vincent de Paul (kostol sv Vincenta Pavlánskeho)
24 Police Station
26 Former Synagogue
30 Piarist Church (kostol Piaristov)
31 Všeobecná úverová banka
32 NISYS Tourist Office
33 Slovenská sporiteľňa
34 Tesco Department Store
35 Agricultural University
36 District Market (tržnica)
37 Bus Stop to Hotels
38 Satur
39 Bus Station
40 Train Station
41 Agricultural University
42 Agrokomplex Exhibition Hall
Upper Town
(Horné Mesto)
Lower Town
(Dolné Mesto)
Steps
Nitra
To Levice
To Bratislava
To Hotel Agrokomplex
To Trans Motel
Orechová
Sirmá
Mousova
Svatourbanská
Pod
Zlatým brehom
dolina
Kamenná
Panská
Jelenecká
Dobšinského
Chrenovská
Parkové
nábrežie
Podzámska
Jesenského
Lomnický
Žiacka
Lomnická
nábrežie Mládeže
Kmeťkova
Ľ. Okánika
Slančíkovej
Hlinku
Andreja
Výstavná
Akademická
Mostná
Vikárska
J. Kráľa
Schurmanova
Ďurkova
Farská
Radlinského
Párovská
Palánok
Vodná
Hviezdna
Štúrova
Piaristická
Štefánikova
F. Mojtu
Hollého
Vajanského
Cintorínska
Damborského
Chalupkova
Coboriho
Stanićná
Družstevná
Moyzesova
Hodžova
Špitálska
150
300 m
Nitra

left of the original Lower Town (or Old Town). The very large, modernist Municipal Theatre and the 1882 Municipal Hall (Mestský dom) on Svätoplukovo námestie mainly call attention to their charmless surroundings. The latter is home to the **Nitra Museum** (Nitrianské múzeum), displaying an odd mix of Yugoslav folk paintings and local archaeological finds. It's open daily, except Monday, from 9 am to noon and 1 to 4 pm; entry costs 5 Sk.

The neighbourhood is dominated by the gloomy Baroque **Piarist Church** (kostol Piaristov; 1748) and monastery on Piaristická (the Piarists are a secular Roman Catholic order devoted to the instruction of the young). Its unspectacular interior includes a massive colonnaded altar and some faded ceiling murals.

More beguiling are two little churches on lower Farská – the tall, neo-Romanesque **Church of St Vincent de Paul** (kostol sv Vincenta Pavlánskeho), with its former convent, hospital and school, and the tiny Baroque **Church of St Michael** (kostol sv Michala; 1739), originally a parish church. Around the corner on Pri synagoge is a heavy, distinctly Byzantine former **synagogue**.

If you have time, look in on the big **district market** (*tržnica*) on Štúrova, awash with produce and people. The flying saucer visible east down Štúrova is part of the Agricultural University, across the river.

SLOVAK REPUBLIC

Upper Town

At the top of Farská, in the 19th century District Hall (Župný dom), recast in 1908 in handsome Art Nouveau style, is the worthwhile **Nitra State Gallery** (Nitrianská štátna galéria). Exhibits feature charcoal and watercolour graphic art by local artist Stano Dusík, plus some modern oil works by lesser Slovak luminaries. It's open daily from 10 am to 5 pm; entry costs 10 Sk.

Through an arch to the gallery's right you enter the Upper Town, the old clerical district, now a historical reserve. The road bears right past the 17th century Franciscan Church (Františkánsky kostol) and former monastery into **Pribinovo námestie**, a sloping, treeless square with all the warmth of a graveyard, its Baroque and neo-Renaissance façades glowering at a modern statue of Prince Pribina.

Across the whole south side stretches the 18th century **Great Seminary** (Veľký seminár), once again in use as a seminary. Opposite is the Lesser Seminary (Malý seminár; 1884). To the south-east, a lone telamon supports the corner of the **Kluch Palace** (Kluchov palác), an 1820 canons' residence.

From here a path and steps climb to the castle. Outside the castle's single gate are a splendid Baroque Marian plague column, a statue of SS Cyril and Methodius, and a good view north-east to Žibrica Hill.

Nitra Castle

The Baroque fortifications are littered inside with evidence of half-hearted restoration and punctuated with archaeological digs. From the forecourt is an uninspiring view west across a municipal park and south-west over the city.

But up the steps is Nitra's biggest drawcard, three small but beautiful churches that together are called **St Emeram Cathedral** (Katedrálny Biskupský Chram sv Emerama). The oldest is a tiny 11th century Romanesque rotunda, to the right of the anteroom (and not always open). Some sources say bits of Prince Pribina's original church were incorporated into the rotunda.

At the rear of the anteroom and up the stairs is the **Lower Church** (Dolný kostol; 1642), a dark, vaguely lopsided room with a remarkable marble relief of Christ being taken down from the cross. Up more stairs is the **Upper Church** (Horný kostol), completed in 1355 but dripping now with Baroque gilt and red marble, a massive organ gallery, and frescoes and paintings everywhere. No photos are permitted.

West of the cathedral you might get a peek into the courtyard of the 18th century **Bishop's Palace** (Biskupský palác), which is closed to the public.

The castle complex is open daily, except

Monday, from 9 am to 1 pm, but no tours are offered and the hours are rather meaningless. A better option is the daily 7 am Mass in the Lower Church, or Saturday and Sunday Mass in the Upper Church.

Walks

North of the city, Zobor Hill (588m) and Žibrica (617m) beyond it, the last vestiges of the Tribeč range, are part of a regional nature reserve and good for walks and huge views. Bits of old walls around the Zobor summit are remnants of ancient fortifications. A **cable car** once climbed to the summit but was closed indefinitely at the time of writing. If it reopens, take bus No 10 just off Kmeťkova to the end of the line at Zobor.

Places to Stay

Accommodation is hard to find during the annual Agrokomplex expo in the second half of August. The same goes for the garden expo in late April. Nitra has no private rooms, but NISYS knows of cheap hotels and, in summer, even cheaper university dorms.

Best value for money is *Hotel Agrokomplex* (☎ 53 45 41), Vihorlatská 10, 25 minutes by foot from the city centre. Single/double rooms with bath are 220/440 Sk, and there's a good restaurant in the lobby. Take bus No 8, 14 or 15 east from Štúrova to Vystavna (four stops), walk back past the 'Zdravotnícke stredisko' building, and turn right onto Vihorlatská.

Hotel Olympia (☎ 53 67 27; fax 362 25), on Andreja Hlinku, has doubles in 2+2 mini-suites with WC and shower for 800 Sk, and singles for 440 Sk. Take bus No 12, 13, 16 or 23 east on Štúrova.

The central *Hotel Zobor* (☎ 52 53 81) at Štefánikova 5 is convenient but not especially comfortable, with rooms at 500/1000 Sk.

A decent splurge is *Penzión U Grófa* (☎ 41 28 57), at Kamenná 8 in the residential neighbourhood below Zobor Hill. Four plush doubles with shower, WC and TV are about 1300 Sk each, and there's a restaurant. Take bus No 23 or 26 east on Štúrova to lower Jelenecká.

Nitra's overpriced high-rise showpiece is *Hotel Nitra* (☎ 342 42/7), Slančíkovej 1, with rooms with bath for 1900/2000 Sk. Take bus No 2 east on Štúrova.

Places to Eat

The low-key *Furmanská vináreň*, in a cellar on Pri synagoge, serves good Slovak meals for 50 to 70 Sk and is open weekdays from noon to 9 pm. Louder and jollier is the beer hall *Thurzo piváreň*, on Štefánikova near Pri synagoge. Upstairs, the smoke-filled and crowded *Thurzo reštaurácia* has Slovak standard fare from 40 to 90 Sk and is open weekdays only to 9.30 pm.

A classy spot for coffee, beer or full meals is the *Piano Café*, in the courtyard at Farská 46, open daily to 10 pm. Come on a Friday or Saturday night for live piano music.

If you're self-catering, try the fresh, cheap and filling baguette sandwiches at *Gastro 2000*, on Štefánikova, or load up on groceries at the *supermarket* inside the Tesco department store.

Entertainment

Check around for *Leto Nitra* (Summer Nitra), a brochure on summer cultural programmes. These often include church music, exhibitions and films.

The cinema *Kino Palace*, on Radlinského, shows films in their original language (often English). For beer, loud rock and a game of billiards try the *Devil's Pub*, Kmeťkova 2, nightly to 4 am.

Getting There & Away

Buses depart from Bratislava's main station every half-hour (or less) all day for the one to 1½ hour trip. Avoid going by train, which could involve multiple transfers and take up to three hours.

KOMÁRNO

This Danube border town opposite Komárom, Hungary, is a convenient entry/exit point between Slovakia and Hungary.

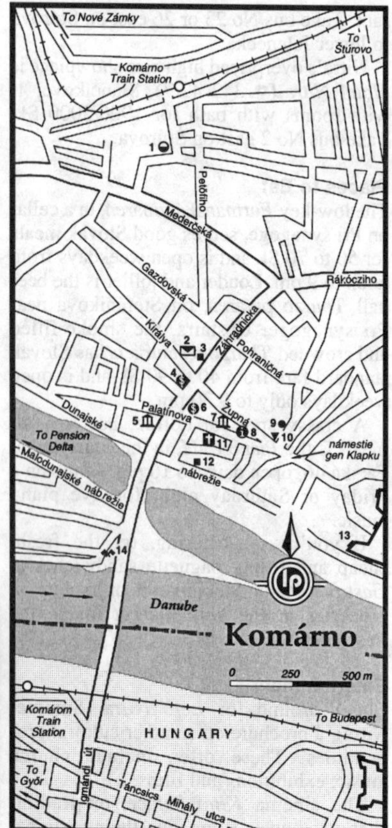

1 Bus Station
2 Post Office
3 Hotel Európa
4 Všeobecná úverová banka
5 Jókai & Lehár Museum
6 Slovenská sporiteľňa
7 Danube Museum (Podunajské múzeum)
8 Aices Tourist Office
9 Town Hall
10 Restaurant Klapka-Vigadó
11 Church of St Andrew
12 Hotel Danubius
13 Fortress
14 Border Checkpoint

Frequent trains (with low domestic fares) run between these twin cities and onwards to Bratislava and Budapest, and it costs nothing to walk across the 1892 bridge linking Slovakia and Hungary.

Komárno (population 38,000) serves as the cultural and political centre of southern Slovakia's large Hungarian community, and two-thirds of local residents are Hungarian. All street signs in Komárno are written in Slovak and Hungarian.

As at Komárom, the Habsburgs erected impressive fortifications here between 1541 and 1592 to hold back the Turks, who never managed to capture the town. The defensive system was rebuilt and greatly expanded during the Napoleonic Wars, eventually to become one of the largest in Europe. The busy shipyards at Komárno, founded in 1898, build both river and ocean-going vessels.

Though Komárno is pleasant enough, it certainly does not merit a special trip – except during the last weekend of April and the first week of May for the Komárno Days festival, with many competitions, folk dances and songs.

Orientation

The train and bus stations are 15 minutes by foot from the town centre, 20 minutes from the international border crossing. Slovak and Hungarian customs are together on a peninsula in the middle of the river.

Information

The helpful Aices office (☎ 73 00 63), Župná 5, arranges accommodation weekdays from 9 am to 5 pm. The Všeobecná úverová banka, with an exchange office and MasterCard ATM, is at Tržničné námestie 1. Slovenská sporiteľňa, on Palatínova, has a Visa ATM. There's also a 24 hour exchange office next to customs on the bridge.

Komárno's area code is ☎ 0819.

Things to See

The two tall towers of the **Church of St Andrew** (1734), on Palatínova, are visible from afar. Directly opposite the church is the relatively small **Danube Museum** (Podunajské múzeum), with a so-so historical and archaeological collection. It's open Tuesday to Saturday from 9 am to 4 pm; entry costs 10 Sk.

East on Palatínova is the main square, námestie gen Klapku, with several attractive monuments and the **town hall** (1875). The small **Komárno Museum**, on the square at No 9, has many old photographs and other collectables from the 19th and 20th centuries. It's open weekdays from 10 am to 4 pm.

Farther east is the massive 18th century **fortress**, near the junction of the Váh and Danube. It's still occupied by the military and inaccessible to the public.

Komárno's most interesting museum is the **Jókai & Lehár múzeum**, dedicated to composer Ferenc Lehár and novelist Jókai Mór, right next to the bridge's approach. Entry includes the adjacent 18th century Serbian Orthodox church and its woodcarvings, though both were temporarily closed at the time of writing.

Places to Stay

The cheapest option is the basic *Hotel Danubius* (☎ 4491), Dunajské nábrežie 12, on the corner of Lehárova. Doubles/triples without bath cost 480/560 Sk. The hotel is in the yellow three storey building with the words 'Spoločenský dom' on the roof.

A better upper-end choice is *Hotel Európa* (☎ 4251), námestie Štefánika 1, with singles/doubles with bath and WC for 650/1000 Sk.

Far more serene is *Pension Delta* (☎ 945 01) at Malodunajské nábrežie 10, on the Slovak side of the island. Rooms with shared facilities are 400 Sk per person, including breakfast.

Places to Eat

Restaurant Klapka-Vigadó, on námestie gen Klapku, is a reasonable mid-range restaurant, but food can be uneven and you should check your bill carefully. *Zlatá Ryba*, Lehárova 12, next to Hotel Danubius, is a cheap stand-up buffet (closed Sunday).

Getting There & Away

Eight buses a day run between Bratislava and Komárno (104km). Or take one of the six local trains to/from Bratislava's Nové Mesto train station (two hours; 94km).

Direct services to Nitra, Trenčín and Žilina are poor and you're probably better off going through Bratislava. Theoretically, there are three buses a day to Nitra and Trnava and one to Trenčín.

A bus to the Komárom train station across the river in Hungary leaves the Komárno train station five times a day.

PIEŠŤANY

Piešťany (population 31,000), beside the Váh river as it descends from the Carpathians, is the Slovak Republic's best known spa resort. Its warm springs and sulphuric mud have been documented since the 12th century and prescribed for aching joints since the 16th century.

The spa pulls in plenty of hard currency for Slovakia, and the international clientele has driven up prices for almost everything – except in winter, when the spa is nearly empty. Like most spa towns, Piešťany is relaxing but fairly boring. Aside from the lavish Thermia Palace, the architecture is no match for the spas of West Bohemia.

Orientation

Shops and tourist hotels are all on or near pedestrianised Winterova. The top-end spas are on Kúpeľný ostrov (Bath Island), reached by the covered Colonnade Bridge (Kolonádový most) with the spa's symbol, a statue of a patient breaking his crutches in half, on it. Between Winterova and the river is a leafy park with bandstand, concert pavilion (Dom umenia) and a footbridge to a smaller island-park.

Drivers beware: illegally parked cars are apt to be clamped, so stick to designated parking lots around the centre.

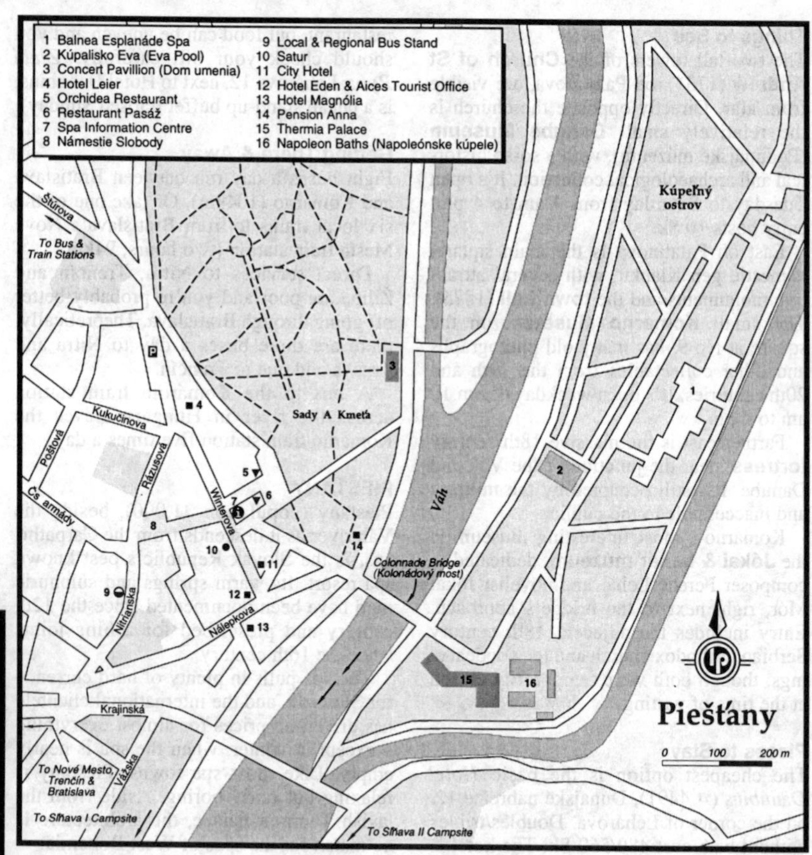

Information

The Aices office (☎ 276 89), inside the Hotel Eden at Winterova 60, has maps and accommodation listings, and it also rents bikes. It's open weekdays from 9 am to 3 pm. For transport questions head to Satur (☎ 215 06) at Winterova 44. Kiosks on the Colonnade Bridge sell international newspapers.

Kúpele Piešťany, the baths information centre and headquarters of Slovthermae, the Slovak spa agency, is at Winterova 29.

Piešťany's area code is ☎ 0838.

Things to See & Do

Winterova is a bland row of hotels and cafés, though it boasts a few modest Art Nouveau buildings. The spa facilities and the springs themselves, are set among gardens on Kúpeľný ostrov. Top of the line is the splendid Art Nouveau **Thermia Palace**, which is worth a look inside.

East of the Thermia Palace are the neoclassical **Napoleon Baths** (Napoleónske kúpele; 1821). North of here three giant, modern Balnea spas stand in a line on the east side of the island. An al fresco exhibition of modern sculpture is dotted around the park.

You can take a dip in the warm **Kúpalisko Eva** (Eva Pool) for 24 Sk, daily from May through September from 10 am to 5 pm (to 6 pm in July and August).

The town hosts a modest music festival in June and July, and the Prix Slovakia auto and motorcycle races in September.

Spa Treatments

The sanatoria here are fit for a Thomas Mann novel, treating a variety of ailments with therapeutic muds, mineral waters and exercise regimes. Check-in for a day or a lifetime, but expect to pay a daily rate of 1800 to 3000 Sk per person, all-inclusive. Three of the better known spas are the Jalta (☎ 51 74 29; fax 241 50), Pro Patria (☎ 51 62 80; fax 240 91) and Balnea Esplanáde (☎ 51 52 95; fax 237 43).

Places to Stay

There are two campsites south of town on the lake – *Sĺňava I* (☎ 943 29), 2km down the west side of the river (from Nitrianska take bus No 13 or 15), and *Sĺňava II* (☎ 235 63), 1.5km down the east side (take bus No 12). Both have bungalows and are open from May through September.

In town, *Pension Anna* (☎ 265 61), in an old spa house within the Sady A Kmeťa park, charges 350 Sk per person. *Hotel Eden* (☎ 247 09), Winterova 60, has singles/doubles for 430/700 Sk without bath, and 1070/1340 Sk with bath.

Up-market options include the intimate *City Hotel* (☎ 254 54), Winterova 35, and the high-rise *Hotel Magnólia* (☎ 262 51), both roughly priced at 1250/1650 Sk with bath, WC and TV.

Hotel Leier is temporarily closed for renovations.

Places to Eat

In addition to decent but pricey hotel restaurants, Winterova abounds in cafés, restaurants and ice-cream stalls. Two standouts are *Orchidea*, with delicious pizzas and pastas, and *Restaurant Pasáž*, an upscale bistro with Slovak and international dishes. Both are on an alleyway off Winterova called Park-Pasáž.

Getting There & Away

Local and regional buses stop on Nitrianska. The train and long-distance bus stations are a 25 minute walk west from the town centre (or take bus No 5 or 11 to/from Nitrianska). About 15 Bratislava-Žilina express trains call at Piešťany every day, taking about an hour from either end. Buses run frequently from Bratislava's main station.

ČACHTICE CASTLE

The fame of this castle, one of several 13th century Hungarian strongholds between Piešťany and Trenčín, springs from its history. In the 17th century a mad Hungarian countess named Alžbeta Nádasdy-Báthory tortured and murdered over 600 peasant women here and in another castle, Beckov, across the Váh. When her grisly doings were finally found out she was imprisoned in Čachtice for the rest of her life.

Since a fire in 1708, there isn't much left of the castle, but it has great views (the surrounding area is a regional nature reserve). There are no roads to the hilltop ruins, just a few scraggy trails.

There are no hotels here, and only a very basic *pivåreň* beside the Višňové train stop.

Getting There & Away

You must change trains or buses at Nové Mesto nad Váhom, a dismal industrial town on the Piešťany-Trenčín road. From there it's a picturesque 15 minute train ride to the whistlestop of Višňové (with half a dozen useful departures during the day) and a 25 minute scramble up the hill to the ruins.

By car, Čachtice village is 7km southwest of Nové Mesto; Višňové and the castle are 5km from there on a side road.

TRENČÍN

For centuries, where the Váh river valley begins to narrow between the White

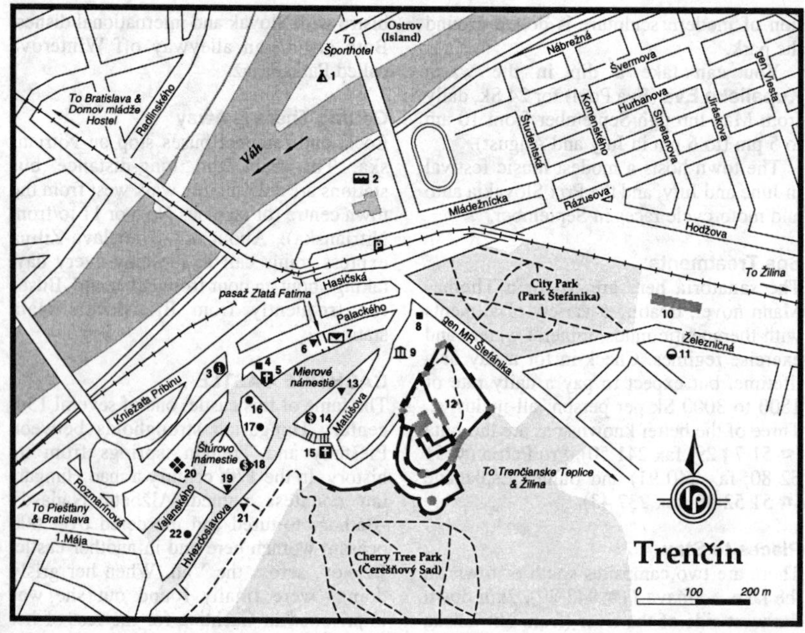

Carpathians and the Strážov hills, Trenčín Castle guarded the south-west gateway to Slovakia. Laugaricio, a Roman military post – the northernmost Roman camp in eastern Europe – was established here in the 2nd century AD. A rock inscription at Trenčín, dated 179 AD, mentions the stay of the Roman 2nd Legion and its victory over the Germanic Kvad tribes.

The mighty castle that now towers above town was first mentioned in 1069 in a Viennese illustrated chronicle. In the 13th century the castle's master Matúš Čák held sway over much of Slovakia, and in 1412 Trenčín obtained the rights of a free royal city. The present castle dates from that period, and although both castle and town were destroyed by fire in 1790, much has been restored.

Modern Trenčín (population 59,000) is an important centre of the Slovak textile industry. Trenčín's main sights – the castle and central square – can be covered in an afternoon, a fortunate thing considering the town's lack of cheap accommodation. In summer it's worth spending the night for the Medieval Days performance at the castle (see below).

Orientation

From the adjacent bus and train stations, walk west through the City Park and follow the Tatra Passage under the highway to Mierové námestie, the main square.

Information

Tourist Office The well-informed staff at Aices (☎ 53 35 05), Štúrova námestie 10, answer transport questions and can help with accommodation, weekdays from 8 am to 6 pm, Saturday to 1 pm.

Money The Prvá komunálna banka, Štúrova námestie, wil change travellers

PLACES TO STAY		OTHER			
1	Vodácky klub na ostrove Camping Ground	2	Swimming Pools	14	Slovenská sporiteľňa
4	Penzión Svorad	3	Aices Tourist Office	15	Parish Church (Farský kostol)
8	Hotel Tatra	5	Piarist Church (Piaristický kostol)	16	Former Synagogue
		7	Post Office	17	Gate Tower (Mestská brána)
PLACES TO EAT		9	Trenčín Museum (Trenčianske múzeum)	18	Prvá komunálna banka
6	Plzeňská pivnica	10	Train Station	20	Prior Department Store
13	Restaurant Lanius	11	Bus Station	22	House of Culture (Dom kultúry)
19	Pizzeria Venezia	12	Trenčín Castle (Trenčiansky hrad)		
21	Gastrocentrum				

cheques and has a MasterCard ATM. Slovenská sporiteľňa, Mierové námestie 4, has a Visa ATM.

Post & Communications The telephone centre in the main post office, Mierové námestie 21, is open weekdays from 7.30 am to 8 pm, Saturday from 8 am to noon. Trenčín's area code is ☎ 0831.

Around Mierové Námestie

This pleasant square lined with Renaissance burghers' houses is dominated at the west end by the old town's only remaining **gate tower** (Mestská brána; 1534) as well as the **Piarist Church** (Piaristický kostol), built in Baroque style in 1657.

In the former monastery, next door at No 7, is the **Oblastná galéria Bazovského**, a beautiful space with work by local artists on the ground floor, plus paintings by Trenčín-born Miloš Bazovský (1899-1968) upstairs. The gallery is open daily, except Monday, from 9 am to 5 pm; entry costs 5 Sk.

In the centre of the square is a **plague column** (morový stĺp) that dates from 1712. On the square's east end, at No 46, is **Trenčín Museum** (Trenčianske múzeum), dedicated to natural history but overpriced even at 4 Sk.

North of the gate tower is the stocky former **synagogue**, in need of serious restoration. Around on Palackého is the rather lavishly renovated **grammar school** (Piaristické Gymnazium) established by the Piarists for the instruction of local youth.

South from the tower a 16th century covered **wooden staircase** (Kryté schody) climbs to a bright-yellow 14th century **Parish Church** (Farský kostol), which has a simple outline bearing Gothic, Renaissance and Baroque traces. The small cemetery chapel beside it is probably the only purely Gothic building in town. From here you can ascend to the castle gate.

Trenčín Castle

The lofty Trenčín Castle (Trenčiansky hrad) provides amazing views over the town and the Váh plain, though the main attraction is the castle itself, an extraordinary fortification now undergoing major restoration. The present layout dates more or less from the 15th century.

The so-called **Well of Love** on the first terrace is a fantastic construction 70m deep. Above is the castle's great **central tower**, with 300 degree views of the area. At night the castle is illuminated with green and purple lights. Nightly in summer between 9 and 11 pm there is a fantastic show called Medieval Days, which includes sword fighting and ghost stories and plenty of fun.

The castle is open daily from 9 am to 4 pm (April through September to 5 pm), and the 50 Sk ticket includes a tour (every 30 minutes).

Other Attractions

South beneath the castle walls, on a footpath off Hviezdoslavova, is the forested **Cherry Tree Park** (Čerešňový sad). North of the city centre are summer and winter swimming pools.

Places to Stay

Camping The *Vodácky klub na ostrove Camping Ground* (☎ 53 40 13) is on Ostrov, an island in the Váh river. Camping is 40 Sk per person, 55 Sk per tent; comfortable two and four-bed cabins are 100 Sk per person. The facility is open from May through to 15 September.

Hostel The comfortable and modern *Domov mládeže* (☎ 52 23 80), Staničná 6, is a year-round hostel 2km north-west of the centre, with two and three-bed suites with shower and WC for 150 Sk per person. It's technically for students only, but the rule is rarely (if ever) enforced. Cross the Váh river and, past the 'Herold Ferm' factory, turn left through an empty lot, go hard left onto a footpath, then take the second right; the hostel is 500m ahead, the second high-rise on the left.

Hotels In the centre of town the only cheap spot is *Penzión Svorad* (☎ 53 03 22), in the gymnasium building (no smoking allowed) at Palackého 4. A bed in twin rooms with shared facilities costs from 180 to 220 Sk. *Športhotel* (☎ 53 19 40) is in the middle of Ostrov island, about a 20 minute walk from Mierové námestie. Doubles with shower and WC are 1000 Sk. The top-of-the-line *Hotel Tatra* (☎ 50 61 11), gen MR Štefánika 2, has singles/doubles with bath and WC at 2200/3200 Sk, including breakfast.

Places to Eat

Plzeňská pivnica, in a damp basement on pasáž Zlatá Fatima, serves basic Slovak meals daily to 10 pm. The buffet *Gastrocentrum*, on the ground floor of a shopping mall, serves cheap and wholesome meals to 6 pm (closed Sunday). The nearby *Pizzeria Venezia*, through an archway at Hviezdoslavova 4, serves tasty pizzas and pastas for less than 60 Sk. *Restaurant Lanius*, Mierové námestie, is a semi-upscale beer hall with an English-language menu.

Cafés For tea in a smoke-free environment try *Čajovná pod hradom*, upstairs in an arcade on Mierové námestie, two doors up from the Slovenská sporiteľňa bank (closed Sunday).

Entertainment

The popular nameless bar in the same arcade as Restaurant Lanius is good for a late-night beer. Or escape reality briefly at the cinema *Kino Metro*, on the main square next to the Slovenská sporiteľňa bank. Special events are sometimes held in the *House of Culture* (dom kultúry), on Hviezdoslavova.

Getting There & Away

All express trains on the main railway line from Bratislava to Košice (via Žilina) stop here. About six buses a day go to Bratislava, Piešťany, Trnava, Košice and Žilina; three a day go to Nitra.

TRENČIÁSKE TEPLICE

This sedate spa in the Teplička valley, 14km north-east of Trenčín, is worth a visit for the good day hikes in the surrounding hills, and a soak at the public thermal pool. Otherwise it's just a complex of huge, impersonal sanatoria. The only building with a hint of character is the opulent 1888 Turkish-style **bath house** (hammam), on Masaryka opposite the Pax sanatorium.

A **thermal swimming pool** at the Zelená žába (Green Frog) restaurant, on the hillside just above the spa, is open daily from May to September until 6 pm and costs 20 Sk. From the train station head east on Šrobárova, left at the Lipa spa, left at the Kúpelná Dvorana spa, and up the left side of the wooded valley. The big pool and a children's pool are both about 28°C.

There are many attractive parks, and from June to September a varied cycle of musical programmes is presented. You can buy circular spa wafers (and see them being made) at Kúpeľné oblátky, Masaryka 14.

Orientation & Information

The train station is near the post office on

PHOTOS BY SCOTT McNEELY

Moravia
Top: Telč's old centre is dominated by the town square, náměstí Zachariáše z Hradce
Bottom: A spa house near Luhačovice

SCOTT McNEELY

SCOTT McNEELY

MARK DAFFEY

Slovakia

Left: St Michael Tower is Bratislava's only surviving watchtower.

Right: Just west of Bratislava is Devín Castle, which was first established by the Romans.

Bottom: A Gypsy caravan on the plain in front of Spiš Castle, Spišské Podhradie.

Šrobárova, which runs north and parallel to the main road, Masaryka.

The Satur office (☎ 55 23 61), inside the Hotel Flora at 17.novembra 14, provides information on the area but does not book accommodation. All the local hiking trails are listed on the map *Trenčín-Trenčianske Teplice* (1:10,000), which is sold by Aices in Trenčin.

Trenčiáske Teplice's area code is ☎ 0831.

Places to Stay & Eat

The inexpensive *Penzión Natalia* (☎ 55 28 58), Bagarova 26, two blocks south of Hotel Jalta, is the best value at 400 Sk per double. *Hotel Jalta* (☎ 55 61 11), a five storey monster on Masaryka, is 800/1280 Sk for a single/double with WC and bath. The fancy *Hotel Flora* (☎ 55 29 81), at the east end of Šrobárova, has doubles with all the trimmings for 1370 Sk.

Hotel Jalta has a *restaurant* and bar. Better value is the *R club reštaurácia*, directly opposite the Jalta and open from 10 am to 2 am. It has a good selection of Slovak dishes, including some vegetarian.

Getting There & Away

Trenčíaske Teplice is accessible via a 6km branch line from Trenčianska Teplá, which is served by frequent local trains on the Trenčín-Žilina line. Electric tram-type trains shuttle back and forth about once an hour. There are also some direct buses from Trenčín (20 minutes).

SLOVAK REPUBLIC

Central Slovakia

HIGHLIGHTS

- Follow the crowd to Bojnice and see why it's the most visited chateau in Slovakia
- The architecturally striking former mining towns of Banská Bystrica and Banská Štiavnica are worth going out of your way for
- See the unusual house decorations at Čičmany
- The Low Tatras has great skiing and hiking areas, as well as the intriguing Demänova Ice Cave

The main attractions of Central Slovakia are geophysical. This is the most mountainous part of a republic appreciated for its mountains – primarily the High and Low Tatras (Vysoké and Nízke Tatry), and the Malá and Veľká Fatra. The ranges are perforated by limestone caves, blanketed with forest (with over 50% coverage, Central Slovakia is the most heavily wooded part of either republic), and carved with deep valleys, the most magical of which are the Vrátna Valley in the Malá Fatra and the Demänova Valley in the Low Tatras. The popular High Tatras is dealt with in the following chapter.

Over 20% of the region is covered with nature preserves of one kind or another, the biggest of which is the Low Tatras National Park. The Malá Fatra probably offers the finest hiking, with the most *chaty* (mountain chalets) along the way.

Other worthwhile stops are the elegant old centre of Banská Štiavnica, one of several former mining towns in the region that together produced 20% of the medieval world's silver and large amounts of its gold; photogenic Orava Castle; romantic Bojnice Chateau; and an excellent *skansen* at Zuberec in the Orava Valley.

The regional economic and administrative centre is Banská Bystrica, though Slovakia's largest domestic and international transport junction (after Bratislava) is not there but at Žilina.

BANSKÁ BYSTRICA

This town of about 85,000, in a valley where three major mountain ranges – the Low Tatras, Veľká Fatra and Slovenské rudohorie – intersect, is the region's administrative capital. German colonists were settled here in the 13th century to extract and refine silver ore, and later copper, from the area's rich veins (*banská* means 'mining'). The town grew fat until the mines began petering out in the 17th century, and faded away until a post-WWII industrial boom.

A traditionally bolshie town and interwar Communist hotbed, Banská Bystrica is best known to Slovaks as the cradle of the Slovak National Uprising (Slovenské národné povstanie, or SNP) against the Nazis and their Slovak puppet state. From here on 29 August 1944, resistance radio announced the start of the uprising.

Although the Slovak fascists gave way, two months later the German army marched in and crushed the revolt. Of German reprisals for the uprising, the worst was the torture and murder of some 900 Slovak men, women and children, along with Russian and French partisans and several members of an Anglo-American military

mission, at Nemecká, 20km east up the Hron Valley.

Banská Bystrica's attraction for visitors is a small but handsome old town centre, including the remnants of a 15th century citadel. You may not want to stay long, though; several industrial combines up the Hron Valley now permanently foul the town's air. Contrary to tourist-office suggestions, this is not a very useful place (nor is there any need) to prebook accommodation for farther north, including the High Tatras.

Orientation

From the bus and train stations, adjacent to 'modern' námestie Slobody and trieda SNP, the old town centre (around námestie SNP) is about 1km away on any westbound bus or trolleybus, plus a walk north on Kapitulská or Národná. A smaller regional train station, Banská Bystrica mesto, is across the river from the city centre.

Information

Tourist Office There is a very good tourist information centre (Informačné stredisko;

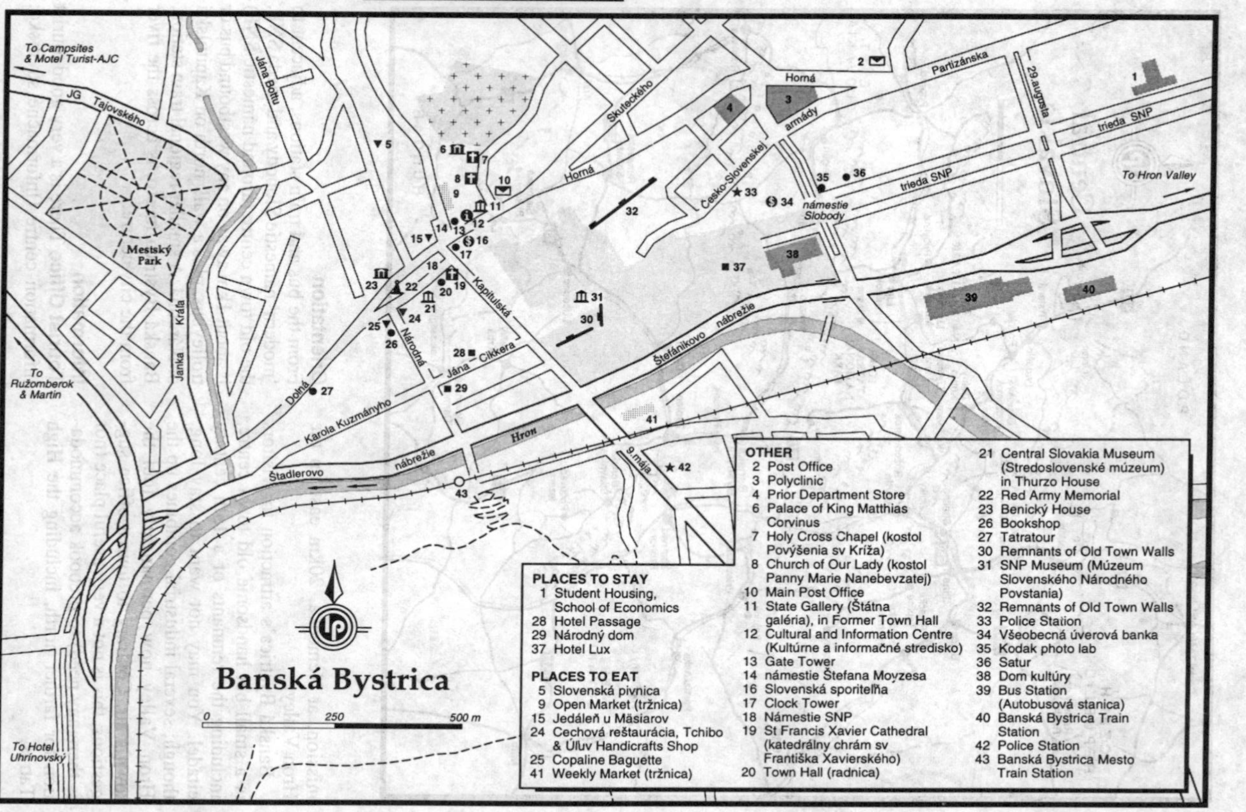
Banská Bystrica
0
250
500 m
PLACES TO STAY
1 Student Housing, School of Economics
28 Hotel Passage
29 Národný dom
37 Hotel Lux
PLACES TO EAT
5 Slovenská pivnica
9 Open Market (tržnica)
15 Jedáleň u Mäsiarov
24 Cechová reštaurácia, Tchibo & Úľuv Handicrafts Shop
25 Copaline Baguette
41 Weekly Market (tržnica)
OTHER
2 Post Office
3 Polyclinic
4 Prior Department Store
6 Palace of King Matthias Corvinus
7 Holy Cross Chapel (kostol Povýšenia sv Kríža)
8 Church of Our Lady (kostol Panny Marie Nanebevzatej)
10 Main Post Office
11 State Gallery (Štátna galéria), in Former Town Hall
12 Cultural and Information Centre (Kultúrne a informačné stredisko)
13 Gate Tower
14 námestie Štefana Moyzesa
16 Slovenská sporiteľňa
17 Clock Tower
18 Námestie SNP
19 St Francis Xavier Cathedral (katedrálny chrám sv Františka Xavierského)
20 Town Hall (radnica)
21 Central Slovakia Museum (Stredoslovenské múzeum) in Thurzo House
22 Red Army Memorial
23 Benický House
26 Bookshop
27 Tatratour
30 Remnants of Old Town Walls
31 SNP Museum (Múzeum Slovenského Národného Povstania)
32 Remnants of Old Town Walls
33 Police Station
34 Všeobecná úverová banka
35 Kodak photo lab
36 Satur
38 Dom kultúry
39 Bus Station (Autobusová stanica)
40 Banská Bystrica Train Station
42 Police Station
43 Banská Bystrica Mesto Train Station
To Hron Valley
To Campsites & Motel Turist-AJC
To Ružomberok & Martin
To Hotel Uhrínovský
Hron
Partizánska
29.augusta
trieda SNP
námestie Slobody
Horná
Skuteckého
Česko-Slovenskej armády
Kapitulská
Jána Cikkera
Národná
Dolná
Karola Kuzmányho nábrežie
Štadlerovo nábrežie
Štefánikovo nábrežie
9.mája
Jána Bottu
Tajovského
JG
Janka Kráľa
Mestský Park

☎ 543 69) at námestie Štefana Moyzesa 26, open weekdays from 9 am to 5 pm. Staff can book accommodation.

Money Change money at Slovenská sporiteľňa near námestie SNP, or Všeobecná úverová banka on námestie Slobody. Both have MasterCard/Visa ATMs.

Post & Communications The main post office is on námestie Štefana Moyzesa; there's another one near námestie Slobody on Horná. Banská Bystrica's area code is ☎ 088.

Travel Agencies The helpful office of Satur (☎ 74 25 75), námestie Slobody 4, is open weekdays from 9 am to 6 pm and Saturday to noon.

Emergency There are police stations across the river on 9.mája, and off námestie Slobody on Česko-Slovenskej armady, plus a polyclinic two blocks north of námestie Slobody.

Námestie SNP

This square lined with brightly painted burghers' houses was once the main market. Among its finest buildings are the **Benický House** on the north side, graced with frescoes and a Venetian-style loggia; **Thurzo House**, opposite at No 4, with sgraffito tracework and round upper windows (and home to the Central Slovakia Museum; see Museums & Galleries); and the **town hall**.

The 16th century **tower** at the east end has two clocks, one right and one wrong. Nearby is the Jesuits' 17th century **St Francis Xavier Cathedral** (katedrálny chrám sv Františka Xavierského). The stodgy black marble **obelisk** to the Red Army now seems wildly out of place, a glum outcast in a square full of cheerful post-1989 private enterprise.

Old Citadel

The sand-coloured buildings north-east of námestie SNP are the remains of the original citadel, a knot of Gothic and

SLOVAK REPUBLIC

RICHARD NEBESKÝ

Námestie SNP and the burgher's houses of Banská Bystrica

Renaissance churches and nobles' and merchants' houses, surrounded at the end of the 15th century with heavy stone walls. You enter the central square, námestie Štefana Moyzesa, past a gate tower and the 16th century former town hall, now a regional art gallery (see Museums & Galleries).

Banská Bystrica's showpiece and oldest building is the 13th century Romanesque (later Gothicised) parish **Church of Our Lady** (kostol Panny Márie Nanebevzatej). Inside, a side chapel dedicated around 1500 to St Barbara, patron saint of miners, boasts a fantastic Gothic carved altar by the master craftsman, Pavol of Levoča. The Baroque interior renovation followed a severe town fire in 1761.

Behind the church is the Gothic (late 15th century) **Holy Cross Chapel** (kostol Povýšenia sv Kríža), plus a small palace built for the Hungarian King Matthias Corvinus, three bastions, and bits of the original citadel walls.

North and south of the SNP Museum are further remnants of 16th century walls erected against the Turks.

Museums & Galleries

You will find the museums and the State Gallery at the following addresses:

Central Slovakia Museum (Stredoslovenské múzeum; ☎ 72 58 97), Thurzo House, námestie SNP 4: ethnographic displays; open daily, except Saturday, from 9 am to noon and 1 to 5 pm

SNP Museum (múzeum slovenského národného povstania; ☎ 232 59), Kapitulská 25: a serious subject approached in over-hyped Soviet style; a booklet with English translations of the captions, sold at the ticket window, helps with the otherwise unenlightening displays of posters, uniforms, weapons and occasionally gripping photos; the multimedia show is apparently switched on only for groups; open daily, except Monday, from 9 am to 6 pm

State Gallery (Štátna galéria; ☎ 72 48 64), former town hall, námestie Štefana Moyzesa 25: changing exhibitions of 20th century Slovak artists; open weekdays, except Monday, from 10 am to 6 pm, and weekends from 10 am to 5 pm

Places to Stay

The information centre can book accommodation. Satur has no hotel contracts, but the staff will give you good advice. It can also arrange private rooms for about 180 to 210 Sk per person (less for more people and/or longer stays). In summer ask both about student housing.

Camping *Autocamping Tajov* (☎ 973 20), just west of the centre on JG Tajovského, is open from mid-May through August. Take bus No 26, 31 or 33 on Štadlerovo nábrežie. A more basic but year-round *campsite* (☎ 972 55) is in the Kremnica Highlands about 10km west on the same road (No 578), beyond Tajov.

Hostels *Hotel Uhrínovský* (☎ 76 12 56), Podháj 57, has doubles for 500 Sk. Take trolleybus No 2 from Štadlerovo nábrežie to the ZVT stop (about 3.5km). The only food is at the plain *Tulipan* restaurant and beer hall by the trolleybus stop.

You might also have some luck on the weekends and during school holidays at student housing of the School of Economics on trieda SNP, 700m east of Satur.

Hotels The *Motel Turist – ATC* (☎ 355 90), at JG Tajovského 68, has beds for 400 Sk as well as a campsite. Take bus No 26, 31 or 33 on Štadlerovo nábrežie. At Národná 11, the *Národný dom* (☎ 72 37 37) has doubles with shower and WC for 600 Sk, including breakfast. Around the corner at Jána Cikkera 5 is the *Passage* (☎ 72 45 56), with singles/doubles for 430/600 Sk, or with shower for 470/680 Sk.

Top-of-the-line here is the boring *Hotel Lux* (☎ 74 41 41/7), námestie Slobody 2, where rooms with bath are 2045/2450 Sk.

Places to Eat

Námestie SNP has a few decent eateries. *Jedáleň u Mäsiarov*, at the north-east corner, has a cheap ground-floor restaurant. *Copaline Baguette* has fast-food type sandwiches, bread, sweets and savouries. Tasty local specialities under 160 Sk can be found at *Cechová reštaurácia* at No 6. Try the vážecká pochúťka, which is pork and smoked pork in a tomato sauce wrapped in a type of potato cake (haruli).

Slovenská pivnica (☎ 537 16), Lazovná 18, north off the square, gets high marks with Slovak specialities at low prices (meals 27 to 99 Sk without drinks) and a wide selection of beers. Try its various good halušky (pasta with cheese) and pirohy (savoury turnovers) too. It is open daily from 10 am to 10 pm.

For self-caterers, there's a small daily *tržnica* (open market) in námestie Štefana Moyzesa, and a big weekly one across the river from Kapitulská on Thursday afternoon and Sunday morning.

Things to Buy

The Úľuv shop, námestie SNP 7, has traditional handicrafts – clothes, wool rugs, wood, ceramics, embroidery – with an upmarket slant.

Getting There & Away

Buses run between Banská Bystrica and Bratislava every one to 1½ hours all day. Train connections from Bratislava are miserable (change at Zvolen), though there are some beautiful local lines west (to Martin) and east (up the Hron Valley towards Košice). To reach Nitra you must change trains at Zvolen and Šurany. Trains run to and from Prague twice a day.

BANSKÁ ŠTIAVNICA

Banská Štiavnica (population 10,500) began as a medieval mining centre, atop some of Europe's richest silver and gold mines in the Štiavnica Highlands (Štiavnické vrchy). Already a showcase town in the 13th century, in its heyday in the 18th century it became Hungary's second largest town.

But then the mines began to dry up, and the town slipped out of the mainstream; today it's less than half its former size. Having missed the 19th century boom that turned Banská Bystrica into a city, it's now an extraordinary mirror of earlier times, with a picturesque old centre full of Gothic and Renaissance houses, churches and two castles, set beautifully in steep, wooded hills.

In 1972 the town was added to the UNESCO World Heritage List. For the moment, slow restoration projects are not keeping up with the disintegration of many of the historical buildings; there are only a handful of visitors to be seen out of season – but it still makes an excellent day trip or overnight stay from Banská Bystrica.

Orientation

From the train and bus stations it's a 2km climb through the factories and housing blocks of the new town, to námestie sv Trojice in the old town. Only local buses and tour coaches stop in the old centre, at námestie Radničné. The hilly, snaky layout can make this a confusing place to find your way around.

Information

The Municipal Information Office (Mestská informačná kancelária; ☎ 218 59), námestie Radničné 1, is open daily from 8 am to 6 pm. It provides all kinds of information, including all the accommodation options in town. The Všeobecná úverová banka is on námestie Radničné (MasterCard ATM) and Slovenská sporiteľňa is at Andreja Kmeťa 7 (Visa ATM). The police are in Rubigallov dom at námestie sv Trojice 3. The post office is on Kammerhofska. Banská Štiavnica's area code is ☎ 0859.

Opening hours of all museums and galleries are Tuesday to Sunday from 8 am to 4 pm, except where mentioned otherwise. Most have the last tour starting an hour before closing, except the Mining Museum, which has a tour 1½ hours before closing. The entry fee is 20 Sk.

Námestie sv Trojice & Námestie Radničné

Námestie sv Trojice (Holy Trinity), the old town's main square, sports a grand **plague column** and is flanked with the old palaces

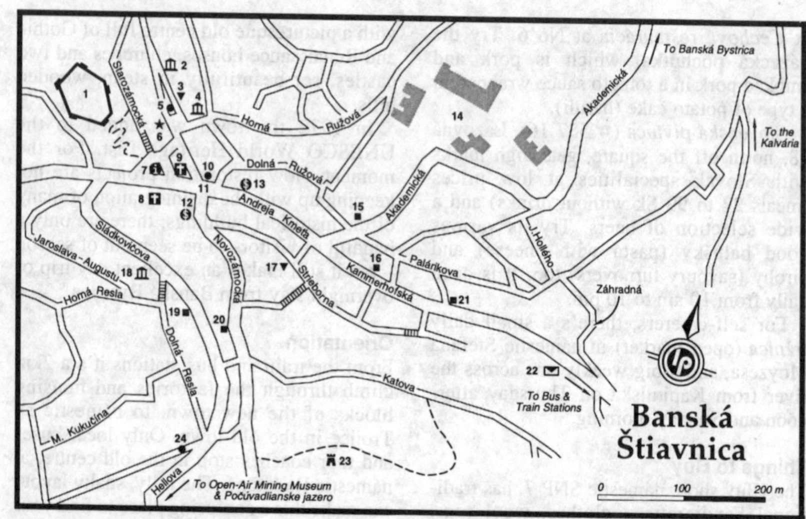

PLACES TO STAY

15 Penzión Matej
16 Hotel Grand
19 Penzión
20 Fond výtvarných umení
21 Hotel Salamander

PLACES TO EAT

3 Reštaurácia pod Galériou
17 Restaurant Paradais

OTHER

1 Old Castle
2 Galéria Jozefa Kollára
4 Geology Museum
5 Námestie sv Trojice
6 Police
7 Municipal Information Office & Town Hall
8 Evangelical Church
9 Church of St Catherine
10 Fritz House
11 Námestie SNP
12 Všeobecná úverová banka
13 Slovenská sporiteľňa
14 Academy of Mining & Forestry
18 'Clapper' House, with Museum of Mining Tools
22 Post Office
23 New Castle & Turkish museum
24 Piarg Gate

of German and Hungarian merchants and mine owners. Behind the bold sgraffito at No 12 is a modern art gallery, the **galéria Jozefa Kollára**. It has the most artistically decorated interior of any house in town. Several rooms have valuable Renaissance wood-cut ceilings and another room has a rich stucco decoration. The one hour tour takes the visitor through exhibits of Gothic to modern art, with the emphasis on local Slovak painter, J Kollár. A few doors down, the former Hungarian Mining Court is now a stuffy **geology museum** (mineralógie).

At the bottom of the square, opposite the bright-yellow Fritz House (Fritzov dom) with its mining motifs, the Gothic parish **Church of St Catherine** (kostol sv Kateríny) still has some original murals and statues among the Baroque furnishings. Behind this is the town hall, with a backwards clock, and across námestie Radničné a very decorated 18th century **Evangelical Church** (Evanjelický kostol).

From here you can explore the centre's back alleys, lined with old miners' houses.

Old Castle

Uphill from the town hall is Banská Štiavnica's ancient heart, the Old Castle (Starý zámok). Between 1546 and 1559 an older Romanesque church was walled in to protect the municipal riches from the Turks. It will reopen when restoration work is completed (which was scheduled to happen in late 1997).

New Castle & Around

Five years after the Old Castle was finished, the burghers evidently decided they needed another one. The strikingly simple New Castle (Nový zámok), a whitewashed block with four corner bastions, now houses a 'Museum of the History of the Struggle against the Turks on the Territory of Slovakia' offering fine views over the town.

On the way up Andreja Sládkoviča, you pass a 'clapper' house (*Klopačka*), once apparently a kind of municipal alarm clock, with a tiny **museum** (múzeum v Klopačke) of mining tools. Near the 18th century Piarg Gate (Piargska brána), a gate for the once-bigger town, and the Church of Our Lady of the Snows (kostol Panny Márie Snežnej), is a footpath to the New Castle.

Other Attractions

Europe's first **mining academy** was founded in Banská Štiavnica in the 1760s. Behind its grand complex above Akademická, now the Slovak Academy of Mining & Forestry, is a large public botanic garden.

The red-and-white hilltop **church,** visible from everywhere, is the topmost in a set of stations of the cross (in the form of Baroque chapels with carved biblical scenes) that make up the Calvary (Kalvária; 1751). The woody summit of the hill, about 1km from the city centre, offers the finest views of the town.

A good open-air **Mining Museum** (Banské múzeum v prírode), at a former old mine camp 1.25km south of the city centre, includes machinery, workshops and a wooden miners' church. Groups of 15 or more can go down into a mine. The museum is closed from December to April. The entry fee is 30 Sk.

Special Events

The annual three day festival of Salamander is on the Friday evening closest to the date of 12 September. According to the staff at the information office this is the best local festival and worth spending a weekend here. The origins of the festival go back to the 19th century when students at the mining academy held their various ceremonies (with some of the traditions going back centuries). Eventually the students combined their ceremonies into one large celebration of which the procession has become the main feature. Many of the townspeople dress up in miners' clothing and perform songs and dances. There are also various rides, food and fireworks.

Places to Stay

Beside Počúvadlianske jazero, one of several artificial lakes originally part of a water-pumping scheme for the mines, 5.5km south-west of the old town on the road to Levice, is a basic *campsite* (☎ 941 12), open in July and August only. It's only convenient by car.

There are inexpensive doubles at *Fond výtvarných umění* (☎ 219 45), Novozámocká 16, for 375 Sk. There is cheaper dormitory accommodation but it's available only at certain times of the year, so check with the information centre about these.

Sunny doubles and triples at *Penzión Matej* (☎ & fax 239 60), Akademická 4, are good value at 500 to 900 Sk, including breakfast served in your room. There are also penzións and private rooms (watch for *'Zimmer frei'* signs) at Kammerhofska 20 and up on Sládkoviča. Walk-in prospects are good at the *Hotel Grand* (☎ 237 82), Kammerhofska 8, where doubles/triples are 500/750 Sk without bath, and 750/1100 Sk with bath. The top-end hotel is the new *Salamander* (☎ 239 92), Palárikova 1, with rooms for 1050/1500 Sk.

Places to Eat

The food is good at *Penzión Matej's* terrace café. Nearby are the fancy-looking *Restaurant Paradais* on Strieborna, the restaurant at the *Hotel Grand*, and a *cukráreň* (patisserie) under the Hotel Salamander on Kammerhofska. The touristy *Reštaurácia pod Galériou* at námestie sv Trojice is OK.

Getting There & Away

There are five direct buses between Banská Štiavnica and Banská Bystrica. The fine, leisurely train ride is only recommended if you're staying the night, as it's two to three hours each way, with changes at Zvolen and Hronská Dubrava.

If you're driving, there's a separate Banská Štiavnica exit from the E571 Highway. To park around the old town you need to buy a parking card (5 Sk per hour), which is available from some hotels, shops or the Municipal Information Office, that can be used in designated spots only.

Malá Fatra & Veľká Fatra

While the High Tatras (Vysoké Tatry) are Slovakia's most dramatic mountains, the modest, forested ranges south-west of them – the Malá (Low) Fatra and Veľká (High) Fatra – are the most user-friendly highlands. They're accessible by road, trail and chair lift for anyone with an urge to walk or ski, or to ride up their tributary valleys (*doliny*) on a bicycle. Cheap chaty (mountain chalets) all over the place make long-distance walking a pleasure.

The historic town of Martin in the broad Turiec Valley (Turčianska kotlina) and Žilina to the north are both convenient bases for exploring.

The Malá Fatra are the more popular of the two mountain groups; despite their name, they also rise higher than the Veľká Fatra. A river, the Váh, and the Žilina-Martin highway slice the Malá Fatra into two parts – the rounded Lúčanská Fatra west of Martin and the craggy Krivánská Fatra to the north-east. Details about the Krivánská Fatra are provided in a separate section later in this chapter.

Most of the Krivánská Fatra is now the Lesser Fatra National Park (Národný park Malá Fatra), centred on the beautiful Vrátna Valley. Both ranges sport numerous protected landscape regions.

MARTIN

In 1861, Turiec St Martin (Turčianský Svätý Martin), a minor town in the broad Turiec Valley separating the Malá and Veľká Fatra ranges, was pushed into the history books when a meeting of intellectuals here issued the so-called *Martin Memorandum*, urging the establishment of a Slovak (and Slovak-language) district within Hungary.

This drew only silence from the authorities, but two years later a private cultural and educational foundation called Matica slovenská ('the kernel of Slovakia') was founded to promote Slovak-language schools, museums, musical societies, publishing etc. During subsequent years of heavy Hungarian cultural domination, Martin became the epicentre of simmering Slovak aspirations. On 30 October 1918 the *Martin Declaration*, in which the Slovaks formally opted to federate with the Czechs, was issued here. Though Bratislava became the capital of Slovakia, Martin remained its sentimental centre.

Except for an impressive ethnographic museum, two pretty-good art galleries and the tasty local beer, the Martin of today is not a very interesting town for tourism and is full of ugly prefabricated buildings. Far more appealing are the trails and rustic chalets in the surrounding mountains.

Orientation

Martin straddles the Turiec river just above its confluence with the Váh. Long-distance trains stop at Vrútky station, in a modern industrial suburb to the north; from there bus No 10 or 12 go the 8km south to námestie SNP, the centre of what there is of 'old' Martin. The train station in the centre of town is only for regional connections.

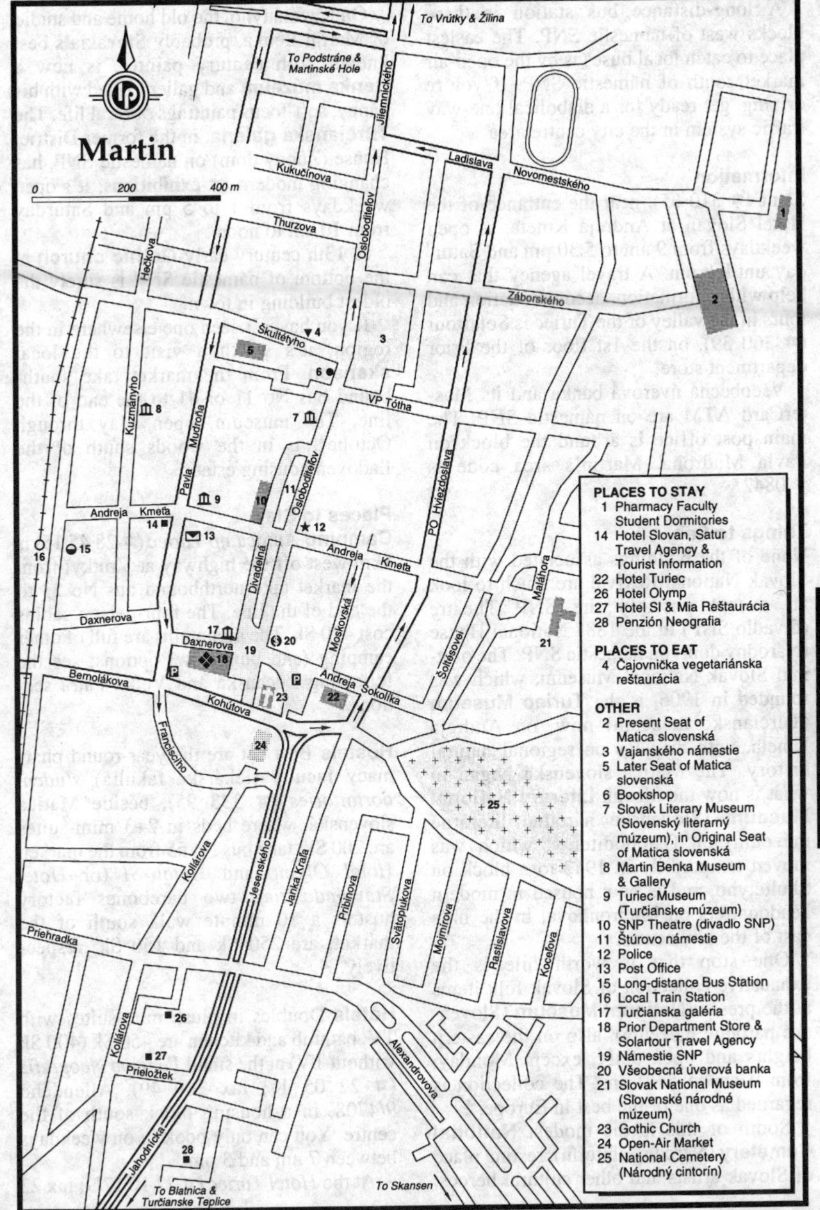
Martin
0
200
400 m
To Vrútky & Žilina
To Podstráne & Martinské Hole
Jilemnického
Ladislava
Novomestského
Kukučínova
Thurzova
Oslobodíteľov
Hečkova
Záborského
Škultétyho
VP Tótha
Kuzmányho
Pavla Mudroňa
P.O. Hviezdoslava
Andreja Kmeťa
Divadelná
Moskovská
Daxnerova
Bernolákova
Kohútova
Andreja Sokolíka
Šoltésovej
Maláhora
Francisciho
Kollárova
Jesenského
Janka Kráľa
Pribinova
Svätoplukova
Mojmírova
Rastislavova
Koceľova
Priehradka
Alexandrovova
Prieložtek
Jahodnícka
To Blatnica & Turčianske Teplice
To Skansen
PLACES TO STAY
1 Pharmacy Faculty Student Dormitories
14 Hotel Slovan, Satur Travel Agency & Tourist Information
22 Hotel Turiec
26 Hotel Olymp
27 Hotel SI & Mia Reštaurácia
28 Penzión Neografia
PLACES TO EAT
4 Čajovnička vegetariánska reštaurácia
OTHER
2 Present Seat of Matica slovenská
3 Vajanského námestie
5 Later Seat of Matica slovenská
6 Bookshop
7 Slovak Literary Museum (Slovenský literárny múzeum), in Original Seat of Matica slovenská
8 Martin Benka Museum & Gallery
9 Turiec Museum (Turčianske múzeum)
10 SNP Theatre (divadlo SNP)
11 Štúrovo námestie
12 Police
13 Post Office
15 Long-distance Bus Station
16 Local Train Station
17 Turčianska galéria
18 Prior Department Store & Solartour Travel Agency
19 Námestie SNP
20 Všeobecná úverová banka
21 Slovak National Museum (Slovenské národné múzeum)
23 Gothic Church
24 Open-Air Market
25 National Cemetery (Národný cintorín)

A long-distance bus station is three blocks west of námestie SNP. The easiest place to catch local buses is by the open-air market south of námestie SNP. If you're driving, get ready for a diabolical one-way traffic system in the city centre area.

Information

Satur (☎ 310 65), near the entrance of the Hotel Slovan at Andreja Kmeťa, is open weekdays from 9 am to 5.30 pm and Saturday until 1 pm. A travel agency that can help with information, accommodation and tours in the valley of the Turiec is Solartour (☎ 360 39), on the 1st floor of the Prior department store.

Všeobecná úverová banka and its MasterCard ATM are on námestie SNP. The main post office is around the block on Pavla Mudroňa. Martin's area code is ☎ 0842.

Things to See

None of the buildings associated with the Slovak National Revival are much to look at, except possibly the SNP Theatre (divadlo SNP) in the 1888 National House (Národný dom) on námestie SNP. The original Slovak National Museum, which was founded in 1906, is the **Turiec Museum** (Turčianske múzeum) now, on Andreja Kmeťa, with displays on regional natural history. The Matica slovenská began in what is now the Slovak **Literary National Museum** (Slovenské národné literarné múzeum) on Osloboditeľov, which was moved temporarily in 1943 to a block on Škultétyho, and is now housed in modern headquarters on Mudronňova, in the hills east of the city centre.

One stop that is worthwhile is the exhaustive collection of Slovak folk items at the present **National Museum** (Slovenské národné múzeum), also on the eastern heights and open daily, except Monday, from 9 am to 5.30 pm. The collection is regarded as one of the best in Europe.

South of this is the modest **National Cemetery** (Národný cintorín), resting place of Slovak artists and other cultural heroes.

On Kuzmányho, the old home and studio of Martin Benka, probably Slovakia's best known 20th century painter, is now a **Benka múzeum** and gallery filled with his happy, soft-focus paintings of rural life. The **Turčianska galéria**, in the former District House (Župný dom) on námestie SNP, has changing modern art exhibitions; it's open weekdays from 1 to 5 pm and Saturday from 10 am to noon.

A 13th century early-**Gothic church** at the bottom of námestie SNP is surely the oldest building in town.

If you haven't seen one elsewhere in the region, it's worth a visit to the local **skansen**. From the market take southbound bus No 11 or 41 to the end of the line. The museum, open May through October, is in the woods south of the Ľadoveň housing estate.

Places to Stay

Camping *Autocamp Turiec* (☎ 28 45 15) is 1km west off the highway at Vrútky; from the market take northbound bus No 23 to the end of the line. The four-person cabins cost 470 Sk. The mountains are full of other camping (and bungalow) options; see the following Lúčanská and Veľká Fatra sections.

Hostels Best bet are the year-round pharmacy faculty (lekárska fakulta) *student dormitories* (☎ 333 95), beside Matica slovenská, where beds in 2+3 mini-suites are 200 Sk; take bus No 55 from the market. *Hotel Olymp* and *Hotel SI* (or *Hotel Stavoindustria),* two barebones factory hostels a 10 minute walk south of the market, are 250 Sk and 150 Sk, respectively.

Hotels Doubles in plush mini-suites with TV, bathtub and kitchen are 450 Sk (400 Sk without TV) at the small *Penzión Neografia* (☎ 22 05 17; fax 349 49), Allendého 9/4708, in a housing block south of the centre. You can only book in on weekdays between 7 am and 3 pm.

At the *Hotel Turiec* (☎ 22 10 17/9; fax 22

05 18), Andreja Sokolíka 2, barren singles/doubles with shower and WC are grossly overpriced from 710/1310 Sk – three times the price for Slovaks. Almost as bad a deal is *Hotel Slovan* (☎ 355 32), on the corner of Vajanského and Andreja Kmeťa, at 800/1100/1400 Sk, including breakfast.

Places to Eat

The Martiner brewery makes a good pale beer and a strong, sweetish porter, but there aren't many appealing places to enjoy them. *Čajovnička vegetariánska reštaurácia* (The Tearoom Vegetarian Restaurant), on the 1st floor at Škultétyho 4, has vegetarian dishes and exotic teas. The uninspiring restaurant at *Hotel Turiec* has good service and an English-language menu (with some macrobiotic dishes) at reasonable prices. By Hotel Olymp and Hotel SI is the plain *Mia reštaurácia.* Fresh produce is available at the small market south of námestie SNP.

Getting There & Away

Many Bratislava-Košice and Prague-Košice express trains stop at Vrútky, about 20 minutes east of Žilina. There are two direct express Prague trains and one Bratislava one that pass through Martin. Local trains go south to Zvolen and Banská Bystrica. There are half a dozen daily direct bus connections to Martin from Bratislava, and hourly ones that connect with Žilina.

LÚČANSKÁ FATRA

The western, non-national park half of the Malá Fatra range gets its name from its dominant peak, Veľká lúka (1476m).

Podstráne & Martinské Hole

Podstráne is a complex of ski chalets and holiday homes west of Martin. From there a year-round chair lift (*lánovka*) climbs to the Martinské hole (Martin Pinnacles) ski area on the slopes of Veľká luka, or you can walk it, a half-day climb up the snaky yellow-marked trail.

Podstráne's big *Horský hotel* (☎ 389 18), 300m beyond the bus stop, has space in summer at 150 Sk per bed, and bungalows at 130 to 150 Sk per bed; half-board is 150 Sk more. Beyond it is the *Hotel Grandis*, and private rooms are available along the road below. There's a mountain chalet, the *Chata na Martinských*, at the top of the chair lift.

To get to Podstráne, take northbound bus No 41 from the centre of Martin, about 4km to the end of the line. The chair lift is 800m from the bus.

Minčol

From the campsite, Autocamp Turiec, west of Vrútky (see Places to Stay in the Martin section) there is also a track to Martinské hole, or you can walk the blue-marked trail up to the 1364m Minčol peak in a couple of hours.

Strečno Castle & Starý Hrad

In summer there are fine hikes on the red-marked trail along the Lúčanská Fatra ridge. About 11km north from Martinské hole on this trail, perched above the Váh gorge, is **Strečno Castle**, built according to some sources by the 14th century warlord Matúš Čák (for more information see the Trenčín section in the West Slovakia chapter). According to local sources it should be opening soon.

Nearby is a bright white memorial to French partisans who died in the Slovak National Uprising. East via a bridge over the Váh, 2.5km away on another ridge, are the brooding 13th century ruins of **Starý** (or Varín) **Hrad**, accessible only on foot.

There's a *campsite* about 4km north at Varín, and there are mountain chalets eastward in the Kriváňská Fatra (see the Kriváňská Fatra section).

Strečno Castle is 500m above the Žilina-Martin road (and a whistlestop on the railway line). Some buses run to Strečno village from Martin and Žilina.

VEĽKÁ FATRA

Numerous valleys (*doliny*) with marked trails drop from the Veľká Fatra ridge line into the river valley south of Martin. Campsites and chaty make for some fairly straightforward overnight trips from Martin; two better known ones are noted here. Serious walkers may want to push up to the red-marked ridge trail.

From Necpaly village, south-east of Martin, it's 13km up the valley of the Necpalsoka to a primitive year-round *chalet* on the peak of Borišov (1510m). An option is to return down the valley of the Belianska to Belá village. Both villages are linked by bus to Martin.

Long and short loop-trails start at the picturesque village of Blatnica, farther south in the valley of the Turiec. A fine long day or overnight trip follows the Gaderská to a *chalet* at the foot of the 1574m Krížna peak, with an option to return down the valley of the Blatnicka past a 13th century castle. The ridges between these two valleys are covered by several nature reserves. Another *chalet*, and a *campsite*, are near Blatnica.

ŽILINA

Žilina (population 86,700) grew around a fortress at the intersection of several impor-

tant trade routes and a ford on the Váh river, on the site of a 6th century Slav settlement. An influential compendium of principles on civic rights and obligations, written here in 1370, may be the oldest existing text in the Slovak language.

Žilina was occupied by the Hussites between 1429-34 and, after being ravaged by the Thirty Years' War, faded away until the railway brought industrialisation in the late 19th century. Today it's one of Slovakia's most important transport junctions.

For tourists it serves mainly as a base for exploring the Malá Fatra, but it's also an upbeat and attractive place in its own right. With an old castle, and a square with cafés spilling out beneath pastel-tinted Renaissance and Baroque façades, it feels like a pocket Prague.

Orientation

From the train and bus stations on Hviezdoslavova, the shopping district of Národná leads into the old market square, Hlinkovo námestie (or námestie A Hlinku). Narrow Farská climbs from here into the old town, centred on Mariánské námestie. Southward, Štúrovo námestie has a concentration of government buildings and tourist offices.

Information

Tourist Offices Satur (☎ 485 11/3), on Štúrovo námestie, has a good accommodation department, and is open weekdays from 9 am to 6 pm and Saturday from 9 am to noon. Tatratour (☎ 62 00 71/2), Mariánské námestie 21, can also help with accommodation. Local bookshops carry only a few regional hiking maps.

Money Všeobecná úverová banka is at Na bráne 1. Slovenská sporiteľňa and its Visa ATM are on Štúrovo námestie.

Post & Communications The main post and telephone office (which is open weekdays from 7 am to 8.30 pm, Saturday from 7 am to 2.30 pm, and Sunday from 8 am to 1 pm) is on Sládkovičova, and another is on Hviezdoslavova. Žilina's area code is ☎ 089.

Emergency There is a police station on Kuzmányho.

Old Town

Comely **Mariánské námestie** is completely surrounded by arcaded burghers' houses, intruded upon by the Jesuits' big 1743 Baroque **St Paul's Church** (kostol sv

PLACES TO STAY

1 Hotel Slovan
2 Hotel Polom
5 Hotel Astoria
11 Penzión Majovej
19 Pension GMK Centrum
32 Hotel Slovakia & Slovakoturist Travel Agency

PLACES TO EAT

4 Gastro
9 Hamburger
14 Arkádia café-pivnice
23 Open-air Market
26 China reštaurácia
27 Reštaurácia & vináreň na bráne
33 Zlatý drak (Chinese) Restaurant
35 Slovenská jedáleň

OTHER

3 Train Station
6 Tesco Department Store
7 Church of St Barbara (kostol sv Barbory)
8 Main Post & Telephone Office
10 Hlinkovo námestie
12 Bus Station
13 Považská Galéria & Atelier Café-Restaurant
15 Bookshop
16 Church of the Holy Trinity (kostol Najsvätejšie Trojice)
17 Burian Tower (Burianova veža)
18 Municipal Theatre
20 Mariánské námestie
21 Tatratour Travel Agency
22 St Paul's Church (kostol sv Pavla), & Považská Galéria in Former Monastery
24 Police Station
25 Bookshop
28 Photo Shop
29 Všeobecná úverová banka
30 Satur & Slovenská sporiteľňa
31 Štúrovo námestie
34 Bookshop

Pavla). In the church's former monastery (at No 23) is a branch of the regional **Považská galéria**, open daily, except Monday, from 9 am to 5 pm (weekends from 10 am). The fountain and several open-air cafés make this a fine place to pause over beer and sausages. The square had its renovation almost complete when we were there.

Once lined with stylish Baroque houses, the lanes called Upper Wall (Horný val) and Lower Wall (Dolný val) ran round the inside of the original town walls. Where the eastern walls once stood, the old parish **Church of the Holy Trinity** (kostol Najsvätejšie Trojice; about 1400) and a Renaissance belfry, the Burian Tower (Burianova veža; 1530), now loom over **Hlinkovo námestie** from atop an overweight marble staircase erected (along with the matching Municipal Theatre) in 1943.

Hlinkovo námestie, the wide former market square, has on the south side at Štefánikova 2 another branch of the Považská galéria. North of the square is the Franciscans' boring Baroque monastery **Church of St Barbara** (kostol sv Barbory).

St Stephen Church

Don't miss this gem, Žilina's oldest building and one of the earliest Romanesque churches in Slovakia. The most ancient bits, and some frescoes rediscovered in the 1950s, date from around 1250. It's 1.25km from the city centre, south-west down Hálkova and across the railway.

Budatín Castle

North across the Váh, above its confluence with the Kysuca, Budatín Castle (Budatín zámok) dates from at least the 13th century (when its Romanesque central tower was built). The Renaissance chateau was part of a face-lift in 1551, with fortifications added in the 17th century. The whole thing was restored in the 1920s.

It now houses the regional **Považské múzeum** (☎ 62 03 06), with an unusual tinkers' trade exhibition featuring 'naïve art' figures of metal and wire, as well as displays on period furniture, church art and early history. It's open daily, except Monday, from 8 am to 4 pm. Take bus No 24 from the bus station; otherwise it's a 20 minute walk from Hviezdoslavova.

SLOVAK REPUBLIC

RICHARD NEBESKÝ

Dating from the 13th century, Budatín Castle now houses an interesting regional museum

Places to Stay

Tatratour can help with places in all price ranges, while Satur can also assist with some accommodation options; see Information for their addresses.

Camping The nearest *campsites* are at Varín (see the Vrátna Valley section later), and near Rajecké Teplice and at Súľovské skaly (see the following Around Žilina section).

Hostels A bottom-end bargain is the *ubytovňa* at Nemocnica Slobodáreň (☎ 687 06 71), Na Hlinách; take bus No 3 from the bus station. The basic rooms with shared facilities cost 160 Sk per person.

Hotels One of the cheapest and most central is *Pension GMK Centrum* (☎ 62 21 36) at Mariánské námestie 3, with single/double rooms from 650/800 Sk that include shower, WC and TV. *Penzión Majovey* (☎ 62 41 52; fax 62 52 39), Jána Milca 3, has new modern rooms from 700/900 Sk, including breakfast. At Hviezdoslavova 22 is the *Hotel Polom* (☎ 62 11 52), which has a high-profile casino and rooms with shower and WC for 800/1300 Sk, including breakfast. Doubles with shower and WC are 1180 Sk with breakfast at *Hotel Slovan* (☎ 62 05 56; fax 62 23 09), on Kálov just off Hlinkovo námestie.

Top of the line is the fading *Hotel Slovakia* (☎ 64 56 71/5; fax 479 75) on Štúrovo námestie, where rooms are 1270/1860 Sk and, for an extra 140 Sk per person, breakfast is included; there's a 25% discount on weekends. The classiest hotel is the *Astoria* (☎ 62 31 73), Národná 1, where new rooms cost 1100/2200 Sk, including breakfast.

Places to Eat

Slovenská jedáleň (☎ 333 68), Bernolákova 2202, serves traditional Slovak meals and good bread, with a bit too much oompah muzak, weekdays from 9 am to 10 pm, Saturday from 11 am to 8 pm (Sunday from noon). It also does breakfast.

Off Mariánské námestie at Štúrova námestie 7, the *China reštaurácia* does fair imitations of Chinese food, but is pricey at 80 to 285 Sk per dish. Another Chinese place is *Zlatý drak* on Bernolákova.

Reštaurácia & vináreň na bráne, Bottova 10, has a cheap downstairs place (open from 8.30 am to 10 pm, Saturday from 9 am) and an upstairs vináreň that smells of ashtrays but has filling Slovak meals at reasonable prices (open weekdays from 10 am to 11 pm, Saturday from 4 to 11 pm).

Just off Mariánské námestie, on the corner of Farská and Hodžova, is a trendy *Arkádia café-pivnice* for coffee, cakes and drinks. In a corner of the Považská galéria on Hlinkovo námestie is the trendy *Atelier Café-Restaurant*. The square also has a few fast-food eateries, such as the *Hamburger* at No 5, where you can try the local version of that American staple. Or try *Gastro*, Jána Milca 1, on the corner of Národná, it's a good place for large sandwiches and inexpensive buffet food.

There is a small open-air *market* on Kuzmányho.

Getting There & Away

Long-distance travel is easiest by train, with 19 daily fast or express connections to Bratislava (2½ hours) and Prague (six hours), over 20 to Poprad (two hours) and Košice (3¼ hours), plus daily trains to Warsaw. Buses are quicker and more frequent to regional destinations. *Informatorium*, a useful booklet available from Satur, includes regional and long-distance train and bus timetables.

SLOVAK REPUBLIC

AROUND ŽILINA

Súľov Highlands

The Súľov Highlands (Súľovské Vrchy) south-west of Žilina offer some modest hiking, handy campsites and several old castles. A good out-of-town base is a beautifully situated *campsite* near a cluster of limestone pinnacles called the **Slnečné skaly**. It lies just beyond Porúbka village, 10km south of Žilina.

From here you can take a short walk north on a green-marked trail to the ruins of

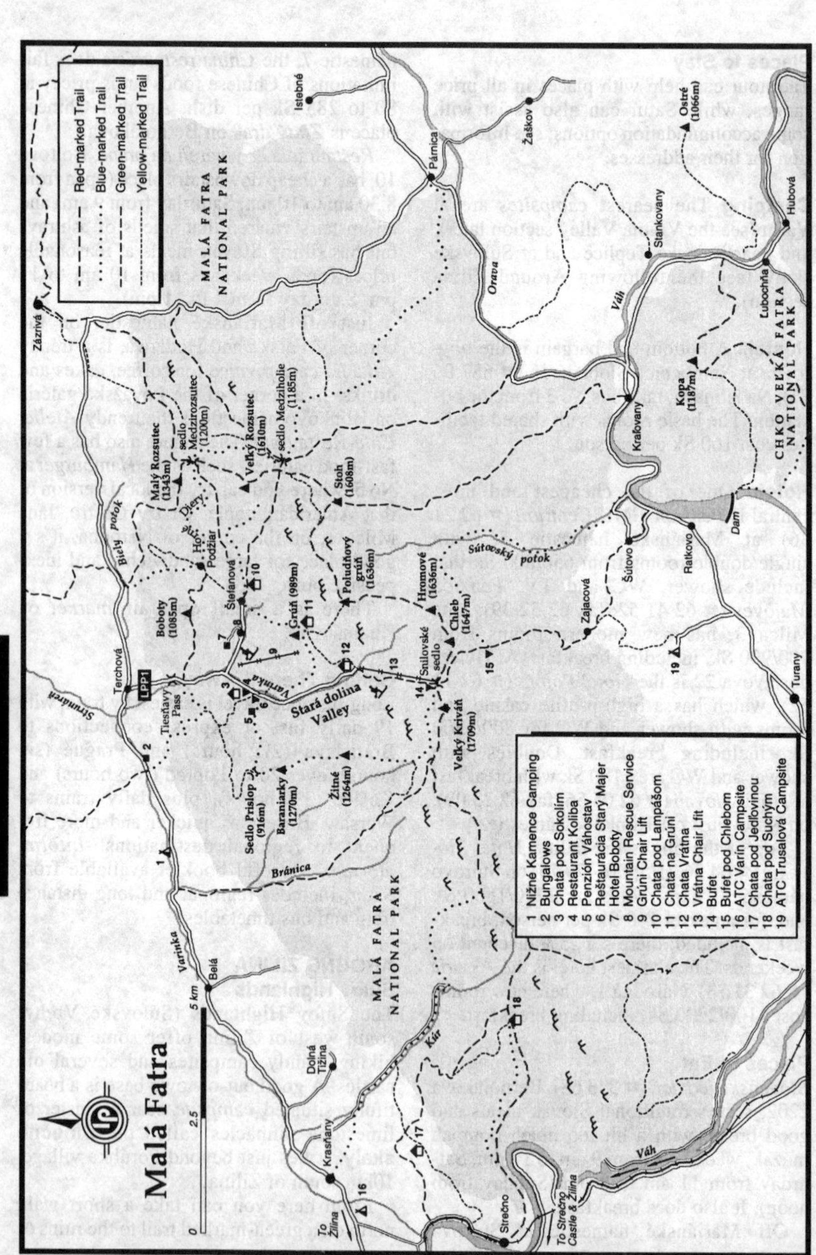
Malá Fatra
0
2.5
5 km
Red-marked Trail
Blue-marked Trail
Green-marked Trail
Yellow-marked Trail
MALÁ FATRA NATIONAL PARK
CHKO VEĽKÁ FATRA NATIONAL PARK
1 Nižné Kamence Camping
2 Bungalows
3 Chata pod Sokolím
4 Restaurant Koliba
5 Penzión Váhostav
6 Reštaurácia Starý Majer
7 Hotel Boboty
8 Mountain Rescue Service
9 Grúni Chair Lift
10 Chata pod Lampášom
11 Chata na Grúni
12 Chata Vrátna
13 Vrátna Chair Lift
14 Bufet
15 Bufet pod Chlebom
16 ATC Varín Campsite
17 Chata pod Jedľovinou
18 Chata pod Suchým
19 ATC Trusalová Campsite
Stará dolina Valley
Tiesňavy Pass
Terchová
Zázrivá
Párnica
Istebné
Žaškov
Stankovany
Kraľovany
Šútovo
Ratkovo
Turany
Hubová
Ľubochňa
Zajacová
Strečno
Krasňany
Dolná Tižina
Belá
Štefanová
Horné Diery
Podžiar
Veľký Rozsutec (1610m)
Malý Rozsutec (1343m)
sedlo Medzirozsutec (1200m)
sedlo Medziholie (1185m)
Stoh (1608m)
Poludňový grúň (1636m)
Grúň (989m)
Boboty (1085m)
Hromové (1636m)
Chleb (1647m)
Snilovské sedlo
Veľký Kriváň (1709m)
Sedlo Prislop (916m)
Baraniarky (1270m)
Žitné (1264m)
Kopa (1187m)
Ostré (1066m)
Váh
Orava
Varínka
Bránica
Kúr
Biely potok
Šútovský potok
Dam
To Žilina
To Strečno Castle & Žilina

Lietavský hrad, above the hamlet of Lietavská Svinná in the next valley, or head south 2km on the green trail to a public thermal pool in the boring spa town of Rajecké Teplice.

Or take a half-day walk west over the Súľov Highlands to some even weirder rocks at Súľovské skaly. Within this protected landscape region is a 15th century castle, **Súľovský hrad**, reduced to ruins by an earthquake in 1763.

Places to Stay In addition to the summer-only campsite *ATC Slnečné skaly* (☎ 0823-49 34 04) in Slnečné skaly, Súľov village has a basic one. The campsite at Slnečné skaly has a snack bar and showers.

Getting There & Away You can get off frequent Rajec-bound buses at Lietavská Lúčka (2.5km east of Lietavský hrad), Slnečné skaly campsite, or Rajecké Teplice. Every few hours, Lietavská Svinná and Babkov buses go right up the valley.

It's a bit harder on the west side. Several buses an hour go from Žilina to Bytča, with a change for Súľov. Drivers can take the E50/E75 road 18km west to the Súľov-Hradná turn-off, then it's 5km to Súľov village.

Rajecká Lesná

If you enjoy moving models of the nativity then stop here on your way to Čičmany. Next to the church and the nearby bus stop is **Slovenský betlehem,** which is a new creation with many moving figures, all carved out of wood, doing their daily chores. The Čičmany and Prievidza-bound buses stop here.

Čičmany

This village up the snug Rajčanka Valley south of Žilina is known for a 200-year-old custom of painting its wooden cottages in patterns based on local archaic embroidery motives. It is now a kind of live-in museum of traditional artistry.

A branch of the regional Považské múzeum in one house features old furnishings and another local speciality, embroidered snow-white folk dresses (which you'll still see on a few older women), along with a low-pressure pitch to buy the local handiwork. Across the road is a reconstructed two-family house. Both are open daily, except Monday, from 8 am to 4 pm.

Places to Stay If you feel like hanging around, there is a choice of several pensions like *Katka* (☎ 0823-921 32), near the museum, where a bed with all meals included is 400 Sk. The more expensive *Hotel Kaštieľ* (☎ 0823-921 97 or 921 19) has a jolly pub and a few plain doubles with shower for about 1100 Sk. You may be able to pitch a tent in a field south-west of the village; ask at the adjacent house.

Getting There & Away A few direct buses leave Žilina by mid-afternoon – three on weekdays, two on Saturday and one on Sunday; or get off any southbound bus (such as to Prievidza) at the Čičmany turn-off after Fačkov and walk or hitch the 7km. For drivers, the turn-off is 33km south of Žilina.

KRIVÁNSKÁ FATRA

The Krivánská Fatra are the eastern half of the Malá Fatra range, so-called after its tallest peak, Veľký Kriváň (1709m). Within this region is the beautiful Vrátna Valley.

Terchová

Terchová, which stands at the mouth of the Vrátna Valley, was the birthplace of one of Slovakia's favourite folk heroes, Juraj Jánošík, in 1688.

After his father was beaten to death by their landlord for taking time off to bury his mother, Jánošík became a kind of Slovak Robin Hood, robbing rich landowners and handing the proceeds to the poor. He was 25 years old when he was captured. He died an excruciating death, being hung up by the ribs in the main square at Liptovský Mikuláš.

Above the village is an immense aluminium statue of the man, and west of the village bus stop next to the town hall (Obecný úrad) is a little museum (Expozícia Jánošík) about him. The Slovakotour office (☎ 089-69 52 22), inside the town hall, can help with accommodation and other information.

Places to Stay *Nižné Kamence camping* (☎ 089-69 51 51) is opposite the Branica turn-off, 3.5km west of Terchová. There are bungalows by the petrol station closer in. The *Hotel Diery* (☎ 089-69 53 22) is about 1km east of the valley turn-off beyond Terchová, in Biely Potok, with a café and doubles/triples with bath for 1000/1220 Sk.

Vrátna Valley

In 1987 a central area of the Krivánská became the 198 sq km Lesser Fatra National Park (Národný park Malá Fatra), largely to protect the Vrátna Valley (Vrátna dolina). This is a thickly forested cul-de-sac that many say is Slovakia's most beautiful valley. It's certainly one of the republic's most accessible mountain regions, with dramatic scenery, bracing hikes, and plenty of summer accommodation along the trails.

Naturally it's overrun with visitors in the high summer and winter seasons, though it can be almost empty in May or September. You can visit it on a long day trip from Žilina, but you're likely to want to linger.

Orientation & Information The valley turn-off is at Terchová, 25km from Žilina, though the real gateway is a slot through teeth-like limestone crags called Tiesňavy Pass. About 2.5km from Terchová, at Zlatý dvor, the road branches – left to the hamlet of Štefanová and right to the head of the valley at Chata Vrátna.

About 1km up the Štefanová road is a turn-off to the Mountain Rescue Service (Horská služba; ☎ 69 52 32), the best source of valley weather and trail information, and to the Hotel Boboty.

On the Chata Vrátna road, it's 1.5km to a bus stop and a side road by the Reštaurácia Starý Majer, and 2.5km more to Chata Vrátna and the chair lift to Veľký Kriváň.

The regional area code is ☎ 089.

Walking the Krivánská Fatra From near Chata Vrátna a year-round chair lift goes to Snilovské sedlo (Snilov Saddle), between Veľký Kriváň and the 1647m Chleb (purists can walk this in two hours on a green-marked trail), from where it's a half-hour climb to either summit. If you're on a day trip, from the chair lift you could walk west on a blue-marked trail and down a side ridge to Reštaurácia Starý Majer (and buses back to Žilina), which is a three hour loop. Take extra layers against the cold wind that howls there even in summer.

For those with more time there are fine, uncrowded hikes all along the 43km, red-marked Hlávný hrebeň (Capital Ridge) trail that stretches the length of the range. In fact you could do it all, from Strečno in the west to Zázrivá village in the east, in three days – the first night could be at Chata pod Suchým, the second at Chata Vrátna or Chata na Grúni in the valley (via the chair lift), and the third in a private home or chata at Zázrivá.

From Snilovské sedlo it's three to four hours down the other side of the range. At Bufet pod Chlebom, on the south face of Chleb, a blue trail branches left (as you face south) via waterfalls to Šútovo village (and a train or bus west to Martin), while a green one branches right to Zajacová with a yellow trail on to Trusalova campsite, 2km from the road to Martin.

Perhaps the most beautiful, but demanding, approach to the mountains is from Štefanová (at about 620m), via the lush Diery gorges to the 1343m Malý Rozsutec and stupendous views from the 1610m Veľký Rozsutec. A sample route, taking six to seven hours, is up the green-marked trail to sedlo Medziholie and the steep red track over Veľký Rozsutec (or the easier blue one behind it) to sedlo Medzirozsutec, then down the blue trail through Horné Diery to Podžiar, and the yellow one back to Štefanová.

For anything more than a day hike, check with Mountain Rescue on weather and trail conditions and chata availability. Carry your own water and some food, even if you have a firm chata booking with meals.

Places to Stay There's a wide selection of accommodation to choose from around the valley.

Campsites The good *ATC Varín* campsite (☎ 69 24 10), 15km east of Žilina on the Terchová road, has bungalows, log cabins, bike rental and a kids' pool. It's open May through September. Closer to Strečno and the park boundary is *Chata pod Jedľovinou*, open at least in summer.

Near Šútovo on the south side of the mountains, about 12km east of Martin and 2km off the highway, is the *ATC Trusalová* campsite.

Mountain Chalets A good chata in the valley but away from the road is *Chata na Grúni* (☎ 69 53 24), a 45 minute walk north-east from Chata Vrátna on a yellow-marked trail, or near the top of a year-round chair lift from the Štefanová road. Recommended on the Capital Ridge trail is the 40 bed *Chata pod Suchým* (☎ 69 73 94), at the western end of the park.

Hostels & Hotels The best deal in the valley is *Chata Vrátna* (☎ 69 52 23), with hostel rooms at 140 Sk per bed, hotel-quality two, three and four-bed rooms with shared facilities for 480/590/680 Sk, and pricey suites. Half-board is 140 Sk more. Summer walk-in prospects are good, but call ahead if possible.

The comfortable *Hotel Boboty* (☎ 69 52 27), up the hill behind the office of Mountain Rescue, has a pool, sauna and doubles with shower but shared WC for 1300 Sk, with breakfast. Štefanová has several private *penzióny*.

Off the Reštaurácia Starý Majer intersection is *Chata pod Sokolím* (☎ 69 53 26) with beds for 456 Sk. Farther up, *Penzión Váhostav* (☎ 69 53 06) has doubles with WC, shower and balconies with a huge view of the valley, for about 600 Sk.

Places to Eat The hotels and bigger chaty have restaurants, and some chaty do meals by arrangement. There is a restaurant and some *buffets* in Štefanová, and there is also the touristy *Reštaurácia Starý Majer* or *Restaurant Koliba* at the turn-off and bus stop 2.5km below the Chata Vrátna.

There is an overpriced *bufet* at the top of the chair lift, and the *Bufet Pod Chlebom* in a former chalet just over the saddle, though the latter keeps unpredictable hours.

Getting There & Away Buses go from Žilina every hour all day, stopping at Terchová, but only about every two hours (only five a day in July and August) into the valley, stopping at Štefanová, Zlatý dvor and Chata Vrátna.

BOJNICE

Bojnice Castle stands out majestically above a wide valley. It is like something straight out of a fairy tale, which should be the first clue it is not the original Gothic version from the 12th century but an early 20th century reconstruction that was modelled on French romantic castles. It belonged to the Pálffy family from 1643 to 1945, when the state took it over. Nevertheless, there are a few remains of the original Gothic and Renaissance sections of the castle incorporated into the present structure.

Orientation

The nearest train and bus stations are 2.5km away in the town of Prievidza. There are municipal buses that regularly depart for Hurbanovo námestie, just below the castle, in Bojnice.

Information

The tourist information centre (☎ 231 35) is in Prievidza at námestie Slobody 14, and is a 500m walk south-east of the stations along A Hlinku. The staff there can give all kinds of good information including suggesting places to stay. In Bojnice the Všeobecná úverová banka, its MasterCard ATM and the post office are on Hurbanovo námestie. Prievidza's and Bojnice's area code is ☎ 0862.

The Castle

Bojnice Castle has the usual exhibits of furniture, paintings, statues, weapons, glass and porcelain in lavishly decorated rooms. There is even a cave underneath it with a well that used to be the castle's only source of water during sieges. This is the most visited castle in Slovakia and the lines do get very long on weekends and holidays, so get there early. You can visit daily, except Monday, between May and September from 8 am to 5 pm (October to April from 9 am to 4 pm); entry costs 40 Sk. The rumours of ghosts are kept alive for a couple of weeks in late April and early May when ghost tours are part of the International Festival of Spirits and Ghosts (entry costs 100 Sk). In the evening there is a light show of the castle's history.

Places to Stay & Eat

The *autocamping* (☎ 338 45) is behind the castle; go along the road to Nitrianske rudno, which takes you past the swimming pool. It's open from May to September.

There are a few priváty and penzióny around Bojnice. The nearest to the castle is *Penzión u Filipa* (☎ & fax 43 03 03) at Sládkovičova 15, with doubles for 700 Sk, including shower, WC and TV. The only hotel is *Hotel Régia* (☎ 43 09 91; fax 43 09 00), on top of a hill south of the castle. It is a typical three-star prefabricated place with not-so-clean singles/doubles for 600/1000 Sk. They both have fairly decent restaurants. There are several eateries on Hurbanovo námestie, including the *Hostinec pod zámkom* at No 25, with meaty main courses for less than 100 Sk.

Getting There & Away

The easiest way to get to Prievidza is by bus. There are five daily buses to Žilina (1½ hours), six to Banská Bystrica (1½ hours) and five to Bratislava (3½ hours). The No 3 bus takes you to the castle from the stations.

Orava Valley

The Orava river rises in Poland, twists down through the highlands west of the High Tatras and eventually flows into the Váh east of Martin.

Hardship and isolation have given the Orava Valley a personality of its own. It suffered an iron feudal grip, Habsburg punishment for Protestant sympathies, crop failure and forced relocation in the early 18th century, and the flooding of the upper basin (and five villages) by the Orava Dam in 1954. Unregulated postwar industrialisation has also blighted great stretches of the lower and upper valley with factories and filthy air.

But the villages from Oravský Podzámok up to Nižná are scenic and relatively unspoilt, with ranks of traditional log house-barns, some with carved fronts, brightly painted and with colourful gardens. Other highlights include one of Slovakia's most photogenic castles, a first-rate skansen, and a hiker's back door into the High Tatras via the Orava's tributary valleys. On holidays and in summer Slovaks flock to Orava Lake.

Trains steam up the valley every hour or two, along with plenty of buses, but bus travel up the side valleys can be tedious. About 6km north of Trstená on Highway 59 is a border crossing to Chyzne in Poland, on the road to Kraków.

DOLNÝ KUBÍN

The only reason to visit the valley's administrative headquarters is for transport connections, accommodation and road and hiking maps, which you may not be able to find up-valley.

Orientation & Information

On Radlinského, about 700m south of the bus and train stations, are Satur (☎ 86 49 17) on the 1st floor at No 29, and Všeobecná úverová banka. A hundred metres farther south is the information and

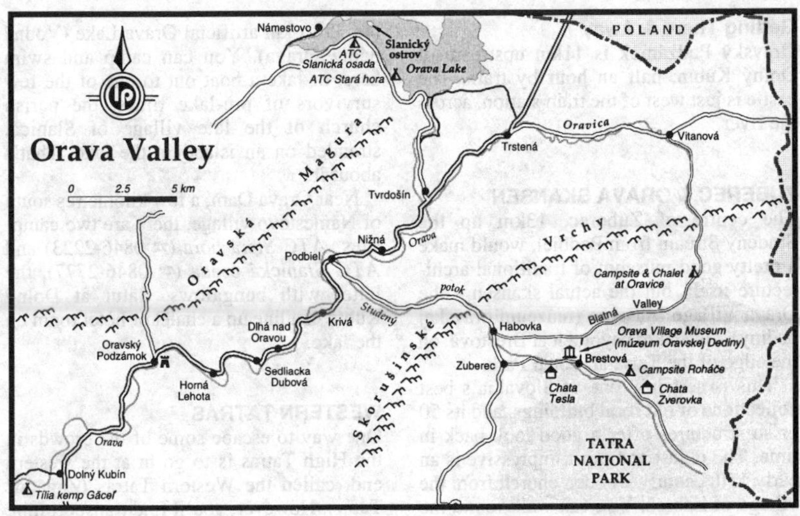

travel agency Slovakotour (☎ 86 54 06), Gäceľská 1. A few hundred metres farther south is the old centre, námestie Hviezdoslava. The new post office is on Aleja Svobody. The area code for Dolný Kubín and the lower valley is ☎ 0845.

Places to Stay

The three-star *Hotel Park* (☎ 86 41 10), Radlinského 21, has singles/doubles from 1030/1350 Sk. The *Hotel Severan* (☎ 86 46 66), just north of Slovenská poisťovňa on Radlinského, has rooms with shower and WC for 300/400 Sk. Beds are 150 Sk per person at the *Kuzmínovo centrum zimných športov* (Kuzmínovo winter sports centre; ☎ 2674), about 500m south-west of the square. About 2km west along the river is the year-round campsite *Tília kemp Gäceľ* (☎ 86 51 10), with bungalows and a restaurant.

ORAVA CASTLE

This massive Gothic castle, perched high above the river and Oravský Podzámok village, was for centuries the seat of regional power. Its oldest parts date from at least 1267, with later improvements by many royal and aristocratic owners. The present storybook look is mainly the result of reconstruction after a fire in 1800.

On your own, you can't get close to it without being hustled into a tedious group tour of rooms full of weapons, tapestries and period furniture, a rococo chapel and some forgettable nature and ethnography exhibits. The castle's main appeal lies in its impressive exterior. It's open daily in June, July and August from 8.30 am to 5 pm, and daily (except Monday) in May, September and October from 8.30 am to 4 pm.

Places to Stay

Imka camping is 1.5km south of the centre of Oravský Podzámok. The *Hotel Oravan* (☎ 0845-89 31 15), across the main valley road from the castle, has 650 Sk beds in rooms with shower and WC, or 450 Sk beds in rooms without facilities, and a restaurant that looks pretty good. It can also organise 180 Sk beds in the dorms at Zámocká ubytovňa.

Getting There & Away
Oravský Podzámok is 11km upstream of Dolný Kubín, half an hour by train. The castle is just west of the train station, across the river.

ZUBEREC & ORAVA SKANSEN
The centre of Zuberec, 13km up the Studený Stream from Podbiel, would make a pretty good museum of traditional architecture itself, but the actual skansen – the Orava Village Museum (múzeum oravskej dediny) – is 3.5km beyond it at Brestová, on the edge of the Tatra National Park.

This is certainly one of Slovakia's best collections of old rural buildings, and its 50 or so structures offer a good look back in time. The oldest and most impressive is an early 15th century wooden church from the village of Zabrež. You can walk round the place by yourself, though with a guide you'll see more interiors and their original furnishings. The ticket office sells a multilingual inventory of the buildings.

The museum is open daily in July and August from 8 am to 5 pm; daily, except Monday, in May, June, September and October until 4 pm; and on weekends only in November and December. Entry costs 40 Sk.

SLOVAK REPUBLIC

Places to Stay
Habovka, just north of Zuberec, and Zuberec itself, have plenty of private rooms. There are two chalets nearby, *Chata Tesla* just below Brestová and *Chata Zverovka* (☎ 0847-39 51 06) about 4km past the museum, both at about 360 Sk per double.

Getting There & Away
Transport is tedious unless you have a car. Many buses run from Dolný Kubín to Podbiel, but there are only about five a day from there to Zuberec and Chata Zverovka.

ORAVA LAKE
Slovaks come up the valley to relax around the 35 sq km artificial Orava Lake (Vodná nádrž Orava). You can camp and swim here, or take a boat out to one of the few survivors of pre-lake times, the parish church of the late village of Slanica, stranded on an island in the lake. That's about it.

Near Orava Dam, a few kilometres south of Námestovo village, there are two campsites, *ATC Stará hora* (☎ 0846-2223) and *ATC Slanická osada* (☎ 0846-2777), the latter with bungalows. Satur at Dolný Kubín can line up a chalet or hotel room on the lake.

WESTERN TATRAS
One way to escape some of the crowds in the High Tatras is to go in at the western end, called the Western Tatras (Západné Tatry). However, you'll find transport thin, facilities limited and trails demanding.

A possible trailhead is at Zverovka (up the valley of the Studený potok), about 4km beyond the Orava Village Museum. The only formal place to stay there is the *Chata Zverovka* (☎ 0847-39 51 06). It's popular so you should book ahead in the high season. Getting there is a bit tedious; see the previous Zuberec & Orava Skansen section.

Another route is up the valley of the Oravica river, which leaves the Orava at Tvrdošín. From Trstená (which you can get to easily by bus or train) it's about 15km, with a turn-off at Vitanová, to the end of the road at Oravice, where there's a *chalet* and a very popular campsite, *ATC Oravice* (☎ 0847-941 14). Buses make the run from Trstená about half a dozen times a day. An alternative would be to walk the 8km green-marked trail from the Orava Village Museum, up the Blatná Valley and down the Mihulčie Valley.

Trails from these points quickly get up into some the highest mountains in central Europe (see the High Tatras chapter), so they are no picnic. You should not attempt any long-distance treks here unless you have experience with high-altitude walking and climbing.

Low Tatras

The Low Tatras (Nízke Tatry) is one of Slovakia's favourite and most frequented mountain recreational areas. The 80km east-west crest, framed between the valleys of the upper Váh and the small Hron river, is most dramatic where it pushes above the tree line, though the lower eastern half is the wildest, with significant numbers of brown bears, wildcats and other animals.

Since 1978 most of this area has been part of the 810 sq km Low Tatras National Park (Národný park Nízke Tatry), but considerable recreation and tourism development continues in the western half. Excellent hiking trails criss-cross the range, though with fewer chaty than in the Malá Fatra.

Of the many deep lateral valleys, the most popular and most developed – as Slovakia's best known ski resort – is Jasná in the Demänova Valley (Demänovská dolina), dropping northward below Chopok peak (2024m), near the town of Liptovský Mikuláš. In summer the crest zone between Chabenec (1955m) and Ďumbier (2043m), which is the highest peak in the range, is easily accessible by chair lift from both Jasná in the Demänova Valley and its southern counterpart, Bystrá Valley. Other tourist development is at Donovaly, at the western end of the range.

The Low Tatras are breached once, by a road over the 1238m sedlo Čertovica between Liptovský Hrádok and Brezno.

LIPTOVSKÝ MIKULÁŠ

Liptovský Mikuláš' main claim to historical fame is as the place where Juraj Jánošík, the 'Slovak Robin Hood' (see the earlier Terchová section), was hung up by his ribcage to die in 1713.

The town is useful only as a base for visiting the Low Tatras, if you can't find a place to stay in the Demänova Valley. Its own marginal attractions include the dungeon where Jánošík was held, and a beautiful wooden church in the nearby village of Svätý Kríž.

Orientation

The mighty Váh doesn't look so mighty here, pooling into a 24 sq km reservoir called Liptovská Mara, the 'Liptov Sea', just west of town. Jánošík was executed in the small main square, námestie Osloboditeľov. The bus and train stations are beside one another, 500m up Hurbanova.

Information

The place to go for maps and information about the town and the mountains is the Municipal Information Centre (Informačné centrum mesta; ☎ 224 18), opposite the Hotel El Greco. It's open weekdays from 8 am to 7 pm, Saturday until 2 pm, and Sunday from noon to 7 pm. A useful reference for regional transport is a booklet called *Informátor Liptova*.

Satur, on námestie Osloboditeľov, is open weekdays from 8 am to 6 pm, Saturday from 8.30 to 11.30 am.

The Liptovský Mikuláš area code is ☎ 0849.

Janko Kráľ Museum

The Illéshazyovská kúrla at námestie Osloboditeľov 31 houses the Literary and Historical Museum of the poet Janko Kráľ (múzeum Janka Kráľa) who is regarded as the leading poet of the Slovak Romanticism era. It also now has the quaint exhibits of 19th and 20th century town life that were moved here from Jánošík's Dungeon. The Baroque Illéshazyovská kúrla is also known as Stoličný or Seligovský House and is where Juraj Jánošík was sentenced on 17 March 1713.

The museum is open Tuesday to Friday from 8 am to 4 pm, weekends from 10 am to 4 pm.

Petr Michal Bohúň Gallery

In the last century there was an Evangelic public school here and today it houses the second largest art collection in the country (the National Gallery in Bratislava is the

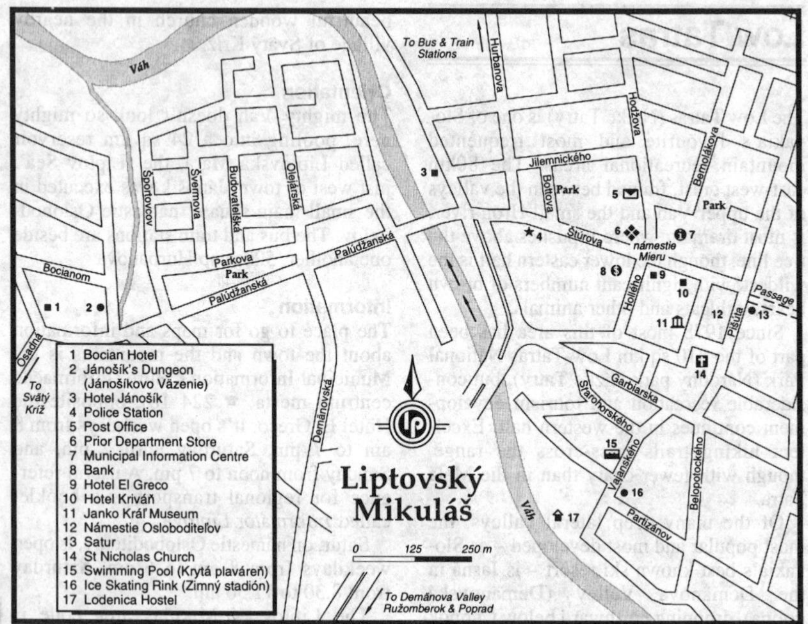

largest) of Gothic, Baroque, and 19th and 20th century art. The Petr Michal Bohúň Gallery (galéria Petra Michala Bohúňa) is at Tranovského 2 and open daily, except Monday, from 9 am to 5 pm.

Jánošík's Dungeon

About 1.5km west of the centre in Palúdzka district is the fortified house of the feudal landlord in whose cellar Jánošík was held and tortured before his execution. It's a 20 minute walk, with lousy bus connections (No 2 or 11 from the centre or No 7 from the bus station, every hour or two). There is not much to see here as the museum exhibits that were inside have been moved to the Janko Kráľ Museum.

Church at Svätý Kríž

In the 17th century a huge, beautiful wooden Protestant church was built in Palúdzka, allegedly without any nails, and an onion-dome belfry was added later. In about 1980 it was moved to the village of Svätý Kríž, 8km south-west of Liptovský Mikuláš, to keep it from being drowned by the Liptovská Mara. Bus No 90423 runs to the village from the main bus station about five times a day.

Places to Stay

A summer-only campsite, *ATC Liptovský Trnovec* (☎ 973 00), is on the north side of the lake at Liptovský Trnovec; others are around the Demänova Valley (see the following section). The *Lodenica* hostel is south of the centre on Vajanského.

In the centre, doubles/triples at the *Hotel Kriváň* (☎ 852 24 14), Štúrova 5, are good bottom-end value from 220/410 Sk with shared facilities, or from 300/680 Sk with private facilities. Noisy doubles at the adjacent *Hotel El Greco* (☎ 852 27 13) are 800 Sk with shower, WC and TV. *Hotel Jánošík*

(☎ 227 21), west of the centre at Jánošíkovo nábrežie 1, has doubles without/with bath for 380/1026 Sk.

The *Bocian Hotel* (☎ 54 12 76), at Polučanská 38, is a renovated manor-house with quiet singles/doubles/triples/quads with shower and WC for 640/1200/1680/2080 Sk. Getting there is a problem; it's near Jánošík's Dungeon, a long walk with poor bus connections, and there's no alternative to its up-market restaurant.

Getting There & Away

Poprad is an hour away by trains that leave every hour or two. The bus journeys are tedious unless you're going to Starý Smokovec (eight buses a day).

AROUND LIPTOVSKÝ MIKULÁŠ

Pribylina

About 21km north-east of Liptovský Mikuláš, just past the village of Pribylina, is another very good skansen, called the Museum of Liptov Village (múseum Liptovskej dediny). Most of the buildings are from the area of Liptovská Mara Lake and were relocated here just before the dam was completed and the valley flooded. Apart from a good collection of local wooden houses (some full of period furniture, tools and clothing), there is also a wooden church and a fire station, as well as a small chateau. It is open daily from mid-June through to mid-September from 9 am to 5.30 pm, from mid-May to mid-June and in October until 4 pm, and from November through April until 3 pm. Entry costs 30 Sk. The only way to get here by public transport is by bus from Poprad (six a day).

DEMÄNOVA VALLEY

Slovaks know the Demänova Valley's (Demänovská dolina) village of Jasná as the republic's best ski resort, and from January through April it overflows with people clunking around in their ski boots. In the summer it reveals itself as a pretty, forested valley, under relentless development (including a mega-hotel and commercial complex) but featuring Slovakia's most accessible limestone caves, and with easy access by foot or chair lift to windswept walks along the crest of the Low Tatras.

Orientation

The valley, and the national park, begin near the village of Pavčina Lehota, 7km from the centre of Liptovský Mikuláš. At the head of the valley is a diffuse collection of chalets and hotels called Jasná, about 1200m high and 15km from Liptovský Mikuláš.

Information

The Slovakotour agency (☎ & fax 234 14), not to be confused with Slovakoturist, is just past the Pavčina Lehota turn-off, and has park information and a foreign exchange desk. Staff can also help with private and chata accommodation. It's open weekdays from 7 am until at least 4 pm, and sometimes on weekends.

The park's Mountain Rescue Service (Horská služba), by the valley road just below the Hotel Družba, is the place to go for trail and weather information if you're planning overnight walks in the mountains.

Demänova Valley's area code is ☎ 0849.

Caves

Two limestone caves in the lower valley are part of Slovakia's biggest continuous cave system. About 2km of passages in the **Demänova Freedom Cave** (Demänovská jaskyňa Slobody) stay open from January to October, while the smaller **Demänova Ice Cave** (Demänovská ľadová jaskyňa), with ice formations at the lowest level, are open from mid-May to mid-September. They're open daily from May through August (closed Monday at other times) from 9 to 11 am and 12.30 to 2 pm. The entry fee is 50 Sk. Take an extra layer against the subterranean chill.

Walks

Better than going below ground is rising above it, on fine ridge walks with long views across the Low Tatras and even north to the High Tatras on a clear day.

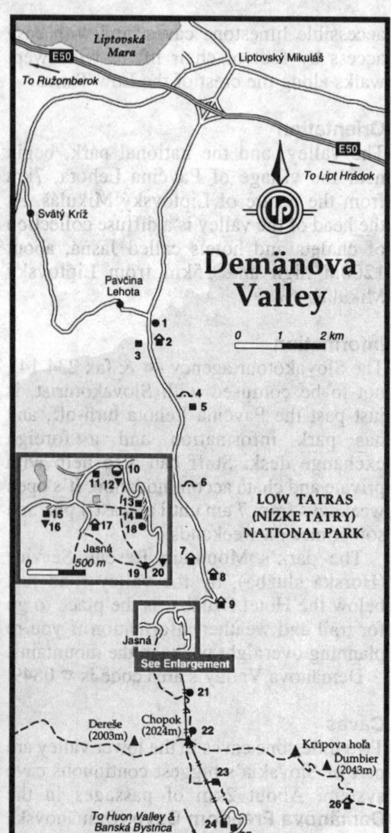

PLACES TO STAY
2 Bystrina Hotel & Campsite
3 Hotel Tri Studničky
5 Chata Odboj
7 Chata Lúčky
8 Chata na Lúčkach
9 Chata Záhradky
11 Hotel Grand
13 Hotel Junior
14 Hotel Družba
15 Hotel Liptov
17 Chata Björnson
23 Hotel Kosodrevina
24 Hotel Srdiečko
25 Hotel Trangoška
26 Chata Štefánika

PLACES TO EAT
12 Bistro Jasná
16 Koliba Restaurant
20 Koliesto Restaurant

OTHER
1 Slovakotour Agency
4 Demänova Ice Cave (Demänovská ľadová jaskyňa)
6 Demänova Freedom Cave (Demänovská jaskyňa Slobody)
10 Bus Terminus
18 Mountain Rescue Service (Horská služba)
19 Koliesto Chair Lift Station
21 Luková Chair Lift Station and Bufet
22 Chopok Chair Lift Station and Bufet

From the end of the bus line at Jasná it's a 20 minute walk up to the Koliesto Restaurant. From there a summer chair lift makes a 20 minute ascent (with a change halfway, at Luková) almost to the top of Chopok (2024m), every half-hour from 9 am to about 4 pm, for 120 Sk.

Visiting Chopok is feasible even for families and couch-potatoes, and there are small buffets at the Luková and Chopok terminals. Take extra layers even in summer. The crowds are thick at Chopok, but just walk 200m in any direction to lose most of them. Check the last return time if you don't want to walk back down.

From Chopok a blue-marked trail returns via Luková to Jasná. Alternatively, you can continue down the other side into the less-developed Bystrá Valley by chair lift, or a 1½ hour walk down a yellow trail to the road, where there are several hotels and the occasional bus out, via Brezno, to Banská Bystrica.

A rocky, red-marked trail teeters along the crest, west for 35 minutes to Dereše (2003m), for 3½ to four hours to Chabenec (1955m), or for two or three days down to the tourist village of Donovaly (with campsite and chaty) on the Banská Bystrica-Ružomberok road.

This trail also runs east to Ďumbier (2043m) in two hours, and to another north-south road at sedlo Čertovica in six hours, with two chaty en route. The wildest and least developed part of the range is east of Čertovica; the red crest-trail offers another three or four days of walking (with no chaty, so you'll need a tent) down to a small hotel at Telgárt, from where you can take a bus or the beautiful train ride west down the Hron Valley to Banská Bystrica.

These and plenty of other routes are marked on Slovenská kartografia's two page *Nízke Tatry* map. Mountain Rescue in the valley can give further advice.

Skiing

This is the best skiing in both republics. It is possible to ski both the northern Jasná and the southern (Chopok Juh) sides of Chopok mountain. There is a good range of runs to satisfy skiers of all levels. The Jasná runs are north-facing and thus tend to have a prolonged season beyond the mid-December to March season, especially if it is a harsher and longer winter. The rental ski equipment is of a reasonable standard for the average skier, and priced at around 200 Sk per day. During peak season, lift passes are 400 Sk per day, 1800 Sk per week.

Places to Stay & Eat

The odds of finding a room without a booking are pretty good in summer but nil in winter. Prices noted are for winter; prices are 40 to 60% less in summer, but in some cases prices could be similar to those of winter during July and August. Most places have their own restaurants, and some bigger ones accept credit cards.

To book ahead, talk to Slovakotour or agencies in Liptovský Mikuláš. Slovakotour can also help with private accommodation in the valley, at about 170 to 300 Sk per person.

Mountain Chalets There are chaty of all sorts in and above the valley; those open in summer have beds for about 120 to 200 Sk, and can do meals by arrangement. Satur and other agencies in Liptovský Mikuláš, Banská Bystrica and elsewhere can book many of them.

Among those near the valley road are *Chata Odboj* at the Ice Caves, *Chata Lúčky*, *Chata na Lúčkach* and *Chata Záhradky* below the bus terminus, and *Mikulášská chata* (☎ 916 72) in Jasná. More spartan ones are along high-country trails – such as *Chata Štefánika* near Ďumbier peak and *Chata Čertovica* a day's walk east at sedlo Čertovica.

Lower Valley On the valley road just after the Pavčina Lehota turn-off is the friendly *Hotel Tri Studničky* (☎ 222 85), where doubles/triples with shower and WC are good value at 1120/1430 Sk (rear rooms face the stream and woods).

About 200m off the road on the other side are the *Bystrina Hotel* and its comfortable summer *campsite* (☎ 75 91 63/4; fax 75 91 65). The hotel has plain doubles for 750 Sk (including breakfast in winter and in July and August, when it's usually full), and two restaurants.

Jasná The giant *Hotel Junior* (☎ 915 71/3; fax 915 75) has a pool, sauna, two restaurants, ski hire, and double rooms with WC and shower for 2850 Sk, with breakfast – but it's invariably full in every season. A far better deal is *Chata Björnson* (☎ 916 77; fax 916 89), a good walk-in bet in summer, with rooms with shared facilities for about 380 Sk per bed, and access to the Hotel Junior's facilities. Student-card holders get 30% off at both places.

Another recommended hotel is the *Družba* (☎ 916 85; fax 915 56), where doubles with shared WC are 1045 Sk with shower, 825 Sk without, including breakfast and dinner. The huge *Hotel Liptov* (☎ 915 06) has doubles with shower but shared WC for 540 Sk, and with their own WC for 1500 Sk. Behind it is the *Koliba* restaurant.

The new four-star *Hotel Grand* (☎ 84 99 14 41; fax 84 99 14 54) is just above the bus terminus. The clean and spacious single/double rooms are 1690/2320 Sk, including a buffet breakfast in July and August. It also has a reasonable up-market restaurant.

Bystrá Dolina Several hotels in the upper Bystrá Valley are within reach. The pleasant *Srdiečko* (☎ 0867-956 21; fax 956 22) at the roadhead, an hour's walk from Chopok on a yellow-marked trail, has doubles with shared facilities for about 520 Sk, and with shower for about 730 Sk. The *Trangoška* is more expensive. There are plenty of other options down the valley too.

Getting There & Away

Bus No 90419 runs to Jasná about hourly from the Liptovský Mikuláš bus station. Two direct buses a day come from Poprad, via Starý Smokovec.

High Tatras

The Tatras mountains (Tatry) are Slovakia's biggest attraction for most foreign tourists – and with a splendid, jagged central massif rising abruptly out of a green plain, it's easy to see why, even from a distance.

Geologically speaking, there are actually three ranges – the Western Tatras (Západné Tatry), High Tatras (Vysoké Tatry) and the small eastern Belianské Tatry. The High Tatras, the tallest (and only genuinely alpine) mountains in either republic, and indeed in the entire Carpathian chain, take centre stage in every sense. At 2655m, Gerlachovský štít is the tallest of some 25 peaks over 2500m, with the 2632m Lomnický štít in second place.

For all their majesty, the High Tatras are surprisingly compact – about 25km from west to east. They're relatively young, their sharp summits and broad valleys carved by glaciers. Three dozen valleys contain over 100 *plesy*, or tarns (small glacial lakes), and dense pine forest skirts the range below 1600m.

Naturally, they are a magnet for fresh-air enthusiasts from all over Europe. They're heavily developed, and in high summer and winter densely crowded – some five million people a year come to walk, climb, cycle, ski or just breathe deeply. You'll need to climb farther than in Slovakia's other mountains to have some of it to yourself, but a bit of sweat brings some fine rewards.

The Tatras are part of the 795 sq km Tatra National Park (Tatranský národný park), Czechoslovakia's first national park, founded in 1949. The range also extends into Poland, where there is also a national park.

The park's administrative centre, and the main gateway to the Tatras, is Poprad. At the foot of the central range is a string of resort 'villages' that began as sanatoria centres, to which Europeans flocked for the 'climate cure'. Starý Smokovec was the first, founded in the 1870s. They're administered from Poprad, though Starý Smokovec now has some administrative independence.

HIGHLIGHTS

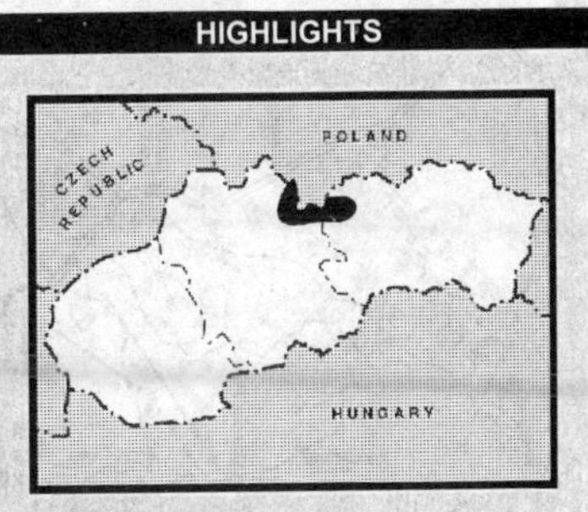

- Catch the cable car up to the lake, Skalnaté pleso, and then continue on up to the summit of Lomnický štít
- Go take a hike, ride a bike, ski down a slope, climb a mountain ... or just breathe deeply
- And when you're exhausted, or if the weather is bad, grab a sauna and massage at Starý Smokovec's Grand Hotel

Stretching up across the mountains are hundreds of kilometres of trails, with enough day hikes and superb long walks to keep you here for years. You can enjoy Lomnický štít without walking at all, thanks to an audacious cable car to the summit.

The main east-west regional highway passes through Poprad, while an upper road joins all the resorts in a line. Starý Smokovec, at 990m, is the biggest resort centre, with the most facilities and connections. To the west is the touristy Štrbské Pleso (1350m), and to the east the more peaceful Tatranská Lomnica (850m). Poprad is linked to all the resorts by road and a convenient *električka* train (see the Getting Around section).

SLOVAK REPUBLIC

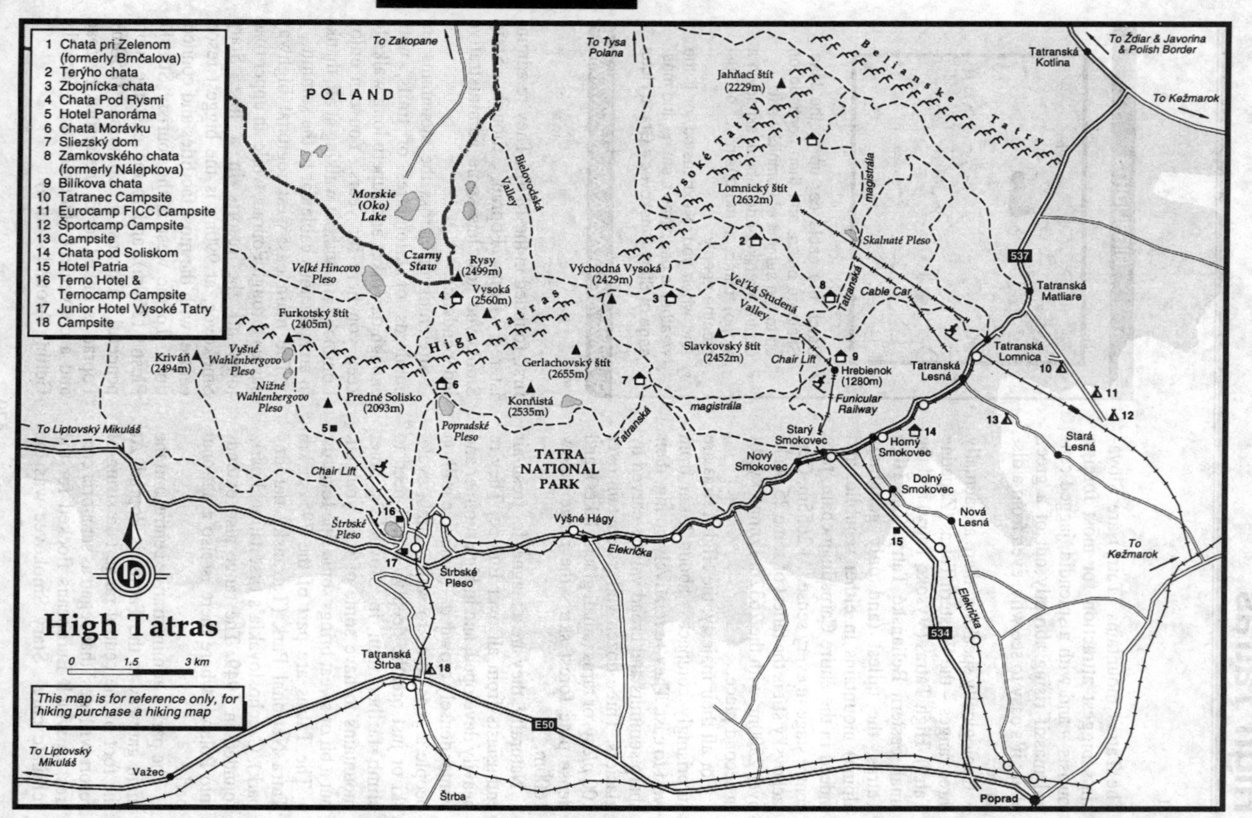

ALL PHOTOS BY MARK DAFFEY

High Tatras

Top Left: Bungee jumping is one of the vast range of activities available in the High Tatras.
Top Right: A walking bridge for hikers in the Mengusov Valley.
Bottom: Zbojnicka Chata is a welcome sight after a long day's hike in the High Tatras.

ALL PHOTOS BY RICHARD NEBESKÝ

A	B
C	D
E	F

East Slovakia

A The walled town of Spišská Kapitula
B A wooden church near Tročany
C Krásna Hôrka Castle
D Thurzov House, Levoča
E Levoča town hall
F Nižný Komárnik's impressive church

Taking exercise is the main thing to do here, and you'll go mad from boredom if the weather confines you for long to the antiseptic resorts. Some bad-weather ideas include low-level hikes, a sauna and massage at Starý Smokovec's Grand Hotel, a look at the National Park Museum in Tatranská Lomnica, and trips to Spišská Sobota near Poprad and to the handsome Spiš town of Kežmarok.

For minimal crowds and decent weather, the best times to visit the High Tatras are late spring or early autumn, with August and September best for walking. Prices are like Bratislava's, considerably higher than elsewhere in Slovakia. Little English is spoken; foreigners are all assumed to speak German.

Information

For anything more than a day hike, you'll need a decent map (see the Books & Maps section). The main artery of trails in this region is the 65km, red-marked Tatranská magistrála, which runs just beneath the southern crest of the High Tatras, and is accessible on dozens of branches.

A few of the most popular walks are noted in this section under each of the resorts – Štrbské Pleso, Starý Smokovec, and Tatranská Lomnica. But with a map and advice from Mountain Rescue, those with the experience and gear can invent their own walks. Don't overlook further treks in the Polish Tatras – you can spot Polish walkers on this side of the border by their ready greetings of a smile and a quiet '*cześć*' (hello).

Some trails are only open from July through October. In June you'll still find melting snow and swollen streams; November sees the autumn snowfalls begin again.

Precautions Carry your own water and some food, even if you have a *chata* booking with meals. Summer weather can be punctuated with sudden, chilling afternoon thunderstorms, so take a waterproof jacket on any walk, no matter how fine the day. The summits can be very cold (occasionally snowy), even in summer. Long hikes on the difficult, rocky upper trails demand durable shoes. Other suggestions are sun-block cream, moleskin for blisters, and a whistle for emergencies (six blasts is an internationally recognised distress call).

Keep the park regulations in mind: stay on the trails, don't pick the flowers, take out your rubbish, and don't cut wood or build open fires. For overnight trips, check the weather forecast in the newspaper or with Mountain Rescue Service. Stay off the ridge tops if they're in the clouds. You'll need a guide to do ascents of the very highest peaks, with the exception of Lomnický štít, which is accessible by cable car (see the Tatranská Lomnica section).

There's snow by November (on some of the highest passes as early as September) and avalanches are a danger from November to June when the higher trails will be closed – ask someone to translate the notices at the head of the trails for you.

Tourist Offices & Weather Information

A recommended source of information on sights, recreational possibilities and accommodation are the Tatry information offices in Starý Smokovec and Štrbské Pleso, and the Poprad Information Agency (PIA) in Poprad. Satur has offices in Poprad and Starý Smokovec. For weather and trail updates, go to the park's Mountain Rescue Service (Horská služba) in Starý Smokovec.

Post & Communications International calls and telegrams are easy from the post offices in Štrbské Pleso, Starý Smokovec and Tatranská Lomnica. The area codes for the region are ☎ 092 for Poprad and ☎ 0969 for all the resorts.

Books & Maps One of the best hiking maps is Vojenský kartografický ústav's (VKÚ) 1:50,000 tourist map No 113, *Vysoké Tatry* (the German version is called *Hohe Tatra).* There are also more detailed 1:25,000 maps. The Združenie cestovného ruchu Vysoké Tatry (Association of High

Tatry Tourist Authority) publishes a booklet every summer and winter with street plans of the main resort villages, accommodation and other services.

A good investment is the current edition of the annual booklet, *Everyman's Guide to the High Tatras* (also suitable for women), packed with information on history, sights, short and long hikes, accommodation and transportation (including *električka* and funicular railway timetables). Another booklet, *The Tatra National Park – the Guide by Nature*, is good on natural features, flora and fauna, and has walking and cycling routes and cable-car timetables.

Booklets and maps are available from kiosks, travel agencies and top-end hotels.

Media Several western newspapers are available, two or three days late, from kiosks. Along with good music, Radio Tatry (102.5 FM) has English-language 'tourist bulletins' daily at 7.20 and 9.20 am and 8.30 pm, with mountain conditions and other tips.

Shops & Laundry Each of the bigger villages has a shopping complex (*dom služieb*) near the centre; some have a laundry service (*čistiareň*). Hotels can arrange washing for about 15 Sk per piece.

SLOVAK REPUBLIC

Accommodation

Frequent, cheap transport means you can stay almost anywhere, but Starý Smokovec and Tatranská Lomnica are the most convenient and attractive centres. Summer accommodation is tight, although you can always find something modest on the spot through PIA in Poprad, Slovakoturist in Horný Smokovec, or Satur or T-Ski in Starý Smokovec. All of them add their own surcharges – Satur's is around 10%!

Rates given here are for high winter unless noted. Prices are highest from July through September, January through mid-March, and around Easter and Christmas, but they dip in spring and autumn.

There are at least six campsites in the park, including top-class ones near Dolný Smokovec and east of Tatranská Lomnica, and a cheap one at Stará Lesná. The best hostel bargain is the *Juniorhotel Vysoké Tatry* in Horný Smokovec, but it's usually full during the high summer/winter seasons. Several agencies arrange private rooms; typical rates per bed at the time of writing were about 180 Sk with shared facilities or 250 Sk with private bath and WC.

Chaty The chaty (*ch.* on maps) in the Tatras run the gamut from plain alpine hostels at around 350 Sk per bed plus 150 Sk per meal, to full-scale *horské hotely* (mountain hotels) at 500 Sk per bed and up. Many are accessible only on foot.

Chaty are open year-round unless noted, and should be booked in advance (although if you arrive without a booking and there are no beds, they'll let you crash on the floor for a small charge). PIA in Poprad, and Satur and Slovakoturist in Horný Smokovec, can help you book accommodation at most of them, at about 350 Sk per bed and 150 Sk per meal. Satur can book the big hotel-chalets, *Sliezsky dom* and *Chata pri Popradskom plese* (*kpt Morávku*), at about 300 Sk per bed (at least 950/1150 Sk in hotel-grade double/triple rooms).

The following are the main chaty on the upper trails, from west to east:

Chata pod Soliskom – 1800m
Chata pri Popradskom plese (also known as Chata kpt Morávku) – restaurant, 1500m
Chata Pod Rysmi – dormitory style, open June through October, highest of all at 2250m
Sliezsky dom – restaurant and cafeteria, 1670m
Zbojnícka chata – 1960m
Téryho chata – 2015m
Zamkovského chata (formerly Nálepkova*)* – 1475m
Bilíkova chata (☎ 42 24 39; fax 42 22 67) – can only be booked directly with the chata, 1220m
Chata pri Zelenom plese (formerly Brnčalova) – 1540m

Food

Hotel restaurants abound. The ones in lower-end places, though plain, can be good value. Top-end hotel eateries are an expensive way to put food in your mouth.

Getting There & Away

There are frequent domestic bus and rail connections in and out of Poprad, as well as domestic and limited international bus connections out of Smokovec. Train bookings out of Poprad in the high season are said to be hard to get without some waiting. An alternative if you're heading east is the ordinary train out of Tatranská Lomnica.

Satur can do international bookings, though the only direct scheduled international connections to the Tatras region is by bus from Poland.

Poland Local buses make the tedious trip between Poprad and the Lysá Poľana border crossing, via Starý Smokovec, about hourly until early evening. On the Polish side there are buses to Zakopane (where you can pick up a long-distance coach) about hourly until early evening. There are direct Poprad-Zakopane coaches (2½ hours) on Wednesday, Thursday and Saturday, leaving Poprad at 6 am or Zakopane at 2.30 pm. Perhaps more convenient is the daily Smokovec-Zakopane bus that departs at 10.23 am and 5.08 pm. Note that customs, passport control and the Slovak bank are all on the Polish side.

Slovak and Polish hikers and skiers routinely ignore the border altogether, though this is not a legal way to cross. You won't get the usual entry stamp on entering Poland; and though Slovak immigration doesn't always stamp passports in any case, you could be fined if you're caught entering Slovakia this way.

Getting Around

The so-called *električka* or 'Tatra-train' – the Tatranská električká železnica or TEŽ – is just a rural tram, built before WWI, frustratingly slow and subject to breakdowns, but cheap and scenic (the stretch near Poprad provides first-class views of the entire front range of the High Tatras).

The minuscule fares depend on distance. Bigger stations have ticket windows and exact-change ticket machines, or you can buy a ticket from the conductor.

Local buses between the resorts are usually more frequent (typically every 10 to 20 minutes) and certainly faster, though with fewer intermediate stops.

If you're driving, the *Everyman's* booklet (see the Books & Maps section earlier) includes petrol stations and auto repair shops. Hitching is easy, especially if you have a sign showing your destination.

You can hire a bicycle in Starý Smokovec, and the Eurocamp campsite near Tatranská Lomnica is said to have repair facilities. In addition to the park's public roads, there are paved service roads, which are closed to traffic, from Starý Smokovec up to Hrebienok and from Tatranská Polianka up to Sliezsky dom.

If you are interested in seeing the mountains from above and can afford the 2200 Sk (maximum three people) for a 30 minute flight in a Cessna 172, contact TLS Air at Poprad-Tatry airport (*letisko*; ☎ 638 75).

POPRAD

Despite a bit of Spiš architecture and a central square that's cheerful at the end of the day, Poprad is not a place to go out of your way visiting. However, it's a handy gateway to the High Tatras, a source of provisions at ordinary Slovak prices, and a possible base for visiting the Spiš region and the Slovenský raj (see the East Slovakia chapter).

Orientation

From the train and bus stations (and the električka terminal upstairs in the train station) it's a five minute walk to the main square, námestie svätého Egídia, lined with shops and eateries. A good street map is available at PNS kiosks, such as at the train station. The Poprad-Tatry airport, the highest in Europe, is about 4km west of town.

Information

The Poprad Information Agency (Popradská informačná agentúra, or PIA, ☎ 72 17 00 or 636 36), námestie svätého Egídia 2950, is the place for local and Tatras information of all kinds, including a very good

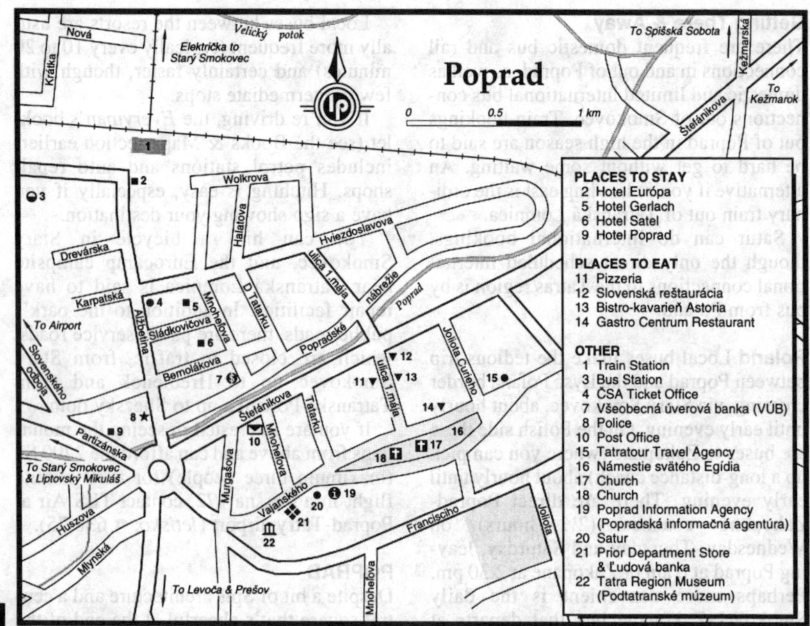

accommodation service. It's open weekdays from 9 am to 1 pm and 1.30 to 6 pm, Saturday from 9 am to 1 pm (and in summer on Sunday afternoons).

Around the corner is Satur (☎ 72 34 30), open weekdays from 9 am to noon and 1 to 4 pm (until 6 pm on Tuesday and Thursday), but about the only thing it does better than PIA is bus and train tickets.

Ľudová banka, in the Prior department store at Vajanského, and VÚB, at the corner of Mnoheľova and Popradské nábrežie, have exchange counters.

Things to See

In the middle of námestie svätého Egídia are two **churches**, one sporting Spiš-style 'gablets'. Natural history, town history and ethnography feature at the **Tatra Region Museum** (Podtatranské múzeum) on Vajanského, open daily, except Monday, from 9 am to 4 pm.

Spišská Sobota If you're coming from the Spiš region, this village (now a Poprad suburb) will be of little interest; otherwise the Germanic, broad-gabled **wooden houses** with heavy front eaves and decorative carving may come as a surprise. The name comes from the Saturday (*sobota*) market once held here.

Renaissance merchants and artisans' houses line the leafy central square, Sobotské námestie. In the late-Gothic interior of the **parish church** is an altar made by Master Pavol of Levoča in 1516. A little **museum** on the square, open daily, except Sunday, from 9 am to 4 pm, features archaeology and church art.

Spišská Sobota is a 20 minute walk from námestie svätého Egídia, north-east on Štefánikova and north on Kežmarská, or you can take bus No 2 or 4. For a better look at Spiš architecture, take a day trip to Kežmarok.

Places to Stay

Although Poprad is about 10km from the mountains, it's worth the trip, if you don't have accommodation already arranged, to PIA – it's probably the region's best accommodation office for budget travellers. Tatratour, at námestie svätého Egídia 19, can also arrange private accommodation.

The town has several hotels. At the bottom end is the damp *Európa* (☎ 72 18 83) beside the train station, where a single/double/triple with shared facilities is 440/550/850 Sk. The *Gerlach* (☎ 72 19 45; fax 636 63), on Hviezdoslavova, has clean rooms with WC and bath for 500/850 Sk. Rooms with bath and TV at the prefabricated *Hotel Satel* (☎ 47 11 11; fax 620 75), Mnoheľova 826/5, are 1250/1960 Sk with breakfast. The best hotel in town is the new *Poprad* (☎ 72 12 60; fax 72 12 84), Partizánska 677/18, where deluxe rooms with bath, WC and TV cost up to 1150/1930 Sk, including breakfast.

Places to Eat

Gastro Centrum is a good fish restaurant, on námestie svätého Egídia, with main courses for less than 162 Sk. Ulica 1.mája has a concentration of eateries, including the *Bistro-kavarieň Astoria* at No 5, the touristy *Slovenská reštaurácia* (☎ 72 28 70) at No 9 (with Slovak main courses under 150 Sk, plus tacky Slovak decor), and a *pizzeria* opposite at No 4. A small open-air *market* percolates all day on Joliota Curieho.

Getting There & Away

The most convenient way in and out of Poprad is by train. There are about six fast trains (including two with overnight sleepers; about nine hours) daily from Prague, eleven from Bratislava (about four hours) and about 16 from Košice (1¼ hours).

Only Air Ostrava flies to and from Prague; on most days of the week (3000 Sk one way, 3500 Sk return). You can buy tickets from the ČSA ticket office (☎ 72 12 09), which is on Alžbetina. At the time of writing there were no flights to/from Bratislava.

Getting Around

There is no airport bus. A taxi to/from the airport is about 120 Sk.

ŠTRBSKÉ PLESO & TATRANSKÁ ŠTRBA

Štrbské Pleso is the Tatras' main ski resort; it's up the mountain from Tatranská Štrba. Its finest feature is a beautiful, 20 hectare alpine lake of the same name, the second-biggest *pleso* in the park. But the lake and its surroundings have been defaced by billboards and giant hotels, so the best thing to do here is overtake the skateboarding kids and tourists in *lederhosen* (those funky German leather shorts), and get up onto the Tatranská magistrála trail.

Orientation & Information

The red-marked Tatranská magistrála actually dips down around the southern end of the lake here. To pick it up in the easterly direction, walk north from the station and after 500m bear right towards the Helios sanatorium; the trail is on the left, just past a small stream.

There is a smaller branch of the useful Tatry Information Office (Tatranská informačná kancelária; ☎ 923 91) next to the Toliar department store (Obchodný dom Toliar), both of which are opposite the train station. Not much farther north is the post office.

Walks from Štrbské Pleso

A relatively easy (and crowded) walk is up the magistrála to Popradské pleso (1494m), which will take one to 1½ hours. A more demanding blue trail climbs to Velké Hincovo pleso (1946m), the biggest and deepest of the park's tarns. From Popradské pleso you can also head east to the Sliezsky dom mountain hotel and down to Starý Smokovec, in a long, day hike or overnight trip.

From the FIS ski resort, beyond the north end of the lake, a year-round chair lift climbs to Solisko, which has a chata. From there it's a one hour walk on a red trail to the 2093m summit of Predné Solisko. A demanding all-day option from the top of the chair lift is via an orange trail to the Lower (Nížné) and Upper (Vyšné) Wahlenbergovo tarns and Furkotský štít (2405m), then down the valley of the Mlynica past the Skok waterfalls back to the resort.

Places to Stay
All the cheap options are down the mountain at Tatranská Štrba; take the funicular railway (see the earlier Getting Around section). *Hotel Junior Rysy* (☎ 926 91/2), near the Tatranský Lieskovec stop, has a restaurant and singles/doubles/triples for 600/800/950 Sk. Half a kilometre south along the road is a basic *campsite*.

Everything at the resort is pricey. The weird 10 storey *Hotel Panoráma* (☎ 49 21 11), just beyond the električka station, charges 2700 Sk for a double with bath and breakfast. Brochures for the *Hotel Patria* (☎ 49 25 91/5) promise that it will 'provide all kinds of joys to its guests', but its triangular bulk is a blot on the lake's splendid landscape. Rooms cost 1781/2418 Sk, including breakfast. It's a 1km walk from the station.

At Solisko is a mountain chalet, the *Chata pod Soliskom*.

Getting There & Away
Štrbské Pleso is at the west end of the električka line. To get straight to the Poprad-Liptovský Mikuláš road from here, you can take the funicular railway that creeps up and down between here and Tatranská Štrba about every 45 minutes, for 15 Sk.

SMOKOVEC RESORTS

Smokovec is the collective name for Old (Starý), New (Nový), Upper (Horný) and Lower (Dolný) Smokovec – all close by one another but isolated by dense woods.

Information
The main Tatry Information Office (☎ 3440) in Dom služieb, north-west of the Starý Smokovec train station, has plenty of information on the region. It's open weekdays from 8 to 11.30 am and noon to 4 pm, Saturday from 8 am to noon.

The T-Ski agency (☎ 3200), behind the Hotel Grand, has bike rental, ski hire, photo

SLOVAK REPUBLIC

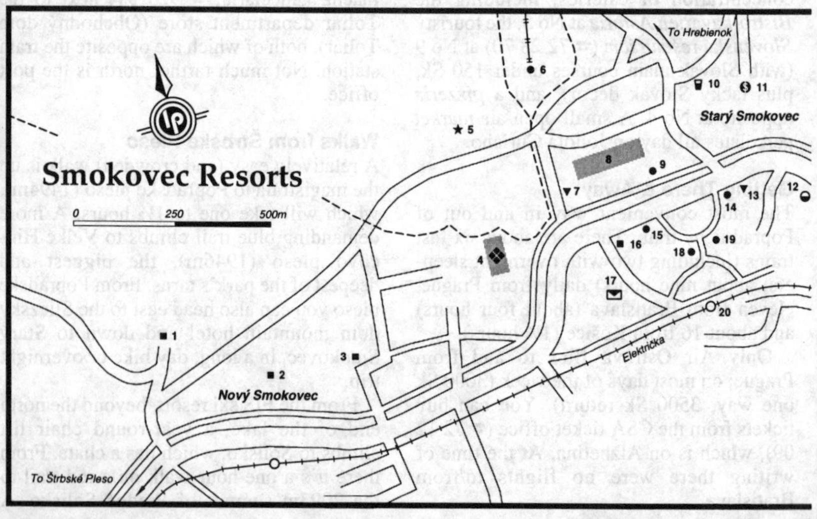

processing, an accommodation service and a good Tatras map selection.

Satur (☎ 2568 or 2414), on the main road above the električka station, is open weekdays from 8 am to 6 pm, Saturday from 8 am to noon.

For information on weather and trail conditions, go to the Mountain Rescue Service (Horská služba; ☎ 2820 or 2855) beside Satur. It's open weekdays from 8 am to 4 pm, Saturday from 8 am to noon.

Guides Mountain Rescue has limited guide services, but private guide agencies fill in the gaps. Across the road at the Start sport shop (☎ 2761; fax 2236) you can arrange for one. Expect to pay about 2000 Sk a day.

Money Všeobecná úverová banka is behind the Mladosť department store, across the road from the bus stop. It has a 24-hour MasterCard ATM. Slovenská sporiteľňa, in the shopping complex, has a Visa ATM.

PLACES TO STAY
1 Hotel MS-70
2 Hotel Park
3 Vila Dr Szontagh
8 Hotel Grand
16 Hotel Crocus
21 Hotel Šport
22 Hotel Bellevue
23 Penzión Poľana
24 Hotel Panda
26 Penzión Marta
27 Junior Hotel Vysoké Tatry

PLACES TO EAT
7 Taverna Reštaurácia
13 Tatranská Kuria & Reštaurácia Tatry

OTHER
4 Shopping Complex, Tatry information office & Slovenská sporiteľňa
5 Police
6 T-Ski Agency & Funicular Railway
9 Start sport Shop
10 Café Albas & Laser Disco
11 Všeobecná úverová banka
12 Bus Stand
14 Tatrasport Bicycle Rental
15 Supermarket
17 Post Office
18 Mountain Rescue Service (Horská služba)
19 Satur
20 Starý Smokovec električka Station
25 Slovakoturist Travel Agency

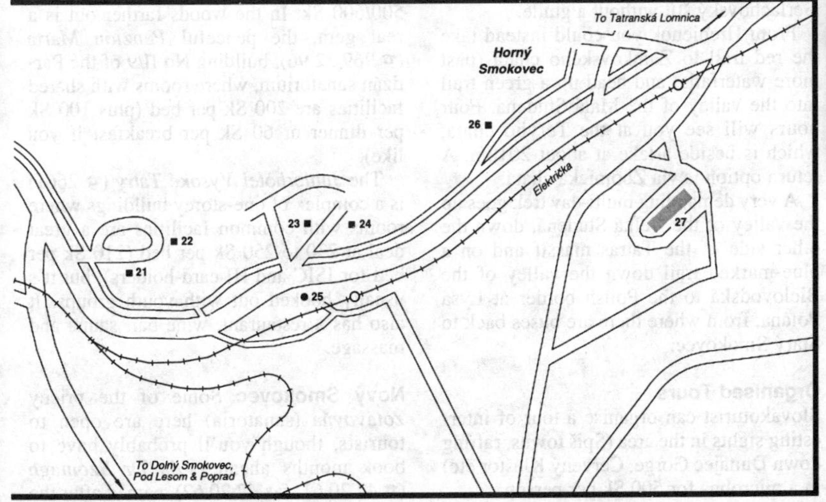

SLOVAK REPUBLIC

Funicular Railway

From behind the Hotel Grand, a funicular railway climbs to Hrebienok (a winter ski area at about 1280m) every 30 to 45 minutes from 6 am to 7.30 pm; it costs 30 Sk. It's very popular; to avoid the queues go early or at dinner time.

The funicular railway is good not only for getting to high trails but for day trips, such as grabbing a beer at the Bilíkova chata (a few minutes along the green-marked path from the upper terminus).

Walks from Starý Smokovec

A good day trip is up the funicular railway from Starý Smokovec to Hrebienok, west on the magistrála to the Sliezsky dom mountain hotel, and down an orange-marked trail back to Starý Smokovec.

If you're fit, a recommended option from Hrebienok is up the green path past the Bilíkova chata, from where it's about 1km to waterfalls on the Studený potok. From there it's a four to five hour climb on a blue trail up the valley of the Veľká Studená to a (prebooked) hot meal and warm bed at the Zbojnícka chata. An extra day allows for an ascent of Východná Vysoká (2429m) peak, offering the park's best close-up look at Gerlachovský štít without a guide.

From Hrebienok you could instead take the red trail to Zamkovského chata (past more waterfalls) and head up a green trail into the valley of the Malá Studená. Four hours will see you at the Téryho chata, which is beside a lake at about 2010m. A return option is via Zbojnícka chata.

A very demanding multi-day trek goes up the valley of the Veľká Studená, down the other side of the Tatras massif and on a blue-marked trail down the valley of the Bielovodská to the Polish border at Lysá Poľana, from where there are buses back to Starý Smokovec.

Organised Tours

Slovakoturist can organise a tour of interesting sights in the area (Spiš towns, rafting down Dunajec Gorge, Červený Kláštor etc) in a microbus for 500 Sk per person.

SLOVAK REPUBLIC

Places to Stay

Slovakoturist (☎ 2031 or 2827; fax 2482), in Horný Smokovec, is a good place to go to find a hotel, chata or private room. Satur and T-Ski also have accommodation services. Below are places to stay in the four resorts.

Starý Smokovec The run-down *Hotel Grand* (☎ 46 79 41/5 or 46 78 91), in the centre of Starý Smokovec, makes a good landmark but is pricey at 1640/2440 Sk for a shabby single/double with bath. Across the road, the *Hotel Crocus* is being renovated.

Horný Smokovec Plain rooms with shared facilities are about 510/890 Sk at the friendly *Hotel Šport* (☎ 42 23 63). Behind it, the stodgy *Hotel Bellevue* (☎ 42 29 41/3; fax 42 27 19) has rooms with WC and shower for 1470/2260 Sk.

Down the road at the modern *Hotel Panda* (☎ 42 26 14; fax 42 34 18), comfortable doubles with bath and WC are reasonable value at 2400 Sk, with breakfast and dinner. Next door, *Penzión Poľana* (☎ 42 25 18; fax 42 21 63) has plain doubles/triples with shared facilities for 500/600 Sk. In the woods farther out is a real gem, the peaceful *Penzión Marta* (☎ 969 32 96), building No II/9 of the Partizán sanatorium, where rooms with shared facilities are 200 Sk per bed (plus 100 Sk per dinner or 60 Sk per breakfast if you like).

The *Juniorhotel Vysoké Tatry* (☎ 2661) is a complex of one-storey buildings where rooms with common facilities are a great deal at 230 to 250 Sk per bed (210 Sk per bed for ISIC and HI card-holders), but it's usually booked out with youth groups. It also has a restaurant, wine bar, sauna and massage.

Nový Smokovec Some of the pricey *zotavovňa* (sanatoria) here are open to tourists, though you'll probably have to book months ahead. *Vila Dr Szontagh* (☎ 42 20 61; fax 42 20 62), named after the physician who founded Nový Smokovec before WWI, has doubles with bath and satellite TV for 1600 Sk with breakfast (about half that in October and November).

Doubles with shower and WC at the *Hotel Park* (☎ 42 23 42; fax 42 23 04) are about 2700 Sk. The *Hotel MS-70* ski centre (☎ 42 29 72) is a bargain during the off-season, with basic, rustic rooms with shower for 400 Sk per bed, or 460 Sk with shower and WC.

Dolný Smokovec The big, clean *Ternocamp* campsite (☎ 2406 or 3159), open from mid-June to mid-September, is good value at about 80 Sk per person, including vehicle and tent. Part of the same complex is the new *Terno Hotel*, with rooms with WC, shower and satellite TV for 500 Sk per person, plus it has a restaurant. Take the električka to Pod Lesom, from where it's a five minute walk.

Hrebienok At the top of the funicular, the *Bilíkova chata* (☎ 42 24 39; fax 42 22 66) has plain doubles for about 500 Sk per person, and there are sometimes off-season rooms available on the spot.

Places to Eat

A bargain in Starý Smokovec is the cheap and cheerful *Tatranská Kuria* near the bus stop; try their guľašová polievka (goulash soup) with halušky (cheese dumplings), or rezeň kuria (chicken cutlet), and fill up for 100 Sk plus beer. Next door the plain *Reštaurácia Tatry* serves adequate, cheap (30 to 90 Sk) daily specials until 8 pm. The restaurant in the *Hotel Šport* is good value, with plain meals for just 30 to 100 Sk.

The *Taverna Reštaurácia*, left of the Hotel Grand, is good and relatively cheap (meals 46 to 120 Sk plus drinks). The restaurant at the *Hotel Grand* is said to be very good, but expect to pay up to 500 Sk for dinner.

Locals like the *To-Ja* Chinese restaurant (☎ 3207), on the way from the Pod Lesom električka station to the Ternocamp campsite; reservations are recommended. Up at Hrebienok, the restaurant at the *Bilíkova chata* is open from 7 am to 6 pm, and the patio has smashing views of Lomnický štít.

Entertainment

There isn't much. The Grand Hotel has the *Cristal disco bar* (open Wednesday to Sunday). The *Laser disco* is at Café Albas, behind the town hall. There are also bars at the Grand and Park hotels.

Getting Around

You can rent a mountain bike for about 250 Sk per day from T-Ski, or from Tatrasport, near Satur.

TATRANSKÁ LOMNICA

This is the quietest of the Tatra resorts, dotted with old trade-union hostels. It's also headquarters for the national park. The only real attraction is the cable car up to Lomnický štít.

Information

The Tatra National Park Information Office (Združenie cestovného ruchu Vysoké Tatry, or TANAP; ☎ 46 79 51) is in the same building as the Tatra National Park Museum (see below), to the right of the entrance. It has plenty of hard-to-get brochures about the Tatra mountain range. Tatratour (☎ 96 72 04) is in obchodný dom Javor.

National Park Museum

The Tatra National Park Museum (múzeum Tatranského národného parku; ☎ 46 79 51 ext 281) is open weekdays from 8.30 am to noon and 1 to 5 pm, and weekends from 8 am to noon, with unexciting displays on flora, fauna and regional ethnography.

Cable Car

A highlight of any visit is the astonishing cable-car journey from Tatranská Lomnica up to the lake (and winter ski area) called Skalnaté pleso (1751m), plus the second, white-knuckle ride to the 2632m summit of Lomnický štít, with views right across the Tatras' jagged crest.

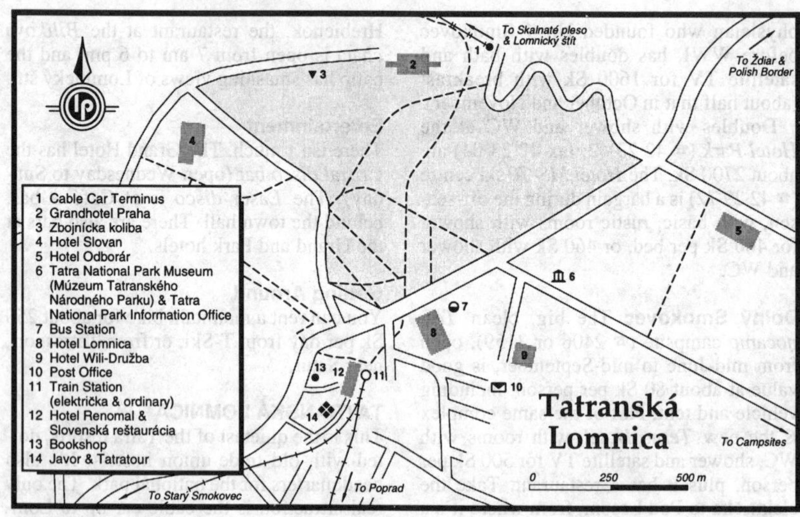

When it's fine everybody else wants to do it too, so the queues are huge. The day's tickets to Skalnaté usually sell out by early morning, and there are no advance bookings. The ticket office opens at 6.45 am, and the cars run daily, except Tuesday, from 7 am to 8 pm in June, July and August, and until 6.30 pm for the rest of the year. Skalnaté is 70 Sk each way and the summit an additional 300 Sk each way, but it's worth every *halier*. Kids from five to 10 years travel for half that price.

One way to beat the queues is to walk up to Skalnaté. There is also an ordinary chair lift from Skalnaté to Lomnické sedlo, a 2190m saddle below the summit, which runs daily from June through October from 8 am to 5 pm. The narrow summit (site of a meteorology research station) will be crowded. Pack warm clothing – it's very cold, even most days in midsummer.

Walks from Tatranská Lomnica

An easy (and popular) all-day loop starts with an early cable-car ascent to Skalnaté pleso (with a detour by cable car to the summit of Lomnický štít). From Skalnaté pleso the red-marked magistrála offers grand views on its way to Hrebienok, where you can catch the funicular railway down to Starý Smokovec and the električka back to Tatranská Lomnica. An alternative is to descend to Tatranská Lomnica on a blue trail from the valley of the Veľká Studená.

Places to Stay

Camping The most sensible accommodation is at one of three campsites east of town. The grandest is the year-round *Eurocamp FICC* (☎ 46 74 41/5), with swimming pool, tennis, sauna, massage and a jolly restaurant. Its hotel doubles are 570 Sk. The others are *Autocamping Tatranec* (☎ 46 77 03/4) and *Športcamp* (☎ 46 72 28), both open from June into September. All three charge about 90 Sk for each person, tent, vehicle etc; Eurocamp and Tatranec also have bungalows for about 1600 Sk. Buses and non električka trains from Tatranská Lomnica pass the campsites about hourly.

A decent bottom-end campsite in Stará Lesná is *Autocamping Jupela* (☎ 46 74 93), a short walk from the Stará Lesná električka stop; it's open from May to September.

Hotels Tatranská Lomnica's cheapest hotel rooms appear to be at the *Hotel Wili-Družba* (☎ 46 77 61/2), in the woods east of the station, where single/double rooms with shower and WC are 720/1200 Sk. Doubles at the run-down *Hotel Lomnica* (☎ 46 72 51) are 625 Sk with shared facilities, 865 Sk with their own (but breakfast is 150 Sk).

The *Hotel Odborár* (☎ 46 73 51/3) is a huge recreational sanatorium with zero character and doubles with WC are a pricey 1290 Sk. Also characterless, the giant *Hotel Slovan* (☎ 46 78 51), where doubles/ triples with shower and WC are 1170/1550 Sk.

At the upper end of both the town and the price scale is the *Grandhotel Praha* (☎ 46 79 41), a Swiss confection with doubles from at least 2305 Sk.

Places to Eat

The *Slovenská reštaurácia*, by the train station, has adequate but pricey Slovak courses for 54 to 269 Sk, and halušky and pirohy for less. For true Slovak entertainment try *Zbojnícka koliba* with its typical Slovak Tatra food and Romany band, which plays at your table. It is open from 4 pm to midnight and there is a 30 Sk music charge. The restaurant is just off the road that leads to the Grandhotel Praha. Many travellers appreciate the *Tatranská Koliba reštaurácia* at Eurocamp FICC, with reasonably priced spit-roasted chicken, plenty of beer and staff who break into song with the house band.

Entertainment

Oáza disco bar is in the Kultúrne stredisko, on the road to Poprad.

Getting There & Away

In addition to the električka, you can catch a regular train from here to Poprad, Kežmarok or Prešov.

BELIANSKÉ TATRAS

This small (64 sq km) eastern arm of the Tatras has until recently been off-limits, to protect its ecosystem (or old state secrets?), but trails are slowly being opened to the public. Limestone prevails here, and there is a large cave system at Tatranská Kotlina.

Tatranská Kotlina

Over 1km of **caves** (Belianské jaskyňa) are open to the public, with tours daily (60 Sk), except Monday, hourly from mid-May to mid-September from 9 am to 5 pm, and every 1½ hours from 9.30 am to 3.30 pm the rest of the year. There is said to be a small *hostel* about 1km east of the bus stop.

Ždiar

Little Ždiar is the only substantial settlement predating the Tatra resorts, though its picturesque timbered and decorated cottages, and a tradition of bright costumes and ceremonies, are being rapidly eroded by tourism. Several sections of the village are now historical reservations, and one house has been done up as the **Ždiar House Museum** (Ždiarská dom múzeum), which is open weekdays from 9 am to 4 pm, weekends to noon, but during the off-season it has irregular opening hours. At the east end of the village there is the small Galéria Jana Zoričáka.

You can eat in another cottage, now the *Reštaurácia Protežka*, on the road by the bus stop. The *Penzión Slovakia Ždiar* has rooms for 350 Sk per bed (500 Sk with three meals), and there are other penzióny and private rooms.

Getting There & Away

There are only seven buses a day between Starý Smokovec/Tatranská Lomnica and Ždiar, and fewer on the weekends.

East Slovakia

HIGHLIGHTS

- Take in the museums and churches, not to mention the bars and cafés, of Košice
- Shoot the rapids at Dunajec Gorge in traditional wooden rafts called *pltě*
- Get an up-close look at traditional folk architecture at the superb skansen in Bardejovské Kúpele
- Hike one of a dozen pristine trails in the Slovenský raj National Park

East Slovakia is the country's remotest and poorest region, but the most interesting to visit. Its isolation has for centuries preserved many traditions (best appreciated during the region's festivals and pilgrimages), as well as protecting Rusin's wooden churches from the ravages of progress. Other highlights include the medieval town centres of Bardejov and Levoča, and the splendid Spiš and Krásna Hôrka castles.

This mostly mountainous region offers some world-class landscapes, most spectacularly the east end of the High Tatras mountains. The adjacent Pieniny National Park is known for its dramatic Dunajec gorge. South of this lie the deep ravines and waterfalls of the Slovenský raj (Slovak Paradise), the grottoes of the Slovak Karst (Slovenský kras), and the eastern extension of the Slovenské rudohorie range. Along most of the border with Poland runs the Nízke Beskydy range, part of the Carpathian chain. Only the East Slovak lowlands (Východoslovenská nížina) in the south-east corner are flat.

Three main rivers, the Hornád, Ondava and Laborec, flow north-south in parallel, with one large artificial lake, Veľká Domáša, on the Ondava, and another, Zemplínska šírava, near the Ukrainian border.

Special Events

There are folk festivals throughout the year in East Slovakia. The best known are in June and include:

Svidník – Rusin-Ukrainian Cultural Festival, late June
Košice – East Slovak Folk Festival, mid-June
Červený Kláštor – Zamaguria Folk Festival, mid-June
Gombasek – Hungarian Folk Festival, late June

Throughout July and August there are Marian pilgrimages in many Slovak villages, starting with one at Levoča on the first weekend of July. A Uniate (Greek Catholic) pilgrimage is held around the third weekend in August near the village of Ľutina, 40km north-east of Levoča.

KOŠICE

This modern, upbeat town of 235,000 is the administrative capital of East Slovakia, not to mention the second-biggest and most important Slovak city after the capital, Bratislava.

Although now a major steel-making city with vast residential districts built by the Communists, there is much in the old town to interest travellers. Churches and museums abound, and there's an active state theatre – plus a vast, painstakingly restored main square that rivals anything in Bratislava. With extensive train and bus connections, Košice is also a good base for excursions to other eastern Slovak towns.

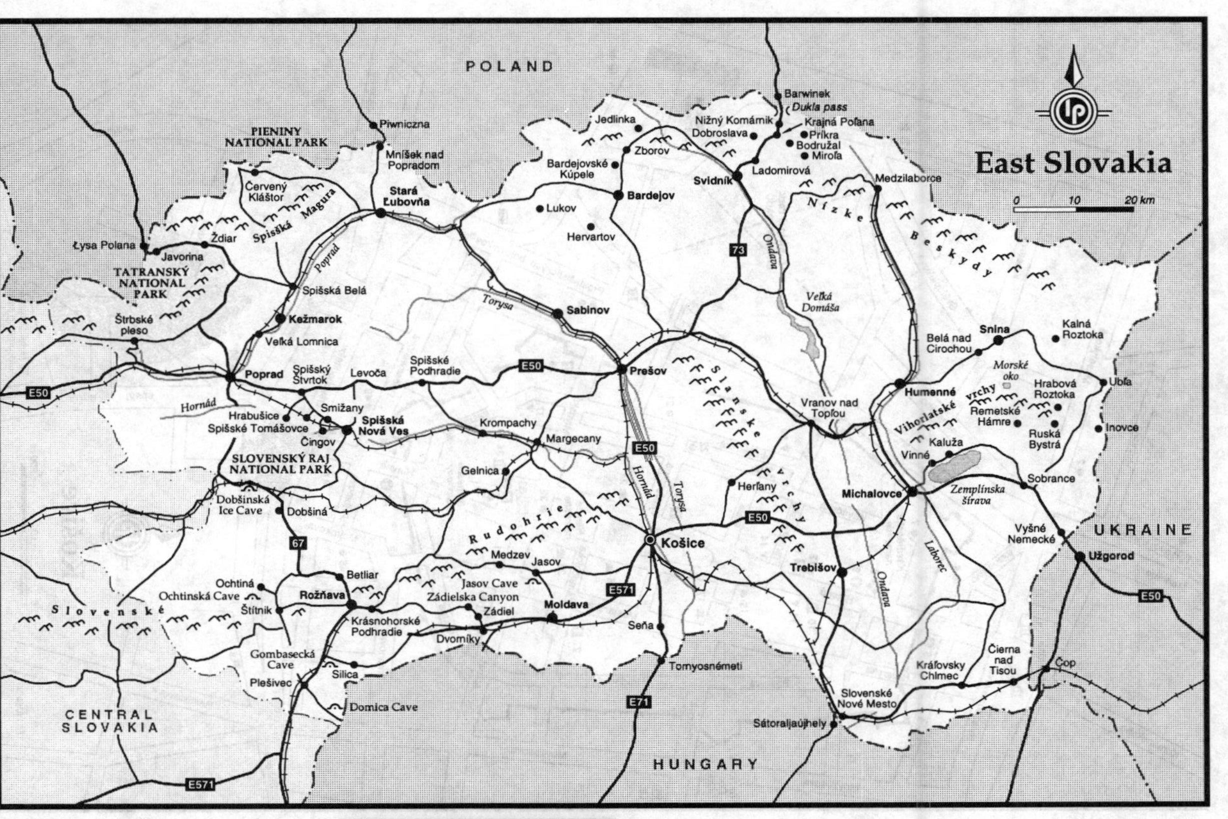
East Slovakia
0 10 20 km
POLAND
UKRAINE
HUNGARY
CENTRAL SLOVAKIA
PIENINY NATIONAL PARK
TATRANSKÝ NATIONAL PARK
SLOVENSKÝ RAJ NATIONAL PARK
Nízke Beskydy
Slanské vrchy
Vihorlatské vrchy
Spišská Magura
Slovenské Rudohorie
Piwniczna
Mníšek nad Popradom
Červený Kláštor
Stará Ľubovňa
Łysa Polana
Javorina
Ždiar
Poprad
Spišská Belá
Štrbské pleso
Kežmarok
Veľká Lomnica
E50
Spišský Štvrtok
Levoča
Spišské Podhradie
Hornád
Hrabušice
Smižany
Spišská Nová Ves
Spišské Tomášovce
Čingov
Krompachy
Margecany
Gelnica
Dobšinská Ice Cave
Dobšiná
67
Torysa
Sabinov
Prešov
Jedlinka
Zborov
Bardejovské Kúpele
Bardejov
Lukov
Hervartov
Barwinek
Dukla pass
Nižný Komárnik
Dobroslava
Krajná Poľana
Príkra
Bodružal
Miroľa
Svidník
Ladomirová
Medzilaborce
73
Ondava
Veľká Domaša
Belá nad Cirochou
Snina
Kalná Roztoka
Morské oko
Humenné
Hrabová Roztoka
Ubľa
Vranov nad Topľou
Remetské Hámre
Ruská Bystrá
Inovce
Kaluža
Vinné
Michalovce
Zemplínska šírava
Sobrance
Herľany
Košice
Vyšné Nemecké
Užgorod
Laborec
Medzev
Jasov
Jasov Cave
Zádielska Canyon
Zádiel
Moldava
E571
Ochtiná
Ochtinská Cave
Rožňava
Betliar
Štítnik
Krásnohorské Podhradie
Dvorníky
Seňa
Trebišov
Gombasecká Cave
Silica
Plešivec
Domica Cave
Tornyosnémeti
E71
Slovenské Nové Mesto
Sátoraljaújhely
Kráľovsky Chlmec
Čierna nad Tisou
Čop

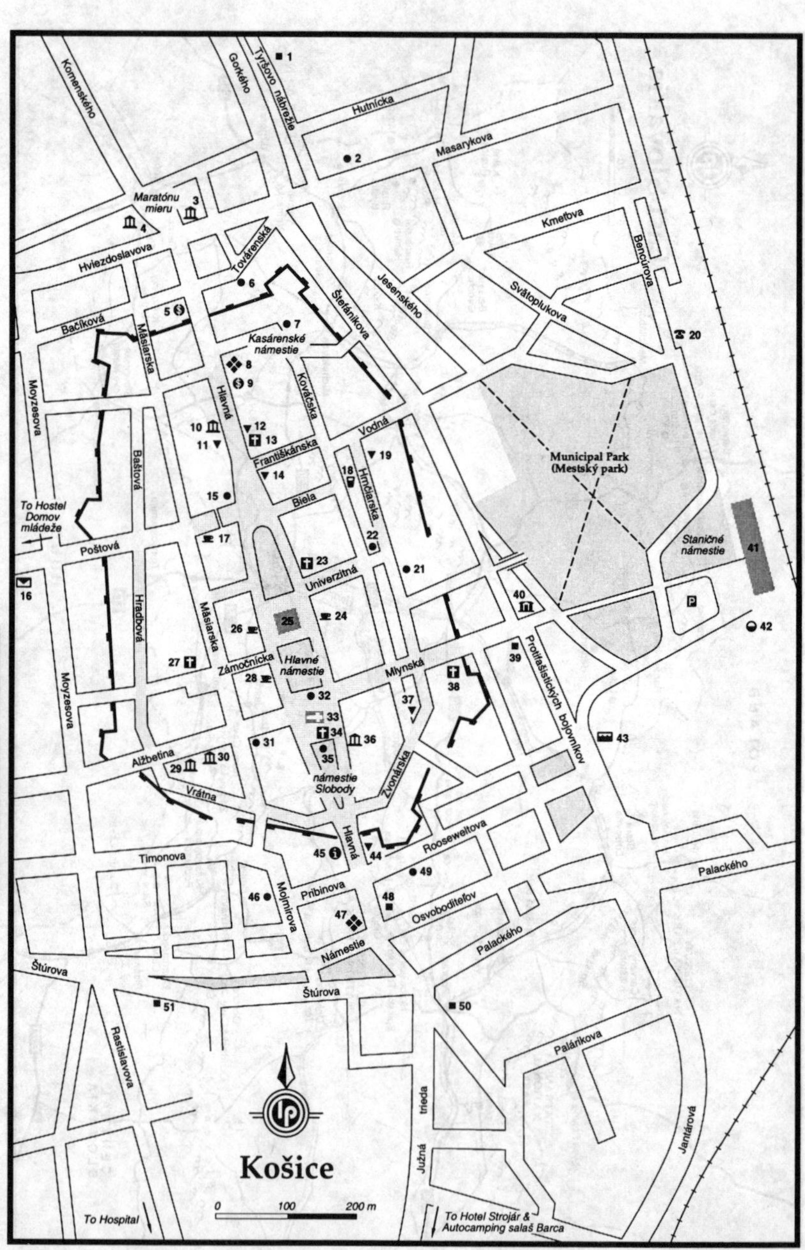
Komenského
Gorkého
Tyršovo nábrežie
Hutnícka
Masarykova
Maratónu mieru
Kmeťova
Benčurova
Hviezdoslavova
Továrenská
Štefánikova
Jesenského
Svätoplukova
Bačíková
Mäsiarska
Kasárenské námestie
Kováčska
Moyzesova
Hlavná
Vodná
Františkánska
Hrnčiarska
Biela
Baštová
Municipal Park
(Mestský park)
To Hostel Domov mládeže
Poštová
Staničné námestie
Univerzitná
Hradbová
Mäsiarska
Zámočnícka
Hlavné námestie
Mlynská
Protifašistických bojovníkov
Moyzesova
Alžbetina
Vrátna
námestie Slobody
Zvonárska
Timonova
Hlavná
Rooseweltova
Palackého
Mojmírova
Pribinova
Osvoboditeľov
Námestie
Palackého
Štúrova
Štúrova
Rastislavova
Paláriková
Južná trieda
Jantárová
Košice
0 100 200 m
To Hospital
To Hotel Strojár & Autocamping salaš Barca

PLACES TO STAY
1 Hotel Hutník
39 Hotel Európa
48 Hotel Slovan
50 Hotel Centrum
51 TJ Metropol turistická ubytovňa

PLACES TO EAT
11 Bakchus
12 Šomoši Veverička grill & Valtická vináreň
14 Pizzeria Milano
17 Aida Espresso
19 Reštaurácia U vodnára
24 Kaviáreň Slavia
26 Čitáreň čajovná
28 Carpano
37 Reštaurácia Ajvega
44 Bomba Klub

OTHER
2 Dom kultúry & Kino Capitol
3 East Slovak Museum
4 East Slovak Museum (Východoslovenské múzeum)
5 Všeobecná úverová banka
6 Autoturist
7 Kino Úsmev
8 Tesco Department Store
9 Visa ATM
10 Slovak Technical Museum (Slovenské technické múzeum)
13 Franciscan Church (kostol Františkánov)
15 Štúdio SMER
16 Post Office
18 Jazz Pub
20 Telephone Office
21 Hangman's Bastion (Katova bašta)
22 Mikluš Prison (Miklušova väznica)
23 Jesuit Church (kostol Jezuitov)
25 State Theatre (Štátne divadlo)
27 Dominican Church (kostol Dominikánov)
29 Július Jakoby Gallery (branch)
30 Múzeum Löfflera
31 Tatratour
32 Urban Tower (Urbanova veža)
33 Cathedral of St Elizabeth (dom sv Alžběty)
34 Chapel of St Michael (kaplinka sv Michala)
35 Fountain
36 Július Jakoby Gallery (Galéria Júliusa Jakobyho)
38 Evangelical Church (Evanjelický kostol)
40 Jakabov Palace (Jakabov palác) & British Council
41 Train Station
42 Bus Station
43 Swimming Pool
45 Aices Tourist Office
46 Thália Hungarian Theatre
47 Dargov Department Store
49 Puppet Theatre (Bábkové divadlo)

History

The oldest record of Košice is from 1230, the town having begun as a Slav settlement, and it received a charter in 1241. After the first Tatar invasions German settlers began to arrive. In 1342 it became an independent royal town, and grew into an important trade and manufacturing centre.

Košice was fortified in the 16th century, when Europe was invaded by the Turks; some of the fortifications survive. Its importance as a commercial centre declined as the invasion pushed trading routes westward, though in 1657 a university was founded here. In an uprising in 1682, Count Imre Thököly, siding with the Turks against the Habsburgs, captured Košice for a short period, proclaiming himself king of Upper Hungary.

The Transylvanian prince Ferenc Rákóczi II had his headquarters at Košice during the Hungarian War of Independence against the Habsburgs (1703-11). Even today Košice has a strong Hungarian flavour, thanks to the 20,000 ethnic Hungarians who live here; Košice's Hungarian name is Kassa.

The town became part of Czechoslovakia in 1918 but was again occupied by Hungary from 1938 to 1945. From 21 February to 21 April 1945, Košice served as the capital of liberated Czechoslovakia. Thus it was here that, on 5 April 1945, the so-called Košice Government Programme (Košický vládny program) was declared, setting out the form of the postwar Czechoslovak government. Since the declaration promised four key ministries to Communists, a Communist future for Czechoslovakia then became a virtual certainty.

Orientation

Košice is clustered largely on the west bank of the Hornád river. From the train and bus stations it's a 10 minute walk farther west to Hlavná, which splits the city centre in half and is wide enough to include two park-like squares, námestie Slobody and Hlavné námestie. Most sights, shops, banks and restaurants are on or near this long, largely pedestrianised street.

The left-luggage office in the train station is open 24 hours, except for three 45-minute breaks.

Information

Tourist Offices The Aices office (☎ 186), Hlavná 8, can answer any questions. It sells maps and guidebooks, changes money and books concert tickets and accommodation, weekdays from 8 am to 5 pm, Saturday from 9 am to 1 pm.

Visa Extensions Apply for visa extensions, complete police registration or report a lost passport or visa at the Úradovňa cudzineckej polície a pasovej služby (police and passport office), across the street from the huge Košice-Mestský municipal administration building on trieda Slovenského Národného Povstania. It's open Monday and Wednesday from 10 am to noon and 12.30 to 6 pm; Tuesday, Thursday and Friday from 7 am to noon. Take bus No 19 west from the corner of Hlavná and Štúrova.

Money The Investičná banka exchange office, upstairs in the train station, charges no commission and is open weekdays from 8 am to 5 pm (Tuesday and Friday to 4 pm, Wednesday to 2 pm). The Všeobecná úverová banka, Hlavná 112, changes travellers cheques for 1% commission and has a MasterCard ATM. There's a Visa ATM near the Tesco department store at Hlavná 103.

For American Express cash advances and the like, the local agent, Tatratour (☎ 622 13 34), is at Alžbetina 6, and is open weekdays from 9 am to 5 pm.

Post & Communications The main post office is on Poštová, west of Hlavná. There's a 24 hour telephone centre inside a second post office at Poštová 18, about 500m north of the train station at the end of the park.

The BBC World Service is available on FM 103.2. Košice's area code is ☎ 095.

Bookshops Petit, Hlavná 41, has a good selection of hiking maps and town plans. Hotel Slovan sells international newspapers and magazines.

Travel Agencies Satur (☎ 622 31), in the Hotel Slovan at Hlavná 1, reserves sleepers and couchettes and sells international train tickets. The 'Pokladnica Ares' office upstairs in the train station also arranges these tickets. Satur sells international bus tickets to many European cities.

Cultural Centre The British Council (☎ 622 51 53; fax 622 51 56), inside Jakabov Palace at Mlynská 30, is an English-language resource centre where visitors can curl up in the library with British newspapers and magazines.

Emergencies The police (*polícia*; ☎ 622 02 37, emergencies ☎ 158) are at Hlavná 105. The hospital (Fakultná nemocnica; ☎ 622 52 51) is at Rastislavova 43. A 24 hour pharmacy is at Toryská 1; take bus No 19 west from the corner of Hlavná and Štúrova.

Things to See

Just outside the relaxing Municipal Park (Městský park) is the **Jakabov Palace** (Jakabov palác), where President Beneš lived in early 1945; today it's partly occupied by the British Council.

Walk along Mlynská, past the Evangelical Church (Evanjelický kostol), and turn right into Hrnčiarska to a museum in the **Hangman's Bastion** (Katova bašta), at No 7. This has exhibits of weapons and medieval miscellany. There is also a replica of a house with some genuine items that belonged to Ferenc Rákóczi II, a Transylvanian-Hungarian rebel leader in the early

18th century. Rákóczi took up a family tradition of fighting the house of Habsburg, carrying on the Protestant struggle against the Hungarian king until his defeat in 1717, whereupon he was exiled in Turkey. The bastion is open Tuesday to Saturday from 9 am to 5 pm, Sunday to 1 pm. Entry costs 20 Sk (minimum five people for tour).

Nearby at Pri Miklušovej väznici 10 is the **Mikluš Prison** (Miklušova väznica). This connected pair of 16th century houses once served as a prison equipped with medieval torture chambers and cells. It's open the same hours as the Hangman's Bastion, which is also where you buy tickets (20 Sk) for Mikluš Prison.

Walk up Kováčska and left into Františkánska, where you'll find the **Franciscan Church** (kostol Františkánov), built at the beginning of the 15th century and 'Baroquefied' in 1724.

Turn left on Hlavná for Košice's top sight, the **Cathedral of St Elizabeth** (dom sv Alžběty), a magnificent late-Gothic edifice built in 1345. In a **crypt** on the left side of the nave is the tomb of Ferenc Rákóczi. Prince Rákóczi II was exiled to Turkey after the failed 18th century Hungarian insurgency against Austria and only in 1905 was he officially pardoned and his remains reburied here. At the time of writing both the crypt and adjacent **Urban Tower** (Urbanova veža) – but not the church itself – were closed due to the massive and ongoing renovation of Hlavné námestie. On the cathedral's south side is the 14th century **Chapel of St Michael** (kaplinka sv Michala).

South-east of the cathedral, at Hlavná 27, is the main branch of the **Július Jakoby Gallery** (galéria Júliusa Jakobyho). This and another at Alžbetina 22 have permanent collections of 19th century eastern Slovak painters, works by local painter Július Jakoby (1903-85), and changing exhibits. Both galleries are open daily, except Monday, from 10 am to 6 pm (Sunday to 2 pm); entry costs 5 Sk for each.

The Jakoby Gallery on Hlavná forms part of a larger building called the Stoličný dom, also known as the **House of the Košice Government Programme** (dom Košického vládného programu). The blueprint for the new Czechoslovak government plan was presented here in 1945.

Most of Košice's other historic sites are north along Hlavné námestie and Hlavná. In the centre of the square is the ornate and recently renovated **State Theatre** (Štátne divadlo), built in 1899. Beside it at Hlavné námestie 59 is the rococo former **town hall** (1780), now a cinema, and north of the theatre is a large **plague column** (1723). Also on the square is a small Jesuit Church (kostol jezuitov).

Farther north at Hlavná 88 is the **Slovak Technical Museum** (Slovenské technické múzeum), full of old machines and wrought-iron ornamental work, for which eastern Slovakia is well known. It's open Tuesday to Friday from 9 am to 5 pm, Saturday to 2 pm, and Sunday from 1 to 4.30 pm; entry costs 20 Sk.

RICHARD NEBESKÝ

The ornate State Theatre building in Hlavné námestie, Košice

SLOVAK REPUBLIC

The **East Slovak Museum** (Východoslovenské múzeum) has two branches on námestie Maratónu mieru at the northern end of Hlavná, both open Tuesday to Saturday from 9 am to 5 pm, Sunday from 1 pm. The main branch on the square's west side is dedicated to archaeology and prehistory; entry costs 20 Sk. A highlight is the stunning **Košice Gold Treasure** (Košický zlatý poklad), with 2920 gold coins minted in Kremnica that were stashed in the wall of a house called the Spiš Chamber at Hlavná 74, and discovered in 1935 by a construction crew during renovations.

Across the square there's a small zoological display with live snakes and bugs (20 Sk), plus art and furniture from the Middle Ages to the present (20 Sk).

Last, but absolutely not least, is the **Löffler Museum**, Alžbetina 20, which is really a gallery showing off the Löffler family's collection of early 20th century portraits and sculptures, plus some good B&W photography by contemporary Slovak artists. It's open Tuesday to Saturday from 10 am to 6 pm, Sunday from 1 to 5 pm; entry costs 5 Sk.

Special Events

In Košice the annual East Slovak Folk Festival takes place up and down Hlavná in mid-June. On the first Sunday in October, runners from many countries participate in an International Marathon Race for Peace.

Places to Stay

Camping Just over 5km south of the city is *Autocamping salaš Barca* (☎ 623 33 97). Take tram No 3 south along Južná trieda from the train station until the tram turns left at an underpass, then walk west on Alejová (the Rožňava Highway) for about 800m till you see the camping ground on the left. It's open from 15 April through September and there are cabins (doubles/triples for 290/445 Sk) and tent spaces (40 Sk per person, 30 Sk per tent). The cabins are available year-round, and there's also a restaurant.

Hostels The *Domov mládeže* (☎ 42 93 34), on the western side of town at Medická 2, has two and three-bed rooms for 130 Sk per person. Follow Poštová west past Moyzesova and Kuzmányho and continue straight after it becomes Vojenská; a stairway 300m ahead on the left leads to Medická.

The proletarian *Hotel Strojár* (☎ 544 06), Južná trieda 93, has double and triple rooms (with a bathroom shared between every two rooms) for 210 Sk and 185 Sk per person, respectively. Apartments are 750 Sk for a double. This workers' dormitory is a little run-down but usually has vacancies. From the train station take tram No 3 south to the 'Hotel Strojár' stop.

Hotels The basic *Hotel Európa* (☎ 622 38 97), a grand old three storey building just across the park from the train station, has singles/doubles/triples at 330/570/770 Sk with shared bath.

The *TJ Metropol turistická ubytovňa* (☎ 559 48), Štúrova 32, is an attractive sports complex where cheerful rooms with shared bath are 250 Sk per person. It's an easy walk from town but is often full with groups, and is prone to tram noise in the very early morning.

The bleak, depressing, 12 storey *Hotel Hutník* (☎ 633 77 80), Tyršovo nábrežie 6, is a last resort, priced at 780/1260 Sk with bath.

Business travellers are the usual clientele at *Hotel Slovan* (☎ 623 27 16; fax 622 84 13), Hlavná 1, with fully equipped rooms for 1620/2510 Sk.

In the same category – but not as nice – is *Hotel Centrum* (☎ 76 31 01), Južná trieda 2A, priced at 1600/2200 Sk.

Places to Eat

Reštaurácia Ajvega, Orlia 10, is an inexpensive, friendly vegetarian restaurant with an English menu, open daily from 11 am to 11 pm. The portions are medium sized and the meals are tasty; try the Moshi-Moshi, a mild curry with rice and potatoes (50 Sk).

Pizzeria Milano, Hlavná 83, serves inexpensive pizzas.

The *Šomoši Veverička grill*, Hlavná 95, is good for grilled meats and fish.

A better choice for more leisurely dining is *Reštaurácia U vodnára*, on Hrnčiarska, a semi-formal spot with above-average Slovak meals. It's open daily to 11 pm.

A popular spot to eat or have a drink is *Bakchus*, Hlavná 8. Through the passageway is an open courtyard with tables, perfect on sunny days. Try the Bakchus chicken.

Another bar-restaurant is the *Bomba Klub*, Hlavná 5, with hearty beer-hall food plus live music on Friday and Saturday nights. Come early to avoid the crowds.

Cafés One of the better spots for espressos and reading the newspaper is *Carpano*, at Hlavná 42. The up-market *Kaviáreň Slavia*, Hlavná 63, has a decent selection of cakes. *Čitáreň čajovná* is a smoke-free teahouse at Hlavná 52. *Aida Espresso*, on Poštová through the passage at Hlavné námestie 74, has the best ice cream in town.

Entertainment

Classical Music & Theatre The renovated *State Theatre* (Štátne divadlo), on námestie Slobody, holds regular performances.

The *Thália Hungarian Theatre* and the *State Philharmonic dom umenia* are both in the south-west corner of the old town, but performances are held only once or twice a week. Recitals are sometimes given at the *Konzervatórium*, Hlavná 89.

You can buy tickets from Aices or at Štúdio SMER, Hlavná 76.

Puppet Theatre The *Bábkové divadlo*, Rooseveltova 1, puts on puppet shows for children on weekday mornings and Sunday afternoons.

Cinemas There are three cinemas in the city centre: *Kino Úsmev* on Kasárenské námestie, *Kino Tatra* in the courtyard behind Aices, and *Kino Capitol* in the dom kultúry by Hotel Hutník.

Bars & Clubs The *Valtická vináreň*, upstairs at Hlavná 97, functions as a disco on Friday from 9 pm to 2 am, but it's better known for its pub (piváreň) downstairs in the courtyard, open nightly until midnight.

More fun is the snazzy *Jazz Pub*, Kováčska 39, with a bar on the ground floor plus an adjacent cellar with live jazz twice weekly (20 Sk cover). Ring the buzzer for both – the doors are locked in a successful effort to be 'exclusive'.

Getting There & Away

Air ČSA (☎ 622 68 71) has daily flights to and from Prague. Tatra Air (☎ 76 05 06) flies five times a week, and ČSA twice a week, between Košice and Bratislava. Both have offices at the Hotel Centrum.

Bus Buses are best for Prešov (36km; several an hour), Bardejov (1¾ hours; 77km; 14 daily), Bardejovské Kúpele (83km; six daily) and Spišské Podhradie (64km; eight daily). A bus to Užgorod, Ukraine (130 Sk; three hours; 200km) leaves Košice up to eight times a day.

Train Overnight trains with sleepers and couchettes are available between Košice and Prague (708km), Brno (493km), Bratislava (445km), Děčín (807km), Karlovy Vary (897km), Plzeň (896km) and Františkovy Lázně (1081km). Daytime express trains connect Košice to Prague (via Poprad and Žilina) and Bratislava (via Banská Bystrica or Žilina).

The daily *Cracovia* and *Karpaty* express trains between Budapest and Kraków pass through Košice (reservations required). Two evening trains depart from Košice for Kiev (1450 Sk; 1013km) and Moscow (2600 Sk; 1880km). The ticket price includes the compulsory sleeper charge.

Car Autoturist (☎ 622 40 66), Továrenská 1, represents Europcar. Tatratour or Satur may be able to help with cheaper vehicles.

Border Crossings About 20km south of Košice at Hraničná pri Hornáde is a 24 hour vehicle and pedestrian crossing to Tornyosnémeti, Hungary. Another crossing is eastward at Slovenské Nové Mesto, which joins Sátoraljaújhely. Neither has a foreign exchange office. At the latter you walk across the border between the Slovak and Hungarian railway systems.

AROUND KOŠICE

The one claim to fame of **Herľany** is that it has Slovakia's only geyser (*gejzír*), which, from a depth of 400m, erupts 15 to 20m every 36 hours. Check with Aices in Košice to find when it will next spout.

There are frequent bus connections from Košice on weekdays, but fewer on weekends, when only two buses depart, at 8.10 and 10.30 am, for the 29km journey.

MICHALOVCE

There's little reason to stop here except to change buses or stay the night en route to Humenné, Medzilaborce or the Vihorlatské Highlands. If you have a couple of hours between buses, the **Zemplínske múzeum**, in the chateau behind the bus station on námestie Červenej armády, has exhibits on regional history and folklore. It is open daily, except Monday, from 10 am to 4 pm. Entry costs 10 Sk.

Orientation & Information

From the bus station, cross the road and turn left past Hotel Družba onto the main drag, námestie Osvoboditeľov. The Aices tourist office (☎ 186) is 300m ahead at No 77, and open weekdays from 9 am to 4 pm.

The train station is 1km south-west of the centre; follow Staničná to Humenská and turn right, then go left on Štefánikova.

Michalovce's area code is ☎ 0946.

Places to Stay

Single/double rooms with the works at the modern *Hotel Družba* (☎ 44 10 69), námestie Osvoboditeľov 1, are 650/830 Sk with breakfast. Otherwise you can pester Aices about private rooms.

Getting There & Away

By bus there are several connections an hour to Košice, and at least four a day to Sobrance. By train there's frequent service to Humenné and Medzilaborce.

VIHORLATSKÉ HIGHLANDS

The Vihorlatské Highlands (Vihorlatské vrchy) east of Košice have some scenic areas for walking, particularly around the popular lake of Morské oko. There is also a major, though not very interesting, resort at the artificial lake of Zemplínska šírava, centred on the towns (really little more than rows of hotels) of Vinné and Kaluža.

Wooden Churches

Near the Ukrainian border are some beautiful examples of traditional Rusin architecture, mainly wooden churches plus the odd barn and weathered cottage. Transportation is the main problem: buses run regularly from Sobrance to Snina (via Ubľa), but the churches are all a few kilometres off the main road.

About 16km north-east of Sobrance, on a hill below the tiny village of **Inovce**, is a three-domed church (1840). Halfway through the village of **Ruská Bystra** is another church in fairly good repair. To reach the church at **Hrabová Roztoka**, head 2km off the main road to Šmigovec and turn left (the road is poorly signposted).

The church at **Kalná Roztoka** is in poor condition with peeling whitewash and a few broken windows. Perhaps to compensate, there's a snack bar at its base – the only eatery of any sort in the area (the nearest hotels are in Snina and Sobrance).

Walks

Hiking is the reason to come here. A vigorous walk starts from **Remetské Hámre** on a red-marked trail, which intersects a yellow trail to the lake (it is prohibited to swim in Morské oko). From Morské oko you can continue north to **Sninský kameň** (1005m), where you climb a series of ladders to fine views from the summit. From there you can continue three hours to

SLOVAK REPUBLIC

Snina along a green trail and catch a train to Humenné, Michalovce or Košice. A less scenic, green trail goes to Zemplínske Hámre, from where it is 5km to either Snina or Belá nad Cirochou, both of which have train stations. It is, of course, possible to do these walks in reverse from Snina.

The map to have is Slovenská kartografia's Edícia turistických series *Vihorlatské vrchy* (1:100,000), with clearly marked walking trails.

Places to Stay

If you're bound for the lake of Zemplínska šírava, try *Hotel Lom* (☎ 0946-921 82) in Vinné, or *Hotel Poštár* (☎ 0946-922 89) in Kaluža. Both charge about 1100 Sk for doubles with bath.

The only choice in tiny Sobrance is the year-round *Hotel Maňa* (☎ 0947-3280), on the main square and priced at 250/400 Sk for single/double rooms with shared bath.

Snina is little more than a ring of high-rise apartments. In the centre of the ring, on Vihorlatska, is the town's only accommodation, the basic *Hotel Vihorlat* (☎ 0932-2704), with rooms that have a bath for 440/600 Sk.

Getting There & Away

Buses run frequently from Michalovce to Vinné, Snina and Sobrance. From Sobrance there are two daily buses to Snina (via Ubľa). The easiest way to reach Morské oko is by bus via Sobrance and Remetské Hámre (outside July and August the buses go only to Remetské Hámre, so you must walk the remaining 9km – two hours on a blue-marked trail). Trains run all day between Snina and Humenné (about 50 minutes), and between Michalovce and Humenné (1½ hours).

Border Crossings There are two border crossings to Ukraine from Slovakia. A 24 hour road crossing is 11km east of Michalovce at Vyšné Nemecké, and joining Užgorod. A rail-only crossing is farther south at Čierna nad Tisou, going to Chop.

The quickest way to or from Uzhgorod is on a Slovak bus, which is allowed to jump the queues in both directions. Entering Ukraine this way you can be through customs and immigration in half an hour. Slovak buses can be booked at the SAD agency in the Michalovce bus station or in Košice.

You can walk into Ukraine at Vyšné Nemecké, but you can only leave Ukraine in a vehicle.

Spiš Region

The Spiš region in north-western Slovakia contains one of the country's most appealing pockets of traditional culture, as well as some outstanding escapes into nature – most notably hiking in the vast Slovenský raj (Slovak Paradise) national park and river trips down the Dunajec gorge. The region's finest architectural landmarks are Levoča's old town, the stoic ruins of Spiš Castle (Spišsky hrad), and the monastery at Červený Kláštor.

The towns in this area were already part of a sturdy, independent-minded region by the late 12th century. From then until the 15th century it was colonised by Saxon settlers, first coaxed in by offers of tax breaks from the Hungarian King Béla III. It was these so-called Spiš Saxons who formed their own union, a defensive alliance of several towns, in 1412. The old royal towns of Levoča and Kežmarok were the region's two most important until the 20th century; today they're simply quiet, photogenic reminders of a more glorious past.

ČERVENÝ KLÁŠTOR

The main attraction in Červený Kláštor, on the banks of the Dunajec river in the region known as Zamaguria ('beyond the Magura mountains'), is a chance to float down the Dunajec gorge on a raft. You needn't even go into town, since everything worth seeing is on the eastern outskirts, right where the buses from Stará Ľubovňa stop.

While waiting for your raft trip, or the bus, visit the once-powerful 14th century **Carthusian Monastery & Church**, which is at the gorge's mouth. Inside is a museum with folk crafts and some superb 16th century frescoes. It's open daily, except Monday, from May through September from 9 am to 5 pm; and Tuesday to Saturday from October through April from 10 am to 4 pm. Entry costs 20 Sk.

Across the bridge from the monastery is an information centre (open mid-May through September) with hiking maps and river-trip details.

Dunajec Gorge

Pieniny National Park (21 sq km), created in 1967, combines with a similar park in Poland to protect the 9km Dunajec river gorge between Červený Kláštor and Szczawnica, Poland. The river here forms the international boundary between the two countries.

Pieniny means 'foam' – not caused by pollution, but a result of the river rushing over its limestone bed. Towering over the river are the gorge's tree-clad, 500m-tall cliffs, at their most impressive when shrouded in mist (which they often are).

From June to mid-September, Dunajec raft trips (150 Sk) depart from two locations at Červený Kláštor: a landing opposite the monastery and a newer landing 1.2km upriver (west of the village). All raft trips end near Lesnica.

It makes little difference which landing you embark from, though the newer one is less crowded in peak season (August). A raft will set out only when 12 passengers gather, and when business is slow you may have to wait around. The rafts themselves are called *pltě*, long and uncomfortably narrow yet more stable than they first appear.

The 5km journey beneath the towering walls of the gorge takes one to 1½ hours. The river is quite calm except for a few shallow rapids – great fun, but you won't get wet (a downright shame on scorching summer days).

From the downriver terminus near Lesnica, you can hike back to the monastery in a little under two hours, take a taxi (around 300 Sk) or rent a bicycle (100 Sk) and peddle back along the river. You could even walk 6km via Lesnica to Veľký Lipník, from where buses go all day to Stará Ľubovňa (25 minutes) and Červený Kláštor. In summer there are also direct buses from Lesnica to Stará Ľubovňa at 11.45 am and 3.20 and 6.15 pm.

Even if you don't go rafting, it's still worth coming to Červený Kláštor to hike through the gorge on the Slovak side (no such trail exists on the Polish side). In midsummer a 20 Sk 'trail fee' is charged to enter the national park.

Special Events

The annual Zamaguria Folk Festival (Zamagurský folklórny festival) in the middle of June is mainly held on the grounds of a nearby campsite (see the Places to Stay & Eat section). Each September the International Pieniny Canoe Slalom (Medzinárodný pieninský slalom) is held on the river here.

Places to Stay & Eat

In July and August hotels – and even camping sites – fill quickly on weekends, when you may have to fall back on a private room in Červený Kláštor; there are a few by the new landing west of the monastery. Also note that it's nearly impossible to find accommodation outside the rafting season (June through September); your best chances are Pieniny chata (see below), which opens earlier and closes later than the competition.

Just across a small stream from the monastery is a *campsite* open from mid-June to mid-September. No bungalows are available. The *monastery* has a children's dormitory and some travellers have managed to stay here (200 Sk per person) when it is not full.

About 1km up the road to Veľký Lipník from the monastery is *Hotel Dunajec*, with some bungalows (100 Sk per person) across

Rafting in Poland

The Dunajec river divides Slovakia and Poland, though once on the river it's something like an international free-for-all, with rafts from both countries competing for customers.

At the moment the Poles are winning the contest – they have better guides, are better organised, and offer much longer trips, including a two day, 50km voyage from Katy to Krościenko.

Depending on your stamina and visa status, it may be worthwhile to cross over into Poland and do your rafting from there. There's a pedestrian-only border crossing (to the Polish town of Szczawnica) on the river 200m beyond the Lesnica raft landing, open daily from 8 am to 10 pm (to 5 pm from November through April). Visas are not issued here, which means Australians, Canadians and New Zealanders cannot cross without pre-arranged visas (also make sure your Slovak visa allows re-entry).

From Szczawnica there are 25 daily buses to Nowy Targ (38km), from where there are six daily buses to the main Polish rafting centre at Katy (31km). By car, you can cross the Slovak-Polish border at Lysá nad Dunajcom (6km west of Červený Kláštor), or Mnišek nad Popradom (46km east of Červený Kláštor). ■

the road. Around 2km farther in the same direction, at Haligovce, is the more up-market *Dunajec Motorest* camping ground, with bungalows at 200 Sk per person. Both are dependably open June through September only.

Near Lesnica, 200m inland from where the raft trips end, is the inexpensive and very friendly *Pieniny chata* (☎ 0963-975 30), with two, three and four-bed dorms for 150 Sk per person. The walls are thin and the bathrooms communal, but the rustic setting scores top marks. Sharing the premises are a restaurant, basic grocery store and bike-rental shop. The chata is open early May through September.

Getting There & Away

Direct buses go frequently to Červený Kláštor from Poprad and, via Stará Ľubovňa, to Bardejov, Prešov and Košice. In summer there are four daily buses to Lesnica from Stará Ľubovňa (via Veľký Lipník).

STARÁ ĽUBOVŇA

This town of 12,000 in the heart of the Spišská Magura region is worth visiting only for its castle, on a hilltop overlooking the Poprad river 3.5km north of town, and for the ordinary skansen at the castle's base.

Stará Ľubovňa itself was made a royal town in 1364. Being so close to the border, from 1412 to 1772 it belonged to the Polish crown, whose representative lived in the castle.

Orientation & Information

From the adjacent bus and train stations, walk up to the main road and turn right for the town's main square, námestie sv Mikuláša (1km), or left for the castle and skansen (2.5km via the red-marked trail).

The Aices tourist office (☎ 217 13), upstairs at námestie sv Mikuláša 12, is supposedly open weekdays from 9 am to 4 pm, but seems permanently and inexplicably closed. The post office is at námestie Gen Štefánika 5. Všeobecná úverová banka, next door, has an exchange counter. Stará Ľubovňa's area code is ☎ 0963.

Ľubovňa Castle

Ľubovňa Castle (Hrad Ľubovňa), thought to date from the 14th century, was the site of battles between Poles and both Hungarians or Austrians, and was also the site of their subsequent peace negotiations.

It's half in ruins but still makes an interesting tour, and has a good view across the valley to the Magura. There are exhibits of leatherwork and woodwork, forging and candlemaking, and a gruesome well, left as a memorial, that contains the skeletons of 150 Slovak partisans dumped there by the Nazis. The castle is open daily from May through September from 9 am to noon and from 12.45 to 5.30 pm, in April and October it's closed Sunday and its hours are from 10 am to 3 pm. Entry costs 20 Sk.

Skansen

Below the castle is a large, rather inorganic arrangement of traditional wooden houses, and a church. It is in a blend of the styles – Slovak, Polish, Rusin and German – typical of the Spišská Magura region. The domestic icons are clearly Russian Orthodox in flavour. It's open daily, except Monday, from 10 am to 5 pm. Entry costs 20 Sk, plus 20 Sk if you want to take snaps.

Places to Stay & Eat

The only hotel in town is the dog-eared *Vrchovina* (☎ 233 11) on námestie Gen Štefánika, priced at 400/580 Sk for a single/double with bath. Downstairs there's a very ordinary restaurant, open until 9.30 pm. From the main square, walk down Obchodna past the decaying Obchodný dom shopping centre.

Opposite the skansen, the *Hostinec Peters pod hradom* (☎ 213 01) has dorm beds for 150 Sk but was closed for much-needed repairs at the time of writing.

Getting There & Away

Buses are quick and frequent to most destinations, including Červený Kláštor (45 minutes), Bardejov (1½ hours), Kežmarok, Poprad (1¼ hours), Prešov (two hours) and Košice. There are eight trains a day between Stará Ľubovňa, Kežmarok and Plaveč, where you must change if you're bound for Poland.

Getting Around

A town bus travels every hour to and from the main square and the train and bus stations. In summer buses go from the bus station to the castle at 8.35 am and 1 and 3.45 pm. Services are rare in the evening and on weekends.

KEŽMAROK

Colonised by Germans in the 13th century and granted free royal town status in 1380,

Kežmarok was the second-most important Spiš town after Levoča from medieval times until the 19th century.

These days it's a quiet, fairly unremarkable town with a well-preserved old centre and one of the Spiš region's finest wooden churches. Kežmarok makes an easy day trip from Poprad and the High Tatra resorts, though you'll probably find Levoča a more rewarding excursion.

Orientation

The bus may drop you either beside the train station or more conveniently at the Zlatý Bažanť stop on Toporcerova. Don't confuse the two central squares, Hlavné námestie and Hradné námestie.

Information

The Aices tourist office (☎ 4047), Hlavné námestie 46, has a good selection of private rooms starting at 350 Sk per person. Staff also sell maps and arrange day trips to the High Tatras. It's open weekdays from 8.30 am to 5 pm, Saturday in summer from 9 am to 2 pm.

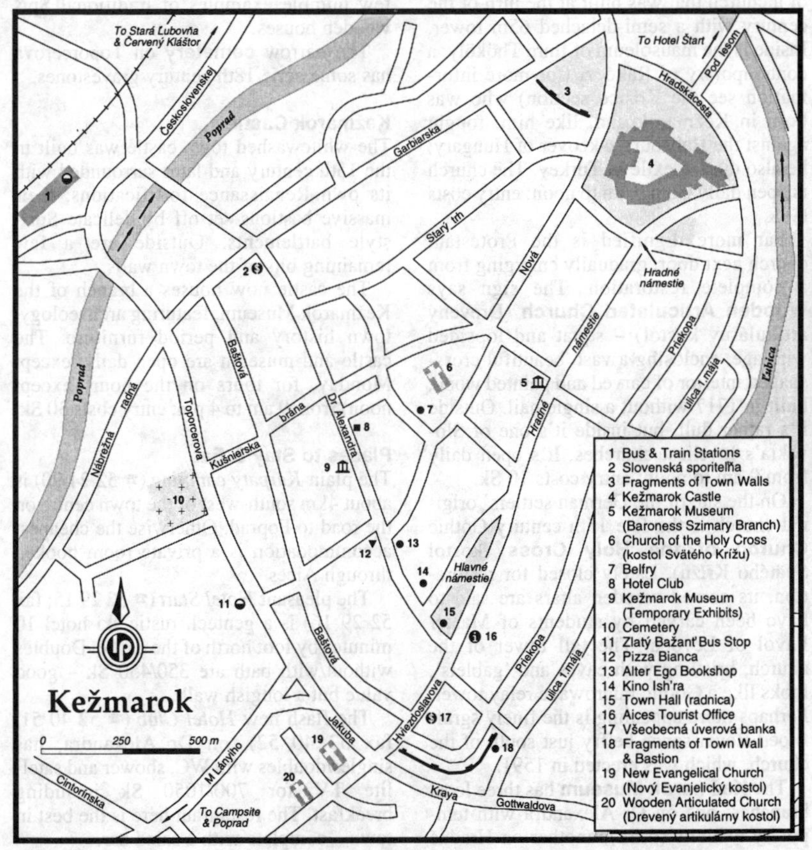

There's a MasterCard ATM at Všeobecná úverová banka on Hviezdoslavova, and a Visa ATM at Slovenská sporiteľňa on Dr Alexandra. The Alter Ego bookshop on Hlavné námestie has a few English-language novels.

Kežmarok's area code is ☎ 0968.

Things to See

The building you may remember the longest has little to do with ancient Kežmarok: the massive pea-green and red **New Evangelical Church** (Nový Evanjelický kostel), a pseudo-Moorish fortress of a church that was built at the turn of the century with a semi-detached 65m tower. Inside is the mausoleum of Imre Thököly, a contemporary of Rákóczi (for more information see the Košice section) who was born in Kežmarok and, like him, fought against the Habsburg takeover of Hungary; he also died in exile in Turkey. The church is open daily from 9 am to noon; entry costs 6 Sk.

Far more dignified is the Protestant church next door, gradually emerging from a complete restoration. The sign says **Wooden Articulated Church** (Drevený artikulárny kostol) – squat and lopsided with age, enclosing a vast, beautiful cross-shaped interior of carved and painted wood, built in 1717 without a single nail. Outside it's rather dull, but inside it's one of Slovakia's loveliest churches. It's open daily from 9 am to noon; entry costs 10 Sk.

SLOVAK REPUBLIC

On the site of the German settlers' original church is the late 15th century Gothic **Church of the Holy Cross** (kostol Svätého Krížu). Lately closed for restoration, its carved wooden altars are said to have been carved by students of Master Pavol of Levoča. The tall tower of the church, bristling with eaves and 'gablets', looks like a Gothic microwave relay tower. Perhaps more appealing is the finely sgraffitoed Renaissance belfry just south of the church, which was erected in 1591.

The **Kežmarok Museum** has three local branches: one on Dr Alexandra with temporary exhibits (6 Sk), another on Hradné námestie in the former home – furniture and all – of Baroness Szimary, who lived here until her death in 1973 (10 Sk), and yet another in the castle (see below). The first two are open daily, except Monday, from 9 am to noon and 1 to 5 pm.

The centre of town shifted towards Hlavné námestie when the Gothic **town hall** (*radnica*) was built there in 1461. At the southern corner of the old town, along Priekopa, are further fragments of the 14th century **town walls**, and a Gothic **bastion**. In the street called Starý trh (Old Market), farther north and leading to the castle, are a few humble examples of traditional Spiš wooden houses.

The narrow **cemetery** on Toporcerova has some eerie 18th century gravestones.

Kežmarok Castle

The whitewashed town castle was built in the 15th century and later surrounded with its own Renaissance fortifications, their massive bastions set off by delicate Spiš-style battlements. Outside are a few remaining bits of the town walls.

The castle now houses a branch of the Kežmarok Museum, featuring archaeology, town history and period furniture. The castle and museum are open daily, except Monday, for tours on the hour (except noon) from 9 am to 4 pm; entry costs 30 Sk.

Places to Stay & Eat

The plain *Karpaty camping* (☎ 52 24 90) is about 4km south-west of the town centre on the road to Poprad. Otherwise the cheapest accommodation is a private room booked through Aices.

The pleasant *Hotel Štart* (☎ 52 29 15; fax 52 29 16) is a genteel, rustic ski hotel 10 minutes by foot north of the castle. Doubles without/with bath are 350/450 Sk – good value but a longish walk.

The flash new *Hotel Club* (☎ 52 40 51; fax 52 40 52), on Dr Alexandra, has singles/doubles with WC, shower and satellite TV for 700/1050 Sk including breakfast. The restaurant here is the best in town – complete with a salad bar.

A good spot for pizza and pasta is *Pizza Bianca* at Hlavné námestie 8; open daily to 10 pm.

Entertainment

Except for the occasional concert in Kežmarok Castle (ask Aices for performance dates), the only late-night option that doesn't involve beer is a film at *Kino Ish'ra*, Hlavné námestie.

Getting There & Away

Buses are faster and more plentiful than trains from the High Tatras – about hourly from Poprad, almost as often from Starý Smokovec. There are also four daily buses to Červený Kláštor.

LEVOČA

Levoča (population 13,000) rivals Bardejov as the region's most historically impressive town, full of fine, predominantly Renaissance buildings. It also has an almost complete set of original fortifications. Levoča is an easy stop on the way to/from Poprad, Prešov and Košice, and there are plenty of reasonably priced hotels here.

History

The first mention of Levoča in writing was in 1249, not long after the Tatars nearly destroyed it. In common with other Spiš towns, Levoča (Leutschau in German) was settled and enriched by a wave of Saxon artisans beginning in the 12th century. By 1271 it was the Spiš administrative seat.

It broke away from the union of Saxon Spiš towns in 1323 to become a free royal town, prospering from trade in gold and woodcarving, and founding its own nine-city union with Košice, Prešov, Bardejov, Sabinov and several other towns for mutual protection. Much of its present Renaissance personality comes from a building boom after a huge fire in the 16th century.

In the 17th century Levoča's fortunes collapsed after an anti-Habsburg uprising. Its isolation was accentuated when it was bypassed by the railway in the 19th century (now it's at the end of a branch line).

A Slovak army garrison from here joined in the Slovak National Uprising in 1944. The town was occupied by German troops until its liberation by the Soviets in February 1945.

Orientation

The bus and train stations are 1km south of the town centre, down the road beside the Hotel Faix. Note that most buses also stop at námestie Slobody, a few blocks east of the main square, námestie Majstra Pavla.

Information

Tourist Office The Kultúrno-informačné centrum (KIC; ☎ 51 37 63), námestie Majstra Pavla 58, provides town and regional information, as well as accommodation assistance. It's open weekdays from 7.30 am to 5 pm, weekends in summer from 9 am to 4.45 pm.

Money Outside the KIC office there's a MasterCard ATM. The Všeobecná úverová banka, námestie Majstra Pavla 28, changes travellers cheques for 1% commission. Slovenská sporiteľňa, on the main square next to Hotel Satel, has a Visa ATM.

Post & Communications The telephone centre in the post office at námestie Majstra Pavla 42 is open weekdays from 7 am to 8 pm, Saturday from 8 am to 1 pm.

Levoča's area code is ☎ 0966.

Things to See

Levoča's main square is crammed with fine Renaissance buildings, though the jewel of the town is Gothic – the **Church of St James** (kostol sv Jakuba), dating from around 1400. It's Slovakia's second largest Gothic church.

An extraordinary piece of craftsmanship is the 19m-high and 6m wide **wooden altar**, which is actually the largest in the world. It was carved by the renowned Master Pavol (Majstra Pavla) of Levoča, after whom the town square is named, between 1507-18. The Madonna on this altar appears on the new 100 Sk banknote.

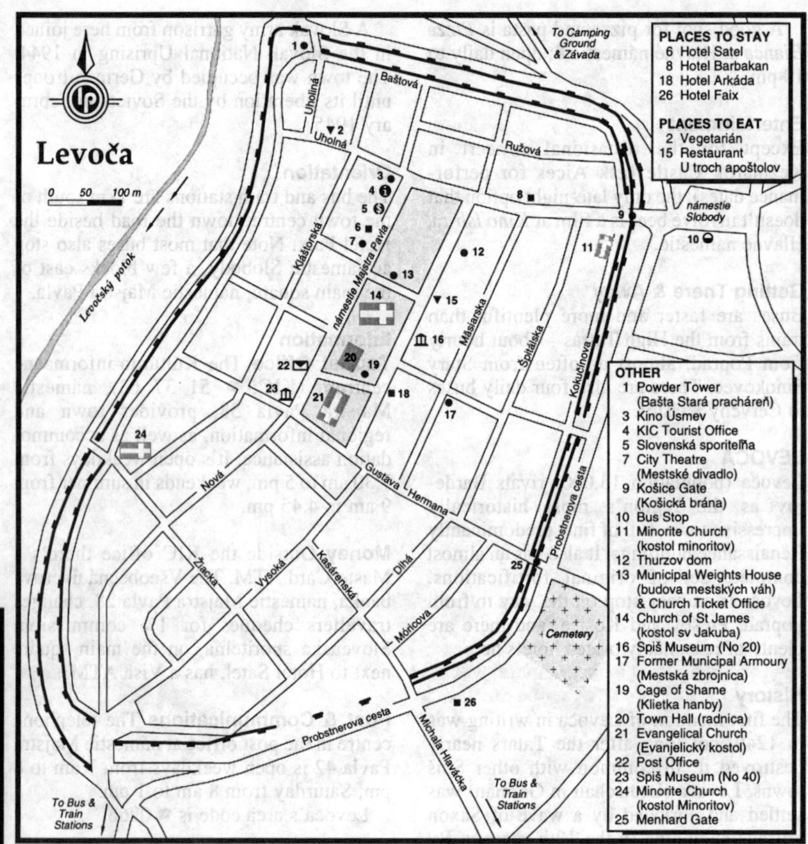

The entire church is a museum of medieval religious art, which is open Tuesday to Saturday from June through September from 9 am to 5 pm, Sunday from 1 pm, and Monday from 2 pm; the rest of the year it's open Tuesday to Saturday on the hour from 8 am to 4 pm. Entry costs 20 Sk, and tickets are available opposite the church in the former Municipal Weights House (budova mestských váh).

The originally Gothic **town hall** (radnica) and tower got a Renaissance facelift in 1551; the town hall is now one of the Levoča's most beautiful buildings. Inside is the first (and best) of three **Spiš Museum** (Spišské múzeum) branches, with folk dresses and town artefacts displayed in stunning wood-panelled chambers. It's open daily, except Monday, from 8 am to 4 pm; entry costs 15 Sk.

South of the town hall is the **Cage of Shame** (Klietka hanby), originally a place of public humiliation for criminals.

In the second branch of the **Spiš Museum**, at No 40 on the main square, are religious and secular art, ceramics in regional styles, and some handsome wood-beamed rooms with hints of Renaissance frescoes. It's open daily, except Monday, from 9 am to 5 pm; entry costs 15 Sk.

Across the square at No 20 is the third and final **Spiš Museum** branch, this one is dedicated to the works of Master Pavol, and is open daily, except Monday, from 8.30 am to 4 pm; entry costs 15 Sk.

The houses on the square were the homes of rich artisans and traders. Finest is the **Thurzov dom** (1532) at No 7, with its characteristic Spiš Renaissance attic. Another well-preserved beauty is **Mariássyho dom** at No 43, notable for its interior. Others to look at are Spillenbergov dom at No 45, Krupekov dom at No 44 and Hainov dom at No 41.

Special Events

On the first weekend in July each year, a Marian Pilgrimage (Marian púť) is held in a church on top of Marianska hora (hill), about 2km north of town. This is one of the most popular religious pilgrimages in Slovakia, with up to a quarter of a million pilgrims converging on the place. Masses are said hourly from 6 pm on Saturday, but the one to wait for is at 10 am on Sunday.

Places to Stay

Camping *Levočská Dolina Autocamp* (☎ 51 27 05) is 5km north of námestie Slobody on the road to Závada. Bungalows are available. The site is open from mid-June through August.

Autocamping Starý mlyn (☎ 36 51), with deluxe bungalows and a restaurant on the premises, is more convenient, about 5km west of Levoča on the road to Poprad.

Hotels The inexpensive 25 room *Hotel Faix* (☎ 51 23 35), Probstnerova cesta 22, between the train station and the old town, has basic singles/doubles from 440/540 Sk with shared bath, and 680/720 Sk with private bath. The hotel restaurant is good.

The mid-range and newly renovated *Hotel Arkáda* (☎ 51 23 72; fax 51 22 55), námestie Majstra Pavla 26, has large, bright rooms with TV, bathroom and toilet at 730/1050 Sk. Breakfast is an extra 60 Sk.

Hotel Barbakan (☎ 51 43 10; fax 51 36 09), Košická 15, offers comfortable, clean and bright rooms with private bath and breakfast for 960/1350 Sk (less 30% off-season).

Top of the line is *Hotel Satel* (☎ 51 29 43; fax 51 44 86), on the main square at No 55, with all the amenities you'd expect at 1250/1900 Sk.

Places to Eat

Levoča's best eatery is the smoke-free *Restaurant U troch apoštolov*, upstairs at námestie Majstra Pavla 11. For coffee and cakes try *Mliečne lahodky*, námestie Majstra Pavla 9.

A good spot for a vegetarian lunch is the popular, simple *Vegetarián* at Uholná 137, open weekdays from 11 am to 3 pm.

Entertainment

The *City Theatre* (Mestské divadlo), near Hotel Satel, puts on drama (mostly in Slovak) plus the occasional musical. *Kino Úsmev*, on Uholná, is the place to see a film.

Getting There & Away

Levoča is connected by 11 daily local trains to Spišská Nová Ves, which is 13km south on the main line from Bratislava to Prague and Košice. Bus travel is more practical as there are frequent services to Poprad (26km), Spišské Podhradie (15km), Spišský Štvrtok (12km) and Prešov (58km). All buses stop at námestie Slobody.

SPIŠSKÝ ŠTVRTOK

This village on the Poprad-Levoča road 12km west of Levoča is marked by a wooden church spire. The main attraction in the originally Gothic church, altered in Baroque style in the 17th and 18th centuries, is a 1473 side chapel built by local noble Štefan Zápoľský in the manner of French palace chapels of the time. There is also a 13th century stone baptismal font.

The church is open every morning except Sunday.

Unless you're driving it's not worth a special trip, though frequent buses take only 30 minutes to Spišský Štvrtok from Poprad, Spišská Nová Ves or Levoča.

SPIŠSKÉ PODHRADIE & AROUND

Spišské Podhradie is 15km east of Levoča in the centre of East Slovakia. In the 12th century a settlement appeared below the neighbouring castle, developing into an artisans' town in the 13th century. The town itself is completely boring, but the adjacent Spiš Castle (Spišský hrad) and Spišská Kapitula are both sights of prime importance.

Spišská Kapitula was built by the clergy and from the 13th century an abbot resided there. After 1776 it became the seat of a bishop. Arrive early to Spišské Podhradie and give yourself at least 4½ hours (including walking time) to see both the castle and Spišská Kapitula – and plan to sleep somewhere other than Spišské Podhradie, if at all possible.

Orientation & Information

Most long-distance buses stop in the main square, Marianské námestie. The train station is 1.5km north-east of town, nearer to the castle.

The unofficial tourist office is Area Tour (☎ 8154), at No 22 on the main square. Staff sell town maps and may help in finding accommodation. It's open from May to September only, weekdays from 9 am to 5 pm.

Spišské Podhradie's area code is ☎ 0966.

Spišská Kapitula

If you're arriving by bus from Levoča, ask the driver to drop you at Spišská Kapitula, on a ridge 1km west of Spišské Podhradie. This 13th century ecclesiastical settlement is completely encircled by a 16th century wall, and the single street running between the two medieval gates is lined with picturesque Gothic houses. Until their eviction in 1948, the residents here were nearly all clergy; in fact, as the name hints, this was once the Spiš region's religious capital, the seat of the regional bishopric.

At the upper end of the main street is the magnificent **Cathedral of St Martin** (katedrála sv Martina), originally built in 1273, with twin Romanesque towers and a Gothic sanctuary. Inside are three folding Gothic altars (1499), a 1317 Gothic fresco of the coronation of King Karol Róbert and, near the door, a Romanesque white lion. Unfortunately, the church is often closed. On opposite sides of the cathedral are the seminary and the Renaissance bishop's palace (1652).

Spiš Castle

Two kilometres south-east of Spišské Podhradie, standing out like a beacon, are the spectacular and photogenic ruins of Spiš Castle (Spišský hrad), the biggest castle in Slovakia. The ridge-top fortress, founded by Hungarian kings in 1209, burned down in 1780 and has been deserted ever since. There is a tour of restored bits of the interior, including torture instruments in the dungeon, though there isn't a lot to see up close – the best views are definitely from afar. The highest castle enclosure contains a round Gothic tower, a cistern, a chapel and a rectangular Romanesque palace perched over the abyss.

The castle is open daily, except Monday, May through October from 9 am to 5 pm; entry costs 40 Sk. The castle is directly above and east of the Spišské Podhradie train station; turn left into the carpark and follow the yellow markers 30 minutes up a steep hill. The first gate you see is always locked, so continue anticlockwise to the main gate (there's a snack bar here). By car, the easiest approach is via the main highway from the east (Prešov) side of the castle.

Places to Stay & Eat

The only place to stay is the ageing dormitory-style *Hotel Alf* (☎ 8619), sídlisko Hrad 1, with beds at 360 Sk per person. The hotel

SLOVAK REPUBLIC

is a three storey red building behind some apartment blocks. From the column on Spišské Podhradie's main square, turn right towards the white Catholic church and, directly behind the church, right again down an unmarked alleyway; the Alf is 200m ahead, on your right.

Hotel Alf has a restaurant, although its menu is very basic. Pickings are not much better at the *Pohostinstvo*, on the main north-eastern road towards the castle.

Getting There & Away

A secondary railway line connects Spišské Podhradie to Spišské Vlachy (9km), a station on the main line from Poprad to Košice. Departures are scheduled to connect with the Košice trains. You can leave your bags at the left-luggage office in the Spišské Podhradie train station (ask the stationmaster).

Buses to and from Prešov (43km), Levoča (15km), Spišská Nová Ves (25km) and Poprad (41km) are quite frequent, and most stop on the main square.

SPIŠSKÁ NOVÁ VES

This old Saxon town (population 32,500) on the Hornád river is little more than a convenient jumping-off point for the nearby Slovenský raj (Slovak Paradise) national park (see the following section). Self-catering travellers should stock up on food here, as there are few markets within the national park's boundaries. Otherwise there's no reason to dawdle in Spišská Nová Ves – you're better off catching the first bus out.

Orientation

The bus station is 200m south-west of the Spišská Nová Ves train station, which has a 24 hour left-luggage office. To reach the centre from the train station, walk south on Odborárov and turn left on Dulianska; the tourist office is 250m ahead on the right.

Information

Tourist Offices The helpful and knowledgeable staff at Aices (☎ 42 82 92), námestie MR Štefánika 10, can assist with accommodation and have lots of national park information, including hiking maps. It's open weekdays from 7.30 am to 3.30 pm.

Satur (☎ 226 21), opposite the dom kultúry, can help with transport queries and has a list of private rooms that cost from 300 to 400 Sk per person, with breakfast included.

Money Change travellers cheques or use the 24 hour MasterCard ATM at Všeobecná úverová banka, Radničné námestie 33.

Post & Communications There's a telephone centre in the main post office at námestie MR Štefánika 7, opposite the dom kultúry.

Spišská Nová Ves' area code is ☎ 0965.

Things to See

The long main square, Radničné námestie, is lined with Renaissance houses with mostly Baroque or neo-classical façades. At No 58 is the **Natural History Museum** (Vlastivedné múzeum), which is open daily, except Monday, from 8.30 am to 5 pm. The building was once the administrative headquarters for the union of towns in the region in the 18th and 19th centuries; its stucco rococo façade dates from 1763-65.

Other buildings worth a look are the **town hall** and the Art Nouveau **Reduta** building.

Attached to the 14th century Gothic **Parish Church** (Farský kostol) is an 86m tower, the highest church tower in Slovakia, added in the 19th century. Inside the church are Stations of the Cross carved by Master Pavol of Levoča around 1520.

Places to Stay & Eat

The modern, 10 storey *Metropol Hotel* (☎ 42 22 41), námestie MR Štefánika 2, three blocks south of the train station, is rather fancy and geared towards business travellers. Singles/doubles cost 1080/1580 Sk with bath and breakfast.

The *Šport Hotel* (☎ 267 53), which is on

T Vansovej next to the Zimný štadión, is 320 Sk per person with shared bath. From the Metropol Hotel continue south a few blocks and you'll see this ramshackle five storey building off to the left. The hotel restaurant is very basic.

Getting There & Away

Bus Buses can take considerably longer than the train to/from Levoča, but they're the only easy way to the Slovenský raj towns like Čingov (at 7 and 9.10 am, noon, 1.35 and 3.40 pm, as well as 5.40 and 7.30 pm from July to September), Dedinky (at 7.45 and 10 am, 1.05, 2.30, 3.30 and 6.15 pm), as well as to Spišský Štvrtok, Rožňava and Prešov.

Train Spišská Nová Ves lies on a main line served by 15 daily express trains between Žilina (2¼ hours away) and Košice (an hour away), with a stop at Poprad, as well as connections all day from Levoča.

SLOVENSKÝ RAJ

The Slovak Paradise National Park (Národní park Slovenský raj, or NPSR) boasts the finest mountain scenery in eastern Slovakia. It is 90% covered in dense pine and deciduous forests, has several rare wildflower species, and is inhabited by eagles, lynx, bears and wolves. Its peaks and gorges, waterfalls and rapids, and wide choice of well-marked trails make it an extremely popular area for outdoor enthusiasts – mostly Slovak and Polish families in pursuit of peace and BBQs. Ideal for summer walking and winter cross-country skiing, the Slovenský raj is perhaps at its most beautiful in winter under a blanket of snow.

Orientation

The park is west of Spišská Nová Ves, at the eastern end of the Low Tatras. The closest convenient bases with accommodation are Čingov, in the north-east of the park and only a short bus ride from Spišská Nová Ves, and Dedinky in the south of the park, approachable by bus from Rožňava or Spišská Nová Ves.

From these towns you can do day or overnight loop hikes, or an overnight hike between them. There's an excellent camping ground at Podlesok, but it's harder to reach without a car.

Maps Don't waste your money on MAPA Slovakia's *Slovenský raj-stredný Spiš* (1:75,000). Hiking trails are far better rendered on VKÚ's *Slovenský raj* (1:50,000), map No 124 in its series and coloured bright green and yellow.

Information

For those planning a hike, the best sources of trail and weather information – and help in booking a chata along the way – are the park's Mountain Rescue Service (Horská služba) stations. The main one (☎ 0965-911 82) is at Čingov, and another (☎ 0942-981 10) is at Dedinky.

The park admission fee – 20 Sk per day – is collected only during peak season.

Walks

The trails through the park's rugged gorges include some challenging sections with ladders and walkways. If the trails are wet, the logs, metal walkways and ladders will be very slippery. And note that certain very steep trails (marked with arrows on all maps) are one way, so plan ahead.

We list here only some of the most popular walks. Other destinations with gorges, rapids and waterfalls on the way are Kyseľ, Vernárska tiesňava and Zejmarská roklina.

Loop Trail from Čingov via Sokolia Valley From Čingov take the blue trail to Biely Potok (40 minutes), then the green trail to the base of Sokolia valley (1½ hours). From here it's a steep two hour hike on a one-way trail to the top of this rugged ravine, where a yellow trail leads down to Klauzy (one hour) and a photogenic lake. Another two hours and 15 minutes on a green trail – following the riverbed of the

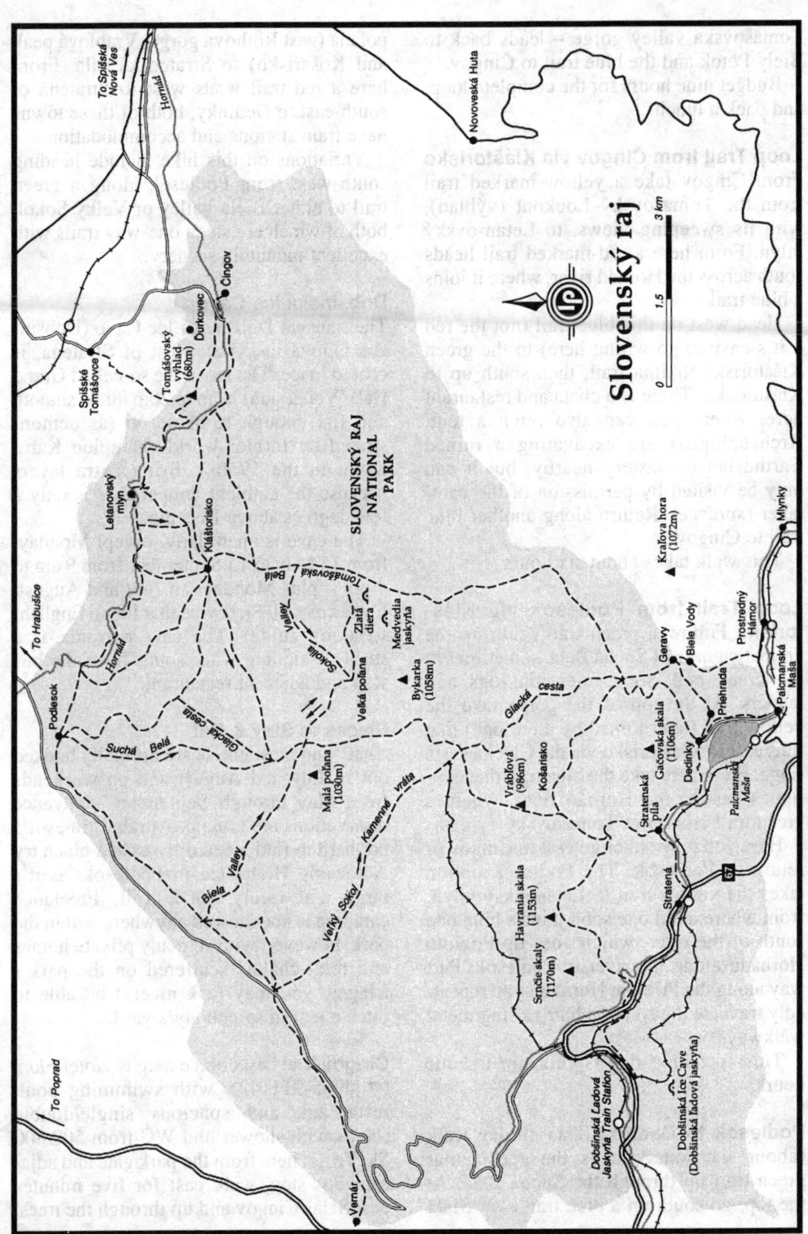
Slovenský raj
0
1.5
3 km
To Spišská Nová Ves
Hornád
Novoveská Huta
Čingov
Ďurkovec
Spišské Tomášovce
Tomášovský výhlad (680m)
Letanovský mlyn
Kláštorisko
SLOVENSKÝ RAJ NATIONAL PARK
To Hrabušice
Podlesok
Suchá Belá
Glacká cesta
Tomášovská Belá
Sokolia Valley
Zlatá diera
Medvedia jaskyňa
Veľká poľana
Bykarka (1058m)
Malá poľana (1030m)
Biela Valley
Kamenné vráta
Veľký Sokol
To Poprad
Vernár
Vrabľová (986m)
Košarisko
Havrania skala (1153m)
Srnčie skaly (1170m)
Stratenská píla
Gačovská skala (1106m)
Dedinky
Priehrada
Geravy
Biele Vody
Kráľova hora (1072m)
Prostredný Hámor
Palcmanská Maša
Mlynky
Stratená
67
Dobšinská Ľadová Jaskyňa Train Station
Dobšinská Ice Cave (Dobšinská ľadová jaskyňa)

Tomášovská valley gorge – leads back to Biely Potok and the blue trail to Čingov.

Budget nine hours for the complete loop, and pack a lunch.

Loop Trail from Čingov via Kláštorisko
From Čingov take a yellow-marked trail from the Tomašovský Lookout (výhlad), with its sweeping views, to Letan-ovský mlyn. From here a red-marked trail heads south across the Hornád river, where it joins a blue trail.

Head west on this blue trail (not the red – it's easy to go wrong here) to the green Kláštoriská roklina trail, then south up to Kláštorisko. There is a chata and restaurant here, where you can also pitch a tent. Archaeologists are excavating a ruined Carthusian monastery nearby, but it can only be visited by permission of the caretaker (*správce*). Return along another blue trail to Čingov.

This walk takes about six hours.

Loop Trail from Podlesok via Kláštorisko Follow a green trail south up the dramatic gorge of Suchá Belá, sometimes in the creek bed, sometimes via logs and ladders. At the top of the gorge take the yellow trail (later joined by a red one) that runs east to Kláštorisko via the Glacká cesta ridge. From here take the blue trail that continues east to the Hornád river, where a green trail crosses to Tomašovský výhlad.

Here you may either go east to Čingov or return to Podlesok. The Podlesok option takes the yellow trail to Letanovksý mlyn, from where a red one soon joins a blue one south of the river, which goes up Prielom Hornádu along the river to Podlesok. Part way along the Prielom Hornádu you repeatedly traverse the river on hair-raising metal walkways.

This is a long day's walk, up to nine hours.

Podlesok to Dedinky This all-day walk (about six hours) takes the spectacular green trail up through the Suchá Belá. At the top, go south on a blue trail over Malá poľana (past Rothova gorge, Vrabľová peak and Košarisko) to Stratenská píla. From here a red trail leads west to Stratená or south-east to Dedinky, both of these towns have train stations and accommodation.

Variations on this hike include heading south-west from Podlesok along a green trail to either Biela valley or Veľký Sokol, both of which are steep one-way trails with excellent mountain scenery.

Dobšinská Ice Cave
The unusual Dobšinská Ice Cave (Dobšinská ľadová jaskyňa), west of Stratená, is coated in ice. The ice in the so-called Grand Hall (Veľká sieň) is up to 20m thick, smooth and flat enough to skate on (as demonstrated by former world champion Karol Divín in the 1950s). Bring extra layers because the ambient temperature is only a few degrees above freezing.

The cave is open daily, except Monday, from 15 May to 15 September from 9 am to 4 pm – plus Mondays in July and August. Entry costs 40 Sk (twice that for an English-speaking guide). The cave entrance is a steep 20 minute walk south from the bus stop and adjacent restaurant.

Places to Stay & Eat
Chaty and most hotels are normally booked out in July and August and on weekends from May through September – advance reservations are crucial. At other times it's not hard to find a bed or two. In a pinch try Autocamp Hrabušice in Podlesok, as it's large and rarely 100% full. Freelance camping is not allowed anywhere within the park, however, with so many private homes and mini-chalets scattered on the park's fringes, you may (ask nicely) be able to pitch a tent in somebody's yard.

Čingov The best choice here is *Hotel Flora* (☎ 0965-911 42), with swimming pool, restaurant, and spacious single/double rooms with shower and WC from 500/800 Sk. To get here from the park gate and adjacent bus stop, walk east for five minutes past Salaš Čingov and up through the trees.

SLOVAK REPUBLIC

Five minutes farther east is the *Hotel Čingov* (☎ 0965-336 63; fax 336 30), with clean modern rooms with bath priced at 540/800 Sk.

Salaš Čingov, just east of the park gate, serves up good home-style meals from 10 am to 7.30 pm. Near the carpark at Čingov there's also a small supermarket and a food kiosk.

Podlesok The year-round *Autocamp Hrabušice – Podlesok* (☎ 0965-902 81; fax 902 37) has comfy bungalows without/with bath for 280/350 Sk per person, plus tent space for 70 Sk. There are also two nearby *restaurants*.

Kláštorisko The lone *restaurant* here also rents chata year-round for 150 Sk per person. If you'd like to stay in midsummer, call ahead (☎ 0965-49 33 07) to check availability.

Dedinky By the lake outside Dedinky, on the north side, is the *Hotel Priehrada* (☎ 0942-981 62), with rooms for 210 Sk per person and bungalows for 100 Sk. In the village itself, on the green trail, is the excellent five room *Pension Pastierňa* (☎ 0942-981 75), priced at 300 Sk per person. It's dependably open from mid-May through September. The restaurant here is very good.

Stratená The only place to stay in this handsome, tiny village is *Chata Stratenka* (☎ 0942-981 67), on the main road 300m west of the bus stop. Rooms are 250 Sk per person, and reception is open from 11 am to 6 pm.

Dobšinská Ice Cave On the main road above the carpark, at the head of the trail to the ice cave, is *Hotel Jas* (☎ 0092-981 72), which has doubles for 250 Sk. It was closed (temporarily?) at the time of writing. The modern *Hotel Ruffiny* (☎ & fax 0942-982 27), on a side road 300m west of Hotel Jas, charges 860 Sk for fully equipped double rooms.

Getting There & Away

Bus From Spišská Nová Ves (see Getting There & Away in the previous section) there are semi-frequent buses to Čingov and Dedinky. There's also a regular bus service from Rožňava to the Dobšinská Ice Cave via Dobšiná (but not Dedinky).

Train The last part of the train journey from Košice is beautiful. For the Dobšinská Ice Cave, Dedinky and the south side of the Slovenský raj you must change at Margecany. Note that a separate railway line comes up from Rožňava to Dobšiná but ends there, without going as far as the ice cave. From the Dobšinská Ľadová Jaskyňa train station it's a 30 minute walk to the cave.

Slovak Karst

The Slovak Karst (Slovenský kras) is a region of limestone canyons and caves at the eastern end of the Slovak Red Mountains (Slovenské rudohorie), a major range that reaches to the border with Hungary. Its most spectacular landscapes are within the 440 sq km Slovak Karst Protected Landscape Region (Chránená krajinná oblast Slovenský kras).

The region's highlights include Domica Cave (Domica jaskyňa), said to be one of the biggest caves in the world, Zádielska canyon near the Hungarian border, and the dramatic Krásna Hôrka Castle.

Public transportation is poor throughout the region, making it nearly impossible to see more than one cave a day, usually by bus from Rožňava.

ROŽŇAVA

A good base for exploring the Slovak Karst, Rožňava is otherwise a drab former mining town of 19,000 with a big Hungarian-speaking minority. It was the region's main gold, silver and iron-mining centre until the 17th century when manufacturing took over as the town's main industry.

Orientation

The train station is 2.5km south of námestie Baníkov, the town centre, and connected by an hourly bus service. On foot, walk to the main road (Šafárikova) and turn right; námestie Baníkov is 30 minutes dead-ahead. The SAD bus station is also on Šafárikova, halfway between the town and the train station.

Information

The Turistické informačné centrum (☎ 328 10), námestie Baníkov 32, books private rooms and has plenty of information about the caves. It's open weekdays from 8 am to noon and 1 to 4 pm, plus summer Saturdays from 9 am to noon.

Slovenská sporiteľňa, if you need to change money, is in a shopping complex at Šafárikova 1704, near the corner with Košická. The main post and telephone office is on Čučmianska, just north of námestie Baníkov. Rožňava's area code is ☎ 0942.

Things to See

Námestie Baníkov's Baroque structures include the former **town hall**, and the 1654 **tower** standing in the middle of the square. At the north-west end of the square is the **Bishops' Cathedral** (Biskupská katedrála), with a Renaissance altar depicting miners at work.

South of the centre at Šafárikova 31 is the plain **Mining Museum** (Baníckе múzeum), featuring the history of local efforts.

Places to Stay

The tourist office books private rooms starting at 300 Sk per person. The only hotel around is *Hotel Kras* (☎ 242 43), on Šafárikova near the corner with Štítnická, with singles/doubles priced at 600/800 Sk without bath or WC. At the time of writing *Hotel Šport*, beside the stadium, was closed indefinitely.

Places to Eat

There isn't much to praise here. The shopping centre opposite the bus station has a cheap self-service cafeteria, *Jedáleň samoobsluha*. On námestie Baníkov, the modern *Vináreň Tři růže* has good meals for up to 170 Sk per dish and is open daily to 10 pm. Far plainer is *Pizzeria Sabi*, on the square at No 12.

Getting There & Away

Rožňava is on a railway line between Košice (1¼ hours away) and Zvolen (2½ hours away), with four fast trains on the whole route and further local services to Košice.

Buses are the only way to the caves, though they aren't very frequent. There are hourly buses to Krásna Hôrka Castle (10 minutes), up to eight a day to Dedinky (one hour) and six to Ochtiná (45 minutes).

AROUND ROŽŇAVA

Krásna Hôrka Castle & Krásnohorské Podhradie

Krásna Hôrka Castle, on a hill above the village of Krásnohorské Podhradie, was built as a feudal residence in 1320. In the 16th century it was bought by the Andrássy family, renovated in Renaissance style, and further fortified against the Turks. The building burned down in 1817, but in the early part of this century the last of the line, Count Dionysius Andrássy, restored it and turned it into a family museum. Tours are given daily, except Monday, April through September from 8 am to noon and 12.30 to 4.30 pm, and cost 30 Sk.

The old village of Krásnohorské Podhradie below the castle has little to offer that isn't Andrássy-related. The **Andrássy Gallery** has a collection of 20 paintings, including Andrássy family portraits. An arresting one is of a woman breast-feeding her father, who had been imprisoned by a king and sentenced to death by starvation, but who was allowed daily visits; when the king learned why the man had not yet died, he pardoned him. The gallery is open daily, except Monday, June through September from 9 am to 4 pm.

The 1904 Art Nouveau **mausoleum** of Dionysius Andrássy and his wife, Františka, is out on the road to Košice, surrounded by a pleasant park. The sumptuous interior includes marble from all over the world.

Places to Stay & Eat Out on the road from Rožňava, before the mausoleum, is the *Jednota Motel* (☎ 0942-238 38), where decent doubles/triples with shower and toilet are 300/450 Sk. Its restaurant is much frequented by travellers between Rožňava and Košice.

Getting There & Away Krásnohorské Podhradie is about 8km east of Rožňava, with buses almost hourly. Many (up to 11 daily) continue to Košice, 1¼ hours away. The train station is about 1km south of the town at Lípovník. The castle, visible from everywhere, is a 3km walk east of the village.

Betliar

The attraction of this town, 4km north of Rožňava, is a grand chateau built in the 18th century for the Andrássy family. It's stuffed with their belongings and furnishings, relics collected in Africa and Asia, and a library of 20,000 books. It was under restoration at the time of writing, though the leafy gardens – full of pavilions, grottoes and fountains – are open.

There are hourly buses through here from Rožňava. At least half a dozen trains stop daily at the station, south of the village.

CAVES OF THE SLOVAK KARST

The whole of the Slovak Karst region contains 47 known caves (*jaskyňa*), as well as 55 gorges, but only a few of the caves are open to the public. Below are four of the major ones. Unfortunately, public transport in the district is a bit scarce, especially on weekends.

Ochtinská Aragonitová Jaskyňa

Ochtinská is one of the more striking caves – though one corner shows the effects of vandalism by a squad of drunken soldiers. Delicate aragonites, which are basically 'inside-out stalactites' made up of thin limestone tubes that water passes through leaving deposits at the growing end, twist in all directions, some resembling flowers.

This cave is open daily, except Monday, for hourly tours from April through to 10 October from 9 am to 2 pm (extended to 4 pm from May through August); the tour costs 60 Sk.

Getting There & Away By train from Rožňava, you must change at Plešivec, from where seven daily trains make the 40 minute trip to Ochtiná. Buses from Rožňava go via Štítnik, sometimes with a change for Ochtiná, in under an hour if your connection is good. There are not many buses on the weekend. The cave is a 3km, one hour walk south along a blue-marked trail from Ochtiná.

Gombasecká Jaskyňa

Gombasecká, with its white and red-brown walls, and stalagmites and stalactites of all shapes and sizes, is perhaps the most accessible cave. It's open daily, except Monday, for hourly tours from May through September from 9.30 am to 4 pm, but only until 2 pm in April and October; the tours cost 40 Sk.

Places to Stay & Eat Near the cave entrance are a *restaurant* and *chalet*, which has beds for 250 Sk.

Getting There & Away The cave is 11km south of Rožňava and best reached by bus, which takes 15 minutes and stops 200m from the cave. If you take the train it's a 2km walk from the Slavec Jaskyňa stop.

Domica Jaskyňa

Domica is the biggest, best known and most beautiful cave, full of colour and with some stalactites as thick as tree trunks. Almost 2km of the 5km length of the so-called Gothic House (Gotický dôm) is accessible by boat along the underground river Styx.

This cave is part of a 22km cave system, most of which is in Hungary (where it's

SLOVAK REPUBLIC

called Baradla). There is talk of future tours taking in the Hungarian caves too.

Domica is open daily, except Monday, from February to 23 December, with six tours a day from 1 May to 15 September and four a day the rest of the year; the tours cost 90 Sk (including the boat trip). The tours leave at 9 and 10.30 am, and 12.30, 2, 3 and 4 pm.

Places to Stay & Eat The *Hotel Pri Jaskyni* (☎ 0942-92 82 15) by the cave entrance has singles/doubles for 300/500 Sk, and cheaper chalets, plus a restaurant.

Getting There & Away Domica is 28km south of Rožňava, via Plešivec. Buses depart from Rožňava only at 11.20 am, and 12.30 and 4.55 pm.

Jasovská Jaskyňa

The small and less visited Jasov Cave has been open to visitors since 1846, but it bears some graffiti apparently left by Hussites in the 15th century. Over 2km long, about a quarter of its extent is open daily, except Monday, for hourly tours from April through October from 9 am to 4 pm (until 2 pm in April and September-October); entry costs 40 Sk.

Places to Stay & Eat The only place to stay is *Autokemping Jasov* (☎ 0943-942 42), on the north side of Jasov past a closed chateau. It also has bungalows for 150 Sk per person, and a bistro with meals. Slovak standard fare is available at the cavern-like *Zámecká pivnice*, two minutes walk from the campsite, for less than 50 Sk.

Getting There & Away This cave is just south of Jasov, which means a 40km trip east of Rožňava to Moldava nad Bodvou, then 10km north. It's fairly easily reached by train from Rožňava, with a change at Moldava nad Bodvou; six trains a day go from Moldava to Jasov.

ZÁDIELSKA CANYON

Over 2km long, hemmed in by 250m cliffs, and at its narrowest just 10m wide, Zádielska Canyon (Zádielska tiešnava, or Zádielska dolina) has been carved by the little Blatnica potok from the limestone tablelands at the eastern edge of the Slovenský kras Protected Landscape Region, of which it is a part. The canyon itself was declared a nature reserve in 1986. Mountain climbers regularly train on its sheer walls.

From the village of Zádiel it's an easy but dramatic 2km walk up through the wooded canyon on a red-marked trail. At the top you can backtrack or, if you take the blue-marked trail along the rim of the canyon east and south to Turnianske Podhradie, it's just over a 4km walk back to the Košice road.

Places to Stay & Eat

At the entrance to the canyon is the basic but homely *Turistický penzión Zádiel*, open at least on weekends. Rooms with shared kitchen, bath and toilet are 100 Sk per person.

Getting There & Away

Košice-Rožňava buses and local trains stop at Dvorníky, from where it's 1km to Zádiel, on foot or by the rare local bus. By train, Dvorníky is 40 minutes from Rožňava, 1¼ hours from Košice.

Šariš Region

PREŠOV

Prešov (Preschau in German) is a sprawling industrial centre with a population of 88,000. Many of the historical buildings along Hlavná have been renovated (most were heavily damaged during WWII), making the square once again picturesque. Prešov is definitely cosmopolitan, but frankly there's not much to see. One day is plenty here.

History

Archaeologists say there was a Slav settlement in Prešov by the end of the 8th

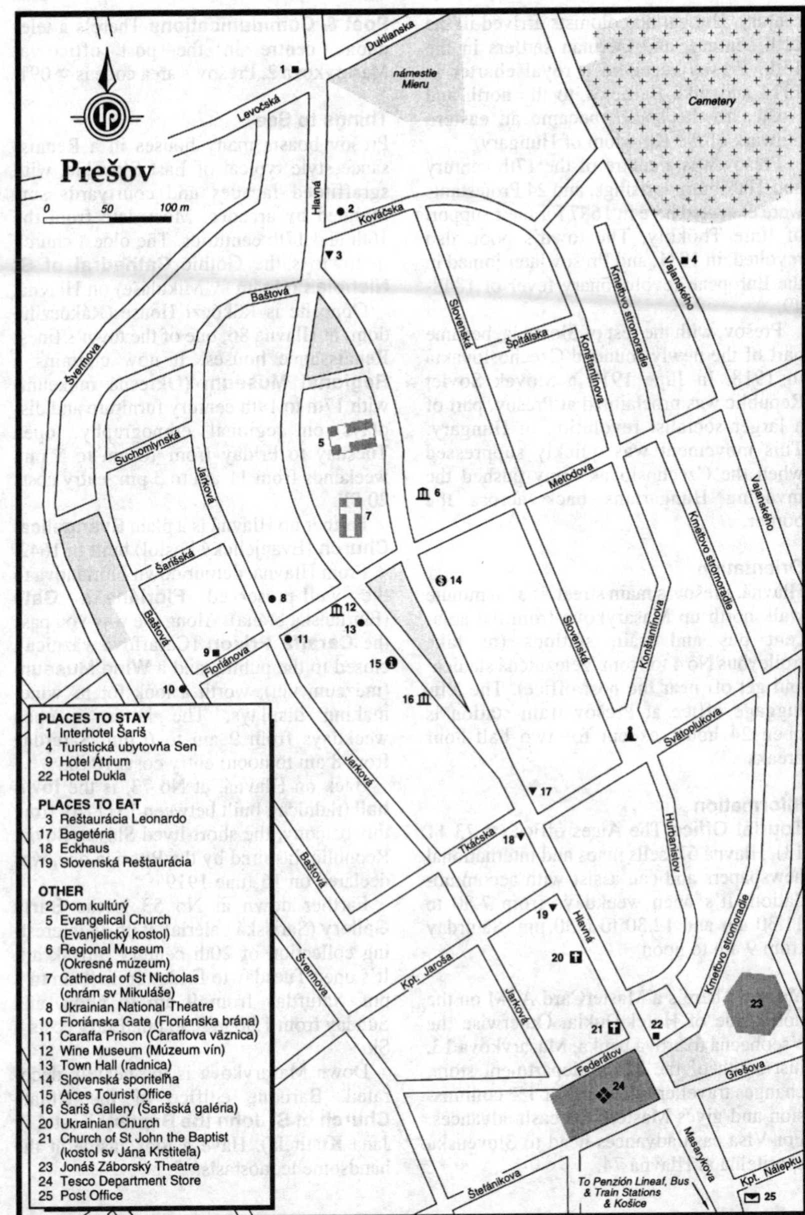

SLOVAK REPUBLIC

century. Hungarian colonists arrived in the 11th century, and German settlers in the 13th. Prešov received a royal charter in 1374 and, like Bardejov to the north and Košice to the south, became an eastern bulwark of the Kingdom of Hungary.

Prešov was a centre of the 17th century anti-Habsburg uprisings, and 24 Protestants were executed here in 1687 for their support of Imre Thököly. The town's poor also revolted, in 1831, and Prešov later joined in the European revolutionary fever of 1848-49.

Prešov, with the rest of Slovakia, became part of the newly founded Czechoslovakia in 1918. In June 1919 a Slovak Soviet Republic was proclaimed at Prešov, part of a larger socialist revolution in Hungary. This movement was quickly suppressed when the Czechoslovak army pushed the invading Hungarians back across the border.

Orientation

Hlavná, Prešov's main street, is a 20 minute walk north up Masarykova from the adjacent bus and train stations (or take trolleybus No 4 to/from 'železničná stanica' and get off near the post office). The left-luggage office at Prešov train station is open 24 hours except for two half-hour breaks.

Information

Tourist Office The Aices office (☎ 73 11 13), Hlavná 67, sells maps and international newspapers and can assist with accommodation. It's open weekdays from 7.30 to 11.30 am and 12.30 to 6.30 pm, Saturday from 9 am to noon.

Money There's a MasterCard ATM on the north side of Hotel Dukla. Otherwise the Všeobecná úverová banka, Masarykova 13, just south of the Tesco department store, changes travellers cheques for 1% commission and gives MasterCard cash advances. For Visa cash advances head to Slovenská sporiteľňa at Hlavná 74.

Post & Communications There's a telephone centre in the post office at Masarykova 2. Prešov's area code is ☎ 091.

Things to See

Prešov boasts many houses in a Renaissance style typical of East Slovakia, with sgraffitoed façades and courtyards surrounded by arcades. Most date from the 16th and 17th centuries. The oldest church in town is the Gothic **Cathedral of St Nicholas** (chrám sv Mikuláše) on Hlavná.

Opposite is Rákóczi House (Rákócziho dom) at Hlavná 86, one of the town's finest Renaissance houses. It now contains a **Regional Museum** (Okresné múzeum) with 17th to 19th century furniture and displays on regional ethnography, open Tuesday to Friday from 10 am to 5 pm, weekends from 11 am to 3 pm; entry costs 20 Sk.

Farther up Hlavná is a plain **Evangelical Church** (Evanjelický kostol) built in 1642.

From Hlavná, detour down Floriánova to the well-preserved **Floriánska Gate** (Floriánska brána). Along the way you pass the **Caraffa Prison** (Caraffova väznica), closed to the public, and a **Wine Museum** (múzeum vín), worth a look for its wine-making displays. The latter is open weekdays from 9 am to 6 pm, Saturday from 8 am to noon; entry costs 10 Sk.

Back on Hlavná, at No 73, is the **town hall** (radnica), built between 1511-20; from this balcony, the short-lived Slovak Soviet Republic, inspired by the Russian one, was declared on 16 June 1919.

Farther down at No 53 is the **Šariš Gallery** (Šarišská galéria), with an interesting collection of 20th century Slovak art. It's open Tuesday to Friday from 9 am to 5 pm, Saturday from 9 am to noon, and Sunday from 1.30 to 5.30 pm. Entry costs 6 Sk.

Down Masarykova is the heavily decorated, Baroque edifice of the Uniate **Church of St John the Baptist** (Kostol sv Jána Krstiteľa). Have a look inside at the handsome iconostasis.

Places to Stay

The central *Turistická ubytovňa Sen* (☎ 73 31 70), Vajanského 65, has beds in two, three and five-bed dorms for 140/130/120 Sk per person, respectively.

The nine storey *Penzión Lineaf* (☎ 72 33 25), Budovatelská 14, has rooms with bath from 240 to 320 Sk per person. It's about 10 minutes from the train station: walk north on Masarykova and turn left on Škultétyho, which crosses the railway line. The second street on the left is Budovatelská.

A good central choice is *Hotel Átrium* (☎ 73 39 52; fax 73 39 15), Floriánova 4, which has clean modern rooms with bath and TV for 650/800 Sk. The restaurant here gets top marks.

Prešov has two mediocre tourist hotels, the cheaper of which is the 39 room *Hotel Dukla* (☎ 72 27 41), Hlavná 2, charging 760 Sk for singles without bath, and 930/1700 Sk for singles/doubles with bath, including breakfast.

Avoid the overpriced *Interhotel Šariš* (☎ 71 63 51), on the corner of Salinovská and Levočská, priced at 960/1890 Sk with bath and breakfast.

Places to Eat

Large sandwiches, baguettes and fresh croissants are hallmarks of *Bagetéria*, Hlavná 36. *Eckhaus*, Hlavná 21, is a decent, very cheap stand-up buffet, open weekdays to 5 pm, weekends to 1 pm. The *Slovenská Reštaurácia*, Hlavná 13, has a menu of above-average Slovak dishes (closed Sunday). *Reštaurácia Leonardo*, Hlavná 144, is a semi-formal spot with typical meat and fish dishes from 100 to 150 Sk (closed Monday).

Entertainment

The *Jonáš Záborský Theatre*, opposite Hotel Dukla, has occasional music and drama performances. Also check the *Ukrainian National Theatre*, Jarková 77, for plays (often in Ukrainian). For films try *Kino Intersonic* in the dom kulturý, or *Kino Panoráma* at Masarykova 7, opposite the post office.

Getting There & Away

Prešov is 36km north of Košice, on the Kraków-Budapest train line (with a daily express between them). There are also daily trains to Košice and Bardejov, though buses are faster and more frequent. Other useful buses with a dozen or more departures a day are to and from Svidník (1½ hours), Levoča, Michalovce (1¾ hours), Spišské Podhradie (1¼ hours), Poprad (two hours) and Stará Ľubovňa (two hours). There are up to three daily connections to Humenné.

BARDEJOV

Bardejov (population 23,500), in the foothills of the Lower Beskydy mountains, is one of the major towns of the Šariš region, together with Prešov. Bardejov's small, impeccably well-preserved centre can be covered in a leisurely afternoon, but consider staying a day or two to visit the superb skansen in nearby Bardejovské Kúpele (see the following section).

The town hosts several festivals, one of the liveliest being The Market (*jarmork*), when Radničné námestie turns into one big marketplace.

History

Bardejov received municipal privileges in 1320 and became a free royal town in 1376. Trade between Poland and Russia passed through the town and in the 15th century the Bardejov merchants grew rich, mainly through the production of cloth and fabrics.

The Thirty Years' War stopped the town's development in its tracks, but saved its fine Renaissance and Gothic centre from being renovated away. This town centre, a total of 84 buildings, was painstakingly restored between 1970 and 1990 at a cost of almost US$9 million. The result is a contribution to Europe's architectural heritage that earned Bardejov a gold medal in 1986.

Orientation

The joint bus and train stations (with a left-luggage office open every day from 7 am to 7 pm) is a five minute walk from Radničné námestie, the town's main square.

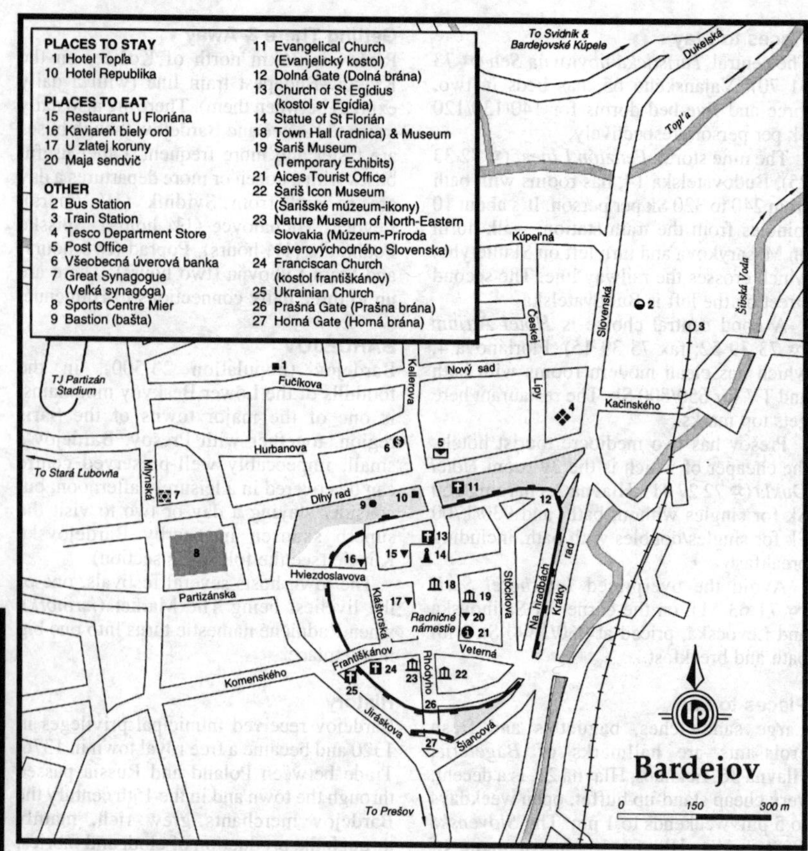

Information

Tourist Office The helpful Aices office (☎ 180), at Radničné námestie 21, can assist with guides, accommodation and guided tours, weekdays from 8 am to 4 pm, weekends in summer from 11 am to 3 pm.

Money The Všeobecná úverová banka, Kellerova 1, changes travellers cheques and has a MasterCard ATM that's open daily from 6 am to 10 pm. Slovenská sporiteľňa, Radničné námestie 22, has an exchange office and gives Visa cash advances.

Post & Communications The telephone centre in the main post office is open weekdays from 7.30 am to 9.30 pm, Saturday from 7.30 am to 8 pm, Sunday from 8 to 11 am. Bardejov's area code is ☎ 0935.

Things to See

On the way from the station you pass a chunky 14th century **bastion** (*bašta*), part of the original town walls. Among the many old town gates, **Dolná brána** and **Prašná brána** are the best preserved; they are east and south, respectively.

At the northern end of cobbled Radničné námestie is the 15th century **Church of St Egídius** (kostol sv Egídia), with one of central Europe's most splendid Gothic interiors, full of paintings, carved wood and stone, and 11 altars. Note the beautifully carved main column.

The former **town hall** (radnica) in the middle of Radničné námestie, built in 1509, is a unique piece of early Renaissance architecture; the bay staircase, the carved stone portals and the wooden inlay ceiling in the Meeting Room are all worth a look. The town hall also has an historical **exhibition** on the Šariš region, with paintings, coins, weapons and handwritten books (20 Sk). It's open – as are all museums in Bardejov – daily, except Monday, from 8 am to noon and 12.30 to 4 pm.

More impressive as collections go is the **Šariš Icon Museum** (Šarišské múzeum-ikony), on Rhodyho south off the square. Highlights include the church icons and models of wooden churches; entry is 25 Sk.

Across the street is another branch of the Šariš Museum, the not-so-enthralling **Nature Museum of North-Eastern Slovakia** (múzeum-Príroda severovýchodného Slovenska); entry costs 10 Sk. A third branch of the Šariš Museum, this one at Radničné námestie 13, has **temporary exhibits** and is free.

Two of the best Renaissance and Baroque houses on the square are the municipal building at No 16 and a former inn at No 42. The 18th century **Great Synagogue** (Veľká synagóga), on Mlýnská, is boarded up and sadly falling to pieces.

Places to Stay

The ageing *Hotel Republika* (☎ 72 27 21), right next to the parish church, has singles/doubles at 450/610 Sk with shared bath.

The smaller *Hotel Topľa* (☎ 72 40 41), Fučíkova 25, has rooms at 330/400 Sk. It does not look much from the outside but the rooms are fine. Reception is on the 3rd floor, and there's a cheap beer hall downstairs.

The *Športhotel* (☎ 72 49 49), Kutuzovova 31, a modern two storey hotel overlooking the Topľa river, has 20 rooms with bath for 350 Sk per person. From the post office walk north on Kellerova and, after crossing the river, make the first left onto Kutuzovova.

Places to Eat

Restaurant U Floriána, Radničné námestie 44, is a small café-restaurant with some vegetarian options, open daily to 6 pm.

U zlatej koruny, upstairs at Radničné námestie 41, serves good if typical Slovak meals daily to 10 pm.

For a quick lunch try *Maja sendvič*, on the main square at No 15; freshly made baguette sandwiches are 30 Sk.

Kaviareň biely orol, Kláštorská 22, is a popular wine bar.

Getting There & Away

Local trains run between Bardejov and Prešov (1¼ hours; 45km), but if you're coming from Prešov, Svidník or Košice, buses are faster. If you're bound for the Vysoké Tatry, take a bus to Poprad (125km; 11 daily). There are also three direct buses a day to Starý Smokovec, four to Bratislava (457km) and two to Žilina (278km).

BARDEJOVSKÉ KÚPELE

Just 4km north of Bardejov is Bardejovské Kúpele, one of Slovakia's most beautiful spas, where diseases of the alimentary and respiratory tracts are treated. Bardejovské was founded in the 13th century but only developed as a spa in the 1920s. Because of a big fire early in this century, there's not much history to look at – a deficiency amply filled by Slovakia's best skansen, set in the spa's foothills. A good time to visit is mid-July for the annual two day Rusin-Šariš folk festival.

Orientation & Information

The bus station is at the spa's south-east end; turn left onto the main road and keep straight for the Hotel Minerál (300m) and skansen (800m).

There's no tourist office here, but the map *Bardejov a Bardejovské Kúpele Mapa mesta*, available at Aices in Bardejov, has an inset map of the spa.

Bardejovské Kúpele's area code is ☎ 0935.

Things to See

Even if you haven't booked a spa cure, you're welcome to partake of the drinking cure. Crowds of locals constantly pace up and down the modern **colonnade** (1972), where an unending supply of hot mineral water streams from eight different springs (bring your own cup).

Near the colonnade is the **Šarišské múzeum**, dedicated to local history and ethnography. Buy tickets (10 Sk) at the skansen.

Alongside the museum is a superb **skansen**, with 24 full-scale buildings ranging from old barns and smithy workshops to rustic houses and wooden churches, all brought here from villages across Slovakia. The skansen's layout has a snug village feel, and there are plenty of nice touches, like beehives made of straw, and frilled domes on the church. Admission is 25 Sk, plus 40 Sk for cameras. Both the museum and skansen are open daily, except Monday, year-round from 8 am to noon and 12.30 to 4 pm.

Places to Stay

Most of the hotels at the spa are reserved for patients undergoing medical treatment, but there are two that do accept tourists: *Hotel Mier* (☎ 72 28 07) and *Hotel Minerál* (☎ 72 41 22; fax 72 41 24), both of which charge about 500/750 Sk for singles/doubles with shower and WC.

Getting There & Away

There's no train station here. Instead Bardejovské Kúpele is connected hourly to Bardejov by city bus Nos 1, 2, 6, 7, 10 and 11. The last bus back is at around 7 pm. Otherwise it's an easy 90 minute walk from Bardejov, with the last 1.5km meandering through wooded countryside.

SLOVAK REPUBLIC

Eastern Borderlands

Slovakia's eastern borderlands are home to a large Rusin minority. The area covers much of the Lower Beskydy mountains along the Polish and Ukrainian border, centreing on Svidník and Humenné.

The Rusin people (Rusíni) are a subgroup of Ukrainians who over many centuries developed a distinct culture and dialect, as well as their own brand of Orthodox Christianity. For centuries they were an isolated group, first within Lithuania, then Poland and finally the Austro-Hungarian Empire, though never acquiring a self-governing territory of their own.

When Czechoslovakia was founded after WWI, a large part of Hungarian Ruthenia called Podkarpatská Rus was included in the new state, but this was lost again to Hungary in 1939. The Czechoslovak state ceded part of Ruthenia to Stalin's Russia in 1945, leaving a minority of Rusins in Slovakia. Today most of historical Ruthenia is under the aegis of Ukraine.

According to the 1990 census, only 40,000 Slovaks called themselves Rusin, though there are thought to be over 100,000.

The skansens in Svidník and Humenné are worth a look and easy to reach. The region's other cultural treasures – mostly wooden Rusin churches – are a bit harder to see unless you have a car or plenty of patience for the infrequent buses.

SVIDNÍK

This bland town of 12,800 is of limited interest except that it's one of Slovakia's main centres of Rusin culture, with a museum and an above-average open-air museum.

The town evolved from Vyšný and Nižný Svidník, both of which were destroyed in heavy fighting between German and Soviet forces in November 1944. The Germans knew that if the Soviets breached German defenses around the Dukla Pass they could

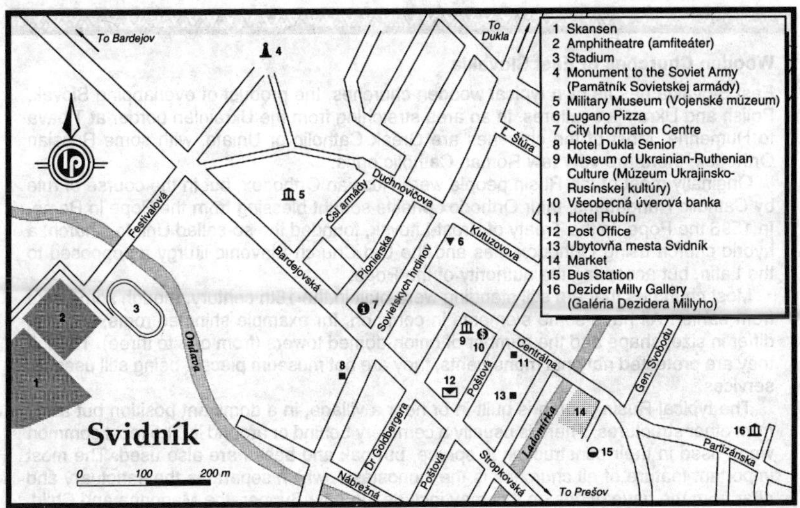

easily advance on the plains to the south, and as a result some of the most ferocious fighting of WWII took place here.

Orientation & Information

There is no train station here. The SAD bus terminal is 500m east of town, just off Centrálna.

The City Information Centre (Mestské informační centrum; ☎ 186), on Sovietskych hrdinov, sells maps but is otherwise unhelpful. It's open weekdays from 7.30 am to 3.30 pm. The Všeobecná úverová banka, on Centrálna, has an exchange desk and MasterCard ATM.

Svidník's area code is ☎ 0937.

Museum of Ukrainian-Rusin Culture

The múzeum Ukrajinsko-Rusínskej kultúry, Centrálna 258, offers a good look at traditional Rusin culture and history.

Unfortunately, everything is labelled in Slovak and Rusin only; the best bits are the folk dresses and painted Easter eggs. Open year-round, Tuesday to Friday from 8.30 am to 4 pm, weekends from 1 pm; entry costs 9 Sk.

Skansen

This outdoor museum of Rusin culture has traditional architecture and furnishings, with old houses, barns, a school, fire station, mill and wooden church built in 1776. It's off Bardejovská behind the amphitheatre, and is open daily, except Monday, May through September from 8.30 am to noon and from 12.30 to 6 pm (weekends from 10 am). Entry costs 9 Sk, and it's an extra 30 to snap photos.

Dezider Milly Gallery

A five minute walk, following the signs from the bus station on Partizánska, brings you to the Dezider Milly Gallery (Galéria Dezidera Millyho) with its excellent collection of icons from the 16th to 19th centuries, plus paintings by contemporary Rusin artists. It's open the same hours as the skansen, and entry costs 6 Sk.

War Memorials

Opposite the skansen, on the other side of Bardejovská, stands a 37m-tall **Monument to the Soviet Army** (Pamätník Sovietskej armády) and a common grave for 9000

Wooden Churches of East Slovakia

East Slovakia has its own typical wooden churches, the product of overlapping Slovak, Polish and Ukrainian cultures, in an area stretching from the Ukrainian border at Tibava to Humenné. Most of the churches are Greek Catholic or Uniate, with some Russian Orthodox; there are very few Roman Catholic ones.

Originally most of the Rusin people were Russian Orthodox, but in the course of rule by Catholic Hungarians, their Orthodox priests sought blessing from the Pope in Rome. In 1596 the Pope, in the Treaty of Brest-Litovsk, founded the so-called Uniate Church, a hybrid church using Orthodox rites and the Old Church Slavonic liturgy as opposed to the Latin, but accepting the authority of the Pope.

Most churches that are still standing were built in the 18th century, though some date from earlier. All have some elements in common, for example shingled roofs, but they differ in size, shape and the number of onion-domed towers (from one to three). Though they are protected national monuments, they are not museum pieces, being still used for services.

The typical Rusin church is built in or near a village, in a dominant position but away from other structures. There is usually a cemetery behind or around it. The most common wood used in their construction is spruce, but oak and beech are also used. The most important feature of all churches is the iconostasis, which separates the sanctuary and altar from the nave. Icons on this may include the Last Supper, the Madonna and Child, the Last Judgement, and St Nicholas or other saints, including the one to whom the church is dedicated.

The most accessible of these churches are in the *skansens* at Svidník, Humenné and Bardejovské Kúpele; however, while these are open to the public, services are not held in them. Many of the ones which are used for worship are north of Svidník.

The following churches around Bardejov are relatively easy to reach:

Jedlinka Here there is a small three-tower Greek-Catholic church built in 1763 in honour of the Mother Mary, of whom there is a highly prized icon. The rococo iconostasis was made in 1780. The church is 14km north of Bardejov, and frequent buses between Svidník and Bardejov stop here.

Lukov – Venecia The Orthodox church of SS Cosmas & Damian here was built between 1708-09. The very fine iconostasis was made in two different eras: the lower part is from 1736, and is by the Bardejov artist Andrej Gajecký; the top part is from the second half of the 18th century. The church is 14km west of Bardejov; several daily buses pass through so you shouldn't have any trouble getting there.

Hervartov The Roman Catholic Church of St Francis of Assisi at Hervartov is the oldest wooden church in Slovakia, and was built around 1500. The interior of the nave is from 1665, and is richly decorated with frescoes. ■

RICHARD NEBESKÝ

Soviet soldiers. On Bardejovská in the park, closer to the town centre, is a **Military Museum** (Vojenské múzeum), which includes photographs and maps of the Dukla battle. Outside, like a military skansen, is a collection of tanks, armoured vehicles and a US-made Dakota transport aircraft with Soviet markings. The museum is open Tuesday to Thursday from 8 am to 4 pm, Friday to 3 pm, and weekends from 10 am to 2 pm; entry costs 8 Sk.

Special Events

Each year in late July Svidník hosts the Rusin-Ukrainian Cultural Festival (Slavnosti kultúry Rusínov-Ukrajincov Slovenska), with music and dance troupes not only from Slovakia but from Ukraine, Germany, Scandinavia and elsewhere.

Places to Stay

Cheapest is the basic workers' hostel *Ubytovňa mesta Svidník* (☎ 220 96), Nábrežná 498, with dormitory beds for about 200 Sk.

More appealing is the new, modern *Hotel Rubín* (☎ 242 10; fax 242 11), on Centrálna, priced at 400/800 Sk for singles/doubles with bath and toilet. The only drawback is early-morning street noise.

Slightly farther afield is the plain but pleasant *Hotel Dukla Senior* (☎ 233 88) on Sovietskych hrdinov, priced at 400/800 Sk with shared bath.

Places to Eat

The selection is grim – both hotels have decent restaurants, or you can dine on pizza and calzones at *Lugano Pizza*, on Sovietskych hrdinov and open daily to 11 pm.

Getting There & Away

There are regular connections to and from Bardejov (up to 10 a day), Prešov, Košice, Humenné, Dobroslava, Dukla (35 minutes) and Medzilaborce.

AROUND SVIDNÍK

The road north of Svidník leads to the Polish border and the Dukla Pass, where there is a monument. This area is an inadvertent open-air museum of WWII weaponry – mainly Soviet, some German – left where it was abandoned in the battle for the pass. Rather more pleasing to the eye are the many 18th century Rusin wooden churches. To have a look inside one of these, you will need to ask around for the priest (*kňaz*).

Valley of Death

The Valley of Death (Údolí smrti) is the first major road to the left, north from Svidník on the road to Ladomirová; at the crossroads is a monument made of a Soviet and a German tank. This road leads to the village of **Dobroslava** and its wooden three-domed church. Along the road are many tanks and other weapons. There are two daily buses to Dobroslava from Svidník (none on Sunday).

Valley of Death to Dukla Pass

Head back to the main road and turn left towards **Ladomirová**, the first village north-east of Svidník, with a handsome, onion-domed church built in 1742. Take the Krajná Poľana turn-off to reach a second church at **Bodružal** and, on a brief detour almost to the Polish border, the three-domed church at **Príkra**, built in 1777. A few kilometres south of Bodružal is a photogenic three-domed church at **Miroľa**.

Back on the Svidník-Dukla road, in **Nižný Komárnik**, is one of the region's more striking wooden churches, with bright-yellow doors, bits of stained glass and unusually broad towers.

The last village with a church before the Dukla Pass is **Vyšný Komárnik**. A few hundred metres before the Vyšný Komárnik turn-off, on the left (west) side of the highway, is a marker for a 30 minute loop trail past foxholes and anti-aircraft guns. From the same spot a red-marked trail leads 5½ hours back to Svidník through largely untouched forests.

Buses run to the wooden churches along the main Svidník-Dukla road at regular intervals, but the churches off the road are virtually unserviced.

Dukla Pass

The Dukla Pass (Dukliansky priesmyk), about 20km from Svidník (35 minutes by bus), is the lowest point in the Laborec range, and named after the Polish town of Dukla on the other side. Czechoslovak units fighting with the Soviets crossed here and liberated Vyšný Komárnik on 6 October 1944. The battle for the pass lasted from 8 September to 27 November 1944, during which 85,000 Soviet soldiers and 6500 Czechoslovaks died or were wounded.

About 1km from the border is a 49m stone monument, on the spot where the Czechoslovak General Svoboda had his observation post; you can climb to the top from June to 6 October. The surrounding area is littered with rusting machine guns, mortars and other weapons.

The border here is a 24 hour crossing for vehicles and pedestrians.

MEDZILABORCE

This plain town of 6500 in the Lower Beskydy, in the far north-east corner of Slovakia, has exactly one, strange claim to fame: the **Andy Warhol Family Museum** (Múzea Moderného umenia rodiny Warholovcov).

Though the artist was born in the USA (in Pittsburgh, as Andrej Varchola), his parents came from the village of Miková, 8km north-west of here. They emigrated early in this century, as had other Rusins since the 19th century. Warhol never acknowledged his roots, though he could speak Rusin. He used to joke, 'I came from nowhere'. The museum was founded after his death in 1987 by his US and Slovak relatives, especially his brother John.

The museum on Andyho Warhola, the town's main street, shares the tall white building with a cinema; from the train station turn left onto Andyho Warhola and keep straight for 800m. Inside are family memorabilia and at least 17 Warhol paintings, including *Campbell Soup II*, *Hammer & Sickle* and *Ingrid Bergman* (as a nun in the film *Bells of St Mary*). There are also paintings by his nephew James Warhol. The museum is open daily, except Monday, from 10 am to 1 pm and 1.45 to 6 pm. Entry costs 15 Sk, which is about as little as you'll ever pay to see an original Warhol.

Places to Stay & Eat

The *Hotel Laborec* (☎ 0939-213 07), 200m past the museum on Andyho Warhola, has singles/doubles with shared bath for 210/420 Sk and a cheap restaurant.

Getting There & Away

Medzilaborce is 1¼ hours up a rail spur from Michalovce, with regular connections. Coming from Prešov, you need to change trains at Strážské. Buses are faster from Prešov and Košice, though less frequent. Buses come from Svidník (1½ hours away) no more than three times a day.

HUMENNÉ

This peaceful town of 37,000 on the Laborec river has a French-style Baroque chateau which began as a Gothic castle, and which now houses a **Museum of Local History** (Vlastivedné múzeum), with exhibits on archaeology, local history and feudal housing.

Considerably more interesting is a **skansen** of about 10 Rusin wooden houses from around the region, dating from the 19th and early 20th centuries. Pride of place goes to a wooden church built in 1754.

Both the skansen and museum are open daily, except Monday, from May through October from 9 am to noon and 1 to 5 pm; entry costs 10 Sk each.

Orientation & Information

The adjacent bus and train stations are 500m due west of the vast, pedestrianised main square, námestie Slobody (really a 600m-long rectangle). Turn right onto Staničná and walk below the overpass; the skansen and museum are at námestie Slobody's northern end (turn left), the Hotel Chemes at its southern end.

C3M (☎ 75 71 36), námestie Slobody 8,

is a semi-official tourist office, but it's only useful for buying maps. Humenné's area code is ☎ 0933.

Places to Stay & Eat

At *Hotel Karpatia* (☎ & fax 75 20 38), Staničná 1 on the other side of the square from the bus station, basic singles/doubles are 350/650 Sk.

Far cheaper is the hostel *Ubytovacie zariadenie SOU* (☎ 75 28 71) at Mierová 5; from the stations turn left onto Družstevná, right on Tolstého and right on Mierová.

The upper-end option is *Hotel Chemes* (☎ 626 09; fax 78 49 53), námestie Slobody 51, with fully equipped rooms at 500/950 Sk.

Restaurant Dukla at námestie Slobody 27 serves above-average Slovak meals daily to 11 pm.

Getting There & Away

Humenné is 50 minutes from Michalovce, on the same rail spur as Medzilaborce. Trains to and from Košice, Prešov and Bardejov require at least one change. Buses are better for other destinations; there are up to eight a day from Svidník, three from Prešov, and up to four from Bardejov and Košice.

Food Guide

Czech cuisine is basically central European, with German, Hungarian and Polish influences. There's usually lots of meat, big portions of either dumplings, potatoes or rice topped with a thick sauce, and a heavily cooked vegetable or sauerkraut; the standard quick meal is *knedlo-zelo-vepřo* (dumplings, sauerkraut and roast pork). Caraway seed, bacon and lots of salt are the common flavourings. Despite spicy Hungarian influences, Slovak food is on the whole not much different though dumplings are not as common as in the Czech Republic. Most restaurants have big menus, but in the end you will come across the same dishes again and again. There is a vast difference between restaurant and home-cooking, so if you have a chance to eat in a local's home don't pass it up.

Two names separated by a slash (/) in this section are the Czech and Slovak terms; those without a slash are the same in both languages.

Where to Eat

Prague and other tourist centres offer a wide variety of local, international and 'ethnic' food. Most sizable towns will have at least one respectable Czech/Slovak restaurant. Even in most of the smallest places you can find a pub, if you don't leave it too late. And for vegetarians and do-it-yourselfers, every sizable town has an open-air produce market somewhere, at least on some weekdays.

Breakfast A typical breakfast (*snídaně/raňajky*) in a typical Czech or Slovak home is bread with butter, cheese, eggs, ham or sausage, jam or yoghurt, and tea or coffee. Commuters in a hurry gobble down soup and frankfurters at a *bufet* and also bring a sandwich for their 10 am snack.

Those on the move can start the day with a Bohemian pastry (*koláče*) topped with poppy seeds, cottage cheese or plum jam from a bakery (*pekárna* or *pekařství/pekáreň*). Bigger tourist towns now also have French and Viennese-style bakeries, with croissants or smaller, heavier local cousins called *loupáčky/lúpačky*.

A hotel breakfast is typically a cold plate or buffet with cheese, eggs, sausage or meat, bread, butter, jam, yoghurt and coffee or tea. Some also offer cereal and milk, pastries, fruit and cakes. Only at top-end hotels and a few restaurants can you get an American or English-style fry-up.

Lunch & Dinner For Czechs and Slovaks, lunch (*oběd/obed*) is the main meal, except on Sunday when it's a hurried affair. Dinner (*večeře/večera*) is usually no more than a cold plate of meats and condiments.

A *bufet* or *samoobsluha* is a self-service, cafeteria-style place with zero atmosphere but cheap soups and stodge for lunch on the run. Common items are *obložené chlebíčky* (open sandwiches) with a great variety of tasty salads, *klobásy* (spicy sausages), *buřt/špekačky* (mild pork sausages), *párky/párok* (frankfurters), *guláš* (goulash), and of course knedlo-zelo-vepřo. Some of these places are tucked to the side of *potraviny* (food shops).

A *pivnice/pivnica* is a pub or beer hall serving no food. *Hospoda* or *hostinec* is a pub or beer hall that serves basic meals. Many of these also tend to be non-smoking for lunch, which usually ends about 3 pm. A *vinárna/vináreň* (wine bar) may have anything from snacks to a full-blown menu. The occasional *kavárna/kaviareň* (coffee shop) has a full menu but most serve only snacks. A restaurace/reštaurácia is any restaurant. As a general rule a restaurant calling itself *restaurace/reštaurácia* is usually cheaper than a 'restaurant'.

Koliba refers to a Slovak-style rustic country restaurant specialising in BBQ chicken and sometimes other lunch-time items; there are now kolibas right across both republics. The Slovak *salaš* is a basic, usually rural, place, originally a shepherd's summer hut, serving standard Slovak fare.

Protocol

When to Go Restaurants may start serving lunch as early as 11.30 am and carry on till 3 pm. They're usually open again for dinner from 5 or 6 pm until at least 8 or 9 pm, sometimes later. Main dishes may stop being served well before the advertised closing time, with only snacks and drinks after that.

Opening hours are volatile, so don't be surprised if they're different from what we found. Most restaurants seem to stay open on national holidays.

Hazards Most restaurants right across both republics are honest, though of course it pays to watch out for mistakes. Prague is a different matter; see Places to Eat in the Prague chapter, for ways to cope with restaurants there. Expect a *couvert,* or cover charge, in the pricier restaurants everywhere.

Even in the best restaurants waiters tend to remove your plate as soon as you finish your meal, despite the fact that everyone at your table is still eating.

And one final point: on average the Prague waiter is an unfriendly and/or indifferent character who suffers from that famous Communist-era service industry disease – surliness. It is nothing personal; it's just the manner they developed during 40 years of only state-owned restaurants and shops. Czechs are used to this behaviour and just ignore it. New and young waiters tend to be more pleasant and professional.

Tipping A tip of 5 to 10% is reasonable in all but the cheapest places, but don't just leave it behind on the table. The usual protocol is for them to show you the total for food and drink, and for you to then reply with what you intend to pay – food and drink plus tip.

Meat

biftek	beef steak
hovězí (maso)/hovädzie (mäso)	beef
játra/pečeň	liver
karbanátek/karbonátka	hamburger
kuře/kura	chicken
kotleta/rebierko (karé)	cutlet, chop
řízek/rezeň	wiener schnitzel
ryba	fish
šunka	ham
svíčková/sviečková	sirloin
telecí (maso)/teľacia (mäso)	veal

Fruit & Vegetables

brambory/zemiaky	potato
česnek/cesnak	garlic
cibule/cibuľa	onion
citrón	lemon
fazole/fazuľa	beans
houby/hríby	mushrooms
hranolky	chips, French fries
hrášek/hrášok	peas
křen/chren	horseradish
květák/karfiol	cauliflower
mrkev/mrkva	carrot
okurka/uhorka	cucumber or pickle
ovoce/ovocie	fruit
paprika	capsicum
pepř/čierne korenie	pepper
rajče/rajčina	tomato
špenát	spinach
sterelizované zelí/sterelizovaná kapusta	pickled cabbage
žampiony/šampiňóny	mushrooms
zelenina	vegetables
zelí/kyslá kapusta	sauerkraut

Other Items

chléb/chlieb	bread
cukr/cukor	sugar
džem	jam
hořčice/horčica	mustard
knedlíky/knedľe	dumplings
máslo/maslo	butter
kmín/rasca	caraway

med	honey
rýže/ryža	rice
smetana/smotana	cream
sůl/soľ	salt
těstoviny/cestoviny	pasta
sýr/syr	cheese
tvaroh	cottage cheese
vejce/vajco	eggs
vejce na tvrdo/ vajca na tvrdo	hard-boiled egg
vejce na měkko/ vajco na mäkko	soft-boiled egg
míchaná vejce/ praženica	scrambled egg
smažená vejce/ volské oko	fried egg
omeleta	omelette
vejce se slaninou/ vajco so slaninou	egg with bacon

Cooking Terms

čerstvý	fresh
domácí/domáci	home-made
dušený/dusený	steamed
grilovaný/na rošte	grilled or on the spit
pečený	roasted or baked
roštěná (na roštu)/ roštěnka (na ražni)	broiled
sladký	sweet
smažený/vypražený	fried
uzený/údené	smoked
vařený/varený	boiled

Utensils

lžíce/lyžica	spoon
nůž/nôž	knife
vidlička	fork
šálek/šálka	cup
sklenice/pohár	glass
talíř/tanier	plate
párátko/špáradlo	toothpick
popelník/popolník	ashtray

Soups

Most Czechs and Slovaks automatically order soup (*polévka/polievka*) first. This can be either broth with bits of meat, bacon, vegetables or noodles, or fairly thick and heavy. Some soups are:

bramborová/ zemiaková	potato, sometimes with vegetables and mushrooms
bujón	broth with egg
dršťková/držková	sliced tripe with spices
gulášová	a thick, spicy beef and potato soup
houbová/hríbová	mushroom
hovězí/hovädzia	beef in broth
hrachová	thick pea soup with bacon
rajská/rajčinová	tomato and rice
zeleninová	vegetables

Cold Starters

Here are some favourite cold starters (*studené předkrmy/studené predjedlá*):

obložené chlebíčky
open sandwiches on French bread, with cold meat, eggs, cheese, or mayonnaise salads like lobster, fish, potato or ham and peas

Pražská šunka s okurkou (uhorkou)
Prague ham with gherkins

ruská vejce/ruské vajcia
hard-boiled egg, potato and sometimes salami, with mayonnaise

sýrový nářez/syrový nárez
a cheese-board

tlačenka s octem a cibulí/ tlačenka s octom a cibulou
jellied meat loaf with vinegar and onion

uherský salám s okurkou/ maďarský salám s uhorkou
Hungarian salami with gherkin

utopenec
literally 'the drowned one' – sliced pickled pork sausage, usually with a slice of rye bread

zavináče
rollmops – herring fillets rolled around onion and/or gherkin and pickled

Warm Starters

The best warm starters (*teplé předkrmy/ teplé predjedláse*) include:

ďábelská topinka/hrianka
a piquant toast with meat and cheese
míchaná vejce s klobásou/ miešané vajcia s klobásou
scrambled eggs with spicy sausage
omeleta
omelette
pečená šunka s vejci/ šunka pečená s vajcem
fried ham with egg

Main Dishes

This category is usually subdivided as *hotová jídla/hotová jedlá* (ready-to-serve dishes) and *jídla na objednávku/jedlá na objednávku* (dishes prepared as they're ordered); the latter in turn sometimes has a main listing plus separate ones for *ryby* (fish), *drůbež/hydina* (poultry), *zvěřina/ divina* (game) and foreign dishes.

Most main dishes are based on meat, though, especially at home, Czechs and Slovaks may cook with only vegetables or even fruit – some can even be sweet. Many Czech meals seem to be anchored with dumplings (*knedlíky/knedle*), made from potato (*bramborové/zemiakové*) or bread (*houskové*). Potatoes, French fries, rice or noodles also accompany dishes, especially in Slovakia.

By far the most common main dish in the Czech Republic – one which you will probably learn either to love or hate – is roast pork with dumplings and sauerkraut. Another, common in both republics, is roast beef with goulash (*guláš*), mushroom sauce (*houbová/hríbová omáčka*) or dill cream sauce (*koprová omáčka/kôprová omáčka*). A delicious Czech speciality is *svíčková na smetaně* – roast beef and bread dumplings in sour cream sauce, with lemon and cranberries.

Other popular meat dishes are:

Dumplings, dumplings, and more knedlíků

Most Czechs and Slovaks are incredibly fond of dumplings (*knedlíky*), which look and taste nothing like the American, Austrian or Bavarian versions. Czech bread dumplings (*houskové*) are made with two stale white bread rolls that have been cubed, two parts continental (or instantized) flour, one part semolina (or farina), and some milk and/or water. The tastier potato dumplings (*bramborové*) is made from cooked potatoes (about 500g), two parts continental flour, one part semolina, one egg, salt to taste and some milk and/or water. Another version of the potato dumpling is made from raw grated potatoes and called hairy dumplings (*chlupaté*).

The king of the dumplings is made with fruit. Many types of dough, and any type of plum, apricot or berry can be used. One of the most popular is made with cottage cheese dough. For these you need 250g of soft cottage cheese, 500g of continental flour, two tablespoons of butter, one egg, salt, one tablespoon of sugar and 200ml to 300ml of milk. Mix to a doughy consistency, then roll out the pastry to a thin pizza-like thickness and cut pieces large enough to cover the plum or apricot. Czechs prefer plum dumplings sprinkled with crushed poppy seeds and apricot dumplings with hard cottage cheese, both mixed with sugar. Either version has melted butter generously poured over it. All knedlíky should be boiled for about 20 minutes.

And yes, Czechs are fiercely proud of their dumplings, a fact celebrated at annual cooking and eating competitions around the country. In 1996 at the Plum Picking Festival (*trnkovraní*) in Vizovice, South Moravia, the winner managed to stuff down 136 plum dumplings at one sitting. This was still far short of the festival record set in 1992 when František Pohorský ate a gut-busting 155 dumplings. ■

dušená roštěňka/dusené hovädzie
braised beef slices in sauce
hovězí guláš/hovädzí guláš
beef chunks in brown sauce
karbanátky/karbonátky
a kind of beef hamburger with bread crumbs, egg, a sliced roll and onion
plněné papriky/plnená paprika
capsicum stuffed with minced meat and rice, served with tomato sauce
přírodní řízek/prírodný rezeň
pork or veal schnitzel without the breadcrumbs
rizoto
a mixture of pork, onion, peas and rice
segedínský guláš/kološárska kapusta
goulash with beef, pork, lamb and sauerkraut (in Slovakia, it's mainly just beef) in a cream sauce
sekaná pečeně
baked minced meat
svíčková na smetaně/ sviečková na smotane
roast beef served with a sour cream sauce and spices
svíčkové řezy/sviečkové rezy
sliced roast or fried beef
tatarský biftek
raw steak
telecí pečeně/telacie pečené
roast veal
telecí řízek/telačí rezeň
veal schnitzel
vepřová játra/bravčová pečeň
pork liver fried with onion
vepřová pečeně/bravčové pečené
roast pork with caraway seeds
vepřový řízek/bravčový rezeň
pork schnitzel
vídeňský biftek/viedensky biftek
beef steak
znojemská pečeně/znojemská roštenka
sliced roast beef in gherkin sauce

Poultry – chicken (*kuře/kura*), duck (*kachna/kačica*), goose (*husa/hus*) and turkey (*krůta/moriak*) – is usually roasted (*pečená*) with dumplings and sauerkraut, or with rice or potatoes in Slovakia. *Kuře* (*kurča*) *na paprice/kurači na paprikáš* is chicken boiled in spicy paprika cream sauce.

Roast turkey is the traditional Christmas Day lunch, and is served with bread dumplings and sauerkraut.

A few restaurants specialise in game, mainly venison (*jelení/jelenina*), pheasant (*bažant*), rabbit (*králík*), hare (*zajíc/zajac*) or boar (*kanec/divá sviňa*), fried and served in a mushroom sauce. A common dish is *zajíc na smetaně/zajac na smotane*, which is hare in cream sauce.

Most fish dishes are of carp (*kapr/kapor*) or trout (*pstruh*). Pike (*štika/šťuka*) and eel (*úhoř/úhor*) are on some specialist menus. Seafood is found only in a handful of places. Be aware that for a dish with a whole fish, usually trout, the menu price is per 100g; ask how much it weighs before you order it!

A summer speciality is fruit dumplings (*ovocné knedlíky/ovocné knedle* or *guľky*)

What Is It?

Many dishes come with names that don't offer a clue as to what's in them. One that all Czechs and Slovaks know is *Španělský ptáček/Španielsky vtáčik*, which is literally translated as 'Spanish Birds' but is actually beef rolled up with bacon and gherkins, served with rice and sauce.

Another is *Moravský vrabec* ('Moravian Sparrow'), which is a fist-size piece of roast pork. A couple of other common ones are *Katův šleh* ('The Executioners Lash'), which is thinly sliced pieces of pork, capsicum and tomato in a sauce, or *Tajemství/tajemstvo* ('A Secret'), which is ham wrapped around a slice of cheese in breadcrumbs.

But even Czechs and Slovaks will need to ask about the following: *Meč krále Jiřího* ('King George's Sword'), *Tajemství Petra Voka* ('Peter Voka's Mystery'), *Bašta nadlesního Karáska* ('Ranger Karásek's Meal'), *Kotlík rytíře Řimbaby* ('The Kettle of Řimbaba the Knight'). ■

– most commonly it'll be plum dumplings sprinkled with crushed poppy seeds mixed with sugar and melted butter (*švestkové knedlíky/slivkové knedle*). Others are *meruňkové/marhuľové* (apricot) and *borůvkové/čučoriedkové* (blueberry), served with cottage cheese and melted butter.

Meatless Dishes

Meatless dishes (*bezmasá jídla/bezmäsité jedlá*) are found on many menus, though some may be cooked in animal fat or even with pieces of ham or bacon! If you ask, most chefs can whip up something genuinely vegetarian. Some of the common vegetarian dishes are:

knedlíky s vejci/knedle s vajcem
fried dumplings with egg
omeleta se sýrem a bramborem
cheese and potato omelette
smažené žampiony/vysmažené šampióny
fried mushrooms with potatoes
smažený květák/smažený karfiol
fried cauliflower with egg and onion
smažený sýr/vysmážaný syr
fried cheese with potatoes and tartare sauce

In fact the Slovak national dish is vegetarian: *bryndzové halušky*, which is sheep's cheese with pasta. A sheep's whey, called *žinčica*, is traditionally drunk with it but you are only likely to find it served at homes in remote villages. Another common dish consists of *pirohy*, which are turnovers – a pastry filled with cheese or jam.

Side Dishes

Side dishes (*přílohy*) are usually dumplings – *houskové/žemlové* are made from bread, *bramborové/zemiakové* from potato, and *chlupaté* from raw potatoes. Other side dishes are potatoes (*brambory/zemiaky*) or French fries (*hranolky*), steamed rice (*dušená rýže/dusená ryža*), and noodles (*nudle/rezance*). Some side dishes are:

bramborový salát/zemiakový šalát
potato salad
chlupatý knedlíky
dumplings made from raw potatoes
dušené fazole/dušená fazuľa
steamed beans
dušená mrkev/dušená mrkva
steamed carrots
okurka/kyslá uhorka
dill pickle
smažené žampiony
fried mushrooms
špenát
finely chopped spinach, cooked with onion, garlic and cream
tatarská omáčka
a creamy tartar sauce

Bread (*chléb/chlieb*) in both countries is good and comes in all styles, mostly rye. Most common is *šumava*, which is made of rye and wheat, and also sometimes comes with caraway seeds (*kmínový/rascový*). A big favourite in Slovakia is sourdough (*moskva*). *Rohlík* is a long roll, and *houska/žemla* or *pletenička* is a plaited roll or bun, usually made of wheat.

Salads

Salads (*saláty/šaláty*) can be either fresh or pickled. If you just ask for *salát/šalát* you may get *sterilizovaný salát/čalamáda*, which is pickled cabbage, capsicum and onion. If you want fresh salad, ask for it – *čerství salát/čerstvý šalát*. These will probably be sweeter, smaller and more watery than you expect. Some common salads are:

míchaný/miešaný	mixed
okurkový/uhorkový	cucumber
rajský/rajčinový	tomato and onion
šopský/balkánský	lettuce, tomato, onion and cheese
hlávkový	lettuce

Desserts

Pubs and bottom-end restaurants may serve only *zmrzlina* (ice cream), *palačinky* or *lívance/dolky* (pancakes), or *kompot* (tinned fruit), either on its own or *pohár*, with ice cream and whipped cream. The more up-market the restaurant, the better the desserts (*moučník/múčnik*).

Only the best will have decent cakes and pastries. The best source for these is a café (*kavárna/kaviáreň*) or cake shop (*cukrárna/cukráreň*). Ice-cream flavours include:

čokoládová	chocolate
kávová	coffee
punčová	fruit punch
oříšková/orieškova	nut
vanilová/vanilková	vanilla

Fruit toppings for your ice cream or pancakes may include:

ananas	pineapple
borůvky/čučoriedky	blueberries
hrušky	pears
jahody	strawberries
maliny	raspberries
meruňky/marhule	apricots
švestky/slivky	plums
třešně or *čerešne*	cherries or sour cherries

Other desserts you may come across are:

jablkový závin or *štrůdl/štrudla*
apple strudel
makový koláč
poppy seed cake
ovocné koláče
fruit slices
rakvička
literally 'coffin'; a meringue in the shape of a coffin topped with whipped cream

In Slovakia, a cheesy pastry dessert that is served hot is *tvarohový koláč*.

Snacks

The most popular Czech snacks are *buřt/vuřt* or *pekačka* (thick sausages, usually pork) and *klobása* (spicy pork or beef sausages), fried or boiled, served with mustard on rye bread or a roll. Other snacks are *párky* (frankfurters), *langoše* (a Hungarian snack of fried pastry coated with garlic, cheese, butter or jam), *bramborák/zemiakové placky* (a patty made from strips of raw potato and garlic) and *hranolky* (chips or French fries) or *brambůrky* (fried sliced potatoes).

Bílý jogurt/biely jogurt is a natural, locally made white yoghurt that beats the pants off the sweetened Austrian and German products dumped on the market; *Grand Míša* or *Eskymáček* (a frozen yoghurt ice cream on a stick, covered in chocolate) is good too.

A favourite sweet sold in spa towns is *lázeňské oplatky* (spa wafers), sold individually either warm or cold, or in a box of half a dozen. If you don't fancy the plain ones there are also chocolate, nut, strawberry, banana, coffee, vanilla and other flavours to choose from.

In the autumn, pavement vendors sell roasted *kaštany* (chestnuts).

Language Guide

This Language Guide contains pronunciation guidelines and basic vocabulary to both the Czech and Slovak languages that will help you get around each country. For background information on the Czech language see the Language section in the Facts about the Country chapter. For a glossary of common terms refer to the Glossary.

For more useful Czech and Slovak phrases and words than we have room for in this section, see Lonely Planet's *Central Europe phrasebook*. If you're serious about studying either language in-country see the Language Courses section in the Facts for the Visitor chapter.

Czech Pronunciation

Vowels There are short and long vowels, the long ones just stretched out for a longer time. Long vowels are indicated by an accent.

a as the 'ah' sound in 'cut' (British pronunciation)
á as in 'father'
e as in 'bet'
é as in 'air'
i/y as the 'u' in 'busy'
í/ý as in 'see'
o as in 'pot' (British pronunciation)
ó as in 'saw'
u as in 'pull'
ú/ů as in 'zoo'

Diphthongs Common vowel combinations are:

aj as the 'i' in 'ice'
áj as in 'eye'
au an 'ow' sound as in 'out'
ej as in 'day'
ij/yj (short), **íj/ýj** (long) – an 'eey' sound
oj as the 'oi' in 'void'
ou as the 'o' in 'note', though each vowel is more strongly pronounced than in English
uj (short) and **ůj** (long) – a short 'u' sound as in 'pull' followed by 'y'

Consonants Some of these also take some getting used to:

c as the 'ts' in 'lets'
č as the 'ch' in 'chew'
ch a 'kh' sound, like the 'ch' in Scottish 'loch' or German 'ich'
f as in 'fever', not as in 'of'
g a hard sound like the 'g' in 'get'
h always voiced, like 'h' in 'hand'
j as the 'y' in 'year'
r a rolled 'r', made by the tip of the tongue
ř no English equivalent; a rolled 'rzh' sound, as in the composer, Dvořák
s as in 'sit', not as in 'rose'
š as in 'ship'
ž a 'zh' sound, as in 'treasure'

The letters **ď**, **ň** and **ť** are very soft palatal sounds. There is a momentary contact between the tongue and the hard palate, as if a 'y' is added, such as the 'ny' in canyon. The same sound occurs with **d**, **n** and **t** followed by **i**, **í** or **ě**.

All other consonants are similar to English, though **k**, **p** and **t** are unaspirated, ie pronounced with no puff of breath after them.

Slovak Pronunciation

Vowels Vowels may be short – **a, ä, e, i, y, o, u** – or long – **á, é, í, ý, ó, ú.** They're like Czech except for **ä,** which is like the 'a' in 'act'.

Diphthongs The combinations **ia**, **ie**, and **iu** are best pronounced by running the vowel sounds together as one syllable. The

ô sound is like linking the 'u' in 'pull' and the 'o' in 'pot' to make one syllable. Other diphthongs are pronounced as in Czech.

Consonants Consonants are similar to Czech. The letters **l**, **d**, **n** and **t** become soft palatal sounds when followed by **e** or **i**, indicated in our phonetic transcription by *ly*, *dy*, *ny* and *ty*. Thus 'ni' sounds like the 'ny' in 'canyon'.

These consonants exist only in Slovak:

ľ, ď, ň, ť	soft palatal 'ly', 'dy', 'ny', 'ty'
dz	like 'th' in that
dž	like 'j' in 'jean'

Stress

In Czech and Slovak the first syllable of a word is usually stressed, but syllables are pronounced the same way, stressed or not.

ENGLISH	CZECH	SLOVAK
Greetings & Civilities		
Hello.	*Dobrý den.*	*Dobrý deň.*
Goodbye.	*Na shledanou. (na-skhle-da-nou)*	*Do videnia.*
Hello/Goodbye. (informal)	*Ahoj* and *čau. (ciao)*	*Ahoj* and *čau. (ciao)*
Yes.	*Ano* or *Jo.*	*Áno or Hej.*
No.	*Ne.*	*Nie.*
Excuse me.	*S dovolením.*	*Prepáčte mi.*
May I? (Do you mind?)	*Mohu? (S dovolením?)*	*Smiem? (S dovolením?)*
Sorry. (excuse me, forgive me)	*Promiňte.*	*Prepáčte.*
Please.	*Prosím.*	*Prosím.*
Thank you (very much).	(*Mockrát) děkuji.*	*Ďakujem.(pekne).*
That's fine. (You're welcome)	*Neni zač.* (*Prosím*)	*Nie je za čo.* (*Prosím*)
Good morning.	*Dobré jitro* or *Dobré ráno.*	*Dobré jitro* or *Dobré ráno.*
Good afternoon.	*Dobré odpoledne.*	*Dobrý deň.*
Good evening.	*Dobrý večer.*	*Dobrý večer.*
Good night.	*Dobrou noc.*	*Dobrú noc.*
How are you?	*Jak se máte?*	*Ako sa máte?*
Fine, thanks.	*Děkuji, dobře.*	*Ďakujem, dobre.*
Useful Phrases		
Do you speak English?	*Mluvíte anglicky?*	*Hovoríte anglicky?*
Does anyone speak English?	*Mluví někdo anglicky?*	*Hovorí tu niekto anglicky?*
I speak a little ...	*Mluvím trochu ...*	*Hovorím trochu ...*
I don't speak ...	*Nemluvím ...*	*Nehovorím ...*
I understand.	*Rozumím.*	*Rozumiem.*
I don't understand.	*Nerozumím.*	*Nerozumiem.*
Please could you write that down?	*Můžete mi to napsat, prosím?*	*Mohli by ste mi to napísat, prosím?*
Could you speak slower please?	*Můžete mluvit pomaleji?*	*Hovorte pomalšie, prosím?*
Can I have my change back, please?	*Můžete mi vrátit drobné, prosím?*	*Můžete mi vrátit drobné, prosím?*
What time is it?	*Kolik je hodin?*	*Koľko je hodín?*
May I take your photo?	*Můžu si vás vyfotit?*	*Možem si vás odfotiť?*
Do you have a boyfriend/girlfriend?	*Máte známost?*	*Máte priateľa/priateľku?*
Are you married?	*Jste ženaty?* (m) *Jste vdaná?* (f)	*Ste ženatý?* (m) *Ste vydatá?* (f)
I'm single.	*Jsem svobodný.* (m) *Jsem svobodná.* (f)	*Som slobodný.* (m) *Som slobodná.* (f)

ENGLISH	CZECH	SLOVAK
Emergencies		
Help!	*Pomoc!*	*Pomoc!*
Please call a doctor.	*Prosím zavolejte doktora.*	*Prosím zavolajte lekára.*
ambulance	*sanitku*	*sanitku*
police	*policii*	*policiu*
I am ill.	*Jsem nemocný* (m).	*Som chorý* (m).
	Jsem nemocná (f).	*Som chora* (f).
Where is the police station?	*Kde je policejní stanice?*	*Kde je policajná stanica?*
Where is the toilet? (men/women)	*Kde je záchod? (muži/ženy)*	*Kde je záchod? (muži/ženy)*
Could you help me please?	*Prosím, můžete mi pomoci?*	*Môžete mi prosím pomôcť?*
I wish to contact my ...	*Přeju si mluvit s mým ...*	*Chcel by som hovoriť s mojím ...*
embassy (consulate)	*velvyslanectvím (konzulátem)*	*veľvyslanectvom (konzulátom)*
dentist	*zubní lékař* or *zubař*	*zubný lekár* or *zubár*
doctor	*doktor*	*lékar*
hospital	*nemocnice*	*nemocnica*
Getting Around		
What time does the train/bus leave?	*Kdy odjíždí vlak/autobus?*	*Kedy odchádza vlak/ autobus?*
What time does the train/bus arrive?	*Kdy přijíždí vlak/autobus?*	*Kedy prichádza vlak/ autobus?*
Excuse me, where is the ticket office?	*Prosím, kde je pokladna?*	*Prosím, kde je pokladna?*
Go straight ahead.	*Jděte přímo.*	*Choďte rovno.*
I want to go to ...	*Chci jet do ...*	*Chcem ísť do ...*
Where is ...?	*Kde je ...?*	*Kde je ...?*
I'm looking for ...	*Hledám ...*	*Hľadám ...*
Turn left.	*Zatočte vlevo.*	*Zatočte vľavo.*
Turn right.	*Zatočte vpravo.*	*Zatočte vpravo.*
entrance/exit	*vchod/východ*	*vchod/východ*
behind/in front of	*za/před*	*za/pred*
far/near	*daleko/blízko*	*ďaleko/blízko*
opposite	*naproti*	*naproti*
Buying Tickets		
I would like ...	*Rád* (m) *bych ...*	*Chce* (m) *by som ...*
	Ráda (f) *bych ...*	*Chcela* (f) *by som ...*
a one-way ticket	*jednosměrnou jízdenku*	*jednosmerný lístok*
a return ticket	*zpáteční jízdenku*	*spiatočný lístok*
two tickets	*dvě jízdenky*	*dva lístky*
a student's fare	*studentskou jízdenku*	*študentský lístok*
1st class	*první třídu*	*prvá trieda*
2nd class	*druhou třídu*	*druhá trieda*
dining car	*jídelní vůz*	*reštauračný vozeň*
express	*rychlík*	*rýchlik (expresný vlak)*
local	*místní*	*osobný vlak*
sleeping car	*spací vůz*	*lôžkový vozeň*

ENGLISH	CZECH	SLOVAK
Places to Stay		
Do you have any rooms available?	*Máte volné pokoje?*	*Máte voľnú izbu?*
I would like ...	*Přál* (m) *bych si ...*	*Chcel* (m) *by som ...*
	Přála (f) *bych si ...*	*Chcela* (f) *by som ...*
a single room	*jednolůžkový pokoj*	*jednoposteľovú izbu*
a room with a bathroom	*pokoj s koupelnou*	*izbu s kúpeľňou*
We would like a double room.	*Přáli by jsme si dvoulůžkový pokoj.*	*Chceli by som dvojposteľú izbu.*
How much is it per night?	*Kolik stojí jedna noc?*	*Koľko stojí na noc?*
accommodation	*ubytování*	*ubytovanie*
bed	*postel*	*posteľ*
cheap hotel	*levný hotel*	*lacný hotel*
good hotel	*dobrý hotel*	*dobrý hotel*
nearby hotel	*blízký hotel*	*blízký hotel*
bathroom	*koupelna*	*kúpeľňa*
room number	*číslo pokoje*	*číslo izby*
key	*klíč*	*kľúč*
shower	*sprcha*	*sprcha*
soap	*mýdlo*	*mydlo*
toilet	*záchod or WC*	*záchod or WC*
toilet paper	*toaletní papír*	*toaletný papier*
towel	*ručník*	*uterák*
blanket	*pokrývka*	*deka*
cold water	*studená voda*	*studená voda*
hot water	*horká voda*	*horúca voda*
window	*okno*	*okno*
clean/dirty	*čistý/špinavý*	*čistý/špinavý*
dark/light	*tmavý/světlý*	*tmavý/svetlý*
quiet/noisy	*tichý/hlučný*	*tichý/hlučný*
cheap/expensive	*levný/drahý*	*lacný/drahý*
Around Town		
art gallery	*umělecká galérie*	*umelecká galéria*
bank	*banka*	*banka*
building	*budova*	*budova*
city centre	*centrum*	*centrum*
disco	*diskotéka*	*diskotéka*
embassy	*velvyslanectví*	*veľvyslanectvo*
information centre	*informační centrum*	*informačné centrum*
laundry	*čistírna* or *prádelna*	*práčovňa*
main square	*hlavní náměstí*	*hlavné námestie*
market	*tržiště or trh*	*tržnica, trhovisko or trh*
museum	*muzeum*	*múzeum*
monument	*pamatník* or *pomník*	*pamätník*
old city/town	*staré město*	*staré mesto*
post office	*pošta*	*pošta*
public toilet	*veřejné záchody*	*verejné záchody*

ENGLISH	CZECH	SLOVAK
ruin	*zřícenina*	*zrúcanina*
souvenir	*suvenýr*	*pamiatkovy predmet*
stadium	*stadión*	*štadión*
statue	*socha*	*socha*
synagogue	*synagóga*	*synagóga*
telephone centre	*telefonní ústředna*	*telefónna ústredňa*
theatre	*divadlo*	*divadlo*
train station	*železniční nádraží* or *ČD*	*železničná stanica* or *ŽSR*
village	*vesnice, obec* or *dědina*	*dedina* or *obec*
Food & Drink		
Some more ..., please.	*Ještě ..., prosím.*	*Eště ..., prosím.*
drinking water	*pitná voda*	*pitná voda*
boiled water	*vařící voda*	*vriaca voda*
Does it cost extra?	*Platí se zato zvlášť?*	*Platí zato zvlášť?*
Table for ..., please.	*Stůl pro ... osob, prosím.*	*Stôl pre ... osôb, prosím.*
We have booked a table.	*Zamluvili jsme si místo.*	*Objednali sme si miestoli.*
May I have the menu please?	*Jídelní lístek, prosím?*	*Jedálny lístok, prosím?*
I'm a vegetarian.	*Jsem vegetarián/ka (m/f).*	*Som vegetarian/ka (m/f).*
I don't eat meat.	*Nejím maso.*	*Nejem mäso.*
I don't eat chicken/fish/ham.	*Nejím kuře/rybu/šunku.*	*Nejem kura/rybu/šunku.*
What is today's special?	*Jaká je specialita dne?*	*Aká je dnešná špecialita?*
Bon appétit.	*Dobrou chuť.*	*Dobrú chuť.*
Cheers!	*Nazdraví!*	*Nazdravie!*
The bill, please.	*Účet, prosím.*	*Účet, prosím.*
Family		
brother	*bratr*	*brat*
sister	*sestra*	*sestra*
mother	*matka*	*matka*
father	*otec*	*otec*
daughter	*dcera*	*dcéra*
son	*syn*	*syn*
grandfather	*dědeček*	*starý otec*
grandmother	*babička*	*stará matka*
wife	*manželka*	*manželka*
husband	*manžel*	*manžel*
family	*rodina*	*rodina*
Surrounding Countries		
Austria	*Rakousko*	*Rakúsko*
Germany	*Německo*	*Nemecko*
Hungary	*Maďarsko*	*Maďarsko*
Poland	*Polsko*	*Poľsko*
Ukraine	*Ukrajina*	*Ukrajina*
Time & Dates		
When?	*Kdy?*	*Kedy?*

ENGLISH	CZECH	SLOVAK
in the morning	*ráno*	*doobeda*
in the afternoon	*odpoledne*	*poobede*
in the evening	*večer*	*večer*
today	*dnes*	*dnes*
now	*teď*	*teraz*
yesterday	*včera*	*včera*
tomorrow	*zítra*	*zajtra*
next week	*příští týden*	*budúci týždeň*
day(s)	*den (dny)*	*deň (dni)*
night	*noc*	*noc*
week	*týden*	*týždeň*
month	*měsíc*	*mesiac*
Monday	*pondělí*	*pondelok*
Tuesday	*úterý*	*útorok*
Wednesday	*středa*	*streda*
Thursday	*čtvrtek*	*štvrtok*
Friday	*pátek*	*piatok*
Saturday	*sobota*	*sobota*
Sunday	*neděle*	*nedeľa*
January	*leden*	*január*
February	*únor*	*február*
March	*březen*	*marec*
April	*duben*	*apríl*
May	*květen*	*máj*
June	*červen*	*jún*
July	*červenec*	*júl*
August	*srpen*	*august*
September	*září*	*september*
October	*říjen*	*október*
November	*listopad*	*november*
December	*prosinec*	*december*
summer	*léto*	*leto*
autumn	*podzim*	*jeseň*
winter	*zima*	*zima*
spring	*jaro*	*jar*
year	*rok*	*rok*
century	*století*	*staročie*
millennium	*milénium* or *tisíciletí*	*tisícročie*
beginning of ...	*začátek ...*	*začiatok ...*
first half of ...	*první polovina ...*	*prvá polovica ...*
middle of ...	*polovina ...*	*stred ...*
second half of ...	*druhá polovina ...*	*druhá polovica ...*
end of ...	*konec ...*	*koniec ...*
around ...	*kolem ...*	*okolo ...*

Numbers

	CZECH	SLOVAK
0	*nula*	*nula*
1	*jeden*	*jeden*
2	*dva*	*dva*
3	*tři*	*tri*
4	*čtyři*	*štyri*
5	*pět*	*päť*
6	*šest*	*šesť*
7	*sedm*	*sedem*
8	*osm*	*osem*
9	*devět*	*deväť*
10	*deset*	*desať*
11	*jedenáct*	*jedenásť*
12	*dvanáct*	*dvanásť*
13	*třináct*	*trinásť*
14	*čtrnáct*	*štrnásť*
15	*patnáct*	*pätnásť*
16	*šestnáct*	*šestnásť*
17	*sedmnáct*	*sedemnásť*
18	*osmnáct*	*osemnásť*
19	*devatenáct*	*devätnásť*
20	*dvacet*	*dvadsať*
21	*dvacet jedna*	*dvadsaťjeden*
22	*dvacet dva*	*dvadsaťdva*
23	*dvacet tři*	*dvadsaťtri*
30	*třicet*	*tridsať*
40	*čtyřicet*	*štyridsať*
50	*padesát*	*päťdesiat*
60	*šedesát*	*šesťdesiat*
70	*sedmdesát*	*sedemdesiat*
80	*osmdesát*	*osemdesiat*
90	*devadesát*	*deväťdesiat*
100	*sto*	*sto*
200	*dvě stě*	*dvesto*
300	*tři sta*	*tristo*
400	*čtyři sta*	*štyristo*
500	*pět set*	*päťsto*
600	*šest set*	*šesto*
700	*sedm set*	*sedemsto*
800	*osm set*	*osemsto*
900	*devět set*	*deväťsto*
1000	*tisíc*	*tisíc*
1 million	*milión*	*milión*

It's quite common for Czechs to say the numbers 21 to 99 in reverse, so that, for example, *dvacet jedna* (21) becomes *jedna dvacet.*

Glossary

You may encounter the following terms and abbreviations in your travels throughout the two republics. Where relevant, the Czech/Slovak terms are separated by a slash (/). See also the Language section at the end of the Facts about the Region chapter, and the Food section in the Facts for the Visitor chapter.

acid rain – rain made sulphurous by factory smoke that destroys trees
atd – etc

bouda or boudy – mountain hut
boží muka/božie muky – wayside column or shrine

ČSAD – Czech Bus Lines
ČD – Czech Railways
Čedok – Czech Travel Agency
celnice – customs
chata or chalupa – mountain hut
CHKO (chráněná krajinná oblast/chránená krajinná oblasť) – Protected Landscape Region
chrám/dóm – cathedral
cizinci/cudzinci – foreigners
ČSA – Czech Airlines
ČTK – Czech Press Agency
cukrárna/cukráreň – cakeshop

dolina – dale
dům kultury/dom kultúry – house of culture, for concerts and music practice
dům umění/dom umĕnia – house of art, for exhibitions and workshops

h.(hod) – hours
hora – mountain
hospoda or hostinec – pub
hrad – castle
HZDS, Hnutie za democratické slovensko – Movement for Democratic Slovakia

jeskyně/jaskyňa – cave
jezero/jazero – lake

JZD – state farm (during Communist rule)

kavárna/kaváriеň – café
Kč (koruna česká) – Czech crown
KDH, Kresťansko democratické hnutie – Christian Democratic Movement
knihkupectví/knihkupectvo – bookshop
koloniál – mixed goods shop
kostel/kostol – church
koupaliště/kúpalisko – swimming pool
KSČM, Komunistická strana Čech a Moravy – Czech & Moravian Communist party

les – forest
lístek/lístok – ticket

město/mesto – town
mlékárna/mliekáreň – dairy
most – bridge

n.l (př.n.l)/n.l (pr.n.l) – AD (BC)
nábřeží (nabř.)/nábrežie (nábr.) – embankment
náměstí/námestie (nám.) – square
nemocnice – hospital

ODA, Občanská democratická aliance – Civic Democratic Alliance
ODS, Občanská democratická strana – Civic Democratic Party
OF, Občanské forúm – Civic Forum
OSN – UN
ostrov – island
otevřeno/otvorené – open
ovoce & zelenina – fruit & vegetables, greengrocer

pekárna/pekáreň – bakery
pivnice/piváreň – (small) beer hall
pivovar – brewery
pleso (Slovak only) – mountain lake, tarn
potok – stream

rokle – gorge
rybník – pond

SAD – Slovak Bus Lines
Satur – Slovak travel agency
sady – park
samoobsluha – supermarket
SDĽ, Strana democratické ĺavice – Democratic Left party
sedlo – saddle (in mountains)
sgraffito – mural technique in which the top layer of plaster is scraped away or incised to reveal the layer underneath
Sk (Slovenská koruna) – Slovak crown
skansen – open-air museum of traditional architecture
SR – Slovak Railways
svatý/svätý – saint

tel. č – telephone no.
toalet – toilet
třída/trieda – avenue

ubytovna/ubytovňa – dormitory accommodation
údolí/údolie – valley

V. Brit. – UK
'Velvet Divorce' – separation of Czechoslovakia into fully independent Czech and Slovak republics in 1993
'Velvet Revolution' – Bloodless overthrow of the Communist regime in 1989
vesnice/dedina – village
věž/veža – tower
vinárna/vináreň – wine bar
vrchy – hills
vstup zakázán – no entry

záchod – toilet
zámek/zámok – castle
zavřeno/zatvorené – closed
železniční zastávka/železničná stanica – railway stop
zelenina & ovoce – vegetables & fruit, greengrocers
zimmer frei – room free (for rent)

Index

ABBREVIATIONS

CR – Czech Republic
SR – Slovak Republic

MAPS

TEXT

Map references are in **bold** type.

Thanks

Many thanks to the travellers who used the first edition and wrote to us with helpful hints, useful advice and interesting anecdotes:

Roger Allnutt, AG Armstrong, Natalie Baker, Diane Baker, Dr Bruno Bubna-Kasteliz, Michael Burden, Eric Carlson, Helene Cincebeaux, Nicola Clark, Brian Coupol, George Crosse, Russell Crumrine, R Dacia, Cole Davis, Nick Diovouniotis, Suzanne Donnelly, Honda Eiki, David Evans, Nick Fischer, Ed Fogden, Ida Freer, Jill Goulder, Libby Grawith, Tapio Hakamaki, Faye Hallett, Alan Harrison, Tim Haughton, Joan Holland, Petr Hruska, GA Hughes, Lyndsay & Juliet Hurn, Carol Ince, Dr Eric Janousek, Nick Jenkin, Peter Jones, Pamela Jordan, Katerina Kotherova, Kevin Knifton, Martin Kriz, Tiffany Kubaugh, David Kucera, R & Sarah Lambert, Diane & Ben Lapinski, Sophie Le Sueur, Vera Macek, Christopher Marks, Selby Martin, Damien Meadows, Ian Mitchell, Timothy Maw, Kathleen Murphy, Hayley Nicholas, Kevin O'Connor, Paul O'Dwyer, Sarah O'Mahony, Paul Orum, Magnus Ostland, Rhonda Payget, Janos Pfannenwald, M Pino, Tony Pitman, IG Pool, Annell Presbie, D Quinn, Rob Ray, K Reineker, Gaynor Roberts, Monica Robinson, John Rogers, David Ruchman, Martin Schmidt, Richard Scott, Deborah Stuart, Karin Spelbrink, Charlotte Strandgaard, Daniel Stuckey, Alberto Such, Matthew Trump, E van der Peijl, Frank Vergona, Everton Walsh, Heather Watson, Lynette Whitaker, MA Wright, Elad Yom Tov, Michael Yovino-Young, Marek Zielinksi, Peter & Maggie Zimmerman

LONELY PLANET JOURNEYS

JOURNEYS is a unique collection of travel writing – published by the company that understands travel better than anyone else. It is a series for anyone who has ever experienced – or dreamed of – the magical moment when they encountered a strange culture or saw a place for the first time. They are tales to read while you're planning a trip, while you're on the road or while you're in an armchair, in front of a fire.

JOURNEYS books catch the spirit of a place, illuminate a culture, recount a crazy adventure, or introduce a fascinating way of life. They always entertain, and always enrich the experience of travel.

THE GATES OF DAMASCUS

Lieve Joris

Translated by Sam Garrett

This best-selling book is a beautifully drawn portrait of day-to-day life in modern Syria. Through her intimate contact with local people, Lieve Joris draws us into the fascinating world that lies behind the gates of Damascus. Hala's husband is a political prisoner, jailed for his opposition to the Assad regime; through the author's friendship with Hala we see how Syrian politics impacts on the lives of ordinary people.

Lieve Joris, who was born in Belgium, is one of Europe's leading travel writers. In addition to an award-winning book on Hungary, she has published widely acclaimed accounts of her journeys to the Middle East and Africa. *The Gates of Damascus* is her fifth book.

'Expands the boundaries of travel writing' **– Times Literary Supplement**

KINGDOM OF THE FILM STARS

Journey into Jordan

Annie Caulfield

Kingdom of the Film Stars is a travel book and a love story. With honesty and humour, Annie Caulfield writes of travelling in Jordan and falling in love with a Bedouin. Her book offers fascinating insights into the country – from the traditional tent life of nomadic tribes to the first woman MP's battle with fundamentalist colleagues. *Kingdom of the Film Stars* unpicks some of the tight-woven Western myths about the Arab world, presenting cultural and political issues within the intimate framework of a compelling love story.

Annie Caulfield, who was born in Ireland and currently lives in London, is an award-winning playwright and journalist. She has travelled widely in the Middle East.

'Annie Caulfield is a remarkable traveller. Her story is fresh, courageous, moving, witty and sexy!' **– Dawn French**

LONELY PLANET TRAVEL ATLASES

Lonely Planet has long been famous for the number and quality of its guidebook maps. Now we've gone one step further and in conjunction with Steinhart Katzir Publishers produced a handy companion series: Lonely Planet travel atlases – maps of a country produced in book form.

Unlike other maps, which look good but lead travellers astray, our travel atlases have been researched on the road by Lonely Planet's experienced team of writers. All details are carefully checked to ensure the atlas corresponds with the equivalent Lonely Planet guidebook.

The handy atlas format means no holes, wrinkles, torn sections or constant folding and unfolding. These atlases can survive long periods on the road, unlike cumbersome fold-out maps. The comprehensive index ensures easy reference.

- full-colour throughout
- maps researched and checked by Lonely Planet authors
- place names correspond with Lonely Planet guidebooks – no confusing spelling differences
- legend and travelling information in English, French, German, Japanese and Spanish
- size: 230 x 160 mm

Available now:
Chile & Easter Island • Egypt • India & Bangladesh • Israel & the Palestinian Territories •Jordan, Syria & Lebanon • Kenya • Laos • Portugal • South Africa, Lesotho & Swaziland • Thailand • Turkey • Vietnam • Zimbabwe, Botswana & Namibia

LONELY PLANET TV SERIES & VIDEOS

Lonely Planet travel guides have been brought to life on television screens around the world. Like our guides, the programmes are based on the joy of independent travel, and look honestly at some of the most exciting, picturesque and frustrating places in the world. Each show is presented by one of three travellers from Australia, England or the USA and combines an innovative mixture of video, Super-8 film, atmospheric soundscapes and original music.

Videos of each episode – containing additional footage not shown on television – are available from good book and video shops, but the availability of individual videos varies with regional screening schedules.

Video destinations include: Alaska • American Rockies • Australia – The South-East • Baja California & the Copper Canyon • Brazil • Central Asia • Chile & Easter Island • Corsica, Sicily & Sardinia – The Mediterranean Islands • East Africa (Tanzania & Zanzibar) • Ecuador & the Galapagos Islands • Greenland & Iceland • Indonesia • Israel & the Sinai Desert • Jamaica • Japan • La Ruta Maya • Morocco • New York • North India • Pacific Islands (Fiji, Solomon Islands & Vanuatu) • South India • South West China • Turkey • Vietnam • West Africa • Zimbabwe, Botswana & Namibia

The Lonely Planet TV series is produced by:
Pilot Productions
The Old Studio
18 Middle Row
London W10 5AT UK

For video availability and ordering information contact your nearest Lonely Planet office.

Music from the TV series is available on CD & cassette.

PLANET TALK

Lonely Planet's FREE quarterly newsletter

We love hearing from you and think you'd like to hear from us.

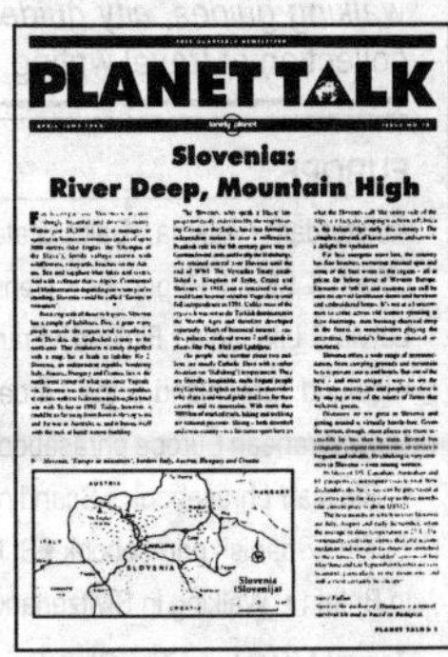

When... is the right time to see reindeer in Finland?
Where... can you hear the best palm-wine music in Ghana?
How... do you get from Asunción to Areguá by steam train?
What... is the best way to see India?

For the answer to these and many other questions read PLANET TALK.

Every issue is packed with up-to-date travel news and advice including:

- a letter from Lonely Planet co-founders Tony and Maureen Wheeler
- go behind the scenes on the road with a Lonely Planet author
- feature article on an important and topical travel issue
- a selection of recent letters from travellers
- details on forthcoming Lonely Planet promotions
- complete list of Lonely Planet products

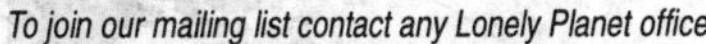

To join our mailing list contact any Lonely Planet office.

Also available: Lonely Planet T-shirts. 100% heavyweight cotton.

LONELY PLANET ONLINE

Get the latest travel information before you leave or while you're on the road

Whether you've just begun planning your next trip, or you're chasing down specific info on currency regulations or visa requirements, check out Lonely Planet Online for up-to-the minute travel information.

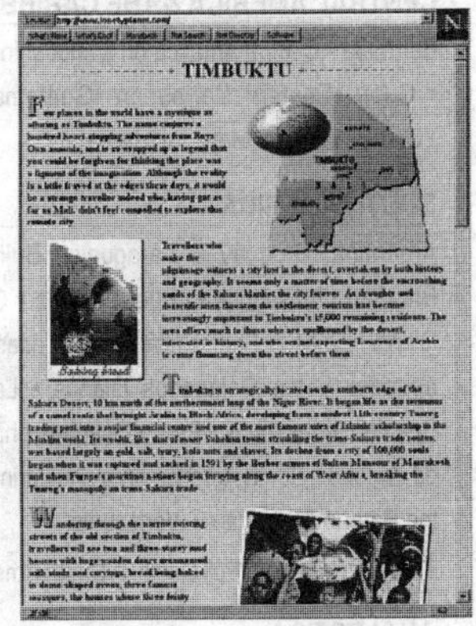

As well as travel profiles of your favourite destinations (including maps and photos), you'll find current reports from our researchers and other travellers, updates on health and visas, travel advisories, and discussion of the ecological and political issues you need to be aware of as you travel.

There's also an online travellers' forum where you can share your experience of life on the road, meet travel companions and ask other travellers for their recommendations and advice. We also have plenty of links to other online sites useful to independent travellers.

And of course we have a complete and up-to-date list of all Lonely Planet travel products including guides, phrasebooks, atlases, Journeys and videos and a simple online ordering facility if you can't find the book you want elsewhere.

www.lonelyplanet.com
or
AOL keyword: lp

LONELY PLANET PRODUCTS

Lonely Planet is known worldwide for publishing practical, reliable and no-nonsense travel information in our guides and on our web site. The Lonely Planet list covers just about every accessible part of the world. Currently there are eight series: *travel guides, shoestring guides, walking guides, city guides, phrasebooks, audio packs, travel atlases* and *Journeys* – a unique collection of travel writing.

EUROPE

Amsterdam • Austria • Baltic States phrasebook • Britain • Central Europe on a shoestring • Central Europe phrasebook • Czech & Slovak Republics • Denmark • Dublin • Eastern Europe on a shoestring • Eastern Europe phrasebook • Estonia, Latvia & Lithuania • Finland • France • French phrasebook • German phrasebook • Greece • Greek phrasebook • Hungary • Iceland, Greenland & the Faroe Islands • Ireland • Italian phrasebook • Italy • Mediterranean Europe on a shoestring • Mediterranean Europe phrasebook • Paris • Poland • Portugal • Portugal travel atlas • Prague • Russia, Ukraine & Belarus • Russian phrasebook • Scandinavian & Baltic Europe on a shoestring • Scandinavian Europe phrasebook • Slovenia • Spain • Spanish phrasebook • St Petersburg • Switzerland • Trekking in Spain • Ukrainian phrasebook • Vienna • Walking in Britain • Walking in Switzerland • Western Europe on a shoestring • Western Europe phrasebook

Travel Literature: The Olive Grove: Travels in Greece

NORTH AMERICA

Alaska • Backpacking in Alaska • Baja California • California & Nevada • Canada • Florida • Hawaii • Honolulu • Los Angeles • Mexico • Miami • New England • New Orleans • New York City • New York, New Jersey & Pennsylvania • Pacific Northwest USA • Rocky Mountain States • San Francisco • Southwest USA • USA phrasebook • Washington, DC & the Capital Region

CENTRAL AMERICA & THE CARIBBEAN

Bermuda • Central America on a shoestring • Costa Rica • Cuba • Eastern Caribbean • Guatemala, Belize & Yucatán: La Ruta Maya • Jamaica

SOUTH AMERICA

Argentina, Uruguay & Paraguay • Bolivia • Brazil • Brazilian phrasebook • Buenos Aires • Chile & Easter Island • Chile & Easter Island travel atlas • Colombia • Ecuador & the Galápagos Islands • Latin American Spanish phrasebook • Peru • Quechua phrasebook • Rio de Janeiro • South America on a shoestring • Trekking in the Patagonian Andes • Venezuela

Travel Literature: Full Circle: A South American Journey

ANTARCTICA

Antarctica

ISLANDS OF THE INDIAN OCEAN

Madagascar & Comoros • Maldives• Mauritius, Réunion & Seychelles

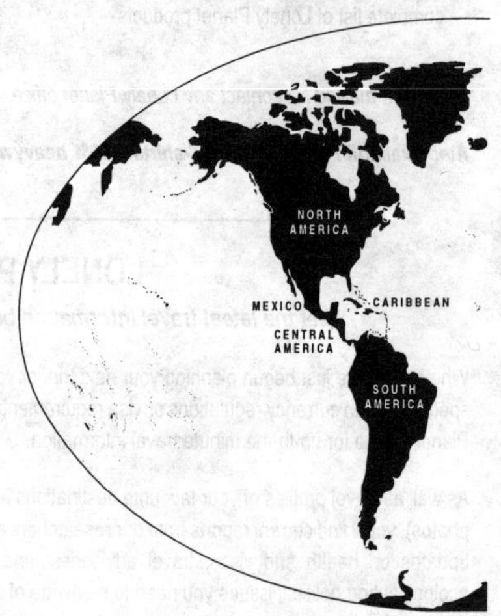

AFRICA

Africa - the South • Africa on a shoestring • Arabic (Moroccan) phrasebook • Cape Town • Central Africa • East Africa • Egypt • Egypt travel atlas• Ethiopian (Amharic) phrasebook • Kenya • Kenya travel atlas • Malawi, Mozambique & Zambia • Morocco • North Africa • South Africa, Lesotho & Swaziland • South Africa, Lesotho & Swaziland travel atlas • Swahili phrasebook • Trekking in East Africa • West Africa • Zimbabwe, Botswana & Namibia • Zimbabwe, Botswana & Namibia travel atlas

Travel Literature: The Rainbird: A Central African Journey • Songs to an African Sunset: A Zimbabwean Story

MAIL ORDER

Lonely Planet products are distributed worldwide.They are also available by mail order from Lonely Planet, so if you have difficulty finding a title please write to us. North American and South American residents should write to Embarcadero West, 155 Filbert St, Suite 251, Oakland CA 94607, USA; European and African residents should write to 10a Spring Place, London NW5 3BH; and residents of other countries to PO Box 617, Hawthorn, Victoria 3122, Australia.

NORTH-EAST ASIA

Beijing • Cantonese phrasebook • China • Hong Kong • Hong Kong, Macau & Guangzhou • Japan • Japanese phrasebook • Japanese audio pack • Korea • Korean phrasebook • Mandarin phrasebook • Mongolia • Mongolian phrasebook • North-East Asia on a shoestring • Seoul • Taiwan • Tibet • Tibet phrasebook • Tokyo

Travel Literature: Lost Japan

MIDDLE EAST & CENTRAL ASIA

Arab Gulf States • Arabic (Egyptian) phrasebook • Central Asia • Central Asia phrasebook • Iran • Israel & the Palestinian Territories • Israel & the Palestinian Territories travel atlas • Istanbul • Jerusalem • Jordan & Syria • Jordan, Syria & Lebanon travel atlas • Lebanon • Middle East • Turkey • Turkish phrasebook • Turkey travel atlas • Yemen

Travel Literature: The Gates of Damascus • Kingdom of the Film Stars: Journey into Jordan

ALSO AVAILABLE:

Travel with Children • Traveller's Tales

INDIAN SUBCONTINENT

Bangladesh • Bengali phrasebook • Delhi • Hindi/Urdu phrasebook • India • India & Bangladesh travel atlas • Indian Himalaya • Karakoram Highway • Nepal • Nepali phrasebook • Pakistan • Rajasthan • Sri Lanka • Sri Lanka phrasebook • Trekking in the Indian Himalaya • Trekking in the Karakoram & Hindukush • Trekking in the Nepal Himalaya

Travel Literature: In Rajasthan • Shopping for Buddhas

SOUTH-EAST ASIA

Bali & Lombok • Bangkok • Burmese phrasebook • Cambodia • Ho Chi Minh City • Indonesia • Indonesian phrasebook • Indonesian audio pack • Jakarta • Java • Laos • Lao phrasebook • Laos travel atlas • Malay phrasebook • Malaysia, Singapore & Brunei • Myanmar (Burma) • Philippines • Pilipino phrasebook • Singapore • South-East Asia on a shoestring • South-East Asia phrasebook • Thailand • Thailand's Islands & Beaches • Thailand travel atlas • Thai phrasebook • Thai audio pack • Thai Hill Tribes phrasebook • Vietnam • Vietnamese phrasebook • Vietnam travel atlas

AUSTRALIA & THE PACIFIC

Australia • Australian phrasebook • Bushwalking in Australia • Bushwalking in Papua New Guinea • Fiji • Fijian phrasebook • Islands of Australia's Great Barrier Reef • Melbourne • Micronesia • New Caledonia • New South Wales • New Zealand • Northern Territory • Outback Australia • Papua New Guinea • Papua New Guinea phrasebook • Queensland • Rarotonga & the Cook Islands • Samoa • Solomon Islands • South Australia • Sydney • Tahiti & French Polynesia • Tasmania • Tonga • Tramping in New Zealand • Vanuatu • Victoria • Western Australia

Travel Literature: Islands in the Clouds • Sean & David's Long Drive

THE LONELY PLANET STORY

Lonely Planet published its first book in 1973 in response to the numerous 'How did you do it?' questions Maureen and Tony Wheeler were asked after driving, bussing, hitching, sailing and railing their way from England to Australia.

Written at a kitchen table and hand collated, trimmed and stapled, *Across Asia on the Cheap* became an instant local bestseller, inspiring thoughts of another book.

Eighteen months in South-East Asia resulted in their second guide, *South-East Asia on a shoestring*, which they put together in a backstreet Chinese hotel in Singapore in 1975. The 'yellow bible', as it quickly became known to backpackers around the world, soon became *the* guide to the region. It has sold well over half a million copies and is now in its 9th edition, still retaining its familiar yellow cover.

Today there are over 240 titles, including travel guides, walking guides, language kits & phrasebooks, travel atlases and travel literature. The company is the largest independent travel publisher in the world. Although Lonely Planet initially specialised in guides to Asia, today there are few corners of the globe that have not been covered.

The emphasis continues to be on travel for independent travellers. Tony and Maureen still travel for several months of each year and play an active part in the writing, updating and quality control of Lonely Planet's guides.

They have been joined by over 70 authors and 170 staff at our offices in Melbourne (Australia), Oakland (USA), London (UK) and Paris (France). Travellers themselves also make a valuable contribution to the guides through the feedback we receive in thousands of letters each year and on our web site.

The people at Lonely Planet strongly believe that travellers can make a positive contribution to the countries they visit, both through their appreciation of the countries' culture, wildlife and natural features, and through the money they spend. In addition, the company makes a direct contribution to the countries and regions it covers. Since 1986 a percentage of the income from each book has been donated to ventures such as famine relief in Africa; aid projects in India; agricultural projects in Central America; Greenpeace's efforts to halt French nuclear testing in the Pacific; and Amnesty International.

'I hope we send people out with the right attitude about travel. You realise when you travel that there are so many different perspectives about the world, so we hope these books will make people more interested in what they see. Guidebooks can't really guide people. All you can do is point them in the right direction.'

– Tony Wheeler

LONELY PLANET PUBLICATIONS

Australia
PO Box 617, Hawthorn 3122, Victoria
tel: (03) 9819 1877 fax: (03) 9819 6459
e-mail: talk2us@lonelyplanet.com.au

USA
Embarcadero West, 155 Filbert St, Suite 251,
Oakland, CA 94607
tel: (510) 893 8555 TOLL FREE: 800 275-8555
fax: (510) 893 8563
e-mail: info@lonelyplanet.com

UK
10a Spring Place,
London NW5 3BH
tel: (0181) 742 3161 fax: (0181) 742 2772
e-mail: lonelyplanetuk@compuserve.com

France:
71 bis rue du Cardinal Lemoine, 75005 Paris
tel: 1 44 32 06 20 fax: 1 46 34 72 55
e-mail: 100560.415@compuserve.com

World Wide Web: http://www.lonelyplanet.com
or *AOL keyword: lp*